THE ESSENTIAL GUIDE
TO COLLECTIBLES

To the men in my life,
Paul, Chris and Alex, all intrepid museum goers.
Cathy Giangrande

With love to Alice Neave, an enthusiast for museums.
Alistair McAlpine

THE ESSENTIAL
GUIDE
TO COLLECTIBLES

A SOURCE BOOK OF PUBLIC
COLLECTIONS IN EUROPE
AND THE U.S.A.

Alistair McAlpine & Cathy Giangrande

VIKING STUDIO

VIKING STUDIO
Published by the Penguin Group
Penguin Putnam Inc., 375 Hudson Street,
New York, New York 10014, U.S.A.
Penguin Books Ltd, 80 Strand,
London WC2R ORL, England
Penguin Books Australia Ltd, Ringwood,
Victoria, Australia
Penguin Books Canada Ltd, 10 Alcorn Avenue,
Toronto, Ontario, Canada M4V 3B2
Penguin Books (NZ) Ltd, 182-190 Wairau Road,
Auckland 10, New Zealand

Penguin Books Ltd, Registered Offices:
Harmondsworth, Middlesex, England

First published in 2001 by Viking Studio,
a member of Penguin Putnam Inc.

10 9 8 7 6 5 4 3 2 1

CIP data available
ISBN 0–670–03032–5

Set in Lexicon
Designed by Anikst Design, London
Printed in Singapore by CS Graphics PTE, Ltd

The authors' photograph (right) was taken by Liz McAlpine.

Cathy Giangrande & Alistair McAlpine

ANTIQUITIES AND ETHNOGRAPHY

BOOKS, MANUSCRIPTS AND PRINTED MATTER

CHILDHOOD MEMORABILIA

DECORATIVE ARTS

MILITARY COLLECTIONS

NATURAL WORLD

POPULAR COLLECTIBLES

SCIENCE AND TECHNOLOGY COLLECTIONS

SPORTING MEMORABILIA

TEXTILES, COSTUMES AND ACCESSORIES

TRANSPORT

UNIQUE AND CURIOUS COLLECTIONS

APPENDICES

FOREWORD

When the renowned scientist, physician and antiquarian, Sir Hans Sloane, set about amassing his drawers full of precious stones, tables of gold and silver, large animals preserved in skin, and a host of curious and rare antiquities, little did he know that his collections, acquired by the nation at the time of his death in 1753, would act as the catalyst for the founding of two great museums and a library: the British Museum, The Natural History Museum in South Kensington, and the British Library. Since then, thousands of other private collections have seeded museums across the globe, from those amassed by the wealthiest of bankers to amateurs who have gone without their next meal to secure a prize specimen for their quarries. It's a pattern which continues today, as collectors feverishly gather a whole range of fascinating objects which run the gamut from fossils and ancient coins to milk bottles and matchbox covers, many of which open as small private museums or later are donated or sold to larger museums for safe-keeping and maximum accessibility.

Collecting has become as normal as shopping in a supermarket and, social psychologists say, has enormous benefits for happiness, health, and mental stability to counter the pressures of modern living. Collecting, in fact, is big business. One in three people in the Western world collect, and the numbers are growing daily. This surge is being fuelled by on-line auctions of a whole range of collectibles, from fine ceramics to the humble antique bead. Our aim is to assist collectors in their quests. There is no better way to learn than from looking at the best; it hones the eye, reveals the range of possibilities, and it challenges and inspires. And there is no better place to see the best than in museums, libraries, and other institutions – guardians and repositories of a limitless diversity of objects made accessible to the public.

Among the world's first museums was an institution in Alexandria dedicated to the Service of the Muses. Founded by Ptolemy Philadelphus, his idea was then, as it is of museums now, to educate people. Museums, however, also have other purposes. They are an indispensable part of a civilized nation. They record the past, preserve the remains of lost cultures, and are an essential ingredient in the task of creating better societies.

Go to most travel or guidebooks and you'll find lists of museums arranged by location, with an overall description of the collections. In this book, we chose to catalogue museums by subject rather than geographically. Massive collections, such as those in major national museums and libraries, have been dissected to reveal their often hidden contents. Where the majority of a collection is in store and only a sliver is on view, we have teased out the reserves from hiding which are accessible by appointment but which are rarely seen usually due to a lack of space. Some museums have already made visible their stores and many others are in the process of doing so, and at the same time are connecting people with the scientific and educational aspects of their work. But the fact remains that in some museums only 1% of their total collections have ever been exposed. Some of the collections we include have been discovered by speaking to specialists, others were suggested by friends or gleaned from books on the subject in question, still others we encountered on our travels through Europe and the USA. The majority, however, were revealed by speaking directly to the curators or keepers in charge of the collections, and we would like to thank them for their help.

Space has precluded certain topics. Paintings, drawings and modern sculpture, to name a few of the most obvious ones, were all simply too large to do justice to in a book of this size, the scale of which is already formidable. Space also does not allow us to be all-inclusive, nor has it allowed us to incorporate as much detail as we would have wished. In each section are highlighted collections which we feel have exceptional holdings, are distinctive in their manner of presentation, or which are simply outright jewels. Often the larger and more famous institutions which are well known for certain parts of their collections, have given way to ones which are less well known. The United States alone has some 12,000 museums, and Britain over 2,500, not including historic homes, libraries, or other repositories. Norway, with over 800 museums, are custodians to over 600,000 fine art objects, 3.6 million objects of cultural history, 10 million natural history specimens, and 9 million photographs – and those numbers are growing with great rapidity. What were once museum backwaters are now awash with museums. Bilbao's new Guggenheim draws crowds the like of which are unprecedented. These new museums, often designed by the best and most famous architects, have become art objects in their own right, their buildings as much if not more of an attraction than their contents. Museums are clearly undergoing a renaissance, and their pulling powers provide a much-needed boost for tourism.

In this guide we have focused on museums with real collections rather than interactive ones. Although technology is often used to support collections, museums that rely solely on such devices are more about entertainment. People go to museums to access objects they cannot see anywhere else, to marvel at the unusual, to learn from what they have not come across before, and to leave with their imaginations racing. This guide is a means of seeking out, amongst the vast sea of holdings, the collections that interest you, and hopefully, as you turn the pages, a phrase or two might catch the imagination and spark the beginnings of yet another great collection. Sloane himself wrote that 'the collection and accurate arrangement of these curiosities constituted my major contribution to the advancement of science'. His surviving legacy is a testimony to his resounding achievement – the establishment of the most magnificent treasure houses in the world.

ACKNOWLEDGEMENTS

Our travels over thousands of miles have taken us to countless institutions where we have spoken to many people who have generously given their help. We owe our greatest thanks to them and to the staff at the museums, libraries, and historic institutions who provided us with information about their collections and with images to illustrate them; without them this book could not have been written. We would also like to thank the various experts who assisted us by suggesting collections and providing us with useful contacts. They include: Kathryn Berenson, Val Berryman, Bluey Brattle, Frank Barraclough, Piers Crocker, Jen Cruse, Penny Dolnick, Helen Farnsworth, Merri Ferrell, Maria Antonietta Fontano Angioy, Gerald Gurney, Jenny Hall, Jennifer Harris, Hélène La Rue, David Moulson, Adrian Norris, Jim Pilistead, Brian Steptoe, Francesco Torre, Thomas E. Weil, Jr., Janet West, Anne Williams, and Ben Williams.

Our outstanding team of researchers and translators did a superb job translating what was often quite technical information: Céline Marquaille and Stéphane Burkhard-Sommer took on the most formidable part of this task and were particularly brilliant. Others include Maria Alieva, Betina Andersen, Hannah Lohijoki, Julia Markowski, Marianna Nagy, Radek Plavnicky Alessandra Rupena, and Robbert van Hulzen. Additional assistance came via Kelly Hetherington, Mary-Ann Gallagher, Hulton Gunter, and Annie Thomson.

Our thanks to Everyman Publishers and the team there who worked so hard on the book. They include, among others, Sandra Pisano, Clémence Jacquinet, and a host of freelance editors, among whom Matthew Tanner was exceptional. Our warmest thanks go to David Campbell, who backed us until the finish. Creative Director, Misha Anikst, and his team deserve special praise and thanks for their efforts in designing the book.

Cathy would personally like to thank several friends who provided her with flashes of inspiration: Philippe Garner, Leslee Holderness, Errol Fuller, David Mindell, Beverly Perkins, Dorothy Twining Globus and Sally Thatcher. Last but not least, she is most grateful to her mother, Irene Giangrande, to her husband Paul, and to their sons, Chris and Alex, for enduring endless museum visits.

AFRICAN ART

ANCIENT GLASS AND CERAMICS

ANCIENT MOSAIC AND WALL PAINTINGS

ANCIENT NEAR EAST AND CYPRIOT ANTIQUITIES

EARLY CHRISTIAN AND MEDIEVAL ANTIQUITIES

EGYPTIAN ANTIQUITIES

ETRUSCAN AND ROMAN ANTIQUITIES

GREEK ANTIQUITIES

INDIAN AND ASIAN ARTEFACTS

ISLAMIC ANTIQUITIES

NORTH AMERICAN INDIAN ARTEFACTS

OCEANIC ART

PRE-COLUMBIAN AND LATIN AMERICAN ARTEFACTS

PREHISTORIC AND BRONZE AGE ARTEFACTS

SAXON, CELTIC AND VIKING ARTEFACTS

The collections described in shaded boxes are the collections which we feel have exceptional holdings, are distinctive in their manner of presentation, or are outright jewels.

Bwa plank mask
The Horniman Museum and Gardens

AFRICAN ART

Afrika Museum
The Africa Museum
Postweg 6, 6571 CS Berg en Dal, The Netherlands
Tel. (31) 24 6842044 www.afrikamuseum.nl
Apr-Oct: Mon-Fri 10am-5pm, Sat-Sun & public holidays 11am-5pm. Nov-Mar: Tue-Fri 10am-5pm, Sat-Sun & public holidays 11am-5pm

The only museum in the Netherlands devoted exclusively to collecting and exhibiting African art, providing a complete survey of Africa's history. A majority of the exhibits focus on the ritual and spiritual aspects of African culture and were collected by the missionaries of the Congregation of the Holy Spirit. Five African compounds have been recreated to give you an idea of how African communities were organized.

Ivory, iron and copper wire mask, Benin, Nigeria, 16th century
British Museum

Musée des Antiquités nationales
The Museum of National Antiquities
Château de Saint-Germain-en-Laye, 78103 Saint-Germain-en-Laye, France
Tel. (33) 1 39 10 13 00
Mon, Wed-Sun 9am-5.30pm

Some of the oldest known African stone tools in the world can be found here, featuring those from Melka Kunture (Ethiopia) around two million years old, and other more recent examples which are placed alongside African and Eurasian examples. There is also the Morgan Brothers' collection of clay, ivory and Egyptian stone statuettes.

Musée d'Arts africains, océaniens, amérindiens
Museum of African, Oceanic and American-Indian Arts
Centre de la Vieille Charité, 2 rue de la Charité, 13002 Marseille, France
Tel. (33) 4 91 14 58 80
Sep-May: Tue-Sun 10am-5pm. Jun-Aug: Tue-Sun 11am-6pm

An award-winning collection, the highlights of which belonged to Pierre Guerre, a native of Marseille. He donated his collection of 87 masks and sculptures, mostly from West Africa, the most famous of which are the Marka masks from Mali and the three Fang reliquaries from Gabon.

Musée des Arts d'Afrique et d'Océanie
The Museum of African and Oceanic Art
293 ave. Daumesnil, 75012 Paris, France
Tel. (33) 1 44 74 84 80 www.afric-network.fr
Mon, Wed-Sun 10am-5.30pm

An encyclopaedic collection covering virtually every region of Africa. West Africa is represented by art from Mali, Burkina, and the Ivory Coast, with masks and sculptures by the Dogon and Bambara tribes from Mali. There is the Do mask with buffalo horns belonging to the Senoufo tribe of the Ivory Coast and the Gouro-Bete Mask from the Tristan Tzara collection with a triangular human face complete with hair and beard made from monkey hair. Twenty of the pieces of Grassland art from the Cameroon are considered to be masterpieces and there are 107 exceptional Nigerian works.

Musée Barbier-Mueller
The Barbier-Mueller Museum
10 rue Jean-Calvin, 1204 Geneva, Switzerland
Tel. (41) 22 3120270
Daily 11am-5pm

The African section is particularly rich in items from Mali, Guinea, Liberia, Burkina-Faso, the Ivory Coast, Gabon, and the French Congo. From Zaire there is gold jewellery of the Akan people.

British Museum
Great Russell Street, London WC1B 3DG, UK
Tel. (44) 20 7636 1555 www.thebritishmuseum.ac.uk
Mon-Sat 10am-5pm, Sun noon-6pm

The newly opened Sainsbury African Galleries display a selection of 600 items from one of the finest collections of African artefacts in the world comprising over 200,000 objects. They encompass both archaeological and contemporary material from northern and sub-Saharan Africa and Madagascar. Highlights include the magnificent brass head of a Yoruba ruler from Ife, Nigeria and Afro-Portuguese ivories of the 15th and 16th centuries, together with selected pieces from the Talbot collection of masks and carvings from southern Nigeria. From the Torday collection of Central Africa are textiles, sculpture, and weaponry.

The Sainsbury African
Galleries
British Museum

Field Museum of Natural History
1400 S Lake Shore Dr, Chicago, Illinois 60605, USA
Tel. (1) 312 922 9410 www.fieldmuseum.org
Daily 9am-5pm

This large collection of African art displays nearly 20,000 objects, not including the 140,000 prehistoric archaeological items. The Madagascar Ethnographic Collection, famous for its outstanding traditional textiles, is the most important and best provenanced collection of Madagascan art in the US. The African collections are strong in art from Angola (especially from the Ovimbundu tribe) and Cameroon, which were mostly gathered in the 1920s. The museum's valuable collection of Benin objects comprises 400 pieces, including wood sculptures, hide fans, and brass and ivory objects.

UCLA Fowler Museum of Cultural History
405 Hilgard Avenue, Los Angeles, California 90095, USA
Tel. (1) 310 825 4361 www.fmch.ucla.edu
Wed-Sun noon-5pm (Thu until 8pm)

The African collection is notable as one of the largest and finest in the world and includes a headdress from Hemba in Zaire, a Bamilke mask from Cameroon, an Ejagham head-dress from Nigeria, a Benin Belt Mask, and a Charm Post from Yaka or Nkanu in Zaire.

Musée de l'Homme
The Museum of Mankind
Palais de Chaillot, 17 place du Trocadéro, 75016 Paris, France
Tel. (33) 1 44 05 72 72 www.mnhn.fr
Mon, Wed-Sun 9.45am-5.15pm

A collection filled with many superb pieces, including a white mask from Gabon, gold jewellery from the Ivory Coast, and magnificent bronzes from Benin. Other exceptional pieces include a horizontal wooden drum in the form of a cow from Yangere and a wooden throne which belonged to the Sultan Bamoum Njoya, made at the beginning of the 20th century by Nji Nkome.

The Horniman Museum and Gardens
100 London Road, London SE23 3PQ, UK
Tel. (44) 20 8699 1872 www.horniman.demon.co.uk
Mon-Sat 10.30am-5.30pm, Sun 2-5.30pm

The African Worlds Gallery offers displays of objects of art from Africa, including a remarkable collection of masks. Among the masterpieces are eight Benin bronze plaques, four Ethiopian crowns of unknown date, and altars from the republics of Benin, Haiti, and Brazil showing Africa's influence on these cultures.

Koninklijk museum voor Midden-Afrika
The Royal Museum of Central Africa
Leuvensesteenweg 13, 3080 Tervuren, Belgium
Tel. (32) 2 7695211 www.africamuseum.be
Tue-Fri 10am-5pm, Sat-Sun 10am-6pm

An extraordinary collection containing over 250,000 pieces, begun in the interest of economics rather then fuelled by curiosity or love. To arouse public interest in the Congo Free State and their exports, King Leopold II arranged a major exhibition in 1897. The result was a new building, the Palais Colonial, containing animals, ethnographic objects, and the principal export products of the Congo. A year later, these collections became a permanent museum. World famous are its well-documented exhibits illustrating the wealth of traditional African culture, many of which were amassed between 1890 and 1940. The Teke, Lega, Luba, and Kuba displays are probably the best in the world.

Liverpool Museum
William Brown Street, Liverpool, Merseyside L3 8EN, UK
Tel. (44) 151 4784399 www.nmgm.org.uk
Mon-Sat 10am-5pm, Sun noon-5pm

Unfortunately, most of the African collection has not been on display since the 1980s despite being one of the most interesting in this category. A quarter of the collection was given to the museum by Arnold Ridyard, an enthusiastic maritime engineer who brought back to Liverpool approximately 2,500 objects at regular intervals from his trips to coastal Africa between 1895 and 1916. Unlike other British collections in the 19th century, the museum holds objects from regions administered by the French, including the French Congo and other colonial powers. The Ridyard collection features a rare collection of Babo figures from Cameroon and a selection of Benin bronzes and ivories, as well as Yoruba and Igbo sculptures.

Haitian voodoo altar (top)
The Horniman Museum and Gardens

Bwa mask from Burkina Faso (above)
The Horniman Museum and Gardens

Kongonese mat woven from palm leaves, 19th century (right)
Náprstkovo muzeum asijských, afrických a amerických kultur

Náprstkovo muzeum asijských, afrických a amerických kultur
Náprstek Museum of Asian, African and American Cultures
Betlémské námesti 1, 110 00 Prague 1, Czech Republic
Tel. (420) 2 22 22 14 16 www.aconet.cz
Tue-Sun 9am-noon, 1.45-5.30pm

This diverse collection of over 15,000 objects was amassed by Emil Holub during his two trips to South Africa, Botswana, Zambia, and Zimbabwe, and includes unique material from a number of southern African tribes, such as the Tswana, Sotho, Lozi, and Matabele. Of significance are the items collected by Antonín Stecker from Libya (then Tripolitania and Abyssinia) including those he received as a gift from the Abyssinian Emperor John IV. There is also a phenomenal resource of over 3,000 priceless photographs taken by Bedrich Machulka who spent his life in Africa as a professional big-game hunter, collector of specimens and safari organizer.

National Museum of African Art

950 Independence Avenue, SW, Washington, DC 20560-0708, USA
Tel. (1) 202 357 4600 www.si.edu
Daily 10am-5.30pm

One of the few museums in the US to be entirely devoted to African art, it now
ranks as one of the best museums in the world. Among the first acquisitions were a
group of Benin court sculptures, an array of seventeen remarkable royal heads, altar
works including a Benin Palace ancestral altar dedicated to Oba Ovonramwen, and eight
wall plaques from the royal palace. Later additions include 1,500 carefully documented
textiles, 85 vessels from Central Africa, and objects from the Ancient city of Kerma in
Nubia. The museum houses the Eliot Elisofon Photographic Archives consisting of
photographic prints and transparencies, together with unedited film footage and documentary films on African art and culture.

Painted wooden Geleda,
Nigeria,
19th century (above)
Národní muzeum
asijských, afrických a
amerických kultur

Sainsbury Centre for Visual Arts

University of East Anglia, Norwich, Norfolk NR4 7TJ, UK
Tel. (44) 1603 592467 www.uea.ac.uk
Tue-Sun 11-5pm

The Sainsbury collection, started in the 1930s, is one of the most remarkable private
collections in Europe, covering modern Western art, African, Pre-Columbian, and
Oceanic art, as well as ancient art from Egypt, the Cyclades, and the Mediterranean. It
was given to the University of East Anglia in 1973 and is now housed in a fine building
designed by Norman Foster. The Sainsbury Centre's African collection shows the dramatic influence of African art on 20th-century European artists. (Nigeria and Zaire are
particularly well represented.) The museum also houses some of the precious bronze
plaques from Benin, and a glorious mid 18th-century Benin armlet.

Sudanese wooden
figures representing
family ancestors,
20th century (below)
Národní muzeum
asijských, afrických a
amerických kultur

Museum für Völkerkunde
Museum of Ethnography

Neue Hofburg, Heldenplatz, 1014 Vienna, Austria
Tel. (43) 1 534300 www.ethno-museum.ac.at
Mon, Wed-Sun 10am-4pm

Over 37,000 African objects, half of which entered the collection before 1927. Of great
interest are the Afro-Portuguese ivory carvings which came from Archduke Ferdinand
II's 'art cabinet' at Ambras Castle. The museum also owns three salt cellars, horns, and
several 15th- and 16th-century spoons. The chalice-like lidded vessels were used as decorative salt cellars at the Renaissance courts in Europe, manufactured in Africa as commissioned pieces that reflected European models. For many, it will be the internationally
important Benin Bronzes, acquired around the turn of the century, that will warrant a
visit to this museum.

ANCIENT GLASS AND CERAMICS

Musée des Beaux-Arts et d'archéologie
The Museum of Fine Arts and Archaeology

1 place de la Révolution, 25000 Besançon, France
Tel. (33) 3 81 87 80 49
Mon, Wed-Sun 9.30am-noon, 2-8pm

Built in 1694, this is one of the oldest museums in France. The building was completely
renovated between 1967 and 1970 by architect, Louis Miquel, and houses an impressive
collection of Greek, Italian, Etruscan, and Roman antiquities featuring items brought

back from Italy by collector, Pierre-Adrien Paris. It contains an ancient Greek ceramic collection representing all the major styles and includes a piece attributed to Master Chairippos (early 5th century BC). There are also early vases with white bases believed to be from Corinthe.

Bristol City Museum and Art Gallery
Queen's Road, Bristol, BS8 1RL, UK
Tel. (44) 117 922 3571 www.bristol-city.gov.uk
Daily 10am-5pm

Holds the entire collection of ancient glass assembled by James Bomford representing the various techniques employed in early glass making and dating from around 1500BC-AD500. Outstanding objects include a Mesopotamian pendant from Nuzi (c.1500BC), which is an example of an exceptionally early glass object. Glorious too is the rare trulla; a free-blown wine ladle in cobalt blue and opaque white, it is an extremely rare form of Roman vessel, with few recorded parallels.

Museo civico archeologico
The City Museum of Archeology
Via dell'Archiginnasio 2, 40124 Bologna, Italy
Tel. (39) 051 233849 www.comune.bologna.it
Tue-Sat 9am-6.30pm, Sun & public holidays 9am-6.30pm

This museum owns a priceless collection of Roman glass as well as numerous objects dating from pre-Roman times. The Bolognese exhibition illustrates the evolution of glass manufacturing techniques. There is a selection of everyday and ornamental objects from the Egyptian and Roman collections (dating from the 14th century BC to the 4th century AD). The complex technique of cameo glass is illustrated by the magnificent panel representing Arianna and scenes from the Dionysiac mysteries, which comes from the Pompei domus by Fabio Rufo as an exceptional loan from the Naples National Archaeological Museum.

Amphora showing eleven dancing figures worshipping Dionysus, Rhodos, mid 6th century BC
Lindenau-Museum

The Corning Museum of Glass
One Museum Way, Corning, New York 14830, USA
Tel. (1) 607 974 8274 www.cmog.org
Daily 9am-5pm (Aug 9am-8pm)

This encyclopaedic collection exceeds 30,000 pieces from ancient Mesopotamia to the present day. Glass from early civilizations includes objects from Mesopotamia, Egypt, the Roman Empire, and the Islamic Near East. The collection of glass from the Roman Empire is especially impressive as it includes the only Roman *Cage Cup* in the Americas (a hanging lamp, c. AD300); *The Morgan Cup*, which is the only complete Roman cameo vessel known (c. AD1-50); and the unique *Disch Kantharos*, an almost complete Roman gold glass vessel. The collection of Islamic cut vessels is the best in the US and rivals those in Europe, including as it does *The Corning Ewer* (c. AD1000), and the *Falcon and Ibex bowl*. There are also several enamelled and gilded pieces from Syria (c. 1350-1400).

Ermitazh
The Hermitage
Dvortsovskaia naberezhnaia 34-36, 191065 Saint Petersburg, The Russian Federation
Tel. (7) 812 1109079 www.hermitage.ru
Tue-Sat 10.30am-6pm, Sun 10.30am-5pm

The collection of ancient ceramics here boasts 15,000 ancient Greek, Etruscan, and Roman vases and is given pride of place in the Twenty-Columned Hall which was inspired by Greek temples. Etruscan ceramics illustrate the influence of Greek tradition on pre-Roman Italy. The *Queen of the Vases*, a black-lacquered hydria from Cumae (4th

century BC), which depicts a procession of wild beasts and various gods and deities, is only one of the numerous masterpieces. The collection of Greek vases is unique, particularly the Attic black-figure examples. Many famous artists contribute to the excellent quality of the collection: Amasis, Epiktetos, Duris, Euphronios, and Keophon, among others. The collection gathers examples from Classical Greece to the Black Sea coast.

Ethnikó arkhaiologikó mouseío
The National Archaeological Museum
Odós Tosítsa 1, 10682 Athens, Greece
Tel. (30) 1 8217717
Summer: Mon 12.30-7pm, Tue-Sun 8am-7pm
Winter: Mon 10.30am-5pm, Tue-Sun 8.30am-3pm

The examples of Greek ceramics illustrate ceramic development through products found during excavations in Greece, whereas many of the most beautiful examples of 5th- and 6th-century vases in other museums were found in the magnificent tombs of rich Etruscan nobles. The museum's vase collection is particularly important due to its geometric vases of the 7th century from Vari, and vases of the Lekythos type.

Piece of mosaic glass with the bird Isis representing the god, Thot (top)
Allard Pierson Museum

Kelsey Museum of Archaeology
University of Michigan, 434 South State Street, Ann Arbor, Michigan 48109, USA
Tel. (1) 734 764 9304, www.umich.edu
Tue-Fri 9am-4pm, Sat-Sun 1-4pm

Terracotta figurine of woman playing the tambourine, c. 350BC (above)
Allard Pierson Museum

Thanks to controlled excavations in Egypt (Dime and Karanis), Syria, Palestine (Sepphoris), and Iraq (Seleucia-on-the-Tigris), this remarkable collection of Hellenistic, Roman, and Islamic glass is especially noteworthy for its Hellenistic and Roman glass pieces from Karanis in the Fayoum.

Amphora showing Greek hero Aias carrying Achilles from battle, and the Athenian hero, Theseus fighting with the bull-headed Minotaur
Lindenau-Museum

Lindenau-Museum
Gabelentzstrasse 5, 04600 Altenburg, Germany
Tel. (49) 3447 2510
Tue-Sun 10am-6pm

The museum was founded by the Saxon-Thuringian statesman, scientist and art collector, Bernhard August von Lindenau. Apart from works of art from the 19th and 20th centuries, the museum contains a selection of 600 antique ceramics – mainly Greek and Etruscan vases from the 7th to the 2nd century BC. One of the finest items is a Corinthian Alabastron from the 7th century BC decorated with animal motifs.

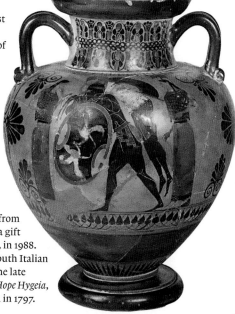

Los Angeles County Museum of Art (LACMA)
5905 Wiltshire Boulevard, Los Angeles, California 90036, USA
Tel. (1) 323 857 6000 www.lacma.org
Mon, Tue, Thu noon-8pm, Fri noon-9pm,
Sat-Sun 11am-8pm

The museum's outstanding holdings of ancient glass from the Eastern Mediterranean were greatly enhanced by a gift from museum trustee, Hans Cohn and his wife, Varya, in 1988. The majority of Roman marble sculpture, Attic and South Italian vases were gifts of William Randolph Hearst during the late 1940s. Two superb examples are the *Hope Athena* and *Hope Hygeia*, both 2nd-century AD Roman works excavated at Ostia in 1797.

19

Panathenaic amphora, late 5th century BC
Musée Antoine Vivenel

Other notable areas are Cypriot pottery, Greek and Roman metalwork, and ceramics from the Cohn collection, as well as examples of Greek, Roman, Etruscan, and Celtic jewellery.

Musée du Louvre
The Louvre
Palais du Louvre, 34-36 quai du Louvre, 75001 Paris, France
Tel. (33) 1 40 20 53 17 www.louvre.fr
Mon, Wed 9am-9.15pm, Thu-Sun 9am-5.30pm

The collection of Greek vases at the Louvre is the richest, most prestigious, and diverse collection illustrating this ancient art form. Two key collections in this area are the 2,000 Greek vases donated by Antoine Durand in 1825 and that of the Marquess Campana, acquired by Napoleon III in 1861. Campana sponsored many excavations in Etruscan funerary sites, in particular the necropolis of Cerveteri. Vases acquired by the museum in the 19th and 20th centuries include the exceptional Attic cup in red figures, which was decorated by the Brygos painter with scenes from the destruction of Troy, and the Milo Amphora, whose gigantomachia was probably inspired by the shield of Athenas Parthenos by Phidias.

Museo Giovanni F. Mariani del Vetro e della Bottiglia
The Giovanni F. Mariani Museum of Glass and Wine
Castello Poggio alle Mura, 53024 St. Angelo Scalo, Montalcino, Italy
Tel. (39) 0577 81 60 01 www.castellobanfi.com
Summer: daily 10am-7pm. Winter: daily 10am-6pm

The displays reflect periods of glass making from the 15th century BC to the present day. Exhibited in six rooms in the west wing of the fortress is the evolution of this art from the ancient Egyptians to the Phoenicians, from Assyrian-Babylonians to Imperial Rome, and from Venetian art to modern day. The museum's most significant display is of ancient Roman glassware which is generally considered to be among the most comprehensive collection in the world of ampules, plates, goblets, and pitchers.

Museo Martini di Storia dell' Enologia
Martini Museum of the History of Oenologia
Frazione Pessione, piazza Luigi Rossi, 1, 10023 Chieri, Italy
Tel. (39) 011 94191
Wed-Fri 2-5pm, Sat-Sun 9am-noon, 2-5pm

A fine collection of Attic vases and other ancient pottery. The vast Roman amphora used for storing wine is truly impressive, while the krater in the red-figure style attributed to the Painter of Bologna from Apulia (360-345BC) is the essence of sophistication.

The Metropolitan Museum of Art
1000 Fifth Avenue, 82nd Street, New York, New York 10028 , USA
Tel. (1) 212 535 7710 www.metmuseum.org
Tue-Thu, Sun 9.30am-5.30pm, Fri, Sat 9.30am-9pm

The museum houses one of the world's most important and diverse collections of Egyptian glass, with 2,000 objects dating from 1500 BC to the 4th century AD. The early objects come from the museum's expeditions to Malkata and Lisht, as well as from the royal tombs at Thebes. The Greek and Roman Glass collection is one of the most comprehensive in the world. The collection of Luigi Palma di Cesnola, purchased by the museum in 1874, provided the museum with 1,200 pieces. The collection was also enriched with the gift by Henry G. Marquand in 1881 of a fine collection of French glass assembled by Jules Charvet. Not to be outdone are the Bothmer Galleries, devoted primarily to Attic black-figure and red-figure vase painting.

Musée municipal
City Museum
32 rue Georges Ermant, 02000 Laon, France
Tel. (33) 3 23 20 19 87 www.perso.wanadoo.fr
Oct-Mar: Mon, Wed-Sun 10am-noon, 2-5pm. Apr-Sep: Mon, Wed-Sun 10am-noon, 2-6pm

This museum houses the best collection of Greek vases in France after the Louvre. It was assembled in the 19th century by the son of a local manufacturer, Paul Marguerite de la Charlonie. Objects have been meticulously chosen to present a complete history of Greek art and the result is astonishing. It includes 600 Greek vases as well as Hellenistic figurines. Highlights of the collection include the group of Corinthian vases, a large black- figure canthara, and the amphora by Fikellura of Rhodes (6th century BC).

Attic lecythus, c. 480BC
(above)
Musée Antoine Vivenel

Attic psykter, c. 500BC
(below)
Musée Antoine Vivenel

The Newark Museum
49 Washington Street, Newark, New Jersey 07101, USA
Tel. (1) 973 596 6550 www.newarkmuseum.org
Wed-Sun noon-5pm (Thu until 8.30pm)

The Classical Collections contain a remarkable array of ancient glass amassed during the 1920s by the New Jersey collector, Eugene Schaefer. Consisting of 1,000 pieces, the collection illustrates glass making from 1500BC to AD1000 and contains vessels, fragments and glass jewellery. The earliest pieces are from New Kingdom Egypt and the Ancient Near East. There is an extensive range of Greek core formed and moulded glass from the 6th-1st centuries BC, and a comprehensive assortment of Roman and late-antique glass of all types. Highlights include an Ennion cup from Sidon or North Italy (c. AD50-75), a unique Egyptian pomegranate flask from the 12th century BC, a broad selection of all types of blown and mould-blown glass from the Eastern Mediterranean region, and a representative selection of Islamic glass.

Allard Pierson Museum
Oude Turfmarkt 127, 1012 GC Amsterdam, The Netherlands
Tel. (31) 20 5252556 www.uba.uva.nl
Tue-Fri 10am-5pm, Sat-Sun 1-5pm

The Greek vase collections consist of 1,000 examples along with 1,650 sherds. A large number of vases were brought together at the beginning of the 19th century by C.W. Lunsingh Scheurleer. A notable recent acquisition is a kylix decorated with the seated god Apollo playing the kithara, a stringed instrument (c. 440-430BC).

Musée Pincé
Pincé Museum
32 bis rue Lenepveu, 49100 Angers, France
Tel. (33) 2 41 88 94 27
Mid Jun-mid Sep: daily 9am-6.30pm
Mid Sep-mid Jun: Tue-Sun 10am-noon, 2-6pm

Among the Greek, Roman, and Etruscan antiquities there is an outstanding collection of Greek vases in geometrical style with black and red figures, together with amphoras.

Museum of Reading
Blagrave Street, Reading, RG1 1QH, UK
Tel. (44) 118 939 9800
www.readingmuseum.org.uk
Tue-Sat 10am-4pm (Thu until 7pm), Sun 11am-4pm

The Silchester Annexe focuses on the Roman pottery discovered at the site and is located next to the main Silchester Gallery. Approximately 200 pieces are displayed in open storage, allowing the visitor to study the variety and beauty of Roman and Romano-British pottery.

Attic bowl, c. 470BC
Musée Antoine Vivenel

Römisch-Germanisches Museum
The Roman-Germanic Museum
Roncalliplatz 4, 50667 Cologne, Germany
Tel. (49) 221 221 2 4438 www.museenkoeln.de
Tue-Sun 10am-5pm

Glasshouses were in operation in Cologne as early as the middle of the 1st century BC. This collection of ancient glassware is unrivalled and includes cameo vessels, discs and plates, together with bottles decorated with coils dating from the 2nd century AD. Highlights include the unique colourful diatreta (4th century AD) which illustrate well why Cologne glass was so coveted throughout Europe. The diatretum technique was the tour de force of Roman glass making. It consisted of a blank vessel which cut back to reveal a complex design connected only by narrow reserve struts to the remaining solid wall. One type of diatretum found almost exclusively in the Rhineland was the cage cup variety carved as a lace network around the exterior of the vessel.

Royal Ontario Museum - University of Toronto
100 Queen's Park, Toronto, Ontario M5S 2C6, Canada
Tel. (1) 416 586 5549 www.rom.on.ca
Mon-Sat 10am-6pm (Fri until 9.30pm), Sun 11am-6pm

The museum boasts the remarkable Sturge collection of Greek vases, including a magnificent black-figured amphora showing on one side a four-horse chariot and on the other the combat between Ajax and Hector (6th century BC). The museum also displays a large collection of archaic Cypriot sculpture and figurines.

Toledo Museum of Art
2445 Monroe Street at Scottwood Avenue, Toledo, Ohio 43620, USA
Tel. (1) 419 255 8000 www.toledomuseum.org
Tue-Sat 10am-4pm (Fri until 10pm), Sun 11am-5pm

This collection was founded on one of the most significant and comprehensive private collections of ancient glass ever assembled. When Edward Drummond Libbey transferred his glass company from Cambridge, Massachusetts, to Toledo he bought the collection of ancient and Islamic glass of the New York financier, Thomas E. H. Curtis, and presented it to the museum. In addition to Libbey's other acquisitions, the museum continued to enrich its ancient glass collection, and significant donations in the 1960s and 1970s enabled the museum to put on display a large majority of its exhibits and to appoint the acclaimed scholar, David F. Grose, as its first Curator of Glass in 1976.

Musée Vendéen
The Vendée Museum
Place du 137e Régiment d'Infanterie, 85200 Fontenay-le-Comte, France
Tel. (33) 2 51 69 31 31,
Mid Jun-mid Sep: Tue-Fri 10am-noon, 2-6pm, Sat-Sun 2-6pm
Mid Sep-mid Jun: Wed-Sun 2-6pm

This provincial museum, founded in 1875 thanks to the donation of a local aristocrat, houses one of the finest collections of Roman glassware in France. The objects were found in two different tombs and include some remarkable examples of glass production imports from the Germanic area.

Musée du Verre
The Glass Museum
Quai de Maastricht 13, Liège 4000, Belgium
Tel. (32) 4 2219404
Mon, Thu 2-5pm, Wed, Fri, Sat 10am-1pm

The glass collection covers the universal history of glass making and is widely
acknowledged to be one of the best in the world thanks to the acquisition in 1952 of
Armand Baar's remarkable collection. It features 1,800 pieces of ancient glass, some of
them from famous collections like Spitzer or Rothschild. Egyptian glass is well represented with glass from Pharaonic times but there is also an Alexandrian production
on display. Roman glass is illustrated with millefiori from the Mediterranean as well
as Gallic/ Gaulish glass. In the latter category, there is a rare glass service which was
found in a tumulus tomb near Vervoz in Belgium.

Inside of decorated drinking cup showing Apollo
playing the lyre, Greece,
c. 440BC (above)
Allard Pierson Museum

Goblets with appliqué
decoration and blue and
white moulded shells,
Rhenan production, 3rd-
4th century, found in
Bouillé-Courdault (left)
Musée Vendéen

Shell-shaped flask, 2nd
century, found in Bouillé-
Courdault (far left)
Musée Vendéen

Musée Antoine Vivenel
Antoine Vivenel Museum
2 rue d'Austerlitz, 60200 Compiègne, France
Tel. (33) 3 44 20 26 04
Apr-Oct: 9am-noon, 2-6pm. Nov-Mar: daily 9am-noon, 2-5pm. Closed Sun & Mon am

Antoine Vivenel, a building contractor and architect, devoted his wealth to the acquisition of art objects that he donated to the city of Compiègne in 1843. His aim was to create a research museum where students could study ancient and decorative arts. He nevertheless gathered a remarkable collection of 250 Greek vases, including several pieces
uncovered during excavations that had been commissioned by Lucien Bonaparte, Prince
of Canino, in the necropolis of the ancient Vulci. The collection of vases includes a
Corinthian olpe (late 7th century BC); pieces with red figures such as a psyker, lecytha,
and cratera of various shapes; and three beautiful panathenaic amphoras with black
figures. There are also Etruscan bowls in Bucchero style (6th-5th century BC).

ANCIENT MOSAICS AND WALL PAINTINGS

Museo archeologico nazionale
The National Archaeological Museum
Via Museo 19, 80135 Naples, Italy
Tel. (39) 081 440166
Mon, Wed-Fri 9am-7.30pm, Sat 9am-midnight, Sun 9am-8pm

The museum houses an enormously rich collection of Roman antiquities, mosaics, and wall paintings acquired from excavations in Pompeii and Herculaneum and from the collections of the Farnese family. From still life to mythological representations, the paintings and mosaics in the museum give you an insight into the surroundings of the wealthy Romans, as well as their intellectual and spiritual background.

Museo archeologico nazionale di Paestum
The National Archaeological Museum of Paestum
Magna Grecia, 84047 Capaccio, Italy
Tel. (39) 0828 811023
Oct-early Jul: daily 9am-7pm. Early Jul-Sep: daily 9am-10pm

Central roundel from the *Cupid on a Dolphin* mosaic, mid 2nd century BC *Fishbourne Roman Palace and Gardens*

Most impressive is the museum's collection of wall paintings, especially those from the Tomb of the Diver. The tomb was discovered in 1968 at Tempa del Prete and was dated as 480BC. Painting was the only Greek art form for which almost no evidence existed, until this extraordinary discovery. The museum also displays around 100 other paintings dating from 380-300BC, including paintings by the Lucanians of their chariot races.

Musée archéologique
The Archaeological Museum
Palais des Archevêques, 11100 Narbonne, France
Tel. (33) 4 68 90 30 54
Apr-Sep: daily 9.30am-12.15pm, 2-6pm. Oct-Mar: Tue-Sun 10am-noon, 2-5pm

Narbonne is the oldest town in the south west of France. Founded as Narbo Martius by the Romans in the 2nd century BC, it became the capital of Southern Gaul. At the time, it was a major port although it now lies some 20 km from the sea. Although there are virtually no Roman remains above ground, there seems to be an endless supply of fragments. The museum is housed in the Archbishop's Palace and has, apart from a large collection of statuary and pottery, several beautiful examples of magnificent, richly coloured Roman wall paintings and mosaics recovered from excavations in the city.

Arkhaiologikó mouseío
The Archaeological Museum
Odós Xanthoudidou 1, 712 02, Heraklion, Crete, Greece
Tel. (30) 81 22 60 92
Summer: Mon 12.30-7pm, Tue-Sun 8am-7pm. Winter: Tue-Sun 8.30am-5pm

Three rooms are devoted to the wall paintings uncovered in the palaces at Knossos and Ayia Triada, and the megara of Amnisos, Tylissos and Pseira. It seems that during the Minoan period Crete saw the construction of huge palatial complexes, of which the Palace of Knossos is the best restored thanks to Sir Arthur Evans. These wall paintings constitute one of the most impressive forms of Minoan art in the famous fresco from Knossos, known as *La Parisienne*. Wall paintings such as the dolphin fresco from the Queen's Megaron in Knossos, the white lilies and red irises from Amnisos, and the intriguing bull-leapers from Knossos challenge the common idea that antiquity is characterized by cold, marble surroundings.

Il Museo della Ceramica 'Manlio Trucco'
The Manlio Trucco Ceramics Museum
Villa Trucco, corso Ferrari, 191, 17011 Albisola Superiore, Italy
Tel. (39) 019 482741 www.comune.albisola-superiore.sv.it
Mon-Sat 10am-noon, Sun by appt. only

Apart from a fine ceramic and maiolica collection, the museum also contains the Schiappapietra Collection, displaying objects from the excavation of the Roman villa, Alba Docilia. The exhibition shows fragments of painted and decorated plaster as well as black and white tessera mosaics and frescoes. Don't miss the torso of a marble statuette that was found in a wall of the San Pietro Church in Albisola.

Seahorse from the *Cupid on a Dolphin* mosaic
Fishbourne Roman Palace and Gardens

Dominikanermuseum Rottweil
The Dominican Museum of Rottweil
Am Kriegsdamm 4, 78617 Rottweil, Germany
Tel. (49) 741 494330 www.uni-tuebingen.de
Tue-Sun 10am-1pm, 2-5pm

The museum opened in 1992 and offers an insight into the rich history of the Roman town, Arae Flaviae. The first excavation in Rottweil was organized in 1784 by Johann Babtist Hofer who found the *Sol Mosaic*. In 1834, the 2nd-century AD *Orpheus Mosaic* was uncovered. Composed of 570,000 small stones, it depicts Orpheus playing his lyre to an array of birds and beasts. The museum, which is located in the Dominican Forum, contains 24 showcases of the most recent finds from the excavations at Arae Flaviae.

Fishbourne Roman Palace and Gardens
Salthill Road, Fishbourne, Chichester, Sussex PO19 3QR, UK
Tel. (44) 1243 785859 www.sussexpast.co.uk
Feb-mid Dec: daily 10am-4pm. Times may vary, please call for details.

Not only is this the largest collection of in-situ mosaic floors in Britain, but some of them, laid when the Palace was constructed around AD75-80, are also among the oldest in Britain. Originally containing over 100 rooms, most of which had mosaic floors, the Palace was the royal seat of the local British tribe, the Atrebates. Although not all are displayed, what can be seen is a remarkable sequence of mosaics, from the earliest ones in black geometric patterns to the later ones of the early 2nd and 3rd centuries consisting of polychrome tesserae.

Hotel Villa Real
Plaza de las Cortes 10, 28014 Madrid, Spain
Tel. (34) 91 4203767

Border of polichrome mosaic with Horn of Plenty motif
1st-3rd century AD
Hotel Villa Real

Designed to embody the splendour of 19th-century Spanish classical architecture, this beautiful hotel also houses a magnificent collection of 3rd-century AD Roman mosaics, mainly originating from Asia Minor. Arranged individually or in more complex combinations, mosaics with geometrical motifs largely predominate. However, there is also a fine selection of figurative representations, such as one depicting two people at a banquet, as well as mosaics of animals, floral motifs, and the 'horn of plenty'.

Mosaïques romaines de Boscéaz
The Boscéaz Roman Mosaics
Boscéaz, 1350 Orbe, Switzerland
Tel. (41) 24 441 52 66
Apr-Oct: Mon-Fri 9am-noon, 1.30-5pm, Sat-Sun & public holidays 1.30-5pm

Here are an exceptional and rare group of mosaics uncovered in the northern Alps near the small city of Orbe. The fine mosaics, which are on display in-situ in four pavilions, belonged to a rich 2nd-century AD Roman villa and depict famous mythological scenes such as Theseus and the Minotaur. There is also a group of medallions representing the seven planets after which the days of the week were named in Latin.

Musée national du Bardo
The National Museum of Bardo
2000 Le Bardo, Tunisia
Tel. (216) 1513 842
Summer: Tue-Sun 9am-5pm. Winter: Tue-Sun 9.30am-4.30pm

Tunisia has one of the finest collections of mosaics in the world and the majority of them can be seen here in this former Moorish palace. The Roman mosaics date from the 3rd and 4th centuries and are classified by regions including Sousse, Carthage, Dougga, and Bulla Regia. The El Jem Room contains a mosaic of the *Triumph of Baccus* and the exquisite *Nine Muses*. On the first floor there is a real gem – a 3rd century mosaic of the poet Virgil, possibly the only known representation of this Augustan figure. In addition to the mosaics there are statues and amphora found on a shipwreck off the coast in 1907, as well as a collection of Islamic art.

Museo nazionale romano - Palazzo Massimo alle Terme
The Roman National Museum - Maximum Palace at the Baths
Largo di Villa Peretti 1, 00185 Rome, Italy
Tel. (39) 06 48903500
Tue-Sat 9am-10pm, Sun 9am-8pm

The Palazzo holds collections of ancient Roman works of art, coins, and jewellery belonging to the National Roman Museum. Items deserving special mention are the frescoes and stucco-designs from a Roman villa found on the grounds of the villa Farnesina on the via Lungara, dating from the early 1st century AD. Equally outstanding is the barrel-vaulted chamber containing the frescoes from an underground room of Livia's villa at Prima Porta, which includes one of the best conserved illustrations of an ancient Roman garden.

Museu nacional arqueològic de Tarragona
National Archaeological Museum of Tarragona
Plaça del Rei, 5, 43003 Tarragona, Spain
Tel. (34) 977 23 62 09 www.mnat.es
Oct-May: Tue-Sat 10am-1.30pm, 4-7pm, Sun & public holidays 10am-2pm. Jun-Sep: Tue-Sat 10am-8pm, Sun & public holidays 10am-2pm

The museum came into existence during the first half of the 19th century, making it the oldest museum of its kind in Catalonia. Most of its contents have been recovered in the last century as a consequence of the building of the modern port and of the city's extraordinary urban growth. The mosaics come mainly from Roman dwellings in the area known as the Pedrera del Port (the Port Quarry). Remarkable is the *Mosaic of the Fish of La Pineda* depicting 47 marine species. It was discovered in 1955 in the remains of a Roman villa in La Pineda.

Mouseío proistorikés théras
Museum of Prehistoric Thera
Phira 847 00, Cyclades, Greece
Tel. (30) 286 23 217
Tue-Sun 8.30am-3pm

In the 1960s the famous, extremely well-preserved Minoan site was discovered on the Akrotiri of Thera, uncovering some of the most remarkable ancient wall paintings in Europe. They show a wide range of compositions depicting everyday life, ritual ceremony, flora and fauna, as well as decorative patterns of surprising colour and creative form reflecting the heyday of the city in the Bronze Age. Four wall-paintings are displayed in this new museum, while others are at the National Archaeological Museum, Athens, or awaiting a suitable location.

The city of Ravenna
Ravenna, Italy

The late Roman mosaics of Ravenna are a must for any mosaic enthusiast, in particular the mosaics of San Vitale, the Tomb of Galla Placidia and Sant' Appolinare Nuovo (lit every Friday night). The most beautiful mosaics can be seen in the Mausoleo di Galla Placidia (Tomb of Galla Placidia, c. AD450), Battistero Neoniano, and in San Appolinare Nuovo.

Museum of Reading
Blagrave Street, Reading, RG1 1QH, UK
Tel. (44) 118 939 9800
www.readingmuseum.org.uk
Tue-Sat 10am-4pm (Thu until 7pm), Sun & public holidays 11am-4pm

Ten miles south west of Reading was the Roman town of Calleva Atrebatum at Silchester in Hampshire. The ruins of this important early Romano-British site were undisturbed until they were excavated in the 1860s. Thirteen mosaic pavements from the excavations are on display in the naturally-lit atrium of the museum.

Rheinisches Landesmuseum Trier
The Rhenish Regional Museum of Trier
Weimarer Allee 1, 54290 Trier, Germany
Tel. (49) 651 97740 www.uni-trier.de
Tue-Fri 9.30am-5pm, Sat- Sun 10.30am-5pm

Two thirds of all Roman mosaics in Germany come from Trier and the surrounding area, and are all in this museum. They demonstrate the remarkable skills of the mosaic workshops on the Rhine and Mosel from the middle of the 1st century AD. The mosaics from the 2nd century AD, when Trier became the capital of the province, are impressive, as well as the later ones, when it was one of the imperial residences of the late Roman Empire.

Römisch-Germanisches Museum
The Roman-Germanic Museum
Roncalliplatz 4, 50667 Cologne, Germany
Tel. (49) 221 221 2 4438 www.museenkoeln.de
Tue-Sun 10am-5pm

Geometrical mosaic
(polichrome tessera),
4th century AD (above)
Hotel Villa Real

Roman country house
wall painting, Trier,
c. AD200 (below)
*Rheinisches Landesmuseum
Trier*

The museum's displays reveal the past prosperity of this former Roman colony. Built on the remains of a Roman villa, the museum displays a 75-metre-square ceramic and glass mosaic made from approximately 1.5 million tiny tessera, which dates back to AD220-230. Its central picture depicts a young, drunken Dionysus leaning on a satyr. Don't miss the outstanding swastika mosaic, as well as the *Philosophers' Mosaic* which represents the Seven Sages of Greece.

Monnus mosaic with Muses, poets and months of the year personified, Trier, c. AD300 Rheinisches Landesmuseum Trier

Musées royaux d'Art et d'Histoire
The Royal Museums of Art and History
10 parc du Cinquantenaire, 1000 Brussels, Belgium
Tel. (32) 2 7417211   www.kmkg-mrah.be
Tue-Fri 9.30am-5pm, Sat-Sun 10am-5pm

The Salle d'Apamée houses one of the world's finest mosaics, found in 1935 at Apamea inside the remains of a building thought to have been the palace of the governor of the Roman province of Second Syria. The *Grande Chasse* mosaic depicts a hunting scene and dates from the second half of the 5th century AD. Its technique has been compared to the mosaics uncovered in the Byzantine Emperors' Palace in Constantinopolis.

Verulamium Museum
St Michaels, St Albans, Hertfordshire AL3 4SW, UK
Tel. (44) 1727 751 810
Mon-Sat 10am-5.30pm, Sun 2-5.30pm

These considerable collections concentrate on the material excavated from the Roman town of Verulamium. The third largest in Britain, it is one of the few Roman towns where the geographic spread of the town can be dated. Verulamium has one of the finest collections of artefacts relating to daily life on display in Britain. Particularly notable are the mosaics and wall paintings. The mosaics were mostly found in the Wheeler and Frere excavations and range from the 2nd century AD (when mosaic-laying was at its height in the town) to the end of the 4th century. The wall paintings on display are almost exclusively from the Frere excavations. These were originally painted on a lime-based plaster while still wet, allowing limewater in the plaster to rise to the surface to form a translucent protective layer of calcium carbonate over the painting. The technique also keeps the colours fast and bright, meaning that the preserved sections at Verulamium are still as vibrant as when first applied.

Worcester Art Museum
55 Salisbury Street, Worcester, Massachusetts 01609, USA
Tel. (1) 508 799 4406   www.worcesterart.org
Wed-Fri, Sun 11am-5pm, Sat 10am-5pm

The mosaic collections rank among the most significant in the world. They come from the once flourishing city of Antioch, also known as the Athens of the Near East, founded in 300BC. The city was destroyed by earthquakes and it was not until excavations in the 1930s that the discovery was made. The collection dates from AD120-520 and is of the highest quality found anywhere in the Mediterranean.

ANCIENT NEAR EAST AND CYPRIOT ANTIQUITIES

Allard Pierson Museum
Oude Turfmarkt 127, 1012 GC Amsterdam, The Netherlands
Tel. (31) 20 5252556   www.uba.uva.nl
Tue-Fri 10am-5pm, Sat-Sun 1-5pm

Objects in the collection span across several cultures in the region between Turkey and Iran and include Mesopotamian clay tablets and beautifully carved cylinder seals. Iran is represented by a pottery collection from Amlash (1350-1000BC), together with a substantial collection of gold jewellery set with carnelian and lapis lazuli. The University of Amsterdam conducted excavations in the 1970s in Selenkahiye, a settlement in Syria from 2400-1900BC. A portion of the finds, including terracotta idols, jewellery, and pottery, was allotted by the Syrian authorities to the museum.

Anadolu Medeniyetleri Müzesi
The Museum of Anatolian Civilizations
Mahmud Pasha Bazaar, 06240 Ankara, Turkey
Tel. (90) 312 3243160
Please call for opening times

This small museum is one of the country's best, with collections that rank among the most important in the world. Here there are some of the best Hittite reliefs, Phrygian pottery, Urartian metalwork, and masterpieces of ancient jewellery and glasswork. Pride of place is naturally given to the Hittite civilisation, including reliefs from Karatepe and sculptures showing hunting and domestic scenes. The collection of bronze pieces from the Hatti and the early Bronze Age period, some bearing cosmological symbols, should not be overlooked since they are among the greatest works of art produced in antiquity.

Terracotta statuette of Eros playing the lyre, Asia Minor, 1st century AD
Allard Pierson Museum

Bijbels Museum
The Bible Museum
Herengracht 366-368, 1001 AK Amsterdam, The Netherlands
Tel. (31) 20 6242436 www.bijbelsmuseum.nl
Mon-Sat 10am-5pm, Sun 1-5pm

This is one of the oldest museums in Holland and displays the private collections of Dr. Schouten in two canal houses built in 1662, with ceilings painted by Jacob de Wit. Amid an array of bibles, there are numerous archaeological finds from the Near East, including a Palestinian ceramic vase from Iron II (930-586BC) found at Tell Sichem, north of Jerusalem, as well as everyday objects excavated there. Mesopotamian cuneiform tablets which date King Nebukadnezar (604-562BC) are on display, along with a Dead Sea roll (1st century AD), written in Hebrew and found in caves near Qumran, and a facsimile of the roll of Jesaja.

Portrait of Gudea, King of the Sumerian city of Lagasj, South Iraq, c.2100BC
Rijksmuseum van Oudheden

British Museum
Great Russell Street, London WC1B 3DG, UK
Tel. (44) 20 7636 1555 www.thebritishmuseum.ac.uk
Mon-Sat 10am-5pm, Sun noon-6pm

One of the world's leading collections. Four rooms are devoted to ancient Near Eastern culture. The Early Mesopotamia Gallery displays Sumerian and Babylonian objects, with outstanding pieces of jewellery from the Royal Cemetery of Ur, excavated by Sir Leonard Woolley in the 1920s and 1930s. In the Gallery of later Mesopotamia, Babylonian boundary stones representing kings and astronomical signs are among the prize exhibits, together with a group of clay cylinders inscribed with royal records. Two rooms are devoted to ancient Anatolia and include pottery from prehistoric Turkey and

from the Yortan cemetery, Assyrian merchants' archives on clay tablets, and seals from Kultepe. Cypriot galleries display endless finds, many from excavations carried out by the museum, including those at Enkomi and the sanctuary of Apollo at Idalion.

Cyprus Museum
Museum Avenue, P.O. Box 2024, Nicosia, Cyprus
Tel. (357) 2 302191
Mon-Sat 9am-5pm, Sun 10am-1pm

Faience tile with fragment from the Koran, Iran, first half of 14th century
Náprstkovo muzeum asijských, afrických a amerických kultur

The museum is an exquisite treasure house of Cypriot art specializing in prehistory. The stellar collection of neolithic figurines are reminiscent of the idols of the Cyclades and also of modern art. Cross-shaped figurines, whose high artistic level is remarkable, feature from the Chalcolithic period. An intriguing red and black polished bowl with the rim surrounded by plastic heads of animals and other projections comes from the second phase of the early Bronze Age. Examples of Mycenaean art are equally enchanting, especially the group of votive figurines excavated by the Swedish Cyprus Expedition in 1929 in the village of Ayia Irini. They uncovered an open-air shrine in which were found 2,000 clay votive figurines dating from 625-500BC and ranging from lifesize statues to diminutive statuettes.

Ermitazh
The Hermitage
Dvortsovskaia naberezhnaia 34-36, 191065 Saint Petersburg, Russian Federation
Tel. (7) 812 1109079 www.hermitagemuseum.org
Tue-Sat 10.30am-6pm, Sun 10.30am-5pm

An outstanding collection of items is housed here, including a stone tablet with a pictographic inscription (late 4th to early 3rd millennium BC) from the Sumerian town of Uruk, regarded as one of the most ancient written documents ever to be uncovered. Important, too, are the zoomorphic bronzes from Luristan (2nd millennium BC) and the incredible collection of Iranian jewellery, especially the pieces from the 5th to the 2nd centuries BC, the era of the Achaemenid dynasty.

Eski Sark Eserleri Müzesi
Museum of the Ancient Orient
Osman Hamdi Bey Yokusu, Gülhane, Istanbul, Turkey
Tel. (90) 212 520 77 74 40
Wed, Fri, Sun 9.30am-5pm

Although only a small number of artefacts are on display in this recently re-opened museum, what can be seen is astounding. The collections consist of pre-Islamic works from the Arabian peninsula, Egypt, Mesopotamia, and Anatolia, with most of the particularly fine Mesopotamian collection excavated between the Tigris and the Euphrates before World War I. The Anatolian collection (4000-1000BC) also includes finds from excavations prior to World War I. The Late Chalcolithic Period, Early Bronze Age Hattian Culture, Middle Bronze Age Colony Period settlements, Old Hittite, Hittite Empire, and Late Hittite Kingdoms are all well represented in the collections.

Horn Archaeological Museum – Institute of Archaeology
Andrews University, Berrien Springs, Michigan 49104-0990, USA
Tel. (1) 616 471 3273 www.andrews.edu
Mon-Thu 9am-noon, 2-5pm, Fri 9am-noon, Sat 2-5pm

Donations and current excavation material from Tell Hesban, Tell el-Umeiri, and Tell Jalul in Jordan, as well as Tel Gezer in Israel, make up these collections. Particularly noteworthy are the Cuneiform tablets ranging from the Third dynasty of Ur (*c.* 2100BC) until the Neo-Babylonian Period (*c.* 600BC).

Musée du Louvre
The Louvre
Palais du Louvre, 34-36 quai du Louvre, 75001 Paris, France
Tel.(33) 1 40 20 53 17   www.louvre.fr
Mon, Wed 9am-9.15pm, Thu-Sun 9am-5.30pm

The Department of Oriental Antiquities holds objects dating back to 600BC retracing the history of Mesopotamia, Anatolia and North Syria, Iran, and Levant. The bulk of the collection comes from the Assyrian museum, founded in 1847, with objects collected by French archaeological excavations of the first known Assyrian monuments. The birth of the Mesopotamian civilisations is illustrated by ceramics from Hassuna, Samarra, Halaf, and Obeid. The next great advance, the appearance of writing, is illustrated by clay and limestone tablets bearing cuneiform inscriptions, including the oldest known written documents (*c.* 3300BC) found in the town of Uruk in Sumer, Iraq. There is a remarkable group of objects from Mari, including the treasures from the Ishtar temple (*c.* 2400BC). One of the highlights of the museum is the stele from the reign of Sargon. The Victory Stele of Naram-Sin, whose reign represents the heyday of artistic production in Agade, is also noteworthy. From the first Babylonian dynasty is the so-called Hammurabi's Code, a collection of judicial rulings and one of the greatest examples of Babylonian literature. From the Assyrian civilisation are the spectacular remains from the palace of Sargon II in Khorsabad, discovered by the French consul Paul-Emile Botta in 1843. The collections from Cyprus, Syria, Phoenicia, and Palestine are equally impressive.

Enamel belt buckle with inlaid corals, Turkey, late 19th-early 20th century
Náprstkovo muzeum asijských, afrických a amerických kultur

Terracotta male statue, Merisinaki, Cyprus, *c.*500-475BC
Medelhavsmuseet

Medelhavsmuseet
Museum of Mediterranean Antiquities
Fredsgatan 2, 103 21 Stockholm, Sweden
Tel. (46) 8 5195 5380   www.medelhavsmuseet.se
Tue 11am-8pm, Wed-Fri 11am-4pm, Sat-Sun noon-5pm

Outside Cyprus, this is the next best place to examine Cypriot archaeological material amassed from excavations of 300 rock-cut chamber tombs conducted by Swedish archaeologists. Thousands of sculptures were found in the temples or sanctuaries, as well as coins, jewellery, and objects made of metal, ivory, glass, and stone. A large showcase reminds the visitor of the importance of the rich Cypriot copper mines. Swords and small daggers of red arsenic copper or yellow bronze were found in a necropolis near Lapithos, together with an extensive collection of magnificent red polished pottery. On display is a unique cuirass from the 6th century BC composed of 6,800 iron splints found close to a sanctuary at Idalion. Scholars also come to examine the collection of around 6,000 Cypriot vases, ranging from Chalcolithic to Roman.

The Metropolitan Museum of Art
1000 Fifth Avenue at 82nd Street, New York, New York 10028 , USA
Tel. (1) 212 535 7710   www.metmuseum.org
Tue-Thu, Sun 9.30am-5.30pm, Fri-Sat 9.30am-9pm

The department's collection has been acquired by donation, purchase, and participation in archaeological excavations at sites including Nippur, Nimrud, and Ctesiphon in Iraq; and Hasanlu, Yarim Tepe, and Qasr-i Abu Nasr in Iran. It has also been enriched by long-term loans from other museum collections. Among the most famous pieces in the collection are a gold, lapis lazuli and carnelian headdress discovered on a young female attendant who had been sacrificed in the royal cemetery at Ur in Mesopotamia (*c.* 2600-2500BC); a Hittite silver drinking vessel in the form of a stag from Central Anatolia, dating to the Empire period (*c.* 15th-13th century BC); the imposing glazed

Statuette of a praying
man, limestone, South
Iraq (former Sumeria),
*c.*2600BC
Rijksmuseum van Oudheden

brick lions created to decorate the walls of the street between the Ishtar Gate and the
Festival House in Babylon during the reign of Nebuchadnezzar in the 6th century BC;
and a remarkable and extensive collection of Sasanian silver-gilt vessels. The central
part of the Raymond and Beverly Sackler Gallery for Assyrian Art recreates an audience
hall in the north west Palace of Ashurnasirpal II (883-859BC) at Nimrud in present day
Iraq. The colossal lamassu (or guardian figures) and monumental stone reliefs in this
space are among the most prized objects in the collection. The Cesnola collection comprises works from Cyprus dating from around 2500BC to AD300, focusing on sculpture,
bronze, terracotta, and precious metals.

Michael C. Carlos Museum

Emory University, 571 South Kilgo Street, Atlanta, Georgia 30322, USA
Tel. (1) 404 727 4282 www.cc.emory.edu
Mon-Sat 10am-5pm, Sun noon-5pm.

This comprehensive collection was originally begun in 1920 when William A. Shelton,
an Emory professor, became involved in the American Scientific Mission, one of the
first university expeditions to the Near East. Objects from major sites (Ur, Lagash and
Babylon) were brought back to the US, together with a significant collection of clay
tablets inscribed with cuneiform characters. The collection was further enriched in
the 1950s with the finds uncovered by Dame Kathleen Kenyon in Jericho, as well as
with the objects recovered during Edward A. Link's underwater excavation in the
harbour of Caesarea Maritima, and the donation of a large collection of ancient
lamps by the collector, Ruth Schloessinger.

Morgan Library

29 East 36th Street, New York, New York 10016, USA
Tel. (1) 212 685 0610 www.morganlibrary.org
Tue-Thu 10.30am-5pm, Fri 10.30am-8pm, Sat 10.30am-6pm, Sun noon-6pm

Libraries are not the usual places to find collections of cylinder seals, but this is no
ordinary library. Its founder, Pierpont Morgan, had funds to spread his collecting
interests far and wide. There is an extensive collection of carved semiprecious stones
which trace a continuous artistic sequence of ancient Mesopotamia from the end of the
5th millennium BC to the time of the Persian Empire in the 5th century BC.

Náprstkovo muzeum asijských, afrických a amerických kultur
Náprstek Museum of Asian, African and American Cultures

Betlémské námesti 1, 110 00 Prague 1, Czech Republic
Tel. (420) 2 22 22 14 16 www.aconet.cz
Tue-Sun 9am-noon, 1.45-5.30pm

The ancient Near East collections contain documentation from the Czech excavations
in Syria and Turkey in 1924 and 1925 by Bedrich Hrozn, dating from the second and
first millennium BC. It also features surface Paleolithic surveys from Palestine by
J. Petrbok and an assortment of items from the collection of Bedrich Forman.

Oriental Institute Museum of the University of Chicago

1155 East 58th Street, Chicago, Illinois 60637, USA
Tel. (1) 312 7029520 www.oi.uchicago.edu
Tue, Thu, Sat 10am-4pm, Wed 10am-8.30pm, Sun noon-4pm

The recently opened Persian Gallery displays approximately 1,000 objects dating from
the Archaic Susiana Period (*c.* 6800BC) to the Islamic Period (*c.* AD1000). Half of the gallery
is devoted to artefacts from Persepolis, which thrived from approximately 520-33BC,
and was destroyed by Alexander the Great and his troops. This portion of the gallery
is dominated by a series of colossal sculptures made of polished black limestone,

including the head of a bull that once guarded the entrance to the Hundred-Column Hall, and column capitals in the forms of bulls and composite creatures. In addition to the ceramics, the gallery also displays elaborate bronze and bone votive pins from the isolated mountain shrine at Surkh Dum-i Luri (1000-500BC).

Rijksmuseum van Oudheden
The National Museum of Antiquities
Rapenburg 28, 2301 EC Leiden, The Netherlands
Tel. (31) 71 5163163 www.rmo.nl
Tue-Fri 10am-5pm, Sat-Sun & public holidays noon-5pm

Cylinder-shaped document with cuneiform characters, earthenware, South Iraq (former Mesopotamia), *c.*580BC
Rijksmuseum van Oudheden

The museum offers a wide variety of exhibits from the Near East, especially Iran and Syria. On display are funerary and dedicatory reliefs, ritual statuettes, figurines of priests, and terracottas. The collection of tablets comprises some fine examples of Mesopotamian tablets found in South Iraq, and a Sumeric document in clay from around 2050BC. Another section is dedicated to valuable archaeological finds from present Armenia, including treasures of the famous Urartu civilisations. Artefacts such as jewellery, warfare, and metallurgy from exceptionally rich graves reflect the wealth of these societies from 2300-600BC.

Musées royaux d'Art et d'Histoire
The Royal Museums of Art and History
10 parc du Cinquantenaire, 1000 Brussels, Belgium
Tel. (32) 2 7417211 www.kmkg-mrah.be
Tue-Fri 9.30am-5pm, Sat-Sun 10am-5pm

The exhibits are displayed both in geographical and chronological order, and range from prehistory to the pre-Islamic period. Cyprus and Anatolia are represented by pre-

historic axes, Hacilar vases, Yortan black ceramic, and Urartean bronze belts. Palestinian works include everyday objects as well as ceramics from tombs in Jericho and Lakish and a white marble sarcophagus from Christian times. Statuettes from Syria and Phoenicia, and ceramics from Petra make up the Arab peninsula and there is also a letter from King Ini-Teshub from Karkemish (14th-13th century BC). From Elam there are bronze arms, plates, and architectural items with inscriptions dating back to 3000-2000BC. There is a relief fragment from the Persian capital Persepolis and a collection of cylindrical seals in Achemenid style. The museum also houses one of the most important collections of Luristan bronzes.

Dagger with shaft, Balkans, 19th century
Náprstkovo muzeum asijských, afrických a amerických kultur

Bronze water jug, Iraq, *c.* mid 13th century
Náprstkovo muzeum asijských, afrických a amerických kultur

Semitic Museum
Harvard University, 6 Divinity Avenue, Cambridge, Massachusetts 02138, USA
Tel. (1) 617 495 4631
www.fas.harvard.edu
Mon-Fri 10am-4pm, Sun 1-4pm

The museum, founded in 1889, is home to Harvard's Department of Near

Eastern languages and civilizations and to the University's collection of Near Eastern archaeological artefacts. These collections comprise over 40,000 items, including pottery, cylinder seals, sculpture, coins, and cuneiform tablets. Most are from museum-sponsored excavations in Iraq, Jordan, Israel, Egypt, Cyprus, and Tunisia. They also hold a portion of the famous Cesnola Collection of Cypriot antiquities. The museum is dedicated to the use of these collections for teaching, research, and publication purposes.

The University of Pennsylvania Museum of Archaeology and Anthropology
33rd and Spruce Streets, Philadelphia, Pennsylvania 19104, USA
Tel. (1) 215 8984000 www.upenn.edu
Tue-Sat 10am-4.30pm, Sun 1-5pm

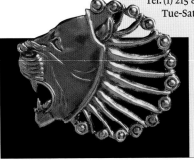

The spectacular discovery excavated by a team of archaeologists headed by Sir Leonard Woolley uncovered some 1,800 burial sites on the west bank of the Euphrates River at the Royal Tombs of Ur in what is now southern Iraq. Most astounding were the tombs of the kings and queens of the city of Ur from the mid 3rd millennium BC, famed in the Bible as the home of Biblical patriarch, Abraham. A gold vessel in the form of an ostrich egg is among the many Sumerian composite art objects in a range of precious and semiprecious materials that rank as amongst the highest masterpieces of Sumerian art.

Gilded silver lion's head,
Iran (former Persia)
c. 400BC
Rijksmuseum van Oudheden

Vorderasiatisches Museum
Ancient Near East Museum
Pergamon Museum, Bodestrasse 1-3, 10178 Berlin, Germany
Tel. (49) 30 209050 www.smb.spk-berlin.de
Tue-Sun 10am-6pm (Thu until 10pm)

This collection ranks alongside those to be found in the Louvre and the British Museum. The main asset is undoubtedly the spectacular reconstruction of part of the Processional Way and the Ishtar Gate of Babylon (named after the divine protectress of Babylon), built by Nebuchadnezzar II (c. 600BC). In the adjoining room are models showing the buildings in context, alongside fragments of earlier construction phases. Other exhibits include the facade of the Temple of Innin from Uruk, the oldest find on show in the museum (15th century BC), as well as the beautiful relief showing a spearbearer, from the palace of the legendary King Darius I in Susa.

EARLY CHRISTIAN AND MEDIEVAL ANTIQUITIES

Musée de l'Arles antique / Institut de Recherche sur la Provence antique
Museum of Ancient Arles / Institute of Ancient Provence Studies
Ave. de la 1ère Division France Libre, 13200 Arles, France
Tel. (33) 4 90 18 88 88
Daily 9am-7pm

The ancient monuments of Arle and its immense archaeological wealth have led UNESCO to make it a world heritage site. The impressive collection of Christian sarcophagi and funerary art in the new museum, which rates only second to the Vatican collections, completes an unforgettable walk along the 'Alyscamps', one of the finest Christian necropolises in Europe. The sarcophagi collection is a highlight and includes the Sarcophagus of Phaedra and Hyppolitus from Attica. Of equal note is the Sarcophagus of Hunting (or the Sarcophagus of the Trinity) which is a masterpiece of early Christian funerary art, adorned with biblical and evangelical scenes and the portrait of the buried couple sculpted in a medallion.

Museo arqueológico de Jerez
The Archeological Museum of Jerez
Plaza del Mercado s/n, 11408 Jerez de la Frontera, Spain
Tel. (34) 956 333316 www.ctv.es
Tue-Fri 10am-2pm, 4-7pm, Sat-Sun 10am-2.30pm. (Mid Jun- mid Aug: Sat-Sun only)

All throughout the Moorish period, Jerez was a city of special importance and even today its medieval configuration still remains evident in its Moorish castle, the 'Alcazaba', the remains of the fortified wall, and many of its streets. The museum displays material from the excavation works in the old part of the city together with architectonic elements and Arabic letterings. One of the most important pieces is a caliphal bottle with epigraphic decoration found in the nearby site of Mesas de Asta.

Museo d'Arte Nazionale d'Abruzzo
The National Museum of Art of the Abruzzi
Castello Conquecentesco, Viale Benedetto Croce, 67100 L'Aquila, Italy
Tel. (39) 0862 64043 www.webaq.it

The small city of L'Aquila boasts the extremely rich Museum of Abruzzo which houses the medieval artistic treasures of this once economically strategic city on the trade route between Naples and Florence. The Madonna and the Child (14th century), formerly in the church of San Silvestro, is one of the museum's numerous masterpieces. Religious art of Abruzzo is well represented by some of the region's finest examples of polychrome wood sculpture and silverwork, as well as Romanesque-Byzantine Madonna icons. One of the greatest treasures here is the splendid embossed and engraved silver processional cross, signed and dated by Nicola da Guardiagrele in 1434.

Augustinermuseum
Museum of the Augustinians
Augustinerplatz 1-3, 79098 Freiburg im Breisgau, Germany
Tel. (49) 761 201 25 21 www.augustinermuseum.de
Daily 10am-5pm

The former Augustinian monastery in Freiburg's Old Town displays a remarkable medieval art collection. Highlights include outstanding examples of 14th-15th century statuary, a Grünewald altarpiece panel depicting the Miracle of the Snow, and the Adelhauser Kreuz, an impressive crucifix from the 14th century. Other notable items include rich goldwork, embroidered and knitted textiles from the Early and Late Middle Ages, and original ornamental sculptures from Freiburg Cathedral.

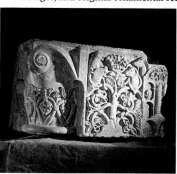

Musée des Augustins
The Museum of the Augustinians
21 rue de Metz, 31000 Toulouse, France
Tel. (33) 5 61 22 21 82 www.augustins.org
Mon, Thu-Sun 10am-6pm, Wed 10am-9pm

The Tree of Life; nook-shaft romanesque detail
Museet i Erkebispegarden

The sumptuous medieval setting of the church and the chapter houses of the old Augustins convent is home to a fine sculpture collection especially rich in medieval pieces, including a collection of exceptional Romanesque capitals from the region. These are mostly mortuary epitaphs which accompany the tombstones, bearing inscriptions which recall the obituary foundations and the foundation stones in chapels, and which originate from the surrounding area of Toulouse.

Bitsantinoú mouseío
The Byzantine Museum
Leofóros Vassilissis Sophias 22, 10675 Athens, Greece
Tel. (30) 1 7237211027
Tue-Sun 8.30am-2pm

The museum's collection, which contains some outstanding pieces, has a pronounced
local character. It includes early Christian works, pieces from the Ilisos basilica, the
remarkable funerary group of Orpheus, the precious objects of the Mytilene Treasure,
examples from the Middle Byzantine period in Greece (8th-12th century) including the
rich collection of marble architectural decorative pieces of the post-Iconoclast period,
and examples from the Frankish occupation and the Palaiologan period (1204-1453). The
museum also houses a comprehensive collection of portative icons, as well as icons dating from after the fall of Constantinople, which were produced in Crete.

Bonnefantenmuseum
Ave. Ceramique 250, 6221 kx Maastricht, The Netherlands
Tel. (31) 43 3290910 www.bonnefanten.nl
Tue-Sun 11am-5pm

This stunning building, designed by Aldo Rossi and completed in 1995, is named
after the museum's former location, the Bonnefanten Monastery, located in the city
centre. Clad partially in zinc with facades in red brick and Irish hardstone, it contains
both contemporary and ancient collections. The important collection of medieval
sculpture includes Maasland wood carvings by the Master of Elsloo and Jan van
Steffeswert. Note, also, The Neutelings Collection of alabaster, wood, Limoges enamels,
and ivory objects dating from the 9th to the 15th centuries.

British Museum
Great Russell Street, London wc1b 3dg, UK
Tel. (44) 20 7636 1555 www.thebritishmuseum.ac.uk
Mon-Sat 10am-5pm, Sun noon-6pm

Some extremely fine ivory objects at the British Museum were acquired as early as the
18th century, including a diptych representing Archangel Michael and the large, early-
medieval panel with subjects from the Gospels. But it was during the 19th century,
with the increasing interest in medieval art, that the largest and most significant
series was acquired – that of William Maskell – whose collection ranged from the 5th
century to his own times and included Early Christian panels (one of which has upon
it the first representations of the Crucifixion), unique medieval and Romanesque
ivories, and a panel by Christoph Angermair.

The Byzantine Fresco Chapel Museum
4011 Yupon at Branard, Houston, Texas 77006, USA
Tel. (1) 713 521 3990 www.menil.org
Wed-Sun 11am-6pm

Intimate in scale (4,000 square feet), the Chapel Museum is the repository in the US for
the only intact Byzantine frescoes in the entire western hemisphere. Dating from the
13th century, they were stolen out of a chapel near Lysi in the Turkish occupied section of

Cyprus and rescued from the thieves by The Menil Foundation. With the approval of their rightful owners, the Church of Cyprus, they have been restored and are on long-term loan.

Museum Catharijneconvent
The Museum of the Catherine Convent
Lange Nieuwstraat 38, Nieuwegracht 63, 3512 LG Utrecht, The Netherlands
Tel. (31) 30 2313835 www.catharijneconvent.nl
Tue-Fri 10am-5pm, Sat-Sun & public holidays 11am-5pm (tours on request)

This museum contains the largest collection of medieval art in the Netherlands, and includes altar pieces, statues, liturgical vestments, reliquaries, and illuminated manuscripts such as the Book of Hours that clearly shows how daily life in the Middle Ages was influenced by Christianity. Concentrate on the ivories and liturgical textile pieces. A jewel is the ivory diptych (*c.* 1375) with scenes from the life of Christ which was made in northern France or Flanders. Find time to take in the Limoges, enamel, and gilded copper reliquary of St Thomas à Becket (*c.* 1190). The death of the martyr is shown on the side of the shrine and behind him an angel appears over the altar. On the lid angels are seen taking his soul to heaven.

The Cloisters
Fort Tryon Park, New York, New York 10040, USA
Tel. (1) 212 535 7710 www.metmuseum.org
Tue-Thu, Sun 9.30am-5.30pm, Fri-Sat 9.30am-9pm

This magical setting overlooking Manhattan is home to one of the greatest medieval collections in the world. The collections' nucleus was originally formed by J. Pierpont Morgan, whose son bequeathed nearly half of his father's collection to the museum. The building incorporates elements from five medieval French cloisters and from other monastic sites in southern France. Several of these reconstructions also feature medieval gardens set according to horticultural information gleaned from medieval treatises. Inside are approximately 5,000 works of art from medieval Europe, dating from about AD800, with particular emphasis on the 12th-15th centuries. There are Burgundian carvings, endless illuminated manuscripts, and a famous set of tapestries known as *The Hunt of the Unicorn*. Particular strengths of the works shown in the main building are early Byzantine and early European tomb decorations, a series of silver plates of the 17th century representing scenes of David, the Antioch Treasure, the Avar hoard, and Byzantine ivory carvings and enamels. Also displayed are later European ivory carvings and sumptuous objects made of precious metals and gems between the 9th-16th century. There are masterpieces of Gothic sculpture and stained glass from key monuments such as the royal abbey of Saint-Denis outside Paris, Notre-Dame in Paris, and Amiens Cathedral.

Dumbarton Oaks
1703 32nd Street, NW, Washington, DC 20007, USA
Tel. (1) 202 339 6410 www.doaks.org
Tue-Sun 2-5pm

The Byzantine collection ranks among the most important in the world. Drawn from the imperial, ecclesiastical, and secular realms, it is comprised mainly of small, luxurious objects (gold, silver, bronze, cloisonné enamel, and ivory), and several illuminated manuscripts. It also includes large-scale materials such as pavement mosaics from Antioch and sculptures from the late Roman and early and middle Byzantine periods, as well as a small but choice collection of textiles and post-Byzantine icons. Although its primary focus is on the Byzantine period proper (4th-15th century) the collection includes several pieces of Western medieval art.

Museet i Erkebispegarden
The Museum in the Archbishop's Palace
Kongsgardsgate 1, 7013 Trondheim, Norway
Tel. (47) 73 53 91 60
Tue-Sat 11am-3pm, Sun noon-4pm (20 Jun-20 Aug: Mon-Sat 10am-5pm,
Sun noon-5pm)

When in 1983 fire ravished the Archbishop's Palace standing adjacent to Trondheim's cathedral and two of its artefact stores, doom and gloom reigned – but not for long. The city's officials heard opportunity knock and subsequently spent the next five years excavating, uncovering an astounding array of some 150,000 objects. Displayed inside the new museum is a selection of these important finds as well as an exceptional group of sculptures from Nidaros Cathedral – in fact, some of the finest sculptures created in Scandinavia in the Middle Ages. Through the course of several hundred years, the Cathedral was also burnt and plundered, requiring sections of it to be torn down and rebuilt. Wagon loads of moulded stonework in a variety of motifs, including dragons with snake-like bodies, which were replaced during the restoration work, constitute the Cathedral's collection of masonry and sculpture, which today comprises some 5,000 objects.

Hedmarksmuseet og Domkirkeodden
The Hedmark Museum at Cathedral Point
Strandveien 100, 2305 Hamar, Norway
Tel. (47) 62 54 27 00 www.hedmarksmuseet.museum.no
Mid May-mid Sep: daily 10am-4pm (mid Jun-mid Aug until
6pm)

Hamarkaupangen was Norway's only inland town in the Middle Ages and an important administrative centre that perished after the Reformation. Now the area is a museum complex covering 110 acres. At its centre are the ruins of a once imposing cathedral completed in 1200 and subsequently destroyed by fire during the Nordic Seven Years Wars (1567) now protected by a fabulous glass structure. Built around the cathedral and the ruined bishop's palace is the museum building containing exhibitions from the Viking and Middle Ages, along with those of later date. Formerly an 18th-century barn, it has been redesigned by Norway's famous architect, Sverre Fehn, to provide a bird's eye view of the ruins, and displays a small fraction of the 11,000 objects recovered from excavations in medieval Hamar.

The Sculpture Collection
(top)
Museet i Erkebispegarden

The Archaeological
Exhibition (above)
Museet i Erkebispegarden

Herzog Anton Ulrich Museum
The Duke Anton Ulrich Museum
Burg Dankwarderode, Burgplatz 4, 38100 Braunswick, Germany
Tel. (49) 531 12250 www.museum-braunschweig.de
Tue-Sun 10am-5pm

Valuable liturgical works include altars, altar fragments, altar utensils, liturgical books and chasubles, and a reliquary of the arm of St Blaise, the patron saint of the cathedral and protector of the Guelphs. A superb example of a medieval codex are the Gospels from the church of St Aegidius. The manuscript contains several miniatures and dates from around 1160-80 whereas the cover, decorated with precious stones, pearls and walrus-tusk reliefs, dates from around 1200. The imperial robes of King Otto IV (13th century) are on display, a fine example of which is one made in the 'opus anglicanum' technique.

Hunt Museum
Custom House, Rutland Street, Limerick, Ireland
Tel. (353) 61 312833 www.ul.ie
Tue-Sat 10am-5pm, Sun 2-5pm

This personal collection of John and Gertrude Hunt includes fine examples of medieval carving in stone, bronze, ivory and wood, medieval ceramics, stained glass, metalwork, textiles, and paintings. The importance of the collection is such that some items are currently on loan to the British Museum and the Victoria and Albert Museum in London. Of particular note are: the Beverley Crosier; an 11th-century carved ivory Crosier head; a 12th-century carving in ivory representing St Thomas à Becket and four knights; a 12th-century leaf from a book of Pericopes, formerly belonging to the Cathedral Treasury in Hildesheim; and a 12th-century stained glass from Bristol Cathedral. The museum also houses a fine collection of crucifix figures in bronze and ivory, including a 12th-century bronze gilt figure formerly owned by the Hohenzollern family.

Runic box, walrus tusk, second half of 8th century
Herzog Anton Ulrich Museum

Janus Pannonius Múzeum, Régészeti Kiállitás
The Janus Pannonius Museum, Archaeological Department
Széchenyi tér 12, 7621 Pécs, Hungary
Tel. (36) 72 312 719
Tue-Sun 10am-4pm

The showpiece of the exhibition constitutes the most significant findings of recent decades in the country. The bronze head of Marcus Aurelius (ruled between AD161-180) is over double the size of a human head and dominates the room. There are vessels found during the excavation of an Old Christian graveyard from the 4th century. Of course, the painted burial vaults have not been moved, but can be seen at their original location. Tombstones and sarcophagi from the 1st and 2nd centuries AD are arranged in the museum's garden. Relics of the period of the great migrations are diverse, ranging from a distorted female skull to Christian circular fibula, from gilded jewellery of barbarians, to bows. Materials from this period include antiquities of the Huns, Germanic people, the Avars, and the Hungarians of the 9th century. The oriental helmet dating from the 9th century is considered to be a unique find in Hungary.

Magyar nemzeti múzeum
The Hungarian National Museum
Múzeum Körút 14-16, 1088 Budapest, Hungary
Tel. (36) 1 3382122 www.origo.hnm.hu
Mid Mar-mid Oct: daily 10am-6pm. Mid Oct-mid Mar: daily 10am-5pm

The museum's showpiece is the Hungarian medieval Coronation Insignia, which constitutes the most important complete set of regalia in the world. Returned in 1978 from the US, where they had been for 33 years, they consist of a crown, a sceptre, an orb, a sword, and a coronation cope. The lower part of the crown is ornamented with precious stones and cloisonné enamel portraits and is an example of the superior quality of the imperial workshop in Constantinople.

Kunstgewerbemuseum
The Museum of Applied Arts
Kulturforum, Matthäikirchplatz 10, 10785 Berlin, Germany
Tel. (49) 30 2662902 www.smb.spk-berlin.de
Tue-Fri 10am-6pm, Sat-Sun 11am-6pm

This is a great collection of arts from the Middle Ages, which includes the famous Welfenschatz, the treasures of the Guelph family, ancestors of England's Hanoverian dynasty. This unique collection of 35 priceless gold and silver reliquaries made between the 11th and 15th centuries includes the celebrated Domed Reliquary in the form of a Byzantine church adorned with ivory carvings and enamelling (1175) and a Byzantine-style portable altar of Eilbertus, made of rock crystal and semiprecious stones (c. 1150).

Liverpool Museum

William Brown Street, Liverpool, Merseyside L3 8EN, UK
Tel. (44) 151 478 4399 www.nmgm.org.uk
Mon-Sat 10am-5pm, Sun noon-5pm

Joseph Mayer gave his collection, including the Fejérváry collection, to the museum in the 1860s, making its collection of ivories one of the best of its kind. The bulk of the collection consists of objects dating from the classical period to medieval times in Europe, along with some fine Asiatic and African ivories. Examples include a beautiful and historically important diptych representing Asclepius and Hygieia, which might represent not the healing gods themselves but an icon of the neo-Platonist philosophy to which the Roman intelligentsia had adhered in the 5th century.

Virgin and Child, polychromed limestone, Lorraine, France, early 14th century
Musée du Louvre

Museum of London

London Wall, London EC2Y 5HN, UK
Tel. (44) 20 7600 3699 www.museumoflondon.org.uk
Tue-Sat 10am-5.50pm, Sun noon-5.50pm

The medieval collection of around 10,000 items is one of the most celebrated elements of the museum's overall holdings due to its breadth, depth and quality. While significant pieces were published in the 1908 Guildhall Museum catalogue, the publication of the London Museum Medieval Catalogue in 1940 broke new ground in establishing medieval archaeology as a subject worthy of study in its own right. It remained the standard reference work for medieval collections for some fifty years and has recently been republished. The collection of medieval pottery is particularly outstanding as are the pewter pilgrim badges recovered from the Thames.

Musée du Louvre
The Louvre

Palais du Louvre, 34-36 quai du Louvre 75001 Paris, France
Tel. (33) 1 40 20 53 17 www.louvre.fr
Mon, Wed 9am-9.15pm, Thu-Sun 9am-5.30pm

One of the most comprehensive museums in the world, showing collections of Western art from the Middle Ages to the mid 19th century and the antique civilizations that have influenced it. Most of this world-leading collection, both for ivories and medieval art, is located in the Richelieu wing of the Louvre palace. The nucleus of the collection was formed between 1825 and 1828 when Edme-Antoine Durand and Pierre Révoil donated their extensive collections of decorative arts from the medieval and Renaissance periods. The museum's royal treasures, such as those constituted by King Henri III and the Abbaye of Saint-Denis, make it one of the most remarkable collections of decorative arts from the Middle Ages. The collection of ivories from the early Middle Ages is equally outstanding.

Museo nacional d'Art de Catalunya
The National Museum of Art of Catalonia

Palau Nacional, Parc de Montjuïc, 08038 Barcelona, Spain
Tel. (34) 93 6220376 www.gencat.es
Tue, Wed, Fri-Sat 10am-7pm, Thu 10am-9pm, Sun 10am-2.30pm

This museum is the major depository of Catal art, a treasure trove for this region of Spain and probably one of the most important centres for Romanesque art in the world. More than 100 pieces are on display, including stone sculptures, wood carvings, icons, and frescoes. The highlight is the collection of murals from various Romanesque churches. The frescoes and murals are displayed as apses, much as they were in the churches in which they were found. Each is placed in sequential order, providing the viewer with a tour of Romanesque art from its primitive beginnings to the more advanced, late Romanesque and early Gothic eras.

Musée national du Moyen-Age - Thermes et Hôtel de Cluny
The National Museum of the Middle Ages - The Cluny Baths and Hotel
6 place Paul-Painlevé, 75005 Paris, France
Tel. (33) 1 53 73 78 00   www.musee-moyenage.fr
Mon, Wed-Sun 9.15am-5.45pm

Admirably displayed in what used to be the Roman baths of Lutetia, transformed in the Middle Ages, the collection owes much to Alexandre du Sommerard, who assembled an extremely fine collection of medieval and Renaissance objects at the beginning of the 19th century. His son Edmond, the museum's first curator, bought the famous *Lady with the Unicorn* tapestry for the museum, as well as the gold crowns of the Visigothic kings, the altar given by Henry II, and the Golden Rose offered by Pope John XXII to the Count of Neuchâtel. Masterpieces of enamels, stained glass, ivories, statuary, and goldsmiths' works contribute to these medieval collections ranking among the best in the world.

Nationalmuseet
The National Museum
Frederiksholms kanal 12, 1220 Copenhagen, Denmark
Tel. (45) 33 134411   www.natmus.dk
Tue-Sun 10am-5pm

A rich collection of early Christian and medieval antiquities mainly from Denmark but also from other parts of Europe. It houses the largest known collections of medieval aquamaniles (vessels used during Mass by priests for washing hands), censers, crosses, and drinking horns, as well as medieval weapons.

Museo nazionale de Bargello
The National Museum of Bargello
Via del Proconsolo 4, 50122 Florence, Italy
Tel. (39) 55 2388 606
Daily 8.15am-1.50pm (closed 2nd and 4th Mon, and 1st and 3rd Sun of each month)

Along with its masterpieces of Renaissance sculpture, the Bargello houses a fine collection of ivories ranging from the Etruscan period to the 17th century. The Room of the Ivories has been restored to its original Renaissance glory and now houses the 265-piece collection gathered by the wealthy art collector, Louis Carrand, who made a crucial donation to the museum in 1888. A Christian diptych (4th-5th century) depicts scenes from the Life of Saint Paul in Malta and of Adam in Earthly Paradise. Another diptych representing two imperial figures is a precious testimony to the Carolingian period. The museum's most famous exhibit is a rare liturgical Flabellum from the Saint Philibert Abbey in Tournus (Loire valley), dating from the 12th century.

Novgorodskii gosudarstvennyi muzej-zapovednik
Novgorod State Museum Preserve
Kreml 11, 173007 Novgorod, Russian Federation
Tel. (7) 816 22 7 36 08   www.eng.novgorod-museum.ru
Mon, Wed-Sun 10am-6pm (closed last Thu of the month)

The first eight halls of this museum are dedicated to the history of medieval Novgorod. Since the Novgorod compact layer of clay top soil preserves everything which has ever been buried in it, the everyday medieval life of the city can be illustrated down to the smallest detail. An outstanding find is the workshop of icon painter, Olisei Grechin (the Greek), dating from the 12th century. The exhibition is notable for its wide use of birch-bark letters of the 11th-15th centuries. No other museum offers a larger number or a better selection of these unique written documents.

Museo pio cristiano
The Pious Christian Museum
Viale Vaticano, 00120 Città del Vaticano, Vatican City
Tel. (39) 06 69883333
Apr-mid Jun, Sep-Oct: daily 8.45am-4.45pm. Rest of year: daily 8.45am-1.45pm

By offering a well-deserved home to the numerous sarcophagi that were scattered among the palaces and villas of Rome, this museum provides a valuable insight into the early beliefs of the Christian faith. It is the richest and most important collection of its kind, spanning 150 years of artistic evolution, until sarcophagi went out of use. The diversity of representations of biblical scenes is absolutely unique. The sculptured scenes are mostly drawn from the Old and New Testaments, the most frequent representations being that of the Good Shepherd giving his life for the flock, which is the most diffused image in early Christian art.

Saint Augustine's Abbey Museum
Saint Augustine's Abbey, Longport, Canterbury, Kent CT1 1TF, UK
Tel. (44) 1227 767345 www.english-heritage.org.uk
Apr-Sep: daily 10am-6pm. Nov-Mar: daily 10am-4pm. Oct: daily 10am-5pm

The Abbey was founded by St Augustine in AD597 and became famous for its illuminated manuscripts. The museum was built in 1997 by English Heritage to commemorate the arrival of Saint Augustine on the shores of Canterbury and exhibits include artefacts excavated from the ruins of the abbey.

Schnütgen-Museum
Cäcilienstrasse 29, 50667 Cologne, Germany
Tel. (49) 221 2212310 www.museenkoeln.de
Tue-Fri 10am-4pm, Sat-Sun 11am-4pm

Award-winning museum of ecclesiastical art, focusing on medieval art. Admire St George's sword, fine Rhineland carvings, and pieces from the Romanesque churches in Cologne. The most impressive exhibits feature goldsmiths' and silversmiths' work, including reliquaries and caskets. Items made by Christians from the East are also on display.

Skulpturensammlung und Museum für Byzantinische Kunst
Sculpture Collection and Museum of Byzantine Art
Bodenmuseum, Bodestrasse 1-3, 10178 Berlin, Germany
Tel. (49) 30 20905601 www.smb.spk-berlin.de
Tue-Sun 9am-5pm (re-opening 2004)

Recently amalgamated are the Sculpture Collection and the Museum of Byzantine Art, bringing together collections which date back to the Kunstkammer art collection of Brandenburg-Prussia. On display are a collection of masterpieces of Byzantine and European sculpture from the 3rd to the 19th centuries, including the great ivory Berlin Pyxis (4th-century ciborium for consecrated wafers), and the stone and glass mosaic of Christ the Merciful from the 12th century. German statues from the Middle Ages include those from Swabia and High Rhineland such as the Schutzmantelmaria from Ravensburg, the Christ, St John's group, the Madonna of Dangolsheim, and Tilman Riemenschneider's Evangelists and Singing Angels. Examples of French Gothic include a lifesize Maria as the queen of heaven.

Tiroler Landesmuseum Ferdinandeum
The Tyrolean Provincial Museum Ferdinandeum

Museumstrasse 15, 6020 Innsbruck, Austria
Tel. (43) 512 59489 www.tiroler-landesmuseum.at
Tue-Sat 10am-noon, 2-5pm, Sun 10am-1pm

Ship model used as a burial object, Egypt, Middle Kingdom, *c.* 1900-1800BC
Allard Pierson Museum

The museum, named after its patron the emperor Ferdinand, contains one of the best collections of medieval art in the country and includes a collection of Gothic paintings which is one of the best anywhere. The collection of Gothic statues and altarpieces is especially remarkable, reflecting the former political and artistic importance of this Central European region. Highlights include the original bas-reliefs by Nikolaus Türing the Elder used in designing the Goldenes Dachl (Golden Roof) which can be found at the end of the city's Maria Theresien Street. It is a richly decorated Gothic loggia built over an oriel window and protected by a crocketed roof composed of fire-gilt copper tiles. It was constructed in 1494-96 as part of the Neuer Hof or Fürstenberg, a palace previously built by Duke Friedrich of Tyrol and drastically modified in 1822.

Universitetets Kulturhistoriske Museer - Historisk Museum
The University Museum of Cultural Heritage - History Museum

Frederiksgatan 2, 0164 Oslo, Norway
Tel. (47) 22 859912 www.ukm.uio.no
Mid Sep-mid May: Tue-Sun 11am-4pm. Rest of year: Tue-Sun 10am-4pm

The antiquities collection presents Norway's heritage from the Stone Age to the Reformation. It is, however, the medieval collection that is outstanding: capitals, corbals, chancel screens, and furniture, as well as a stellar collection of large carved portals of Norway's stave churches. The Norwegian 'stave churches' are the only remains of a type of church building in wood previously found all over northern Europe. Still standing around Norway's countryside are 28 such churches and one in the Norsk Folkemuseum in Oslo. All dating from 1100-1300, many were demolished in the 19th century, but the large carved, portal frames and other decorations were often preserved. The largest collection in the country can be found here.

Head of an Egyptian coffin lid
British Museum

Ägyptisches Museum und Papyrussammlung
The Egyptian Museum and Papyrus Collection

Schlossstrasse 70, 14059 Berlin, Germany
Tel. (49) 030 320911 www.smb.spk-berlin.de
Tue-Sun 10am-6pm

The museum was founded in 1846 by Frederick William IV, King of Prussia, in order to house the 1,500 pieces brought back from an expedition led by the Egyptologist, Karl Richard Lepsius. To these pieces were added Frederick William III's collection of Egyptian antiquities and now the museum's holdings represent an impressive collection of extremely fine Egyptian antiquities. The most famous piece is the polychrome bust of Queen Nefertiti (Tell el-Amarna, 1350BC) brought back from Tell el-Amarna by Ludwig Borchardt. Equally impressive is the ebony head of the Queen Tiyi, mother of Akhenaten (18th dynasty), the rare and expressive head of a priest, the so-called 'green head' sculpted in green pierre dure (*c.* 300BC), and the Kalabsha Gate (*c.* 20BC).

Museo archeologico nazionale di Firenze
The Museum of Archeology
Via della Colonna 38, 50121 Florence, Italy
Tel. (39) 055 23575
Tue-Sat 9am-2pm, Sun 9am-1pm

This extensive collection, the second most important in Italy after the museum in Turin, displays more than 14,000 items chronologically. It features statues from the reign of Amenhotep III, those from 2625-2475BC of female servants preparing beer and kneading dough, part of the granite statue of a Pharaoh from the 19th century BC, and a wooden Hittite chariot, as well as sarcophagi, mummies, stelae, scarabs, and a rich collection of Coptic textiles.

The Egyptian god Anoebis in the form a jackal, glass, Egypt, 1st century BC (top)
Allard Pierson Museum

Galleries of Ancient Egyptian Funerary (above)
British Museum

Ashmolean Museum
Beaumont Street, Oxford, Oxfordshire OX1 2PH, UK
Tel. (44) 1865 278000 www.ashmol.ox.ac.uk
Tue-Sat 10am-5pm, Sun & public holidays 2-5pm

Lovers of contemporary art will find the simple shapes and bold primary colours of the predynastic period of Egyptian antiquity a source of immense inspiration. The collection is one of the world's most important assemblages of predynastic material and originates from Petrie's finds at Naqada and Ballas. The Naqada material included many of the pots from the type series used by Petrie to construct his celebrated 'Sequence Dating' system which established a relative chronology of prehistoric Egypt. The great attraction of these pots is that similar examples can still be acquired from dealers and sale rooms. Do not miss the artefacts recently added from other cemeteries in Upper Egypt and from the neolithic sites in the Fayum. The two colossal statues of the god Min, discovered by Petrie under the Ptolemaic temple at Koptos, are the earliest surviving monumental stone sculptures, created around 3300-3100BC. A fragmentary third figure is now in the Egyptian Museum in Cairo. Also on display is the earliest and most celebrated representation of a black-topped pot (*c.* 3600BC) of the Red Crown which was later to symbolize the kingship of Lower Egypt.

British Museum
Great Russell Street, London WC1B 3DG, UK
Tel. (44) 20 7636 1555 www.thebritishmuseum.ac.uk
Mon-Sat 10am-5pm, Sun noon-6pm

Although only a fraction of this museum's immense collection of Egyptian antiquities is on show, the list is nevertheless stunning. In the 18th century, Sir Hans Sloane's collection, mainly acquired from two pioneers in Egyptology, George Sandys and Robert Huntington, formed the basis of the museum's collection. Since then it has been enhanced by private donations, scientifically conducted excavations, and the defeat of the French at the Battle of the Nile in 1801, where the British acquired one of the most famous pieces in the British Museum, the *Rosetta Stone*. The Egyptian Sculpture Gallery is noted for the size of the granite figures of King Amemophis II, the red granite lions from the temple at Soleb in the Sudan, the massive head of Amenophis III, and the bust of a colossus of Ramses II

The Brooklyn Museum of Art
200 Eastern Parkway, Brooklyn, New York 11238-6052, USA
Tel. (1) 718 638 5000 www.brooklynart.org
Wed-Fri 10am-5pm, Sat-Sun 11am-6pm (first Sat of each month until 11pm)

Housing one of the finest collections of Egyptian art and artefacts in the world, ranging from the predynastic period to Roman times. An early female figure from El Ma'mariya

(Naqada II, *c.* 3500-3400BC) is an object of unbelievable beauty, representing a slender female raising her arms above her birdlike head. A black granite seated statue of Sesostris III is probably from Hierakonpolis, late 12th dynasty (*c.* 1878-1840BC). The pharaoh's role as protector of Egypt's borders is symbolized by the nine bows beneath Sesostris III's feet, which represent Egypt's nine traditional enemies. Reliefs from the tomb of the Vizier Nespeqashuty (from Thebes, 26th dynasty, 664-661BC) show female mourners whose faces are virtually expressionist.

Terracotta funerary figure, Coptic (above)
Allard Pierson Museum

Decorated coffin lid, clay and gold, Egypt, 1st century BC (left)
Allard Pierson Museum

Cairo Museum

Shari' Mariette, Midan at-Tahir, Cairo, Egypt
Tel. (20) 25 75 42 67
Daily 9am-5pm (closed Fri 11.15am-1.30pm)

Auguste Mariette was instrumental in the creation of the Cairo Museum by founding the Egyptian Antiquities Department in 1859 which aimed at centralizing and supervizing archaeological research in Egypt. It is a museum crammed with huge granite sarcophagi and statues both above and below ground, and although it is in need of excavation itself, it is not to be missed. Recently opened and restored in a nitrogen-rich atmosphere is the mummy room, where at least fourteen are on display. See the 19th-dynasty mummy of Merenptha, the thirteenth son and heir of Ramses II, and Seti II, whose strong features are well preserved. The Tutankhamun exhibit displays the wealth of gold which covered his body, from the gold mask which was placed over his head to the gold tips which surrounded his toes.

Museo civico archeologico di Bologna
The City Museum of Archeology

Via dell' Archiginnasio 2, 40124 Bologna, Italy
Tel. (39) 051 233849 www.comune.bologna.it
Tue-Sat 9am-6.30pm, Sun & public holidays 9am-6.30pm

The new section of Egyptian material in the museum has recently re-opened and is now one of the most important in Europe. Most of it comes from the artist, Pelagio Palati, who bequeathed his collection of antiquities to his native city. Highlights include the various exhibits from the tomb of Horemheb in Saqqara. Before acceding to the royal throne, he had a sumptuous tomb made in the administrative capital, Memphis. His royal tomb is in the Valley of the Kings itself. The museum displays beautiful stelae from the tomb in Saqqara that are still reminiscent of the Amarna style which had not completely disappeared at that period. The stelae show scenes typical of the rural paradise in Egyptian art, but also prisoners being counted, military campaigns, and provisions being accumulated for his journey into the afterlife.

Museum of Egyptian Antiquities

Egypt Centre, University of Wales, Swansea, Singleton Park, Swansea, SA2 8PP, UK
Tel. (44) 1792 295960 www.swan.ac.uk
Tue-Sat 10am-4pm

Opened in 1998, this collection consists of 3,000 artefacts once owned by Sir Henry Wellcome. Important items are a 21st-dynasty wooden coffin of a female musician from Thebes (*c.* 1000BC), and an Old Kingdom reserve head of which only thirty are known. These replica heads were placed in the burial chamber near the corpse in case the process of mummification was unsuccessful and the real head was replaced with the reserve one. Also on display is the historically important stela of the Roman Emperor Commodus (AD190) from the Bucheum at Armant, showing the emperor making an offering to the mother of Buchis bull.

Ermitazh
The Hermitage
Dvortsovskaia naberezhnaia 34-36, 191065 St Petersburg, Russian Federation
Tel. (7) 812 1109079
www.hermitage.ru
Tue-Sat 10.30am-6pm, Sun 10.30am-5pm

The Ancient Egyptian collection here is, together with that of the Pushkin Museum, one of the largest collections in Russia. In 1825 the Egyptian Museum was established in St Petersburg under the auspices of the Academy of Sciences and the nucleus of the collection consisted of 1,000 objects purchased from the Italian collector, Castiglione. It was later transferred to the Hermitage. It was not until the 1960s that a Soviet archaeological expedition first took part in excavation work in Egypt. The collection now contains more than 10,000 items including masterpieces such as the statue of Amenhemet III, the stele of Ipy (the Royal Fan Bearer), and the stele of Horemheb. A significant part is composed of beautiful works of handicraft and jewellery decorations, especially Egyptian faience. It is also particularly rich in rare bronzes including a portrait of Pharaoh Taharqa of the Ethiopian dynasty which brings out the ethnic features of the Ethiopians and yet reconciles them with the canons of Egyptian art.

Museum of Fine Arts, Boston
465 Huntington Avenue, Boston, Massachusetts 02115-5519, USA
Tel. (1) 617 267 9300   www.mfa.org
Mon, Tue 10am-4.45pm, Wed-Fri 10am-9.45pm

The nucleus of the museum's outstanding Egyptian collection was formed by the Lowell and Way Collections, subsequently supplemented by several gifts awarded to the museum by the Egypt Exploration Fund. However, it is the Harvard University Museum of Fine Arts Egypt Expedition which brought the museum the full range of Egyptian art from the predynastic period to the late Roman period. The Old Kingdom's collections are surpassed only by Cairo. It is essential to view the bust of Prince Ankh-haf (Giza, 4th dynasty, *c.* 2600-2500BC), one of the most remarkable and unusual examples of portraiture to have survived from ancient Egypt.

Freud Museum
20 Maresfield Gardens, Hampstead, London NW3 5SX, UK
Tel. (44) 20 7435 2002   www.freud.org.uk
Wed-Sun noon-5pm

The house where Sigmund Freud lived, worked, and died is now home to a remarkable collection of over 2,000 Egyptian, Greek, Roman, and Chinese antiquities collected by the famous psychoanalyst. The collection includes many fine examples of Egyptian bronze gods (Ptah and Imhotep), goddesses (Isis, from the Ptolemaic period), faience shabties, and numerous alabaster and bronze containers.

Gosudarstvennyi muzei izobrazitel'nykh iskusstv im. A Pushkina
The Pushkin Museum of Fine Arts
Ulitsa Volkhonka 12, 121019 Moscow, Russian Federation
Tel. (7) 095 2037412   www.global-one.ru
Tue-Sun 10am-7pm

The Egyptian collection contains some 8,000 pieces covering each significant period of Egyptian history, a large part of which was purchased in 1909 from the Egyptologist and Assyriologist, Vladimir Golenichtchev. An enormous variety is on offer, from the reliefs from the Tomb of Isi, the stelae representing Henenu, and the granite statue of Amenhemat III, to the famous painted toilet spoon with a female bather. Most impressive is the group of two statues representing the priest Amenhotep and the priestess Rannahi (New Kingdom) whose beauty was thought to be unsurpassed.

Museo gregoriano profano
The Secular Gregorian Museum
Viale Vaticano, 00120 Città del Vaticano, Vatican City
Tel. (39) 06 69883333
Daily 8.45am-1.45pm (Apr-mid Jun, Sep-Oct until 4.45pm)

What makes this collection particularly interesting is that the largest part of it is made up of statues which were found in Italy but which had been brought from Egypt in Roman times, as well as the Egyptianized objects produced by admiring Romans. These objects are testimony of the ardent admiration the Roman conquerors had for the ancient civilization of the Nile. (Egypt became a Roman province soon after the Battle of Actium in 31BC where Octavius, the future Emperor Augustus, defeated the fleet of Antony and Cleopatra, the last member of the Macedonian Ptolemaic dynasty.) Among the principal works of sculpture dating from the Old Kingdom to the Christian Era are the famous sandstone head of Mentuhotep, the throne of a seated statue of Ramses II (*c.*1250BC), and a colossal statue of Queen Tiye, mother of Ramses II. Perhaps only the reconstruction of the Canopos Serapeum of Hadrian's Villa gives us a true idea of the Roman fascination for Egyptian art and religion. The edifice symbolically represented Egypt submerged by the flood waters of the Nile and was decorated with imitations of Egyptian statuary, including statues of Osiris-Antinous, a representation in Egyptian dress of Antinous, Hadrian's lover, deified after his drowning in the Nile in AD130.

Necklace with pendant in the shape of a human head, 4th-3rd century BC
Náprstkovo muzeum asijských, afrických a amerických kultur

The Harer Family Trust Collection at the San Bernardino County Museum
2024 Orange Tree Lane, Redlands, California 92374, USA
Tel. (1) 909 798 8570   www.co.san-bernardino.ca.us
Tue-Sun 9am-5pm
R.V. Fullerton Art Museum
California State University Museum, San Bernardino
5500 University Parkway, San Bernardino, California 92407, USA
Tel. (1) 909 880 7373
Sep-Jul: Mon-Fri 10am-4pm, Sat-Sun noon-4pm

The Harer Family Trust Collection consists of over 280 objects, divided into two separate museums. Many of the objects were acquired from an Egyptian collection assembled by Emil Brugsch of the Cairo Museum and the Egyptian Antiquities Organization during the late 19th century. Highlights of the San Bernardino County Museum include the Bust of Bes in green-glazed faience from the late or Ptolemaic periods, fine examples of black-topped terracotta pottery from the predynastic period, and a mirror in copper (11th-13th dynasty) with a pair of celestial falcons sacred to the sun god appropriately flanking the mirror's disk with Hathor at the base. The California State University houses one of the most important works of art in the Harer Family Trust Collection – the standard-bearing statue of a queen, possibly Nefertiti. There is an impressive bronze statuette with inlays of gold and copper representing Osiris (uncommon in Egyptian bronze sculpture), and colourful amuletic inlays in glazed faience depicting various deities and symbols which were intended to decorate a wooden coffin.

Highclere Castle Collection
Highclere, Newbury, Berkshire RG15 9RN, UK
Tel. (44) 1635 253210   www.highclerecastle.co.uk
Please call for opening times

This museum was home to the cursed 5th Earl of Carnarvon. In 1907-11 Lord Carnarvon joined forces with Howard Carter on their first excavation of the private cemeteries of Dra Abu'l-Naga, Asaif, and Deir el-Bahri. They moved into the Valley of the Kings in

Lapis lazuli amulet
shaped as a lying bull,
South Iraq 3100-2900BC`
*Náprstkovo muzeum
asijských, afrických a
amerických kultur*

Faience ring with
inscription: 'nebb-matt-
re' (Amenhotep III),
New Kingdom,
14th century BC
*Náprstkovo muzeum
asijských, afrických a
amerických kultu*

1915, and in 1922 they uncovered the tomb of Tutankhamun. Amid rumours flying around about the curse of Tutankhamun, Carnarvon died in 1923. Much of their collection was sold to the Metropolitan Museum in New York but various pieces were rediscovered in the family home by a butler in the 1980s. Examples of these are two fine, early lotus-flower bowls of bright blue Egyptian faience, some important material from the tomb of Amenophis III (including an archer's wristguard of tooled leather with geometric patterns), and a series of bound captives symbolizing the enemies of the Egyptian state.

Muséum d'Histoire naturelle
The Museum of Natural History
28 blvd des Belges, 69006 Lyon, France
Tel. (33) 4 72 69 05 00 www.museum-lyon.org
Tue-Sun 10am-6pm

The museum boasts a fascinating collection of over 1,000 mummified animals, mainly from Upper Egypt. The collection is among the most important in Europe, both for its size and its diversity, due to the efforts of former museum director, Louis Lortet, who undertook excavations in Egypt between 1901 and 1909 with the support of the famous Egyptologist, Maspero. The collection is composed of mammals, birds, reptiles, and fishes, with the collection of birds being the most important and comprehensive. They probably belong to the Ptolemaic period which saw the development of widespread animal cults.

Musée Georges Labit
The Georges Labit Museum
43 rue des Martyrs de la Libération, 31400 Toulouse, France
Tel. (33) 5 61 22 21 84 www.mairie-toulouse.fr
Jun-Sep: Mon, Wed-Sun 10am-6pm. Oct-May: Mon, Wed-Sun 10am-5pm

The museum is located in an enchanting Moorish pavilion on the peaceful verges of the canal du Midi. A focal point of the exhibition is the collection of funeral steles. Mainly originating from Abydos, they date from the 6th dynasty (end of the Old Kingdom period) onwards. The collection also contains a selection of statues, statuettes, and funeral boats. There are several funeral papyri, including the *Book of the Dead* in the name of Ta-net-Imen. This Alexandre Varille Papyrus (named after its last proprietor) is 410cm long and bears inscriptions in coloured ink. Also on display is a complete mummy with its sarcophagi from the Lybian period (12th-13th dynasty) as well as a sarcophagus mask from the 13th dynasty. The collection of Coptic fragments donated in 1902 is remarkable and includes many pieces from Antinoe such as a *Decorative Sash with Shepherds* (5th century) and a square with Saint Georges (7th century).

Liverpool Museum
William Brown Street, Liverpool, Merseyside L3 8EN, UK
Tel. (44) 151 478 4399 www.nmgm.org.uk
Mon-Sat 10am-5pm, Sun noon-5pm

The nucleus of the collection consists of 5,000 Egyptian artefacts donated in 1867 by Joseph Mayer, a local goldsmith and devoted collector. On display is the most ancient and best preserved textile to be seen anywhere in the world today: the girdle of Ramses III (1193-1162BC), together with an important collection of Coptic tapestry fragments.

Musée du Louvre
The Louvre
Palais du Louvre, 34-36 quai du Louvre, 75001 Paris, France
Tel. (33) 1 40 20 53 17 www.louvre.fr
Mon, Wed 9am-9.15pm, Thu-Sun 9am-5.30pm

The Egypt Expedition, led by Napoleon Bonaparte in 1798, heralded the birth of archae-ology in Egypt, and more precisely, the birth of Egyptology. Several famous European scientists, sixteen cartographers and topographers, and more than 160 artists and tech-nicians contributed to this artistic and scientific mission. Since the foundation of the department, the collection has been considerably enriched by the French excavations carried out by Mariette and the foundation of the Cairo branch of the French Institute in 1880. All aspects of Egyptian life are documented here and you will have the chance to admire the famous Seated Scribe, the sumptuous pectoral of Ramses II made from coloured glass and turquoise, and the large pink granite Sphinx from Tanis (Old Kingdom, 2700-2000bc). Don't leave without wandering through an almost complete interior of a 4th-century Coptic church presented to France by the Egyptian government.

Amulet showing a bird pecking an ibex's back, South Iraq, 3100-2900BC (above)
Náprstkovo muzeum asijských, afrických a amerických kultu

Bead net dress from Qua, dynasty V (below)
Petrie Museum of Egyptian Archaeology

Luxor Museum
Corniche, Luxor, Egypt
Tel. (20) 95 38 02 69
Daily 10am-noon, 4-9pm (summer 5-10pm)

This outstanding museum focuses on quality rather than quantity. In the great basement rooms are the discoveries made in 1989 at the Great Court of Amenhotep III at the Temple of Luxor. These include a quartzite reproduction of a lifesize statue of Amenhotep III and a group depicting Horemheb kneeling before Amun. On the ground floor a basalt statue of Thutmose III shows the Pharaoh as eternally young, posing with the supreme confidence of a deity, while a red granite head of Sesostris III bears the expressionist features of a wise man. A great stele of King Kamose depicts the decisive Theban victory over the Hyskos, which announced the birth of the New Kingdom. On the second floor stands an impressive head of Amenhotep IV (Akhenaten), alongside

scenes reconstructed from the talattat blocks which were taken from the ninth pylon of the Temple of Karnak. The scenes show Akhenaten paying homage to Aten. Various objects found in the Tomb of Tutankhamun are on display, including a majestic head of Mehit-Weret and a gilded aspect of the cow-headed Goddess Hathor. In addition, there is a sculpture made of calcite in a perfect state of preservation, representing Amenhotep III and the god Sobek, one of the greatest finds of the region of Thebes in recent years. Don't miss the fascinating relief from the Coptic period showing how the Coptic cross derived from the Ankh sign of eternity used in Ancient Egypt.

The Manchester Museum
The University of Manchester, Oxford Road, Manchester M13 9PL, UK
Tel. (44) 161 275 2634   www.museum.man.ac
Mon-Sat 10am-5pm

This is a stellar collection which sits proudly among the best in the world. At its core are objects of everyday use from the town-sites of Kahun and Gurob presented to the museum in 1890 by Jesse Haworth, a Manchester textile merchant, and Martyn Kennard. The museum has made international headlines with its Egyptian Mummy Research Project, extracting tissue samples from its human and animal mummies in order to shed light on everything from the spread of infectious disease and the development of agriculture to the origins and migrations of the human race.

The Metropolitan Museum of Art
1000 Fifth Avenue at 82nd Street, New York, New York 10028, USA
Tel. (1) 212 535 7710   www.metmuseum.org
Tue-Thu, Sun 9.30am-5.30pm, Fri-Sat 9.30am-9pm

Hieroglyphics with inscription in cuneiform characters from various cultures around the Mediterranean Sea (top)
Rijksmuseum van Oudheden

The Ebony Egress (above)
Petrie Museum of Egyptian Archaeology

The Met houses a full-scale Egyptian temple – the Temple of Dendur. Originally from Nubia, it would have been submerged as a result of the construction of the Aswan Dam in the 1960s. Egypt gave it to the US in recognition of the American contribution to the Nubian rescue operation. Reassembled as it appeared on the banks on the Nile in a glass pavilion on the edge of Central Park, it looks impressive but more than slightly incongruous. Built by the Roman Emperor Augustus, the temple was dedicated to the goddess Isis, whose cult had largely spread in the Mediterranean in the 3rd century BC. The creation of the department coincided with the first American expeditions to Egypt. The collections were also enriched by the reproductions of more than 400 copies of wall paintings made by the team of epigraphists accompanying the expeditions. Private collectors who considerably contributed to the collections include Lord Carnarvon, Theodore M. Davis and Albert Gallatin.

Museo egizio Torino
The Egyptian Museum of Turin
Via Accademia Delle Scienze 6, 10123 Turin, Italy
Tel. (39) 011 5617776   www.multix.it
Tue-Sun 8.30am-7.30pm (Jun-Sep until 11pm)

Although the nucleus of this collection consists of over 8,000 objects collected by Consul B. Drovetti, the museum is dominated by the donation from Schiparelli and Farina at the beginning of the 20th century, of 17,000 objects from the prehistoric to the Coptic eras. Following the Nubian rescue operation, which was mounted by UNESCO during the 1960s, the museum acquired Nubia's most ancient rock chapel, built at Ellejissa by Thutmose III in 1450BC and restored two centuries later by Ramses II. The museum also displays an intact tomb with furnishings of the architect Kha and his wife Mirit (Deir el Medina, 14th century BC), which features gilded coffins, flower garlands, food offerings, dresses, linen, pottery, and furniture. This tomb, with its modest furnishings, provides a dramatic contrast to the popular idea of an Egyptian tomb. In addition, there is the colossal statue of the seated Ramses II from Karnak, the 'Mine Papyrus' (the oldest topographical map in existence), stelae, coffins, mummies, amulets, reliefs from Heliopolis (3rd dynasty), and the rich paintings from the tomb of Ity at Gebelein (11th dynasty), not to mention the monolithic Colossus of Sethi II which, when moved from Genoa to Turin, had to be mounted on gun carriages drawn by sixteen horses.

Myers Museum
Brewhouse Gallery, Eton College, Windsor, Berkshire SL4 6DW, UK
Tel. (44) 1753 801538   www.etoncollege.com
Tue, Thu, Sat-Sun 2.30-5.30pm

Undeniably one of the world's finest collections of ancient Egyptian decorative arts, consisting of 2,100 individual items. The best part is the collection of the old Etonian army officer, Major William J. Myers. Over the course of his eleven years in Cairo, having been posted there in the 1880s, he amassed a stunning collection which he hoped would act as a source of inspiration for future generations. In 1899 Myers died and the collection was donated to the college to join the Copeland Collection. Myers's colourful diaries form part of the collection. Remarkable pieces include the items of Egyptian faience, 'Egyptian Blue', glazed steatite and glass, a virtually complete series of lotus-design bowls of the 18th dynasty, and the stemmed chalice-like cups and bowls in the shape of lotus flowers.

Náprstkovo muzeum asijských, afrických a amerických kultur
Náprstek Museum of Asian, African and American Cultures
Betlémské námesti 1, 11000 Prague, Czech Republic
Tel. (42) 2 22221416   www.aconet.cz
Tue-Sun 9am-noon, 1.45-5.30pm

The Egyptian collections contain gifts from the excavations of the French Oriental Institute in Cairo consisting mainly of everyday items from Deir el-Medina, a village of artists and labourers working on the pharaohs rock tombs in the Valley of the Kings. Additionally, there are the finds made by the Czech Egyptological Institute in Nubia which were subsequently presented as a gift by the Egyptian authorities as a reward for their participation in the UNESCO organized campaign in the early 1960s to save Nubian monuments. This collection consists of approximately 650 objects mainly from the New Kingdom, Late Period, and Early Byzantine Period. There are also objects found during this Institute's archaeological excavations at the pyramid field in Abusir, including the funeral outfits and articles used by temple priests in the discharge of their everyday duties in obsequial temples.

Faience counterpoise with the head of a goddess, perhaps from Tuna-el-Gebel, Third Intermediate Period, 22nd dynasty, *c.* 945BC (above)
Myers Museum

Bronze Aegis, protective shield, Greco-Roman, 4th century BC (below)
Náprstkovo muzeum asijských, afrických a amerických kultur

Ny Carlsberg Glyptotek
The New Carlsberg Glyptotheque
Dantes Plads 7, 1556 Copenhagen, Denmark
Tel. (45) 33 418141 www.glyptoteket.dk
Tue-Sun 10am-4pm

The Egyptian Collection is extensive and holds several outstanding objects. The jewel of the museum is a black basalt royal head of the 2nd or 3rd dynasty. The eyes, lids, and cheeks are carved with touching realism, and the mouth conveys the majesty of the king. Equally fascinating are the three heads of princesses, probably Akhenaten's daughters, which have been carved in minute detail. It was found in 1910 and was in the possession of Baron von Bissing for years before being displayed at the Glyptotek. Also on show are a group of three unique statues representing Taharka, the last Ethiopian King who reigned over a united Egypt (25th dynasty). Sculpture, stelae, and figurines of the Graeco-Roman period are also well represented and the collection of the so-called Fayum portraits is remarkable.

Oriental Institute Museum of the University of Chicago
1155 E. 58th Street, Chicago, Illinois 60637, USA
Tel. (1) 312 7029520 www.oi.uchicago.edu
Tue, Thu, Sat 10am-4pm, Wed 10am-8.30pm, Sun noon-4pm

The Joseph and Mary Grimshaw Egyptian Gallery opened to the public in May 1999, following a three-year renovation project. The 4,000-square-foot gallery displays

approximately 800 objects dating from the predynastic period (*c.* 5000BC) to the Arab conquest (7th century AD). The installation of climate control systems to the museum enabled many fragile objects of cloth, wood, rush, and papyrus to be exhibited for the first time. Shown here are objects from the Ptolemaic Period (332-30BC) through to the Byzantine era (to the 7th century BC). An exhibition on kingship, dominated by a bust of King Neferhotep (*c.* 1740BC) is another highlight. The Haskell Oriental Museum, a gift of Mrs Caroline E. Haskell, was opened in 1896 and displayed objects from both the Far and the Near East. The Near Eastern collection was later supplemented by acquisitions obtained in return for the contribution Chicago citizens made to the Egypt Exploration Fund and to Sir Petrie's Egyptian Research Account. The Institute took full possession of the Haskell Oriental collections in 1925-26. Of particular interest is an Egyptian Tomb painting on wood from the

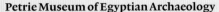

Mummy portrait of woman in blue robe, Hawara, Greco-Roman *Petrie Museum of Egyptian Archaeology*

tomb of Lady Meri at Dishshah (*c.* 2300BC), and a clay tablet fragment written in Babylonian cuneiforms from Tell el-Armana and hence known as the Armana Letters. There are also several scientific instruments including an astronomical instrument made by King Tutankhamun from Luxor (*c.*1300BC) which probably comes from the tomb of Tuthmose IV.

Petrie Museum of Egyptian Archaeology
University College London, Malet Place, London WC1E 6BT, UK
Tel. (44) 20 7679 2884   www.petrie.ucl.ac.uk
Tue-Fri 1-5pm

This jewel of a museum is one of London's best kept secrets. Its collections derive chiefly from the excavations of Sir Flinders Petrie, the doyen of Egyptian archaeology, and it is recognized as one of the most important teaching research collections in the world and is used as such. Through the years, material has been added to it from the Egypt Exploration Society in Nubia and Saqqara, as well as from the collection of Sir Henry Wellcome. It holds over 80,000 objects dating from Palaeolithic to Roman times. The collections of pottery and figurines is extensive; all periods are well represented but the predynastic period is particularly remarkable. Outstanding is the Tarkhan dress, supposedly the earliest garment in the world dating back to the first dynasty (3100-2890BC) and more precisely the reign of Djet (*c.*2800BC).

Allard Pierson Museum
Oude Turfmarkt 127,1012 GC Amsterdam, The Netherlands
Tel. (31) 20 5252556   www.uba.uva.nl
Tue-Fri 10am-5pm, Sat-Sun 1-5pm

Many of the prize pieces in the Egyptian collection have come via Mr C.W. Lunsingh Scheurleer, who bought a large number of objects from the Von Bissing collection. Scheurleer also partially funded Sir Flinders Petrie's excavations and in turn was repaid with many objects. When he became bankrupt his collection was acquired by the museum and since then the collection has grown through gifts and other purchases, including the Van Leer and Boeke-Cadbury collections, and the Dobbor shabti collection. The Egyptian objects represent over 5,000 years of history focusing on the pre- and early dynastic period, the Amarna period, and the Graeco-Roman period. Scale models of the pyramids of Giza and the temple of Edfu are among the attractions.

The earliest known linen dress from Tarljam *c.* 2800BC *Petrie Museum of Egyptian Archaeology*

Rijksmuseum van Oudheden
The National Museum of Antiquities
Rapenburg 28, 2301 EC Leiden, The Netherlands
Tel. (31) 71 5163163   www.rmo.nl
Tue-Fri 10am-5pm, Sat-Sun noon-5pm

One of three places in the world outside Egypt where you can see a complete Egyptian temple, a gift donated to the museum in the 1970s for its exceptional contribution to the conservation of Egypt's cultural heritage. Probably dedicated to the goddess Isis, it dates from the reign of Emperor Augustus. Also noteworthy is a magnificent double-statue of Maya and Merit. This well-kept, over-lifesize chalk statue group shows the couple sitting on a throne waiting for a sacrificial meal. A characteristic Theban mummy from the Late Period (26th dynasty), Ancchor's mummy is one of the museum's most well-known mummies. Ancchor was a Theban priest who died young around 625BC. Placed over his mummified body is a web of blue beads, symbolizing heaven, with amulets including a winged scarab, to guarantee eternal life.

Roemer-und Pelizaeus-Museum
The Roemer and Pelizaeus Museum
Am Steine 1-2, 31134 Hildesheim, Germany
Tel. (49) 5121 93690
www.roemer-pelizaeus-museum.de
Tue-Sun 9am-4.30pm

The museum holds the distinctive Egyptian collection of Herman Roemer and Wilhelm Pelizaeus. The collection grew from 1885 when Pelizaeus acquired a mummy complete with mummy mask and coffin which he sent home to the museum. This was followed by a series of excavation commissions which secured enough items to establish a museum dedicated exclusively to the art of Ancient Egypt. Today, the collection numbers more than 9,000 objects spanning nearly 6,000 years of Egyptian history. The section dedicated to the Old Kingdom (2700-2200BC) displays the huge statue of the Vizier Hem-iunu, who oversaw the building of the Great Pyramid for his uncle, Pharaoh Cheops. The Middle Kingdom (2100-1700BC) is represented through small burial objects as well as painted coffins. The depictions on the lid from the coffin of Nakht, for example, show an astronomical clock with a sequential series of rising stars. The section dedicated to the New Kingdom (1570-1080BC) displays a beautiful relief of Pharaoh Tuthmosis I. He wears an ornate headdress with plumes, ram's horns, a sun-disk, and writhing cobras.

Lifesize double statue of Maya, Tutankhamun's treasurer, and his wife Merit, Egypt, 1333-1323BC (left)
Rijksmuseum van Oudheden

Wooden painted shabti figure, inscribed with traditional shabti formula dynasty XVIII (below)
Petrie Museum of Egyptian Archaeology

Rosicrucian Egyptian Museum
Rosicrucian Park, Park and Naglee Avenues, San José, California 95191, USA
Tel. (1) 408 947 3636 www.rosicrucian.org
Daily 10am-5pm

Designed in authentic Egyptian architectural style, the Rosicrucian Egyptian Museum sits swaddled in the surrounding Rosicrucian Park. Visitors are lead past walls carved with hieroglyphics, and elaborate fountains lined with papyrus. The museum claims to have the largest collection of Egyptian (as well as Babylonian and Assyrian) antiquities on display on the west coast of America.

Sir John Soane's Museum
13 Lincoln's Inn Fields, London WC2A 3BP, UK
Tel. (44) 20 7405 2107 www.soane.org
Tue-Sat 10am-5pm (plus 6-9pm first Tue of each month)

This museum, Sir John Soane's former family home which he bequeathed to the nation in 1833, encompasses the dreams of a man who was one of England's most famous and inventive architects of his age. In the Sepulchral Chamber is one of the most outstanding examples of Egyptian workmanship: a stunning alabaster sarcophagus and fragments of its lid, which was the outermost container of the coffin, of the Egyptian pharaoh Seti I (19th dynasty, c. 1300BC). Discovered in 1817 by Giovanni Belzoni in the Valley of the Kings, it remains one of the most important antiquities ever uncovered. Carved out of one piece of Egyptian Alabaster it was originally inlaid with blue hieroglyphs and tells the story of the soul's passage through the underworld. It was purchased by Soane in 1824, after the British Museum refused to pay £2,000 for it.

University of Michigan Library
Harlan Hatcher Graduate Library, University of Michigan, Ann Arbor,
Michigan, 48109, USA
www.lib.umich.edu
Mon-Fri 10am-5pm, Sat 10am-noon

One of the great treasures housed here is the collection of papyrus manuscripts comprising about 7,000 catalogued items, which is by far the largest in the US. The university's collection of ostraca, which is housed in the Kelsey Museum of Archaeology, is worth a visit in itself. The Michigan papyri range from the earlier part of the 3rd century BC to the 8th century AD. Most are written in Greek, with considerable numbers in Latin, Coptic, Arabic, and even a few in Egyptian Demotic.

Red jasper face inlay, New Kingdom, 19th dynasty, reign of Seti I
c. 1294-1279BC
Myers Museum

The University of Pennsylvania Museum of Archaeology and Anthropology
33rd and Spruce Streets, Philadelphia, Pennsylvania 19104, USA
Tel. (1) 215 898 4000 www.upenn.edu
Tue-Sat 10am-4.30pm, Sun 1-5pm

The museum's collection of Egyptian antiquities is among the finest in the US and especially prized for two unique exhibits. One is the Royal Palace of Merenptah. The monumental gateway and the palace itself are still the finest preserved parts of an ancient palace in the world. They once stood in the vicinity of the sanctuary of Ptah at Memphis and now are part of the museum. The second jewel is a red granite Sphinx bearing the cartouches of Ramses II and Merenptah, also found in the Temple of Ptah at Memphis. It is the third largest sphinx in the world and weighs 12 tons, which is all the more extraordinary as it was quarried at Aswan, some 600 miles away from the Temple.

ETRUSCAN AND ROMAN ANTIQUITIES

Museo di Antichità etrusche e italiche
The Museum of Etruscan and Italic Antiquities
Università La Sapienza, piazzale Aldo Moro 5, 00185 Rome, Italy
Tel. (39) 06 49913721
Mon-Sat (by appt. only)

The museum illustrates the history of pre-Roman peoples. It houses material from the Gorga Collection as well as from two exhibitions, the Etruscan Art and Civilization, held in Milan in 1955; and the Etrurian Sanctuaries, held in 1985.

Musée des Antiquités nationales
The Museum of National Antiquities
Château de Saint-Germain-en-Laye, 78103 Saint-Germain-en-Laye, France
Tel. (33) 1 39 10 13 00
Mon, Wed-Sun 9am-5.30pm

In the Gallo Roman Rooms there are effigies of Celtic gods, funerary objects, day-to-day pieces of silverware (including the *Canthare of Alesia* vase with floral decoration), bronzeware, glassware, ceramics, lamps, jewellery, surgical instruments, and tools. There is also an exceptional merovingien arms collections, as well as two gilt handled swords, and women's jewellery.

Museum of Antiquities
University of Newcastle upon Tyne, Newcastle upon Tyne, Tyne & Wear NE1 7RU, UK
Tel. (44) 191 222 7849 www.ncl.ac.uk
Mon-Sat 10am-5pm

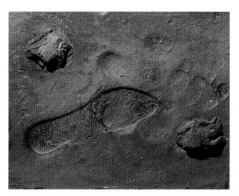

A renowned collection of artefacts, models, and diagrams relating to Hadrian's Wall are housed here, along with a full-scale reconstruction of the Temple to Mithras which was at Carrawburgh. Other displays illustrate the variety of life in the region before and after the Romans, from the early prehistory up to 1600. As the principal museum of archaeology in north east England, it holds enormous archaeological resources.

Samian pottery, 2nd century AD
Museum of London

Footprints on part of a roof tile
Fishbourne Roman Palace

One of the museum's Roman galleries
Ny Carlsberg Glyptotek

Museo archaeologico nazionale di Firenze
The National Museum of Archaeology of Florence
Via della Colonna 38, 50121 Florence, Italy
Tel. (39) 055 23575
Tue-Sat 9am-2pm, Sun 9am-1pm

The museum grew out of the Medicis' interest in antiquity and now represents one of the finest and most important collections of Etruscan art. The collection was begun by Cosimo il Vecchio and Lorenzo il Magnifico and was later enriched by Lorenzo's successors and the grand-dukes of Lorraine. Highlights of the collection include the famous François Vase, a Greek Krater made by Ergotimos and painted by Kleitas in 570BC Athens, the tomb statue Mater Matuta of an Etruscan woman seated on a throne and holding a baby, and the famous Chimera from Arezzo (4th century BC), a fantastical animal with the body of a lion, the head of a ram, and a serpent's tail.

Musée archéologique d'Argentomagus
The Archaeological Museum of Argentomagus
Mersans, 36200 Saint-Marcel, France
Tel. (33) 2 54 24 47 31 www.argentomagus.com
May-Oct: Mon, Wed-Sun 9.30am-noon, 2-6pm. Nov-Apr: Wed-Sun 10am-noon, 2-5pm

This is the first museum in the centre of France to be located on an archaeological site. Argentomagus was an old Gallo-Roman town which, because a vineyard was on top of it, was left virtually intact before it was discovered. Although known since the 16th century, it was not excavated until recently, when archaeologists found three cult temples, a theatre, a fountain, an ampitheatre, and public baths. Among the collection are sculptures and everyday objects such as toiletries and writing implements, a great many of which are made of bone or of deer horn. There are also numerous pots, amphora, and glass bottles. From the commercial side of the town, there are a great number of Spanish amphorae for the transport of oil, as well as a fine coin collection. There are some remains of 2nd-century paintings in the archaeological crypt.

Museo arqueológico de Jerez
The Archaeological Museum of Jerez
Plaza del Mercado s/n, 11408 Jerez de la Frontera, Spain
Tel. (34) 956 333316 www.ctv.es
Tue-Fri 10am-2pm, 4-7pm, Sat-Sun 10am-2.30pm

Three rooms show a wide variety of amphorae and funeral stelae from Asta Regia. One of the highlights is the reproduction of the head of an old man. There is also a fine selection of Roman coins in one of the adjacent rooms.

Arsenale Mediceo
The Medici Arsenal
The Roman Ships of Pisa, Lungarno Simonelli, 561000 Pisa, Italy
www.navipisa.it

Not far from the Leaning Tower of Pisa, archaeologists discovered the remains of a large number of Roman ships. Dating from around 200BC-AD500 (and older ones may still be found) they lie in a plot of land just over six miles from the sea. Pisa in Roman times was like Venice today. It was a city built on an island in a vast lagoon traversed by canals, and the area containing the remains would once have been a small harbour off a large lagoon that has since silted up. What was to become a new railway control station has, since 1998 when they first sampled the site, become a spectacular graveyard packed with a variety of water-craft, from sturdy sail driven boats (with their preserved cargos) to river canoes and possibly Roman warships. One ship is a 35ft boat (*c.* 1st century BC) with seven benches for the oarsmen, fourteen tholepins that held the oars in place, and the futtocks that ribbed the ancient hull. Archaeologists also found, lying near, a winch and hemp lines which were possibly part of the rigging. Another boat's hold is lined with amphorae stacked upright between pieces of lava from Vesuvius. Inside the amphorae are residues of wine, fruits, and nuts. Yet another vessel tells its story through its contents: incense burn-

ers of Punic style point to a stop in Carthage, and a painted vase from the coast of Spain and a gold Celtic clasp were likely to have come on board in southern France. The most remarkable item of this ship's cargo was a single canine tooth, large enough to have come from a lion which might have lost its battle with a gladiator. A new museum is proposed to house this kaleidoscope of everyday objects, wooden dishes, leather sacks, sailors' sandals, and baskets. However, until funds are available, there is a small display in the Arsenal Mediceo. The ships can be viewed by archaeologists only on site at Andrea Pisano.

Museo Capitolino
Capitoline Museum
Piazza del Campidoglio 6, 00186 Rome, Italy
Tel. (39) 06 399 67800
Tue-Sat 9.30am-7pm, Sun 9am-11pm

Greek sculpture
Ny Carlsberg Glyptotek

The collections of the Capitoline Museum were started as early as 1471 by Pope Sistus IV. The museum was inaugurated in 1734 by Clement XII and in the following years it acquired the *Capitoline Venus*, the *Red Faun*, the *Centaurs from Hadrian's Villa* and the *Mosaic of the Doves*. You will be welcomed to the museum by Marforio, a river divinity who proudly lies in a fountain in the entrance hall. The room of the Dying Galatian is particularly moving. It houses a beautiful copy of the *Amazon of Phidias*, the Parthenon's 'maître d'œuvre', and the expressive and touching statue of the *Dying Galatian* who stands in the middle of the room.

Museo civico archaeologico
The Town Museum of Archaeology
Via dell'Archiginnasio 2, 40124 Bologna, Italy
Tel. (39) 051 233849   www.comune.bologna.it
Tue-Fri 9am-2pm, Sat-Sun & public holidays 9am-1pm, 3-7pm

One of the most important archaeological museums in Italy gives pride of place to the Etruscan civilization, which is the best documented period of Bologna. The collection gives a comprehensive view of the development of the ancient town of Felsina from the 9th to the 4th century BC when the town was invaded by Gauls. The Hoard of St Francesco uncovered an 8th-century BC foundry store containing 14,838 bronze objects and also letters and carved alphabets. Among the famous and most remarkable pieces are the *Askos Benacci* (askos meaning leather bottle in Greek); the *Certosa Situla*, a hammered bronze

vase with rich decorations representing parades, banquets, and hunting, and ploughing scenes (early 5th century BC); and the head of Atena Lemnia, a marble Roman copy of the bronze statue by Phidias. There are a large amount of treasures from the 'Tomba Grande' of the Giardini Margherita, dating from the 5th century BC, including a sumptuous banqueting service and Attic ceramics, in particular a krater attributed to the Niobid Painter.

The Neumagen wine boat, c. AD200 Rheinisches Landesmuseum Trier

Musée de la Civilisation gallo-romaine
The Museum of Gallo-Roman Civilization
17 rue Cléberg, 69005 Lyon, France
Tel. (33) 4 72 38 81 90
Wed-Sun 9.30am-noon, 2-6pm

Located in the heart of the ancient city of Lugdunum and surrounded by the oldest theatre in France (10,000 seats), an odeum, the sub-foundations of a temple to Cybele, and the remains of a craftsmen's quarter, this museum is a fascinating place to visit. The jewel is the historically important Claudian Table, discovered in the 16th century on the slopes of the Croix-Rousse quarters in Lyon. On this bronze table is inscribed the speech of the Emperor Claudius which he gave in front of the Senate in 48BC to request access for Gaul chiefs to Roman magistratures. It is one of the best preserved inscriptions known to us. The museum is organized by themes such as the army, religions in ancient Gaul and drama. The rich collection of artefacts and objects illustrate the various activities of everyday life in a Roman province, while statuettes and portraits testify to the Imperial presence in the ancient capital of Gaul. The museum also houses fine mosaics, including the masterpiece mosaic of the *Jeux du cirque* which was discovered in 1806 in Lyon and is one of the rare representations of games in antiquity.

Ermitazh
The Hermitage
Dvortsovskaia naberezhnaia 34-36, 191065 Saint Petersburg, Russian Federation
Tel. (7) 812 1109079 www.hermitage.ru
Tue-Sat 10.30am-6pm, Sun 10.30am-5pm

Housed in the recreated inner courtyard of a Roman villa, the collection of Roman sculptural portraits has a worldwide reputation and represents one of the best of its kind. From emperors to private individuals, the collections span five centuries. Among the museum's jewels are the bronze expressive bust of a Roman man (1st century BC), the bust of Philip the Arab (3rd century AD), the statue of Augustus represented as Jupiter (1st century BC-AD), and the melancholic portrait of the emperor Lucius Verus. The collection of Etruscan art is also famed outside Russia. One of the masterpieces is the splendid black-lacquered hydria from the 4th century BC known as the *Queen of the Vases,* found in the town of Cumae.

Museo etrusco Guarnacci
The Etruscan Guarnacci Museum
Via Don Minzoni 11, 56048 Volterra, Italy
Tel. (39) 0588 86347
Mid Mar-Oct: daily 9am-7pm. Nov-mid Mar: daily 9am-4pm

The museum's ground floor exhibits the Archaic and Classic eras, while the second floor illustrates the economic and artistic splendour of Etruscan Volterra from the 4th-1st centuries BC. Reconstructed tombs are on display with a magnificent cinerary urn typical of Volterra, as the rite of cremation was almost exclusive to this area. Its lid represents a recumbant figure attending a luxurious banquet feast. On display is also a reconstruction of an artisan workshop exhibiting the utensils used by the alabaster artisans in Volterra and a collection of alabaster urns of exquisite workmanship. There is also an impressive collection of coins, with rare examples of Etruscan coins in gold, silver and bronze, as well as more than 3,000 Greek, Roman Republican and Imperial coins. The votive figure of a young boy known as *Ombra della sera* (*Shadow of the Evening*) is an exquisite example of 3rd-century Etruscan sculpture.

Museo e Galleria Borghese
The Borghese Museum and Gallery
Piazza Scipione Borghese 5, 00197 Rome, Italy
Tel. (39) 06 8548577 www.galleriaborghese.it
Tue-Sat 9am-7pm, Sun 9am-1pm

Immediately outside the Aurelian Walls, surrounded by a huge park, is one of the most beautiful Roman villas commissioned by Cardinal Scipione Borghese and built between 1613 and 1614. Although famous for its statues by Bernini, it is the early 4th-century mosaics set in the floor of the entrance hall, depicting gladiatorial and animal combat in larger-than-life detail, that are of interest to the classicist. There are also many Roman sculptures, a sarcophagus with the battle of Romans against northern Barbarians, and in the hall, marble busts of Roman emperors by G. B. Della Porta.

Interior of a gallery
Ny Carlsberg Glyptotek

Museo gregoriano etrusco
The Etruscan Gregorian Museum
Viale Vaticano, 00120 Vatican City, Italy
Tel. (39) 06 69883333 www.christusrex.org
Apr-mid Jun & Sep-Oct: daily 8.45am-4.45pm. Rest of year: Mon-Fri & last Sat-Sun each month 8.45am-1.45pm

This museum was opened by Gregory XVI in 1837. It houses one of the few large Italiot bronzes that have survived, the so-called *Mars of Todi* (5th century BC). It represents a young warrior armed with helmet, leaning on a lance with his left hand and offering a libation with the cup held in his outstretched right hand before going to battle. There is also a very fine collection of candelabra, one of which is 1.5 metres high. Among the museum's key objects is a pyriform ink pot in 'bucchero' with inscribed alphabet on the base and graffito syllabary on the sides, showing the introduction of writing in Etruria through the Greek colonies of 'Magna Graecia' (southern

Glass cremation group, Roman, 1st-early 2nd century AD
Museum of London

Italy). You will not be able to miss one of the most monumental products of Corinthian art – a large krater, known as the Astarita Krater, depicting Ulysses and Menelaus setting out to rescue Helen – and a stunning gold fabula.

Museum of London
London Wall, London EC2Y 5HN, UK
Tel. (44) 20 7600 3699
www.museumoflondon.org.uk
Tue-Sat 10am-5.50pm, Sun noon-5.50pm

Londinium became the capital city of the most northern province of the Roman Empire around AD100. Part of the local excavations have been put on display in the museum and the daily life of the city has been recreated through domestic interiors and workshops. There is a reconstructed living room (AD300) which contains reproduction furniture and original objects from Roman London. The collection also includes a Roman jug found in Southwark, inscribed with the words 'Londini Ad Fanum Isidis' ('In London, by the Temple of Isis') which was possibly a temple offering. It is the earliest example of an inscription using the Roman name for London. The best-known group of Roman material is the metalwork derived from the bed of the Walbrook stream in 1956. The superb preservation of this collection and the wide range of domestic, industrial, and religious artefacts rivals in quality and quantity even that of the British Museum.

Roman pottery ware
found at Brockley and
Highgate
Museum of London

Musée du Louvre
The Louvre
Palais du Louvre, 34-36 quai du Louvre, 75001 Paris, France
Tel. (33) 1 40 20 53 17 www.louvre.fr
Mon, Wed 9am-9.15pm, Thu-Sun 9am-5.30pm

The quality and quantity of the old royal collection was greatly enhanced by the prizes of
war seized by Napoleon. The triumphal procession in 1798, reminiscent of the Imperators'
processions in Rome, included many famous sculptures obtained by the Treaty of Tolentino
in 1797 (the Laocoon group, the *Dying Gaul*, the *Apollo Belvedere* etc). Some of them have now
returned to their original home country, but the Roman collections remain one of the
world's leading and most comprehensive collections. The Louvre houses several masterpieces of Etruscan art, including the sarcophagus of a man and a woman showing the
surprising image, for antiquity, of the woman as equal to the man. *The Muses from Pompeii*,
a 1st-century AD wall painting, is stunning. The sculpture and bronze collections are
equally impressive, and include a marble statue of Trajan exalting the power of Rome,
from the Borghese collection; a bronze colossal head of Hadrian; a cuirassed bust of
Caracalla in marble; and a portrait of Herodes from the 2nd century. Thanks to a Rothschild
donation, the Louvre displays one of the richest collections of Roman silverware. A large
hoard of Roman silver plate found in a villa at Boscoreale, near Pompeii, includes a superb
emblema bowl thought to represent Alexandria, and a cup showing skeletons at a feast.

Musée luxembourgeois
The Luxembourg Museum
13 rue des Martyrs, 6700 Arlon, Belgium
Tel. (32) 63 22 61 92 www.ial.be
Tue-Sat 9am-noon 1.30-6pm, Sun & public holidays 2-6pm

Orolanum was, in Roman times, a trading post at the crossroads between the trade roads
from Reims to Trier, and from Tongeren to Metz. Its archaeological museum, one of the
best in Belgium and Luxembourg, is based mainly on archaeological finds uncovered in
the area. Take a walk to the Archaeological park off the rue des Thermes, to see the foundations of the oldest church in Belgium, a basilica from the 5th century AD, surrounded
by a cemetery where many of the ancient tombstones, including some Merovingian
ones, are still present. There are also the remains of the Roman Thermae and bathhouses.
The museum boasts more than 450 statues from tombstones and from the Roman baths.

Museo nacional de Arte romano
The National Museum of Roman Art
José Ramón Melida s/n , 06800 Mérida, Spain
Tel. (34) 924 311690 www.mcu.es
Tue-Sat 10am-2pm, 4-6pm, Sun 10am-2pm. Times may vary, please call for details.

Mérida was the Roman capital of the western half of the Iberian peninsula, which fell to
victorious Rome over Hannibal and Carthage in 202BC. The museum recounts the roman-
ization of Hispania. Among the most impressive ruins at Mérida are an amphitheatre, a
Diana temple, and a forum's portico. Parts of these excavations are now on display in the
museum and include Roman glass, ceramics and jewellery, coins, mosaics, reliefs and
murals, collections of epigraphs, stelae, and several busts. There is also a large collection
of sculptures, including statues of Venus, Ceres, Proserpina, Oceanus and a bust of Augustus.

Il Museo Navale Romano
The Roman Naval Museum
piazza San Michele, 11, 17031 Albenga, Italy
Tel. (39) 0182 51215 www.emmeti.it
Jun-Sep: Tue-Sun 10am-noon, 4-7pm. Oct-May: Tue-Sun 10am-noon, 3-6pm

The Palazzo Peloso Cepolla (14th-16th century) houses one of Italy's most important naval antiquities exhibitions. The centrepiece of the collection are some thousand or so amphorae and other objects from the wreck *Artiglio* which was recovered near Albenga. Apart from amphorae containing wine from France and Spain, the shipload also included ceramics which are on display along with a number of personal objects belonging to the crew and the armed escort.

Museo nazionale tarquiniese
The National Museum of Tarquinia
Palazzo Vitelleschi, piazza Cavour 1, 01016 Tarquinia, Italy
Tel. (39) 0766 856036
Tue-Sun 9am-7pm

Situated at the lower end of the River Marta, Tarquinia was one of the centres of the Etruscan area, a pacesetter of Etruscan civilization, culture, and religion. With its 200 or so painted tombs, the necropolis of Tarquinia was already unique in the Etruscan as well as the ancient world. After fluctuating fortunes, it rose to new splendour thanks to the lordship of the Vitelleschi (whose mansion is now the home of the National Museum of Tarquinia), and then sank into decay as a result of a disastrous earthquake in the 16th century. Apart from their beauty, the tomb frescoes are important for their documentation of myths, traditions, and family clans. The collection's sarcophagi recount genealogies, events, and the roles of entire families such as the Pulena and the Camna. Everyday objects like pottery, tools, weapons, and ornaments inform the visitor about Etruscan life. There are several Etruscan ceramic masterpieces, a large vase by Nikosthenes (5th century BC), and an amphora by Phintias (late 6th century BC).

Gold coin, 10-aureus piece, struck in Trier in AD297 (top)
Rheinisches Landesmuseum Trier

Central Hall (middle)
Ny Carlsberg Glyptotek

Roman sarcophagi (above)
Ny Carlsberg Glyptotek

Roman figure of a young boy (right)
Allard Pierson Museum

Ny Carlsberg Glyptotek
The New Carlsberg Glyptotheque
Dantes Plads 7, 1556 Copenhagen, Denmark
Tel. (45) 33 418141 www.glyptoteket.dk
Tue-Sun 10am-4pm

The collection of late-Etruscan funerary art is particularly extensive and ranks among the finest in the world. The sarcophagus from Vulci depicting a divine Lasa, whose wings associate her with Vanth, the Etruscan demon of death, was Jacobsen's first purchase through Helbig in 1887. The sarcophagus lid dating from 250-180BC supporting an Etrurian man lying on a mattress is quite remarkable. There is also a collection of drawings of tombs collected by Danish archaeologists or commissioned by Jacobsen during his trips in Rome and Tarquinia. Greek influence on sculpture is particularly noticeable on a head of Athena from a Greek original model. A painted woman's head that was probably found in Etruria is also a fine example of the kinds of carved heads that were later inserted on lids for funerary urns.

Allard Pierson Museum
Oude Turfmarkt 127, 1012 GC Amsterdam, The Netherlands
Tel. (31) 20 5252556 www.uba.uva.nl
Tue-Fri 10am-5pm, Sat-Sun 1-5pm

The masterpiece of the Roman department is a large marble sarcophagus with the god Dionysus and his followers. The sarcophagus was made in Rome in the early 3rd century AD. Another important piece of Roman sculpture from the middle of the 1st century AD is a statue of a boy personifying Autumn. The figure is a half life-size representation of a child aged about four years old. Other notable objects come from the earliest period of the Etruscan culture, known as the Villanovan period (900-675BC) and include pottery and cinery urns, as well as metal belts and clothes-pins.

Rheinisches Landesmuseum
The Rhenish Regional Museum
Colmanstrasse 14-16, 53115 Bonn, Germany
Tel. (49) 228 72941 www.lvr.de
Tue, Thu-Fri 9am-5pm, Wed 9am-10pm, Sat-Sun 10am-5pm

Gold coin, 10-aureus piece, struck in Trier in AD 297
Rheinisches Landesmuseum Trier

The museum was founded in 1820 and is one of the oldest museums in Germany. Its Roman section shows the cultural development in the Rhineland during the first 400 years after the birth of Christ. Some of the most important exhibits include the tombstone of the Roman captain, Marcus Caelius, who died in the battle of Varus; the impressive rock altar of Hercules Saxanus; and the sun-god motif from the mid-3rd century. This mosaic shows the sun god in his chariot surrounded by the signs of the zodiac. There is a fine collection of helmets as well as glasses.

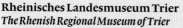

Rheinisches Landesmuseum Trier
The Rhenish Regional Museum of Trier
Weimarer Allee 1, 54290 Trier, Germany
Tel. (49) 651 97740 www.uni-trier.de
Tue-Fri 9.30am-5pm, Sat-Sun 10.30am-5pm

A walk through the town gives some indication as to the extent of its importance as the capital of the province of Gallia Belgica from the 2nd century AD, and as one of the imperial residences of the late Roman Empire in the 4th century. Sites such as the audience chamber of the Roman palace remain, as does the Elector's Palace, along with the Kaiserthermen (Imperial Baths), attesting to the city's power which climaxed under Constantine in the early 4th century, and Valentinian I and Gratian in 367-383. The museum's collections reveal the merging of native Celtic elements with the new Roman culture to produce the Gallo-Roman culture. One of the many religious sculptures illustrating this fusion shows the old Celtic god Esus and the Roman god Mercury. Agriculture and wine-making have left not only buildings and tools, but are themes illustrated on a number of funeral reliefs. One of the best known is the Neumagen wine boat (*c.* AD220) showing a local product, possibly wine, being rowed downstream for export. A wide range of assorted vessels points to the intensive production of pottery in the city and nearby centres, while jewellery, glass fragments, and mosaic panels all attest to the sophisticated skills of the artists and the importance of the city.

Fishbourne Roman Palace and Gardens
Salthill Road, Fishbourne, Chichester, Sussex PO19 3QR, UK
Tel. (44) 1243 785859 www.sussexpast.co.uk
Feb-mid Dec: daily from 10am (closing times vary). Rest of year: Sat-Sun 10am-4pm

Many visitors come to see the largest and most superb collection of in-situ mosaics in Britain, but adjacent to these covered remains is a gallery containing the most important items from the excavations of this Roman site, believed to have been active several decades before the conquest in AD43. Some objects might not seem particularly exotic or impressive, but all have a story to tell. The marble head of a boy is certainly a portrait of someone important and may depict a young Tiberius Claudius Togidubnus who was the probable owner of the palace. A child's gold ring set with a green stone showing a small bird was made for either a wealthy woman or child.

Marble head of a boy, suggested to be the young Tiberius Claudius Togidubnus, probable owner of the palace later in his life
Fishbourne Roman Palace and Gardens

Römisch-Germanisches Museum
The Roman-Germanic Museum
Roncalliplatz 4, 50667 Cologne, Germany
Tel. (49) 221 2214090
Tue-Sun 10am-5pm

Beside the cathedral is this famous museum with treasures from the time when there were two Germanic tribes in Cologne on opposite sides of the river. On display are objects of Roman everyday life, ancient jewelry, glass arts, oil lamps, Roman cult statues, games, keys, and a suprisingly modern-looking four wheeled chariot.

Musée Saint-Rémi
The Saint-Rémi Museum
53 rue Simon, 51100 Reims, France
Tel. (33) 3 26 85 23 36
Mon-Fri 2-6.30pm, Sat-Sun 2-7pm

Following the conquest of Gaul by Julius Caesar, the small Gallic village of Durocortorum became an important city in less than two years and stood as the headquarters of the Roman governor. The Porte de Mars, which used to stand at the end of one of the two main routes that traversed the city in a right angle, is one of the largest surviving monumental arches in the Roman world. The collections here are testimony to the past splendour of Durocortorum. The altar of Cernunnos, the deer-god, illustrates religious syncretism with the Gallic god surrounded by Apollo and Mercure. One of the most impressive tombs ever unearthed houses the marble sarcophagus of Jovin, the general of the Roman Cavalry in Gaul. There are official portraits of famous emperors such as Marcus Aurelius and Antonin the Pious, as well as portraits of anonymous local people, which illustrate Reims society under the rule of imperial Rome.

Sir John Soane's Museum
13 Lincoln's Inn Fields, London WC2A 3BP, UK
Tel. (44) 20 74052107 www.soane.org
Tue-Sat 10am-5pm (plus 6-9pm on first Tue each month)

For the passionate collector this museum is a must. Highlights include a bronze lamp with an early Christian monogram (4th-5th century AD) and an antique Roman vase found at Cologne which can be seen in the library. In the crypt, a marble relief of a lion-footed griffin from the end of a Roman sarcophagus (*c.* 2nd century AD) is an interesting example of a much stereotyped item. One of the most impressive ancient items is a marble statue of the Ephesian Artemis or Diana, which is an antique Roman adaptation of a wooden cult-figure which may have once stood in the Temple of Artemis at Ephesus (*c.* second half of 2nd century AD). The visitor cannot miss the cast of the Apollo Belvedere, ostensibly put on display by Soane as one of his favourite pieces. The original is at the Vatican and is a Roman copy (*c.* AD135) after a Greek bronze. Among the great treasures of Soane's collection of architectural fragments is a marble capital of a pilaster from the interior of the Pantheon at Rome, erected by Hadrian between AD118-128.

Staatliche Antikensammlungen and Glyptothek
The State Collections of Antiquities and Glyptotheque
Königsplatz 1-3, 80333 Munich, Germany
Tel. (49) 89 598359 www.stmukwk.bayern.de
Tue, Thu-Sun 10am-4.30pm, Wed noon-8.30pm

Located next door to each other, the Glyptotheque and the State Collections of Antiquities complement each other perfectly. Both have their roots in the collection of over 600 Greek vases amassed by King Ludwig I, but there is also a fine display of

Etruscan art, including bronzes and glass, of which a centrepiece is the Etruscan golden jewellery (680-539BC). In addition, there are outstanding Roman copies of Greek statues, such as Kephisodot's Eirene or Praxiteles's naked Aphrodite. There are several important original tomb reliefs from the 4th century BC and a collection of Roman portraits ranging from Alexander the Great as a young man to various fine examples from the period of Augustus up to late antiquity.

Museum het Valkhof
The Falcon Court Museum
Kelfkensbos 59, 6501 BL Nijmegen, The Netherlands
Tel. (31) 24 3608805   www.museumhetvalkhof.nl
Tue-Fri 10am-5pm, Sat-Sun & public holidays noon-5pm

Nijmegen is the largest and most important Roman site in the Netherlands, having been continuously occupied from around 15BC until the end of the 4th century. In the modern city remains can still be found of several military camps and civilian settlements. Prominent among these are the fortress of the Tenth Legion which was occupied from AD71 until the second half of the 2nd century. The museum was built on the site of the civilian settlement of Batavodurum (1st century AD) and houses a large archaeological collection, in which Roman finds from the city of Nijmegen and the province of Gelderland predominate. Its collections consist of military paraphernalia such as inscriptions, weaponry, and equipment (both infantry and cavalry) as well as a prominent collection of helmets, including a number of unique cavalry sports helmets. Fine glass vessels and a series of small sculptures made from amber, as well as jewellery and coins, a large collection of bronze vessels used for cooking, dining and bathing and a few pieces of furniture such as folding stools document the Romans' everyday life. In a separate room of the museum the pottery collections are on display.

Worthing Museum and Art Gallery
Chapel Road, Worthing, West Sussex BN11 1HP, UK
Tel. (44) 1903 239999
Mon-Sat 10am-5pm

The Archaeology Gallery shows finds from the Roman shrine at Muntham Court. Among the votive offerings is a beautifully made bronze boar. The Avisford cist burial, finds from a local cemetery, a bath house, and a villa are displayed beside several large coin hoards. The jewel in the crown has to be the Patching Gold Hoard, found in 1997. It is the largest hoard of Roman gold and silver ever found in this country and most of the gold coins are in near mint condition. The latest dates from around AD461 and there are also a number of Visigothic copies of Roman coins. The hoard also includes two gold thumb rings, fifty silver coins and a quantity of silver bullion. It was buried around AD465, when Roman coins no longer circulated in this country.

Fragment of a red-figure terracotta vase, Greek, c. 390BC
(left)
Allard Pierson Museum

Greek red-figure ware vase (right)
Allard Pierson Museum

GREEK ANTIQUITIES

Allard Pierson Museum
Oude Turfmarkt 127, 1012 GC
Amsterdam, The Netherlands
Tel. (31) 20 5252556   www.uba.uva.nl
Tue-Fri 10am-5pm, Sat-Sun 1-5pm

The oldest objects in the Greek collections date from the Bronze Age (300BC). Of particular note are the so-called *Idols* from the Cycladic Islands fabricated from local marble and given to sanctuaries or entombed in graves. The imagery of painted pottery and of the statues made of stone, clay and bronze reveal the world of the Greeks, ranging from gods and heroes to everyday life in Greece and overseas colonies. The museum has an important collection of Greek pottery decorated in the black-figure and red-figure technique.

Archaeological Museum
Sarayiçi Osman Hamdi Yokusü, Istanbul, Turkey
Tel. (90) 212 5 20 77 40
Tue-Sun 9.30am-5pm

The museum was founded in 1881 by Hamdi Bey, Turkey's first archaeologist of international status, and was the first building in Turkey ever to have been constructed expressly as a museum. The museum's architect was influenced by the decorative elements of the Sarcophagus of Alexander and the Sarcophagus of the Mourners, which are among the highlights to be found here. Once thought to be the sarcophagus of the great conqueror himself, it has since been identified as belonging to the king Abdalonymus of Sidon (the place it was found). The museum also holds a superb head of Alexander, probably a copy after the famous original by Lysippus, who was the only sculptor allowed to make personal representations of the Macedonian conqueror. The Archaeological Museum was named as the Best Museum of the Year in 1992 by the European Council.

Attic amphora with red figures, attributed to Andokides' painter, *c*. 530-520BC (above)
Musée du Louvre

Pergamon altar, built under Eumenes II, marble, *c*. 170BC (below)
Pergamon Museum

Arkhailogikó mouseío Delphón
The Delphi Archaeological Museum
33054 Delphi, Greece
Tel. (30) 265 82312
Summer: Mon noon-5pm, Tue-Sun 8am-7pm. Winter: daily 8.30am-3pm

In Ancient Greece, people travelled to Delphi from far and wide to consult the famous oracle or participate in the Pythian games. The museum houses a collection of Greek antiquities essentially assembled through the successive excavations in the sanctuary and includes remains from the Temple of Apollo and reconstitutions of Treasuries, as well as examples of private or public offerings to the god Apollo. Among the highlights are the majestic *Sphinx of the Naxians* that used to stand at the top of a 10-metre column (570-560BC); the *Twins of Argos*, two identical Archaic kouroi sculpted in Paros marble (6th century BC), and a statue of Antinoüs, Hadrian's favourite, who drowned in the Nile and was subsequently deified by the Emperor.

Musée Barbier-Mueller
The Barbier-Mueller Museum
10 rue Jean-Calvin, 1204 Geneva, Switzerland
Tel. (41) 22 3120270
Daily 11am-5pm

This collection of sixty marble sculptures from the Cyclades is among the finest of its type and one of the largest in Europe. Josef Müller became interested between the two world wars and acquired several significant items from the Jouvenel collection, including a famous violin-shaped marble statuette. There is also a rudimentary but delicate Kusura-type marble idol from the Turkish coast.

Museo Barracco
The Barracco Museum
Corso Vittorio Emanuele II 166A,
00186 Rome, Italy
Tel. (39) 06 68806848
Tue, Thu 9am-1pm, 5-10pm, Wed,
Fri-Sun 9am-1pm

This small, cosy museum contains a fine collection of Assyrian, Egyptian, and Greek artefacts. The second floor is given over to Greek art and includes ceramics, sculptures, portraits of reliefs, and statuettes, as well as rare original Attic works by Myron, Phidias, and Lysippus. Sculptures in the collection are mainly from the 5th and 4th centuries BC. Of special importance is a fragment of an Attic funerary stele depicting a horseman. Dating from 520BC, it is the oldest piece in this section.

Detail of Pergamon altar
Pergamon Museum

Collezioni Ludovisi Boncompagni in Palazzo Altemps, Museo nazionale romano
Ludovisi Boncompagni Collection at the Altemps Palace, Roman National Museum
Piazza Sant' Apollinare 46, Rome, Italy
Tel. (39) 06 6833759
Tue-Sun 9am-7.45pm

Fifty yards from the end of the Piazza Navona in the Piazza de Sant'Apollinare stands the Palazzo Altemps, the austere Renaissance residence that now houses the great Roman noble families' collections of ancient statuary. Inside you find the Ludovisi Boncompagni collection of stunning sculpture which was, in past centuries, a point of pilgrimage for artists, students, and scholars during their stay in Rome. The collection, housed in a garden of 75 acres reached its high point during the 19th century when it contained 339 sculptures. In 1883 Prince Rodolfo Ludovisi sold the estate to property developers, much to the annoyance of those scholars who had enjoyed visiting the place. Urged on by educated opinion in 1901, the Italian government purchased 104 of the sculptures from this 17th-century collection which have since been added to by the Altemps Collection (sadly only sixteen works dating from the 16th century are on show), and the 17th-century Mattei Collection.

British Museum
Great Russell Street, London WC1B 3DG, UK
Tel. (44) 20 7636 1555   www.thebritishmuseum.ac.uk
Mon-Sat 10am-5pm, Sun noon-6pm

The museum acquired its first pieces of Greek sculpture in 1815 from the Temple of Apollo at Bassae in Arcadia (450-400BC). A year later, the British Government bought the sculptures and other antiquities acquired by the Earl of Elgin in Greece, including the controversial *Frieze of the Parthenon*, better known as the *Elgin Marbles*. Carved in about 440BC to decorate Athena's temple on the Acropolis, they depict a festival to commemorate Athena's birthday which includes a grand procession of chariots, musicians, pitcher bearers, sacrificial victims, and beautiful women, as well as the gods Hermes and Dionysus. Visitors to the museum can also see a royal tomb (*c.* 400BC) from Xanthus in Lycia, one of the Caryatids from the Erechtheion (the remaining five still support the monument in Athens), and the colossal figures of Mausolus and his wife Artemisia from the Mausoleum at Halicarnassus, which was considered one of the Seven Wonders of the World in antiquity. In addition, there is a well-documented collection of Greek vases and an extensive collection of small sculptures, including the Tanagra figures of 325-200BC which rank as some of the finest examples of the minor arts of the Hellenistic period.

Ny Carlsberg Glyptotek
The New Carlsberg Glyptotheque
Dantes Plads 7, 1556 Copenhagen, Denmark
Tel. (45) 33 418141   www.glyptoteket.dk
Tue-Sun 10am-4pm

Among the most interesting displays to be found here is the splendid colossal-sized Naxian head from the 6th century BC, which was probably inspired by Egyptian art. Although true portraiture developed with the habit of immortalizing illustrious citizens, idealization remained a key-feature in Greek portraits, whose most significant achievement may be the famous head of Alexander the Great held by the Glyptotek. The oriental idea of divine kingship is perfectly rendered in the contemplative pose of the Macedonian hero.

Aphrodite; cult statue of a Goddess, unknown artist working in Magna Grecia, limestone and marble 425-400BC
The J. Paul Gettty Museum

Ethnikó arkhaiologikó mouseío
The National Archaeological Museum
Odós Tosítsa 1, 10682 Athens, Greece
Tel. (30) 1 821 7717
May-Sep: Mon 12.30-7pm, Tue-Sun 8am-7pm
Oct-Apr: Mon 10.30am-7pm, Tue-Sun 8.30am-3pm

The museum is an obvious place to go for anyone interested in Greek antiquities, though the collection is not one of the world's best thanks to the rampant pillaging of Greek treasures over the years. Nevertheless, it remains a significant collection and

contains a number of rare pieces including the superb *Poseidon of Artemision* in bronze. However, what makes this museum unique is its collection of Mycenaean art. The importance of this collection is enhanced by its central position in the museum. It consists of a panorama of all the arts practised by the Mycenaeans and the other Greeks who shared the Mycenaean culture, which spread from approximately 1600-700BC. Among the items on display are gold masks, including the famous mask of Agamemnon, finds from the Palace of Nestor, and frescoes from the Palace at Tiryns, whose walls were decorated with a large colourful procession of women.

The J. Paul Getty Museum
The Getty Centre, 1200 Getty Center Drive, Los Angeles, California 90049-1679, USA
Tel. (1) 310 440 7300   www.getty.edu
Tue-Wed 11am-7pm, Thu-Fri 11am-9pm, Sat-Sun 10am-6pm

The collection of antiquities at the museum is one of the finest in the US and includes a valuable number of Greek sculptures including a remarkable life-size head of Apollo (probably a Greek imperial copy of the 2nd century AD), a statue of Herakles after an original of *c.* 340BC found near Hadrian's Villa, and a Graeco-Roman Aphrodite crouching at her bath.

Musée du Louvre
The Louvre
Palais du Louvre, 34-36 quai du Louvre, 75001 Paris, France
Tel. (33) 1 40 20 53 17   www.louvre.fr
Mon, Wed 9am-9.15pm, Thu-Sun 9am-5.30pm

Like the museum's other collections of antiquities, the ancient Greek exhibits at the Louvre rank among the best in the world. Of special interest is the collection of Hellenistic art (*c.* 323-31BC). One of the main acquisitions of the 19th century was the famous *Venus de Milo*, together with the *Gladiator of Agasias*, and the *Sleeping hermaphrodite*, who lies on a mattress added by Bernini. These sculptures feature among the most beautiful works of art ever to be produced. The powerful wings of the *Victory of Samothrace*, a Rhodian dedication celebrating a naval victory in the 2nd century BC, also illustrate the new aesthetics which flourished at the time. The bronze statuette of *Alexander with a Spear* was mentioned by ancient authors, while the stunning example of the *Crouching Aphrodite* was also to become a popular subject in Hellenistic times. The museum also holds one of the richest collections of Tanagra statuettes, the painted figurines whose name comes from the tombs excavated at Tanagra in Beotia. The famous group of 500 statuettes donated by Gaudin from the cemetery of Myrina in Asia Minor illustrates well small-scale sculpture from the Hellenistic period.

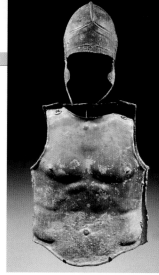

Nationalmuseet
The National Museum
Frederiksholms kanal 12, 1220 Copenhagen, Denmark
Tel. (45) 33 134411 www.natmus.dk
Tue-Sun 10am-5pm

The collections of Greek and Roman antiquities to be found here are the richest in Denmark, thanks in part to the Crown Prince who participated in the
opening of several ancient tombs in the towns of Nola and Cumae. The collection of Greek pottery is especially fine and illustrates numerous themes from
antiquity which enable the visitor to imagine the life of the ancient Greeks or
to admire famous scenes from Greek mythology. Among the items on display
are a wine jar from Athens (c.530BC) depicting an athlete who has just won a
bronze tripod, a jug representing girls fetching water at the fountain house inside
which young men are bathing, and a wedding vase from Apulia (350-300BC) which bears
exquisite motifs and female figures.

Complete Greek bronze
suit of armour, 350-300BC
Rijksmuseum van Oudheden

Natsionalen arkheologicheski muzei
The National Archaeological Museum
Buyuk Dzhamiia, ulitsa Saborna 2, 1000 Sofia, Bulgaria
Tel. (359) 2 882405
Tue-Sun 10am-noon, 1.30-6pm

The museum is housed in the 'Big Mosque' which dates from 1494. Although Bulgaria's
most valuable treasures are in the National History Museum, this museum still possesses
some individual items that stand out, such as an 8th-century BC bronze figurine of a stag
found at Sevlievo near Pleven. There are plenty of Greek finds from around the country,
the most famous of which is the Stela of Anaximander, a 6th-century BC gravestone from
the ancient Greek colony of Apollonia (now Sozkopol) on the Black Sea coast.

Pergamon-Museum - Antikensammlung
The Pergamon Museum - Collection of Antiquities
Bodestrasse 1-3, 10178 Berlin, Germany
Tel. (49) 30 209050 www.pergamon-museum.de
Wed-Sun 9am-5pm

The Pergamon houses one of the largest and most astonishing collections of Graeco-
Roman antiquities in the world, including the massive Altar of Zeus from Pergamon,
known as Pergamonaltar, and the treasures excavated by Heinrich Schliemann in the
city he identified with ancient Troy. The collection of Greek and Roman sculpture
includes masterworks of the Archaic, Classical, Hellenistic, and Roman periods, such as
the *Goddess of Berlin*, the seated *Goddess of Tarantum*, and a good selection of Roman
copies of Greek sculptures.

Rijksmuseum van Oudheden
The National Museum of Antiquities
Rapenburg 28, 2301 EC Leiden, The Netherlands
Tel. (31) 71 5163163 www.rmo.nl
Tue-Fri 10am-5pm, Sat-Sun & public holidays noon-5pm

This is the leading archaeological museum in the Netherlands and has a good store of
Greek antiquities. Star exhibits include a complete set of armour from the 4th century
BC, complete with a chest plate, helmet with cheek protectors, fragments of a bronze
belt, and two leg protectors. The department is mainly famous for its large collection of
Greek vases. In 1839, the museum bought the vases from the collection of Napoleon I's
brother, Lucien Bonaparte. These 100 vases include the Antimedes vase, bearing the

Rabbit, wood with traces
of plaster, polychrome,
Japan, Edo Period,
18th century
Le Musée des Arts Asiatiques

inscription 'kalos Antimenes' (beautiful Antimenes). Its centre shows a temple-shaped bathing place where young athletes shower under gargoyles.

Staatliche Antikensammlungen und Glyptothek
The State Collections of Antiquities and Glyptotheque
Königsplatz 1-3, 80333 Munich, Germany
Tel. (49) 89 598359 (Antiquities) / 286100 (Glyptotheque)   www.stmukwk.bayern.de
Antiquities: Tue, Thu-Sun 10am-4.30pm, Wed noon-8.30pm
Glyptotheque: Tue, Wed, Fri-Sun 10am-4.30pm, Thu noon-8.30pm

The collection boasts an outstanding number of Greek antiquities ranging from the 14th century BC to the 4th century AD. Highlights of the collection are the superb Greek decorative vases and urns including a collection of painted Attic black- and red-figure vases by some of the best practitioners of this art including Exekias, Andokides, and Euphronios. Centrepieces include the famous cup depicting Dionysus, the god of wine and ecstasy, making a voyage across the sea, and a vase depicting the poet Sappho. The adjacent Glyptotheque is the setting for a museum devoted to statuary and sculpture including the east and west pediment of the Temple of Aphaia on the Greek island of Aegina (505-485BC), which were sculpted from Paros marble. Highlights include the Medusa Rondanini or the Barberinian Faun. These artefacts were removed from the temple in 1811 by a group of German archaeologists who sold them to King Ludwig I of Bavaria.

INDIAN AND ASIAN ARTEFACTS

Museo d'Arte orientale Edoardo Chiossone
The Eduardo Chiossone Museum of Oriental Art
Villetta di Negro, piazzale Mazzini 1, 16122 Genoa, Italy
Tel. (39) 010 542285
Tue-Sat 9am-1pm, 2-7pm (plus every alternate Sun 9am-12.30pm)

Rhino horn cup
decorated with scholar
under a pine tree,
Chinese, Ming dynasty,
early 17th century
*The Museum of East
Asian Art*

A fascinating mass of Oriental art collected by the painter Edoardo Chiossone during his stay in Tokyo, to which acquisitions by the town of Genoa have been added. There are thousands of Japanese pieces from various historical periods, including 11th-century paintings, suits of armour, ceramics, lacquerwork, and theatre masks.

Le Musée des Arts Asiatiques
The Museum of Asian Art
405 promenade des Anglais - Arénas, 06200 Nice, France
Tel. (33) 4 92 29 37 00   www.arts-asiatiques.com
Mid May-mid Oct: Mon, Wed-Sun 10am-6pm. Mid Oct-Apr: Mon, Wed-Sun 10am-5pm

This museum's collection reads like a history lesson. The sculpted and painted items in the Indian section illustrate the Hindu presence in 18th-century South India. The exceptional and complete set of throne legs made of sculpted ivory reveal the long tradition of magnificent Indian court furniture. The art of Cambodia is represented through statues and reliefs made of sandstone, as well as a rich collection of iconographic art. Among the Far Eastern antiquities are Chinese bronze objects (vases etc.) which evoke twelve centuries of cultural history (1600-256BC). The section dedicated to Japan includes a clay statue representing a horse (6th century AD), recounting Japan's origins as a feudal and aristocratic warrior society.

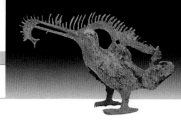

Bronze cormorant with
fish in its beak, Chinese,
Eastern Han dynasty
25–220AD
*The Museum of East
Asian Art*

Ashmolean Museum

Beaumont Street, Oxford, Oxfordshire OX1 2PH, UK
Tel. (44) 1865 278000 www.ashmol.ox.ac.uk
Tue-Sat 10am-5pm, Sun & public holidays 2-5pm

The Indian collections (which include Tibetan and South East Asian artefacts) are of
international importance, and with the help of several benefactors, have continued to
grow around the nucleus of the Old Indian Institute collection which was begun in
1897. Even before that, Oxford University was acquiring art from India and elsewhere
(the earliest recorded acquisition is of an Indian sculpture which was purchased for the
University in 1686). Among the items on display are a number of sculptures including a
Seated Bodhisattva from Gandhara, India (1st century AD) and a monumental head of
Siva from the Gupta dynasty. There are also outstanding examples of gold coinage,
including a gold muhur from Agra (1611), and an example of one of the earliest series of
manuscripts illustrating Amir Hamza overthrowing Amir 'Imad Karuba (*c.* 1562). The
E. M. Scratton collection of Tibetan Buddhist art is on long-term loan to the museum
and includes rich examples of thangka-paintings, bronze casting, metalwork, and
bone- and ivory-carving. There is also a good representation of textiles from Burma.

Asia Society Museum

725 Park Ave., New York, New York 10021, USA
Tel. (1) 212 288 6400 www.asiasociety.org
Tue-Sat 10am-6pm, Sun noon-5pm

In 1979, Mr and Mrs John D. Rockefeller III granted the Asia Society a collection of
nearly 300 works which they had acquired over 25 years of exploring Asia. This
collection of masterworks dates from 2000BC to the 19th century and includes
bronzes, paintings, ceramics, and sculpture. The Asia Society now selectively adds
objects to this core collection. The collection of Hindu and South East Asian sculpture
is one of the major highlights and includes a copper statue of Rama from the Chola
period, and pages of the Ashtasahsrika Prajnaparamita manuscript (c. 1073) from the
Nalanda monastery in Bihar, India.

Asian Art Museum

Golden Gate Park, near 10th Ave. S and Fulton Street, San Francisco,
California 94118, USA
Tel. (1) 415 379 8800 www.asianart.org
Mon, Wed-Sun 10am-6pm

Virtually every facet of Asian art is represented in this museum which was founded by
Avery Brundage, long-serving president of the International Olympic Committee. Of
particular merit are the collections of Chinese jades, ceramics and ritual bronzes which
span thousands of years and account for over half the museum's holdings. In addition,
the museum has a superlative collection from India and other South East Asian countries. The majority of the Indian sculptures come from the central part of the country,
but Indian bronzes from the south are also well represented. Several notable recent
additions have placed this collection in a special league. These include works of exceptional quality from the Christensen Fund from a broad range of cultures throughout
Asia. Another highlight is 61 ceremonial kris (Javanese-style swords) from Indonesia,
Malaysia, Thailand, and the Philippines. In addition, Dr. Narinder S. Kapany, a collector of Sikh, has donated over ninety works of Sikh art from his personal collection,
resulting in a display unique in North America. These collections are due to be exhibited along with other highlights from the permanent collection in specially designed
galleries at the museum's new, expanded facility at San Francisco's Civic Center (sched-
uled to open in the autumn of 2002).

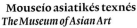

Mouseío asiatikés texnés
The Museum of Asian Art
49 100 Kérkura, Corfu, Greece
Tel. (30) 661 30443
Jul-Mar: Tue-Sun 8.30am-3pm

The nucleus of this collection was the donation in 1927 of 10,500 items by Gregorios Manos which included mainly Chinese and Japanese art. Later additions from Central Asia broadened the scope of the museum and today the collection covers the whole of Asia. Housed in a building designed by the British architect, George Whitmore, it started life as the Residence of the Lord High Commissioner, later becoming the headquarters of the Knights of the Order of St Michael and St George, and finally the summer residence of the Greek royal family before it eventually became a museum. Among the most important items are statuettes from China (T'ang dynasty), bronze ritual vases (Chueh) of the Shang dynasty, examples of Samurai armour from Japan's Han dynasty, and Japanese theatrical masks from the Edo period.

Bronze crossbow trigger mechanism inlaid with gold foil, Chinese, Eastern Zhou, Warring states period, 3rd century BC
The Museum of East Asian Art

Musée Barbier-Mueller
The Barbier-Mueller Museum
10 rue Jean-Calvin, 1204 Geneva, Switzerland
Tel. (41) 22 3120270
Daily 11am-5pm

This museum's South East Asian collection is particularly strong and well known for the large number of megalithic sculptures from Indonesia, Nias, Sumba, and the Barak regions of Sumatra, as well as from Flores, Timor, Sulawesi, and Northern Luzon. Some of the pieces are on permanent loan to the Dallas Museum of Art and the Metropolitan Museum.

British Museum
Great Russell Street, London WC1B 3DG, UK
Tel. (44) 20 7636 1555   www.thebritishmuseum.ac.uk
Mon-Sat 10am-5pm, Sun noon-6pm

A world-class collection of Chinese artefacts from the Neolithic period. Among the collection are finds from Bampo, stone and jade tools, and ritual vessels from the Shang dynasty, with examples of bronze vessels from the early Shang and Eastern Zhou period (770-221BC). There is also a fine collection of tomb figures of horses and camels from the T'ang period, as well as Chinese paintings including *Admonitions of the Instructress to Court Ladies* by Gu Khaizi (c. AD345). Among the most important Korean objects is the Koryo-period manuscript of the Amitabha Sutra in gold and silver paint, while the Japanese collection of 24,000 treasures includes examples of Jomon pottery, funerary material from the Kofun period, and a comprehensive collection of Japanese prints.

Le Musée Cernuschi
The Cernuschi Museum
7 ave. Vélasquez, 75008 Paris, France
Tel. (33) 1 45 63 50 75
Tue-Sun 10am-5.40pm

Fleeing Paris in 1871 during its popular uprising, the wealthy financier Pierre Cernuschi embarked on a long trip to Asia and returned laden with bronzes, lacquers, ceramics, and other artefacts. Bequeathed to the city of Paris in 1896, the collection is today considered to be one of the most important assemblages of ancient Chinese art in Europe. It includes a large number of tomb figurines, remarkable porcelains from the T'ang dynasty, and (the museum's prize exhibit) a celebrated painted scroll, *Horses and Grooms*, attributed to one of China's greatest court painters, Han Kan.

The Corning Museum of Glass

One Museum Way, Corning, New York 14830, USA
Tel. (1) 607 974 8274   www.cmog.org
Daily 9am-5pm (Jul & Aug until 8pm)

This museum holds 1,500 glass vessels from the Far East, ranging from ancient Chinese pieces to examples from present-day Japan. Most of the Chinese pieces are from the Qianlong period (1736-1795). A Warrior's Vase, made of bubbly white glass, overlaid with red, and carved with a representation of warriors on horseback, is one of the finest Chinese carved vessels in existence. The Japanese collection was partially formed by Dorothy Blair who, besides writing the first monograph on the history of Japanese glass (published in 1973), was the original curator of the museum's Far Eastern collection.

The Crow Collection of Asian Art

2010 Flora Street, Dallas, Texas 75201-2335, USA
Tel. (1) 214 979 6430   www.crowcollection.org
Tue-Sun 11am-6pm (Thu until 8pm)

Gallery Three is devoted to the arts of India, South East Asia, Tibet, and Nepal and features a number of Hindu, Buddhist, and Jainist religious sculptures. These include a huge stone head of a Bodhisattva which demonstrates Graeco-Roman influences on Buddhist sculpture, and a number of Hindu sculptures representing popular deities such as Ganesha, the elephant-headed son of Shiva. In Cambodia, Khmer kings identified themselves as living gods and embraced both Hinduism and Buddhism, and a wide array of statues and religious objects are set against a vast photographic backdrop of the temple of Angkor Wat. The most impressive piece is a large section of Mughal wall worked in red sandstone, which fuses elements of Indian and Islamic architecture. Tibet and Nepal were heavily influenced by esoteric Buddhism and there are a number of fearsome, multi-limbed deities including a 16th-century gilt bronze image of Vajradhara, the thunderbolt thrower, inset with turquoise and rubies. The museum's collection of Far Eastern antiquities includes painting, sculpture, porcelain, lacquer, objects carved in jade and horn, crystal and glass, and focuses mainly on works from China's last empire, the Qing dynasty (1644–1911). Several of the pieces were evidently created for Imperial use and display exquisite workmanship. The Japanese collection includes a number of fine scrolls and screens as well as objects made of rock crystal, lacquer, ceramics, and bronze.

The Museum of East Asian Art

12 Bennett Street, Bath, Somerset
BA1 2QL, UK
Tel. (44) 1225 464640
www.east-asian-art.co.uk
Tue-Sat 10am-5pm, Sun noon-5pm

Founded in 1993 by Brian McElney, a retired solicitor who practised in Hong Kong for over 35 years, the museum is housed in a refurbished Georgian building and displays objects dating from 500BC to the 20th century. The collection is predominantly Chinese and ceramic based with examples from all parts of East Asia. There are also some fine examples of Chinese ritual bronzes and enamelled metalwork. The comprehensive collection of jades (200 examples) is accompanied by information on how the pieces were used and produced.

Tall vase, cloisonné enamel on cast bronze, China, Qing dynasty (1644-1911), Quianlong period (1735-95) (top)
The Crow Collection of Asian Art

White glazed jar with carved lotus leaves, porcelain, Chinese, Northern Song dynasty, 10th-11th century (above)
The Museum of East Asian Art

Makie lacquer dowry box with hill and waterfall design and interior tray, Japanese, early 18th century (left)
The Museum of East Asian Art

Roof tile in moulded
earthenware
British Museum

Field Museum of Natural History

1400 S. Lake Shore Dr, Chicago, Illinois 60605, USA
Tel. (1) 312 922 9410 www.fieldmuseum.org
Daily 9am–5pm

The museum has exhibits from across India and South
East Asia. There are, for instance, some 5,000 secular
and religious objects from Tibet which were acquired
by Berthold Laufer in 1908–09. Nearly all date from the
17th to the 19th century. The highlights of the collection
include more than 1,000 traditional Tibetan books, printed and hand written woodblocks, 850 costumes and personal accessories, 800 ritual containers and images, and 350
tangka paintings. The museum's Indonesian and Malaysian collection numbers over
6,000 objects and includes textiles, iron and steel weapons, wayang drama items, and
one of the finest sets of gamelan musical instruments outside Java. In addition, there is a
particularly valuable collection of textiles from the Philippines and a unique
collection of Andamanese wood, bamboo, and rattan utilitarian and ritual objects.

Museum of Fine Arts, Boston

465 Huntington Avenue, Boston, Massachusetts 02115-5519, USA
Tel. (1) 617 2679300 www.mfa.org
Mon, Tue 10am-4.45pm, Wed-Fri 10am-9.45pm

This is a stellar collection of Oriental art, partly as a result of the close trading connections
between New England and the Far East and also thanks to the subsequent donations by a
number of benefactors including Edward Sylvester Morse, Ernest Francisco Fenellosa,
Okakura Kakuzo, William Sturgis Bigelow, and Charles Goddard Weld in the early years,
to later benefactors including John Ware Willard, Frederick L. Jack, Marshall H. Gould,
and Keith McLeod whose donations allowed the Museum's collections of Chinese art to
be considered on a par with those in Japan. The collection includes Chinese glazed earthenware, stoneware, and richly decorated furniture.

Freer Gallery of Art

Jefferson Drive at 12th Street, SW, Washington, DC 20560, USA
Tel. (1) 202 357 4880 www.asia.si.edu
Daily 10am-5.30pm

The Gallery was founded in 1923 by Charles Lang Freer. As the collection grew, the
museum began to lack space and in the 1980s it expanded thanks to the financial assistance of Arthur M. Sackler, a psychiatrist and researcher who had made his fortune as a
publisher of medical books. Since 1987, the gallery's collections have expanded further
to include the Vever Collection, an important assemblage of Islamic manuscripts from
the 11th to the 19th century. More than 5,000 objects from the collection of Paul Singer
were also recently presented to the Sackler Gallery. A passionate collector, Singer's most
important artefacts are from the state of Chu in southern China and, like much of his art,
reflected life in the provinces. With the combined bequests the Freer Gallery's collection
is now world renowned and includes art from China, Japan, and Korea, combining masterpieces of paintings, jades, bronzes, and lacquerworks. The museum's collection of
sculpture from South and South East Asia is particularly remarkable and includes 10th-
13th-century Cambodian stone sculptures and Hindu stone, bronze, brass and terracotta
sculptures from South India dating from the 8th to the 14th century. Ceramics include
pieces from the Hauge donation, with large storage vessels such as glazed and unglazed
'Martaban' jars from Thai and Burmese kilns. The most prized Martaban jars were
considered by their owners in the highlands of insular South East Asia to be able to move
on their own over long distances, and even to marry and produce offspring.

Musée Guimet – Musée national des Arts asiatiques
The Guimet Museum – The National Museum of Asian Art
6 place d'Iéna, 75016 Paris, France
Tel. (33) 1 56 52 53 00
Mon, Wed-Sun 10am-6pm

Black lacquer box inlaid
with wood and mother-of-
pearl, Japan, 1590-1620
*Náprstkovo muzeum
asijských, afrických a
amerických kultur*

The Indian collections are on show on the ground floor, with pride of place given to the
Khmer art collection. Several masterpieces illustrate Angkorian art from the 9th to the
11th century, such as the Koki lintel and two statues of Vishnu in Phnom Kulen style.
There are statues, reliefs, and bronzes from Champa, and more material from Laos,
Burma, and Bali. The group of thang-ka prints and a gold-illuminated manuscript on
black background, recording the secret visions of the fifth Dalai Lama (1617-82), feature
among the most precious pieces in the museum. Artefacts from the ancient civilizations
that lived along the Indus reveal how trade relations with the West flourished under the
Roman period. The Mathura School from northern India is represented by a statue in
pink sandstone of the Snake-god (2nd century), while several bas-reliefs from the Amaravati
School illustrate the art of southern India. There is also a superb head in pink sandstone
from the Gupta period, alongside another high relief representation of Buddha. Among
the Cola period's collection of bronzes stands a very fine statue of Çiva Natarâja performing a cosmic dance. Thanks to a number of donations the museum also has a fine selection of art from Nepal and Tibet which includes 11th-century illuminated manuscripts
and a gold-plated copper Bodhisattva from the 13th century. In addition, there are some
exceptional ceramics from China, Japan, and Korea which include pieces from the Han
dynasty (2nd century BC to 3rd century AD) and T'ang pottery from the 7th to 10th centuries.

Honolulu Academy of Arts
900 South Beretania Street, Honolulu, Hawaii 96814-1495, USA
Tel. (1) 808 532 8700 www.honoluluacademy.org
Tue-Sat 10am-4.30pm, Sun 1-5pm

Developed from founder Anna Rice Cooke's initial gift of approximately 4,500 works of
art, the academy's collection now totals over 34,000 pieces divided between Western and
Asian art. The collection of Asian art is particularly strong and consists of over 16,000
objects by artists and craftspeople from China, Japan, Korea, South East Asia, and India.
The largest sections are the Chinese and Japanese holdings which include paintings,
sculpture, ceramics, lacquerware and prints.

Musée Jacquemart-André
Abbaye royale de Chaalis, 60 300 Fontaine-Chaalis, France
Tel. (33) 3 44 54 04 00 www.ac-amiens.fr
Mar-Oct: Mon-Fri 2-6.30pm, Sat-Sun 10.30am-
12.30pm, 2-6.30pm. Nov-Feb: Sun & public holidays
1.30-5.30pm

Polychrome ceramic
horse figure, China,
T'ang dynasty,
AD618-907
*Náprstkovo muzeum
asijských, afrických a
amerických kultur*

Madame Jacquemart-André, a wealthy widow, spent
much of her life travelling in India and Burma. This led
to the acquisition of precious furniture, as well as
Oriental carpets and objects from Buddhist temples which
are today displayed in the house she bought especially to
house her expanding collection. The Salon Indien is
filled with ancient gilded altars, polished bronze
Buddhas, bronze temple gongs, and votives, as well as a
panoply of Indian and Singhalese arms, richly woven
Oriental rugs, and a white marble throne set on a carpeted dais
which is surrounded by silver chairs and stools inlaid with
mother-of-pearl from India.

Selection of Yangshao-Banshan jars, painted terracotta, *c.* 2500BC
Musée Georges Labit

Museum für Kunst und Gewerbe
The Museum of Decorative and Applied Arts
Steintorplatz 1, 20099 Hamburg, Germany
Tel. (49) 40 24862732 www.mkg-hamburg.de
Tue-Sun 10am-6pm (Thu until 9pm)

The museum's collection ranges from antiquity to the Ming and Qing dynasties. The Chinese collection contains ceramics, jade, bronzes, and paintings. One of the highlights is a Buddha from the Xixia dynasty (11th-12th century). There is also a fine example of a ceremonial receptacle of the 'Ding' type which dates from 1300-1027BC (the Shang-Yin period). A bronze, three-legged basin, it was used for cooking sacrificial food offerings in order to worship ancestors.

Musée Georges Labit
The Georges Labit Museum
43 rue des Martyrs de la Libération,
31400 Toulouse, France
Tel. (33) 5 61 22 21 84 www.mairie-toulouse.fr
Mon, Wed-Sun 10am-5pm (Jun-Sep until 6pm)

The founder of the museum, Georges Labit, travelled the world in search of objects and tokens of unknown peoples and civilizations. A century after its establishment and following many additional contributions, the museum offers a complete panorama of 3,000 years of Asian art. Highlights from the Indian collection include a Buddha sitting in meditation (Ghandara) and busts of Buddha from the 8th and 12th centuries. There is also a selection of Dravidian Bronzes from South India. Further highlights include Chinese urns and receptacles from the Yangshao culture (*c.* 2500BC) and an 18th-century Tibetan white Târâ.

Vajravàràhi 'the adamantine path', gilded copper, Tibet, 16th-17th century
Musée Georges Labit

Head of Buddha, Afghanistan, 1st-3rd century AD
Musée Georges Labit

Los Angeles County Museum of Art (LACMA)
5905 Wiltshire Boulevard, Los Angeles, California 90036, USA
Tel. (1) 323 857 6000 www.lacma.org
Mon, Tue, Thu noon-8pm, Fri noon-9pm, Sat-Sun 11am-8pm

The museum has extensive holdings of arts and ceramics from China, Korea, and South East Asia. Its collection of lacquers takes up ten rooms and is among the finest in the US. There are examples from the Song, Yuan, Ming, and Qing dynasties (some of which were created for emperors) which together represent the full range of decorative techniques employed in lacquerwork.

Musée chinois
Chinese Museum
Château, 77300 Fontainebleau, France
Tel. (33) 1 60 71 50 70
Mon, Wed-Sun 9.30am-5pm

This is Empress Eugenie's personal collection of objects collected from the Far East, through wars, as the result of political gifts, or through donations. There are over 400 pieces including jades, porcelain, silks, vases, and perfume burners which were pillaged from the Summer Palace in Peking during one of the French campaigns of 1860. Other items were donated by Siamese ambassadors who gave Napoleon III some 48 boxes containing gifts. The objects are displayed according to the original arrangement devised by the Empress herself.

Painted paper screen, China, 18th century
Náprstkovo muzeum asijských, afrických a amerických kultur

Náprstkovo muzeum asijských afrických a amerických kultur
Náprstek Museum of Asian, African and American Cultures
Libechov Castle Betlémské náme sti 1, 110 00 Prague 1, Czech Republic
Tel. (420) 2 22 22 14 16   www.aconet.cz
Tue-Sun 9am-noon, 1.45-5.30pm

Although part of the museum, these collections are shown in the striking baroque castle at Libechov near Melník, about 45 kilometres north of Prague. The collections number 50,000 objects, although the castle's 22 halls of permanent exhibition space can only show around 2,500 items at any one time. Nevertheless, the variety is considerable and includes stone and wooden sculptures, weapons, textiles, and folk and ethnographic items. The Indonesian collection has examples of tribal art from the islands of Nias, Sumatra and Kalimantan (called Borneo by Europeans). The section of artefacts from India consists of 19th-century decorative art exhibits, including Bidri items inlaid with silver or gold. These are shown alongside an evocative array of classical sculpture and decorations from Jainist temples. Shawls, embroidery, and hangings produced in Kashmir and Punjab are equally outstanding, as is the collection of lacquerware, ablaze with colour, from Savantvadi. Another highlight of this collection is a permanent exhibition of over thirty examples of Chinese ceramic work from the first millennium BC to stoneware from the Sung period (10th-13th centuries). The Japanese section deals mainly with woodblock prints, porcelain, swords, and lacquerware and dates from the Edo period. Among these are two distinct collections worthy of attention: one of wicker baskets, bowls, and trays woven from bamboo, the other of stencils used for decorating kimono fabrics.

Copper box with lid decorated with rosette spirals, Kashmir, India, second half of 19th century
Náprstkovo muzeum asijských, afrických a amerických kultur

The Newark Museum
49 Washington Street, P.O. Box 540, Newark, New Jersey 07101, USA
Tel. (1) 973 596 6550   www.newarkmuseum.org
Wed-Sun noon-5pm (Thu until 8.30pm)

Among the early donors to this museum were the Jaehne brothers whose business activities in the Far East greatly enriched the collections with several thousand Japanese and Chinese objects, as well as decorative works from India, Burma, Siam, and elsewhere. Over the years, these have been added to through purchases and donations resulting in Japanese art holdings that are encyclopaedic. Most famous, however, are the collections of Tibetan art and artefacts, the most complete outside the Himalayas. Recently the Tibetan Galleries were reinstalled as part of the major exhibition based on their holdings. Only a fraction of the collection is on permanent display, but they encompass the breadth of religious and lay culture in Tibet from the 13th to the mid-20th century, a large part of which were brought back by American missionaries including Dr. Albert Shelton. There is an 11th-century gilt copper image of the goddess Tata, silver vessels, painted tangkas, script volumes from the royal palace of the Prajnaparamita, hair ornaments of silver and coral, and a leather apron decorated with a net of human bones. Amounting to thousands of pieces, they are a superb record of a rich culture that is now truly lost.

Museum für ostasiatische Kunst
The Museum of East Asian Art
Universitätsstrasse 100, 50674 Cologne, Germany
Tel. (49) 221 9405180
Tue-Sun 11am-5pm (Thu until 8pm)

Founded in 1913 to exhibit the private collection of Adolf and Frieda Fischer, the original building was destroyed during World War II and replaced in 1977 by the current Japanese-inspired construction and landscape garden designed by Kunio Maekawa. The museum's extensive collection covers all aspects of Chinese, Japanese, and Korean arts, craft and sculpture from 1500BC to the 19th century. Special emphasis is given to Chinese ritual bronzes from the 16th to the 11th century BC. Other focus is on Korean ceramics of the Koryp dynasty (10th-14th century), lacquerware and Japanese screen painting, and woodblock prints.

Rijksmuseum
The State Museum
Stadhouderskade 42, 1071 ZD Amsterdam, The Netherlands
Tel. (31) 20 6732121 www.rijksmuseum.org
Daily 10am-5pm

Thanks to 300 years of trading with the Far East, the Rijksmuseum boasts an important collection of Asiatic art, including ceramics, lacquerwork, and textiles from Japan, and Javanese sculpture and religious works from China, India, and Burma. Among the highlights are a 12th-century dancing Shiva in bronze and a Chinese Buddhist saint, the Bodhisattva Avalokitesharva (13th century).

Rijksmuseum voor Volkenkunde
The National Museum of Ethnology
Steenstraat 1, 2300 AE Leiden, The Netherlands
Tel. (31) 71 5168800 www.rmv.nl
Tue-Fri, Sun 10am-5pm, Sat noon-5pm

The collection contains objects from areas as far flung as Siberia, Oceania, and Central and South America. Its Indonesian collection is particularly strong and includes stone statues from the Singasari empire which give an impression of the power of old Javanese and Balinese principalities, terracotta statuettes from the Majapahit empire, jewellery, puppets, and a variety of musical instruments. In addition, the museum has a collection of over 6,000 Japanese objects brought back by the scholar Philip von Siebold after he was sent as an ambassador to Japan by William I. The collection includes fans, colossal Buddha statues, and other artefacts. Thanks to other 19th-century scholars, such as Blomhoff and Overmeer Fischer, this is now one of the most comprehensive collections of Japanese art in the world, with displays of complete suits of Samurai armour and ancient tea ceremony items.

Royal Museum of Scotland
Chambers Street, Edinburgh EH1 1JF, Scotland, UK
Tel. (44) 131 225 7534 www.nms.ac.uk
Mon-Sat 10am-5pm (Tue until 8pm) Sun noon-5pm

In the recently opened Ivy Wu Gallery there is a sumptuous array of treasures from China, Japan, and Korea including a large number of Japanese archaeological objects donated at the turn of the century by Gordon Munro, a Scottish doctor who became Medical Director of Yokohama Hospital in Japan. Munro also donated a collection of about 350 Ainu objects, including ritual and domestic clothing and accessories. The collection also includes Japanese ceramics, textiles, costumes, musical instruments, and armour. Asian textiles are well represented with over 2,000 Chinese items including court robes.

Royal Ontario Museum
100 Queen's Park, Toronto, Ontario M5S 2C6, Canada
Tel. (1) 416 586 5549 www.rom.on.ca
Mon-Sat 10am-6pm (Fri until 9.30pm), Sun 11am-6pm

Porcelain incense burner,
Japan, 1720-60
*Náprstkovo muzeum
asijských, afrických a
amerických kultur*

This museum is best known for its Chinese collections which were mainly gathered by
Bishop William C. White and George Crofts at the beginning of the 20th century. The
collection includes pieces dating from the Neolithic and early Bronze Age. The ceremonial
bronze vessels are particularly important, as are the funerary objects, especially pottery
miniatures of living creatures and models of residences found in the tombs of important
personages. Among these is a colourful group of tomb figurines from the cemetery of
Mang Shan near Lo-yang in the Honan province (*c*. AD693).

Musées royaux d'Art et d'Histoire
The Royal Museums of Art and History
10 parc du Cinquantenaire, 1000 Brussels, Belgium
Tel. (32) 2 7417211   www.kmkg-mrah.be
Tue-Fri 9.30am-5pm, Sat-Sun & public holidays 10am-5pm

The Indian and South East Asian collections are presented in seven new rooms which are
divided geographically. The room devoted to Tibet and Nepal exhibits more than 200
tanka prints, as well as hundreds of Buddhas and other examples of statuary art. The
Indian collection is also particularly strong in sculpture. Four wood columns from
Kerala in southern India surround a bronze statue of Shiva Nataraja from the Cola
period and a stone linga of the god Shiva. The extensive collection of 3,000 ceramics
from Vietnam and Laos is displayed alongside thirteen bronze drums dating from 200BC
to the 19th century.

Arthur M. Sackler Museum
Harvard University, 32 Quincy Street, Cambridge, Massachusetts 02138, USA
Tel. (1) 617 495 9400   www.artmuseums.harvard.edu
Mon-Sat 10am-5pm, Sun 1-5pm

Superb collections of Chinese jades, Korean ceramics, and Chinese cave temple painting
and sculpture, as well as an important collection of Chinese bronzes all feature in this
museum designed by the architect James Stirling and funded by the late physician,
collector, and philanthropist Arthur M. Sackler. The Gregory Henderson Collection of
Korean ceramics is one of the largest and most representative collections of such material
in the world. Equally significant are the collections of archaic Chinese jades, ritual bronze
vessels, and early stone and gilt bronze sculptures. The best collection of carved rhinoceros horn in the US, and a selection of Japanese calligraphy round off these prized holdings.

Seattle Asian Art Museum
1400 E Prospect Street, Volunteer Park, Seattle, Washington 98112, USA
Tel. (1) 206 654 3255   www.seattleartmuseum.org
Tue-Sun 10am-5pm (Thu until 9pm)

This small but growing collection of South East Asian artefacts includes Buddhist and
Hindu sculpture in stone and bronze, painting, decorative arts, and a premiere collection of early Thai ceramics. With over 7,000 objects, the museum's collection of Far
Eastern antiquities is considered to be one of the top five in the US and among the most
distinguished outside Japan. The extensive holdings include significant examples of
ink painting, calligraphy, Buddhist sculpture, metalwork and folk textiles. The Chinese
collection spans the Neolithic period to the 19th century and includes tomb figures,
ceramics, ritual bronzes, sculpture, painting, lacquers, jade carvings, snuff bottles, and
over 350 Chinese puppets.

Victoria and Albert Museum
Cromwell Road, South Kensington, London SW7 2RL, UK
Tel. (44) 20 7942 2000   www.vam.ac.uk
Daily 10am-5.45pm (Wed until 9.30pm)
The Indian and South East Asian collections rank among the best in the world. Only five

Ceremonial axe (Yue type) bronze, China, Shang dynasty, 13th century
Museum für ostasiatische Kunst

per cent of the 35,000 Indian artefacts are actually on show. The Mughal period is particularly well represented and includes pages of a royal copy of the Akbarnama commissioned by the Emperor Akbar, with 116 miniatures. Indian sculpture is also very strong and includes the Hindu deity Shiva performing the nadanta dance (*c.* AD900), and a cult image of the 23rd Jina Parshvanatha, with a rare inscription on its base recording the names of both the sculptor and the sponsor. From Nepal there are rare 16th-century gateway reliefs from a Hindu temple and metalwork from South East Asia including a stunning gold container in the form of a bird, inlaid with rubies and emeralds, given to the museum by the Government and people of Myanmar. The museum inherited the large collection of decorative arts which once belonged to the East India Company. Among this collection was Tippoo's Tiger – a mechanical organ hidden inside a man-eating tiger. There are also some of the finest examples of Korean, Chinese, and Japanese art. The Chinese collection is displayed chronologically from the Neolithic period to the present day. Of particular note are some fine T'ang tomb figure horses, as well as a porcelain pagoda 2.7 metres high (one of only ten in existence). There is also a fine collection of Chinese hardwood furniture and rare examples of Chinese woven silk and embroidery. Much of the Japanese collection was donated by the novelist and prolific collector William Beckford, and includes a magnificent lacquer Japanese screen (in the Toshiba Gallery) which was presented as a gift to Sir Harry Parkes, the British minister to Japan, by the Meiji emperor himself.

ISLAMIC ANTIQUITIES

Prayer niche, moulded faience decorated with metallic reflections, Persia, 13th-14th century
Museu Calouste Gulbenkian

British Museum

Great Russell Street, London WC1B 3DG, UK
Tel. (44) 20 7636 1555 www.thebritishmuseum.ac.uk
Mon-Sat 10am-5pm, Sun noon-6pm

Probably the largest and finest outside the Middle East are these prized examples of Islamic works across all media. Besides the Godman collection of Islamic ceramics, precious metalwork includes the *Vaso Vescovali*, a bronze bowl with an inlaid lid bearing astrological symbols (*c.*1200), and delicate specimens of fluted brass ewers, including one inscribed with the name of the decorator, the date, and also the city, Mosul, where it was made. It is the only North Mesopotamian object whose provenance is known for certain. Equally superb are the inkwells from the province of Khurasan in Iran and an incense burner inscribed with two Mamluk rulers. There are fine examples of mosque lamps from the Mamluk period and an excellent collection of miniature paintings, the most important of which dates from the Mughal period in India. Remarkable is a glass pilgrim flask made in Syria during the Ayyubid period. It is a piece of technical wizardry, combining no less than eight coloured enamels with gilding.

The Corning Museum of Glass

One Museum Way, Corning, New York 14830, USA
Tel. (1) 607 974 8274 www.cmog.org
Daily 9am-5pm (Jul & Aug until 8pm)

The Islamic arts are well represented by a group of carved and engraved rock crystal vessels (thought to be as valuable as gold and silver in medieval times) made between the 8th and the 12th century. Not to be overlooked is a Near Eastern blue-turquoise fluted bowl (9th-10th century). Also on display are gilded and enamelled glasses from the 12th - 14th century which illustrate one of the most flourishing periods in Islamic glass making. A good example is the mosque lamp, of which the museum has several.

Davids Samling
The David Collection
Kronprinsessegade 30-32, 1306 Copenhagen, Denmark
Tel. (45) 33 73 49 49 www.davidmus.dk
Daily 1-4pm

Hidden away in intimate rooms containing a European col-
lection of fine and applied art from the 17th to the early 19th century, is by far the largest
collection of Islamic antiquities in Scandinavia. Pieced together by the museum's
founder, Christian Ludvig David, the collection includes calligraphy, a large collection
of miniatures, ceramics, glass, metalwork, wood, stone, and textiles.

Silk fragment, Persia, first
half of 17th century
Museu Calouste Gulbenkian

Museum für frühislamische Kunst
The Museum of Early Islamic Art
Austrasse 29, 96047 Bamberg, Germany
Tel. (49) 951 25954 www.uni-bamberg.de
By appt. only

This private museum contains a unique and valuable collection of early Islamic bronzes
belonging to the Bumiller Art Foundation. Objects originate from what is now modern
Iran, Afghanistan, and Turkmenistan. Apart from works made from stone, ceramics,
wood, and glass, the collection comprises metalwork from the 8th to the 11th centuries as
well as a rich collection of bottles, incense burners, oil lamps, mirrors, and jewellery.

Jade jug, Samarkand,
1417-49
Museu Calouste Gulbenkian

Museu Calouste Gulbenkian
The Calouste Gulbenkian Museum
Avenida de Berna 45a, 1067 Lisbon, Portugal
Tel. (35) 1 21 7823000 www.gulbenkian.pt
Tue 2-6pm, Wed-Sun 10am-6pm

Calouste Gulbenkian had a passion for Persian carpets and one of the highlights of his
collection is an exquisite Persian silk fragment from the first half of the 12th century. Its
motif depicts a youth, symmetrically shown twice, sitting in a garden wearing a turban.
Elsewhere, there are examples of Islamic glass, ceramics, lamps, textiles, and illuminated
manuscripts from the 12th century up to the 18th, from Syria, India, Persia, and Turkey.
Highlights include a white-jade jar which once belonged to Sultan Ulag Bag
(Samarcand, 1417-49); a spectacular gilt-and-enamel glass vase from Syria, depicting
fantastic birds in flight; a Turkish decorative textile made from velvet, brocaded with
silver threads (16th-17th century); and a fantastic selection of Islamic tiles.

Musée de l'Institut du Monde Arabe
The Museum of the Institute of the Arabic World
1 rue des Fossés Saint Bernard, 75005 Paris, France
Tel. (33) 1 40 51 38 38 www.imarabe.org
Tue-Sun 10am-6pm

Jean Nouvel's modern building on the banks of the Seine is the perfect jewel case for this
fascinating museum dedicated to Arab-Islamic culture. The museum's collection
focuses on the cultural exchanges that characterized the making of an Arab-Islamic
area. Many pieces on display are precious exhibits on permanent loan from the Louvre.
They include several sumptuous ceramics such as rare examples from the Umayyad
period, and a dish with polychrome decoration which betrays a Chinese influence (9th-
10th century). Architectural fragments also find pride of place in the collection, with a
13th-century carved wood fragment from Toledo, and everyday objects illustrate the
life of both princes and more humble people.

Museum für Kunst und Gewerbe
The Museum of Decorative and Applied Arts
Steintorplatz 1, 20099 Hamburg, Germany
Tel. (49) 40 24862732 www.mkg-hamburg.de
Tue-Sun 10am-6pm (Thu until 9pm)

The Islamic section consists of a precious collection of tiles, ceramics, glass, and bronzes. There is a fine selection of textiles including a fragment of Iranian silk which dates from the beginning of the 16th century and depicts a wide range of animals including a lion, tigers, panthers, and the mythical creature, Kilin. Among the collection of sculptures and statues is an Iranian (Kashan or Rayxy) statuette of a horseman made from glazed clay dating from the 14th century. The horse carries a musician with two big drums on each side of the saddle. This Seldshuk figurine is very rare as imagery of animated objects is forbidden in Islamic culture.

Musée du Louvre
The Louvre
Palais du Louvre, 34-36 quai du Louvre, 75001 Paris, France
Tel. (33) 1 40 20 53 17 www.louvre.fr
Mon, Wed 9am-9.15pm, Thu-Sun 9am-5.30pm

The Islamic collections, unlike the Near Eastern sections, stem from the popularity of Orientalism in the 19th century rather than from archaeological excavations. Some of the most prestigious objects come from the royal collections and include a remarkable 11th-century Egyptian ewer in carved rock crystal and several bowls in jade, gold and precious stones, which featured in Louis XIV's inventories. The bulk of the collection, however, dates from 1890 thanks to the Sauvageot donation. In 1905 a room devoted to Muslim art was inaugurated. Among the highlights are ceramics, metal objects such as a bronze perfume-burner on a tripod, and numerous little bottles and glass recipients from the Umeyyades, founders of the first Islamic dynasty (AD661-750). From the Abassides in the 8th and 10th centuries AD there are examples of imperial art such as textiles, lamps, and ceramics. From the Fatimides dynasty of the 10th and 15th centuries there are examples of rock crystal engravings, wooden sculpture, and ceramics. From Iran there is a fascinating collection of inventions produced mainly in Kurdistan (10th-13th century).

Mpenaki mouseío
The Benaki Museum
Odós Koumbari 1, 10674 Athens, Greece
Tel. (30) 1 367 1000 www.benaki.gr
Mon, Wed, Fri-Sat 9am-5pm, Thu 9am-midnight, Sun 9am-3pm

Antonis Benakis began this collection in Egypt in the early 20th century and it has since grown to become one of the most important collections of Islamic art in the world, with more than 8,000 works of art including pottery, gold, metalwork, textiles, glass, bone objects, inscribed funerary steles, and weaponry. Among the most important objects in the collection are two carved wooden memorial door leaves from 8th-century Mesopotamia, a small brass box dated 1200 with the signature of Ismail ibn al-Ward al-Mausili, the bronze astrolabe of Ahmad ibn al-Sarraj dated 1328-29, and a beautiful 16th-century velvet saddle from Bursa. Also on display is an intricately carved marble-faced interior of a reception room from a 17th-century mansion in Cairo.

Museo nacional de Arte hispano-musulmán
The National Museum of Hispano-Moresque Art
Palacio de Carlos v Alhambra, Colina de Alhambra, 18009 Granada, Spain
Tel. (34) 958 226279
Tue-Sat, 9am-2.30pm

This museum owns some 10,000 objects, of which around 300 are on view at any one time. Dating from the 8th to the 16th centuries, they represent the various Muslim cultures which dominated much of the Iberian peninsula for eight centuries, among them the Caliphate of Córdoba, the Almoravids, the Almohads, and the Nasrids (the dynasty that converted Granada into a grand metropolis that became the last stronghold of Islam in Spain). Artisans from all corners of Al Andalus converged on Granada to transform the Alhambra into a jewel of Islamic architecture, and many of the museum's treasures are from the grounds of the palace itself, including the famous *Vase of the Gazelles*, an exquisite lustreware jar dating from the 14th century. Also from the Alhambra proper are marble capitals inscribed with intricate Arabic lettering; lace-like plaster architectural decorations; richly coloured azulejos (tiles); and a selection of toys including ceramic horses and whistles shaped like fish and reptiles which were unearthed during excavations.

Pergamon-Museum - Museum für Islamische Kunst
The Pergamon Museum - Museum of Islamic Art
Bodestrasse 1-3, 10178 Berlin, Germany
Tel. (49) 30 209050   www.pergamon-museum.de
Wed-Sun 9am-5pm

The museum's permanent exhibition is dedicated to the art of Islamic peoples from the 8th to the 19th century, originating from an area stretching from Spain to India. However, the collection's main focus is on the Middle East including Egypt and Iran. The broad spectrum of art includes applied arts and crafts, a superb collection of Oriental rugs, jewellery, and rare books, including the calligraphic works and miniatures from albums of Mogul times. The architectural items represent one of the major attractions and consist of entire houses and streets as well as parts of desert fortifications, gates, and mosaics. Highlights include the stone façade of Omayyade Castle in Mshatta (8th century BC), stuccoes (archaeological finds from Samarra), and painted and lacquered wooden panelling from an early 17th-century house in Aleppo.

Arthur M. Sackler Museum
Harvard University, 32 Quincy Street, Cambridge, Massachusetts 02138, USA
Tel. (1) 617 495 9400   www.artmuseums.harvard.edu
Mon-Sat 10am-5pm, Sun 1-5pm

A recent gift of more than 300 works from the Stuart Cary Welch Collection of Indian and Islamic Art means that the museum's collection of Islamic and later Indian art is now one of the foremost in the US. Among the most important works are two folios from a famous manuscript produced in Safavid Iran, the *Divan* (Collected Works) of Hafiz (*c.* 1525), which features the painting *Scandal in a Mosque* signed by the great master Shaykh Zada. Also from the Welch collection is a splendid and powerful painting, *Bhoj Singh of Bundi Slays a Lion*. Attributed to the Kotah Master, the painting was produced in one of the Rajput states of India (*c.* 1725). This gift has been added to the core collection and consists primarily of works of art on paper from Iran, India, and Turkey; holdings of carpets from Iran, Turkey, and the Caucasus; and ceramics from Iran and Turkey.

Museum of Turkish and Islamic Art
Ibrahim Pasa Sarayi, Sultanahmet, Istanbul, Turkey
Tel. (90) 212 518 1805
Tue-Sun 9.30am-5pm

The dark stone building that houses the museum was built in 1524 by Ibrahim Pas, a Grand Vizier to Süleyman the Magnificent. Today, it displays a superb collection of ceramics, metalwork, miniatures, calligraphy, textiles, and woodwork, as well as some of the oldest carpets in the world.

Two folios from the *Divan* of Hafiz signed by Shaykh Zada
Arthur M. Sackler Museum

Victoria and Albert Museum

Cromwell Road, South Kensington, London sw7 2RL, UK
Tel. (44) 20 7942 2000 www.vam.ac.uk
Daily 10am-5.45pm (Wed and last Fri of each month 10am-10pm)

With the world famous Ardabil Carpet hanging in the background, the Islamic Gallery presents one of the finest collections of Islamic art in the world. This is completed by the extraordinary collection of Islamic glass, which includes rare examples of rock crystal vessels from Caliph Mostansir-Billah's treasure in Cairo, of which only a few pieces have survived.

NORTH AMERICAN INDIAN ARTEFACTS

Alaska State Museum

395 Whittier, Juneau, Alaska 9980, USA
Tel. (1) 907 465 2901 www.museums.state.ak.us
Mid May-mid Sep: Mon-Fri 9am-6pm, Sat-Sun 10am-6pm
Mid Sep-mid May: Tue-Sat 10am-4pm

Over half of the 27,000 objects in this collection are Native Alaskan, fashioned by the Eskimos, Athabaskans, Aleuts, and Northwest Coast Indian tribes, including the Haida and Tlingit. Besides these, there are objects relating to exploration of the area, the Klondike Gold Rush, the whaling and fishing industries, and the Russian explorers who inhabited the area prior to 1867, along with natural history collections. The Native Alaskan collections are especially worth visiting. The range is enormous and includes ceremonial textiles, carved masks of curious animals, objects decorated with beadwork and dyed porcupine quills, tools, and eating utensils fashioned from bone or pieces of driftwood found on the banks of the mighty Yukon. It is hard to miss the painted wooden ceremonial helmet stacked with basketry rings, called the 'Frog Hat' because the front is decorated with a finely carved frog. Made by the Tlingit Frog Clan, it is jointly owned by them and the museum, and still goes out on loan for special ceremonies.

Mask from the Northwest coast of America, 19th century
British Museum

British Museum

Great Russell Street, London wc1b 3DG, UK
Tel. (44) 20 7636 1555
www.thebritishmuseum.ac.uk
Mon-Sat 10am-5pm, Sun noon-6pm

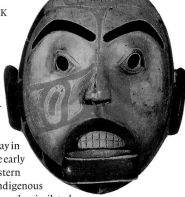

The Chase Manhattan Gallery of North America holds an extensive collection of Native American Indian artefacts and contains an impressive spread of apparel and artefacts formerly held in the Museum of Mankind, where most of it was hidden away in storage. The gems in this collection are the early items made before 'contamination' by Western cultures, as well as those made when the indigenous peoples first encountered European goods and assimilated European artistic traditions into their work. There are also artefacts from the burial mounds of the Hopewell culture who populated the Ohio valley from around 400BC, bold masks carved by the tribes of the Northwest coast, and Plains Indian headdresses and beaded clothing.

The Brooklyn Museum of Art
200 Eastern Parkway, Brooklyn, New York 11238, USA
Tel. (1) 718 638 5000 www.brooklynart.org
Wed-Fri 10am-5pm, Sat-Sun 11am-6pm (first Sat of each month 11am-11pm)

Chase Manhattan Gallery
of North America
British Museum

In 1903, when the museum announced in the Brooklyn *Daily Eagle* that they were to embark on 'building up great ethnological collections, sending out expeditions for acquiring of antiquities, first over all America, then over the entire world', they chose as head of the program, R. Stewart Culin. Self-taught and without much professional experience, Culin was not the most obvious choice. He had however the knack of a born collector, and seemed able to root out the rare and unusual and acquire it at rock bottom prices. By 1912, he had crisscrossed the country, systematically acquiring more than 9,000 objects representative of Native American India emphasizing the Zuni, Navajo, and Pueblo of the Southwest; the California tribes and those of the Northwest Coast; and several regional tribes, including the Osage collection amassed in Oklahoma. Travel diaries record both his acquisitions and the process of collecting, making the collection unique for its level of documentation. Besides outstanding collections of Native American textiles, ceramics, basketry, and masks, the theme of games runs through the collection, a subject of special interest to Culin and one with which his name is still closely associated.

Burke Museum of Natural History and Culture
University of Washington Campus, Seattle, Washington 98195, USA
Tel. (1) 206 543 5590 www.washington.edu
Daily 10am-5pm (Thu until 8pm)

There is a good collection of dinosaurs, but one of the real gems is the Northwest Coast Indian collection, which is the fifth largest in the US, with approximately 9,400 items. Among these are exceptional examples of cedar canoes and totem poles. Highlights are the Anne Gerber Collection of Kwakwaka'wakw masks (forty-plus examples) and a 45-foot canoe donated by Mrs Thomas Burke from the same Northwest Coast tribe. George Emmons, in the latter part of the 1800s, collected Tlingit material including a number of bentwood boxes, while Myron Eells and Janice Swan put together a well-documented collection (also at the end of the 1800s) of western Washington groups, including the first peoples of the Puget Sound. Equally strong is the Alaskan Arctic collection which includes over 6,500 pieces.

Eiteljorg Museum
500 West Washington Street, Indianapolis, Indiana 46204, USA
Tel. (1) 317 636-9378 www.eiteljorg.org
Tue-Sat 10am-5pm, Sun noon-5pm

Harrison Eiteljorg first went West in the 1940s in search of coal. Soon, however, he found the art of Native Americans to be a far greater draw and the avid collector travelled thousands of miles to attend exhibitions and to visit museums devoted to Western art. Today this collection has become the Eiteljorg Museum. The collection is particularly rich in objects from the Plains and the Southwest. Many of these are now familiar items – totem poles, a feathered headdress, a tomahawk. Others, such as the wooden masks of the Haida tribe, wooden whistles used by the shaman to accompany their songs and dances, and wooden snow goggles, are less well known.

Fenimore Art Museum
PO Box 800, Lake Road, Route 80, Cooperstown, New York 13326, USA
Tel. (1) 607 547 1400 www.fenimoreartmuseum.org
Apr-May, Oct-Dec: Tue-Sun 10am-4pm. Jun-Sep: daily 10am-5pm

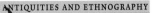

This museum is filled with memorabilia relating to one of the town's heroes – James Fenimore Cooper, author of *Last of the Mohicans*. The lower floor galleries are crammed with choice examples of North American Indian artefacts, the core of which were collected by Eugene and Clare Thaw. The quality of the workmanship and the spirit which went into producing the painted bowls and masks is astounding. The fine carving of totem poles and the intricacy of the woven baskets, made by tribes which once upon a time inhabited the plains and mountains of North America, are equally impressive. The total collection stands at 780 items and includes a horse mask by the Nez Perce Indians. Made from bright red trade cloth and decorated with dyed horse hair, glass beads, ribbons, mirrors, leather, and flicker feathers, it is an awesome piece.

Central Yup'ik Mask, Alaska, *c.* 1890
Fenimore Art Museum

Canoe model with Indian figurine by Mary Kooyik, Ontario, Canada, 1847-53
Fenimore Art Museum

Gilcrease Museum

1400 Gilcrease Museum Road, Tulsa, Oklahoma, 74127-2100, USA
Tel. (1) 918 596.2700 www.gilcrease.org
Tue-Sat 9am-5pm, Sun & public holidays 11am-5pm

Objects from 19th- and early 20th-century American Indian communities residing on the Great Plains are especially well represented in the Gilcrease anthropology collections. Kiowa, Comanche, Lakota (Sioux), Osage, Arapaho, and Cheyenne are among the groups from which important collections of moccasins, parfleches (rawhide containers), clothing, tools, and other items have been preserved.

Haffenreffer Museum of Anthropology

Brown University, 300 Tower Street, Bristol, Rhode Island 02809, USA
Tel. (1) 401 253 8388 www.brown.edu
Jun-Aug: Tue-Sun 11am-5pm. Sep-May: Sat-Sun 11am-5pm

This museum has an astounding collection of 10,077 native North American objects including a strong collection of Plains Indian art dating from the late 19th and early 20th century. Current facilities limit the number of objects on display, but a computerized database allows access, and those wishing to conduct research should contact Barbara Hail, whose knowledge is extensive.

Hastings Museum and Art Gallery

Johns Place, Bohemia Road, Hastings, East Sussex TN34 1ET, UK
Tel. (44) 1424 781155
Mon-Sat 10am-4.45pm, Sun 2-4.45pm

Two galleries devoted to displaying a collection of artefacts from two of the main cultural areas of the North American continent: the Plains, including the Sioux and Blackfoot; and Woodlands, particularly the tribes associated with Gray Owl, a local man turned conservationist. The core of the collections is based on material gathered over 60 years by an Eastbourne man, Edward Blackmore, who became fascinated from an early age by American Indians through books and visits to the cinema and who went on to become not just a collector, but one of the foremost exponents of Indian culture in Britain, teaching himself how to ride and make Indian crafts (he even used a tepee on his honeymoon). Besides Blackmore's material, there are items amassed by Clare Sheridan, sculptress and friend of Blackmore who moved onto a Blackfoot reservation in 1937 and later to Blood Indian country, building up a collection of historic items which she eventually

gave to Blackmore. Her small collection contains two scalps taken as trophies by Chief Crazy Crow, a Blackfoot deerskin dress, and a Crow Indian belt decorated with brass studs and beadwork given to her father by Chief Sitting Bull himself.

Beacon Lights, degikup,
Lousa Keyser,
c. 1850-1925
Fenimore Art Museum

George Gustav Heye Center, National Museum of The American Indian

Smithsonian Institution, Alexander Hamilton US Custom House, One Bowling Green, New York, New York 10004, USA
Tel. (1) 212 514 3700   www.nmai.si.edu
Daily 10am-5pm (Thu until 8pm)

The Alexander Hamilton US Custom House, designed by architect Cass Gilbert, is an apt setting for displays drawn from what is the finest and most comprehensive collection of Indian cultural materials in the world, assembled by George Gustav Heye over a 54-year period beginning in 1903. Originally located in the heart of Harlem where only the most intrepid dared to venture, the 800,000 items sat languishing in poor conditions until they were rescued by the Smithsonian in Washington, DC, which established this outpost as well as a new museum on the mall in Washington. Heye collected obsessively, not only with his eye, but he also saw the value in articles produced for everyday use. The result is a collection of extraordinary aesthetic, religious and historical significance, as well as of utilitarian use, spanning the Western Hemisphere from the tribes of the Arctic Circle to Tierra del Fuego. Space here limits the number of objects on view, but exhibitions feature artefacts selected for their beauty and rarity across a diverse range of cultures, rotating with those chosen by indigenous peoples of the Western Hemisphere, fulfilling the museum's aim to keep alive the vital link between itself and native communities across the Americas.

Diorama in the Edward Blackmore Gallery of American Indian Art
Hastings Museum and Art Gallery

Hood Museum of Art

Dartmouth College, Hanover, New Hampshire 03755, USA
Tel. (1) 603 646 2808   www.dartmouth.edu
Tue-Sat 10am-5pm (Wed until 9pm), Sun noon-5pm

A diverse collection comprising nearly 60,000 works of art and artefacts of which nearly half constitute the College's ethnographic collection. Of these, there are nearly 8,000 objects representing the artistic and cultural traditions of Native North America. Strong in pottery, basketry and beadwork, highlights include an early Haida wood, bone and painted missionary figure (*c.*1820-60) and an Athabaskan jacket (pre 1879) made from buckskin and decorated with red wool cloth, pink, green, and red silk cloth, glass beads, and brass buttons.

The Horniman Museum and Gardens

100 London Road, London SE23 3PQ, UK
Tel. (44) 20 8699 1872   www.horniman.demon.co.uk
Mon-Sat 10.30am-5.30pm, Sun 2-5.30pm

An extensive collection of North American Indian artefacts which includes a 19th-century beaded shoulder bag from Delaware; a pair of 18th-century buckskin moccasins from the Huron; a colourful saddle blanket, dyed red with cochineal (*c.* 1850); and a late 19th-century ceremonial headdress decorated with horns, ermine, feathers, and bells belonging to one of the Blackfoot. These and other items including woven baskets, hats, blankets, cutlery, trophies, and children's toys are testimony to a culture now all but dead.

Institute for American Indian Studies

38 Curtis Road, Washington, Connecticut, USA
Tel. (1) 860 868 0518   www.amerindianinstitute.org
Mon-Sat 10am-5pm, Sun noon-5pm (Jan-Mar closed Mon and Tue)

This massive study collection of artefacts from the Algonkian speaking peoples of southern New England is primarily made up of objects fashioned from stone and bone. Dating back 10,000 years, the life of the Indians stretches into the Stone Age, and is clearly represented here, particularly in the collection of tools, weapons, and cooking equipment made from stone, wood, and bark. Formerly known as the American Indian Archaeological Institute, the Institute's main function for its first fifteen years was to carry out archaeological excavations and research. Now, however, it has taken on a full museum function, with changing exhibitions, educational workshops and camps.

Montana Historical Society
225 North Roberts, Helena, Montana 59620, USA
Tel. (1) 406 444 2694   www.his.state.mt.us
Summer: Mon-Fri 8am-6pm, Sat-Sun 9am-5pm. Winter: Mon-Fri 8am-5pm, Sat 9am-5pm

Central Yup'ik parka,
Alaska, *c.*1890-1910 (top)
Fenimore Art Museum

Child's vest back, Teton
Sioux (Lakota), *c.*1890-1910
(above)
Fenimore Art Museum

Wooden war helmet,
Tlingit, Southeastern
Alaska, *c.* 1750-1800
(right)
Fenimore Art Museum

The Native American collection (3,900 pieces) contains artefacts from each of the many tribes who have called Montana home. Strengths of the collections are their early reservation-era Blackfoot, Sioux, and Salish materials. The society's archaeological collection (2,500 pieces) is relatively small, but contains artefacts from the Anzick Site, the most complete known Clovis Cache of the Paleolithic Period in the United States. The Historical Society is the official repository for archaeological materials found on State-owned lands.

Musée de l'Homme
The Museum of Mankind
Palais de Chaillot, 17 place du Trocadéro, 75016 Paris, France
Tel. (33) 1 44 05 72 72   www.mnhn.fr
Mon, Wed-Sun 9.45am-5.15pm

A number of the choice artefacts to be found here can be traced back to several cabinets of curiosities, including that of François I, as well as of Fayolles who amassed the exotic holdings from the Marquis of Sérent to assist in educating the children of the Count of Artois. Among these items are beautiful examples of painted bison skins. Additional bison and reindeer skins were commissioned by Louis XVI in 1776 from the tribes in northern Canada for use in educating the princes, and these early pieces are rarities. The collections have since been augmented by a number of acquisitions including those collected by Raoul d'Harcourt in 1964 and those of Claude Lévi-Strauss. The Arctic collections contain significant numbers of Inuit artefacts, including 3,752 objects gathered by explorer Paul-Emile Victor in 1934 on behalf of the museum.

Museon
Stadhouderslaan 41, 2517 HV The Hague, The Netherlands
Tel. (31) 70 338 1338   www.museon.nl
Tue-Sun 11am-5pm

The Inuit collection of the museum is exceptional, with 1,500 objects from forgotten centuries of the old world, paying homage to the exquisite craftsmanship still evident in the objects they produce today. Many of the earliest items were collected by Niko Tinbergen in 1932 on a Dutch expedition to East Greenland. On display are clothing, masks, and sculptures. In addition there are a number of wooden boxes decorated with bone and ivory. A particularly fine example is a small riveted casket for tools and personal belongings carved by a hunter, with ivory figures in relief of bears, dogs, and a man on a sledge.

National Cowboy & Western Heritage Museum
1700 NE 63rd Street, Oklahoma City, Oklahoma 73111, USA
Tel. (1) 405 478 2250 www.nationalcowboymuseum.org
Daily 9am-5pm

A new Native American Indian gallery contains both fine contemporary art and traditional, historic Indian objects such as pottery, carvings, and basketry. It focuses on the
Indians of the southern Plains of the United States. Considerable holdings have come via
the J. H. Bratley Collection with well-documented provenance.

Blackfeet Tepee camp
The Plains Indian Museum

National Museum of American Indian
Smithsonian Institution, The National Mall, Washington, DC, USA
Tel. (1) 202 287 2020 www.nmai.si.edu
Please call for opening times

Currently under construction is the Smithsonian's newest addition
dedicated to Native American cultures. Due to open in 2004, the core
of this collection was amassed by George Gustav Heye, whose hobby
was collecting everything related to the Indian tribes from the entire
Western Hemisphere. Around 800,000 objects are augmented by
photo archives of 86,000 prints and negatives. The majority come
from North America, although about thirty per cent are from Central
and South America. Besides the new Mall location, they have a
remarkable array of holdings displayed at their satellite site in downtown New York (see separate entry). However, the bulk of the collection
is housed in a state-of-the-art Cultural Resources Center in Suitland,
Maryland, where the collection is accessible to researchers.

The Plains Indian Museum
Buffalo Bill Historical Center, Cody, Wyoming, USA
Tel. (1) 307 587 4771 www.bbhc.org
Nov-Mar: Tue-Sun 10am-3pm. Apr: daily 10am-5pm. May: daily
8am-8pm. Jun-Oct: daily 9am-5pm

A full-size tepee and expansive murals greet you as you walk into the wing of the
Buffalo Bill Historic Center complex, established to display one of the finest collections
of Plains Indian art and artefacts to be found anywhere. Early reservation period artefacts
(*c.* 1880) and crafts from tribes such as the Arapaho, Cheyenne, Kiowa, Crow, Comanche,
Blackfoot, Sioux, Shoshone, and Pawness are stunningly exhibited. The sections
devoted to clothing and artefacts decorated with beads and quill work are extensive,
detailing dyeing processes and methods of application.

Reservation Era House
The Plains Indian Museum

Royal Museum of Scotland - National Museums of Scotland
Chambers Street, Edinburgh EH1 1JF, Scotland, UK
Tel. (44) 131 225 7534 www.nms.ac.uk
Mon-Sat 10am-5pm (Tue until 8pm), Sun noon-5pm

The holding of over 2,000 items includes internationally important collections amassed
in the early 19th century by explorers in the Arctic and Subarctic, as well as significant
collections of Great Lakes and Plains material. Of the Northwest Coast collections there
are a few items collected by Captain Cook as well as star items such as a selection of beautifully carved domestic utensils, tools, masks and ceremonial material, and a full-size
totem pole carved by Nishga'a carver, Oyea, in 1855. Other artefacts include a significant
group of early 19th-century Beothuck grave material (1854) and the Plains collection
containing the costume of the Sioux chief, Wanatak, who died in 1837.

Nepcetat mask,
1840-60 (above)
Fenimore Art Museum

Crow shield, *c.* 1860
(below)
Fenimore Art Museum

Seattle Art Museum

100 University St, Seattle, Washington 98101, USA
Tel. (1) 206 654 3255 www.seattleartmuseum.org
Tue-Sun 10am-5pm (Thu until 9pm)

In 1991, the museum was fortunate enough to acquire a small but desirable collection of 188 artefacts amassed by artist-cum-collector John H. Hauberg. The majority of these are Tlingit (34), Haida (23), and Kwakwaka'wakw (22) and the collection is considered to be one of the finest of its kind in the world. Other highlights are the collection of almost 200 native American masks, sculpture, textiles, and decorative and household objects from the Pacific Northwest, British Columbia, and Alaska.

Yosemite Museum

Indian Cultural Exhibit, Yosemite National Park, Yosemite Valley, Yosemite, California, 95389 USA
Tel. (1) 209 372 0281
Daily 8.30am-noon, 1-5pm

Looming large on the right side of the entrance to the museum is a cross-section of a 1,000-year-old sequoia, its rings highlighted by significant dates including the landing of Columbus in the New World and the American Civil War, hinting perhaps at the size and scope of the museum's collections: an estimated 1,700,000 items including all manner of natural and cultural materials relating to Yosemite and its environs. Within this mass is the ethnographic collection of 5,000 objects which contains the largest extant group of documented artefacts of the region's native Miwok and Paiute people dating from the 1880s to the present. These people came to be called the Ahwahnichi ('people who live in the valley shaped like a big mouth'). Strengths of the collection are its examples of Miwok dance regalia dating from 1920 to 1950 and its made-for-sale Miwok and Mono Lake Paiute baskets woven from 1910 to 1960. The

majority of the collection is in store but can be accessed by appointment, while in the small exhibition area are remarkable examples of ceremonial headdresses, jewellery, and capes superbly decorated with feathers, beads, and shell ornaments.

Staatliches Museum für Völkerkunde
The State Museum of Ethnology
Maximilianstrasse 42, 80538 Munich, Germany
Tel. (49) 89 2101360 www.stmukwk.bayern.de
Tue-Sun 9.30am-4.30pm

Georg Heinrich von Langsdorff, who participated in Ivan von Krusenstern's first Russian circumnavigation of the earth (1803-06), amassed a collection of curiosities from the Aleutians and the Pacific Inuits during his stay in Alaska between 1805 and 1806. In 1823 he offered King Maximilian I, Joseph of Bavaria, his 'Krusenstern Collection' which became one of the two original collections forming the basis of the Royal Ethnographic Collections founded in 1868. Today the collection comprises some 2,000 exhibits and focuses mainly on early objects from Alaska. On display are clothes made from fur, leather, and skin as well as everyday objects such as eating utensils, train oil lamps, and combs made from clay, wood, bone, or ivory. Bags, baskets, and receptacles made from leather, fabric or woven grass are also on display, as are a number of everyday items decorated with glass pearls. There is a beautiful example of a small kayak, probably used by a child in order to hunt birds and sea mammals, as well as several kayak models used as toys, burial, or ceremonial objects. Weapons include harpoons, spears, and arrows. The museum also possesses a remarkable selection of Inuit sculpture, including the Lorne Balshine collection.

Museum für Völkerkunde
Museum of Ethnology
Neue Burg, 1014 Vienna, Austria
Tel. (43) 1 534 30 00 www.ethno-museum.ac.at
Mon, Wed-Sun 10am-4pm

Masks from the
Northwest coast of
America, 19th century
British Musuem

This vast collection of 250,000 ethnographical and archaeological objects comes from
Asia, Africa, Oceania-Australia and America. Among the jewels here are artefacts
acquired by Captain James Cook on his voyage to the Northwest coast of North America
in 1778. Items worth noting are a portrait mask from Nootka Sound, Canada, possibly
representing death, and a thread-woven blanket from British Columbia that represents
the transitional phase between cedar bast capes and the famous chilkat blankets.

Museum für Völkerkunde
Museum of Ethnology
Lansstrasse 8, 14195 Berlin, Germany
Tel. (49) 30 8301226 www.smb.spk-berlin.de
Tue-Fri 9am-5pm, Sat-Sun 10am-5pm

A move to larger premises and the return of objects confiscated by the Soviet Union
after World War II allowed a large selection of over 30,000 objects relating to North
American Indians to be exhibited after years of being hidden away in storage rooms.
Items range from those of the Inuit, collected by Captain Corner, to those acquired by
Adrian Jacobsen from the Haida tribe in 1882 including a superb example of a carved
and painted chest with lid. Among the many highlights of the collection are the valuable
buffalo robes which Prince Maximilian zu Wied brought back from his journey to the
Missouri River between 1832 and 1834.

George Woodruff Indian Museum
Bridgeton Free Public Library, 150 E Commerce Street, Bridgeton, New Jersey 08302, USA
Tel. (1) 856 451 2620
Mon-Sat 2-4pm. Other times by appt. only

The basement of the library displays artefacts from the Nanticoke Lenni-Lenape tribe
(also known as the Delawares) given to them by the English settlers in the mid 17th century who named the river. The core of this collection, numbering tens of thousands, is
the work of one man, George Woodruff, a local businessman whose hobby was amassing
artefacts relating to this tribe. All the artefacts come from within a 30-mile radius of the
city and each of them, whether they were collected by Woodruff, bought by him or
donated to him, have accurate and detailed records of their places of origin. Thousands
of arrow and spear heads, parts of tomahawks, grinding stones and an extensive array of
clay cooking pots are on display, along with several new additions recently teased from
the damp soil of local ongoing excavations.

OCEANIC ART

Musée d'Aquitaine
The Museum of Aquitaine
20 cours Pasteur, 33000 Bordeaux, France
Tel. (33) 5 56 01 51 00 www.mairie-bordeaux.fr
Mon, Thu-Sun 11am-6pm, Wed 11am-8pm

Marseilles sailors, officials, merchants and missionaries returned from exotic ports
laden with Oceanic art in the 19th century. Particularly well represented in this collection
are ethnographic objects from New Caledonia, primarily from the Reverend Lambert's

collection, and those from Polynesia. The museum offers a brief introduction to the
Kanak culture, displaying everyday objects such as stone tools, examples of tidi and
masks, but it also has several prize items. One is the statue-mask from Vanuatu (Bank
Islands), made of painted bark. Other noteworthy items include those from Polynesia,
such as ornamental drop earrings, bracelets made of human hair, and an outstanding
full suit of armour from the Gilbert Islands made of plaited coir consisting of a breastplate, trousers, and helmet. It is displayed alongside lethal weapons fitted with
sharks' teeth.

Musée des Arts d'Afrique et d'Océanie
The Museum of African and Oceanic Art
293 ave. Daumesnil, 75012 Paris, France
Tel. (33) 1 44 74 84 80
Mon, Wed-Fri 10am-noon, 1.30-5.20pm, Sat-Sun 12.30-5.50pm

This very important collection from the Pacific region contains extensive holdings of
Australian art, including a handsome group of carved and decorated funerary poles
made by the Tiwi tribe, and a precious collection of 300 bark paintings painted with
shades of ground earth by the Aborigines from Arnhem Land.

Musée Barbier-Mueller
The Barbier-Mueller Museum
10 rue Jean-Calvin, 1204 Geneva, Switzerland
Tel. (41) 22 312 02 70
Daily 11am-5pm

An important collection, of which the finest pieces can often be seen in temporary exhibitions worldwide. The Melanesian section is comprehensive, while New Guinea is particularly well represented with a selection from all its stylistic centres (the Biwat of the
Sepik river, the Sentani lake region, the Huon and Papua Gulf, and the Torres Trait
region). There are statues and ritual masks from the Bismarck Archipelago which were
brought back by explorers such as Parkinson (including a sumptuous 'Kepong'- wood
polychrome mask), Festetics de Tolna, Biró, and others.

Musée des Beaux-Arts
29 cloître Notre-Dame, 28000 Chartres, France
Tel. (33) 2 37 36 41 39
May-Oct: 10am-noon, 2-6pm. Nov-Apr: 10am-noon, 2-5pm

These remarkable Oceanic collections came to the museum through the generosity of
Louis-Joseph Bouge in the 1970s, who was a French official stationed in the French possessions of the Pacific which included New-Caledonia, New-Hebrides, Tahiti, Wallis,
and Futuna. The New-Caledonian collection reigns supreme, with the majority represented by the Kanaks in the form of masks, arms and costumes.

Bernisches Historisches Museum
The Historical Museum of Berne
Helvetiaplatz 5, 3000 Berne, Switzerland
Tel. (41) 31 350 77 11
Tue-Sun 10am-5pm

The museum houses the ethnographic collection of Johann Wäber, a Bernese painter
who accompanied Captain Cook on his third expedition. Illustrating and supplement-
ing Cooks' written records, his documentation consists of over 200 drawings, etchings,

watercolours, and oil paintings, of which 64 engravings were used to illustrate the official expedition report. Like other crew members, Wäber collected ethnographic memorabilia and acquired some 100 objects from the South Seas and Alaska. His personal collection is of importance for two reasons. First, although smaller than Cook's, his is the only one from this voyage which has not been dispersed over the years. Secondly, Wäber was not showered, like Cook, with splendid gifts. He acquired more simple, everyday objects by bartering with the natives. From New Zealand there are needles, a nose flute and a club. From Tonga there are utilitarian objects such as combs, clubs, and a wooden headrest, as well as a fine collection of textiles, bags, and mats.

Bernice Pauahi Bishop Museum - The State Museum of Natural and Cultural History
1525 Bernice Street, Honolulu, Hawaii 96817, USA
Tel. (1) 808 847 3511   www.bishopmuseum.org
Daily 9am-5pm

Founded in 1889 by Charles Reed Bishop in honour of his late wife, Princess Bernice Pauahi Bishop (the last descendant of the royal Kamehameha family), the museum's original function was to show the Princess's Hawaiian artefacts and other heirlooms. Since then it has expanded to include over two million objects, documents, and photographs, not only about Hawaii but other Pacific island cultures too. Its outstanding collections of artefacts include ceremonial and domestic objects, and rarities such as bowls made from human teeth and dance anklets of dogs' teeth. Displayed in the Kahili Room are symbols of early 19th-century Hawaiian royalty, including royal feather standards and capes, along with the ceremonial carriage of the last ruling monarch of Hawaii, Queen Lili'uokalani.

Burke Museum of Natural History and Culture
University of Washington Campus, Seattle, Washington 98195, USA
Tel. (1) 206 543 5590   www.washington.edu
Daily 10am-5pm (Thu until 8pm)

The museum's Oceanic collections consist of approximately 5,000 objects, the largest of which includes material collected from Papua New Guinea from the Sepik and Highland areas. The anthropologists, Virginia and James Watson, amassed well-documented collections from the Highlands in the 1950s, while items collected by Roland Beck in the 1920s (around 100-150 artefacts) also contain material from Papua New Guinea, Fiji, and Samoa. Highlights include a rare canoe prow ornament in the form of a Frigate bird from Micronesia, a recent (1950s) but fine example of a Sepik river dugout canoe, and an extensive collection of tapa cloths (around 400) from Fiji, Samoa and Tonga dating from the last 100 years.

Palm leaf basket, Samoa Islands
Náprstkovo muzeum asijských, afrických a amerických kultur

University of Cambridge Museum of Archaeology and Anthropology
Downing Street, Cambridge, Cambridgeshire CB2 3DZ, UK
Tel. (44) 1223 333516   www.cumaa.archanth.cam.ac.uk
Tue-Sat 2-4.30pm (extended hours during summer)

This museum has a large and unparalleled Pacific collection of over 35,000 objects which consists of many high quality items collected in the 18th century. Objects from this period come from Cook's first and third voyages to the South Pacific which arrived at the museum through a number of circuitous routes over the years. Other items from the 19th and 20th centuries have come via expeditions led by Bateson to New Guinea and by Haddon to the Torres Straits region in 1898, among others. Stunning items from the Cook Collection include a crescent-shaped gorget from Tahiti composed of bans of feathers, pearl shells and sharks' teeth, a headrest of wood also from Tahiti, and a circular wooden drinking bowl in the form of a human figure on all fours.

ANTIQUITIES AND ETHNOGRAPHY

New Guinean limestone
spoons
*Náprstkovo muzeum
asijských, afrických a
amerických kultur*

Kuka'ilimoku, breadfruit
wood, late 18th-early 19th
century, Hawaii
Peabody Essex Museum

Vessel carved from a
coconut, Solomon Islands
*Náprstkovo muzeum
asijských, afrických a
amerických kultur*

Château-Musée
The Castle Museum
rue de Bernet, 62200 Boulogne-sur-Mer, France
Tel. (33) 3 21 10 02 20
Please call for opening times

Four Oceanian collections hidden in northern France have been recently catalogued by
Sylviane Jacquemin from the Museum of African and Oceanic Arts in Paris. Many outstanding pieces were uncovered, illustrating the historic links of this region's harbours
with England and its famous explorers who ventured to the Pacific. The collection in
Boulogne is comprehensive and consists of 450 objects formed by the local scholar, Dr
Hamy. This is the only one on public display. Lille, however, contains the most impor-
tant group, consisting of 750 objects which they eventually hope to make public. These
include a rare series of body ornaments from the Cook Islands, New Ireland, and the
Trobiand Islands, with original labels revealing their provenance via English explorers.
The other museums open by appointment are: Musée d'histoire naturelle, géologique
et d'ethnographie, 19 rue de Bruxelles, 59000 Lille Tel. (33) 3 20 85 28 60; Musée des
Beaux Arts, Place du Général de Gaulle, 59140 Dunkerque Tel. (33) 3 28 59 21 65; Musée
de l'Hôtel Sandelin, 14 rue Carnot, 62500 Saint-Omer Tel. (33) 3 21 38 00 94.

Musée de l'Homme
The Museum of Mankind
Palais de Chaillot, 17 place du Trocadéro, 75016 Paris, France
Tel (33) 1 44 05 72 72   www.mnhn.fr
Mon, Wed-Sun 9.45am-5.15pm

Within one of the world's most prestigious institutions of anthropological, ethnographic,
and archaeological holdings, are 22,500 examples of Oceania of which around half have
been collected in Melanesia, over 2,000 in Polynesia, and the rest in Micronesia and
Australia. Material has entered the collections from 1880 through donations, expeditions,
and missions, including a large number of items in 1934 (1,495) collected by du père
O'Reilly in the Solomon Islands. Considerable material comes from the 1955 and 1957
expeditions to New Guinea when excellent examples of house crochets, masks, wooden
plates, and a double wooden sculpted bowl from Tami in Eastern New Guinea were
added. From the Ambryn Islands there is a monumental drum with a fantastical bird's
head, a large engraved arrow from New Caledonia, and superb masks. Hawaiian material includes a feathered warrior's mask, and from the Carolinas Islands there is an
anthropomorphic statuette carved from Tino wood, which is one of just ten objects from
these islands on display in any museum in the world.

Náprstkovo muzeum asijských afrických a amerických kultur
Náprstek Museum of Asian, African and American Cultures
Libechov Castle Betlémské náme sti 1, 110 00 Prague 1, Czech Republic
Tel. (420) 2 22 221416   www.aconet.cz
Tue-Sun 9am-noon, 1.45-5.30pm

Collections from Australia and Oceania shown in the exhibition hall alongside the collections of the Americas, contains predominantly Aboriginal tree-bark paintings from
Australia, items from Melanesia collected from 1886-88, and wood carvings and masks
from New Guinea collected in the 1880s. The collection from New Zealand comes from
B. Lindauer and consists of portraits of Maori tribesmen, Maori robes, and weapons
from the end of the 19th century. Auxiliary material includes photographs taken by the
prominent explorer Enrique Stanko Vráz's (1860-1932) expeditions to Borneo and New
Guinea, along with those gathered by Josef Korensk between 1900-1901 on his expedition
to Australia, New Zealand and the Pacific Islands, taken by professional photographers
who had studios in every major tourist centre.

New Guinean wooden
figure
*Náprstkovo muzeum
asijských, afrických a
amerických kultur*

Peabody Essex Museum

East India Square, Salem, Massachusetts 01970, USA
Tel (1) 978 745 9500   www.pem.org
Tue-Sat 10am-5pm, Sun noon-5pm (Apr-Oct also open Mon)

Internationally recognized, the Pacific art and culture collection is linked to the explorations of Salem's merchant seamen and whalers. The collection includes more than 22,000 objects from more than 36 island groups in Polynesia, Melanesia, and Micronesia, and the collection of 5,000 Hawaiian objects ranks among the best outside Hawaii. Equally significant are the 19th-century woven cloaks, weapons and carvings from New Zealand, as well as the Fijian collection, and Dr Gajdusek's collection from New Guinea.

The Pitt Rivers Museum

South Parks Road, Oxford, Oxfordshire OX1 3PP, UK
Tel. (44) 1865 270927   www.prm.ox.ac.uk
Mon-Sat 1-4.30pm, Sun 2-4.30pm

As with the collection to be found at Göttingen University (see separate entry), the nucleus of this extraordinary collection was amassed in the South Pacific by the German scholar and scientist, Johann Reinhold Forster and his son, Georg, during their second voyage with Captain Cook in 1772-75. Donated originally to the Ashmolean Museum in 1776, after J. R. Foster received an honorary degree, it was subsequently transferred here but remained hidden away for almost two centuries before a substantial part of it was permanently displayed. A large number of the objects come from the Marquesas Islands, Tonga, Tahiti, and New Zealand, but the Forsters also acquired objects in Rapa Nui (Easter Island), the New Hebrides, and New Caledonia. Undoubtedly, one of the most spectacular objects in the collection is the mourning dress (heva) from Tahiti, worn by the chief mourner during funerary rituals for high-ranking men and women. It consists of a mantle formed of feathers, a crescent-shaped breastplate ornamented with large circular pieces of mother-of-pearl, a cloak made from bark cloth, and a fantastic headpiece made of shells decorated with pieces of tortoiseshell fastened to pinna shells from which spring rows of black and white tail feathers from tropical birds.

Royal Albert Memorial Museum

Queen Street, Exeter, Devon EX4 3RX, UK
Tel. (44) 1392 665858   www.exeter.gov.uk
Mon-Sat 10am-5pm

These collections are of international importance and are based upon those of the Devon and Exeter Institution (founded 1813). The earliest Polynesian and Melanesian items in the museum were collected on the 18th-century voyages of Cook, Vancouver, Bligh and others: a unique barkcloth from central Polynesia; clubs from Tonga and New Caledonia; a staff from Easter Island; fish-hooks, knife, and adze from Hawaii; a magnificent Tahitian mourning dress and gorget; and clubs and items of regalia from New Zealand. There are other outstanding late 18th-and early 19th-century items, including a Hawaiian spear rest, an Easter Island standing figure, stilt steps and an ornately carved club from the Marquesas Islands. There is a comprehensive collection of barkcloth from all parts of Polynesia and Melanesia. Outstanding among the Australian items are a painted wood shield and sword club from Queensland, tools from the Warramunga people of the central desert, and spears and throwing sticks from Queensland.

Royal Museum of Scotland - National Museums of Scotland

Chambers Street, Edinburgh EH1 1JF, Scotland, UK
Tel. (44) 131 225 7534   www.nms.ac.uk
Mon-Sat 10am-5pm (Tue until 8pm), Sun noon-5pm

New Guinean miniature
mask
*Náprstkovo muzeum
asijských, afrických a
amerických kultur*

Many of the 20,000 items in the ethnographic collections were collected by Scottish missionaries, traders, and explorers. Of these, 6,012 items are from Oceania, including late
18th-century pieces collected in Polynesia and New Zealand by Captain Cook which are
of international importance. Items from all regions of Australia date from the late 19th
and 20th century and consist of clothing and ornaments, ceremonial and religious material, domestic equipment, musical instruments, tools, and weapons. Almost every island
in Polynesia is represented by artefacts and, beside the Cook material, there are examples
collected by the traveller and writer, Constance F. Gordon Cumming, in Fiji in 1875. A
highlight from New Zealand is a full-size 19th-century fishing canoe, but perhaps the
most poignant item on display is the fine mat donated by the family of Robert Louis
Stevenson after his death in Samoa in 1894. Made of freycenetia leaf and decorated with
bright red and green Fijian parrot feathers, it was placed over Stevenson's body as it lay
in state, by Chief Tupuola of Upolu (the island Stevenson settled on).

Saffron Walden Museum
Museum Street, Saffron Walden, Essex CB10 1JL, UK
Tel. (44) 1799 510333 www.uttlesford.gov
Mar-Oct: Mon-Sat 10am-5pm, Sun 2-5pm. Nov-Feb: Mon-Sat 10am-4.30pm,
Sun 2-4.30pm

There are some real gems from Polynesia, Micronesia, Melanesia, and Australia in this
collection of some 3,500 objects, of which around 20 per cent are on display. Significant
early collections include objects from George Bennet's tour of Polynesian missionary
stations in the 1820s, Australian aboriginal weapons collected by John Helder Wedge in
Victoria before 1840, and the Lord Charles Hervey bequest of objects from Hawaii. A
number of items also came via purchases from other museums, including a number of
important items (some from Cook's third voyage) from the sale of the contents of the
Leverian Museum in 1806.

Museum für Völkerkunde
Museum of Ethnology
Neue Burg, 1014 Vienna, Austria
Tel. (43) 1 534 30 00 www.voelkerkundemuseum.com
Mon, Wed-Sun 10am-4pm

A highly important historic collection dating back to 1806 when, thanks to the initiative
of Emperor Franz I, a collection of ethnological objects (most of them dating back to
James Cook's voyages of discovery) was obtained at the auction of Parkinson's (previously
Sir Ashton Lever's) museum in London. They were further enriched as the result of
expeditions undertaken by Austrian ethnologists, including those by Karl Freiherr von
Hügel (1839). The museum is fortunate enough to own a feather sculpture (made before
1778) acquired by Cook on the Hawaiian Islands. This bust represents the god of war,
Kukailimoku, and was made by knotting brightly coloured feathers into a wicker shape.

Museum für Völkerkunde
Museum of Ethnology
Lansstrasse 8, 14195 Berlin, Germany
Tel. (49) 30 8301226 www.smb.spk-berlin.de
Tue-Fri 9am-5pm, Sat-Sun 10am-5pm

A large number of the objects come from Captain Cook's expeditions and include painted
masks and wooden sculptures from New Guinea, and a superb feathered cloak worn by
the King of Hawaii. The Boat Hall contains a variety of vessels including a twin-hulled
boat from Tonga which visitors can board. A significant proportion of the museum's collection dates back to the 'Cabinet of Art and Rarities' belonging to the Electors of
Brandenburg, and includes objects dating back to French explorer Louis Bougainville's
global circumnavigation, such as an exquisite mourning dress from Tahiti.

Museum für Völkerkunde
The Museum of Ethnology
Rothenbaumchaussee 64, 20148 Hamburg, Germany
Tel. (49) 40 44195524
Tue-Sun 10am-6pm (Thu until 9pm)

A portion of this collection was gathered by large expeditions organized by the museum at the beginning of the 20th century and is diverse and well documented. Besides an important collection of Melanesian masks, to which a whole gallery is devoted, there are also traditional tattoo patterns and various nose ornaments from these islands. A considerable number of storage pots, fire bowls, fish traps, weir baskets, and fishing spears illustrate everyday life in Papua New Guinea.

Hawaiian barkcloth
'tapu' (above)
*Náprstkovo muzeum
asijských, afrických a
amerických kultur*

Moche portrait head
vessel (below)
*El Museu Barbier-Mueller de
Arte Precolombino*

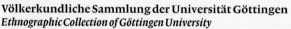

Völkerkundliche Sammlung der Universität Göttingen
Ethnographic Collection of Göttingen University
Institut für Ethnologie, Theaterplatz 15, 37073 Göttingen, Germany
Tel. (49) 551 397894   www.gwdg.de
Sun 10am-1pm

Although Captain Cook actively discouraged members of his crew from collecting curiosities, some 2,000 ethnographic items from his voyages are known and traceable in collections around the world. Of these the university owns around 500, collectively known as the Cook/Forster Collection. It is the most comprehensive accumulation of 18th-century creations from the South Seas anywhere. It originates from two sources: Johann Reinhold Forster and his son Georg (German scientists who went along on Cook's second voyage and systematically collected objects); and George Humphrey, a London dealer, whose collection originates from the second and third voyages. Although the most important part of the collection amassed by the Forsters is at the Pitt Rivers Museum (see separate entry), this is the next most significant selection and consists of items primarily from the Tongan and Society Islands, as well as New Zealand, with individual items from the New Hebrides, New Caledonia, and the Marquesas.

Whaling Museum Nantucket Historical Association
13 Broad Street, Nantucket Town, Nantucket, Massachusetts 02554, USA
Tel. (1) 508 228 1894   www.nha.org
Oct: daily 11am-3pm. Nov: Sat-Sun 11am-3pm

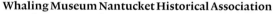

As larger whaleships became the norm, the Nantucketers traversed the oceans of the world on their mammoth voyages in search of 'greasy luck'. The exotic Polynesian and Micronesian islands of the Pacific were frequent watering holes for the ships during the early 1800s and the whalers who landed there were intrigued by these cultures, bringing home clubs, model canoes, paddles, and jewellery. Although the museum's collection numbers only several hundred items, they all stem from early contact with these islands.

PRE-COLUMBIAN AND LATIN AMERICAN ARTEFACTS

Musée d'Arts africains, océaniens, amérindiens
Museum of African, Oceanian and American-Indian Arts
Centre de la Vieille Charité, 2 rue de la Charité, 13002
Marseille, France
Tel. (33) 4 91 14 58 80
Sep-May: Tue-Sun 10am-5pm. Jun-Aug: 11am-6pm

A Chupicuaro terracota
figure, Mexico, 500-100BC
*El Museo Barbier-Mueller de
Arte Precolombino*

The core of the collections were uncovered in the 1990s from the cellars of the Chambre de Commerce where they had been stored for years after the local colonial museum closed in 1962. Like the other great French harbours, Marseille has benefited from years of trade with distant contacts. Prized are its collection of human heads gathered by Professor Henri Gastaut, a local brain surgeon. These heads are sculpted, painted, or engraved and come from the Sepik Valley in Papua New Guinea, the Solomon Islands and, the most celebrated of all, the Mundurucu Head, from the Amazon. Also fascinating is a new room housing the Reichenbach Collection of 3,000 objects of popular art from Mexico. It includes masks and ceramics from Ocumichu gathered by the acclaimed French film director, Reichenbach, who himself filmed the objects in their original and festive context.

El Museo Barbier-Mueller de Arte Precolombino
The Barbier-Mueller Museum of Pre-Colombian Art
Montcada 14, 08003 Barcelona, Spain
Tel. (34) 93 3104516 www.bcn.es
Tue-Sat 10am-8pm, Sun 10am-3pm

This is one of the most prestigious collections of pre-Columbian Art in the world, which the Barbier-Mueller Museum in Geneva ceded to Barcelona City Council. The museum is housed in a building of medieval origin, the Palau Nadal. The collection illustrates most of the styles corresponding to pre-Hispanic cultures with sculptures, ceramics, jade, goldsmithery, textiles, and ritual objects from Meso-America, Central America, the Andes, and the Amazon. Olmecas, Mayas, and Aztecs represent the main cultures in the Meso-American section, whereas the Andes include the Incas and Mochicas as well as the Chavin cultures. The exhibition focuses on the last 1,700 years before the first contacts with Europe. Three stone objects from the area of Guanacaste-Nicoya, Costa Rica, represent the oldest exhibits in the collection which date from around 200BC. However, the majority of exhibits date from AD300-1500 and illustrate the social, religious, and military hierarchies present in the societies of this period.

British Museum
Great Russell Street, London WC1B 3DG, UK
Tel. (44) 20 7636 1555 www.thebritishmuseum.ac.uk
Mon-Sat 10am-5pm, Sun noon-6pm

The move of the ethnographic collections from the Museum of Mankind to the British Museum allowed the pre-Hispanic collections to find their rightful place alongside the other great cultures. In the 1990s, the Mexican government financed a permanent exhibition of ancient Mexican and Central American art in a new gallery designed by a Mexican architect. It is now possible to admire what stands as the third best collection after those in Mexico City and Berlin.

The Brooklyn Museum of Art
200 Eastern Parkway, Brooklyn, New York 11238, USA
Tel. (1) 718 6385000 www.brooklynart.org
Wed-Fri 10am-5pm, Sat-Sun 11am-6pm (first Sat of each month until 11pm)

The Arts of the America portion of this collection includes some of the most important Andean textiles in the world, including the famous *Paracas Textile* (200-100BC). Other notable works include a 15th-century Aztec stone jaguar, and a new presentation of Peruvian art including textiles, ceramics, and gold objects. A major acquisition was recently made for this portion of the collection of an extremely rare set of fourteen mid 18th-century portraits of the kings of the Inca Empire, painted by anonymous artisans of the Cuzco School in the highlands of Peru.

Dumbarton Oaks

1703 32nd Street, NW, Washington, DC 20007, USA
Tel. (1) 202 339 6410   www.doaks.org
Tue-Sun 2pm-5pm

Arranged in an enclosed glass pavilion designed by Philip Johnson is the exquisite
Robert Woods Bliss Collection of Pre-Columbian Art which was lovingly amassed by

Robert Bliss and, after his death, expanded by his wife.
Objects in the collection were all produced before the
Spanish conquest of the New World and range from Central
Mexican Aztec stone sculptures and gold jewellery by the
artisans of Oaxaca, to carved shell and stone adornments. In
addition, there are exceptional objects of the great Maya
civilizations (AD250-900), stone sculptures from the Classic
and Post-Classic periods in Veracruz (AD250-1519), and a
wide range of Andean art including fine ceramics, shell
mosaics, gold and silver objects, textiles, and featherwork.

North Chilean woollen
bag, 20th century (above)
*Náprstkovo muzeum
asijských, afrických a
amerických kultur*

Brazilian feather head-
dress, 19th century (left)
*Náprstkovo muzeum
asijských, afrických a
amerických kultur*

Museum of Fine Arts, Boston

465 Huntington Avenue, Boston, Massachusetts 02115, USA
Tel. (1) 617 267 9300   www.mfa.org
Mon-Tue 10am-4.45pm, Wed-Fri 10am-9.45pm

Andean textiles were among the first pieces to enter this museum's textile collections at
the end of the 19th century, and the collection of Pre-Columbian textiles now constitutes
one of the museum's most notable strengths and is a leading collection in the field. It was
acquired mostly through gifts, the first one being the group of early Peruvian textiles
given by Edward Hooper in 1876.

Musée de l'Homme
The Museum of Mankind

Palais de Chaillot, 17 place du Trocadéro, 75016 Paris, France
Tel. (33) 1 44 05 72 72   www.mnhn.fr
Mon, Wed-Sun 9.45am-5.15pm

This museum has a good mix of Latin American artefacts including ceramics made by
Kaduveo Indians, arrows with emblematic decorations from Bororo in Brazil, together
with feather ornaments and hairpieces. Other items include the famous 'tsenta', which
are shrunken heads worn as trophies by warriors; painted ceramics from Nazca on the
south coast of Peru; anthropomorphical funerary urns from the northern Andes,
Colombia and the Equator; and Inca objects including ceramic and wooden goblets
decorated with people called 'keros'.

Musée des Jacobins
The Museum of the Jacobins

4 Place Louis-Blanc, 32000 Auch, France
Tel. (33) 5 62 05 74 79
Apr-Oct: Tue-Sun 10am-noon, 2-6pm. Nov-Mar: Tue-Sun 10am-noon, 2-5pm

One of the largest collections of objects from the Americas in France, the core of the collection was formed by a bequest from Guillaume Pujos who gathered an impressive
number of ceramic pieces, religious sculptures, and archaeological objects at the end of
the 19th century. After World War II, the museums of Annercy and Les Eyzies added
their own substantial American holdings to the museum. Archaeological artefacts
dominate the collection and Meso-America is most strongly represented with a number
of ceramic figurines. These figures illustrate the artistic and religious beliefs of three

Meso-American cultures: the Huastec, Teotihuacan, and Aztec. Central America and the Caribbean are less comprehensively represented, but there is a large and interesting collection of Peruvian ceramic art which is derived from eight cultures or regions: Paracas, Mochica, Nazca, Huari, Chimu, Chancay, Inca, and North Chile. Latin America is mainly represented by several pieces of decorated riding paraphernalia made in Argentina. There is a small folk art collection, with musical instruments, carved gourds, and weapons, most of which originated in Argentina and Chile. The museum's showpiece, however, comes from Central America: a feather mosaic or 'painting' representing Saint-Gregory's mass which was made by pasting thousands of exotic birds' feathers onto a support.

Náprstkovo muzeum asijských afrických a amerických kultur
Náprstek Museum of Asian, African and American Cultures
Libechov Castle Betlémské náme sti 1, 110 00 Prague 1, Czech Republic
Tel. (420) 2 22 221416   www.aconet.cz
Tue-Sun 9am-noon, 1.45-5.30pm

Tiahuanancan ceramic cup (top)
Náprstkovo muzeum asijských, afrických a amerických kultur

Chancay textile female figure (above left)
Náprstkovo muzeum asijských, afrických a amerických kultur

Bolivian silver goblet from the colonial era (above right)
Náprstkovo muzeum asijských, afrických a amerických kultur

Americas First Peoples Collections are an amalgamation of many notable collections of artefacts and photographs gathered by prominent explorers and naturalists. One is the small, but outstanding collection of wood carvings and baskets amassed by the Bohemian naturalist, Thaddäau Haenke, one of the most important explorers of the 18th century. It was amassed as he accompanied the Sicilian explorer Alessandro Malaspina in 1789 (on behalf of Carlos IV of Spain) around Central America and up through California to Alaska. Other significant collections include the Pre-Columbian, Meso-American, and Peruvian Ceramic holdings; the ethnographical collection of native Mexican costumes, ceramic, and dance masks; and the superb ethnographical collections from equatorial America gathered by Enrique Stanko Vráz in the 1890s as he navigated the Orinoko and Amazon rivers and transversed the Andes on foot. The museum also holds a large body of expedition photographs taken by Vráz between 1883-1904.

Peabody Museum of Natural History
Yale University, 170 Whitney Avenue, New Haven, Connecticut 06520, USA
Tel. (1) 203 432 3750   www.peabody.yale.edu
Mon-Sat 10am-5pm, Sun noon-5pm

In 1911, after encountering vampire bats and enduring mountain sickness, American explorer Hiram Bingham III was lead by local Peruvians to the heart of the long-hidden Inca empire, high in the Andes of Peru in the shadow of a mountain called Machu Picchu. His first expedition, as well as subsequent ones, was sponsored by the National Geographic Society and Yale University. A few objects from the site have been on display in the museum for a number of years, but the majority of the objects Bingham brought back have been kept behind closed doors. For the first time since their discovery a new exhibit displays over 100 specimens from Bingham's collection which consists mostly of pottery fragments. There is also a computer-driven virtual tour of the site. This is only a small part of the museum's holdings which include extensive Meso-American and Caribbean South American archaeological collections.

Museum für Völkerkunde
Museum of Ethnology
Lansstrasse 8, 14195 Berlin, Germany
Tel. (49) 30 8301226   www.voelkerkundemuseum.com
Tue-Fri 9am-5pm, Sat-Sun 10am-5pm

This museum presents the great diversity of pre-Hispanic cultures in Meso-, Central, and South America from 2000BC to the first half of the 16th century. Exhibits include unique stelae from Guatemala with carved reliefs, painted stoneware vessels, and steles of the Maya; sacred and secular Aztec statuary; and a selection of gold objects from Central America, Colombia, and Peru. In the Gold Room you will find superb jewels and cult objects from the 7th century BC to the 11th century AD.

Museum für Völkerkunde
The Museum of Ethnology
Rothenbaumchaussee 64, 20148 Hamburg, Germany
Tel. (49) 40 44195524
Tue-Sun 10am-6pm (Thu until 9pm)

The Americas section houses several archaeological rarities, including an extensive costume collection from the Guatemala Indians. The museum also has a famous Gold Room comprising Central and South American gold treasures, including pre-Columbian jewellery.

Chilean dried udder bag (above)
Náprstkovo muzeum asijských, afrických a amerických kultur

Nazcan ceramic vessel (below)
Náprstkovo muzeum asijských, afrických a amerických kultur

Museum für Völkerkunde
Museum of Ethnology
Neue Burg, 1014 Vienna, Austria
Tel. (43) 1 534 30 00 www.ethno-museum.ac.at
Mon, Wed-Sun 10am-4pm

The so-called 'Mexican Treasures' collection in Vienna are among the prized objects of this enormous ethnographic collection. Dating back to the period of the Conquista, they are the oldest ethnographic artefacts that have been collected for a museum in Austria and can be traced back to the 16th century. Among the highlights are numerous feather artefacts including a fine feather headdress consisting of over 450 tailfeathers of the quetzal bird that have been fixed to a fibre net. Another important group in the collection is the Johann Natterer's Brazilian Collection (1817-35) which was assembled by the zoological explorer Johann Natterer who, at the request of Emperor Franz I, went to the New World to carry out scientific research and establish collections for the imperial museums, zoos, and gardens. During a series of expeditions, Natterer, a natural scientist, collected 12,294 birds, 32,825 insects, thousands of seeds, and specimens of minerals and wood. Almost as an afterthought he added more than 2,000 ethnographic artefacts from over sixty different tribes of 'savage and tamed Indians' and also from 'whites'. The centre of his ethnographic activity was in the Mato Grosso region and along the Rio Negro and the Rio Blanco. Today, his ethnographic collection represents a unique treasure as the objects come from tribes who are now either extinct or have more or less lost their cultural identity.

Wereldmuseum
Willemskade 25, 3016 DM Rotterdam, The Netherlands
Tel. (31) 10 270 71 72 www.wereldmuseum.rotterdam.nl
Tue-Sun & public holidays 10am-5pm

The museum's primary aim is to show the contribution of all cultures to the history of mankind. It is through its collection of everyday objects and textiles that we can acquire such an overall view. Interesting highlights include a well documented collection of jade from Costa Rica. The Surinam collection (lent by Queen Beatrix), and a recently expanded collection of archaeological ceramics and textiles from Peru adds to a collection numbering some 9,000 items from the Americas.

PREHISTORIC AND BRONZE AGE ARTEFACTS

Musée des Antiquités nationales
The Museum of National Antiquities
Château de Saint-Germain-en-Laye,
78103 Saint-Germain-en-Laye, France
Tel. (33) 1 39 10 13 00   www.culture.fr
Mon, Wed-Sun 9am-5.30pm

Early Bronze Age beaker,
c. 1300BC
Dover Museum

Bronze 'Picardy' pin,
c. 1400BC
Dover Museum

The museum is situated in an old castle which used to be a royal residence for many of the kings of France. Offering a cross-section of the history of mankind from its origins to the Middle Ages, it has one of the world's richest collections of prehistoric implements. It was created by Napoleon III in 1862 in order to illustrate mankind's technical and artistic evolution. The Archeological room, located in the old ballroom, displays items from all the archeological periods. Highlights of the exhibition include a reconstruction of the famous Lascaux Caves and a 22,000-year-old 'Dame' (the first representation of a human face known to us) found at Brassempouy. Finds in the Palaeolithic room date back to 20,000BC and include incredibly fine sculptures and drawings of animals and people. From the Neolithic period there are items of pottery, polished stones and, menhirs. The Bronze Age room contains arms, clothes, and jewellery such as bracelets, brooches, and torcs often made from gold. Here, also is the famous *Avanton* of Vienne, a curious cone-shaped vessel from the middle Bronze Age, and two cuirasses (8th or 9th century BC).

Musée d'Aquitaine
The Museum of Aquitaine
20 cours Pasteur, 33000 Bordeaux, France
Tel. (33) 5 56 01 51 00   www.mairie-bordeaux.fr
Tue-Sun 11am-6pm

This museum's interest in prehistory dates back to the very origins of the institution. The first prehistoric collection to reach the museum was donated by François Jouannet in 1845. It was then called the Musée des Antiquités. When Jean-Bernard Gassies donated his collection of 280 prehistoric objects to the City of Bordeaux, the municipal council decided to establish a museum of prehistory and ethnography, of which Gassies would be the first curator. In less than ten years the museum's collections were enriched with more than 15,000 objects and it has been growing ever since. The highlight of the collection is undoubtedly the outstanding donation by Jean-Gaston Lalanne of objects found in Laussel. These have been named by the museum as though they were modern sculptures and include a female figure carved on a block of scree known as *Venus Holding a Horn*, and *Scene with Two Characters* which probably represents childbirth. Another similar figure to the Venus has prominent breasts and possibly represents a pregnant woman, while a relief on limestone depicts a hunter. Among the other precious acquisitions made by the museum is a set of 77 works of art from the Upper Magdalenian period, which were uncovered in a rock-shelter, and include a number of finely engraved animals such as horses, reindeer, and a bison, which date back to 10,000BC.

Museo archeologico nazionale delle Marche
National Archaeological Museum of Marche
Ferretti Palace, Via Ferretti 6, 60100 Ancona, Italy
Tel. (39) 071 202602
Daily 8.30am-1.30pm

The museum underwent significant refurbishment after it was forced to close following the disastrous earthquake of 1972. Since 1988 the prehistoric and protohistoric collections, which form the museum's core, have re-opened to the public. Two rooms are dedicated to the Palaeolithic period, three to the Neolithic period, and another to the Eneolithic period. The collections illustrate human activities in prehistoric times from sites excavated in the Marches region and include artefacts from the Monte Conero area which are thought to date back to 300,000BC.

Museo archeologico regionale Eoliano
Aeolian Regional Archaeological Museum
Via del Castello, 98055 Lipari, Aeolian Islands, Italy
Tel. (39) 090 9880174   www.museolipari.org
Daily 9am-1.30pm, 3-7pm

In the various buildings of the Aeolian Museum, created in 1954 by Luigi Bernabò Brea and Madeleine Cavalier, are systematically displayed collections of artefacts from the excavations carried out by the two archaeologists in the Aeolian archipelago from the 1940s onwards. Among the items on display are Neolithic weapons and tools fashioned from black volcanic glass, middle Neolithic pottery, 11th- and 12th-century BC bronzeware, and Neolithic grave goods and pottery. As well as numerous finds from the Bronze and Iron Ages, the museum has, in its Marine Archaeology room, the outstanding remains from the *Ciabatti-Signorini* wreck which was discovered at Pignataro di Fuori in Lipari. One of the oldest naval cargoes of the Mediterranean ever discovered, the haul includes impasto pottery of the Early Bronze Age which was produced in Lipari during the second millennium BC and loaded onto a vessel which was bound for one of the other islands of the archipelago.

Arkhaiologikó mouseío
The Archaeological Museum
Odós Xanthoudidou 1, 712 02 Heraklion, Crete, Greece
Tel. (30) 81 22 60 92
Summer: Mon 12.30-7pm, Tue-Sun 8am-7pm. Winter: Tue-Sun 8.30am-5pm

The museum houses excavated finds from all over Crete, covering the ancient history of the island from the Neolithic period until Crete became a Roman province in 58BC. From approximately 2700BC, Crete began a new era known as the Minoan period, a golden age of prosperity that lasted until 1200BC. The period is named after the king Minos, who had ordered Daedalus to build the famous labyrinth to hide the no-less famous Minotaur, a creature with the body of a man and the head of a bull. From the finds uncovered at Knossos, the bull seems to be everywhere. They include an ivory figurine of an acrobatic bull and an outstanding bull's head with gilded horns. The museum also holds the oldest sculptures made from hammered bronze ever to be discovered in Greece.

Museo arqueológico de Jerez
The Archeological Museum of Jerez
Plaza del Mercado s/n, 11408 Jerez de la Frontera, Spain
Tel. (34) 956 333316   www.ctv.es
Tue-Fri 10am-2pm, 4-7pm, Sat-Sun 10am-2.30pm (mid Jun-Aug: Sat-Sun only)

The archaeological finds of the museum come almost entirely from the sites within the area of Jerez. The prehistoric section is certainly one of the biggest of the exhibition. The earliest items date from the Palaeolithic period (Stone Age), and include carved tools coming from the terraces above the Guadelete river. Reproductions of paintings and engravings from the Motilla cave illustrate the cave art of this epoch. The use of pottery with different decoration techniques are among the innovations brought about during the Neolithic period. Objects include excavations from the Dehesilla and the Parralejo caves. A further section displays a wide variety of Copper Age objects including pottery, stones, bones, and metals which originate mostly from farmland settlements.

Iron Age gold stater,
c. 57-45BC
Dover Museum

Early Bronze Age spear
head, *c.* 2000BC
Dover Museum

Museo arqueológico nacional
The National Museum of Archaeology
Calle Serrano 13, 28001 Madrid, Spain
Tel. (34) 91 5777912 www.man.es
Tue-Sat 9.30am-10.30pm, Sun 9.30am-2.30pm

This museum's collection includes skulls and tusks from early elephants in Toledo; Palaeolithic artefacts from the San Isidro Hill; and finds from caves on the coast including bones, Neolithic ceramics, knives, and an alabaster idol. Among the Megalithic objects from the Balearics are three bronze bull heads. Bronze and Iron Age objects include goddess figures from Los Millares; necklaces made of shells, bone, and bronze; and weapons and glass from Ciempozuelos. One of the highlights is the 'Altamira bison', a reproduction of the roof in the Altamira cave. These Cantabrian cave paintings show a group of bison together with a deer and numerous geometric symbols which have never been fully explained. The museum also boasts several Axtroki bowls. These beaten and repoussé gold containers are decorated with circles and were perhaps intended for religious use in a cult connected with sun worship. Like other Hispanic treasures, they show the influence of Atlantic metalwork in the Iberian peninsular at the end of the Bronze Age.

British Museum
Great Russell Street, London WC1B 3DG, UK
Tel. (44) 20 7636 1555 www.thebritishmuseum.ac.uk
Mon-Sat 10am-5pm, Sun noon-6pm

Although the museum houses one of the most extensive collections of prehistoric objects in the world, a separate department was not created until 1969. The earliest objects are more than two million years old and include chopping tools from the Olduvai Gorge in Tanzania. The Quaternary collection is one of the finest in the world, covering a period spanning more than two million years from all over the world. Late Neolithic beakers are well represented from widely separated European sites, and the Bronze Age by tools, weapons, and other articles in bronze and gold. The Agean Bronze Age Galleries (*c.* 3200-1100BC) cover the Cycladic Cultures in the Bronze Age to the Mycenaean culture in the later part of the period.

Mouseio kykladikis tekhnis
Museum of Cycladic Art
Odós Neophytou Douka 4, 106 74 Athens, Greece
Tel. (30) 172 28 321 www.cycladic-m.gr
Mon, Wed-Fri 10am-4pm, Sat 10am-3pm

This museum was founded in 1986 in order to house the collection of Cycladic and Ancient Greek art belonging to Nicholas and Dolly Goulandris. Starting in the early 1960s, and with a permit by the Greek state, the couple collected Greek antiquities, with special interest in the prehistoric art from the Cycladic islands. Until the opening of the museum, their collection had been exhibited in major American and European museums. The collection consists of more than 350 artefacts made on the Cycladic islands between 3200-2000BC. The abundance of white, good quality marble on most of the islands encouraged its wide use in the creation of artefacts and implements of a functional or symbolic nature. Among these, Cycladic figurines are by far the most distinctive Cycladic creation. The majority of figurines are women, who might have been mortals or deities, but as the 3rd millennium progressed, male figurines made their appearance. A seated man 'proposing a toast' is one of the collection's key exhibits.

Dover Museum
Market Square, Dover, Kent CT16 1PB, UK
Tel. (44) 1304 201066 www.dover.gov.uk
Apr-Sep: daily 10am-6pm. Oct-May: daily 10am-5.30pm

Set over three floors, displays tell the story of the development of this town and, since medieval times, its importance as a port. Key objects, graphics, and models take you from the Stone Age to World War II. Without a doubt, the cornerstone of the collection is the Dover Bronze Age Boat discovered in 1992 during road works in Dover town centre. This large wooden prehistoric boat is about 3,550 years old and ranks as one of the most important prehistoric discoveries to be made in this century, shedding new light on early seafaring and woodworking skills in northern Europe.

Ermitazh
The Hermitage
Dvortsovskaia naberezhnaia 34-36, 191065 Saint Petersburg, Russian Federation
Tel. (7) 812 1109079   www.hermitagemuseum.org
Tue-Sat 10.30am-6pm, Sun 10.30am-5pm

This museum has a large prehistoric and Bronze Age collection. Palaeolithic items are represented by artefacts from the Caucasus, Crimea, Russian Steppes, Siberia, and Altai. From the Stone Age there are female figurines from Malta dwellings, including some exceptionally rare early Palaeolithic examples wearing garments of some kind. Neolithic art is represented by a number of large and varied collections of objects found in vast isolated areas in Eastern Europe, Siberia, and Central Asia. Most fully represented are archaeological complexes discovered in the forest regions of European Russia between the rivers Volga and Oka, the Urals, and southern areas of the Pskov region including settlements in Karelia. Among these are a number of articles probably intended for tribal cults which include polished stone axe-hammers and other ceremonial weapons. Materials from the mid 3rd-century BC Maikop burial mound in the Northern Caucasus are regarded as among the most important pieces in the archaeological collection. A lavishly dressed nomadic chief was found in this burial mound, his head crowned with two gold diadems, and with a heavy necklace consisting of several rows of beads in gold and turquoise.

Small decorated hanging urn
Dover Museum

Muséum d'Histoire naturelle
The Museum of Natural History
13 bis blvd Admiral Courbet, 30000 Nîmes, France
Tel. (33) 4 66 673914
Tue-Sun 11am-6pm

Two rooms of this museum are dedicated to prehistory, especially the Neolithic period. The focal point of the exhibition is undoubtedly the collection of menhir-statues from the Languedoc area. They appeared alongside the megaliths around 2500-3500BC. These intriguing statues are steles of an anthropomorphic character, relief sculptures applied on a megalith which was to be driven into the earth. Their purpose remains unknown; they could have been manifestations of magical rites or religious, schematic representations referring to a common ancestor.

Hollufgård
Archaeological Museum of Fünen
Hestehaven 201, 5220 Odense SØ, Denmark
Tel. (45) 66 13 13 72   www.odmus.dk
Tue-Sun 10am-4pm

The recently-added Open Store galleries display the museum's entire collection of archaeological finds, excluding scientific examples and potsherds, which are still kept in the closed storage areas. This collection, the second largest of its kind in Denmark, is divided into three periods (the Stone, Bronze and Iron Ages) and consists of the most important finds from Funen prehistory. Although currently it is without descriptions of any type, the sheer volume of material arranged systematically without distracting labels will be especially rewarding for those who know what they are looking at. One of the highlights of the collection is the skeleton of Denmark's (until recently) eldest human being, the Koelbjerg woman, who is approximately 10,000 years old.

Horse gear, 2nd-1st century BC (above)
Museum of London

Flint, bone, and copper knives, 2200-1500BC (right)
Museum of London

Musée de l'Homme
The Museum of Mankind
Palais de Chaillot, 17 place du Trocadéro,
75016 Paris, France
Tel. (33) 1 44 05 72 72   www.mnhn.fr
Mon, Wed-Sun & public holidays 9.45am-5.15pm

When the ethnographic collections of the museum move to the new Museum of Primary Arts in 2004, it will call for a complete rearrangement of the museum's prehistoric and anthropological collections, which have long been hidden from public view. The collections were formed at the end of the 18th century and considerably enlarged in the 19th. The collections of physical anthropology are very important and include ritual preparations of skulls from Peru and reduced heads. The museum holds the largest collection of human fossils, from the Homo Erectus and famous Neandertalian specimens from La Quina and La Chapelle-aux-Saints in France, to modern men from Cro-Magnon and the Mesolithic and Neolithic populations from Mali, Israel, and France. The collections of prehistoric objects benefited early from the research of Jacques Boucher de Perthes in Abbeville, considered the father of prehistory, and Isodore Geoffroy Saint-Hilaire. A donation by Prince Albert of Monaco in 1920 led to the creation of the Institute of Human Palaeontology, which housed the works of some of the greatest scholars in prehistoric sciences, including Marcellin Boulle, Henri Breuil, Robert Verneau, Pei Wen Chung, and many more, who all donated their collections to the museum. These collections are now reference collections, with objects from La Madeleine donated by Lartet and Christy, material from the Volp caves that came to the museum thanks to Count Bégouën, as well as worldwide Palaeolithic objects from Sidi Abderrahman in Morocco, Kenya, and South Africa. Among the museum's treasures feature the Venus statuette, uncovered in 1864 by the Marquis of Vibraye in Laugerie-Basse in France, and the famous *Lespugue Venus*, the largest and most renowned statue from the Paleolithic period in France. The Neolithic zoomorphic statuettes from central Sahara, along with the large group of paintings and drawings brought back by Henri Breuil from Africa, place these collections among the best in the world.

The Kentucky Museum
The Kentucky Building, Western Kentucky University, One Big Red Way, Bowling Green, Kentucky 42101, USA
Tel. (1) 270 745 2592   www.wku.edu
Tue-Sat 9.30am-4pm, Sun 1-4pm

A majority of the 100,000 pieces in the archaeological holdings consist mainly of lithic materials such as projectile points, scrapers, hoes, axes, belts, gorgets, mortars, and pestles. They are composed primarily of materials collected in the Mammoth Cave System, the longest recorded cave system in the world, with more than 336 miles explored and mapped.

Langelands Museum
Langeland's Museum
Jens Winthersvej 12, 5900 Rudkøbing, Denmark
Tel. (45) 63 51 10 10   www.rudkom.dk
Mon-Thu 10am-4pm, Fri 10am-1pm

Founded and furnished by the merchant-cum-archaeologist, Jens Winther, who was born in Rudkøbing in 1863, the museum was established in 1900. Two thirds of the exhibition is made up by the large and distinguished prehistoric collection from Langeland which included finds from the well-known large Stone Age settlements of Troldebjerg, Klintebakke, Blandebjerg, and the new site at Stengade. Important Stone Age finds from settlements in the Langeland area (now beneath the sea) include implements of flint, wood, bone, and antler. Finds from two longhouses dating from the beginning of the Neolithic period are also rarities.

La grotte de Lascaux (Lascaux II)
The Cave of Lascaux
Montignac-Lascaux, France
Tel. (33) 5 53 35 50 10   www.culture.fr
Please call for opening times

Discovered in 1940 when several young boys tumbled down a hole, are cave walls covered in bulls and prancing horses painted by Cro-Magnon man. The real caves are now closed because of the damage caused by carbon dioxide exhaled by millions of tourists. Instead, faithful replicas of ninety per cent of the paintings are nearby in Lascaux II. Exhibits include painters' tools such as reindeer tallow lamps and animal hair brushes. Two hours southeast of Lascaux is a prehistoric cave called Pech-Merle, still open to the public, containing black outlines of handprints and dancing ponies.

Horse gear
2nd-1st century BC
Museum of London

Museum of London
London Wall, London EC2Y 5HN, UK
Tel. (44) 20 7600 3699   www.museumoflondon.org.uk
Mon-Sat 10am-5.50pm, Sun noon-5.50pm

The museum holds an archive of finds and associated records from some 2,000 archaeological sites excavated in Greater London from 1908 to 1995. The archive consists of individual objects, large assemblages of ceramics and building materials, human and animal bones, elements of waterlogged wooden structures, samples of environmental material such as seeds and pollen, together with paper, photographic, and computer records. It

A cascade of bronze
weaponry, 1300-650BC
Museum of London

represents the most extensive database of urban excavations in Europe, if not the world, and makes London probably the most intensively studied archaeological site in the world. One of the most important elements of the prehistoric material, which includes axes and picks, pottery, bone and metalware, mace heads, and a huge number of other items, is the collection of 900 or so pieces of Bronze Age and Iron Age metalwork which was mostly recovered from the Thames. Included in this collection are two unparalleled items found in Brentford, a copper alloy chariot fitting or 'horn cap' which is a superb example of the Celtic art style, and a wooden stove-built tankard in bronze.

Musée national de Préhistoire
The National Museum of Prehistory
Château de Eyzies, 24620 Les Eyzies-de-Tayac, France
Tel. (33) 5 53 06 45 45
Sep-Jun: Mon, Wed-Sun 9.30am-noon, 2-6pm (Jul-Aug until 7pm)

Pantheological art is one of the earliest existing pieces of evidence of artistic tendencies. This museum has a unique collection of limestone blocks and paving stones, carved and sculpted between 30000 and 12000BC. Some are associated with burial sites and others, such as the engravings, are more mysterious. Among the early animal paintings are scenes depicting herbivores from surrounding areas while there are also a number of feminine profiles without heads from the Roche de Lalinde. This area of France has also uncovered some of the earliest sculptures, including two large bison made from red clay discovered in 1912. A variety of other animals including tortoises, fish, and horses are also on display.

National Museum of Archaeology
Republic Street, Valetta CMR 02, Malta
Tel. (356) 230711
Oct-mid Jun: daily 8.15am-5pm (Sun until 4.15pm). Mid Jun- Sep: 7.45am-2pm

The Megalithic temples on the islands of Malta are on the prestigious World Heritage Sites list. Pre-dating the Pyramids of Egypt and Stonehenge, these awe-inspiring structures were constructed between 3000 and 2500BC by an extraordinary people who inhabited the islands. The sheer size of the stone blocks used, and in many cases (such as in the temples of Hagar Qim, Tarxien, and Mnajdra) the perfect interlocking between them to produce a solid structure, is a remarkable achievement. Displayed in the museum are pottery, stone tools, beads, and figurines of people and animals, including numerous plumply rounded figures, possibly fertility idols, discovered inside the temples and prehistoric underground burial chambers. Some, like the *Venus of Malta*, stand upright, while the famous statue of a sleeping woman found in the underground Neolithic temple, the Hypogeum, is lying down.

National Museum of Ireland
Kildare Street, Dublin 2, Republic of Ireland
Tel. (353) 1 677 7444
Tue-Sat 10am-5pm, Sun 2-5pm

In the museum's treasury room, the Ireland's Gold exhibition presents one of the best collections of Bronze and Iron Age gold artefacts in Europe. The collection was started in the early 18th century, but finds continue to be unearthed, including the Derrynaflan Hoard near Killenaule. The provenance of Irish gold is still not completely clear, but there is evidence that metals such as gold, copper, and bronze were being worked as early as 2000BC. The *Glenisheen Gorget*, a gold collar discovered in 1932, shows that by 800-700BC, the goldsmiths' skills in Ireland were undoubtedly at their peak. Another permanent exhibition, Prehistoric Ireland, covers the period from Mesolithic to Iron Age and complements the ironwork on display.

Natsionalen istoricheski muzei
The National Museum of History
2 bulevard Vitosha, 1000 Sofia, Bulgaria
Tel. (359) 2 9816600   www.historymuseum.org
Nov-Apr: daily 9.30am-5.15pm. May-Oct: daily 10.30am-6.15pm

Evidence of the first European civilization which existed in the Bulgarian lands are illustrated by finds from the 294 graves from the Varna Chalcolithic Necropolis. These include over 3,000 gold ornaments as well as copper, clay, bone, and stone objects. The collection contains fine examples of cult objects and power insignia. The cult of the Sun, Moon and natural elements was extremely important among the first Europeans and evidence of this can be seen in the solar symbols on altars, loom weights, and clay vessels in the collection. Most significant is the depiction of a cult scene unearthed at the village of Ocharovo in the Turgivishte district (5000-4100BC). The scene represents a model of a solar temple devoted to the Sun, the Moon, and the Elements and consists of three altars, four priestess figures, three tables, eight chairs, three vessels with covers, two bowls, and three drums.

Norwich Castle Museum
Castle Meadows, Norwich, Norfolk NR1 3JU, UK
Tel.(44)1603 223624 www.norfolk.gov.uk
Mon-Sat 10-5pm, Sun 2-5pm

Displayed in the refurbished Archaeology Gallery is the largest collection of Iron Age gold neck rings (torcs) to be found anywhere in Europe. Discovered in 1948 and known as the Snettisham Treasure, it dates to around 70BC and may be related to East Anglia's Queen Boadicea and her tribe, the Iceni. Many examples of Roman craftsmanship found in the region are also exhibited.

Janus Pannonius Múzeum, Régészeti Kiállitás
The Janus Pannonius Museum, Archaeological Department
Széchenyi tér 12, 7621 Pèçs, Hungary
Tel.(36)72 312 719
Tue-Sun 10am-4pm

This museum collects relics of the county Baranya, South of Hungary, from prehistoric times onwards. Among the Neolithic objects on display are painted dishes and metal jewellery which show the importance of the territory in the first half of the 5th millennium BC. Artefacts from the Bronze Age include over-decorated encrusted ware, swords, and bronze treasures. Rarities include a dish with the first known letter of the Carpathian Basin engraved on it, and another, from the period of the great migrations, bearing the only known contemporary portrayal of a Hun found in Europe.

Views of the Mnajdra Megalithic Temple
National Museum of Archaeology

Musée de la Préhistoire
The Museum of Pre-History
Château du Grand-Pressigny,
37350 Le Grand-Pressigny, France
Tel.(33)2 47 94 90 20
Mid Mar-Sep: daily 9am-noon,
2-6pm Oct-mid Mar: Mon, Tue,
Thu-Sun 9am-noon, 2-5pm

Together with Eyzies, Carnac, and Ariège, the region of Le Grand Pressigny represents one of the biggest prehistoric sites in France. It is famous worldwide for its sites spanning from the paleolithic to historic ages. The museum's prehistoric room illustrates the diversity and quality of the local craftsmanship executed by the prehistoric men who occupied this area for a period of 400,000 years. The region contains a great quantity of flint, which they knapped into superb tools for their use and for trade. Evidence points to le Grand-Pressigny as being one of the first centres of international trade in history. The museum displays a fine collection of flint tools and weapons, especially blades and daggers, dating back as far as 300,000BC.

Musée de la Préhistoire Miln – Le Rouzic
The Miln – Le Rouzic Museum of Prehistory
10 place de la Chapelle, 56340 Carnac, France
Tel. (33) 2 97 52 22 04 www.ot-carnac.fr
Oct-Apr: Mon, Wed-Sun 10am-noon, 2-5pm. May-Sep: Mon-Fri 10am-6.30pm, Sat-Sun
& public holidays 10am-noon, 2-6.30pm

The museum at Carnac houses the world's most important collections from the
Megalithic period. They include more than 500,000 objects from more than 300 sites,
with 6,600 objects on display. The collection was started by a rich Scottish scholar,
James Miln, who lived in Carnac and excavated an important number of sites with the
help of a local boy, Zacharie Le Rouzic, who later became a prehistorian with a special
interest in the area around Carnac. When Miln died he bequeathed his collections to the
city of Carnac and a museum was opened in 1985. The displays are organized both
chronologically, from the Paleolithic to the Gallo-Roman periods, and thematically
within each period. From the Paleolithic period, the museum displays chopping tools
made by Homo Erectus (450,000BC). From the Middle Paleolithic period, there are
objects made by Neanderthal man including scrapers. From the Mesolithic period,
there are objects from two sites in Brittany, Téviec, and Hoedic, which include the
reconstructed tomb of a woman and a child. A group of windows presents the development of Megalithic architecture (4500-2000BC) which was a remarkable phenomenon
in this part of France. There are also jewels and ritual objects from tombs, as well as
tools, ceramics, food, and weaving material.

Museu de Prehistòria i de les Cultures
The Museum of Pre-History and Cultures
Carrer de Corona 36, 46003 Valéncia, Spain
Tel. (34) 96 388 3633 www.xarxamuseus.com
Mid Oct-mid Mar: Tue-Sun 10am-8pm. Mid Mar-mid Oct: Tue-Sun 10am-9pm

This museum, founded in 1927, presents the evolution of mankind in the Valencian area,
from the first prehistoric communities up to the end of the Roman period. The museum
contains some fine examples of the first testimonies of man's presence on earth. The oldest
trace of this presence in the local region are a series of stone implements and animal
remains from the lower levels of the Bolomor cave in Tavernes de Valldigna, which date
back 350,000 years. The exhibition's selection of post-Palaeolithic art corresponds to the
first farmers and livestock herders, as well as the hunting groups still active at the start of
the neolithisacion process. Apart from parietal mural art, there are also examples of
portable art on ceramic wares. Fragments of Neolithic ceramic vases and bear incised or
impressed cardial or combtooth decorations are also on display. The collection of finds
from the Bronze Age focuses on local culture beginning in the 2nd millennium BC and
lasting about ten centuries, and includes flat copper axeheads, arms and blades with rivets, and bronze espirals from funeral offerings, as well as ceramic bowls and vases.

Museo di Preistoria
Museum of Prehistory
Via Torre Ligny, 91100 Trapani, Sicily, Italy
Tel. (39) 0923 22300
Daily 9.30am-1pm, 4.30-7pm

This small museum located at the Torre di Ligny, a fortress built in 1671 by the Spanish
Viceroy, devotes two floors to its prehistoric and protohistoric collection, which illustrate
the region's outstanding wealth in prehistoric finds. The province is famous for the discovery of the so-called 'pebble culture', attested by the presence of choppers and chopping
tools between Trapani and Marsala that probably date back to the Bronze Age. Exhibits
in the museum range from stone artefacts from the Lower paleolithic period, Mesolithic

finds from the Uzzo cave, which rank among the oldest evidence for funerary rites, and Neolithic flints and cave paintings from the island of Levanzo. Underwater finds include the museum's most remarkable exhibit: a Punic bronze helmet.

Rheinisches Landesmuseum
The Rhenish Regional Museum
Colmanstrasse 14-16, 53115 Bonn, Germany
Tel. (49) 228 72941 www.lvr.de
Tue, Thu, Fri 9am-5pm, Wed 9am-10pm, Sat-Sun 10am-5pm

Impressive examples of the museum's collection of Rhenish prehistory include some remnants of the people from the Cromagnon period (*c.* 12th century BC). Probably the museum's most famous exhibit is the first recognized Neanderthal skull ever discovered. It is believed to be 50,000 years old.

Early Saxon jewellery from Mitcham and Hanwell
Museum of London

Musée Schwab
The Schwab Museum
50 Faubourg du Lac, 2502 Bienne, Switzerland
Tel. (41) 32 3227603 www.bielstar.ch
Tue-Fri 10am-noon, 2-5pm, Sat-Sun 11am-5pm

The museum is housed in a charming 19th-century building, built in 1876 thanks to a legacy of Frédéric Schwab. Having served first as a museum of natural sciences and art, since 1947 the museum has held solely prehistoric and archeological objects. The museum boasts an archeological collection of artefacts found in a pile village. This unique collection shows how communities in this part of the world built houses on stilts above the water. There is an especially fine collection of pendants and axes from the Neolithic period, and pins, axes, hatchets and bowls from the Bronze Age. From the Iron Age there are swords and sheaths found at the site of La Tène.

Tanums Hällristningsmuseum
The Tanum Museum of Rock Carvings
Vitlycke, 457 00 Tanumshede, Sweden
Tel. (46) 525 29555 www.ssfpa.se
Summer: daily 10am-5pm

These remarkable rock carvings represent a unique artistic achievement due to their cultural and chronological unity as well as for their rich and varied motifs of humans and animals, weapons, boats, and other objects. The diminutive figures and symbols roam across the rocks telling tales of battles, longboat voyages, and encounters with deer and snakes, illustrating the life and beliefs of the people of Bronze Age Europe. The 3,000-year-old pictures are carved into smooth granite rocks, with a visual language so rich and intense that the carvings are now included in UNESCO's World Heritage List. The museum documents these carvings, which are disintegrating at an alarming rate.

Museum für Vor- und Frühgeschichte
The Museum of Pre- and Early History
Schloss Charlottenburg, Langhansbau, Spandauer Damm 22, 14059 Berlin, Germany
Tel. (49) 30 32 674811 www.smb.spk-berlin.de
Tue-Fri 10am-6pm, Sat-Sun 11am-6pm

This is one of the largest collections specializing in the pre- and early history of the Old World. The exhibition, which occupies six galleries, covers the prehistoric cultures of Europe and the ancient Near East from their beginnings to the Middle Ages. The gallery tour begins with the history of the development of Man and his early culture. It focuses on Stone Age tool-making techniques and the art of the Ice Age. Another major theme is the development of agricultural societies and the evolution of urban settlements in the

Near East. The beginnings of agriculture in Europe during the Neolithic period are illustrated by numerous items from a variety of cultures which flourished during the 6th-3rd century BC. Insights are given into early developments in the production and use of metal, forms of settlement, and methods of burial during the late Bronze Age. The tour finishes with finds from ancient Troy including weaponry and works in gold ceramics, which are some of the museum's major attractions.

Worthing Museum and Art Gallery
Chapel Road, Worthing, West Sussex BN11 1HP, UK
Tel. (44) 1903 239999
Mon-Sat 10am-5pm

Few people know that the hills in the south east of England, known as the South Downs (north of Worthing), are the site of the oldest Neolithic flint-mines in the country. Hundreds of shafts were dug into the Downs to extract flint for tool-making, 5-6,000 years ago. Finds from excavations at a number of these sites are displayed in the museum together with a scale model of one of the mines. From the Bronze Age there are a number of hoards which have been found around Worthing. The objects in them include three Sussex Loops, a type of bronze armring found only in this part of Sussex; a cauldron; and a twisted gold torc (necklace). The sheer numbers of objects are impressive, as is the quality of workmanship.

SAXON, CELTIC AND VIKING ARTEFACTS

Musée des Antiquités nationales
The Museum of National Antiquities
Château, 78100 Saint-Germain-en-Laye, France
Chieftain's gold jewellery   Tel. (33) 1 39 10 13 00
Keltenmuseum Hochdorf   Mon, Wed-Sun 9am-5.30pm

Sumptuous vases, jewellery, and arms conjure up the lives of the first Celtic princes and warriors, largely thanks to material uncovered at the famous site of Alesia. Among the museum's highlights are a magnificent helmet made of gold, iron, enamel, and bronze, as well as a funerary boat. Statues of Celtic gods, however, bear testimony to the resistance of the Celtic religion after the Roman invasion. Even the tombs of the first Frank kings show the permanence of Celtic tradition and reveal that the development of Christianity in the 6th century did not stop the royal warriors being buried with their arms and jewellery.

British Museum
Great Russell Street, London WC1B 3DG, UK
Tel. (44) 20 7636 1555 www.thebritishmuseum.ac.uk
Mon-Sat 10am-5pm, Sun noon-6pm

The history of Britain has been significantly marked by the successive influences of the Scandinavian, Anglo-Saxon, and Celtic cultures, so it is quite natural to find some of the best collections in the world at the British Museum. You will find gold and silver jewellery from the Goths, the Ostrogoths, the Franks, and the Lombards; treasures showing the skills of the Scandinavian Vikings; as well as objects found in Norwegian burials. The Anglo-Saxon collection is the best in the UK (probably in the world) with goods unearthed in the graves of the early Anglo-

Saxon settlers who came from the North German Plain and southern Scandinavia. The highlight from the Saxon collection is an extraordinary group of objects from royal and princely burials, including the famous Sutton Hoo ship burial of an East Anglian king, which unearthed examples of some of the finest ancient jewellery alongside well-preserved pieces of armour. The collection also includes a very fine series of 10th- and 11th-century ivory carvings, sculpture, weaving and metal working implements, pottery, and iron knives. The early Celtic collection is the largest outside Ireland, with fascinating hanging-bowls, and a large group of material from Ireland, including a comprehensive series of 'penannular' brooches. There is also a significant group of ecclesiastical metalwork, as well as domestic objects and sculptured stones such as the memorial stone from Llywel, Wales, inscribed in both Ogham and Latin.

Roman pottery ware found at Brockley and Highgate (above)
Museum of London

Saxon pins, late 8th-early 9th century (left)
Museum of London

Musée du Châtillonnais
Museum of the Châtillon Region
Rue du Bourg, 21400 Châtillon-sur-Seine, France
Tel. (33) 3 80 91 24 67 www.mairie-chatillon-sur-seine.fr
Apr-mid Nov: 9am-noon, 2-6pm. Mid Nov-Mar: 10am-noon, 2-5pm

The museum's highlights are the finds uncovered at the Tomb of the Vix Princess, which has been reconstructed in the museum. Vix was located in the middle of the La Tène area, near the Seine river, at a crossroads for trade between the Seine and the Rhône. In 1929 a fortified oppidum and a Celtic settlement were discovered at Lassois Mount near Vix. Valuable objects were unearthed but it was not until 1952 that one of the most important Celtic discoveries was uncovered. A farmer found what he first thought was a horse saddle; this happened to be the handle of the *Vix Vase*, the largest bronze krater ever found. It was made in South Italy and dates from the middle of the 6th century. It belonged to a woman's burial, where a large amount of ceramics and jewellery, including a gold torc, lay alongside a woman's body on a four-wheeled chariot. Although some of the material is not of local provenance but comes from Greece and Etruria, it shows the important relations of the site with distant areas.

Musée de la Civilization celtique
Museum of Celtic Civilization
71990 Saint-Léger-sous-Beuvray, France
Tel. (33) 3 85 86 52 39 www.bitracte.tm.fr
Mid Mar-mid Nov: daily 10am-6pm (Jul & Aug until 7pm)

Bibracte, the Gaulish capital of the Aedui, which Caesar confronted during his first campaign in Gaul in 58BC, is thought to have stood on the actual site of Mont-Beuvray. The museum, housed in a beautifully designed building that won the French National Architecture Award in 1997, is part of the Centre archéologique européen du Mont Beuvray, and is one of the few museums to be entirely devoted to the Celtic and Romano-Celtic civilizations in Europe. The majority of the exhibits come from the site of Bibracte itself and are on loan from other European museums, although the real emphasis is on educating visitors on Celtic civilization in the region and Europe, through interactive displays and models. The collection is comprehensive and particularly strong for the late Gallic period, with weapons, tools, ceramics, and stone and wooden architectural items.

Ermitazh
The Hermitage
Dvortsovskaia naberezhnaia 34-36, 191065 Saint Petersburg, Russian Federation
Tel. (7) 812 1109079   www.hermitagemuseum.org
Tue-Sat 10.30am-6pm, Sun 10.30am-5pm

Exterior of the museum
Keltenmuseum Hochdorf

On their journeys east, the Vikings sailed into the Gulf of Finland, up the river Neva to the huge Lake Ladoga, and on to the mouth of the river Volkhov. Some way up this river is the settlement Aldeigjuborg, known today as Staraia (Old) Ladoga. Finds from this area indicate a Scandinavian presence from as early as AD750 and herald a significant chapter in Viking history. Among the Viking objects on display are combs from the 8th to the 10th centuries, draughtsmen and glass necklaces, and typical examples of personal ornamentation. Of particular interest is a 9th-century wooden rod with a runic inscription, intended for exorcism.

Hedmarksmuseet og Domkirkeodden
The Hedmark Museum at Cathedral Point
Strandveien 100, N-2305 Hamar, Norway
Tel. (47) 62 54 27 00
www.hedmarksmuseet.museum.no
Please call for opening times

Burial Chambers
Keltenmuseum Hochdorf

Viking battle axes and
spears from the Thames
Museum of London

The Åker exhibition in the converted Sorharmer barn traces the area's history from the powerful line of wealthy farmers who ruled this area in AD550 to the end of the Viking Age, around 1050. Stunning artefacts were unearthed in the Viking chieftain's grave found on the Åker farm in Vang, a few kilometres east of the modern town centre (the gilt objects are on display in Oslo). A large collection of richly decorated weapons, clothing, and riding gear, including a gold plated harness ornamented with semprecious stones from the late 6th century AD, attests to the power the seat of Åker must have held. It is likely that the chieftains acquired their riches and status both through warfare and trade with neighbouring countries and Central Europe, using the local iron-ore deposits, as well as furs, as commodities which could be bartered. Other cases contain grave finds from the Early Iron Age (*c.* AD200-400) including weapons and jewellery, a large bronze cauldron, and remains of early iron production (*c.* AD200).

Christianity came to this area around AD900 and one of the earliest symbols marking its arrival is a small pendant cross unearthed near the spot where Hamar Cathedral now stands.

Keltenmuseum Hochdorf
The Hochdorf Celtic Museum
71735 Eberdingen-Hochdorf, Germany
Tel. (49) 7042 78911
www.keltenmuseum.de
Tue-Sun 9.30am-noon,
1.30-5pm

On display are the archaeological finds from a Celtic chieftain's grave dating from

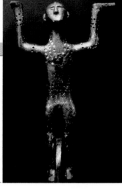

around 540BC, including the chieftain's items of personal adornment, such as a gold bracelet, a gold torc, and a gold-foil belt covering. Also nine drinking horns, of which the best preserved is a fine bronze and iron horn with gold ornament. Several serpentine fibulae, a gold bowl, and a cauldron decorated with lions can be also be seen, along with several fine shoe ornaments which once were probably sewn onto leather, although this is not preserved. Other items include a gold-foil covered dagger with an iron blade, a bronze scabbard, and an 'antenna' hilt.

Museum of London

London Wall, London EC2Y 5HN, UK
Tel. (44) 20 7600 3699   www.museumoflondon.org.uk
Tue-Sat 10-5.50 pm, Sun noon-5.50pm

Female figure carrying the chieftain's couch
Keltenmuseum Hochdorf

From the Saxon period the archive holds finds and records relating to early Saxon sites in outer west London, Battersea, Clapham, and Hammersmith. In addition, the museum holds the archives for the highly significant series of sites excavated around the area of Covent Garden and the Strand, which showed that mid-Saxon Lundenwic was located in this area. Excavations in the City reveal its re-occupation from the 9th century, with a planned street pattern and port installations.

Museu nacional de Arqueologia
The National Museum of Archaeology

Praça do Império, 1400 Lisbon, Portugal
Tel. (351) 21 362 0000
Tue 2-6pm, Wed-Sun 10am-6pm

This museum was established in 1893 and contains some remarkable Portuguese archaeological artefacts. Of particular interest is a fine collection of Celtic gold and silver jewellery. Although there are some primitive examples, the majority of this collection consists of more elaborate pieces, such as several outstanding bracelets from the late Bronze Age decorated with increasingly sophisticated geometric patterns and animal and floral motifs.

National Museum of Ireland

Kildare Street, Dublin 2, Republic of Ireland
Tel. (353) 1 677 7444
Tue-Sat 10am-5pm, Sun 2-5pm

The museum houses a fascinating collection of Viking artefacts in the Dublin 1000 exhibit. Case upon case displays items unearthed from Wood Quay (the area between Christchurch Cathedral and the River Liffey) that tell the story of Dublin's Viking history from around 800 -1150AD .

Nationalmuseet
The National Museum

Frederiksholms kanal 12, 1220 Copenhagen, Denmark
Tel. (45) 33 13 4411   www.natmus.dk
Tue-Sun 10am-5pm

These quite naturally rank among the best Viking collections in the world. In a room exhibiting the largest and richest hoards of the Viking period, you will find a perfect demonstration of why the period is also called the Silver Age, due to the extensive amount of silver objects found in Viking burials. The Ladby Ship Burial is even more impressive, where the body of a Viking chief was found lying in a dedicatory ship. He had been buried together with horses and dogs, who all wore beautifully worked harnesses. Though the burial had been later re-opened, several objects were left behind, including arrows, a shield, and fine utensils.

Neck rings and bracelets
from Erstfeld Gold
Treasure, *c.* 300 BC
*Schweizerisches
Landesmuseum*

Prähistorisches Abteilung Naturhistorisches Museum
Natural History Museum Department of Prehistory
Burgring 7, 1014 Vienna, Austria
Tel. (43) 1 52 177
www.nhm-wien.ac.at
Mon, Wed-Sun 9am-6.30pm
(Wed until 9pm)

One of the secrets of the museum is its outstanding Celtic finds from Hallstatt and its wealthy tombs. Dating from around 600 BC, the collection was originally in the royal collections of the Habsburg family. However, continuous excavations both there and at other Celtic sites have further enriched the collections. The finds at Hallstatt range from clothes and leather caps to ceremonial objects and arms, including a high quality bronze bowl. Discovered in the cemetery, the bowl, with its handle designed as a cow and pommel made of ivory inlaid with amber, was probably used at ceremonial banquets. Other sites provided the museum with an extremely well-preserved conical bronze helmet from the 4th-3rd century, and examples of La Tène swords in iron scabbards brought back from Yugoslavia and Hungary when those regions were linked to the Austrian crown. One of the museum's most precious Celtic objects is a fine gold torc from Oploty, Bohemia (4th-3rd century).

Musée de la Préhistoire Miln – Le Rouzic
The Miln – Le Rouzic Museum of Pre-History
10 place de la Chapelle, 56340 Carnac, France
Tel. (33) 2 97 522204   www.ot-carnac.fr
Oct-Apr: Mon, Wed-Sun 10am-noon, 2-5pm. May-Sep: Mon-Fri 10am-6.30pm, Sat-Sun & public holidays 10am-noon, 2-6.30pm

The collections here are divided into four distinct sections; funerary art, Celtic art in the Armoric region, dwellings, and salt production. One of the museum's finest pieces is a gold archer's brace, while Celtic art is further illustrated through coinage, with an example showing a curled hair on the obverse and an androcephal horse on the reverse. There are also ceramics with spiral motifs and objects attesting to Celtic trade with the Romans.

Royal Museum of Scotland - National Museums of Scotland
Chambers Street, Edinburgh EH1 1JF, Scotland, UK
Tel. (44) 131 225 7534   www.nms.ac.uk
Mon-Sat 10am-5pm, Tue 10am-8pm, Sun noon-5pm

These Viking holdings can be divided into three major areas: settlements, burials, and fine metalwork. Excavated finds from settlements in Scotland remain comparatively rare, although the situation is gradually improving. Holdings include important groups from Jarlshof, Shetland (1957), and Broch of Birsay, Orkney (1982) as well as material from Westness with important associated burial assemblages (1966 and 1992). The acquisition of the Westness cemetery material and a recent grave from Balnakeil (1991) further strengthen what is the dominant collection of Viking burial material from Scotland.

Schweizerisches Landesmuseum
The Swiss National Museum
Museumstrasse 2, 8023 Zurich, Switzerland
Tel. (41) 1 218 65 11   www.simnet.ch
Tue-Sun 10am-5pm

The museum holds the Golden Treasure of Erstfeld, a Celtic treasure that was found in 1962 during civil engineering excavations carried out at the foot of the Gotthard. It includes two torcs, four richly decorated necklaces, and three bracelets dating from around 300BC. Their ornamental work is magnificent, illustrating the degree to which gold processes and its use were already developed and specialized at the time of the Helvetians.

Universitetets Kulturhistoriske Museer - Vikingskipshuset
The University Museum of Cultural Heritage - Viking Ship Museum
Huk aveny 35, 0287 Oslo, Norway
Tel. (47) 22 43 83 79   www.ukm.uio.no
Please call for opening times

A separate building houses three Viking ships excavated between 1867 and 1903. Most well-known is the ship from Oseberg (late 9th century), decorated with elaborate wood carving. When found, it contained a large collection of objects both for religious and everyday use. Also found were textiles showing mysterious processions and the bodies of two women. The other two ships are less well preserved, but of immense interest particularly for their construction details.

Detail of neck ring, from Erstfeld Gold Treasure, 4th century BC
Schweizerisches Landesmuseum

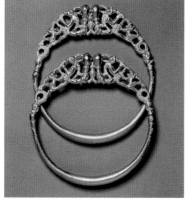 

Bracelets from Erstfeld Gold Treasure, *c.* 300BC
Schweizerisches Landesmuseum

Vikingeskibsmuseet i Roskilde
The Viking Ship Museum in Roskilde
Vindeboder 12, 4000 Roskilde, Denmark
Tel. (45) 46 300 20
May-Sep: daily 9am-5pm. Oct-Apr: daily 10am-4pm

The museum accommodates five different Viking ships from the 11th century which were excavated in Roskilde inlet near Skuldelev in 1962. Throughout the years since their discovery, the museum has created a prominent collection of working vessels of Nordic type, among which are copies of the Skuldelev ships. Today these lie in the harbour at the new museum lake where the archaeological workshop, the shipbuilding yard, and the workshops for visitors are located.

Glass goblet from
Anglo-Saxon cemetery at
Highdown Hill, Ferring,
c. AD400
*Worthing Museum and Art
Gallery*

Worthing Museum and Art Gallery

Chapel Road, Worthing, West Sussex BN11 1HP, UK
Tel. (44) 1903 239999
Mon-Sat 10am-5pm

A selection of artefacts from all periods is displayed in the
Archaeology Gallery. Others, along with the paper records of
the excavations, are available to researchers in the Reserve
Collections. One of the highlights is the collection of finds
from the early pagan Saxon cemetery at Highdown, west of
Worthing. First found in the 1890s, this Saxon cemetery was
in use by the mid 5th century and is the earliest yet known in
Sussex. A highlight among the grave goods has to be the
inscribed glass beaker which is thought to have been made in
Egypt in AD400, brought all the way to Sussex and buried in
a grave some years later.

Yorkshire Museum

Museum Gardens, York, North Yorkshire YO1 7FR, UK
Tel. (44) 1904 551800   www.york.gov.uk
Daily 10am-5pm

One of the finest archeological collections in Europe, ranging from prehistoric times to
the Roman, Anglo-Saxon, Viking, and Medieval periods. Anglo-Saxon artefacts include
an 8th-century silver gilt bowl from Ormside, the Gilling sword, and sculptures and
personal ornaments. The famous Viking collection includes decorated metalwork, a
spectacular warrior stone, swords, battle-axes, and a silk cap.

BOOKS, MANUSCRIPTS AND PRINTED MATTER

AMERICAN AND EUROPEAN
18TH–20TH CENTURY BOOKS

BOOK AND MAGAZINE ILLUSTRATORS

BOTANICAL BOOKS AND PRINTS

COMICS AND MAGAZINES

COOKBOOKS

JAPANESE WOODBLOCK PRINTS

PHOTOGRAPHS

PLAYING CARDS

POSTERS

RARE AND SPECIAL COLLECTIONS OF BOOKS
AND MANUSCRIPTS

AMERICAN AND EUROPEAN 18TH – 20TH CENTURY BOOKS

Muzei Anny Akhmatovy
The Anna Akhmatova Museum
Naberezhnaia reki Fontanki 34, 191104 Saint Petersburg, Russian Federation
Tel. (7) 812 272 2211 www.md.spb.ru
Tue-Sun 10.30am-6.30pm

Founded in 1989, the museum consists of six rooms documenting different stages in
Akhmatova's life and work. As well as manuscripts and rare editions, the great poet's
bleak but dazzlingly creative life is evocatively conjured up through photographs,
posters, works of art (including Modigliani's famous portrait), and original furniture.

A selection of Balzac's
books and manuscripts
La Maison de Balzac

La Maison de Balzac
Balzac's House
47 rue Raynouard, 75016 Paris, France
Tel. (33) 1 55 74 41 80
Tue-Sun 10am-5.40pm

Now with a ground floor library containing over
10,000 books and manuscripts, Balzac's house
provides a fascinating glimpse into the 19th-century
novelist's life and working methods. The study has
been furnished with memorabilia and preserved
almost exactly as it was when the novelist was
working. A comprehensive genealogy of *La Comédie
humaine* is displayed in the museum's basement.

Brontë Parsonage Museum
Haworth, Keighley, West Yorkshire BD22 8DR, UK
Tel. (44) 1535 642323 www.bronte.org.uk
Apr-Sep: daily 10am-5.30pm
Oct-Mar: daily 11am-5pm

Set in the Yorkshire moorlands, the Haworth
Parsonage is where the Brontë sisters grew up and wrote most of their novels. Built in
1778-79 the house remained in the family from 1820-61, opening as a museum run by the
Brontë Society in 1928. The dining room, kitchen and bedrooms are filled with the family's original furniture plus a collection of books of the period, manuscripts of their
earliest writings, clothes, and Emily's writing desk, complete with contents as she left it.

Dickens' House Museum
48 Doughty Street, London WC1N 2LF, UK
Tel. (44) 20 7405 2127 www.dickensmuseum.com
Mon-Sat 10am-5pm

Dickens lived in this handsome Georgian house for two years from 1837-39, during
which time he completed *Oliver Twist*, *Nicholas Nickleby*, and the final six installments of
The Pickwick Papers. Besides portraits, letters, and memorabilia, the museum has one of
the greatest collections of Dickens' manuscripts in the world, highlights of which
include Dickens' own reading copies (and the prompt books used by him for readings),
first editions, foreign translations, and a large number of critical works.

Dove Cottage and the Wordsworth Museum
Grasmere, Cumbria LA22 9SH, UK
Tel. (44) 1539 435544 www.wordsworth.org.uk
Daily 9.30am-5.30pm

Enlarged in 1981, this award-winning museum and library houses one of the greatest collections of manuscripts, books, and paintings relating to Wordsworth and the Romantic poets. It is a collection of national pre-eminence and contains Wordsworth's grandson's collection, which includes ninety per cent of the poet's working manuscripts.

Astronomic clock in the Goethe House
Goethe-Haus und-Museum

Goethe-Haus und -Museum
The Goethe House and Museum
Großer Hirschgraben 23-25, 60311
Frankfurt, Germany
Tel. (49) 69 138800
www.goethehaus-frankfurt.de
Apr-Sep: Mon-Fri 9am-6pm
Oct-Mar: Mon-Fri 9am-4pm,
Sat-Sun 10am-4pm

Exterior view of Dr Johnson's house
Dr Johnson's House

Joyce death mask
James Joyce Museum

Reconstructed after the war, Goethe's paternal home is maintained in a state of suspended animation. Paintings on the walls evoke memories of his family and friends, while the pots and pans in the kitchen and a toy marionette theatre vividly summon up the Goethe household's everyday life. The museum next door displays documents and manuscripts by Goethe, as well as paintings by Tischbein, Fuseli, Hackert and other artists.

Dr Johnson's House
17 Gough Square, London EC4A 3DE, UK
Tel. (44) 20 7353 3745 www.drjh.dircon.co.uk
May-Sep: Mon-Sat 11am-5.30pm. Oct-Apr: Mon-Sat 11am-5pm

This Queen Anne house was home to Samuel Johnson who compiled the first comprehensive dictionary of English ('lexicographer = a writer of dictionaries, a harmless drudge') in the attic room of this house, perched on a three-legged stool while he barked out orders at his six hired clerks. The museum has a small but significant collection of Johnsonian books and manuscripts, including the third edition of the *Dictionary*, Johnson's own copy of Homer, and books from the library of Johnson's friend Elizabeth Carter, including her translations of Epictetus and Euripides.

The James Joyce Museum
The Joyce Tower, Sandycove, Dublin, Ireland
Tel. (353) 1 2809265 www.visit.ie
Apr-Oct: Mon-Sat 10am-5pm, Sun & public holidays 2-6pm

Built in 1804 by the British Army as a defence against Napoleon and the backdrop for the opening chapter of *Ulysses*, this Martello tower is now home to a museum of James Joyce memorabilia ranging from personal items to rare and first editions of his books. Joyce's most cherished possession was his waistcoat, given to him by his father and embroidered by his grandmother with hunting scenes of stags and packs of dogs.

Keats' House
Wentworth Place, Keats Grove, Hampstead, London NW3 2RR, UK
Tel. (44) 20 74352062
Apr-Oct: Mon-Fri 10am-1pm, 2-6pm, Sat 10am-1pm, 2-5pm, Sun & public holidays 2-5pm. Nov-Mar: Mon-Fri 1-5pm, Sat 10am-1pm, 2-5pm, Sun 2-5pm

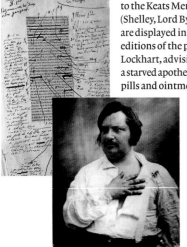

Keats composed his *Ode to a Nightingale* at this London literary shrine which is now home to the Keats Memorial Library and some 8,000 volumes devoted to Keats and his circle (Shelley, Lord Byron, Leigh Hunt, Wordsworth). Some of the most precious manuscripts are displayed in the museum itself: Keats' last sonnet *Bright Star*; the rare first three editions of the poems; and the notoriously damning review of *Endymion* by John Gibson Lockhart, advising Keats to go back to being a surgeon: 'It is a better and wiser thing to be a starved apothecary than a starved poet; so back to the shop, Mr. John, back to the "plasters, pills and ointment boxes."'

Keswick Museum & Art Gallery

Fitz Park, Station Road, Keswick, Cumbria CA12 4NF, UK
Tel. (44) 1768 773 263
Apr-Oct: daily 10am-4pm

Superb original manuscript collection devoted to prose, poetry and letters by Wordsworth, Coleridge, de Quincey, and other writers associated with the Lakes, particularly Southey, Walpole, and Ruskin.

Literaturno-memorial'nyi muzei F. M. Dostoevskogo
The F. M. Dostoevsky Literary and Memorial Museum

Corrected proofs of
La Vieille Fille
La Maison de Balzac

Portrait of Balzac by
Bisson, 1842
La Maison de Balzac

Kuznechnyi pereulok 5/2, 191002 Saint Petersburg, Russian Federation
Tel. (7) 812 3114031 www.md.spb.ru
Tue-Sun 11am-5.30pm

The seven-roomed flat where Dostoevsky spent the last three years of his life (1878-81) reflects a stable period when, tired of gambling, Dostoevsky lived as a quiet family man with his wife and two children while working on perhaps the greatest of his novels, *The Brothers Karamazov*. There is a library of 24,000 volumes (including some of the original manuscripts), a small art gallery, and memorabilia.

Herman Melville Memorial Room

Berkshire Athenaeum, Pittsfield Public Library, 1 Wendell Avenue, Pittsfield, Massachusetts 01201, USA
Tel. (1) 413 499 9486 www.berkshire.net
Mon 9am-5pm, Tue-Thu 9am-9pm, Sat 10am-5pm

A massive archive of material connected with Melville. There is a 'vault room' where visitors can sift through a mass of uncatalogued material (by appointment), a large collection of his letters on microfilm, an extensive library of books about Melville, and other memorabilia, including a collection of the pipes he smoked, the dishes he ate from, and one of his desks. There is even a case of scrimshaw containing some pieces dating from the period when Melville wrote *Moby Dick*.

Mugar Memorial Library

Special Collections, Boston University, 771 Commonwealth Avenue, Boston, Massachusetts 02215, USA
Tel (1) 617 353 3696 www.bu.edu
Mon-Fri 9am-5pm

This is a large and very extensive collection of 18th- and 19th-century English and American literature. There are two outstanding archives of original manuscripts and first editions by Joseph Conrad and Walt Whitman. On display are holographed letters, manuscripts, translations, inscribed critical works, and a first edition of *Leaves of Grass*. Also photographs, engravings, and other memorabilia, including Whitman's correspondence with biographers and collectors. Truly outstanding is the vast 20th-century archive consisting of works and papers collected by well-known modern authors. Over 1,600 collectees make up this cache, which includes the entire archive of Isaac Asimov.

National Steinbeck Center

1 Main Street, Salinas, California, 93901, USA
Tel. (1) 831 775 4720   www.steinbeck.org
Daily 10am-5pm

This interactive tribute has an abundance of multi-sensory displays documenting Steinbeck's life and works. At its core is an archive (open for research by appointment only) of over 40,000 items including manuscripts, first editions, posters, and photographs.

D. H. Lawrence and
Frieda Lawrence in
Chapala, Mexico, 1923
*University of Nottingham
Library*

Ruskin Library

Lancaster University, Bail Rigg, Lancaster, Lancashire LA1 4YH, UK
Tel. (44) 1524 593587   www.lancs.ac.uk
Gallery: Mon-Sat 11am-4pm, Sun 1-4pm. Reading room by appt. only.

Recently re-housed in a striking new building at Lancaster University is a wide-ranging collection bringing together the writings, correspondence, daguerreotypes and prints of the 19th-century art critic and social reformer, John Ruskin. The collection comprises more than 350 of Ruskin's books and 200 manuscripts, including 29 volumes of Ruskin's diaries as well as his vast, and so far unpublished, correspondence.

D. H. Lawrence in Santa
Fe, New Mexico, 1922
*University of Nottingham
Library*

University of Nottingham Library

Manuscripts and Special Collections, The University of Nottingham, University Park, Nottingham, Nottinghamshire NG7 2RD, UK
Tel. (44) 115 9515151   www.mss.library.nottingham.ac.uk
Mon-Fri 9am-5pm

This library is home to over two million rare books and documents, with the world's finest archive devoted to the great English novelist and poet, D. H. Lawrence: original manuscripts of *Women in Love*, *The Rainbow* and *Lady Chatterley's Lover*, plus letters, publications, biographical and a wealth of critical material. Lovingly built up over a period of seventy years, it was bequeathed to the university by George Lazarus. Due to open in 2002 is a new exhibition pavilion located across the road from the art museum where the library will display some of their important holdings.

Vserossiiskii muzei A. S. Pushkina
The All-Russian Museum of A. S. Pushkin

Naberezhnaia reki Moiki 12, 191186 Saint Petersburg, Russian Federation
Tel. (7) 812 3113531   www.pushkin.ru
Mon, Wed-Sun 10.40am-5pm

This hallowed literary shrine is the world's largest repository of relics, books, and works of art connected to the life of Alexander Pushkin. He lived here with his wife, four children, his wife's two sisters and some fifteen staff, editing his journal *The Contemporary* and finishing *The Captain's Daughter*. As well as thousands of rare publications, many autographed by Pushkin's contemporaries, the museum houses some evocative memorabilia, such as the bullet-punctured waistcoat worn by Pushkin as he lay bleeding in the snow.

One of Kjell Aukrust's
illustrations (right)
Aukrust Senter

The Aukrust Centre
(below)
Aukrust Senter

Interior of museum
(bottom)
Brandywine River Museum

Walt Whitman House and Library

328 Mickle Boulevard, Camden, New Jersey 08103-1126, USA
Tel. (1) 856 964 5383
Wed-Sun (please call for opening times)

Whitman's sales from *Leaves of Grass* enabled the purchase of this, his first and only house, in 1844. Whitman lived here until his death in 1892, and the house is crammed with personal possessions including original correspondence and the earliest known image of the poet. At the core of the extensive library is the Colonel Richard Gimbel collection of over 100 rare books by and about Whitman, including the 1855 first edition of *Leaves of Grass*. Adjacent to the house is the library, open by appointment only (two weeks notice required).

BOOK AND MAGAZINE ILLUSTRATORS

Aukrust Senter
Aukrust Centre
2560 Alvdal, Norway
Tel. (47) 62 48 78 77   www.aukrust.no
Sep-May: daily 10am-4pm. Jun-Aug: daily 10am-6pm

Designed by Sverre Fehn, this stunning slate, shingle, and concrete exhibition space over-looking snow capped mountains and wheat fields is dedicated to the much loved Norwegian author and graphic artist, Kjell Aukrust. A large and stylish oblong gallery space inside evokes the quirky imagination of an artist whose work spans many disciplines, including illustration, painting, writing, theatre, and film. (Aukrust's *Flåklypa Grand Prix* was one of the greatest box office hits in the history of Norwegian film.) As well as displays of Aukrust's drawings and book illustrations the centre has a library, auditorium, and inventor's corner devoted to crazy contraptions (such as Aukrust's ballistic hydromobile and chocolate machine).

Beinecke Library

Yale University, New Haven, Connecticut 06520-8240, USA
Tel. (1) 203 432 2972   www.library.yale.edu
Mon-Fri 8.30am-5pm

This superb collection comprises several hundred volumes of exquisitely bound and printed French illustrated books dating from the 18th century onwards. Illustrators represented include Bonnard, Boucher, Braque, Daumier, Doré, Gavarni, Gravelot, Lepère, Moreau, Picasso, and Steinlen.

Brandywine River Museum

US Route 1, Chadds Ford, Pennsylvania 19317, USA
Tel. (1) 610 388 2700   www.brandywinemuseum.org
Daily 9.30am-4.30pm

This beautiful riverside gristmill dating from the 1850s has been converted with floor-to-ceiling windows into a magnificent exhibition space showing works by many of the region's famous illustrators, including Howard Pyle (called 'the Father of American Illustration') and many of his students such as N.C. Wyeth and Harvey Dunn. Hundreds

of other early-20th-century giants of illustration are represented such as Edwin Austin Abbey, Winslow Homer, Maxfield Parrish, and Rockwell Kent. A shuttle bus takes visitors a mile down the road to the 1911 studio where N.C. Wyeth worked for many years illustrating such children's classics as *Drums, Kidnapped* and other Scribners' classics.

California Palace of the Legion of Honor

100 34th Avenue, Lincoln Park, San Francisco, California 94122, USA
Tel. (1) 415 863 3330 www.thinker.org
Tue-Sun 9.30am-5pm (first Wed of each month until 8.45pm)

This magnificent collection of contemporary American artists' books dates from the 1960s onwards and ranges across the spectrum of *livres d'artiste*, from sumptuously produced leather-bound editions, to works that stretch the definition of the book itself; from the Flockophobic Press' *Human House* (1990), to poetry printed on sheets of pasta. Highlights include *Fêtes*, wonderfully illustrated by Alexander Calder (1971), mass-produced counterculture publications such as Ed Ruscha's *Twenty-six Gasoline Stations* (1962), and a host of recent books produced by California-based artists and publishers.

Dickens' House Museum

48 Doughty Street, London WC1N 2LF, UK
Tel. (44) 20 7405 2127 www.dickensmuseum.com
Mon-Sat 10am-5pm

Some of Kjell Aukrust's comic characters (above)
Aukrust Senter

Ex Libris Vitalija Keblys: one of the collection's bookplates (left)
Fredikshavn Kunstmuseum og exlibrissamling

Original illustrations from the novels, including work by Frederic George Kitton.

Frederikshavn Kunstmuseum og exlibrissamling
The Frederikshavn Museum of Art and Ex Libris Collection

Parallelvej 14, 9900 Frederikshavn, Denmark
Tel. (45) 98 431663
Tue-Fri 10am-5pm, Sat-Sun 10am-4pm

One of the largest *ex-libris* collections in the world, with 400,000 bookplates dating from the 16th century to the present day, and a library of handbooks, journals and catalogues covering graphic techniques from the first woodcuts to modern computer art. Items worthy of note include 400 years of Swedish Royal *ex-libris*, theme collections (such as flora, fauna, mythology, and erotica), and Japanese colour woodcuts.

Princeton University Library

Department of Rare Books and Special Collections, Firestone Library, One Washington Road, Princeton, New Jersey 08544-2098, USA
Tel. (1) 609 258 3197 www.princeton.edu
Mon-Fri 9am-5pm by appt. only

It's hard to do justice to these collections which are as deep as they are broad. Highlights include the Sinclair Hamilton Collection of American Illustrated Books 1670-1870 containing the work of more than 700 illustrators, engravers, and firms, and a superb collection of over 600 prints by the illustrator and caricaturist, George Cruikshank. Born in 1792, Cruikshank's hand-coloured etchings amused, astounded and scandalized an increasingly prosperous and well-informed audience, with targets ranging from the foibles of high society to the imperial pretensions of Napoleon, and the dissipated conduct of the Regent.

Ex Libris Carl Asp:
one of the collection's
bookplates
Fredikshavn Kunstmuseum
og exlibrissamling

Harry Ransom Humanities Research Center

The University of Texas at Austin, Austin, Texas 78713-7219, USA
Tel. (1) 512 471 4663   www.hrc.utexas.edu
Mon-Fri 9am-5pm, Sat 9am-noon

There are watercolours by E. H. Shepard, Eric Kennington's original illustrations for the
works of T. E. Lawrence, and Arthur Rackham's original illustrations for Edgar Allen
Poe's *Tales of Mystery and Imagination*. The George Macy Limited Editions Club Collection
has over 6,000 pieces of art prepared for their deluxe editions by over 100 internationally
known artists and nearly 1,000 woodblocks, intaglio plates, prints, and drawings by
artists from the Golden Cockerell Press. By far the largest part of the collection are the
works by Eric Gill (1882-1940) with over 3,000 drawings, prints, and stone carvings.

The Norman Rockwell Museum at Stockbridge

Route 183, Stockbridge, Massachusetts 01262, USA
Tel. (1) 413 298 4100   www.nrm.org
May-Oct: daily 10am-5pm. Nov-Apr: Mon-Fri 11am-4pm, Sat-Sun 10am-5pm

As Norman Rockwell so rightly said, 'I showed the America I knew and observed to
others who might not have noticed'. Located in the small New England village that was
his home for the last 25 years of his life is this stunning wood, slate, and fieldstone
museum. Exhibited within are the largest public collections of artwork by America's
favourite illustrator. His works are exhibited all year round, along with those of other
illustrators. It also houses the artist's papers and archives.

University of Surrey

George Edwards Library, Shepard Archive, Guildford, Surrey GU2 7XH, UK
Tel. (44) 1483 873325   www.surrey.ac.uk
Please call for opening times

Botanical prints
Hunt Institute for Botanical
Documentation

Best known for his illustrations for A. A. Milne's *Winnie-the-Pooh*, Ernest Shepard was a
prolific contributor to *Punch* and worked on 57 books including an illustrated autobiography. The excellent archive on Shepard includes the drawings he produced on active
service in World War I, 37 sketchbooks, the contents of his studio and study, and a choice
selection of his masterly pen-and-ink line drawings.

BOTANICAL BOOKS AND PRINTS

Bibliothèque des Conservatoire et Jardin botaniques
Library of the Botanical Academy and Botanical Garden
Chemin de l'Impératrice 1, C. P. 60, 1292 Chambésy, Switzerland
Tel. (41) 22 418 52 00   www.cjb.unige.ch
Mon 1.30-4.30pm, Tue-Fri 10am-noon, 1-4.30pm

With over 225,000 volumes, this is one of the most remarkable and comprehensive private collections of botanical
works in the world, including 16th- and 17th-century
plant illustrations made on wood and beautifully
illustrated botanical works from the 18th century. The
pre-Linnean collection of 680 titles from the 16th and
17th centuries includes works by Bauhin, de l'Ecluse
and Dalechamps, and the Linnean Collection includes
all the reference texts published by Linnaeus, including
revisions of both his own works and those of his students.

Hunt Institute for Botanical Documentation

Carnegie Mellon University, 5000 Forbes Avenue, Pittsburgh,
Pennsylvania 15213, USA
Tel. (1) 412 268 2434   www.huntbot.andrew.cmu.edu
Mon–Fri 9am–noon, 1–5pm

One of the world's largest botanical art collections, with over 30,000 original
paintings (mostly 20th-century watercolours), drawings, and original prints
dating from the Renaissance to the present day. Among the prized possessions is
the Hitchcock-Chase Collection, containing over 4,700 ink drawings of grasses
assembled by the 20th-century Smithsonian agrostologists, Albert S. Hitchcock
and Agnes Chase. An international nexus for bibliographical research on botany,
horticulture, and all aspects of the history of plant sciences, highlights range from
early horticultural works and 17th- and 18th-century colour plate books, to early
accounts of travel and exploration relating to plant discovery.

John Innes Foundation Collection of Rare Botanical Books

John Innes Centre, Norwich Research Park, Colney, Norwich NR4 7UH, UK
Tel. (44) 1603 450674   www.jic.bbsrc.ac.uk
By appt. only

Founded in 1910 by the City of London merchant John Innes, this small but exquisite
collection of rare plant books covers some of the landmark discoveries in plant science
as well as four centuries of botanical literature. Under the directorship of the genetics
pioneer, William Bateson (who coined the word 'genetics' in a letter to Adam Sedgwick
in 1905) the foundation became the UK's leading research centre on plant breeding and
genetics (the collection includes Gregor Mendels' original paper on the science of genetics). The many treasures in the rare books collection include a hand-coloured 1570 herbal
by L'Obel, after whom lobelia was named; Philip Miller's *Catalogue plantarum* (published
for the Society of Gardeners in 1730); and a Dutch edition of Weinmann's *Phytanthoza
Iconographia* (1737-45).

Botanical prints (top)
*Hunt Institute for Botanical
Documentation*

Tulip illustration from
Hortus Floridus by Crispin
de Pas, 1614-17 (above)
*John Innes Foundation
Collection of Rare
Botanical Books*

Lindley Library at the Royal Horticultural Society Library

80 Vincent Square, London SW1P 2PE, UK
Tel. (44) 20 7821 3600   www.rhs.org.uk
By appt. only

Founded in the early 19th century, the collection started with a volume of drawings by
William Hooker documenting fruits exhibited at RHS meetings. It has since grown into
a library of over 18,000 drawings and Chinese prints, along with gems such as: Dean
Herbert's crocus drawings; F. Bauer's illustrations for Lindley's *Digitalium Monographia*
of 1820; an unpublished florilegium by Pieter van Kouwenhoorn dating from the 1630s;
pencil drawings by Aubriet; an album of vellums by Turpin, with a copy of his *Leçons de
Flore* which he made for King Louis XVIII; and some of Ehret's drawings.

Nationaal Herbarium Nederland Library
The Library of the Dutch National Herbarium

University of Leiden , Branch Einsteinweg 2, Leiden, The Netherlands
Tel. (31) 71 5273513   www.nhncml.leidenuniv.nl
Mon–Fri 8.15am–12.30pm, 1–4.45pm

Founded in 1590, the Leiden Botanic Garden is the earliest scientific garden in Western
Europe. It has since played a significant role in botanical research and its rich historical
collection of books, periodicals, plant illustrations, and reprints of the library are a vital
research resource. The collection comprises some 45,000 books, 100,000 journal volumes,
100,000 reprints, and 90,000 microfiches and plant illustrations.

Linden tree illustration from Kräuterbuch by Hyeronmus Bock, 1516
John Innes Foundation Collection of Rare Botanical Books

Natural History Museum Library

Cromwell Road, London SW7 5BD, UK
Tel. (44) 20 7942 5011 www.nhm.ac.uk
By appt. only

One of the most significant and wide-ranging collections of botanical watercolours, drawings, and prints in the world, as well as over 800,000 books, including 21 incunabula. There are also maps (especially geological), manuscripts, the archives of the Natural History Museum itself, and the natural history collections of Sir Hans Sloane, the British Museum's founder.

The New York Botanical Gardens Library at the LuEsther Mertz Library

New York Botanical Gardens, Bronx, New York, New York 10458-5126, USA
Tel. (1) 718 817 8604 www.nybg.org
Tue-Thu noon-6pm, Fri-Sat noon-5pm

Established in 1972, this is a very broad-ranging collection of over 13,000 line drawings, prints, watercolours, oil paintings and sculptures, including illustrations commissioned for the Botanical Garden's own research publications. Some of the oldest works document early US expeditions, and regional flora from around the world is well represented with original illustrations from taxonomic works such as Britton and Brown's *Illustrated Flora of Northeastern United States and Adjacent Canada.*

Royal Botanic Gardens

Kew, Richmond, Surrey TW9 3AB, UK
Tel. (44) 20 8332 5000 www.rbgkew.org.uk
Feb-Mar: 9.30am-5pm. Apr-Oct: 9.30am-5.30pm. Nov-Feb: 9.30am-3.45pm.

Kew's exhaustive library of over 175,000 botanical prints and drawings from the 17th century onwards incorporates the private collections of Sir Joseph Banks and the garden's first official director, Sir William Hooker. Showstoppers include Ruiz's *Florae Peruvianae et Chilensis* (1794) and Besler's *Hortus eystettensis* (1613) plus exquisite examples of work by G. D. Ehret, Ferdinand and Franz Bauer (18th century) and Walter Hood Fitch (19th century). The botanical material includes a special collection devoted to works by Carolus Linnaeus and his contemporaries, and some seven million sheets of unpublished work on plants and fungi.

The Royal Collection

Windsor Castle, Windsor, Berkshire SL4 1NJ, UK
Tel. (44) 1753 868286 www.the-royal-collection.org.uk
By appt. only

Windsor Castle's excellent botanical prints collection includes 159 folios (28 of tulips and 22 of gillyflowers) painted in the 17th century by Alexander Marshal (a friend of John Tradescant the Younger) and recently documented in Prudence Leith-Ross and Henrietta McBurney's *Florilegium of Alexander Marshal at Windsor Castle* (2000).

UJ Biblioteka Instytutu Botaniki

Jagiellonian University Institute of Botany Library
31-501 Kraków, Kopernika 27, Poland
Tel. (48) 12 421 02 77 www.ib.uj.edu.pl
Please call for opening times

One of the oldest centres of plant science, with books, journals and booklets, early illustrated atlases of flora, rare works by G. Wahlenberg, and a small collection of 736 old prints collected by botanists and bibliophiles from the Kraków region.

COMICS AND MAGAZINES

Musée de la Bande dessinée
The Museum of the Comic Strip
121 rue de Bordeaux, 1600 Angoulême, France
Tel. (33) 5 45 38 65 65
May-Sep: Tue-Fri 10am-7pm, Sat-Sun 2-7pm
Oct-Apr: Tue-Fri 10am-6pm, Sat-Sun 2-6pm

The museum displays only a fraction at a time of its massive
collection of 4,000 drawings and original plates spanning
150 years of French, Belgian, and North American comic
book production. The collection also includes 200,000
periodicals dating back to the 19th century.

Wilhelm-Busch-Museum / Deutsches Museum für Karikatur und kritische Grafik
The Wilhelm Busch Museum / German Museum of Caricature
Georgengarten 1, 30167 Hanover, Germany
Tel. (49) 511 714076   www.wilhelm-busch-museum.de
Tue-Sat 10am-5pm, Sun 10am-6pm

Morris's 'Lucky Luke'
entering the Belgian
Comic Strip Centre
*Centre belge de la
Bande dessinée*

The core collection is devoted to the works of Wilhelm Busch, the 19th-century cartoonist
and creator of Max and Mortiz. Since 1950, it is has been considerably extended, with 150
cartoons and 16,000 drawings (also oil paintings, drawings, cartoon stories, letters, and
poems) by other prominent German and international cartoonists. The museum publishes its own journal, *Schriften zur Karikatur und kritischen Graphik.*

Centre belge de la Bande dessinée
The Belgian Comic Strip Centre
20 rue des Sables 20, 1000 Brussels, Belgium
Tel. (32) 2 219 1980   www.tintin.be
Tue-Sun 10am-6pm

This stunning Art-Nouveau textiles warehouse, designed by Victor Horta in 1906, has
been converted into a museum celebrating the draughtsmanship of the many great
cartoonists produced by Belgium in the 20th century. As well as exhibitions on cartoon
drawing, animation, and the latest trends, the collection includes a trove of original
works by Hergé (Tintin), Franquin (Gaston Lagaffe), and Edgar-Pierre Jacobs (Blake and
Mortimer) among others. An auditorium shows animations and documentaries, the

library is crammed with 30,000 albums by 700
authors, and the excellent museum bookstore has
a choice selection of cult and mainstream comics.

Cover of *Tintin and the
Picaros* by Hergé
*Centre belge de la
Bande dessinée*

The Centre for the Study of Cartoons and Caricature
Templeman Library, University of Kent at
Canterbury, Canterbury, Kent CT2 7NU, UK
Tel. (44) 1227 764 000   www.library.ukc.ac.uk
Mon-Fri 9.30am-4.30pm

This excellent 85,000-strong collection of (mostly)
British newspaper and magazine cartoons taps into
a rich vein of humour and biting satire dating back
to the early days of *Punch* and ending with Steve Bell,
Ralph Steadman, Gerald Scarfe and Bill Tidy. The
library holds 2,000 books on cartoonists and cartoons

(both British and foreign), anthologies and reference works, and an almost complete run of Giles from 1945 onwards.

Centre Tomi Ungerer
The Tomi Ungerer Centre
4 rue de la Haute-Montée, 67000 Strasbourg, France
Tel. (33) 3 88 32 31 54
By appt. only

A vast collection of works donated by Tomi Ungerer, the Strasbourg cartoonist, writer, and illustrator who regarded caricature as candour without malice. The collection's 7,000 original drawings covering a range of subjects from the nature of eroticism to the fear of death, takes in forty years of creative endeavour, from books for children and adults, to posters, sculptures, and other precious memorabilia.

Comic Art Collection
Michigan State University Libraries, 100 Library, East Lansing, Michigan 48824, USA
Tel. (1) 517 355 3770   www.lib.msu.edu
Please call for opening times

The collection focuses on published work rather than original drawings. Over 110,000 comic books, newspaper strips, books, and periodicals make the archive a hugely valuable resource for collectors, scholars, and artists. The broad categories include US comic books, newspaper strips, historical and critical materials, and international comics, with smaller sub-collections covering propaganda and movie tie-ins. Most of the collection is American (over 300,000 daily comic strips from 1940-80 have been pasted into 534 scrapbooks), but there is a first-class international collection with excellent examples of comics from all over the world including Europe, Brazil, Canada, Korea, Mexico, and Sweden. Many, such as the fotonovelas from Latin America or erotic stories from Spain and France, offer a refreshingly satirical perspective on real life, in contrast to the superheroes and cuddly cartoon characters.

Meeting Paul Klee by Luiz Caulos, 1987 (top) *Karikatur und Cartoon Museum*

No title by Gin, 1980 (above) *Karikatur und Cartoon Museum*

Beethoven by Erich Sokol, 1978 (right) *Karikatur und Cartoon Museum*

International Museum of Cartoon Art
Mizner Park, 201 Plaza Real, Boca Raton, Florida 33432, USA
Tel. (1) 561 391 2200   www.cartoon.org
Tue-Sat 10am-6pm, Sun noon-6pm

Founded in 1974, this superb collection comprises some 160,000 original cartoons in every medium: animation, comic books, comic strips, greetings cards, caricature, and graphic novels. The emphasis is on American cartoonists and there are extensive archives on Al Capp (the lampooning pen behind Lil' Abner), Stan Lee (Spiderman and assorted superheroes), Charles Schulz, and Walt Disney. Over 10,000 books on cartoons and thousands of hours of film and video of animated cartoons plus interviews and documentaries make this one of the world's most comprehensive cartoon collections.

Karikatur und Cartoon Museum
The Caricature and Cartoon Museum
St Alban-Vorstadt 28, 4002 Basle, Switzerland
Tel. (41) 61 271 1346   www.cartoonmuseum.ch
Wed, Sat 2-5.30pm, Sun 10am-5.30pm

Founded by Dieter Burckhardt in 1979, this vast museum has amassed over 3,000 humorous drawings by 700 artists from forty countries, including Caran d'Ache, Charles Addams, Peter Arno, Albert Dubout, and George Grosz. Displays in the medieval building which has been brilliantly converted by Herzog & de Meuron (the two Swiss architects behind the Tate Modern conversion in London) focus on individual artists or themes, with parodies on art, portraits, gag-cartoons without captions, and cartoons with captions.

The National Art Library at The Victoria and Albert Museum

Cromwell Road, London SW7 2RL, UK
Tel. (44) 20 7942 2397 www.nal.vam.ac.uk
Tue-Sat 10am-5pm

The Island of Death
by Borislav Sajtinac
Karikatur und Cartoon Museum

This recently established collection includes the Krazy Kat Arkive (named after the famous George Herriman strip cartoon and curated by the Scottish artist Eduardo Paulozzi) of over 40,000 comic strips and cartoons, and the Ian Rakoff Collection of newspaper strips and New Wave comics (mostly four-colour books, such as the famous Marvel series).

Statue of Liberty
by Jack Davis
Karikatur und Cartoon Museum

The Ohio State University Cartoon Research Library

27 West 17th Avenue Mall, Columbus, Ohio 43210, USA
Tel. (1) 614 292 0538 www.lib.ohio-state.edu
By appt. only

The largest cartoon-related research facility in the US, with a state-of-the-art multimedia collection documenting cartoon art, film posters and stills, historic photographs, and magazine illustrations. There are some original works and related manuscript materials and more than 10,000 published works on cartoon art.

Storm P Museet
The Storm P Museum

Pile Allé 2, 2000 Frederiksberg, Denmark
Tel. (44) 38 860523
May-Sep: Tue-Sun 10am-4pm. Oct-Apr: Wed, Sat-Sun 10am-4pm

More than 50,000 Heath Robinson-style drawings and paintings by the famous Danish humorist, cartoonist, painter and actor Storm P, including social-critical drawings from his early years and a collection of more than 450 pipes and material chronicling the cartoonist's acting career.

Caroline and Erwin Swann Collection of Caricature and Cartoon

Library of Congress Rare Books & Special Collections ,Rm LJ-206 Thomas Jefferson Building, 1st Street and Independence Avenue, SE Washington, DC 20540, USA
Tel. (1) 202 707 3448 www.lcweb.loc.gov
Mon-Fri 8.30am-5pm

An advertising executive working in New York, Erwin Swann began collecting original cartoon artwork in the early 1960s. Today the collection has swelled to 2,085 drawings, prints, and paintings dating back to the French Revolution which use a mix of biting satire and gentle banter to give illuminating insights into life at the time. About 25 per cent of the work is by American artists.

Tegneseriemuseet i Denmark
The Danish Museum of Comics

Kirkevangen 22, 4281 Gørlev, Denmark
Tel. (45) 58 855141 www.kulturnetvestsj.dk
Mon-Thu 11am-4pm

Danish comic book art from Storm P (the creator of Peter & Ping and one of Denmark's first fully fledged cartoonists) to the present day. There are also pristine examples of work by Oscar Knudsen (fairy stories and classic adventure yarns like *The Count of Monte Christo* retold in comic book form), 'Mik' (the creator of Ferd'nand), and Willy Nielsen (whose 1950s strip published in *Skipper Skraek* was set in prehistoric Denmark with Danish history and folklore as its theme).

COOKBOOKS

Musée de l'Art culinaire – Auguste Escoffier
Auguste Escoffier Museum of Culinary Art
3 rue Escoffier, 06270 Villeneuve-Loubet, France
Tel. (33) 4 93 20 80 51 www.fondation-escoffier.org
Jan-Oct, Dec: Tue-Sun 2-6pm

This fascinating museum dedicated to the great chef, Auguste Escoffier, has a library filled with ancient and modern cookbooks, many of which are on open shelves. His titles include *Le Guide Culinaire*, *Livres des Menus*, and *Ma Cuisine*, some of which are still used by professional chefs.

Cookery Collection, Michigan State University Libraries
Special Collections Division, 100 Library, East Lansing, Michigan 48824, USA
Tel. (1) 517 355 3770 www.lib.msu.edu
Mon-Fri 9am-5pm

An enormous collection of 2,000 cookbooks spanning five centuries which provide fascinating insights into society and the social mores of the time. Among the rare 17th-century holdings some giants stand out: Hannah Glasse's *The Art of Cookery* (1747), Elizabeth Raffald's *The Experienced English Housekeeper* (1769), William King's *The Art of Cookery* (1712), Penelope Bradshaw's *The Family Jewel and Compleat Housewife's Companion* (1751), Ann Cook's *Professed Cookery* (1755), and the first cookery book to be published in America, Eliza Smith's *Compleat Housewife* (1727).

Museum library (top)
Musée de l'Art culinaire – Auguste Escoffier

La Cuisinière de la Campagne cookbook, first published Paris, 1818 (above)
The Culinary Collection

The Cookery Collections
Special Collections, The Brotherton Library, University of Leeds, Leeds, West Yorkshire LS2 9JT, UK
Tel. (44) 113 233 5518 www.leeds.ac.uk
By appt. only

Three core collections of around 2,000 books covering medieval, Victorian and 20th-century cookery and household management.

The Culinary Archives & Museum, Johnson & Wales University
315 Harborside Boulevard, Providence, Rhode Island 02905, USA
Tel. (1) 401 598 2805 www.culinary.org
Tue-Sat 10am-4pm (by guided tour)

Food history from ancient times to the present day, represented by a massive collection of over half a million items: rare cookbooks, cooking tools (from a 5,000-year-old Scythian bronze trade knife to a 17th-century cannibal dish and fork from Fiji), antique kitchen appliances, 19th-century stoves, the first electric toaster (produced by General Electric in 1906), graphic prints of chef's uniforms, and menus and food-related correspondence signed by emperors, kings and US presidents.

The Culinary Collection
Newcomb College Center for Research on Women, Nadine Vorhoff Library, Caroline Richardson Hall, Tulane University Libraries, New Orleans, Louisiana 70118, USA
Tel. (1) 504 865 5762 www.tulane.edu
Mon-Tue 9am-9pm, Wed, Fri 9am-5pm, Thu 9am-8pm

Over 2,000 cookbooks, other books, and periodicals relating to culinary history dating from the 1850s to the present. Areas of specialisation include writing on the history of food; New Orleans and Southern regional cookbooks; manuscript housekeeping papers; and such rarities as *Bon Mélange*, a home-made community cookbook created in

1976 by the Amigas Club of Thibodaux and featuring original Louisiana specialities. Also an impressive collection of international cookbooks (Polish, Jewish, Italian, Scandinavian, Caribbean, Indian, Chinese and French), many of which are published in their original languages.

Deutsches Kochbuch-Museum
German Cookbook Museum
An der Buschmühle (im Westfahlenpark), 44139 Dortmund, Germany
Tel. (49) 231 502 5741 www.museendortmund.de
Mar-Oct: Tue-Sun 10am-5pm. Oct-Mar: Tue-Fri 1-5pm, Sun 10am-5pm

From J. J. Weber's *Universal Encyclopedia of Cooking*, published in 1913
Deutsches Kochbuch-Museum

Over 3,000 cookery and household management books and encyclopaedias shed new light on the status of women and the social history of the family in the 19th and 20th centuries. The museum includes a bakery, herb garden, and some 600 exhibits (cookers, kitchen equipment and dishes etc.)

The Husted Collection
Special Collections and Archives, Penrose Library, University of Denver, Denver, Colorado 80208, USA
Tel. (1) 303 871 3428 www.penlib.du.edu
Mon-Fri 8.30am-5pm

Over 7,000 books, magazines, and pamphlets amassed by Margaret Husted of Alexandria, Virginia, and donated to the University of Denver in 1985. Though the collection is international in scope, the emphasis is on American regional cuisine and the history of American domestic and culinary practices over four centuries.

Kansas State University
Hale Library, Special Collections, Manhattan, Kansas 66502, USA
Tel. (1) 785 532 7455 www.lib.ksu.edu
Mon-Fri 8am-5pm

One of the leading cookery book collections of the US, with 10,000 cookbooks dating from the 16th century to the present. Gems in the collection include the first folio (1747) of Hannah Glasse's *Art of Cookery,* an 1812 edition of Amelia Simmons' *American Cookery* (the first cookbook published in the US that was not a whole or partial reprint of an English work), and an outstanding collection of juvenile cookery books dating back to the 1890s.

The New York Public Library
5th Avenue and 42nd Street, New York, New York 10018, USA
Tel. (1) 212 930 0830 www.nypl.org
Mon, Tue, Fri noon-6pm, Wed noon-8pm, Thu 10am-6pm, Sat noon-5pm

Books by Auguste Escoffier
Musée de l'Art culinaire – Auguste Escoffier

Since it was founded, the library has collected culinary materials from all over the world and now has an extensive collection of 16,000 volumes, 20,000 menus, and rare 15th-19th-century English cookery books and manuscripts.

Peabody Essex Museum
Phillips Library, East India Square, Salem, Massachusetts 01970, USA
Tel. (1) 978 745 9500 www.pem.org
Tue, Wed, Fri 10am-5pm, Thu 1-8pm

Approximately 500 volumes of early cookbooks and works on domestic economy, all printed before 1900, which according to the staff, deserves more research and publicity.

Szathmary book plates;
copies of woodblock
prints (above and right)
*The Szathmary
Culinary Archives*

Peacock-Harper Culinary Collection

Special Collections, Newman Library, Virginia Tech, Blacksburg, Virginia 24062, USA
Tel. (1) 540 231 6308 www.spec.lib.vt.edu
Mon noon-4.30pm, Tue-Fri 10am-4.30pm

Two centuries of culinary arts, from Eliza Leslie's *Seventy-five Receipts for Pastry, Cakes, and
Sweetmeats by a lady of Philadelphia* (1829) to Margaret McWilliams' *Experimental Foods
Laboratory Manual* (1994). Laura Jane Harper was Dean of Virginia Tech College of Home
Economics from 1960-80 and a prominent researcher into nutrition in international
development.

Joseph and Elizabeth Robins Pennell Collection

Library of Congress, Rare Books and Special Collections Division, Thomas Jefferson
Building, 1st Street and Independence Avenue SE, Washington, DC 20540, USA
Tel. (1) 202 707 3448 www.lcweb.loc.gov
Mon-Fri 8.30am-5pm

Elizabeth Pennell wrote extensively on gastronomy and during her life amassed a large
collection of 433 European cookbooks, in particular 16th-18th-century French and
Italian cookbooks (including a rare, fully illustrated edition of Bartolomeo Scappi's
Opera dating from 1574).

Schlesinger Library

Radcliffe Institute for Advanced Study, 3 James Street, Cambridge,
Massachusetts 02138, USA
Tel. (1) 617 495 8647 www.radcliffe.edu
Mon-Fri 9am-5pm (Wed until 8pm)

This is the foremost library in the US on the history of women, and its holdings include
a special collection supporting research in culinary history, the history of domestic life,
and the role of food in history and culture. It includes 12,000 books, periodicals, microforms
of rare or fragile items, and the manuscript collections of Julia Child, M. F. K. Fisher,
Alice Bradley, Lydia Child, Corner Book Shop Records (Eleanor Lowenstein), and others
concerned with food, cooking, and domestic economy.

The Szathmary Culinary Archives

Special Collections Department, University of Iowa
Libraries, Iowa City, Iowa 52242-1420, USA
Tel. (1) 319 335 5921 www.lib.uiowa.edu
Mon-Fri 9am-5pm

An eclectic mix of 8,600 books, menus, and other items
relating to the art and science of cooking and eating.
Collected by the Hungarian chef Louis Szathmary from
1951, the focus is on national, regional, and ethnic cuisine, beverages, and gastronomy. As well as cookbooks
there are pamphlets and menus autographed by kings
and queens, presidents, politicians, actors, musicians,
and Nobel Prize winners (including Winston
Churchill, Enrico Caruso, Juan and Evita Peron). The
wonderful manuscript collection has letters from just
about every president or first lady in American history,
including 'thank you' notes for gifts of food. In addition, there is a long letter from Walt
Whitman itemising two recent meals, a note by Ernest Hemingway to a condiment
company in New York requesting a recipe booklet, and a plea from Benjamin Franklin
for Betsy Franklin's help in getting rid of some maggots in salt pork.

JAPANESE WOODBLOCK PRINTS

The Art Institute of Chicago

111 South Michigan Avenue, Chicago, Illinois 60603, USA
Tel. (1) 312 443 3600   www.artic.edu
Mon-Fri 10.30am-4.30pm (Tue until 8pm), Sat 10am-5pm, Sun noon-5pm

Frank Lloyd Wright, Fredrick William Gookin, and
Clarence Buckingham all exhibited their collections
of ukiyo-e (or 'pictures of the floating world') for the
first time at the Chicago Art Institute. Clarence
Buckingham donated his prints to the Institute on
his death in 1917. The majority of the 15,000 prints
date from the classical period (1625-1880) but there
are also 3,500 prints from the 20th century.

Museo d'Arte orientale Edoardo Chiossone
The Eduardo Chiossone Museum of Oriental Art

Villetta di Negro, piazzale Mazzini 1, 16122 Genoa, Italy
Tel. (39) 010 542285
Tue-Sat 9am-1pm, 2-7pm, Sun 9am-12.30pm

The museum contains a fine selection of ukiyo-e
prints, many of which reflect the daily life, habits,
and amusements of mercantile and artisan classes
which flourished during the Edo epoch (1603-1869).
The collection also includes numerous 20th-century
prints and wood engravings.

Bristol City Museum and Art Gallery

Queen's Road, Bristol BS8 1RL, UK
Tel. (44) 117 922 3571   www.bristol-city.gov.uk
Daily 10am-5pm by appt. only

*Ladies at New Year's
preparations* by Toyohiro
(top)
*Museum für Ostasiatische
Kunst (Cologne)*

Most of the 500 Japanese prints were purchased from Professor Curnall Punnet in the
1950s. Early 18th- and 19th-century masters are well represented, especially Moronobu,
Utamaro, Hiroshige, Kunisada, and Hokusaï.

*View of the Eight Sights of
Kanazzwa by Night*
by Hiroshige (above)
*Museum für Ostasiatische
Kunst (Cologne)*

British Museum

Great Russell Street, London WC1B 3DG, UK
Tel. (44) 20 7636 1555   www.thebritishmuseum.ac.uk
Mon-Sat 10am-5pm, Sun noon-6pm

One of the finest collections of Japanese woodblock prints in the world, with a comprehensive group of Maruyama-Shijo prints and 8,000 ukiyo-e woodblock prints dating
from the 1780-1800 golden age. They include gems such as Kiyonaga's *Asukayama at
Cherry Blossom Time*. The museum also collects recent prints, with works by Unichi, one
of the founders of the Sōsaku Hanga movement.

The Brooklyn Museum of Art

200 Eastern Parkway, Brooklyn, New York, New York 11238-6052, USA
Tel. (1) 718 6385000   www.brooklynart.org
Wed-Fri 10am-5pm, Sat-Sun 11am-6pm

This eclectic collection of Asian art works from Cambodia, China, India, Iran, Japan,
Thailand, Tibet, and Turkey includes the only complete set in the country of Utawaga
Hiroshige's *One Hundred Famous Views of Edo*.

Scenes from a drama
by Toyohiro (left)
Museum für Ostasiatische
Kunst (Cologne)

The beautiful Okita
by Utamaro (right)
Museum für Ostasiatische
Kunst (Cologne)

Collections Baur
The Baur Collections
8 rue Munier-Romilly, 1206 Geneva, Switzerland
Tel. (41) 22 346 17 29   www.baur-collections.ch
Tue-Sun 2-6pm

After making his fortune in Colombo, Alfred Baur spent the next half century amassing a stupendous oriental collection which comprises netsuke, sword-fittings, lacquer, Chinese ceramics, over 600 Japanese ukiyo-e prints dating from the 18th century, and 19th-century tryptichs of Kunisada, Kuniyoshi, and Hiroshige.

The Chester Beatty Library
Dublin Castle, Dublin 2, Ireland
Tel. (353) 1 407 0750   www.cbl.ie
Oct-Apr: Tue-Fri 10am-5pm. May-Sep: Mon-Fri 10am-5pm. Sat 11am-5pm, Sun 1pm-5pm

An exceptional collection of late 18th-century and early 19th-century Japanese surimono prints. Meaning 'printed object', the intricately produced prints combined images and poems, most of which were privately published. They were used to mark special events or distributed to friends as gifts on festive occasions, particularly at the New Year.

Museum of Fine Arts
465 Huntington Avenue, Boston, Massachusetts 02115-5519, USA
Tel. (1) 617 267 9300   www.mfa.org
Mon-Tue 10am-4.45pm, Wed-Fri 10am-9.45pm

One of the largest and most representative Japanese print collections in the world, with 60,000 prints and works by all the major artists including Hiroshige, Kiyochika, Gekko and, Nobukazu. In 1921 the museum acquired William S. and John T. Spaulding's collection of 6,495 woodblock prints, purchased for the brothers by the architect Frank Lloyd Wright. The museum owns a unique collection of 657 Japanese colour woodblock prints from the Meiji era (1868-1912), many depicting scenes from the two Meiji wars.

Minneapolis Institute of Arts
2400 Third Avenue South, Minneapolis, Minnesota 55404, USA
Tel. (1) 612 870 3131   www.artsmia.org
Tue, Wed, Sat 10am-5pm, Thu, Fri 10am-9pm, Sun noon-5pm

One of the best collections in the US with masterpieces by Hokusai, Toyokuni, Toshinobu, Utamaro, and Hokusai.

Musée Monet
Monet Museum
Fondation Monet, 27620 Giverny, France
Tel. (33) 2 32 51 28 21   www.fondation-monet.com
Daily 10am-6pm (Apr-Nov closed Mon)

Claude Monet's small but valuable collection of Japanese woodblock prints provides a fascinating insight into both his paintings and Japanese-inspired garden. Japanese prints were first exhibited in Europe at the Venice World Fair of 1862.

Museum für Ostasiatische Kunst
The Museum of East Asian Art
Universitätsstrasse 100, 50674 Cologne, Germany
Tel. (49) 221 9405180
Tue-Sun 11am-5pm (Thu, Sat until 10pm)

The Riese Collection of 177 Japanese woodblock prints from the Edo period is one of the museum's highlights. Although the ukiyo-e technique began as a cheap way of reproducing images, it developed to become a highly skilled and respected art form. Works by masters such as Sharaku, Utamaro, Haronobu, Masanobu, and Hiroshige are well represented in the collection. The collection also includes two images from Hokusai's famous *Thirty-Six Views of Mount Fuji*.

Museum für Ostasiatische Kunst
The Museum of East Asian Art
Lansstrasse 8, 14195 Berlin, Germany
Tel. (49) 30 8301382
Tue-Fri 9am-5pm, Sat-Sun 10am-5pm

Over 7,000 Japanese prints constitute the largest collection in Germany and include excellent works by many of the great masters, including some formerly owned by the famous Paris dealer, Hayashi Tadamasa. Also noteworthy are 500 illustrated books. On permanent loan is the first-rate collection of Mr Klaus Naumann, consisting of ten Nikuhitsue (paintings of beautiful women), as well as lacquer and Japanese ceramics.

Girl with a Cat by Isoda Koryusai, *c.* 1770 (above) *Museum für Ostasiatische Kunst* (Berlin)

Actors, S. Ichimatsu and I. Tomienin by Tôshusai Sharaku, 1794 (above left) *Museum für Ostasiatische Kunst* (Berlin)

Musée Pincé
Pincé Museum
32 bis rue Lenepveu, 49100 Angers, France
Tel. (33) 2 41 88 94 27
Daily noon-6.30pm. Times may vary, please call for details.

A rare and beautiful collection of Japanese prints by Utamaro, Hiroshige, and Hokusaï. Also Chinese art, including mirrors from the Han to Ming dynasties.

The Rijksmuseum
The State Museum
Stadhouderskade 42, 1071 ZD Amsterdam, The Netherlands
Tel. (31) 20 6747047   www.rijksmuseum.nl
Daily 10am-5pm

The core of this collection, numbering 1,500 prints, is relatively young, although early additions came from the private collections of artists such as the Dutchman, Hendrik George Breitner who donated a polyptych by Utagawa Toyokuni, several prints amassed by Vincent van Gogh, and Meiji prints gathered by Barbara van Houten. The museum purchased the considerable collection of Ferdinand Lieftinck consisting of first-class prints by the great masters, including forty superb early sheets by Harunobu and some of the finest prints by Utamaro. Later, surimono were added and recently 200 more have followed from J. H. W. Goslings.

Rijksmuseum voor Volkenkunde
The National Museum of Ethnology
Steenstraat 1, 2300 AE Leiden, The Netherlands
Tel. (31) 71 5168800   www.rmv.nl
Tue-Fri, Sun 10am-5pm, Sat noon-5pm

Following the French occupation of the Netherlands, King Willem, who reigned from 1815 to 1840, dispatched several professors to the Dutch East Indies to extract Japanese and Chinese objects. Those amassed by the Master of the Warehouse in Deshima, Jan Cock Blomhhoff, consisted of several hundred prints probably collected during his visits to the imperial court in Edo in 1818 and 1829. Others the King purchased from those working in Deshima, while a third important contingent came via von Siebold. Notable items of this collection were the first ten parts of the *Hokusai manga* and the 1823 reprint of Utamoro's *Book of Insects*. In 1885, the Paris collector Louis Gonse's donations greatly enriched the museum's holdings. Gaps in the collection were filled with the purchase of C. Vogel's entire collection. There are now 7,000 prints including several groups which few museums possess in large numbers, namely those by the Osaka designers, and a series of earthquake prints.

Royal Museum of Scotland
Chambers Street, Edinburgh EH1 1JF, Scotland, UK
Tel. (44) 131 225 7534 www.nms.ac.uk
Mon-Sat 10am-5pm (Tue until 8pm), Sun noon-5pm

The largest collection of Far Eastern art in the UK, including almost 4,000 pristinely preserved 19th-century prints.

Arthur M. Sackler Museum
Harvard University, 32 Quincy Street, Cambridge, Massachusetts 02138, USA
Tel. (1) 617 495 9400 www.artmuseums.harvard.edu
Mon-Sat 10am-5pm, Sun 1-5pm

On display are almost 4,000 18th- and 19th-century Japanese woodblock prints which include one of the largest and finest collections of surimonos in the world.

Victoria and Albert Museum
Cromwell Road, South Kensington, London SW7 2RL, UK
Tel. (44) 20 7942 2000 www.vam.ac.uk
Daily 10am-5.45pm (Wed & last Fri of every month 10am-10pm)

Although there are some 20,000 prints, it is a mixed bag in terms of quality. A cache of aesthetically valuable images is accompanied by many less wonderful examples. Nevertheless, the size of this secondary material forms an invaluable documentary resource on numerous themes, including Japanese theatre. Fan prints by Hiroshige number around 100 examples and have recently been published by the museum in *Hiroshige Fan Prints* by Rupert Faulkner.

Worcester Art Museum
55 Salisbury Street, Worcester, Massachusetts 01609, USA
Tel. (1) 508 799 4406 www.worcesterart.org
Wed-Fri, Sun 11am-5pm, Sat 10am-5pm

The renowned John Chandler Bancroft Collection includes a rare 17th-century single-sheet print by Kiyonobu depicting the star Onnagata in the play *Kanto Koroku*, as well as more recent acquisitions such as Koshiro's 1943 *Portrait of the Author of Ice Island* and *Hagiwara Sakutaro*.

PHOTOGRAPHS

Aerial Photography at Cambridge
The Committee for Aerial Photography, Mond Building, Free School Lane, Cambridge, Cambridgeshire CB2 2RF, UK
Tel. (44) 1223 334578 www.aerial.cam.ac.uk
Mon-Fri 9am-1pm, 2-5pm (Fri until 4pm)

This unique university collection was the brainchild of Dr J. K. St Joseph, a lecturer in Geology at Cambridge whose wartime experiences convinced him that many subjects could be better studied from the air. In archaeology, for instance, Roman encampments and garrison forts have been discovered. In agriculture, patterns in growing crops observed from the air reveal variations in the soil or the spread and nature of plant disease. The university owns its own aircraft for taking photographs and its collection of over 400,000 images has become an invaluable historical record of how the landscape has altered over the years.

Birmingham Central Library

Floor 6, Local Studies and History, Chamberlain Square, Birmingham, West Midlands
B3 3HQ, UK
Tel. (44) 121 303 4549 www.ramesis.com
Mon-Fri 9am-8pm, Sat 9am-5pm

The library houses several interesting collections: the work of Francis Bedford, one of England's foremost landscape photographers; the archive of Benjamin Stone, who in 1895-1914 took and amassed a collection of 22,000 prints and 17,000 glass negatives documenting views, folk costumes, and dress in Britain and across the world; and the pioneering work of Francis Frith, who tried to photograph every town and site of interest in the British Isles, creating an archive of 300,000 negatives dating from 1870 to the mid 1960s.

The Amon Carter Museum

3501 Camp Bowie Boulevard, Fort Worth, Texas 76107-2695, USA
Tel. (1) 817 738 1933 www.cartermuseum.org
Re-opening end of 2001

Photograph by Pirotte, 1947
Musée de la photographie

The Texan publisher and philanthropist, Amon Carter, had a passion for the frontier and spent some of his vast fortune amassing a collection of rare photographs reflecting his love affair with the Wild West. It contains some 300,000 prints and includes the first known photo of a North American Indian in existence – an 1845 calotype of the Ojibway Indian, Peter Jones. Also on display is a series of daguerreotypes documenting the 1846-48 Mexican-American War and 1860s landscapes by photographers who accompanied railroad survey teams into the uncharted West. Virtually all of the big names in 20th-century American photography are represented, from the vast landscapes of Ansel Adams to Dorthea Lange's gritty dustbowl series.

Chrysler Museum of Art

245 West Olney Road, Norfolk, Virginia 23510, USA
Tel. (1) 757 664 6200 www.chrysler.org
Tue-Sat 10am-5pm, Sun 1-5pm

From the earliest daguerreotypes to the latest digital imagery, this eclectic collection covers an unusually broad range of themes and subjects, from Civil War photography to 19th-century French photography and images documenting the Civil Rights movement in the 1950s-70s. Works by Harold Edgerton, who developed a stroboscopic light in the 1930s to photograph objects moving faster than the human eye could discern, mingle with those by Adolphe Bertsch, who used a microscope in the 1850s to investigate another world.

George Eastman House

International Museum of Photography and Film, 900 East
Avenue, Rochester, New York 14607, USA
Tel. (1) 716 271 3361 www.eastman.org
Tue-Fri 10am-5pm by appt. only

A collection of nearly half a million negatives and photographs
trace the medium from its earliest technological breakthroughs
to its modern developments. Virtually every major figure is
represented. Special collections are devoted to early British
and French photography, and 19th-century images of the
American West (including important work by Alvin Langdon
Coburn and William Jennings). The hoard of 3,500 daguerreotypes is one of the largest in the world, and includes images
made by the inventor of the process, Louis Jacques Mandé
Daguerre. There are also whole plate views by the great
American dageurreotypists Samuel Bemis and Albert Sands
Southworth.

Portrait of René Magritte by
Leirens, 1959
Musée de la Photographie

Musée de l'Elysée
The Elysée Museum

18 ave. de l'Elysée, 1014 Lausanne, Switzerland
Tel. (41) 21 316 9911 www.elysee.ch
Tue-Sun 10am-6pm (Thu until 9pm)

Founded in the 1970s by Charles-Henri Favrod, the Elysée provides an overview of photography and its different processes from its earliest technological breakthroughs to the
development of lightweight wide-angle lenses, roll film, and onwards to the cameras of
the modern digital era. Though most of the photographers on show in the 18th-century
mansion are Swiss, there are also works by photographers of other nationalities such as
the documentary images of Walker Evans, examples of early Magnum photography, and
early experimental work by László Moholy-Nagy and Man Ray.

Museo Fratelli Alinari di Storia della Fotografia
The Fratelli Alinari Museum of the History of Photography

Palazzo Alinari, Largo Alinari 15, 50123 Florence, Italy
Tel. (39) 055 23951 www.alinari.com
Moving to new premises, please call for details

The museum houses 350,000 vintage and contemporary prints by some of the great
masters of the 19th and 20th centuries. As well as documenting every kind of photographic process the museum has a large collection of over 1,000 old cameras, lighting,
enlargement and developing equipment, and an extensive library.

Imperial War Museum

Lambeth Road, London SE1 6HZ, UK
Tel. (44) 20 7416 5320 www.iwm.org.uk
Daily 10am-6pm

Over five million photographs covering virtually every 20th-century conflict involving
Britain and the Commonwealth. As well as the work of official war photographers (post
1916) the collection has been supplemented by work from press and amateur photographers, and material from Germany, the US and other countries. Subject matter ranges
from portraits of famous figures to images reflecting the lives of ordinary people in the
context of war.

Museum Ludwig
The Ludwig Museum
Bischofsgartenstrasse 1, 50667 Cologne, Germany
Tel. (49) 221 2212375 www.artworks.de
Tue 10am-10pm, Wed-Fri 10am-6pm, Sat-Sun 11am-6pm

An outstanding collection of over 9,000 prints and negatives by some of the world's most important photographers. Experimental trends are represented by the likes of Maholy-Nagy, Man Ray, and Otto Steinert; fashion photography by Cecil Beaton and Irving Penn; reportage by Eve Arnold, Alfred Eisenstaedt, Henri Cartier-Bresson, and Robert Doisneau; American portrait and landscape photography by Ansel Adams and Walker Evans; and contemporary conceptual art by Bill Brandt and Robert Mapplethorpe.

Magyar Fotográfiai Múzeum
Hungarian Museum of Photography
Katona József tér 3, 6000 Kecskemét, Hungary
Tel. (36) 76 483221
Wed-Sun 10am-5pm

Founded in 1989 in a small synagogue in Kecskemét, this remarkable collection of half a million photographs dates from 1839 onwards and incorporates a large photographic history collection first set up by the Association of Hungarian Photographers in 1958. The museum showcases work by Hungary's foremost photographers (Pécsi József, Balogh Rudolf, Angelo) as well as international photography and work by photographers of Hungarian origin (André Kertész, Moholy-Nagy László, Kepes György, Brassaï and Munkácsi Márton). There museum also houses collections of photographic equipment, library materials, and video and sound recordings.

Three sumo wrestlers in ceremonial aprons, *c.* 1870-90 (below)
Peabody Essex Museum

Photograph by Guidalevich, *c.* 1933 (bottom)
Musée de la Photographie

The Museum of Modern Art
11 West 53rd Street, New York, New York 10019, USA
Tel. (1) 212 708 9400 www.moma.org
Mon, Tue, Thu-Sun 10.30am-5.45pm (Fri until 8.15pm)

MoMA's founding director, Alfred H. Barr, believed that all mediums of the visual arts were interdependent and that none could be studied in isolation. The museum's photographic collection was started in 1930, two years after the museum opened, and today its holdings number more than 25,000 dating from 1840 to the present. The diverse spread includes work by journalists, scientists, entrepreneurs, and amateurs recording every aspect of American life.

National Monuments Record Centre
Great Western Village, Kemble Drive, Swindon, Gloucestershire SN2 2GZ, UK
Tel. (44) 1793 414600 www.english-heritage.org.uk
Tue-Fri 9.30am-5pm, third Sat of each month 10am-4pm

Housing some twelve million photographs, drawings, and maps covering every aspect of English architecture from townscapes and farm buildings to former hospitals, local shops and even slagheaps, this enormous archive paints a unique topographical portrait of England past and present. A gallery space in a railway shed designed in 1842 by Isambard Kingdom Brunel showcases the cream of the collection and there is also an extensive on-line catalogue.

National Museum of Photography, Film & Television
Pictureville, Bradford, West Yorkshire BD1 1NQ, UK
Tel. (44) 1274 202030 www.nmpft.org.uk
Tue-Sun 10am-6pm

Crammed with two centuries of work, the recently revamped museum has an archive
holding of more than one million prints, including daguerreotypes, negatives, and glass
plates. Lesser known photographers are represented alongside pioneering work by
William Henry Fox Talbot, Juliet Margaret Cameron, David Octavius Hill and Robert
Adamson, Roger Fenton, and Lewis Carroll. The museum also owns a collection of over
100,000 objects and 150,000 images donated by Kodak in the 1980s, highlights of which
include the world's first negative created by Fox Talbot, and Conan Doyle's fake fairies
photographed at nearby Cottingley.

Peabody Essex Museum
East India Square, Salem, Massachusetts 01970, USA
Tel. (1) 978 745 9500 www.pem.org
Nov-Mar: Tue-Sat 10am-5pm, Sun noon-5pm
Apr-Oct: Mon-Sat 10am-5pm, Sun noon-5pm

This massive holding consists of half a million photographs
and includes a unique collection of 17,000 early 19th-century
images from Japan, Korea, China, Cochin China (Vietnam),
the Philippines, Java, the South Seas, Siam, Malaya, Burma,
and the British Indian Empire. In addition, the museum has
14,000 glass lantern slides and a remarkable collection of 110
signed mammoth-plate exhibition prints of Native
Americans which were produced by Edward Sheriff Curtis
during his travels through America and Canada between
1904-05.

Chief Joseph – Nez Perce
by Edward S. Curtis, 1903
(above left)
Peabody Essex Museum

A Hopi mother and child
by Edward S. Curtis, 1900
(above right)
Peabody Essex Museum

Anonymous
by Launae, 1853 (right)
Musée de la Photographie

Museum of Photographic Arts
1649 El Prado, San Diego, California 92101, USA
Tel. (1) 619 238 7559 www.mopa.org
Daily 10am-5pm

The museum's collection reflects the central role photography plays in our image-based
culture, both as a medium of expression and as a documentary record. Its holdings
currently include more than 4,000 photographs spanning the history of the medium.

Musée de la Photographie
The Museum of Photography
11 ave. Paul Pastur, 6032 Charleroi,
Belgium
Tel. (32) 71 435810
www.musee.photo.infonie.be
Tue-Sun 10am-6pm

A fine collection tracing the development of photography through work
by pioneers such as Poitevin, Fenton,
Du Camp, Baldus, pictoralists such as
Misonne, Dubreuil and Marissaiaux, and techniques such as photogenic drawing,
daguerreotypes, salt prints, albumen prints, and autochromes. The collection also
includes work by 20th-century photographers.

Royal Geographical Society
1 Kensington Gore, London SW7 2AR, UK
Tel. (44) 20 7591 3060 www.rgs.org
Mon-Fri 10am-1pm, 2pm-5pm by appt.

The picture library provides an unrivalled source of over half a million images of peoples and landscapes from around the globe. Photographs date from the 1830s onwards and cover a variety of subjects including climbing, Colonial Empire, deserts, exploration, indigenous peoples, landscapes, remote destinations, and travel. The focus of the collection is not the generic stock shot, rather the portrayal of man's resilience, adaptability, and mobility in remote places of the world.

The Royal Photographic Society
The Octagon, Milsom Street, Bath, Somerset BA1 1DN, UK
Tel. (44) 1225 462841 www.rps.org
Please call for opening times

This superb cache of over a quarter of a million photographs and holographs includes some of the rarest in the world. Highlights include Fox Talbot's *The Pencil of Nature*, early photographic equipment, and important bodies of work by Coburn, Evans, Demachy, Stieglitz, and Steichen. From the Niépce Heliograph of the Cardinal d'Amboise, made on pewter in 1826, to a Linda McCartney self portrait platinum print, the collection encompasses a diversity of media and forms.

Victoria and Albert Museum
Cromwell Road, South Kensington, London SW7 2RL, UK
Tel. (44) 20 7942 2000 www.vam.ac.uk
Daily 10am-5.45pm (Wed & last Fri of each month 10am-10pm)

The long, long night by Frank Hurley; Imperial transantarctic expedition led by Sir Ernest Shackleton, 1910-16 (top)
Royal Geographical Society

The Beaconsfield statue, 1907 (above)
Victoria and Albert Museum

Founded in 1856 by the museum director, Sir Henry Cole, this is one of the earliest and largest photography collections in the world. A permanent gallery chronicles the history of the medium, from masterpieces of early photography by Fox Talbot and Julia Margaret Cameron through to innovators such as Cecil Beaton and on to technically sophisticated, often highly experimental contemporary work by photographers such as David Hockney, Don McCullin, and Gabriel Orozco. The recent transfer of 4,500 photographs from the British Museum include images by Gustave Le Gray (1850s-60s) and *The Fruits of the Spirit* – the first photographs by Cameron to enter any museum. A large portion of this collection is the National Photographic Record, begun in 1895 for the purpose of recording the British way of life at the turn of the 20th century.

Cards in a fake (hollow) book, Gent, c. 1785
Nationaal Museum van de Speelkaart

PLAYING CARDS

Beinecke Library
Yale University, New Haven, Connecticut 06520-8240, USA
Tel. (1) 203 432-2972 www.library.yale.edu
Reading Room: Mon-Fri 8.30am-5pm
Exhibition area: Mon-Fri 8.30am to 5pm, Sat 10am-5pm

The Cary Playing Card Collection comprises about 2,600 decks, 40 sheets, and 150 wood blocks representing five centuries of card production from Germany (over 900 packs), the United States (300 packs), and China, Japan, Persia, Russia, Scandinavia, the Netherlands, Spain, Portugal, Mexico, and Latin America. In addition,

Jeu de Panama, French card game satirizing the Panama Scandal, 1890
Nationaal Museum van de Speelkaart

there are over 200 books on playing cards plus engravings, several made in the 15th century, of cards and card games. There is also a smaller Fisher Collection of Playing Cards.

Bibliothèque nationale de France - Département des Estampes et de la Photographie
National Library of France - Drawing and Photography Department
58 rue de Richelieu/ 2 rue de Louvois, 75002 Paris, France
Tel. (33) 1 47 03 81 26   www.bnf.fr
Please call for opening times

One of the oldest playing card collections in the world. Some of the most significant items were donated in the 20th century, but the highlight of the 5,000-piece collection is a set of seventeen gilded Venetian tarots belonging to Charles VI and bequeathed to the Royal Library by Roger de Gaignères in 1711.

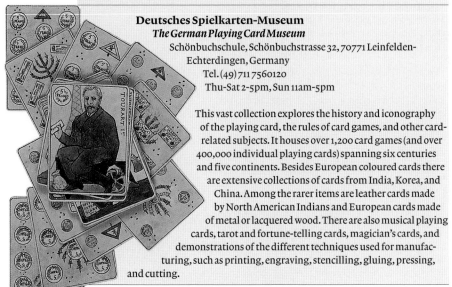

Deutsches Spielkarten-Museum
The German Playing Card Museum
Schönbuchschule, Schönbuchstrasse 32, 70771 Leinfelden-Echterdingen, Germany
Tel. (49) 711 7560120
Thu-Sat 2-5pm, Sun 11am-5pm

This vast collection explores the history and iconography of the playing card, the rules of card games, and other card-related subjects. It houses over 1,200 card games (and over 400,000 individual playing cards) spanning six centuries and five continents. Besides European coloured cards there are extensive collections of cards from India, Korea, and China. Among the rarer items are leather cards made by North American Indians and European cards made of metal or lacquered wood. There are also musical playing cards, tarot and fortune-telling cards, magician's cards, and demonstrations of the different techniques used for manufacturing, such as printing, engraving, stencilling, gluing, pressing, and cutting.

Museo 'Fournier' de Naipes, de Alava
The 'Fournier' Playing Card Museum of Alava
Palacio de la Bendaña, Cuchillería 54, 01001 Vitoria-Gasteiz, Spain
Tel. (34) 945 181920
Tue-Fri 10am-2pm, 4-6.30pm, Sat 10am-2pm, Sun 11am-2pm

This historic collection was started in 1916 by the grandson of Don Heraclio Fournier, the owner of a large card factory founded in Vitoria in 1868. In 1986 Félix Fournier's original collection was put on public exhibition in the beautiful Bendaña Palace and expanded from 3,150 decks to 20,300. The vast collection documents the history of playing cards from their origins to the 19th century, when new developments in lithography significantly improved the quality and variety of cards available, to the 20th century, when cards reached an even more sophisticated level both in terms of raw materials (cardboard, inks and varnishes) and printing, cutting and finishing techniques.

Musée français de la Carte à jouer
The French Museum of Playing Cards
Galerie d'Histoire de la ville, 16 rue Auguste Gervais, 92130 Issy-les-Moulineaux, France
Tel. (33) 1 46 42 33 76   www.issy.com
Wed, Sat-Sun 10am-7pm (groups on Thu & Fri by appt.)

This stunning museum documents the history of the playing card from its earliest beginnings. The collection includes rare examples of some of Europe's first tarot cards, satirical playing cards from the French Revolution, four of the playing card ballet costumes produced by André Derain for the *boutique fantasque* performed by Diaghilev in 1919, and a 'Wall of 1,000 Cards' charting the latest in contemporary card design. This well-presented collection won the European Museum of the Year Award in 1999.

Guildhall Library
Aldermanbury, London EC2P 2EJ, UK
Tel. (44) 20 7332 1839 www.ull.ac.uk
Mon-Fri 9.30am-5pm

Founded in 1907 by H. D. Phillips, a Master of the Worshipful Company of the Maker of Playing Cards, this collection is rich in English pictorial cards of the late 17th and early 18th centuries, and includes over 300 examples of the packs issued annually by the Company. The collection now comprises over 1,100 packs of cards, including some very rare Japanese items and some fine decks from Spain and Germany.

Nationaal Museum van de Speelkaart
The National Museum of the Playing Card
Druivenstraat 18, 2300 Turnhout, Belgium
Tel. (32) 14 415621
Re-opening in 2002

This museum is housed in the former workshop belonging to Mesmaekers, a paper manufacturer renowned for the fine playing cards it produced from 1859-1968. The collection includes classic examples of cards from Turnhout and the Low Countries, as well as company archives and books about cards and graphic techniques. There is also a unique collection of tools and pressing machines.

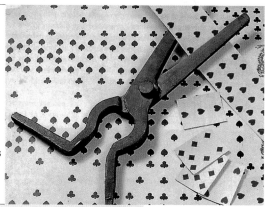

Schloss- und Spielkartenmuseum
The Castle and Playing Card Museum
Schloss 2, 04600 Altenburg, Germany
Tel. (49) 3447 315193 www.abg.shuttle.de
Tue-Sun 9am-5pm

Playing cards have been manufactured in Altenburg since 1832 and legend has it that the city was the birthplace of the popular German card game, Skat. An exhibition of playing cards was mounted in the castle's Skat Room in 1923, which was painted with a series of exuberant Skat motifs by Otto Pix. The collection contained over 6,000 cards, but during World War II it was taken by the Russians and is now lost. After the war the museum re-opened (in 1950) with items donated by private collectors and the Altenburg Playing Card Factory, including cards, card presses, copper printing plates, and card tables.

POSTERS

Dansk Plakatmuseum
The Danish Poster Museum
J. M. Mørks Gade 13, DK-8000 Århus C, Denmark
Tel. (45) 86 15 33 45 www.plakatmuseum.dk
Tue-Sun 10am-5pm

(Left to right)

Proof-prints for a playing card game
Nationaal Museum van de Speelkaart

'Goldsmith' card, Italy, c. 1450
Deutsches Spielkarten-Museum

Omi card, 1900-25
Deutsches Spielkarten-Museum

German Unification card, Saxony, c. 1830
Deutsches Spielkarten-Museum

Scissors for cutting playing cards
Nationaal Museum van de Speelkaart

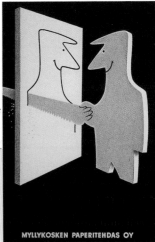

Amassed over the last 25 years by the Århus sculptor and collector, Peder Stougård, this is of the world's largest and most diverse collections of posters. It holds around 120,000 items from 116 countries dating from 1885 onwards. The museum arranges changing themed exhibitions of domestic and international poster design.

Deutsches Historisches Museum
The German Historical Museum
Zeughaus Unter den Linden 2, 10117 Berlin, Germany
Tel. (49) 30 215020   www.dhm.de
Re-opening in 2002

This trove of over 60,000 posters from 1890 to the present focuses on domestic and international political propaganda, from early placards and World War I posters to propaganda material produced during the Weimar Republic, Nazi, World War II, GDR, and German Federal Republic periods. One of the highlights is a collection of pre-1920s posters by artists such as Chéret, Mucha, and Steinlen amassed by the Jewish dentist Hans Sachs over thirty years and confiscated by the Nazis in 1938.

Imperial War Museum
Lambeth Road, London SE1 6HZ, UK
Tel. (44) 20 7416 5000 www.iwm.org.uk
Daily 10am-6pm

Poster by W. Walkuski
(top)
Dansk Plakatmuseum

'Let us go forward together' poster
Imperial War Museum

'Never was so much owed by so many to so few' poster
Imperial War Museum

Kipsonit lithography by Per-Olof Nyström, 1954 (right)
Julistemuseo

Highlights in this collection of over 3,000 war propaganda posters include the 'Women of Britain say "Go!"' Kitchener poster designed by Alfred Leete, the 'Never was so much owed by so many to so few' Battle of Britain poster, and the famous 'Keep mum... she's not so dumb! - careless talk costs lives' poster.

Musée d'Ixelles
The Museum of Ixelles
71 rue Jean van Volsem, Ixelles, 1050 Brussels, Belgium
Tel. (32) 2 515 6421
Tue-Fri 1-6.30pm, Sat-Sun 10am-5pm

The museum houses approximately 1,000 posters, half of which were donated to the museum by the passionate poster collector, Joseph Botte; Botte's close connections with artists and printing companies allowed him to obtain many rare and valuable first editions. The collection also includes 31 of the 32 posters produced by Toulouse-Lautrec as well as first editions by Privat Livemont, Meunier, Donnay, Chéret, Ibels, Aubrey Beardsley, Dudley Hardy, and W. H. Bradley. Outstanding examples include Chéret's *La danse du feu* (1897), Toulouse-Lautrec's *Divan japonais* (1893), Steinlein's *A la bodinière* (1894), and Alphonse Mucha's *Bières de la Meuse* (1897).

Julistemuseo
Poster Museum
Vesijärvenkatu 11 A, 15111 Lahti, Finland
Tel. (358) 3 814 4546
Please call for opening times

Founded in 1975, this Finnish poster museum is a valuable resource for social and art historians as well as graphic artists. In addition to 55,000 posters from forty countries dating from 1852 to the present, the collection includes *ex libris* and advertising labels.

London's Transport Museum

Covent Garden, London WC2E 7BB, UK
Tel. (44) 20 7379 6344   www.ltmuseum.co.uk
Daily 10am-6pm

Frank Pick, the design genius of the interwar Underground in London, commissioned many of the original pictorial posters to advertise the services of the Underground Group. The great variety of artistic styles and techniques used over the years by some of the finest graphic artists can be seen in the museum's collection of over 5,000 posters on computer in the Resource Centre. Travel to London Zoo proved to be one of the most popular subjects and the holdings of these posters are considerable.

Muchovo Museum
Mucha Museum

Kaunicky Palác, Panská 7, 110 00
Prague 1, Czech Republic
Tel. (420) 2 628 41 62 www.mucha.cz
Daily 10am-6pm

Circus poster advertising the clown, Charlie Rivel (right)
Dansk Plakatmuseum

Poster by Stasys Eidrigevicius (left)
Dansk Plakatmuseum

Set in an immaculately restored 18th-century palace, this collection is devoted to work by the celebrated Czech Art-Nouveau artist, Alphonse Mucha (1860-1939). Mucha made his first poster for Sarah Bernhardt in 1894 when she was appearing in *Gismonda*, and the series of posters which he went on to produce for her over the next six years made him internationally famous. Personal memorabilia and Mucha's work in other media including lithographs, sculptures, and jewellery is also on display.

Österreichische Nationalbibliothek
The Austrian National Library

Josefsplatz 1, 1015 Vienna, Austria
Tel. (43) 1 534 10   www.onb.ac.at
Mon-Wed, Fri 9am-3.45pm

Nearly 10,000 posters documenting Austrian history, politics, and arts from World War I onwards. The 3,000 political posters from 1918-38 are a rich resource for historians as well as art historians, and the library also holds a remarkable collection of 3,000 film posters produced for Austrian, German, and American silent films from 1910-29.

Muzeum Plakatu w Wilanowie
The Poster Museum At Wilanów

Ulica St. Kostki Potockiego 10-16, 02-958 Warsaw, Poland
Tel. (48) 22 8422606   www.webmarket.com
Tue-Sun 10am-4pm

Poster by Finn Hjernøe
Dansk Plakatmuseum

DANSK
PLAKATMUSEUM

*Plakat til Dansk Plakat Museum
Aarhus Finn Hjernøe*

Housing 54,000 posters dating from 1892 to the present, this museum was one of the first collections of its kind in the world. The collection of Polish posters dates from 1892 to the present day (30,000 items) and is the most complete set of Polish works in the world. Emphasis is placed on the aesthetics of poster design and every two years the museum hosts an internationally important poster competition and show.

Musée de la Publicité
The Museum of Advertising
Palais du Louvre, 107 rue de Rivoli, 75001 Paris, France
Tel. (33) 1 44 55 57 50 www.ucad.fr
Tue-Fri 11am-6pm (Wed until 9pm)
Sat-Sun 10am-6pm

On the third floor of the Louvre, this museum shows a constantly changing exhibition of posters from its superb holding of 85,000 posters dating from the early 18th century to the present. Highlights include advertisements produced in the early 18th century by one of the world's first poster designers, Jean-Michel Papillon, and works by some of the greatest names in French poster design including Jules Chéret (who introduced a faster colour printing process to the medium), Mucha, Cappiello, Loupot, and Carlu. The excellent website gives a comprehensive panorama of both the collection and the history of poster making in general.

Muzeum Sportu i Turystyki
The Museum of Sports and Tourism
Ulica Wawelska 5, Stadion, 02-034 Warsaw, Poland
Tel. (48) 22 8254851
Tue-Sun 10am-4pm (Thu until 6pm)

This Warsaw sports museum houses a unique collection of several hundred summer and winter Olympic Games' posters, from the famous poster designed by Olle Hjortzberg for the Stockholm Olympic Games of 1912 to examples from the present day.

Victoria and Albert Museum
Cromwell Road, South Kensington, London SW7 2RL, UK
Tel. (44) 20 7942 2000 www.vam.ac.uk
Daily 10am-5.45pm (Wed & last Fri of each month until 10pm)

A collection of over 10,000 posters ranging from the sublime artistry of Toulouse-Lautrec, to advertisements and protest and propaganda posters of the war years. These powerful forms of visual imagery have been actively collected by the museum for over 125 years.

The Wolfsonian–Florida International University
1001 Washington Avenue, Miami Beach, Florida 33139, USA
Tel. (1) 305 531 1001 www.wolfsonian.fiu.edu
Mon, Tue, Fri, Sat 11am-6pm, Thu 11am-9pm, Sun noon-5pm

The largest collection in the country of American, German, Italian, and Dutch political propaganda, including prints, posters, drawings, books, and serial holdings as well as items documenting the rise and demise of these various nations' Fascist movements. The collection includes graphic arts from Russia, Czechoslovakia, and Hungary, and Spanish Civil War posters.

RARE AND SPECIAL COLLECTIONS OF BOOKS AND MANUSCRIPTS

The Chester Beatty Library
Dublin Castle, Dublin 2, Ireland
Tel. (353) 1 407 0750 www.cbl.ie
Oct-Apr: Tue-Fri 10am-5pm. May-Sep: Mon-Fri 10am-5pm, Sat 11am-5pm, Sun 1pm-5pm

Sir Alfred Chester Beatty was an American-born mining engineer who started his career at the bottom of a mine and was a millionaire by the age of 32. He was a passionate collector, acquiring treasures from around the world including a particularly rich collection of early manuscripts. Among the holdings are a vast Islamic collection (with 270 superb copies of the Koran), Chinese and Japanese painted scrolls, lavishly illustrated Turkish manuscripts, and an especially strong selection of Biblical material including Syrian, Armenian, Ethiopian, and Coptic texts.

Carp Swimming among Water Weeds, Japanese print, Taito, 1832 (above) *The Chester Beatty Library*

The God Daikoky as a Woman with a Rat, Japanese print, 1827-28 (left) *The Chester Beatty Library*

Beinecke Library
Yale University, New Haven, Connecticut 06520-8240, USA
Tel. (1) 203 432 2972 www.library.yale.edu
Mon-Fri 8.30am-5pm, Sat 10am-5pm

Some 3,100 incunabula are held at this major rare books repository, including the Melk Gutenberg Bible, Greek and Latin classics, Italian humanist literature, historical texts, biblical literature and exegesis, and Hebrew printing.

Biblioteca Apostolica Vaticana
The Vatican Apostolic Library
Viale Vaticano, 00120 Vatican City
Tel. (39) 06 6988 3333
Apr-Jun, Sep-Oct: Mon-Sat 8.45am-4.45pm
Rest of year: 8.45am-1.45pm

One of the richest manuscript depositories in the world. Little is known about the ancient library until the 13th century, when it was greatly enlarged in the Renaissance under Popes Nicholas V (who added the remnants of the imperial library of Constantinople), Sixtus IV, and Julius II. The present building was built in the 1580s by Domenico Fontana. Today, the library possesses some 65,000 manuscripts (mostly in Latin or Greek) and more than 900,000 printed volumes.

Bibliotheca Bodmeriana - Fondation Martin Bodmer
The Bodmer Library - Martin Bodmer Foundation
19-21 route de Guignard, 1223 Cologny-Geneva, Switzerland
Tel. (41) 22 7362370 www.ville-ge.ch
First Tue of each month 6-8pm, Thu 2-6pm

This literary shrine holds a pristine collection of rare books, manuscripts, and ancient papyri, many of which are completely unique to the collection. The library's founder, Martin Bodmer, believed that books contributed to man's salvation and in an attempt to create a temple of 'Weltliteratur' (universal literature) he categorised some 160,000 volumes into five pillars of wisdom: Homer, the Bible, Dante, Shakespeare, and Goethe. The Goethe collection alone includes more than 1,000 different versions of *Faust*. In the Bible section there are gospels by Saint John (written in the 2nd and 4th centuries), Saint Luke (3rd century), Saint Matthew (4th century), part of Saint Paul's Epistle to the Romans, and some of Saint Augustine's sermons. One of the library's most precious

possessions is the only copy in the world of the *Celestina* or *Calisto y Melibea*, a comedy attributed to Fernando de Rojas and printed in Toledo in 1500.

Bijbels Museum
The Bible Museum
Herengracht 366-368, 1001 AK Amsterdam, The Netherlands
Tel. (31) 20 6242436 www.bijbelsmuseum.nl
Mon-Sat 10am-5pm, Sun 1-5pm

Double page with title and woodblock print by W. Morris (Syr Perecyvelle of Gales. Hammersmith: Kelmscott Press 1895) Deutsches Buch-und Schrift-Museum

Housed in a townhouse designed by the Dutch architect, Philip Vingboon in 1660-62, and decorated with a stunning ceiling painting by Jacob de Wit, this excellent museum includes examples of Bibles in every language, from the earliest (Hebrew, Aramaic, and Greek) to the Statenvertaling of 1637, the first edition of the authorised Dutch translation.

The British Library
96 Euston Road, London NW1 2DB, UK
Tel. (44) 20 7412 7332 www.bl.uk
Mon-Fri 9.30am-6pm (Tue until 8pm) Sat 9.30am-5pm, Sun & public holidays 11am-5pm

St Mark the Evangelist; the Last Judgement Miniatures from the Bernold Codex, Reichenau, c. 1040, *Museum Catharijneconvent*

Behind the brutal, post-modern exterior of Colin St John Wilson's controversial £500m new British Library is one of the world's most sumptuous book collections. A six-storey glass-walled tower in the centre of the building serves as both a book stack and exhibition space for the vast King's Library, assembled by George III and comprising over 65,000 volumes and 20,000 pamphlets covering almost every field of human knowledge, and written in all European and many other languages. Other collections include Thomas Grenville's collection of 20,000 volumes donated in 1847; Sir Hans Sloane's library of books, manuscripts, and antiquities; and the Old Royal Library of books of the kings and queens of England which was donated by George II in 1759.

Museum Catharijneconvent
The Museum of the Catherine Convent
Lange Nieuwstraat 38, Nieuwegracht 63, 3512 LG Utrecht, The Netherlands
Tel. (31) 30 2313835 www.catharijneconvent.nl
Mon-Fri 10am-5pm by appt. only

Based in a late-medieval convent, this museum library houses a pristine collection of over 3,600 antiquarian books and illuminated manuscripts, many obtained from 16th- and 17th-century Roman Catholic seminaries. Outstanding pieces include the Lebiun and Ansfrid codices, written on parchment (*c.* AD840 and 975) and richly bound and decorated with filigrain crosses, carved cameos, and medallions of gilded silver. A stunning breviary made for Beatrice of Assendelft in 1495 consists of eleven full-page miniatures, initials, and other decorations by various artists.

Musée Condé
The Condé Museum
Château, 60500 Chantilly, France
Tel. (33) 3 44 62 62 62 www.ville-chantilly.fr
Daily 9am-12.30pm, 2-5pm (plus private guided tours in the evenings)

This breathtaking library is probably one of the most valuable in the world. Among the 13,000 volumes are 1,500 illuminated manuscripts, incunabula, and precious bindings ranging from medieval goldsmithery to 18th-century gold-tooled Marocain. The unrivalled jewel of the collection is the exquisitely illuminated *Très Riches Heures du Duc de Berry* (1413-16) by the Limbourg brothers. There is another library on the estate, donated to the Institut de France in 1906 by Viscount Spoelberch de Lovenjoul, which specialises in 19th-century French literature. The Viscount wanted his collection to be part of the Condé Museum without losing its original character, and it is now housed in one of the Pelouse houses. Pride of place is given to writers such as Balzac, Théophile Gautier, and George Sand. In addition, there is a fine collection of 19th-century newspapers and journals.

Deutsches Buch- und Schrift-Museum
The German Museum of Books and Writings
Die Deutsche Bibliothek, Deutscher Platz 1, 04103 Leipzig, Germany
Tel. (49) 341 2271324   www.ddb.de
Mon-Sat 8am-4pm

New Newspaper of Scholarly Things by Christian Martini Leipzig, 1718 *Deutsches Buch-und Schrift-Museum*

Founded in 1884, this is one of the oldest specialist museums of its kind, with more than half a million items documenting the history of books, writing, and paper. The special collections include 21,000 manscripts and prints dating from the 15th to the 19th centuries, historic book jackets, 400,000 watermarks, writing appliances, and materials for book and paper production.

East Asian Library
Durant Hall, 8 Durant Hall, University of California, Berkeley
California 94720-6000, USA
Tel. (1) 510 642 2556   www.lib.berkeley.edu
Mon-Fri 9am-7pm (Fri until 5pm), Sat-Sun 1-5pm

One of the most comprehensive research collections of Chinese, Japanese, Korean, Manchu, Mongolian, and Tibetan works in the West. A spectacular array of special collections includes the Ho-Chiang Collection of Buddhist scriptures (documenting the evolution of Buddhist works in China, Japan, and Korea and containing many medieval manuscripts written in gold or silver); the Asami Library of 4,000 volumes of classical Korean imprints; and the Mongol and Manchu Collections (the highlight of which is the exceedingly rare Manchu title of 1673, *Tai sang-ni acabume karulara bithe*). The 8,850-volume Murakami Library is almost without rival, even in Japan, and contains writings of the Meiji Period (1868-1912), many of which are first editions.

Grolier Club
47 East 60th Street, New York, New York 10022, USA
Tel. (1) 212 838 6690   www.grolierclub.org
Mon-Sat 10am-5pm (closed Aug)

Founded in 1884, the Grolier was set up to promote every aspect of the art of bookmaking, from bookbinding to papermaking and illustration. The club has a small but choice permanent collection: two Gutenberg leaves printed on vellum; illuminated manuscripts; and some very beautiful examples of the 'Grolier bindings' commissioned by the French book-lover Jean Grolier in the 16th century. Other treasures include the private library of Madame de Pompadour, and a fascinating collection of ancient and modern bookbindings created in all styles and every conceivable material.

Gutenberg-Museum
The Gutenberg Museum
Liebfrauenplatz 5, 55116 Mainz, Germany
Tel. (49) 6131 122640   www.gutenberg.de
Tue-Sat 9am-5pm, Sun 11am-3pm

5th anniversary of Lenin's
death, early Soviet poster
Marx Memorial Library

Gutenberg invented the first moveable type printing press in 1440, producing 180 Bibles printed on paper and parchment from 1452-55. The Gutenberg Museum owns two of 48 surviving Bibles, beautifully printed in Gothic typeface and with 42 lines per page.

Herzogin Anna Amalia Bibliothek
The Dutchess Anna Amalia Library
Platz der Demokratie 1, 99423 Weimar, Germany
Tel. (49) 36 43 54 5200 www.weimar-klassik.de
Please call for opening times

The intelligent and cultivated duchess, Anna Amalia Regent of Saxe-Weimar-Eisenach, converted the 16th-century Grünes Schloss into a library in 1761 to house the duchy's remarkable collections of books and manuscripts. This architectural gem is lined with bookcases interspersed with plinths supporting busts of famous men and women. When Goethe became director of the library (a position he held for 35 years) not only were scholars and officials permitted to borrow books, but also craftsmen and school children. He added to the collections, which grew to 120,000 volumes, focusing on German literature from 1750-1850. Today, the library is part of the Weimar Classics Foundation which comprises 900,000 works, including 500 incunabula, collections of Bibles, globes and maps, the largest *Faust* collection in the world, the entire libraries of Liszt, Nietzsche, the von Arnim family and the German Shakespeare Society, as well as books from the 20th century.

Duke Humfrey's Library
Bodleian Library, Broad Street, Oxford, Oxfordshire OX1 3BG, UK
Tel. (44) 1865 277158 www.bodley.ox.ac.uk
Please call for opening times

Founded in the 17th century by the scholar and diplomat, Sir Thomas Bodley, this famous copyright library is the second largest library in the UK and one of the world's most important and comprehensive research centres. The historic 15th-century Duke Humfrey's Library has recently been magnificently restored (and also given a starring role as Hogwarts School Library in the film of *Harry Potter*).

The Huntington Library Art Collections
1151 Oxford Road, San Marino, California 91108, USA
Tel. (1) 626 405 2100 www.huntington.org
By appt. only

The library's hoard of 5,400 incunabula is the largest in the US after the Library of Congress. Highlights include the Ellesmere manuscript of Chaucer's *The Canterbury Tales* (c.1410), the Gutenberg Bible (c.1455), and a vast holding of scientific and medical literature published in the 15th century including such landmarks as the first edition of Euclid, the Ulm Ptolemy (1482), the Aldine Aristotle (1495-98), and the first editions of Pliny's *Historia naturalis* (1469).

Knihovna - Strahovsky kláster
The Strahov Monastery Library
Strahovské nádvorí 132, Hradcany, 11838 Prague, Czech Republic
Tue-Sun 9am-5pm

This magnificent baroque monument was home to the Premonstratensian monks from 1140-1848. In the late 18th century, during Joseph II's clampdown on religious institutions, the monks set themselves up as an educational establishment, buying up the libraries of other monasteries and convents as they closed down. Not surprisingly, most of the 830,000 volumes in the collection are ecclesiastical. Highlights include the famous

Kralice Bible (16th century) and writings of the Fathers of the Church and leaders of the Counter-Reformation. But the monks by no means confined their collecting to religious works and the Philosophy Room contains some 50,000 volumes ranging from philosophy through to history and philology.

Library of Canna House

2 Canna House, Isle of Canna PH44 4RS, UK
Tel. (44) 1687 462473
By appt. only.

Situated in the heart of the Hebrides, this exceptional Celtic Studies archive was donated to Canna by the Gaelic scholar, Dr J.L. Campbell and his wife, in 1981. The collection encompasses books on Scottish, Gaelic, and Irish languages and folklore; a unique oral record of Gaelic folksongs and folktales; and objects including lepidoptera relating to Scottish natural history. At the end of 2002, a visitor's accommodation and education centre will open in the newly renovated church of St Edwards, Lincoln Cathedral Library.

Lincoln Cathedal Library

Lincoln, Lincolnshire LN2 1PZ, UK
Tel. (44) 1522 544544 www.lincolncathedral.com
Reading room and group visits to the Medieval and Wren Libraries by appt.

This outstanding Norman cathedral houses a library that has been an integral part of the life of the cathedral from its earliest days. The oldest manuscript is a 10th-century copy of the sermons of the Venerable Bede, which was probably brought to the Cathedral as it was being built. The library comprises three areas: part of the original Medieval Library

Photograph of Karl Marx (top)
Marx Memorial Library

Females as they work at the pit banks in James Klugmann's collection of books (above)
Marx Memorial Library

Lincoln Cathedral library, Sir Christopher Wren, 1674 (left)
Lincoln Cathedral Library

(1420s); the Wren Library, designed by Sir Christopher Wren in 1660; and the Reading Room built in 1914. Dean Honywood bequeathed his vast library of over 5,000 early printed books to fill Wren's stunning interior. While a royalist exile in Holland, Honywood bought classics, literature, and mathematical works in Dutch, English, French, and Latin. Most of the library's medieval manuscripts (270) are kept at Nottingham University where they can be assessed by permission.

Musée Marmottan

2 rue Louis-Boilly, 75016 Paris, France
Tel. (33) 1 44 96 50 33 www.marmottan.com
Tue-Sun 10am-5.30pm

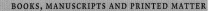

A Pageant of working-class history in Clerkenwell by Dan Jones *Marx Memorial library*

International brigade banner, Spain, 1938 (right) *Marx Memorial library*

Best known for its stunning collection of Impressionist masterpieces, this magnificent museum is also home to Georges Wildenstein's exquisite collection of illuminated manuscripts, amassed by the legendary art dealer during his travels across Europe. Themes are mainly religious (Girolamo di Giovanni dei Corradi da Cremona's symbolic *Christening of Constantine* of 1451), or else humanist or naturalistic.

Marx Memorial Library

37a Clerkenwell Green, London EC1R ODU, UK
Tel. (44) 20 7253 1485
Mon 1-6pm, Tue-Thu 1-8pm, Sat 10am-1pm

Established in 1933 to mark the fiftieth anniversary of the death of Karl Marx, this building has housed radical reform clubs and the printing presses which pumped out such seminal underground journals and papers such as Lenin's 1902-03 *ISKRA* (or *The Spark*). A tradition of radical didacticism is continued in the library with its 20,000 volumes covering a range of subjects including works on Marx, Engels, Lenin, and Marxist economic theory. The reference room has an excellent collection of journals dating from the 1850s, including *The Red Republican* (which carried the first English translation of The Communist Manifesto), the Suffragette journal *Votes for Women*, and William Morris' *Common Weal*. Early radical and Chartist books, pamphlets and tracts can be found in the Klugmann Special Collection.

Monasterio de San Lorenzo del Escorial

The Monastery of San Lorenzo del Escorial
Avenida Juan de Borbon y B. s/n, 28200 San Lorenzo del Escorial, Madrid, Spain
Tel. (34) 91 8905902
Apr-Sep: daily 10am-6pm
Oct-Mar: daily 10am-5pm

Spaniards routinely refer to Philip II's 'El Escorial' as the Eighth Wonder of the World. Built from 1563-84 by Juan Bautista de Toledo and his brilliant pupil Juan de Herrera, the immaculate Renaissance building is crammed with 1,150 works of art, and combines a palace with a monastery, royal mausolea and a library filled with some 40,000 volumes. An esoteric mix of Greek, Hebrew, and Arabic philosophical and mystical texts, it is one of the largest of its kind in Europe.

The Morgan Library

29 East 36th Street, New York,
New York 10016-3403, USA
Tel. (1) 212 685 0610   www.morganlibrary.org
Tue-Fri 10.30am-5pm, Sat 10.30am-6pm, Sun noon-6pm

Filling a grand Renaissance-style palazzo designed in 1902 by McKim, Mead & White, this rare collection spanning four millennia and a score of civilizations was amassed in the 19th century by the banking billionaire, Pierpont Morgan. The collection comprises over 1,300 priceless medieval and Renaissance manuscripts, printed books and bindings, literary and historical manuscripts, autographed music manuscripts, and early children's books. Highlights include the Lindau Gospels, the Hours of Catherine of Cleves (Utrecht, *c.* 1440), the Farnese Hours (Giulio Clovio, 1546), and three copies of the Gutenberg Bible.

Mundaneum
76 rue de Nimy, 7000 Mons, Belgium
Tel. (32) 65 31 53 43 www.mundaneum.be
Tue-Fri 10am-6pm, Sat-Sun noon-8pm

A visionary lawyer turned bibliographer, Paul Otlet was a pioneer of information science. In 1895 he co-founded, with Henri La Fontaine, the International Institute of Bibliography and later developed the Universal Decimal Classification. Their utopian vision was to make all recorded knowledge available to those who needed it, which in turn would encourage mutual understanding and therefore peace. Thanks to the obstinate efforts of these two men this collection was formed, embracing all forms of printed matter and including the important collections of the Press Museum: 10,000 boxes of archival material dedicated to feminism, anarchy, and pacifism; 12,000 posters; 200,000 postcards; illustrated books; 20,000 negatives; the collections of the Book Museum founded by Otlet in 1906; the nucleus of the International Press Museum (with their original holdings of 7,000 newspapers from all over the world); and 500 works related to press history. A total of over six kilometres of printed matter, some of which can be accessed by computer.

Illustration *Whale sinking a Ship* from *Historia Animalium* by Conran Gesner, 1551-58
Lincoln Cathedral Library

Natsionalen istoricheski muzei
The National Museum of History
2 bulevard Vitosha, 1000 Sofia, Bulgaria
Tel. (359) 2 9816600 www.historymuseum.org
May-Oct: daily 10.30am-6.15pm. Nov-Apr: daily 9.30am-5.15pm

A priceless collection of early Bulgarian writings, including the country's only preserved medieval chronicle (and an essential source of information about the First Bulgarian Kingdom) by Ioannes Scylitzes. Other highlights include the Boyana Psalter (1240-1300) found during restoration works in the Boyana Church near Sofia; richly decorated copies of the Tomitchov Psalter (1360-65); and Tsar Ivan Alexander's Gospel, produced in 1365 with 366 miniatures.

Nemzeti Széchény Könyvtár
The National Széchény Library
Special Collections, budavári Palota Fépület, 1827 Budapest, Hungary
Tel. (36) 1 2243741 www.oszk.hu
Mon 1-5pm, Tue-Fri 9am-5pm, Sat 9am-1pm

Founded by Count Ferenc Széchényi in 1802, the collections span a vast and eclectic range of subjects from incunabula to contemporary history. The early books collection includes King Matthias' collection of 33 Corvina codices, a selection of books written and published in Hungary before 1711, and such rarities as the *Halotti Halotti Beszéd* (or *Funeral Oration*), the earliest written text in any Finno-Ugric language. The antiquities collection includes the 1546 Basel edition of the works of Hippocrates, publications by the early Slavic Old Church, and the complete illustrated works of Albrecht Dürer.

Museo dell'Opera del duomo
The Cathedral Museum
Piazza Duomo 8, 54100 Siena, Italy
Tel. (39) 0577 283048
Mid Mar-Oct: daily 9am-7.30pm. Nov-mid Mar: daily 9am-1.30pm

Decorated with a spectacular series of frescoes by Pinturicchio (a disciple of Raphael) the Piccolomini Library was built in 1495 to house the magnificent Renaissance library of the poet, diplomat, collector, geographer, and religious reformer, Pope Pius II. Prized possessions include two parchment rolls from the 12th and 13th centuries, and 13th-century anthem books illuminated by Lippo Vanni (1340-45).

The Parker Library

Corpus Christi College, University of Cambridge, Cambridgeshire CB3, UK
Tel. (44) 1223 338025   www.corpus.cam.ac.uk
Mon-Fri 9.30am-12.30pm, 2-4.15pm (to visiting scholars)

España Lucha, Spanish anti-Fascist war poster, 1936-39
Marx Memorial Library

Established by Matthew Parker, Archbishop of Canterbury under Elizabeth I and author of the Thirty-nine Articles and the Bishop's Bible, this is one of the finest Renaissance libraries. Among the 600 medieval manuscripts and 20,000 books are such treasures as: the Gospels of St Augustine (the oldest book in Britain sent to Canterbury by Pope Gregory in the 590's); the 8th-century Northumbrian Gospel Book (the oldest decorated manuscipt in the UK); a 1415 edition of Chaucer's *Troilus and Creseyde* with an illuminated frontispiece depicting Chaucer at the court of Richard II; and the Bury Bible, illustrated in breathtakingly rich colours by England's first known professional artist, Master Hugo.

Pepys' Library

Magdalene College Library, Cambridge, Cambridgeshire CB3 0AG, UK
Tel. (44) 1223 332187   www.magd.cam.ac.uk
Please call for opening times

Samuel Pepys was an avid book collector, arranging his library with military precision and scouring the market for books in every known script (his Chinese book has its bookplate at the back and upside down). Pepys worked as a secretary to the Admirality for many years, and the 3,000-volume collection is especially strong on naval history, with highlights including maps and topographical prints, an armament roll depicting the navy of Henry VIII, shipbuilding manuscripts, and Sir Francis Drake's autographed tidal almanac. The library's prize possession is Pepys' Diary, written in code and finally deciphered and published in 1825.

Plantin-Moretus Museum

Vrijdagmarkt 22, 2000 Antwerp, Belgium
Tel. (32) 3 221 1450   www.dma.be
Tue-Sun 10am-4.45pm

A room in the museum is devoted to the life's work of Christoffel Plantin's: the *Biblia Polyglotta* which he produced in Latin, Greek, Hebrew, Chaldean, and Syriac. Among the museum's other treasures are 150 incunabula including Belgium's only Gutenberg Bible, the *Carmen Paschale* by Sedulius, the *Epigrammata* by Prosperus, and the *De Consolatione* by Boethius (all 9th century).

Public Record Office

Kew, Richmond, Surrey TW9 4DU, UK
Tel. (44) 20 8392 5200   www.pro.gov.uk
Please call for opening times

Kew's 97 miles of records includes such fascinating documents as the Domesday Book of 1086 (the first ever survey of an entire country); the Magna Carta of 1215; Shakespeare's will (bequeathing his 'second-best bed' to Anne Hathaway); Guy Fawkes' confession; and the telegram announcing the sinking of the Titanic.

The Rosenbach Museum & Library

2010 DeLancey Place, Philadelphia, Pennsylvania 19103, USA
Tel. (1) 215 732 1600   www.rosenbach.org
Tue–Sun 11am–4pm (Library by appt. only)

The successful rare books dealer, Dr A. S. W. Rosenbach, lived with his art dealer brother
at this elegant 1865 townhouse until his death in 1952. In 1954 a museum and library was
founded, and Dr Rosenbach's impressive collection of rare books and manuscripts was
significantly augmented with a rich and eclectic mix of British and American literature, including the handwritten 800-page manuscript for James Joyce's *Ulysses*. Other
treasures include a rare copy of the Bay Psalm Book (1640), the first book ever to be
printed in what is now the USA; Lewis Carroll's personal copy of the 1865 edition of
Alice's Adventure's in Wonderland; Marianne Moore's literary papers and library; and the
largest surviving sections of Dickens' *Pickwick Papers* and *Nicholas Nickleby*.

Book illustration *Youth in a Fur Trimmed cap* by Riza Abbasi, Iran, 17th century *The Chester Beatty Library*

Rossiiskaia natsional'naia biblioteka,
The Russian National Library

Sadovaia ulitsa 18, 191069 Saint Petersburg, Russian Federation
Tel. (7) 812 110 6253
Mon–Fri 11am–5pm

With its striking ionic columned façade embellished with statues of philosophers and
Minerva, this Rossi-built extension to Saint Petersburg's original public library now
holds an astonishing 26 million items. The massive rare books collection encompasses
Voltaire's library (originally purchased by Catherine the Great) and an edition of Krylov's
Fables the size of a postage stamp, which can be read with the naked eye.

John Rylands University Library of Manchester

Special Collections, 150 Deansgate, Manchester M3 3EH, UK
Tel. (44) 161 834 5354   www.rylibweb.man.ac.uk
Mon–Fri 10am–5.30pm, Sat 10am–1pm

English printers are especially well represented in this stupendous collection of over
3,000 incunabula from Germany, Italy, France, Spain, and England. Alongside over sixty
Caxtons (of which four are unique) the university library owns editions of works by John
Lettou, William de Machlinia, Richard Pynson, Julian Notary, the Schoolmaster printer
of St Albans, and Wynkyn de Worde (whose 1498 *Morte D'Arthur* is unique in the world).
Outstanding works in the German collections include the Letters of Indulgence of Pope
Nicholas V; 36- and 42-line Gutenberg, Fust and Schöffer Bibles; and the UK's only complete editions of the books produced in Bamberg by Albrecht Pfister. Italy is represented
by 253 printers from fifty different Italian towns. In addition, there are over 100 works by
the first Parisian printers, including Gering, Friburger, and Crantz.

Staatsbibliothek zu Berlin - Preussischer Kulturbesitz
The Berlin State Library - Prussian Cultural Heritage

Potsdamer Strasse 33, 10785 Berlin, Germany
Tel. (49) 30 266 2235 www.sbb.spk-berlin.de
Mon–Fri 10am–7pm, Sat 10am–1pm

Founded in 1661 by the Great Elector, Friedrich-Wilhelm of Brandenburg, this vast state
library contains nearly ten million books and periodicals. Among the special collections
of early books, rare manuscripts, maps, and pieces of music are original texts by Hegel,
Herder, and Fichter; a valuable 9th-century Psalter of Ludwig the German; a highly
decorated Gutenberg Bible; and a Coptic codex of the Biblical Book of Proverbs from the
3rd century. Also worthy of note are early printed versions of Bach's Mass in B Minor,
Beethoven's 4th, 5th and 9th symphonies, and almost all of Mozart's great operas.

The Women's Library

Old Castle Street, London E1 7NT, UK
Tel. (44) 20 7320 1189 www.lgu.ac.uk
Please call for opening times

Focusing on the history of women (and particularly women's suffrage) this collection
spans a broad body of writings by and about women. It ranges from 19th-century books
on household economy to first editions of Mary Wollstonecraft and such early feminist
stirrings as a Venetian publication of 1621 entitled *The Nobility and Excellence of Women
with the Defects and Failings of Men*. One of the library's prized possessions is the purse
and return ticket to Victoria held by Emily Wilding Davison, the suffragette who was
crushed beneath the hooves of the king's horse on Derby Day in 1913.

Map of colony of Virginia
from *La theatre du monde* by
Willem and Jan Blaeu,
Amsterdam, 1647 (right)
Lincoln Cathedral Library

Nobleman, from a volume
of the works of Richard
Rolle, *c*.1400 (far right)
Lincoln Cathedral Library

BOARD GAMES, PUZZLES AND TRADITIONAL TOYS

Museum of Childhood at Bethnal Green
Cambridge Heath Road, London E2 9PA, UK
Tel. (44) 20 8 983 5200 www.vam.ac.uk
Mon-Thu, Sat-Sun 10am-5.50pm

The core structure of this museum was the old Iron Museum. Its interest in children dates back to 1915, when the directors recognized the plight of wartime children who had to spend the summer in London. Renamed as the Museum of Childhood in 1974, it has a huge collection of games and puzzles, for the most part organized by manufacturer (Chad Valley, Spears, and John Waddington Ltd. have their own showcases), or by type of game. Displayed are such forgotten favourites as The Famous Game of Military Tactics (1925) and Tiddly Tennis (1935). Numerous puzzles are exhibited, including jigsaw puzzles, first introduced in 1873, as well as puzzles by Raphael Tuck such as Please Spare me a Penny (c. 1920). In addition, there is an excellent collection of mid 19th-century games where marbles were used as counters.

Pyramid of dice game (above)
Deutches Spiele-Museum Chemnitz

Braunes Haus (Brown House): toy from the Nazi period, 1933 (below)
Deutsches Historisches Museum

Birmingham Central Library
Arts, Language and Literature Department,
Chamberlain Square, Birmingham, West Midlands B3 3HQ, UK
Tel. (44) 121 303 4227 www.ramesis.com
Mon-Fri 9am-8pm, Sat 9am-5pm

Along with their collection of children's books, the Parkers amassed early educational board games, jigsaws, wooden pictorial blocks, peepshows, alphabet tiles and cards, and building bricks. The jigsaw collection contains examples from the 19th century, mainly with religious, geographical or historical themes. One example, entitled The Principal Events in English History from the Landing of Caesar to William the Fourth (Wallis, 1830) consists of a set of wooden pictorial blocks showing the kings and queens of England, their dates, the chief events of their reigns, and a comment on their characters (e.g. 'cruel' for Henry the VIII).

The Corning Museum of Glass
One Museum Way, Corning, New York 14830, USA
Tel. (1) 607 974 8274 www.cmog.org
Daily 9am-5pm

Although this museum is partially supported by Corning Inc., a manufacturing company, it is not a museum of Corning glass but a museum of the art, history, and science of glass making worldwide. Included among its holdings is a display of European and American marbles, most of them handmade, which was a gift from the Marble Collectors Society of America. Few museums in the world give display space to this once popular childhood game, now a serious collector's item.

Deutsches Historisches Museum
The German Historical Museum
Zeughaus Unter den Linden 2, 10117 Berlin, Germany
Tel. (49) 30 215020 www.dhm.de
Mon, Tue, Thu-Sun 10am-6pm

The toy section in this museum does not concentrate on rare or unique objects but on specific epochs, and on the differences between toys from East and West Germany. Many of the toys and games from World Wars I and II reveal how politics and ideology invaded children's lives. A West German dice game, Dein Volkswagen

(Your Volkswagen) by O. and M. Hausser, Ludwigsburg (*c.* 1952), features the Volkswagen Beetle, the symbol of West Germany's 'economic miracle'. Compare this to the East German dice game, Sandmann, lieber Sandmann (Sandman, dear Sandman), produced by Spika in 1965, in which this popular figure of GDR children's television served as a model for 'good' children. Don't miss the fascinating examples of the 'Emergency-production-toys' that were manufactured shortly after the end of World War II.

Deutsches Spiele-Museum Chemnitz
The German Games Museum of Chemnitz
Im Solaris Technologie- und Gewerbepark, Neefestrasse 78 A, 09119 Chemnitz, Germany
Tel. (49) 371 306565   Wed-Fri 1-6pm, Sat-Sun 1am-7pm

The Tower: wooden ball game by Piet Hein
Deutches Spiele-Museum Chemnitz

Unique Monopoly board, *c.* 1934
Deutches Spiele-Museum Chemnitz

The 20-year-old dream of J. Peter Lemcke has amounted to a collection of more than 10,000 games spanning three centuries (1660-1960), with another 6,000 games having been added since 1960. Lemcke firmly believes in the importance of playing games if you want to succeed in life. What better way is there to learn the strategies of planning, decision-making, and risk-taking than through games? The games on display are divided into four groups: games of skill; games of chance; games of strategy; and war games. Taking pride of place is the 3,000-year-old Parchessi game, which has, along with chess, puzzles and a few others, stood the test of time. Other highlights include the chess computer once used by Erich Honecker, chief of East Germany's Communist Party.

Germanisches Nationalmuseum
The German National Museum
Kartäusergasse 1, 90402 Nuremberg, Germany
Tel. (49) 911 13310   www.gnm.de
Tue-Sun 10am-5pm (Wed until 9pm)

Toys and the city of Nuremberg are inextricably linked. It has been producing toys for more than 600 years, the trade in these items having played a large part in the city's industrial history. Clay was used to produce the first dolls, while the establishment of the first German paper mill in 1390 in Nuremberg supplied paper for the papier-mâché dolls produced in the mid-17th century. The size of this collection reflects these close links, with some 19,000 objects illustrating the historical development of toys and the production processes involved in their manufacture. Highlights include a very impressive collection of board games dating from the Middle Ages to the present day. There are over 1,000 pieces and boards for chess, checkers, and Nine Men's Morris, including thirty beautifully enamelled board pieces by Christian Wermuth from the early 18th century. A further seventy paper games and boards are held in the graphics collection.

Hampshire County Council Museums Service

Chilcomb House, Chilcomb Lane, Winchester, Hampshire SO23 8RD, UK
Tel. (44) 1962 846304 www.hants.gov.uk
By appt. only

There are over 4,000 items in the council's toy collection, of which only several dozen are displayed at any one time in their various branches. To see the main holdings, consisting of 450 jigsaws and numerous board games, you must make arrangements in advance with the main office. A limited selection of these items, around a dozen, are usually on show in the Curtis Museum in Alton, as well as in their new Living History Museum, Milestones.

Der Weltkrieg (The World War): dice game, Germany, *c.* 1915
Deutsches Historisches Museum

Incredibly Fantastic Old Toy Show

26 Westgate, Lincoln, Lincolnshire LN1 3BD, UK
Tel. (44) 1522 520534
Tue-Sat 11am-5pm, Sun & public holidays noon-4pm.
(Times may vary, please call for details)

Board games were first offered by publishers of jigsaws as educational and moral toys. Early examples on display taught the benefits of living a 'good' life. Later they became more concerned with play, and the museum has examples incorporating targets to shoot at, points to score, and the chance to beat fellow players. The museum also has a number of dexterity puzzles which involved positioning small ball bearings in prescribed holes, and picture bricks which were popular with Victorian and Edwardian children. In religious households children were only allowed to play with certain toys on a Sunday. Many of these 'Sunday toys' are on display and include Noah's Arks, crèche figures, and building bricks, particularly those that could be made into churches and chapels.

National Yo-Yo Museum

320 Broadway, Chico, California 95928, USA
Tel. (1) 530 8930545 www.nationalyoyo.org
Mon-Sat 10am-5.30pm, Sun 11am-4pm

The yo-yo craze goes up and down much like the toy itself, but few have escaped its popularity at some point in their childhood. The collection is worth seeing regardless of your interest in this 'spinning return top' because it belonged to the D. F. Duncan family who ran the Duncan Yo-Yo Company from 1928-65. It was Donald F. Duncan who bought the right to market the yo-yo in 1928 after it had been introduced to America in the 1920s by the Filipino, Pedro Flores. The 1950s baby boom kids took to it immediately. The evolution of the toy and the marketing techniques that were responsible for its popularity are documented here, as are eighty years of yo-yo artefacts.

Nationalmuseet
The National Museum

Ny Vestergade 10, 1471 Copenhagen, Denmark
Tel. (45) 3313 4411 www.natmus.dk
Daily 10am-5pm

Unfortunately, the permanent exhibition space within the Prince's Palace cannot always accommodate a display of Denmark's finest collection of traditional toys, but for those who love wooden toys, this is the place to come. Collections include those produced by prisoners and sold by The Danish Toy Company between 1905 and 1977. On display are examples of Kay Bojesen's wooden blocks, model animals and ships, as well as modern unpainted wooden toys such as building blocks. More recent producers include the company KREA, and not surprisingly, there are vast holdings of Lego.

Speelgoedmuseum Mechelen
The Mechelen Toy Museum
Nekkerspoel 21, 2800 Mechelen, Belgium
Tel. (32) 15 55 70 75 www.speelgoedmuseum.be
Tue-Sun 10am-5pm

Coming here is like stepping into the 16th-century painting, *Kinderspiel*, by Pieter Bruegel. Within this giant toy chest there are approximately twenty showcases full of games and jigsaws, primarily from the 19th and 20th centuries. See board games such as the game of goose, published by Phobel in Brussels in 1930, and the game of fishing by Diabolo from the 1950s, among countless others. There are hundreds of jigsaws and puzzles, including charming block puzzles from as early as 1890 in their original wooden boxes, and early German jigsaws from the 1850s. A huge variety of construction toys include kits by Meccano, Distler, Trix, Bral, Erector, and Lego. There is also a vast collection of spinning tops, yo-yos, and marbles. The showpiece of the collection is the two-wheeler gold painted bicycle which belonged to the future King Leopold III of Belgium.

Het Brugse Zwanenspel: game of goose, Bruges, *c.* 1980 (above)
Speelgoedmuseum Mechelen

Musée suisse du Jeu
The Swiss Museum of Games
Château de La Tour-de-Peilz, 1814 La Tour-de-Peilz, Switzerland
Tel. (41) 21 944 4050 www.msj.ch
Tue-Sun 2-6pm

Het echt Gansenspel; Rondreis in België: game of goose, Brussels, *c.* 1930 (below)
Speelgoedmuseum Mechelen

A beautiful 13th-century castle, left to languish, became home to an eclectic collection of games. The collection is particularly strong in ancient board games, and includes a Coptic game from the 6th century AD called, The Game with 58 holes, similar to the example at the British Museum in London. To this day, the rules of the game are still unknown. There is a game thought to be the ancestor of chess, consisting of pieces from the 6th century AD, as well as others from late antiquity.

CHILDREN'S BOOKS AND ILLUSTRATIONS

Arbeitsstelle für Leseforschung und Kinder-und Jugendmedien
The Research Centre on Reading and Children's and Youth Media
Universität zu Köln, Bernhard-Feilchenfeld-Strasse 11, 50969 Cologne, Germany
Tel. (49) 221 4704069 www.aleki.uni-koeln.de
Mon-Thu 10am-4pm (by appt. only)

The centre is dedicated to historical research concerned with children's and young adult's literature, with special emphasis on female writing. There are 5,000 historical works from the 15th century up to 1950, as well as an additional 1,000 first editions of fairy tales. The contemporary collection covers books collected since 1989 and mainly focuses on German, Swiss, and Austrian works.

Biblioteca Juvenil Santa Creu
The Children's Library of Santa Creu
Centro de Documentació del Libre Infantil, carrer de l'Hospital 56, 08001 Barcelona, Spain
Tel. (34) 93 302 5348
Mon, Tue, Fri 1.30-8.30pm, Wed, Thu, Sat 10am-noon, 1.30-8.30pm

A centre for the documentation of children's literature containing 20,000 volumes, including collections of books, magazines, and periodicals in both Catalan and Castilian from the end of the 19th century up to 1962.

Girl's portrait by Kate Greenaway (not used in a book)
The de Grummond Children's Literature Collection

Bibliothèque de Nantes – Centre de recherche sur l'édition francophone pour la jeunesse
The Library of Nantes – Research Centre on Francophone Youth Literature
Médiathèque – Espace Jacques Demy, 24 quai de la Fosse, 44000 Nantes, France
Tel. (33) 2 40 41 95 95 www.mairie-nantes.fr
By appt. only

The centre was founded in 1996 when the city received an exceptional donation from Monique Bermond and Mr Boquié. Both literary critics, they wrote on children's literature, and from 1964 onwards they catalogued and entered on a database every press copy sent to them by the publishing houses. The advantage of collecting children's books in this way is that they are all in pristine condition. Part of the Bermond-Boquié donation included a complete series of recordings of their programmes on radio.

Birmingham Central Library
Arts, Language and Literature Department, Chamberlain Square, Birmingham, West Midlands B3 3HQ, UK
Tel. (44) 121 303 4227 www.ramesis.com
Mon-Fri 9am-8pm, Sat 9am-5pm

The nucleus of this collection was originally part of Mr and Mrs Parker's private museum of British rural life at Tickenhill, near Bewdley, consisting of children's books published after 1830. Over the years the collection has expanded and now holds approximately 11,000 books dating from 1538 to the present day. Most of the early examples in the collection are educational and reflect the Renaissance revival of interest in the study of classical Greek and Latin. In addition, there are arithmetic books, as well as a facsimile of one of the earliest English primers, the *ABC both in Latyn & Englyshe* (c. 1538). As well as a large number of books designed to teach children, the collection also has a rich vein of fairy tales, including early editions of Perrault and Andersen. One of the great strengths of the collection is its comprehensive collection of illustrated, moveable, and pop-up books.

Brüder-Grimm Museum
The Museum of the Grimm Brothers
Palais Bellevue, Schöne Aussicht 2, 34117 Kassel, Germany
Tel. (49) 561 787203 www.museumsnacht.de
Daily 10am-5pm

As fairy-tale authors go, the brothers Jacob and Wilhelm Grimm are among the most famous. By far the most important of their works is the *Kinder-und Hausmärchen*, a collection of fairy tales for children and adults published in 1812, still one of the most translated, illustrated, and read books today. Besides writing 200 fairy tales and ten children's legends, the brothers collected folklore from other countries, including around 600 sagas and 600 folk songs. Founded in 1959, the museum is located at the back of the Palais Bellevue in a historical building (1714) and is filled with Grimm memorabilia, works by the brothers, and a collection of fairy tales from all over the world.

The Centre for the Children's Book
Pendower Hall Education Development Centre, West Road, Newcastle-upon-Tyne NE15 6PP, UK
Tel. (44) 191 2743941
Due to open in 2003. Please call for details.

Set up in 2001 as a national centre devoted entirely to the preservation of British postwar children's books, manuscripts, and original artwork. The centre's first purchase was the Kaye Webb archive containing correspondence, photographs, and promotional material, as well as copies of virtually every Puffin book published from 1961-79 during her remarkable editorship there. Another highlight is a collection of work by the renowned British illustrator, Faith Jacques. A house-clearer who was too late for the local rubbish dump decided to have a look inside the sacks abandoned in a Bath house. Inside he found hundreds of drawings, letters, and annotated books by Jacques who collaborated with best-selling authors on many books, including Roald Dahl's *Charlie and the Chocolate Factory*. Besides these two acquisitions, the centre has been offered material by over ninety authors and illustrators, including the late poet laureate, Ted Hughes.

The Children's Literature Research Collections, University of Minnesota
113 Elmer L. Andersen Library, 222 21st Avenue South, Minneapolis, Minnesota 55455, USA
Tel. (1) 612 6244576   www.special.lib.umn.edu
Mon-Fri 9am-4pm

Several key collections make up this outstanding resource of children's literature. Among these are the Laura Jane Musser Oziana Collection: an accumulation of material (400 items) relating to the book and its author, L. Frank Baum, collected by Musser throughout her life. The largest source of children's literature to be found here however, is the massive Kerlan Collection, begun in 1949 when Dr Irvin Kerlan generously donated his collection of children's books to the university. It now contains 75,000 children's books, primarily by 20th-century American writers, along with manuscripts and illustration materials for more than 9,000 titles. A recent addition is the original, preliminary, and final drawings for Wanda Gág's *Snow White and the Seven Dwarfs*, first published in 1938.

The Connecticut Historical Society
1 Elizabeth Street, Hartford, Connecticut 06105, USA
Tel. (1) 860 236 5621   www.chs.org
Tue-Sat 10am-5pm

Several distinguished collections of American books and periodicals for children can be found here. Comprising 3,000 items is the Caroline Hewins Collection which focuses on the period 1820-1918, with strengths in the area of juvenile periodicals and gift books. Three issues of an otherwise unknown children's magazine issued in 1841 by Harriet Beecher Stowe (the novelist best known for her anti-slavery publication, *Uncle Tom's Cabin*) is one of the highlights. The Connecticut Printers' Archive Collection includes samples of books by all the prominent producers of mid 20th-century children's books.

The Roald Dahl Children's Gallery
Church Street, Aylesbury, Buckinghamshire, UK
Tel. (44) 1296 331441
Mon-Sat 10am-5pm, Sun 2-5pm

Though Roald Dahl thought 'museums were awfully boring.... entertainment for adults, torture for children', his widow Liccy Dahl, believed he 'would have loved this.' An interactive museum, it is filled with objects relating to his books, along with copies of the books themselves. Make your way through the entrance where the Great Glass Elevator from *Charlie and the Chocolate Factory* dominates the atrium, planets swirl around the domed roof, and gigantic sweets decorate the windows around you.

The de Grummond Children's Literature Collection
McCain Library and Archives, The University of Southern Mississippi, Southern Station, Hattiesburg, Mississippi 39406, USA
Tel. (1) 601 2664345   www.lib.usm.edu
Mon-Fri 8am-5pm

One of North America's leading research centres in the field of children's literature, the focus is on American and British works, both historical and contemporary. Founded by Dr Lena Y. de Grummond in 1966, the collection has grown from its original holdings of 1,200 items to a collection of over 55,000 books and related holdings dating from 1530 onwards. The collection includes the archive of Hans and Margaret Rey, authors of the Curious George series, as well as a large selection of work by the British illustrator Randolph Caldecott. Kate Greenaway is represented by over 100 volumes illustrated with her work, as well as 300 original illustrations, unpublished artwork and verse, woodblocks used in printing, and an extensive selection of her greeting cards. There is a great deal besides, including extensive holdings of fairy tales, folktales, and folklore dating from the early re-tellings in the 18th century up to the modern reinterpreted editions of the 1990s.

The Royal Primer printed for J. Newbery, London, c.1760
The de Grummond Children's Literature Collection

Internationale Jugendbibliothek
The International Youth Library
Schloss Blutenburg, 81247 Munich, Germany
Tel. (49) 89 801 2110 www.ijb.de
Mon-Fri 2-6pm

The library, founded in 1948 by Jella Lepman, has since 1983 been housed in the 15th-century Blutenburg Castle (the 'book castle'). Its collection numbers 460,000 volumes and contains books in more than 100 languages. Every year the library receives donations of new books from 1,000 publishing houses all over the world. Approximately 12,000 books as well as 250 journals are available to readers in the research library; other works are available on request.

Det Kongelige Bibliotek
The Royal Library
The Manuscript Department, 1016 Copenhagen, Denmark
Tel. (45) 33 474747 www.kb.dk
Mon-Fri,10am-9pm, Sat 10am-7pm

The Royal Library is one of the oldest Danish museums and dates back to the 17th century, when Frederik III acquired three Danish private libraries. Among its holdings are the archives of Denmark's most important children's authors including, of course, Hans Christian Andersen who wrote 168 stories and fairytales, the first of which was *The Tinder Box* in 1835.

The Lilly Library, Indiana University
1200 East 7th Street, Bloomington, Indiana 47405, USA
Tel. (1) 812 855 2452 www.indiana.edu
Mon-Fri 9am-6pm, Sat 9am-1pm (times may vary, please call for details)

A collection primarily made up of two major donations: those from the private library of J. K. Lilly. Jr, given to the University in 1956; and the majority of its 10,000 books from Elisabeth Ball, of the Ball glass manufacturing family of Muncie, Indiana, which came to the library in 1983. Holdings are mainly English language books of the 18th and 19th centuries, but also include 20th-century books in French and German. Some of the treasures include *A Little Pretty Pocket-Book* (John Newberry, 1744). Though the earliest surviving copy from the tenth edition is in the British Library, the next earliest edition from 1763 resides here. Here, too, you will find chapbooks galore; hornbooks of silver, ivory, wood, leather, brass, and paper; mechanical books; thumb Bibles; miniature libraries; and original art work by all the greats in children's literature including Kate Greenaway, Walter Crane, and Ernest Howard Shepard.

Milner Library

University, Normal, Illinois 61761, USA
Tel. (1) 309 438 7450 www.mlb.ilstu.edu
Mon-Fri 10am-noon, 1-3pm (other times by appt.)

Holds several excellent collections of children's literature. The Lois Lenski Collection contains autographed first editions of most of her books, as well as foreign editions, manuscripts, and original illustrations. There is a large historical textbook collection of elementary school primers, readers, and texts covering all areas of study primarily from the late 19th century. A large selection of historical children's literature, with early editions by a number of authors and illustrators including Louisa May Alcott, Randolph Caldecot, and Kate Greenaway is also held here.

Puss in Boots from Charles Perrault's *The Tales of Mother Goose*
The Morgan Library

The Morgan Library

29 East 36th Street, New York, New York 10016 -3403, USA
Tel. (1) 212 6850610 www.morganlibrary.org
Tue-Thu 10.30am-5pm, Fri 10.30am-8pm, Sat 10.30am-6pm,
Sun noon-6pm

This is one of the world's greatest libraries. Its first director remarked that it 'contains everything but the original tablets of the Ten Commandments'. Their collection of children's literature reflects the scale of the holdings. Here, original manuscripts are one-a-penny and include Charles Perrault's manuscript for *The Tales of Mother Goose* (1685), Twain's *Pudd'nhead Wilson*, and Charles Dickens' *A Christmas Carol*.

National Art Library (Victoria and Albert Museum)

Cromwell Road, South Kensington, London SW7 2RL, UK
Tel. (44) 20 7942 2400 www.nal.vam.ac.uk
Tue-Sat 10am-5pm

Formerly held at the Museum of Childhood at Bethnal Green, The Renier Collection has recently been returned here. Consisting of over 80,000 books, including its famous editions of Hans Christian Andersen, it contributes greatly to a collection now numbering some 100,000 volumes dating from the 16th century to the present day. Other collections are soon to be returned here, including the Saekel-Jelkmann Collection of 20th-century pop-up books, the Vyvien Newton Collection, and the Patrick Hardy Archive.

The Elizabeth Nesbitt Room, University of Pittsburgh

Room 305, Information Sciences Building, 135 North Bellefield Avenue, Pittsburgh, Pennsylvania 15260, USA
Tel. (1) 412 624 4710 www.library.pitt.edu
Mon-Fri 12.30-5pm (other times by appt.)

Begun by Miss Nesbitt, a children's librarian and later the dean of Carnegie Library School, this particularly fine collection contains around 250 chapbooks printed in England and America between 1650 and 1850. These little chapbooks ('chap' meaning cheap) were sold for sixpence from the late 1600s to the late 1800s. Rarities such as the stories of Robin Hood, Dick Whittington, Jack the Giant Killer, Tom Thumb, Bluebeard and countless others can be found among them. A first edition of J. M. Barrie's 1906 *Peter Pan in Kensington Gardens*, illustrated by Arthur Rackham, is a prize possession, along with a very respectable collection of Rackham illustrations. Also a copy of Beatrix Potter's privately printed 1902 *Tailor of Gloucester*, whose text and pictures are different from the copy of the book known to millions today.

Five Girls on a Fence, an unfinished illustration by Kate Greenaway
The de Grummond Children's Literature Collection

The Beatrix Potter Gallery

Main Street, Hawkshead, Cumbria LA22 0NS, UK
Tel. (44) 1539 436355
Apr-Nov: Mon-Thu, Sun 10.30am-4.30pm

Housed in what were once the offices of Beatrix Potter's solicitor husband, William Heelis, is an annually changing exhibition of a selection of Beatrix Potter's original drawings and illustrations. The 17th-century building remains largely as it was in Potter's day, complete with a reconstruction of part of her husband's office and a display about her life.

Princeton University Cotsen Children's Library

Main Floor, Firestone Library, Department of Rare Books and Special Collections, One Washington Road, Princeton, New Jersey 08544, USA
Tel. (1) 609 2581148   www.princeton.edu
Mon-Fri 9am-4.45pm, Sat-Sun noon-5pm (by appt. only)

Founder of the Neutrogena empire, Lloyd Cotsen is a passionate collector of children's books, educational toys, and games. It started out simply as an activity for his four children, but soon the collection expanded to include more than 22,000 items. Pledging $8 million, he created a new facility within this fine library, where research on children's books can be undertaken. The oldest items in the library date from the 15th century, when printing began, and continue through to the present day, with illustrated books predominating. One of its strengths are the 3,500 English books and toys from the period 1700-1839 (a key period in the development of children's literature), including imprints by Newbery, Harris and Darton. Highlights include a privately printed first edition of Beatrix Potter's *The Tale of Peter Rabbit*, inscribed as a Christmas present to Potter's cousin.

The Rosenbach Museum and Library

2010 DeLancey Place, Philadelphia, Pennsylvania 19103, USA
Tel. (44) 215 7321600   www.rosenbach.org
Tue-Sun 11am-4pm (by appt. only)

This extraordinary private collection contains, among other items of children's literature, two noteworthy holdings: an extensive Lewis Carroll collection, and over 3,000 illustrations and manuscripts by the author Maurice Sendak. Over his fifty year career, Maurice Sendak has illustrated more than eighty children's books, including ten that he wrote himself. Best known for his book *Where the Wild Things Are* (1963), his talents extend to contributions for opera and theatre, as well as set designs for several productions. Among the items in the Carroll collection are some three dozen of John Tenniel's original drawings for *Alice in Wonderland* and *Through the Looking-Glass* (1820-1914). There is also a first edition of *Alice's Adventures in Wonderland*, published by London Macmillan and Co. in 1865. This is especially rare as Carroll withdrew the first edition of *Alice* due to the poor quality of the printing.

Musée de la Comtesse de Ségur
The Museum of the Countess of Ségur

3 rue Abbé Derry, 61270 Aube, France
Tel. (33) 2 33 24 60 09
Mon 2-6pm, Wed, Thu 4-5pm, Fri-Sun 2-6pm

The Comtesse de Ségur, born over 200 years ago in St Petersburg, started writing novels for her grandchildren at the age of 57 and success soon followed. Although her books would probably seem dated today, they used to feature on every girl's bookshelf. The most famous one, avant-garde for its time, was *Les Malheurs de Sophie*, telling of the adventures of a mischevious little girl. Having spent fifty years in Aube, the museum displays documents relating to the author's life and family, as well as early editions from the Bibliothèque Rose, the most famous pocket edition of children's books in France.

Staatsbibliothek zu Berlin – Preussischer Kulturbesitz
The Berlin State Library – Prussian Cultural Heritage
Kinder- und Jugendbuchabteilung III K, Unter den Linden 8, 10102 Berlin, Germany
Tel. (49) 30 2661394 www.sbb.spk-berlin.de
Mon-Fri 9am-6pm, Sat 9am-1pm

The Children's and Youth Book Section was founded in 1951 with the aim of collecting old German children's books, but has since extended its remit to include books published worldwide dating from 1501 onwards. German and European literature form the core of the collection but increasing numbers of children's books from Africa and Asia are being acquired in collaboration with the Oriental and East Asian sections of the library. To date, the collection contains more than 145,000 volumes of which some 45,000 are old German children's books published before 1945 (7,000 before 1860), as well as 7,000 reference works and forty specialized periodicals. There is also a selection of original illustrations by a number of German artists, along with an important collection of works by the Grimm brothers.

Svenska barnboksinstitutet
The Swedish Institute for Children's Books
Odengatan 61, 11322 Stockholm, Sweden
Tel. (46) 8 545 42050 www.sbi.kb.se
Mon-Thu noon-5pm (Wed until 7pm) (closed Jul)

A library and information centre whose aim is to collect, catalogue, and promote Swedish juvenile literature. Begun in 1967, its research and reference library contains around 55,000 catalogued volumes comprising books originally published in Swedish, those which have been translated into Swedish, and those published in Sweden in other languages. The collection is complete in its early works and relatively complete for the whole of the 20th century.

Tampereen Taidemuseon Muumilaakso
The Moominvalley of the Tampere Museum of Art
Hämeenpuisto 20, 33101 Tampere, Finland
Tel. (358) 3 31466578 www.tampere.fi
Tue-Fri 9am-5pm, Sat-Sun 10am-6pm

The core of the collection consists of Tove Jansson's illustrations for the Moomin series which covers five decades. The majority are original illustrations and sketches for his Moomin books and comics, but there are over 200 other children's story illustrations by authors such as J. R. R. Tolkien and Lewis Carroll. There are forty three-dimensional tableaux depicting adventures of the Moomintrolls, most made by Tuulikki Pietilä (a co-founder of the museum) between 1976-90.

University of South Florida
Special Collections Department, LIB 407, 4202 East Fowler Avenue,
Tampa, Florida 33620, USA
Tel. (1) 813 9742731 www.lib.usf.edu
Mon-Thu 9am-9pm, Fri 9am-6pm, Sat 10am-7pm

Much of this collection owes its thanks to Miss Margaret Louise Chapman (the first Special Collections Librarian) and her various successors. The library is one of the nation's major centres for 19th-century American juvenilia, including collections containing the Dime Novel (8,000 items), American Toybook (700 items), and American

Carousel giraffe by the
Gustav Dentzel
Company, *c.* 1903
Shelburne Museum

Textbook Collections. In addition, the library has a huge collection of American boys' series books and other 20th-century juvenile books which were amassed by private collector, Harry K. Hudson. Building on this came a collection of girls' series books. A pre-1865 American schoolbook collection, which began with 300 volumes purchased from the John Jay Bookshop's stock, has subsequently grown to number approximately 1,000 volumes.

Musée Jules Verne
The Jules Verne Museum
3 rue de l'Hermitage, 44100 Nantes, France
Tel. (33) 2 40 69 72 52
Mon, Wed-Sat 10am-noon, 2-5pm, Sun 2-5pm

A fascinating museum where the writings of Jules Verne come to life through sets and characters recreated from his novels. Come face to face with the flying boat from *Robur the Conqueror* and the characters Blériot and Gagarine. Be sure to visit the room containing the objects that inspired Verne, as it attempts to explain the workings of his unbounded imagination. Serious Verne fans should also visit the Bibliothèque municipale (City Library) of Nantes, where 5,000 volumes of his works, as well as his letters and studies devoted to him, have been gathered.

Wilhelm-Busch-Museum
The Wilhelm Busch Museum
Georgengarten 1, 30167 Hanover, Germany
Tel. (49) 511 714076 www.wilhelm-busch-museum.de
Tue-Sat 10am-5pm, Sun 10am-6pm

This museum was first opened in 1937 to honour the 19th-century cartoonist, Wilhelm Busch. The building was destroyed in the war, but fortunately the collection was saved, and in 1949 the Wilhelm Busch Society moved it to its current location. The permanent exhibition primarily shows the work of this artist and creator of the childhood characters, Max and Moritz, although it also includes famous cartoons and caricatures by other well-known artists. Besides the displays of oil paintings, drawings, cartoon stories, letters, and poems there is a large archive and a library containing many early editions of Busch's work.

CAROUSEL, ANIMAL AND AMUSEMENT PARK COLLECTIBLES

Musée des Arts Forains
The Museum of Travelling Arts
Les Pavilions de Bercy, 53 ave des Terroirs de France, 75012 Paris, France
Tel. (33) 1 43 40 16 22 www.pavilons-de-bercy.com
By appt. for groups of fifteen or more

Twenty years of hard work and a passion for theatre has resulted in this collection of antique carnival art amassed by Jean-Pierre Favand. The collection primarily includes objects from the second half of the 19th century and the *belle époque*: items such as games of chance, shooting-gallery targets, carousels, mechanical musical instruments, decorations, and scenery. Among them the various schools of carnival artists are represented, including Frederich Heyn from Neustadt and Alexander Devos from Ghent. An invaluable store of period archives complement this truly amazing collection.

Ecomusée d'Alsace
The Alsace Eco-Museum
68190 Ungersheim, France
Tel. (33) 3 89 74 44 74 www.ecomusee-alsace.com
Daily 10.30am-4.30pm

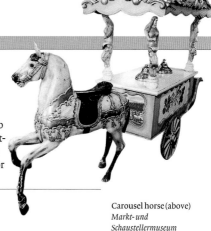

This museum houses the last surviving Carousel-Salon in Europe. It is preserved in its original state and has been the museum's showpiece since it was acquired in 1990. Built by Gustava Bayol in 1909, the owner Maurice Demeyer attempted to re-ignite dwindling interest in carousels in the 1930s by accelerating the pace and inverting the rotation in the ceiling. His efforts were ineffective as it was put in storage in 1937, where it stayed for over forty years. It is, however, an enchanting piece of work.

The Herschell Carousel Factory Museum
180 Thompson Street, North Tonawanda, New York 14120, USA
Tel. (1) 716 693 1885 www.carousel.org
Apr-mid Jun, Sep-Dec: Wed-Sun 1-5pm. Mid Jun-end Aug: daily 1-5pm

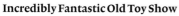

The city of North Tonawanda was home to both the famous Herschell factory and the Wurlitzer Company, maker of band organs for carousels. This was one of the main American carousel companies specializing in making portable carousels that travelled between country fairs. The history of the Herschell-Spillman and Allan Herschell companies is well documented, with photographs depicting carvers at work in 1919 producing carousel figures and chariots. Ride ponies on the Allan Herschell carousel or the 1916 Special Herschell carousel, complete with Lover's tubs, and in the Lockman exhibit see some rare carousel mounts close up.

Carousel horse (above)
Markt- und Schaustellermuseum

Fairground organ
(below)
Markt- und Schaustellermuseum

Incredibly Fantastic Old Toy Show
26 Westgate, Lincoln, Lincolnshire LN1 3BD, UK
Tel. (44) 1522 520534
Tue-Sat 11am-5pm, Sun & public holidays noon-4pm (times may vary, please call for details)

Adding tremendous colour and zest to this already lively museum is a fine collection of fairground art. Here, too, are endless examples of penny and slot machines, all in working order, allowing visitors to experience the lost world of the British seaside. The machines range from the very earliest known clockwork examples from the 1880s through to the electro-mechanical versions of the 1960s which began to decline due to the introduction of the decimal coinage system.

International Museum of Carousel Art
304 Oak Street, Hood River, Oregon 97031, USA
Tel. (1) 541 387 4622 www.carouselmuseum.com
Wed-Sun noon-4pm

This is one of the world's largest and most comprehensive collections thanks to the preservation and restoration work of the Perron family over the past 25 years. The exhibition space is in the most breathtaking setting, crammed with English, French, and German carousel figures, armoured horses, mythical menagerie figures, domestic and exotic carved animals, chariots, rounding and centre board panels. Among these are Big Brother, a gorgeous outside row Muller horse with his original paint (*c.* 1905); Catnip, a Dentzel cat by Salvator Cernigliiaro (*c.* 1907); and several great scenery panels featuring the work of the Looff, the Herschell-Spillman, and the English painters.

Markt- und Schaustellermuseum
The Market and Fairground Museum
Hachestrasse 68, 45127 Essen, Germany
Tel. (49) 201 228749 www.divio.de
By appt. only (please call 201 884 5200)

Erich Knocke started collecting ephemera related to fairgrounds and markets thirty years ago. The 20,000 or so items he has amassed comprise everything and anything that could once either be ridden, bought, or won at shooting and other competitions at fairs or markets. There is a matchless collection of more than 200 carousel animals from the 19th and 20th centuries, by the master carvers Muller, Heyn, Dare, and Limonaire. Also on display is a caravan used by fairground artists and workers, made by Schuman in 1904; market-vehicles by Citroën dating from the 1930s-50s; and other vehicles that were once used to transport the huge carousels. There is also an extensive library.

Exterior view of museum (above)
The Merry-Go-Round Museum

Carousel horses (right)
The New England Carousel Museum

Stargazer, the lead horse on the 1939 Allan Herschell carousel (below)
The Merry-Go-Round Museum

The Merry-Go-Round Museum
W. Washington and Jackson Streets, Sandusky, Ohio 44870, USA
Tel. (1) 419 626 6111 www.carousel.org
Wed-Sat 11am-5pm, Sun noon-5pm

The carousel, purchased in 1991, features Stargazer (*c.* 1915), the famous lead horse which is an excellent example of the supreme workmanship which companies like its maker, C.W. Parker, produced. The pièce de résistance is the Dentzel Carving Shop, which has on display the actual tools as they appeared in the shop in the 1920s before it closed. They include both wood carving and leather working tools, materials and partially finished pieces.

The New England Carousel Museum

95 Riverside Drive, Bristol, Connecticut 06010, USA
Tel. (1) 806 585 5411 www.carousel.org
Mon-Sat 10am-5pm, Sun noon-5pm (closed Mon-Wed from Dec-Mar)

The museum's aim is to display items representative of every master carver and carving style. Its collections are constantly being added to. Some of the most magnificent pieces include figures by the Russian wood carver, Marcus Charles Illions, an inside row prancer with original paint by Dentzel, others by C.W. Parker, and a horse known as Sweet-faced Looff named after its carver, Charles I.D. Looff.

Shelburne Museum
US Route 7, Shelburne, Vermont 05482, USA
Tel. (1) 802 985 3346 www.shelburnemuseum.org
Late May-late Oct: daily 10am-5pm. Rest of year: walking tour of selected buildings at 1pm daily

Displayed alongside circus art, the collection of carousel figures is enchanting. The park carousel, whose mounts were manufactured by the Gustave Dentzel Company of Philadelphia (1902), are shown inside the building, while outside there is a portable carousel from about 1910, made by the Allan Herschell Company of North Tonawanda, NY. Forty animals created by Dentzel and his master carvers are on show. Originally a three-row machine, it carried 29 horses, four chariots and a collection of menagerie figures. The mounts to see are the Dentzel giraffe which is in the Muller style. All the animals are in their original factory paint (almost unheard of!).

The Thursford Collection
Thursford Green, Thursford, Near Fakenham, Norfolk NR21 0AS, UK
Tel. (44) 1328 878477
Daily noon-5pm

A museum packed with fascinating items. Visitors will probably be drawn to the lights, the movement, and the beauty of the Gondola switchback, the oldest steam machine in the collection, dating from 1889. This magnificent round-about, possibly the last of its kind in existence, was created in the King's Lynn factory of Frederick Savage, an inspired inventor of steam-powered machines

and merry-go-rounds. Today, this opulent gold and gilt Gondola is run by electricity, its steam engine having been replaced by a Gavioli pipe organ with 98 keys. A magnificent collection of mechanical fairground organs includes the huge Marenghi organ bought by George Cushing in Ireland. Having started its life in 1905 in Paris, its colourful front houses a 98-key instrument. Equally stunning is the Mortier, a 1930s-styled instrument with a massive 112 keys, made for Brussels just before the war, . The prize exhibit is the 1,339-key Wurlitzer.

CIRCUS MEMORABILIA

Barnum Museum
820 Main Street, Bridgeport, Connecticut 06604, USA
Tel. (1) 203 331 1104   www.barnum-museum.org
Tue-Sat 10am-4.30pm, Sun noon-4.30pm

Gavioli pipe organ
The Thursford Collection

The flamboyant impresario, Phineas T. Barnum, and his friends, are immortalized here. Other features include items relating to those Barnum employed in his side shows, including Tom Thumb his infamous dwarf, and Jumbo the African elephant.

The Circus and Applied Arts Collection
Milner Library Special Collections and Rare Book Room, Illinois State University, Normal, Illinois 61761, USA
Tel. (1) 309 438 7450   www.mlb.ilstu.edu
Mon-Fri 10am-noon, 1-3pm when classes are in session. Other times by appt.

The emphasis is on circus memorabilia but the collection also includes items relating to carnivals, carousels, conjuring and vaudeville, among them posters, photographs, videotapes, and band scores. A notable donation consisted of 1,500 circus posters dating from the 1930s-50s covering a broad range of subjects. Book holdings number over 6,000 volumes dating from the 16th century to the present. The archives of the Dobritch International Circus (numbering 20,000 items) are also located here.

Circus Museum Rapperswil
The Rapperswil Circus Museum
Fischmarktplatz 1, 8640 Rapperswil, Switzerland
Tel. (41) 55 220 5757   www.rapperswil.ch
May-Oct: daily 10am-5pm. Nov-Apr: daily 1-5pm

Founded in Rapperswil, the winter home to Switzerland's most famous circus (Zirkus Knie) this collection comes from the Knie family who have a long tradition of circus performing. Examples from the collection include the oriental costume of Karl Knie (1919), a costume of a maharaja (*c.* 1925-30), and an original costume belonging to the famous clown, Grock.

Circus World Museum
426 Water Street, Baraboo, Wisconsin 53913, USA
Tel. (1) 608 356 8341 24   www.circusparade.com
Daily 9am-6pm. Mid Jul-mid Aug: 9am-9pm

This was the original winter quarters of Ringling Brothers Circus (1884-1918), not to mention more than 100 other travelling tent shows, its not surprising that this collection and its library are massive. The collection consists of 150 antique circus parade wagons and circus vehicles. In the museum's restoration centre you can witness the work involved in transforming the antique circus wagons which are rescued from farm fields and leaky

barns. Examples include the 1903 Spain Float, with gilded wooden griffins, an 1883 British RV wagon complete with iron stove, and a steel sea lion's cage. In July, sixty of the best wagons are paraded through Milwaukee in a recreation of an old-time procession. It also heralds thousands of posters, photographs and films, as well as other rare pieces of circus memorabilia.

Cirkusmuseet
The Circus Museum
Østerled 1, Rold, 9510 Arden, Denmark
Tel. (45) 98 510555
Apr-Oct: Tue-Sat 11am-5pm

A distinctive dodecagonal wooden building (30ft high and 60ft in diameter) is the stunning setting for this museum. This former riding stable, built in 1912, was reconstructed and transformed into a small museum for memorabilia relating to the Miehe Circus. It is the only wooden circus building preserved in Denmark.

Musée du Cirque
The Circus Museum
Place de la Liberté, 36150 Vatan-en-Berry, France
Tel. (33) 2 54 49 77 78 www.musee-du-cirque.com
Jan-mid Jun, mid Sep-Dec: Sat-Sun & public holidays 10am-noon, 2pm-6pm
mid Jun-mid Sep: daily 10am-noon, 2pm-6pm

This first museum of circus art in France displays the unique collection of Alain Frère. Among its gems is a selection of beautiful circus posters by Antoine Magne and Gustave Soury which offer a unique insight into French and international circus history. Then there are the colourful original costumes once worn by the clowns Achille Zavatta, Roger Lanzac, and the Fratellini brothers, as well as by the trapeze artist, Gérard Edon. A complete folk-art miniature circus and the smallest bicycle in the world sit alongside music stands from the famous orchestra, Piste aux Etoiles.

Clowns Gallery, Archives & Museum
1 Hillman Street, Hackney, London E8, UK
Tel. (44) 20 7608 0312 www.staffordr.freeserve.co.uk
First Fri of each month noon-5pm, or by prior appt.

The original St. Francis Clown Portrait Gallery was opened by Billy Smart, a legend of the British circus, in 1960. It was based around clown ephemera originally collected and donated by Stan Bult. Don't miss the famed collection of eggs painted with trademark clown faces.

Erstes Circus-Museum in Deutschland
The First Circus Museum in Germany
Mühlenstrasse 14, 24211 Preetz, Germany
Tel. (49) 4342 1869 www.circus-museum.de
Apr-Aug: Wed 5-8pm, Sat 3-6pm, Sun 10am-noon, 3-6pm

Founded in 1974, the holdings here are based on the private collection of the journalist, Friedel Zscharschuch. Posters, programmes, props, and original costumes compete for your attention among a vast collection of photographs and documents charting the historic development of the circus.

Merle Evans Papers, University of Maryland Libraries
Hornbake Library, University of Maryland, College Park, Maryland 20742-7011, USA
Tel. (1) 301 4059256 www.lib.umd.edu
Mon-Thu 8.30am-10pm, Fri 8.30am-6pm, Sat 10am-5pm, Sun 1-10pm
(advisable to book ahead)

Merle Evans, one of the most famous American circus bandmasters, is remembered in this museum. Correspondence, diaries, scrapbooks, business records, awards, books, articles, circus band music, magazines, programs, posters, route books, even items of his clothing can all be seen here. There are also materials pertaining to the Ringling Brothers Barnum and Bailey Circus, the S. W. Brundage Carnival Band, the Cole Brothers Circus, and an incredible collection of over 1,500 photographs dating from 1880 to 1989 of Evans and other circus performers, bands, equipment, and memorabilia.

The Harvard Theater Collection
The Houghton Library, Harvard University Library, Cambridge, Massachusetts 01238, USA
Tel. (1) 617 4952445 www.htc.harvard.edu
Mon-Fri 9am-5pm

George Beal's collection includes paper ephemera relating to circus performing and includes prints and engravings, rare books on the history of the circus, photographs, broadsides, advertisements, and circus posters. Other key holdings are the Lyndon Phifer Collection of photographs and books relating to acrobats and contortionists, and the Marian Hanna Winter collection of popular entertainment with documents and books covering 400 years of history.

Hertzberg Circus Collection & Museum
210 W. Market Street, San Antonio, Texas 78205, USA
Tel. (1) 210 2077810 www.sat.lib.tx.us
Sep-May: Mon-Sat 10am-5pm. Jun-Aug: Mon-Sat 10am-5pm, Sun 1-5pm

A fanatical collector, Harry Hertzberg gathered together what is perhaps the largest collection of 19th- 20th-century American circus artefacts ever assembled by one person. European circus history and artefacts also feature in the collection. Among the posters, books, letters, diaries, tickets, and photographs is the tiny carriage of General and Mrs Tom Thumb. Equally fascinating is the 1835 route book of a pioneer show called the Zoological Institute. The book, a diary of the yearly travels of the show, is considered by some collectors to be the greatest of all circus treasures, and is the only copy known to exist.

International Circus Hall of Fame
154 N, Peru, Indiana 46970, USA
Tel. (1) 765 4727553 www.circushalloffame.com
May-Oct: Sun 10am-4pm

Clown shoes
Cirkusmuseet

Over the past 100 years, Peru has seen endless circus activity, being the winter home to some of the most famous shows including Hagenbeck-Wallace, Sells-Floto, Terrell Jacobs, and John Robinson. Photographs, uniforms and costumes of famous performers, trapeze apparatus, rigging, harnesses, guns, mouthpieces, and furniture from the Wallace Circus Train and the Ben Wallace Home are also on display.

International Clown Hall of Fame
Grand Avenue Mall, 161 W. Wisconsin Avenue, Suite LL700, Milwaukee,
Wisconsin 53203, USA
Tel. (1) 414 319 0848 www.webdom.com
Mon-Fri 10am-4pm

The aim of this museum is to keep the tragi-comic aspect of clowning alive. The museum not only displays clown memorabilia, artefacts, costumes and props, but also hosts live performances by clowns from around the world. There is a collection of some 500 hand-painted goose eggs which exhibit trademark clown faces registered with the Department of Clown Registry.

Internationales Artistenmuseum
The International Artists Museum
Liebenwalderstrasse 2, 16348 Klosterfelde, Germany
Tel. (49) 33 396272 www.niederbarnim.com
Thu-Sun 2-6pm. Groups by appt. at other times

Of special note among the array of paraphernalia relating to the lives of various circus performers and other performing artists is the stuffed polar bear that killed the husband of Ursula Boettcher, the famous German animal trainer. Another remarkable object is a model of the Sarrasani Circus, founded in 1901 by Hans Stosch-Sarrasani and built by the circus collector, Erich Brauer. It is a perfect copy of the original, showing the beautiful oriental style entrance decorated with ornaments, as well as the caravans used as living quarters for the staff, and the animals' stables.

Clowns and
miniature clowns
*Österreichisches Circus und
Clown Museum*

Emmett Kelly Museum
Main Street, Sedan, Kansas 67361, USA
Tel. (1) 316 725 3470
May-Sep: Mon-Sat 9am-noon, 1-5pm, Sun 1-5pm

Here among the quilts, Civil War memorabilia, and Native American artefacts, you'll find memorabilia relating to Kelly's circus career and information on the role of the clown in circus performances.

National Fairground Archive
University Library, University of Sheffield, Sheffield, South Yorkshire s10 2TN, UK
Tel. (44) 114 222 7231 www.shef.ac.uk
Mon-Fri 9.30am-4.30pm

Every aspect of the lives of travelling showpeople is documented here via photographic images, audio and visual material, journals and monographs, and a body of ephemera which includes programmes, handbills, posters, charters, proclamations, plans, and drawings. The George Tucker Collection comprises 1,400 photographs of circus shows in the south of England. A recent donation via the family of the ringmaster, Billy Smart (1920-90) of the notable English circus, Billy Smart Circus, includes hours of interviews he filmed as an amateur home movie buff in the 1950s.

Clowns and tiger
*Österreichisches Circus und
Clown Museum*

Österreichisches Circus und Clown Museum
The Austrian Circus and Clown Museum
Karmelitergasse 9, 1020 Vienna, Austria
Tel: (43) 1 369 1111
Wed 5.30-7pm, Sat 2.30-5pm, Sun 10am-noon

Originating from the private collection of Heino Seitler, the Viennese writer and editor, this museum houses such treasures as the estate of Tom Belling, who created the figure of the foolish clown 'der dumme August' in the Renz Circus in Berlin. Remembered too are the famous tamer Miss Senide and the clowns, Charlie Rivel and Grock, with their original costumes. Also on display are the belongings of other famous clowns including the Fratellinis, Bonos, Bronetts, Morenos, and Chickys. Of particular interest are the props and equipment from the turn of the century, many of them works of art.

John and Mable Ringling Museum of Art

5401 Bay Shore Road, Sarasota, Florida 34243, USA
Tel. (1) 941 359 5700   www.ringling.org
Daily 10am-5.30pm

Circus poster by the
Strobridge
Lithographing Company,
c. 1890
Shelburne Museum

After John Ringling left his spectacular Italian Renaissance villa crammed with works of art to the State of Florida, they decided to honour him by establishing a circus gallery. It contains an astounding selection of memorabilia, from rare 18th-century prints and coloured drawings to glittering costumes and loudly-painted carved circus wagons. The best of the 19th- and early 20th-century posters can be seen, as well as circus curiosities such as Tom Thumb's walking stick and wardrobe. The excellent library contains circus history ephemera and literature, including newspaper clippings dating as far back as 1816.

Shelburne Museum

US Route 7, Shelburne, Vermont 05482, USA
Tel. (1) 802 985 3346   www.shelburnemuseum.org
Late May-late Oct: daily 10am-5pm. Rest of year: walking tour of selected buildings at 1pm daily

Circus specialists are drawn to this museum for its 500-plus vintage circus advertising posters, with many rare early examples from all the major players of America's golden circus age including Barnum and Bailey, Adam Forepaugh, John B. Doris, and the Sells Brothers. Housed here are three carved miniature circuses, one of which, The Circus Parade, was conceived in 1925 by Roy Arnold of Hardwick, Vermont. Equally impressive is the three-ringed folk art circus by Edgar Kirk of Pennsylvania.

Somers Historical Society & Museum of the Early American Circus

Elephant Hotel, Routes 100 and 202, Somers, New York 10589, USA
Tel. (1) 914 277 4977
Fri 2-4pm. Additional weekend hours during summer.

Memorials to elephants are few and far between, but here is one of them. Built between 1820 and 1825 by Hachaliah Bailey, father of the American circus, this three-storey red brick building had the words 'Elephant Hotel' painted across the front to commemorate Old Bet, the elephant responsible for his success. It was here in Somers around 1804 that Bailey purchased the famous elephant and exhibited her locally. Success led to the acquisition of an exotic menagerie. Over two decades these shows were a national phenomenon. It took the establishment of the railroad, east of the city in 1840, to curtail Somers' popularity. However, the hotel remained a social centre until the early years of the 20th century when it was purchased by the town. The collection of 10,000 items include rare menagerie posters, paintings by folk portrait artist, Ammi Phillips, an 1840 pianoforte given as a wedding gift by the Keeper of the Royal Menagerie at the Tower of London, and a suit worn by Tom Thumb during an audience with Queen Victoria. Allow enough time to see the Rowell miniature circus, constructed and assembled by the avid circus collector, Dr Hugh Grant Rowell in 1910. It is a superb representation of a travelling three-ring circus. Serious collectors should take advantage of the library and research facility.

Theatre Museum

Hippisley Coxe Circus Collection, Study Room, Russell Street, London WC2E 7PA, UK
Tel. (44) 20 7943 4700   www.theatremuseum.vam.ac.uk
Tue-Fri 10.20am-4.30pm by appt. only

Buried within its enormous holdings is the Hippisley Coxe Circus Collection of over 1,000 volumes, covering all subjects from clowns and animal training to the history of fairgrounds.

Muzei tsirkovogo iskusstva
The Museum of Circus Art
Naberezhnaia reki Fontanki 3, 191011 Saint Petersburg, Russian Federation
Tel. (7) 812 3134413
Mon-Fri 10am-5pm

Russia has had a strong relationship with the circus since the 18th century. The original idea for a permanent circus here was the brainchild of the Italian circus performer, Gaetano Ciniselli, who played an important role in the development of circus art in Russia. For years the only establishment of its kind in the world, the Museum of Circus Art contains an enormous amount of memorabilia recalling its famous circus artists, along with items and documents recounting the history of other domestic and foreign circuses.

Tyne & Wear Archives
Blandford House, Blandford Square, Newcastle upon Tyne, Tyne & Wear NE1 4JA, UK
Tel. (44) 191 232 6789   www.thenortheast.com
Mon-Fri 9am-5.15pm, Tue 9am-8.30pm

Of special note here is the Fenwick Collection of Circus and Fairground Material and the circus poster collection, spanning the mid-1860s to the mid-1930s. The collection reflects the personal fascination of Arthur J. Fenwick with the entertainment world and the nomadic life of circus performers. The collection was transferred from the Laing Art Gallery, Newcastle, to the Archives Service in 1978, but the gallery has retained some artefacts from the collection.

The University of Memphis Libraries
Special Collections Department, Campus Box 526500, The University of Memphis, Memphis, Tennessee 38152, USA
Tel. (1) 901 6788242   www.lib.memphis.edu
Mon-Fri 8am-4.30pm, Sun 1-5pm during academic terms

The extensive Dyer Marion 'Ichabod' Reynolds Circus Collection (1878-1980) is part of the Mississippi Valley Collection (MVC), housed here in the Ned R. McWherter Library. On display is memorabilia documenting the life and multi-faceted operations of many circuses from the late 1870s to 1980, particularly Ringling Brothers Barnum and Bailey Circus, and the Al B. Barnes Circus.

DOLLS AND DOLLS' HOUSES

Museo della Bambola
The Doll Museum
Rocca Borromeo, via alla Rocca, 21021 Angera, Italy
Tel. (39) 0331 931 300
Apr-Sep: daily 9.30am-12.30pm, 2-6pm. Oct: daily 9.30am-12.30pm, 2-5pm

The collection of Princess Bona Borromeo Arse, housed in a 13th-century fortress dominating Lake Maggiore, is remarkable for its encyclopaedic coverage of the development of dolls from the beginning of the 19th century to the early 20th century. There are Italian-made, sculpted and jointed wooden figures from the 18th century reflecting iconographic religious traditions, and French and German dolls from the 19th-20th centuries including character dolls. A rare example of the latter is the doll by Simon & Halbig dressed in its original clothing with a delicately painted bisque head. There is also an important collection of Japanese dolls from the Edo, Meiji, and Taisho periods together with a collection of African and South American pieces. A significant addition to the museum is the entire collection of doll costumes from the Tours museum in France.

Museum of Childhood at Bethnal Green

Cambridge Heath Road, London E2 9PA, UK
Tel. (44) 20 8983 5200   www.vam.ac.uk
Mon-Thu, Sat-Sun 10am-5.50pm

An impressive collection of over fifty dolls' houses ranging from 18th-century English examples to a rare German dolls' house made in Nuremberg in 1673. Many of the later examples (1760 to the present) were constructed with the accuracy of architectural models. The oldest doll (*c.* 1680) originally belonged to James II and sits proudly on a walnut chair. Equally stunning is the fashion doll made by Charles Ernest Pierotti in 1903. She wears a Hamley's silk and lace costume and a hat made by Kate Reily of Dover Street. Princess Daisy, an English wax doll, was a medal winner at the Amsterdam International Exhibition of 1895, and was subsequently given to Queen Mary in 1899.

Museum of Childhood

42 High Street, Edinburgh, Scotland EH1 1TG, UK
Tel. (44) 131 529 4142
Mon-Sat 10am-5pm, Sun 2-5pm during the Edinburgh Festival.

Besides the wax, porcelain, and wooden dolls by all the noted makers, there are amusing character dolls of Shirley Temple, Rex Harrison, and three prime ministers. Don't miss the collection of around 600 'emergency dolls' donated by the London collector, Edward Lovett. His collection is comprised of dolls made by tribes in Africa and elsewhere which played a role in magic, fertility, or voodoo. Some of the most enchanting dolls he collected were on expeditions to the slum areas in the east end of London. He exchanged a box full of new dolls for those which he found being played with and made by children on the streets. A charming example is one made from an old shoe; the foot forms the doll's body and the heel becomes the head. The doll's arms and legs are modelled by wrapping old rags around the shoe, while odd bits of paper are used to form its features.

Museum of the City of New York

Fifth Avenue at 103rd Street, New York, New York 10029, USA
Tel. (1) 212 534 1672   www.mcny.org
Wed-Sat 10am-5pm, Sun 1-5pm. Tue 10am-2pm for pre-booked school and group tours

One of the best known exhibits in the Toy Gallery here is the permanent Dolls' House Gallery exhibiting period houses and miniature furniture. True treasures include the Ann Anthony's Pavilion (1769), Shelton-Taylor (1835), Brett (1838), Goelet (1845), Elder (1865), and Altadena's (1895), all made and played with by New York society families of the time. Another significant holding is the Stettheimer Doll House (1920) decorated by Carrie Stettheimer who was active in the artistic movement of the period. She commissioned popular artists like Marcel Duchamp and Gaston Lachaise to produce miniature works for the house. The dolls even represent artistic notables including the writer Gertrude Stein and the photographer Edward Steichen.

Biscuit-porcelain
dolls, Thuringia, *c.* 1880
Deutsches Spielzeugmuseum

Coburger Puppenmuseum
The Coburg Doll Museum

Rückertstrasse 2-3, 96450 Coburg, Germany
Tel. (49) 956 174047   www.spielzeugfreunde.de
Apr-Oct: daily 9am-5pm. Nov-Mar: Tue-Sun 10am-5pm

The former home of poet and orientalist Friedrich Rueckert is overflowing with more than 600 dolls, many from the golden age of German doll making spanning the mid 19th century to the first quarter of the 20th century. Also included is a great collection of half-dolls and rare French dolls. Period furniture, clothing, and accessories complement the exhibits in more than fifty miniature rooms.

Horse and carriage with
dolls, probably
Sonneberg, *c.* 1900-10
Deutsches Spielzeugmuseum

Musée du Costume
The Costume Museum
Place de L'Eglise, Hauteville-Gondon, 73700 Bourg-Saint-Maurice, France
Tel. (33) 4 79 07 09 01
Mon, Wed-Sun 2-6pm

A specialist collection of dolls dressed in traditional costumes made by the needleworkers of the village between 1890 and 1910. Both an important record of traditional dress and a delight to behold.

Dagmar's Museum of Dolls and Toys
Sakrisóy, 8390 Reine i Lofoten, Norway
Tel. (47) 76 09 21 43 www.lofoten-info.no
Please call for opening times

Rare German makers are represented in this collection of over 1,500 dolls, but what makes this museum truly unique is its Lofoten Room containing dolls and toys collected from the surrounding area and from across Norway.

The Delaware Toy & Miniature Museum
Route 141, Wilmington, Delaware 19807, USA
Tel. (1) 302 427 8697 www.thomes.net
Tue-Sat 10am-4pm, Sun noon-4pm

Porcelain Oliver doll by
H.E. Thomicny
*Museum der Deutschen
Spielzeugindustrie*

A historical and contemporary collection of dolls' houses, miniatures, and toys founded by Gloria R. Hinkel and Beverly J. Thomes. On display are 100 dolls' houses and period rooms from Europe and America from the 18th to the 20th centuries. Many of these come from private collections, including those of Jean Austin du Pont, Miriam Wentworth, Helena Rubenstein, and the Strassburger family. An outstanding example is the Mount Pleasant dolls' house (1912), a reproduction of the famous Georgian masterpiece in Philadelphia's Fairmount Park.

Museum der Deutschen Spielzeugindustrie
The Museum of the German Toy Industry
Hindenburgplatz 1, 96465 Neustadt bei Coburg, Germany
Tel. (49) 9568 5600 www.museen-in-bayern.de
Daily 10am-5pm

A region renowned for toy making, the art of carving wooden toys is thought to have been brought to this area in the 14th or 15th century by traders from Nuremberg, while pre-industrial toy production started in the late 17th and early 18th century. To mark and preserve the region's heritage of doll making, the museum was founded in 1929 after the local toy industry was threatened following World War I. Today, around 800 dolls show off their costumes from over 100 countries and regions around the world, standing proudly among the museum's permanent collection of more than 1,500 dolls.

Deutsches Historisches Museum
The German Historical Museum
Zeughaus Unter den Linden 2, 10117 Berlin, Germany
Tel. (49) 30 215020 www.dhm.de
Mon, Tue, Thu-Sun 10am-6pm

Two collections have been brought together here from East and West Germany and reflect the different attitudes to toys in their political and historical contexts. There are dolls from around 1840 to the present day, from delicately worked papier-mâché dolls with leather bodies, made in Thuringia (*c.* 1840), to robust bathing dolls made of glazed porcelain (*c.* 1870). The patriotic soldier dolls from World War I made by Steiff from felt, leather, and wood are fascinating. A large three-room dolls' house reflects the spirit of National Socialism in the kitchen wallpaper which displays scenes from the life of the Hitler Youth and the German Girls' Association.

Deutsches Spielzeugmuseum
German Toy Museum
Beethovenstrasse 10 ,96515 Sonneberg, Germany
Tel. (49) 3675 702856 www.sonnebergonline.de
Tue-Sun 9am-5pm

Among the treasures are wooden toys made in Sonneberg in the 18th and 19th centuries, papier-mâché figures, and masks and dolls from Thuringia and East Asia (Indonesia, India, China, and Japan). Also of importance is the large collection of pattern books for toys made in Sonneberg, as well as catalogues by the firms Spindler and Nick & Bähring, and original negative and positive dolls' heads moulds from the 19th century made of plaster of Paris or gypsum. A remarkable piece is the Thüringer Kirmes, which was first shown in Brussels in 1910 during the World Exhibition, and returned to Sonneberg in 1912. It was originally designed by the sculptor Reinhard Möller, and furnished by 37 different toy firms. This huge fair has 67 human figures, nearly all lifesize, which were modelled after various well-known people from Sonneberg.

Musée de l'Enfance
The Museum of Childhood
Domaine de Lacroix-Laval, 69280 Marcy-L'Etoile, France
Tel. (33) 4 78 87 87 00
Mid Feb-mid Nov: Tue-Sun 10am-5pm. Mid Nov-mid Feb: Wed-Sun 10am-5pm

The former Château de la Poupée, now a childhood museum, is a paradise for any French doll collector. The collection of Denise Sambrat reflects the golden age of French doll production (1850-90). Improvements were due to Adélaïde-Calixte Huret, who first conceived of a doll that would change doll production forever. Even the introduction of Japanese dolls, which were copied by the Germans, did not stop the innovative wave in France. Bru, Jumeau, and many others became household names. Unfortunately this quality was not to last after the creation of the Société Française de Fabrication des Bébés et Jouets (SFBJ), and eventually French doll production ceased to exist. Among the most remarkable examples are: a very rare doll by Huret, with a wooden body and a red costume; a Parisian by Rohmer, with original costume and a head made after a license registered in 1858; and a remarkable Bébé Bru from the Girard period with its original dress, table, and Bébé Bru 'téteur'.

Exterior view of museum
(top)
Deutsches Spielzeugmuseum

Doll in traditional Upper
Bavarian costume,
Berchtesgaden, 1932
(middle)
*Museum der Deutschen
Spielzeugindustrie*

Upper Franconian bride
doll, *c.* 1930 (above)
*Museum der Deutschen
Spielzeugindustrie*

Germanisches Nationalmuseum
The German National Museum
Kornmarkt 1, 90402 Nuremberg, Germany
Tel. (49) 911 1331116 www.gnm.de
Tue, Thu-Sun 10am-5pm, Wed 10am-9pm

Remarkable are the five large 17th-century dolls' houses, four with their original interiors, belonging to families from Nuremberg. The oldest has a courtyard surrounded by a stunning golden balustrade. There are another 42 dolls' rooms and kitchens originating from the 18th and 19th centuries, as well as over 200 miniature pieces for dolls' houses. A collection of 195 dolls illustrates the development of the doll from the 18th through to the early 20th century.

Heimatmuseum Schloss Tenneberg
The Regional Museum of Castle Tenneberg
Schloss Tenneberg, 99880 Waltershausen, Germany
Tel. (49) 3622 691 70   www.waltershausen.de
Daily 9am-4pm

Housed in a 12th-century fortress, among the collection's main features are the
'Kugelgelenkpuppen', or ball-jointed dolls (manufactured here), along with the many
examples of the character baby doll, first made by one of the leading doll makers from
Waltershausen, Kämmer, and Reinhardt. Worth viewing is the hand-carved wooden
bust of Hilda, produced by Johannes Daniel Kestner Jr.. Most impressive is the only
surviving example of a doll to be fitted with a miniature record player to make it talk.
It was Emile Berliner who around 1890 struck a deal with Kämmer and Reinhardt to
produce one of the world's first dolls fitted with a commercial disc record. Sitting
right next to her is a gramophone from the same date, complete with a record the size
of a CD.

Hessisches Puppenmuseum
The Hessian Doll Museum
Parkpromenade 4, 63454 Hanau-Wilhelmsbad, Germany
Tel. (49) 6181 86212   www.museen-hanau.de
Tue-Sun 10am-noon, 2-5pm

Situated in the birthplace of the Grimm Brothers, this doll museum opened in 1983 and
houses the collection of its founder, Gertrud Rosemann. Dolls from her 2,000-strong
collection present clearly, and with style, the development of the European doll from
antiquity through to the present day.

Historisches Museum Basel
The History Museum of Basle
Steinenberg 4, 4051 Basle, Switzerland
Tel. (41) 61 205 8600   www.historischesmuseumbasel.ch
Mon, Wed-Sun 10am-5pm

The galleries here are filled with twelve dolls' houses and rooms. The oldest dates from
about 1680 and is a prototype of the dolls' houses kept in lockable cupboards. These
rooms, called 'Doggetekänschterli' (dolls' boxes), were built into a cupboard because
tradition dictated that children should only play with these expensive toys under strict
supervision. In one such cupboard sits a silver dish with an engraved lid presented in
1709 by Peter Biermann. Of special note are the collections of dolls complete with their
wardrobes and table services.

Musée du Jouet de Poissy
The Toy Museum of Poissy
2 Enclos de l'Abbaye, 78300 Poissy, France
Tel. (33) 1 39 65 06 06
Tue-Sun 9.30am-noon, 2-5.30pm

Opened in 1974 and housed in the remains of a 14th-century royal monastery, this is an
exhaustive collection containing many precious dolls, including examples made by Bru
and Jumeau. There is also a selection of related objects such as layettes, houses, paintings,
and illustrations.

Kinderland- und Spielzeugmuseum
The Museum of Toys and Children
Ritscherstrasse 4, 37431 Bad Lauterberg im Harz, Germany

Tel. (49) 5524 92040 www.badlauterberg.de
Tue, Thu, Sat-Sun 10.30am-noon, 2.30-5.30pm, Wed, Fri 2.30-5.30pm

An amalgamation of two private collections containing mainly German-made items, this museum offers an insight into the lives of children between 1860 and 1960. An enormous dolls' house dating from 1900, has Birgit, a Käthe-Kruse doll, setting the table in the kitchen, while in the living room a children's birthday is being celebrated. Other highlights are the 'artist's dolls' by Käthe-Kruse and a rare selection of handmade felt dolls from the Italian company Lenci.

Milwaukee Public Museum
800 W Wells St, Milwaukee, Wisconsin 53233, USA
Tel. (1) 414 278 2732 www.mpm.edu
Daily 9am-5pm

This museum is in the rare position of owning a fine collection of 'used' Milwaukee W. P. A. (Works Progress Administration) dolls in very good condition and with their original clothes intact. The Milwaukee W. P. A Handicraft Project was set up in 1935 to help the Milwaukeeans through unemployment during the Great Depression. The dolls are especially noteworthy as they were made to the highest standards. Their main function was educational, helping to teach children how to dress themselves.

Barn-woman, Tierijärvi, Finland, 1600s (above)
Nukke-ja pukumuseo

Fancy dolls knitted by Gunver Ekroos, 1960s (below)
Nukke-ja pukumuseo

Musée national de Monaco
The National Museum of Monaco
17 ave. de la Princesse Grace, 98000 Monte Carlo, Principality of Monaco
Tel. (377) 97 707475 www.monte-carlo.mc
Easter-Sep: daily 10am-6.30pm. Oct-Easter: daily 10am-12.15pm, 2.30-6.30pm

Princess Grace of Monaco offered the Principality as a home to the collection of the Princess of Galéa. The collection reflects the personality of Madeleine de Galéa. She would acquire the dolls in specific shops, then antique dealers who knew her tastes would present her with their most unusual finds. She would then ask artists such as Wakevitch or Christian Bérard to provide her with the suitable furniture. She collected biscuit dolls, dolls with bisque heads attached to gusseted, stuffed leather bodies, or papier-mâché dolls from Germany. She also owned several rare examples of wooden dolls from the 18th and 19th centuries.

Nukke-ja pukumuseo
The Museum of Dolls and Costumes
Hatanpään kartano, Hatanpään puistokuja 1, 33900 Tampere, Finland
Tel. (358) 3 222 6261 www.user.sgic.fi
May-Aug: Tue-Sat 10am-5pm,
Sun noon-5pm
Sep-Apr: Wed-Sun noon-5pm

A massive collection ranging from a Peruvian Inca rag doll dating from the 12th century, to quirky Mexican flea dolls in festive attire. The museum was founded in 1966 by the owner of the Haihara Mansion, Gunvor Ekroos, and since 1982 has been run by the Haihara Museum Foundation. The collection is outstanding, with magic dolls, religious and paper dolls, as well as dolls' houses. The setting is breathtaking.

Poppen en Speelgoedmuseum
The Doll and Toy Museum
Telefoonstraat 13-15, 5038 DL Tilburg, The Netherlands
Tel. (31) 13 543 6305
Summer: Wed-Fri, Sun 1-4pm. Winter: Sun, Wed 1-4pm

This monumental textile warehouse has been transformed into a home for over 3,000 dolls and a selection of doll accessories. The displays document the various methods and materials used in doll manufacturing, covering everything from wood to modern-day plastics.

Porvoon nukke- ja lelumuseo
The Porvoo Doll and Toy Museum
Jorma Söderlund, Jokikatu 14, 06100 Porvoo, Finland
Tel. (358) 19 582941 www.kolumbus.fi
Summer: Mon-Sat 11am-3.30pm, Sun noon-3.30pm

Every doll on display was collected individually by the owner on her travels. They range from a Kämmer & Reinhardt walking doll dating from 1891, to Ideal's Shirley Temple dolls, as well as dolls from Finland. Don't miss the group of six Biedermeier dolls dating from 1860-90 seated expectantly around a dining table.

Ideal's Shirley Temple dolls, 1930 (top)
Porvoon nukke- ja lelumuseo

German dolls, 1900-05 (above)
Porvoon nukke- ja lelumuseo

Musée de la Poupée
The Doll Museum
Impasse Berthaud, 22 rue Beaubourg, 75003 Paris, France
Tel. (33) 1 42 72 73 11 www.pariserve.tm.fr
Tue-Sun 10am-6pm

The story of the French doll begins around 1860 with Jumeau at the heart of the industry. Founded in 1842 by Pierre François Jumeau, the business continued to flourish. As competition increased many of the French companies banded together to form the Société Française de Fabrication de Bébés et Jouets (SFBJ). Quality declined, and the heyday of French doll making drew to a close at the beginning of the 20th century. This superb exhibition has the best of the French dolls of this period, complete with hand-painted porcelain heads. All the famous French manufacturers are represented, including Fernand Gaulthier, Leon Casimir Bru & Son, J. N. Steiner, A. Thuillier, and Jumeau. The collection now numbers over 1,000 items. Rarities include the Bébé Halopeau, and another made by Thuillier which is said to be one of the finest ever made.

Musée de la Poupée et du Jouet ancien
The Doll and Ancient Toy Museum
23 rue de Saillé, 44350 Guérande, France
Tel. (33) 2 40 15 69 13
May-Nov: Tue-Sun 10.30am-1pm (Jul-Aug: 2.30pm-7pm). Nov-Apr: Tue-Sun 2-6pm

This beautiful collection was amassed over 30 years by Mrs Brisou. It is housed in the 12th-century Chapelle St Jean and includes dolls, accessories, and furniture by all the famous French manufacturers from the 19th and 20th centuries including Jumeau, Bru, Schmitt, and Gaultier. The museum also has a very good representation from the SFBJ.

Musée de la Poupée et du Jouet ancien
The Doll and Ancient Toy Museum
Château de Robersart, Wambrechies, France
Tel. (33) 3 20 39 69 28
Sun & public holidays 2-6pm (Mon-Fri on request)

Most of the displays reproduce scenes from daily life from the beginning of the 20th century to the 1960s. All the notable manufacturers are represented: Bru, Jumeau, SFBJ, François Gaultier, Armand Marseille, Steiner, Simon & Halbig. Famous examples include many Bleuette and Mignonette dolls, and dolls from Napoleon III's time. There is also an extensive collection of early Barbies, with costumes dating from the 1960s.

Musée des Poupées
The Museum of Dolls
3 rue des Trente, 56210 Josselin, France
Tel. (33) 2 97 22 36 45
Jul & Aug: daily 10am-6pm. Jun & Sep: daily 2-6pm. Apr & May: Wed, Sat-Sun 2-6pm

The old stables of the Château of Josselin provide a wonderful setting for this collection of more than 1,000 dolls gathered by several generations of the Rohan family. The collection includes ancient dolls; 17th- and 18th-century wax, wooden, and papier-mâché dolls; porcelain dolls with accessories and furniture; ethnographic examples; and dolls in local costume. Rare and unique dolls by manufacturers such as Bru, Jumeau, and Huret, many of which were donated by Emile Zola, the Prince of Wales, and Princess Bibesco, sit alongside ordinary dolls from all over the world.

Puppen und Spielzeugmuseum
The Doll and Toy Museum
Schulhof 4, 1010 Vienna, Austria
Tel. (43) 1 535 6860 www.magwien.gv.at
Tue-Sun 10am-6pm

A fascinating collection of 20th-century 'exotic dolls' or South Sea babies. The Biedermeiers or 'black spot' china are also there to be admired, as are dolls' houses with elaborate interiors, a dolls' toy shop, and grocers. Originally a private museum, it was opened to the public in 1989.

Puppen und Spielzeugmuseum
Doll and Toy Museum
Hofbronnengasse 11-13, 91541 Rothenburg, Germany
Tel. (49) 9861 7330 www.spielzeugmuseum.rothenburg.de
Daily 9.30am-6pm (Jan, Feb: 11am-5pm)

Over 800 dolls from the last 200 years are on display, including many by the noted manufacturers, among them Heubach, Kling, Hurét, Simon & Halbig, Lecomte, and Steiner. An unusual addition is a doll called Karolin (c. 1885) with a biscuit-porcelain head, blond curls, and leather body. Her extreme elegance set a perfect example for upper-class girls of the period. Among the highlights is a copy of the Petit Trianon built in 1995 on a scale of 1:12. The building has six rooms, all exact replicas of the interiors at Versailles.

The Rijksmuseum
The State Museum
Stadhouderskade 42, 1071 ZD Amsterdam, The Netherlands
Tel. (31) 20 6732121 www.rijksmuseum.nl
Daily 10am-5pm

Two of the most beautiful houses in Amsterdam can be found in this museum and they are dolls' houses. One has a cabinet of oak veneered with tortoise shell and inlaid with tracery of pewter. The house was commissioned following the marriage of Petronella Oortman to Johannes Brandt in 1686 and took fifteen years to complete. The other,

'Washing Day'. Doll with joints made by the Heuer brothers, 1916 (below)
Puppen und Spielzeugmuseum (Rothenburg)

Papier-mâché doll, 1800 (middle)
Puppen und Spielzeugmuseum (Rothenburg)

Danish doll, Karolin, c. 1885 (left)
Puppen und Spielzeugmuseum (Rothenburg)

German doll, Kämmer &
Reinhardt / Simon &
Halbig, 1935 (top)
Speelgoedmuseum Mechelen

German doll, 1900 (above)
Speelgoedmuseum Mechelen

Parisian doll, biscuit-
porcelain head (below)
Musée national de Monaco

from 1676, is the earliest dolls' house in the collection and has its date embroidered onto a pincushion in one of the rooms which also bears the initials P. D., for the then 26-year old Petronella Dunois. The daughter of a high official, when she married in 1677 the house was accorded a special mention in a list of her contributions to their household. The workmanship is outstanding. Bed linen bears the monograms of the owners and the silver, glass, and pottery matches both the style and quality of the workmanship of the great craftsmen of 17th-century Holland. It is, however, the domestic quarters that are of most interest, with perfect copies in miniature of the items used by the owners' families. The larders have barrels for wine and beer, each marked accordingly, as well as glass bottles and clay pots, plates of food, and pewter flagons.

Schweizer Kindermuseum
The Swiss Children's Museum
Oelrainstrasse 29, 5401 Baden, Switzerland
Tel. (41) 56 222 1444 www.kindermuseum.ch
Wed, Sat 2-5pm, Sun 10am-5pm

The largest part of this museum's toy collection is made up of dolls, including a comprehensive selection of paper dolls. There are sixteen paper figures from Roman mythology by H. F. Müller of Vienna (1841), along with more recent examples which include paper Barbies (1967), a paper Snow White from Denmark (1950), and an Italian paper Mickey Mouse (1978). Also worth noting are the porcelain dolls with real hair and glass eyes by Gaultier (1860). Others include the 'swimming dolls' (1-50cm in height) which became very popular because they could actually float. One of the highlights of the wooden doll section is a doll dating from 1850, 48cm in height with a wooden head and limbs, coloured eyes, and real hair. One of the turned wooden dolls, which signified the beginning of mass production for wooden toys, is the Wickelkindl: 12cm in height, its hollowed centre is filled with crockery. Also of note are the Japanese Kokeshi turned wooden dolls and the Russian Marushkas (manufactured around the second half of the 19th century), which have several smaller dolls inside and whose origins are mostly peasant or religious.

Shelburne Museum
US Route 7, Shelburne, Vermont 05482, USA
Tel. (1) 802 985 3346 www.shelburnemuseum.org
Late May-late Oct: daily 10am-5pm. Rest of year: walking tour of selected buildings at 1pm daily

A collection of over 1,000 dolls, 27 dolls' houses, and accessories is housed in the Variety Unit, a brick farmhouse built in 1835. There are examples of some of the first commercial dolls made in America by Joel Ellis of Springfield, Vermont, with wooden bodies, jointed limbs, and pewter hands and feet. The famed makers Bru, Jumeau, Steiner, Kestner, and Simon & Halbig are all represented. The English peddler dolls and the fine collection of American Indian dolls shouldn't be missed either.

Speelgoedmuseum Mechelen
The Mechelen Toy Museum
Nekkerspoel 21, 2800 Mechelen, Belgium
Tel. (32) 15 557075 www.speelgoedmuseum.be
Tue-Sun 10am-5pm

The substantial collection of Belgium dolls has been improved further due to the acquisition of a wonderful collection of French and German dolls from the former Musée de la Poupée in Saint-Malo, France. Dolls from the US, Italy, and several other countries are represented, including folk art examples from Argentina, Egypt, and South Africa.

Pierrot writing, by Vichy,
Paris, late 19th century
Musée national de Monaco

Spielzeugmuseum
The Toy Museum
Wettsteinhaus, Baselstrasse 34, 4125 Riehen, Switzerland
Tel. (41) 61 641 2829   www.riehen.ch
Wed-Sat 2-5pm, Sun 10am-5pm

The museum's large collection of dolls' houses, formerly belonging to
the wealthy families of Basle, are enthralling. One such house became an important
document of Basle's culture. Built in 1872 by Louise Burckhardt, it represents her own
house (the Württembergerhof) with seven rooms over four floors, and part of the garden
with its dog kennel, pond, and animals. The paintings in the windows, executed by Mrs
Burckhardt herself, are of the original views outside her home. Other charming examples include a fashion shop from the mid 19th century, a German dolls' kitchen from
around 1900, and a dolls' school.

Spielzeugmuseum Nürnberg
The Toy Museum of Nuremberg
Kalrstrasse 13-15, 90403 Nuremberg, Germany
Tel. (49) 911 231 3164   www.nurenberg.de
Tue-Sun 10am-5pm, Wed 10am-9pm

Dolls' kitchen from the
family of Hugo Steiff,
c. 1920-21
Spielzeugmuseum Nürnberg

Nuremberg boasts a 600-year-old tradition of toy making and is host to the
International Toy Fair once a year. Lydia and Paul Bayer began building this collection in
the early 1920s and the museum (opened in 1971) now consists of over 1,500 dolls, as well
as the dolls' houses for which it is so famous. One of the highlights is a kitchen originating
from the royal family of Bavaria, the 'Wittelsbacher' Princesses, made by Bing (1882), the
biggest toy factory in the world at that time. Another exquisite piece is a huge kitchen
dating from 1920-21 which once belonged to the family of Hugo Steiff, a nephew of
Margarete Steiff (the founder of the firm).

The Strong Museum
One Manhatten Square, Rochester, New York 14607, USA
Tel. (1) 716 263 2700   www.strongmuseum.org
Mon-Thu, Sat 10am-5pm, Fri 10am-8pm, Sun noon-5pm

The collection of over 20,000 dolls amassed by Margaret Woodbury Strong is breathtaking. Numerous rag-dolls and one-of-a-kind homemade dolls stuffed with sawdust,
rags or even grass, jostle for space with masterpieces by all the main French and German
makers. Among the earliest examples are the English Queen Anne-style 'lady' dolls
with carved wooden bodies and jointed, pegged-on-arms and legs. Dolls with wax heads
include one made by Dressel, Cuno & Otto (*c.* 1893-95), the major German manufacturer.
There is also a pedlar doll in the dress of a 19th-century street merchant, with its face and
hands made of painted white kid. This was made by C. & H. White of Milton in
Hampshire, England. The dolls' houses and furniture are equally stunning. One special
example to look out for is a lithographed paper doll house by McLoughlin Brothers of
New York City.

The Toy and Miniature Museum of Kansas City
5235 Oak Street, Kansas City, Missouri 64112, USA
Tel. (1) 816 333 9328   www.umkc.edu
Wed-Sat 10am-4pm, Sun 1-4pm

For lovers of dolls' houses look out for the Victorian Fancies (miniatures made in the
1800s). Classed as a type of folk art, the creations were often crafted at home from any
available materials; particularly whimsical is the lounge seat made from a series of wish-
bones from chickens. There is also a nine-foot-tall house which was made in the 1860s for

Pierrot with Dogs, by
Vichy, Paris, late 19th
century
Musée national de Monaco

the children of George Coleman, with ceilings high enough to accommodate French fashion dolls standing eighteen to twenty inches high. The cabinet miniatures are exquisite, intricately carved and hand-crafted from ivory, silver, and ormolu. See a contemporary room setting of the Powel House parlour in Philadelphia (*c.* 1765) created by Harry Cooke. In this 1:12 scale reproduction, the furniture is carved in the popular Philadelphia Chippendale style, while the draperies and upholstery are by Thelma Cooke.

Washington Dolls' House and Toy Museum

5236 44th Street, NW. Chevy Chase, Washington,
DC 20015, USA
Tel. (1) 202 244 0024
Tue-Sat 10am-5pm, Sun noon-5pm

This extensive collection is never all out on display at once, though there is still an impressive array of dolls' houses and related buildings including shops, stables, school rooms, and even dolls' ships. Unusual offerings include a 1903 New Jersey seaside hotel; Bliss Street, a collection of turn-of-the-century houses of lithographed paper on wood, manufactured by R. Bliss of Rhode Island; a miniature Mexican mansion (*c.* 1890) in Puebla, Mexico; and an exquisite toy shop from Zurich (*c.* 1800). The doll collection is smaller and includes five long-face Jumeaus, which were a gift from Mrs Nancy Petrikin Menoni in 1981.

Wenham Museum

132 Main Street, Wenham, Massachusetts 01984, USA
Tel. (1) 978 468 2377 www.wenhammuseum.org
Tue-Sun 10am-4pm

This rotating permanent exhibit features 1,000 of the 5,000 dolls in this world-famous doll collection. The exhibit focuses on the history of dolls and doll making with examples of European and American dolls ranging from the late 18th century to the present day. Among the many highlights are a late 18th-century wooden Suzanna Holyoke doll with original costume and wig in her original wallpaper storage box; a late 19th-century bisque costumed mechanical doll; dolls by Joel Ellis, Grenier, and Izannah Walker; and examples of 20th-century collectible dolls by Vogue, Madame Alexander, and the Ideal Toy Company. There is an important group of American cloth dolls, and rare 19th-century Native American and Inuit dolls. On permanent display is the International Doll Collection. Exhibited for charity around the world, it forms the nucleus of the museum's original doll collection. Noteworthy is the peg wooden doll from 1897, donated by Queen Victoria and believed to have been one of her childhood dolls; a doll carved of walrus ivory and brought from Greenland by the Perry Relief Ship in 1900; African figures sent by Cecil Rhodes; and dolls from the personal collection of Elizabeth of Romania. A significant sub-collection in the 20th-century holdings is that of the Medford, Massachusetts firm founded by Jenny Graves, the producer of one of the most popular dolls of the postwar period. The dolls' houses, miniature rooms, settings, and playsets are equally exceptional, making this collection one not to be missed.

Rosalie Whyel Museum of Doll Art

1116 108th Avenue NE, Bellevue, Washington 98004, USA
Tel. (1) 425 455 1116 www.dollart.com
Mon-Sat 10am-5pm, Sun 1-5pm

The emphasis here is on the history of the doll from prehistoric through to contemporary times, with over 1,200 dolls of all nationalities on permanent display. In 1994 it was awarded the prestigious French Jumeau Trophy for Best Private Doll Museum in the world. Most fascinating perhaps are the dolls made from animal skulls. There is also an extensive library.

Windsor Castle

Windsor, Berkshire SL4 1NJ, UK
Tel. (44) 1753 868286 www.royalresidences.com
Daily 10am-5.30pm

A miniature mansion
from Puebla, Mexico,
c. 1890
*Washington Dolls' House
and Toy Museum*

Designed by Sir Edward Lutyens in the 1920s for Queen
Mary, this is certainly one of the most impressive dolls'
houses in the world. Built to a 1:12 scale with the help of
1,000 craftspeople, it was presented to the Queen to help
raise funds for charity. It is a wonder of minuscule engineering, complete with electric lights, two working lifts,
plumbed closets, a gramophone, running water, and even
miniature bottles of wine in its cellar.

PUPPETS

Alfa Teatro
The Alfa Theatre
Via Casalborgone, 16/1, 10132 Turin, Italy
Tel. (39) 011 8193529
Mon-Sat 3.30-7pm

This theatre is home to over 5,000 puppets from the collection of Augusto Grilli,
founder and president of the Alfa Association. Made from every conceivable material,
several belonged to famous artists including Lupi, Colla, Gambarutti, and Lauro. Some
date from as early as 1600 and include the traditional marionette puppets. Also featured
are those from other parts of the world where puppetry is popular such as Greece,
Turkey, France, and Indonesia. A vast library is filled with books, paper theatres, costumes,
and related accessories.

Ballard Institute and Museum of Puppetry
University of Connecticut, School of Fine Arts, Depot Campus, 6 Bourn Place, U-212,
Storrs, Connecticut 06269, USA
Tel. (1) 860 486 4605 www.sp.uconn.edu
Apr-Nov: Fri-Sun noon-5pm. Groups at other times by appt.

The treasures in this museum include puppets made by the university students, and
donations from world-famous puppeteers from all over the world. Miniatures of the
original puppets, Spebiel and Hurvinek, created by Josef Skrupa, the leading puppeteer
in Czechoslovakia in the 1930s, are on display. Don't miss the dramatic examples of
Javanese shadow puppets belonging to Wayang drama performances such as the Demon
King and the Prince with the Pink Face.

Museum of Childhood at Bethnal Green
Cambridge Heath Road, London E2 9PA, UK
Tel. (44) 20 8983 5200 www.vam.ac.uk
Mon-Thu, Sat-Sun 10am-5.50pm

This extensive puppet collection features a magnificent 18th-century Venetian marionette
theatre with characters from the Commedia dell'Arte and a rare example of hand puppets,
carved and painted by David Jones in 1922 for Eric Gill's children. Punch and Judy are
well represented, along with many examples of work by English puppet-makers such as
Gair Wilkinson, Mary Bligh Bond, and John Bickerdike. String-puppets from Burma,
examples from Eastern Europe, German shadow puppets by Lotte Reiniger, bunraku
puppets from Japan, and hide puppets from Turkey make up this international collection.

Center for Puppetry Arts
1404 Spring Street at 18th, Atlanta, Georgia 30309, USA
Tel. (1) 404 8733089 www.puppet.org
Mon-Sat 9am-5pm

One of the largest centres in the US devoted to this art offers daily workshops and adult education classes. All the well-known names and characters are represented here, including Punch and Judy, Jim Henson's Muppets, Madame of 'Wayland', and hundreds of others from around the world.

Château Musée de Nohant – Maison de George Sand
The Castle Museum of Nohant – The George Sand House
Château de Nohant, 36400 Nohant-Vic, France
Tel. (33) 2 54 31 06 04
Summer: daily 9am-12.15pm, 2-6.30pm. Winter: daily 10am-12.15pm, 2-4.30pm

A fascinating collection of 150 puppets made by George Sand's son, fashioned from lime wood and with delicately designed costumes and natural hair.

Cheltenham Art Gallery and Museum
Clarence Street, Cheltenham, Gloucestershire GL50 3JT, UK
Tel. (44) 1242 237431 www.cheltenham.gov.uk
Mon-Sat 10am-5.20pm

Home to a small but fine collection of puppets by the painter and wood carver, William Simmonds who began making puppets around 1912, and together with his wife held professional puppet shows in the 1920s and 30s. A superb example of his talent is the horse and wagon puppet. The wagon is a working model of oak and plywood. The horse, carved in wood, has a mane, tail, harness, and saddle made of leather, fabric, and string.

The Chicago Historical Society
Clark Street at North Avenue, Chicago, Illinois 60614-6099, USA
Tel. (1) 312 642 4600 www.chicagohistory.org
Mon-Sat 9.30am-4.40pm

Puppets from the 1950's daily television show featuring Kukla, Fran, and Ollie created by Burr Tillstrom are on display here. These puppets were the inspiration for later programs such as the Muppets and Sesame Street.

Deutsches Ledermuseum / Schuhmuseum Offenbach
The German Leather Museum / Shoe Museum of Offenbach
Frankfurter Strasse 86, 63067 Offenbach, Germany
Tel. (49) 69 8297980 www.dhm.de
Daily 10am-5pm

A superb collection of shadow puppets from Thailand, India, China, Indonesia, Egypt, and Turkey. Cut with precision from the finest parchment and often vividly painted, these one-dimensional puppets are operated by rods from below, and set against a translucent back-lit screen. Don't miss the set of Chinese shadow puppets that belonged to the 18th-century Emperor Qian-long, or some of the very large Thai shadow figures.

Dockteaterbiblioteket i Västra Frölunda
The Puppet Theatre Library in Västra Frölunda
Frölunda Arts Centre, 42121 Västra Frölunda, Gothenburg, Sweden
Tel. (46) 31 851760 www.frolunda.kulturhus.goteborg.se
Mon-Thu 10am-7pm, Fri 10am-4pm

Annette Cegrell-Sköld spent years fund-raising and gathering books from specialist shops, publishers, and museums to put together this superb puppet book collection and the Figure and Puppet Theatre Centre. The historical classics in new editions are fascinating, such as Heinrich von Kleist's 19th-century essay on marionette theatre, or Charlie Magnin's book on the history of European marionette theatre.

Mouseío ellenikís laïkís tekhnis
Museum of Greek Folk Art
Kydathinaion 17, Plaka, 10558 Athens, Greece
Tel. (30) 1 3229031
Tue-Sun 10am-2pm

Richly traditional, the museum displays shadow puppets with their backdrops. Puppet theatre originated in the east and was adapted by the Karaghioze, taking their inspiration from Greek mythology and history, popular stories, and everyday life. There is an exhibition room with a reconstructed karaghiozis' screen, showing the central figures of the art.

Museo etnografico Siciliano Pitrè
The Pitrè Ethnographical Sicilian Museum
1 viale Duca degli Abruzzi, parco della Favorita, 90146 Palermo, Italy
Tel. (39) 091 7404890
Daily 8.30am-1pm, 3.30-6.30pm

This museum was founded in 1910 by Giuseppe Pitrè, considered to be the greatest scholar of Sicilian popular traditions and a distinguished author on the subject. There is a section devoted to chivalric traditions where you can find a theatre devoted to the Opera dei Pupi which includes a display of around twenty traditional puppets.

Il Museo del Falegname Tino Sana
The Tino Sana Carpentry Museum
Via Aldo Moro 6, 24030 Almenno San Bartolomeo, Italy
Tel. (39) 035 554411 www.tinosana.com
Sat 3-6pm, Sun 9.30am-noon, 3-6pm (closed Aug)

Spanning the last four centuries and carved primarily from wood, the puppets line the walls of this reproduction theatre. Among the latest acquisitions are puppets by the artist, Benedetto Ravasio, who performed on several occasions in the museum's theatre.

Historisches Museum Basel
The History Museum of Basle
Steinenberg 4, 4051 Basle, Switzerland
Tel. (41) 61 205 8600 www.historischesmuseumbasel.ch
Mon, Wed-Sun 10am-5pm

Samurai Bunraku
puppet, Japan
*The Horniman Museum
and Gardens*

On display are the painted, wooden hand puppets of Kasperl and his ghost companion, made by Carlo Böcklin, a pioneer of puppet art. The character of Kasperl was first created as a figure on the stage by Johann Joseph Laroche in the late 18th century, and was modelled on the satirist-cum-jester, Hanswurst.

The Horniman Museum and Gardens
100 London Road, London SE23 3PQ, UK
Tel. (44) 20 8699 1872 www.horniman.ac.uk
Mon-Sat 10.30am-5.30pm, Sun 2.30-5.30pm

Of special note here is the collection of ethnographic puppets. One showcase features a Christmas crib and rod puppets from Poland (20th century) complete with a cardboard crib decorated with sweet wrappings; a Samurai Bunraku puppet from Japan; several excellent examples of shadow puppets from Java, Greece, Turkey, and China; rod puppets from Java; and a pair of amusing articulated puppets from Nigeria representing the newly married Prince Charles and Princess Diana.

Musée international de la Marionnette
The International Puppet Museum
Musée Gadagne, 14 rue Gadagne, place du Petit-Collège, 69005 Lyon, France
Tel. (33) 4 78 42 03 61

Daily 10.45am-6pm

Benjamin puppet by Michael Meschke
Marionettmuseet

Guignol, the famous puppet character, was created in Lyon by Laurent Mourguet in the 19th century and the museum pays tribute to the local hero. The collection documents the art of puppet making worldwide, including English puppets and examples from the George Sand theatre. In 1955, the collection was significantly enriched with the exceptional collection of Léopold Dor.

Museo internazionale delle Marionette
The International Puppet Museum
Via Butera 1, 90100 Palermo, Italy
Tel. (39) 091 328060   www.comune.palermo.it
Mon-Fri 9am-1pm, 4-7pm, Sat 9am-1pm.

This island has long been famous for its puppet theatres. Well represented are the Sicilian puppets from Palermo, Catania, and Naples. These marionettes are controlled by an iron rod coming from the head, another rod to the sword arm, and a string to the opposite arm. The legs dangle freely and their distinctive movement is produced by a twisting and swinging of the main rod. The collection includes marionettes from Vietnam, a collection of Greek (karaghiozis) and Turkish (karagöz) shadow figures made of parchment and wood, eastern shadow figures and marionettes, and even contemporary puppets made by famous artists such as Renato Guttuso, Enrico Baj, and Tadeusz Kantor. The superb library holds books and videos on traditional puppetry from around the world.

Muzeum loutkárskych kultur
The Museum of Puppet Culture
Bretislavova 74, 53760 Chrudim, Czech Republic
Tel. (420) 455 620310   www.coprosys.cz
Apr-May, Sep: daily 9am-noon, 1-5pm. Jun-Aug: daily 9am-noon, 1-6pm
Oct-Mar: Mon-Fri 9am-noon, 1-5pm, Sat-Sun 1-5pm

Open since 1972 and housed in a magnificent Renaissance building, the core of this museum's collection is made up of the formerly private puppet collection of Professor Jana Malíka, an assiduous promoter of the art of puppeteering. He assisted in organizing key national centres for the international puppet organization UNIMA, securing several puppets from these various collections for the museum. The collection numbers around 6,000 puppets and includes 60,000 related items such as billboards, publications, programmes, manuscripts, photographs, and paintings.

Charles H. MacNider Art Museum
303 2nd Street SE, Mason City, Iowa 50401, USA
Tel. (1) 515 4213666   www.macniderart.org
Tue, Thu 10am-9pm, Wed, Fri, Sat 10am-5pm, Sun 1-5pm

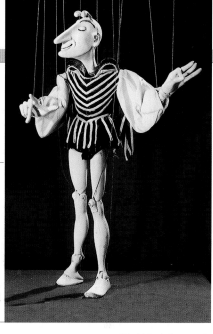

The highlight here is the collection of master puppeteer Bil Baird. During his fifty years in the business, Baird, with his wife Cora, took his puppetry art around the world, to places such as Russia, India, Nepal, and Afghanistan. He also ran a puppet theatre in Greenwich Village, New York.

Museu das Marionetas
The Puppet Museum
Largo do Rodrigo Freitas 19A, 1100 Lisbon, Portugal
Tel. (351) 22 8882841
Tue-Fri 10am-1pm, 2-7pm, Sat-Sun 11am-1pm, 2-7pm

This small, charming museum displays some 800 traditional puppets from all over the world, with special emphasis on antique Portuguese puppets. As well as guided tours, there are puppet shows in the museum's theatre which are complemented by a small library.

Museo della Marionetta
The Puppet Museum
Teatro Gianduja, via Santa Teresa 5, 11100 Turin, Italy
Tel. (39) 011 530238   www.comune.torino.it
Mon-Fri 9am-1pm, 3-5pm (by appt. only)

Mephistopheles puppet by H. Siegel 'Faust', c.1950 (above)
Marionettmuseet

Baptiste puppet by Michael Meschke, 1953 (below)
Marionettmuseet

This outstanding marionette collection was once owned by the renowned puppeteers, the Lupis family. You will find beautifully carved wooden puppets with Murano glass eyes and others with real hair wigs. Located in the Gianduja Theatre, the museum also houses a collection of stage material, backdrops, costumes, equipment, and furniture from the late 18th to the early 20th century.

Marionettmuseet
The Marionette Museum
Brunnsgatan 6, 11138 Stockholm, Sweden
Tel. (46) 8 103061
Tue-Sun 1-4pm (closed Jun & Jul)

Two floors beneath the Marionette Theatre is its museum, full of fantastic puppets. The core of the collection consists of puppets from the theatre's past performances and are primarily the work of Dr Michael Meschke, who has more than forty years experience in the art. The collection has grown steadily since the theatre began travelling the world in the 1970s, and the museum is now home to over 4,000 examples (some gifts, some purchases) from India, Japan, Indonesia, and Thailand.

Mostra dei Pupi Siciliani
The Sicilian Puppet Exhibition
c/o the old Teatro Stabile dell'Opera dei Pupi di Caltagirone,
via Discesa Verdumai 4, 95041 Caltagirone, Italy
Tel. (39) 0933 54085
Daily 10am-1pm, 3.30-9pm.

Guided tours take you around an outstanding collection of about fifty puppets belonging to the Scuola Pupara of Catania. Taller and heavier than those made in Palermo, they are constructed without articulated knees, giving them a distinctive movement. Alongside these displays are scenery boards dating from around the early 1950s, as well as pulleys, keys, and history books. There is a good selection of posters (cartelli) dating from around 1918.

Musée national des Arts et Traditions populaires
The National Museum of Folk Art and Traditions
6 ave. du Mahatma Gandhi, 75116 Paris, France
Tel. (33) 1 44 17 60 00   www.culture.fr
Mon, Wed-Sun 9.45am-5.15pm

This museum's collection of local and traditional arts was amassed after World War II by Georges-Henri Rivière. Famous puppets include the French Guignol with his son Guillaume, Gnafron, the Mère Gigogne, the Police Officer, and the Gendarme – all from the Mourguet Theater in Lyon. There are also local puppets such as Lafleur from Amiens, Jacques from Lille, and Barbizier from Besançon. A puppet theatre is on display and an audio-visual performance of the Vrai Guignolet Theatre which could once be found on the Champs Elysées.

Poppenspeelmuseum
The Puppetry Museum
Kerkweg 38, 8193 KL Vorchten, The Netherlands
Tel. (31) 578 631329   www.poppenspelmuseum.nl
Wed, Sat-Sun noon-5pm. Other times by appt.

In the small town of Vorchten, situated close to the banks of the river Ijssel between Deventer and Zwolle, is this fabulous museum. All the well-known characters are here, displayed amid illustrations, posters, photographs, slides, and an impressive collection of books on puppet-related topics. There is an extensive selection of Indonesian Wayang puppets, marionettes from several continents, glove puppets, string and rod puppets, as well as miniature paper cut out theatres and shadow theatres.

Puppentheatermuseum
The Puppet Theatre Museum
St Jakobs-Platz 1, 80331 Munich, Germany
Tel. (49) 89 23322370   www.stadtmuseum-online.de
Tue-Sun 10am-6pm, Wed 10am-8pm

Kreon doll by Michael Meschke, 1977 *Marionettmuseet*

An international collection containing around 13,000 figures, including hand puppets, marionettes, and stick and shadow figures complete with their sets, theatre decorations, and books. Founded in 1939, the museum covers all puppet-related topics from the 18th century onwards, focusing on the traditional and artistic puppet plays of Germany. There are a large number of puppets from other parts of Europe, as well as Asia and Africa.

Spatháreio mouseío theátriou skión
Spatharion Museum of Shadow Theatre
Vass Sofias & Dim Ralli Streets, Kastalias Square, 15125 Maroussi, Athens, Greece
Tel. (30) 1 6127245
Mon, Wed 10am-1.30pm, 5.30-7.30pm
Tue, Thu, Fri, Sun 10am-1.30pm

The founder of this museum, Eugenios Spatharis, and his father are puppeteers and their own work is exhibited together with shadow figures collected from Thailand, Bali, Java, and Turkey. The museum is filled with Greek shadow theatre accessories dating from around 1860 to the present. There are black and white shadow theatre figures belonging to the traditional shadow theatre of the period 1900-30, as well as shadow puppets representing deities from Greek mythology, and historical figures such as Alexander the Great.

Musée suisse de la Marionnette
The Swiss Puppet Museum
Rue de la Samaritaine 34, 1701 Fribourg, Switzerland
Tel. (41) 26 3228513 www.mcnet.ch
Jan-Jun, Sep-Dec: Sat-Sun 2-5pm. Jul-Aug: Fri-Sun 2-5pm
Mon-Fri for groups by appt.

A truly international collection of 2,000 pieces of which 200 are
displayed at any one time. Highlights include a pair of Swiss
puppets made of Ascona threads representing mermaids (20th
century); a contemporary hand and rod puppet from the Fribourg Puppet Theatre; an
Italian rod puppet, the Lady of the Camorra from Naples (19th century); a French
'castelet' with two hand puppets from the Guignol theatre, and a giant articulated bird
from Burma.

Karl Liebknecht doll by
Arne Högsander, 1972
Marionettmuseet

Musée du Théâtre Forain
The Museum of the Travelling Theatre
Quartier du Paradis, 45410 Artenay, France
Tel. (33) 2 38 80 09 73 www.coeur-de-france.com
Jun-Sep: 10am-noon, 2-5.30pm. Oct-May: 2-5.30pm

Housed in a recently refurbished farm set in the heart of Artenay, this museum documents
the cultural heritage of fairgrounds through artefacts relating to travelling puppet
theatres. Over 86 marionettes are on display including 700 costumes formerly worn by
fairground entertainers, posters, and an extensive archive of written documents.
Unique pieces include panoramas belonging to the famous Pajot puppet theatre from
the end of the 19th century; the full-size caravan of the comedian Aimé Clariond; and
etchings by Callot, representing characters and plays from the Commedia dell'Arte Balli
Sfessani (Animals' Ball).

Theatro Del Drago
The Dragon Theatre
via S. Alberto 297, 48100 Ravenna, Italy
Tel. (39) 0544 483461 www.teatrodeldrago.it
Please call for opening times

Fifty string puppets, over 100 glove puppets and around 150 paper backdrops form the
core of this collection, mainly the property of the Monticelli Family, the oldest puppeteering family in northern Italy. Many of the puppets are from the region of Piemonte, while
others are from Agostino Galliano Serra who collaborated with the Monticelli Family.
Some formerly belonged to the famous puppet theatre group, Fantocci Lirici Yambo,
founded in 1919 by Enrico Novelli.

The University of New Mexico
Fine Arts Library, Albuquerque, New Mexico 87101-1501, USA
Tel. (1) 505 2772357 www.unm.edu
Please call for opening times

The McPharlin Puppet History Collection is considered to be one of the world's largest
private libraries on the subject. The Punch and Judy section contains six early editions
of Collier Cruikshank's illustrated volumes. In addition, are works on the history of the
puppet duo as they first emerged as hero figures in Turkey and were then adopted in
Italy as Pulcinella, in France as Scarmouche, by the Russians as Petrouchka, and as the
German Kasperle. The lives of puppeteers from Mexico, Peru, Bolivia, and Argentina
are also documented.

TEDDY BEARS AND OTHER STUFFED ANIMALS

A selection of the
museum's toys
Puppenhausmuseum

The Bear Museum
38 Dragon Street, Petersfield, Hampshire GU31 4JY, UK
Tel. (44) 1730 265108   www.bearmuseum.co.uk
Tue-Sat 10am-5pm

This world-renowned collection of antique teddy bears is a widely visited reference source for arctophiles from across the globe. Mr Fluffy by the British toy company, Chad Valley, is one of the earliest bears carrying the Aerolite trademark, indicating it is stuffed with kapok, a silky fibre which comes from the seed pod of a tropical tree. This is also home to Bertie, made by Britain's oldest existing soft toy manufacturer, Dean's Rag Book Company, founded in 1903.

Museum of Childhood at Bethnal Green
Cambridge Heath Road, London E2 9PA, UK
Tel. (44) 20 8983 5200   www.vam.ac.uk
Mon-Thu, Sat-Sun 10am-5.50pm

Many English makers are represented here including the Chad Valley Company, the House of Nisbet Ltd, and Dean's & Company. As well as one of the earliest Paddington Bears, there are several wonderful examples of wartime teds dressed in uniforms identical to those of the soldiers who had left for the front. The centrepiece of the collection is the display of nine teddy bears which originally belonged to the Cattley family's five children. The family not only created all the various bear outfits themselves, including full sets of underwear from lace and velvet, but also photographed and painted them in various settings.

British Bear Collection at Banwell Castle
Banwell Castle, Banwell, Somerset BS29 6NX, UK
Tel. (44) 1934 822263
Easter-Sep: daily 11am-5pm. Oct-Easter: Sat-Sun 11am-5pm

Part of this collection was amassed by Felix Sear who spent years collecting historical information on British bear making by searching behind the scenes at factories, including Chad Valley, Dean's, Merrythought, Nisbet, and Chiltern. He gathered a representative selection of mint-condition bears from each of the ten major makers. These have joined fifteen years worth of bears of a more recent vintage collected by Carolyn Parsons.

Canterbury Heritage Museum
Poor Priests' Hospital, Stour Street, Canterbury, Kent CT1 2JE, UK
Tel. (44) 1227 452747   www.canterbury.gov.uk
Jun-Oct: Mon-Sat 10.30am-5pm, Sun 1.30-5pm

Surprising to find a Rupert Bear Gallery among Roman remains, but this is the home town of Mary Tourtel, a children's book illustrator and Rupert's creator. Her husband was an editor on the *Daily Express* and he turned to her in search of a comic strip to outdo those in the other national papers. Introduced by the paper in 1920, Rupert had become a national institution by 1932. Original artwork by the creator, along with early and modern merchandise relating to Rupert can be found here.

Museum of the City of New York
Fifth Avenue at 103rd Street, New York, New York 10029, USA
Tel. (1) 212 534 1672   www.mcny.org
Wed-Sat 10am-5pm, Sun 1-5pm, Tue 10am-2pm for booked tours

Morris Michtom was the first to name and make the teddy bear with moveable limbs and button eyes in honour of President Roosevelt, and within a year he had established himself as the Ideal Novelty and Toy Company, which was to become one of the biggest toy manufacturers in America. Among the museum's collection of over 100,000 toys and amusements are numerous stuffed toys and teddy bears. One bear, of olive-coloured mohair with green paws, dates from 1925 and was given to the museum by Paul Ludwig in memory of Renée Forsyth.

Wool plush teddy bear, Germany, *c.* 1929-40 (below)
Deutsches Historisches Museum

Teddy Clowns, 1926-28, Steiff (bottom)
Puppenhausmuseum

Deutsches Historisches Museum
The German Historical Museum
Zeughaus Unter den Linden 2, 10117 Berlin, Germany
Tel. (49) 30 215020 www.dhm.de
Mon, Tue, Thu-Sun 10am-6pm

No toy museum in Germany would be complete without stuffed toys. This collection is particularly strong on bears from the 1920s, 30s, and 40s, but the one not to pass by is the brown and beige plush mascot bear, Mischa, made in Korea for the 1980 Olympic Games in Moscow.

Donnell Library Center
20 West 53rd Street, New York, New York 10019, USA
Tel. (1) 212 621 0618 www.nypl.org
Mon, Wed-Fri noon-6pm, Tue 10am-6pm, Sat noon-5pm, Sun 1-5pm

Winne-the-Pooh, Tigger, Kanga, Eeyore, and Piglet have entertained children for generations, but the original stuffed toys from which the illustrator Ernest Howard Shepard based his inspired drawings now stare out of a glass case in New York. Although they are viewed by thousands every year, the various heritage sectors in Britain have lobbied for them to be repatriated; many feel that the famous five deserve to be closer to Christopher Robin's home in Ashdown Forest, East Sussex.

House on the Hill Toy Museum
Stansted, Essex CM24 8SP, UK
Tel. (44) 1279 813237 www.gold.enta.net
Daily 10am-4pm

The largest privately-owned toy museum in Europe oozes with the passion of its owner and founder, Mr Gold. Of the fifty or so bears housed here, a large number are by the famous English makers, there is at least one example from all of the ten major workshops.

Puppenhausmuseum
The Dolls' House Museum
Steineck-Foundation, Steinenvorstadt 1, 4051 Basle, Switzerland
Tel. (41) 61 225 9595 www.puppenhausmuseum.ch
Daily 11am-5pm. Thu 11am-8pm

Of the 2,000 teddies dating mostly from before 1950, Steiffs in cinnamon, white, brown and blonde covering several decades of manufacture are well represented, as are bears from other traditional manufacturers from America and Europe. A place of honour is given to those bears who had their heyday shortly after the turn of the century. The oldest of these dates back to 1904, and is accompanied by another especially attractive bear which was presented as a gift to a friend by President Theodore Roosevelt.

Margarete Steiff Museum

Alleenstrasse 2, 7928 Giengen-Brenz, Germany
Tel. (49) 7322 131204 www.steiff.com
Mon-Fri 1-4pm, Sat 8.30am-noon, Sun 8.30am-4pm

Steely Germanic determination took Margarete Steiff from Giengen, a small town on the River Brenz in southern Germany, and made her a household name. Polio confined her to a wheelchair so she took up sewing and needlework. She started a dressmaking company, but in 1879 it was the pattern for a toy elephant which caught her imagination and launched her second career. The company was well established by 1897, and in 1902 came up with the idea for jointed monkeys and bears. At this time an incident involving President Theodore Roosevelt was immortalized when he refused to shoot a young bear and the bear become known as 'Teddy's Bear'. The Steiffs could not have asked for more favourable circumstances. By 1907 a million teddy bears had been produced by the company. Today the museum, situated in the company headquarters, is filled with old and new animals and memorabilia associated with this success story.

The Teddy Bear Den

Dancing Bear Folk Center, 119 S. 6th Street, Highway 20, Termopolis,
Wyoming 82443, USA
Tel. (1) 307 864 9396 www.dancingbear.org
Mid May-mid Sep: daily 9am-7pm. Rest of year: daily 10am-5pm

The bears come from all over the world, and although the major manufacturers such as Steiff, Hermann-Spielwaren, Hermann-Coberg, Sigikid, Canterbury, and Merrythought are represented, the emphasis here is on artist-made bears. The Scottish Highlands display has Rob Roy and William Wallace by Kathi Burch-Snyders. There's Teddy Roosevelt and bear cub by Linda Nelson, and Buffalo Bill Cody on his favourite horse by Bev White. The history of early German, English, and American bear companies are documented, along with replica bears and historical photographs.

Teddy Bear Museum

19 Greenhill Street, Stratford-upon-Avon, Warwickshire CV37 6LF, UK
Tel. (44) 1789 293160 www.teddybearmuseum.uk.com
Daily 9.30am-6pm

Hundreds of bears from over twenty different countries are exhibited in various themed rooms. The Best of British collection has four fine old bears from three pioneer companies – Chiltern Toys, Chad Valley, and J. K. Farnell. Dean's Means Bears!, the oldest British teddy bear company, is represented, as is Merrythought of Ironbridge in Shropshire, with three examples of one of their most loved bears, Cheeky. Five Steiff bears dating from 1903-06 are among the oldest in the world.

Teddy Bear Museum of Naples

2511 Pine Ridge Road, Naples, Florida 34109, USA
Tel. (1) 941 598 2711 www.teddymuseum.com
Wed-Sat 10am-5pm, Sun 1-5pm. Times may vary, please call for details.

The museum opened in 1990 with a collection of 1,500 bears amassed by its founder, Frances Pew Hayes. Now with over 4,000 bears accompanied by paintings, sculptures, posters, and other collectibles, it must be one of the largest of its kind in the world.

Teddy Bear Shop Museum

The Ironbridge Gorge Museums, Ironbridge, Telford, Shropshire TF8 7NJ, UK
Tel. (44) 1952 433029 www.merrythought.co.uk
Daily 10am-5pm

A collection of around fifty antique bears, most made by Merrythought, are on display at the home of the prestigious toy manufacturer. In 1919, Mr Holmes went into partnership with Mr Lax and established a mill to spin mohair. As demand for the fabric declined, they needed to find something to do with their product and set up a new company with three employees from Chad Valley and J. K. Farnell, calling it Merrythought toys. Together they designed the entire first range for the company in 1930, including their now famous line of teddy bears. The factory, housed in the building adjoining the shop, opens once a year but only to members of the Merrythought International Collectors Club.

Teddy Museum Berlin
The Teddy Bear Museum of Berlin
147 Kurfürstendamm, 10709 Berlin, Germany
Tel. (49) 30 8933965
Wed-Fri 3-6pm

The Guinness Book of World Records lists this museum as the largest teddy bear museum in the world. It is the result of Florentine C. Bredow's childhood love of stuffed animals. When her family fled the country during World War II, they took only her father's bears with them, and it is these that form the core of the 3,000-strong collection.

Teddymuseum Klingenberg
The Klingenberg Teddy Museum
In der Alstadt 7, 63911 Klingenberg, Germany
Tel. (49) 9372 921167   www.t-bear.de
Mon-Fri 2-6pm, Sat-Sun 10am-6pm

This museum, established by Wolfgang and Renate Koenigh in an old inn, is a paradise for obsessed collectors. Included are Winnie the Pooh, Rupert, Petzi, Bamse, and many others by all the famous makers such as Steiff, Hermann, Bing, and Peggy Nisbet.

Toy & Teddy Bear Museum
373 Clifton Drive North, St Annes, Lytham St Annes, Lancashire FY8 2PA, UK
Tel. (44) 1253 713705
Mar-Oct: Mon, Wed-Sun 11am-5pm. Nov-Feb: Sun 10am-5pm

A small, private museum packed floor to ceiling with bears by all the leading English and German companies including Steiff, Gebruder, Chad Valley, and Bing. One of the museum's famous donations is Ernest James, a teddy purchased in 1923 at Wembley Stadium. It came via Bolton, in the year when the Cup Final was played between Bolton Wanderers and West Ham. Since its arrival at the museum its fame has not diminished.

'General Store' cupboard, *c.* 1840
Puppenhausmuseum

Wiener Teddybärenmuseum
The Vienna Teddy Bear Museum
1 Drahtgasse 3, 1010 Vienna, Austria
Tel. (43) 1 533 4755   www.teddybear.org
Mon-Sat 10am-6pm, Sun 2-6pm

A stunning private collection of antique teddies from all over the world, spanning the period 1905-60. The usual stuffed variety share space with somersaulting wind-up bears, china bears, and one of the very earliest battery-operated bears made before World War I. Located in a baroque house five minutes walk from Saint Stephen's cathedral, it is well worth a visit.

TIN AND CAST-IRON TOYS

Tin figures with
suitcases
Museu do Brinquedo

Musée des Arts et Métiers
The Museum of Arts and Crafts
60 rue Réaumur, 75003 Paris, France
Tel. (33) 1 53 01 82 00   www.cnam.fr
Tue, Wed, Fri-Sun 10am-6pm, Thu 10am-9.30pm

Designed by Fernand Martin, this collection of over 100 mechanical tin toys displays his knowledge and skill to perfection. In 1878 he founded a toy company which produced simple, inexpensive mechanical tin toys. Some were driven by twisted rubber bands or wheels that had to be wound by hand, but gradually Martin developed more sophisticated clock mechanisms to bring his figures to life.

Museum of Childhood at Bethnal Green
Cambridge Heath Road, London E2 9PA, UK
Tel. (44) 20 8983 5200   www.vam.ac.uk
Mon-Thu, Sat-Sun 10am-5.50pm

A fine selection of clockwork toys, with items by the German firms Bing, Märklin, Lehmann, and Carette dominating the collections. Notable examples include the marvellous engine and tender by Carette of Nuremberg (*c.* 1910), and the clockwork car made by Bing in the 1920s. Die-cast toys include examples by Hornby and Lesney, famous for their Dinky and Matchbox vehicles. A must-see is an early die-cast model of the racing car *Bluebird* (William Britain and Co., 1935), which the English driver Malcolm Campbell made famous when he broke the land speed record.

Museu do Brinquedo
The Museum of Toys
Rua Visconde de Monserrate, 2710 Sintra, Portugal
Tel. (351) 21 910 6016   www.museu-do-brinquedo.pt
Tue-Sun 10am-6pm

Arbués Moreira's obsession with toys has grown into a collection which now stands at over 20,000 items. An outstanding tin toy collection includes everything from simple, wind-up toys to battery-operated ones. A fleet of German tin battleships from World War I reflects Portugal's close links with Germany. Thousands of Dinky toys on display include substantial Bugattis and Ferraris, as well as various model Citroëns which the company used in the 1930s to attract potential buyers – by offering their children a miniature version.

Centre Tomi Ungerer
The Tomi Ungerer Centre
4 rue de la Haute-Montée, 67000 Strasbourg, France
Tel. (33) 3 88 32 31 54   www.musees-strasbourg.org
Thu 10am-noon, 2-6pm by appt. only.

Alongside works relating to the career of Tomi Ungerer, the Strasbourg cartoonist, writer and illustrator, is a vast collection of about 6,000 toys and games amassed by the artist himself. Highlights among the mechanical and cast-iron toys are the battleship Oregon, manufactured by Märklin in 1898, a fine selection of tin toys by Lehmann and Martin, and an enchanting range of toys made by the artist himself for his children.

Museum of Childhood Memories
1 Castle Street, Beaumaris, Anglesey, Gwynedd LL58 8AP, Wales, UK
Tel. (44) 1248 712 498   www.nwi.co.uk
Apr-Nov: daily 10.30am-5.30pm

Robert Brown, a former mechanical engineer turned antique collector and dealer, has a remarkable collection including over 200 banks, around forty of which are mechanical (mainly of cast iron), the rest made of tin. Of the clockwork tin-plate toys, German and English makers dominate, although there are several exquisite items by French makers and some by the better known American firms. Two of the owner's favourites pieces are an American sand toy complete with buckets and a weight; and the *Golden Arrow* racing car made to commemorate Major Seagrave's historic race in 1933.

Scooter, 1955 (below)
Deutsches Historisches Museum

Levy motocycle with side-car, 1930-35 (bottom)
Holstebro Museum

Museum of the City of New York

Fifth Avenue at 103rd Street, New York, New York 10029, USA
Tel. (1) 212 534 1672 www.mcny.org
Wed-Sat 10am-5pm, Sun 1-5 pm, Tue 10am-2pm for booked tours

This massive collection, ranging from the Colonial period to the present day, includes a plethora of tin and cast-iron toys of all types. The US was a pioneer in the field of tin toy production. This collection is rich in examples of the wheeled horse-drawn vehicles made famous by the firm Stevens & Brown. In the late 19th and early 20th centuries the US began to use cast iron. Examples representing this are experimental iron banks by Stevens & Brown which incorporated figures activated by the insertion of a coin.

Deutsches Historisches Museum
The German Historical Museum
Zeughaus Unter den Linden 2, 10117 Berlin, Germany
Tel. (49) 30 215020 www.dhm.de
Mon, Tue, Thu-Sun 10am-6pm

It was the advent of firms such as Hess, Bing, and later Gebrüder Märklin of Göppingen who radically transformed the tin toy industry. Once cottage-based, it soon became a factory-based, mass-production industry adopting methods of cutting and stamping, along with new methods in decorative techniques, including the introduction of stencils and the application of chromolithography to the tin. After 1880 these changes allowed the German manufacturers to eclipse the American firms and to become the leading players in the market. Tin models of steam engines with accessory figures include the splendid example, Arbeiter mit Säge (Worker with Saw), a 1920s lacquered tin-plate figure made by Märklin of Göppingen. There are examples of tin toys from other countries too, such as the tin-plate, plastic, lithographed VW Beetle made by Bandai of Tokyo around 1965.

Holstebro Museum
The Museum of Holstebro
Museumsvej 2, Postboks 1240, 7500 Holstebro, Denmark
Tel. (45) 97 42293 www.holstebro-museum.dk
Jul-Aug: Fri-Sun 11am-5pm.
Sep-Jun: Fri 11am-5pm, Sat-Sun noon-4pm

Donated by the Danish architect Hans Dissing, this prize collection of 700 tin toys stands together with 3,000 items consisting mostly of tin cars, motorbikes, trains, and ships dating from the late 1800s to the 1950s. Of special interest are the mechanical tin toys by the German, Paul Lehmann, dating from around 1920. There are also examples by Märklin, Günthermann, Meccano, Hess, Hornby, Wells, Arnold, Wittrock, and a fine collection of Tekno from 1935. Robots and space toys produced by the Japanese are also well represented.

Incredibly Fantastic Old Toy Show
26 Westgate, Lincoln, LN1 3BD, UK
Tel. (44) 1522 520534
Tue-Sat 11am-5pm, Sun & public holidays noon-4pm. (times may vary, please call for details)

Robots dominate in this 1950-60 collection, including Robby from *The Forbidden Planet*, Starstrider, High Gear, Mr Machine, and a giant shop display model made from Meccano. Mainly battery-powered and made from tin-plate (some in plastic) they show a wonderful inventiveness and style. There are also space items from *Buck Rodgers*, *Flash Gordon* and *Dan Dare*, as well as more modern sci-fi toys such as those from *Dr Who* and *Star Wars*.

The Kentucky Museum
The Kentucky Building, Western Kentucky University, One Big Red Way, Bowling Green, Kentucky 42101, USA
Tel. (1) 270 745 2592   www.wku.edu
Tue-Sat 9.30am-4pm, Sun 1-4pm. (researchers may view archives by appt. only)

Based on the collection donated by Orbra E. King are an impressive number of still banks, including 75 cast-iron, glass, and ceramic examples. Collectors will find a model of Independence Hall patented in 1875 by Enterprise Manufacturing Company of Philadelphia, and Buster Brown & Tige, probably made by the A.C. Williams Company between 1910 and 1930. The lithographed tin toys date from the 1930s-50s, with examples from Louis Marx & Company and the Unique Art Company, among others. Examples from the 1930s include the Charleston Trio and Hercules Ferris Wheel, with postwar toys featuring Lil' Abner and the Dogpatch Band, and Shoot-a-Loop.

Museum of London
London Wall, London EC2Y 5HN, UK
Tel. (44) 20 7600 3699   www.museumoflondon.org.uk
Tue-Sat 10am-5.50pm, Sun noon-5.50pm

Lehmann mechanical monkey, string operated with articulated arms, Aben Tom, 1945-50
Holstebro Museum

This museum houses a collection of toys of national importance – the 1918 Ernest King collection of 1,703 penny toys which were bought by King directly from street pedlars. The importance of this collection lies partly in the detailed documentation that came with it. The toys themselves are charming – small tin figures of people and animals produced very cheaply for a mass market. Most were made by German firms and some bear German inscriptions, but the trade came to an end during World War I when all commercial links with that country were severed. Only a small selection are on display; others can be seen by appointment.

Porvoon nukke- ja lelumuseo
The Porvoo Doll and Toy Museum
Jorma Söderlund, Jokikatu 14, 06100 Porvoo, Finland
Tel. (358) 19 582941   www.kolumbus.fi
Mon-Sat 11am-3.30pm, Sun noon-3.30pm

Founded in 1974 by Evi Söderlund, this collection includes mechanical tin toys and cast-iron banks, among them American wind-up tin toys and German hand-painted and lithographed tin and sheet metal toys.

David Pressland's Collection of Tin Toys
London W2, UK
Tel. (44) 20 7262 2701   www.artofthetintoy.com
Registered groups or serious collectors by appt. only.

An exceptional collection amassed over forty years by the avid collector and dealer in tin toys, David Pressland. It consists primarily of toys manufactured by German companies (because they possess 'not only quality, but soul'), with rare and whimsical examples of cars, boats, carousels, trains, and train accessories by Märklin, Bing, Rock & Graner, Lutz, Günthermann, and Plank. Author of three definitive works on tin toys, Pressland is generous with his vast knowledge of the subject and his enthusiasm for these diminutive works of art is boundless.

Passengership *Nederland*, probably Märklin
c. 1910
Speelgoed en Blikmuseum

Casige miniature sewing machine, Germany, 1950-60
Speelgoedmuseum Mechelen

Rockwell Museum

Cedar Street at Denison Parkway, Corning, New York 14830, USA
Tel. (1) 607 937 5386   www.stny.com
Mon-Sat 9am-5pm, Sun noon-5pm

American and European cast-iron and tin toys grace the galleries of this museum founded by Robert and Hertha Rockwell. Look out for the rail pump car with a wind-up mechanism made by Girard Model Work (Girard, Pennsylvania), as well as the amusing lithographed tin-plate wind-ups by Lehmann Co. (Brandenburg, Germany). There are numerous cast-iron banks and a printed cast-iron and steel Stichwell miniature sewing machine with its original box (*c.* 1923). Other beauties include the Buddy 'L' fire trucks (*c.* 1925) and a Schoenhut circus by the American wooden toy manufacturer.

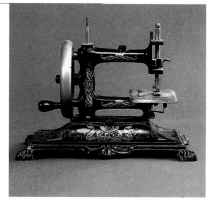

Speelgoed en Blikmuseum
The Toy and Tin Museum
Brink 47, 7411 BV Deventer, The Netherlands
Tel. (31) 570 69 37 86   www.deventer.nl
Please call for opening times

The firm of Thomassen en Drijver Verblifa maintained a historical tin packing collection, now on permanent display. See the stunning example of a tin-plate passenger boat by Märklin. Several notable pieces by Lehmann include the Echo clockwork motorcyclist. At the turn of the 20th century, the French and the Germans ingeniously concealed clockwork mechanisms within tin-plate bodies. This golden age produced whimsical toys with several motions, achieved by incorporating cams and cranked shafts. Some were hand-enamelled and later, lithographed. After 1930 the novelty tin toy took off, influenced by popular cartoon characters. The firm Schuco produced a range of clockwork animals, an example of which is featured in the collection, as is the key wind figure of Pinocchio on a bike by the Italian firm INGAP (Industria Nazionale Giocattoli Automatici Padua), and the clown doing a handstand by the firm Köhler.

Speelgoedmuseum Mechelen
The Mechelen Toy Museum
Nekkerspoel 21, 2800 Mechelen, Belgium
Tel. (32) 15 55 7075   www.speelgoedmuseum.be
Tue-Sun 10am-5pm

Around 3,400 mechanical tin toys and cast-iron objects are on display by German makers such as Issmayer, Kiensberger & Co, Plank, and Märklin. Modern toys include examples by Tucher & Walther who started making mechanical toys in 1979, as well as some Japanese and American companies who were among several of the dominant tin-toy producing countries of the 20th century. Cast-iron banks, miniature sewing machines, and typewriters are well represented.

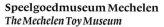

Early motor car
Museu do Brinquedo

Spielzeugmuseum
The Toy Museum
Alten Rathausturm, Marienplatz 15, 80331 Munich, Germany
Tel. (49) 89 294001
Daily 10am-5.30pm

Opened in 1983, this is part of the private collection of the caricaturist, Ivan Steiger. Highlights include the beautiful and rare collection of hand-painted clockwork toys from the US, Germany, and France. A vast display of old technical toys includes steam engines, carousels, and tin figures. There are tin cars by Lehmann, Schuco models, Märklin construction kits, clockwork planes, zeppelins and cars, technical toys from World War I and the postwar era, and toy trains with steam and electric engines by Märklin and Bing.

Spielzeugmuseum
The Toy Museum
Haus 'Zum Schwarzen Garten', Stüssihofstatt 9, 8001 Zurich, Switzerland
Tel. (41) 1 2514777   www.zurichtourism.ch
By appt. only

Christian and Claudia Depuoz's collection, dating from the 19th century onwards, covers all varieties of toy making. The collection of tin-plate toys contains examples from the big German makers, including Ernst Paul Lehmann of Brandenburg, the best known early producer of lithographed tin-plate novelty toys. There is a rare steam-driven fire hose on wheels by Jean Schoenner of Nuremberg (*c.* 1895) complete with a brass boiler, spoked flywheels, and a single burner on a cast-iron base. A 1900 Günthermann model Peugeot car with driver and real rubber tyres commissioned by the company to assist with selling their full-size vehicles is also of note, as is the fine selection of flat tin toy figures.

Spielzeug-Museum Nürnberg
The Toy Museum of Nuremberg
Kalrstrasse 13-15, 90403 Nuremberg, Germany
Tel. (49) 911 2313164   www.nuremberg.de
Tue-Sun 10am-5pm, Wed 10am-9pm

In the heart of Nuremberg's Old Town lies the product of several decades of collecting by Lydia and Paul Bayer. Along with an immense doll collection the museum boasts a great selection of technical toys from a cross-section of Nuremberg's tradition of toy making. Examples of iron toys include magic lanterns, film projectors, dancing figures, steam engines, and toy trains. All of the big names connected to tin toy production are represented here.

The Strong Museum
One Manhatten Square, Rochester, New York, 14607, USA
Tel. (1) 716 263 2700   www.strongmuseum.org
Mon-Sat 10am-5pm (Fri until 8pm), Sun noon-5pm

Margaret Woodbury Strong's eccentric collection focuses on toys made in the US from 1820-1996, as well as those from the larger manufacturers based in Germany, France, England, and Japan. The collection of tin and cast iron includes lithographed tin-plate clockwork-powered trains and stations by Ives Manufacturing Company of Bridgeport, Connecticut; tin and sheet metal toy trolley cars by Clark & Boyer of Dayton, Ohio (*c.* 1905); and lithographed wind-up toys by J. Chein & Company, Harrison, NY (*c.* 1932). Of particular note is the toy battleship manufactured by Gebrüder Märklin (*c.* 1912) and the tin toys made in America between 1920 and 1940 by the innovative firm Louis Marx. For many collectors the prize cast-iron toys are vehicles, especially the horse-drawn ones produced from the 1880s-1930s; impressive examples held here are those by Hubley.

Toy Museum

Whitefriars Gate, Much Park Street, Coventry, West Midlands CB1 2LT, UK
Tel. (44) 1203 227560
Apr-Oct: daily noon-6pm. Nov-Mar: Sat-Sun noon-5pm.

The history of this building, constructed in 1352 and part of the Whitefriars Gate, is as intriguing as the collections held within it. Queen Elizabeth I and King James I were both received here. It later became a dwelling house for the poor, then a weaver's house, a butcher's, and a draper's. A diverse range of toys including a great selection of tin-plate toys are now housed here. Boats, battleships, motorcycles, wind-up walking figures, aeroplanes, roundabouts, and cars jostle for space. The majority are by the famous German makers Bing, Hess, and Märklin, with some by English and American companies. Alongside are modern examples of tin-plate toys from Spain, Czechoslovakia, Hungary, and Japan, including a number of Japanese robots.

Museo valenciano del Juguete de Ibi
The Valencian Toy Museum of Ibi
Caballero, 4, 03440 Ibi, Alicante, Spain
Tel. (34) 9 66 55 02 26
Tue-Sat 10am-1pm, 4-7pm, Sun & public holidays 11am-2pm

The Payá tinsmith family history is documented here in their outstanding collection. Ice suppliers by trade, they travelled around Europe looking for popular toys, buying two of each and bringing them home to copy. They would dissect one to discover how it was constructed and keep the other as a sample. By 1909 not only were they a profitable tin toy-making company, but owners of a valuable collection of toys, too. There are locomotives with spring-loaded mechanisms (*c.* 1920) and electric trains from the 1940-50s, many made by Spanish companies including Electrotren of Madrid. The ingenuity behind these toys is demonstrated by the charming fire truck of Tip & Company (Germany 1920s) – a hidden hone is connected with the mechanism so that as it rotates sparks fly into the air.

Wenham Museum

132 Main Street, Wenham, Massachusetts 01984, USA
Tel. (1) 978 468 2377   www.wenhammuseum.org
Tue-Sun 10am-4pm

An important subcollection here is the group of mechanical toys, many of tin and cast-iron banks. The bulk of the collection came from Mrs E. H. Osgood and consists of pre-1914 clockwork toys and battery-operated ones from the 1940s onwards. The cast-iron bank holdings from the 19th century is small, but all are in mint condition. Most of the important tin-plate toys from American manufacturers date from the 20th century, as do those made in Japan. Important items include Powerful Katrinka and Little Jimmy from the Toonerville Trolley comics, the key-wind Charlie Chaplin, and the Japanese-made Space Scout. Several key items of automata include an example of the 'Autoperitapakos'; a walking doll that pushes a carriage; a French swimming doll; and two dancing dolls by the New England manufacturer Ives.

Toy car, 1910
Speelgoed en Blikmuseum

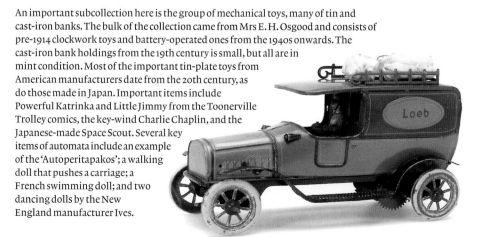

TOY SOLDIERS

Musée de l'Armée
The Army Museum
Hôtel National des Invalides, 129 rue de Grenelle, 75007 Paris, France
Tel. (33) 1 44 42 37 72 www.invalides.org
Apr-Sep: daily 10am-6pm. Oct-Mar: daily 10am-5pm

Knight on horse by
Engels, Verden
*Deutsches Zinnfiguren
Museum*

One of the richest known collections of figurines, unfortunately not shown en masse but scattered among the museum's other collections. Along with the Germans, the French were major manufacturers of toy figures, producing fully rounded, solid lead figures as early as 1790. Examples by the best of the French firms are here, among them Lucotte and CBG Mignot of Paris (who took over the firm of Lucotte in 1825). The collection is especially strong on French and German figurines from the second half of the 19th century, highlights of which include: the Würtz Collection of approximately 16,000 'petits soldats d'Alsace', representing soldiers of the First Republic; the De Ridder Collection of 93,000 lead soldiers, made in Heinrichsen in Nuremberg and Allegeyer in Fürth; and the Leclercq Collection of 1,300 soldiers and thirteen carriages manufactured by CBG Mignot from 1920-1940, representing French armies from the 17th-20th centuries.

Museum of Childhood at Bethnal Green
Cambridge Heath Road, London E2 9PA, UK
Tel. (44) 20 8983 5200 www.vam.ac.uk
Mon-Thu, Sat-Sun 10am-5.50pm

A wonderful collection of soldiers and other lead figures by Heinrichsen of Nuremberg (1850-70) and the UK firm Britains, who revolutionized the field with the introduction of hollow-cast figures. Lighter and cheaper than solids and far more realistic than flats, these figures were soon being exported throughout the world – even to Germany. There are forts, too, including one made of wood and printed paper probably manufactured in Germany around 1910. Keep in mind that these figures were not only used as toys but often employed in war games by kings and generals for replaying famous battles or for working out war strategies.

Blenheim Palace
Woodstock, Oxfordshire OX20 1PX, UK
Tel. (44) 1993 811325 www.blenheimpalace.com
Mar-Oct: daily 10.30am-5.30pm

Home of the 11th Duke of Marlborough and birthplace of Sir Winston Churchill, this fine English baroque palace was designed by Vanbrugh, with 2,100 acres of parkland landscaped by 'Capability' Brown. Among the fine tapestries, paintings, and sculptures is a unique collection of Napoleonic troops by the French firm of Lucotte. Capitalizing on the demand for more realistic figures, Lucotte became known for their solid, fully rounded toy soldiers depicting units of the French Imperial Army (made in the later half of the 18th and early 19th centuries). They issued a wide range of troops representing various conflicts from the Napoleonic wars (1792-1815). Identified by the Imperial bee which is stamped on the underside of the base, the figures are highly collectable.

The British Model Soldier Society's National Collection
Hatfield House, Hatfield, Hertfordshire AL9 5NQ, UK
Tel. (44) 1707 26 28 23 www.eastbournemuseums.co.uk
End Mar-beg Oct: Tue-Sat noon-5pm, Sun 1-4.30pm

A grand setting for one of the finest collections of model soldiers in the world. In 1986 the collection received the Bamford bequest, an immense collection of soldiers featuring large numbers of mint-condition Britains. Look out for the monumental display of the

Trooping of the Colour Ceremony made by the National Collection Curator, which took two and a half years to complete. Other major bequests have come from the collections of the late Robert John Grazie and Jack Higgs. The enormous display of Britains is complemented by items from other well-known makers such as Heyde and Elastolin. A smaller part of the collection is housed at the Sussex Combined Services Museum and Redoubt Fortress in Eastbourne (see next entry).

The British Model Soldier Society's National Collection
Sussex Combined Services Museum and Redoubt Fortress, Royal Parade, Eastbourne, East Sussex BN22 7AQ, UK
Tel. (44) 1323 41 03 00 www.eastbournemuseums.co.uk
Please call for opening times

A museum which preserves uniforms, medals, and other military artefacts telling the history of the local regiments and the Queen's Royal Irish Hussars. Themes are wide ranging, from ancient Roman and medieval armies to the American infantry. The Royal Navy is represented, as are items from the Bamford collection of Britains. The new gloss toy soldiers can be seen here, several types of which are no longer available. Flats are on display, and recently a display of naval uniform models was added.

The Anne S. K. Brown Military Collection
The John Hay Library, 20 Prospect Street, Brown University, Providence, Rhode Island 02912, USA
Tel. (1) 401 863 2414 www.brown.edu
Mon-Fri 9am-5pm

It was while she was on honeymoon in Europe in 1930 that Mrs Brown purchased a number of lead soldiers which she intended to display in her house. The majority were by the famous makers of the day, including Britains, Heyde, and Mignot. By the time the museum inherited the collection in 1981-82, it consisted of more than 5,000 figures. A donation of 66 sets of Britains' miniatures have recently been added. Among this swirl of toy soldiers are commissioned items depicting units of the United States Militia of the 1830s and 1840s, modelled after Huddy and Duval from plates in the *United States Military Magazine*.

Century Village Museum
Geauga County Historical Society, 14653 East Park Street, Burton, Ohio 44021, USA
Tel. (1) 440 834 1492
May-Oct for guided tours (please call for times)

Knight by Engels, Verden
Deutsches Zinnfiguren Museum

A glorious collection of over 7,000 toy soldiers housed in the Hickox Brick House (named after its owner Eleazer Hickox whose association with Burton goes back to 1805). The collection of soldiers were a gift from Mr and Mrs Lyle Thoburn, many of them hand painted by Mr Thoburn himself over the forty years he collected them. The soldiers represent troops from Greek and Roman days through to World War II.

Deutsches Zinnfiguren Museum
The German Tin Figure Museum
Plassenburg, 95326 Kulmbach, Germany
Tel. (49) 9221 95880 www.zinnfigurenmuseum.de
Daily 10am-5pm

Housed in the Plassenburg Castle is the largest collection of tin figures in the world: more than 300,000 pieces arranged in some 250 three-dimensional dioramas. Founded in 1926 by a group of local enthusiasts, the collections contain metal figures produced by almost all the important makers. The Parisian Mignot donated their entire collection to the museum in 1988. Look out for the figures made by Heinrichsen (1806-88) and those by Allgeyer in Bavaria.

'Tradition' figures by
Cornelius Fraser (above)
*Nationaal Tinnen Figuren
Museum*

A Dutch hussar officer by
Cornelius Fraser,
c. 1900 (below)
*Nationaal Tinnen Figuren
Museum*

Le Musée de la Figurine historique
The Museum of the Historical Figurine
28 place de l'Hôtel de Ville, 60200 Compiègne, France
Tel. (33) 3 44 40 72 55
Tue-Sat 9am-noon, 2-6pm, Sun 2-6pm (times may vary, please call for details)

This collection of 100,000 figurines started with a bequest from Alfred Ternisien in 1927 and steadily grew to include tin, lead, wood, plastic, cardboard, and papier-mâché figures from the 18th-20th centuries. Some of the most important dioramas focus on Napoleon's military movements, the highlight of which is a model of the Battle of Waterloo containing 12,000 figures by Charles Laurent made between 1905 and 1923. There are dioramas representing the Battle of Dettinghem and the Battle of Austerlitz. Escorts of antique soldiers represent the Scythian, Parthian, Mede, and Egyptian cavalries. Also, the King's armies: the Lansquenets (15th century) and the Pikeman (early 16th century).

Le Musée de la Figurine-Jouet
The Toy Soldier Museum
Cave Gratien & Meyer, 22 Route de Montsoreau, 49400 Saumur, France
Tel. (33) 2 41 83 13 32 www.gratienmeyer.com
Mid Sep-mid Jun: daily 9am-noon, 2-6pm. Mid Jun-mid Sep: daily 9am-6.30pm

The collection of Edouard Pemzec, which today stands at around 40,000 pieces, was previously shown in the Château de Saumur. When Pemzec retired in 1994 he bought the CBG Mignot & Lucotte company, the last French manufacturer of toy soldiers. Most of the collections focus on soldiers produced in France, with examples by the figurine maker Alexandre. The manufacturers Quiralu and Boersch are also particularly well represented. There are figurines made of lead, aluminium, wood, paper, and skin. Highlights include a display devoted to Vertunni, containing the entire range of the company's products, and a group of German wood figurines which are thought to have once belonged to Louis II of Bavaria. Other collections featuring foreign figurines such as the English-made Britains and Marlborough, the German-made Heyde, and those by the Spanish firm Palomeque can be seen by appointment.

Forbes Magazine Galleries
62 Fifth Avenue at 12th Street, New York, New York 10011, USA
Tel. (1) 212 206 5548
Tue, Wed, Fri, Sat 10am-4pm

This collection contains an eccentric display of over 12,000 toy soldiers of different styles and eras set in an elaborate tableaux and accompanied by music. It was organized by the late Malcom S. Forbes, the editor-in-chief and chairman of *Forbes* magazine, who purchased his first set of figures at auction in the late 1960s and who went on to assemble a collection unlike any other. There are military and civilian figures from Britains, dimestore figures from America, and examples by Heyde, Elastolin, Heinrichsen, and Minot of France.

Germanisches Nationalmuseum
The German National Museum
Kartäusergasse 1, 90402 Nuremberg, Germany
Tel. (49) 911 13310 www.gnm.de
Tue, Thu-Sun 10am-5pm, Wed 10am-9pm

Within this general museum is an extensive collection of tin figures from the 18th and 19th centuries, many by Ernst Heinrichsen dating from 1840 to 1910. As early as 1578, the business of producing toy soldiers had become so massive that the Council of Nuremberg had to step in and impose regulations. By the 1840s it was Heinrichsen, one of Nuremberg's most famous manufacturers, who obtained more or less universal agreement on the present standard height of 30mm for figures, opening the way for collectors who wanted to amass soldiers from various manufacturers.

Guards Museum

Wellington Barracks, Birdcage Walk, London SW1E 6HQ, UK
Tel. (44) 20 7414 3271
Mon-Thu, Sat-Sun 10am-4pm

By one of the most glorious of London's parks, St James's, is this museum dedicated to the history of the five Guards regiments of the British Army. Dating back to the founding of the regiments and to the reign of Charles II (1660-85), it is predominantly concerned with the everyday life of the soldier. Among the museum's extensive collection of paintings, uniforms, and medals there is a unique collection of model soldiers commissioned by the late Sir John Horlick (of the British bedtime drink company). In total there were around 300 figures representing the various Scottish regiments. Obsessed with detail, Horlick himself researched the colours of the regiments and their uniforms, selecting just the elite officers from each regiment to be modelled. A great collection for those yearning to know more about King Solomon's body guards and Scottish regiments today.

Heritage Plantation of Sandwich, Americana Museum and Gardens

Grove Street, Sandwich, Massachusetts 02563, USA
Tel. (1) 508 888 3300   www.heritageplantation.org
May-mid Oct: daily 10am-5pm

An officer of the Dutch artillery by Cornelius Fraser, *c.* 1900
Nationaal Tinnen Figuren Museum

A collection of Americana located in the oldest town on Cape Cod. It includes 2,000 hand-painted lead figures representing the uniforms, arms, and insignia of the colour guards of various regiments from Colonial times to the Spanish-American War. Three dioramas are especially worth viewing: the Surrender at Yorktown, the Boxer Rebellion, and the Battle of New Orleans.

Incredibly Fantastic Old Toy Show

26 Westgate, Lincoln, Lincolnshire LN1 3BD, UK
Tel. (44) 1522 520 534
Tue-Sat 11am-5pm, Sun & public holidays noon-4pm (times may vary, please call for details)

This jewel of a museum has a wonderful selection of toy soldiers. A large display case (not permanent, so call ahead if it is only soldiers you are interested in) holds hundreds of soldiers of every kind and every material: wood, cardboard, bisque, tin, plaster, lead, and fabric. The British Line Infantry and Grenadier Guards Band were made of paper by McLoughlin Bros of America in 1898. The bisque soldiers are worth a good look and include French infantry men by SFBJ of France (1900), and British Officers by Simon & Halbig (*c.* 1910). There is an extensive display of exquisitely painted flats and a selection of flat knights made by Heinrichsen of Germany in 1900.

The Kentucky Museum

The Kentucky Building, Western Kentucky University,
One Big Red Way, Bowling Green, Kentucky 42101, USA
Tel. (1) 270 745 2592   www.wku.edu
Tue-Sat 9.30am-4pm, Sun 1-4pm

The William H. McLean Toy Soldier Collection is remarkable. Composed of 1,350 military miniatures and vehicles, the soldiers date mainly from the 1920s through to the mid 1960s, with some from as late as 1985. You'll find examples by many of the well-known names including Barclay, Britains, Grey Iron, Lincoln Logs, and Manoil. Barclay and Manoil are the best known manufacturers of dimestore figures, so-called because they were sold for five or ten cents at stores like Krege, Neisner, and Woolworths (known as 'five and dime stores'). Grey Iron made their contribution producing dimestore figures using a cast-iron process, and Barclay became one of the largest manufacturers of toy soldiers and figures in the US, having started in 1924.

Blenheim models of Indian Army Sappers and Miners with pack mules, 1980s (right)
Nationaal Tinnen Figuren Museum

A Jemadar of the 3rd Bengal Lancers, 1914 (below)
Nationaal Tinnen Figuren Museum

Nationaal Tinnen Figuren Museum
The National Tin Figure Museum
Markt 1, 7731 DB, Ommen, Overijssel, The Netherlands
Tel. (31) 529 454500 www.tinfigmuseum.nl
Mon-Sat 10am-5pm, Sun 2-5pm

One of the features here is the diorama of Waterloo, containing 6,000 figures spread over 25 square metres. It was presented to the museum by Professor Dr Diederich in 1985. A superb display charts the history of flat figure making. The collection of flats revolves around the sixty or so dioramas of 30mm flats originally amassed and painted by Dr Wieringa, a mathematician who lectures in Haarlem. For those keen to see the fully rounded figures, there are two major collections to view. One is a large bequest from Cornelius Fraser which includes the Camel Corps of the Nizam of Hyderabad (India) 1850, manufactured by Marlborough of England. The other is even larger and cannot be displayed all at once. It contains an excellent cross-section of pre- and postwar figures by various manufacturers. Don't miss one of the earliest figures in the museum: a Prussian Hussar from around 1760.

Museo nazionale del Soldatino Mario Massaccesi
The Mario Massaccesi National Museum of the Toy Soldier
Villa Mazzocorati, via Toscana 19, 40141 Bologna, Italy
Tel. (39) 051 623 4703 www.imprese.com
Mon-Sat 8am-12.30pm, Sun 9.30am-12.30pm

An astounding collection of over 70,000 toy soldiers featuring numerous examples of the famous Nuremberg tin 'flat' soldiers. These were cast in small factories around the city from lead (or alloys of lead) in shallow moulds engraved by artists, and became known as 'flats' because of their less than rounded shape. Thematic displays include dioramas of Carabinieri and the Foreign Legion. Curiosities include the collection of cardboard soldiers once belonging to Giacomo Leopardi, the Italian poet.

Porvoon Museo
The City Museum of Porvoo
Välikatu 11, 06100 Porvoo, Finland
Tel. (358) 19 5747589 www.porvoo.fi
May-Aug: daily 11am-4pm. Sep-Apr: Wed-Sun noon-4pm

The model soldiers can be found in the museum's pewter collection. Highlights include three moulds used by Erik Lodin in Lovisa (a neighbouring town) for casting soldiers. One is signed and dated 1789 and is thought to represent a Swedish Cossack of a short-lived unit created during the war against Russia of the same year. The soldiers cast from these early moulds, which are extremely rare, would have been 'flats'.

Museo del Soldatino e della Figurina storica
The Museum of the Toy Soldier and Historical Figurine
Via Giotto, 5, Calenzano, 50121 Florence, Italy
Tel. (39) 055 883 3421
Mon, Wed-Fri 9am-1pm, Tue 4-7pm

Only part of this museum's collection of 14,000 items is on display at any one time. Not to be missed is the maquette representing the siege in 1325 of Callenzano's Castle, complete with hand-painted figures and peasant scenes. Examples from the 14th-18th centuries are made from various materials including wood, paper, plastic, and lead alloys. The Nuremberg flats dating from the 19th century are definitely worth seeing.

Spielzeugmuseum
The Toy Museum
Wettsteinhaus, Baselstrasse 34, 4125 Riehen, Switzerland
Tel. (41) 61 641 2829 www.riehen.ch
Wed-Sat 2-5pm, Sun 10am-5pm

Most of the museum's figures originate from the famous Nuremberg manufacturer E. Heinrichsen and date from around the 1880s. Heinrichsen introduced a standard size, called the 'Nürnberger Grösse' (Nuremberg Size); the foot soldier figurines measured 30mm in height and the horsemen 40mm. These historical figurines, as opposed to toy soldiers, are displayed in over thirty dioramas covering events of national and international importance. Dioramas featuring solid lead rather than tin figures include the landing of Blériot after his flight over the channel, and an elephant hunt (both scenes from the Georg Heyde manufacture in Dresden). A special collection focuses on the production of 19th-century toy soldiers in Aarau, Switzerland.

A Captain of Probyn's Horse by Cornelius Fraser, 1901
Nationaal Tinnen Figuren Museum

Musée suisse de la Figurine historique
The Swiss Museum of Historic Toy Soldiers
Château de Morges, 1110 Morges, Switzerland
Tel. (41) 21 804 85 56 www.swisscastles.ch
Feb-Dec: Tue-Fri 10am-noon, 1.30-5pm, Sat-Sun 1.30-5pm (Jul-Aug: daily 10am-5pm)

The chateau was originally built as a fort on Lake Geneva in 1286 by Louis de Savoie, and in the 16th century it became a manorial castle. Some 10,000 figurines selected from the outstanding collection of Raoul Gérard are displayed in fifty dioramas, illustrating some of the greatest battles in history: see Darius against Alexander at Arbeles, after the famous mosaic in Naples; the siege of Alesia; and the crossing of the Berezina.

The Toy Soldier
Paradise Falls, RR No.1, Cresco, Pennsylvania 18326, USA
Tel. (1) 570 629 7227 www.the-toy-soldier.com
By appt. only (no children under 12)

A collection of 35,000 soldiers amassed by James Hillestad, a history buff with a penchant for the British Colonial Period. Displayed in a series of action dioramas, battle scenes include the Siege of Vicksburg, Cornwallis at Yorktown, the Defence of Hougemont, and the Charge up San Juan Hill. There are also regiments of Indian sepoys, a set piece from Britains' Ashanti wars, and even a rendering of President Kennedy's funeral cortege.

Wenham Museum
132 Main Street, Wenham, Massachusetts 01984, USA
Tel. (1) 978 468 2377 www.wenhammuseum.org
Tue-Sun 10am-4pm

The museum's collection of soldiers, primarily the gift of William B. Osgood, contains one of the finest sets of Britains currently on display in the US. Many of the sets are complete, in pristine condition, and have retained their original boxes. Some even have their original price stickers attached. The most notable are three collections from the '1900' series in 1940, produced only in that year. Descriptions of them do not appear in company records, reference materials list them as 'sets unknown', and the museum believes they may well have the only known examples. Besides this core of Britains, they have representations of soldiers from the American Revolution through to World War II by other European and American manufacturers.

The West Point Museum

United States Military Academy, Building 2110, West Point, New York 10996, USA
Tel. (1) 914 938 2203 www.usma.edu
Daily 10.30am-4.15pm

The museum's collections actually predate the founding of the Military Academy (1802), the original materials having been brought to West Point after the British defeat at Saratoga in 1777. Among the numerous dioramas is one depicting the Roman invasion of Avaricum in 59BC – an excellent three-dimensional example of siege warfare.

Zinnfiguren Museum
The Museum of Tin Figures
Münzstrasse 11, 38640 Goslar, Germany
Tel. (49) 5321 25889
Daily 10am-5pm

JEP miniature train,
France, *c.* 1900
Speelgoedmuseum Mechelen

Situated in a former post office built in 1644 is this stunning collection of toy figures displayed in over 100 dioramas. Take a trip through history from Neanderthal man and Moses to the battlefields of the Thirty Years War. The manufacturing process of the tin figures is documented, illustrating the precision and intensity of the work, all of which can be seen in the on-site workshop.

TRANSPORT IN MINIATURE

Chester Toy and Doll Museum

13a Lower Bridge Street, Chester, Cheshire CH1 1RS, UK
Tel. (44) 1244 346297
Mon-Sat 10am-5pm, Sun 11am-5pm (times may vary, please call for details)

Home to a collection featuring every toy or model made by Matchbox from 1947 to the present day, with examples of Lesney toys, Models of Yesteryear, and Miniatures. In 1948, Matchbox began making large toys such as the Road Roller, and designed a large model Coronation Coach with a miniature to match for the coronation of Queen Elizabeth II. The co-owner, Jack Odell, followed this up with a design of a tiny road roller for his daughter which was an immediate success. A mould was fabricated and the company focused on the production of miniatures. The Meccano company was set up by Frank Hornby, a metal worker in Liverpool who, with the help of his sons, created a crane on his kitchen table out of odd pieces of copper. A factory was set up making tin-plate, clockwork trains and they launched a range of 'o' gauge trains, marketing them under Hornby. He then introduced a range of die-cast, non motorized miniature train sets and road vehicles, calling them 'Dinky'. The models in the Hornby room are all shop display items and were originally built by a special department of Meccano for the purpose.

Museum of Childhood Memories

1 Castle Street, Beaumaris, Anglesey, Gwynedd LL58 8AP, Wales, UK
Tel. (44) 1248 712 498 www.nwi.co.uk
Apr-Nov: daily 10.30am-5.30pm

Vehicles of all kinds fill every piece of available space here. They range from the very best cars by Lehmann to motorcycles and submarines by Bing and Märklin, and trains (both steam and stationary steam) by Lionel and Hornby. An early 1906 Lehmann clockwork Zeppelin and a selection of plastic Japanese transport toys of the 1960s compete with die-cast model cars by Lesney. A British cast-iron locomotive with tender and carriages by Wallwork's of Manchester, and motor coaches by the same maker, sit alongside cases full of tinplate toy boats, including a whole case by Sutcliff.

The Children's Museum of Indianapolis
3000 N. Meridian St., Indianapolis, Indiana 46208-4716, USA
Tel. (1) 317 334 3322 www.childrensmuseum.org
Daily 10am-5pm

A 35-foot-long, 55-ton steam engine greets you as you enter this museum. It was made for the Jefferson, Madison, and Indianapolis Railroad in 1868 to conquer the steepest railroad grade in the United States. More than 100 toy train sets and a 'G'-gauge model train layout make up the rest of the collection.

The Delaware Toy & Miniature Museum
Route 141, Wilmington, Delaware 19807, USA
Tel. (1) 302 427 8697 www.thomes.net
Tue-Sat 10am-4pm, Sun noon-4pm

Prize specimens of planes, boats, and trains from the 18th-20th centuries, by both European and American manufacturers, fill this museum: wonderful boats by Keller & Coudray and Märklin; iron horse-drawn wagons; fire engines; and the magnificent roadster by Hubley. Steam-driven toys and accessories form part of the collection and true steam enthusiasts will love the realistic model steam plant, complete with a single cylinder incorporating an imitation regulator, pressure gauge, and whistle.

Forbes Magazine Galleries
62 Fifth Avenue at 12th Street, New York, New York 10011, USA
Tel. (1) 212 206 5548
Tue, Wed, Fri, Sat 10am-4pm

There are fleets of model boats (500 or so) manufactured between 1870 and 1955, including ocean liners, warships, rowboats, and even Noah's Ark, all set on glassy seas accompanied by nautical music. All the notable German, French, and American firms are represented.

Museum Hracek
The Castle Museum
Na Prazském Hrade, Jirská 6 11901 Prague, Czech Republic
Tel. (420) 2 2437 2294
Please call for opening times

The Toy Museum is housed in the Old Count's Chambers of the castle and includes the collection of the Ivan Steiger family. Steiger's collection concentrates on traditional toys from the past 150 years, mainly focusing on the valuable tin toy clockwork toys, a large number of which are transport wonders from French, German, and American makers. There are coaches drawn by teams of tin horses, cars and motorcycles, aircraft, paddle steamers, and ocean-going liners. Toy trains, stations, and accessories include some of the oldest Märklin engines.

Incredibly Fantastic Old Toy Show
26 Westgate, Lincoln, Lincolnshire LN1 3BD, UK
Tel. (44) 1522 520534
Tue-Sat 11am-5pm, Sun & public holidays noon-4pm (times may vary, please call for details)

The toys here reflect developments made in transport from the 19th century to the present day. They range from hand-painted clockwork models from makers like Bing, to tin lithographed ones by Carette, Citroën, JEP, and Tipp and Distler. Also included are the battery-powered copies of the American 'gas guzzlers' of the 1950s by Japanese makers such as Bandai and Alps. Toy trains include examples of the first simple, pull-along models of the 1840s to the real steam locomotives of the 1870s, and an example of the last model made by Hornby of an electric pantograph. Complementing these are railway accessories by makers such as Märklin, Carette, Bing, and Kibri.

Kinderland und Spielzeug Museum
The Museum of Toys and Children
Ritscherstrasse 4, 37431 Bad Lauterberg im Harz, Germany
Tel. (49) 5524 92040 www.badlauterberg.de
Tue-Sun 10.30am-noon, 2.30-5.30pm (Wed, Fri 2.30-5.30pm only)

A highlight here is the great selection of technical toys. They include model steam engines by Bing, Karl Bub, Fleischmann, Märklin, and Piko; racing cars by Schuco; and model cars by Wiking. There are outdoor toys such as pedal cars, and even a small plane. Don't miss the selection of miniature toys, some of which are electrically powered.

Märklin Museum
The Märklin Museum
Holzheimer Strasse 8, 73037 Göppingen, Germany
Tel. (49) 7161 608289 www.maerklin.de
Mon-Fri 9.30am-5pm, Sat 9am-2pm

The Märklin company turned their headquarters into a museum to demonstrate the development of toy trains from 1891 to the present. The earliest toys the company produced were cooking utensils and kitchens for dolls, which are well represented here. The company was renamed Gebrüder Märklin and the focus of production became tin boats, trains, and horse-drawn vehicles. As you might expect from the oldest manufacturer of model trains in the world, the toy train installations are magnificent. Highlights include a clockwork-engine (Storchbein). Manufactured in 1891, it is the oldest engine in the museum.

Musée de la Poupée et du Jouet ancien
The Doll and Ancient Toy Museum
Château de Robersart, 59118 Wambrechies, France
Tel. (33) 3 20 39 69 28
Wed, Sun & public holidays 2-6pm

Highlights among the toy trains, cars, and boats are three Hornby trains, including the *Flèche d'Or 221* with two Pullman coaches and rails. There is also a Hornby station with three platforms and a turntable. The German company Bing, who started making trains in 1882 and produced sheet-steel carpet runners and sophisticated steam engines, is well represented, as is JEP. The collection of toy cars is dominated by rare Citroën models, first produced in 1923 as promotional items. A small collection of boats includes three splendid examples by Hess.

Tippico motorcycle, Nuremberg, 1930-40
Speelgoedmuseum Mechelen

Musée Rambolitrain
The Rambolitrain Museum
4 place Jeanne d'Arc, 78120 Rambouillet, France
Tel. (33) 1 34 83 15 93
Wed-Sun 10am-noon, 2-5.30pm

The museum traces the fabulous history of the railway and toy trains, from toys made of sheet metal and zamac, to models cast in brass and bronze. Four hundred metres of track with miniature stations, travellers, and goods bring the collection to life. The Central Station by Märklin (1904) with accessories and figures, is a particularly fine example. A vast panorama of industrial and small-scale models from 1885 to the present day includes a unique piece – the engine *Pacific 231* from the film starring Jean Gabin and Julien Carette.

Schlossmuseum Aulendorf
The Castle Museum of Aulendorf
Hauptstrasse 35, 88326 Aulendorf, Germany
Tel. (49) 7525 934203 www.schloss-museum.de
Tue–Fri 1–5pm, Sat–Sun 10am–5pm

The accessories belonging to a stunning toy train collection form the focal point of the museum, featuring manufacturers such as Rock & Graner, Ludwig Lutz, Märklin, and Kindler & Briel (Kibri). Covering some 100 years of Kindler & Briel production, the collection includes the oldest known Kibri station accessory from 1900. Founded in 1895, it is, together with Märklin, the only 19th-century manufacturer still in operation. Märklin trains from 1912–29 are a feature, along with examples of the 1935 new miniature 'oo' gauge trains that were precisely twice as small as the previous 'o' gauge ones. Prototypes, hand-drawn sketches, and plans beautifully complement the collection.

Speelgoedmuseum Mechelen
The Mechelen Toy Museum
Nekkerspoel 21, 2800 Mechelen, Belgium
Tel. (32) 15 557075
www.speelgoedmuseum.be
Tue–Sun 10am–5pm

Every form of transport is represented in this international collection. Especially impressive are the wooden Lego trucks from 1940; postwar lithographed tin-plate keywind motorcycles by Tippco; tin-plate lithographed racing motorcycles by Technofix; and Corgi toys from the 1960s and 70s. The toy train collection includes fine examples of train engines by Märklin (such as *George the Fifth* from 1938-39), as well as Bing, Fleischmann, Wilesco, Hornby-Meccano, and Mamod from Great Britain.

Spielzeugmuseum
The Toy Museum
Wettsteinhaus, Baselstrasse 34, 4125 Riehen, Switzerland
Tel. (41) 61 6412829 www.riehen.ch
Wed–Sat 2–5pm, Sun 10am–5pm

A wonderful collection of cast-iron and tin toys, many driven by sophisticated brass and steel steam engines, others which were operated by hand, and even some that relied on the dangerous camphene or burning fluid used in contemporary lamps. Steam engines abound, including a scale model commemorating the first German steam-driven train from Nuremberg to Fürth that opened in 1835. Clockwork toys include a paddle steamer from around 1890, a Tipp and Company fire engine from Nuremberg (*c.* 1925), and a Rapide train from Paris (*c.* 1870).

Spielzeugmuseum im Stadtmuseum Ingolstadt
The Toy Museum in the Town Museum of Ingolstadt
Auf der Schanz 45, 85049 Ingolstadt, Germany
Tel. (49) 841 3051885 www.ingolstadt.de.tourism
Tue–Sat 9am–5pm, Sun 10am–5pm

A collection of around 1,900 tin transport toys with accessories; tin dolls' ovens and kitchens; and key-wind tin-plate animals. Highlights include a vast number of steam engine models of the actual trains of the time. Superb Märklin examples are the Wuppertaler Schwebebahn (a suspension railway), and the highly detailed, small-scale models of trains made in the 1930s with their new gauge of 'oo'. Ships include a paddle steamer with a clockwork mechanism by Bing (1898), and a copy of a war ship produced by Märklin as a construction set.

Märklin train,
1898-1904 (above)
*Spielzeugmuseum im
Stadtmuseum Ingolstadt*

Technofix motorcycles,
Nuremberg, 1950-60
(middle)
Speelgoedmuseum Mechelen

Toy train by Rock &
Graner, *c.* 1875 (below)
Schlossmuseum Aulendorf

George the Fifth train by
Märklin, Göppingen,
1938-39 (above)
Speelgoedmuseum Mechelen

Model of Boston and
Maine Locomotive no.
1498, built by Wilbur Frey
(below)
Wenham Museum

Technorama der Schweiz
The Technorama of Switzerland
Technoramastrasse 1, 8404 Winterthur, Switzerland
Tel. (41) 52 243 0505 www.technorama.ch
Tue-Sun 10am-5pm

A museum of technology with an outstanding selection of toy trains and tin-plate accessories. Engines are powered by steam, clockwork, and electricity, the oldest piece being a
Lutz engine from 1885 with a clockwork mechanism. Another rarity is the cable car from
1908 by Carette. Found unassembled in a box in Duisburg in 1985, it took two years to
assemble.

The Toy and Miniature Museum of Kansas City
5235 Oak Street, Kansas City, Missouri 64112, USA
Tel. (1) 816 333 9328 www.umkc.edu
Wed-Sat 10am-4pm, Sun 1-4pm

Trains, planes, boats, and automobiles of tin and cast iron fill this museum. Many were
gifts from the late Jerry Smith, a Kansas City businessman and philanthropist who
began his collecting career in the 1950s. By the time of his death, he had amassed over
11,000 items of American memorabilia, many of which were toys.

Tretauto-Museum - Zentrum für Aussergewöhnliche Museen
The Pedal Car Museum - Centre of Extraordinary Museums
Westenriederstrasse 41, 80331 Munich, Germany
Tel. (49) 89 2904121 www.faszination-oldtimer.de
Daily 10am-5pm

Everything you need to know about the pedal cars which appeared after the first horseless
carriages. Originally marketed for children, today it is the adult collector who regularly
puts these vintage beauties on their list. Like their full-size counterparts they came complete with bright enamel paint and leatherette upholstery. Exhibits include those made
at the turn of the 20th century such as mini-Bugattis, Buicks and Morgans, Noddy cars,
and contraptions from as early as the 1880s.

Wenham Museum
132 Main Street, Wenham, Massachusetts 01984, USA
Tel. (1) 978 468 2377 www.wenhammuseum.org
Tue-Sun 10am-4pm

The model and toy train room features operating layouts of various gauges, with as
many as twelve trains ready to be operated at the push of a button. The depot at Salem,
Massachusetts, with its stone arch flanked by Norman towers, is exquisitely modelled.
The museum's latest acquisition is the model railroad by the late Peter Arnott, a noted
modeller who spent over twenty years on its construction.
The manufacturing methods
employed in pre- and post-World War
II models are compared with
those of today, with explana-
tions relating to gauge and
scale. There are also toy cars,
aeroplanes, ships, horse
drawn carts, and cast-
iron circus wagons.

AMERICAN POTTERY AND GLASS (1790-1895)

Cascade and *Sweetheart*
pitchers, United States
Pottery Co., 1854-55
(right)
Bennington Museum

Water Cooler by J. & E.
Norton, Bennington,
Vermont, 1850 (below)
Bennington Museum

Museum of American Glass at Wheaton Village
1501 Glasstown Rd, Millville, New Jersey 08332, USA
Tel. (1) 856 825 6800   www.wheatonvillage.org
Apr-Dec: daily 10am-5pm (Jan-Mar: please call for opening times)

Wheaton Industries, once the largest family-owned glassworks in the world, was
founded in 1888 by Dr T.C. Wheaton. In 1970, Wheaton Village was established by
Wheaton's grandson and is home to a museum which contains the finest and largest
collection of American glass in the US (over 7,000 pieces), particularly 18th- to 20th-
century examples, including the world's largest bottle.

Bennington Museum
West Main Street, Bennington, Vermont 05201, USA
Tel. (1) 802 447 1571   www.benningtonmuseum.com
Nov-May: daily 9am-5pm. Jun-Oct: 9am-6pm

The museum houses more than 7,000 objects, most of
them American, including a large collection of Vermont glass produced by the Vermont
Glass Factory and the Lake Dunmore Glass Company. There are fine examples of blown
glass and mercury glass, all manufactured in the country's well-known 19th-century
glass making areas of New England, New Jersey, and Ohio. Its collection of Bennington
Pottery is unsurpassed, including over 4,000 pieces produced by the United States
Pottery Company (1847-58). It traces the history of Norton Pottery from 1785, when
Captain John Norton began to produce utilitarian earthenware and stoneware,
through its period of growth in the 19th century, to its brilliantly decorated stoneware.

Chrysler Museum of Art
245 West Olney Road, Norfolk, Virginia 23510, USA
Tel. (1) 757 664 6200   www.chrysler.org
Tue-Sat 10am-5pm, Sun 1-5pm

The Chrysler collection boasts a few early examples of glassware from the late 1700s.
Much of the work on display, however, is 19th-century tableware, including such
pressed glass rarities as the *Cape Cod Lily* vase (*c.* 1830) and a beautiful *Lacy Compote*
in electric blue glass. In addition, the collection includes many examples of work
from the New England Glass Company of Cambridge, Massachusetts, founded by
Deming Jarves in 1818.

The Corning Museum of Glass
One Museum Way, Corning, New York 14830, USA
Tel. (1) 607 974 8274   www.cmog.org
Daily 9am-5pm (Jul-Aug 9am-8pm)

This collection of nearly 11,500 pieces includes the earliest known American piece, a
wine bottle made for Richard Wistar in his own glass factory shortly before the
American Revolution. This is the only known piece definitely produced in the legendary glass house of H.W. Stiegel at Manheim, Pennsylvania. An adjacent gallery,
'Crystal City', shows the elaborate cut glass that was so popular in the US from 1880
until 1915, much of it made in Corning.

Dorflinger Glass Museum
Dorflinger-Suydam Wildlife Sanctuary, White Mills, Pennsylvania 18473, USA
Tel. (1) 570 253 1185   www.dorflinger.org
May-Oct: Wed-Sat 10am-4pm, Sun 1-4pm

The museum houses a collection of 600 pieces of Dorflinger glass made famous by its exquisite crystal and cut glass, which supplied the tableware for eight presidents of the US, and the future Edward VII. In the 1860s, French glassmaker Christian Dorflinger purchased 600 acres of spectacularly beautiful land in White Mills and constructed a glass factory where he was to design and produce some of the finest lead crystal in the country. Theodore Roosevelt ordered the first highball glasses from here.

The Lightner Museum
Museum-City Hall Complex, King Street, St Augustine, Florida 32084, USA
Tel. (1) 904 824 2874 www.lightnermuseum.org
Daily 9am-5pm

During the Great Depression, Otto C. Lightner of Chicago snapped up houses full of massive furnishings, paintings, and ornate glassware. He established this vast assemblage of 19th-century decorative arts, natural sciences, industry and anthropology. There is a major exhibit of late 19th-century American cut glass and crystal, including a magnificent punch bowl crafted by Pitkin & Brooks of Chicago; an enormous variety of Victorian glass; Tiffany windows, lamps, and art glass; English, Daum and Schneider cameo glass; pressed World's Fair souvenirs; and even an 1850 glass steam engine made by William H. Allen, the master scientific glass blower of his generation. Complementing the collection is a library of over 6,000 volumes on 19th-century decorative arts.

The Metropolitan Museum of Art
1000 Fifth Avenue at 82nd Street, New York, New York 10028, USA
Tel. (1) 212 535 7710 www.metmuseum.org
Tue-Thu, Sun 9.30am-5.30pm, Fri-Sat 9.30am-9pm

Standing stag by Daniel Greatbach, United States Pottery Co., c. 1852
Bennington Museum

The collection spans from 1740 to 1920 and includes more than 2,000 objects. There are free-blown table articles, including examples of South Jersey and New York State lily-pad vessels, as well as pieces from the Christian Dorflinger factory of New York. The museum includes important presentation pieces such as a covered goblet bearing the arms of the city of Bremen, Germany, from the New Bremen Glass Manufactory established at the end of the 18th century by John Frederick Amelung. There is also pressed glass from the Lacy period (1830-45) and later pressed pattern glass (1845-1900), with an extensive collection of blown glass by Tiffany.

The Charles Hosmer Morse Museum of American Art
445 North Park Avenue, Winter Park, Florida 32789, USA
Tel. (1) 407 645 5311 www.morsemuseum.org
Tue-Sat 9.30am-4pm, Sun 1-4pm (times may vary, please call for details)

This museum is known for its extensive collection of works by Tiffany, but it also contains about 300 pieces from the Rookwood Pottery. Established in 1880 in Cincinatti, the pottery marked an important chapter in the American Arts and Crafts movement. Among the pieces are some early examples of the earthy 'Standard ware' developed in 1884, along with some of the designs in new colours – Iris, Sea Green, Aerial Blue – that were introduced in the 1890s. There are some ceramic pieces by Tiffany, who began to design pottery in 1900, as well as about 500 works by other members of the richly creative 19th-century American Art Pottery movement.

The National Heisey Glass Museum
Veterans Park, corner of Sixth and Church Streets, Newark, Ohio 43055, USA
Tel. (1) 740 345 2932 www.heiseymuseum.org
Tue-Sat 10am-4pm, Sun 1-4pm

On display are more than 4,500 pieces of handmade glassware produced by A. H. Heisey & Company in Newark from 1896 to 1957. Displays of moulds, tools, etching plates and experimental pieces take you through the production process. A library facility is open to Heisey Club of America members. This is one of the most highly prized collections of glass to be seen in the US.

New Bedford Whaling Museum
18 Johnny Cake Hill, New Bedford, Massachusetts 02740-6398, USA
Tel. (1) 508 9970046 www.whalingmuseum.org
Daily 9am-5pm (until 9pm every 2nd Thu of the month)

There are more than 3,500 examples of glass owned or manufactured in the New Bedford area, including examples from the Mt Washington, Gundersen Glass Works, and Pairpoint Glass companies. When the New Bedford Glass Museum closed in 1991, part of its important collections of locally-made art glass of the 19th and 20th centuries, metalware, and archival materials were entrusted to the museum.

Sandwich Glass Museum
129 Main Street, Route 130, Sandwich, Massachusetts, USA
Tel. (1) 508 888 0251 www.sandwichglassmuseum.org
Apr-Dec: daily 9.30am-5pm. Feb-Mar: Wed-Sun 9.30am-4pm

Deming Jarves founded the Boston & Sandwich Glass Company in 1825 and employed hundreds of factory workers, including European glass artisans, to perfect the techniques of mould-blown and pressed glass. Almost all of the museum's collection of 5,800 pieces of glass, produced by the company from 1825-88, is on display, adding up to the best collection of its type anywhere. Around 100 of the wooden patterns still survive, but the bronze moulds were melted down for their metal during the war.

Art Nouveau glasses by Lötz Witwe, Klostermuhle, c. 1900 Museum Kunst Palast

Winterthur Museum, Garden & Library
Route 52, Winterthur, Delaware 19735, USA
Tel. (1) 302-888 4600 www.winterthur.org
Mon-Sat 9am-5pm, Sun noon-5pm

Glass was one of Mr du Pont's earliest collecting interests and the collection is one of the very few formed between 1920 and 1950 that is still intact. It dates from 1650 to 1850 and includes a healthy selection of 18th-century American made glass, especially of pocket flasks attributed to Henry W. Stiegel's glassworks near Manheim, Pennsylvania, and sugar bowls made by the glassworks of John Frederick Amelung at New Bremen, Maryland. The 19th century is represented by the kinds of glass that American factories produced, and includes one of the largest known pressed glass bowls.

ART NOUVEAU CERAMICS AND GLASS

Musée des Arts décoratifs
The Museum of Decorative Arts
Palais du Louvre, 107 rue de Rivoli, 75001 Paris, France
Tel. (33) 1 44 55 57 50 www.ucad.fr
Due to open 2003

This is considered to be one of the best collections of decorative arts in the world. Many, if not all of the Art Nouveau artists of any merit are represented, with glass by Daum, Dammouse, Gallé, Decorchemont, and Tiffany, as well as ceramics by Delaherce, Jean Carriès, and Dalpayrat. The museum owns most of the Chapelet collection, including the blood red 'sang de Boeuf' models and the jug (1887) made by Gauguin in his studio. There is a display of faïences by Eugène Rousseau, porcelain by Georges de Feure, and glasswork by Henry Cros. There is jewellery by Fouquet, Henri Vever,

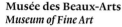

and Lalique. The Lalique collection includes rare pieces such as the bowl *Deux Sirènes*, the vase *Quatre Scarabées*, and the vase *Quatre feuilles de rhubarbe*. Some of the pieces were given by the artist himself. Other exceptional pieces include an 1880-85 fireplace made from sculpted oak with enamelled faïence decorations, from the Gillot Hotel in Paris, and outstanding examples of Tiffany. Also in the museum are two doors that Lalique designed for his pavilion at the Exhibition of 1925 in Paris, as well as his *Fontaine aux Poissons* from the 1937 Exhibition.

Musée des Beaux-Arts
Museum of Fine Art
3 place Stanislas, 54000 Nancy, France
Tel. (33) 3 83 85 30 72
Mon, Wed-Sun 10am-6pm

This superb Daum collection began with just 160 pieces but now numbers around 600 pieces, after an important private donation in 1999. The collection's nucleus was formed thanks to donations by the Daum Frères glassworks in Nancy along with items from family members and private collectors. It reflects the development of techniques and experiments carried out by the brothers, Auguste and Antonin.

Chrysler Museum of Art
245 West Olney Road, Norfolk, Virginia 23510, USA
Tel. (1) 757 664 6200 www.chyrsler.org
Tue-Sat 10am-5pm, Sun 1-5pm

Decorative glasses by
Koepping, Berlin,
*c.*1896-99 (top)
Museum Kunst Palast

Bowl vase by Daum
Frères, Nancy, *c.*1893
(above)
Museum Kunst Palast

The museum's collection of Tiffany Favrile, the exotic blown glass from the Tiffany studios, is stunningly beautiful. Inspired by the ancient technique of colouring the glass while it is being fired rather than painting it afterwards, Tiffany experimented with oxides of iron until he was able to manufacture any colour and lustre that he desired. The resulting flower forms, lava vases, paperweight-style vases (which involved sandwiching a decoration between two layers of hot, molten glass), and peacock glass made him one of the biggest names in Art Nouveau.

The Corning Museum of Glass
One Museum Way, Corning, New York 14830, USA
Tel. (1) 607 974 8274 www.cmog.org
Daily 9am-5pm (Jul-Aug: daily until 8pm)

This small museum boasts an exceptional selection of works by Tiffany, including the earliest documented Tiffany vessel (a vase exhibited at the Chicago World's Fair in 1893), and stained-glass windows by Tiffany, John LaFarge, and Frank Lloyd Wright. The exceptional collection of French Art Nouveau glass includes several masterpieces from the workshop of Gallé and the factory of Lalique.

Musée de l'Ecole de Nancy
Museum of the School of Nancy
36-38 rue du Sergent Blandan, 54000 Nancy, France
Tel. (33) 3 83 40 14.86
Mon 2-6pm, Wed-Sun 10.30am-6pm

The group known as the Ecole de Nancy flourished from 1901 through to 1935. Exhibits include Gallé's surreal mushroom table lamp, *Les Coprins,* and his famous chest of drawers, *Les parfums d'autrefois* (1894). There is the whimsical bedroom suite and grand piano with fir cone decorations by Majorelle, also the extraordinary dining room by Vallin (1904), which includes designs and creations by Prouvé. The museum also has a garden with a funerary chapel designed by the architect Gérard and decorated with sculptural works by Pierre Roche.

Vase by Glassworks,
Ferdinand von
Poschinger, Buchenau,
*c.*1902 (above)
Museum Kunst Palast

Vase by Gallé, Nancy,
*c.*1900 (below left)
Museum Kunst Palast

Decorative glass by
Tiffany, New York,
1897-1900 (below right)
Museum Kunst Palast

Haworth Art Gallery

Haworth Park, Manchester Road, Accrington, Lancashire BB5 2JS, UK
Tel. (44) 1254 233782
Due to reopen late 2001 (please call for opening times)

This is the largest public collection of Tiffany glass outside the US, brought back from
New York in 1933 by Joseph Briggs. The collection includes mosaics, tiles, and over
seventy superb examples of the handmade Favrile glass vases.

Cecil Higgins Art Gallery and Museum

Castle Close, Bedford, Bedfordshire MK40 3NY, UK
Tel. (44) 1234 211222
Tue-Sat 11am-5pm, Sun 2-5pm

Cecil Higgins died in 1941, leaving an outstanding collection of European glass, a hefty
endowment, and instructions to the trustees to purchase new acquisitions. In 1972,
they acquired 102 pieces of glass from the 19th and 20th centuries, including examples
from the Gothic revival, the Arts and Crafts Movement and Art Nouveau. Two Favrile
vases and candlesticks by Tiffany, and inlaid vases by Gallé are noteworthy

Museum Kunst Palast
The Museum Art Palace

Ehrenhof 5, 40479 Düsseldorf, Germany
Tel. (49) 211 8992460
www.museum-kunstpalast.de
Tue-Sun 11am-6pm

The Hentrich Collection documents the development of glass making from pre-Roman times to
contemporary studio glass. Art Nouveau is particularly well represented with a display of all its main
trends, including works by Gallé, Tiffany, Koepping,
and Lötz among others, and is considered one of the
finest of its kind. There are also beautiful collections of Persian, Indian and, most of
all, Chinese glass, which illustrates the influence of Oriental glass art on European
designers, as well as medieval and French Art Deco glass.

Maison du Verre et du Cristal
The Glass and Crystal House

Place Robert Schumann, 57960 Meisenthal, France
Tel. (33) 3 87 96 91 51
Easter-early Nov: Mon, Wed-Sun 2-6pm (groups by appt. all year)

The museum in Meisenthal's former glassworks, active between 1704 and 1969, contains a reconstructed workshop with tools and equipment as well as various types of
moulds. There is a fine selection of works by Lalique, Müller, Argental, Gallé, and
Daum, and some other wonderful Art Nouveau pieces.

The Charles Hosmer Morse Museum of American Art

445 North Park Avenue, Winter Park, Florida 32789, USA
Tel. (1) 407 645 5311 www.morsemuseum.org
Tue-Sat 9.30am-4pm, Sun 1-4pm (times may vary, please call for details)

This is one of the most comprehensive collections of Tiffany art in the world. Along
with seventeen stained-glass pieces, the Byzantine chapel which showcased many of
his innovations at the 1893 Chicago World Columbian Exposition has been re-erected

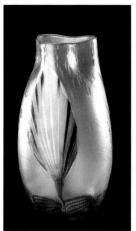

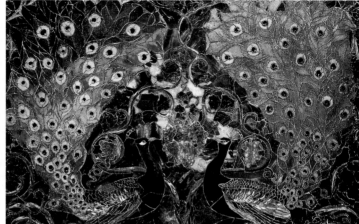

here. One of the finest pieces is a vase in the form of a 'Jack-in-the-Pulpit' in full bloom, a huge open flower on top of a slim, elegant stem.

Detail of *Chapel Reredos*, favrile glass mosaic, Tiffany, 1892 (above)
The Charles Hosmer Morse Museum of American Art

Vase by Lötz Witwe, Klostermühle, *c.*1900 (left)
Museum Kunst Palast

Musée d'Orsay
The Orsay Museum
62 rue de Lille, 75007 Paris, France
Tel. (33) 1 40 49 48 14 www.musee-orsay.fr
Tue, Wed, Fri, Sat, 10am-6pm, Thu 10am-9.45pm, Sun 9am-6pm.
(Mid June-mid Sep: opens 9am)

On the second floor, six rooms are dedicated to Art Nouveau. Horta, Guimard, and Van de Velde are represented and there are remarkable collections of ceramics by Chapelet, Delaherche, and Carriès, as well as glass by Gallé and Lalique.

Österreichisches Museum für angewandte Kunst
The Austrian Museum of Applied Arts
Stubenring 5, 1010 Vienna, Austria
Tel. (43) 1 71136 www.mak.at
Tue-Sun 10am-6pm (Thu until 9pm)

A remarkable collection of lamp-blown Bimini glass filled with filigree opaque swirls and strips, incorporating mythical creatures and animal figures, graceful dancing female forms, as well as hunting and musical scenes.

Rockwell Museum
Cedar Street at Denison Parkway, Corning, New York 14830, USA
Tel. (1) 607 937 5386 www.stny.lrun.com
Mon-Sat 9am-5pm, Sun noon-5pm

The most comprehensive collection of Carder Steuben glass in the world, with 2,500 pieces dating from 1903 to 1933. The Diatreta technique using the lost wax method of cast glass resulted in the most stunning vases that were made during the Art Nouveau period, including the green, blue and white *Diatreta* vase, the famous blue and gold *Aurenes*, and the yellow *Florentia* vase.

Sainsbury Centre for Visual Arts
University of East Anglia, Norwich, Norfolk NR4 7TJ, UK
Tel. (44) 1603 592467 www.uea.ac.uk
Tue-Sun 11am-5pm

Receptacles,
Klostermuhle, *c.* 1907
(below)
Museum Kunst Palast

Porcelain birdcage vase,
Japan, *c.* 1700 (middle)
Porzellansammlung-
Staatliche
Kunstsammlungen Dresden

Blue and white lotus bowl,
15th century (bottom)
Durham University Oriental
Museum

The Anderson Collection of Art Nouveau contains glass by Gallé, Tiffany and Lalique, fine Dutch Rozenburg porcelains, Liberty metalwork, and impressive pieces of jewellery by Lalique and Georges Fouquet. Additionally, there is glassware from the Austrian firm Loetz, and work attributed to the country's best designers, Graf Harrach and Wihelm Kralik Sohn.

Museum voor Sierkunst en Vormgeving
The Museum of Decorative Arts and Design
Jan Breydelstraat 5, 9000 Gent, Belgium
Tel. (32) 9 2256676 www.design.museum.gent.be
Tue-Sun 9.30am-5pm

This superb Art Nouveau collection includes an outstanding group of ceramics by Félix Bracquemond, Ernest Chaplet, Albert Dammousse, and Bernard Moore as well as glass by Eugène Rousseau and Jean Auguste.

CHINESE AND JAPANESE CERAMICS

Ashmolean Museum
Beaumont Street, Oxford, Oxfordshire OX1 2PH, UK
Tel. (44) 1865 278000 www.ashmol.ox.ac.uk
Tue-Sat 10am-5pm, Sun & public holidays 2-5pm (except the Cast Gallery)

Various colleges of Oxford University deposited their Eastern collections here. There is a unique collection of early Chinese ceramics, and Reitlinger's collection of Japanese export porcelain. Combined with purchases from the Story Fund (specific to Japan) this museum perhaps holds the most comprehensive collection in the West.

Barlow Collection of Chinese Art
University Library, University of Sussex, Falmer, Brighton, East Sussex BN1 9QL, UK
Tel. (44) 1273 873506 www.susx.ac.uk
Tue, Thu 11.30am-2.30pm

Presented to the University by Sir Alan Barlow and Lady Barlow, this small but fine collection contains many gems. Its 400 examples cover every period of China's history, from the 12th century BC to the 18th century. The collection is rich in Chinese green-glazed wares (celadons) of the Song dynasty, extremely rare Ru ware, and several examples of Guan celadons made for the Imperial palace. A statuette of the goddess Guanyin (Dehua kilns, Fujian province, *c.*1700) is one of the most perfect surviving specimens of its type.

Bristol City Museum and Art Gallery
Queen's Road, Bristol BS8 1RL, UK
Tel. (44) 117 922 3571 www.bristol-city.gov.uk
Daily 10am-5pm

The Eastern Art Collections, consisting of around 8,000 items, are considered of international importance. The greatest strength of the Schiller collection are the Chinese ceramics, ranging from neolithic vessels from *c.*2000BC to the 20th century. Particularly important are the T'ang (AD618-906) and Sung (song) (AD960-1279) ceramics, including a rare Ru ware bowl made for an Emperor in the early 12th century. The museum holds the largest collection of Chinese glass tableware outside China, some dating from the 2nd-3rd centuries AD, with stunning examples of large decorated glasses from the Manchu Qing dynasty.

Burghley House

Stamford, Lincolnshire PE9 3JY, UK
Tel. (44) 1780 52451
End Mar-early Oct: daily 11am-5pm

Punchbowl, Chinese,
c.1735 (far left)
Burghley House

Two wrestlers, Japanese,
c.1670 (left)
Burghley House

Burghley houses the earliest inventoried collection of Japanese ceramics in the West which were exported only between 1659 and 1711. An important group of 17th-century Japanese wrestlers painted in the Kakiemon style were discovered in the house where they had been used as doorstops until 1982. Besides these, there are several other pieces of rare Japanese porcelain and a beautiful Ming dynasty bowl known to have been presented by Queen Elizabeth I to her godchild, Walsingham.

Collections Baur
The Baur Collections

8 rue Munier-Romilly, 1206 Geneva, Switzerland
Tel. (41) 22 3461729 www.baur-collections.ch
Tue-Sun 2-6pm

One of the world's most interesting collections of Chinese ceramics dating from the 8th to the 19th centuries. Highlights include monochrome porcelains of the Qing dynasty, Chinese snuff bottles with a variety of decorations, as well as a remarkable collection of Japanese earthenware and porcelain from the Edo period.

The Percival David Foundation of Chinese Art

53 Gordon Square, London WC1H OPD, UK
Tel. (44) 20 7387 3909 www.soas.ac.uk
Mon-Fri 10.30am-5pm

Widely regarded as the most important collection of Chinese ceram-ics outside China, surpassed only by the former imperial collection in the National Palace Museum, Taipei. The core collection of 1,400 pieces consists of near-perfect examples of Chinese stoneware and porcelain primarily of the Song, Ming, and Qing dynasties. These include the most important and valuable pair of Chinese porcelains in the world, the so-called 'David vases' which are made from blue and white porcelain and are dated by inscription to 1351. Among the most important earlier works are a group of exception-ally rare Ru wares, which are the earliest ceramic vessels made exclusively for the imperial court. The collection is also distinguished by the large number of pieces with important inscriptions, including reign marks, poems, and auspicious sayings. The collection is a key point of reference for all those interested in Chinese ceramics.

Figure of a cockerel,
Japanese, c.1660-80
(above)
Burghley House

Pilgrim flask with
underglaze decoration,
18th century (below)
*Durham University
Oriental Museum*

Durham University Oriental Museum

Elvet Hill, South Road, Durham DH1 3TH, UK
Tel. (44) 191 374 7911 www.dur.ac.uk
Mon-Fri 9.30am-1pm, 2-5 pm, Sat-Sun 2-5pm

Over 400 pieces of Chinese ceramics dating from prehistory to the 19th century. Outstanding objects include a porcelain pil-grim bottle with a copper red underglaze dating from 1736; a selection of pieces with marks indicating their imperial kiln origins; a T'ang Dynasty woman polo player; and a number of interesting tomb figures and fine vessels. The jade collection contains over 4,000 pieces dating from the 13th to 15th centuries. There is also a gallery of Chinese ceremonial robes, an important imperial hanging from a palace, and a collection of tiny shoes.

Groninger Museum
The Museum of Groningen
Museumeiland 1, 9700 ME Groningen,
Netherlands
Tel. (31) 50 3666555 www.groninger-museum.nl
Tue-Sun 10am-5pm

The nucleus of the Oriental ceramic collection comprises Chinese and Japanese export porcelain shipped to the Netherlands by the Dutch East India Company in the 17th and 18th centuries. A recent focus of the collection are porcelains recovered from shipwrecks connected with the Dutch porcelain trade, especially from the *Hatcher* wreck (*c.*1645), ceramics from the Vung Tau (*c.*1690), and those from the Geldermalsen or Nanking Cargo (1752). There are holdings of export porcelain made according to European shapes and decorations (so-called *Chine de Commande*), specially ordered from models supplied by the VOC and private individuals. Also a fine selection of porcelain, stone- and earthenware from Korea, Vietnam, and Thailand.

Keramiekmuseum het Princessehof
The Princess Court Ceramics Museum
Grote Kerkstraat 11, 8911 DZ Leeuwarden, The Netherlands
Tel. (31) 58 2127438 www.home.wxs.nl
Daily 10am-5pm, Sun 2-5pm

The collection of Chinese ceramics is exceptionally important, showing how the nation's industry developed from early terracotta pieces (3rd millennium BC) leading up to objects manufactured during the Qing dynasty.

Musée national Adrien Dubouché
The National Museum Adrien Dubouché
8 bis, place Winston Churchill, 87000 Limoges, France
Tel. (33) 5 55 330850
Mon, Wed-Sun 10am-noon, 1.30-5.15pm

Thousands of masterpieces illustrate the history of ceramics, porcelain and glass from antiquity to the present day. Blue and white porcelain from 17th and 18th century China; outstanding examples of white and green celadon monochromes from the Song Dynasty; a fine collection of white porcelain from the To Houa factories in southern China; and porcelain from the so-called Green and Pink Families. The Japanese collection is particularly strong in examples of Imari from the 17th and 18th centuries, and Kakiemon from the 18th century.

Porcelain dish, Japan, c.1680 (top) Porzellansammlung-Staatliche Kunstsammlungen Dresden

Exterior view of the museum (middle) Keramiekmuseum het Princessehof

Interior view of the museum (bottom) Keramiekmuseum het Princessehof

Musée national de la Céramique
The National Museum of Ceramics
Place de la Manufacture, 92310 Sèvres, France
Tel. (33) 1 41 14 04 20
Mon, Wed-Sun 10am-5pm

This collection, covering the history of ceramics to the 19th century, includes numerous Chinese works such as grey pottery for domestic or funerary use from the Ziou period, unglazed grey pottery, and red ceramics with glazing based on lead from the Han Dynasty, Ming celadons from the 15th century, and two beautiful Chinese plates from the 13th and 14th centuries. There is also a fine selection of pottery from the 17th and 18th centuries with pure blue and white decoration. Japanese ceramics include momoyama pottery for tea ceremonies, mainly found in Mino, east of Kyoto.

Pavillon chinois
The Chinese Pavilion
44 avenue Van Praet, 1020 Brussels, Belgium
Tel. (32) 2 2681608   www.kmkg-mrah.be
Tue-Sat 10am-4.45pm

Housed in a spectacular traditional Chinese building commissioned by King Leopold II after his visit to the Universal Exhibition in Paris in 1900, is a remarkable collection of Japanese and Chinese export porcelain mainly from the 17th and 18th centuries.

Two Arita ware wrestlers, Kakiemon style, c.1680 (below)
Peabody Essex Museum

Peabody Essex Museum
East India Square, Salem, Massachusetts 01970, USA
Tel. (1) 978 745 9500   www.pem.org
Nov-Mar: Tue-Sat 10am-5pm, Sun noon-5pm
Apr-Oct: Mon-Sat 10am-5pm, Sun noon-5pm

Seventy per cent of the holdings of 20,000 objects in the department devoted entirely to Asian material are porcelains from Japan, China, and India, exported to the West between the 15th and 20th centuries. A large number include export armorial and special order wares made for the American, English, French, Russian, Dutch, and Portuguese markets. Mrs. Lamont du Pont Copland recently bequeathed her remaining collection of over 300 Chinese figures to the museum. Consisting of all manner of animals and birds, it is on view in its entirety in the Copland Gallery.

Porzellankabinett – Schloss Charlottenburg
The Porcelain Cabinet – Charlottenburg Palace
Luisenplatz, 14059 Berlin, Germany
Tel. (49) 30 32091
Tue-Fri 9am-5pm, Sat-Sun 10am-5pm

The Porcelain Cabinet is one of the highlights of the palace, with Chinese porcelain from the 17th and 18th centuries, as well as blue and white porcelain works from the Ming Dynasty. The walls of the chamber are decorated from floor to ceiling with 3,000 pieces including jars, plates, and sake bottles.

Porzellansammlung – Staatliche Kunstsammlungen Dresden
The Porcelain Collection - State Art Collections of Dresden
Zwinger Entrance 'Glockenspielpavillon', 01067 Dresden, Germany
Tel. (351) 14627   www.staatl-kunstsammlungen-dresden.de
Mon-Wed, Fri-Sun 10am-6pm

Porcelain garniture, Chian Qing Dynasty, 1644-1911 (above)
Porzellansammlung-Staatliche Kunstsammlungen Dresden

White porcelain vase, Korea, c.1500s (left)
Royal Museum of Scotland

Augustus the Strong was so obsessed by porcelain that at one point he owned over 25,000 individual pieces. Part of the collection is on view, arranged much as he would have organized it, in large radiating patterns on the walls. Among the collection are some wonderful blue and white vases which the pottery-mad monarch procured from the Prussian king, Frederick-William I, in exchange for 600 dragoons. Since 1900, the collections have been enriched with Chinese tomb figures from the T'ang period, Chinese stoneware in the style of the Song period, and other items of Ming porcelain.

Art Deco stork and
bowl by Lötz Witwe,
c.1905
Glasmuseum Frauenau

Royal Museum of Scotland
Chambers Street, Edinburgh EH1 1JF, UK
Tel. (44) 131 225 7534 www.nms.ac.uk
Mon-Sat 10am-5pm (Tue until 8pm), Sun noon-5pm

Ceramics make up part of the museum's significant collections of Far Eastern material. The earliest pieces come from Japan's Jomon period, continuing through with pottery of the later Tumulus period, and a range of contemporary Japanese acquisitions. There are 1,600 Chinese ceramics on display, dating from the neolithic period to the 20th century, including important pieces made for export and a large collection of blue and white china from the Kangxi period.

CONTEMPORARY CERAMICS AND GLASS

Musée Ariana
The Ariana Museum
10 ave. de la Paix, 1202 Geneva, Switzerland
Tel. (41) 22 4185450 www.mah.ville-ge.ch
Mon, Wed-Sun 10am-5pm

One of the most important ceramics museums in Europe. All the main ceramic techniques are represented: pottery, stoneware, earthenware, porcelain, and china. There is a large exhibition space devoted to work from the early 20th century to the present.

Musée des Arts décoratifs
The Museum of Decorative Arts
Palais du Louvre, 107 rue de Rivoli, 75001 Paris, France
Tel. (33) 1 44 55 57 50 www.ucad.fr
Due to open in 2003

The best of 20th-century ceramics are represented by La Borne, Joulia, Mohy, and works from Ratilly by Pierlot, Leach, Georges Jouve, and crystal by the Baschet brothers. From the 1980s, there are examples of ceramics by Jean Girel, Deblander, Marc Emerie, and Adrien Saxe, as well as by Lambercy and Aline Favre from Switzerland. More recent works from the 1980s and 1990s include ceramics from Champy, Bayle, Bottagisio, and Decoux, with glass objects by Pierre Baey and Patrice Alexandre.

Museo de Ceràmica
The Ceramics Museum
Palau de Pedralbes, avengida Diagonal 686, 08034 Barcelona, Spain
Tel. (34) 93 2801621
Tue-Sat 10am-6pm, Sun 10am-3pm

Special attention is given to contemporary ceramics. Important pieces include Filter's porcelain vases; works by Josep Llorens Artigas, among them the famous *Moonlight* vase; Antoni Cumella's vases and sculptural panels; Picasso's jugs twisted into human forms; and Miró's vast platters decorated with his ebullient and very personal symbolism. Among the finest of the contemporary Spanish artists are examples of delicate porcelain work by Maria Bofill, and some wonderful sculptural ceramics by Rosa Amorós and Enric Mestre. Among the artists from other countries who are represented in the collection are the Italian Carlo Zauli and Emilio Galassi and the British Elisabeth Raeburn and Gordon Baldwin.

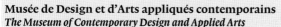

Musée de Céramique et d'Art moderne
Museum of Ceramics and Modern Art
Place de la Libération, 06220 Vallauris, France
Tel. (33) 4 93 64 16 05
Mon, Wed-Sun 10am-noon, 2-6pm (Jul-Aug: 10am-12.30pm, 2-6.30pm)

This rich and diverse collection housed in a 16th-century castle has a number of works
by Picasso, who lived here from 1948 until 1955. Other contemporary artists represented include Yves Mohy, Hans Hedberg, and Alain Bresson.

Vase with metal
setting by Kralik,
c. 1900
Glasmuseum Frauenau

The Corning Museum of Glass
One Museum Way, Corning, New York 14830, USA
Tel. (1) 607 974 8274 www.cmog.org
Daily 9am-5pm (Jul-Aug until 8pm)

The contemporary glass collection is displayed in two galleries: the Sculpture Gallery,
which shows large-scale pieces made since 1980, and the Modern Glass Gallery, which
includes pieces from the 20th century.

Musée de Design et d'Arts appliqués contemporains
The Museum of Contemporary Design and Applied Arts
6 place de la Cathédrale, 1005 Lausanne, Switzerland
Tel. (41) 21 3152530 www.lausanne.ch
Tue 11am-9pm, Wed-Sun 11am-6pm

An important exhibition of some 450 objects of contemporary glass, including works
by Egidio Costantini de la Fucina degli Angeli after drawings by Picasso, Max Ernst,
Jean Arp, Jean Cocteau, Marc Chagall, and others. Highlights include: an important
group of pieces by Libensky; *Birdman* by Naoto Yokoyama (1985); *New York, New York* by
Paul Schulze (1984); *Red/Blue Object* by Bretislav Novak Jun. (1985); *Garden of Eden* by
Jay Musler (1998) and *Elemental Rythm* by Stephen Procter (1984).

Fundación Centro nacional del Vidrio
The National Centre of Glass Foundation
Real Fábrica de Cristales de la Granja, 40100 La Granja de San Ildefonso, Segovia, Spain
Tel. (34) 921 471712 www.fcnv.es
Tue-Sat 10am-6pm, Sun 10am-3pm

A vast collection of contemporary glass art by over 100 designers from across the world,
including Higuchi, Vesa Varrela, Ana Thiel, Pavel Homolka, and Javier Gómez.

Glasmuseet
Glass Museum
Strandvejen 8, 8400 Ebeltoft, Denmark
Tel. (45) 86 341799 www.glasmuseet.dk
Jan-Jun: daily 10am-5pm

Regularly changing displays exhibit one of Europe's largest collections of contemporary glass consisting of approximately 1,500 works which are either on loan or have
been donated by more than 600 glass artists and craftsmen from all over the world.

Glasmuseum Frauenau
The Frauenau Glass Museum
Am Museumspark 1, 94258 Frauenau, Germany
Tel. (49) 9926 940035 www.eisch.de
Mid May-Oct: Tue-Sun 9am-5pm. End Dec-mid May: Tue-Sun 10am-4pm

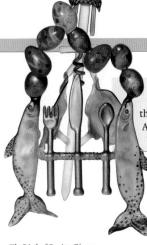

An amazing collection of glass spanning centuries. It contains an exemplary array of around 1,000 pieces of international studio glass, including pieces by the pioneer Finnish artists, Tapio Wirkala and Kai Franck, the Dutch designer A.D. Copier, Erwin Eisch in Germany, and the Italians Archimedo Seguso and Venini.

Museum het Kruithuis
The Kruithuis Museum
5211 LX 's-Hertogenbosch, The Netherlands
Tel. (31) 73 612 21 88   www.fku.nl
Wed-Sun 1-5pm
(moving to new premises in 2002/3)

The Birth of Caviar, Ginny Ruffner, 1987 (top)
Musée de Design et d'Arts appliqués contemporains

Founded in 1955, the museum features one of the best and largest collections of ceramic works by major 20th-century artists. From early masters such as Picasso, Braque, Chagall, Miró, and Léger, through to great artists of the 1980s including A.R. Penck and Mimmo Paladino.

Museo internazionale delle Ceramiche
The International Ceramics Museum
Via Campidori 2, 48018 Faenza, Italy
Tel. (39) 0546 21240   www.micfaenza.org
Nov-Mar: Tue-Fri 9am-1.30pm, Sat-Sun 9.30am-1pm, 3-6pm
Apr-Oct: Tue-Fri 9am-7pm, Sat-Sun 9.30am-1pm, 3-7pm

Garden of Eden, Jay Musler, 1988 (above right)
Musée de Design et d'Arts appliqués contemporains

A must for ceramic collectors of any period. It houses *La Paloma* by Picasso alongside stunning examples of works by Chagall, Matisse, Rouault, Léger, Gropius, Wirkkala, Martini, Fontana, Burri, Melotti, Arman, and Matta, and local artists such as Pietro Melandi and Ricardo Gatti.

Plate by Constant, 1948 (above)
Museum het Kruithuis

Los Angeles County Museum of Art (LACMA)
5905 Wiltshire Boulevard, Los Angeles, California 90036, USA
Tel. (1) 323 857 6000   www.lacma.org
Mon, Tue, Thu noon-8pm, Fri noon-9pm, Sat-Sun 11am-8pm

A collection of contemporary studio ceramics unrivaled in its depth, diversity, and quality. It includes vessels and large-scale sculptures by internationally acclaimed artists.

Museum für modernes Glas
The Museum of Modern Glass
Orangerie Schloss Rosenau, 96472 Rödental bei Coburg, Germany
Tel. (49) 9561 8790   www.kunstsammlungen-coburg.de
Apr-Oct: Tue-Sun 10am-1pm, 1.30-5pm. Nov-Mar: Tue-Sun 1-4pm

The Orangerie is a branch of the Veste Coburg Art Collections, presenting its magnificent collection of contemporary glassware from the 1950s to the present day in a sun-lit glass conservatory. At any one time there are around 300 works on display from a collection numbering over 1,000 pieces and growing daily.

Musée national de la Céramique
The National Museum of Ceramics
Place de la Manufacture, 92310 Sèvres, France
Tel. (33) 1 41 14 04 20
Mon, Wed-Sun 10am-5pm

A collection of Art Deco vases from 1925, as well as works by such artists as Rapin, Ruhlmann, Mayodon and Aubert. Also a superb 1931 coffee service by Litron. The series of works from 1965 to 1970 features contemporary artists such as Beaudin, Fiorini, Mathieu, Guitet, and Calder. Also exquisite vases and plates by Hajdu, five cylindrical vases by Alicia Penalba, four plates by Gilioli, and a dinner service by Zao Wouki. Other noteworthy pieces include Lalanne's *Egg Ice Bucket*, Georges Jenclos's *Sleeper,* and Anne and Patrick Poirier's *Ruins of Egypt.*

Opaline and Oxblood Persian Set, blown glass, Dale Chihuly, 1988
Musée de Design et d'Arts appliqués contemporains

Musée national Picasso
The National Picasso Museum
Hôtel Salé, 5 rue de Thorigny, 75003 Paris, France
Tel. (33) 1 42 71 25 21
Apr-Sep: Mon, Wed-Sun 9.30am-6pm. Oct-Mar: Mon, Wed-Sun 9.30am-5.30pm

There are paintings, drawings, engravings, and manuscripts, as well as 191 sculptures and 107 ceramics from Picasso's major periods. Especially notable are the sculptures and ceramics from his stay at Vallauris in southern France at the beginning of the 1950s.

New Walk Museum and Art Gallery
53 New Walk, Leicester, Leicestershire LE1 7EA, UK
Tel. (44) 116 255 4100 www.leicestermuseums.ac.uk
Mon-Sat 10.30am-4pm, Sun 1-4pm

This pottery collection includes important early works by Bernard Leach, Hamada, and Staite Murray. There are some good examples of post-1945 material, ranging from Hans Coper and Lucy Rie to young contemporary potters.

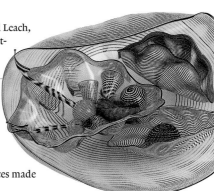

Museo Picasso
The Picasso Museum
Carrer de Montcada 15-19, 08003 Barcelona, Spain
Tel. (34) 93 3196310
Tue-Sat 10am-8pm, Sun 10am-3pm

Spain's most significant Picasso museum includes 41 ceramic pieces made between 1947 and 1965.

The Potteries Museum and Art Gallery
Bethesda Street, Hanley, Stoke-on-Trent, Staffordshire ST1 3DW, UK
Tel. (44) 1782 232323 www.stoke.gov.uk
Mon-Sat 10am-5pm, Sun 2pm-5pm

A world-class collection of ceramics containing over 30,000 pieces of pottery dating from the medieval period to the present. Their 20th-century collection is the largest in the UK and contains both industrial and studio pottery from several collections, among them the Bergen Collection of pioneer studio pottery and works by Bernard Leach, Michael Cardew, and Shoji Hamada.

Sainsbury Centre for Visual Arts
University of East Anglia, Norwich, Norfolk NR4 7TJ, UK
Tel. (44) 1603 592467 www.uea.ac.uk
Tue-Sun 11am-5pm

Includes works by Lucie Rie, Hans Coper, Bernard Leach, and Coper and Rie's students Ian Godfrey, Ewen Henderson, and John Ward. Altogether there are over 400 pieces by 27 artists. The collection of Coper is the best to be found anywhere and includes 43 pots from his studio acquired upon his death in 1981. Although the entire collection is not always on show, there is a permanent display of both Coper and Ries' works in the Crescent Wing Lobby.

Tierra del Fuego Series
1991, Toots Zynsky, 1991
(above)
*Musée de Design et d'Arts
appliqués contemporains*

Work by Hans van Hoek
(below)
Museum het Kruithuis

Museum voor Sierkunst en Vormgeving
The Museum of Decorative Arts and Design
Jan Breydelstraat 5, 9000 Gent, Belgium
Tel. (32) 9 2256676 www.design.museum.gent.be
Tue-Sun 9.30am-5pm

The museum has a remarkable collection of French Art Deco, with ceramics by Jean Mayodon, André Metthey, Henri Semmen, Raoul Lachenal, Auguste Delaherche, Emile Lenoble, and Pierre-Adrien Dalpayrat. Glass works are by Lalique, Marcel Goupy, and Maurice Marinot.

Il Museo del Vetro
The Glass Museum
Oratorio di San Sebastiano, piazza san Sebastano, 117041 Altare, Italy
Tel. (39) 019 584734 www.italianriviera.com
Mon-Sat 3-6pm
(Location change in 2002 to the Villa Rosa, Altare)

The collection contains over 2,500 objects, of which some 600 are on display, focusing mainly on glass art of the 20th century.

Victoria and Albert Museum
Cromwell Road, South Kensington, London SW7 2RL, UK
Tel. (44) 20 7942 2000 www.vam.ac.uk
Daily 10am-5.45pm (Wed & last Fri of every month 10am-10pm)

Among the more unusual holdings are modern Korean ceramics by Shin Sang-ho, reflecting a commitment to interpreting native ceramic traditions within a modern context. There is a range of Japanese crafts dating from the 1970s onwards. The Glass Gallery tends to concentrate on British work, but this is by no means exclusive. It shows work by Peter Aldridge, Colin Reid, Alison Knead, Galia Amsel, Debrah Fladgate, Dale Chihuly, and the celebrated Czech modern artists, Libensk and Brychtová.

York City Art Gallery
Exhibition Square, York, Yorkshire YO1 2EW, UK
Tel. (44) 1904 551861 www.york.gov.uk
Daily 9.30am-4.30pm

There is a remarkable collection of British pioneer and 20th-century studio pottery with fine examples by Leach, Cardew, Hamada and Staite Murray. Highlights include Leach's well-known ceramics, *Leaping Salmon* and *Tree of Life* bottle.

Yorkshire Museum
Museum Gardens, York, Yorkshire YO1 7FR, UK
Tel. (44) 1904 551800 www.york.gov.uk
Daily 10am-5pm.

The collection of several thousand pots belonging to W.A. Ismay (a collector and writer on studio ceramics), which includes work by many of the leading British ceramists such as Bernard Leach, Lucie Rie, Hans Coper, and the Japanese potter Shoji Hamada, has recently been bequeathed to the museum. Ismay amassed a meticulously catalogued collection representing the work of over 500 potters including work by northern potters who may have been missed by other collectors.

CONTINENTAL POTTERY AND PORCELAIN

Apsley House, The Wellington Museum
Hyde Park Corner, London W1V 9FA, UK
Tel. (44) 207 499 5676   www.vam.ac.uk
Tue-Sun 11am-5pm

The house contains the greatest collection of early 19th-century continental porcelain in England. From the Sèvres collection, an Egyptian service of 1809-19 contains a centrepiece made from hard-paste porcelain mounted on tôle peinte. An extensive Prussian service made at the Berlin factory in 1816-19 was given to the Duke of Wellington in 1818 by Louis XVII, and contains 64 plates showing scenes from the Duke's life. There are also the Austrian and Saxon Services, respectively presented by Francis I of Austria and Frederick Augustus IV of Saxony in 1820. These services also bear Egyptian motives recalling Napoleon's expedition to Egypt.

Musée d'Art et d'Industrie
Museum of Art and Industry
24 rue de l'Espérance, 59100 Roubaix, France
Tel. (33) 3 20 69 23 60
Daily 1-6pm

The museum boasts a collection of 19th- and 20th-century Sèvres porcelain that rates as one of the most important of its kind in France. It includes services, vases, and unique monumental pieces such as the portico designed by Sandier for the Universal Exhibition in 1913.

Musée des Arts décoratifs
Museum of Decorative Arts
39 rue Bouffard, 33000 Bordeaux, France
Tel. (33) 5 56 00 72 51
Mon, Wed-Sun 2-6pm

The faïence collection has many examples of Nevers faïence, including the blue and white Chinese style. The Bordeaux faïence is very good, the best piece being a monumental fountain with female figures.

Musée des Arts décoratifs
The Museum of Decorative Arts
Palais du Louvre, 107 rue de Rivoli, 75001 Paris, France
Tel. (33) 1 44 55 57 50   www.ucad.fr
Due to re-open in 2003

The French porcelain services on display include those of Madame du Barry (1770) and that of Marie Caroline, Queen of Naples (1773).

Musée des Beaux-Arts
The Museum of Fine Arts
22 rue Paul Doumer, 62000 Arras, France
Tel. (33) 3 21 71 26 43
Apr-mid Oct: Mon, Wed-Sun 10am-noon, 2-6pm
Rest of year: Mon, Wed-Sun 10am-noon, 2-5pm (Sat-Sun closes 6pm)

A rich collection of Tournai porcelain, ranking just behind those of Brussels and Mariemont. Particularly noteworthy is a beautiful service with birds from 1787 by Buffon, and purple camays from Duvivier made between 1762 and 1781.

Musée des Beaux-Arts
The Museum of Fine Arts
Place Charles-de-Gaulle, 59140 Dunkerque, France
Tel. (33) 3 28 59 21 65
Mon, Wed-Sun 10am-noon, 2-6pm

Meissen porcelain dishes
Suomen merimuseo

There is an extensive collection of Dutch Delftware. The pirate Jean Bart's portrait is represented in a tableau made from 540 Delft tiles.

Museo de Ceràmica
The Ceramics Museum
Palau de Pedralbes, avengida Diagonal 686, 08034 Barcelona, Spain
Tel. (34) 93 2801621
Tue-Sun 10am-3pm

This vast collection gives a comprehensive overview of Spanish ceramics between the 12th and 19th centuries. The collection is divided into separate displays from the best-known areas of ceramic production: Andalucia, Valencia (especially Paterna and Manises), Catalonia, Aragon, and Alcora. The pieces are chronologically displayed and begin with Islamic and Mudéjar pieces from the 11th to the 15th centuries.

Il Museo della Ceramica 'Manlio Trucco'
The Manlio Trucco Ceramics Museum
Villa Trucco, corso Ferrari, 191, 17011 Albisola Superiore, Italy
Tel. (39) 019 482741 www.comune.albisola-superiore.sv.it
Mon-Sat 10am-noon, Sun on request

Exhibits on the production of ceramics in Albisola, showing around 1,400 pieces, from the excavation of ancient kilns to 19th-century pottery and pharmacy jars.

Château-Musée
The Castle Museum
49400 Saumur, France
Tel. (33) 2 41 40 24 40
Mon, Wed-Sun 9.30am-noon, 2-5.30pm (times may vary, please call for details)

One of the best ceramics collections in France, showing the development of the main centres of production. Also featured are pharmaceutical pots and Delft faïences.

Ethnographic Exhibition
Ràkòczi Ferenc utca 15, 7621 Pèc, Hungary
Tel. (36) 72 315629
Tue-Sun 10am-6pm

A display of 17th- to 19th-century ceramics made in the region, including a richly ornamented pitcher and a jug (*c.* 1781) made by the guild of potters of Mohács, in the south of Hungary.

Fries Aardewerkmuseum De Waag
The De Waag Museum of Earthenware
Pruikmakershoek 2, 8754 ET Makkum, The Netherlands
Tel. (31) 515 231 341
Apr-Oct: Mon-Sat 10am-5pm, Sun 1.30-5pm

The collection is housed in a 1698 weighing house and features an overview of four centuries of ceramics with tin glaze, mainly a product of Frysian companies.

Gemeentemuseum
The City Museum
Stadhouderslaan 41, 2501 CB The Hague, The Netherlands
Tel. (31) 70 3381111 www.gemeentemuseum.nl
Tue-Sun 11am-5pm

An outstanding collection of Dutch Delftware. Many pieces are decorated in blue, but there is also rare white Delftware as well as polychrome items, including the red and gold pieces for which Delft became so famous. Some pieces are very simple while others are sophisticated and highly decorated. There is also an excellent collection of Rozenburg porcelain, including the magnificent 'eggshell porcelain' which won first prize at the Paris World's Fair of 1900.

Gosudarstvennyi muzei-zapovednik Oranienbaum
The State Museum-Preserve Oranienbaum
Iunogo Leninsa 8, 189510 Oranienbaum, Russian Federation
Tel. (7) 812 4231625
Mon, Wed-Sun 11am-5pm

Catherine the Great commissioned forty allegorical figures of Saxe porcelain from the Meissen works to decorate her palace. These exquisite heroic figurines, modelled by Kändler and Acier, are held on leafy stucco consoles, some supported by monkeys and birds. There are further porcelain displays in the Menshikov Palace, the Katalnaia Gorka Pavilion, and residential rooms in the China Palace.

Grossherzogliche Porzellansammlung
The Grand Ducal Porcelain Collection
Prinz-Georg-Palais, Schlossgartenstrasse 7, 64289 Darmstadt, Germany
Tel. (49) 6151 781414
Mon-Thu 10am-1pm, 2-5pm, Sat-Sun 10am-1pm

Most pieces in Grand Duke Ernst Ludwig von Hessen's remarkable porcelain collection were gifts from Europe's royal and imperial families. One of the largest collections of Hesse-Darmstadt porcelain from the ducal factory at Kelsterbach, there are exquisite examples from the Russian Imperial manufactory of St Petersburg. An encyclopaedic cross section of European manufacturers, with some Chinese and Japanese examples, makes this an excellent starting point for new and experienced collectors alike.

Musée de l'Hôtel Sandelin
The Sandelin Hotel Museum
14 rue Carnot, 62500 Saint-Omer, France
Tel. (33) 3 21 38 00 94 www.musenor.org
Wed, Sat-Sun 10am-noon, 2-6pm, Thu, Fri 10am-noon, 2-5pm

The museum contains a 750-piece collection of Delft porcelain, as well as remarkable paintings, sculptures, and over 40,000 shells. The showpiece is a dining table complete with turquoise-blue porcelain and plates made from 18th-century Saint-Omer faïence. There are octagonal bottles and vases from the 17th and 18th centuries with chinoiseries, pieces with floral motifs in blue camaieu, statuettes, and polychrome pieces including a large vase in 'Cachemire' style.

Il Museo dell' Istituto Statale d' Arte De Fabris per la Ceramica
The Museum of Ceramics of the De Fabris School of Art
Istituto d' Arte De Fabris, via Giove, 1, 36055 Nove, Italy
Tel. (39) 0424 590022
Mon-Sat 8am-noon (Tue, Thu by appt. only)

The museum has a vast collection of ceramics and porcelain from the 18th and the 19th centuries as well as a collection of contemporary pottery.

Koninklijke Porceleyne Fles
The Royal Delft
Rotterdamseweg 196, 2600 AA Delft, The Netherlands
Tel. (31) 15 2512030 www.royaldelft.com
Apr-Sep: Mon-Sat 9am-5pm, Sun 9.30am-5pm. Oct-Mar: Mon-Sat 9am-5pm

This is the only 17th-century factory left in Delft where the world-famous earthenware is still entirely painted by hand. It displays a fine selection of pieces from the 17th century onwards.

Museum für Kunsthandwerk
The Museum of Applied Arts
Schaumainkai 15-17, 60594 Frankfurt am Main, Germany
Tel. (49) 69 2123 4037
Tue-Sun 10am-5pm (Wed until 8pm)

The Islamic section includes faïence from the 9th to 15th centuries. The Eastern Asian section includes Chinese porcelain from the Ming and Qing periods and white and blue porcelain from the 17th and 18th centuries. The museum also houses an outstanding collection of porcelain from the leading European manufacturers such as Meissen, Berlin, Fürstenberg, Nymphenburg, Vienna, and Sèvres.

Kunstsammlungen zu Weimar
The Art Collections of Weimar
Burgplatz 4, 99423 Weimar, Germany
Tel. (49) 3643 546130 www.kunstsammlungen-weimar.de
Apr-Oct: Tue-Sun 10am-6pm (mid Oct-end Oct: Tue-Sun 10am-4.30pm)

A fine collection of German and European china, faïence from Meissen, Berlin, Vienna and Thuringian factories, as well as 16th- to 19th-century glassware.

Musée national Adrien Dubouché
The Adrien Dubouché National Museum
8 bis, place Winston Churchill, 87000 Limoges, France
Tel. (33) 5 55 33 08 50
Mon, Wed-Sun 10am-noon, 1.30-5.15pm

Remarkable examples of Limoges porcelain with items manufactured by the famous Pouyat family, such as the trompe l'oeil Folded Paper. There are pieces from the Blancs (which cemented the fame of Limoges porcelain) that were first acclaimed at the 1878 Universal Exhibition, including an Etruscan Coffee Service by Edme Pouyat. Not to be missed are the examples of porcelain from Vienna by Claudius-Innocentus Du Paquier, which sit alongside rare statuettes by Wegely.

Musée national de la Céramique
The National Museum of Ceramics
Place de la Manufacture, 92310 Sèvres, France
Tel. (33) 1 41 14 04 20
Mon, Wed-Sun 10am-5pm

Reputed to be the world's largest and oldest museum dedicated to the ceramic arts, it is justifiably overwhelming. The collection traces the history of the Sèvres factory and reveals shifts in French royal taste, from biscuit figures to tableware and tea services. There are exquisite figurines, including Boucher's Les trois graces, Falconet's

Baigneuse and *L'amour Falconet*. The vase collection includes pieces like the *Duplessis* vase and works by Jean-Louis Morin. Tableware includes the service designed for Madame du Barry in 1770 and part of the Buffon service. Clocks are well represented, as are pieces inspired by ancient ceramics and ancient Egypt, such as the thirteen-piece Egyptian service sent to the Russian Tsar by Napoleon. Other masterpieces include an Etruscan scrolled vase (1813) showing the Entry into Paris, and a Chinese teapot and gilded bronze vase by Fragonard. There is also a stunning lady's cabinet consisting of porcelain plaques supported by bronze frames (1825-27). Other 19th-century items testify to the innovative techniques developed at the factory, including the 'B' violet vase with copper-red decoration (1883). A group of 320 pieces from the end of the 19th century are made in Art Nouveau style. There are life-sized animals made from white Meissen porcelain by the sculptors Käendler and Kirchner, rare pieces of blue and white Dutch Delftware and a group of blue and white 'Medici' porcelains, regarded as the earliest of their type made in Europe.

Meissen table
decorations, 1740s
Suomen merimuseo

Museé National de la Renaissance
National Museum of the Renaissance
Château d'Ecouen, 95440 Ecouen, France
Tel. (33) 1 34 38 38 63   www.musexpo.com
Mon, Wed-Sun 9.45am-12.30pm, 2-5.15pm

Among the most celebrated Renaissance ceramists were Masséot Abaquesne, Bernard Palissey, and the group of unknown artists working from Saint-Porchaire. Abaquesne was responsible for much of the ornamental tiling which decorates the Château d'Ecouen, and which is clearly influenced by Italian maiolica work.

Musée national du Moyen-Age – Thermes et Hôtel de Cluny
The National Museum of the Middle Ages – The Cluny Baths and Hôtel
6 place Paul-Painlevé, 75005 Paris, France
Tel. (33) 1 53 73 78 00
Mon, Wed-Sun 9.15am-5.45pm

One of the richest medieval collections in the world, housed in the Gothic Cluny Abbey. There is a remarkable collection of Spanish lustre ceramics and some very rare pieces such as the three early 15th-century *bassins creux à bélières* (hollow bowls), two large pharmacy pots, as well as a decorated bowl and plate (1430).

Nationalmuseum
The National Museum
S. Blasieholmshamnen, 103 24 Stockholm, Sweden
Tel. (46) 8 5195 4300   www.nationalmuseum.se
Tue 11am-8pm, Wed-Sun 11am-5pm (Sep-Dec also Thu 5pm-8pm)

Items here were manufactured in Germany (Meissen, Höchst, Nymphenburg, Berlin), Austria, Holland, Italy, Spain, France (Saint-Cloud, Chantilly, Sèvres, Verneuilh), Belgium, and Russia (with a plate from Catherine the Great's Yacht Service).

Museo nazionale della Ceramica 'Duca di Martina'
The National Museum of Ceramics 'Duca di Martina'
Via Cimarosa 77, 80100 Naples, Italy
Tel. (39) 081 5788418
Tue-Sat 9am-2pm, Sun 9am-1pm

A priceless collection of porcelain and maiolica, uniting works by Meissen, Limoges, Capodimonte, and Sèvres. Among the collection of Renaissance earthenware are works by Gubbio, Deruta, Faenza, and Palermo. The museum also boasts precious examples of Chinese and Japanese porcelain and a collection of enamel and ivory.

Musée Nissim de Camondo
The Nissim de Camondo Museum
63 rue de Monceau, 75008 Paris, France
Tel. (33) 1 53 89 06 50
Wed-Sun 10am-noon, 2-5pm

This museum is a jewel box of elegance and refinement, evoking the days of Louis XVI and Marie Antoinette. There is an extensive collection of rare hand-painted Sèvres, Meissen, and Chantilly services.

Palacio Real
The Royal Palace
Calle Bailén s/n, 28071 Madrid, Spain
Tel. (34) 91 5420059
Apr-Sep: Mon-Sat 9am-6pm. Oct-Mar: Mon-Sat 9.30am-5pm. All year: Sun 9am-3pm

One of the finest European collections of porcelain is housed in the Salon de Porcelanas. It includes porcelain from the best Spanish furnaces, most from the Royal Factory of the Granja.

Porzellansammlung – Staatliche Kunstsammlungen Dresden
The Porcelain Collection – State Art Collections of Dresden
Zwinger Entrance 'Glockenspielpavillon', 01067 Dresden, Germany
Tel. (49) 351 4627   www.staatl-kunstsammlungen-dresden.de
Mon-Wed, Fri-Sun 10am-6pm

Collectors of fine porcelain should not bypass this museum. Don't miss the massive porcelain animals designed by Johann Joachim Kaendler at Meissen or the porcelain glockenspiel which played rows of unglazed white porcelain bells. There is a special exhibit dedicated to Johann Fredrich Böttger, who in 1708 created the first European porcelain modelled on that of the Far East. Some of his first attempts at coloured glazes are on display.

Porzellansammlung Schloss Nymphenburg
The Porcelain Collection of the Nymphenburg Palace
Schloss Nymphenburg 1, 80638 Munich, Germany
Tel. (49) 89 179080
Apr-mid Oct: daily 9am-6pm (Thu 9am-8pm). Rest of year: daily 10am-4pm

The Bäuml Collection of Nymphenburg porcelain, housed in the south wing of the palace, boasts some extraordinary examples, including painted figurines by Franz Anton Bustelli, master modellist of the Nymphenburg factory between 1754 and 1763.

Queen's Gallery, Buckingham Palace
Buckingham Palace Road, London SW1A 1AA, UK
Tel. (44) 20 7839 1377   www.royal.gov.uk
Reopening in 2002

The royal holdings of porcelain are vast and of superb quality. Even with the expansion of the galleries, there will be barely enough space to display the holdings which come from many of the well-known European factories, including Sèvres.

Rijksmuseum
The State Museum
Stadhouderskade 42, 1071 ZD Amsterdam, The Netherlands
Tel. (31) 20 6732121 www.rijksmuseum.nl
Daily 10am-5pm

The museum's Meissen collection is among the finest in the world, after that in Dresden. On show is a vast array of high-quality ornamental pieces, figures, and porcelain services from such famous Dutch factories as Weesp, Oud-Loosdrecht, and Ouder-Amstel. Highlights include the *Temple of Venus*, by Johann Gottlob Kirchner (1727), an ice-pail decorated with birds in a landscape from Friedrich Daeuber's porcelain factory (c. 1790), and a crockery set from Joannes de Mol's factory (c. 1776).

Schauhalle der staatlichen Porzellanmanufaktur
The Showroom of the State Porcelain Manufactory
Talstrasse 9, 01662 Meissen, Germany
Tel. (352) 1 468208 www.meissen.de
Exhibition: daily 9am-5pm. Workshops: daily 9am-noon, 1-5pm

The Meissen tradition is well illustrated in the museum. It holds over 20,000 pieces of which about 3,000 are displayed in annually rotating exhibitions. It was here, as a virtual prisoner under Augustus the Strong, that Johann Friedrich Böttger discovered the secret of porcelain in 1707 (the precious ceramic that the Chinese had been making for almost 1,000 years). Visitors can also watch the preparation of paste and the designs being painted on by hand in the demonstration workshop.

Suomen merimuseo
The Maritime Museum of Finland
Hylkysaari, 00570 Helsinki, Finland
Tel. (358) 9 40501 www.nba.fi
May-end Sep: daily 11am-5pm. Mar-Apr: Sat-Sun 10am-3pm

The museum is a repository for submerged ancient relics found around Finland, including over 100 unbroken porcelain dishes belonging to the early period of production of the Meissen porcelain factory. Among the dishes there is Böttger porcelain from the 1720s and 1730s.

Villa Ephrussi de Rothschild
06230 Saint-Jean-Cap-Ferrat, France
Tel. (33) 4 93 01 33 09 www.villa-ephrussi.com
Mid Feb-Oct: daily 10am-6pm(Jul-Aug until 7pm)
Nov-mid Feb: Sat-Sun & public holidays 10am-6pm

The pieces that come from the Royal Manufactory are stunning: China Sèvres pieces of lapis lazuli and royal blue, Bordaloue vases, and the 'vases aux antiques ferrés' with designs by Boucher. Also on display are the precious yellow Sèvres from Vincennes. A service of Sèvres porcelain with love motifs, also by Boucher, monopolizes an entire window. In the Square Drawing Room is a collection of Fürstenberg porcelain which stands next to a remarkable group of yellow Du Barry sky-blue or pink Sèvres china.

Musée de la Ville de Bruxelles
The Museum of the City of Brussels
La Maison du Roi, Grand-Place, 1000 Bruxelles, Belgium
Tel. (32) 2 2794350 www.brussels-online.be
Apr-Sep: Mon-Thu 10am-12.30pm, 1.30-5pm
Oct-Mar: Mon-Thu 10am-12.30pm, 1.30-4pm. All year: Sat-Sun 10am-1pm

A beautiful collection of porcelain and Brussels faïence. Shapes are simple and the decor ranges from polychrome flowers to landscapes, medallions, and garlands. There is an 18th-century soup tureen shaped like a green cabbage, with a bird on top of the lid and three slugs for its feet. There is also a fine collection of porcelain inspired by the Empire and Louis-Philippe styles.

Staffordshire figurine of 'The Red Barn', scene of the infamous murder of Maria Martin (above)
Saffron Walden Museum

Sugar box, rock pattern
c. 1795-1800 (below)
Spode Museum

Waddesdon Manor – The Rothschild Collection
Waddesdon, near Aylesbury, Buckinghamshire HP18 0JH, UK
Tel. (44) 1296 653211 www.waddesdon.org.uk
Please call for opening times of manor. Grounds: Wed-Sun 11am-5pm

This collection of Sèvres porcelain is matched in the UK only by that at the Wallace and Royal Collections. Waddesdon houses a series of Sèvres garnitures and vases, many of impressive size. It is also home to three of the rare 'masted ship' vases of 1761 (only eleven of which are known to survive in the world). In the Sèvres Exhibition Rooms are the Starhemberg Service, a dinner and dessert service of 300 pieces presented in 1766 by Louis XV to the Austrian ambassador, Prince Starhemberg. There are also superb examples of Meissen porcelain displayed on the dining-room table.

The Wallace Collection
Hertford House, Manchester Square, London W1M 6BN, UK
Tel. (44) 20 7563 9500 www.the-wallace-collection.org.uk
Mon-Sat 10am-5pm, Sun 2-5pm

The elegance and ostentatious luxury of the *ancien régime* in France is well illustrated by this 18th-century Sèvres porcelain collection. The 4th Marquess was an astute and careful purchaser and favoured items in a perfect state and with royal connections. The setting, among remarkable examples of French 18th-century furniture, allows you to fully appreciate who the items were designed for.

Zsolnay Múzeum
The Zsolnay Museum
Káptalan utca 2, 7621 Pécs, Hungary
Tel. (36) 72 324822 www.pserve.hu
Tue-Sun 10am-6pm

The museum chronologically displays the most beautiful examples of the Zsolnay factory's decorative potteries, from earthenware dishes and decorative pottery (1853) through to 'porcelain-faïence' (1858), and frost-resistant pyrogranite that could be coloured with either a glazed or an unglazed finish. Eosin decoration can be seen on Art Nouveau ornamental dishes that were displayed at the Universal Exhibition in Paris in 1900.

ENGLISH POTTERY AND PORCELAIN

Allen Gallery
10-12 Church Street, Alton, Hampshire
GU34 1BA, UK
Tel. (44) 1420 82802 www.hants.gov.uk
Tue-Sat 10am-5pm

One of southern England's most outstanding ceramics collections. Comprising English, Continental, and Oriental pottery, porcelain, and tiles illustrating the history of ceramics from 1250 to the present day.

Clifton Park Museum

Clifton Lane, Rotherham, South Yorkshire S65 2AA, UK
Tel. (44) 709 823635
Mon-Sat 10am-5pm, Sun 2.30-5pm

The most comprehensive public collection of Rockingham porcelain in the country. A highlight of the collection is the Rhinocerous vase.

Harris Museum and Art Gallery

Market Square, Preston, Lancashire PR1 2PP, UK
Tel. (44) 1772 258 248   www.preston.gov.uk
Mon-Sat 10am-5pm

An important holding of British ceramics. It shows the development of pottery and porcelain from the 17th to the early 20th centuries, including slipware, tin-glazedware, salt-glazed stoneware, creamware, dry bodyware, and porcelain by the major factories.

Martinware Pottery Collection

Southall Library, Osterley Park Road, Southall, Middlesex UB2 4BL, UK
Tel. (44) 20 8574 3412   www.ealing.gov.uk
Tue-Sat 9.30am-5pm

This collection of over 300 pieces is made up solely of the work of the Martin brothers who specialized in producing a salt-glazed stoneware. They drew their inspiration from the fields and hedgerows along the canals.

De Morgan Foundation

15 Codman Close, London SW15 6RG, UK
Tel. (44) 20 8785 6450
Relocation in 2001/2 to Wandsworth, south London

The Foundation's collection of Arts and Crafts pots and tiles by William De Morgan is by far the largest anywhere. See the results of his experiments with glazes that produced intense greens and blues more commonly seen in maiolica wares, and view his tiles based on a range of design motifs from medieval figures to the elegant and decorative Art Nouveau style. An added bonus is the extensive archive pertaining to the De Morgans and their circle.

Pair of Queen's ware vases decorated by Emile Lessore, c.1870
The Wedgwood Museum

Nelson-Atkins Museum of Art

4525 Oak Street, Kansas City, Missouri 64111-1873, USA
Tel. (1) 816 751 1278   www.nelson-atkins.org
Tue-Thu 10am-4pm, Fri 10am-9pm, Sat 10am-5pm, Sun 1-5 pm

The exceptional Burnap Collection illustrates the complete history of English pottery. It has over 1,600 objects with particularly strong holdings of 17th- and 18th-century slipwares and Delftware.

The Potteries Museum and Art Gallery

Bethesda Street, Hanley, Stoke-on-Trent, Staffordshire ST1 3DW, UK
Tel. (44) 1782 232323   www.stoke.gov.uk
Mon-Sat 10am-5pm, Sun 2pm-5pm

One of the largest and finest collections of pottery and porcelain in the world, its collection contains an unparalleled representation of some 30,000 Staffordshire wares

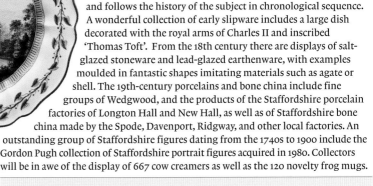

and follows the history of the subject in chronological sequence. A wonderful collection of early slipware includes a large dish decorated with the royal arms of Charles II and inscribed 'Thomas Toft'. From the 18th century there are displays of salt-glazed stoneware and lead-glazed earthenware, with examples moulded in fantastic shapes imitating materials such as agate or shell. The 19th-century porcelains and bone china include fine groups of Wedgwood, and the products of the Staffordshire porcelain factories of Longton Hall and New Hall, as well as of Staffordshire bone china made by the Spode, Davenport, Ridgway, and other local factories. An outstanding group of Staffordshire figures dating from the 1740s to 1900 include the Gordon Pugh collection of Staffordshire portrait figures acquired in 1980. Collectors will be in awe of the display of 667 cow creamers as well as the 120 novelty frog mugs.

Rienzi House

1406 Kirby Drive, Houston, Texas 77019, USA
Tel. (1) 713 639 7800 www.mfah.org
Mon, Thu-Sat, 10am-4pm (tours only), Sun 1-5pm

A Palladian-style home packed with 17th- and 18th-century Italian and Spanish paint-ings, 18th- century English furniture, and one of North America's best collections of soft paste Worcester porcelain amassed by Harris Masterson III. Numbering several hundred pieces, the collection consists of items from the first period of production (1751-83), although there is a significant number of late 18th- early 19th-century works. Star pieces include seven of the eight figures known to be made by Worcester, with armorials and pieces decorated with patterns designed by James Giles.

Queen's Ware polychrome enamel decorated plate featuring a central view of Moore Park, c.1775-76 (top)
The Wedgwood Museum

Staffordshire figure, 'Astbury' type, c.1745 (above)
Saffron Walden Museum

The Royal Crown Derby Museum

Royal Crown Derby Porcelain Co., 194 Osmaston Road, Derby, Derbyshire DE23 8JZ, UK
Tel. (44) 1332 712800 www.royal-crown-derby.co.uk
Please call for opening times

An encyclopaedic collection of Derby porcelain with examples from the foundation of the factory in 1748 to the present day. The cornerstone of the collection are the early figures in the Meissen style. Rarities include a George III Coronation Tankard, the famous Kedleston vase commissioned by Lord Scarsdale (c. 1790), and a mug of 1820 by William Dixon painted with a panel showing grotesque men fighting. Besides the famous brightly coloured and gilt Imari ware, there is a room dedicated to the Raven Bequest – an exemplary collection of Derby Porcelain donated by Ronald Raven. The factory tour is highly recommended but must be arranged by appointment in advance.

Royal Doulton Visitor Centre

Nile Street, Burslem, Stoke-on-Trent, Staffordshire ST6 2AJ, UK
Tel. (44) 1782 292434 www.royal-doulton.com
Mon-Sat 9.30am-5pm, Sun 10.30am-4.30pm

Visitors walk through original refurbished factory buildings dating back to the mid 19th century, with the world's largest public collection of a group of Royal Doulton figures. Examples include pottery and terracotta sculptures by George Tinworth; salt-glazed incised wares by Hannah Barlow; and elaborate modelled wares by C.J. Noke. There is work by Phoebe Stabler, Albert Toft, and Charles Vyse, with representative coverage of the complementary character jugs and Toby jugs.

Royal Museum of Scotland

Chambers Street, Edinburgh, Scotland, EH1 1JF , UK
Tel. (44) 131 225 7534 www.nms.ac.uk
Mon-Sat 10am-5pm (Tue until 8pm), Sun noon-5pm

This large collection includes extensive numbers of Wemyss Ware from Kirkcaldy and transfer-printed earthenware by J. & M. P. Bell & Co, as well as fine pieces of Delftfield and West Pans pottery.

Saffron Walden Museum
Museum Street, Saffron Walden, Essex CB10 1JL, UK
Tel. (44) 1799 510333 www.uttlesford.gov.uk
Mon-Sat 10am-5pm, Sun & public holidays 2-5pm

The ceramics collection focuses on English pottery and porcelain, together with European and Chinese imports. The English ceramics collection covers earthenwares and stonewares, and includes a number of Staffordshire figures. There is soft paste porcelain from Worcester, Bow, Derby, and Caughley. Also a small collection of Castle Hedingham pottery, a highly ornamented ware produced by Edward Bingham.

Staffordshire figure, 'Astbury' type, *c.*1745 (above)
Saffron Walden Museum

Garden seat, leg bath & cheese cradle (below)
Spode Museum

Schloss Wörlitz
The Wörlitz Castle
Schloss Wörlitz, 06786 Wörlitz, Germany
Tel. (49) 34905 4090 www.hom.t-online.de
Please call for opening times

The collection comprises some 105 pieces of Wedgwood pottery and includes vases, tea sets, and assorted tableware, much of which was displayed in porcelain cabinets by Prince Franz von Anhault-Dessau. There is a notable sculpture of Somnus in Princess Luise's bedroom, which was ordered from Wedgwood in 1774 and is one of the largest pieces ever to be made by the factory. More modest but no less beautiful is the 23-piece Wörlitz tea set in black basalt with enamel painting which has thirteen motifs representing the eternal themes of love and music.

Spode Museum
Church Street, Stoke-on-Trent, Staffordshire ST4 1BX, UK
Tel. (44) 1782 744011 www.spode.co.uk
Mon-Sat 9am-5pm, Sun 10am-4pm (factory visits by appt. only)

Spode's signature was the fine underglazed blue and white printed earthenware. He adopted classical images, producing multi-centred pattern earthenware and china covered with mythological images. Every facet of the company is represented by superior work, from richly painted and gilded dessert dishes (*c.* 1801) in Stoke China, to Parian figures. The main galleries focus on early work from 1770 to 1833, and the Blue Room can be visited by appointment, where underglazed blue printedware is displayed on antique furniture. The archives, open to serious researchers only, hold all the original copper plates used for plain printing (25,000) and pattern books (1800 onwards) recording 75,000 designs used at the factory.

The Wedgwood Museum
Josiah Wedgwood & Sons Ltd, Barlaston, Stoke-on-Trent, Staffordshire ST12 9ES, UK
Tel. (44) 1782 282818 www.wedgwoodmuseum.org.uk
Mon-Fri 9am-5pm, Sat-Sun 10am-4pm

This is the largest and most varied assemblage of early Wedgwood in the world. It ranges from a unique collection of Josiah Wedgwood's original trials for the perfection of the Queen's Ware service made for Catherine the Great of Russia in 1774, to a rare two-metre-high Exhibition Vase, decorated by Emile Lessore, the only one of its kind in Britain. On display is an exquisite reproduction of the Portland or Barberini

Vase (the original is made from cameo-glass and dates from around 25BC). The *Sydney Cove Medallion*, a small circular commemorative medallion made from clay was sent from Sydney Cove itself. Another distinctive piece is the *Slave Medallion*, one of Wedgwood's most important contributions to the Movement for the Abolition of Slavery.

Yorkshire Museum
Museum Gardens, York, Yorkshire YO1 7FR, UK
Tel. (44) 1904 551800 www.york.gov.uk
Daily 10am-5pm

A nationally important collection of ceramics which includes tin-glazed Delftware, Leeds creamware, and Rockingham porcelain. There are also pieces from most Yorkshire potteries, examples of county pottery, late-Victorian art pottery production and work by York silversmiths.

EUROPEAN GLASS (1500-1880)

Goblet, Venice, c. 1500
Kunstsammlungen der
Veste Coburg

The Art Institute of Chicago
111 South Michigan Avenue, Chicago, Illinois 60603, USA
Tel. (1) 312 443 3600 www.artic.edu
Mon, Wed-Fri 10.30am-4.30pm, Tue 10.30am-8pm, Sat 10am-5pm, Sun noon-5pm

An important collection of German and Dutch glass. It includes a Nuremberg goblet by Georg Friedrich Killinger, dated 1723, and a goblet attributed to Franz Gondelach of Kassel.

Musée Atelier du Verre
The Glass Studio Museum
1 rue du General de Gaulle, 59216 Sars-Poteries, France
Tel. (44) 3 27 61 61 44
Mon, Wed-Fri 3-6pm, Sat-Sun & public holidays 3-7pm

A collection of 2,000-3,000 *bousillés*, the pieces the glassblowers made during their breaks for their own use, displaying their experiments and personal creations.

Musée Baccarat
Baccarat Museum
30 bis rue du Paradis, 75010 Paris, France
Tel. (33) 1 47 70 64 30 www.baccarat.fr
Mon-Sat 10am-6pm

This exceptional collection of rare crystal glassware illustrates the best of this world-famous French crystal factory, which still produces high-quality crystal glass. There are collections of glassware engraved with coats-of-arms, monograms, and emblems, formerly owned by the Imperial House of Japan, King Farouk of Egypt, and President Franklin D. Roosevelt, among many others.

Bergstrom-Mahler Museum
165 North Park Avenue, Neenah, Wisconsin 54956, USA
Tel. (1) 920 751 4658
Tue-Fri 10am-4.30pm (Thu until 8pm), Sat-Sun 1-4.30pm

The collection includes around 300 pieces of quality Germanic glass, mainly drinking vessels from the late 16th to the late 19th centuries, from Bohemia, Austria, Silesia, Saxony, and Germany. The earliest example, dated 1573, is a large ceremonial drinking vessel known as a Stangenglas, decorated with painted enamels. Later examples (*c.* 1700s) of engraved covered goblets and beakers with inscriptions made in Bohemia demonstrate the technical brilliance of engravers using wheel engraving.

Bristol City Museum and Art Gallery
Queen's Road, Bristol BS8 1RL, UK
Tel. (44) 117 922 3571 www.bristol-city.gov.uk
Daily 10am-5pm

Bristol is best known for the production of lead blue glass, which became known as 'Bristol Blue'. Besides this, the museum has pieces of green glass and works by the most important 'Bristol Blue' glassmakers, Lazarus and Isaac Jacobs.

Broadfield House Glass Museum
Compton Drive, Kingswinford, West Midlands DY6 9NS, UK
Tel. (44) 1384 812 745 www.dudley.gov.uk
Tue-Sun 2-5pm. Public holidays 10am-5pm

An internationally important collection of British glass from the 17th century to the present day. Works by Varnish, Pellat, and Monart; good examples of enamelled decoration on glasses from the workshop of William and Mary Beilby at Newcastle-upon-Tyne; a splendid and rare baluster vase with its cover painted by the artist known as P.P. or P.F.; and the best collection of locally-made cameo glass in the country.

Chrysler Museum of Art
245 West Olney Road, Norfolk, Virginia 23510, USA
Tel. (1) 757 664 6200 www.chyrsler.org
Tue-Sat 10am-5pm, Sun 1-5pm

The museum is especially rich in European glass, with French Art Nouveau and Art Deco particularly well represented. There are some 255 examples from such famous names as Gallé and Daum, with unique pieces such as a 'verrerie parlante' ('talking glass') engraved with a poem by Maurice Rollinat (*c.* 1892). The French pâte de verre collection ranges from turn-of-the-century pieces by George Despret, through to vases and bowls by Gabriel Argy-Rousseau. There are examples of exquisite glass from Venice, including bowls laced with white filigree patterns and fanciful glasses with dragon stems. Also pieces of German Zwischengold glass (two layers with gold foil in between) and the glittering results of diamond-point stippling from the Netherlands. Amongst the examples of English cameo glass are a number of notable pieces, including two pendant vases titled *Happy Child* and *Unhappy Child* made by Joseph Locke in 1877, a richly detailed *Antarctic Vase* designed and carved by George Woodall (*c.* 1909-10) and a recently acquired *Milton Vase* (1878) by John Northwood.

The Corning Museum of Glass
One Museum Way, Corning, New York 14830, USA
Tel. (1) 607 974 8274 www.cmog.org
Daily 9am-5pm. Jul-Aug: 9am-8pm

The collection of European glass is encyclopaedic, with more than 10,000 examples of Venetian, Germanic, Bohemian, French, Dutch, Spanish, Scandinavian, Russian, English, and other glasses. There are nearly 1,000 Venetian and Façon de Venise glasses with all types of decorative techniques including latticino, millefiori, dragon-stem, applied decoration, gilded, gold-painted, enamelled, diamond-point engraved, and other elaborate decorations. The collections of dated German enamelled glass and copper-wheel engraved vessels are particularly outstanding. The collection of English glass contains nearly 2,000 pieces, including two goblets attributed to the glasshouse of Giacorno Verzelini. Both of these pieces are dated and the earlier one, which bears the date 1577, is the first known dated piece of English glass. The collection also includes two vessels with the raven's head seal of George Ravenscroft, the developer of lead glass who founded the English table glass industry.

Musée du Cristal
The Museum of Crystal
93 bis cour Cristalleries, 54120 Baccarat, France
Tel. (33) 3 83 76 60 06
Apr-Oct: daily 9.30am-12.30pm, 2-6.30pm. Nov-Mar: daily 10am-noon, 2-6pm

This is one of France's most celebrated glass factories, set up in 1764 by Louis XV to provide a national product that would halt imports of rival glass from Bohemia.

Danske Kongers Kronologiske Samling Rosenborg
The Rosenborg Royal Collection
Øster Voldgade 4A, 1350 Copenhagen, Denmark
Tel. (45) 33 153286 www.kulturnet.dk
Please call for opening times

Goblet with the bust of Duke Ernst I, 1830 (above)
Kunstsammlungen der Veste Coburg

Cut goblet from Silesia, c.1750 (below)
Glasmuseum Frauenau

Room 22 is known as The Glass Cabinet and contains an exquisite collection of glass presented to King Frederik IV of Denmark by the City of Venice during his stay there in 1709. Porcelain cabinets were fashionable at this time, but this is the only known glass cabinet. The Venetian section includes mainly 17th-century pieces of clear glass inlaid with white threads, blue glass with white wavy lines, and yellow and red coloured glass. There are examples of engraved glass from Saxony (c.1700); red ruby glass with gold, most likely made in South Germany and glass inherited by the King, including Frederik II's humpen from 1598.

Fundación Centro nacional del Vidrio
The National Centre of Glass Foundation
Real Fábrica de Cristales de la Granja, 40100 La Granja de San Ildefonso, Segovia, Spain
Tel. (34) 921 471712 www.fcnv.es
Tue-Sat 10am-6pm, Sun 10am-3pm

The museum contains a fine collection of some 500 pieces of Granja glass dating from the 18th and 19th centuries. There is also a magnificent collection of European bottles and vases from the 16th to the 19th centuries, many of which bear the distinctive stamp of the proprietor, manufacturer, or the dealer.

Glasmuseum Frauenau
The Frauenau Glass Museum
Am Museumspark 1, 94258 Frauenau, Germany
Tel. (49) 9926 940035 www.eisch.de
Mid May-Oct: Tue-Sun 9am-5pm. End Dec-mid May: Tue-Sun 10am-4pm

Galleries cover the history of glass making. Ranging from Egyptian vessels, Roman glasses, Venetian items and cut-glass goblets of the Baroque era, to later periods such as Jugendstil and Art Deco. Also an extensive array of glass from postwar Europe.

Glasmuseum Rheinbach
The Rheinbach Glass Museum
Himmeroder Wall 6, 53359 Rheinbach, Germany
Tel. (49) 2226 14224
Tue-Fri 10am-noon, 2-5pm, Sat 2-5pm, Sun 11am-5pm

Outstanding exhibits of Bohemian glassware include the well-known hollow glass that was a specialization of Northern Bohemia. Exhibits range from the Baroque period, Biedermeier and Historicism to contemporary studio glass, with special emphasis on 19th-century glassware.

Harris Museum and Art Gallery
Market Square, Preston, Lancashire PR1 2PP, UK
Tel. (44) 1772 258 248   www.preston.gov.uk
Mon-Sat 10am-5pm

The local optician, Dr Harry Taylor, collected 18th-century drinking glasses and donated them to the museum in 1964. These, combined with the J.B. Hide collection of drinking glasses, and the Laura Seddon collection of jewel-like coloured drinking glasses, jugs, and bowls from the 18th and 19th centuries, form a very fine collection.

Cecil Higgins Art Gallery and Museum
Castle Close, Bedford, Bedfordshire MK40 3NY, UK
Tel. (44) 1234 211222
Tue-Sat 11am-5pm, Sun 2-5pm

*Goblet with lid, Venice, c.1600
Kunstsammlungen der Veste Coburg*

Wealthy, bored brewer, Cecil Higgins, amassed a wide range of quality glass in the 1930s. Although there are a few Roman and Egyptian items, the earliest glass represented is façon de Venise made in Europe, based on the famed recipe for clear glass that the Venetians had tried to keep secret. The real prize, however, is the collection of glass from the reigns of William and Mary, and Queen Anne, illustrating the development of English lead glass from complicated Venetian patterns, which turned out to be a failure. Don't miss the drinking glasses manufactured between 1688 and around 1760, when the Jacobites and anti-Jacobites were debating their political stance and drinking to the Sovereign's health with glasses decorated according to their chosen allegiance.

Kunstsammlungen der Veste Coburg
The Art Collections of the Coburg Citadel
Veste Coburg, 96450 Coburg, Germany
Tel. (49) 9561 8790 www.kunstsammlungen-coburg.de
Apr-Oct: Tue-Sun 10am-5pm. Nov-Mar: Tue-Sun 1-4pm

The museum displays a small selection of Venetian glass for the banquet table and enamel, millefiori, agate, lozenge and threaded glass from Venice itself, alongside façon de Venise glass from Hall and Innsbruck, Spain, the Netherlands, and Germany. The oldest pieces include an early 15th-century ribbed goblet painted with enamel, and a jug of milky and blue glass, dated late 15th century. In the adjoining room, there is baroque cut glass from Nuremberg, Thuringia, Saxony, Potsdam, Bohemia, and Silesia.

Museum of London
London Wall, London EC2Y 5HN, UK
Tel. (44) 20 7600 3699 www.museumoflondon.org.uk
By appt. only

The Garton Collection of English table glass is encyclopaedic and of outstanding quality. Formed between 1927 and 1934 by Sir Richard Garton (1857-1934), it comprises 437 pieces ranging from the mid 17th century to the beginning of the 19th century. Its focus is on goblets and wineglasses, although there are also bowls, candlesticks, jelly glasses, and sweetmeat baskets. The gem is the Chesterfield Flute, the only known specimen of English mid 17th-century glass of this type.

Glass beaker, Germany,
1716
Royal Museum of Scotland

Mompesson House
The Close, Salisbury, Wiltshire SP1 2EL, UK
Tel. (44) 1722 335659
Apr-Oct: Mon-Wed, Sat-Sun noon-5.30pm

The Turnbull collection of 18th-century drinking glasses includes an
Amen glass (of which there are only 26 known examples) and Belby
enamelled glasses.

Museé national de la Renaissance
National Museum of the Renaissance
Château d'Ecouen, 95440 Ecouen, France
Tel. (33) 1 34 38 38 63 www.musexpo.com
Mon, Wed-Sun & public holidays 9.45am-12.30pm, 2-5.15pm

Among the pieces on display are a Venetian dish of dense blue, flecked with gold (16th century), a gilded dish with the insignia of Anne of Brittany (late 15th century), and a finely detailed depiction of the Birth of Bacchus on Venetian glass (16th century).

Passauer Glasmuseum
The Passau Glass Museum
Hotel Wilder Mann, Am Rathausplatz, 94032 Passau, Germany
Tel. (49) 851 35071
Daily 10am-4pm (times may vary, please call for details)

A survey of Bohemian glass manufacturing, embracing 250 years of history, marks out
this collection as the largest of its kind. There are 30,000 pieces, from the Baroque
period to the 20th century. Most impressive is the collection of Biedermeier glass,
much of it reverse hand painting of scenic subjects. There are also agate and glass perfume bottles and boxes alongside hand-painted opaline glass, and a cut and gilded
goblet with a portrait of Napoleon.

Royal Museum of Scotland
National Museums of Scotland
Chambers Street, Edinburgh EH1 1JF, Scotland, UK
Tel. (44) 131 225 7534 www.nms.ac.uk
Mon-Sat 10am-5pm (Tue until 8pm), Sun noon-5pm

A small collection of approximately 1,000 items, with several outstanding early exam-
ples such as the Pitfirrane goblet, traditionally said to be the stirrup cup of James VI.
Eighteeneth-century wine glasses illustrate the vigorous tradition of conviviality, and
Jacobite glass provides a sumptuous indicator of fashions and shifts in political life.
Most remarkable are the early 18th-century Amen glasses.

Sklârské Muzeum
Museum of Glass
Nov Svet, 512 46 Harrachov 96, Czech Republic
Tel. (420) 432 52 81 41 2
Tue-Sun 9am-5pm

This factory, started in 1712, is famous for engraved, cut crystal, along with glass in
shades of ruby red, yellow (created using uranium), and green. Tours of the factory
include the 1895 engraving rooms where you can still see original grinding and cutting equipment powered by water turbines (the only place in Europe). The museum
next door exhibits the history of Bohemian glass making, including red and black
Hyalith glass, and work by Dominik Biman.

Smålands Museum – Sveriges Glasmuseum
The Museum of Småland – Swedish Glass Museum
Södra Järnvägsgatan 2, 351 04 Växjö, Sweden
Tel. (46) 470 704200 www.smalandsmuseum.g.se
Mon-Fri 10am-5pm, Sat-Sun 11am-5pm (Jun-Aug closed Mon)

This is Sweden's oldest provincial museum, with collections dating from 1792. The
heart of the collection is its internationally renowned glass, with exhibits tracing the
development of Swedish glass from its late 16th-century origins to modern studio glass.

Umeleckoprumyslové museum v praze
Museum of Decorative Arts in Prague
Ulice 17. listopadu 2, 110 00 Prague, Czech Republic
Tel. (42) 02 5109 3111
Tue-Sun 10am-6pm

The Czech Republic has been known for it glass production since the Middle Ages,
but is particularly famous for works produced in Bohemia from the end of the 16th
century. Displayed are glass objects from the Middle Ages to the 19th century drawn
from the Lanna collection, and from a collection of 2,400 glass objects donated by the
director of the Provincial Museum in Stuttgart.

Museo vetrario di Murano – Sezione antico
The Murano Glass Museum – Antique Section
Palazzo Giustinian, Fondamenta Giustinian 8, 30141 Venice, Italy
Tel. (39) 041 739586
Apr-Sep: Mon, Tue, Thu-Sun 10am-5pm. Oct-Mar: Mon, Tue, Thu-Sun 10am-4pm

The museum possesses some of the oldest examples of Muranese glass from the first
half of the 14th century. It also boasts the famous *Coppa Nuziale* (also known as *Coppa
Barovier*) by Angelo Barovier, who died in 1460. There are some outstanding examples
of Filigrana Glass from the 15th-16th centuries; some fine examples of Opalino Glass
with its changing colour (dark blue in reflected light, or brown-yellow in transmitted
light); and Calcedonio Glass (16th century), a vitreous paste with coloured stripes imitating natural marbles.

Victoria and Albert Museum
Cromwell Road, South Kensington, London SW7 2RL, UK
Tel. (44) 20 7942 2000 www.vam.ac.uk
Daily 10am-5.45pm (Wed & last Fri of every month 10am-10pm)

The Glass Gallery displays a large, representative selection of glass
from a collection numbering over 8,000 pieces dating from ancient
times to the present day. There is a large section devoted to
Renaissance Venetian enamelled glass and Venetian glass of later
periods, particularly the 16th, 17th and 18th centuries. Also wheel-
engraved German goblets, the earliest English lead-glass, and
remarkable High Victorian glass.

Fabergé Easter Egg, St
Petersburg, 1895
*Hillwood Museum
and Gardens*

FABERGE

Cleveland Museum of Art
University Circle, 11150 East Boulevard, Cleveland, Ohio 44106, USA
Tel. (1) 216 421 7340 www.clevelandart.org
Tue-Sun 10am-5pm (Wed, Fri until 9pm)

Although the collection has only one Imperial Easter Egg, *The Red Cross Egg with Resurrection Triptych* (1915), it has an amazing variety of pieces in most of the areas Fabergé worked, including the masterpiece rhodonite Tower Clock.

Ermitazh
The Hermitage
Dvortsovskaia naberezhnaia 34-36, 191065 St Petersburg, Russian Federation
Tel. (7) 812 1109079 www.hermitage.ru
Tue-Sun 10.30am-6pm, Sun 10.30am-5pm

There are a number of magnificent items, including miniature copies of the Imperial Regalia, and a large quantity of archival materials. The collection mainly comprises pieces executed by masters from the workshop rather than by Fabergé himself. Such an example is a table seal with the Grand Ducal Coat-of-Arms by Julius Rappoport. Highlights also include a dipper (*kovsh*), and covered mustard pot made from silver, gilt, nephrite and enamel, executed by Andres Johann Nevalainen. This small *kovsh* has a silver rouble of 1775 soldered into it.

Forbes Magazine Galleries
62 Fifth Avenue at 12th Street, New York, New York 10011, USA
Tel. (1) 212 206 5548
Tue, Wed, Fri, Sat 10am-4pm

The collection here is packed with treasures, including twelve Imperial Easter Eggs (the largest collection in the world) and other luxurious items created by Fabergé for Russian royalty. The displays include the first Imperial Egg and the *Cross of St George Egg* (1916), which originally belonged to Maria Feodorovna, the wife of Alexander III. The *Orange Tree Egg* is a masterpiece of goldsmith and mechanical art, with jade leaves and diamond-centred enamel blossoms, amethyst and citrine oranges, and a mechanical bird hidden in its branches, which sings when one of the oranges is turned. Equally breathtaking are the Fabergé-designed jewellery, cigarette holders, and picture frames. They include the Big Bad Wolf lighter, made of silver and glazed earthenware; the Imperial Diadem, made of diamonds, platinum, gold, and cobalt blue enamel; jewelled cufflinks; vodka glasses with gold and enamel decoration; and even a luxurious pair of knitting needles in ebony, gold, enamel, and rubies.

Pink Imperial Egg, Fabergé, Russia, 1914 *Hillwood Museum and Gardens*

Gosudarstvennyi istoriko-kul'turnyi muzei-zapovednik 'Moskovskii Kreml''
The State Historical-Cultural Museum-Preserve 'Moscow Kremlin'
Krasnaia ploshchad', 103073 Moscow, Russian Federation
Tel. (7) 095 2023776 www.kremlin.museum.ru
Mon-Wed, Fri-Sun 10am-4pm

Of the 56 Imperial Easter Eggs commissioned and created between 1885 and 1917, ten are in the Kremlin Museum. The picturesque miniatures are splendidly decorated with tiny models of palaces, monuments, yachts and trains, as well as birds, figures and flower bouquets. Some of these astounding creations even have 'surprises' inside, with intricate and delicate mechanisms, such as the *Memory of Azov Egg* (1891) containing an exact replica of the cruiser *Memory of Azov*, executed in gold and platinum, with windows set with small diamonds. The *Trans-Siberian Railway Egg* (1900) contains a working model of the train, whereas the *Romanov Tercentary Egg* (1913) bears eighteen miniature portraits of the Romanov Tzars and Emperors. A rotating steel globe of dark blue enamel is secured inside, showing the territories of Russia in 1613 and 1913.

Imperial Pelican Easter Egg,
Peter Carl Fabergé, 1898
Virginia Museum of Fine Arts

Hillwood Museum and Gardens
4155 Linnean Avenue NW, Washington, DC 20008, USA
Tel. (1) 202 6865807   www.hillwoodmuseum.org
Tue-Sat 9am-5pm (closed Feb)

One of the most important assemblages of Russian imperial art outside Russia. Besides icons, silver, and textiles, there is a huge collection of Fabergé, with eggs that belonged to the Tsars in the late 19th century. There are also music boxes and clocks by Fabergé.

New Orleans Museum of Art
1 Collins Diboll Circle, New Orleans, Louisiana 70124, USA
Tel. (1) 504 488 2631   www.noma.org
Tue-Sun 10am-5pm

The museum has one of the four largest collections of Fabergé objects in the US. The pride of the collection is its three dazzling Imperial Easter eggs, the *Caucasus Egg* (1893), the *Danish Palaces Egg* (1895), the *Napoleonic Egg* (1912), and the breathtaking *Imperial Lilies of the Valley Basket* (1896), recognized as Fabergé's finest floral creation.

Queen's Gallery, Buckingham Palace
Buckingham Palace Road, London SW1A 1AA, UK
Tel. (44) 20 7839 1377   www.royal.gov.uk
Re-opening in 2002

The British Royal Collection of Fabergé is one of the three greatest in the world. The first pieces in the collection were gifts from various friends and family members to Queen Victoria, King Edward VII, Queen Alexandra, King George V, and Queen Mary, all purchased directly from the Fabergé firm. The collection contains three Imperial Easter Eggs, the *Colonnade Egg* (1905), the *Flower Basket Egg* (1901) and the *Mosaic Egg* (1914), as well as one of the Kelch Eggs, the *Twelve Panel Egg*.

Virginia Museum of Fine Arts
2800 Grove Avenue at the Boulevard , Richmond, Virginia 23221, USA
Tel. (1) 804 3401400   www.vmfa.state.va.us
Tue-Sun 11am-5pm (Thu until 8pm)

The museum's Fabergé Gallery offers one of the grandest public collections outside Russia, with a priceless collection of jewelled Fabergé objects of fantasy from the court of the Russian Tsars. It includes five beautifully detailed Imperial Easter Eggs: the *Peter the Great Egg* (1903), the *Rock Crystal Egg* (1896), the *Czarevitch Egg* (1912), the *Pelican Egg* (1898), and the *Red Cross Egg with Folding Miniatures* (1915).

The Walters Art Museum
600 North Charles Street, Baltimore, Maryland 21201, USA
Tel. (1) 410 5479000   www.thewalters.org
Tue-Sun 11am-5pm

This museum, founded by Henry Walters, contains a number of Fabergé animals and parasol handles. The collection also includes two of the Imperial Easter Eggs, the *Gatchina Palace Egg*, and the *Rose Trellis Egg*.

FAIENCE

A round faced clock and a pair of vases covered in colourful glazes, c. 1900
Musée de Sarreguemines

Musée des Arts décoratifs
The Museum of Decorative Arts
2 place du Château, 67000
Strasbourg, France
Tel. (33) 3 88 52 50 00
Mon, Wed-Sat 10am-noon, 1.30-6pm,
Sun 10am-5pm

This museum is situated on the ground floor of the Palais Rohan, the former bishops' residence built between 1731 and 1742. Displayed in the splendid cardinals' apartments is the world-renowned faïence by Charles Hannong. There are also several priceless trompe l'oeil pieces by his son Paul Hannong, including the famous terrine in the shape of a turkey (1750-53), and one in the shape of a boar. There is a faïence inkpot and the service ordered in 1753 for the marriage of the Prince of Condé.

Musée des Beaux-Arts
The Museum of Fine Arts
Place de la République, 59000 Lille, France
Tel. (33) 3 20 06 78 00
Mon 2-6pm, Wed-Sun noon-8pm

This is one of the great regional museums founded by Napoleon to display his country's treasures and those seized from elsewhere. Its share of paintings and other objects is staggering. Displayed are 400 ceramic pieces including Delft faïence and exceptional ceramics from Lille and Saint-Armand-les-Eaux. Equally astonishing is the early 18th-century embroidered style (*lambrequin*) faïence, characteristic of the famous production at Rouen. Also, early 16th-century faïence pieces including apothecary jars and architectural features, as well as *faïence parlante* and *faïence patriotique* pieces decorated with satiric and political scenes. There are also wares from Sainceny, Moustiers, and Sèvres.

Musée des Beaux-Arts et d'Archéologie
The Museum of Fine Arts and Archaeology
1 place de la Révolution, 25000 Besançon, France
Tel. (33) 3 81 87 80 49
Mon, Wed-Sun 9.30am-noon, 2-8pm

One of the oldest museums in France (1694) houses a fine collection of 16th-, 17th- and 18th-century faïence from Delft, Hanau, Nevers (including the famous Persian Blue), Rouen, Lille (18th-century works), and the Hannong manufacturers in Strasbourg.

Musée de la Céramique
Museum of Ceramics
4 rue de la Pie, 76000 Rouen, France
Tel. (33) 2 35 07 31 74
Mon, Wed-Sun 10am-1pm, 2-6pm

This collection of 6,000 items of Rouen ceramics has faïence from the 16th to 19th centuries. There are pieces by Masséot Abaquesne from the mid 16th century, Edme and Louis Poterat from the 17th century, a round plate of Chinese inspiration signed Brument (1699), two terrestrial and celestial globes by Pierre Chapelle (1725), and white faïence from the 18th century. The museum houses the biggest collection of Revolutionary faïence in France outside Roanne, along with faïence from Rhodes, Chinese and Japanese porcelain, and popular faïences from the 18th century.

Musée de la Faïencerie
Museum of Faïence
Place de la Victoire, 45500 Gien, France
Tel. (33) 2 38 67 00 05
Mon-Sat 9am-noon, 2-6pm, Sun 10am-noon, 2-6pm. Factory visits by appt. Mon-Thu.

The museum contains 600 pieces of fine faïence made in the Gien factory from 1821.

Musée de l'Hôtel Sandelin
The Hotel Sandelin Museum
14 rue Carnot, 62500 Saint-Omer, France
Tel. (33) 3 21 380094 www.musenor.org
Wed, Sat-Sun 10am-noon, 2-6pm (Thu, Fri closes at 5pm)

This magnificent 18th-century mansion is home to a fine collection of over 4,000 pieces of French faïence from Saint-Omer's local Levesque and Saladin factories, as well as from Rouen, Sinceny, Nevers, Moustiers, and Marseilles.

Museo internazionale delle Ceramiche
The International Ceramics Museum
Via Campidori 2, 48018 Faenza, Italy
Tel. (39) 0546 21240 www.micfaenza.org
Nov-Mar: Tue-Fri 9am-1.30pm, Sat-Sun 9.30am-1pm, 3-6pm.
Apr-Oct: Tue-Fri 9am-7pm, Sat-Sun 9.30am-1pm, 3-7pm

Started in 1908, this collection contains 30,000 pieces. The core collection presents the historic evolution of Faenza ceramics from the early Middle Ages onwards. There is a fine collection of 12th- and 13th-century household items, on which the potters devised, developed, and perfected two techniques for covering their products: tin glaze (vitreous white) and engobe (earthy white). The Renaissance section illustrates the changes that took place in the late 15th and early 16th centuries. Production of the gothic and oriental motifs characteristic of the late medieval 'archaic' and the early Renaissance 'severe' phase, was slowly abandoned, and the transition to a new, purely Italian decorative language took place. Having reached a zenith shortly after the middle of the 16th century, Faenza's craftsmen then turned to the production of objects commonly called Faenza White Ware, also known as Compendiario Style. The museum offers a wonderful selection of these pieces.

Musée Mandet
The Mandet Museum
14 rue de l'Hôtel-de-Ville, 63200 Riom, France
Tel. (33) 4 73 38 18 53
Mon, Wed-Sun 10am-noon, 2.30-6pm

The last three centuries of Europe's main faïence centres – France, Italy, Spain, and Germany – as well as the Far East are well represented, especially Faenza, Urbino, and Iznik. There is a rare Faenza plate with Michelangelo decorations, and a plate by Bernard Palissy.

Musée national Adrien Dubouché
The Adrien Dubouché National Museum
8 bis place Winston Churchill, 87000 Limoges, France
Tel. (33) 5 55 3308 50
Mon, Wed-Sun 10am-noon, 1.30-5.15pm

The collection includes several examples of 16th- and 17th-century Spanish faïence from Talavera de la Reyna in Castilla. From Limoges there is a particularly noteworthy circular plate with allegorical decorations (1741), and an ornamental fountain with grotesque

A decorative plate of fine yellow faïence, *Terre de Naples*, with printed decoration, *c*. 1830 (top)
Musée de Sarreguemines

A faïence vase with painted decoration, *c*. 1865-70 (above)
Musée de Sarreguemines

251

decorations from 1739. Faïences from Marseilles include works by the renowned Joseph Fauchier Louis Leroy (18th century).

Musée national de la Céramique
The National Museum of Ceramics
Place de la Manufacture, 92310 Sèvres, France
Tel. (33) 1 41 14 04 20
Mon, Wed-Sun 10am-5pm

The faïence collection contains items produced by Hispano-Moresque potters in the 14th century, with decorations in green copper, violet magnesia, or yellow silver oxide and with Near Oriental designs. The collection also includes two yellow lustre plates with the coat-of-arms of Marie de Castille, and Blanche de Navarre, Queen of Sicily. There is a life-sized faïence statue of a Madonna and Child (16th century), as well as a reconstruction of a 17th-century apothecary containing hundreds of jars.

Musée de Sarreguemines
The Museum of Sarreguemines
15-17 rue Poincaré, 57200 Sarreguemines, France
Tel. (33) 3 87 98 93 50 www.sarreguemines-museum.com
Mon, Thu-Sun 2-6pm, Wed 9am-noon, 2-6pm

The picturesque Salon des Faïences, a magnificently reconstructed winter garden from the 1880s, houses a good collection of richly decorated and coloured 19th- and 20th-century faïences from Sarreguemines.

St George, tempera on wood, two transverse profiled splines, 18th century *Suomen ortodoksinen kirkkomuseo*

Musée de la Ville de Bruxelles
The Museum of the City of Brussels
La Maison du Roi, Grand-Place, 1000 Brussels, Belgium
Tel. (32) 2 2794350 www.brussels-online.be
Mon-Thu 10am-12.30pm, 1.30-5pm, Sat-Sun 10am-1pm

Philippe Mombaer is considered to be the real founder of the Brussels' faïence industry, with his copper-green decor of butterflies, caterpillars, and seaweed which became typical of the capital. The museum boasts a very fine collection of elegant objects such as sauce dishes, chocolate pots, hampers, and plates.

ICONS

Agion Oros
Mount Athos
Agion Oros, 63075 Halkidiki, Greece

(Only adult males are allowed to visit the monastery, with a special permit.)

The monasteries of the Holy Mountain possess the greatest wealth of Byzantine and post-Byzantine art anywhere in Greece, including some 15,000 icons of great significance for the Orthodox world. The oldest known icon, dated to the end of the 11th century, is at the Monastery of Great Lavra, depicting the Five Saints of Sebasteia. From the Palaeologan era, there are superb icons from important centres such as Constantinople or Thessaloniki, and some mosaics with tiny tesserae and usually a gold background. In the 16th century, painters created triptychs, including a unique creation by Michael Damaskinos which can be found in the Monastery of Stavronikitas. From the late 18th century come the icons signed 'Makarios' from Galatista in Chalkidiki.

Bitsantinoú mouseío – Kentro politistikis klironomias
The Byzantine Museum – Centre of Cultural Heritage
Pláteia Archiepiskopou Kyprianou, 1515 Nicosia, Cyprus
Tel. (357) 2 456781
Mon-Fri 9am-1pm, 2pm-5pm, Sat 9am-1pm

The museum houses 220 Cypriot icons dating from the 5th to the 19th centuries. Masterpieces include the icons of Christ and the Virgin Mary (12th century) from the Church of the Virgin Mary of Aracas at Laghoudera, and The Resurrection (13th century) from the Church of St John Lambadistis Monastery at Kalopanayiotis.

Our Lady Orante, cloisonné on 22-carat gold plate, 12th century
Suomen ortodoksinen kirkkomuseo

Bitsantinoú politismoú mouseío
The Museum of Byzantine Civilization
Leofóros Stratou 2, 54 640 Thessaloniki, Greece
Tel. (30) 31 868 5704
July-Oct: Mon noon-7pm, Tue-Sun 8am-7pm. Nov-Jun: Tue-Sun 8am-2.30pm

There are many remarkable examples of icon art here, including an icon of the Virgin holding Christ in her arms and the icon *Christ Pantokrator, The Wisdom of God*, both dating from the Palaeologan period.

Muzei drevnerusskoi kul'tury i iskusstva im. Andreia Rubleva
The Andrei Rublev Museum of Early Russian Culture and Art
Spaso-andronikov monastyr', Andronevskaia ploshchad 10, 107120 Moscow, Russian Federation
Tel. (7) 095 2781489   www.moscow.lvl.ru
Mon, Tue, Thu-Sun 11am-5pm

Opened in 1960, the museum is named after its most celebrated monk, Andrei Rublev, who lived here in the 15th century. There is a vast collection of works from the Moscow, Tver, Rostov, and Novgorod schools from the 14th to the 16th centuries. There are also five impressive 17th-century icons from Suzdal and some fragments of the earliest 12th-century icons.

Ermitazh
The Hermitage
Dvortsovskaia naberezhnaia 34-36, 191065 St Petersburg, Russian Federation
Tel. (7) 812 1109079   www.hermitage.ru
Tue-Sat 10.30am-6pm, Sun 10.30am-5pm

The important collections at this museum include over 500 Byzantine and post-Byzantine icons. Of exceptional value are the 12th-century icons *St Gregory Thaumaturge* and *The Transfiguration*. Another highlight is an icon of Christ the Almighty (1363) with representations of the donors. The old Russian icons on display include wonderful examples of the Novgorod, Moscow, and Yaroslavl Schools, and works from the Northern Schools.

Gosudarstvennaia Tret'iakovskaia Galereia
The State Tretiakov Gallery
Lavrushinskii pereulok 10, 109017 Moscow, Russian Federation
Tel. (7) 095 230 7788   www.tretyakov.ru
Tue-Sun 10am-8pm

This is the largest collection of Russian art in Russia. A section is dedicated to early Russian art from the 9th to the 17th centuries, with icons like the *Virgin of Vladimir* (Constantinople, 12th century) that were brought to Russia from Byzantium. The gallery boasts Andrei Rublev's famous *Trinity* (wood, tempera, 1420s), as well as his *Saviour and Archangel Michael* (both c.1394).

Our Lady of Kazan, tempera on wood, 18th century (below)
Suomen ortodoksinen kirkkomuseo

St George, tempera on wood Russia, 16th century (bottom)
Hillwood Museum and Gardens

Gosudarstvennyi istoriko-kul'turnyi muzei-zapovednik 'Moskovskii Kreml
The State Historical-Cultural Museum-Preserve 'Moscow Kremlin'
Krasnaia ploshchad', 103073 Moscow, Russian Federation
Tel. (7) 095 2023776   www.kremlin.museum.ru
Mon-Wed, Fri-Sun 10am-4pm

The Kremlin has a rich collection of ancient Russian icons, from the monumental icons of the late 11th and early 12th centuries to the elegant and decorative works of the late 17th and early 18th centuries. Apart from works by Russian artists such as Andrei Rublev, Theophanes the Greek, Dionisius, and Simon Ushakov, the museum also contains icons from Byzantium and the South Slavonic countries. One of the museum's oldest icons is the pre-Mongol period Novgorod icon *Our Lady of Tenderness*.

Gosudarstvennyi russkii museum
The State Russian Museum
Mikhailovskii dvorets,
Inzhenernaia ulitsa 4/2, 191011 St Petersburg, Russian Federation
Tel. (7) 812 318 3448   www.rusmuseum.rus
Mon, Wed-Sun 10am-6pm

The collection offers a great cross-section of Russian religious art over many centuries. The earliest works, such as mosaics, frescoes, and icons, represent the holy images venerated in Orthodox churches and households. There are also some fine examples from the bolder and brighter Russian style which emerged at Novgorod from the 12th century onwards, and which was developed in Moscow by Theophanes the Greek.

Jebel Musa St Catherine's Monastery – Mount Sinai
Jebel Musa, St Catherine's, Egypt
Mon-Sat 9.30am-noon

Located at the foot of Mount Sinai, St Catherine's Monastery is a spectacular natural setting for priceless works of art, including a collection of icons that is second in size only to the Vatican's. Most of the icons native to St Catherine were created between the 10th and 15th centuries, following the Sinaitic School. Russian Tsars made significant donations, as did leaders from Crete, Byzantium, and Palestine.

The Menil Collection
1515 Sul Ross, Houston, Texas 77006, USA
Tel. (1) 713-525-9400   www.menil.org
Wed-Sun 11am-7pm

There is an impressive collection of Byzantine artefacts and icon paintings from the Mediterranean world, Asia Minor, and Russia. Highlights include a 13th-century icon of Saint Marina, *The Entry into Jerusalem* (Constantinople, *c*. 1400), and *Saint Onuphrius* by Emmanuel Lambardos (Crete, first half of 17th century).

Novgorodskii gosudarstvennyi muzei-zapovednik
The Novgorod State Museum Preserve
Kreml' 11, 173007 Novgorod, Russian Federation
Tel. (7) 816 2273608   www.eng.novgorod-museum.ru
Mon, Wed-Sun 10am-6pm

The icon collection here is as important as that in the Tretyakov
in Moscow and the Russian Museum in St Petersburg. It numbers
over 1,500 exhibits from the 11th to the early 20th centuries. The
core of the collection consists of unique examples of Novgorod
art dating back to the 11th to 15th centuries.

Museum für Spätantike und Byzantinische Kunst
The Museum of Late Antique and Byzantine Art
Bodestrasse 1-3, 10178 Berlin, Germany
Tel. (49) 30 20355503   www.smb.spk-berlin.de
Due to open 2004

The museum possesses a first-class collection of early Christian,
Byzantine, and post-Byzantine works of art dating from the 3rd to
the 19th centuries. The icons range from the Novogorod School
around 1400 to the Muscovite paintings of the 19th century.

Golgotha, tempera on
wood, two profiled
splines, 17th century
*Suomen ortodoksinen
kirkkomuseo*

Suomen ortodoksinen kirkkomuseo
The Orthodox Church Museum of Finland
Karjalankatu 1, 70110 Kuopio, Finland
Tel. (358) 17 287 2244   www.ort.fi
Please call for opening times

The museum's collection consists of 800 icons amassed from the Monasteries of Valamo,
Konevitsa, and Petsamo; the Karelian parishes in Viborg; and from Finnish private collectors. The 19th-century burial icon *Our Lady* is exquisite. Equally beautiful is the icon
entitled *A Group of Saints* depicting a group of 46 Saints from north of Novgorod, with St
Andrew as its central figure. Researchers wishing to see icons not on display may do so
by appointment.

Sveta Aleksandar Nevski
The Alexander Nevsky Memorial Church
Ploshchad Aleksandar Nevski 1, 1000 Sofia, Bulgaria
Tel. (359) 2 877697
Wed-Sun 10.30am-12.30pm, 2pm-6.30pm

The church's crypt contains a superb collection of icons from all over the country, dating
from the 9th to the 19th centuries. Look out for some medieval gems from the town of
Nesebâr, home to a prolific icon-painting school.

Timken Museum of Art
1500 El Prado, Balboa Park, San Diego 92101, USA
Tel. (1) 619 2395548
Tue-Sat 10am-4.30pm, Sun 1.30pm-4.30pm

The museum preserves a collection of Russian icons. Highlights include *The Ascension*
(Moscow School, 16th century), *St Basil the Great and Scenes from His Life* (Central Russia, late
16th- early 17th centuries), *Our Lady of Jerusalem* (Moscow School, 17th century), and *The
Last Judgement*, a monumental icon divided into five registers (Russia, School of
Dionisius, 16th century).

ISLAMIC CERAMICS

Ashmolean Museum
Beaumont Street, Oxford, Oxfordshire OX1 2PH, UK
Tel. (44) 1865 278000 www.ashmol.ox.ac.uk
Tue-Sat 10am-5pm, Sun & public holidays 2-5pm

Many items are among the most important outside the Islamic world, including a rare
bowl by the potters of Kashan, produced by painting in black and blue under a turquoise
glaze. Also a delightful Persian dish with carved and incised decoration under a transparent blue glaze, a technique used both in Egypt and Persia to great effect. Also on display is the only known example of a tin glazed cup of the Abbasid period, decorated
with a band of palmette motifs. A diverse collection with encyclopaedic coverage.

British Museum
Great Russell Street, London WC1B 3DG, UK
Tel. (44) 20 7636 1555 www.thebritishmuseum.ac.uk
Mon-Sat 10am-5pm, Sun noon-6pm

The collection of Islamic art includes the largest and finest collection of Islamic pottery
outside the Middle East, thanks to the donation of the Godman Collection. Highlights
include a group of 200 pieces of Iznik pottery, with a pear-shaped bottle of 'Golden Horn
ware' bearing the Armenian date of 978 (AD1529) and made in Kutahya, together with the
mosque lamp from the Dome of the Rock in Jerusalem, dated 1549. The museum owns
the only three dated pieces of 16th-century Iznik pottery, and the best examples of grand
architectural lustre tiles, including a group of star- and cross-shaped wall tiles with animal decorations, made in Kashan (c. 13th century).

Museu Calouste Gulbenkian
The Calouste Gulbenkian Museum
Avenida de Berna 45a, 1067 Lisbon, Portugal
Tel. (351) 21 7823000 www.gulbenkian.pt
Tue 2-6pm, Wed-Sun 10am-6pm

Calouste Gulbenkian's collection of vessels and tiles is outstanding. A must for lovers of
Turkish tiles and pottery, as well as collectors of medieval Persian ceramics.

Museu de Ceràmica
The Ceramics Museum
Palau de Pedralbes, avengida Diagonal 686, 08034 Barcelona, Spain
Tel. (34) 93 2801621
Tue-Sun 10am-3pm

The palace offers an overview of ceramic work in Spain from the 12th to the 19th centuries. The collection begins with 139 pieces discovered in Palma de Mallorca, including
a number of small amphorae, two- and four-handled jugs, and a delightful pair of animals (a lioness and a camel).

Cinili Kosk – Istanbul Arkeoloji Müzerleri
The Tiled Pavilion – Archaeological Museum of Istanbul
Gülhane-Sultanhamet, 34400 Istanbul, Turkey
Tel. (90) 212 5207740
Tue-Sun 9.30am-5pm

The Tiled Pavilion was originally part of the Topkapi complex built in 1472 for Mehmet
the Conqueror. The walls of the entrance façade are covered with geometric compositions and a blue and white calligraphic frieze. The collection contains beautiful Iznik

Hispano-Moorish
ceramic bowl
Musée Hyacinthe Rigaud

tiles from the 16th century and fine examples of Seljuk and Ottoman tiles and ceramics. Highlights include, Miletus ware from the late 14th and early 15th centuries; blue and white tiles and ceramics including a 15th-century charger; a group of four ceramic mosque lamps probably commissioned by Selim I for the Mausoleum of his father Bayesit II in Istanbul; and an interesting blue and white jug bearing buildings topped with domes or towers and struck with gilded dots (16th century). There is a fine selection of 16th-century Golden Horn ware; Blue and Turquoise ware, including a group of seven hexagonal tiles; and Damascus ware.

Davids Samling
The David Collection
Kronprinsessegade 30-32, 1306 Copenhagen, Denmark
Tel. (45) 33 73 49 49 www.davidmus.dk
Daily 1-4pm

An expansive collection that includes some of the world's finest pieces of Islamic pottery. An early example of lustre used as a pigment on opaque white tin glaze is demonstrated on a Mesopotamian bowl, with decorations of interlocking half-palmettes. There is an unusual dish from the Abbasid period with an inscription around the rim blessing its owner, and several 12th-century lustre-painted pots from Syria. The massive mihrab is composed of two tiles with blue and green in-glaze colours decorated with lustre, showing the technique of underglazed painting in its most superb form.

Musée Hyacinthe Rigaud
The Hyacinthe Rigaud Museum
16 rue de l'Ange, 66000 Perpignan, France
Tel. (33) 4 68 35 43 40
Mid Jun-mid Sep: Mon, Wed-Sun 9.30am-noon, 2.30-7pm
Mid Sep-mid Jun: Mon, Wed-Sun 9am-noon, 2-6pm

This museum owns an important collection of 12th- to 13th-century Hispano-Moorish lustre ceramics that were found during excavations in Collioure.

The L. A. Mayer Museum of Islamic Art
Ha-Palmakh 2, Jerusalem, Israel
Tel. (972) 2 5661292
Mon-Thu, Sun 10am-3pm, (Tue until 6pm), Fri, Sat & public holidays 10am-2pm

An outstanding collection of Islamic art dating from the 7th to the 19th centuries, from Egypt, Syria, Iraq, Turkey, India, Afghanistan, Spain, and Iran. The pottery examples illustrate work ranging from the early Umayyads to the master Ottoman potters of the 19th century. Superb Kashan tiles from the Seljuk period that would have decorated mosques, palaces, and private homes are displayed alongside fine Nishapur and Samarkand bowls.

Musée national de la Céramique
The National Museum of Ceramics
Place de la Manufacture, 92310 Sèvres, France
Tel. (33) 1 41 14 04 20
Mon, Wed-Sun 10am-5pm

The museum possesses a fine collection of Islamic ceramics, with examples of tin-glazed faïence and lustreware, as well as siliceous pottery. Its 17th-century ceramics from the Middle Orient include pieces from Syria, Mesopotamia and Byzantium. There are whole panels of tiles that once decorated mosque façades, as well as a rare collection of 15th-century Hispano-Moorish gold and cream lustre ceramics from Malaga, Valencia, and Manisa.

Musée national de la Renaissance
The National Museum of the Renaissance
Château d'Ecouen, 95440 Ecouen, France
Tel. (33) 1 34 38 38 50   www.musexpo.com
Mon, Wed-Sun 9.45am-12.30pm, 2-5.15pm

The castle houses a superb collection of some 430 Iznik ceramics and is especially rich in ceramics from 1550 and 1570, the so-called 3rd period of Iznik. Highlights of the collection include a wall panel of square tiles from the Rustem Pasha Mosque in Istanbul (1561).

Plate, blue glazed maiolica, Albisola, 1683 (above)
Il Museo della Ceramica 'Manlio Trucco'

Italian maiolica from the donation of Galeazzo Cora (below)
Museo internazionale delle Ceramiche

Pergamon-Museum – Museum für Islamische Kunst
The Pergamon Museum – Museum of Islamic Art
Bodestrasse 1-3, 10178 Berlin, Germany
Tel. (49) 30 209050   www.pergamon-museum.de
Wed-Sun 9am-5pm

This encyclopaedic collection of Islamic art contains many exemplary ceramics which demonstrate technological advances in the production of Islamic wares. There are early pieces, including a 9th-century dish with mould formed decoration from Mesopotamia, and painted bowls in lustre by Egyptian potters of Fatimid Egypt. Marking yet another advance is a dish with incised decoration painted with blue and aubergine under a transparent glaze. It is a wonderful example of Lakabi ware, where the potter attempts to stop the colours running together by using deeply incised lines.

Rüstem Pasa Cami
The Rüstem Pasha Mosque
Hasircilar Cad. 90 Unkapani, Eminönü, Istanbul, Turkey

The hundreds of thousands of tiles that cover the walls, the mihrab, the mimbar, and the columns of the mosque illustrate the heyday of Iznik ceramics. Here is a perfect use of brilliant cobalt blue and turquoise, together with novel scarlet red. The floral theme of the tiles and their stunning realism, beautifully arranged near geometric motifs, are a spectacular sight.

MAIOLICA

Bottle, blue glazed maiolica, 16th century (right)
Il Museo della Ceramica 'Manlio Trucco'

Ashmolean Museum
Beaumont Street, Oxford, Oxfordshire
OX1 2PH, UK
Tel. (44) 1865 278000   www.ashmol.ox.ac.uk
Tue-Sat 10am-5pm, Sun & public holidays 2-5pm

One of the best collections of Renaissance maiolica in the world, with examples of different Italian fabrics, and works of the master potters. The core was donated by Drury Fortnum (1820-99) and augmented by later pieces from the Fortnum collection.

Castello Sforzesco: Collezione d'arti applicati
Collection of Applied Arts in the Sforzesco Castle
Castello Sforzesco, Piazza Castello, Milan, Italy
Tel. (39) 02 62 08 39 40
Tue-Sun 9.30am-5.30pm

This stunning collection, housed in a Romanesque castle, is one of the largest in Italy. There are galleries devoted to pieces from the 16th century and to the 'Compendiare' pieces from Faenza, with a large and unusual collection of pottery from the late 17th to early 18th centuries. These were once thought to have been created in Angarano (Bassano) but have recently been linked to the kilns of Lombardy. Next is Milan's contribution to maiolicas, including 18th-century pieces from the Clerici and Rubati manufacturers. Finally, a range of objects from Lodi, Pesaro, Faenza and Venice. There is also a substantial collection of modern works including pieces by Melotti and Ponti, some delightful 17th-century maiolicas from Abruzzo and Savona, and a collection of wonderful Hispanic-Moorish lustreware from the 15th to 18th centuries.

Plate decorated in manganese and copper green maiolica, second half of 18th century
Il Museo della Ceramica 'Manlio Trucco'

Il Museo della Ceramica 'Manlio Trucco'
The Manlio Trucco Ceramics Museum
Villa Trucco, corso Ferrari, 191, 17011 Albisola Superiore, Italy
Tel. (39) 019 482741 www.comune.albisola-superiore.sv.it
Mon-Sat 10am-noon, Sun on request

This beautiful collection documents the area's production from the end of the 17th and beginning of the 18th century, including the trademark monochrome blue maiolica of Savona.

Il Museo delle Ceramiche
The Museum of Ceramics
Basilica di San Nicola, piazza San Nicola, 62, 62029 Tolentino, Italy
Tel. (39) 0733 969996 www.sannicola.sinp.net
Daily 9.30am-noon, 4-7pm

A range of local ceramics, including Faenza maiolicas with their typical mixture of red and blue on an enamel white background, and ceramics from Savona with decorations in light and dark blue.

Fitzwilliam Museum
Trumpington Street Cambridge, Cambridgeshire CB2 1RB, UK
Tel. (44) 1223 332900 www.fitzmuseum.cam.ac.uk
Tue-Sat 10am-5pm, Sun 2.15-5pm

A representative collection of more than 500 pieces of Italian maiolica with medieval, Renaissance and later examples. Items from most major manufacturing centres can be found, charting the improvements in kilns and glazes.

Museum entrance hall
The J. Paul Getty Museum

The J. Paul Getty Museum
17985 Pacific Coast Highway, Malibu, California, USA
Tel. (1) 310 459 7611 www.getty.edu
Tue-Wed 11am-7pm, Thu-Fri 11am-9pm, Sat-Sun 10am-6pm

Although small, this collection has items of extreme rarity and the highest quality. From Spain there is a remarkable pavement of interlinked octagonal units from Manises (15th century), with devices written in Gothic style.

Il Museo dell'Istituto Statale d'Arte De Fabris per la Ceramica
The Museum of Ceramics of the De Fabris School of Art
Istituto d'Arte De Fabris, via Giove, 1, 36055 Nove, Italy
Tel. (39) 0424 590022
Mon-Sat 8am-noon (Tue, Thu on request)

The collection ranges from plates, cutlery, trays, and tiles to vases and figurines. Works date from the 17th to the early 20th centuries.

Museo internazionale delle Ceramiche
The International Ceramics Museum
Via Campidori 2, 48018 Faenza, Italy
Tel. (39) 0546 21240   www.micfaenza.org
Nov-Mar: Tue-Fri 9am-1.30pm, Sat-Sun 9.30am-1pm, 3-6pm
Apr-Oct: Tue-Fri 9am-7pm, Sat-Sun 9.30am-1pm, 3-7pm

A superb collection of maiolicas consisting primarily of Italian
Renaissance pieces and numbering around 960 items bequeathed by
Galeazzo Cora. A collector and scholar, Cora purchased not only rare
and beautiful pieces, but also understood the significance in amassing
fragments for study.

Renaissance ceramics
(above)
*Museo internazionale delle
Ceramiche*

Italian maiolica from the
donation of Galeazzo
Cora (above right)
*Museo internazionale delle
Ceramiche*

Musée du Louvre
The Louvre
Palais du Louvre, 34-36 quai du Louvre, 75001 Paris, France
Tel. (33) 1 40 20 53 17   www.louvre.fr
Mon, Wed 9am-9.15pm, Thu-Sun 9am-5.30pm

Around 800 pieces representing all periods and provenances. Items from the Della
Robbia workshop; albarelli from the famous Orsini-Colonna pharmacy; a superb disk of
St George; pieces from Urbino; and a plaque of the Virgin with Child with the brand of
'Maestro Prestino', dated 1536.

Musée national de la Céramique
The National Museum of Ceramics
Place de la Manufacture, 92310 Sèvres, France
Tel. (33) 1 41 14 04 20
Mon, Wed 10am-5pm

The oldest pieces of maiolica include a cup from Faenza (*c*.1525) dedicated to the story of
Joseph, and a bowl (*c*.1540) from the 'bottega' of Guido Di Merlino at Urbino. There are
several coveted items from the Della Robbia workshop, including the *Christ in Pain*, and
the large group entitled the *Virgin with Child*. Also rare pieces from Montelupo and Sicily,
as well as superb examples of French maiolica.

Museo nazionale del Bargello
The National Museum of Bargello
Via del Proconsolo 4, 50122 Florence, Italy
Tel. (39) 055 2388606
Tue-Sat 8.30am-3pm

The museum boasts works from the Deruta, Montelupo, Faenza and Urbino potteries,
and part of a service which belonged to Guidobaldo II della Rovere, Duke of Urbino.
Particularly noteworthy is the beautiful *Garland* with the Bartolini-Salimbeni and
Medici emblems by Giovanni della Robbia.

Victoria and Albert Museum
Cromwell Road, South Kensington, London SW7 2RL, UK
Tel. (44) 20 7942 2000   www.vam.ac.uk
Daily 10am-5.45pm (Wed & last Fri of every month 10am-10pm)

An extraordinarily diverse and comprehensive collection. The range is from primitive
maiolica and Renaissance wares from every pottery centre in Italy, to maiolica using different kinds of techniques and styles (istoriato, bianchi di Faenza, stile compendiario).
The collection also includes later productions from the 17th and 18th centuries.

The Wallace Collection

Hertford House, Manchester Square, London W1M 6BN, UK
Tel. (44) 20 7563 9500 www.the-wallace-collection.org.uk
Mon-Sat 10am-5pm, Sun 2-5pm

The Renaissance collections contain numerous masterpieces including a
Gubbio maiolica dish decorated with maidens, and the Urbino wine cooler
probably by Flaminio Fontana. Among many other wonders is a dish by
Giorgio Andreoli featuring decorations after Raphael.

OBJECTS OF DEVOTION

The American Museum in Britain

Claverton Manor, Bath, Somerset BA2 7BD, UK
Tel. (44) 1225 460503 www.americanmuseum.org
Museum: Tue-Sun 2-5pm. Gardens: Tue-Fri 1-6pm, Sat-Sun noon-6pm

The museum's displays represent the range of religions in the US. There are santos and
retablos from the Spanish colonies of the South; angels, trees of life, and other religious
images adorning the handiwork of Mennonites, Amish, Lutherans, and many other
denominations. There is also a gallery devoted to the Shakers, who held the belief
'Hands To Work and Hearts to God'.

Composite gold earrings,
late 4th c century BC
(above)
Mpenaki mouseío

Reliquary of St Thomas à
Becket, *c.* 1190 (below)
Museum Catharijneconvent

Musée d'Art et d'Histoire du judaïsme
Museum of the Art and History of Judaism
71 rue du Temple, 75003 Paris, France
Tel. (33) 1 53 01 86 60
Mon-Fri 11am-6pm, Sun 10am-6pm

This museum traces the history of Jewish communities in Europe and North Africa from
the Middle Ages to the present day. One of the most important items on display is the
Sacred Arch of Modene dated 1472, representing two carved and painted bodies with
coloured wood inlay. There are textiles, cups, lamps, illustrated prayers, wedding rings,
and all kinds of decorative religious items.

Musée d'Art religieux et d'Art mosan
Museum of Religious and Mosan Art
Rue Mère-Dieu 11, 4000 Liège, Belgium
Tel. (32) 4 221 42 79
Tue-Sat 1pm-6pm, Sun 11am-4pm (times may vary, please call for details)

The museum presents the development of religious art in the old Liège diocese, from the
Middle Ages to the beginning of the 20th century. There is a beautiful
series of bronze Crucifixions from the 12th century, and the reliquary triptych from the Eglise Sainte Croix, made of gilt copper with enamels. The
neo-Gothic period is particularly well represented as the museum inherited the archives from two goldsmiths' workshops in Liège.

Museum Catharijneconvent
The Museum of the Catherine Convent
Lange Nieuwstraat 38, Nieuwegracht 63, 3512 LG Utrecht,
The Netherlands
Tel. (31) 30 2313835 www.catharijneconvent.nl
Tue-Fri 10am-5pm, Sat-Sun & public holidays 11am-5pm

The museum's collections include 42,000 objects and 17,000 devotional prints, a large proportion of which are medieval. The holdings of richly embroidered liturgical vestments of the Roman Catholic Church are extensive. Some of the finest devotional objects include two silver reliquaries with triangular bases, formerly possessions of the Old Catholic Church Museum in Utrecht. Another exemplary object is the crozier from the Bishop's crook of Aegidius de Monte, made in Antwerp in 1570.

Monstrance, Michiel Esselbeeck, Amsterdam, 1656
Museum Catharijneconvent

Museu Diocesà de Barcelona
The Diocesan Museum of Barcelona
Avengida Catedral 4, 08002 Barcelona, Spain
Tel. (34) 93 3152213
Tue-Sat 10am-2pm, 5-8pm, Sun 11am-2pm

The museum contains works of art donated by the parish churches of the city's diocese. Of particular interest are the items from the Romanesque, Gothic, Renaissance and Baroque periods, especially the 12th-century murals from Polinyà, the carved Virgin from Santa Maria de Toudell, and the Romanesque silver cross from Riells del Fai.

Museo ebraico di Venezia
The Jewish Museum of Venice
Campo del Ghetto Nuovo 2902/b, 30121 Venice, Italy
Tel. (39) 041 715359
Mon-Fri, Sun 10am-5pm (Jun-Sep until 7pm)

The collections include rare and precious textiles and silverwork, ritual items, paintings, manuscripts, and other relics. Especially noteworthy is the embroidered Paroket donated by the Levantina Community in 1804, representing the Jewish encampment in the desert, the manna, the quail, and the hand of Moses drawing water from the rock.

The Jewish Museum
Raymond Burton House,
129/131 Albert Street, Camden Town, London NW1 7NB, UK
Tel. (44) 20 7284 1997   www.jewmusm.ort.org
Mon-Thu 10am-4pm, Sun 10am-5pm.

The collection specializes in Jewish ceremonial art and Jewish history, and includes an Italian 16th-century carved and gilded walnut synagogue Ark, and a Sabbath lamp by Abraham Lopes d'Oliveyra. Their other location (The Sternberg Centre, 80 East End Road, London N3 2SY) houses the museum's social history collections.

The Jewish Museum
1109 Fifth Avenue at 92nd Street, New York, New York 10128, USA
Tel. (1) 212 423 3200   www.jewishmuseum.org
Mon, Wed, Thu, Sun 11am-5.45pm, Tue 11am-8pm

The largest Jewish museum in the Western hemisphere, and one of the three top collections in the world, now houses more than 28,000 objects covering the history and art of the Jewish people. There is a collection of Jewish coins and medals, including a *bar kokhba* coin from Israel (133-34CE) and ceremonial objects interpreting Jewish religious life. There is a foundation stone from the fortification wall of Jerusalem (41-70CE) and a group of Hanukkah lamps. A Torah ark made for the Jews of Urbino in 1533 is a masterpiece.

Musée du Louvre
The Louvre
Palais du Louvre, 34-36 quai du Louvre, 75001 Paris, France
Tel. (33) 1 40 20 53 17   www.louvre.fr
Mon, Wed 9am-9.15pm, Thu-Sun 9am-5.30pm

The superb collections include Western religious objects from antiquity to the 20th century. There are reliquaries of St Francis of Assisi and St Luke, tomb sculptures and tapestries from Roman times to the 16th century, stained-glass window fragments from Reims, and cathedral statues. Don't miss the gold and bronze *Virgin of the Annunciation* from Limoges, the *Heretic Angel* from Cluny Abbey, and *St Michael Slaying the Dragon* from the Notre Dame Abbey of Nevers.

Phelonion of an Igumen; a liturgical vestment used by the leader of a monastery, early 19th century
Suomen ortodoksinen kirkkomuseo

Musée marial
Museum of the Virgin
Rue de l'Aubépine, 17, 5570 Beauraing, Belgium
Tel. (32) 82 71 33 04
By appt. only

This most unusual museum houses about 800 statues or replicas of the Virgin Mary, commemorating a number of apparitions that took place in the area in 1932-33.

The Metropolitan Museum of Art
1000 Fifth Avenue at 82nd Street, New York, New York 10028, USA
Tel. (1) 212 535 7710   www.metmuseum.org
Tue-Thu 9.30am-5.30pm, Fri, Sat 9.30am-9pm, Sun 9.30am-5.30pm

The Mary and Michael Jaharis Galleries for Byzantine Art contain superb religious art from across the Byzantine Empire. Some of the earliest Christian images are on display, as well as works from the surviving Greco-Roman tradition and examples of Judaic art.

Mpenaki mouseío
The Benaki Museum
Odós Koumbari 1, 10674 Athens, Greece
Tel. (30) 1 361 1000   www.benaki.gr
Mon, Wed-Sat 9am-5pm, (Thu until noon), Sun 9am-3pm

The collection of post-Byzantine ecclesiastical art comprises a selection of sacred and service vessels, liturgical vestments, jewellery and accessories, and church furnishings in carved wood. The objects date mostly from the end of the 16th century to the early 20th century, and were collected from as far afield as Russia, Venice, and Asia Minor. The 17th- and 18th-century icons are especially fine and include: a golden St Mark the Evangelist seated on a lion by Theodorous Poulakis, and a composite many-figured icon of 1774 with the *Akathasistos Hymn* and the *Second Coming* by Athanasios Doudas.

Museo nacional de Escultura
The National Museum of Sculpture
Calle Cadenas de San Gregorio 1, 47011 Valladolid, Spain
Tel. (34) 983 250916
Tue-Sat 10am-2pm, 4pm-6pm, Sun 10am-2pm

The museum contains an outstanding collection of religious sculpture made of wood from the 13th to the 18th centuries. Exhibits include altarpieces, choir stalls, sepulchres, and processional floats (pasos).

Musée de L'Oeuvre
Palais du Tau, 2, Place du Cardinal Luçon, 51100 Reims, France
Tel. (33) 3 26 47 81 79
Mid Mar-Jun, Sep-mid Nov: daily 9.30am-6.30pm. Jul-Aug: 10am-noon, 2-5pm

Epitaphios with gold
thread embroidery,
dated 1599
Mpenaki mouseío

The museum displays a number of ceremonial objects
from French kings' coronations now kept as part of the
Cathedral treasure. The rest were melted down during the
French Revolution, They include a 12th-century coronation chal-
ice, an 11th-century reliquary of Sainte Epine made of Egyptian rock crystal, and a talisman
that was found on Charlemagne's body when he was exhumed in 1166.

Museo dell'Opera del duomo
The Cathedral Museum
Piazza del Duomo 9, 50122 Florence, Italy
Tel. (39) 055 2302885
Apr-Oct: daily 9am-7.30pm. Nov-Mar: daily 9am-6pm

A collection of works of art gathered from the major religious monuments of Florence,
featuring sculptures from the Cathedral's ancient Gothic façade by Arnolfo di Cambio,
and works by masters such as Nanni di Banco, Donatello, and Luca della Robbia. There
are two large statues from the Bell Tower, by Andrea Pisano and Donatello; bas reliefs of
the Biblical Stories and the Labours of Man by Pisano; the Sciences by Luca della Robbia;
and the Sacraments by Alberto Arnoldi.

Museo dell'Opera del duomo
The Cathedral Museum
Piazza Duomo 8, 54100 Siena, Italy
Tel. (39) 0577 283048
Mid Mar-end Oct: daily 9am-7.30pm. Nov-mid Mar: daily 9am-1.30pm

The most precious works of art from the cathedral are preserved in this museum, including
the outstanding *Maestà* by Duccio di Boninsegna. There is also the reliquary of the head
of Saint Galgano in gold-embossed silver with filigree and enamels(12th century), as well
as a silver Renaissance-style urn for the arm of Saint John the Baptist.

Santuario di Madonna dell'Arco
The Shrine of our Lady of dell'Arco
Via Romani 3, 80043 Madonna dell'Arco, Italy
Tel. (39) 081 5517611
Daily 6.45am-1pm, 3.30-6.30pm

The shrine houses tens of thousands of ex-votoes encrusted in the walls or hung from
long metal poles. In the treasury there are silver and gold offerings in the form of eyes,
heads, hearts, ears, bellies, or breasts, offered in thanks for the intervention of the Madonna.

Santuario della Madonna del Rosario
The Shrine of our Lady of the Rosary
Basilica del Rosario, piazza B. Longo 1, 80045 Pompei, Italy
Tel. (39) 081 8610744
Daily 9am-1pm, 3-6.30pm

The shrine of the Madonna del Rosario was originally built to counteract the crowded
and noisy assemblies at the neighbouring shrine of the Madonna dell'Arco. The church
was gradually filled with all kinds of ex-voto, body parts or figurines in gold and silver,
and countless painted panels.

Museo Sefardi
The Sephardic Museum
Calle Samuel Levi s.n. 45002 Toledo, Spain
Tel. (34) 25 223665
Tue-Sat 10am-1.45pm, 4pm-5.45pm, Sun & public holidays 10am-1.45pm

A collection that aims to show the Sephardic cultural legacy as part of the Spanish heritage, with objects reflecting the culture of the Jews when they lived in Spain. Items include gravestones with Hebraic inscriptions from Jewish necropolises and an excavation of a vaulted building which was probably the Jewish quarter's public baths.

Ivory panaghiario (pectoral), 1624-39 (below)
Mpenaki mouseio

Baroque chasuble, Amsterdam, second quarter of 18th century (bottom)
Museum Catharijneconvent

Suomen ortodoksinen kirkkomuseo
The Orthodox Church Museum of Finland
Karjalankatu 1, 70110 Kuopio, Finland
Tel. (358) 17 287 2244   www.ort.fi
May, Jun, Aug: Mon-Fri noon-3pm, Sat-Sun noon-5pm
Jul: Tue-Sun 10am-5pm. Rest of year: Tue-Sun 9.30am-4pm

The museum collects, maintains, researches, and exhibits sacred and liturgical objects which relate to the history of the Orthodox Church in Finland. There are 3,000 objects dating back to the 18th and 19th centuries (with icons dating back to the medieval period). One of the most remarkable objects in the museum is the cenotaph of the founding fathers of the Monastery of Valamo, weighing over 200kg and made of gilded silver.

Topkapi Sarayi Müzesi
The Topkapi Palace Museum
Sultanahmed, 34410 Istanbul, Turkey
Tel. (90) 212 5120480
Mon, Wed-Sun 9.30am-6pm

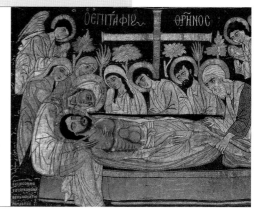

In the Chamber of the Sacred Relics are displayed some of the most precious Islamic relics in the Western world. Among them are the Mantle of the Prophet, the Banner of the Prophet, and two swords that previously belonged to Mohammed. Other relics of the Prophet include a print of his right foot, a hair from his beard, a letter and his seal, and a bow. There is also a small fragment of his tooth in a silver box.

Trésor du Prieuré d'Oignies
The Treasure of the Priory of Oignies
c/o Soeur Suzanne Vandecan, rue Julie Billiart, 17, 5000 Namur, Belgium
Tel. (32) 81 23 03 42
Daily 10am-noon, 2pm-5pm(times may vary, please call for details)

In the convent of the Sisters of Notre-Dame is a beautiful art treasure of the early 13th century which is characteristic of the exquisite Mosan style. Highlights include a reliquary of St Peter's rib, the relic holder of St Martin, a silver-gilt chalice, a superb double-cross with enamels, and phylacteries.

Trésor de la Cathédrale de Sens
Treasure of the Cathedral of Sens
135 rue des Déportés de la Résistance , 89100 Sens, France
Tel. (33) 3 86 64 46 22
Daily 10am-noon, 2-6pm. Jul-Aug: Mon, Wed-Sun 10am-6pm

A very important collection of precious objects, including medieval chalices and the *tau de Saint Loup*, one of the oldest known pastoral canes in the shape of a 'tau'. Thomas à Becket spent several years in Sens and left relics including the remarkable reliquary of *La Vraie Croix de Charlemagne* (14th century), made of lapis lazuli, precious stones, and mother-of-pearl.

The University of Pennsylvania Museum of Archaeology and Anthropology
33rd and Spruce Streets, Philadelphia, Pennsylvania 19104, USA
Tel. (1) 215 898 4000   www.upenn.edu
Tue-Sat 10am-4.30pm, Sun 1-5pm

This fine comprehensive collection focuses on monumental art and Chinese Buddhist art. There are pieces of sculpture from early Chinese tombs and temples, including two chimera from the Han Dynasty; a huge stone carving of the historical Buddha, Shakyamuni, bearing the dedication of a district chief in AD516; and four stone stelae on which were carved scenes from two important Buddhist texts, the *Lotus Sutra* and the *Vimalakirti Nirdesa Sutra*.

Zidovské Muzeum V Praze
The Jewish Museum in Prague
Jáchymova 3, 110 00 Prague, Czech Republic
Tel. (420) 2 248 10099   www.jewishmuseum.cz
Apr-Oct: Mon-Fri, Sun 9am-6pm. Nov-Mar: daily 9am-4pm

One of the most extensive collections of Jewish art in the world exclusively from the territory of Bohemia and Moravia. The synagogue textiles include almost 2,500 temple curtains and 4,000 mantles, binders, and draperies, some dating from the end of the 16th century. The collections of silver include decorated Torahs, crowns, filials, shields, and pointers from the 18th and 19th centuries. Also domestic objects, including goblets, spice boxes, and Hanukkah candles. The library contains more than 100,000 books. Among the most priceless examples are the Hebraic and Judaic volumes dating from the 12th and 13th centuries, and rare Prague Hebrew prints from the beginning of the 16th century. The museum oversees several of the city's synagogues and the Jewish cemetery.

PAPERWEIGHTS

Baccarat (French) paper-weight, mid 19th century
Bergstrom-Mahler Museum

Museum of American Glass at Wheaton Village
1501 Glasstown Rd, Millville, New Jersey 08332-1566, USA
Tel. (1) 856 825 6800   www.wheatonvillage.org
Apr-Dec: daily 10am-5pm. Jan-Mar: please call for opening times

The museum holds examples of clear glass paperweights with whimsical features inside, including the famous *Millville Rose* by Ralph Barber and Emil Larson (1920-30).

The Art Institute of Chicago
111 South Michigan Avenue, Chicago, Illinois 60603, USA
Tel. (1) 312 443 3600   www.artic.edu
Mon-Fri 10.30am-4.30pm (Tue until 8pm), Sat 10am-5pm, Sun noon-5pm

The famous Arthur Rubloff Collection of over 1,000 paperweights is one of the largest and most famous in the world. Comprised primarily of French 19th-century weights, it also includes both English and American examples together with weights by contemporary makers.

Bergstrom-Mahler Museum
165 North Park Avenue, Neenah, Wisconsin 54956, USA
Tel. (1) 920 751 4658
Tue-Fri 10am-4.30pm (Thu until 8pm), Sat-Sun 1-4.30pm

Probably the world's most comprehensive collection of glass paperweights, with over 2,000 pieces representing the classic to modern periods of paperweight making. There are millefiori and lampwork-styled paperweights, sulphides from the French factory of Baccarat, as well as 20th-century designs by artists including Paul Ysart and Charles Kaziun.

Bristol City Museum and Art Gallery
Queen's Road, Bristol BS8 1RL, UK
Tel. (44) 117 922 3571 www.bristol-city.gov.uk
Daily 10am-5pm

An array of around fifty French 19th-century paperweights donated by Conrad Fry, said to be the finest collection in the country.

The Corning Museum of Glass
One Museum Way, Corning, New York 14830, USA
Tel. (1) 607 974 8274 www.cmog.org
Daily 9am-5pm (Jul-Aug until 8pm)

The paperweight collection has nearly 1,000 pieces, most of them made in France in the 'classic' period from 1845-65. There are millefiori, sulphide weights, floral weights, overlay weights from the Baccarat, Pantin, and St. Louis glasshouses in France. Also displayed are modern weights by famous American makers like Paul J. Stankard.

The Currier Gallery of Art
201 Myrtle Way, Manchester, New Hampshire 03104, USA
Tel. (1) 603 669 6144 www.currier.org
Mon, Wed, Thu, Sun 11am-5pm, Fri 11am-8pm, Sat 10am-5pm

Remarkable examples come from the French glass houses of Clichy, Baccarat, and Saint-Louis. These are exhibited together with very fine contemporary pieces from great 20th-century glass artists such as Paul Ysart, Charles Kaziun, Rick Ayotte, Paul Stankard, and Delmo and Debbie Tarsitano.

Degenhart Paperweight and Glass Museum, Inc.
165323 Highland Hills Road, Intersection of Route 22 and I-77, Cambridge, Ohio 43725, USA
Tel. (1) 740 432 2626
Mar-Dec: Mon-Sat 9am-5pm, Sun 1pm-5pm. Rest of year: Mon-Fri 10am-5pm

Besides the rose and celebratory paperweights that the factory became well known for, Elizabeth Degenhart collected paperweights by the most sought-after manufacturers. Many of these are made in France by the prestigious houses of Baccarat and St Louis, as well as by firms elsewhere such as Whitefriars, Hanson, and Murano.

The Strong Museum
One Manhattan Square, Rochester, New York, 14607, USA
Tel. (1) 716 263 2700 www.strongmuseum.org
Mon-Sat 10am-5pm (Fri until 8pm), Sun noon-5pm

Nearly 500 examples including French makers Clichy, Baccarat, and St Louis, some dating from the 1840s-50s. Also, items by the Boston & Sandwich Glass Works and the New England Glass Company, with later pieces by contemporary 20th-century glass makers.

Millville Rose paperweight, *c.* 1905 (top)
Museum of American Glass at Wheaton Village

Basket paperweight by Jim & Nontas Kontes of Vineland, NJ, 1999 (above)
Museum of American Glass at Wheaton Village

PERFUME BOTTLES AND PERFUME INDUSTRY

Museum of American Glass at Wheaton Village
1501 Glasstown Rd, Millville, New Jersey 08332 1566, USA
Tel. (1) 856 825 6800   www.wheatonvillage.org
Apr-Dec: daily 10am-5pm. Jan-Mar: please call for opening times

Just after World War II, Wheaton made the majority of commercial perfume bottles in the US. The museum's collection contains examples of the bottles they manufactured for, among others, Elizabeth Arden, Coty, Max Factor, Corday, Guerlain, and Schiaparelli, between 1945 and 1951.

Musée Baccarat
Baccarat Museum
30 bis rue du Paradis, 75010 Paris, France
Tel. (33) 1 47 70 64 30   www.baccarat.fr
Mon-Sat 10am-6pm

Amulet, Flowers of Devonshire by Mary Dunhill (above)
Alfred Dunhill Museum

Advertisement for Escape perfume (below)
Alfred Dunhill Museum

The perfume bottles exhibited here are splendid works of art, many of which reflect the cultural trends of their time, such as the bottle in the shape of a pyramid made for Sybmée by Cottan in 1917. The collection also includes the surrealistic Roi Soleil, designed by Salvador Dali for Elsa Schiaparelli in 1945.

Museum der Düfte – Zentrum für Aussergewöhnliche Museen
The Museum of Scent – Centre for Extraordinary Museums
Westenriederstrasse 41, 80331 Munich, Germany
Tel. (49) 89 2904121
Daily 10am-5pm

The museum comprises 5,000 items covering over 200 years of the industry. Besides kitsch American bottles in the shape of golliwogs, there are bottles by Dali, Saint Phalle, and Lalique, along with tiny miniatures, perfume lamps, and powder jars.

Alfred Dunhill Museum
48 Jermyn Street, London sw1y 6DL, UK
Tel. (44) 20 7838 8233
Mon-Fri 9.30am-6pm (Sat 10am-6pm by appt. only)

Not just a museum for men who love gadgets, but also for women who want to see the bottles used to hold the ladies fragrance introduced to the company by Mary Dunhill, daughter of Alfred, in the 1930s. Along with original bottles there are adverts and related advertising ephemera pertaining to Dunhill's perfumes, most of which is held in the company's archives.

Musée du Flacon à Parfum
Museum of the Flask of Perfume
33 rue du Temple, 17000 La Rochelle, France
Tel. (33) 5 46 41 32 40
Daily (except Mon morning) 10am-12.30pm, 2-7pm

Over 1,000 perfume bottles and related items from more than nine countries, many designed by famous artists. The collection includes such treasures as bottles commemorating the first trip of the *Normandie* and the crowning of the Emperor of Japan.

A selection from the
collection of Mrs French
*Harris Museum and Art
Gallery*

Annette Green Museum

The Fragrance Foundation, 145 East 32nd Street, New York, New York 10016, USA
Tel. (1) 212 725 2755 www.fragrance.org
By appt. only

Opened under the auspices of the Fragrance Foundation, this is the first fragrance museum in the US. In beautiful 18th-century Adam cabinets are a selection of vintage and antique perfume flacons shown in exhibitions that change three times a year.

Harris Museum and Art Gallery

Market Square, Preston, Lancashire PR1 2PP, UK
Tel. (44) 1772 258 248 www.preston.gov.uk
Mon-Sat 10am-5pm

A remarkable collection of 2,700 scent bottles amassed by Mrs Idonea French. The earliest ones date from the 18th century and are mostly clear glass with silver mounts. Of particular interest is a mould-blown Negro's head bottle attributed to Bernard Perrot (early 18th century). The collection is largely of 19th-century bottles made in Britain, France, Bohemia, Italy, the Netherlands, and China. Many are glass, but there are also smaller numbers of porcelain and silver bottles, as well as those made from more unusual materials like polished stone, nuts, and mussel shells.

Musée international de la Parfumerie
The International Museum of Perfume

8 Place du Cours, 06130 Grasse, France
Tel. (33) 4 93 36 80 20 www.museesdegrasse.com
Jun-Sep: daily 10am-7pm. Oct-May: Mon, Wed-Sun 10am-12.30pm, 2-5.30pm

The collections cover 3,000 years of perfume making with remarkable displays of ancient objects, from a terracotta bottle from the Near East (4th century BC) representing the sacrifice of Mithra, to a strange kohl receptacle in the shape of a fish, and a hedgehog from the 6th century BC. Other gems are white porcelain bottles from Meissen, engraved crystal ones from Italy and France, a stunning bottle in white porcelain from the imperial manufacturer for Alexander I in St Petersburg, and exotic bottles from India, Morocco, Turkey, and Iran.

Magie du Parfum
The Magic of Perfume

61 rue du Docteur Caral, 05400 Veynes, France
Tel. (33) 4 92 57 14 50 www.magieduparfum.fr.fm
Tue-Sun 10am-7pm

This museum comprises a collection of some 8,000 objects including perfume bottles, powder cases, and lipsticks, from antiquity to the present day. On show are works of art from Lalique, Baccarat and Viard among others. They were produced for the likes of Guerlain, Molinard, Rigaud, Dior, Nina Ricci, and Yves Saint-Laurent.

(Left to right):
Gold encrusted and
etched perfumizer 1924
Wicker demijohn 1830-60
Cintra cologne, red and
blue, 1927-31
Cameo cologne, red flowers & green leaves, 1903
Gold Aurene, 1924-29
Prince Matchabelli
Beloved perfume blue &
gold, 1950
Realities Eau de Toilet
Spray, 1990
*Museum of American Glass at
Wheaton Village*

Manor House Museum

Honey Hill, Bury St Edmunds, Suffolk IP33 1HF, UK
Tel. (44) 1284 757072 www.stedmundsbury.gov.uk
Tue, Wed, Sat, Sun noon-5pm

There are 230 scent and perfume bottles dating primarily from the late 18th to the early 19th centuries, bequeathed by Mrs John Greene. There are also examples of Oxford Lavenders, manufactured as cheap disposable containers for lavender water in the 19th century.

Nederlands Parfumflessen Museum
The Dutch Museum of Perfume Bottles
Bosstraat 2, 1731 SE Winkel, The Netherlands
Tel. (31) 224 541578
Wed, Fri 2-5pm, Sat 11am-5pm (Jul-Aug: Thu 2-5pm)

A staggering 7,000 perfume bottles from all the well-known commercial perfume houses, including Shalimar by Guerlain and the ubiquitous Chanel No. 5. By far the most fascinating examples are the older scent flasks by, for example, René Lalique and Salvador Dali. See the table fitted with 300 bottles, each filled with a different scent, where the perfumer sat when creating new fragrances.

Bottle top in the shape of a black head
Harris Museum and Art Gallery

Osmothèque
36 rue du Parc de Clagny, 78000 Versailles, France
Tel. (33) 1 39 55 46 99
By appt. only

This is not a museum in the traditional sense, but rather a 'house of perfumes' set up in 1990 and managed by the French Perfumers' Society and the French Perfume Committee, where both professionals and amateurs can rediscover obsolete fragrances, or learn about those currently being produced. It includes Paul Poiret's Arlequinades Pierrot, and the eau de cologne used by Napoleon I on St Helena.

Musée de la Parfumerie Fragonard
Museum of the Fragonard Perfumery
9 rue Scribe, 75009 Paris, France
Tel. (33) 1 47 42 04 56 www.fragonard.com
Daily 9.30am-5.30pm. Mid Mar-mid Oct: 10am-2pm

Founded by the perfume maker Fragonard, the museum traces 3,000 years of perfume history through flasks, travel necessities, distillation equipment, engravings, and perfume packaging. Among the perfume bottles on display is a box with more than sixty pieces in vermeuil-silver-gilt, decorated with crystal and mother-of-pearl, that was presented by the Duc de Berry as a gift to his first wife when he left her. A vinaigrette with its tiny 'sponge' used by ladies in the 18th century when they felt faint, and a gold ring capable of releasing fragrance are fascinating. They also own the Museé du Parfum, housed in a magnificent factory from the end of the 18th century (20 blvd Fragonard, 06130 Grasse, France, Tel. (33) 4 93 36 44 65), as well as two factories that are open to visitors by tour: La Fabrique des fleurs (Route de Cannes, Les 4-Chemins, 06130 Grasse Tel. (33) 4 93 77 94 30) and at Eze-Village located between Nice and Monaco (Tel. (33) 4 93 41 05 05).

Museo del Perfum
Perfume Museum
Passeig de Gracia, 39 Barcelona, 08007, Spain
Tel. (34) 93 216 0121 www.perfum-museum.com
Mon-Fri 10am-2pm, 4.30-8pm, Sat 10.30am-2pm

A collection of 5,000 bottles spanning all cultures and civilizations, from Egyptian containers and Greek ceramic scent bottles to Roman and Punic glass ones, along with Arabic and Oriental flasks. The majority are French bottles from the 18th and 19th centuries in porcelain, glass, and silver.

Promenade du Parfum
The Perfume Walk
Château de Chamerolles, 45170, Chilleurs-aux-Bois, France

Tel. (33) 2 38 39 84 66 www.coeur-de-france.com
Feb-Mar, Oct-Dec: Mon, Wed-Sun 10am-noon, 2-5pm. Apr-Sep: daily 10am-6pm (closed Tue except in Jul, Aug)

The collection, displayed throughout the castle, now numbers some 400 perfume bottles. The oldest piece is a 16th-century pomander. There are examples in Sèvres porcelain for Baccarat and bottles made by Lalique for Roger & Gallet.

Rare Essence Perfume Bottle Museum
757 Sutter Street, San Francisco, California 94109, USA
Tel. (1) 415 447 9772 www.rareessence-sf.com
Mon-Sat 10am-6.30pm

A perfumery with a museum attached containing rare and unusual perfume bottles dating back to the 1900s.

The Ruth Warner Collection
Kent, UK
Tel. (44) 1233 636185
By appt. only

Ruth Warner's collection of scent bottles fills 43 large drawers and includes counter displays, books, old adverts, dummy bottles, and antique display cabinets. It is internationally renowned and draws visitors from all over the world, including experts on fashion, perfumers, glass manufacturers, and historians.

Two small Communion flagons by Jeremias Wolsdorf
Städtisches Museum Göppingen

PEWTER

The American Museum in Britain
Claverton Manor, Bath, Somerset BA2 7BD, UK
Tel. (44) 1225 460503 www.americanmuseum.org
Museum: Tue-Sun 2-5pm. Gardens: Tue-Fri 1-6pm, Sat-Sun noon-6pm

Romano-British wine or water carafe excavated from the Thames,
c. 250-350AD
The Museum of British Pewter

The museum contains a sizeable collection of American pewter from the 18th and 19th centuries, including tankards, jugs, and other dishes and utensils. Hallmarks, like those used on silver, came into use in the second half of the 18th century. Popular motifs included the rose and crown and the rampant lion, but these were superseded by and eagle after the American Revolution.

Arlington Court
Arlington, near Barnstaple, Devon EX31 4LP, UK
Tel. (44) 1271 850296 www.nationaltrust.org.uk
Apr-mid Sep: daily 11am-5.30pm. Mid Sep-end Oct: daily 11am-4pm (Sun 11am-5.30pm)

Rosalie Chichester's pewter collection consists of nearly 400 pieces, of which the majority are British, and several pieces have the crest or arms of the Chichester family. There are some Irish and Continental examples, a Romano-British flagon dating from AD300, a 14th-century spoon, and fine examples of a salt cellar and candlestick from the 16th century.

The Museum of British Pewter
High Street, Stratford upon Avon, Warwickshire CV37 6HB, UK
Tel. (44) 1789 204507
Daily 10am-4.30pm

Left to right:
Octagonal flask by
Jeremias Wolsdorf
Bowl by Friedrich August
Wolsdorf
Tankard by Chrisian
Friedrich Wolsdorf
(above)
*Städtisches Museum
Göppingen*

Rosewater dish by
Richard Weir of
Edinburgh, *c.* 1600
(below)
*The Museum of British
Pewter*

This splendid Elizabethan house displays a first-class collection of 1,200 pewter pieces including the recently donated Neish Pewter Collection and 20th-century British work. The Neish Collection ranges from Romano-British pieces made and excavated in Britain, up to and including items from the 19th century. All periods are represented except the Dark Ages (500-1200AD) when no pewter was produced. Among the many highlights are a 3rd-century charger decorated with sunbursts and various patterns; a fine collection of flat-lidded tankards with royal portraits; and various Irish and Scottish pieces, including a rosewater bowl with an enameled brass boss dating from 1605.

Musée d'Etains
The Pewter Museum
Hôtel de Ville, 3960 Sierre, Switzerland
Tel. (41) 27 4520111
Mon-Fri 9-11am, 3-5pm

A small but fine collection of pewter containing 173 objects, mainly French and Swiss, from the 17th to 19th centuries. Most items are service sets consisting of pewter dishes and utensils. Traditional local items, with their distinctive styles, also include plates and tankards produced by the local guilds, alongside religious pewter items and medical instruments.

Historisches Museum Basel
The History Museum of Basle
Steinenberg 4, 4051 Basle, Switzerland
Tel. (41) 61 2710505   www.historischesmuseumbasel.ch
Mon, Wed-Sun 10am-5pm

The 'Tüllenkannen', a trio of three pewter pots with long spouts, are the highlights of this collection and are among the oldest pewter vessels in the world. Other pieces include a plump bow-handled pot (*c.*1500), the oldest secular piece in the pewter collection; a late 17th-century plate with an allegory of Temperance in relief; and a pretty claw-footed 'Ohrenshüssel' ('ear-dish') from the early 18th century.

Museum of London
London Wall, London EC2Y 5HN, UK
Tel. (44) 20 7600 3699   www.museumoflondon.org.uk
Tue-Sat 10am-5.50pm, Sun noon-5.50pm

The museum's pewter collection is unparalleled for provenanced pieces with specific local associations.

Pewter cups and flagons,
c. 1870s (right)
Royal Museum of Scotland

Royal Museum of Scotland
Chambers Street, Edinburgh EH1 1JF, Scotland, UK
Tel. (44) 131 225 7534   www.nms.ac.uk
Mon, Wed-Sat 10am-5pm, Tue 10am-8pm,
Sun noon-5pm

A small but interesting collection of over 300 pewter items, some from the 16th century, but concentrating on the 18th and 19th centuries, with a good representation of the work of Scottish pewterers. Some remarkable early pieces include the Rosewater dish by Richard Weir of Edinburgh (*c.* 1604), made for James I, and an early 17th-century pilgrim's bottle by Patrick Walker of Edinburgh.

Shelburne Museum
U.S. Route 7, Shelburne, Vermont 05482, USA
Tel. (1) 802 9853346 www.shelburnemuseum.org
Late May-late Oct: daily 10am-5pm

A collection of pewter that offers an overview of French, German, Dutch, English, and American styles. Look out for examples of Vermont-made pewter by Richard Lee of Springfield (active 1802-20) and Ebenezer Southmayd (1775-1831) of Castleton.

Städtisches Museum Göppingen
The Town Museum of Göppingen
Im Storchen, Wühlestrasse 36, 73033 Göppingen, Germany
Tel. (49) 7161 686375
Wed, Sat, Sun 10am-noon, 2-5pm

Pewter casting in Göppingen dates back to as early as 1516, and its pewterware is one of the most beautiful products of the town's craftmanship. The collection contains bottles, flagons, chalices, tankards, measures, plates, and many more. Highlights include two beautiful pewter flagons on a bell-shaped base, one of them dating from 1735, probably given as a christening gift. Equally fine are a flagon from 1729, and a goblet from 1686, both from the weaver-guild in Göppingen.

Muzeum Uniwersytetu Jagielloñskiego
The Jagiellonian University Museum
Collegium Maius, ulica Jagielloñska 15, 31-010 Cracow, Poland
Tel. (48) 12 4220549
Daily 11am-3pm, Sat 11am-2pm

Octagonal can with screw top by Johannes Berner
Städtisches Museum Göppingen

A small but important collection of around 200 objects, the majority made in the German towns of Frankfurt, Nuremberg, and Saxony. There is Nuremberg pewter, a jar and plate with relief cast decoration made by Hans Sigmund Geisser, and two other plates from this city, again with relief cast motifs by Hans Spatz II (1636) and Georg Schmauss (1630). There are 48 objects made in the Polish pewter centres from the 16th century onwards. One piece, in the form of a baluster, was made by Michel Hoppe in Wschowa at the beginning of the 18th century. Other items come from Russia, Czechoslovakia, and Switzerland.

Victoria and Albert Museum
Cromwell Road, South Kensington, London SW7 2RL, UK
Tel. (44) 20 7942 2000 www.vam.ac.uk
Daily 10am-5.45pm (Wed & last Fri of every month 10am-10pm)

An extensive collection of secular and non-secular pieces covering most of Europe, as well as China and the US. Particularly well represented are wares from France, Germany, Switzerland, and the Low Countries. Many of the British pieces are post 1600, but there are some important medieval items as well. There are contemporary works designed for the London department store Liberty's by Archibald Knox.

Winterthur Museum, Garden and Library
Route 52, Winterthur, Delaware 19735, USA
Tel. (1) 302 888 4600 www.winterthur.org
Mon-Sat 9am-5pm, Sun noon-5pm

A collection which displays work by several of the best-known American pewterers, including William Will and Frederick Bassett. There are particularly stunning examples of Will's coffee pots and flagons, and Bassett's quart tankards based on English designs of the late 17th and early 18th centuries.

English hammerhead baluster wine measure, *c.*1450-1500
The Museum of British Pewter

The Worshipful Company of Pewterers
Oat Lane, London EC2V 7DE, UK
Tel.(44) 20 7606 9363 www.pewterers.org.uk
By appt only

An encyclopaedic collection of antique British pewter which includes many first-class examples made in London. Outstanding is a lager charger from 1676, a beaker with relief decoration incorporating the initials and motto of Henry Prince of Wales (1610), and a double-eared porringer with relief decoration (*c.*1690-1702). Retained by the Company are five touch plates containing over 1,000 Master Pewterers' trade marks.

SILVER

The American Museum in Britain
Claverton Manor, Bath, Somerset BA2 7BD, UK
Tel.(44) 1225 460503 www.americanmuseum.org
Museum: Tue-Sun 2-5pm. Gardens: Tue-Fri 1-6pm, Sat-Sun noon-6pm

Two cases in the Central Hall contain examples of American silver from the 18th and 19th centuries. One of the finest pieces is a baroque porringer by William Jones of Massachusetts, and a tall creamer with a sweeping handle dating from around 1790. There are two pieces by Tiffany: an ornate silver-gilt cake knife decorated with an extravagantly florid motif, and a late 19th-century Mackay service made with silver from the Comstock lode.

Apsley House, The Wellington Museum
Hyde Park Corner, London W1V 9FA, UK
Tel.(44) 207 499 5676 www.vam.ac.uk
Tue-Sun 11am-5pm

Apsley House contains several outstanding pieces of silverwork, all presented to the Duke by European monarchs. The huge Wellington shield in the China Room was designed by Thomas Sothard (*c.*1822). Do not miss the two magnificent candelabra by Benjamin Smith of 1816-17. The highlight of the collection is the spectacular silver service (1,000 pieces) designed by Domingos Antonios de Sequiera and presented to Wellington by the Prince Regent of Portugal in recognition of the British help to the Portuguese against Napoleon. The centrepiece runs the length of the dining room table and bears dramatic mythological representations from Greece and Egypt.

Museo degli Argenti
The Silver Museum
Palazzo Pitti, Piazza Pitti, 50125 Florence, Italy
Tel.(39) 055 2388 709
Daily 8.30am-1.50pm (times may vary, please call for details)

The museum houses an important collection of silverware, vases, jewels, and precious objects gathered by the Medicis and the Grand Dukes of Tuscany. Remarkable vases and cups belonging to Lorenzo the Magnificent are made from silver and semiprecious stones such as amethyst, onyx, and jasper, and were assembled in the 15th century by Florentine goldsmiths.

Musée Bouilhet-Christofle
Bouilhet-Cristofle Museum
9 rue Royale, 75008 Paris, France
Tel.(33) 1 49 33 43 00
Mon-Tue, Thu-Sun 2-6pm

A collection of 400 Christofle pieces dating from 1830 to the present day, showing the evolution of different techniques.

Cabinet des Médailles et Antiquités
Cabinet of Medals and Antiques
Bibliothèque nationale de France, 58 rue de Richelieu, 75002 Paris, France
Tel. (33) 1 47 03 83 40
Mon-Fri 1-6pm, Sat 1-5pm, Sun & public holidays noon-6pm

A unique group of more than 100 silver objects from antiquity, the Treasure of Berthouville was found in 1830 in Normandy and given to the Cabinet by the Comte de Caylus. It consists of a silver table set, made in Italy in the 1st century AD, and of votive pieces from 2nd-century Gaul, including statuettes, and votive inscriptions.

Ewer by Paul de Lamerie,
London, 1742-43 (above)
The Gilbert Collection

Cooper-Hewitt National Design Museum
Smithsonian Institution, Fifth Avenue at 91st Street, New York, New York 10028, USA
Tel. (1) 212 849 8400 www.si.edu
Tue 10am-9pm, Wed-Sat 10am-5pm, Sun noon-5pm

Vase, Austria, c. 1920
(below)
*Cooper-Hewitt National
Design Museum*

A diverse selection of silver- and goldsmiths' work, including 17th- and 18th-century German presentation pieces, fine rococo examples from France, and a number of English works of the 18th and early 19th centuries. Other silver, much of it peasant work, comes from China, Turkey, Russia, Scandinavia, Central Europe, Mexico, and the US.

Danske Kongers Kronologiske Samling Rosenborg
The Rosenborg Royal Collection
Øster Voldgade 4A, 1350 Copenhagen, Denmark
Tel. (45) 33 15 32 86 www.kulturnet.dk
Please call for opening times

The Castle collections include many unusual silver objects. There is a life-sized lion in silver and gold made by Ferdinand Køblich in Copenhagen between 1665 and 1670; this lion and two other replicas were commissioned to guard the throne, which was made of a narval tooth. Another surprising object is the armchair in wood entirely covered in silver.

Ermitazh
The Hermitage
Dvortsovskaia naberezhnaia 34-36, 191065 St Petersburg, Russian Federation
Tel. (7) 812 110 9079 www.hermitage.ru
Tue-Sat 10.30am-6pm, Sun 10.30am-5pm

The Hermitage possesses one of the most important collections of silver- and goldsmith art in the world, with pieces from Russia and Western Europe. Highlights include a ship goblet from the 17th century made in Nuremberg by Jesaia zur Linden; the Nécéssaire with Châtelaine and Two Pendants by Thomas Tearle (18th century): and the salver by Marx Weinold (Augsburg, 17th century).

Fenimore Art Museum
Lake Road, Route 80, Cooperstown, New York 13326, USA
Tel. (1) 607 547 1400 www.fenimoreartmuseum.org
Apr-May, Oct-Dec: Tue-Sun 10am-4pm. Jun-Sep: daily 10am-5pm

For almost 200 years the city of Albany was a regional centre of silver manufacturing, producing a variety of outstanding silver items, from spoons and tankards to teapots and plates. This collection of several hundred items is complemented by photographs and ephemera providing insights into the silversmiths and their customers of the period.

Focke-Museum – Bremer Landesmuseum für Kunst und Kulturgeschichte
The Focke Museum – Museum of Bremen's Cultural History
Schwachhauser Heerstrasse 240, 28213 Bremen, Germany
Tel. (49) 421 361 3575 www.bremen.de
Tue-Sun 10am-6pm

This museum concentrates on articles produced in local workshops and the city's important silverware factories. The two oldest pieces of Bremen civic silverware are a flagon (1562-63) and a large, heavy bowl (1535-36) of the type that was used to rinse the hands at table in the 16th century.

Fogg Art Museum
The Harvard University Art Museums,
32 Quincy Street, Cambridge, Massachusetts 02138, USA
Tel. (1) 617 495 9400 www.artmuseums.harvard.edu
Mon-Sat 10am-5pm, Sun 1pm-5pm

The collection comprises approximately 3,750 works, including several very important 17th-century pieces, as well as later fine works by Huguenot goldsmiths working in London, such as Paul de Lamerie.

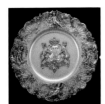

Henry Ford Museum and Greenfield Village
20900 Oakwood Blvd., Dearborn, Michigan 48124-4088, USA
Tel. (1) 313 271 1620 www.hfmgv.org
Daily 9am-5pm

Many of the best-known American silversmiths of the 1700s and 1800s are represented in this exhibition, from Paul Revere to Tiffany. Highlights include one of the oldest silver sports racing cups to survive, made by Jesse Kyp (c.1690), and a sterling silver set made in 1888 by the Gorham Manufacturing Company of Providence, Rhode Island, with all the handles made to look like the heads and trunks of elephants.

Dish by Paul de Lamerie, London, 1742-43 (top)
The Gilbert Collection

Basket, silver-gilt, Paul Storr, London, 1797-98 (above)
The Gilbert Collection

Monteith Bowl, silver-gilt, Edward Farrell, London, 1820-21 (right)
The Gilbert Collection

The Gilbert Collection
Gilbert Collection, Somerset House, Strand, London WC2, UK
Tel. (44) 20 7240 4080 www.gilbert-collection.org.uk
Mon-Sat 10am-6pm, Sun noon-6pm

The silverware dates from the 15th to the 19th centuries with works by the great English masters of the Georgian period especially well represented. Among the earliest pieces are a silver-gilt and rock crystal cup and cover (c.1568). Several pieces come from the Spencer family collection at Althorp, including a small bowl and stand by the refugee Huguenot goldsmith, Paul de Lamerie. There are examples of almost every kind of silver utensil, including silver sauce boats, tea kettles, coffee pots, plates, bowls, sconces, tureens, even chamber pots. Perhaps the most noteworthy item, if only for its sheer bulk, is a wine cistern which weighs in at nearly 36 kilos. It was bequeathed to the nation by London-born property developer, Arthur Gilbert.

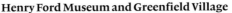

Gosudarstvennyi istoriko-kul'turnyi muzei-zapovednik 'Moskovskii Kreml'
The State Historical-Cultural Museum-Preserve 'Moscow Kremlin'
Krasnaia ploshchad', 103073 Moscow, Russian Federation
Tel. (7) 095 2023776 www.kremlin.museum.ru
Mon-Wed, Fri-Sun 10am-4pm

This rich and diverse collection of metalwork contains secular and ecclesiastical objects, many of unique artistic and historical significance. There is an exceptional example of a pre-Mongol (12th century) silver vessel, a chalice created by craftsmen from the Vladimir-Suzdal principality. Another remarkable example forms a 13th-century pectoral cross. Its silver front bears an engraved cross with six arms, with a heart-shaped filigree pattern on the gold reverse. One of the many treasures is a small manuscript of the Gospels from the late 16th to the early 17th century. This is a fine example of the opulent artistic book design of Russia's Middle Ages. Its wooden binding is covered in gold brocade with silver-gilt plaques which depict both the Crucifixion and the Evangelists. Apart from holy water basins, diptychs, and censers the museum also possesses a wide range of everyday objects. Amongst these items are bowls, such as the typical Russian vessel, the bratina or toasting bowl, which was an indispensable accessory at the banquet table.

Double trophy, made after the model drawing of Albrect Dürer in, 1526
Hiekan taidmuseo

Gruuthuse Museum
Dijver 17, 8000 Bruges, Belgium
Tel. (32) 50 448711
Apr-Sep: daily 9.30am-5pm. Oct-Mar: Mon, Wed-Sun 9.30am-12.30pm, 2-5pm

The museum's extensive collection of silverware is chiefly local in origin. Apart from the numerous ecclesiastical and liturgical objects in precious metal, and the table-silver, it is the 'guild-silver' from the 16th, 17th, 18th and 19th centuries that gives the collection its special importance. Especially noteworthy is the Great Shield of the Bruges Bakers' Guild, dating from 1769.

Interior of the museum
Hiekan taidmuseo

Hiekan taidemuseo
Hiekka Art Museum
Pirkankatu 6, 33210 Tampere, Finland
Tel. (358) 3 212 39 73 www.vip.fi
Wed, Thu 3-6pm, Sun noon-3pm

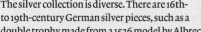

The silver collection is diverse. There are 16th- to 19th-century German silver pieces, such as a double trophy made from a 1526 model by Albrect Dürer; 18th-century Baltic silver; and Finnish and Swedish silver from the 17th century onwards. The 19th-century Russian silver focuses mainly on objects produced in St Petersburg, including some enamel-patterned objects such as a tea glass holder and a spoon by Pavel Ovtshinnikov.

The Huntington Library, Art Collections, and Botanical Gardens
1151 Oxford Road, San Marino, California 91108, USA
Tel. (1) 626 405 2100 www.huntington.org
Tue-Fri noon-4.30pm, Sat-Sun 10.30am-4.30pm

More than 430 silver objects dating from the early 18th century through to the antebellum period. The collection is remarkable for the 34 forms of silver that it contains, its representation of the work of over 160 American silversmiths, and the large number of pieces made before 1800. You'll see everything from pap boats to porringers, and tea sets to tankards. Makers include Nathaniel Hurd, Paul Revere, Philip Syng, and Jacob Lansing.

Twenty-piece toilet
service, silver-gilt, Philip
Rollos, c. 1695
The Gilbert Collection

Kunstgewerbemuseum
The Museum of Applied Arts
Schloss Köpenick, Schlossinsel, 12557 Berlin, Germany
Tel. (49) 30 6572651 www.smb.spk-berlin.de
Tue-Fri 10am-6pm, Sat, Sun 11am-6pm

This branch of the museum houses a remarkable collection of silverware. It includes a 33-piece set of Councillors' silverware from Lüneburg, with scenes and symbols from the Old and the New Testament, as well as mythological deities. A further focal point is the great silver sideboard from the Knight's Room in the old castle of Berlin, made by J. Ludwig and A. Biller between 1695 and 1698.

The Library and Museum of Freemasonry
Freemasons' Hall, 60 Great Queen Street, London WC2B 5AZ, UK
Tel. (44) 20 7395 9251 www.grandlodge-england.org
Mon-Fri 10am-5pm

The plate collection includes presentation pieces in silver, silvergilt and Sheffield plate, with salvers, loving cups and candelabra. There is also an important silver centrepiece of 1838 by Robert Garrard, an Indian silver presentation casket to the Prince of Wales of 1875 and a Dutch parcel gilt beaker.

Musée du Louvre
The Louvre
Palais du Louvre, 34-36 quai du Louvre, 75001 Paris, France
Tel. (33) 1 40 20 53 17 www.louvre.fr
Mon, Wed 9am-9.15pm, Thu-Sun 9am-5.30pm

The Louvre houses an unparalelled number of important masterpieces and objects of great historical significance, with the world's largest collection of pieces by Louis XV's famous goldsmith Germain, whom Voltaire said had a 'divine hand'. Highlights include Napoleon's knife; the gold coffin of Anne of Austria, probably a gift from Cardinal Mazarin; Marie-Antoinette's silverware, including cutlery, plates, boxes, and inkstands; plus Napoleon's tea service in gilded silver by Biennais.

Musée Mandet
The Mandet Museum
14 rue de l'Hôtel-de-Ville, 63200 Riom, France
Tel. (33) 4 73 38 18 53
Jun-Sep: Wed-Mon 10am-noon, 2.30-6pm. Oct-May: Wed-Mon 10am-noon, 2-5.30pm

The majority of the silverware collection originates from the donation of Edouard and Marie-Josèphe Richard. Its balance of Parisian, provincial and foreign pieces from the 17th and especially from the 18th century provides an excellent study of styles and techniques.

Museé national de la Renaissance
National Museum of the Renaissance
Château d'Ecouen, 95440 Ecouen, France
Tel. (33) 1 34 38 38 63 www.musexpo.com
Mon, Wed-Sun 9.45am-12.30pm, 2-5.15pm

Displays include a beautifully worked pendant in the form of a swan, a delightful snail-shaped goblet, tankards and caskets covered in tiny figures set in extravagant pastoral scenes, and an Italian mirror elaborately decorated with flowers, garlands, and fabulous creatures.

Nederlands Goud-, Zilver- en Klokkenmuseum
The Dutch Gold, Silver and Clock Museum
Kazerneplein 4, 2871 CZ Schoonhoven, The Netherlands
Tel. (31) 182 385612
Tue-Sun noon-5pm

Schoonhoven is known as Silvertown, taking its name from the silver industry which flourished there in the 18th and 19th centuries. The museum shows an exclusive collection of Dutch silverware, including candlesticks, coffee and tea sets, little 'l'eau de reine' boxes, and sewing kits.

Österreichisches Gold- und Silberschmiedmuseum
Austrian Gold- and Silversmith Museum
Zieglergasse 221070 Vienna, Austria
Tel. (43) 1 523 40 96
Wed 3-6pm

This museum demonstrates the techniques of gold- and silversmiths, with an original smithy, and information on the history of the crafts. There is a fine collection of handcrafted silver objects from Empire, Classicism, Biedermeier, Art Nouveau, and Art Deco, mainly consisting of cutlery, bowls, trays, powder-boxes, and lighters.

Musée d'Orfèvrerie
The Museum of Goldsmithery
9 rue Royale, 75008 Paris, France
Tel. (33) 1 49 33 43 00
Mon, Tue, Thu-Sun 4-6 pm (closed Aug)

A collection of 400 Christofle pieces from the beginning of the company in 1830 through to present day, showing the evolution of different techniques. Of special interest are the tea and coffee services, as well as plates and soup bowls made for Louis Philippe at the Tuileries. Also on display is a tea urn measuring 1 metre high, said to be able to hold 35 litres of tea, which was made in 1873. There is a selection of Japanese teapots and several examples of Art Nouveau and Art Deco by Gio Ponti, Fjerdinstad, Sue and Mare, and Luc Lanel. Later items include works by Lino Sabaitni, Deluol, Yencesse, and engraved plates by Man Ray, Jean Cocteau, and Marie Laurencin.

Royal Albert Memorial Museum
Queen Street, Exeter, Devon EX4 3RX, UK
Tel. (44) 1392 665858   www.exeter.gov.uk
Mon-Sat 10am-5pm

The museum's collection of West Country silver is of international importance. It also has some important early church silver on indefinite loan from churches within the diocese.

Royal Museum of Scotland
Chambers Street, Edinburgh EH1 1JF, Scotland, UK
Tel. (44) 131 225 7534   www.nms.ac.uk
Mon-Sat 10am-5pm (Tue until 8pm), Sun noon-5pm

An encyclopaedic collection of Scottish silver (3,000 pieces) unsurpassed by any collection anywhere. It concentrates on the major centres of production: Edinburgh, Glasgow, Dundee, Perth, and Inverness. One piece not to miss is the Galloway mazer by James Grey of the Canongate (1569). Recently acquired

Goldsmith's worktop (below)
Österreichisches Gold und Silberschmiedmuseum

Silver presentation casket, 1894 (bottom)
Royal Museum of Scotland

was an eighteen-piece 17th-century silver communion set, described as one of the most precious and important collections of church silver in Britain.

Coffee pot, silver and enamel, Gerald Benney, 1997
Worshipful Company of Goldsmiths

Temple Newsam House
Temple Newsam Road, off Selby Road, Leeds, West Yorkshire LS15 0AE, UK
Tel. (44) 113 264 7321 www.leeds.gov.uk
Apr-Oct: Tue-Sat 10am-5pm, Sun 1-5pm. Nov-Dec, Mar: Tue-Sat 10am-4pm, Sun noon-4pm

The silver collection is one of the finest in England, presenting a comprehensive history of the main forms and stylistic trends in English silver between the 17th and late 19th centuries. Early pieces include the ornately engraved silver-gilt Mostyn flagon (1601) and the Thirkleby flagon (1646), which formed part of the church plate at Thirkleby church in Yorkshire and is delicately engraved with trailing garlands and fabulous creatures. Eighteenth-century silver is particularly well represented. Among the finest exhibits is a Rococo 'tea equipage' from 1735 by Paul Lamerie.

Tønder Museum
Kongevej 51, 6270 Tønder, Denmark
Tel. (45) 74 72 26 57 www.tonder-net.dk
Jun-Aug: daily 10am-5pm. Sep-May: Tue-Sun 10am-5pm

The collection illustrates the works of gold- and mainly silversmiths in the Tønder area between 1700 and 1900. It is characterized by the objects that were most popular at the time: spoons, buttons, buckles, a few sugar trays, sugar bowls, and smaller cups.

UCLA Fowler Museum of Cultural History
405 Hilgard Avenue, Los Angeles, California 90095-1549, USA
Tel. (1) 310 825 4361 www.fmch.ucla.edu
Wed-Sun noon-5pm (Thu until 8pm)

The collection comprises objects from 16th- to 19th-century Europe and the US. The most important acquisitions of English silver were made in 1947 with the dispersal of the J. Pierpont Morgan collection. There are items from the workshops of British silversmith Paul de Lamerie (*c.*1800), Fabergé (*c.*1900), and Paul Revere (*c.*1760). Earliest pieces include important Elizabethan silver such as twelve engraved and parcel gilt spice or fruit plates struck with the maker's mark of the hooded falcon and the London hallmark for 1567.

Victoria and Albert Museum
Cromwell Road, South Kensington, London SW7 2RL, UK
Tel. (44) 20 7942 2000 www.vam.ac.uk
Daily 10am-5.45pm (Wed & last Fri of every month 10am-10pm)

A dazzling suite of galleries are devoted to both the National Collection of English silver (1300-1800), with a display of over 800 objects, and the International Silver Collection (1800-2000) displaying a further 1,100 objects. Set in their social and historic context, and arranged in chronological and thematic displays, are the grandest of Victorian silver unmatched anywhere. Also a collection of ecclesiastical and domestic plate which demonstrates its development since the 16th century, and an extensive array of small scale 19th-century commercial silver from shoehorns to silver theatre tickets. Not content with providing just labelled cases crammed with stellar examples, the curators have embarked on an ambitious programme illustrating the versatility of the material; hall-marking; fakes; forgeries; and decorative techniques.

Worshipful Company of Goldsmiths
Goldsmiths' Hall, Foster Lane, London EC2V 6BN, UK
Tel. (44) 20 7606 7010 www.thegoldsmiths.co.uk
Please call for opening times

By far the most comprehensive part of the collection is that of 20th-century British silver, their 1,700 pieces far exceeding most museums. They range in style from 1930s Art Deco to recent millennium commissions. The earliest piece, gifted in 1561, is the Bowes Cup, believed to have been used by Queen Elizabeth I at her Coronation banquet in 1558.

The Millennium Bowl,
silver, 1999
Worshipful Company of Goldsmiths

STAINED GLASS

The Burrell Collection

2060 Pollokshaws Road, Glasgow G43 1AT, Scotland, UK
Tel. (44) 141 649 7151
Mon-Sat 10am-5pm, Sun 11am-5pm

With 700 panels, this is the second largest museum collection of stained glass in Europe. Half of them are English, ranging from complete panels to fragments, and dating from the 12th to the 19th centuries. Highlights include a 13th-century medallion window of the Marriage of Cana, probably from Clermont-Ferrand Cathedral, and the fine heraldic glass from the pre 16th-century glass-painting schools of Flanders, the Rhineland, and Cologne.

Hammersmith Library

Shepherds Bush Road, London W6 7AT, UK
Tel. (44) 20 8576 5055
By appt. only

A superb library full of fine stained glass. There are medallions of Spenser and Chaucer, among others, and a splendid full-length portrait of Dean Colet, friend of Erasmus and founder of St Paul's School, gracing the east window. In the music library there is the Bennett Window, consisting of eighty panels of 16th- and 17th-century stained and painted glass of Flemish and Dutch origins, originally part of Horace Walpole's Strawberry Hill collection.

Musée historique lorrain
Lorraine History Museum

Palais ducal, 64 Grande Rue, 54 000 Nancy, France
Tel. (33) 3 83 32 18 74
May-Sep: Tue-Sun 10am-6pm. Oct-Apr: Mon-Sat 10am-noon, 2-5pm
Sun & public holidays 10am-noon, 2-6pm

A remarkable collection of civil stained glass, with the armorial bearings of the dukes René II and Antoine or Jean de Lorraine, is exhibited in the old palace of the Dukes of Lorraine, together with glass from various churches in and around Nancy.

Historisches Museum Basel
The History Museum of Basle

Steinenberg 4, 4051 Basle, Switzerland
Tel. (41) 61 2710505
Mon, Wed-Sun 10am-5pm

More than 200 glass-paintings and fragments of windows from the last eight centuries have been gathered, although sadly some of the most beautiful panels from the Charterhouse in Freiburg have been draped in order to prevent light damage. Among the earliest items are two roundels from Chartres Cathedral (early 13th century).

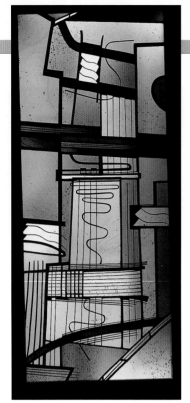

Composition, by Georg
Meistermann, 1957
Suermondt Ludwig Museum

The Metropolitan Museum of Art

1000 Fifth Avenue, 82nd Street, New York, New York 10028, USA
Tel. (1) 212 535 7710 www.metmuseum.org
Tue-Thu 9.30am-5.30pm, Fri, Sat 9.30am-9pm
Sun 9.30am-5.30pm

The most comprehensive collection of Renaissance glass in the US.
Not to be missed are two large windows and four oculi, including one
signed by the famous Valentin Bousch, from the Abbey of Flavigny;
the twelve stained-glass panels by Franz Fallenter, originally painted
for the Swiss Cloister at Rathausen (end 16th century); and panels for
the cloister of the Carthusian monastery at Louvain (16th century).
There are stunning Tiffany stained-glass windows in the courtyard of
the American Wing.

The Charles Hosmer Morse Museum of American Art

445 North Park Avenue, Winter Park, Florida 32789, USA
Tel. (1) 407 645 5311 www.morsemuseum.org
Tue-Sat 9.30am-4pm, Sun 1-4pm

Devoted to the end of 19th- and beginning of 20th-century American
art, the collection includes an extraordinary number of stained-glass
windows by Tiffany. He had registered a patent for a radical glass-
manufacturing technique in 1881 which created a new opalescent glass, and allowed an
unprecedented range of colours and three-dimensional effects. There is also an extensive collection of stained-glass pieces by other artists of the period, including Sir Edward
Burne-Jones, William Morris, Louis Sullivan, Frank Lloyd Wright, John La Farge, and
Arthur Nash.

William Morris Gallery

Lloyd Park, Forest Road, London E17 4PP, UK
Tel. (44) 20 8527 3782 www.lbwf.gov.uk
Tue-Sat 10am-1pm, 2-5pm

Among the examples in the gallery's collection is a stained-glass panel of Angels, originally designed by Burne-Jones as a window in Salisbury Cathedral. Another stunning
example is of the figure of St Cecilia, originally designed in 1867 by Burne-Jones for St
Saviour's church, Leeds.

Museé national de la Renaissance
National Museum of the Renaissance

Château d'Ecouen, 95440 Ecouen, France
Tel. (33) 1 34 38 38 63 www.musexpo.com
Mon, Wed-Sun 9.45am-12.30pm, 2-5.15pm

Among the fine examples of stained glass is a mid 16th-century piece showing the insignia
of Anne de Montmorency, formed by the king's sword piercing a golden knot. Also a fiery,
exquisitely detailed depiction of the Earth and Mars, possibly imported from Italy.

Musée de L'Oeuvre Notre-Dame
Museum of the Good Work of our Lady

3 Place du Château, 67000 Strasbourg, France
Tel. (33) 3 88 52 50 00
Tue-Sat 10am-noon, 1.30-6pm, Sun 10-5pm

The collection of stained glass ranges from the 11th century to present times, with the core of the collection coming from Notre-Dame Cathedral in Strasbourg. The museum's prize is the earliest well-preserved figurative window representing the head of Christ, the so-called Christ of Wissenburg.

The Stained Glass Museum

South Triforium Gallery, Ely Cathedral, Ely, Cambridgeshir CB7 4DL, UK
Tel. (44) 1353 660 347   www.stainedglassmuseum.org
Mon-Fri 10.30am-4.30pm, Sat 10.30am-5.30pm, Sun noon-6pm

The museum displays around a hundred pieces of mainly British glass tracing the history of the craft from the Middle Ages to recent times, rescued from over sixty redundant churches. The reserve collection of around 300 windows (open to researchers by appointment) supports the main collections, as does a library.

Isabella Stewart Gardner Museum

280 The Fenway, Boston, Massachusetts 02115, USA
Tel. (1) 617 566 1401   www.boston.com
Tue-Sun 11am-5pm

Among the endless highlights is a fragment of a window from Soissons Cathedral, which represents scenes from the Martyrdom of Saints Nicasius and Eutropia. There are also In the Chapel and the Gothic Room there are six potmetal and stained panels probably from Milan Cathedral (*c.* 1500). In the Spanish Chapel there are three German potmetal and stained *kabinettscheiben* from the 15th and 16th centuries. St. Benedict Lying in the Briars was one of the series designed by Dürer.

Interior of the musuem
Suermondt Ludwig Museum

Suermondt Ludwig Museum

Wilhelmstrasse 18, 52070 Aachen, Germany
Tel. (49) 241 479800   www.heimat.de
Tue-Fri 11am-7pm (Wed until 9pm) Sat-Sun 11am-5pm

Vast collections spanning three millennia include late Gothic sculpture, glorious Dutch 17th-century paintings, as well as objects from classical antiquity. Modern glass paintings include works by Otto Dix, Johannes Schreiterm, Pierre Soulages, and a sandblasted glass pane from Ludwig Schaffrath.

Musée suisse du Vitrail
The Swiss Museum of Stained Glass

Châteaude Romont, 1680 Romont, Switzerland
Tel. (41) 26 6521095   www.romont.ch
Apr-Oct: Tue-Sun 10am-noon, 2-6pm. Nov-Mar: Sat-Sun 10am-noon, 2-6pm

Romont Castle houses this comprehensive collection of stained glass from the Middle Ages to contemporary works.

Victoria and Albert Museum

Cromwell Road, South Kensington, London SW7 2RL, UK
Tel. (44) 20 7942 2000   www.vam.ac.uk
Daily 10am-5.45pm (Wed & last Fri of every month 10am-10pm)

This collection is probably the most important in the world. The collection was significantly increased during the 20th century by the donations of private benefactors. Before that, Henry Vaughan had given some of the most important items to the museum. In 1919 the collection benefited from the gift by John Pierpont Morgan of his father's collection, which had been on loan for many years.

TILES

Allen Gallery
10-12 Church Street, Alton, Hampshire GU34 1BA, UK
Tel. (44) 1420 82802   www.hants.gov.uk
Tue-Sat 10am-5pm

The gallery's collection of ceramic tiles includes a charming series made in the late 1770s, showing actors and actresses in roles they were famous for.

Birmingham Museum & Art Gallery
Chamberlain Square, Birmingham, West Midlands B3 3DH, UK
Tel. (44) 121 303 2834   www.birmingham.gov.uk
Mon-Thu, Sat 10am-5pm, Fri 10.30am-5pm, Sun 12.30-5pm

The museum houses a remarkable and extensive collection of William De Morgan tiles.

Gekachelter Saal – Residenz Ansbach
The Tiled Hall – Ansbach Residence
Promenade 27, 91522 Ansbach, Germany
Tel. (49) 981 953 8390
Apr-Sep: Tue-Sun 9am-6pm. Oct-Mar: Tue-Sun 10am-4pm

This beautiful Renaissance castle's stunning interior is especially remarkable for its Tiled Hall with some 2,800 faïence tiles from the local manufacture, lightly and delicately designed with rural motifs.

Museum für islamische Fliesen und Keramik
The Museum of Islamic Tiles and Ceramics
Westerhof-Klinik, Olaf-Gulbransson-Strasse 19, 83684 Tegernsee Germany
Tel. (49) 8022 1810
Guided tour by appt. only.

Four tiles, The Netherlands, *c.* 1625
Keramiekmuseum het Princessehof

Displayed in a corridor between two buildings of the Westerhof Hospital are about 300 Islamic ceramics, principally tiles from the 10th to the 19th centuries collected by Dr Theodor Sehmer. The tiles originate mainly from Turkey, Iran and Iraq.

Jackfield Tile Museum
Jackfield, Telford, Shropshire, UK
Tel. (44) 1952 882030
www.vtel.co.uk
Daily 10am-5pm

A remarkable collection of Victorian tiles housed in an 1874 factory. Most of the collection is devoted to the work of Maw and Craven Dunhill whose tiles were produced in the factory until 1952.

Keramiekmuseum het Princessehof
The Princess Court Ceramics Museum
Grote Kerkstraat 11, 8911 DZ
Leeuwarden, The Netherlands
Tel. (31) 58 2127438
www.home.wxs.nl
Mon-Sat 10am-5pm,
Sun 2-5pm

Ceramic tile, Persia, 17th-18th century
Österreichisches Museum für angewandte Kunst

As well as Dutch tiles, the collection includes tiles from the Iberian peninsula, France, England, Italy, Syria, Iran, and Iznik tiles from Turkey. Several large tiled floors have been brought together and there are also some large groupings arranged on the walls.

Leighton House Museum & Art Gallery
12 Holland Park Road, London W14 8LZ, UK
Tel. (44) 20 7602 3316
Mon-Sat 11am-5.30pm

Leighton House's Arab Hall, intricately decorated with Iznik tiles, is based on the reception hall of the Muslim Palace of La Zisa in Palermo. Persian and Syrian tiled panels and a magnificent gilt mosaic frieze containing verses from the Koran cover the walls. In spite of its original pieces, the Arab Hall is an original creation of Victorian art rather than a true copy of an Arab interior.

Moravian Pottery and Tile Works
130 Swamp Road, Doylestown, Pennsylvania 18901, USA
Tel. (1) 215 345 6722   www.go.to
Daily 10am-4.45pm

Thanks to the visionary Henry Mercer, this pottery and tile works became the leading producer of Arts and Crafts tiles, producing floor tiles for the rotunda and halls of the Pennsylvania Capitol. The Tile Works themselves are a testimony to Mercer's unerring eye. Still functioning, they are filled with young artisans who replicate Mercer's original designs. The tiles and their moulds are displayed throughout the Spanish Mission-inspired building.

William Morris Gallery
Lloyd Park, Forest Road, London E17 4PP, UK
Tel. (44) 20 8527 3782   www.lbwf.gov.uk
Tue-Sat 10am-1pm, 2-5pm

William Morris formed Morris, Marshall, Faulkner & Co. in 1861 (later renamed Morris & Co), which was well-known for its stained glass, tiles, and other decorative items. Fine panels are on display from a series illustrating The Labours of the Months (c. 1862/3) designed by Ford Madox Brown; tiles hand-painted for the company by Lucy J. Faulkner; and the zodiac sign of Cancer the crab, designed by Philip Webb. Look carefully at the tile for January, represented by a figure of the Roman god Janus. In the corner there is a caricature of William Morris carrying pails of water, representing the zodiac sign of Aquarius.

Museu nacional do Azulejo
The National Museum of Tiles
Rua da Madra de Deus 4, 1900 Lisbon, Portugal
Tel. (361) 21 8147747
Tue 2-6pm, Wed-Sun 10am-6pm

Glazed tiles (azulejos) are a typical Portugese art form. The museum contains thousands of examples, covering a span of 500 years ranging from tiles made in 16th-century Antwerp to contemporary examples. One of the highlights is a 25 metre-long panel by Xábregas do Cruz Quebrada, showing Lisbon before the earthquake of 1755.

Nederlands Tegelmuseum
The Dutch Tile Museum
Eikenzoom 12, 6731 BH Otterlo,
The Netherlands
Tel. (31) 318 591519
Tue-Fri 10am-12.30pm, 1-5pm, Sat-Sun 1-5pm

Located in a national park, the museum houses what is considered to be one of the largest collections of Dutch tiles. On show are a vast collection of multicoloured tiles popular in the 16th century, up to around 1620, when the vogue seemed to favour primarily blue tiles depicting typical Dutch scenes, ships, biblical passages, landscapes, and

Animal-decorated tile (top left) and blue and white tiles, Rotterdam, 1700-50
Nederlands Tegelmuseum

flowers. Around the 18th century, purple tiles became fashionable, particularly in Rotterdam. There is a beautiful selection of ornamental tiles as well as Art Nouveau and post-1900 tiles. The library specializes in Dutch ceramic floor and wall tiles, but also contains general works on the subject and documentation on individual manufacturers and designers.

Österreichisches Museum für angewandte Kunst
The Austrian Museum of Applied Arts
Stubenring 5, 1010 Vienna, Austria
Tel. (43) 1 71136 www.mak.at
Tue-Sun 10am-6pm (Thu until 9pm)

The museum's Oriental section possesses a fine collection of late 16th-century Iznik tiles, mainly faïence in cobalt blue, green, and red under glaze, some of them from the Omar mosque in Jerusalem. On display are some fine late 13th-century faïence tiles from Kashan.

Philadelphia Museum of Art
26th Street and the Benjamin Franklin Parkway, Philadelphia, Pennsylvania 19130, USA
Tel. (1) 215 763 8100 www.philamuseum.org
Tue-Sun 10am-5pm (Wed until 8.45pm)

Although there is a small group of Mexican 18th-century tiles, the most comprehensive collection consists of approximately 900 decorative Dutch tiles of the 17th and 18th centuries, amassed by the notable collector, Francis P. Garvan.

Musée de Sarreguemines
The Museum of Sarreguemines
15-17 rue Poincaré, 57200 Sarreguemines, France
Tel. (33) 3 87 98 93 50 www.sarreguemines-museum.com
Mon, Thu-Sun 2-6pm, Wed 9am-noon, 2-6pm

This winter garden is completely covered with faïence tiles and has a monumental fountain in the middle. Stoves and fireplaces illustrate the expertise and excellent technical skills of the Sarreguemines faïence workers. There are some magnificent pieces covered in richly coloured enamels, with some tiles enlivened by figures in relief.

WALLPAPER AND PRINTED TEXTILES

Busch-Reisinger Museum
Harvard University, 32 Quincy Street, Cambridge,
Massachusetts 02138, USA
Tel. (1) 617 495 2338 www.artmuseums.harvard.edu
Mon-Sat 10am-5pm, Sun 1pm-5pm

The most important collection of Bauhaus fabric in
the US, displayed alongside Bauhaus paintings, wallpaper, furniture, work in metal and glass, and architectural designs. The archives of Lyonel Feininger and
Walter Gropius are also held here, along with smaller
holdings of printed Vienna Secession textiles.

Cooper-Hewitt National Design Museum
Smithsonian Institution, Fifth Avenue at 91st Street, New York, New York 10028, USA
Tel. (1) 212 849 8400 www.si.edu
Tue 10am-9pm, Wed-Sat 10am-5pm, Sun noon-5pm

Detail of panoramic wall-
paper, Battle at Austerlitz,
France, 1827-29 (above)
Deutsches Tapetenmuseum

Wallpaper with flower
motif by Jules Desfossé,
Paris, 1862 (below)
Deutsches Tapetenmuseum

The largest and most comprehensive survey of wallcoverings in the US, with over 10,000
examples. It is rich in French floral compositions from the 19th century, William Morris-
inspired patterns, and early block-printed papers. There is an archive of over 1,500 drawings in the museum's Wiener Werkstätte collection, documenting the designs of
Dagobert Peche. There are wallpapers designed by students at the Bauhaus in 1929; some
by Frank Lloyd Wright from 1956; and Jhane Barnes's 1992 designs made with acrylic
resin powders.

Deutsches Tapetenmuseum – Hessisches Landesmuseum
The German Wallpaper Museum – The Hessian Regional Museum
Brüder-Grimm-Platz 5, 34117 Kassel, Germany
Tel. (49) 561 78460 www.kassel.de
Tue-Sun 10am-5pm

The collection contains 18,000 objects illustrating the history of wallcoverings
from the 16th to the 20th centuries. A great variety of techniques feature, from
Spanish and Dutch embossed leather (16th to 18th centuries), to oil cloth or
Japanese silk. Highlights include a hand-printed 19th-century French
panoramic mural depicting the Battle of Austerlitz, dating from 1827-29.
Another exhibit, a Chinese panoramic wallpaper from the 1780s, shows a hand-
painted Chinese funeral procession. The collection of printed papers ranges
from the 18th century to the newest designer wallpapers, with designs from
famous workshops in Germany and France, like Réveillon in Paris. There is
also a selection of East Asian wall decorations made of tree-bark fabrics.

The Museum of Domestic Design & Architecture
Middlesex University, Cat Hill, Barnet, Hertfordshire EN4 8HT, UK
Tel. (44) 20 8411 5244 www.moda.mdx.ac.uk
Tue-Sat 10am-5pm, Sun 2pm-5pm

An outstanding collection of wallpapers and textiles dating from the 1870s to the 1960s containing 20,000 designs, 2,000 wallpapers, fifty wallpaper-pattern books and about 400 textile samples. Meticulous record-keeping means that designs can be traced back to designers
and buyers, and there is a complete photographic archive of designs sold from 1890 to 1963.
Many of these are the work of the Silver Studio. Other parts of the collection include
trade catalogues of furnishers and interior decorators, the Crown Wallpaper Archive,
and an extensive library of books on design, architecture, and town planning.

The Drawing Room,
c. 1911 (above)
*The Museum of Domestic
Design & Architecture*

Textile, *c.* 1900 (below)
*The Museum of Domestic
Design & Architecture*

The Museum at the Fashion Institute of Technology

27th Street at Seventh Avenue, New York, New York 10001, USA
Tel. (1) 212 217 5700 www.fitnyc.edu
Tue-Fri noon-8pm, Sat 10am-5pm

The Textile Collection is an extensive resource of more than 30,000 textiles dating from the 17th century to the present day. These include apparel and home furnishing fabrics, laces and embroideries, printed and woven textiles, beaded pieces, and shawls. There are more than 15,000 jacquard point wallpapers in the collection, and velvets spanning a 125-year period are housed in the J. B. Martin Company Velvet Room. The Françoise de la Renta Color Room contains solid swatches from which members can take cuttings.

Musée de l'Impression sur Etoffes
Museum of Printed Fabrics

14, rue Jean-Jacques Henner, 68072 Mulhouse, France
Tel. (33) 3 89 46 83 00 www.musee-impression.com
Daily 10am-6pm

Built in 1858 in one of the international textile centres, the museum was first established to promote local production and to provide inspiration. Completely refurbished in 1996, it contains over three million examples of designs on file and is devoted to printed textiles as well as to printing technology. It covers all types of printing and dyeing, from the 18th century up to the present day, in Europe, Asia, Africa, Japan, the Pacific, and the US, and is the largest of its kind in the world. It also includes an impressive database of over 200,000 printed designs on paper, together with an enormous collection of sample books.

William Morris Gallery

Lloyd Park, Forest Road, London E 17 4PP, UK
Tel. (44) 20 8527 3782 www.lbwf.gov.uk
Tue-Sat 10am-5pm

The museum holds over 400 designs created either by Morris or his associates, and 85 textiles designed by A. H. Mackmurdo. It has a study room and a library of about 1,000 volumes on applied arts of the period.

Museé National de la Renaissance
National Museum of the Renaissance

Château d'Ecouen, 95440 Ecouen, France
Tel. (33) 1 34 38 38 63 www.musexpo.com
Mon, Wed-Sun 9.45am-12.30pm, 2-5.15pm

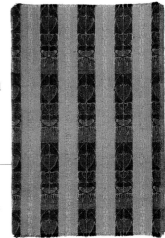

Only about a dozen leather wall hangings from the end of the 16th century survive in France, and two of them hang at the Château d'Ecouen. They depict great Roman heroes: Rome herself, looking on as Romulus and Remus suckle at the boar; and Manlius and Curius astride fierce horses.

Musée du Papier peint
The Wallpaper Museum

La commanderie, 28 rue Zuber, 68170 Rixheim, France
Tel. (33) 3 89 64 24 56
Oct-May: Mon, Wed-Sun 10am-noon, 2-6pm. Jun-Sep:
Mon-Fri 9am-noon, 2-6pm, Sat-Sun 10am-noon, 2-6pm

The basis of the large collection consists of wallpapers made by Zuber & Co. from 1800 to the present. Examples have been added from other sources in order to provide comparative material, and an outstanding collection of block-printed scenic wallpaper is also on display. Printing machinery is exhibited, as are 130,000 documents which provide an accurate account of the manufacturing of wallpaper from 1791 to the present.

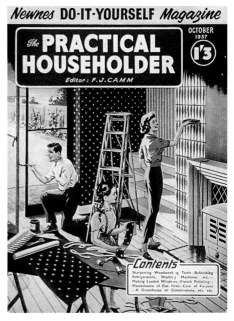

Philadelphia Museum of Art
26th Street and the Benjamin Franklin Parkway, Philadelphia, Pennsylvania 19130, USA
Tel. (1) 215 763 8100 www.philamuseum.org
Tue-Sun 10am-5pm (Wed until 8.45pm)

The collection of 17th- to 19th-century European and American printed textiles, block prints, plate prints and roller prints is one of the finest in North America. Comprising over 600 designs and some 200,000 swatches from American and European mills. The earliest European printed textiles are several 17th-century woodblock prints from Holland and Germany, while the largest number of French printed textiles are those manufactured at the Oberkampf factory in Jouy-en-Josas near Versailles.

Temple Newsam House
Temple Newsam Road, off Selby Road, Leeds, West Yorkshire LS15 0AE, UK
Tel. (44) 113 264 7321 www.leeds.gov.uk
Apr-Oct: Tue-Sat 10am-5pm, Sun 1-5pm. Nov-Dec, Mar: Tue-Sat 10am-4pm, Sun noon-4pm

The Practical Householder magazine, c. 1957
The Museum of Domestic Design & Architecture

An extraordinary collection of fabrics, that divides roughly into three categories: silks, both for dressmaking and furnishings; a substantial group of printed cottons; and a number of heavyweight fabrics used for furnishings. They all provide an illuminating insight into the decoration of interiors over the last 500 years. There are tapestries and brocatelle wall coverings; 18th- and 19th-century loose covers for furniture upholstered in decorative fabrics such as velvet, damask or fine needlework, and 16th- to 17th-century embroidered wool and linen hangings for beds.

Toijalan Tapettimuseo
The Wallpaper Museum of Toijala
Satamatie 8, Toijala, Finland
Tel. (358) 3 54 21090 www.tapettitalo.fi
Mon-Fri 9am-4.30pm, Sat 9am-noon

The only wallpaper museum in the Nordic countries was founded by Finland's oldest continuously working wallpaper factory, Pihlgren and Ritola Oy. It exhibits the factory's collections of machinery, photographs and wallpaper designs covering a period of seventy years since the founding in about 1930. The museum boasts a collection of over 2,000 wallpaper designs, including the famous Night of the Skylarks design by Birger Kaipiainen from the 1950s. Also designs by Tapio Wirkkala, Ritva Kronlund, Mirja Vänni, and others.

Musée de la Toile de Jouy
The Museum of Toile de Jouy
Château de L'Eglantine, 54 rue Charles-de-Gaulle, 78350 Jouy-en-Josas, France
Tel. (33) 1 39 56 48 64
Mar-Oct: Tue-Fri 10am-6pm. Nov-Feb: 10am-5pm, Sat-Sun & public holidays 2-6pm

Wallpaper design, 1941
(below)
*The Museum of Domestic
Design & Architecture*

Wallpaper design
(bottom)
*The Museum of Domestic
Design and Architecture*

Toile de Jouy was used for clothing, upholstery and decorative textiles. There is a wide collection of print designs in the museum, including the *indienne* inspired by Asian and floral motifs in the early 19th century, and scenes with characters following Jean-Jacques Rousseau's works on naturalism in the 18th century.

Victoria and Albert Museum

Cromwell Road, South Kensington, London sw7 2rl, UK
Tel. (44) 20 7942 2000   www.vam.ac.uk
Daily 10am-5.45pm (Wed & last Fri of every month 10am-10pm)

This is the UK's national collection of wallpapers. Like the collection of decorative textiles, it is massive in size and scope and embraces a wide variety of historical designs and designers.

The Whitworth Art Gallery

University of Manchester, Oxford Road, Manchester,
Greater Manchester m15 6er, UK
Tel. (44) 161 275 7450   www.man.ac.uk
Mon-Sat 10am-5pm, Sun 2-5pm

The gallery has an unusual collection of around 1,000 pieces of wallpaper. There are 18th-century embossed and gilt leather hangings; French 19th-century wallpapers; an enormous number of patterns by William Morris, Voysey, and Crane; and 20th-century examples showing the inventiveness of early postwar designers, the exuberance of the 1970s, and the work of late 20th-century artists using wallpaper in a fine art context (like Terence Conran, Audrey Levy, Roger & Robert Nicholson, and Zandra Rhodes). Recent acquisitions include a heavily embossed and decorated wallcovering from a property associated with the Colman's Mustard family. There is the original artwork for the 1970s *Flintstones* wallpaper, and several pictorial commemorative papers, including one depicting the founding of the Rifle Volunteers (forerunners of the Territorial Army). Another features motifs from the French Revolution, and there are two rolls printed with a design by a Palestinian-born artist based on photographs of bullet-riddled masonry.

Winterthur Museum, Garden & Library

Route 52, Winterthur, Delaware 19735, USA
Tel. (1) 302-888 4600   www.winterthur.org
Mon-Sat 9am-5pm, Sun noon-5pm

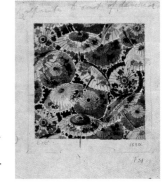

Over 100 rooms document furnishings from the 17th to the 19th centuries, displaying many examples from their vast textile collection which specialises in home furnishing fabrics made in the US and those which have been imported. Among the imported textiles is one of the most important collections of printed and painted cottons in the US. The Library contains a very good collection of sample books.

ARTILLERY, MILITARY AIRCRAFT AND SUBMARINES

EDGED WEAPONS AND BOWS

EUROPEAN ARMOUR

FIREARMS

ISLAMIC AND FAR EASTERN ARMOUR

MILITARY APPAREL

ARTILLERY, MILITARY AIRCRAFT AND SUBMARINES

The Crew of HMS
Thunderbolt on their return
to Britain from service in
the Mediterranean,
'March 1942
Imperial War Museum

Musée de l'Air et de l'Espace
The Air and Space Museum
Aéroport du Bourget BP 173, 93352 Le Bourget, France
Tel. (33) 1 49 92 71 99 www.mae.org
May-Oct: Tue-Sun 10am-6pm. Nov-Apr: Tue-Sun 10am-5pm

This is the oldest and one of the richest collections of aircraft in the world. As well as civilian aircraft developed by the early pioneers, the museum houses an outstanding collection of military planes from both World Wars and later, including the Mirage III, the first French aircraft to reach Mach2 in 1958.

Musée de l'Armée
The Army Museum
Hôtel National des Invalides, 129 rue de Grenelle, 75007 Paris, France
Tel. (33) 1 44 42 37 72 www.invalides.org
Apr-Sep: daily 10am-6pm. Oct-Mar: daily 10am-5pm

This 200-year-old collection houses more than 1,000 pieces of small artillery, including cannons, swivel guns, mortars, howitzers, and mounts, dating from the 17th century to the present day. Among the most remarkable are a 17th-century twelve-pounder basinet cannon and carriage, and a 1743 emblazoned and decorated eight-inch howitzer by Jean Maritz, foundry commissioner of the French artillery.

Aviatsionnyi muzei v Monino
The Air Force Museum at Monino
141170 Monino, near Moscow, Russian Federation
Tel. (7) 095 526 3327
Mon, Tue, Thu, Fri 9.30am-1pm, 2.30-5pm, Sat 9.30am-2pm

This vast collection of more than 160 aircraft, laid out over fifty acres, covers the history of Russian aviation from its earliest beginnings to the present day. Alongside the usual array of military planes, helicopters, and gliders are some more unusual flying machines such as Tatlin's flapflyer, Rafaelynts's turboflyer, and the orbital spaceship developed under the 'Spiral' programme.

Brooklands Museum
Brooklands Road, Weybridge, Surrey KT13 0QN, UK
Tel. (44) 1932 857381 www.motor-software.co.uk
Summer: Tue-Sun 10am-5pm. Winter: Tue-Sun 10am-4pm

This famous aeroplane hangar contains more than thirty Brooklands-built aircraft, a number of Barnes Wallis 'bouncing bombs', and one of only two surviving Wellington bombers, rescued from the depths of Loch Ness in 1985.

Firepower – The Royal Artillery Museum
Repository Road, Woolwich, London SE18 4DN, UK
Tel. (44) 20 8855 7755 www.firepower.org.uk
Daily 10am-5pm

Established in 1716, Woolwich's Royal Laboratory Department was part of the historic Royal Arsenal and was responsible for the design, manufacture, testing, and distribution of ammunition for many years. The artillery collection was set up in 1778 as a teaching aid for cadets, but has only recently been opened up to the public. As well as artillery, the museum displays more than 7,000 medals including 62 Victoria Crosses.

Fleet Air Arm Museum

Royal Naval Air Station, Yeovilton, Near Ilchester, Somerset BA22 8HT, UK
Tel. (44) 1935 840565   www.fleetairarm.com
Apr-Oct: daily 10am-5.30pm. Nov-Mar: daily 10am-4.30pm

The Royal Naval Air Service is the most technically advanced branch of the British armed forces. Since 1914 it has created many of military aviation's most innovative devices. Opened in 1963, the air station museum has grown into a 6.5 acre complex showing more than forty restored aircraft, together with an exhibition tracing the development of British aircraft from wooden biplanes through to the supersonic Concorde, and the world-famous Sea Harrier.

Forsvarsmuseet på Bornholm
The Defence Museum on Bornholm
Arsenalvej 8, 3700 Rønne, Denmark
Tel. (45) 56 956583
May-Oct: Tue-Sat 10am-4pm

This museum exhibits a variety of artillery, from 17th-century wrought iron muzzle-loading cannons to anti-aircraft guns used up until 1996. In the grounds are four heavy cannons used to protect Bornholm against naval attacks in the 18th and 19th centuries, as well as a few armoured vehicles including tanks and jeeps.

Military aircraft from the aeroplane exhibition (top)
Imperial War Museum, Duxford

A crew at action stations (above)
Imperial War Museum

John P. Holland, the American inventor of the first submarine to be tried out by the Royal Navy (left)
Imperial War Museum

Fort Nelson

Down End Road, Fareham, Hampshire PO17 6AN, UK
Tel. (44) 1329 233734   www.armouries.org.uk
Apr-Oct: Thu-Sun 10am-5pm. Nov-Mar: Thu-Sun 10.30am-4pm

One of the great forts built around Portsmouth in the 1860s to guard the dockyards from a French invasion, Fort Nelson provides an outstanding space for displaying an extraordinary collection of artillery. Brought here from its original home at the Tower of London, the collection covers artillery for land and sea from all periods. Pride of place goes to a piece of heavy artillery, the Great Turkish Bombard, which was cast for Mehmet II and used to flatten Constantinople in 1453.

Hubschraubermuseum Bückeburg
The Bückeburg Helicopter Museum
Sabléplatz, 31665 Bückeburg, Germany
Tel. (49) 5722 5533   www.hubschraubermuseum.de
Daily 9am-5pm

The brainchild of the German pilot, Werner Notemeyer, this museum traces the technological evolution of the helicopter. The collection consists of mostly military helicopters, including several interesting prototypes such as the BO-46 which was designed to fly at nearly 250mph.

Imperial War Museum

Lambeth Road, London SE1 6HZ, UK
Tel. (44) 207 416 5000
Mon-Sat, 10am-5.50pm, Sun 2am-5.50pm

The collection of World War II aircraft is remarkable and includes a Supermarine Spitfire Mark 1A. Other exhibits relate to air warfare and include anti-aircraft guns and a BAC Thunderbird 2 missile. There is an also an extensive display of tanks, including a British Infantry Mark II and an American M4 Sherman. Unusual examples of World War II submarines include the German one-man *Biber* and the Italian 'human torpedo'.

Imperial War Museum, Duxford

Duxford Airfield, Duxford, Cambridgeshire CB2 4QR, UK
Tel. (44) 1223 835000   www.iwm.org.uk
Mar-Oct: daily 10am-6pm. Nov-Feb: daily 10am-4pm

Built during the early part of World War I, this famous RAF base went on to play a vital role in the Battle of Britain. With much of the airfield preserved as it was in the early 1940s, the station makes an ideal backdrop for the UK's finest collection of military and civil aircraft, vehicles, tanks, and naval exhibits (including midget submarines). From 1943-45 Duxford was also a US air base, and the complex includes a striking new building housing American military aircraft and uniforms of historical note.

Intrepid Sea-Air-Space Museum

Pier 86, Twelfth Avenue and 46th Street, New York, New York 10036, USA
Tel. (1) 212 245 0072   www.intrepidmuseum.com
Oct-Mar: Tue-Sun 10am-5pm (please call for summer opening times)

Launched in 1943, the USS *Intrepid* saw 31 years in service and was responsible for shooting down 650 enemy planes and sinking 289 ships. Now docked at New York's Pier 86, the eighteen-deck aircraft carrier displays the full spectrum of gruesome military hardware. Star exhibits include a Polish Mig 21, a McDonnell Douglas F-4N Phantom fighter bomber, and a Blackbird spyplane flown by the CIA during the Cold War. The museum also houses one of the first guided-missile submarines, the *Growler*. Launched in 1958, the submarine carried a crew of 88 men in a space just over 300ft long.

Spitfire Mark 1A (top)
Imperial War Museum

A submariner testing escape equipment (above)
Imperial War Museum

Two French three-barrelled bronze guns captured at the battle of Ramilles, 1706 (below)
Fort Nelson

Kristiansand Kanonmuseum
The Kristiansand Cannon Museum

Møvik, near Kristiansand, Norway
Tel. (47) 38 085090
May-Jun: Thu-Sun 11am-6pm. Jul-Aug: daily 11am-6pm

Constructed in the spring of 1940, Møvik Fort was part of a chain of military installations along the coast designed to prevent British warships from entering German or Danish waters, and to protect German supply ships. Now a museum, the pristinely preserved machine rooms, crew's quarters, furnaces, and ammunition and shell rooms, filled with their original armaments, charts, and pictures, provide a fascinating glimpse into the workings of a battery during World War II.

Legermuseum
The Army Museum

Korte Geer 1, 2611 CA Delft, The Netherlands
Tel. (31) 15 2150500   www.uitindelft.nl
Mon-Fri 10am-5pm, Sat-Sun noon-5pm

Historical guns and other armaments, including a rare bronze twenty-inch howitzer cast by Johannes Nieport in 1694, are displayed on the first floor of this 17th-century building. The ground floor is devoted to exhibitions documenting the history of the Dutch forces and their allies and opponents from World War II to the Cold War. The Study Collection of the Ministry of Defence is included in the estimated 90,000 objects in the museum.

Spitfire IX EN199
(above)
Malta Aviation Museum

One of the two sections of
the Iraqi Supergun
(below)
Fort Nelson

Muzeum Lotnictwa Polskiego
The Polish Aviation Museum
Aleja Jana Pawla II 39, 30-969 Cracow, Poland
Tel. (48) 12 412 9000 www.muz-lotnictwa.krakow.pl
Mon-Fri, Sun 9am-3pm, Sat 10am-3pm

Originally built for the balloon detachment of the Polish Garrison Artillery, the historic
Rakowice-Czyzyny aerodrome is one of the oldest military airfields in Europe. More
than 100 planes, gliders, helicopters, and anti-aircraft missiles are now shown at the
museum, as well as 200 aviation engines dating from 1908 to the present. The museum
also holds examples of almost every variant of jet warplane used by the Polish Air Force,
Polish-flown helicopters, and a vast array of world-famous Polish-built gliders.

Malta Aviation Museum
Huts 161/2, Crafts Village, Ta'Quali, Rabat RBT, Malta
Tel. (356) 416 095 www.digigate.net
Daily 9am-5pm

This aviation museum tells the full story of the 'island fortress' which was of vital strategic
importance to the British during the final years of World War II. There are planes, including
Spitfires, Hurricanes, a Douglas DC-3 Dakota, and a jet-engined De Havilland Vampire;
uniforms, including the white drill worn by Earl Mountbatten while he was captain of
HMS *Kelly* in Malta in 1941; insignia; and anti-aircraft guns. There are also exhibits
chronicling the German air bombardments which began in June 1940 and reduced most
of the island to rubble.

Militaire Luchtvaart Museum
The Military Aircraft Museum
Kamp van Zeist, Kampweg, 3769 ZK Soesterberg, The Netherlands
Tel. (31) 3404 34222 www.mlm.mindef.nl
Tue-Fri 10am-4.30pm, Sun noon-4.30pm

This comprehensive display of aircraft used by the Dutch Royal Air
Force and Navy is housed in two hangars and includes thirty immaculately restored aircraft ranging from a 1917 Farnham to a 1994 F-15 Eagle.

National Air and Space Museum
Smithsonian Institution, Seventh and Independence Avenue, SW, Washington, DC
20560, USA
Tel. (1) 202 357 2700 www.nasm.si.edu
Daily 10am-5.30pm

Although the main museum building includes an excellent selection of American aircraft, the best examples, with a reserve collection of hundreds of military planes, are
held at the Paul E. Garber Facility in Suitland, Maryland. (Tours can currently be booked
in advance, but in 2003 many of the planes will be exhibited in the new Dulles annexe.)

The Naval Undersea Museum
610 Dowell Street, Keyport, Washington 98345, USA
Tel. (1) 360 396 4148 num.kpt.nuwc.navy.mil
Oct-May: Mon, Wed-Sun 10am-4pm. Jun-Sep: daily 10am-4pm

As an official Navy museum, this houses the largest number of artefacts relating to naval
undersea science and operations in the US. The undersea weapons and submarines
collection contains displays showing the first diving bells and aqua-lungs, mine warfare
from the American Revolution onwards, and modern submersibles. Prized exhibits

Fenian Ram, experimental submarine built by John P. Holland and launched in 1881
Paterson Museum

include an 1890 brass Howell torpedo, a Whitehead torpedo, and various US torpedoes from World War II. The library contains a collection of interviews with US naval leaders.

New Jersey National Guard Militia Museum

National Guard Training Center, Sea Girt Ave, Building 66, Sea Girt, New Jersey 08750, USA
Tel. (1) 732 974 5966 www.state.nj.us
Tue, Thu, Sat-Sun 10am-1pm (times vary in summer, please call for details)

One of the highlights is the *Intelligent Whale*, the prototype wrought-iron, hand-cranked submarine conceived by Scovel Merriam during the Civil War and finally completed by Nathaniel Halstead (five years before his murder) in 1866.

Paterson Museum

2 Market Street, Paterson, New Jersey 07501, USA
Tel. (1) 973 881 3874
Tue-Fri 10am-4pm, Sat-Sun 12.30-4.30pm

Situated in the Rogers Locomotive Erecting Shop (where eighty per cent of America's locomotives were built), this fascinating museum houses the shell of the original fourteen-foot prototype submarine built in 1878 by the Irish mathematician and father of the modern submarine, John Holland. The museum also contains the *Fenian Ram*, a true submersible which Holland built in New York City in 1881. The 31-foot boat contained all the elements that make a modern submersible, including a tube which could discharge a six-foot torpedo.

Miniature bronze statue of an artillery officer by C. Marochetti, 1859
Museo storico nazionale d'Artiglieria

Picatinny Arsenal Museum

ARDEC Historical Holding, Building 2, Picatinny Arsenal, New Jersey 07806-5000, USA
Tel. (1) 201 724 3222 www.pica.army.mil
Tue-Thu 9am-3pm

After World War II, Picatinny's army powder factory was turned into a weapons development and research centre, and over the years it has churned out weapons for use in a succession of bitter conflicts, including the Korean War. The museum was established in an adjacent 19th-century arsenal in 1920 and today its holdings chronicle the development of weapons and ammunition from the 1800s onwards. Exhibits range from bullets to bombs, with themed displays on topics such as the development of smokeless gun powder, and the manufacture of chemical weapons and projectiles.

Pima Air and Space Museum

6000 East Valencia Road, Tucson, Arizona 85706, USA
Tel. (1) 520 574 0462 www.pimaair.org
Daily 9am-5pm

With more than 250 aircraft displayed on eighty acres of land, this is one of the largest air museums in the world. Star exhibits range from presidential aircraft to a Martin B-57 E Canberra bomber used by Britain in the Falklands War. Among the attractions is the museum's eerie aerospace graveyard, where more than 5,000 aeroplanes, neatly arranged in rows, wait for restoration. There is also a useful research library.

The Royal Air Force Museum

Grahame Park Road, Hendon, London NW9 5LL, UK
Tel. (44) 20 8205 2266 www.rafmuseum.org.uk
Daily 10am-6pm

More than seventy pristinely restored historic aircraft document the story of aviation from its earliest pioneering days to the present. Among the several hundred thousand exhibits are engines, propellers, armaments, instruments, navigation aids, models, photographs, uniforms, decorations, memorabilia, and trophies, with separate sections devoted to bomber planes and the Battle of Britain.

Royal Gunpowder Mills

Beaulieu Drive, Waltham Abbey, Essex EN9 1JY, UK
Tel. (44) 1992 767022   www.royalgunpowdermills.com
Daily 10am-6pm

Gunpowder was first manufactured here in 1665, and by the 1730s the powder mills had grown into 'the largest and compleatest works in Britain'. The mills went on to lead the way in British explosives development and production over the next three centuries. Cordite propellant was produced here in the 1880s, and in the 20th century the bouncing bomb and many other secret materials were developed at the site. In 1991 the works were decommissioned and a museum was opened tracing the evolution and impact of gunpowder technology over the centuries.

From the Large Exhibits
Gallery (top)
Imperial War Museum

Concorde (above)
*Imperial War Museum,
Duxford*

Museo storico nazionale d'Artiglieria
The National Historical Artillery Museum

Corso G. Ferraris o, 10121 Turin, Italy
Tel. (39) 011 5629223
Tue-Thu, Sat-Sun 9am-7pm, Fri 9am-11pm

Housed in the keep which is all that remains of Turin's fort, the museum contains a world-class weaponry collection, from slings, clubs, and spears dating from the Stone, Iron, and Bronze Ages to 20th-century tanks and firearms. Important pieces in the artillery collections include the first rifled breech-loading cast iron cannon (made by Cavalli in 1832) and a series of exquisitely worked 18th-century French and Genoese cannons decorated with saints or patrons, florid patterns, and fabulous animals.

Tank Museum

Bovington Camp, Dorset BH20 6JG, UK
Tel. (44) 1929 405096   www.tankmuseum.co.uk
Daily 10am-5pm

Situated in Bovington tank training camp, this is one of the world's largest and most comprehensive armoured fighting vehicle collections. Artefacts and over 300 vehicles from 26 countries chronicle the history of the tank from the earliest prototypes to now. Among the oldest examples are a Hornsby Tractor 'Little Caterpillar' built in 1909 and possibly the oldest surviving tracked vehicle, and a Mark I, Mark II, and Mark V dating from World War I. From World War II are German and French tanks and a British Sherman Crab used on D-Day in 1944. Postwar examples include a Soviet T-72, an American M46 from the Korean War, and a Chinese Norinco armoured ambulance from the Gulf War.

Titan Missile Museum

1580 West Duval Mine Road, Sahuarita, Arizona, USA
Tel. (1) 520 791 2929   www.pimaair.org
Nov-Apr: daily 9am-5pm. May-Oct: Wed-Sun 9am-5pm

In the desert 25 miles south of Tucson, Titan II was one of 54 massive nuclear warheads constructed in the 1960s and then phased out by the US government in 1987. Now a National Historic Landmark, the surreal 'Bond movie' warhead interior is visible through a set of picture windows set into its launch duct.

The YF-22, the Air Force's next generation air superiority fighter
U.S. Air Force Museum

Tøjhusmuseet
The Defence Museum
Tøjhusgade 3, 1214 Copenhagen K, Denmark
Tel. (45) 33 11 60 37 www.thm.dk
Tue-Sun noon-4pm

Housed in an enormous armoury hall built by Christian IV in 1604, this museum chronicles the history of Danish artillery from the 16th century to the present day. It includes a unique collection of small arms dating from the Middle Ages onwards.

Tykistömuseo
The Artillery Museum
Linnankasarmi, 13100 Hämeenlinna, Finland
Tel. (358) 3 68 4600 www.tiko.sci.fi
May-Sep: daily 10am-6pm. Oct-Apr: Sat-Sun noon-5pm

Housed near Häme castle in barracks built under Russian rule from 1910-13, this unique museum chronicles the development of Finnish artillery from the 15th to the 21st centuries. Hundreds of exhibits and a multimedia theatre recreate the battle of Tali-Ihantala, one of the biggest artillery battles of World War II. An additional artillery hall by Vanajanvesi Lake houses the museum's collection of ninety guns from thirteen countries (in particular Russia and Japan) dating mainly from the 1870s to the 1940s.

U.S. Air Force Museum
Wright-Patterson Air Force Base, 1100 Spaatz Street, Dayton, Ohio 45433-7102, USA
Tel. (1) 937 255 3284 www.wpafb.af.mil
Daily 9am-5pm

Beginning with pioneering aircraft such as those belonging to the Wright brothers, this museum covers the history of American aviation from its earliest days to the present. The vast and chilling Cold War missile collection is currently in storage, but from 2003 it will be shown off once again in a grisly Cold War 'Missile Mall'.

Voenno-istoricheskii muzei artillerii
The Military-Historcial Artillery Museum
Aleksandrovskii park 7, 193015 St Petersburg, Russian Federation
Tel. (7) 812 2330382
Wed-Sun 11am-5pm

Fronted by tanks and missile launchers, this enormous horseshoe-shaped arsenal houses a vast display of artillery from medieval times to World War II. Some of the most interesting pieces include the pike carried by Peter the Great as a foot soldier, the ornate coach from which Suvorov harangued his troops at Borodino, the armoured car on which Lenin rode in triumph from Finland in 1917, the Red Army uniforms designed by a Futurist who was killed in the purges, a Katiusha multiple-rocket launcher from World War II, and a diorama of Kursk, where the biggest tank battle in history took place.

EDGED WEAPONS AND BOWS

Musée de l'Archerie
The Archery Museum
Château des Ducs de Valois, rue Gustave Chopinet, 60800 Crépy-en-Valois, France

Tel. (33) 3 44 59 21 97
Mon, Wed-Sat 10am-noon, 2-6pm, Sun & public holidays 10am-noon, 3-7pm

The display of bows and crossbows from across the globe celebrates this city's historic tradition of training archers for war, yet also focuses on the history of archery as a sport. The collection benefits greatly from the bequest of the Bertier de Sauvigny collection.

Turkish sabre, mid-16th century (far left)
Royal Armouries Museum

Nepalese *kukri* with an ivory hilt carved in the form of a lion, 19th century (left)
Royal Armouries Museum

Chinese sword probably made for presenation by an early Ming emperor to one of the Buddhist monasteries in Tibet, *c.*1420 (below)
Royal Armouries Museum

Château Musée de l'Empéri
The Empéri Castle Museum
Château de l'Empéri, 13300 Salon-de-Provence, France
Tel. (33) 4 90 56 22 36 www.invalides.org
Sep-Jun: Mon, Wed-Sun 10am-noon, 2-6pm
Jul-Aug: Mon, Wed-Sun 10am-6pm

The outstanding Brunon collection includes an important group of French swords from the 18th and 19th centuries. Alongside the thirty swords and knives which were used during the Italian campaigns of the Revolutionary Army, there are some remarkable pieces in a section devoted to the Algerian Army.

Collections Baur
The Baur Collections
8 rue Munier-Romilly, 1206 Geneva, Switzerland
Tel. (41) 22 3461729 www.baur-collections.ch
Tue-Sun 2-6pm

This outstanding collection of Japanese sword-furniture consists of 2,600 high-quality pieces produced by more than 800 different craftsmen, including works by Natsuo, Ichijo, and Ikkin. The majority date from the 18th and 19th centuries, but older pieces include the work of one of the early Jingo masters.

Cooper-Hewitt National Design Museum
Smithsonian Institution, Fifth Avenue at 91st Street, New York, New York 10028, USA
Tel. (1) 212 849 8400 www.si.edu
Tue-Sat 10am-5pm (Tue until 9pm), Sun noon-5pm

One of the gems among this metalwork collection is the display of 1,400 Japanese sword fittings. The pieces date from the 17th to the 19th centuries and include examples of *tsuba*, *fuchi* (a ring which strengthens the guard), and *kashira* (the pommel).

Dean Castle
Dean Road, Kilmarnock, Ayrshire, Scotland, UK
Tel. (44) 1563 554704
Easter-end Oct: daily noon-5pm. Nov-Easter: Sat-Sun noon-5pm. (Also by appt.)

This collection of Lord Howard de Walden, an expert swordsman and a member of the British Olympic fencing team, includes edged weapons from late medieval war swords and massive two-handed ceremonial swords from the 16th century. The skills of

Indian punch-dagger or
katar with a double blade,
confiscated in 1858 after
the Indian Mutiny
Royal Armouries Museum

decorative metalworkers are revealed in the collection, especially in the civilian small swords with their Regency and Rococo ornamentation.

Deutsches Klingenmuseum Solingen
The German Blade Museum of Solingen
Klosterhof 4, 42653 Solingen, Germany
Tel. (49) 212 59822 www.solingen.de
Tue-Thu, Sat-Sun 10am-5pm, Fri 2-5pm

For centuries, Solingen was a world-famous centre for blade making, and the great collections here recount the history of a variety of blades. From diverse origins, they span from the Bronze Age to the Renaissance and Baroque periods. On view are elegant 19th-century swords used as status symbols, some from the Nazi period; a fantastic collection from the Thirty Years War; Asian and African hunting weapons; and Asian weapons.

Museo del Ejército
The Army Museum
Calle Méndez Nuñez 1, 28014 Madrid, Spain
Tel. (34) 91 5228977
Tue-Sun 10am-2pm

This museum, in the Buen Retiro Palace, houses outstanding exhibits from Spanish military history, including El Cid's original Tizona sword and a large collection of the famous Toledon swords decorated in the Mudéjar tradition.

Gettysburg National Military Park
Visitor Center, 97 Taneytown Road, Gettysburg, Pennsylvania 17325-1080, USA
Tel. (1) 717 334 1124 www.nps.gov
Daily 8am-5pm (summer until 6pm)

A vast array of swords ranging from standard issues, Cavalry pattern swords, surgeons' swords, those for specific branches of the service, and elaborately decorated inscribed presentation swords. A fine collection of artillery and a variety of bayonets are also on view.

Fortezze medievale del Monte Titano
The Medieval Forts of Mount Titano
San Marino City, Republic of San Marino
www.inthenet.sm

Perched upon the cliffs of the majestic Mount Titano are three medieval forts with breathtaking views of the Adriatic. Two of these are filled with an impressive collection of crossbows and other weapons used for centuries to defend the Republic. To see archery in action visit the week-long medieval celebration.

The National War Museum of Scotland
Edinburgh Castle, Edinburgh EH1 2NG, Scotland, UK
Tel. (44) 131 2257534 www.nms.ac.uk
Apr-Oct: daily 9.45am-5.30pm. Nov-Mar: daily 9.45am-4.30pm

One of this museum's main strengths are the distinctive late 18th-century Scottish military swords. Although the focus is on British edged weapons, there are some notable exceptions acquired by servicemen overseas.

Royal Armouries Museum
Armouries Drive, Leeds, West Yorkshire LS10 1LT, UK
Tel. (44) 1132 201999 www.armouries.org.uk
Daily 10.30am-5.30pm

Ranging from the Middle Ages to the 20th century, this collection of swords includes numerous fine treasures of great historical interest. Among the booty are items that belonged to members of the English Royal family, the 1st Duke of Wellington, and Oliver Cromwell. There is also an extensive array of Asian and Indian daggers and swords.

Armour of the military writer and commander Sir John Smythe, *c.*1585
Royal Armouries Museum

Saint-Joris Gilde
St George's Guild
Stijn Struvelsstraat 59, 8000 Bruges, Belgium
Tel. (32) 5 033 5408
Wed, Sat-Sun 2-6pm

Founded in 1321, this was one of the medieval guilds of archers that protected the city. Below 17th-, 18th-, and 19th-century portraits of guild dignitaries, princes, and kings are displayed the magnificent ancient crossbows ranging from plain target crossbows with a wind-up system to those inlaid with ivory. Also of note are the numerous guild emblems and mementoesm, and the standard and miniature artillery.

Victoria and Albert Museum
Cromwell Road, South Kensington, London SW7 2RL, UK
Tel. (44) 20 7942 2000 www.vam.ac.uk
Daily 10am-5.45pm (Wed & last Fri of every month 10am-10pm)

A superb collection of Japanese swords and sword-furniture dating from the 14th to the early 20th centuries is displayed alongside an exceptional collection of Japanese art. Highlights include a sword made by Tomomitsu in 1335, and one given to Queen Victoria in 1860. These superb cutting weapons were believed to be imbued with a spirituality obtained during their manufacture.

The Wallace Collection
Hertford House, Manchester Square, London W1M 6BN, UK
Tel. (44) 20 7563 9500 www.the-wallace-collection.org.uk
Mon-Sat 10am-5pm, Sun 2-5 pm

In 1870, Sir Richard Wallace bought collections belonging to Comte de Nieuwerkerke and Sir Samuel Rush-Meyrick. The resulting exhibition now has one of the finest collections of Renaissance swords and rapiers in the world. Magnificent examples include swords made for Cosimo de'Medici and Henry Prince of Wales.

EUROPEAN ARMOUR

Musée de l'Armée
The Army Museum
Hôtel National des Invalides, 129 rue de Grenelle,
75007 Paris, France
Tel. (33) 1 44 42 37 72
www.invalides.org
Apr-Sep: daily 10am-6pm. Oct-Mar: 10am-5pm

The museum houses a remarkable range of 15th- and 16th-century defensive and offensive arms, including chainmail armour from Italy and Germany. Exceptional pieces include suits of armour made by Filipo Negroli for the future Henri II, by Jorg Seusenhofer for Francis I, and by Lorenz Helmshmied of Augsbourg for Maximilian I and II. The museum also holds a fine collection of helmets.

Armeria Reale
The Royal Armoury
Piazza Castello, 191 Turin, Italy
Tel. (39) 011 543889
Tue, Thu 2.30-7.30pm, Wed, Fri-Sun 9am-2pm

This huge and sumptuously decorated palace houses the former Royal Armoury set up by King Alberto of Savoy in 1837. One of the most important and comprehensive collections of weaponry and armoury in Europe, it contains some splendid examples from the 13th century onwards. Of special interest are the armouries of Charles V, Napoleon, and the Savoy.

Horned helmet by Konrad Seusenhofer of Innsbruck for presentation to King Henry VIII by the Holy Roman Emperor Maximilian I (above)
Royal Armories Museum

King Henry VIII's armour for man and horse, c.1515 (below)
Royal Armouries Museum

Musée d'Art et d'Histoire
The Museum of Art and History
Palais Masséna, 65 rue de France, 06 000 Nice, France
Tel. (33) 4 93 88 11 34
May-Sep: Tue-Sun 10am-noon, 3-6pm. Oct-Apr: Tue-Sun 10am-noon, 2-5pm

The museum houses a remarkable collection of arms, helmets, arquebuses, and crossbows. It includes some spectacular armour made for Maximilian I, a very rare helmet from the Bronze Age, and items belonging to Philip II of Spain and Charles V.

The Art Institute of Chicago
111 South Michigan Avenue, Chicago, Illinois 60603, USA
Tel. (1) 312 443 3600   www.artic.edu
Mon, Wed-Fri, 10.30am-4.30pm, Tue 10.30am-6pm, Sat 10am-5pm, Sun noon-5pm

One of the best collections of its kind in the US, the Harding Collection of Arms and Armour comprises more than 1,500 primarily European pieces, with several examples from the Middle East and the US. More than 200 pieces, ranging from entire and partial suits of armour to horse equipment, swords and daggers, polearms, firearms, and other accessories are on permanent display. One of the gems in the collection is a selection of beautifully etched and gilded three-quarter field armour produced in Milan in the 16th century.

Museo Bagatti Valsecchi
The Bagatti Valsecchi Museum
Via Santo Spirito 10/via Gesù 5, Milan 20121, Italy
Tel. (39) 02 76006132   www.museobagattivalsecchi.org
Tue-Sun 1-5pm

This beautiful Milanese palace was renovated and refurbished in the 19th century by two brothers, Fausto and Giuseppe Bagatti. Their extraordinary collection of swords, arms, and armour from the Renaissance period onwards is displayed in an arms gallery on pedestals (in keeping with the late 19th-century fashion for historical reconstruction). One of the finest pieces is a breastplate featuring a Lion of St Marks made in Breschia in the 17th century and worked in intricate gold leaf and thread on an engraved background.

Museo Stephano Bardini
The Stephano Bardini Museum
Piazza dei Mozzi 1, 50125 Florence, Italy
Tel. (39) 055 2342427
Mon, Tue, Thu-Sun 9am-2pm, public holidays 8am-1pm

This eclectic collection, amassed by the well-known art dealer, Stefano Bardini, includes a small but exquisite holding of arms and armour dating from the 5th century BC to the 17th century. Among its features are 16th-century swords, crossbows and other infantry weapons, a helmet from the 6th century BC, halberds, pikes, spears, painted shields, tournament weapons, and firearms.

Musée des Beaux-Arts
The Museum of Fine Art
29 cloître Notre-Dame, 28000 Chartres, France
Tel. (33) 2 37 36 41 39
Nov-Mar: Mon, Wed-Sat 10am-noon, 2-5pm

Housed in an Episcopal palace built in various stages between the Middle Ages and the 18th century, this is one the finest arms collections in France. The spectacular armour collection features a series of exquisitely worked 16th- and 17th-century helmets, armlets and breastplates, as well as eight impressive 19th-century reproduction plate-armours integrating original elements. The group of weapons is equally excellent, with pikes and a selection of halberds, mounted on modern staffs, dating from the 16th to the 18th centuries, .

Dean Castle
Dean Road, Kilmarnock, Ayrshire, Scotland, UK
Tel. (44) 1563 554704
Easter-end Oct: daily noon- 5pm. Nov-Easter: Sat-Sun noon-5pm

While serving as a soldier in the Boer War, Lord Howard de Walden inherited a fortune, including land and property, in Ayrshire. His new-found wealth enabled him to indulge his fascination with the Middle Ages and he began assembling this extraordinary collection of European late medieval and Renaissance arms and armour. Today, the castle's great hall displays full and half suits of armour for the field and parade, plus a representative array of helmets ranging from 14th-century bascinets to a 16th-century close helmet of the Greenwich type.

Deutsches Historisches Museum
The German Historical Museum
Zeughaus Unter den Linden 2, 10117 Berlin, Germany
Tel. (49) 30 215020 www.dhm.de
Mon, Tue, Thu-Sun, 10am-6pm (due to re-open Jan 2002)

This medieval and early modern collection of weapons and armour from the arsenals and armouries of the Bradenburgs is one of the best of its kind in Europe. Amongst a collection of rare helmets and pieces of armour are some unique pieces, including two princely 'Spangenhelme' from the 6th century and a 13th-century great helmet.

Gosudarstvennyi istoriko-kul'turnyi muzei-zapovednik 'Moskovskii Kreml'' - Oruzheinaia palata
The State Historical-Cultural Museum-Preserve 'Moscow Kremlin' - The Armoury
Krasnaia ploshchad', 103073 Moscow, Russian Federation
Tel. (7) 095 2023776 www.kremlin.museum.ru
Mon-Wed, Fri-Sun 10am-4pm

The earliest written reference to the Kremlin's armoury dates back to the 16th century, when the collection was not only an arsenal but also a centre for the manufacture of

Gauntlets belonging to Philip II of Spain (top left)
Higgins Armory Museum

Tail piece of a horse armour by Kunz Lochner of Nuremberg, c.1550 (top right)
Royal Armouries Museum

Armour for Prince Henry and James II, early 17th century (above)
Tower of London

armaments. Today the collection encompasses objects acquired by foreign ambassadors and merchants from all over the world, as well as treasures made on site. Many of the exhibits are connected with Russian statesmen or crucial historical events. Gems in the collection include a Shishak helmet commissioned by Ivan the Terrible in 1557 for his three-year-old son, and a coat of chain mail belonging to Boris Godunov dating from the late 16th century.

Higgins Armory Museum

100 Barber Avenue, Worcester, Massachusetts 01606, USA
Tel. (1) 508 853 6015   www.higgins.org
Tue-Sat 10am-4pm, Sun noon-4pm

The owner of a pressed steel company in Worcester, Massachusetts, John Woodham Higgins developed a passionate interest in medieval and Renaissance weapons during his childhood. In 1931, he finally opened his 'Steel Museum'. A splendid glass and steel Art Deco building houses a monumental medieval Great Hall displaying dozens of suits of armour by Renaissance master craftsmen such as Anton Peffenhauser, Pompeo della Cesa, and Stefan Rormoser.

Burgundian Bard horse armour, *c*.1510 (top)
Royal Armouries Museum

Gladiator helmet (above)
Higgins Armory Museum

Hofjagd- und Rüstkammer - Kunsthistorisches Museum
The Armoury - Art Historical Museum
Neue Burg, 1010 Vienna, Austria
Tel. (43) 1 52524460   www.khm.at
Mon-Wed, Fri-Sun 10am-6pm, Thu 10am-10pm

This vast and diverse collection was created in the 19th century, when almost all the armouries of the Austrian branch of the House of Habsburg were united in Vienna. Among the wonderful pieces of craftsmanship are a steel and gold parade helmet made in Milan for Archduke Ferdinand II in 1550, and the museum's prize piece, a magnificent 16th-century Medusa shield embossed with a series of highly complex historical and mythological scenes.

Kunstsammlungen der Veste Coburg
The Art Collections of the Coburg Citadel
Veste Coburg, 96450 Coburg, Germany
Tel. (49) 9561 8790   www.kunstsammlungen-coburg.de
Apr-Oct: Tue-Sun 10am-5pm. Nov-Mar: Tue-Sun 1-4pm

The castle's banqueting hall (*c*. 1501) features an outstanding display of weaponry and court armour. Among the many remarkable pieces is an ornate half-suit made by Anton Pfeffenhauser (*c*. 1570), two jousting sabatons owned by Duke Johann Philipp of Weimar, and sections of a suit (1537) made by Jörg Seusenhofer for the future Emperor Ferdinand I.

Landeszeughaus Graz
The Provincial Armoury of Graz
Herrengasse 16, 8010 Graz, Austria
Tel. (43) 316 8017   www.viaimperalis.at
Apr-Oct: Tue-Sun 9am-5pm. Nov-Mar: by appt. only

The Provincial Armoury is one of the very few early modern armouries still in existence anywhere in the world, housing an outstandingly well-preserved collection of 15th- to 18th-century arms and armour. By 1699, the Styrian State Armoury housed an incredible

185,000 items, and while it no longer needed to defend itself, it became, and remains today, a symbolic memorial to the history of Styria and an extraordinary repository of Austrian Renaissance, and baroque artistry and history.

The Metropolitan Museum of Art
1000 Fifth Avenue at 82nd Street, New York, New York 10028, USA
Tel. (1) 212 535 7710   www.metmuseum.org
Tue-Thu, Sun 9.30am-5.30pm, Fri, Sat 9.30am-9pm

This encyclopaedic collection consists of more than 15,000 pieces from Europe, North America, the Middle East, and Asia, dating from the 5th century onwards. Among the many masterpieces are a set of 15th-century armours made at the English royal workshops in Greenwich; various Renaissance parade pieces (including a helmet dated 1543) by the Milanese armourers Filippo Negroli; and a 1555 suit of armour worked in bas relief for Henry II of France.

Muzeum Narodowe - Muzeum Czartoryskich
The National Museum - Czartoryski Museum
Ulica Swietego Jana 19, 31-017 Cracow, Poland
Tel. (48) 12 4225566   www.muz-nar.krakow.pl
Mon, Tue, Sat-Sun 10am-3.30pm, Fri noon-5.30pm

Amassed by the aristocratic Czartoryski family, this stunning collection includes a host of national relics, royal jewels, documents, arms and armour, ivories and Italian, Dutch, and Flemish paintings. Among the star items is a set of 17th-century Hussar armour with its Zischägge iron helmet, iron and brass breastplate, knight's cross, chain mail of riveted, oval-shaped iron rings, silver-gilt iron 'karvash' forearms, and original silk-lined leopard skin and reconstructed eagle feather wings.

Model of Italian export armour, *c.*1453
Royal Armouries Museum

Musée national du Moyen-Age - Thermes et Hôtel de Cluny
The National Museum of the Middle Ages - The Cluny Baths and Hotel
6 place Paul-Painlevé, 75005 Paris, France
Tel. (33) 1 53 73 78 00   www.musee-moyenage.fr
Mon, Wed-Sun 9.15am-5.45pm

A gallery documenting the role of the knight in medieval society includes some superb 13th- to 15th-century enamelled harnesses, warriors' arms, and a unique collection of shields.

Museo nazionale del Bargello
The National Museum of Bargello
Via del Proconsolo 4, 50122 Florence, Italy
Tel. (39) 05 52388606
Tue-Sat 8.30am-3pm

The museum contains a magnificent display of arms and armour from the Medici, Carrand, and Ressman Collections. It includes saddles decorated with gold, silver, and ivory, and a 17th-century shield by Gaspare Mola. Among the numerous examples of dress armour is the breastplate of steel and gold by Filippo Negroli produced for Guidobaldo II della Rovere, Duke of Urbino. It ranks as one of the masterpieces of Italian Renaissance metalwork.

Ostfriesisches Landesmuseum und Emder Rüstkammer
The East Frisian Museum and Emden Armoury
Rathaus am Delft, 26721 Emden, Germany
Tel. (49) 4921 872058   www.landesmuseum-emden.de
Apr-Sep: Tue-Sun 10am-5pm. Oct-Mar: Tue-Sun 10am-4pm

Earl of Worcester armour,
c.1570
Tower of London

This Renaissance town hall and armoury was bombed during World War II. It was rebuilt in 1962 to house a remarkable collection of objects documenting the history of arts and culture of East Frisia and Emden, from ancient times to the beginning of the 20th century. Apart from a remarkable gallery of fine arts, the museum contains the old burgher's arsenal and around 2,500 splendid 16th- to 18th-century sidearms, suits of armour, and reproductions illustrating the history of the arsenal.

Real Armería - Palacio Real
The Royal Armoury - Royal Palace
Calle Bailén s/n, 28071 Madrid, Spain
Tel. (34) 91 5420059
Apr-Sep: Mon-Sat 9am-6pm, Sun 9am-3pm
Oct-Mar: Mon-Sat 9.30am-5pm, Sun 9am-3pm

One of Europe's largest collections of 16th-century German, Italian, and Spanish armour, as well as a fine selection of historically significant swords. Highlights include Charles V's famous 'KD' armour, made in Augsburg in 1525, featuring an etching of the Order of the Golden Fleece on the upper breast and backplates. Equally stunning are a helmet and shield made by Filippo Negroli in 1533 for Charles V, and the Roman-style armour, complete with imitation Roman sandals, made by Bartolomeo Campi in 1546 for the Duke of Urbino.

Royal Armouries Museum
Armouries Drive, Leeds, West Yorkshire LS10 1LT, UK
Tel. (44) 113 2201999 www.armouries.org.uk
Apr-Oct: daily 10.30am-5.30pm
Nov-Apr: Mon-Fri 10.30am-4.30pm, Sat-Sun 10.30am-5.30pm

Moved to this purpose-built space from the Tower of London, this is the best and most comprehensive collection of arms and armour to be found in the world. The vast collection of armour made from the 15th to the 17th centuries encompasses a resplendent spectrum, from the tonlet armour worn at the Field of Gold tournament by Henry VIII, to the tremendous horse armours, including the 'Burgundian' Bard given to Henry VIII by Maximilian I in 1510. A gallery devoted to the craftsmanship of the armour-makers includes the bizarre 'horned helmet' presented to Henry VIII by Maximilian I and made by Konrad Seusenhofer of Innsbruck in 1511-14. Sporting horns and a grotesque human mask with spectacles, the helmet was intended to be frightening and was made for use in court pageants. Last, but not least, the extensive holdings of the museum's library include numerous rare pattern books used to fashion guns, swords, and armour; a unique 13th-century German illustrated fencing manual; and a parchment Store Ledger dating from 1675 which lists the entire inventory of Henry VIII's armour at the Tower.

Rüstkammer
The Armoury
Semperbau am Zwinger, Theaterplatz 1, 01067 Dresden, Germany
Tel. (49) 351 4914626 www.staatl-kunstsammlungen-dresden.de
Tue-Sun 10am-6pm

This huge and very fine collection includes suits of armour by the famous Augsburg armourer, Anton Peffenhauser, and a superb set of ceremonial and horse armour made for Erik XIV of Sweden by Libaert of Antwerp. Also on display is a unique collection of children's armour, and a superb collection of jousting weapons.

Museo Stibbert
The Stibbert Museum
Via Federigo Stibbert 26, 50134 Florence, Italy
Tel. (39) 055 475520 www.fionline.it
Mon-Wed 10am-1pm, Fri-Sun 10am-6pm

Armour for man and
horse in German Gothic
style, late 15th century
Royal Armouries Museum

The enormous armour and firearms holdings date from the beginning of the 16th to the
end of the 18th centuries, and also include early Etruscan, Roman, and Lombard armour.
Outstanding pieces include the costume and shoes worn by Napoleon at his coronation
in Milan in 1805, and a display of life-sized horsemen decked in full armour from the
16th century.

Tower of London
Tower Hill, London EC3N 4AB, UK
Tel. (44) 20 7709 0765 www.hrp.org.uk
Mar-Oct: Mon-Sat 9.30am-6pm, Sun 2-5.30pm. Nov-Feb: Mon-Sat 9.30am-4.30 pm

Although a large part of the Royal Armouries' collection has moved to Leeds, the Tower
of London still houses one of the world's finest collections of European and Oriental
armour and weaponry from the Middle Ages to the 20th century. Among the many
unmatched highlights is a collection of royal armour, including the personal armour of
Henry VIII (made in the Royal Workshop at Greenwich, around 1520), those of several
prominent Tudor courtiers and soldiers, and a collection of Stuart royal armour, in particular the splendid gilt armour of Charles I.

The Wallace Collection
Hertford House, Manchester Square, London W1M 6BN, UK
Tel. (44) 20 7563 9500 www.the-wallace-collection.org.uk
Mon-Sat 10am-5pm, Sun 2-5 pm

Displayed over three rooms, this is one of the richest collections of 'princely' arms and
armour from the Middle Ages and Renaissance in the world. The unique collection
numbers some 1,300 items, a large portion of which came from Comte de Nieuwekerke,
Director of the Louvre under Emperor Napoleon III. Highlights include a magnificent
gilt close-helmet made in Augsburg for the Habsburg Emperor and his three sons, and
16th-century Italian parade armour attributed to Lucio Piccinino of Milan.

FIREARMS

American Precision Museum
196 Main Street, Windsor, Vermont 05089, USA
Tel. (1) 802 674 5781 www.americanprecision.org
Daily 10am-5pm (times may vary, please call for details)

Dedicated to the history of precision manufacture and housed in an historic armoury
building, this extensive gun collection traces the history of firearm design and manufacture in the Connecticut Valley including those manufactured in the building by
Robbins & Lawrence. The birth of the 'American System', making possible the concept
of interchangeable parts and revolutionizing production, is also celebrated.

Musée d'Armes anciennes
The Museum of Ancient Arms
Château de Joux, 25300 La Cluse-et-Mijoux, France
Tel. (33) 3 81 69 47 95 www.chateaudejoux.com
Mid Feb-Sep: 10-11.30am, 2-4.30pm (Jul & Aug: daily 9am-6pm). Oct-mid Feb: tours only

This important collection of guns from the 17th to the 19th centuries includes a rare example of the regulation model adopted in 1717 and used by the entire French Royal Infantry from then onwards. Special strengths of the collection are the 17th-century handheld arquebus and muskets used during the *ancien régime*.

Parker side-by-side, 1873
Springfield Carbine, Colt.
Revolver composite shot
(above)
The Cody Firearms Museum

Sharps M1851, composite
shot (right)
The Cody Firearms Museum

Exhibition 'Turning
Point: The American Civil
War' (below right)
Atlanta History Center

Musée d'Armes de Liège
The Arms Museum of Liège
8 quai de Maestricht, 4000 Liège, Belgium
Tel. (32) 4 221 9416 www.museedarmes.be
Mon, Thu, Sat-Sun 10am-1pm,
Wed, Fri 2-5pm

Established in the heart of one of the most historic gunmaking centres in the world, this collection offers a wealth of craftsmen's tools, samples of work from the Liège Gunmaking School (est.1897), gunmakers' signs, trade memorabilia, banners, photographs, and regional and international arms. The arms range from prehistory through to modern machine guns and artillery, with an outstanding variety of small arms for both military and personal use.

Atlanta History Center
130 West Paces Ferry Road NW, Atlanta, Georgia 30305-1366, USA
Tel. (1) 404 814 4000 www.atlhist.org
Mon-Sat 10am-5.30pm, Sun noon-5.30pm (other collections by appt.)

A stunning collection of more than 5,000 objects connected with America's most pivotal conflict, the American Civil War. It consists of more than 175 firearms, including a series of Union carbines and rows of sharpshooters, as well as uniforms, bullet moulds, and memorabilia. What is not on display can be accessed in the study-storage collection.

The Cody Firearms Museum
Buffalo Bill Historical Center, Cody, Wyoming 82414, USA
Tel. (1) 307 587 4771 www.bbhc.org
Apr: daily 10am-5pm. May: daily 8am-8pm. Jun-mid Sep: daily 7am-8pm. Mid Sep-Oct: daily 8am-5pm. Nov-Mar: Tue-Sun 10am-3pm

This 4,000-strong exhibition is based upon the collection of the Winchester Repeating Arms Company, but also documents the development of other American-manufactured firearms and its inventors, including Colt, Evans, Remington, Sharps, and Stevens. Also worth viewing is the Connecticut valley arms factory with its late 19th-century machinery, and the replica hunting lodge crammed full of animal trophies.

Corps of REME Museum of Technology
Isaac Newington Road, Arborfield, Berkshire RG2 9NJ, UK
Tel. (44) 118 8763375 www.rememuseum.org.uk
(By appt. only)

The Royal Electrical and Mechanical Engineers (REME) are responsible for the examination and repair of all mechanical, electrical, and optical equipment of the British Army. In storerooms there is civil engineering plant and machinery equipment; radio, telegraph, and telephone equipment; guidance systems; all forms of motor transport; and weaponry illustrating every type of equipment the army has used, tested, or modified.

Deutsches Historisches Museum
The German Historical Museum
Zeughaus Unter den Linden 2, 10117 Berlin, Germany
Tel: (49) 30 215020 www.dhm.de
Mon, Tue, Thu-Sun 10am-6pm

These vast holdings of handguns and small firearms date back to the
end of the 15th century and contain about 4,500 civil and military
examples. Among the outstanding individual pieces from the 16th
century are wheel-lock pistols owned by Colonel Andreas Teuffel von
Gundersdorf (1556), and a breech-loading wheel-lock rifle manufactured in Augsburg or Nuremberg in 1540.

Erickson case Derringers
composite shot
The Cody Firearms Museum

Ermitazh
The Hermitage
Dvortsovskaia naberezhnaia 34-36, 191065 St Petersburg, Russian Federation
Tel. (7) 812 1109079 www.hermitage.ru
Tue-Sat 10.30am-6pm, Sun 10.30am-5pm

Some 15,000 examples of first-class works by both Russian and western European
craftsmen give a comprehensive idea of the development of arms and armour from the
early Middle Ages to the early 20th century. Of particular note is the large holding of
French weaponry gathered from various famous collectors and historical figures,
including the Duke of Leichtenbergsky.

Gettysburg National Military Park
Visitor Center, 97 Taneytown Road, Gettysburg, Pennsylvania 17325-1080, USA
Tel. (1) 717 334 1124 www.nps.gov
Daily 8am-5pm (summer 8am-6pm)

Displayed within the museum are more than 40,000 objects relating to the Battle of
Gettysburg. There are displays of firearms from the period of the American Revolution
up to the Civil War which trace the evolution of weaponry, from the flintlock musket to
the percussion rifle and the invention of rifling. Also on display are weapons from
Enfield in Britain and from Austria, that were imported to make up the shortages.

Harpers Ferry National Historic Park
Harpers Ferry, West Virginia 25425, USA
Tel. (1) 304 535 6223 www.nps.gov
Daily 8.30am-5pm

This town was chosen by George Washington as a second national armoury in 1799. It
churned out arms until the Civil War destroyed most of the stock, machinery, and buildings. More than two dozen historic houses and museums can be explored by using a self-
guided map, or join the ranger-led tour to learn about types and stages of arms production.
In the Industry Museum you can view operating examples of 19th-century armoury
machinery and learn about gunmaker John H. Hall's patented Hall Rifle and his introduction of the mechanized production of interchangeable rifle components.

Kongsberg Våpenfabrikks Museum
The Kongsberg Weapon Manufactory Museum
Hyttegata 3, 3602 Kongsberg, Norway
Tel. (47) 32 723200 www.bvm.museum.no
Mid May-Jun: daily 10am-4pm. Jul-mid Aug: daily 10am-5pm. Sep: daily noon-4pm
Oct-mid May: Sun noon-3pm

Newly re-housed, the collections trace the development of the firearm industry in Kongsberg from 1814, when 'Kongsberg Våpenfabrikk' was established by royal decree to save the local economy. The production processes of the famous 'Krag-Jørgensen rifle', developed here in the 1890s, are explained in detail.

Museu militar
The Military Museum
Largo do Museu do Artilharia, Santa Apolónia, 1100 Lisbon, Portugal
Tel. (351) 21 888 2131 www.geira.pt
Tue-Sun 10am-5pm

The museum is housed in a former 17th-century weapons factory whose walls and ceiling are covered with tiles and paintings depicting battle scenes. There are two rooms entirely devoted to the Napoleonic invasions, a display on World War I, and a comprehensive display of Portuguese arms from prehistory to the 20th century.

Prussian orderly percussion pistol, 1851
Waffenmuseum Suhl

Royal Armouries Museum
Armouries Drive, Leeds, West Yorkshire, UK
Tel. (44) 113 220 1999 www.armouries.org.uk
Apr-Oct: daily 10.30am-5.30pm. Nov-Mar: Mon-Fri 10.30am-4.30pm, Sat-Sun 10.30am-5.30pm

This collection has unique and historically significant guns from various parts of Europe spanning the last four centuries, as well as the outstanding English Civil War armoury from Littlecote House. Subjects covered include the development of the bayonet, the earliest repeating magazine rifles, and the birth of automatic weapons.

Springfield Armory National Historic Site
1 Armory Square, Springfield, Massachusetts 01105-1299, USA
Tel. (1) 413 734 8551 www.nps.gov
Wed-Sun 10am-4.30pm

This town held America's first federal arsenal, created in 1794, and was a centre for the manufacture of US Military small arms until 1968. The Armory's 'Industry' area highlights many important technological advances made here. The original Main Arsenal Building displays just a sliver of its 7,000 weapons, including a fine collection of confederate weapons and examples of experimental and standard US military arms.

Tsentral'nyi voenno-morskoi muzei
The Central Navy Museum
Birzhevaia ploshchad' 4, 199034 St Petersburg, Russian Federation
Tel. (7) 812 328 2701 www.museum.navy.ru
Wed-Sun 11am-6pm

There are more than 10,000 weapons and firearms from various countries here which date from the Middle Ages to the present day. There is an especially rich collection of artillery, mine, and torpedo weapons of the 20th century. The collection boasts personal weapons of famous admirals such as Admiral Nelson, Great Prince Konstantin Nikolaevich, and admirals of the Soviet Fleet.

Waffenmuseum Suhl
The Suhl Museum of Weapons
Friedrich-Koenig-Strasse 19, 98527 Suhl, Germany
Tel. (49) 3681 720698 www.waffenmuseumsuhl.de
Apr-Oct: Tue-Sun 9am-5pm, public holidays 10am-5pm
Nov-Mar: Tue-Sat 9am-4pm, Sun & public holiday 10am-4pm

A beautiful 17th-century malt house contains an exhibition which traces the
history of firearms production in Suhl back to 1535. The town was an important
centre for weapon making within Europe, and most of the firearms on display
were produced here. All emphasise the techniques and fine engraving characteristic of the town's gunsmiths.

Exterior of the museum
Waffenmuseum Suhl

Japanese gift armour
given by Tokugawa
Ieyasu to King James I
in 1613 (below)
Royal Armouries Museum

The Wallace Collection
Hertford House, Manchester Square, London W1M 6BN, UK
Tel. (44) 20 7563 9500 www.the-wallace-collection.org.uk
Mon-Sat 10am-5pm, Sun 2-5pm

This collection is justifiably famous for its fabulous array of early firearms. Among the
most magnificent is the wheel-lock gun by Daniel Sadeler and Hieronymous Borstorffer
(*c.*1620), and the French flintlock pistols made for presentation to Louis XIV.

Muzeum Wojska Polskiego
The Museum of the Polish Army
Aleje Jerozolimskie 3, 00-496 Warsaw, Poland
Tel. (48) 22 6295271
Wed-Sun 10am-4pm

The museum lost much of its collection through plundering in World War II. However, a
detailed inventory secretly made by the museum staff during this time enabled the
museum to replace or recover much of its collection and, at the same time, to acquire
new objects relating to the last war. The collection of firearms, including an outstanding
selection of hunting firearms and edged weapons, is of great importance.

ISLAMIC AND FAR EASTERN ARMOUR

Musée de l'Armée
The Army Museum
Hôtel National des Invalides, 129 rue de Grenelle,
75007 Paris, France
Tel. (33) 1 44 42 37 72 www.invalides.org
Apr-Sep: daily 10am-6pm. Oct-Mar: daily 10am-5pm

This outstanding collection of Oriental armour features
exceptional objects such as a helmet belonging to the
Ottoman sultan Bajazet II (end of the 15th century),
armour of the Japanese Odoshi Yokohagi do Tosei Gusoki
(19th century), and an 18th-century war dress belonging to the
Emperor K'ien Long of China.

The L.A. Mayer Museum of Islamic Art
Ha-Palmakh 2, 91040 Jerusalem, Israel
Tel. (972) 2 5661292
Mon, Wed, Thu, Sun 10am-3pm, Tue 10am-6pm,
Fri, Sat & public holidays 10am-2pm

311

The extensive collection of Islamic arms and armour focuses on helmets and body armour from the 15th- and 16th-century Ottoman Empire. There is also an array of fine Mughal swords and shields, many inlaid with gold and decorated animal motifs or inscriptions, confirming the importance given to arms and armour.

The Metropolitan Museum of Art

1000 Fifth Avenue at 82nd Street, 10028 New York, USA
Tel. (1) 212 535 7710 www.metmuseum.org
Tue-Thu, Sun 9.30am-5.30pm, Fri, Sat 9.30am-9pm

This collection of Islamic arms sparkles with jewelled swords, jade hilted daggers, gold inlaid axes, and silver mounted pistols, all symbols of wealth and prestige, as well as testaments of war. The Japanese armour (the finest and most comprehensive collection outside Japan) includes a significant group of early swords and an important helmet of lamellar construction from the Kofun period. Important armour from the late Kamakur period can also be found here.

Muzeum Narodowe - Muzeum Czartoryskich
The National Museum - Czartoryski Museum

Ulica Swietego Jana 19, 31-017 Cracow, Poland
Tel. (48) 12 4225566 www.muz-nar.krakow.pl
Mon-Tue, Sat-Sun 10am-3.30pm, Fri noon-5.30pm

An impressive collection amassed by Princess Isabel Czartoryska and her husband in the 18th century. Among its treasures are arms, armour, seals, costumes, and war trophies, including the hoard of Ottoman booty taken in 1683 from the Battle of Vienna where the King of Poland halted the Turkish advance into Central Europe.

The Pitt Rivers Museum

South Parks Road, Oxford, Oxfordshire OX1 3PP, UK
Tel.(44) 1865 270927 www.prm.ox.ac.uk
Mon-Sat 1-4.30pm, Sun 2-4.30pm

Shield (top)
The L.A. Mayer Museum of Islamic Art

Indian quilted armour of Tipu Sultan of Mysore (above)
Royal Armouries Museum

Among the museum's weird and wonderful collections is this fine collection of Japanese arms and armour, which are presented as objects of art as well as of battle. The eight-foot bow, decorated with lacquer and cane strips, is of exquisite quality, as are the sword blades and Samurai armour from around 1750. The Samurai collection includes the box used to transport the armour on a servant's back.

Royal Armouries Museum

Armouries Drive, Leeds, West Yorkshire LS10 1LT, UK
Tel. (44) 113 2201999 www.armouries.org.uk
Apr-Oct: daily 10.30am-5.30pm. Nov-Apr: Mon-Fri 10.30am-4.30pm, Sat-Sun 10.30am-5.30pm

An exceptional collection of Oriental and Indian arms and armour, featuring a unique example of 17th-century Indian elephant armour captured by Lord Clive during his great victory at the Battle of Plassey in 1757. Islamic displays include some remarkable medieval pieces such as a 'turban' helmet decorated with Arabic verses complete with its *mail aventail*. China is well represented, but most impressive are the holdings of Japanese armour, represented by pieces such as an armour of haramaki type (c. 1560) which belonged to the Christian convert, Naito Yukiyasu.

George Walter Vincent Smith Art Museum

220 State Street, Springfield, Massachusetts 01103, USA
Tel. (1) 413 263 6800   www.quadrangle.com
Wed-Sun noon-4pm

The Japanese Arms and Armour Gallery is arranged around a late 18th-century Shinto wheel shrine, with case after case of samurai arms and armour. Some of the swords are simple, elegant blades of steel with a signature on the unpolished tang. Others are trimmed with multi-coloured metal mountings, hilts wrapped in ray fish skin and bound with silk cord, and scabbards of beautifully designed lacquer, chased silver, or polished wood.

Snowshill Manor

Snowshill, Broadway, Gloucestershire WR12 7JU, UK
Tel. (44) 1386 852410   www.ntrustsevern.org.uk
Apr-Oct: Wed-Sun noon-5pm (open public holidays Jun-Jul)

Charles Paget Wade, the last owner of the manor, devoted his life to amassing curios, antiquities, and fine objects, creating an environment to fuel the imagination of both old and young. His collecting fervour led him to the pursuit of Far Eastern objects in such bizarre locations as a plumber's shop in Cheltenham and a cellar off Charing Cross Road, London, in order to assemble this dazzling collection of Japanese armour, which includes 26 suits of Samurai armour.

Museo Stibbert
The Stibbert Museum

Via Federigo Stibbert 26, 50134 Florence, Italy
Tel. (39) 055 475520
Mon-Wed 10am-1pm, Fri-Sun 10am-6pm

Displayed in a spectacular setting are European and Oriental weapons, clothes and accessories, tapestries, period paintings, and porcelain. The comprehensive collection of Islamic and Oriental arms and armour offers typical examples from Japan, Persia, India, and Indonesia, and includes excellent examples of Japanese swords.

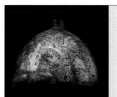

Topkapi Sarayi Müzesi
The Topkapi Palace Museum

Sultanahmet, 34410 Istanbul, Turkey
Tel. (90) 212 5120480
Mon, Wed-Sun 9.30am-6pm

Undeniably the best collection of late Mamluk arms and armour, consisting of both ceremonial and utilitarian weapons which date from the reign of Qaitbay to the end of the Mamluk period. Not to be missed is the 18th-century Topkapi dagger whose hilt bears three walnut-sized emeralds. Crafted as a gift to the Persian King Nadir Shah, the dagger never reached its intended recipient, who was killed in an uprising before the Ottoman emissary crossed the border into Iran.

The Wallace Collection

Hertford House, Manchester Square, London W1M 6BN, UK
Tel. (44) 20 7563 9500   www.the-wallace-collection.org.uk
Mon-Sat 10am-5pm, Sun 2-5pm

One of the largest collections in the museum is dedicated to arms and armour and includes approximately 1,000 pieces of Oriental arms and armour, collected by Lord

Quoit turban or *dastar bungga*, India, 18th century (below)
Royal Armouries Museum

Mongol helmet (bottom)
Royal Armouries Museum

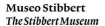

313

Hertford largely for decorative purposes. Rich in Indian, Middle-Eastern (especially Persian) and Ottoman weapons, the swords and edged weapons are especially prized. Items not displayed in the main gallery can be seen in the new reserve collection displays on the lower ground floor.

Muzeum Wojska Polskiego
The Museum of the Polish Army
Aleje Jerozolimskie 3, 00-496 Warsaw, Poland
Tel. (48) 22 6295271
Wed-Sun 10am-4pm

Apart from the main collection relating to Poland's and Europe's history, the museum owns a valuable international collection of arms and armour. Most impressive are exhibits from Japan, the Ottoman Empire, Persia, India, Arabia, and China.

MILITARY APPAREL

Musée de l'Armée
The Army Museum
Hôtel National des Invalides, 129 rue de Grenelle, 75007 Paris, France
Tel. (33) 1 44 42 37 72   www.invalides.org
Apr-Sep: daily 10am-6pm. Oct-Mar: daily 10am-5pm

Mughal Indian elephant armour, *c*.1600
Royal Armouries Museum

The museum has a vast selection of uniforms from the ancient monarchy to the present, and of German, Austro-Hungarian, British, American, Belgian, and Russian origin. An excellent collection of uniforms from the campaigns of Louis XIV and XV show magnificent examples of prestigious apparel. The collection of 19th-century uniforms is equally outstanding, with several key items worn by Napoleon.

The Black Watch Regimental Museum
Balhousie Castle, Hay Street, Perth PH1 5HR, Scotland, UK
Tel. (44) 131 310 8530
May-Sep: Mon-Sat 10am-4.30pm. Oct-Apr: Mon-Fri 10am-3.30pm

Treasures here cover over two-and-a-half centuries of the 42nd and 73rd Highland Regiments' role in the British Army. Among the highlights is the complete scarlet number one dress uniform worn by King George V when he visited the regiment as their Colonel and Chief.

Forsvarsmuseet på Bornholm
The Defence Museum on Bornholm
Arsenalvej 8, 3700 Rønne, Denmark
Tel.(45) 56 956583
May-Oct: Tue-Sat 10am-4pm

The collection of uniforms here is among the largest in Denmark and covers the period 1801-1964. All the uniforms are second-hand, many with the names of the wearers still visible inside.

Household Cavalry Museum
Combermere Barracks, Windsor, Berkshire SL4 3DN, UK
Tel. (44) 1753 75512   www.householdcavalry.co.uk
Mon-Fri 10am-4pm

On display is a unique collection of horse furniture, weapons, and uniforms devoted to the history of the Cavalry in Britain over the last three centuries. Items include cuirasses and gauntlets from 1678, flamboyant 18th- and 19th-century uniforms, and their quieter 20th-century counterparts. The highlight is undoubtedly the pair of silver kettledrums presented to the 2nd Life Guards by William IV in 1831.

Hrvatski povijesni muzej
The Croatian History Museum
Matoseva 9, 10000 Zagreb, Croatia
Tel. (385) 1 431065
Mon-Fri 10am-5pm, Sat-Sun 10am-1pm

There are around 100 uniform parts here, mostly coats, caps, and trousers. There are also more than 300 accessories such as insignia, epaulettes, belts, belt buckles, buttons, and satchels, most of them dating from the second half of the 19th century.

Musée international des Hussards
The International Hussar Museum
Jardin Massey, 65000 Tarbes, France
Tel. (33) 5 62 36 31 49
Sep-Jun: daily 10am-noon, 2-6pm. Jul-Aug: Wed-Sun 10am-noon, 2-6.30pm

The collections trace five centuries of the history of the Hussars and contain an exceptionally rich number of uniforms dating back as far as 1474. The core of the collection, however, is made up by 131 uniforms worn by other French divisions, as well as those from abroad (seventeen items) dating from 1783 to 1976.

National Army Museum
Royal Hospital Road, London SW3 4HT, UK
Tel. (44) 20 7730 0717   www.national-army-museum.ac.uk
Mon-Sat 10am-5.30pm

One of the largest collections of military costumes in the world, with thousands of examples, including beautifully embroidered 18th-century grenadier caps displayed alongside Baden-Powell's army uniform.

National Maritime Museum
Romney Road, Greenwich, London SE10 9NF, UK
Tel. (44) 20 8858 4422   www.nmm.ac.uk
Daily 10am-5pm

A rich collection of clothing worn at sea, from the purely functional to ceremonial and regulation uniforms. Prized among the collection is Lord Nelson's undress coat worn at the Battle of Trafalgar, with the bullet hole from the musket ball which killed him clearly visible on the left shoulder.

The National War Museum of Scotland
Edinburgh Castle, Edinburgh EH1 2NG, Scotland UK
Tel. (44) 131 2257534   www.nms.ac.uk
Apr-Nov: daily 9.45am-5.30pm. Dec-Mar: daily 9.45am-4.30pm
(Reference Library by appt. only)

More than 15,000 items represent the dress and personal equipment of all three Scottish armed services since their establishment in the 17th century. Strengths include the uniforms of the Scottish regiments of the British regular army, especially those of the 19th century, and the insignia of the various auxiliary military units raised during the Revolutionary and Napoleonic Wars of 1793-1815.

Royal Navy; Gold Medal glazed with ribbon (above left)
The National War Museum of Scotland

Glengarry Fencibles, colours of the regiment, 1794-1802 (above right)
The National War Museum of Scotland

Various medals,
Argyll and Sutherland
Highlanders
*The National War Museum
of Scotland*

The New York Public Library

Fifth Avenue and 42nd Street, New York, New York 10018-2788, USA
Tel. (1) 212 930 0830   www.nypl.org
Mon, Thu 10am-6pm, Tue, Fri noon-6pm, Wed noon-8pm, Sat noon-5pm

The archive of military uniforms is a unique resource based on two major donations.
The first, the Vinkhuizen Collection, comprises 32,236 illustrations and watercolour
drawings, documenting uniforms from early times up to 1909. The second donation
came from the library of General DeWitt Clinton Falls and contains pictures, drawings,
and photographs of United States uniforms, notably from the Spanish-American War
until World War I.

US Army Quartermaster Museum

Building 5218, A. Avenue and 22nd Street, Fort Lee, Virginia 23801-1601, USA
Tel. (1) 804 734 4203   www.qmmuseum.lee
Tue-Fri 10am-5pm, Sat-Sun 11am-5pm

The Quartermaster Corps, dating back to 1775, had the task of supporting the individual
combat soldier in the field. Their jobs ranged from bakers to typewriter specialists, shoe
repairmen and suppliers of uniforms. The collection includes significant numbers of
army uniforms and accessories from the early 19th century to currently issued uniforms.

Voenno-istoricheskii muzei artillerii
The Military-Historical Artillery Museum

Aleksandrovskii Park 7, 193015 St Petersburg, Russian Federation
Tel. (7) 812 2330382
Wed-Sun 11am-5pm

The general museum exhibit includes a small number of uniforms. In the special
'Crown and Cloak' exhibition there are several fascinating garments, including a selec-
tion of military uniforms and uniform portraits of Russian tsars and their families, from
Peter I to Nicholas II.

Muzeum Wojska Polskiego
The Museum of the Polish Army

Aleje Jerozolimskie 3, 00-496 Warsaw, Poland
Tel. (48) 22 6295271
Wed-Sun 10am-4pm

In 1920, the role of the museum was cast by Marshal Józef Piłsudski's decree which
stated that it should be ' a temple of fame of Polish arms and the treasure store of eternal
knightly chivalry'. Paintings of battles, sidearms, bridles, saddlery, and firearms are
held with a unique collection of pre-1830 Polish uniforms.

ANIMAL, FISH AND BIRD COLLECTIONS

ENTOMOLOGY

FOSSILS, ROCKS, MINERALS AND GEMS

PLANT MODELS AND RELATED COLLECTIONS

SHELLS

ANIMAL, FISH AND BIRD COLLECTIONS

Grus leucogeranus (right)
Musée cantonal de Zoologie

Booth Museum of Natural History

194 Dyke Road, Brighton, East Sussex BN1 5AA, UK
Tel. (44) 1273 292777
Mon-Wed, Fri-Sat 10am-5pm, Sun 2-5pm

Over half a million natural specimens from around the world are held in what was formerly called Mr Booth's Bird Museum, named after its founder Edward Booth. Like most Victorians, he preferred to view the natural world through a glass case. The collection began with his 300 cases of stuffed birds, and specimens from the city's art museum were added later. Virtually every bird in the original collection was shot by Booth, who aimed to bag all the birds of Britain before he passed away. Besides the stuffed specimens, including controversial ones prepared by the taxidermist George Bristow, there are bird skins, nests, and extensive egg collections comprising five major worldwide collections and several smaller ones from Australasia and the Indo/Australian region. The osteological collections are extremely important and comprise disarticulated and articulated skeletons of all vertebrate classes. The skeletons of the sturgeon, green turtle, dodo, monk seal, African rhinoceros, and some rare primates are especially noteworthy.

The British Library

National Sound Archive, Wildlife Sounds, 96 Euston Road, London NW1 2DB, UK
Tel. (44) 20 7412 7402 www.bl.uk
Mon-Thu 9.30am-6pm (Tue, Wed until 8pm), Fri-Sat 9.30am-5pm

Tucked away in this massive archive are 130,000 recordings of animal sounds, from the mating call of the haddock and the noisy crackling made by a snapping shrimp, to a chaffinch alarm call. There are recordings of bats, whales, egrets, earthworms (yes, they make faint noises), frogs, and distinct sounds from fish underwater. Users of these audible treasures include film producers, naturalists, museums, and zoos. Those keen to contribute to this resource can attend the annual one-day training workshop on wildlife sound recording (see website for details).

Preserved specimen of
the unusual-looking
Limulus or horse-shoe
crab (above)
*Grant Museum of Zoology
and Comparative Anatomy*

Musée cantonal de Zoologie

Cantonal Museum of Zoology
Palais de Rumine, 6 place de la Riponne, 1005 Lausanne, Switzerland
Tel. (41) 21 316 34 60 www.lausanne.ch
Tue-Thu 11am-6pm, Fri-Sun 11am-5pm

Holdings include a considerable number of birds, an important osteological collection, and 2,000 vertebrates. At the heart of the collection are the library and archives of Bernard Heuvelmans, founder of cryptozoology, who is well known for his publication *On the Track of Unknown Animals*. The archives include rare books, Heuvelmans' original research, 25,000 photos, letters, bones, and skulls of species he investigated.

Grant Museum of Zoology and Comparative Anatomy

University College London, Darwin Building, Gower Street, London WC1E 6BT, UK
Tel. (44) 20 7679 2647 www.collections.ucl.ac.uk
Wed, Fri 1-5pm

Within the buildings of University College, London, is a Victorian Aladdin's cave, with shelf upon shelf crammed with around 30,000 exotic specimens, articulated skeletons, and oddities, including a box of bones from the dodo, the skeleton of a Quagga (one of only half a dozen known to exist), and a Thylacine skeleton. The museum is named after its founder, Professor Robert Edmond Grant, who was one of the pioneers of evolutionary theory and a great influence on Charles Darwin. On his death in 1874, he bequeathed his considerable holdings of books, journals, and natural history specimens to the University.

Musée d'Histoire naturelle
The Natural History Museum
19 rue de Bruxelles, 59000 Lille, France
Tel. (33) 3 28 55 30 80
Mon, Wed-Fri 9am-noon, 2-5pm, Sun 10am-5pm

Over 60,000 specimens of mammals, local and exotic birds, insects, and arachnids. The specimens of birds, partly assembled from 1820 to 1855 by Côme Damien Degland, a doctor from Lille, are outstanding. The collection gives an overview of ornithology, particularly of the region, and assists in population studies.

Exhibition Room
Musée cantonal de Zoologie

Iisalmi Luontomuseo
Iisalmi Nature Museum
Kirkkopuistonkatu 9, 74100 Iisalmi, Finland
Tel. (358) 17 818387   koti.mbnet.fi
Please call for opening times

24,984 skulls, indigenous to Finland and from over 45 species, amassed over decades by Uolevi Skarén. Two are extinct – *Eliomys quercinus* and *Rattus rattus*. The main purpose of the collection is to assist population biologists, but a small number of skulls are on display.

Institut royal des Sciences naturelles de Belgique
The Royal Institute of Natural Sciences of Belgium
29 rue Vautier, 1000 Brussels, Belgium
Tel. (32) 2 627 4211   www.sciencesnaturelles.net
Tue-Sat 9.30am-4.45pm, Sun 9.30am-6pm

This exceptionally rich, diverse collection contains over thirty million specimens, making it one of the top ten zoological collections in the world. In the hall devoted to mammals, eighty out of the 107 present-time families are represented, with special attention being paid to primates, carnivores, ungulates, and bovidae.

Luonnontieteellinen keskusmuseo
Finnish Museum of Natural History
Pohjoinen Rautatiekatu 13, Helsinki, Finland
Tel. (358) 9 191 28800   www.fmnh.helsinki.fi
Mon-Fri 9am-5pm, Sat-Sun 11am-4pm

The vertebrate collections comprise 75,000 specimens of native species, including several that have long been extinct, like the *Castor fiber* (beaver) and *Hydrodamalis gigas* (Steller's sea cow). Many of them were gathered by government officials serving in parts of the Russian Empire. Avon Nordmann worked as a professor in Odessa and collected recent and fossil vertebrates in the Ukraine, Moldova, and the Caucasus. R. F. Sahlberg brought back vertebrates from South and North America and Asia during expeditions from 1839-43 and 1849-51. Other collections were bought, like V. Pousar's bird collection and A. Gallen-Kallela's African mammals.

Mergus cucullatus (above)
Musée cantonal de Zoologie

Haeliaeetus leucocephalus (left)
Musée cantonal de Zoologie

Museo nacional de Ciencias naturales
The National Museum of Natural Sciences
C. José Gutiérrez Abascal 2, 28006 Madrid, Spain
Tel. (34) 91 5646169   www.mncn.csic.es
Tue-Fri 10am-6pm, Sat 10am-8pm, Sun 10am-2.30pm

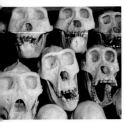

The collection of birds and mammals has its origins in the Royal Cabinet of Natural History, which was founded at the end of the 18th century by Carlos III. Some of these early exhibits, still preserved, include an Indian elephant (*Elephas maximus*) and the skull of a sperm whale (*Physeter macrocephalus*). Additions to the collection, including 30,000 birds and 27,000 mammals from Spain, Latin America, North Africa, the Philippines, and Equatorial Guinea, have created one of Spain's best study collections. They are of an outstanding quality due to taxidermists, Luis and José Benedito, who worked at the museum at the beginning of the 20th century.

Musée national d'Histoire naturelle
The National Natural History Museum
57 rue Cuvier, 75005 Paris, France
Tel. (33) 1 40 79 30 00 www.mnhn.fr
Please call for opening times

With more than 76 million species, this is one of the leading collections and research institutes in the world. The displays focus on the theory of evolution, with rare historical and extinct species given pride of place. Exhibits include the only preserved skeleton of the black emu, the Seychelles turtle, the famous dodo, and the great mammoth discovered in Siberia in 1905. The vertebrate section includes examples of a paleotherium, a chalicotherium, and the rare *Maastricht mosasaurus* studied by Georges Cuvier. Spread over three levels in the basement are millions of specimens accessible to researchers and scholars.

The Natural History Museum
Cromwell Road, London SW7 5BD, UK
Tel. (44) 20 7942 5011 www.nhm.ac.uk
Mon-Sat 10am-5.50pm, Sun 11am-5.50pm

The museum's origins date back to the collection of Sir Hans Sloane, a physician who, in 1753, bequeathed his vast and curious holdings of some 80,000 items to the nation, including substantial natural history specimens. Later, the voyages of Captain Cook, Darwin, and others, contributed to the museum's holdings. Entire museums were bought, and by the late 19th century it was bursting at the seams. The collections now number some 68 million specimens, which has necessitated a major rethink regarding how to exhibit them. Phase one of the new Darwin Centre attempts to bring some of these tremendous holdings out of store. Shelves lined with some twelve million or so wet specimens (including a sea bass brought back by Cook, such pickled rarities as an Oarfish, plus thousands of reptiles and small mammals) will fill half of the six floors of

Gorilla skulls (top)
The Powell-Cotton Museum and Quex House & Gardens

Elephant diorama (middle)
The Powell-Cotton Museum and Quex House & Gardens

Artist's impression of the Atrium (Four IV Design) (bottom)
The Natural History Museum

this purpose-designed science and collection facility. The other half, with glazed internal partitions, allows visitors to watch scientists at work and examine specimens. Opening in 2005 is the second phase for the equally massive insect and plant collections.

Natural History Museum of Los Angeles County
900 Exposition Boulevard, Los Angeles, California 90007, USA
Tel. (1) 213 763 3466 www.nhm.org
Mon-Fri 9.30am-5pm, Sat-Sun 10am-5pm

A world leader in research, with more than 34 million specimens and artefacts from Africa. The collections of marine mammals (ranked second in the world), ornithology, and fish are particularly comprehensive. The collections of fish include seven million specimens and contain a large portion of the ocean's bounty, particularly from the Pacific Rim regions and the freshwaters of North, Central, and South America. The museum's Antarctic and Central American collections are especially rare. The only megamouth shark on display in North America is a prize piece. The Schreiber Hall of Birds, where animated birds walk through various habitats, is excellent.

The Powell-Cotton Museum and Quex House & Gardens
Quex Park, Birchington, Kent CT7 0BH, UK
Tel. (44) 1843 842168
Apr-Oct: Tue-Thu, Sun & public holidays, 11am-5pm
Nov-Mar: Sun 11am-4pm

A great repository of well-documented African mammals and material collected between 1885 and 1939 by the great hunter and explorer, Major Powell-Cotton (1866-1940). Powell-Cotton returned from his first visit to the African continent intoxicated by the beauty of both its animal life and the artefacts produced by its indigenous cultures. Over the next half century, he embarked on 28 expeditions to Africa (spending some 26 years on African soil), amassing several thousand study skins of mammals, thousands of skeletal specimens, massive holdings of ethnographic objects, and photographic and cinematographic documentation. Realizing the importance of accurate recording, his specimens were collected with data, including longitude and latitude map references, which added to their importance scientifically and served as an indicator of ecological change. He also travelled to Asia and the Indian sub-continent, peppering his collections with both animal specimens and objects from these countries. Five hundred beasts in action poses are exhibited over eight save dioramas, pioneered by the Major, against backdrops of their natural habitats. The 438 skeletal specimens of chimpanzee gorillas come with full body measurements, external pathology, and even the local name of the disease the animal died from. Underpinning the collections are fifty years of the Major's diaries and paperwork relating to transport and costs of preparing the collections.

The Walter Rothschild Zoological Museum
Akeman Street, Tring, Hertfordshire HP23 6AP, UK
Tel. (44) 20 7942 6171 www.nhm.ac.uk
Mon-Sat 10am-5pm, Sun 2-5 pm

This was once the private museum of the eccentric collector, Lionel Walter Rothschild, whose wealth enabled him to send agents all over the world in search of rare and beautiful specimens. He kept an array of live animals including giant tortoises which he rode and zebras which he harnessed to his carriage and drove through the streets of London. His speciality was rare birds, and his collection numbered hundreds of skins. It was considered the most comprehensive in the world, and contained an unparalleled collection of birds of paradise of which he was particularly proud. Fears of blackmail necessitated the sale of these skins to the American Museum of Natural History in New York. He parted with many rarities but kept his cassowaries, which are now part of the national bird collections held here. Over 4,000 items are displayed, including a bewildering array of odd- and even-toed mammals, and Victorian curiosities. His massive library contains rare ornithological works, atlases, and travel literature.

Carriage drawn by four zebra driven by Lord Rothschild
The Walter Rothschild Zoological Museum

Saffron Walden Museum
Museum Street, Saffron Walden, Essex CB10 1JL, UK
Tel (44) 1799 510333 www.uttlesford.gov.uk
Mar-Oct: Mon-Sat 10am-5pm, Sun & public holidays 2-5pm
Nov-Feb: Mon-Sat 10am-4.30pm, Sun & public holidays 2-5pm

Wallace the Lion, born in 1816, guards the natural history galleries where the nature of the woodlands, hedgerows, and ponds of northwest Essex are displayed alongside examples of Victorian zoology. The bird collection contains a wealth of fine artistic Victorian taxidermy, with examples from South America, Asia, and Australia. There are important collections of birds' eggs, insects, shells, and plant material from around the world.

Museo di Storia Naturale
Museum of Natural History
Santa Croce 1730, 30135 Venice, Italy
Tel.(39) 041 5240885
Due to re-open in 2004

This collection will be arranged like a cabinet of curiosities, with oddities from the natural world including 15th- to 16th-century 'mermaids' made by fixing the top half of a small monkey to the lower half of a large fish.

Vänersborg Museum
Regionmuseum Västra Götaland,
462 21 Vänersborg, Sweden
Tel.(46) 521 264100
Sep-May: Tue, Thu, Sat-Sun noon-4pm
Jun-Aug: Tue, Wed, Thu, Sat-Sun noon-4pm

A staggering collection of birds, eggs, mammals, and insects collected in South West Africa (Namibia), with the world's largest exhibition of South West African birds (1,000 specimens) and a diverse array of extinct fauna. They were donated in 1883 by the Vänersborg-born trader, hunter, and ornithologist, Axel W. Eriksson (1846-1901). Eriksson came to southern Africa in 1865 to assist the explorer, Charles John Andersson (1827-67), who was one of the first Europeans to venture into the interior of what today is Namibia. When Andersson died two years later, Eriksson took over his natural history research, funding it through a trading company he started in the 1870s.

'Noctifer' – a creation by Charles Waterton (top)
Wakefield Museum

'Martin Luther after his fall' – a creation by Charles Waterton (above left)
Wakefield Museum

'The Nondescript' – a creation by Charles Waterton (above right)
Wakefield Museum

A bird from the collection (right)
Wakefield Museum

Wakefield Museum
Wood Street, Wakefield , West Yorkshire WF1 2EW, UK
Tel.(44) 1924 305351
Mon-Sat 10am-4.30pm, Sun 2-4.30pm

The explorer and eccentric naturalist, Charles Waterton (1782-1865), travelled far and wide but is best known for his wanderings in South America, particularly British Guiana, where he made accurate observations on New World wildlife and brought back rare specimens. His eccentricities led many to consider him mad. He is known to have climbed up the lightening rod on St Peters in Rome only to leave his gloves on top (which enraged the Pope), and in South America he spent weeks trying to be bitten by a vampire bat. An excellent naturalist, he was among the first to set aside land for the sole purpose of a wildlife sanctuary. Waterton is best remembered for his grotesque taxidermic mounts of imaginary animals, created by sewing together the head of one creature to the body of another. He frequently took this one step further, producing cartoon-like creations with an odd mixture of humanoid and anthropoid traits, often modelled in the likeness of a politician he particularly disliked.

Zoologicheskii muzei
The Zoological Museum
Universitetskaia naberezhnaia 1, 199034 St Petersburg, Russian Federation
Tel.(7) 812 3280112 www.zin.ru
Mon-Thu, Sat-Sun 11am-6pm

Over 100,000 specimens including a set of stuffed animals that once belonged to Peter the Great. Among the collection of extinct animals, the mammoths discovered in the permafrost are particularly impressive.

ENTOMOLOGY

American Museum of Natural History
Central Park West at 79th Street, New York,
New York 10024-5192, USA
Tel. (1) 212 769 5100 www.amnh.org
Daily 10am-5.45pm (Fri, Sat until 8.45pm)

Around eighteen million specimens, among them some of
the thousands of butterflies Vladimir Nabokov captured
while in America (1940-60). The museum also has massive holdings of termites, bees,
spiders, gall wasps, moths, and South American blackflies, to name just a few. The collection of fossil amber insects is the best and most important anywhere, and research on
extracting DNA from 'frozen' specimens has made the popular press in recent years.

Booth Museum of Natural History
194 Dyke Road, Brighton, East Sussex BN1 5AA, UK
Tel. (44) 1273 292777
Mon-Wed, Fri-Sat 10am-5pm, Sun 2-5pm

The entomology collections consist of over half a million lepidoptera and 70,000 non-lepidoptera. Most British insects are represented, and there is a good smattering of foreign specimens as
well, especially from South and Central America. There is specialist
coverage of the family *Lycaenidea*, with specimens of the Large Blue
and Large Copper, now extinct in the UK, and the critically endangered species of Birdwings, among others. Excellent swallowtails,
both rare and extinct, from Papua New Guinea are displayed along
with endangered Bird Wing butterflies.

Musée cantonal de Zoologie
Cantonal Museum of Zoology
Palais de Rumine, 6 place de la Riponne, 1005 Lausanne,
Switzerland
Tel. (41) 21 316 3460 www.lausanne.ch
Tue-Thu 11am-6pm, Fri-Sun 11am-5pm

The museum houses Vladimir Nabokov's famous collection of 4,323
butterflies, gathered between 1961 and 1975 while he lived in Montreux.
Among them are 195 species, of which 157 are from the 200 or so known in
Switzerland (*Rhopalocera* butterflies). The entomology collections also contain several million other specimens, mainly coleoptera, lepidoptera, hymenoptera
(ants and ichneumonidae in particular), ephemeroptera, plecoptera, and diptera from
across the globe. The museum library holds around 5,000 volumes.

Top to bottom:
Morpho didius Hopffer
(Didius Morpho)

Semomesia, probably
croesus

Prepona praeneste bucklyana
Hewitson

Hebomia leucippe (Cramer)

Ornithoptera goliath
(Goliath Birdwing)

Florida Museum of Natural
History

Florida Museum of Natural History
Powell Hall, Hull Road and SW 34th Street, University of Florida, Gainesville, Florida
32611-2710, USA
Tel. (1) 904 392 1721 www.flmnh.ufl.edu
Mon-Sat 10am-5pm, Sun & public holidays 1-5pm (by appt. only until 2003)

The new lepidoptera research facility, due to open in 2003, will be the second largest collection of lepidoptera in the world. It will be one of the most significant regional,
national, and international research resources in North America, with more than
1,032,000 specimens representing 92-95 per cent of all known butterfly genera. The
majority of specimens are derived from North America (especially the western US),
Central and South America (including the West Indies), and Africa.

Insectarium
8046 Frankford Avenue, Philadelphia, Pennsylvania 19136, USA
Tel. (1) 215 338 3000 www.insectarium.com
Mon-Sat 10am-4pm

Here there is a roach kitchen filled with thousands of hissing cockroaches from Madagascar, live tarantulas, emperor scorpions, Goliath beetles, Indian walking sticks, human face stink bugs, waterbugs, and a collection of mounted insect specimens, including 68,000 mounted butterflies. Watch bees at work in hives and termites tunnelling nests.

Teinopalpus imperialis
(male) (above left)
Musée des Papillons

Argema mittrei (male)
(above right)
Musée des Papillons

Butterflies (below)
Booth Museum of Natural History

Library of Canna House
Secretary, 2 Canna House, Isle of Canna PH44 4RS, Scotland, UK
Tel. (44) 1687 462473
By appt. only

This Hebridean collection of butterflies and moths consists of some thirty cabinet drawers containing 283 species of macrolepidoptera, including the first recorded specimen of the noctuid moth *Dianthoecia caesia*. It was amassed by the Gaelic scholar, Dr J. L. Campbell, who started the collection on Barra in 1936.

Luonnontieteellinen keskusmuseo
Finnish Museum of Natural History
Pohjoinen Rautatiekatu 13, Helsinki, Finland
Tel. (358) 9 191 28800 www.fmnh.helsinki.fi
Mon-Fri 9am-5pm, Sat-Sun 11am-4pm

With eight million insect specimens from all over the world, this is one of the largest collections in Europe. There are substantial collections of coleoptera, diptera, hymenoptera, and lepidoptera, plus extensive collections of spiders from Finland and Newfoundland.

Magyar Természettudományi Múzeum
Hungarian Natural History Museum
Department of Zoology, Baross utca 13, 1088 Budapest, Hungary
Tel. (36) 1 2677100 www.nhmus.hu
Please call for opening times

Three million insects, including many rare species like the darkling beetle of Vietnam (*Artactes vietnamensis Kaszab*) and the blind ground beetle (*Duvalius gebharti*). Edmund Reitter (1845-1920) was probably the greatest coleopterist of the temperate zone of Eurasia and North Africa, and his formidable collection of 200,000 specimens includes the rare beetle from the *byturiadae* family, first described by him in 1905. The extensive butterfly collection contains the best reference collection of the winter noctuid moth species of the Himalayas.

Museo nacional de Ciencias naturales
The National Museum of Natural Sciences
C. José Gutiérrez Abascal 2, 28006 Madrid, Spain
Tel. (34) 91 5646169 www.mncn.csic.es
Tue-Fri 10am-6pm, Sat 10am-8pm, Sun 10am-2.30pm

This important collection has about 2.5 million insects

preserved dry, 25,000 microscopic preparations of entire specimens and anatomical parts, as well as almost 5,000 containers that hold vials with examples in alcohol. Most of the material comes from the Iberian Peninsula and the Canary Islands.

Left – top to bottom:
Southern Hawker
(*Aeshna cyanea*)

Migrant Hawker
(*Aeshna mixta*)

Musée national d'Histoire naturelle – Galerie d'Entomology
The National Museum of Natural History – the Entomology Gallery
45 rue Buffon, 75005 Paris, France
Tel. (33) 1 40 79 30 00   www.mnhn.fr
By appt. to researchers only

Brown Hawker
(*Aeshna grandis*)

Broad-Bodied Chaser
(*Libellula depressa*)

The National Dragonfly Bio Museum

Undoubtedly one of the world's leading collections, with some thirty million insects including subsections of type specimens which rank among the largest anywhere. Historic collections loom large and include the sub-tropical butterflies collected by A. Fournier and the beetles amassed by Sir J. Thompson in the 19th century – presented in hollow leather bound books with rows of pin-mounted insects instead of pages.

The National Dragonfly Bio Museum
Ashton Mill, Near Oundle, Peterborough, Cambridgeshire
PE8 5LZ, UK
Tel. (44) 1832 272427   www.natdragonflymuseum.org.uk
Mid Jun-mid Oct: Sat, Sun & public holidays 10.30am-5pm

One of only two museums in the world (the other is in Japan) dedicated to the dragonfly. View live dragonfly larvae in tanks, and displays about conservation and encouraging the digging of ponds. At feeding time, a special camera allows visitors to watch dragonfly larvae devour bloodworm and mosquito larvae, which turns the water bright red.

Ornithoptera Hippolytus, East Indonesia (below)
Wellesley Historical Society

Oxford University Museum of Natural History
Parks Road, Oxford, Oxfordshire OX1 3PW, UK
Tel. (44) 1865 272950   www.oum.ox.ac.uk
Daily noon-5pm

Bursting with historically important collections and over three million specimens, comprising 20,000 insect type specimens, and more than 3,000 specimens of arachnids, and other arthropods. The most important single collection of diptera anywhere in the UK is held here, as is a rich collection of spiders and other arthropods (including specimens from Palestine and Syria), and butterflies, especially from the Palaearctic, Ethiopian, and Oriental regions. The museum recently added 20,000 specimens of water bug from Australia and Papua New Guinea (around thirty new species), and over half a million insect specimens from Acacia trees in the East African savannahs.

Musée du Papillon
Butterfly Museum
7 rue de Sluse, 4000 Liège, Belgium
Tel. (32) 425 23468
By appt. only
More than 20,000 butterflies, with many species exclusively from Belgium

Interior of the museum
Musée des Papillons

(there are over 1,000 native species), and others from Africa and Asia. They were collected by Dr Paul Houyez, who in 1919, turned a hobby into a scientific endeavour.

Musée des Papillons
Museum of Butterflies
Espace Saint-Jacques, 14 rue de la Sellerie,
02100 Saint-Quentin, France
Tel. (33) 3 23 06 93 93
Mon, Wed-Sat 2-6pm, Sun 3-6.30pm

This is one of the most significant collections of butterflies and insects in Europe, with over 11,000 specimens permanently displayed out of a collection numbering some 600,000. There are large numbers of tropical butterflies, including a *Thysania* from Guyana, metallic blue morphos from Central and South America, and the Argema from Madagascar. Equally impressive is the phyllodes which mimics the leaf of a tree.

Royal Entomological Society
41 Queen's Gate, London SW7 5HR, UK
Tel. (44) 20 7584 8361 www.royensoc.demon.co.uk
Mon-Fri 9.30am-5pm to Fellows, members and their guests only. Non-members can apply for a one day 'taster membership'

Set over three floors, there are some 11,000 books and 750 journal titles, with strengths in the general biology and taxonomy of insects, particularly with reference to the Western Palaearctic Region. An invaluable collection of reprints dating back to 1700 includes the Rothschild papers on Siphonaptera. Equally impressive are the rare editions, including several volumes illustrated with watercolours of insects and butterflies by the Dutch entomologist, Maria Sybilla Meriaen (1647-1717). There is also a small selection of rare books on spiders, and a significant collection of several hundred arachnids. The Society's archive contains many unique hand-written diaries, letters, and manuscripts by eminent entomologists such as Charles Darwin, the noted German lepidopterist, Jacob Hübner, and the former British prime minister, Neville Chamberlain.

Exotic beetles (above)
Musée des Papillons

Papilio Tamilana, Malabar coast, India (from the Denton Collection) (right)
Wellesley Historical Society

Wellesley
Historical Society
229 Washington Street, Wellesley Hills,
Massachusetts 02481, USA
Tel. (1) 781 235 6690 www.wellesleyhsoc.com
Mon, Wed 2-4.30pm, Thu 4.30-7.30pm, Sat 1.30-3.30pm. (By appt. at other times.)

A collection of 1,500 moths and butterflies from many parts of the world. A large number of New England specimens, known as the Denton Brothers' Butterfly Collection, is a fine example of a natural history collection formed by early 20th-century collectors. Avid collectors, the Denton brothers turned butterfly hunting into a business, developing novel methods of display and supplying both private clients and notable museums with specimens.

FOSSILS, ROCKS, MINERALS AND GEMS

Bärnstensmuseet
Amber Museum
Leif Brost, Mariavagen 4, 236 35 Höllviken, Sweden
Tel. (46) 40 450861   www.brost.se
May–Sep: daily 11am–5pm. Rest of year: weekends only

Amber artefacts from all ages are on display, from Stone Age beads to those traded during the Roman period and later. There are also Viking and Medieval items. The museum is best known, however, for its unique collection of over 1,000 rare specimens of inclusions in amber, some of them insects more than forty million years old.

Big Pit National Mining Museum of Wales
Blaenafon, Torfaen, South Wales NP4 9XP, UK
Tel. (44) 1495 790311   www.nmgw.ac.uk

The role this area played in the Industrial Revolution has recently earned it World Heritage status. Covering 25 square miles are the museum, the preserved iron-works, the town of Blaenavon, and part of the Brecknock and Abergavenny Canal. You can descend 90m to the coal face for a first-hand experience.

A mating pair of scavenger flies in Dominican amber (above)
Bärnstensmuseet

Inside the coal mine (left)
Big Pit National Mining Museum of Wales

Spider and fly in amber (below)
Bärnstensmuseet

Booth Museum of Natural History
194 Dyke Road, Brighton, East Sussex BN1 5AA, UK
Tel. (44) 1273 292777
Mon–Wed, Fri–Sat 10am–5pm, Sun 2–5pm

The particular strengths of the fossil collections are the chalk fossils, especially vertebrates; the Lower Cretaceous fossils, particularly plants, dinosaurs, and insects; and the Pleistocene fossils, including the Ice Age cave fauna mammals. The bulk of the collection originates from Sussex and southeast England, although other parts of the British Isles are represented. There is also material from further afield including Russia, France, and North Africa. Three centuries of scientific endeavour are documented, with the earliest material dating from the 1796 White Watson petrology and mineralogy cabinet, and many others from the 'heroic age' of geology (the first half of the 19th century). Internationally important are the Lower Cretaceous insect fossils which have been collected in Britain more recently (1987- present) by Edward Jarzembowski and Andrew Ross.

Bristol City Museum & Art Gallery
Queen's Road, Bristol BS8 1RL, UK
Tel. (44) 117 9223571   www.bristol-city.gov.uk
Daily 10am–5pm

This collection is among the best and oldest in the British Isles. Approximately half a million geological specimens include minerals, rocks, building and decorative stones, and fossil remains of plants and animals, many from the rich deposits of the surrounding areas including the Mendip Hills and the nearby colliery at Lower Writhlington. There is a large collection of Jurassic invertebrates (especially Sea Dragons), two massive Pliosaurus skulls, the skull of the marine crocodile Metriorhynchus from Wiltshire, the most complete Grendelius skeleton, and an ichthyosaur bearing the earliest stage in the growth of an unborn infant.

Ice crystal(below)
Tampereen Kivimuseo

Spectrolite(middle)
Tampereen Kivimuseo

Fossilised coral (bottom)
Tampereen Kivimuseo

Collection de Minéraux de l'Université Pierre et Marie Curie
The Mineral Collections of the Pierre and Marie Curie University
34 rue Jussieu, 75005 Paris, France
Tel.(33)1 44 27 52 88   www.lmcp.jussieu.fr
Mon, Wed-Sun 1-6pm

Only the best specimens are on display among a collection of 25,000 minerals which rank among the best in the world. They include the most beautiful cumengite crystals known, an exceptional group of kunzite crystals, the stunning tetraedrite crystal found in Ariège, a group of carbonates including the finest reticulate cerusite ever found at Tsumeb, and the world's finest group of rhodochrosite crystals from Tennessee.

Esbjerg Museum – Vestjyllands Ravmuseum
Esbjerg Museum – The Amber Museum of Western Jutland
Torvegade 45, 6700 Esbjerg, Denmark
Tel.(45)75 127811
Sep-May: Mon, Wed-Sun 10am-4pm

A large exhibition on the cultural and natural history of amber, containing several hundred unique amber objects covering 10,000 years.

Franklin Mineral Museum
32 Evans Street, Franklin, New Jersey 07416, USA
Tel.(1) 973 827 3481   www.franklinmineralmuseum.com
Apr-Nov: Mon-Sat 10am-4pm, Sun 11am-4.30pm. Mar: by appt. only

The most comprehensive display of Franklin-Sterling Hill fluorescent minerals in the world, with many of the 88 varieties of fluorescent minerals shown under ultraviolet light. The massive collections number some 7,000 local specimens. The sister deposits of Franklin and nearby Sterling have, to date, revealed 353 mineral species (more than anywhere else on earth). The Jensen Annex displays 5,500 minerals, fossils, and Native American stone tools donated by Mr and Mrs Wilfred R. Welsh. Behind the museum is the Buckwheat Dump, where budding mineralogists can try their hands at finding prize specimens. Last year, three new mineral species were discovered.

Geologisk Museum – Københavns Universitet
The Geological Museum – University of Copenhagen
Øster Voldgade 5-7, 1350 Copenhagen, Denmark
Tel.(45)33 3135001   www.geol.ku.dk
Tue-Sun 1-4pm

This museum houses remarkable collections of vertebrate and invertebrate fossil specimens, meteorites, rocks, and minerals, several dating back to the 17th and 18th centuries. Highlights include the cases of Kongsberg silver; the world's most spectacular examples of cryolite from the mine at Ivigtut; large twinned crystals of pachnolite; octahedral magnetite crystals; and the largest crystals of perovskite ever recorded. The meteorite collection includes the massive Cape York specimens.

Institut royal des Sciences naturelles de Belgique
The Royal Institute of Natural Science of Belgium
29 rue Vautier, 1000 Brussels, Belgium
Tel.(32)2 627 4211   www.sciencesnaturelles.net
Tue-Sat 9.30am-4.45pm, Sun 9.30am-6pm

One of the highlights here is a unique collection of thirty (almost complete) iguanodon skeletons which were discovered in 1878 in a coal mine at Bernissart. Also on display are some beautiful fossil crinoids and mosasaurs, and a representative array of finds from the village of Messel. These include rare discoveries such as the elytra of beetles, flower buds, and the spectacular 'horses', which, unlike the horses of today, were stocky forest dwellers.

A fossilissed ammonite
Tampereen Kivimuseo

Kultamuseo
Gold Prospector Museum
Kultakylä, 99695 Tankavaara, Finland
Tel. (358) 16 626171 www.urova.fi
May-Sep: daily 9am-5pm. Oct-Apr: Mon-Fri 10am-4pm

Situated about 230 km north of the Polar Circle, this museum houses an exhibition on the history of Finnish gold prospecting and on the most well-known prospecting sites of over twenty other countries. Alongside the museum's mineral collection, consisting of 2,600 samples, are artefacts such as prospecting pans, postcards, stamps, and 300 travelling badges. The library and photo archives are extensive.

Luonnontieteellinen keskusmuseo
Finnish Museum of Natural History
Pohjoinen Rautatiekatu 13, Helsinki, Finland
Tel. (358) 9 191 28800 www.fmnh.helsinki.fi
Mon-Fri 9am-5pm, Sat-Sun 11am-4pm

The mineralogy section contains about 45,000 specimens and 35,000 rock and ore samples, while the collections of the Geological Museum hold about 500 meteorites and 6,000 fossils. The Palaeontology Division displays fossils discovered in the Ukraine and Central Europe, as well as large mammoth tusks found in Alaska.

Lyme Regis Philpot Museum
Bridge Street, Lyme Regis, Dorset DT7 3QA, UK
Tel. (44) 1297 443370 www.lymeregismuseum.co.uk
Apr-Oct: daily 10am-5pm (closed Sun noon-2.30pm)

Watercolour of Mary Anning by de la Beche
Lyme Regis Philpot Museum

The geology collection is of international standing, with extensive exhibits of fossils discovered along the coast. Many were found in the early 19th century by Mary Anning (widely regarded as Britain's first female geologist) and her brother Joseph. Shrewd and highly intelligent, Anning made an astounding series of discoveries and is credited with a number of spectacular finds. Besides selling directly to the public, she supplied the fossil collections to museums at Bristol, London, Cambridge, Paris, and even the US. Joining her on collecting forays were a constant stream of professional geologists, from Richard Owen (later head of the Natural History Museum, London) to Henry de la Beche (who founded the Geological Survey of Great Britain in 1835). The museum, built on her birthplace, is a good starting point for those wishing to try their luck along the fossil-rich coastline.

Winding machine no. 1,
Siemens - Schuckert, 1912
Památkovy Ústav v Ostrave-
Dul Michal

Magyar Természettudományi Múzeum
Hungarian Natural History Museum
Department of Mineralogy and Petrology, Ludovika tér 2, 1083 Budapest, Hungary
Tel. (36) 1 3130842 www.nhmus.hu
Please call for opening times

Collections of minerals, precious stones, and fossils from the Carpathians and the
Carpathian Basin. The outstanding collection of Italian ornamental stone gathered by
Victor Emmanuel II (King of Italy 1849-78) comprises 400 brick-shaped pieces. Rarities
include the 'Grandpa' (a large piece of quartz crystal 69cm in height, with a circumference of 122cm, and weighing 133.5kg), a desk-sized amethyst, and a piece of moon rock.

Museo di Mineralogia e Petrografia
The Museum of Mineralogy and Petrography
Università di Bologna, Piazza Porta S. Donato, 40126 Bologna, Italy
Tel. (39) 051 2094926 www.bo.astro.it
Mon-Sat 9am-1pm

Currently houses around 50,000 specimens, with approximately a fifth on display at
any one time. Most remarkable are the collection of meteorites, the Sarti Collection of
ornamental stones, the precious and semiprecious stones, a 230g gold nugget, an array
of fluorescent minerals, and the collections of amber from the Marches, several of which
date back to the Etruscan period.

Mineralogicheskii muzei im. A. E. Fersmana
The Fersman Museum of Mineralogy
Leninskii prospekt 18, 117071 Moscow, Russian Federation
Tel. (7) 095 9520067 www.fmm.ru
Wed-Sun 11am-5pm

This museum's collection consists of some 135,000 items from all over the world,
including natural crystals, geodes, druzes, and other kinds of material treasures, as well
as meteorites and articles made by 18th- to 20th-century jewellers. It includes the
collection of Peter the Great and other tsars, with a magnificent example of wire silver
called the 'Silver Horn', which is about 16cm long and weighs 277kg.

Musée de Minéralogie de l'École des Mines de Paris
Museum of Mineralogy and the Mining Schools of Paris
60 blvd Saint Michel, 75005 Paris, France
Tel. (33) 1 40 51 91 39   www.ensmp.fr
Mon-Fri 9am-6.30pm, Sat 10am-12.30pm, 2-5pm

This museum holds one of the top five best collections in the world, with titanite minerals from Maevatanana and Franklin Furnace's Willemite, as well as recent acquisitions including the fersmite from Kandreho. It was established with the assistance of R. Haüy, 'the father of modern mineralogy and crystallography'.

Museo nacional de Ciencias naturales
The National Museum of Natural Sciences
C. José Gutiérrez Abascal 2, 28006 Madrid, Spain
Tel. (34) 91 5646169   www.mncn.csic.es
Tue-Fri 10am-6pm, Sat 10am-8pm, Sun 10am-2.30pm

The museum's geology collection contains some 14,000 objects, about half of which originated in Spain. Included is a vast range of fluorites, carbonates, sulphates, phosphates, and quartzes, as well as gold and native silver from Europe and the Americas. Obsidians from Italy and Mexico, basalts from the Vesuvius, and a collection of granites from Galicia are also exhibited. Other geology sections include a meteorite collection of some 230 items, and a lapidary collection comprising over 800 items, mainly marbles and agates.

Musée national d'Histoire naturelle – Galeries de Minéralogie et de Géologie
The National Museum of Natural History – the Mineralogy and Geology Galleries
36 rue Geoffroy Saint-Hilaire, 75005 Paris, France
Tel. (33) 1 40 79 30 00   www.mnhn.fr
Apr-Oct: Mon, Wed-Sun 10am-5pm

Housed here are more than 600,000 minerals, including a unique collection of giant crystals such as a rare stalactite quartz in an amethyst quartz 'géode' from Brazil, and a beautiful series of sculpted gems from Louis XIV's collection. One of the collection's highlights is a magnificent cane head in rock crystal, inlaid with diamonds, citrine, and mother-of-pearl, mounted in gold and silver (Germany, 18th century).

Naturhistoriska riksmuseet (Sektionen för mineralogi)
National Museum of Natural History (Department of Mineralogy)
Frescativägen 40, 104 05 Stockholm, Sweden
Tel. (46) 8 51954032   www.nrm.se
Tue-Sun 10am-6pm (Thu until 8pm)

The 'Fahrkunst' lift in the King's Mine (above)
Norsk Bergverksmuseum

The mine train in the Christian VII audit (below)
Norsk Bergverksmuseum

Among the peculiarities is a 25,000kg boulder of native iron, found at Uivfaq on Qertarsuaq (Disko Island) in 1870. There are around 1,000 samples from 300 different meteorites among the 145,000 catalogued specimens, of which about half are from Swedish localities. A cornerstone is the collection of 25,000 minerals from the Långban mines and related satellite occurrences in the Filipstad district, Värmland.

Norsk Bergverksmuseum
The Norwegian Mining Museum
Hyttegata 3, 3602 Kongsberg, Norway
Tel. (47) 32 723200 www.bvm.museum.no
Daily 10am-4pm (times may vary, please call for details)

Legend has it that in 1623 two children were tending their herd of cattle when one of the oxen rubbed its horns against a crag and exposed a vein of silver. What followed is the story of the biggest silver rush the world has ever known. Word spread to the king in Copenhagen, Christian IV, who claimed the silver for the Crown and chose a site for the new mining town, naming it Konningsberg (the king's mountain) in his honour. The mining museum is located on two different premises: the first is the old smeltery in the centre of the town, and the second the mines at Saggrenda (about 8km outside the town centre). The greatest attraction at the museum is the collection of 1,500 specimens of native silver, displayed in rows of twisted silver lumps, from tiny wire specimens to enormous crystals. Included is the famous silver twin crystal standing at 3.5cm tall, which is considered the world's finest crystal of native silver.

Machine drilling (top)
Norsk Bergverksmuseum

Silver miners in the lift at the King's Mine (above)
Norsk Bergverksmuseum

The silver mines at Saggrenda (above right)
Norsk Bergverksmuseum

Norsk Bremuseum
The Norwegian Glacier Museum
6848 Fjærland, Norway
Tel. (47) 57 693288 www.bre.museum.no
Jun-Aug: daily 9am-7pm. Apr-May, Sep, Oct: 10am-4pm
Nov-Mar: by appt only

Entering through a crevasse between flights of stairs, visitors find themselves in a dramatic and imaginative interior, where the mystery of glaciers unfolds through models, films, and interactive exhibits that demonstrate how ice forms and alters the landscape. A visit to the museum will answer such questions as why ice appears blue, how melted water from glaciers is harnessed to produce hydropower, and how glaciers play an important role in climatic studies.

Exterior of the museum (right)
Norsk Bremuseum

Interior of the museum (below)
Norsk Bremuseum

Hermann Ottó Múzeum Ásványtára
Ottó Herman Museum Mineral Collection
Kossuth utca 13, 3525 Miskolc, Hungary
Tel. (36) 46 560178
Tue-Sun 10am-6pm

The mineral collections consist of 15,850 items, making it the largest in the country. Some of the collections date back to the 19th and beginning of the 20th centuries. Among the most spectacular specimens are native copper, cuprite, malachite, and azurite from Rudabánya; galena, sphalerite, and wurtzite from Gyöngyösoroszi; whewellite from Recsk; and calcite from Tornaszentandrás.

Oxford University Museum of Natural History
Parks Road, Oxford, Oxfordshire OX1 3PW, UK
Tel. (44) 1865 272950 www.oum.ox.ac.uk
Daily noon–5pm

Highlights include the most complete remains anywhere of a single dodo, as well as a marvellous skeleton of an Iguanodon. At the core of the geological collections, which are of national and international significance (500,000 specimens), are those of William Buckland (1784-1856), Professor of Geology at Oxford. A notable dinosaur hunter, he was the first to name and scientifically describe the Megalosaurus (in 1824). Besides the Jurassic vertebrates, the Lias fishes described by Louis Agassiz are well worth seeing, as are the Cretaceous invertebrates from Africa and North America (the largest, most important collections outside those continents). The mineral collections are outstanding, comprising 30,000 specimens, many originating from fine 19th-century collections.

The mine train entering the Christian VII audit
Norsk Bergverksmuseum

George C. Page Museum & Rancho La Brea Tar Pits
5801 Wilshire Boulevard, Los Angeles, California 90036, USA
Tel. (1) 323 934 7243 www.tarpits.org
Park: all year round (pit 91 in progress during summer). Museum: Tue-Sun 10am-5pm

In the La Brea tar pits, hot tar has been bubbling from the earth for more than 40,000 years. It enticed animals during the Pleistocene era, capturing now-extinct animals such as the ancient bison, giant sloth, and sabre-toothed cats. Since 1908, more than one million bones, representing over 231 species of vertebrates, 159 kinds of plants, and 234 species of invertebrates, have been recovered. In the museum, holography transforms into flesh and blood the skeletons of a sabre-tooth cat and the 9,000 year-old La Brea Woman, while robotics move reconstructed skeletons. A fifteen-minute film documenting the finds runs continuously, providing a wonderful introduction to the site.

Paleontologicheskii institut rossiiskoi akademii nauk
Paleontological Institute of the Russian Academy of Sciences
Profsoyuznaya ulitsa, 123, 117868 Moscow, Russian Federation
Tel. (7) 095 339 0577 www.paleo.ru
Please call for opening times

Massive collections amassed from all over the former Soviet Union and the world. The exhibits are particularly rich in Mongolian dinosaurs, synapsids from the Perm region of Russia, and Precambrian fossils from Siberia.

Museo paleontologico e geologico G. Capellini
The G. Capellini Museum of Palaeontology and Geology
Università di Bologna, via Zamboni 63, 40126 Bologna, Italy
Tel. (39) 051 2094555
Mon-Fri 9am-12.30pm

Considered to be the biggest palaeontological museum in Italy, both for its size and for the number and importance of the collections. Among the most impressive is a perfectly preserved example of the ichtyosaurus quadriscissus, along with the colossal model of the diplodocus dinosaur from the Jurassic period, measuring 26 metres in length.

Model of the magnolia
flower (top)
*Botanischer Garten und
Botanisches Museum Berlin*

Pride of California flower
(above)
*The Botanical Museum-
Harvard Museum of Natural
History*

Památkovy Ústav V Ostrave- Dul Michal
Institute for National Heritage in Ostrava- The Michal Mine
Korejská 12, 70200 Ostrava, Czech Republic
Tel. (420) 69 6133481
Please call for opening times

One of the most beautiful and best preserved mines, located in Ostrava, north Moravia.
The exhibits of mining machinery include a unique collection of electric winding
machines and compressors from the very beginnings of electrification.

Patterson Museum
2 Market Street, Patterson, New Jersey 07501, USA
Tel. (1) 973 881 3874
Tue-Fri 10am-4 pm, Sat-Sun 12.30-4.30pm

Two major basaltic lava flows exist in the world: one is on the Deccan Plateau in India
and the other lies adjacent to Patterson in the three Watchung Ridges. When the lava
came into contact with swamps and pools of water, it cooled rapidly, forming large
round masses of rock around which beautiful crystalline minerals formed, such as
prehnite. Besides exhibits of crystals from these deposits, there are many high-quality
gems and minerals from around the world.

Peabody Museum of Natural History
Yale University, 170 Whitney Avenue, New Haven, Connecticut 06520-8118, USA
Tel. (1) 203 432 3750   www.peabody.yale.edu
Mon-Sat 10am-5pm, Sun noon-5pm

A tremendous collection of dinosaur fossils, including one of the best brontosaurus
skeletons outside the Smithsonian, amassed mainly through the efforts of the great
American dinosaur hunters of the 19th century. A collection that spans the world, it comprises over 55,000 catalogued specimens, as well as Princeton University's fossil vertebrate collection, numbering 15,000 catalogued specimens.

The Sedgwick Museum of Earth Sciences
Downing Street, Cambridge, Cambridgeshire CB2 3EQ, UK
Tel. (44) 1223 333456   www.sedgwick.esc.cam.ac.uk
Mon-Fri, 9am-1pm, 2pm-5pm, Sat 10am-1pm

Over one million specimens including fossils, minerals, sort sediments, and building
and decorative stones. These range from the earliest life forms (over 3,000 million years
old) to giant marine reptiles and a hippopotamus from a nearby gravel pit (a mere
125,000 years old). The original core collection came from the notable fossil collector,
John Woodward (1665-1728), who, unlike his contemporaries, set about building a comprehensive 'scientific' collection of mainly fossils, rocks, and minerals. Carefully
documented and used by him to establish pioneering classification systems, they
included around 9,400 specimens that are still displayed in their original walnut cabinets.

Tampereen Kivimuseo
The Tampere Mineral Museum
Hämeenpuisto 20, 33211 Tampere, Finland
Tel. (358) 3 2196046   www.tampere.fi
Tue-Fri 9am-5pm, Sat-Sun 10am-6pm

The collection contains some 4,000 objects from 64 countries, including some Russian
rarities and Finnish rocks, ballstones, and spectrolites. There are gemstones in cut and
rough form, minerals, ores, metals, and decorative stones, as well as meteorites.

Teylers Museum
The Teylers Museum
Spaarne 16, 2011 CH Haarlem, The Netherlands
Tel. (31) 23 531 9010 www.teylersmuseum.nl
Tue-Sat 10am-5pm, Sun noon-5pm

The geological collections consist of tens of thousands of specimens, many bought in
the 18th century before palaeontology and mineralogy were well-defined sciences.
There is an important collection of Cretaceous fossils, including the jawbones of a
mosasaurus found in 1766, the first of its kind to be discovered. More than 12,000 minerals are displayed in their original cases, lined with black velvet, in the Oval Room.
This is the oldest part of the museum, originally commissioned as an arts and book
room where the public would have watched scientific demonstrations. There is also a
fine collection of 18th- and 19th-century literature on botany, zoology, and geology.

PLANT MODELS AND RELATED COLLECTIONS

Bibliothèque centrale du Musée national d'histoire naturelle
Central Library of the National Museum of Natural History
38 rue Geoffroy Saint-Hilaire, 75005 Paris, France
Tel. (33) 1 40 79 36 27 www.mnhn.fr
Mon-Fri 9.30am-7pm, Sat 9.30am-5.30pm

Gaston d'Orléans founded this stunning collection in 1630, with the idea of decorating
his cabinet with representations of plants and birds from the gardens and aviary of his
chateau at Blois. After his death the collection was handed over to Louis XIV (d'Orléan's
nephew) and assimilated into the Royal Gardens Collection. The museum houses a
huge collection of herbaria, with more than eight million items, including the priceless
collections of Jean-Baptiste Lamarck and Sébastien Vaillant. It also includes spectacular
examples of 7,000 *vélins* or vellums (watercolours of botanical and animal specimens
painted on stillborn veal skin) by Nicolas Robert, Claude Aubriet, the Belgian painter
Pierre-Joseph Redouté, and his student Marie-Firmin Bocourt.

The Botanical Museum – Harvard Museum of Natural History
26 Oxford Street, Cambridge, Massachusetts 02138, USA
Tel. (1) 617 495 3045 www.hmnh.harvard.edu
Mon-Sat 9am-5pm, Sun 1-5pm

Seed specimen(below)
Millennium Seed Bank

Wakehurst Place(bottom)
Millennium Seed Bank

Commissioned for teaching purposes by the first director of the museum, George Goodale, is a remarkable collection of life-size glass flowers, plants, and fruits. Produced from 1887 to 1936 by glass blowers, Leopold Blaschka and his son Rudolf, in Dresden, the collection is popularly known as 'the Glass Flowers' and is the only one of its type in the world. The 3,000 life-size replicas represent over 840 plant species, mostly from the North Temperate region, and are incredibly precise renderings of real plants, accurate to the most minute detail.

Botanischer Garten und Botanisches Museum Berlin
Botanic Garden and the Botanic Museum-Berlin

Tropical Pavilion
Botanischer Garten und
Botanisches Museum Berlin

Man collecting seeds
Millennium Seed Bank

Königin-Luise-Strasse 6-8, 14195 Berlin, Germany
Tel. (49) 30 83850191 www.bgbm.fu-berlin.de
Daily 10am-6pm

The exceptional herbarium of three million specimens, one of the best in the world, has flowering and spore plants, large dried fruits, seeds, cones, wood samples, wet (spirit) collections, and microscope slides of specimens and small items. A unique collection of models from fossilized plants to more recent plant life, highlights the morphological details of flowers, fruits, seeds, algae, and other cryptogams. The vast life-size models of toadstools and mushrooms are exceptional. There is also a library with precious, rare books collected over five centuries.

Musée de l'Ecorché d'Anatomie
Museum of Anatomical Sections
Espace Culturel, 54, Avenue de la Libération, 27110 Le Neubourg, France
Tel. (33) 2 32 35 93 95
Wed-Sun 2-6pm (Wed 10am-noon in Aug, closed Jan)

Doctor Louis Auzoux (1797-1880) made his name by constructing flexible, easy to study anatomical models for doctors and teaching institutions in Europe and the US. Following this success, his models of fauna and flora were soon in demand. Although the collection contains many more of his medical models, it also displays a small group of botanical ones, including models of medicinal plants that were probably used for teaching medical students about plant structure and their use in developing remedies. He produced great bouquets of flowers, fruits, and seeds many times larger than their originals. These could be taken apart to show their internal structures and, like his anatomical models, were labelled with their French and Latin names.

Magyar Természettudományi Múzeum
Hungarian Natural History Museum
Department of Biology, Könyves Kálmán körút 40, 1087 Budapest, Hungary
Tel. (36) 1 2101330 www.nhmus.hu
Please call for opening times

Several important collections from the 18th and 19th centuries consist primarily of flowering plants from all four corners of the world. Mygind's herbarium, containing 3,345 sheets, is the oldest part. Subsequent donations have made this one of the largest collections in Europe. A notable acquisition was Archbishop Lajos Haynald's herbarium of 100,000 sheets in 1892. Besides possessing one of the largest private herbaria in Europe, he actively sought plants and engaged in exchanging and purchasing them all over the world. Miraculously, the collections survived World War I, and grew with further additions of herbaria, seeds, and a collection of wax models of fungi.

Millennium Seed Bank

Royal Botanic Gardens Kew, Wakehurst Place, Ardingly, West Sussex RH17 6TN, UK
Tel. (44) 1444 894066   www.rbgkew.org.uk
Apr-Sep: daily 10am-6.30pm (times may vary, please call for details)

This unique conservation achievement by the Royal Botanic Gardens, Kew, stores the seeds of all 1,442 wild plants, flowers, and trees regarded as properly native to Britain, making it the first country in the world to hold its entire seed-bearing flora in a bank. It aims to carry on collecting seeds of the world's wild plants, concentrating on those that face extinction. Visitors can watch scientists at work in the seed preparation areas and see their microscopic views on monitors in the public display area.

Royal Botanic Gardens

Kew, Richmond, Surrey TW9 3AB, UK
Tel. (44) 20 8332 5000   www.rbgkew.org.uk
The herbarium by appt. only

The gardens comprise follies, carpets of flowers, glasshouses brimming with exotic plants, and a first-rate scientific institution containing the largest collection of historical plant specimens from all regions of the world. There are seven million reference specimens, with 250,000 type specimens, some dating back to the 18th century. Many are the personal herbaria of some of Britain's most celebrated scientists, including Charles Darwin, Joseph Hooker, David Livingstone, John Hanning Speke, and Miles Joseph Berkeley. The Economic Botany Collections display original samples of materials from the beginning of their trials for commercial and industrial production, with thousands of bottles of perfume oils, and a wood collection containing 32,000 samples. There are also extraordinarily colourful floor-to-ceiling paintings depicting exotic fruit and flowers, by the Victorian artist Marianne North.

Floor-to-ceiling display of paintings depicting exotic fruit and flowers by the Victorian artist, Marianne North (top)
Royal Botanic Gardens

Painting by Marianne North (above)
Royal Botanic Gardens

Chicoreus maurus, Durban Bay (Falcon) (below)
National Museum & Gallery

SHELLS

Bailey-Matthews Shell Museum

3075 Sanibel-Captiva Road, Sanibel, Florida 33957, USA
Tel. (1) 941 395 2233   www.shellmuseum.org
Tue-Sun 10am-4pm

This is shell heaven both inside and out, for on the shores of Sanibel and Captiva Islands you can start your own collection with shells washed up from the sea. Fossil shell deposits dating back over twenty million years are on display. For children, there is a live shell tank and the Learning Lab. The museum contains a collection of worldwide and local molluscs, encompassing over 200,000 specimens, with a growing focus on molluscs from the coast of southwest Florida, its barrier islands, and the Gulf of Mexico.

Bernice Pauahi Bishop Museum

1525 Bernice Street, Honolulu, Hawaii 96817-2704, USA
Tel. (1) 808 847 3511   www.bishopmuseum.org
Daily 9am-5pm

A first-rate scientific establishment, with six million specimens from all over the Pacific. This is an irreplaceable resource which contains now-extinct terrestrial molluscs from Hawaii and the Pacific area.

Delaware Museum of Natural History
4840 Kennett Pike, Wilmington, Delaware 19807-0937, USA
Tel. (1) 302 658 9111 www.delmnh.org
Mon-Sat 9.30am-4.30pm, Sun noon-4.30pm

A collection now numbering over two million mollusc specimens, representing more than 17,000 species. It has worldwide scope and covers all seven living classes of molluscs, mostly as dry shells. The core of the collection was amassed by John E. du Pont, an avid amateur shell collector whose wealth and travels to exotic locations, in particular the Philippines, allowed him to collect many rare and unusual specimens. He specialized in collecting volutes, and sponsored an expedition for the rare *Cymbiolacca perplicata*.

Musée Henri Dupuis
The Henri Dupuis Museum
9 rue Henri Dupuis, 62500 St Omer, France
Tel. (33) 3 21 38 24 13
Daily 10am-noon, 2-6pm

Henri Dupuis was both an insatiable traveller and a lover of the natural world. A myriad of stuffed birds collected from all over the world is displayed on the ground floor of his 18th-century home. In the second-floor conchology department there are over 20,000 labelled shells packed in cases and displayed on the walls. This is one of the richest collections of its kind in France.

The Glanford Shell Museum
Glandford, Holt, Norfolk NR25 7JR, UK
Tel. (44) 1263 740081
Feb-Nov: Tue-Sat 10am-12.30pm, 2-4.30pm (times may vary, please call for details)

Specially made whitewashed display cases show off Sir Alfred Jodrell's shell collection in this utterly delightful museum. It consists of just one room decorated with shells which form mirror surrounds and borders. The building still has no electricity, but these natural wonders jumbled together with decorated ostrich eggs, skulls of birds, and sharks' jaws are best seen in natural light.

Interior of the museum
Muséum d'Histoire naturelle

Muséum d'Histoire naturelle
The Museum of Natural History
28 rue Albert 1er, 17000 La Rochelle, France
Tel. (33) 5 46 41 18 25
Tue-Fri 10am-noon, 1.30-5.30pm (mid Jun-mid Sep until 6pm), Sat-Sun 2-6pm

La Rochelle was a hotbed of natural history enthusiasts, greeting the ships returning from far away lands laden with exotica. Assembled here are the natural history collections of the town, as well as a cabinet of curiosities amassed by Clément de Lafaille in the middle of the 18th century. His rare and splendid collection of 2,128 shells from all over the world is displayed on the ground floor, in beautiful purpose-built wooden tables and chests, mixed with other wondrous objects.

Institut royal des Sciences naturelles de Belgique
The Royal Institute of Natural Science of Belgium
29 rue Vautier, 1000 Brussels, Belgium
Tel. (32) 2 627 4211 www.sciencesnaturelles.net
Tue-Sat 9.30am-4.45pm, Sun 9.30am-6pm

Undoubtedly one of the major world malacological collections, with an estimated nine million specimens subdivided, for historical reasons, into what is known as the general collection and the important Dautzenberg collection. In 1929, Philippe Dautzenberg bequeathed to the museum his shell collection, containing some 38,600 species, and his exceptional library. He spent years purchasing items from renowned malacologists, and through his own explorations in France, where he was born. The collection is of great interest because of its rare specimens and the great diversity of species.

Leeds Museum and Art Galleries
Leeds Museum Resource Centre, Moorfield Road, Yeadon, Leeds LS19 7BN, UK
Tel. (44) 113 2146526 www.leeds.gov.uk
Mon-Thu 10am-4pm, Fri 10am-3pm (by appt. only)

Since its foundation in 1819, over 150 sources have contributed to what is now the third largest shell collection in the UK. The largest and most important collection came from Sylvanus Charles Thorpe Hanley, the first person to publish a book on shells using the then new technique of photography (*Photographia Conchology*, 1863). His collection arrived in thirteen cabinets, containing 206 drawers, and like many collections of its day was built up by swapping with major naturalists of the period or by purchasing collections at sales. The Conchological Society of Great Britain and Ireland was founded in Leeds, and this affiliation has benefited the museum enormously. It has added material collected by the survey ship HMS *Porcupine* in 1869, as well as over 100 type specimens and a collection of tropical land snails built up over five generations, starting with specimens collected in Palestine in 1858. There is also an extensive collection of spirited material, including thousands of slugs from all over the world, collected by Senior Curator, Adrian Norris.

Scallop shells
Bailey-Matthews Shell Museum

Children's Learning Lab
Bailey-Matthews Shell Museum

Museo Malacologico
Malacology Museum
Via delle Pinete, 91016 Erice, Italy
Tel. (39) 092 3566312
Please call for opening times

Located in this hilltop town, with stunning views of the coastline, is this small, but very active museum. The collections contain shells from all over the world, with the emphasis on Mediterranean material.

Museo di Malacologia Terrestre
Terrestrial Malacology Museum
Via del Duomo 47, 58010 Sovana, Italy
Tel. (39) 05 646 16582 www.stonet.com
Mon-Fri 9.30am-6.30pm

A unique collection of over 90,000 shells belonging to specimens of terrestrial molluscs from tropical forests, rivers, lakes, swamps, arid areas, and woody areas around the world. Examples from the collection – including rare molluscs, extinct specimens and fossilized items – are arranged geographically with information on their habitats. Delightful exhibits in large aquariums include some giant African snails and other living species.

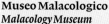

Museo nacional de Ciencias naturales
The National Museum of Natural Sciences
C. José Gutiérrez Abascal 2, 28006 Madrid, Spain
Tel. (34) 91 4111328 www.mncn.csic.es
Tue-Fri 10am-6pm, Sat 10am-8pm, Sun &
public holidays 10am-2.30pm

Shell collection (above)
Muséum d'Histoire naturelle

Siphonaria anneae
specimen with original
label written by Tomlin
(below)
National Museum & Gallery

Carlos III of Spain left a royal cabinet packed with molluscs, insects, birds, and mammals to begin this collection, which now comprises a million mollusc specimens, preserved dry in fluids and as microscope preparations. The collection includes around 2,944 type specimens of 461 taxa from West Africa, the Caribbean, the Mediterranean, the Philippines, and Antarctica.

National Museum & Gallery
Cathays Park, Cardiff, Wales CF10 3NP, UK
Tel. (44) 292 0397951 www.nmgw.ac.uk
Tue-Sun 10am-5pm

At the core of this vast, high-quality conchology collection is the Melvill-Tomlin material, which contains specimens from over 900 collectors and is well documented with letters from conchologists, shell sale catalogues, and numerous annotations. It is the second best collection of molluscs in the UK, numbering some 400,000 lots. The collections continue to grow through NMGW field surveys, both locally and overseas, and from donations by universities, government agencies, and active shell collectors. The staff encourage visitors to use this vast scientific resource, which includes the massive Melvill-Tomlin library.

Wood End Museum of Natural History
The Crescent, Scarborough, North Yorkshire YO11 2PW, UK
Tel. (44) 1723 367326
Tue-Sun 10am-5pm

The mollusc collection contains a remarkable array of approximately 36,000 specimens, representing around 4,000 species, but the nomenclature has not been updated since the 1960s. Further research is required, but so far ten types of figured and cited specimens have been confirmed. Primarily amassed by one man, William Bean II (1787-1866), a local conchologist and geologist, it also includes material presented by other 19th- and early 20th-century collectors.

Zoologisk Museum
Zoological Museum
University of Copenhagen, Universitetsparken 15, 2100
Copenhagen, Denmark
Tel. (45) 35 321001 www.zmuc.dk
Tue-Sun 11am-5pm

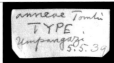

This collection of molluscs is tipped as one of the more important of the large, old collections in Europe. Highlights include the Forsskål 'fish herbarium', containing numerous specimens of molluscs and corals; Lorenz Spengler's famous shell collection; King Christian VIII's magnificent shell cabinet with many of J. H. Chemnitz's types; collections made in Greenland by Otto Fabricius; and, via Fabricius, some remains of O. F. Müller's collections. Further amalgamations and acquisitions have placed this collection in the top ten worldwide.

ADVERTISING AND PACKAGING WARES

Sardine can by Auto,
c. 1915
Norsk Hermetikkmuseum

The Museum of Advertising and Packaging
Albert Warehouse, Gloucester Docks, Gloucester, Gloucestershire GL1 2EH, UK
Tel. (44) 1452 302309 www.themuseum.co.uk
Recently closed, but hoping to re-open if a new home can be found.

Amassed by the packaging and advertising guru, Robert Opie, this huge and fascinating collection of items ranges from enamel signs, packing, and posters to early commercials, and traces the history of ordinary household products from 1880 to the present.

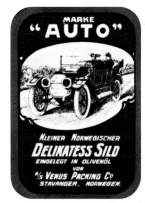

The Museum of Beverage Containers and Advertising
1055 Ridgecrest Drive, Millersville, Tennessee 37072, USA
Tel. (1) 615 859 5236 www.gono.com
Mon-Fri 9am-5pm

Begun by father and son Paul and Tom Bates, this vast collection includes 36,000 beer and soda cans, 9,000 bottles, and other promotional and advertising items such as soda bottle caps, glasses, tray, and match covers – in total more than a quarter of a million items. Coveted trophies include James Bond's 007 Special Blend premium beer cans, camouflaged beer cans sent to US troops during World War II, and rare examples of Coca-Cola and 7-Up bottles.

British Cycling Museum
The Old Station, Camelford, Cornwall PL32 9TZ, UK
Tel. (44) 1840 212811
Mon-Thu, Sun 10am-5pm

As well as masses of antique cycles, the collection includes around 400 enamel signs and posters advertising famous bike manufacturers such as Raleigh, Mohawk, Michelin, Robin Hood, and Swiss Cycles.

Il Museo della Figurina
The Picture Card Museum
Via Scaglia, 941100 Modena, Italy
Tel. (39) 059 344133 www.comune.modena.it
Tue-Thu 3-7.30pm

Over 750,000 picture cards from around the world, based around a core collection of 50,000 picture cards produced by the Liebig meat factory from 1873 to 1975. Others were produced by companies such as Nestlé, Suchard, Van Houten, Kemmeric, and Maggi, and come mostly from France, Germany, Britain, Italy, and Switzerland; Russia, China, and the Americas are also well represented. Fine examples include a mint collection of 240 cigarette cards showing German uniforms, produced by Sturm-Zigaretten in Dresden in 1933.

Museo Fisogni
The Fisogni Museum
Palazzolo Milanese, via Tirano 14, 20030 Milan, Italy
Tel. (39) 029 90013306 www.museo-fisogni.org
Mon-Fri by appt.

Alongside a unique collection of petrol pumps, Guido Fisogni's museum houses a vast collection of packaging and advertising material relating to the golden age of the motor car. Mobiloil, Michelin, Pirelli, Castrol, and Essolube are all excellently represented, and the collection also encompasses oil cans and pumps, metal badges, posters, and 'free' gifts such as lighters, key rings, pocket knives, and flasks.

Henry Ford Museum and Greenfield Village
20900 Oakwood Boulevard, Dearborn, Michigan 48124-4088, USA
Tel. (1) 313 271 1620 www.hfmgv.org
Daily 9am-5pm

A comprehensive chronicle of the early automobile and its marketing, with
product literature, advertising, and promotional material from virtually every US
automobile manufacturer, and selected foreign manufacturers too. The section dedicated to motion pictures includes original Ford advertising films from the 1950s, intro-
ducing some of the great classics such as the Edsel and Thunderbird.

Prince Olav sardine can,
1905
Norsk Hermetikkmuseum

Het emaillebordenarchief
Enamel Advertising Art
Boetiek 'T Winkeltje, Galerij 23, 5401 GC Uden, The Netherlands
Tel. (31) 6 53659365 (10.00-17.00) www.emaillebordenarchief.nl
Mon-Thu, Sun 9.30am-5pm, Fri 9.30am-8pm, Sat 9.30am-4pm

Jack Boelens' collection of enamel signs began as decoration for his jeans boutique in
Uden. Now covering every spare inch of wall and ceiling space, the collection has grown
into one of the best and largest in Europe, and includes examples of 1900-1960 enamel
signs from all over the world.

National Museum of American History
14th Street and Constitution Avenue, N.W., Smithsonian Institution, Washington, DC
20560, USA
Tel. (1) 202 357 2700 www.americanhistory.si.edu
Daily 10am-3.30pm

This massive holding contains advertising and marketing material from a vast spectrum
of well-known US products. The Warshaw Collection of Business Americana comprises a
particularly fine collection of advertising cards, posters, labels, letterheads, trade catalogues, and other ephemera covering the period 1840 - 1900.

Museo Nazionale delle Arti e Tradizioni Popolari
The National Museum of Popular Art and Traditions
Piazza Marconi, 8/10, 00144 Rome, Italy
Tel. (39) 06 5926148 www.popolari.arti.benicultari.it
Mon-Sat 9am-2pm, Sun 9am-1pm

Alongside traditional clothing, musical instruments, puppets, and agricultural objects
is a special section dedicated to advertising and signs produced by craftworkers, shop-
keepers, and professionals (including doctors and lawyers). The collection includes over
100 signs, often of oversized tools or goods, as well as portable work counters set up by
itinerant salesmen as they passed through villages across the countryside.

Sardine cans by Dom or
Chr. Bjelland & Co.
Norsk Hermetikkmuseum

Norsk Hermetikkmuseum
The Norwegian Canning Museum
Øvre Strandgate 88A, 4010 Stavanger, Norway
Tel. (47) 51 534989 www.stavanger.museum.no
Please call for opening times

As well as cataloguing the history of sardine production in Norway from 1873 onwards, the museum has an
important collection of over 30,000 sardine labels,
posters, and packaging, including the well-known
image of a bearded fisherman in a yellow sou'wester,

with a pipe dangling from his mouth. During the early part of the 20th century – the heyday of the sardine canning industry – collecting sardine labels became a popular pastime with children and adults, who swapped and traded them.

Peabody Essex Museum
East India Square, Salem, Massachusetts 01970, USA
Tel. (1) 978 745 9500 www.pem.org
Apr-Oct: Mon-Sat 10am-5pm, Sun noon-5pm
Nov-Mar: Tue-Sat 10am-5pm, Sun noon-5pm

The museum's fascinating collection of over 250 Japanese shop signs was amassed at the curatorial aegis of museum director, Edward S. Morse, who first saw them on a visit to Japan in 1877. Examples on display include giant-sized pipes and tortoise shells, fans, spectacles, and vegetables. Some promote a single product – for example, a red demon holding a club, for stomach medicine, and jars of tea leaves or evocative landscapes, for tea suppliers.

Masseur Giving Therapy, watercolour advertisement by Watanabe Bunzo, *c.* 1880
Peabody Essex Museum

Musée de la Publicité
The Museum of Advertising
107 rue de Rivoli, 75001 Paris, France
Tel. (33) 1 44 55 57 50 www.ucad.fr
Tue-Fri 11am-6pm (Wed until 9pm), Sat-Sun 10am-6pm

The origins and history of advertising are comprehensively documented with a collection of nearly 100,000 French and foreign posters dating from the mid 18th century to the present, and some 20,000 contemporary cinema, radio, and TV commercials. The poster collection is particularly rich and includes a special section devoted to Jules Chéret, the poster pioneer who developed the rapid-colour printing process to print numerous posters at one time. The museum also includes work from the golden age of French poster design, especially those produced by Mucha, Grandville, Raffet, Johannot, Gavarni, and Dore, as well as artists influenced by Chéret, such as Bonnard and Lautrec.

Shelburne Museum
US Route 7, Shelburne, Vermont 05482, USA
Tel. (1) 802 985 3346 www.shelburnemuseum.org
May-Oct: daily 10am-5pm (walking tours rest of the year at 1pm)

Though some craftspeople made their own signs, most 19th-century trade signs were the work of professional sign painters working on wood, iron, or zinc. The museum's entrance hall and a downstairs room have a rich assortment of trade signs, from flat wooden inn signs to oversized locksmiths' keys, opticians' eyeglasses, and skatemakers' skates.

John Springer Collection of Printing and Advertising
Materials Special Collections Department, University of Iowa Libraries, Iowa City, Iowa 52242-1420, USA
Tel. (1) 319 335 5921 www.lib.uiowa.edu
Mon-Thu 8.30am-5.30pm, Fri 8.30am-5pm (Other days by appt.)

John Springer was born in Pennsylvania in 1850, and brought up in Iowa. He worked as a printer's devil for the *State Press* newspaper, becoming its co-owner and editor after its sale at the turn of the century. In the years that followed, he became an avid collector of typographic specimens, advertising or trade cards, merchandising catalogues, calendars, and other ephemera related to printing and advertising. Springer presented his collection to the Iowa Libraries in 1936. Choice examples in the collection include a mechanical trade card with a pop-up hog depicting various products, and some classic posters for Pears' Soap.

The Strong Museum
One Manhattan Square, Rochester, New York 14607, USA
Tel. (1) 716 263 2700   www.strongmuseum.org
Mon-Sat 10am-5pm (Fri until 8pm), Sun noon-5pm

American advertising history from 1840 to the present day is represented
here by 18,000 postcards, 15,000 trade cards, 20,000 advertising signs,
premiums, packages (from toys and microwaves to patent medicine and
food), and thousands of other objects and ephemera.

Museu de la Taronja
The Citrus Museum
Carrer Major, 1012530 Borriana,
Spain
Tel. (34) 964 515415   www.ctv.es
Tue-Sat 10am-1pm, 4-8pm,
Sun 10am-2pm

Surrounded by orange groves,
this museum provides a unique insight into
the Valencian and Spanish citrus fruit trade.
The highlight is a display of over 6,000
beautifully designed brand labels, alongside
19th- and 20th-century trademarks printed
on silk papers used for wrapping individual
oranges.

Export label, 1930s (top)
Museo de la Taronja

Export label, 1920s
(above)
Museo de la Taronja

Export label, 1930s (left)
Museo de la Taronja

The World of Coca-Cola Pavilion
55 Martin Luther King Jr. Dr., Atlanta, Georgia 30303-3505, USA
Tel. (1) 404 676 5151
By appointment only

This shrine to Coke houses an exhibition of advertising from past decades, demonstrations of bottling techniques, and a room for sampling the self-styled 'most successful
product in the history of commerce'.

BOTTLES (INCLUDING CHINESE SNUFF BOTTLES)

The Chester Beatty Library
Dublin Castle, Dublin 2, Ireland
Tel. (353) 1 4070750   www.cbl.ie
May-Sep: Mon-Fri 10am-5pm, Sat 11am-5pm, Sun 1-5pm
Oct-Apr: Tue-Fri 10am-5pm

The mining engineer, Sir Alfred Chester Beatty, collected finely worked art works
carved from semiprecious minerals and innumerable mineral specimens. Along with
Chinese jade books carved by the imperial workshops in the 18th century, Beatty also
amassed a comprehensive collection of over 900 Chinese snuff bottles, many made of
jade and amber or of painted porcelain and ivory. (Only thirty are displayed from the
revolving collection at any one time.)

Lapis Lazuli snuff bottle
decorated with a floral
design in low relief
The Chester Beatty Library

Bottle Cap Museum
4977 Sparr Road, Gaylord, Michigan 49735, USA
Tel. (1) 517 732 1931
Wed-Sat 11am-5pm

This wall-to-ceiling private collection of 4,000 Coca-Cola bottles, tops, and advertising paraphernalia was started after Bill Hicks found a stash of Coke bottles in his hunting cabin. The museum also has a Christmas room filled with Santas and tree ornaments, paying homage to the Swedish artist, Haddon Sundbolm, who created the red and white suited persona of Santa for a 1931 Christmas Coca-Cola advertisement.

Burghley House
Stamford, Lincolnshire PE9 3JY, UK
Tel. (44) 1780 752451 www.stamford.co.uk
Apr-Oct: daily 11am-4.30pm

The visually stunning Chinese and Japanese wares collection includes some 400 snuff bottles, bought by the late sixth Marquess of Exeter from a Welsh missionary doctor stationed in China from 1900 to 1939. Though the collection is personal rather than definitive, it includes eight ivory bottles made in the Beijing Palace workshops in the late 18th century (out of thirty recorded world wide).

Embossed clear bottles, 1930s-50s (above)
Steve Wheeler's Milk Bottle Museum

Beer bottles from the 1930s and 40s (below)
Kansainvälinen Pullomuseo

Wine bottle, c. 1800 (below right)
Kansainvälinen Pullomuseo

The Corning Museum of Glass
One Museum Way, Corning, New York 14830, USA
Tel. (1) 607 974 8274 www.cmog.org
Daily 9am-5pm (Jul-Aug 9am-8pm)

This gigantic museum houses the largest collection of American flasks in the world (660 examples, each from a different mould), and 100 Chinese snuff bottles. The research library has nearly 100,000 books, periodicals, and trade catalogues on glass, as well as advertising ephemera, historical documents, fine art prints, glass batch (recipe) books, and archival materials.

Museum of Fine Arts
465 Huntington Avenue, Boston, Massachusetts 02115-5519, USA
Tel. (1) 617 267 9300 www.mfa.org
Mon, Tue 10am-4.45pm, Wed-Fri 10am-9.45pm (West Wing: Thu, Fri after 5pm only), Sat-Sun 10am-5.45pm

The Chinese collections house a display of Chinese snuff bottles donated by William Sturgis Bigelow and Frederick Jack. Choice examples in the collection include amber snuff bottles with malachite or turquoise stoppers, and an early 19th-century porcelain snuff bottle overglazed with an enamel decoration depicting a cricket match.

Kansainvälinen Pullomuseo
International Bottle Museum
74300 Sonkajärvi, Finland
Tel. (358) 17 761470
Jun-Aug: Tue-Sun 10am-6pm (groups by appt.)

A professor of physiology at the University of Kuopio, Osmo Hänninen started gathering this vast collection of bottles after stumbling on a cache of rare bottles in a remote croft in Paisua village, Sonkajärvi, in the 1970s. Now housed in a former dance house in Oinasjärvi, this exquisite museum displays a huge variety of Finnish bottles, and also has some exceptionally rare examples from further afield, including a 1600 year-old Syrian tear bottle (used to collect tears after the death of a close relative).

The National Bottle Collection

Elsecar Heritage Centre, Elsecar Watch Road, Elsecar, Barnsley,
North Yorkshire S74 8HJ, UK
Tel. (44) 1226 745156
Please call for opening times

This British collection focuses especially on pot lids – prize exhibits include the world's largest pot lid (advertising Gosnell's Cherry Toothpaste), miniature tradesman's samples by Daulton Pottery, and hundreds of coloured pottery lids by F. & R. Pratt of Fenton.

National Bottle Museum

76 Milton Avenue, Ballston Spa, New York 12020, USA
Tel. (1) 518 885 7589   www.family.knick.net
Summer: daily 10am-4pm. Winter: Mon-Fri 10am-4pm

By the mid 19th century there were forty glasshouses in New York State alone, making millions of bottles from blown and moulded glass. This collection recreates a glass factory from the era, complete with furnace, original tools, a miniature model of an early glassworks, and an impressive collection of 2,000 bottles dating back two centuries.

Selection of bottles
National Bottle Museum

Victoria and Albert Museum

Cromwell Road, South Kensington, London SW7 2RL, UK
Tel. (44) 20 7942 2000   www.vam.ac.uk
Daily 10am-5.45pm (Wed and last Fri of every month 10am-10pm)

The Far Eastern Department has a magnificent collection of Chinese snuff bottles, especially overlay glass examples, as well as hardstone bottles carved from agate and turquoise in the 18th and 19th centuries.

Steve Wheeler's Milk Bottle Museum

Malvern, Worcester WR14 1JW, UK
Tel. (44) 01684 569 656
By appt. only

A shrine to the defunct British pint of milk, Steve Wheeler's collection of 14,500 foreign and domestic milk bottles is the largest in the UK. He is the first person to whom historians or film companies come when they need a pint from a certain period or place. An avid hill walker, his passion began when he came across endless old bottles shoved into the ground near gateposts. Last year ('a good year'), he added 2,000 bottles to his collection by scouring rubbish tips and old dairy farms and by befriending dairymen up and down the country who supplied him with rare and unusual examples.

Chess set from Equador
Musée international du Jeu d'échecs

CHESS SETS

British Museum

Great Russell Street, London WC1B 3DG, UK
Tel. (44) 20 7636 1555   www.thebritishmuseum.ac.uk
Mon-Sat 10am-5pm, Sun noon-6pm

Among the highlights are the 67 chessmen from the 1135-75 AD chess set discovered on the Isle of Lewis in 1831 (the remaining eleven pieces from the set are displayed at the Royal Museum of Scotland; see below). Further outstanding chess sets and related games can be found in many other departments of the museum.

Lewis chess figures of
walrus tusk, possibly
Scandinavia, 1135-1175
(above)
Royal Museum of Scotland

Chess set from Peru made
from painted wood
(below)
*Musée international du Jeu
d'échecs*

Cleveland Public Library
The John G. White Collection of Chess and Checkers, Main Library, Main Building
3rd Floor, 325 Superior Avenue, Cleveland, Ohio 44114-1271, USA
Tel. (1) 216 623 2818 www.cpl.org
Mon- Sat 9am-6pm, Sun 1-5pm

The largest chess library in the world, this collection was the creation of John White, an
eminent Cleveland citizen and president of the Cleveland Public Library Board of
Trustees (1884-86 and 1913-28). Among the 32,568 volumes of books and serials are 6,359
volumes of bound periodicals documenting the history, development, and
technical aspects of the game.

Musée international du Jeu d'échecs
The International Museum of Chess
Château de Clairvaux, 86140 Scorbé-Clairvaux, France
Tel. (33) 5 49 93 90 08
Jun-Sep: Mon-Sun 2-4pm (Other times by appt. only)

One highlight of this unique collection of 140 chess sets, made in forty kinds of materials,
is an exquisite 17th-century royal chess set from Tuscany, with 25cm-tall pieces.

Koninklijke Bibliotheek
The Royal Library
Prins Willem-Alexanderhof 5, 2529 BE The Hague, The Netherlands
Tel. (31) 70 3140911 www.kb.nl
Mon-Fri 9am-5pm, Sat 9am-1pm

This collection of around 40,000 books and volumes on chess and draughts is the second
largest in the world. Meindert Niemeijer gave the library 7,000 rare books in 1948, and
this collection is especially rich in titles from Eastern Europe and the Soviet Union.
Equally fascinating is the collection of chess posters advertising exhibitions and competitions, and the portraits of chess grandmasters drawn by Ph. Fokkens during the 1954
Olympiad in Amsterdam.

The L. A. Mayer Museum of Islamic Art
Ha-Palmakh 2, 91040 Jerusalem, Israel
Tel. (972) 2 5661292
Mon-Thu, Sun 10am-3pm (Tue until 6pm), Fri, Sat & public holidays 10am-2pm

Chess was enthusiastically taken up by the Arabs after their conquest of Iran in the 7th
century, and there are fine displays of both simple and elaborate ivory, bone, and wood
chess pieces, including many dating from the Samanid period when the game was particularly popular.

Maryhill Museum of Art
35 Maryhill Museum Drive, Goldendale, Washington 98620, USA
Tel. (1) 509 773 3733 www.maryhillmuseum.org
Mid Mar- mid Nov: daily 9am-5pm

A collection of over 300 sets represented by examples from across the globe and made
from every conceivable substance, including glass, shell, and bone. They date from the
early part of the 17th century to the present day. The ivory presentation chess set carved
in India was intended for export, and therefore favourably depicts the British. There is
also a plastic set commemorating the US election of McGovern versus Nixon, and a
diminutive set of abstract pieces carved from walrus ivory from the Aleutian Islands.

Royal Museum of Scotland
Chambers Street, Edinburgh EH1 1JF, Scotland, UK
Tel. (44) 131 225 7534   www.nms.ac.uk
Mon-Sat 10am-5pm, Tue 10am-8pm, Sun noon-5pm

A highlight of the collection are the eleven pieces from the 'Lewis chess set', a 12th-century set, carved from walrus ivory, which was discovered by a crofter in 1831 in a subterranean chamber on the Isle of Lewis (the other 67 pieces are in the British Museum; see entry). It is thought to have been made in Scandinavia and perhaps owned by a trader, or possibly carved in Britain by an Anglo-Norse craftsman.

Schachmuseum Ströbeck
The Ströbeck Chess Museum
Bahnhofstrasse 210, 38822 Ströbeck, Germany
Tel. (49) 3942 799850   www.stroebeck.de
Tue-Sat 1-3pm, Sun 10am-noon

This museum has an eclectic collection of rare chess sets from various cultures, including a set from Greenland with figures resembling Inuits and igloos, a Chinese set with temples and peasants representing eight immortal gods, and a magnificent chess board donated by the Elector Friedrich Wilhelm in 1651, which bears an inscription and the Brandenburg coat of arms. The annual chess festival at Whitsun draws tourists from far and wide.

Swedish gilded and silvered chess set; ball bearings, 1950 (above)
Maryhill Museum of Art

Chessman of walrus tusk representing two knights back to back, Skye, mid 13th century (left)
Royal Museum of Scotland

Christmas tree with pewter decoration, end of 19th century (below)
Deutsches Weihnachtsmuseum

Musée suisse du Jeu
The Swiss Museum of Games
Château de La Tour-de-Peilz, 1814 La Tour-de-Peilz, Switzerland
Tel. (41) 21 9444050   www.msj.ch
Tue-Sun 2-6pm

The museum owns several beautiful ornamental chess sets, including a proto-chess game dating from the 6th century. The showpiece is one of six special edition sets produced on the occasion of the famous encounter between Fischer and Spassky in 1972.

U.S. Chess Hall of Fame and Museum
U.S. Chess Center, 1501 M Street NW, Washington, DC 20005, USA
Tel. (1) 202 8574922   www.chessctr.org
Mon-Thu 6-10pm, Sat-Sun noon-6pm

This chess centre organizes tournaments, camps, and school programmes, and is the headquarters of the first American Chess Hall of Fame. Exhibits on display include trophies, chess sets, the world's first chess computer, and other memorabilia.

CHRISTMAS DECORATIONS AND NATIVITY FIGURES

La Collezione dei Presepi del Monastero Muri-Gries
The Crib Collection of the Muri-Gries Monastery
Piazza Gris 21, 39100 Bolzano, Italy
Tel. (39) 0471 281116
Please call for opening times

A small but valuable collection of period cribs. The Lofferer Crib from 1750 is probably the most impressive item here. Other fine cribs include a small Prelate Crib showing alpine farm life, and a large Christmas crib with the Kings' procession and Herod's castle. Both are by the Augustin, Alois Probst (1758-1807).

Deutsches Weihnachtsmuseum
The German Christmas Museum
Herrngasse 1, 91541 Rothenburg ob der Tauber, Germany
Tel. (49) 9861 409365 www.weihnachtsmuseum.de
Jan-Apr: Sat-Sun 9am-6pm. May-Dec: daily 9am-6pm

Ten packed rooms recount the history of German Christmas traditions from the 4th century to the present day. On display are more than 20,000 Christmas-related objects, including Christmas trees, angels, *Dresdner pappe* (cardboard wrapped with gold or silver wire), glass ornaments from Gablonz and Lauscha, ornaments (made from wax, cotton, pewter, and porcelain), candleholders, sweet containers, Santas, advent calendars, postcards, pop-up nativities, pyramids, and incense smokers.

A selection of Santa Clauses (above)
Deutsches Weihnachtsmuseum

Holy Family by L. Maio (right)
Il Museo del presepio di Albusciago

Museum für Glaskunst Lauscha
The Lauscha Museum of Glass Art
Oberlandstrasse 10, 98734 Lauscha, Germany
Tel. (49) 3670 220724
Daily 9am-5pm

Lauschan glassblowers invented Christmas tree ornaments in the mid 19th century. The 10,000-piece collection includes brightly coloured glass spheres and figural ornaments, as well as examples of the earlier, heavy glass ornaments blown into round spheres. These were produced before the German glassblowers had perfected the art of blowing the thin-walled ornaments we know today.

Krippenmuseum Mindelheim
The Mindelheim Crib Museum
Ehemaliger Jesuitenkolleg, Hermelestrasse 4, 87719 Mindelheim, Germany
Tel. (49) 82 616964
Tue-Sun 10am-noon, 2-4pm

This tiny museum explores the development of the Christmas crib, from the first known depiction of the birth of Jesus Christ in 1280 through to the present. The crib tradition of Mindelheim dates back to 1618, when the Jesuits displayed their first crib. Today, this same crib scene consists of some eighty figures and is still put up at Christmas in the Jesuit church; during the rest of the year several of these figures are displayed in the museum. The Fackler-Hartmann crib from the first half of the 19th century and the alabaster Pilate group of figures from around 1500 are especially noteworthy.

Michigan State University Museum
Val Berryman Santa Collection, West Circle Drive, East Lansing,
Michigan 48824-1045, USA
Tel. (1) 517 355 0322 www.museum.cl.msu.edu
Mon-Fri 9am-5pm, Sat 10am-5pm, Sun 1-5pm; closed on University holidays

With over 3,000 Santas dating largely from the mid 19th to the mid 20th centuries, the museum also has antique figures, toys, ceramics, sweet containers, postcards, early department store displays, graphic arts, books, and knick-knacks depicting the various transitions from St Nicholas to Santa Claus. It was amassed by the Curator of History, Val Berryman, who plans to donate his collection to the museum. Every Christmas the collection is on display in the Michigan area.

The National Christmas Center

3427 Lincoln Highway East, Paradise, Pennsylvania 17562, USA
Tel. (1) 717 442 7950
Please call for opening times

Priceless antique collections dating back to the early 1800s. Besides a hall hung with over 500 images of Santa, there are early German blown glass *kugels* (balls), turn-of-the-century paper ornaments, and plastic Christmas items from the 1950s.

Musée national de Monaco
The National Museum of Monaco

17 ave. de la Princesse Grace, 98000 Monte Carlo, Principality of Monaco
Tel. (377) 97 707475 www.monte-carlo.mc
Easter-Sep: daily 10am-6.30pm
Oct-Easter: daily 10am-12.15pm, 2.30-6.30pm

Portuguese crib (above)
Il Museo del presepio di Albusciago

The Infant's Dream (below)
Il Museo del presepio di Albusciago

Santon (bottom)
Il Museo del presepio di Albusciago

Madeleine de Galéa's charming collection includes an outstanding group of 200 Neapolitan santons from the the late 18th and early 19th centuries. The santons' hands and heads are made of terracotta, and their bodies are metal and dressed in hemp clothing.

Museo Nazionale di San Martino
The National Museum of San Martino

Largo San Martino, 80129 Naples, Italy
Tel. (39) 081 5781769
Tue-Sun 8.30am-7.30pm

Situated on a hill overlooking the Bay of Naples, this gleaming white monastery was once the privileged home of monks belonging to the Carthusian Order (founded in the 1300s). Collections within tell the story of Naples, however, pride of place is given to the huge and splendid Baroque Nativity scene. Instead of a stable, the Nativity is set in a Roman temple. Colourful Neapolitan street scenes enclose the central figures, and include a bakery, a vintner, and a cart over-flowing with vegetables. Adjacent rooms in the Nativity scene show other figures, which were commissioned by wealthy families from well-known sculptors, including Sammartino and Celebrano.

Il Museo del presepio di Albusciago
The Albusciago Crib Museum

Parrocchia di Albusciago di Sumirago, via
S.G. Bosco 2, 21040 Albusciago, Italy
Tel. (39) 0331 909145
www.freeweb.org/arte/museo
Sun 2.30-5.30pm (other days on request)

This collection contains cribs from all over the world. It also has 21 other scenes from the life of Christ, depicted with figures made of terracotta. Highlights include a beautiful crib from Palestine with a panoramic view of Bethlehem and Mount Judea.

351

Il Museo presepistico
The Museum of Nativity Figures
Basilica di San Nicola, piazza San Nicola 62, 62029 Tolentino, Italy
Tel. (39) 0733 969996   www.sannicola.sinp.net
Daily 9.30am-noon, 4-7pm

The centrepiece of this exhibition is the extensive crib scene displayed over 100 square metres. As well as this, there are 62 biblical scenes illustrating stories from the Old and the New Testaments.

Crib made from fired
papier-mâché by
A. Malecore
*Il Museo tipologico
internazionale del Presepio*

Il Museo tipologico internazionale del Presepio
The International Typological Crib Museum
Via Tor de' Conti, 31/a, 00184 Rome, Italy
Tel. (39) 06 6796146   www.presepio.it
Please call for opening times

This museum has more than 3,000 Nativity figures and thirty cribs from around the world. Some are made by the greatest Nativity artists, including a cast reproduction of the crib by Arnolfo di Cambio from 1289.

Wall clock in Baroque
style with cuckoo, Black
Forest, *c.* 1780
Deutsches Uhrenmuseum

Museo tipologico dei Presepi
The Typological Crib Museum
Via Maffeo Pantaleoni 4, 62100 Macerata, Italy
Tel. (39) 0733 234035
By appt. only

A collection of 4,000 cribs from the 1600s to the present, of which only a small number is on show at any one time. There are cribs from all over the world, including an excellent selection from the Italian regions of Campania, Apulia, Sardinia, Sicily, Calabria, Liguria, and Marche. Don't miss the stunning examples produced by Neapolitan workshops of the 17th and 18th centuries.

CLOCKS

American Clock and Watch Museum
100 Maple Street, Bristol, Connecticut 06010-5092, USA
Tel. (1) 860 583 6070
Apr-Nov: daily 10am-5pm. Dec-Mar: by appt only

No significant moment in American clock manufacturing is overlooked at this museum. There are 3,000 clocks and watches, and a large private library. Among the highlights is a huge striking weight-driven year clock in an Empire cornice top shelf-style case, made by Chauncey Pomeroy of Bristol, Connecticut.

Belmont
Belmont Park, Throwley, Faversham, Kent ME13 0HH, UK
Tel. (44) 1795 890 202
Please call for opening times

With some 340 horological pieces, this is the finest and most extensive range of clocks in private hands in the UK. There are clocks by Edward East, Joseph Knibb, and George Graham, a night clock by Henry Jones, a pair of 1820s amboyna long case regulators made by Benjamin Lewis Vulliamy, and three clocks by Thomas Tompion. There are also novelty and mystery clocks such as the Masonic clock which requires several buttons to be pressed before it will reveal the correct time.

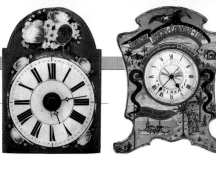

Beyer Museum der Zeitmessung
The Beyer Museum of Time Measurement
Bahnhofstrasse 31, 8001 Zurich, Switzerland
Tel. (41) 1 221 1080   www.beyer-ch.ch
Tue-Fri 9am-noon, 2-6pm, Sat 9am-noon, 2-4pm

Displays of several hundred timepieces, ranging from sundials and hourglasses to a working replica of the remarkable planetary clock created by Giovanni de' Dondi. Don't miss the very early German and Swiss wrought-iron and wooden clocks.

Imperial Colonial Clock, Baden Clock Factory, Furtwangen, c. 1905 (above)
Deutsches Uhrenmuseum

British Museum
Great Russell Street, London WC1B 3DG, UK
Tel. (44) 20 7636 1555   www.thebritishmuseum.ac.uk
Mon-Sat 10am-5pm, Sun noon-6pm

Lacquer clock with floral motif on blue background, c. 1840 (above left)
Deutsches Uhrenmuseum

One of England's truly great horology collections, and one of the most comprehensive in the world. Don't miss the 16th-century clocks, like the 'nef' table clock/automaton made by Hans Schlottheim (c.1580), the carillon clock by Isaac Habrecht (1589), and Nicholas Vallin's carillon clock of 1598 which plays musical quarter chimes on thirteen bells.

Muzeul Ceasului
The Clock Museum
1 Nicolae Simache Str., 2000 Ploiesti, Romania
Tel. (40) 44 142861   www.cimec.ro
Call for opening times

Astronomical clock from the St Peter Monastery, Black Forest, c. 1750
Deutsches Uhrenmuseum,

This museum prides itself on displays of some of the earliest time-measuring devices, including sundials, water clocks, and sand-glasses. There are a number of ornate French clocks, such as an urn-shaped clock made of Sèvres porcelain, and a small table clock suspended between marble colonnades.

Collection and Library of the Worshipful Company of Clockmakers
The Clock Room, Guidhall Library, Aldermanbury, London EC2P 2EJ, UK
Tel. (44) 20 7606 3030   www.clockmakers.org
Mon-Fri 9.30am-4.30pm

English clocks predominate, but there are also clocks by European makers, including a 15th-century domestic clock with foliot escapement, probably made in Germany, and an automaton clock by Johann Schneider (Augsburg, c.1625). The important links between timekeeping and navigation are illustrated by marine timekeepers, including a prototype example by Henry Sully (1724) and John Harrison's personal regulator which contains three of Harrison's most important inventions: oil-free bearings, a friction-free escapement, and a temperature-compensated pendulum.

Deutsches Uhrenmuseum
The German Clock Museum
Gerwigstrasse 11, 78120 Furtwangen, Germany
Tel. (49) 7723 920117   www.deutsches-uhrenmuseum.de
Apr-Oct: 9am-6pm. Nov-Mar: 10am-5pm

The largest clock collection in Germany, covering all periods and manufacturers in Europe and , with a special emphasis on Black Forest clocks. The cuckoo clock is well represented, with examples of the 'Bahnhäusle' clock, inspired by the gatekeepers of the railway in Baden from 1840.

Musée François Duesberg
The François Duesberg Museum
12 Franklin Roosevelt Square, 7000 Mons, Belgium
Tel. (32) 6 536 3164
Tue, Thu, Sat-Sun 2-7pm

A great and unique collection of exotic clocks dating from 1795 to 1815. The highlights are the so-called clocks *au nègre* which illustrate the Romantic theme of the 'noble savage'. Two fascinating clocks by Jean-Simon Deverberie show, respectively, an Indian and a European couple tenderly embraced in a kiss.

Musée d'Horlogerie
The Museum of Watch- and Clock-Making
Château des Monts, 2400 Le Locle, Switzerland
Tel. (41) 32 9311680
Tue-Sun 10am-2pm

There is a splendid selection of 18th-century French clocks with Boulle marquetry, and a unique group of English clocks dating from the late 17th and 18th centuries. Many of these come from the four private collections donated to the museum, including the Sandoz Collection (1892-1958) which mainly focuses on automata. The clock with a singing bird, attributed to Henry-Louis Jacquet-Droz, is one of the most prestigious pieces in the collection. The museum also traces the history of time measuring, and includes Chinese and Japanese clocks.

'Clock Man', painted tin figure as a Blackforest clock tradesman, probably Messkirch, 19th century (top left)
Deutsches Uhrenmuseum

One of the first type of electric clocks, Alexander Bain, mid 19th century (top right)
Collection and Library of the Worshipful Company of Clockmakers

Magnificent table clock (above)
Musée François Duesberg

Musée de l'Horlogerie et de l'Emaillerie
The Museum of Watch- and Clock-Making and Enamelling
15 route de Malagnou, 1208 Geneva, Switzerland
Tel. (41) 22 4186470   www.mah.ville-ge.ch
Mon, Wed 10am-5pm

The collection is one of the best of its kind, with examples by Louis François Gilbert, Jean André Furet, Abraham Louis Beguet, and long case clocks by Louis Simon and Pierre Jacquet-Droz. It includes what was the most valuable astronomical clock in the world, built in Geneva by Jacques Maizière Labaume in 1711.

Musée international d'Horlogerie
The International Museum of Watch- and Clock-Making
29 rue des Musées, 2301 La Chaux-de-Fonds, Switzerland
Tel. (41) 32 9676861   www.mih.ch
Jun-Sep: Tue-Sun 10am-5pm. Oct-May: Tue-Sun 10am-12pm, 2-5pm

With 650 items, the clock collection is smaller than the watch collection but is equally significant. Parisian 18th-century clocks include a splendid 'pendule' by Albert Baillon and André-Charles Boulle, a musical clock by Le Grand, a neo-classical clock by the bronze sculptor Pierre-Philippe Thomire, and wooden clocks by the Huguenin Brothers.

Manor House Museum
Honey Hill, Bury St Edmunds, Suffolk IP33 1 HF, UK
Tel. (44) 1284 757072   www.stedmundsbury.gov.uk
Tue-We, Sat-Sun 10am-5pm

One of the finest horology collections in the world, with a large collection of time measuring instruments and clockmakers' equipment. Don't miss the collection of late Renaissance clocks, including a gilt tabernacle clock by A. Meyer, and a Madonna clock by Jeremias Pfaff, both built around 1600. There are also automata mechanisms,

including a lion clock with eyes that move with the ticking and a mouth that opens and shuts as the clock strikes.

Mathematisch-Physikalischer Salon
The Salon of Mathematics and Physics
Zwinger, Sophienstrasse 2, 01067 Dresden, Germany
Tel. (49) 351 4914622 www.staatl-kunstsammlungen-dresden.de
Fri-Wed 10am-6pm

Clocks form an important part of the museum's collection of scientific instruments. For the construction of the astronomical clock made between 1563 and 1568 by the architect Eberhardt Baldewein and the clockmaker Hans Bucher, special astronomical knowledge and outstanding mastery of 16th-century precision engineering were necessary. Also of note is a tower-shaped table clock made by Paulus Schuster (Nuremberg, 1587), with three separate mechanisms that work individually. A fine collection of sundials, automatons, and pocket watches are also on display.

The National Watch and Clock Museum
514 Poplar Street, Columbia, Pennsylvania 17512-2130, USA
Tel. (1) 717 684 8261 www.nawcc.org
Tue-Sat 10am-5pm, Sun noon-4pm

This is probably the largest and most comprehensive collection in the US, with more than 12,000 pieces. The collection is particularly strong in American clocks and watches. Highlights include the *Engle Monumental Clock* with 48 moving figures, and a three-metre-tall *French Statue Clock* made by Farcot.

Nederlands Goud-, Zilver- en Klokkenmuseum
The Dutch Gold, Silver and Clock Museum
Kazerneplein 4, 2871 cz Schoonhoven, The Netherlands
Tel. (31) 182 385612
Tue-Sun noon-5pm

Starting with tower clockworks from 1543 and ending with the modern atomic clock, there is a varied selection here which provides an insight into the history of time measuring through the ages. Electric clocks form a special part of the exhibition, and there are some 2,000 alarm clocks.

Museum van het Nederlandse Uurwerk
The Museum of Dutch Clockwork
Kalverringdijk 3, Zaanse Schans, 1509 BT Zaandam, The Netherlands
Tel. (31) 75 6179769
www.noord-holland-tourist.nl
Mar-Oct: daily 10am-5pm
Nov-Feb: Sat-Sun noon-4.30pm

A unique collection of historical Dutch clocks dating from 1500 to 1850. There are three early 'Hague clocks' by Salomon Coster, Severijn Oosterwijck, and Pieter Visbagh, along with a Dutch long case clock with a second hand by Anthonius Hoevenaer (1685).

Musée Paul Dupuy
The Paul Dupuy Museum
13 rue de la Pleau, 31000 Toulouse, France
Tel. (33) 5 61 14 65 50
Jun-Sep: Mon, Wed-Sun 10am-6pm
Oct-May: Mon, Wed-Sun 10am-5pm

Four centuries of clocks collected by Paul Dupuy (1867-1944) are arranged chronologically and comprise exceptionally rare pieces. The 17th-century room, with its table clocks, pendulums, and a wall clock, illustrates the progress of clockmaking and includes a notable table clock transformed into a pendulum by Isaac Thuret. A highlight of the 19th-century room is a beautiful planetary pendulum by Janvier. It dates from 1773 and 1806, and indicates time, months, moon phases, and the temperature in Fahrenheit and Réaumur.

Suomen Kellomuseo
Finnish Museum of Horology
Opinkuja 2, Tapeola, 02100 Espoo, Finland
Tel. (358) 9 4520688   www.kelloseppaliitto.fi
Winter hours only, please call for times

A selection of 8,000 Finnish horological items. Remarkable pieces include a Bregut pocket watch with duplex escapement and 1/4 repeater, a precision clock with Riefler escapement made by Lauri Helske, chronometers made by Wäinö Maukonen and August de la Porte, a two-day marine chronometer made by John Arnold, and a table clock made by Johann Sayller.

Magnificent table clock
(top left)
Musée François Duesberg

Table clock by Martinot,
engraved and gilded copper, Paris, *c.* 1580
(top right)
Musée Paul Dupuy

Iron clock, probably
South German,
16th century (above)
Deutsches Uhrenmuseum

Tabley Cuckoo Clock Collection
Nether Tabley Old School House, Chester Road, Tabley, Cheshire WA16 0HL, UK
Tel. (44) 1565 63303   www.cuckooland.uk
By appt. only

The world's largest collection of cuckoo clocks. Among the prize possessions are a 41-key Wilhelm Bruder, a 48-key barrel Wilhelm Bruder, and a 45-key trumpet Hoffbauer.

Uhren-Museum der Stadt Wien
Clock Museum of the City of Vienna
Schulhof 2, 1010 Vienna, Austria
Tel. (43) 1 5332265   www.museum.vienna.at
Tue-Sun 9am-4.30pm

The museum contains more than 1,000 timepieces, many of them centuries old (mainly 15th to 20th century). A focal piece is the big astronomical clock made in 1769 by the Augustinian, Cajetano. Its hands need 20,904 years for one rotation. The world's smallest pendulum clock, tiny enough to fit in a thimble, is also on display here.

The Wallace Collection
Hertford House, Manchester Square, London W1M 6BN, UK
Tel. (44) 20 7563 9500   www.the-wallace-collection.org.uk
Mon-Sat 10am-5pm, Sun 2-5pm

A priceless selection of French 18th-century clocks with many exquisite examples, including a clock face of gilt bronze with white enamel plaques, a pedestal clock by André-Charles Boulle, and a French mantel clock made of gilt bronze, enamel, and Carrara marble, showing the young Louis XVI being instructed by Minerva, goddess of Wisdom.

Willard House and Clock Museum
11 Willard Street, Grafton, Massachusetts 01536, USA
Tel. (1) 508 839 3500 www.nawcc.org
Tue-Sat 10am-4pm, Sun 1-5 pm

To see a collection of objects in the workshops where they were made is
unusual in itself, but the fact that they are displayed in the home of their
makers is really rather special. Here, in what was once a rural suburb in
Massachusetts, is the home of three generations of a clockmaking family.
In 1766, Benjamin Willard began making clocks. Soon after, his three
younger brothers, Simon, Ephraim, and Aaron, took up the trade. Gracing
the walls is almost every Willard-style clock, including Turret, Gallery,
Skeleton, Tall Case, Regulator, Eddystone Lighthouse, Act of Parliament,
Lyre, Massachusetts Shelf, Improved Timepiece, and 30-hour Primitive.

Selection of alarm clocks
Nederlands Goud-, Zilver- en Klokkenmuseum

COINS AND MEDALS

American Numismatic Association Museum
818 North Cascade Avenue, Colorado Springs, Colorado
80903-3279, USA
Tel. (1) 719 632 2646 www.money.org
Tue-Fri 9am-4.30
(Move due in 2002 to new premises currently under construction at 140 William Street)

Founded in 1858, the collection has grown steadily through large numbers of donations
and purchases. Though the Greek and Roman coin collections are especially strong,
there are also significant holdings of Islamic, medieval, and modern coins, and rare
paper money. There is also an extensive library.

Muzeum Archeologiczne i Etnograficzne
Museum of Archaeology and Ethnography
Plac Wolności 14, 91-415 Łódz, Poland
Tel. (48) 42 6328440
Tue, Thu, Fri 10am-5pm, Wed 9am-4pm, Sat 9am-3pm, Sun 10am-3pm

Established in 1948, the museum's magnificent coin collection consists of over 57,000
classical and medieval coins. Highlights include extremely rare coins from the royal
collection of King Stanislas Augustus Poniatowski, along with Greek, Roman, Celtic,
and Arabic treasures (some of which were found on Polish soil). There is also a hoard of
gold and silver coins which were discovered in 1942 in Kisarabad, Iraq.

Ashmolean Museum
Beaumont Street, Oxford, Oxfordshire OX1 2PH, UK
Tel. (44) 1865 278000 www.ashmol.ox.ac.uk
Tue-Sat 10am-5pm, Sun 2-5pm

This collection of nearly a third of a million coins is the second largest in the UK. A
permanent display in the Heberden Coin Room covers the history of English coinage
from the Celts to the Stuarts, Greek and Roman coinage, and Oriental coins from the
cowry shells of the 2nd millennium BC to modern South East Asian currency.

Bank of England Museum
Bartholomew Lane, London EC2R 8AH, UK
Tel. (44) 20 7601 4878 www.bankofengland.co.uk
Mon-Fri 10am-5pm

Opened in 1988, the displays give a particularly lucid overview of the bank's history, using original architectural plans (plus a reconstruction of Sir John Soane's marvellous original Bank Stock Office), interactive multimedia videos, and such resonant real exhibits as the original deeds, bank charter, and lists of subscribers to the 'Lady of Threadneedle Street'. There's a mint collection of British coins first introduced in 1932.

Bodemuseum - Münzkabinett
The Bode Museum - Coin Cabinet
Bodestrasse 1-3, 10178 Berlin, Germany
Tel. (49) 30 20905577   www.smb.spk-berlin.de
Please call for opening times

Gnadenpfenning with the portrait of Maximilian I, Elector of Bavaria
Staatliche Münzsammlung

Originally established by the Electors of Brandenburg, this vast, internationally renowned coin collection covers the complete history of coinage, from its beginnings in Asia Minor in the 17th century BC to the present day. Alongside 102,000 Greek and 20,000 Roman coins are nearly 200,000 European and Islamic medieval coins.

British Museum
Great Russell Street, London WC1B 3DG, UK
Tel. (44) 20 7636 1555   www.thebritishmuseum.ac.uk
Mon-Sat 10am-5pm, Sun noon-6pm

Opened in 1997, the British Museum's HSBC Money Gallery uses pristine examples from the museum's hoard of 500,000 coins to explore the development, manufacture, and cultural role of money from the 3rd millennium BC to the present day. The 230,000-strong classical collection includes some of the earliest known coins, as well as a huge number of Roman coins (54,951 in all) from Mildenhall, Suffolk. (The largest hoard of Roman coins ever found in Britain was discoveed here.) The museum also owns 40,000 medals, including a gold medal with a portrait of Queen Elizabeth I on it, probably by the great miniaturist, Nicholas Hilliard. The medal was struck in 1588 to commemorate the defeat of the Spanish Armada.

Cabinet des Médailles et Antiques
Cabinet of Medals and Ancient Works of Art
Bibliothèque Nationale de France, 58 rue de Richelieu, 75002 Paris, France
Tel. (33) 1 47 03 83 30   www.bnf.fr
Daily 1-5pm

Over 500,000 coins and medals, including more than 200,000 from ancient Greece, Gaul, and Rome, and a mint collection of contemporary medals and coins from France. Highlights in the French collections include the Gold Ecu belonging to Saint Louis (1266-70), the Golden Mantlet of Philippe IV (1305), the Golden Crown of Philippe VI (1340), and the Franc à Cheval, the earliest surviving coin bearing the word 'franc', minted in 1360 to ransom King Jean le Bon.

Museo de Cádiz
The Museum of Cádiz
Plaza de Mina s/n, 11004 Cádiz, Spain
Tel. (34) 956 212281   www.infocadiz.com
Tue 2.30-8pm (earlier by appt. only), Wed-Sat 9am-8pm, Sun 9.30am-2.30pm

The treasures in the numismatic collection originate from excavations in Cádiz (1910s-30s), and excavations in Bolonia undertaken from 1966 to 1980. The main part of the exhibition consists of coins from the Punic and Roman periods (4th century BC-4th century AD).

Museo de la Casa de la Moneda
The Museum of the Mint
Calle Doctor Esquerdo 36, 28009 Madrid, Spain
Tel. (34) 91 5666544 www.fnmt.es
Tue-Fri 10am-2pm, 5-7.30pm, Sat-Sun 10am-2pm

Though the collection mainly covers early Greek and Roman coins, the Hispanic coin collection, with its gold coins minted under the Swabian and Visigoth kings, is particularly noteworthy.

Deutsches Historisches Museum
German Historical Museum
Zeughaus Unter den Linden 2, 10117 Berlin, Germany
Tel. (49) 30 215020 www.dhm.de
Mon, Tue, Thu-Sun 10am-6pm (Closed for re-construction until Jan 2002)

The collection of 7,000 coins, 5,000 medals and commemorative coins, and 60,000 notes incorporates coins from the East German museum, and gives a remarkable overview of Germany's monetary history, from the first Roman minting of coins in the Rhineland to the current Federal Republic financial system. The special collections take in emergency and siege coins from the 16th to the 19th centuries, war money from World War I prisoner of war camps, and emergency money from the inflation era of 1922-23.

Germanisches Nationalmuseum
The Germanic National Museum
Kartäusergasse 1, 90402 Nuremberg, Germany
Tel. (49) 911 13310 www.gnm.de
Please call for opening times

Tetradrachma with the helmeted head of Arethusa, Syracuse, c. 410BC (top)
Staatliche Münzsammlung

This small but rich collection dates from the founding of the museum in 1852. Besides coins, medals, badges, tokens, and jetons, there are dies and seal-matrices (more than 5,000 examples), plus a special collection of Roman gems.

Silver medal by Hans Krafft showing the portrait of Karl V, 1521 (middle)
Staatliche Münzsammlung

Hollufgård
Archaeological Museum of Fünen
Hestehaven 201, 5220 Odense SØ, Denmark
Tel. (45) 66 13 13 72 www.odmus.dk
Apr-Oct: Tue-Sun 10am-4pm. Nov-Mar: Mon-Sat 10am-4pm

Tetradrachma with the helmeted head of Athena, Athens, c. 510BC (above)
Staatliche Münzsammlung

This is one of the largest and most accessible collections in Denmark, with over 17,000 pieces, of which around 5-6,000 are on permanent display. Besides the collection of Greek and Roman coins, there are coins from the Viking period, early Danish bank notes, and portrait medallions from the 15th century onwards.

Septimus Severus, Aureus showing Julia Domna, Caracalla and Gaeta, Rome, c. AD202 (left)
Staatliche Münzsammlung

Hunterian Museum and Art Gallery
The University of Glasgow, University Avenue
Glasgow G12 8QQ, Scotland, UK
Tel. (44) 141 330 4221 www.hunterian.gla.ac.uk
Mon-Sat 9.30am-5pm

Based originally around the cabinet of the great Scottish surgeon and anatomist, William Hunter, the fabulous collections include an impressive numismatic collection. A series of permanent displays chronicles the manufacture and use of coins, forgeries, and methods of engraving. The many highlights include a gold stater of Athens struck in 296BC, once owned by King George III and personally given to Hunter. Scottish coins are well represented, from the first pennies of David I, struck around 1136, to the last pieces bearing an Edinburgh mint mark, which were minted just after the Union with England in 1707.

Den Kongelige Mynts Museum
The Royal Mint Museum
Hyttegata 3, 3602 Kongsberg, Norway
Tel. (47) 32 723200   www.bvm.museum.no
Please call for opening times

Still operating today, Kongsberg's Royal Mint opened in 1686 after it was transferred here from Akershus in Christiana. The first coins struck at Kongsberg were Norwegian 4-marks, using tools fashioned by Casper Barth, who worked at the Christiana old mint but who was a Kongsbergian by birth. The collections include nearly all of the mints coined in Norway since the 17th century.

Kungliga Myntkabinettet - Sveriges Ekonomiska Museum
The Royal Coin Cabinet - National Museum of Monetary History
Slottsbacken 6 i Gamla Stan, 114 84 Stockholm, Sweden
Tel. (46) 8 51955300   www.myntkabinettet.se
Tue-Sun 10am-4pm

Situated opposite the Royal Palace, this is one of Europe's oldest coin cabinets. Nearly half the collection of 500,000 coins consists of Viking coins discovered on archaeological digs. The unique collection also includes the world's earliest coin, dating back to 625BC. The world's biggest coin, a Swedish copper plate weighing 20kg, and Sweden's first banknote, dating from 1661, are also on display here.

Kunsthistorisches Museum - Münzkabinett
The Art-Historical Museum - Coin Cabinet
Maria-Theresien-Platz, 1010 Vienna, Austria
Tel. (43) 1 52524380   www.khm.at
Tue-Sun 10am-6pm (Thu until 9pm)

An extraordinary early 19th-century cabinet of over 700,000 coins, covering three millennia. It owes its existence to the Habsburgs, especially Franz I, and the famous numismatist, Abbé Joseph Ambras. As well as coins, the collection takes in paper money, medals, orders, and other items. The unique Brettauer collection of coins, relating to the history of medicine, is one of the museum's highlights.

Museum für Kunst und Kulturgeschichte
The Museum of Art and Cultural History
Hansastrasse 3, 44137 Dortmund, Germany
Tel. (49) 231 5025525   www.museendortmund.de
Tue-Sun 10am-5pm

The museum houses the Dortmund Treasure, a cache of 444 gold coins dating for the most part from the 4th century AD, and buried by an unknown trader near the city's West Gate.

Landesmünzkabinett - Staatliche Galerie Moritzburg
The Regional Coin Cabinet - State Gallery of Moritz Castle
Friedemann-Bach-Platz 5, 06108 Halle, Germany
Tel. (49) 345 2024751   www.moritzburg.halle.de
Tue 11am-8.30pm, Wed-Fri 10am-6pm

Moritz Castle housed Magdeburg's archiepiscopal mint from 1582 to 1680, and since the mid 19th century the city has amassed a significant coin collection of 35,000 coins and medals from all over the world. Special emphasis is given to modern German medals and the medieval and modern coinages of the Central German states.

Musée de la Monnaie
Money Museum
11 quai de Conti, 75006 Paris, France
Tel. (33) 1 40 46 55 35   www.monnaiedeparis.fr
Tue-Fri 11am-5.30pm, Sat-Sun noon-5.30pm

Opened in 1988, the museum presents the history of French coins from antiquity to modern times, using some magnificent examples from a superb collection of 30,000 coins and 75,000 medals. Beginning with a Philip II of Macedon gold stater, the exhibition chronicles the first coins introduced to Gaul from Rome, the Charlemagne monetary system based on the pound (which lasted a millennium in Europe), and the introduction in 1360 of the first franc (which stood for 'franc des Anglais' or 'freed from the English').

Munt en Penningkabinet Surhuisterveen
Numismatic Cabinet Surhuisterveen
Spaar en Voorschotbank, Jan Binneslaan 9a,
Surhuisterveen, The Netherlands
Tel. (31) 512 369999
Tue-Fri 2-5pm
(Groups visits and coin examination by appt. only)

Jelle Bekkema was a former director of the bank, whose private collection contains some choice examples of coinage from Asia Minor, Greece, Rome, and particularly Frysia. The collection also includes historic medals relating to the northern part of the Netherlands, coins of the 'Society of Beneficence', gold and silver bars from VOC shipwrecks, primitive forms of money from northern Siam, and a first-class research library.

Velvet purse with silver thread embroidery and *jetons* (tokens), 18th century
Musée de la Monnaie

Rheinisches Landesmuseum Trier
The Rhenish Regional Museum of Trier
Weimarer Allee 1, 54290 Trier, Germany
Tel. (49) 651 97740   www.uni-trier.de
Tue-Fri 9.30am-5pm, Sat-Sun 10.30am-5pm

Sadly, only a fraction of this museum's massive holding of 160,000 Treveri and Roman coins, and 50,000 medieval and modern coins, can be displayed at any one time.

Rijksmuseum - Het Koninklijk Penningkabinet
The National Museum - The Royal Coin Cabinet
Rapenburg 28, 2301 EA Leiden, The Netherlands
Tel. (31) 71 5160999   www.penningkabinet.nl
Tue-Fri 10am-5pm, Sat-Sun noon-5pm

Originally a private cabinet assembled by William IV in the 18th century, this museum has grown into the world's most comprehensive survey of Dutch currency and medals. Showstoppers among the 120,000 coins include good examples of Lydian staters and a silver restrike of a Leicester real, which replaced the coinage issued by Philip II. Among the 40,000 medals is a heart-shaped badge depicting the start of the Eighty Years' War and the Dutch Revolt, and an internationally-renowned collection of counters.

Silver medallion with the
portrait of Constantin I,
Ticinum, *c.* 315BC (top)
Staatliche Münzsammlung

Five-Ducat with the por-
trait of Bavarian Elector,
Maximilian I, Munich
mint, 1640 (above)
Staatliche Münzsammlung

Somerset County Museum

Taunton Castle, Castle Green, Taunton, Somerset TA1 4AA, UK
Tel. (44) 1823 355504 www.somerset.gov.uk
Apr-Oct: Tue-Sat 10am-5pm. Nov-Mar: Tue-Sat 10am-3pm

This museum is home to the Shapwick Coin Hoard, a cache of 9,213 pristine Roman silver denarii discovered in 1998 in the corner of a room in a previously unknown Roman
house. Coins range in date from the time of Mark Antony (31-30BC) to emperor Severus
Alexander (AD222-35).

Staatliche Münzsammlung
The State Coin Collection

Residenzstrasse 1, 80333 Munich, Germany
Tel. (49) 89 227221
Tue-Sun 10am-4.30pm

The main focus of the 300,000-strong collection is antique coins from Greece, Rome,
and Byzantium, and medals from the Renaissance onwards.

COWBOY GEAR AND BARBED WIRE

Autry Museum of Western Heritage

4700 Western Heritage Way, Los Angeles, California 90027-1462, USA
Tel. (1) 323 667 2000 www.autry-museum.org
Tue-Sun 10am-5pm, Thu 10am-8pm

Founded by the cowboy actor, Gene Autry, this comprehensive museum
chronicles the people and events that shaped this part of the US. Over
17,000 artefacts (including firearms and personal possessions belonging
to Wyatt Earp, Black Bart, Billy the Kid, and Annie Oakley) trace the
development of California from its early nomadic cultures to its enclo-
sure by Europeans and Americans, using saddles, tools, and firearms.

The Buffalo Bill
Historical Center (above)
The Buffalo Bill Museum

The Family Room, 1992
(right)
The Buffalo Bill Museum

The Buffalo Bill Museum

Buffalo Bill Historical Center, 720 Sheridan Avenue,
Cody, Wyoming 82414, USA
Tel. (1) 307 587 4771 www.bbhc.org
Please call for opening times

Initially a rider for the Pony Express, William Cody
(aka Buffalo Bill) served as a scout in the Civil War,
scalped Chief Yellow Hand in revenge for the massacre of Custer's men at Little
Bighorn, and went on to make millions with his Wild West extravaganza starring
Annie Oakley, Sitting Bull, and himself. Located in the town named in his honour, this
complex of museums displays a wealth of material relating to the early pioneers, with
a fascinating set of displays chronicling the life of Buffalo Bill himself.

Ellwood House Museum

509 North First Street, DeKalb, Illinois 60115 USA
Tel. (1) 815 756 4609 www.bios.niu.edu
Guided tours Tue-Fri 1pm, 3pm; Sat-Sun 1pm, 2pm, 3pm

Dating from 1879, Ellwood House was built by Isaac Ellow, an uneducated hardware store
owner who became a barbed wire baron after he secured a fifty per cent interest in Joseph
Glidden's patent. Today, the small museum houses posters ('Sparks do not set it on fire;

floods do not sweep it away'), fence stretchers, and mounted specimens of classic types of wire, including Scutt's Wooden Block, Dodge Star, Wilkes Two Staple, Wilson Ring Locked Four Point, and Burnell Small Gauge Parallel.

When the Land Belonged to God by Charles M. Russell, 1914
Montana Historical Society

Guitar Museum

Jacksonville Guitar Center 1105 Burman Drive, Jacksonville, Arkansas 72076, USA
Tel. (1) 501 982 4933
Mon-Sat 10am-6pm

Steve Evans began collecting novelty cowboy guitars in the 1930s and 40s, and his Arkansas guitar shop now has a space set aside for displaying 150 rare examples from the collection. Gems include some of the earliest 'singing cowboy' guitars ever produced (the very first – dedicated to Gene Autry – were produced by Sears & Roebuck in 1932).

William S. Hart Museum

24151 San Fernando Road, Newhall, California 91321 USA
Tel. (1) 661 254 4584 www.hartmuseum.org
Please call for opening times

This superb collection of Native American art, housed in a 22-room Spanish colonial ranch, was given to Los Angeles by actor William Hart. 'Two Gun Bill' grew up with the Sioux, and many of the items in his collection were gifts from Sioux friends. Stunning Navajo rugs from the early 1900s, Native American baskets, beaded leather artefacts, costumes, and firearms provide a perfect backdrop for Hart's outstanding collection of Western paintings and sculpture.

The Historical Museum of Barbed Wire and Fencing Tools (aka Devil's Rope Museum)

I-40 and Old Route 66, McLean, Texas 79057 USA
Tel. (1) 806 779 2225 www.barbwiremuseum.com
Tue-Sat 10am-4pm

Along with the windmill, the Winchester rifle, and the six-shooter, barbed wire was a key component in the making of the Old West. There are over 500 patents for barbed wire and some 2,000 variations, but sheriff Joseph Glidden of Illinois has been credited with the invention of the first 'devil's rope', made out of a coffee bean grinder twisted along a smooth wire. This museum includes 700 fencing tools and over 1,500 examples of barbed wire, from the first wires used by cattle ranchers in the Old West to razor-sharp warwire used in World War I.

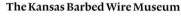

The Kansas Barbed Wire Museum

120 West 1st Street, LaCrosse, Kansas, 67548 USA
Tel. (1) 785 222 9900 www.rushcounty.org
Mon-Sat 10am-4.30pm, Sun 1-4.30pm

Opened in 1991, this collection is one of the largest of its kind, with several thousand varieties of wire on show, ranging from the first patented handmade wire to wire from the Berlin Wall.

'Roy Rogers' guitar, by the Harmony Company of Chicago, mid 1950s
Guitar Museum

Symbol of the Pros, sculpture outside the building (left)
Montana Historical Society

Montana Historical Society

225 North Roberts, Helena, Montana 59620 USA
Tel. (1) 406 444 2694 www.his.state.mt.us
Summer: Mon-Fri 8am-6pm, Sat-Sun 9am-5pm. Winter: Mon-Fri 8am-5pm, Sat 9am-5pm

The Society owns over 200 oil paintings, pen and inks, and bronzes by the Montana 'cowboy artist', Charles M. Russell. Equally significant are the breathtaking photographs by F. Jay Haynes, the official photographer for the Northern Pacific Railroad and Yellowstone National Park, and the 1,000-strong firearms collection (including Jim Bridger's Hawken rifle of 1870 and Sitting Bull's Henry repeating rifle of 1866).

National Cowboy & Western Heritage Museum

1700 NE 63rd Street, Oklahoma City, Oklahoma 73111 USA
Tel. (1) 405 478 2250   www.nationalcowboymuseum.org
Daily 9am-5pm

Buffalo Jump diorama
Montana Historical Society

Exploring the history of the American West, a large part of this museum is devoted to work by 19th-century artists such as Charles Russell, Frederic Remington, Albert Bierstadt, and Thomas Moran. However, the collection is also rich in the 'stuff' of the West, including saddles, firearms, braided rawhide, and a large number of rodeo cups, trophies, and saddles. There is also a private collection, amassed by Robert Campbell, which exhibits the history and uses of barbed wire, comprising 1,300 varieties of the 'rusty stuff'.

'Jerry The Yodeling Cowboy' guitar, by Regal of Chicago, Illinois, early 1940s (near right) *Guitar Museum*

'Red Foley, Smooth Trailin' guitar, by Richter in Chicago, Illinois, early 1940s (middle right) *Guitar Museum*

Vacquero 'Rodeo Scene' guitar, by Kay Musical Instrument Company of Chicago, 1936 (far right) *Guitar Museum*

The National Cowgirl Museum and Hall of Fame

1700 Gendy Street, Fort Worth, Texas 76107 USA
Tel. (1) 817 336 4475   www.cowgirl.net
Opening June 2002

Five galleries and a multi-purpose theatre will chronicle the many unsung female heroes of the West (from ordinary frontierswomen to rodeo cowgirls), as well as a host of famous names including Annie Oakley, Calamity Jane, Vivian White, and Lucille Mulhall. Did you know that rodeo cowgirls were among the first women in the US to achieve recognition as professional athletes?

Panhandle-Plains Historical Museum

West Texas A & M University, 2401 Fourth Avenue, Canyon, Texas, 79016 USA
Tel. (1) 806 651 2244   www.wtamu.edu
Jun-Aug: Mon-Sat 9am-6pm, Sun 1-6pm. Sep-May: Mon-Sat 9am-5pm, Sun 1-6pm
(Research Center Mon-Fri 9am-noon, 1-5pm)

This is the official depository for the papers of the Texas Barbed Wire Collectors Association. Along with barbed wire, the collection comprises anything and everything to do with the panhandle region of the state, including manuscripts, photographs, maps, and papers depicting the settling, ranching, and farming of the area from the 1870s onwards.

Sid Richardson Collection of Western Art
309 Main Street, Fort Worth, Texas 76102 USA
Tel. (1) 817 332 6554 www.sidrmuseum.org
Tue-Wed 10am-5pm, Thu-Fri 10am-8pm, Sat 11am-8pm,
Sun 11am-5pm

Oil tycoon, Sid Richardson, started collecting 19th-century
Western art in 1942, gradually amassing a collection of over
100 paintings. Around sixty are now on permanent display,
alongside a rich mix of cowboy-related paraphernalia.

Roy Rogers-Dale Evans Museum
15650 Seneca Road, Victorville, California, 92392 USA
Tel. (1) 760 243 4547 www.royrogers.com
Daily 9am-5pm

Buffalo Runners - Big Horn Basin by Frederic Remington, oil on canvas, 1909
Sid Richardson Collection of Western Art

Dedicated to the cowboy singer and actor, Roy Rogers, this museum and shrine chronicles the Rogers life story with a glittering array of family photos, costumes, saddles, movie memorabilia, fan mail, comic strips, piped music, novelty toys, and a collection of Frederic Remington paintings amassed by Rogers and his wife, Dale Evans. The star attraction of the museum is the embalmed mummy of Trigger, Rogers' much-loved palomino. He bought Trigger for $2,500 in the 1940s (a vast sum at the time), and on its death had the animal stuffed in a characteristic pose.

Black and silver chaps and vest, Edward H. Bohlin Co., 1947
Sid Richardson Collection of Western Art

CRAFTSMEN'S IMPLEMENTS

Musée des Arts et Métiers
Museum of Arts and Crafts
60 rue Réaumur, 75003 Paris, France
Tel. (33) 1 53 01 82 00 www.cnam.fr
Tue-Sun 10am-6pm (Thu until 9.30pm)

A huge collection covering the history of crafts and tools, with objects dating back to the 18th century. These include lifting machines such as the 'chevrette' by La Garouste (19th century), a chain-making device by Vaucanson (18th century), and a lathe belonging to Louis XVI by Mercklein (1780).

Dorf- und Rebbau-Museum
The Village and Viniculture Museum
Wettsteinhaus, Baselstrasse 34, 4125 Riehen, Switzerland
Tel. (41) 61 641 2829 www.riehen.ch
Wed-Sat 2-5pm, Sun 10am-5pm

A vast collection of agricultural and craftsmen's tools, ornamental door and window mountings, tiles, and household equipment. The museum also has a reconstructed shop from around 1900, and the workshop of cooper Karl Böhme from Basle, founded in 1878 and closed down in 1979.

Museum of Early Trades and Crafts
Main Street at Green Village Road, Madison, New Jersey 07940 USA
Tel. (1) 973 377 2982 www.rosenet.org
Tue-Sat 10am-4pm, Sun 2-5 pm

Edgar Land, founder of this local craft museum, was a passionate collector. When he went to flea markets he didn't see rusty piles of metal but valuable pieces of American

Building, donated by The Stanley Works, displaying the work of Conneticut author and artist, Eric Sloane, and his extensive collection of early American tools (above)
Sloane-Stanley Museum

Eric Sloane's painting *Knox Bridge* hangs in the gallery at the Sloane-Stanley Museum (above right)
Sloane-Stanley Museum

Some of Eric Sloane's Early American tool collection on diplay at the Sloane-Stanley Museum
Sloane-Stanley Museum

history. A developer and builder, he established the museum in his own home, then later in the former town library. He spent hours and days scouring craftsmen's ledger books to track the ownership history for many of the items on display, making this a valuable record not only of American tools but also of the people who worked with them.

Il Museo del Falegname Tino Sana
The Tino Sana Carpentry Museum
Via Aldo Moro 6, 24030 Almenno San Bartolomeo, Italy
Tel. (39) 035 554411 www.tinosana.com
Sep-Jul: Sat 3-6pm, Sun 9.30am-noon, 3-6pm

This unique collection contains over 4,000 objects from the last four centuries, offering a detailed insight into the craft of carpentry and woodwork in northern Italy. There is an enormous selection of implements and tools, as well as carpenters' and joiners' benches, and old-fashioned equipment for carving and planing.

Jokioisten Naulamuseo
The Nail Museum at Jokioinen
Humppilantie 8, 31600 Jokioinen, Finland
Tel. (358) 3 4182420
Jun-Jul: Sat-Sun noon-2pm, 3-6pm (other times by appt.)

Numerous types of nails were produced at the factory, from 'Bombay nails' exported to India, to boat nails, and ones used on the railways.

Museo del Maglio
The Hammer Museum
Localitá Maglio, via Strada del Molino 6,
36042 Breganze, Italy
Tel. (39) 0445 873908 www.didanet.it
Daily by appt.

A beautiful rural complex of medieval origin, which includes a forge, a water-hammer, and a number of simpler machines. The museum displays objects of its own production too, such as axes, spades, and hatchets. Also on show are drills, hammers, tongs, iron poles for the forge, and virtually every other conceivable instrument used in this industry.

The Mercer Museum
84 South Pine Street, Doylestown, Pennsylvania 18901 USA
Tel. (1) 215 345 0210 www.mercermuseum.org
Mon, Wed-Sat 10am-5pm, Tue 10am-9pm, Sun noon-5pm

A seven-storey, reinforced concrete building, conceived by collector, archaeologist, and ceramist, Henry Mercer. It is packed with a vast collection of American pre-industrial tools (to *c.* 1850), which he considered, above all the other items he amassed on his world travels, to be his prize finds. Thousands of examples are on display, from woodworkers' and shoemakers' implements, to those of farmers, weavers, and other tradesmen.

The Nail Mill Museum & Bridgeton Antiquarian League
1 Mayor Aitken Drive, Bridgeton, New Jersey 08302, USA
Tel. (1) 856 455 4100
Tue-Fri 10am-1.30pm, Sat-Sun 11am-4pm

The Cumberland Nail and Iron Company was established in 1815 and became the town's largest industry until 1899. Shown in the former office of the ironworks are associated artefacts, from a model of the *Laura B* which once transported nails down the Cohansey River, to a case filled with nails. Outside in the park is one of only two nail machines known (the other is in the Treemont Nail Company in Massachusetts). Related items include hand-written posters announcing company rules, account books, brass stencils used to label the nail kegs, and early photos of the nail works.

Eric Sloane's Warren studio, recreated at the Sloane-Stanley Museum
Sloane-Stanley Museum

The New Canaan Historical Society
13 Oenoke Ridge, New Canaan, Connecticut 06840 USA
Tel. (1) 203 966 1776   www.nchistory.org
Summer: Tue-Fri, Sun 2-4pm. Winter: Wed, Thu, Sun 2-4pm. It is advisable to call ahead.

This museum is covered wall-to-wall with implements dating from the 18th century, donated by the families of local men who worked as cabinetmakers, wheelwrights, tanners, shoemakers, coopers, and builders. Nearby is a re-creation of a 19th-century printing office, complete with a rare Smith-Hoe Acorn press made in 1822.

Shelburne Museum
US Route 7, Shelburne, Vermont 05482 USA
Tel. (1) 802 985 3346   www.shelburnemuseum.org
May-Oct: daily 10am-5pm. Rest of year: walking tours at 1pm

Most of this comprehensive collection of 18th- and 19th-century hand tools and machinery is exhibited in the Shaker Shed. There are axes used by the early settlers, as well as an astonishing range of planes (each with an individual function), a cabinetmaker's tool chest, and a complete exhibit of cooper's tools.

Eric Sloane believed Early American tools were works of art
Sloane-Stanley Museum

Sloane-Stanley Museum
Route 7, Kent, Connecticut 06757 USA
Tel. (1) 860 927 3849
www.cthistorical.com
May-Oct: Wed-Sun 10am-4pm

The collection of several hundred implements is spread over several barn-like structures located on the site of the Kent Iron Furnace, which was active in producing pig iron from 1826 until the 1890s. The humble silage chopper, wooden snow shovel, and goose-wing axe reflect how carefully early tools were made, while contraptions including the dog-powered butter churn and the rotary corn shellers commemorate American craftsmen's ingenuity.

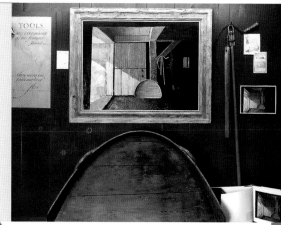

FARM IMPLEMENTS

Musée agricole
The Agricultural Museum
Château de Didonne, 17120 Semussac, France
Tel. (33) 5 46 05 82 26
Jun-Sep: daily 10am-7pm

Palatine Plow, 1750
The Farmers' Museum

This is an exceptional collection of agricultural machines dating from the 1850s onwards. Apart from ploughs, seed drills, rakes, and mowers, there are tractors a-plenty, including an American Titan from 1917 and a 1950s Renault.

Billings Farm & Museum

Route 12 and River Road, Woodstock, Vermont 05091-0489 USA
Tel. (1) 802 457 2355   www.billingsfarm.org
May-Oct: daily 10am-5pm. Winter: please call for opening times

A working farm and a museum, with 19th-century farm implements used for planting, harvesting, milking, cheese and butter making, and maple sugaring. It was founded in 1871 as a scientifically-run farm by one of the America's early conservationists, Frederick Billings. He bred cows imported from the Isle of Jersey, to make butter in what was then a technologically advanced creamery, and established a programme of re-forestation.

Conservatoire de l'agriculture
The Conservatory of Argriculture
Pont de Mainvilliers, 28000 Chartres, France
Tel. (33) 2 37 36 11 30   www.lecompa.com
Tue-Fri 10am-12.30pm, 1.30-6pm, Sat-Sun 10am-7pm

Selection of buckets
Billings Farm & Museum

The collection contains more than 1,000 items, including a collection of tractors. Also on display is the country's first harvester (the MacCormick from 1831), a 1928 locomobile from the Société française de Vierzon, and a unique collection of 19th-century ploughs and swing ploughs from Europe and the US.

Museum of English Rural Life

The University of Reading, Whiteknights Park, Shinfield Road, Reading RG6 6AG, Berkshire UK
Tel. (44) 118 9318660   www.museums.reading.ac.uk
Tue-Sat 10am-1pm, 2-4.30pm

One of the first specialist museums of farming and rural life in England, with a broad range of artefacts relating to farming and rural crafts.

The Farmers' Museum

Lake Road, Route 80, Cooperstown, New York 13326 USA
Tel. (1) 607 547 1400   www.fenimoreartmuseum.org
Apr, May: Tue-Sun 10am-4pm. Jun-Sep: daily 10am-5pm. Oct-Dec: Tue-Sun 10am-4pm

A collection of more than 23,000 artefacts ranging from early trade and craft tools to historically accurate furnishings. They came from the 25 buildings moved to the museum from sites within a 100-mile radius of Cooperstown. Key to the interpretation of the Main Barn exhibition is a collection of over 250 shuttles and bobbins, used in spinning and weaving demonstrations.

Lolland-Falsters Traktor- og Motormuseum
The Tractor and Motor Museum of Lolland-Falster
Nørregade 17 B, 4863 Eskilstrup, Denmark
Tel. (45) 54 43 70 07   www.traktormuseum.dk
May-Oct: daily 10am-5pm (May, Jun, Sep: Tue-Sun 10am-5pm)

The collection contains about ninety tractors dating from 1917 to 1960. Among those on show are a Mogul (1917), a Ferguson Brown (1938), and a Lanz Bulldog (1938).

Maatalousmuseo
Agricultural Museum
Helsinki University, Viikin koetila 00710, Helsinki, Finland
Tel. (358) 9 647 677   www.helsinki.fi
Sun noon-4pm

This is a diverse collection of over 4,000 Finnish agricultural implements, used mainly for teaching purposes. It contains horse- and man-powered implements (such as ploughs, milking apparatus, carpenter's and smithy's tools), and a small number of tractors. Pride of place is given to 100 accurate miniature models of animals produced by the artisan, Ravander-Rauaksen.

Patent model hop kiln, 1876 (above)
The Farmers' Museum

Various farm implements (left)
Billings Farm & Museum

Metz Bicycle Museum
54 West Main Street, Freehold, New Jersey 07728, USA
Tel. (1) 732 462 7363
www.metzbicyclemuseum.com
Please call for opening times

Not content with collecting bikes, pencil sharpeners, and kitchen contraptions, David Metz also has a collection of over 100 early mouse traps, many of which were used in the agricultural industry. The scope of man's ingenuity is apparent in this collection of bizarrely-shaped contraptions, ranging from clear glass vials which were dug into the ground at the base of fruit trees, to an aluminium self-setting mouse trap endorsed by Bing Crosby, and an example of the *Better Mouse Trap*, developed by Dian B. Wirt of Nebraska in 1884 (with the original patent papers).

New Jersey Museum of Agriculture
103 College Farm Road, Rutgers University, New Brunswick, New Jersey 08902, USA
Tel. (1) 732 249 2077   www.agriculturemuseum.org
Tue-Sat 10am-5pm

A collection of three centuries of historic agricultural artefacts, second only to that of the Smithsonian Institution. It includes everything from apple cider presses to market wagons, corn shellers, and cranberry scoops. Highlights include the Deats Plow, patented in 1828, and a rare life-sized reproduction of the McCormick Reaper from the 1920s.

Musée régional du Machinisme agricole
The Regional Museum of Agricultural Machinery
68 bis rue de la Chaussée, 02460 La Ferté-Milon, France
Tel. (33) 3 23 96 29 85
Sat 10am-12.30pm, 3-5.30pm

This museum exhibits a great number of machines, tools, and agricultural implements, some of which have been in use for over a century. There are also prehistoric examples, such as dibbers, lances, and stone blades. Contemporary machinery is also on display, and the section dedicated to tractors shows several brands and types, mainly American, from the end of the 19th century onwards.

Museum of Scottish Country Life
Kittochside, East Kilbride, Scotland, UK
Tel. (44) 131 247 4274   www.nms.ac.uk
Please call for opening times

There are galleries on the environment, rural technologies, and people, with the oldest threshing machine in the world and the best collection of combine harvesters in Europe. A working farm will operate throughout the year showing the range of seasonal work, from ploughing and haymaking to harvesting.

FOLK ART (INCLUDING DECOYS)

One Shoe Off, oil, John
Brewster, 1807
Fenimore Art Museum

Barnegat Bay Decoy and Baymen's Museum

Tuckerton Seaport 120 West Main Street, Tuckerton, New Jersey 08087 USA
Tel. (1) 609 296 8868 www.tuckertonseaport.org
Wed-Sun 10am-4.30pm

Opened in 1993 in a replica hunting cabin, the museum displays a superb collection of
decoys and other Baymen's hunting, fishing, and boat-building artefacts at various
locations in Tuckerton Seaport. One major collection donated to the museum was originally amassed by Dr and Mrs Robert Irvin of Manahawkin, and consists of over ninety
decoys. Local carvers demonstrate their skills in three contemporary carving shops.

Chesapeake Bay Maritime Museum

Mill Street, St. Michaels, Maryland 21663 USA
Tel. (1) 410 745 2916 www.cbmm.org
Jan-Feb: Fri-Sat 9am-5pm. Mar-Dec: daily 9am-5pm

Situated on the largest inland estuary in the west, and in the heart of one of the great
migratory flyways, this Chesapeake museum features an exceptionally fine collection
of decoys and other wildfowl artefacts, including fowling guns and
hunting boats. Gems in the collection include a swan carved by Sam
Barnes, marked with the number 1, and a scaup by the African-
American carver, Pied Jones.

The Craft and Folk Art Museum (CAFAM)

5800 Wilshire Boulevard, Los Angeles, California 90036 USA
Tel. (1) 323 937 4230
Tue-Sun 11am-5pm (Fri until 8pm)

Weather vane in the shape
of a horse, unidentified
maker, end of 19th /
beginning of 20th century
*Abby Aldrich Rockefeller Folk
Art Center*

A vibrant mix of contemporary craftwork, folk art, product design, masks, and traditional
Hispanic and Asian household objects. The folk art collection includes toys, tools, basketry,
and dolls. There are 19th- and 20th-century textiles, and costumes from India,
Indonesia, Uzbekistan, and Eastern Europe. Also, Amish and other American quilts.

Fenimore Art Museum

Lake Road, Route 80, Cooperstown, New York 13326, USA
Tel. (1) 607 547 1400 www.fenimoreartmuseum.org
Apr-May: Tue-Sun 10am-4pm. Jun-Sep: daily 10am-5pm. Oct-Dec: Tue-Sun 10am-4pm

Alongside the excellent American Indian Collection is a comprehensive collection of
American folk art which includes painting, sculpture, textiles, weathervanes, and ships'
figureheads. Among the paintings are some fascinating early 18th-century depictions of
Dutch life along the banks of the Hudson River. Also of interest is work by a range of late
20th-century artists including Grandma Moses, Ralph Fasanella, and Lavern Kelly.

Havre de Grace Decoy Museum

215 Giles St, Havre de Grace, Maryland 21078, USA
Tel. (1) 410 939 3739 www.decoymuseum.com
Daily 11am-4pm

This magnificent collection features 2,250 hunting decoys made by 300 carvers, for the
most part between 1930 and 1960. Alongside the decoys is related paraphernalia such as
guns, duck calls, and boats (including a sinkbox, punt gun skiff, night gunning boat,
sneak boat skill, and bushwhacking boat). The workshop of the carver, Madison
Mitchell, was reconstructed in the museum in the 1980s.

Hedmarksmuseet og Domkirkeodden
The Hedmark Museum at Cathedral Point

Strandveien 100, 2305 Hamar, Norway
Tel. (47) 62 542700
www.hedmarksmuseet.museum.no
Please call for opening times

This superb open-air museum consists of sixty original rural buildings built between the 17th and the 19th centuries, ranging from a humble tenant farmer's cabin to a complete dairy farm. Sverre Fehn's brilliantly converted Sorharmer barn includes folk art items such as sleighs, furniture, farming implements, and fishing and hunting tools.

George Gustav Heye Center - National Museum of The American Indian

Smithsonian Institution, Alexander Hamilton U.S. Custom House, One Bowling Green, New York, New York 10004, USA
Tel. (1) 212 514 3700 www.nmai.si.edu
Daily 10am-5pm (Thu until 8pm)

This superb Smithsonian collection includes eleven of the prehistoric decoys made by Native Americans, which were discovered alongside fish hooks and nets in 1924 in a cave and fossil lake in Nevada.

High Museum of Art, Folk Art and Photography Galleries

133 Peachtree Street, Georgia-Pacific Center, Atlanta, Georgia 30303, USA
Tel. (1) 404 577 6940 www.high.org
Mon-Sat 10am-5pm

Housed in a spectacular building by Richard Meier, where a large-scale expansion by Renzo Piano is currently being added. This museum began collecting contemporary self-taught art in 1975, and has since grown into one of the most important repositories for the genre in the world. Highlights include work by Howard Finster and the Alabama artist, Bill Traylor.

Museum of International Folk Art

Museum of New Mexico, 706 Camino Lejo, Santa Fe, New Mexico 87505, USA
Tel. (1) 505 476 1200 www.moifa.org
Daily 10am-5pm

Unlabelled displays allow you to concentrate on the beauty of over 125,000 objects representing more than 100 countries, all mixed together with what appears to be gay abandon. The core of the collection was donated by the founder of the museum, Florence Dibell Bartlett, and the collection was then greatly enhanced with a gift from Alexander and Susan Girard in 1978. They spent their lives collecting, taking humour, whimsy, and spontaneity as their guides. The result is a wonderful and delightful museum.

Horse with the Longest Hair in the World, oil on canvas, anonymous, *c*.1895-96 (top)
Fenimore Art Museum

Watering can (above)
The National Waterways Museum

Bears and Pears, oil on wood, artist unidentified, *c*.1825-50 (above left)
Fenimore Art Museum

The Long Island Museum of American Art, History and Carriages
1200 Route 25A, Stony Brook, New York 11790-1992, USA
Tel. (1) 631 751 0066 www.longislandmuseum.org
Wed-Sat 10am-5pm, Sun noon-5pm

This huge American art museum comprises a nine-acre complex of exhibition buildings and educational facilities. The collection consists of 40,000 objects, primarily horse-drawn vehicles, along with paintings, drawings, and prints of Long Island by such eminent New York artists as William Sidney Mount. The Margaret Melville Blackwell History Museum includes a major collection of 250 Long Island and regional wildfowl decoys, considered to be one of the top three duck decoy collections in the US.

Milwaukee Public Museum
800 West Wells Street, Milwaukee, Wisconsin 53233, USA
Tel. (1) 414 278 2732 www.mpm.edu
Daily 9am-5pm

Canvasback, by Joseph Sieger, Lake Poygan area, Winsconsin, c. 1925, carved and painted wood with glass eyes (top)
Abby Aldrich Rockefeller Folk Art Center

Eel Spearing at Setauket, oil on canvas, William Sidney Mount, 1845 (above)
Fenimore Art Museum

Canada goose, attributed to Edward James Phillips, Cambridge, Maryland, c.1922, carved and painted wood with lead weights and tack-head eyes (above right)
Abby Aldrich Rockefeller Folk Art Center

The collection of 390 decoys includes a dozen or so reed decoys made by Augusto Francischini in the 1930s-50s, startlingly similar to the prehistoric decoys found in Nevada and presently in the Smithsonian in New York (see entry). The breadth of this collection is its main strength. It contains examples dating from 1890 to the 1940s by most of the major makers from the Eastern and Midwestern schools of decoy carving.

The National Waterways Museum
Llanthony Warehouse, Gloucester Docks, Gloucester, Gloucestershire GL1 2EH, UK
Tel. (44) 1452 318054 www.nwm.org.uk
Daily 10am-5pm

The museum's collection of canal art decoration on narrow boat exteriors, watercans, and other household objects covers a complete history of the distinctive 'Roses and Castles' style, from its origins in the 1840s and 1850s when it was inspired by gipsy folk art found in Scandinavia, Germany, Eastern Europe, Turkey, and Bangladesh.

The Noyes Museum
Lily Lake Road, Oceanville, New Jersey 08231, USA
Tel. (1) 609 652 8848 users.jerseycape.com
Wed-Sun 11am-4pm

Surrounded by pine trees and lakes, this spacious contemporary museum houses a remarkable collection of American folk art, including a substantial collection of 450 duck decoys, consisting mostly of works from carvers on the Atlantic flyway.

Oshkosh Public Museum
1331 Algoma Boulevard, Oshkosh, Wisconsin 54901-2799, USA
Tel. (1) 920 424 4731 www.publicmuseum.oshkosh.net
Tue-Sat 9am-5pm, Sun 1-5pm

This magnificent collection of folk art – crafted by local German, Polish, Russian, and Scandinavian immigrants – is housed in a mansion built in 1908 for the lumber baron, banker, and businessman, Edgar P. Sawyer. One of the prize exhibits is an eight-foot-tall Apostles Clock, built in 1895 by Mathias Kitz.

Abby Aldrich Rockefeller Folk Art Center
307 South England Street, Williamsburg, Virginia 23185, USA
Tel. (1) 757 229 1000 www.colonialwilliamsburg.org
Daily 10am-5pm

One of the largest collections of folk art in the US, the centre houses nearly 3,000 pieces, including a large number of paintings by Edward Hicks, Joseph Hidley, Ammi Philips, and the Prior-Hamblin group. There are carved works by Wilhelm Schimmmel, the sketchbooks of Lewis Miller, superb examples of woven coverlets, and a wide variety of folk art forms ranging from weathervanes (depicting horses, butterflies, and leaping deer) to tobacconist shop figures.

May Day 1948, Ralph Fasanella (above) *Fenimore Art Museum*

Shelburne Museum
US Route 7, Shelburne, Vermont 05482, USA
Tel. (1) 802 985 3346   www.shelburnemuseum.org
May-Oct: daily 10am-5pm. Rest of year: walking tours at 1pm

Rhyton in the shape of a ram's head with red figures (below) *Museo Martini di Storia dell'Enologia*

View of the brewing house at the museum (bottom) *Brauerei-Museum Dortmund*

This wide-ranging collection of early American weathervanes, whirligigs, and decoys is displayed in various buildings in the locality. The decoy collection (nearly 900 examples) is displayed in the Dorset house, along with decorative decoys, miniature bird carvings, wildfowl painting, and prints, and a rare collection of fish decoys used by ice fishermen to lure their prey within spearing range. Over 130 weathervanes and moulds dating from the 18th century onwards are exhibited in the Stagecoach Inn. The Round Barn has a charming display of whirligigs.

Ward Museum of Wildfowl Art
909 South Schumaker Drive, Salisbury, Maryland 21804-8743, USA
Tel. (1) 410 742 4988   www.wardmuseum.org
Mon-Sat 10am-5pm, Sun noon-5pm

Skiffs, hunting paraphernalia, literature on fowling, decorative bird carving, and several thousand decoys have been gathered together at this Mecca for wildfowl art located in the heart of one of America's major flyways (the Atlantic coast). The collection is displayed in ten galleries, with a special emphasis on the hand-carved and painted decoys produced from 1918 to 1980 by Len and Steve Ward.

FOOD, WINE AND BREWING

The Bass Museum
Horninglow Street, Burton upon Trent,
Staffordshire DE14 1YQ, UK
Tel. (44) 1283 511000   www.bass-museum.com
Daily 10am-4pm

This is the largest brewing collection in the country, with a diverse and entertaining range of artefacts and memorabilia, from historic equipment and advertising materials to vintage vehicles and photographs. Learn about the art of barrel-making, visit an Edwardian bar, and see the wonderful Daimler Worthington White Shield Bottle car, constructed in the shape of an enormous beer bottle.

Brauerei-Museum Dortmund
Brewery Museum Dortmund
Märkische Strasse 85, 44141 Dortmund, Germany
Tel. (49) 231 574214
Tue-Sun 10am-2pm

This museum explores the cultural history of beer from its beginnings in antiquity to the present day. Among the

exhibits is a cast of an Egyptian statuette of a beer brewer found in a tomb dating from 2400 BC. There is early brewing equipment and examples of mass production and distribution machinery, including old-fashioned bottling machines, fermenting vats, and a compressed air pump.

Deutsches Technikmuseum Berlin
The German Museum of Technology in Berlin
Trebbiner Strasse 9, 10963 Berlin, Germany
Tel. (49) 30 254840 www.dtmb.de
Tue-Fri 9am-5.30pm, Sat-Sun 10am-6pm

Housed in a former brewery warehouse, this exhibition explains the traditional methods of brewing, using technical equipment from the early 20th century. The brewing room, with its copper vats, handwheels, pipes, and gleaming fittings, dates back to 1909.

Le Musée français de la Brasserie
The French Brewery Museum
62 rue Charles-Courtois, 54210 Saint-Nicolas-de-Port, France
Tel. (33) 3 83 46 95 52
Tue-Sun 2-6pm

This museum offers an insight into the history of brewing, with numerous photographs and documents as well as vats, equipment, and a laboratory. Another part of the exhibition displays collectors' items such as advertising posters, postcards, beer labels, bottles, and beer mats.

Muzei khleba
The Bread Museum
Ligovskii prospekt 73, 191040 St Petersburg, Russian Federation
Tel. (7) 812 164 1110 www.museum.ru
Tue-Fri 10am-5pm, Sat 11am-3pm

Red-figure kantharos (top)
Museo Martini di Storia dell'Enologia

Red figure amphora (middle left)
Museo Martini di Storia dell'Enologia

Small alembic for distilling herbs in infusion (middle right)
Museo Martini di Storia dell'Enologia

Machine for filtering wine (above)
Museo Martini di Storia dell'Enologia

The size of this museum belies its scope. Two of its four rooms house a comprehensive collection of bread-making apparatus, which visitors are encouraged to pick up and touch, along with pictures documenting the history of bread-making in Russia. The third room devotes itself to the role of bread in Russian literature. One case documents Pushkin's references to bread in his works, and even suggests what food the writer might have eaten while composing them. The fourth room contains an exhibition on the Siege of Leningrad, where the visitor is introduced to the various improvised bread substitutes which were the staple diet of St Petersburg's wartime inhabitants.

Museo Giovanni F. Mariani del Vetro e della Bottiglia
The Giovanni F. Mariani Museum of Glass and Bottles
Castello Poggio alle Mura, 53024 St Angelo Scalo, Italy
Tel. (39) 0577 816001 www.castellobanfi.com
Summer: daily 10am-7pm. Winter: 10am-6pm

A delightful museum located in a medieval castle surrounded by vineyards and orchards. It traces the history of wine through the evolution of glassmaking, from Roman bottles made in Italy and the Rhineland through to onion-shaped bottles from the 17th century, and on to the cylindrical bottle and mechanical manufacturing of the 20th century. In addition, the museum has a collection of glassworks by Picasso, Cocteau, and Dali, and an extensive selection of Murano glassware.

Museo Martini di Storia dell' Enologia
The Martini Museum of the History of Oenology
Frazione Pessione, piazza Luigi Rossi 1, 10023 Chieri, Italy
Tel. (39) 011 94191
Sep-Jul: Wed-Fri 2-5pm, Sat-Sun 9am-noon, 2-5pm

From industrial machinery to Roman glass, the methods of
making and consuming wine over the centuries are carefully
documented. Archaeological finds, drinking vessels and fil-
ters, bronzes, cups, and goblets are included, along with
technical equipment such as ebullioscopes and capillarimeters
from the 20th century.

Nationaal Jenevermuseum
The National Genever Museum
Witte Nonnenstraat 19, 3500 Hasselt, Belgium
Tel. (32) 011 241144
Apr-Oct: Tue-Sun 10am-5pm. Nov-Mar: Tue-Fri 10am-5pm, Sat-Sun 1-5pm

Housed in a listed distillery complex, the collection traces the history and manufacture
of Belgian gin since its development in the 14th century from aqua vitae. You also have a
chance to sample a glass at the end of your visit.

Nederlands Wijnmuseum Arnhem
The Dutch Wine Museum in Arnhem
Velperweg 23, 6824 BC Arnhem, The Netherlands
Tel. (31) 26 4424042   www.bosgraaf.nl
Tue-Fri 2-5pm, Sat 11am-5pm

Displays cover thousands of years of wine-making history and include historic casks,
bottles, glasses, wine cellar tools, and corks, as well as a collection of over 750 corkscrews.

Norsk Hermetikkmuseum
The Norwegian Canning Museum
Øvre Strandgate 88 A, 4010 Stavanger
Norway
Tel. (47) 51 534989
Please call for opening times

The history of sardine production
from c.1880 to 1930, with presses, dies,
guillotines for sheet metal, soldering
equipment, a flanging machine, a
machine for making the keys for sardine cans, a machine for cutting off fish-heads, and
a labelling-cum-wrapping machine.

Paprika Múzeum
The Museum of Paprika
Szent István király út 6, 6300 Kalocsa, Hungary
Tel. (36) 78 461819
Apr-Oct: Tue-Sun 10am-5pm. Nov-Mar: by appt. only

The museum examines the history of paprika in Hungary since its introduction to the
country by the Turks. Displays of tools follow the cycle of paprika from planting
through to powdered spice.

Hall displaying goblets
and glasses (top)
*Museo Martini di Storia
dell'Enologia*

Two goblets, Dublin, end
of 18th century (above)
*Museo Martini di Storia
dell'Enologia*

Interior of the production
area (left)
Norsk Hermetikkmuseum

Boerhaave's Apparatus, the reconstruction of the air-cooling cone by the Dutch physician, Ermanno Boerhaave (above)
Poli Museo della Grappa

Late 18th-century copper wari (below)
The National Museum of Gardening

Museum felling and pruning display (below right)
Harlow Carr Museum of Gardening

Musée de la Pêche
The Museum of Fishing
3 rue Vauban, 29900 Concarneau, France
Tel. (33) 2 98 97 10 20
Sep-Jun: daily 10am-noon, 2-6pm. Jul-Aug: 9.30am-8pm

This museum displays tins made by some of the first tuna and sardine companies, of which the highlight is Joseph Colin's sardine tin. He was a sweet-maker who first had the idea of sealing sardines in a box in 1824.

Poli Museo della Grappa
The Poli Museum of Grappa
Ponte Vecchio, 36061 Bassano del Grappa, Italy
Tel. (39) 0424 524426
Daily 9am-1pm, 2.30-7.30pm (closed Mon am)

Set inside a 15th-century palace located at the end of the historic wooden bridge, Ponte Vecchio, the history of the distillation and production of Grappa is told through documents and Grappa-making equipment. Reconstructed stills and historic engravings illustrate the extensive experiments and developments that first produced perfume essences, later pharmacological substances, and before too long pleasurable drinks as well. The library holds rare editions on the art of distillation.

Musée du Tire-bouchon
The Corkscrew Museum
Domaine de la Citadelle, 84560 Ménerbes, France
Tel. (33) 4 90 72 41 58
Please call for details

This collection belongs to the vineyard's owner, Yves Rousset-Rouard, the film-maker responsible for the *Emmanuelle* series. His collection began when he visited the auction house, Hôtel Drouot, in Paris. Intrigued by a corkscrew collection, he decided to buy the lot (approximately 200 pieces). His idea was that it might be good for his business if he opened a quirky museum within his newly acquired Domaine. Today, there are more than 2,200 items on display, including one of the oldest corkscrews in existence, dating from around 1694.

GARDENING TOOLS AND ORNAMENTAL IRONWORK

Musée de l'Abeille
The Museum of the Bee
Esplanade de l'Abeille, 4130 Tilff, Belgium
Tel. (32) 4 3882263
Apr-Jun, Sep: Sat-Sun 2-6pm. Jul, Aug: daily 10am-noon, 2-6pm

Unlike other museums of apiculture, this one focuses on the bee itself, housing not only displays of items used in apiculture, but also exhibits relating to the 'scientific' aspects of bees and their habitats. Exhibits include 19th- and 20th-century beehives, bee-keeping equipment

(including an 18th-century smoke blower), and a 'live section' with two glass-sided hives.

British Lawnmower Museum

106-114 Shakespeare Street, Southport, Lancashire PR8 5AJ, UK
Tel. (44) 1704 501336
Daily 9am-5.30pm

Dozens of lawnmowers in all their glory, including those that belonged to the rich and famous. Prince Charles' lawnmower is in the collection, and while it is possible to believe that he cut his own lawn on occasion, it's hard to imagine that the late Diana Princess of Wales used hers very often.

Tin plate clockwork
child's toy
*The National Museum of
Gardening*

The Brooking Museum of Architectural Detail

University of Greenwich, Dartford Campus, Oakfield Lane, Dartford, Kent DA1 2SZ, UK
Tel. (44) 20 8331 9897
By appt. only

Comprising 8,000 items ranging in date from the 16th century to the present, this museum comprehensively covers window ironmongery, door ironmongery (knockers, bolts, letterplates, and locks), and the principle forms of domestic staircases. It also explores the history of the coal burning grate (from 1700 to 1960), and the development of the rainwater head from the 16th century to the present.

Deutsches Gartenbaumuseum Erfurt
The German Museum of Horticulture of Erfurt

Cyriaksburg, Gothaer Straße 50, 99094 Erfurt, Germany
Tel. (49) 361 223990
Tue-Sun 10am-6pm

The exhibition, in 46 thematic sections, attempts to convey all aspects of gardening as well as imparting recent scientific knowledge. There is an apple cabinet, a winter garden, a medieval herbarium, and a genetics laboratory. Also 'Gardens of the World', ranging from Japanese rock gardens to an English landscape.

Musée de la Ferronnerie
The Museum of Ironwork

Place de L'Eglise, 27160 Francheville, France
Tel. (33) 2 32 32 69 87
Please call for opening times

At the end of the 19th century there were over 400 forges in Francheville. This collection features examples of their work, as well as a large selection of tools.

The Museum of Garden History

Lambeth Palace Road, London SE1 7LB, UK
Tel. (44) 20 7401 8865 www.cix.co.uk
Mid Mar-mid Dec: Mon-Fri, Sun 10.30am-5pm

A remarkable collection of English gardening tools, along with displays on the history of gardens, notable gardeners, and plant hunters. A wonderful array of watering cans line the shelves, including a 17th-century lead-glazed earthenware watering pot. Rows of syringes, spray devices, ceramic tallies or labels, wasp traps, and cucumber straighteners are displayed in cases, along with long-handled edging shears, sickles, and seed packets. One of the more exotic items is the 'Vegetable Lamb of Tartary', a rare fungus with roots resembling a young lamb.

Box set of a Victorian garden syringe and nozzles, c.1870
The National Museum of Gardening

Gartenbaumuseum
The Museum of Horticulture
Kurpark Laaer Berg 10, Laaer-Berg-Strasse 211, 1100 Vienna, Austria
Tel. (43) 1 6881170   www.magwien.gv.at
May-Oct: Wed-Fri 10am-2.30pm, every 1st and 3rd Sat-Sun of the month 1-5pm
Other times by appt.

The collection ranges from greenhouses, garden vehicles, and machines through to clothes, tools, and utensils. Highlights include a Roman waterpipe, and tools from the Renaissance made from wood or stone. There is also a vast collection of original plans for famous landscaped gardens and avenues both in Vienna and in other parts of the country.

Harlow Carr Museum of Gardening
Harlow Carr Botanical Gardens, Crag Lane, Harrogate, Yorkshire HG3 1QB, UK
Tel. (44) 1423 565418   www.harlowcarr.fsnet.co.uk
Daily 10am-4pm

Around 1,000 gardening implements displayed in a gatehouse within 68 acres of magnificent gardens. Budding knives, lawnmowers, hand ploughs, forks, pruners of all sorts, a bilberry picker, and a cucumber straightener are exhibited alongside early gardening magazines and colourful seed packets.

Ceramic plant labels
Harlow Carr Museum of Gardening

Musée horticole
The Horticultural Museum
15 rue du Jardin-Ecole, 93100 Montreuil, France
Tel. (33) 1 48 57 00 86
By appt. only

This small museum offers a very fine collection of gardening tools and documentation of techniques, mainly related to fruit-growing and in particular to peach-growing. On display are tools for grafting and fruit picking, and the typical patterns of the 'tattooist' who 'tattooed' the fruits with the producer's initials. There is also a 19th-century appliance for brushing peaches.

One of many colourful advertising signs
The National Museum of Gardening

Moottorisahamuseo
The Chain Saw Museum
Ainolantie 1, 72401 Pielavesi, Finland
Tel. (358) 17 861 545 / (358) 400 218 191 (for appointments)
Jun, Jul: daily noon-6pm. Rest of year: by appt. only

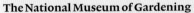

A collection of over 700 chainsaws, as well as nearly 2,000 other objects related to forestry work. Most are from the US, athough the two Finnish chainsaw manufacturers, Hyry and Permit, are fully represented. The collection is probably the largest in the world. A rarity is a German two-man chainsaw from 1932, which is 2.5 metres long and weighs 57 kg.

The National Museum of Gardening
Trevarno Estate Gardens, Trevarno Manor, Helston, Cornwall TR13 0RU, UK
Tel. (44) 1326 574274
Daily 10.30am-5pm

A large and important collection of over 2,000 garden antiques, implements, artefacts, memorabilia, and ephemera, displayed in ten themed areas. There is a bewildering array of watering cans and sprinklers, sprayers, puffers, and wheelbarrows, as well as tools through the ages. Rare seed cabinets form the backdrop to a collection of old seed packets, labels, dibbers, and seed sowers.

Musée Le Secq des Tournelles
The Le Secq des Tournelles Museum
2 rue Jacques-Villon, 76000 Rouen,
France
Tel. (33) 2 35 71 28 40
Wed-Mon 10am-1pm, 2-6pm

This remarkable collection of ironwork includes numerous grilles and
railings, from a 13th-century iron gate
which belonged to the Ourscamp
Abbey, France (decoration consisting
of a close network of twigs, gathered
in bundles and fastened by rings), to
grilles of the 15th century. The majority
of the collection, however, features grilles from
the 18th century, when ornamental ironwork reached its zenith.

Societe Centrale d'Apiculture - Jardin du Luxembourg
The Central Bee-Keeping Society - The Luxembourg Gardens
Blvd. Saint-Michel, rue de Médicis, 75006 Paris, France
Tel. (33) 1 45 42 29 08
Summer: daily 9am-9.30pm. Winter: daily 9am-9pm

Brimming with bee-related manuscripts, engravings, and literature dating back to the
1600s, the Society once held an extraordinary collection of exotic beehives. Although
the documents remain at their headquarters, some thirty hives have found pride of
place in the city's Jardin du Luxembourg, while the majority have been sent to the
secluded Musée apicole de Beautheil (3, route d'Amillis, 77120 Beautheil, France. Tel.
(33) 1 64 04 68 45). Those in the garden include mud-plastered, woven frame hives from
southwest France; the round, rustic willow skeps with pointed tops; the hexagonal
wooden hives with copper roofs; and a host of others embellished with bee motifs.

Rare seed catalogue
(above)
*The National Museum of
Gardening*

Rare seed cabinet,
c. 1900 (above left)
*The National Museum of
Gardening*

Spalding Bulb Museum
Birchgrove Garden Centre, Surfleet Road, Pinchbeck, Lincolnshire PE11 3XY, UK
Tel. (44) 1775 680490
Daily 10am-4pm

At the early part of the 20th century, Spalding's tulip bulb industry gave the Dutch a run
for their money, with over 100,000 acres ablaze with tulips at its peak in 1939. Today, less
than 200 acres remain. A restored 1904 Flower Forcing House displays this collection,
which traces the heyday of tulip cultivation in the area and includes old machinery,
photographs, and equipment.

Victoria and Albert Museum
Cromwell Road, South Kensington, London SW7 2RL, UK
Tel. (44) 20 7942 2000 www.vam.ac.uk
Daily 10am-5.45pm (Wed and last Fri of every month 10am-10pm)

The focal point of the Ironwork Galleries is the choir screen designed by Sir George
Gilbert Scott for Hereford Cathedral. There are hundreds of items (iron chests, biscuit
tins, locks and keys, door furniture, and railings) dating from the 12th to the 20th centuries, representing Britain, Italy, France, Germany, Belgium, and Spain. Don't miss the
elaborate Versailles balcony (*c*.1770) or the flowered candlesticks, filigree iron bracelets,
and satyr masks from Hampton Court. It is one of the most comprehensive collections of
its type in the world.

KITCHENALIA AND EATING UTENSILS

Musée de l'art culinaire – Auguste Escoffier
Auguste Escoffier Museum of Culinary Art
3 rue Escoffier, 06270 Villeneuve-Loubet, France
Tel. (33) 4 93 20 80 51 www.fondation-escoffier.org
Summer: Tue-Sun 2-7pm. Winter: Tue-Sun 2-6pm (closed in Nov)

This museum, housed in Escoffier's birthplace, is a charming blend of professional memorabilia, family souvenirs, photographs, portraits, and mementoes from a long, successful career. There are utensils and cake moulds, porcelain dishes and pottery bowls, a reproduction of a train created entirely from sugar, and a picture of a tiger executed in rice. For the serious enthusiast, the museum has 1,500 menus (some from Escoffier's days at the Savoy hotel).

Bakers at work
Bakkerijmuseum
'Walter Plaetinck'

Bakkerijmuseum 'Walter Plaetinck'
Baking Museum 'Walter Plaetinck'
Zuidgasthoeve Albert I laan 2, 8630 Veurne, Belgium
Tel. (32) 58 313897
Please call for opening times

This baking museum includes a model of a 1900s bakery and a huge assortment of bread paraphernalia, including ration cards from World War II, bread coupons which were handed out by companies in order to keep wages low, and a collection of little coins or 'patakons' which were often put in children's pastries as a surprise. There are also thousands of magazines and books devoted to baking and a beautiful collection of 17th- and 18th-century moulds for the production of *speculaas* (a kind of sweet, spicy biscuit).

Museum of Childhood at Bethnal Green
Cambridge Heath Road, London E2 9PA, UK
Tel. (44) 20 8983 5200 www.vam.ac.uk
Mon-Thu, Sat 10am-5.50pm, Sun 2.30-5.30pm

The museum has an extensive display of child-feeding equipment, from rare antique 'pap boats' to all kinds of sucking bottles. Among the items of particular interest are a nipple shield in silver (1812) and a glass breast pump from 1905, with original packaging.

Cooper-Hewitt National Design Museum
Smithsonian Institution, Fifth Avenue at 91st Street, New York, New York 10028, USA
Tel. (1) 212 849 8400 www.si.edu
Tue 10am-9pm, Wed-Sat 10am-5pm, Sun noon-5pm

One of the many highlights in the Applied Arts Department is the Robert L. Metzenberg Collection of historic cutlery, which comprises approximately 250 items illustrating the evolution of European and American cutlery, from simple utilitarian forms to highly ornate, coveted works of art with handles of engraved silver, porcelain, amber, and even beadwork. There is also modern cutlery design and non-Western eating utensils.

Musée de la Coutellerie
The Museum of Cutlery
Maison des Couteliers, 23 rue de la Coutellerie, 63300 Thiers, France
Tel. (33) 4 73 80 58 86 perso.wanadoo.fr
Please call for opening times

A wide-ranging collection of post-medieval European and local cutlery. There are unique pieces displayed alongside mass-produced examples, illustrating the skills and knowledge of Thiers's craftspeople.

Musée de la Coutellerie - Espace Pelletier
The Pelletier Cutlery Museum

Place de l'Hôtel de Ville, Nogent-en-Bassigny, France
Tel. (33) 3 25 31 89 21
Jun-Sep: daily 10am-noon, 2-6pm. Oct-May: Mon, Wed-Sun 10am-noon, 2-6pm

Ceramic platter for
serving biscuits
*Bakkerijmuseum
'Walter Plaetinck'*

The area is famous for making the best high-class cutlery and scissors in Europe. The museum displays magnificent 18th-century luxuries such as a delicate porcelain-handled knife, in an elegant sheath, with which a lady would cut fruit while travelling in her carriage.

Deutsches Klingenmuseum Solingen
The German Blade Museum of Solingen

Klosterhof 4, 42653 Solingen, Germany
Tel. (49) 212 59822   www.solingen.de
Tue-Thu, Sat-Sun 10am-5pm, Fri 2-5pm

This museum has a great variety of cutlery dating from the Bronze Age to the present day, including a fine collection of forks and spoons from the Roman Empire and Persia. One of the highlights is a set of six knives dating from 1584, with handles made from ivory, ebony, and mother-of-pearl, and blades showing the coat-of-arms of the city of Nuremberg.

Gruuthuse Museum

Dijver 17, 8000 Bruges, Belgium
Tel. (32) 50 448711
Apr-Sep: daily 9.30am-5pm. Oct-Mar: Mon, Wed-Sun 9.30am-12.30pm, 2-5pm

The oldest pieces of silver cutlery date back to the 17th century – two Baroque spoons (Brussels and Amsterdam), and two notable examples of folding spoon-forks (Bruges and

Antwerp). A variety of personalized cutlery displays the original owner's engraved initials or armorial bearings.

Kansainvälinen Kahvikuppimuseo
The International Coffee Cup Museum

97900 Posio, Finland
Tel. (358) 16 3721412   www.posi.fi
Daily 9am-8pm (Sat until 6pm)

Six knives: handles in
ivory, ebony and mother-
of-pearl; blades bear coat
of arms of Nuremberg
and signs of knife-maker;
pommels bear coat of
arms of the Patrician families Stomer and Sheurl
*Deutsches Klingenmuseum
Solingen*

A unique collection of 1,833 coffee cups from 81 countries. The most unusual foreign cup is an English 'moustache cup' from the late 19th century, so-called because it was designed to protect gentlemen's whiskers from coffee stains.

Museum of London

London Wall, London EC2Y 5HN, UK
Tel. (44) 20 7600 3699   www.museumoflondon.org.uk
Mon-Sat 10am-5.50pm, Sun noon-5.50pm

The 16th- and 17th-century collections are particularly strong in base metal artefacts, and the notable cutlery collection contains over 1,500 pieces.

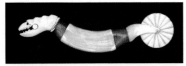

Sea monster crimper (top)
Whaling Museum

Unicorn pie crimper
(above)
Whaling Museum

Metz Bicycle Museum
54 West Main Street, Freehold, New Jersey 07728, USA
Tel. (1) 732 462 7363 www.metzbicyclemuseum.com
Please call for opening times

Along with hundreds of bikes there are household gadgets, including a
spring-steel hot dog fork made in the 1880s, a Michigan geared string
bean slicer (slices four string beans at once), early toasters, an asparagus
buncher, and an 1875 cheese slicer.

Musée de l'Opinel
The Opinel Museum
25 rue Jean Jaurès, 73300 Saint-Jean-de-Maurienne, France
Tel. (33) 4 79 64 04 78
Mon-Sat 9am-noon, 2-7pm

This museum is dedicated to the famous Opinel pocket-knife, itself a trademark for the
wooden-handled knife bearing the symbol of a crowned hand. It has old tools and
machines that were used in the production process, and commemorative items including
knives marking the Albertville Olympic Games and the anniversary of the invention of
cinema by the Lumière brothers.

Musée de la Poeslerie
The Museum of Copperware
Cour du Foyer, 50800 Villedieu-les-Poêles, France
Tel. (33) 2 33 90 20 92
Please call for opening times

The town got its name from the art of making pans. After the Crusades, the Duke of
Normandy, king of England, gave the town to the Malta Knights who had returned
from the Middle East with pan-making techniques. The collection gathers together
copper objects recovered from houses in the neighbourhood. The oldest object is a
16th-century *poêle à bouillie*, which was used for cooking black wheat, and there are
numerous other items of kitchenalia including frying pans, plates, and tools used for
cheese making.

Museum of Reading
Blagrave Street, Reading, RG1 1QH, UK
Tel. (44) 118 939 9800 www.readingmuseum.org.uk
Fri-Sat, Mon-Wed 10am-4pm, Thu 10am-7pm, Sun 11am-4pm

The world's first biscuit gallery recounts the story of the famous Reading biscuit manufacturers, Huntley & Palmers. There are glass cases lined with 300 decorative tins, along
with related artefacts and advertising, including a biscuit cutter, original posters, and a
special biscuit supplied to Captain Scott's ill-fated Antarctic expedition.

Sheffield City Museum
Weston Park, Sheffield S10 2TP, UK
Tel. (44) 114 2782600
Tue-Sat 10am-5pm, Sun 11am-5pm

This collection is worldwide in scope, although at its core is a selection of Sheffield
cutlery. The earliest Sheffield knife in the collection was excavated on the site of
Sheffield castle and dates from Chaucer's time. From the 18th century, there is a set of
twelve silver pistol-handled knives and forks, in a sharkskin case made by Edward Fox.

Whaling Museum

Nantucket Historical Association, 13 Broad Street, Nantucket Town, Nantucket, Massachusetts 02554, USA
Tel. (1) 508 228 1894 www.nha.org
Please call for opening times

A large core of the scrimshaw collection consists of kitchenware. There are several hundred examples of pie crimpers, trimmers, and sealers with intricate convolutions and curves, and often carrying personal messages. There are also rolling pins with handles turned from whale or walrus ivory.

Winterthur Museum

Garden and Library Route 52, Winterthur, Delaware 19735 USA
Tel. (1) 302 888 4600 www.winterthur.org
Mon-Sat 9am-5pm, Sun noon-5pm

The Campbell Collection's soup tureens and soup-related items have many whimsical details, from feet in the shape of dolphins to ornamental handles. Don't miss the porcelain tureen made in Meissen, Germany (1741-43), decorated with the Imperial Russian eagle.

LOCKS AND KEYS

Musée des Beaux Arts
The Museum of Fine Arts
Château, 41000 Blois, France
Tel. (33) 2 54 90 33 33
Mid Mar-mid Jun: daily 9am-6.30pm. Winter: please call for opening times

One of the leading collections of metalwork in France, gathered by Narcisse de la Houssaye in the 19th century. It comprises over 1,000 pieces dating from the Gallo-Roman period to the 19th century, including a 400-piece key collection dating from the 12th to the 19th centuries.

Björkbodan Lukkomuseo
Björkboda Lock Museum
Tullimäentie 7, 25900 Taalintehdas Finland
Tel. (358) 2 466 2200
Summer: Wed-Sun 3-6pm. Winter: by appt. only

Displayed in a former lock-worker's home is a collection of over 1,500 locks, keys, fittings, and bolts, taking you through the history of the local lock-making industry. Highlights include egg locks from the 1920s, which came in several different sizes.

Musée Bricard de la Serrure
The Bricard Lock Museum
1 rue de la Perle, 75003 Paris, France
Tel. (33) 1 42 777962
Mon 2-5pm, Tue-Fri 10am-noon, 2-5pm

The collection contains many rare and precious devices. There is a *serrure prévotale* in the shape of a lion's mouth – put your hand inside the animal's mouth to insert the key in the lock, and the mouth will shut and trap your hand. Other masterpieces include a lock in the shape of a lily, the French royal symbol.

The Albert Lock, made by Carpenter & Tildesley Willenhall, and named after Consort, Prince Albert. The lock was first seen at the Great Exhibition 1851 (top)
The Lock Museum

Dessert service, Paris, c. 1900, C.V. Gilbert and F. Nicoud, silver, gilding, mother-of-pearl (above)
Cooper-Hewitt National Design Museum

Crossbones padlock
(above)
Lock Museum of America

Facsimile key (right)
The Lock Museum

Cooper-Hewitt National Design Museum

Smithsonian Institution, Fifth Avenue at 91st Street, New York, New York 10028, USA

Tel. (1) 212 849 8400 www.si.edu

Tue 10am-9pm, Wed-Sat 10am-5pm, Sun noon-5pm

The museum's extensive metalwork collections range from European furniture mounts made in gilt bronze from the 18th century, to English and American hardware. There are several hundred examples of iron locks, keys, and other hardware of earlier periods, making the collection an important documentary resource.

The General Society of Mechanics and Tradesmen of the City of New York

20 West 44th Street, New York, New York 10036, USA

Tel. (1) 212 840 1840 www.generalsociety.org

Mon-Fri 9am-5pm

The John M. Mossman Lock Collection constitutes the main exhibit, with more than 370 examples. They range from ancient 4000 year-old wooden locks to modern 20th-century time locks. The collection is highly specialized and primarily features made-to-order bank and vault locks.

The Lock Museum

54-56 New Road, Willenhall West Midlands WV13 2DA, UK

Tel. (44) 902 634 542

Tue-Thu, Sat 11am-5pm

An interesting and eclectic collection of locks and keys, as well as lock-making tools. These include the Lighter Lock (used for securing crates to the decks of lighter boats), the Barpadlock (used for securing prison gates and cattle compounds), intricate Egyptian locks, elaborately shaped Roman keys, and wonderfully crafted royal locks.

Lock Museum of America

230 Main Street, Route 6, Terryville, Connecticut 06786-0104, USA

Tel. (1) 860 589 6359 www.lockmuseum.com

May-Oct: Tue-Sun 1.30-4.30pm

A collection of over 20,000 locks, keys, and associated hardware. The Yale Room overflows with locks manufactured by the company from 1860 to 1950, and has the original patent model of the mortise cylinder pin tumbler lock designed by Linus Yale, Jr, on June 25, 1865. The Eagle Lock Company Room contains over 1,000 locks and keys manufactured from 1854 to 1954, while the Corbin-Russwin Room has a large display of gold- and silver-plated hardware.

Harry Miller Lock Museum

Lockmasters Education Center, Lockmasters, Inc., 1014 South Main Street, Nicholasville, Kentucky 40356-9531, USA

Tel. (1) 859 887 9633

Mon, Wed, Fri 1-4pm

Comprising about 7,000 examples, the museum displays locks dating from ancient Egypt, Africa, Europe, Russia, and the US. From state-of-the-art locks to an Arabic mechanism of 1803, the bewildering variety will challenge the most technically minded.

Porvoon Museo
The City Museum of Porvoo
Välikatu 11, 06100 Porvoo, Finland
Tel. (358) 19 5747589
May-Aug: daily 11am-4pm
Sep- Apr: Wed-Sun noon-4pm

An exceptionally large collection of locks. Some are
Oriental, but most are from old buildings in Finland,
including some recovered from burning buildings on
the front line in Eastern Karelia during World War II.

Door lock, steel, made by
Jean Dutartre, Spain,
c. 1700
*Cooper-Hewitt National
Design Museum*

Schlage Antique Lock Collection
IR Sector & Safety Corporation, 111 Congressional Boulevard 200, Carmel, Indiana, USA
Tel. (1) 317 613 8301   www.schlage.com
Open to serious researchers only

This collection of over 200 locks is of great historical significance. It includes a rare
Mesopotamian pin tumbler lock, and a padlock and key belonging to Ivan the Terrible.
Reputed to have been given to Catherine II by a locksmith serving life in a Siberian
prison for the unauthorized picking of chastity belt locks, is a chain of tiny padlocks
forged from platinum. Apparently, Catherine was so pleased with it, she released him.

Musée Le Secq des Tournelles
The Le Secq des Tournelles Museum
2 rue Jacques-Villon, 76000 Rouen, France
Tel. (33) 2 35 71 28 40
Mon, Wed-Sun 10am-1pm, 2-6pm

One of the best collections of locks and keys in the world, with more than 4,000 pieces
on display and another 4,000 in store. There are keys stamped with the crest of Tsar
Nicolas I and the skeleton key used by the Duke of Chartres for Saint Cloud castle.
Another gem is the symbolic key given to England by France when it was dethroned,
featuring the arms of the House of France and the effigy of the Sun King.

STAMPS AND POSTAL HISTORY

Bath Postal Museum
8 Broad Street, Bath BA1 5LJ, UK
Tel. (44) 1225 460333   www.bathpostalmuseum.org
Mar-Dec: Mon-Sat 1-5pm, Sun 2-5pm

The world's first Penny Black stamped letter was posted here on 2 May, 1840. Now a
museum, the exhibitions focus on the history of communications from ancient Egypt
to the present day, with separate sections on uniforms, coaching prints, letters, post
boxes, post horns, and the role of planes and even pigeons in mail delivery.

The British Library
96 Euston Road, London NW1 2DB, UK
Tel. (44) 20 7412 7635   www.bl.uk
Mon-Fri 9.30am-6pm (Tue until 8pm), Sat 9.30am-5pm, Sun 11am-5pm

With eight million stamps, postal stationery, revenue stamps, artwork, covers, philatelic
books, and other archival material from all over the world, this astonishingly comprehensive collection is a first stop for philatelic researchers everywhere. Some 80,000

items, including the Penny Black of 1840 and the Blue Mauritius of 1847, are on permanent display.

Museo de la Casa de la Moneda
The Museum of the Mint
Calle Doctor Esquerdo 36, 28009 Madrid, Spain
Tel. (34) 91 5666544 www.fnmt.es
Tue-Fri 10am-2pm, 5-7.30pm, Sat-Sun 10am-2pm

The collection encompasses every Spanish issue since the creation of the Spanish post office in 1850, as well as a small number of foreign postage stamps. Other philatelic items include first-day covers and postcards, postal stationery, aerogrammes, original drawings, plates, and first samples used in the production of postage stamps.

Museum voor Communicatie
Museum of Communication

Town postman in summer uniform (top)
Museum für Kommunikation

Cashbox, Berne Fischer post, 1830 (above)
Museum für Kommunikation

Posting box, 1918 (right)
Museum für Kommunikation

Zeestraat 80- 82, 2518 AD The Hague, The Netherlands
Tel. (31) 70 3307500 www.ptt-museum.nl
Mon-Fri 10am-5pm, Sat-Sun noon-5pm

The museum's core collection was donated by Pieter Waller in 1924, on condition that a postal museum was founded. Today, four sections cover the history of Dutch communication, from the development of early postal systems at home and in the colonies onwards. The jewel of this two-million-strong stamp collection is an unmarked 1847 Blue Mauritius.

Museum für Kommunikation
Museum of Communication
Helvetiastrasse 16, 3000 Berne, Switzerland
Tel. (41) 31 3575555 www.mfk.ch
Tue-Sun 10am-5pm

This museum houses a vast stamp collection of around 500,000 items, including famous Swiss issues such as the Zurich 4 and 6. As well as displaying gems from the collection on a rotational basis, the museum documents the history of the Swiss Federal Post Office from its creation in 1849, using dioramas, original objects, and models of mail coaches and post buses.

National Postal Museum
The Smithsonian Institute, 2 Massachusetts Avenue, NE Washington, DC 20002, USA
Tel. (1) 202 633 9360 www.si.edu
Daily 10am-5.30pm

Established in 1886 with a donation from M.W. Robertson of a pane of 10-cent Confederate postage stamps, this collection (like so many in the Smithsonian) has expanded beyond comprehension. There are two main core collections: the Master Collection, which includes the museum's best examples of mint, used, and unused (without gum) US federal postage stamps (dating from 1847 to the present); and the Certified Plate Proof Collection, which contains approximately 40,000 proofs printed from the original plates of the Bureau of Engraving and Printing. Alongside these two monstrous archives are interactive exhibits covering such topics as the Pony Express and the art of letter writing. There are also displays of postal vehicles, handstamps, metering machines, and other objects.

The New York Museum of Postal History

James A. Farley Building, General Post Office, 421 Eighth Avenue, New York,
New York 10199, USA

Tel. (1) 212 330 3291

Main building open daily; please call for opening times to see special collections

With its free translation from Herodotus ('Neither snow nor rain nor heat nor gloom
of night stays these couriers from the swift completion of their appointed rounds')
and 'New Deal' murals, the monumental lobby of New York's Post Office headquarters
makes a fitting backdrop for this marvellous collection of post office memorabilia.
Alongside an original 19th-century horse-drawn postal cart (recovered from a restau-
rant in Ohio), a 1940s postal bike, and an Irish post office box, are cases filled with
badges, locks, and keys of every kind, a bee hive twine dispenser, a model of a Russian
mail bus, a 1920s metal egg crate (used to ship eggs from rural farms to schools), and
remains of pneumatic tubing that once connected most post office branches in
Manhattan and Brooklyn, sending mail through the city in minutes.

Posting box from Ste-
Croix (top)
*Museum für
Kommunikation*

Musée Olympique
The Olympic Museum

1 quai d'Ouchy, 1001 Lausanne, Switzerland

Tel. (41) 21 6216511 www.museum.olympic.org

May-Sep: Mon 9am-6pm, Tue-Wed, Fri-Sun 9am-6pm, Thu 9am-8pm

Poster by Rolf Gfeller,
1966 (above)
*Museum für
Kommunikation*

Four horse stagecoach,
type 'Coupé-Berline'
no.1401 (left)
*Museum für
Kommunikation*

Olympic stamps have been issued since the first Modern Olympics were held in Athens
in 1896. This collection has more than 12,000 Olympic stamps and other philatelic
documents commemorating the games.

Musée philatélique des Nations Unies
The United Nations Philatelic Museum

Palais des Nations, ave. de la Paix, 1202 Geneva, Switzerland

Tel. (41) 22 9074882

Mon-Fri 9am-noon, 2-4.30pm

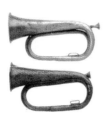

This magnificent museum houses the unique and rare collection of the Genevan teacher, Charles Misteli, who spent thirty years gathering together postage stamps, envelopes, and other items relating to the League of Nations and its successor, the United Nations.

Military telephone (top)
Museo postale e telegrafico della Mitteleuropa

Post horns (above)
Postmuseet

Wall postal Station
'Zellweger', *c.* 1893 (right)
Museum für Kommunikation

Philatelistische Bibliothek
The Philatelic Library
Rosenheimer Strasse 5, 81667 Munich, Germany
Tel. (49) 89 48098291
Mon 10am-8pm, Tue-Fri 10am-7pm

This is the largest public philatelic library in Europe, with an archive of 246 German and 265 current foreign periodicals, and 105 German and 135 current foreign auction catalogues. The special collections include over 45,000 monographs, periodicals, and auction catalogues on stamps and postal history.

Museo postale e telegrafico della Mitteleuropa
The Postal and Telegraphical Museum of Central Europe
Piazza Vittorio Veneto 1, 34132 Trieste, Italy
Tel. (39) 040 4196414
Mon-Sat 9am-1pm

Founded in 1994, this new museum celebrates the postal history of the Austro-Hungarian Empire, and includes items from Austria, Hungary, Slovenia, Croatia, Switzerland, and Italy. The small but excellent stamp collection displays some of the first stamps issued by the empire in 1850, plus postal maps and numerous rare stamps from the 19th century up to 1954. Alongside the stamps are fascinating sections devoted to the post office, from mail boxes (there were different colours for rural and official mail) to letters, post marks, uniforms, and an instrument called a *rastrello*. Between 1839 and 1879 this was used to slice open letters arriving at Trieste harbour, as well as to disinfect them, using sulphur or chlorinefrom contagious diseases.

Musée de la Poste
The Postal Museum
34 blvd de Vaugirard, 75015 Paris, France
Tel. (33) 1 42 79 24 44   www.laposte.fr
Mon-Sat 10am-6pm

This recently re-vamped museum is one of the world's largest devoted to postal history. Now enriched by the collections of the postal museum in Amboise, the magnificent Montparnasse museum houses an archive of over 700,000 items documenting the history of French postage stamp production from 1849 onwards. Laid out over fifteen rooms, the permanent display shows the best of the collection's stamps and other postal service-related material, including postmen's calendars dating from 1854 onwards, road maps, French and foreign postcards, negatives, and production tools used for making French postage stamps.

Post og Tele Museum
The Post and Tele Museum
Købmagergade 37, 1012 Copenhagen K, Denmark
Tel. (45) 33 410900   www.ptt.museum.dk
Tue-Sun 10am-5pm (Wed until 5pm)

This magnificent history of Denmark's postal system charts 400 years of Danish communication, from the first public mail services founded by Christian IV in 1624 to the computerized telecommunications services of today. Organized in three time zones, the museum displays some exquisite examples of Denmark's oldest stamps and letter boxes, and many resonant post-related objects, including a reconstruction of an original *kuglepostvognen* (Danish postal coach).

Museum für Post und Kommunikation
The Museum of Post and Communication
Schaumainkai 53, 60596 Frankfurt, Germany
Tel. (49) 69 60600   www.museumsstiftung.de
Tue-Fri 9am-5pm, Sat-Sun 11am-7pm

One of the world's largest stamp collections, with exhibitions on every aspect of Germany's postal service, from vans and uniforms to aeroplanes. The museum also includes an interactive section dedicated to the development of the Bundespost's telephone service.

Mail car Franz, 1911
*Museum für
Kommunikation*

Museum für Post und Kommunikation
The Museum of Post and Communication
Stephansplatz 5, 20354 Hamburg, Germany
Tel. (49) 40 3576360   www.museumsstiftung.de
Tue-Sun 9am-7pm

Displays tackle every aspect of the history and evolution of Hamburg's postal service from the 16th century onwards, from mail delivered by rail, air, and sea, to tubular post. Historic exhibits include postage stamps, letters, letter boxes and pillar boxes, models of vehicles and ships, franking-machines, and postal uniforms.

Postimuseo
The Post Museum
Helsingin pääpostitalo, Asema-aukio 5, Helsinki, Finland
Tel. (358) 204 511   www.posti.fi
Mon-Fri 10am-7pm, Sat-Sun 11am-4pm

Founded in 1926, this is one of the oldest specialist museums in Finland. Every aspect of the Finnish postal service is represented, in a collection including examples of every stamp issued from 1881 onwards. Rarities include a set of 1856 stamps decorated with pictures of Fabergé, the Finnish Post's first car, and the EPL computer used to start the electronic mail traffic in 1986. There is an archive of 30,000 photos, 200,000 slides and colour negatives, 13,000 postcards, and 800 posters.

Fiat 15 Ter Lorry, 1914 model
Postmuseet

Postmuseet
The Postal Museum
Kirkegata 20, 0107 Oslo, Norway
Tel. (47) 23148162   www.norwaypost.no
Mon-Fri 10am-5pm, Sat 10am-2pm, Sun noon-4pm

The most complete collection of Norwegian stamps in the world, including varieties, proofs, and errors, as well as postmarks and letters from pre-postage stamp times. There are displays on polar philately; Norway's first stamp issue of 1855 (which bore no country name and was printed on unperforated sheets); and the post horn stamps which have been in continuous use since their debut in 1872.

Postmuseum
The Postal Museum
Lilla Nygatan 6, 103 11 Stockholm, Sweden
Tel. (46) 8 7811755   www.posten.postnet.se
Sep-Apr: daily 11am-4pm (Wed until 7pm)

This museum traces the Swedish postal service over the last 350 years, using a mix of dioramas and a choice selection from 90,000 letters and four million stamps. Rarities include an 1840 Penny Black, two of the Post Office Mauritius stamps issued in 1847, and a letter with 6-skilling banco stamps sent from Stockholm to London in 1858.

Rossiiskii gosudarstvennyi muzei arktiki i antarktiki
The Russian State Museum of the Arctic and Antarctic
Ulitsa Marata 24a, 191040 St Petersburg, Russian Federation
Tel. (7) 812 1131998   www.polarmuseum.sp.ru
Wed-Sun 10am-5pm

One of the best collections of polar philately anywhere, with a fine collection of commemorative stamps issued by countries participating in polar exploration. Post offices were organized in the Arctic and Antarctic almost as soon as exploration began.

The Royal Philatelic Collection
Royal Philatelic Society, 41 Devonshire Place, London W1N 1PE, UK
Tel. (44) 20 7486 1044   www.rpsl.org.uk
Please call for opening times

Originally created by King George V, this is the most comprehensive collection of postage stamps devoted to the UK and the Commonwealth. George V was a devoted and knowledgeable collector, and his many trophies included whole collections as well as one-offs, such as the first stamps issued by a colonial post office (1d and 2d Mauritius issue of 1847) and the much prized Penny Orange-red. The collection has continued to grow, and in November 2000 Queen Elizabeth paid £250,000 for a unique set of ten Penny Black stamps, stuck onto a first day cover dated May, 1840.

Spellman Museum of Stamps and Postal History
235 Wellesley Street, Weston, Massachusetts 02193, USA
Tel. (1) 781 768 8367   www.spellman.org
Thu-Sun noon-5pm

Founded in 1960, this illustrious museum brings together the stamp collections of Francis Spellman, Archbishop of New York, and that of the Philadelphia National Philatelic Museum. Further donations have come from President Dwight David Eisenhower, violinist Jascha Heifetz, and General Matthew Ridgway. With some two-million-plus items, the museum is one of the largest in the US after the Smithsonian.

TWENTIETH-CENTURY FURNITURE AND DESIGN

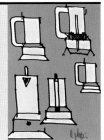

Design and result: coffee pots 9090 and the majestic kettle with a singing whistle (left)
The Alessi Factory

Shaker, ice bucket, and ice thongs from Programme 4 (below)
The Alessi Factory

Coffee maker, La conica, from the Tea & Coffee Piazza project (bottom)
The Alessi Factory

The Alessi Factory
via Privata Alessi 6, 28882 Crusinallo, Italy
Tel. (39) 0323 868 611 www.alessi.it
By appt. only

The history of this company is told through displays of the household products they have given us. There is Philippe Starck's futuristic juice squeezer; the Hot Bertaa kettle; Guido Venturini's loveable, though undeniably phallic, stove lighter, Firebird; and Allessandro Mendini's smiling Anna G corkscrew, which was launched in 1994 and immediately became the company's top selling item.

Musée d'Art moderne de la Ville de Paris
Paris Museum of Modern Art
11 ave. du Président Wilson, 75116 Paris, France
Tel. (33) 1 53 67 40 00
Tue-Fri 10am-5.30pm, Sat-Sun 10am-7pm

The collection of furniture and Art Deco objects includes works by Rhulmann (two secretaires, one with crocodile skin cover from 1926); Arbus (four lacquer and ivory chairs, 1937); Chareau (jewellery box); Dufet (zinc and red lacquer desk from 1929); and many other major figures.

Museu de les Arts decoratives
The Museum of Decorative Arts
Avenida Diagonal 696, 08034 Barcelona, Spain
Tel. (34) 93 280 5024 www.bcn.es
Tue-Sat 10am-6pm, Sun 10am-3pm

The exhibition offers a detailed insight into the history of domestic design in Spain. One of the highlights is a comprehensive selection of Spanish industrial design dating from the Rationalist period.

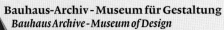

Bauhaus-Archiv - Museum für Gestaltung
Bauhaus Archive - Museum of Design
Klingelhöferstrasse 14, 10785 Berlin, Germany
Tel. (49) 30 2540020 www.bauhaus.de
Daily 10am-5pm

The archive of this monumental German institution documents the non-linear history of the school through extensive studies from the courses, workshop pieces, architectural plans and maquettes, photography, and documents by some of the leading exponents of the Bauhaus, including Van der Rohe, Schlemmer, and Breuer. The museum, in a building drafted by Gropius, holds one of the most complete collections focused on the school.

The 5070 condiment set
The Alessi Factory

Brighton Museum and Art Gallery
Church Street Brighton, Sussex BN1 1UE, UK
Tel. (44) 1273 603005
Mon, Thu-Sat 10am-5pm, Sun 2-5pm

A wonderful collection of modern European furniture and design, with a focus on Art Nouveau and Art Deco. Among outstanding furniture from the 1900s is a screen by Josef Hoffmann; a chair and cabinet by Koloman Moser; a desk by Emile Gallé; and a cabinet, dressing table, and writing table by Louis Majoreile. Postwar and contemporary design includes chairs by Americans Harry Bertoia, Charles Eames, and Frank Gebry; the Danes Arne Jacobsen and Hans Wegner; Andre Dubreuil from France; and the Britons Robin Day, Jasper Morrison, and the Earl of Snowdon.

Bröhan-Museum Schlossstrasse
Bröhan Museum
1a Schlossstrasse, 14059 Berlin, Germany
Tel. (49) 30 32690600   www.broehan-museum.de
Tue-Sun 10am-6pm

A collection of international significance devoted to the Jugendstil and Art Deco movements. There is a selection of furniture, glass, ceramics, paintings, and sculpture from 1889 to the 1930s. Don't miss the furniture made by French cabinetmakers in the 1920s, or the last two rooms dedicated to Henry van de Velde and Josef Hoffmann.

Red lips sofa
Brighton Museum and Art Gallery

Craftsman Farms
2352 Route 10-w, Morris Plains, New Jersey 07950, USA
Tel. (1) 973 540 1165   www.parsippany.net
Apr-mid Nov: Wed-Sun for tours only (please call for times)

The home of the icon of the Arts and Crafts Movement, designer Gustav Stickley, is a synthesis of Stickley's 'Mission' style furniture, his philosophy on architecture, and his ideas of simplicity. Eschewing the Victorian love of embellishing homes with ornaments, he believed women had better things to do with their time than clean. He installed drains in the floors of the kitchen and sleeping porch so they could be hosed down, and filled his log home (built in 1911) with simple, functional furniture, where the joints between the pieces became both the ornament and a way of showing off the craftsmanship of the piece. Tours take you through the main room, where you can view many of his custom-built furnishings, including items recently reclaimed at auction.

Design Museum
28 Shad Thames, London SE1 2YD, UK
Tel.(44) 20 7940 8790   www.designmuseum.org
Mon-Fri 11.30am-6pm, Sat-Sun noon-5pm

The brainchild of style guru, Sir Terence Conran, the Design Museum is devoted to international product and graphic design. It presents everyday items such as radios, televisions, cameras, and vacuum-cleaners as objects to be studied and valued. Included among these are a large number of kitchen items, displayed in the permanent collection, where the history and value of various implements such as kettles, tableware, washing machines, and cutlery are assessed.

Drents Museum
Brink 1-5, 9401 HS Assen, The Netherlands
Tel. (31) 592 312741   www.drentsmuseum.nl
Tue-Sun 11am-5pm

A collection that spans all the branches of Dutch art and applied art from 1885 to around 1935. Represented are Karel Petrus Cornelis de Bazel, who designed glass for the Leerdam Glassworks, and furniture and bookbindings designed by Hendrik Petrus Berlage.

Electropolis - Musée de l'Energie électrique
Electropolis - The Museum of Electrical Energy
55 rue du Pâturage, 68200 Mulhouse, France
Tel. (33) 3 89 32 48 60   www.electropolis.tm.fr
Daily 10am-6 pm

Electropolis is the largest museum in Europe dedicated entirely to electricity. The museum focuses on the history of electricity and how it changed everyday life. Cooking equipment ranges from can openers and coffee grinders to microwave ovens and toasters. There are travel irons dating from the 1930s, a diverse collection of radiators, and a comprehensive collection of lighting systems, from Jablokof's 'candle' to prototypes of induction lamps.

Clock
The Alessi Factory

Musée Horta
The Horta Museum
25 rue Américaine, 1050 Brussels, Belgium
Tel. (32) 2 5371692   www.cbrgroup.com
Tue-Sun 2-5.30pm

During the late 19th and first half of the 20th centuries, Victor Horta was one of Brussels' leading architects. Together with Hankar, Van de Velde, and Serrurier-Bovy, he gave a new impetus to architecture and applied arts. This museum is located in Horta's private house and contains one of his most beautiful creations, the staircase, an exquisite work illuminated with stained glass. Dotted throughout the house there are outstanding examples of furniture owned by the architect himself.

Suomen Jäähdytysalan Museo
The Finnish Museum of Refrigeration
Härkilevontie 77, 33480 Ylöjärvi, Finland
Tel. (358) 3 3491611
Jun-Sep: 1st Sun of the month noon-4pm (groups by arrangement)

Forty years of collecting by Paavo V. Suominen, who founded Huurre, the Finnish flagship of the refrigerator industry, has produced exhibits on Finnish refrigerating history and the development of the industry worldwide. Besides Finnish manufactured compressors, freezers, and refrigerating machinery, there are thirty machines made by foreign manufacturers. Rarities include the German eight-metre Linde refrigerating apparatus and an Audiffren-compressor originally developed by the French monk, Abbe Audiffren.

Kunstgewerbemuseum
The Museum of Applied Arts
Kulturforum, Matthäikirchplatz 10, 10785 Berlin, Germany
Tel. (49) 30 2662902   www.smb.spk-berlin.de
Tue-Fri 10am-6pm, Sat-Sun 11am-6pm

The museum's branch at the Kulturforum houses the largest permanent collection of international design in Germany, including furniture and domestic appliances as well as tapestries and wainscots from all styles and periods. In the New Collection, arts and crafts of the 20th century are complemented by examples of industrial products.

Museum für Kunst und Gewerbe
The Museum of Decorative and Applied Arts
Steintorplatz 1, 20099 Hamburg, Germany
Tel. (49) 40 24862732 www.mkg-hamburg.de
Tue-Sun 10am-6pm (Thu until 9pm)

A Wegner chair
Tønder Vandtårn og
Wegnerudstillingen

One of the most important collections of Art Nouveau. There are works in the style of French Art Deco, German Expressionist graphics and sculpture, furniture by Bauhaus and De Stijl, ceramics and studio pottery of the 1920s and 1930s, Kinetic objects, and modern industrial design.

Miele & Cie. GmbH & Co. Museum
Carl-Miele-Str. 29, 33332 Gütersloh, Germany
Tel. (49) 5241 890 www.miele.deopen
Wed 2-4pm (or by appt.)

The history of Miele started in 1899, when Carl Miele and Reinhard Zinkamm discovered a fabric with which they were able to construct centrifuges. Soon, they were making washing machines, butter-machines, wringers, vacuum cleaners, and refrigerators. About 200 Miele items are on display here, from their earliest days to the present.

Nederlands Kachelmuseum
The Dutch Heater Museum
Bierkade 10, 1811 NJ Alkmaar, The Netherlands
Tel. (31) 72 5159 4181
Oct-Easter: daily noon-4pm
Easter-Oct: Fri, Sun noon-4pm

Housed in the recently restored Baroque residence of a former mayor of Alkmaar, the collection provides an overview of the development of the Dutch stove from 1850 to the present day. It was begun about forty years ago by Cees in't Veld, a local businessman and owner of a stove and heating firm, who would occasionally be given interesting or historic stoves in part exchange for the new ones he was providing. There are now about 75 stoves in the collection, including fancifully decorated Art Nouveau stoves, elegant stoves with Art Deco designs, and emergency stoves from World War II.

Museo Sandretto
Sandretto Museum
Via G. Marconi 30, 10085 Pont Canavese, Turin, Italy
Tel. (39) 0124 862222 www.sandretto.it
Daily by appt.

An old mill-owner's lodge has been renovated to house this vast collection devoted to the history of plastics. It boasts more than 2,500 pieces dating from the end of the 19th century onwards. On the first floor are photographic enlargements of the men who played a vital role in the industry – from John W. Hyatt, an American who was the first to create celluloid, to Giulio Natta, the Italian Nobel prize winner who invented polypropylene. As plastics developed, so did their uses, and items on display include toys, radio sets, musical instruments, cars, shoes, and credit cards.

Staatliches Museum für Angewandte Kunst
The State Museum of Applied Art
Prinzregentenstrasse 3, 80538 Munich, Germany
Tel. (49) 89 227844
Tue-Sun 10am-5pm

This unique collection of over 40,000 items traces the development of industrial design, graphic design, and crafts. Along with everyday objects, it includes mass-produced products of modern industrial design.

Tønder Vandtårn og Wegnerudstillingen
Tønder Water Tower and the Wegner Exhibition
Kongevej 51, 6270 Tønder, Denmark
Tel. (45) 74 722657   www.tonder-net.dk
Jun-Aug: daily 10am-5pm. Sep-May: Tue-Sun 10am-5pm

A Wegner chair
Tønder Vandtårn og Wegnerudstillingen

The upper storey is furnished by the furniture architects, Hans J. Wegner and Marianne Wegner Sørensen, and includes 25 copies of the famous chair (known simply as 'The Chair') placed around a circular table. The seven other storeys house a permanent exhibition of Wegner's chairs, among them his most popular, the 'Y Chair', designed in 1950 and still produced today.

Vitra Design Museum
Charles-Eames-Strasse 1, 79576 Weil am Rhein, Germany
Tel. (49) 7621 7023578   www.design-museum.de
Tue-Sun & public holidays 11am-6pm

The furniture manufacturer Vitra has always produced stimulating products, and when commissioning a design for their museum they looked to architect, Frank Gehry, to come up with a design to create lively discussion. Completed in 1989, it has become a place of architectural pilgrimage, despite its location in a little-known border town. The museum holds temporary exhibitions on furniture design which aim to foster an appreciation for well-designed products.

Wäschepflege-Museum
Museum of Laundering
Pragerstrasse 2, 4261 Rainbach i. M., Austria
Tel. (43) 7949 6880   www.museumstrasse.at
Please call for opening times

Sound washing machine, Bosch, 1930
Wäscheplege-Museum

Washboards, washtubs, wash troughs, and hand-operated mangles show techniques employed at the beginning of the 20th century, together with an account of various precursors to washing powder such as urine and ash-lye. There is a 150-year-old wooden washing machine, antique hand-operated machines, and a number of patents for early machines, including one from the 18th century.

Wharton Esherick Studio
1520 Horseshoe Trail, Paoli, Pennsylvania 19301, USA
Tel. (1) 601 644 5822
Mar-Dec: Mon-Fri 10am-4pm, Sat 10am-5pm, Sun 1-5pm (for groups only)

Just under half an hour from Philadelphia, and only two miles west of the major Revolutionary War site of Valley Forge, is the handcrafted studio-residence of artist and woodworker, Wharton Esherick (known to his contemporaries as the 'Dean of American Crafts'). Originally Esherick settled his family in the farmhouse on the estate, but several years later, in 1926, he began building a studio on the hill above,

Inkstand in pewter and marble with inscription 'Work economy. Help each other'
Scryption Museum

and for over forty years lived and worked there, transforming it into a whimsical space where he designed the sculptural furniture for which he is so well known. Today, it's a museum bursting with examples of his work, including paintings, utensils, woodcuts, and furnishings, as well as the famous furniture which was inspired by the organic forms around him.

VINTAGE FOUNTAIN PENS, PENCILS AND INKWELLS

Birmingham Museum and Art Gallery
Chamberlain Square, Birmingham B3 3DH, UK
Tel. (44) 121 303 2834   www.birmingham.gov.uk
Mon-Thu, Sat 10am-5pm, Fri 10.30am-5pm, Sun 12.30-5pm

The Charles Thomas Collection of writing equipment at the Birmingham Museum and Art Gallery comprises several thousand rare items. As well as pens, the collection includes nibs, dusting pads, quills, and pen knives from India, Asia, China and the West. Unusual objects range from a French quill-cutting machine dating from *c*.1822, to wafer seals made of pink paper and printed with mottoes dating from the introduction of postage stamps in 1840.

British Museum
Great Russell Street, London WC1B 3DG, UK
Tel. (44) 20 7636 1555   www.thebritishmuseum.ac.uk
Mon-Sat 10am-5pm, Sun noon-6pm

Writing implements are scattered throughout the enormous collections, but highlights include a collection of Chinese brushes, ink cakes, pen rests, and pen boxes in the Department of Oriental Antiquities. Bone, iron, and bronze styli feature in the early medieval collections.

The Cumberland Pencil Museum
Southey Works, Greta Bridge, Keswick, Cumbria CA12 5NG, UK
Tel. (44) 17687 73626   www.pencils.co.uk
Daily 9.30am-4pm

Run by the famous Derwent Artists pencil company, this museum documents the complete history of the pencil and its evolution, with displays of machinery, video shows of pencil making and an in-depth study of graphite mining in Borrowdale. The superb pencil collection includes early examples of handmade pencils and pencils fashioned on primitive lathes. There is even an example of a World War II pencil with a tightly rolled map and a miniature compass hidden in its shaft. These were manufactured in secret by the managers of a department of the pencil factory and then smuggled into Germany in an attempt to help POWs escape from German prison camps.

Alfred Dunhill Museum
48 Jermyn Street, London SW1Y 6DL, UK
Tel. (44) 20 7838 8233
Mon-Fri 9.30am-6pm, Sat 10am-6pm

A display of luxury accessories includes examples of pens produced for Dunhill in the 1930s by the Japanese company Namiki. Four different grades of lacquer were introduced, some with the addition of gold dust to create a shimmering luminescence. Dunhill stopped producing the pens in 1939, but recently reintroduced them.

The Fountain Pen Shop

2640 South Myrtle Avenue, Unit 12, Monrovia, California 91016-8204, USA
Tel. (1) 626 294 9974 www.fountainpenshop.com
Please call for opening times

Established in 1922, this family-run Californian pen shop incorporates the superb vintage pens, writing materials, pen parts, and catalogue collection of Fred Krinke. Among the thousands of pens on display are 1920s and 1930s Sheaffers, in virtually every style and colour combination; rare dip pens; a Sterling filigree Swan trench pen; a Parker Spanish Galleon 75; a Sterling 'Tree Trunk' pen; and transparent 'demonstrator' pens.

Silver writing set (above)
Scryption Museum

Dunhill-Namiki
fountain pen (left)
Alfred Dunhill Museum

Musée international du Stylo
The International Fountain Pen Museum
5 rue de Chaillot, 75116 Paris, France
Tel. (33) 1 47 20 87 05
Sun 10am-noon, 2-6pm

Bruno Lussato's enviable collection mixes antique and new pens, presenting them thematically rather than chronologically, in a series of lavish exhibition rooms. As well as snake pens and special displays on companies such as Parker and Waterman, the museum has an excellent collection of handmade papers, books, and other kinds of writing instruments.

Keswick Museum and Art Gallery

Fitz Park, Station Road, Keswick, Cumbria CA12 4NF, UK
Tel. (44) 1768 773263
Apr-Oct: daily 10am-4pm

The most important raw material for pencil manufacture (graphite) was first discovered in the Borrowdale valley near Keswick in the 16th century. Also known as black lead, wad and plumbago, it became a very valuable commodity and was used for marking sheep, as well as for various medicinal purposes, and for casting shells and cannon balls. It became a criminal act to steal it, and consignments to London had armed escorts Pencil manufacturing began in Keswick in the 18th century with numerous cottage industries, which ultimately developed into the large companies of the 19th century and today. The museum has a fine collection of graphite as well as a selection of various pencil types made by local manufacturers, including some made from a tree which stood in the garden of the British poet and author, Robert Southey.

Metz Bicycle Museum

54 West Main Street, Freehold, New Jersey 07728, USA
Tel. (1) 732 462 7363 www.metzbicyclemuseum.com
Please call for opening times

Apart from his fascination with bicycles, David Metz's enduring interest in ingenious inventions prompted him to amass a vast collection of pencil sharpeners. Dating back to 1868, the collection takes in an incredible range of sharpeners with a variety of blades and shavers ranging from metal to sandpaper and glass.

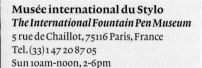

Bird-shaped jagging wheel or pie crimper made from a sperm whale's tooth
New Bedford Whaling Museum

Montblanc-Museum
Hellgrundweg 100, 22525 Hamburg, Germany
Tel. (49) 40 84001860
By appt. only

Montblanc was one of the few survivors (along with Pelikan and Lamy) of Germany's once large and diverse fountain pen industry. The company's superb vintage pen collection documents many of the highlights in the development of Montblanc design, including the flawless, masculine Meisterstück MB149, with its piston-fill mechanism and huge, ornate 18k gold nib with platinum inlay.

Pen Collectors of America Library
P.C.A. Librarian, Glendale, California 91209-3435, USA
Tel. (1) 818 246 7286 www.pencollectors.com
Open to members only, please call for details

This growing library is the largest archive of pen and pen-related materials in the US. PCA members may request copies of any items for a nominal fee. However, currently archived materials are not available online.

Scryption Museum
Spoorlaan 434a, 5038 CH Tilburg, The Netherlands
Tel. (31) 13 5800821 www.tref.nl
Tue-Fri 10am-5pm, Sat-Sun 1-5pm

This superb museum, founded originally by Friar Ferrierius van den Berg, traces the development of script from its earliest beginnings to the development of typewriters and other office machines. As well as countless fountain pens and some 1,200 inkstands, the collection includes writing sets, travel cases, a huge and unique display of typewriters, and a library of some 3,000 technical and historic books on every aspect of writing, from calligraphy to shorthand and modern word processing.

WHALING ARTEFACTS

The American Museum in Britain
Claverton Manor, Bath, Somerset BA2 7BD, UK
Tel. (44) 1225 460503 www.americanmuseum.org
Apr-Oct: Tue-Sun 2-5pm

The importance of the whaling industry to those living on the eastern seaboard is illustrated with a replica of the captain's cabin on the whaler *Charles W. Morgan*. A cabinet of whaling implements and scrimshaw items includes a Susan tooth and a short, bleak poem reading 'Death to the living, long live the killers / Success to sailor's wives and greasy luck to whalers'.

Museu dos Baleeiros
The Whalers Museum
Rua dos Baleeiros 13, 9930 Lajes, Pico, Portugal (Azores)
Tel. (351) 92 672276
May-Sep: Tue-Fri 9.30am-12.30pm, 2-5.30pm
Rest of year: please call for opening times

The first attempts to establish whaling in the small ports of the Azores began in the mid 19th century after several whalers returned from the US. Importing whaling gear and boats, Pico's talented fishermen and merchants took to whaling, and it became a

significant means of earning a living. Displayed in three original 19th-century boat houses are a documentation centre and library, traditional whaling boats, weapons, and a scrimshaw collection.

Broughty Castle Museum

Castle Approach, Broughty Ferry, Dundee DD5 2PE, Scotland, UK
Tel. (44) 1382 436916
Summer: Mon-Sat 11am-5pm, Sun 12.30-5pm. Winter: Tue-Sat 11am-5pm, Sun 12.30-4pm

Dating from 1498, Broughty Castle houses a museum of arms and armour, along with a gallery devoted to the history of Scotland's premier whaling port. Among the many fascinating artefacts is the personal memorabilia of whalers, drawings, paintings, and several early pieces of local scrimshaw, as well as other items made of whale bone, including a walking stick, ladle, and combs. Harpoon guns, flensing knives, jars filled with whale oil, engines used on whaling vessels, whale eardrums, whaling logbooks, and Inuit artefacts, tell the story of ships which for over a century sailed the arctic waters in search of whales.

Hart Nautical Collections

MIT Museum, 265 Massachusetts Avenue, Cambridge, Massachusetts 02139 USA
Tel. (1) 617 253 5942   www.mit.edu
Daily 9am-8pm

This vast archive relating to the technical history of New England ship and small craft design, includes the Allan Forbes Whaling Collection. Donated to MIT in 1940, it comprises a small collection of rare books and manuscripts on whaling, and some 2,000 prints and paintings ranging from 16th-century Dutch engravings to 19th-century Japanese woodcuts. The early charts and maps of Bermuda are quite extraordinary.

Hull Maritime Museum

Queen Victoria Square, Kingston-upon-Hull, East Yorkshire HU1 3DX, UK
Tel. (44) 1482 613902   www.hullcc.gov.uk
Mon-Sat 10am-5pm, Sun 1.30-4.30pm

Using a cross section of 19th-century arctic whaling material, the museum's Whaling Gallery tells the fascinating story of whaling in Hull from its earliest beginnings in 1598 (when the first ship sailed to Greenland) to its demise in the mid 19th century, when prices fell dramatically and a number of ships were wrecked in the treacherous arctic waters. Displays encompass an enormous skeleton of a Greenland Right Whale,

Sperm whale tooth, George O. Hiliott (mid 19th century), American. Polychrome engraved with full figure portrait of a Polynesian maiden in grass skirt and tropical island surroundings; full figure portrait of New-England lady (verso)
c. 1840-50 (above)
The Kendall Whaling Museum

Oil painting by William Bradford of a whaling ship called *Syren Queen* (above left)
New Bedford Whaling Museum

Twisted harpoon
Whaling Museum

399

Africa nova descriptio map,
1644
Hart Nautical Collections

logbooks, nautical art, journals (including the journal of the *Diana* which sank on her homeward journey in 1869), tools, paintings of whaling ships, and the largest collection of scrimshaw this side of the Atlantic.

The Kendall Whaling Museum

27 Everett Street, Sharon, Massachusetts 02067, USA
Tel. (1) 781 784 5642
www.kwn.org
Tue-Sat 10am-5pm,
Sun 1-5pm

Housed in a former sanatorium for tuberculosis sufferers, this world-class museum chronicles five centuries of whaling. It holds an extraordinary collection of around 72,000 objects, 1,500 paintings and drawings, 6,500 prints, ship models, figure heads, tribal art, manuscripts, books and, by a clear margin, the largest and most complete collection of scrimshaw in the world. Fascinating items include an early Dutch painting detailing the capture and cutting-up of a whale in the Arctic, rare Viking scrimshaw, and the world's only known African-American scrimshaw.

New Bedford Whaling Museum

18 Johnny Cake Hill, New Bedford, Massachusetts 02740-6398, USA
Tel. (1) 508 9970046 www.whalingmuseum.org
Please call for opening times

One of the largest collections of its sort in the country, this outstanding collection focuses on the social, economic, and environmental impact of every aspect of the American whaling industry. The collection includes over 500 harpoons and other implements, models of whaling ships, lamps and lighting fixtures which once used whale-oil, paintings, prints and drawings, figureheads, logbooks, and a much prized collection of scrimshaw.

Peabody Essex Museum

East India Square, Salem, Massachusetts 01970, USA
Tel. (1) 978 745 9500 www.pem.org
Apr-Oct: Mon-Sat 10am-5pm, Sun noon-5pm
Nov-Mar: Tue-Sat 10am-5pm, Sun noon-5pm

Founded in 1799 as the East India Marine Society, this is America's oldest museum. Though whaling artefacts are not a focus for the museum, the collection includes hundreds of whaling implements, prints and paintings depicting the whaling industry, and the oldest collection of scrimshaw in existence. Gems include one of the logbooks from the whaler *Acushnet*, which sailed to the South Seas with Herman Melville on board in 1845, and a Susan Tooth by the famed Nantucket scrimshander, Frederick Myrick.

San Francisco Maritime National Historical Park

Hyde Street Pier, San Francisco, California 94109, USA
Tel. (1) 415 556 3002 www.nps.gov
Daily 10am-5pm

This beautiful Art Deco ship-like structure, built as part of an original WPA project, contains a fascinating collection of photographs documenting the hundreds of ships that were abandoned in the American gold rush, plus a modest collection of whaling paraphernalia dating from the last quarter of the century, when San Francisco was one of the most important whaling centres in the world. Exhibits include photos, toggle head harpoons, jars of whale oil, and one delightful case of scrimshaw with four sperm whale teeth decorated in the 1880s by William Gilman.

Scott Polar Research Institute
University of Cambridge, Lensfield Road, Cambridge, Cambridgeshire CB2 1ER, UK
Tel. (44) 1223 336540   www.spri.cam.ac.uk
Mon-Sat 2.30-4pm

This repository for British polar exploration (see other entry) also contains documents and artefacts relating to the whaling industry, and a well-researched collection of scrimshaw, thanks to Dr Janet West. Numbering 78 pieces, it is unusual because it primarily contains items exclusive to sperm whaling, the major industry of Yankee whalers. Highlights include two rare 19th-century examples of sculpted teeth (a technique popular with Antarctic whalers in the 20th century), a fine bone stay-busk with a British Sperm whaling scene, and a stunning tooth with the engraving of the ship *Governor Halkett*.

Interior of the museum
The Kendall Whaling Museum

Shelburne Museum
US Route 7, Shelburne, Vermont 05482, USA
Tel. (1) 802 985 3346   www.shelburnemuseum.org
May-Oct: daily 10am-5pm. Rest of the year: Walking tours at 1pm

One of the museum's farmhouse galleries is used to display a small exhibition of scrimshaw and whaling folk art. Items include a precious Myrick Susan's Tooth, carved on board the *Susan* in the 1830s; a series of ingeniously crafted objects including whalebone corset busks, knitting needles, and a pie-crimper made with red wax, brass, and silver; and an intricate yarn-winder made from a mix of turned and incised ivory and bone.

Valfangstmuseet
The Whaling Museum
Museumsgata 39, 3210 Sandefjord, Norway
Tel. (47) 33 484650
Please call for opening times

Founded in 1917 by Lars Christensen, this is one of the most substantial modern whaling collections in the world. Though the museum includes a superb life-sized model of a blue whale, the star exhibit is probably the *Southern Actor*, an immaculately restored 1950s whale catcher with a fully working 1.800 IHK Triple Steam engine, moored on a nearby wharf. The extensive library and archives include a large collection of photos and film covering whaling in action, whale catchers, life among whalers, and historical archives from several whaling companies.

Whalers Village Museum
2435 Ka'anapali Parkway, Lahaina, Maui, Hawaii 96761, USA
Tel. (1) 808 6614567   www.whalersvillage.com
Daily 9.30am-10pm

Recounted through the eyes of the ordinary sailor is the history of whaling in Lahaina from 1825 to 1860, with displays ranging from the

Half-scale model of the whaling ship *Lagoda*, the largest ship model in the world, which can be boarded and looked over
New Bedford Whaling Museum

401

Pentacle (above)
Museum of Witchcraft

Dowsing pentacle from
the Richel Collection
(right)
Museum of Witchcraft

cramped quarters where the men lived for the duration of voyages, to several hundred artefacts illustrating the horror of the whaling trade, including harpoons, sea chests, sailors' journals, tools, and a large scale model of a whaling ship.

Whaling Museum

Nantucket Historical Association, 13 Broad Street, Nantucket Town, Nantucket, Massachusetts 02554, USA
Tel. (1) 508 228 1894   www.nha.org
Please call for opening times

Housed in a 19th-century spermaceti candle factory, this superb museum documents every aspect of the whaling industry and its impact on Nantucket from the 18th century onwards. Alongside a fully-rigged whaling boat, portraits of sea captains and the skeleton of a 43-foot finback whale, are several original artefacts from the *Essex*, the doomed whaling ship sunk by an enraged sperm whale and which inspired Melville's *Moby Dick*. A collection of whaling implements amassed by Edward Sanderson from the 1920s onwards includes blubber gaffs, double-flued harpoons, and thousands of other tools made by the blacksmiths of Nantucket. The scrimshaw collection features a series of Frederick Myrick's richly decorated Susan's Teeth.

WITCHCRAFT

Museo archeologico nazionale dell'Umbria
The National Archaeological Museum of Umbria
Piazza Giordano Bruno 10, 06121 Perugia, Italy
Tel. (39) 075 5727141
Daily 8.30am-7.30pm

The museum houses the extraordinary charms and amulets collected in the 19th century by Giuseppe Bellucci, a demonologist. The collection encompasses a heady mix of religious and magical traditions, and though the collection was exhibited in Torino in 1898, it was hidden away for most of the 20th century and has only recently been restored to public view. Among the 1,700 items are teeth, rocks, carved dog bones, fetishes encased in wolf intestines, badger tails (worn as a protective charm by children), and polished gem stones (worn by pregnant women s protection during childbirth).

Cleveland Public Library
Main Library, Main Building, 3rd Floor, 325 Superior Avenue, Cleveland, Ohio 44114, USA
Tel. (1) 216 623 2818   www.cpl.org
Mon-Sat 9am-6pm, Sun 1-5pm

Cleveland's 47,040-volume folklore collection covers the spectrum of primitive, peasant, native and folk cultures, and is one of the largest in scope in the US. Subjects include the occult sciences, magic and witchcraft, mythology, legends, and primitive religion.

Museum für Magie und Hexenverfolgungen
The Museum of Magic and Witch-Hunting
Am Wall 15, 17217 Penzlin, Germany
Tel. (49) 3962 210494
May-Oct: Tue-Fri 9am-5pm, Sat-Sun 10am-5pm
Nov-Apr: Tue-Wed 10am-1pm, Sat-Sun 1-4pm

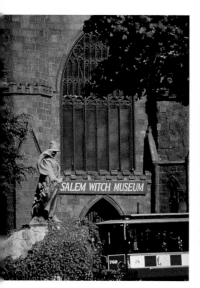

This extraordinary museum is situated in the 16th-century dungeons where witches from Mecklenburg's 4,000 witch-hunt trials were held in chains and tortured. An exhibition on the first floor documents the portrayal of witches in German art and folklore.

Examination of a Witch, Tompkins H. Matteson, 1853, oil on canvas (above) *Peabody Essex Museum*

Musée national des Arts et Traditions populaires
The National Museum of Folk Art and Traditions
6 ave. du Mahatma Gandhi, 75016 Paris, France
Tel. (33) 1 44 17 60 00
Mon–Wed–Sun 9.45am–5.15pm

Exterior of the museum (above left)
Salem Witch Museum

With an extensive library and almost one million objects on permanent display, this unique museum records every facet of French peasant life and craft culture from the Middle Ages to the present day. Exhibits on witchcraft and astrology in the folklore section focus on witches, wise-women, and healers. There is also a reconstruction of a clairvoyant's office, complete with tarot cards and crystal balls.

Peabody Essex Museum
Phillips Library, East India Square, Salem, Massachusetts 01970, USA
Tel. (1) 978 745 9500   www.pem.org
Tue–Fri 10am–5pm (Thu until 8pm)

This fascinating manuscript collection houses 552 documents, written in brown ink on rag paper, from the original 1692 Salem witchcraft trials. Other related items, such as the 'witch pins' used for examining witches, are also kept at the museum. The contents of the legal documents are accessible online at http://etext.virginia.edu/salem/witchcraft.

Salem Witch Museum
Washington Square North, Salem, Massachusetts 01970, USA
Tel. (1) 978 7441692   www.salemwitchmuseum.com
Daily 10am–5pm (Jul, Aug until 7pm)

A show with life-sized figures recounts the story of the 1692 Salem witchcraft trials, in which over nineteen women were sent to the gallows in the space of seven months. Other exhibits explore changing perceptions of witches, magic, and witchcraft, from medieval times to the present day.

Musée de la Sorcellerie
The Museum of Sorcery
La Jonchère, 18260 Concressault, France
Tel. (33) 2 48 73 86 11
Apr-May, Oct: daily 10am-6pm. Jun-Sep: daily 10am-7pm

Wooden pentacle hands from the Richel Collection
Museum of Witchcraft

In a stone barn several hours south of Paris, this eclectic museum uses dioramas, original artefacts, and sound effects to explore the diverse history of magic and sorcery. Displays cover all apects, from witch hunts and the Inquisition, to the beliefs and practices of Celtic druids, and folklore portrayals of such supernatural figures as Mephisto, Merlin, witches, forest elves, and sea dragons.

Drawing from the Richel Collection
Museum of Witchcraft

Museum of Witchcraft
The Harbour, Boscastle, Cornwall PL35 0AE, UK
Tel. (44) 1840 250111 www.museumofwitchcraft.com
Apr-Oct: Mon-Sat 10.30am-6pm, Sun 11.30am-6pm
(other times by appt. only)

Established on the Isle of Man in 1948, this was the first museum in the world devoted to the subject of witchcraft. Now in Cornwall, it is packed with objects associated with the subject, from authentic crystal balls and dousing rods, to Victorian tea leaf cups, Cornish sailors' sea charms made of shell and fish bone, poppets (wax dolls), scourges (ceremonial whips), and talismans. A collection of books and archival materials is available to serious researchers by appointment.

SCIENCE AND TECHNOLOGY COLLECTIONS

CAMERAS AND PHOTOGRAPHICA

COMMUNICATION AND COMPUTING

MEDICAL INSTRUMENTS

MUSICAL INSTRUMENTS

PHONOGRAPHS AND GRAMOPHONES

POLAR AND OCEANOGRAPHIC EXPLORATION

SCIENTIFIC INSTRUMENTS

TECHNOLOGY COLLECTIONS AND LIBRARIES

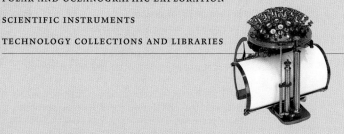

CAMERAS AND PHOTOGRAPHICA

Giroux daguerreotype
camera, 1839
*George Eastman House -
International Museum of
Photography and Film*

The official Eastman
Kodak Co. photo of the
company's founder,
George Eastman, *c.1924*
*George Eastman House -
International Museum of
Photography and Film*

Agfa Foto-Historama
Museum Ludwig, Bischofsgartenstrasse 1, 50667 Cologne, Germany
Tel. (49) 2212 212411 www.cologneweb.com
Tue-Fri 10am-6pm, Sat-Sun 11am-6pm

This small gallery, covering 150 years of photography, shows some of its vast collection of over 20,000 historic cameras, 12,000 photographs, and 3,000 books. Prize items include the Dubroni No.1 (produced in Paris in 1864 and regarded as the world's first instant camera), the first amateur camera made by Eastman Kodak (1888), and a carrier-pigeon camera used for aerial reconnaissance in World War I. Rare miniature toy and spy cameras, mint condition daguerreotypes, ambrotypes, ferrotypes, and calotypes, plus numerous albums and prints by Henry Fox Talbot, David Octavius Hill, Maxime Du Camp, Auguste Salzmann, and Hugo Erfurth are also included.

Deutsches Filmmuseum
The German Film Museum
Schaumainkai 41, 60596 Frankfurt, Germany
Tel. (49) 692 1238830
www.deutsches-filmmuseum.de
Tue-Fri, Sun 10am-5pm (Wed until 8pm), Sat 2-8pm

As well as a host of early cinematographic devices such as magic lanterns, stroboscopic discs, zoetropes, and thaumatropes, the museum houses a vast collection of film memorabilia, posters, and programmes. Various filmic backdrops include the Indian Saloon of the Grand Café in Paris, where the Lumière brothers staged the first film projection in 1895, a 1920s-style cinema lobby, and a room recreating Sam Spade's office in the film version of *The Maltese Falcon*.

George Eastman House - International Museum of Photography and Film
900 East Avenue, Rochester, New York, New York 14607, USA
Tel. (1) 716 271 3361 www.eastman.org
Tue-Fri 10am-5pm by appt. only

One of the most comprehensive collections of photographic and cinematographic equipment in the US, from devices pre-dating the invention of the daguerreotype in 1839 to the most recently produced amateur and professional equipment. The core collections feature hundreds of early French and American cameras, including the unique Bemis daguerreotype camera outfit, built in 1840 and sold by François Gouraud, Daugerre's first sales agent in the US.

Hollywood Heritage Museum
2100 North Highland Avenue, Hollywood, California 90068, USA
Tel. (1) 323 874 2276 www. hollywoodheritage.org
Sat-Sun 10am-4pm

Cecil B. de Mille converted this former barn into a movie studio in 1913. It now houses costumes, props, and an impressive collection of motion picture cameras. Gems include a 1908 Prestwich 35mm, a 1909 Williamson 35mm Tropical Model, and the 1916 Karl Brown Camera which was used to shoot Intolerance. Also, a 1917 Bell & Howell camera owned by the Charlie Chaplin Studio, thought to have been used to film The Great Dictator in 1940. Recently acquired is a collection of projector and atmospheric special effects equipment found in the projection booths at the Pantages and Hollywood Pacific Theatres.

The original Brownie
camera (1900)
George Eastman House -
International Museum of
Photography and Film

Incredibly Fantastic Old Toy Show
26 Westgate, Lincoln, Lincolnshire LN1 3BD, UK
Tel. (44) 1522 520534
Easter-Sep: Tue-Sat 11am-5pm, Sun noon-4pm. Oct-Dec: Sat 11am-5pm, Sun noon-4pm

This small but representative collection of vintage toys includes various 19th-century
devices – the praxinoscope, phenatoscope, and mutoscope, plus shadow theatres and
optical experiments with mirrors – which cumulatively contributed to the development
of cinematography. The collection also encompasses mechanical slides for magic
lanterns, and toy film projectors and viewers.

Kingston Museum
Wheatfield Way, Kingston, Surrey KT1 2PS, UK
Tel. (44) 20 8546 5386 www.kingston.gov.uk
Mon-Tue, Thu-Sat 10am-5pm

The museum owns a priceless collection of equipment and prints donated by the pioneering English photographer, Eadweard Muybridge, on his death in 1904. Among the
many significant pieces are an original zoopraxiscope, a binunial lantern, and a rare
panorama of San Francisco dating from 1878. Additional pieces including zoopraxiscope slides and lantern discs can be viewed by appointment.

Le Musée suisse de l'Appareil Photographique
The Swiss Camera Museum
6 ruelle des Anciens-Fossés, 1800 Vevey, Switzerland
Tel. (41) 21 9252140 www.cameramuseum.ch
Mar-Oct: Tue-Sun 11am-5.30pm. Nov-Feb: Tue-Sun 2-5.30pm

This magnificent camera collection covers the history of photography, its inventors,
and techniques, from the earliest days to the present. As well as cameras, the collection
encompasses laboratory equipment, stereoscopes, magic lanterns, and projectors.
Special displays focus on the history of photography in Switzerland, and the work of
pioneers such as Oscar Barnack, the inventor behind the Leica 35mm still camera. For
younger visitors there are interactive computer games, hands-on models, audiovisuals,
and a video showing how Nicéphore Niépce produced the first photograph.

Musée des Arts et Métiers
The Museum of Arts and Crafts
60 rue Réaumur, 75003 Paris, France
Tel. (33) 1 53 01 82 00 www.cnam.fr/museum
Tue-Sun 10am-6pm (Thu until 9.30pm)

Established by the Société française de la Photographie in 1854, this magnificent collection features some outstanding examples of early French photography. Among the
many highlights are daguerreotypes by Daguerre and examples of his equipment and
camera obscura, Becquerel's photograph of the solar spectrum (1848), Chevalier's Grand
Photographe of 1841, Geymet and Alker's Nicour binoculars (1874), Enjalbert's Photo-
Revolver of 1882, and Bloch's Photo-Cravate (1890). The cinematic equipment collection
includes Chevalier's Megascope, Prazmowski's Heliostat, and the Cinématographe used
by the Lumière brothers for their first public projection.

Musée du Cinéma Henri Langlois
The Henri Langlois Museum of Cinema
Palais de Chaillot, 1 place du Trocadéro, 75016 Paris, France
Tel. (33) 1 45 53 21 86 www.cinematheque.tm.fr
Wed-Sun: guided tours at 10am, 11am, 2pm, 3pm, 4pm, 5pm

Selection of cameras
and photographs
*Musée français de la
Photographie*

Exterior of the museum
*Musée français de la
Photographie*

Opened in 1972, this *maison du rêve collectif* was the first in the world entirely devoted to cinema. Henri Langlois' massive collection traces the origins of cinema back to 13th-century Japanese shadow plays and puppet theatre, and takes in a huge diversity of exhibits including costumes, programmes, posters, and photographs. Highlights include photographic equipment belonging to Eadweard Muybridge, the 75mm camera made by the Lumière brothers and Jules Carpentier for the Universal Exhibition of 1900, and a superb series of exhibits focusing on the first American films, German Expressionist films of the 1920s, and French cinema of the 1940s and 1950s. In spring 2002, the museum is due to move to new premises at the old American Centre in Bercy.

Musée français de la Photographie
The French Museum of Photography
78 rue de Paris, 91570 Bièvres, France
Tel. (33) 1 69 35 16 50
Mon, Wed-Sun 10am-noon, 2-6pm

Founded by Jean and André Fage in 1960, this excellent museum houses a magnificent collection of cameras and photographs, covering artistic as well as technical developments in the history of the medium. Starting with the use of the camera obscura in the Renaissance, the museum chronicles the development of the first mechanical cameras by Niépce and Daguerre – concluding with the story of their mass production by companies such as Leica and Kodak. Among the gems in the early collections are magic laterns, very rare daguerreotypes, and examples of the stereoscopic cameras produced by Jules Richard in the 1880s. Later highlights include miniature spy cameras, early panoramic cameras, and military cameras, including a photographic machine gun. The use of photography in science is illustrated with examples of microphotography, velocigraphy, and underwater photography. The museum also houses a section on cinematography.

Musée Marey
Hôtel de Ville, 21200 Beaune, France
Tel. (33) 3 80 24 56 92
Apr-Nov: Mon-Fri 2-6pm

This unique museum is dedicated to Jules Marey, the father of 'scientific cinema' and one of Beaune's most famous residents. Marey's famous study of the horse's gallop inspired the equally famous stills taken by Eadweard Muybridge of a racehorse galloping at 22mph with four hoofs leaving the ground at once. The project prompted Marey to collaborate on further photographic projects, and the museum includes examples of the chronophotographic gun invented by Marey in 1882, together with original examples of chronophotography, and a priceless copy of the Eadweard Muybridge album published in 1899, which includes 781 plates made between 1884 and 1885.

Musée Nicéphore Niépce
The Nicéphore Niépce Museum
28 quai des Messageries, 71100 Châlon-sur-Saône, France
Tel. (33) 3 85 48 41 98 www.museeniepce.com
Mon, Wed-Sun 9.30-11.30am, 2.30-5.30pm (Jul, Aug 10am-6pm)

The father of modern photography, Nicéphore Niépce, was born in Châlon-sur-Saône in 1765. Among the gems in this superbly well-presented museum is the first piece of equipment used by Niépce, in 1820. The extensive collection comprises over 6,000 early photographic devices and optical objects, including the first daguerreotype (commercialised by Charles Chevalier in 1839), Bertsch's Voiglander machine and Great Photographe of 1861, Damoiseau's Panoramic machine or Cyclographe of 1890, and Herman Casler and Koopman's Presto Camera of 1899. There are also photographic books by Robert Demachy, portraits by Gimel, photos by Lefebvre, Avon, and Ducos de Hauron (possibly the first colour photographs in the world), calotypes by Stephane Geoffray, Julien Vallou de Veilleneuve, and Louis Adolphe Humbert de Molard, and the exceptional Combier collection which comprises over 1.5 million documents and views of France.

Museo del Cinema
The Museum of the Cinema
Palazzo Dugnani, via Manin, 2/b Milan, Italy
Tel. (39) 02 6554977
Tue-Fri 3-6.30pm

This outstanding collection focuses on early cameras and cinema- tography equipment, as well as posters and other evocative memorabilia from the period. Among the earliest pieces on display are magic lanterns with their original hand-coloured slides, early tin toy projectors, and the magnificent Mondo Niovo. This was made in Venice in the 18th century, and showed moving landscapes and architectural views, by candlelight, to up to three viewers at a time. Highlights among the cameras range from Italian country cameras with leather bellows and solar lense, to folding pocket Brownie cameras produced by Kodak (several in mint condition), while the cinematography collection features an original projector made by Louis and Auguste Lumière in 1895 (registration no. 371), and one of the first Lumière films, in a tin box and featuring characteristic round perforations.

Muséum d'Histoire naturelle et de Géologie
The Museum of Natural History and Geology
19 rue de Bruxelles, 59000 Lille, France
Tel. (33) 3 20 55 30 80
Mon, Wed-Fri 9am-noon, 2-5pm, Sat-Sun 10am-5pm

Daguerreotype
(anonymous)
Musée Nicéphore Niépce

The museum's small but unique collection of rare 19th-century photographic equipment was discovered in 1992. Amassed by the editor, publisher, and photographic inventor Louis-Desiré Blanquart-Evrard, the core collection was donated to the former Musée Industriel et Commercial in 1870. The unique collection includes early daguerreotypes, paper negatives, and a significant number of unidentified objects. For the time being it is accessible by appointment only.

Museum of the History of Science
Broad Street, Oxford, Oxfordshire OX1 3AZ, UK
Tel. (44) 1865 277280   www.mhs.ox.ac.uk
Tue-Sat noon-4pm

The museum's fascinating collection of 800 cameras and related equipment includes an 1845 camera designed by Daguerre, a Sutton panoramic camera with a glass-and-water lens (c. 1861), an early wet-plate folding box-camera (c. 1855), Lewis Carroll's Wet-Collodion photographic outfit, and some of the first mass-produced cameras such as the No.2 Kodak box camera (1890), the Kodak 'Brownie', and Kodak Retina I (1946). The museum also displays part of its comprehensive collection of stereoscopic cameras, of which the earliest example is a sliding-box monocular camera designed by Dallmeyer in 1862.

Národní Technické Muzeum
The National Technical Museum
Kostelní 42, 170 78 Prague 7, Czech Republic
Tel. (420) 2 20399111 www.ntm.cz
Tue-Sun 9am-5pm

This vast collection gives a fine overview of the history and development of photography and cinematography. Among the earliest exhibits are magic lanterns, professional hall projectors dating back to the beginning of the 20th century, and the original Lumière camera used by Jan Krizenecky in 1895 to make the first Czech films. The fields of optics, spectrography, X-ray, and photomicrography are also richly represented.

COMMUNICATION AND COMPUTING

AWA Electronic Communication Museum
Village Green, Routes 5 and 20 Bloomfield, New York, New York 14468, USA
Tel. (1) 716 392 3088 www.antiquewireless.org
May-Oct: Sun 2-5pm (Jun-Aug also Sat 2-4pm)

When it comes to the history of wireless communications, curator Edward Gable is a mine of information. The museum covers the spectrum of electronic communications from the earliest telegraph, radios, and televisions, through to their modern descendants. A particular highlight is a collection of original Marconi shipboard equipment, dating back to 1907. Enthusiasts should book to visit the annexe, where additional objects are stored and new ones repaired, or to use the research library.

Enigma Rotor Cypher Machine
Heinz Nixdorf MuseumsForum

Cyberbikes, a virtual model factory (right)
Heinz Nixdorf MuseumsForum

Bletchley Park
The Mansion, Bletchley Park, Milton Keynes, Buckinghamshire MK3 6EB, UK
Tel. (44) 1908 640404 www.bletchleypark.org.uk
Every alternate Sat-Sun 10.30am-5pm

Though plans are afoot to rationalize this enormous site into a 'themed' museum, for the time being the atmosphere remains much as it was during World War II when Bletchley Park was the vital nerve centre of allied intelligence. It was here that Alan Turing, philosopher, mathematician, and computer pioneer, invented the Enigma code-breaking machine. The existence of the 55-acre complex – which once accommodated 12,000 employees – was kept top secret until 1974.

Deutsches Museum
The German Museum
Museumsinsel 1, 80538 Munich, Germany
Tel. (49) 89 21791 www.deutsches-museum.de
Daily 9am-5pm

Six galleries in the museum provide a short but comprehensive history of telecommunications, from the ancient use of beacons and the mechanical optical telegraphs introduced just after the French Revolution, to today's computer-supported multifunctional telecommunications systems. Among the items on display are the earliest surviving electric telegraph, built by Soemmerring in 1811.

Heinz Nixdorf MuseumsForum

Fürstenallee 7, 33102 Paderborn, Germany
Tel. (49) 5251 306600 www.hnf.de
Tue-Fri 9am-6pm, Sat-Sun 10am-6pm

Founded by the computer pioneer Heinz Nixdorf, this vast and fascinating museum
covers the history of information processing, from the emergence of cuneiform writing
in 3000BC to the mass production of a range of communication technologies including
telephones, typewriters, and computers in the 19th, 20th, and 21st centuries. The core
exhibition traces the evolution of computers from Leibniz's four-function calculating
machine, to the creation of the first fully electronic computer (ENIAC)) in 1945. Among
the many remarkable exhibits is a Thomas Arithmometer dating from 1850, a Jacard
loom with punch cards, and modern on-board computers from the Gemini space capsule.

Hansen's 'writing ball',
1878 model
*Heinz Nixdorf
MuseumsForum*

Lizard Wireless Station Bass Point

Lizard Peninsula, Cornwall, UK
Tel. (44) 1209 210900 www.trevithicktrust.com
Jul-Sep: Tue-Fri, Sun 1-4pm. Oct-May: Wed 1-4pm. Jun: Wed, Sun 1-4pm

From this purpose-built wireless station in Cornwall, Marconi established that signals
could be transmitted across long distances after he picked up a broadcast from the Isle
of Wight (196 miles away) on 23 January, 1901. The station has been restored exactly as it
was in Marconi's day, and contains replicas of some of Marconi's pioneering wireless
apparatus.

Museo Guglielmo Marconi
The Guglielmo Marconi Museum

Villa Griffone, via Celestini 1, 40044 Pontecchio Marconi, Italy
Tel. (39) 051 846121 www.fgm.it
Mon-Fri 10am-1pm, 2.30-5pm

The laboratory which the young Marconi set up in an attic at his family home has been
restored exactly as it was in 1895, when Marconi sent the first radio signal to an antenna
and receiver set up by his brother on a nearby hill. The museum houses over fifty working replicas of historical instruments from the Maurizio Bigazzi Collection.

Marconi Collection

Marconi plc, West Hanningfield Road, Great Baddow, Chelmsford, Essex CM2 8HN, UK
Tel. (44) 1245 242390 www.marconicalling.com
By appt. only

Plans are in hand to open up the collection to the public for the first time in its history.
To achieve maximum access the collection will be split – documents will be kept in an
archive at the Essex Records Office in Chelmsford, and artefacts in a new purpose-built
museum. Included in the documents collection are diaries, personal and company
correspondence, press cuttings, photographs, diagrams, and maps dating back to
Marconi's earliest experiments in the 1890s, plus 2,000 wireless messages sent from
the *Titanic* and other ships involved in her final hours. The enormous artefact collection
includes a diverse range of wireless telegraphy equipment made by the Marconi
Com-pany, from the first prototype receivers and transmitters, to communication
equipment which was mass produced in World War II.

The New England Wireless and Steam Museum

1300 Frenchtown Road, East Greenwich, Rhode Island 02818, USA
Tel. (1) 401 885 0545
By appt. only

The original coastal wireless station, built by Walter Wentworth Massie in 1907 on Point Judith, Rhode Island, forms the centrepiece of this out-standing vintage wireless collection. It is the oldest surviving originally equipped wireless station anywhere. Massie's family kept all his original items, including his laths and drawings, and subsequently donated them to the museum. Additional gems include a Marconi distress transmitter, an Edison 1882 diode (the first radio tubes), and an 1881 Professor Dolbear radio receiver.

Pavek Museum of Broadcasting
3515 Raleigh Avenue, St. Louis Park, Minnesota 55416, USA
Tel. (1) 952 926 8198   www.pavekmuseum.org
Tue-Fri 10am-6pm, Sat 9am-5pm

Featuring large in this collection is equipment documenting recorded sound, thanks to Jack Mullin. There are equally massive holdings of radio receivers, transmitters, and televisions, the core of which belonged to Joseph R. Pavek. The main focus is equipment from the first half of the 20th century, including radios built before 1926 (namely battery sets – radios did not run on house current until after 1926).

Postmuseum
The Postal Museum
Stephansplatz 5, 20095 Hamburg, Germany
Tel. (49) 40 35037700
Tue-Fri 10am-3pm (Thu until 6pm)

This museum owns numerous examples of early long-distance transmitting equipment such as telegraphs and telephones created by Bell and Siemens, an exchange keyboard, fax machines, and radio installations.

Musée radar
The Radar Museum
Route de Basly, 14 440 Douvres-la-Délivrande, France
Tel. (33) 2 31 37 74 43
Easter-Nov: daily 10am-5pm

Based in a German World War II radar station, this D-Day museum chronicles the history and development of detection techniques using radar equipment, scale models, maps, and plans. It includes a fully restored command bunker featuring one of the Würzbürg Riese radars, developed for Hitler in 1936.

The Radio-Television Museum
2608 Mitchellville Road, Bowie, Maryland 20716, USA
Tel. (1) 301 390 1020   www.radiohistory.org
Sat-Sun 1-4pm (other times by appt.)

Opened in Maryland in 1999, this energetic museum traces the history of radio and television using vintage radios, televisions, and related memorabilia.

Musée de la Radio
The Radio Museum
Grand'Rue 64, 4870 Trooz, Belgium
Tel. (32) 4 3516947
Sat-Sun 2-6pm

This radio and communications museum houses over 400 items, ranging from early telewriters and 1920s receiving stations, to special devices produced during World War II.

Museum of Radio and Technology

1640 Florence Avenue, Huntington, West Virginia 25701 USA
Tel. (1) 304 525 8890
Sat 10am-4pm, Sun 1-4pm

Conceived and run by a team of devoted volunteers, this eclectic collection
covers every aspect of 20th-century communication, from vintage 1920s
battery sets and wind-powered generators used for charging batteries, to
military radio equipment and TVs from the 1940s.

Löwe economy tubes,
3xLA75, 1926
Radiomuseum

Radio- ja TV-Museo
Radio and TV Museum

Radiomäki, 15111 Lahti, Finland
Tel. (358) 3 81410 www.lahti.fi
Mon-Fri 10am-5pm, Sat-Sun 11am-5pm

Located inside a former radio station belonging to the Finnish Broadcasting Network,
this museum covers the history of Finnish radio and television from its earliest days to
the present. The museum has its own real-time radio station, and the station's broadcasting hall, sound effect and TV studios form an ideal backdrop to the displays of pioneering radio and TV sets.

Radiomuseum
The Radio Museum

Klitzingstrasse 14, 84056 Rottenburg an der Laaber, Germany
Tel. (49) 8781 2862 www.rolaa.de
Every 1st and 3rd Sun of the month 1-5pm

Founded by a group of radio enthusiasts in 1997, this museum features a series of exhibits
on radios and related items, including vintage crystal radio sets, early phonographs and
gramophones, pocket radios, tape players, microphones, and vintage televisions.

The Science Museum

Exhibition Road, London SW7 2DD, UK
Tel. (44) 870 870 4771 www.sciencemuseum.org.uk
Daily 10am-6pm

The museum's 'Computing Then and Now' gallery gives an incisive overview of the
history of computing, from the invention of the first mechanical calculator in 1623, to
the most recent technological advances in analogue and digital computation, data
management and processing, and cryptography. One of the centrepieces is a portion of
the Difference Engine No.1 invented by Charles Babbage, the awkward genius whose
complex calculating machines proved impossible to complete in his lifetime. Other
ground-breaking computers include the only working vacuum tube computer in
Europe (the Ferranti 'Pegasus'), and the Russian computer Elliott 401, currently being
restored. Another of the many treasures is one of the valves used by John Ambrose
Fleming in the first practical thermionic device for detecting radio signals.

Stubbekøbing Motorcykel- og Radiomuseum
The Stubbekøbing Motorcyle and Radio Museum

Nykøbingvej 54, 4850 Stubbekøbing, Denmark
Tel. (45) 54 442222
Please call for opening times

Inventor of the loudspeaker, Peter Jensen was born and lived near to this unusual museum
of motorcycles, vintage radio sets, loudspeakers, and gramophones.

The Museum of Submarine Telegraphy
Porthcurno, Cornwall TR19 6JX, UK
Tel. (44) 1736 810966 www.porthcurno.org.uk
Jan-Mar: Mon 10am-4pm. Apr-Oct: Mon-Fri, Sun 10am-5pm (Jul, Aug: daily 10am-5pm)

Since 1870, when the British end of the first all-submarine telegraph cable to Bombay
was landed at Porthcurno, this tiny Cornish cove has played a distinguished role in the
history of international communications. Additional cables were landed here during
the early years of the 20th century, and in 1941 Cornish tin miners blasted a top secret
communications centre out of the granite hillside. Now a unique museum, the hewn-
out tunnels include a fully working telegraph system demonstrating how the global
telecommunications system operated during the war.

Telegraph from the
Sonera Collection
Telegalleria

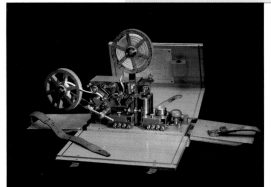

Telegalleria
The Telegallery
Elimäentie 9A, 00510 Helsinki, Finland
Tel. (358) 204 060027 www.sonera.com/telegalleria
Please call for opening times

Based at the headquarters of Sonera (formerly Telecom
Finland), this internationally renowned gallery
spans the history of telecommunications from the
mid-1850s to the present day. Objects on display
range from manual telephones dating from the 1880s,
to the most recent developments in transferring network devices, dialling devices, and mobile phones.

U.S. Army Communications and Electronics Museum
Building 275, Kaplan Hall, Fort Monmouth, Monmouth, New Jersey 07703-5103, USA
Tel. (1) 732 532 2440
Sat-Sun noon-4pm

Built during World War I, this US Army Signal Corps headquarters spearheaded a host
of communications technology advances, from the first radio-equipped weather
balloon to be sent into the upper atmosphere (1928), to sophisticated aircraft detection
radar (it was from here in 1946 that the first radar signals were bounced off the moon).
Edwin H. Armstrong, the radio pioneer responsible for the regenerative circuit (1912),
has a case containing his personal notebook and amplifiers. On the front lawn are
satellite dishes, mortar-locating radar sets, and tank-carrying equipment developed
at the fort. But it's not all about electronics and radar wizardry – there are displays
honouring the work of military carrier pigeons used during the World Wars to carry
messages and supplies into occupied territories. G. I. Joe has a special place in the Army's
'Pigeon Hall of Fame', stuffed and accompanied by all his honours. During World War II
he carried a message from the British 10th Corps Headquarters which resulted in saving
1,000 British soldiers. And he's not alone – there's Geronimo, Eureka, and Scoop among
others, along with displays of carrier pigeon memorabilia dating from the days when
this was a pigeon breeding and training centre.

Vintage Wireless Museum
23 Rosendale Road, West Dulwich, London SE21 8DS, UK
Tel. (44) 20 867 03667
By appt. only

Gerald Wells' enormous private collection consists of several thousand vintage wireless
sets and pre-war televisions, almost all of which are in working order. His museum
also includes an extensive library of wireless and television manuals and books.

U.S. ARMY COMMUNICATIONS ELECTRONICS MUSEUM
Fort Monmouth, New Jersey

Field Telephone 1918,
drawing (far left)
*U.S. Army Communications
and Electronics Museum*

Drawing of a field
telegraph operator (left)
*U.S. Army Communications
and Electronics Museum*

The Glass Woman (below)
Deutsches Hygiene-Museum

MEDICAL INSTRUMENTS

Museo di Anatomia umana normale
The Museum of Human Anatomy
Università di Bologna, via Imerio 48, 40126 Bologna, Italy
Tel. (39) 051 244467
Mon-Fri 8.30am-5.30pm

Established in 1742 by Pope Benedict XIV, this superb anatomy collection contains some exceptional works sculpted in coloured wax by some of the best and most brilliant model makers of the 18th and 19th centuries. Ercole Lelli's life-sized nudes, of both sexes, and his 'skinned' statue showing the disposition of muscles, are outstanding.

Armamentarium obstetricium Gottingense - Georg-August-Universität
The Obstetrics Instrument Collection - Georg-August-University
Department of Ethics and History of Medicine,
Humboldtallee 36, 37073 Göttingen, Germany
Tel. (49) 551 399007   www.gwdg.de
Mon-Thu 9am-4pm, Fri 9am-1pm

Göttingen's first academic obstetrics collection
was established by Albrecht von Haller in 1751. The
museum documents crucial stages in the development
of the science, and among the 1,564 pieces in the collection are
early medical instruments and anatomical specimens dating
from the 18th century.

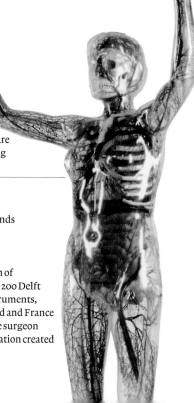

Museum Boerhaave
The Boerhaave Museum
Lange Sint Agnietenstraat 10, 2312 WC Leiden, The Netherlands
Tel. (31) 71 5214224   www.museumboerhaave.nl
Tue-Sat 10am-5pm, Sun noon-5pm

The museum houses a unique and heterogeneous collection of
medical and pharmacological paraphernalia, ranging from 200 Delft
apothecary jars, to a collection of 17th-century surgical instruments,
including ornate amputation saws and knives from England and France
and the more functional instruments adopted by the Hague surgeon
,Cornelis Solingen. (He was the first to recognize that decoration created
unnecessary dirt traps.)

Musée Delmas-Orfila-Rouvière
The Delmas-Orfila-Rouvière Museum
Institut d'Anatomie, Université Paris V, 45 rue des Saints-Pères, 75006 Paris, France
Tel. (33) 1 42 86 2047 www.biomedicale.univ-paris5.fr
By appt. only

Founded by Mathieu Orfila in 1844, this is one of the largest anatomical collections in
France. Though many of the original specimens were lost in the Revolution or melted
down to make candles in World War II, the museum has continued to grow.

Deutsches Apothekenmuseum
The German Pharmaceutical Museum
Heidelberg Schloss, Friedrichstrasse 3, 69117 Heidelberg, Germany
Tel. (49) 6221 25880 www.deutsches-apotheken-museum.de
Daily 10am-5.30pm

Founded in 1937, this fascinating museum contains over 10,000 items chronicling the
history of medicine-making from the 13th century to the present day. Exhibitions inside
ten different galleries range from six complete apothecaries dating from the 17th and
18th centuries (all with their original ornate furniture and apothecary jars), to a unique
collection of 17th- to 19th-century drugs.

Exterior of the museum
Deutsches Hygiene-Museum

Deutsches Hygiene-Museum
The German Museum of Hygiene
Lingnerplatz 1, 01069 Dresden,
Germany
Tel. (49) 351 48460
www.dhmd.de
Tue-Fri 9am-5pm,
(Wed until 8.30pm),
Sat-Sun 10am-5pm

Covering a diverse range of topics including the pill, AIDS, genetic engineering, and
biological functions, this medical collection was founded in 1911 by the Dresden mouth-
wash millionaire, Karl August Lingner. Historically, the museum's emphasis on individual and social 'hygiene' made it an ideal mouthpiece for Nazi and subsequently
Soviet propaganda. In recent years, however, the museum has been free to focus on its
original aims. It is famous for its *Gläserner Mensch* (Transparent Man), a life-sized model
of a human being, built in 1926, that allows us to peer at our the working functions of
our bodies. It was such a success that the Transparent Woman, Horse, Cow, and even the
Transparent Factory followed. The moulage collection of 2,000 wax models of body
parts chronicles a range of unspeakable diseases, and the Schwarzkopf collection has
enriched the museum with more than 2,000 items pertaining to the history of body
care and beauty.

Deutsches Klingenmuseum Solingen
The German Blade Museum of Solingen
Klosterhof 4, 42653 Solingen, Germany
Tel. (49) 212 59822 www.solingen.de
Tue-Thu, Sat-Sun 10am-5pm, Fri 2-5pm

This museum houses a fine collection of medical instruments, in particular early
scalpels, hooks, forceps, saws, specula, catheters, and bronze and silver files gathered
from the tombs of Roman physicians. Among the 17th-century medical instruments
are surgical and especially trepanning tools, bloodletting knives, and bowls for
collecting blood.

Deutsches Medizinhistorisches Museum
The German Museum of the History of Medicine
Anatomiestrasse 18-20, 85049 Ingolstadt, Germany
Tel. (49) 841 3051860
Tue-Sun 10am-noon, 2-5pm

Established in 1973 in a former anatomy hall decorated with a magnificent series of 19th-century allegorical frescoes, the museum presents a fascinating and comprehensive history of medicine from ancient times to the present. Over 1,000 objects on show range from Roman and Greek surgical instruments to exhibits on the history of Egyptian, South American, and Asian medicine and dentistry.

Musée de l'Ecorché d'Anatomie
Museum of Anatomical Sections
Espace Culturel, 54 ave de la Libération, 27110 Le Neubourg, France
Tel. (33) 2 32 35 93 95
Feb-Dec: Wed-Sun 2-6pm (Aug: also Wed 10am-noon)

In 1822, after several years of experimenting, Louis Thomas Jerome Auzoux presented to the Paris Academy of Medicine the first anatomical model that could be taken apart and reassembled. It eliminated some of the need for human corpses, and six years later Auzoux began mass producing the models for sale all over the world at a factory based close to this museum. Renowned for his works, he was received by the king of England, the Pope, and congratulated by the Tsar of Russia. In 1830, he produced a complete human figure that contained 129 individual, labelled sections, an example of which is on display. The *Grand Ecorché* stood 1.8 metres high, and sold for well over a hundred years to schools of medicine around the world.

Pregnancy calendar with the goddess Juno and child depicted on the lid of a snuff box (top)
Medizinhistorisches Museum der Universität Zürich

Painting of a pharmacy, Berne, 1792 (above)
Medizinhistorisches Museum der Universität Zürich

Alpine wooden figure of Roccus, the patron saint of the plague, early 18th century (left)
Medizinhistorisches Museum der Universität Zürich

Musée Fragonard
The Fragonard Museum
Ecole nationale vétérinaire d'Alfort, 7 ave du Général de Gaulle, 94707 Maisons-Alfort, France
Tel. (33) 1 43 96 71 72
Tue, Wed 2-5pm, Sat-Sun 10am-5pm

The National Veterinary School's extraordinary anatomical collection was begun in 1765 by the surgeon, Honoré Fragonard (cousin of the painter Jean-Honoré Fragonard). Crammed into case after case are specimens ranging from teaching aids (a cow's liver infested with worms or the foetus of a horse injected with mercury to highlight its veins) to 21 examples of the famous flayed skin figures produced by Fragonard himself.

History of Medicine Library
Wellcome Trust, Wellcome Building, 183 Euston Road, London NW1 2BE, UK
Tel. (44) 20 7611 8582   www.wellcome.ac.uk
Mon-Fri 9.45am-5.15pm (Tue, Thu until 7.15pm), Sat 9.45am-1pm

This superb library collection, founded by Sir Henry Wellcome, includes literature on an illuminatingly diverse range of topics relating to medicine, including anthropology, ethnology, archaeology, population studies, witchcraft,

Doctor's homeopathic
first-aid kit, *c.*1850
*Medizinhistorisches
Museum der Universität
Zürich*

magic, botany, alchemy, cookery, and eugenics. Superb
Oriental collections comprise 4,000 printed books and
11,000 manuscripts – including the library's most ancient
document – a medical prescription written on papyrus
(*c.*11000BC).

Hunterian Museum

Royal College of Surgeons of England, 35-43 Lincoln's Inn
Fields, London WC2A 3PN, UK
Tel. (44) 20 7869 6560   rcseng.ac.uk
Mon-Fri 10am-5pm

Amassed originally in the 18th century by John Hunter, this
outstanding historic medical collection provides an insight into the work of the brilliant
Scottish surgeon and his pioneering observations on body trauma and disease. The
collection was all but destroyed in World War II, but 3,500 of Hunter's original dissections
and pathological specimens have survived. There are teaching collections of the
Odontological Museum, The Wellcome Museums of Anatomy and Pathology, and the
Historical Surgical Instrument Collection (with instruments from the collection shown
throughout the displays, and others on loan to the Science Museum in London).

Museo internazionale della Croce Rossa
The International Museum of the Red Cross
Palazzo Longhi, via Garibaldi 50, 46043 Castiglione delle Stiviere, Italy
Tel. (39) 0376 638505   www.dsmnet.it
Apr-Sep: Tue-Sun 9am-12.30pm, 3-7pm. Oct-Mar: Tue-Sun 9am-noon, 2-5.30pm

Housed in a large and imposing palazzo, which dates from the mid 18th century,
this venerable museum celebrates the history and work of the Red Cross. The
international volunteer association was established in 1859 in the wake of the Battle
of Solferino, after Swiss businessman Henry Dunant witnessed the townswomen
of Castiglione delle Stiviere rushing to the aid of thousands of mutilated soldiers
streaming into the town.

Johann-Winter-Museum
Frankenstrasse 19, 56626 Andernach, Germany
Tel. (49) 2632 30161
May-Nov: 1st Sun of every month (or by appt.)

The 16th-century humanist and physician, Johann Winter, was born in Andernach and
taught the father of modern anatomy, Andreas Vesalius. The museum gives a complete
account of medicine, from ancient times to the present day, beginning with Egyptian
papyri, illustrations and mummies, and Greek and Roman surgical instruments, and
moving on to displays on the advent of hospitals in the 14th century.

Lääketieteen historian museo
The Museum of Medical History
University of Helsinki, Hämeentie 153 C, 00014 Helsinki, Finland
Tel. (358) 9 7084823   www.helsinki.fi
Tue, Fri noon-3pm, Thu 3-6pm

The collection includes a diverse range of objects relating to the history of the medical,
nursing, and veterinary sciences, acquired from provincial hospitals all over the country
(including Finland's first hospital, the Pyhä Yrjänä hospital for lepers in Turku, which
has records dating back to 1355). Among the highlights are physicians' cupping horns,
axes and bleeding irons, and an array of pharmaceutical equipment.

Lepramuseum
The Museum of Leprosy
Kinderhaus 15, 48159 Münster, Germany
Tel. (49) 251 28510 / 16920   www.muenster.org
Sun 3-5pm

Housed in a former leper's hospital which dates from 1333, this extraordinary museum traces the history of the disease. Alongside historical documentation from the hospital (including handwritten lists of house rules and punishments, and a map locating 1,110 lepers' homes), are displays of medicines prescribed as cures in the Middle Ages, clothes worn by lepers, and rattles carried to warn of their approach. Further exhibitions focus on discrimination against lepers, leprosy today, and the success of modern drugs in combating the disease.

Medizinhistorisches Museum der Universität Zürich
The Museum of the History of Medicine of the University of Zurich
Rämistrasse 69, 8001 Zurich, Switzerland
Tel. (41) 1 6342072   www.mhiz.unizh.ch
Tue-Fri 1-6pm, Sat-Sun 11am-5pm

Established by Doctor Gustav Adolf Wervill in 1915, this eclectic collection has over 100,000 pieces covering every aspect of medicine, from quacks and folk medicine, to the history of diseases such as plague and leprosy.

Mendelianum
Mendelovo námesti 1, 603 00 Brno, Czech Republic
Tel. (420) 5 337854   www.mzm.cz
Jul-Aug: daily 9am-6pm. Sep-Nov, Feb-Jun: Mon-Fri 8am-7pm.
Dec-Jan: Mon-Fri 8am-4pm

The Augustinian monk and father of genetics, Gregor Johann Mendel, lived and worked in this monastery, growing the pea plants in the monastery's courtyard garden that proved vital to his researches into inherited characteristics. A museum in the former refectory is lined with cases containing items commemorating Mendel's life, including his barometer, chair, walking stick, notebooks, manuscripts, photographs, and portrait, as well as books annotated by him.

An early 19th-century
trepanning set
*The Old Operating Theatre
Museum and Herb Garret*

419

The Herb Garret
The Old Operating Theatre Museum and Herb Garret

Mütter Museum
19 South 22nd Street,
Philadelphia, Pennsylvania
19103, USA
Tel. (1) 215 563 3737
www.collphyphil.org
Daily 10am-5pm

This is one of the great
19th-century medical
museums still remaining,
with modern imaging and
preservation techniques having long replaced fluid-preserved anatomical and
pathological specimens. At its core is a collection of preparations amassed by the
pioneering 19th-century plastic surgeon, Thomas Dent Mütter. Today, it houses some
20,000 objects ranging from wax models of faces deformed by wasting skin disease,
to obsolete medical instruments and apparatus. Outstanding among these are
Dr Benjamin Rush's medicine chest, Marie Curie's quartz-piezo electrometer (used
by her and Pierre Curie in the earliest measurements of radium), the Hyrtl Skull
Collection demonstrating variations in cranial development, and the Chevalier Jackson
Collection of Objects Swallowed and Inhaled, ranging from nuts and buttons to coins
and metal toys, elegantly displayed like small treasures in a purpose-made cabinet.

Taxidermic child
Pathologisch-Anatomisches Bundesmuseum

The Old Operating Theatre Museum and Herb Garret
9a St Thomas's Street, London SE1 9RY, UK
Tel. (44) 20 7955 4791 www.thegarret.org.uk
Daily 10.30am-5pm

This pristinely-preserved early 19th-century operating
theatre was discovered by accident in 1957, when historian
Raymond Russell crawled through a hole in the belfry of a
chapel belonging to old St Thomas' hospital. The theatre
predates the discovery of antiseptics and anaesthetics and –
with its original metal saws, knives, pliers, bloodletting
equipment, and bloodspattered floor – vividly evokes a
period when patients opting for surgery had to be grogged
up on ale, blindfolded and gagged, and held down by rope,
with a box of sawdust underneath to catch the blood.

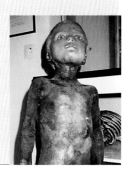

Pathologisch-Anatomisches Bundesmuseum
The Federal Pathological-Anatomical Museum
Altes Allgemeines Krankenhaus, Spitalgasse 2, 1090 Vienna, Austria
Tel. (43) 1 4068672 www.pathomus.or.at
Wed 3-6pm, Thu 8-11am, every 1st Sun of the month 10am-1pm

Founded by Franz I in 1796, this enormous anatomical museum is housed in a former
psychiatric hospital in Vienna. and consists of approximately 50,000 exhibits. Excellent
collections include medical instruments, medical coins, stamps and the trade insignia of
medical professions, and collections on tuberculosis. There are also casts of dermatolog-
ical diseases intended to teach medical students about normal and pathological anatomy.

Pharmazie-Historisches Museum der Universität Basel
The Pharmacy-Historical Museum of the University of Basle
Totengässlein 3, 4051 Basle, Switzerland
Tel. (41) 61 2617940
Mon-Fri 9am-noon, 2-5pm

Established by Swiss pharmacist Josef Haefliger in 1925, this remarkable collection is housed in an historic 14th-century house and spa where Paracelsus von Hohenheim lived from 1526-27. The museum traces the development of modern-day pharmaceuticals from their earliest beginnings. One of the many highlights is the collection of ceramic apothecary jars.

Röntgen-Gedächtnisstätte
The Röntgen Memorial
Röntgenring 8, 97070 Würzburg, Germany
Tel. (49) 931 3511102   www.fh-wuerzburg.de
Mon-Thu 9am-4pm, Fri 9am-3pm

Based in the former University of Würzburg Physics Institute, the memorial hall celebrates the work of Wilhelm Conrad Röntgen, who discovered X-rays here on 8 November, 1895 (the first *Röntgenogram* was an image of his wife's hand). On display are various personal items, a biographical video, and some of the original instruments used in Röntgen's experiments, including induction coils and vacuum tubes.

Empire Pharmacy
Pharmazie-Historisches Museum der Universität Basel

Thackray Medical Museum
Beckett Street, Leeds, West Yorkshire LS9 7LN, UK
Tel. (44) 113 2444343
www.thackraymuseum.org
Tue-Sun 10am-5pm

From the workings of the human body to the medical and public health developments of the last 150 years, this mesmerising exhibition explores, quite literally, what makes us tick – and keep on ticking. Begun in the 1980s by the medical company, Chas F. Thackray Ltd, the collection now numbers some 35,000 items. It includes historical surgical textbooks from the Renaissance to the 20th century, and commercial literature relating to all aspects of the medical supply trade, as well as a huge variety of surgical instruments dating from early Roman times to the present day. The recent addition of the Wilkinson collection of pharmacy ceramics, put together over 75 years, includes a significant number of English Delftware pharmacy pots.

Voenno-meditsinskii muzei
The Military-Medical Museum
Latsaretnyi pereulok 2, 191180 St Petersburg, Russian Federation
Tel. (7) 812 3154225
Mon-Fri 10am-noon, 1-3pm

This is the only medical museum in the Russian Federation. Its collections – illustrating the army's close links with medicine from Peter the Great onwards – are unique. Among the 200,000 pieces in the museum are 6,000 medical instruments, around 3,000 works of art depicting medical themes, 300 medical books (including original editions of Bidloo and Vesalius), and substantial archives.

MUSICAL INSTRUMENTS

Accordeon- en Harmonica-Museum 'De Muse'
The 'De Muse' Accordion and Harmonica Museum
Kerkplein 12, 6581 AC Malden, near Nijmegen, The Netherlands
Tel. (31) 24 3584196 www.accordeonmuseum.nl
Wed-Sun noon-5pm

Pardessus de Viole by Benoist Fleury, Paris, *c.1770*
The Horniman Museum and Gardens

Amalgamating their collections, two collectors – Henk Kuik, an accordion expert, and Art Daane, a mouth organ enthusiast – formed the only museum of its kind in the Netherlands, displaying 300 accordions and some 1,100 mouth organs. The collection gives an historic overview of free-reed instrument innovation. It houses items such as an early 19th-century French accordion, melodeons, concertinas, and three exceptional accordions by the Dutch maker, Bernard Vos.

The Bate Collection of Musical Instruments
Faculty of Music, St Aldates, Oxford, Oxfordshire OX1 1DP, UK
Tel. (44) 1865 276139 www.ashmol.ox.ac.uk
Mon-Fri 2-5pm, Sat 10am-noon during term time

This collection was begun in 1963 by Philip Bate, who gave his collection of European orchestral woodwind instruments to the University of Oxford. One of the collection's prize exhibits is the world famous treble recorder by Pierre Jaillard, who arrived in England from Bresse in France in 1680.

17th-century Venetian spinet from the Lord Howard de Walden Collection *Dean Castle*

Cobbe Collection Trust
Hatchlands Park, East Clandon, Surrey GU4 7RT, UK
Tel. (44) 1483 211474 www.cobbecollection.co.uk
Apr-Oct: Tue-Thu, Sun 2-5.30pm (plus Fri during Aug)

An outstanding collection of historic keyboard instruments, most of which were collected by Alex Cobbe, is displayed in this National Trust Property, along with Cobbe's fine collection of old master paintings. Twelve of the 37 instruments were owned or played by great composers (including Mahler and Chopin), making it the largest group of instruments associated with composers to be seen in one place.

Dean Castle
Dean Road, Kilmarnock, Ayrshire, UK
Tel. (44) 1563 554704
Easter-Oct: daily noon-5pm. Nov-Easter: Sat-Sun for guided tours only. Other times by appt. only.

Displayed in the 14th-century castle keep, Dean Castle houses the Charles van Raalte collection of early musical instruments. It is an exquisite collection set in an awe-inspiring setting. Although it contains several African and Eastern instruments, it is largely European in character and consists of early string and woodwind instruments, and percussion items.

Fenton House - Benton Fletcher Collection of Early Keyboard Instruments
Windmill Hill, Hampstead, London NW3 6RT, UK
Tel. (44) 20 7435 3471 www.nationaltrust.org.uk
Please call for opening times

Bow harp (*Saunggauk*),
Burma (far left)
*The Horniman Museum and
Gardens*

Bell by Johann Gottfried
Ullrich, Apolda, 1764
(left)
Glockenmuseum Apolda

The Benton Fletcher Collection of Early Keyboard Instruments is housed in a charming William and Mary merchant's house. Nineteen keyboard instruments were collected by Major Fletcher between the 1920s and 1940s, with the intention that they be restored to working order so that people could hear music on the original instruments for which they had been written.

Finchcocks Living Museum of Music
Goudhurst, Kent TN17 1HH, UK
Tel. (44) 1580 211702   www.finchcocks.co.uk
Please call for opening times

This is a fabulous collection of nearly 100 historic keyboard instruments amassed by pianist, Richard Burnett. Most of the instruments date from the 18th and 19th centuries, with early square pianos by Bayes & Company and Beyer & Broadwood & Son, alongside grand pianos of slightly later dates.

Germanisches Nationalmuseum
The Germanic National Museum
Kartäusergasse 1, 90402 Nuremberg, Germany
Tel. (49) 911 13310   www.gnm.de
Tue-Sun 10am-5pm (Wed until 9pm)

The nucleus of the collection is made up of the historic musical instruments of the family Rück, which comprised almost 1,550 objects in 1962, including an extensive specialized library and a collection of paintings, as well as numerous photographic negatives and restoration reports. Another impassioned collector, Johann Cristoph Neupert (1842-1921), founder of the Neupert piano company, amassed an historical piano collection numbering 300 instruments, which the Neupert family sold to the museum in 1968.

Glockenmuseum Apolda
The Bell Museum of Apolda
Bahnhofstrasse 41, 99510 Apolda, Germany
Tel. (49) 3644 650331
Tue-Sun 10am-6pm (Nov-Apr: until 5pm)

The collection, founded in 1952 (housed in a 19th-century manufacturer's house), numbers about 150 bells spanning three millennia, whose function and origin vary as much as their size (from 2cm to 1m in diameter). There are bell-foundry tools, casting models, stencils for decorations, prints, stamps, and medals with bell motifs. A particularly beautiful exhibit is a Chinese temple bell from the Ming Dynasty.

Gosudarstvennyi tsentral'nyi muzei musikal'noi kul'tury im. M. I. Glinki
The Glinka State Central Museum of Musical Culture
Ulitsa Fadeeva 4, 125047 Moscow, Russian Federation
Tel. (7) 095 2513143   www.museum.ru
Tue-Sun 11am-7pm

The museum's exhibition displays musical instruments, as well as folk and professional instruments, from more than fifty countries. European instruments include a violin by Antonio Stradivari (17th century), a guitar that once belonged to Fedor Shaliapin, and a rare example of a crystal flute. There is also a fine collection of unique lutes, mandolins, and guitars.

Violin-maker's workshop, c. 1900 (above)
Musikinstrumenten-Museum (Markneukirchen)

Giant piano-accordion, Kligenthal and Zwota, 1938 (above right)
Musikinstrumenten-Museum (Markneukirchen)

Barrel organ by Cocchi, Bacigalupo & Graffigna, Berlin, c. 1895 (below)
Musikinstrumenten-Museum (Markneukirchen)

Harmonium Museum
The Reed-Organ Museum
Widmannstrasse 9a, 4410 Liestal, Switzerland
Tel. (41) 61 9216410   www.datacomm.ch
Groups by appt. only

After more than twenty years of collecting reed organs, the Swiss organ teacher and performing musician, Dieter Stalder, can be proud of his collection of more than 130 reed organs, organs, concertals, cecilial, melophones, pianolas, and celestas. The size of his ever-expanding collection provided the incentive to found Switzerland's first reed organ museum.

The Horniman Museum and Gardens
100 London Road, London SE23 3PQ, UK
Tel. (44) 20 8699 1872   www.horniman.ac.uk
Mon-Sat 10.30am-5.30pm, Sun 2.30-5.30pm

From a collection of more than 6,000 instruments, 2,000 are on display. They have been placed in context using videos, sound recordings, and historic costumes drawn from the museum's ethnographic collections. When he began collecting, the museum's founder, Frederick John Horniman, sought to amass sound reproducing instruments from across the globe and across history. Acquisitions have never stopped pouring in and are still actively sought; one curator has recently returned from the Fergana Valley in Uzbekistan where recordings were made of music used

in ceremonies and weddings. As well as those of non-European origin, there is a notable collection of historic European musical instruments. One of the largest of the many gifts is the collection of over 300 European woodwind instruments, donated in 1947 by Adam Carse, professor at the Royal Academy of Music.

Musée des Instruments de musique
The Museum of Musical Instruments
Rue Montagne de la Cour, 2, 1000 Brussels, Belgium
Tel. (32) 2 5450130 www.mim.fgov.be
Tue-Fri 9.30am-5pm (Thu, until 8pm), Sat-Sun 10am-5pm. Guided tours available.

This diverse collection of over 7,000 instruments remains one of the largest in the world. The museum was founded in 1877, when it was part of the Conservatoire Royal de Musique. Its nucleus consists of two collections: the ancient and ethnic instruments assembled by the Belgian musicologist, François Joseph Fétis (1784-1871), and a collection of several hundred Hindu instruments presented to King Léopold II in 1876 by the Rajah Sourindro Mohum Tagore. Victor-Charles Mahillon, the museum's first director, enhanced the collection of non-Western pieces by securing friendly ties with Belgian diplomats overseas (in China and Mexico) and encouraging them to bring back items from beyond Europe. Among the displays are Vietnamese instruments donated to the museum in the 1890s by the colonial Dumoutier, a rare Chédeville bagpipe from the Coussemaker collection (1877), and several crumhorns, shawms, and bajoncillos from the Barbieri collection (1902).

Violin by Johann Gottlob Heberlein, Markneukirchen, 1851
Musikinstrumenten-Museum (Markneukirchen)

Klaviermuseum Schloss Stoitzendorf
The Piano Museum of Stoitzendorf Castle
Schloss Stoitzendorf, Stoitzendorf 1, 3730 Eggenburg, Germany
Tel. (49) 2984 2733
By appt. only

Any instrument with keys has found a place in this remarkable collection of Hermann Buchner. The collection of keyboard instruments is arranged around the castle, which is also his home. The tour begins in the drawing room where, apart from two grand pianos, you will see a clavichord, a celesta, a spinet, and a vibraphone. The remaining collection consists of some sixty pianos, pianolas, harpsichords, regals, and organs.

Musée de la Lutherie et de l'Archèterie française
The Museum of French Stringed Instruments and Bow Making
Hôtel de Ville, 32 rue du Général Leclerc, 88500 Mirecourt, France
Tel. (33) 3 29 370522
Jun-Aug: Mon, Wed-Sun 2-6pm, Tue 9am-noon, 2-6pm.
Sep-May: Tue 2-6pm, Wed, Fri 9am-noon, 2-6pm

Xylophone, possibly West African
The Horniman Museum and Gardens

The art of lute making is thought to have come to Mirecourt in the 16th century, thanks to a man called Tywersus who had learnt his art in Italy. Mirecourt violin production rapidly became renowned across the whole of Europe, reaching its climax in the 18th century when the term *luthe* first appeared. Professional corporations were created, gathering instrument and bow makers at Mirecourt. The nucleus of this collection was assembled by the GLAAF (the 'groupement des luthiers et arche-

tiers d'art de France'), supplemented by donations from professional musicians and private collectors.

Metropolitan Museum of Art

1000 Fifth Avenue at 82nd Street, New York, New York 10028-0198, USA
Tel. (1) 212 535 7710   www.metmuseum.org
Tue-Sun 9.30am-5.30pm (Fri, Sat until 9pm)

A comprehensive collection of instruments (numbering around 5,000 pieces at last count), containing a superb selection of Western instruments arranged by type or family, and an equally stellar collection of non-Western ones, grouped geographically.

Morpeth Chantry Bagpipe Museum

Bridge Street, Morpeth, Northumberland NE61 1PD, UK
Tel. (44) 1670 519466
Mon-Sat 10am-5pm

This collection of over 200 pipes – everything from small Northumbrian pipes to Irish and Scottish ones, plus a selection from France and Spain – belonged originally to one W. A. Cocks, a master clockmaker who started collecting bagpipes in 1914 and later began making and playing them. On his death in 1971, his collection of pipes and manuscripts was bequeathed to the Society of Antiquaries and is now displayed in a former chantry.

Musikhistorisk Museum
The Museum of the History of Music

Åbenrå 30, 1124 Copenhagen, Denmark
Tel. (45) 33 112726   www.kulturnet.dk
May-Sep: Mon-Wed, Fri-Sun 1-5.50pm. Oct-Apr: Mon, Wed, Sat-Sun 1-3.50pm

There are some 3-4,000 instruments in this collection. Among its holdings is a collection of over 1,000 traditional instruments from Europe, Asia, and Africa (including substantial Scandinavian folk music instruments). Dating from around 1500 to around 1900, the collection was formed by a fusion of two museums – the Carl Claudius' Samling and the Musikhistorisk Museum.

Musikinstrumenten-Museum
The Museum of Musical Instruments

Bienengarten 2, 08258 Markneukirchen, Germany
Tel. (49) 37422 2018   www.markneukirchen.de
Tue-Sun 9am-5pm

Founded in 1883 by teacher and organist, Paul Apian-Bennewitz, the initial aim of this museum was to create a centre for local instrument makers. Today, it houses over 3,000 instruments. Apart from classical European string, plucked string, keyboard, metal, and woodwind instruments, there are also several mechanical instruments with musical-mechanisms, plus instruments from China, Japan, Turkey, Africa, and the Americas.

Musikinstrumenten-Museum
The Museum of Musical Instruments

Tiergartenstrasse 1, 10785 Berlin, Germany
Tel. (49) 30 254810
Tue-Fri 9am-5pm, Sat-Sun 10am-5pm

A journey through 400 years of musical history takes you from the medieval period to the present day, and includes a huge Wurlitzer theatre organ and a computerized Synclavier. The exhibition contains early tools, tuning devices, and string winders, as well as examples of early work benches. Apart from a fine collection of woodwind and brass instruments, the museum owns several harpsichords by all three instrument makers of the Ruckers family – Andreas, Jacob, and Johannes.

Musikinstrumenten-Museum der Universität Leipzig
The Museum of Musical Instruments of the University of Leipzig
Täubchenweg 2c-e, 04103 Leipzig, Germany
Tel. (49) 341 2142120
www.uni-leipzig.de/museum/musik
Tue-Sat 10am-5pm, Sun 10am-1pm

Leipzig is where Johann Sebastian Bach wrote most of his compositions, and traces of his legacy can be seen throughout the city. One not to miss is the collection of musical instruments at the University of Leipzig, containing a furnace plate from his residence in St Thomas's School, the organ bench from St John's School, and countless original musical instruments made in Leipzig during the Bach era. The museum's inventory contains over 5,000 musical instruments, of which some 800 are on display.

Four clarinets, oboe, and a horn, early 19th century
Ringve Museum

Musikmuseet
The Museum of Music
Sibyllegatan 2, 10326 Stockholm, Sweden
Tel. (46) 8 51955490 www.smus.se
Tue-Sun 11am–4pm

Founded in 1899, this museum was largely inspired by the industrial exhibition that took place two years earlier in Stockholm. It now comprises some 6,000 exhibits, with Western music especially well represented. Among its collections are Nordic folk instruments, European wind instruments, keyboards, and modern electronic organs. Of special interest is the collection of folk instruments from Europe, Africa, and Asia.

Musée de la Musique
The Museum of Music
Cité de la Musique, 221 ave Jean-Jaurès, 75019 Paris, France
Tel. (33) 1 44 84 46 46 www.cite-musique.fr
Tue-Fri, Sat noon-6pm (Thu until 9.30pm), Sun 10am-6pm

Based in Paris' Parc de la Villette, the Park of the 21st Century, this museum is a gathering of over 4,500 instruments, spanning virtually the whole history of music. It includes a flute from 2500 BC made from the bone of a vulture, violins by Stradivarius and Guarnieri, Beethoven's clavichord, and an E-mu synthesizer which once buzzed and whined to the mad melodic strains of Frank Zappa. Among the world music collection, numbering some 600 pieces and mainly from Africa and Asia, are an Ethiopian lyre and one of the oldest gamelans in existence.

Muzeum Instrumentów Muzycznych
The Museum of Musical Instruments
Stary Rynek 45/47, 61-772 Poznañ, Poland
Tel. (48) 61 8520857 www.info.poznan.pl
Tue, Sat 11am-5pm, Wed, Fri 10am-4pm, Sun 10am-3pm

A collection awash with superb instruments and related items, including over 160 pianos, illustrating the historical development of the instrument from 1750 onwards. Another room is filled with Frederic Chopin memorabilia and papers. Exhibits display over 2,000 European and non-European instruments by type (such as harmoniums,

Pentagonal spinet,
16th century (above)
*Museo degli Strumenti
musicali (Rome)*

Automatic musical
mechanism, 1627, and
tower clockwork (below)
Nationaal Beiaardmuseum

brass and wooden instruments etc.). Among the notable items is a 1st century BC bronze Celtic carnyx and a collection of lutes by Amati and Guarnieri.

Nationaal Beiaardmuseum
The National Carillon Museum

Ostaderstraat 23, 5721 WC Asten, The Netherlands
Tel. (31) 493 691865 www.carillon-museum.nl
Tue-Fri 9.30am-5pm, Sat-Mon 1-5pm

Used to accompany song in Ancient China; by horsemen in the Near East around the necks of their horses to protect them from impending danger; to proclaim law; to pronounce a sentence; to embellish liturgical services…. what would man have done without the ring, clang, and gong of the bell? Every aspect of the development of this instrument is covered in this museum, which aims to collect and conserve carillons,

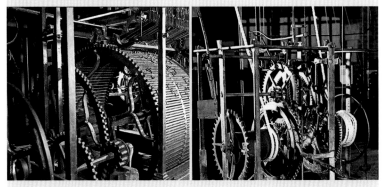

clocks, and chiming mechanisms from the past and present, from the Netherlands, Flanders, and elsewhere.

The Pitt Rivers Museum

South Parks Road, Oxford, Oxfordshire OX1 3PP, UK
Tel. (44) 1865 270927 www.prm.ox.ac.uk
Mon-Sat 1-4.30pm, Sun 2-4.30pm
Please call for opening times

This is one of the most important collections of ethnographic instruments in the world, containing over 6,000 items. The first curator, Henry Balfour, was a particularly assiduous collector. General Pitt-Rivers' core donation, bequeathed in 1883, contained more than 300 instruments. It included a series of musical bows, which Balfour augmented and used as a resource for his monograph *The Natural History of the Musical Bow*. The collection also holds instruments collected by many well known names in anthropology – Evans Pritchard, Hutton, and Mills, among others. The collection of bagpipes, bells, and the virginals made in 1552 by Marcus Jadra, are highlights of this collection.

Ringve Museum

Lade Allé 60, 7441 Trondheim, Norway
Tel. (47) 73 922411 www.museumsnett
By appt. only

In the autumn of 1917, when two young Russian opera stars arrived in Trondheim, the younger one, Victoria, stayed on and married Christian Anker Bachke. She began to amass musical instruments and other related items. This, the only Norwegian museum of musical instruments, is based on her collection and is home to 1,750 instruments from all over the world, including classical, folk, and popular examples. The emphasis is on historical, Western stringed keyboard instruments, including grand pianos made by Stein and Graaf, classic string instruments, and ethnographic (in particular Tibetan) instruments, as well as Norwegian folk instruments.

Royal Academy of Music

Marleybone Road, London NW1 5HT, UK
Tel. (44) 20 7873 7373 www.ram.ac.uk
Please call for opening times

The stunning exterior of this Regency building was originally one of the grand entrances to Regent's Park by John Nash (1822). The string collection on the first floor is extensive and occupies a flexible space designed so that instruments can easily be removed for concert use. Here, too, are items from the violin collection, with starry examples always on view alongside a violin maker's workshop. Above these are twelve pianos displayed to demonstrate how the instrument developed in England during the 19th century. On the top floor, the special collections of the Academy house rare editions and early printed music collections of international significance.

The Beethoven Room (above)
Ringve Museum

Two-wheel cart cylinder piano by Vicente Llinares, Barcelona (below)
Museo degli Strumenti musicali (Rome)

Royal College of Music – Museum of Instruments

Prince Consort Road, London SW7 2BS, UK
Tel. (44) 20 7591 4346 www.rcm.ac.uk
Wed 2-4.30pm during term time (other times by appt.)

This collection includes mainly European keyboard, wind, and stringed instruments from around 1480 to 1980 (500 instruments), as well as 100 instruments from Asia and Africa. Individual gifts plus other collections have come to the college since its foundation in 1883, although the museum was not founded until 1968. The key pieces in the collection include an anonymous South German caicytherium (*c.* 1480), thought to be the earliest surviving stringed keyboard instrument; a harpsichord by Alessandro Trasuntino, made in Venice in 1531; Venetian virginals by G. Celestini of 1593; Handel's spinet; Daydn's clavichord; a Regal organ of 1629; and a chitarrone by Magnux Tieffenbrucker of 1608.

Russell Collection of Early Keyboard Instruments

St Cecilia's Hall, Niddry Street, Cowgate, Edinburgh EH1 1LJ, UK
Tel. (44) 131 650 2805 www.music.ed.ac.uk
Wed, Sat 2-5pm

Raymond Russell collected early keyboard instruments and wanted to see these traditional keyboard instruments played. After his death, nineteen of his choice instruments were presented to Edinburgh University. Among the gems are four Ruckers harpsichords, as well as one by the French maker Pascal Taskin (Paris 1769); an English virginal by Stephen Keene; a North German harpsichord; and a large clavichord of 1763 by Hass; and a single-manual harpsichord by Thomas Hancock (London, 1720).

Sibeliusmuseum

The Sibelius Museum
Turku Åbo, Piispankatu 17, 20500 Turku, Finland
Tel. (358) 2 215 4494 www.abo.fi
Please call for opening times

Two Turkish lutes,
17th century (right)
*Museo degli Strumenti
musicali (Rome)*

The Sibelius Museum is the collective name for the various parts of the Department of Musicology at Åbo Akademi, the Swedish university of Turku. The museum is made up of two parts of equal standing – the instrument collections and the teaching section. It also contains manuscripts, including those written by Sibelius himself. Approximately

300 of the collection's 900 instruments are on display, the majority of which are fine European instruments. The museum also has a small number of folk instruments collected from across the globe.

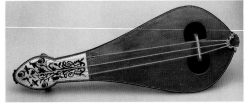

Museo Stradivari
The Stradivari Museum
Palazzo Affaitati, via
Palestro, 17 Cremona, Italy
Tel. (39) 0372 461886
Tue-Sat 8.30am-5.45pm,
Sun 9.15am-12.15pm,
2.30-6pm

A visit to Cremona is a must for serious collectors of stringed instruments, and the first stop should be the Stradivarius Museum. It contains the tools, models, instruments, and drawings of Antonio Stradivari, as well as documentation on the development of the craft in the city.

Museo degli Strumenti musicali
The Museum of Musical Instruments
Piazza S. Croce in Gerusalemme 9/A, 00185 Rome, Italy
Tel. (39) 06 7014796
Tue-Sun 9am-7pm

This collection was begun by Evangelista Gorga, who, after a brief career as a tenor, turned his musical energies to the art of collecting. His most important collection was of musical instruments, which now form the basis of the museum. The instruments are arranged either by theme or by era (from the 11th to the 18th centuries). There are psalteries, guitars, lutes, mandolins, and harpsichords from the 16th and 17th centuries, including one built in 1637 by J. Ruckers. It is one of the few museums to pay any regard to archaeological instruments, and it also contains a rich vein of folk and ethnic instruments. The variety and ingenuity of many of them is staggering, from an Afro-Cuban instrument made from the jaw bone of an ass, to nine examples of a charango (a small guitar using an armadillo as a resonance box).

Chinese *Yueh ch'in*
*Museo degli Strumenti
musicali (Rome)*

Museo degli Strumenti musicali – Collezione Luigi Cherubini
The Museum of Musical Instruments – Luigi Cherubini Collection
Galleria dell'Accademia, via Ricasoli 58-60, 50122 Florence, Italy
Tel. (39) 055 2388609 www.sbas.firenze.it
Mon-Fri 9am-7pm, Sun 9am-1pm

On the Piazza delle Belle Arti, installed in the Palazzo Vecchio, is this magnificent collection of musical instruments, whose origins date back to the 17th century when Ferdinando de' Medici began the collection. Since then, the collection has grown to number some 400 instruments dating from the 17th to the 20th centuries, of which nine are from the Medici collection.

Il Museo degli Strumenti musicali dell'Accademia Musicale Chigiana
The Museum of Musical Instruments of the Chigiana Music Academy
Via di Città 89, 53100 Siena, Italy
Tel. (39) 0577 46152   www.chigiana.it
By appt. only

This museum houses over 10,000 musical instruments in 105 rooms. At the heart of the collection is a series of stringed instruments made by the lutist, Leandro Bisiach, between 1903 and 1915 on behalf of Count Chigi. It contains two violins, one viola, and a violoncello called 'd'amore', so named because the strings would release a particularly 'sweet' sound.

Museo degli Strumenti musicali del Castello Sforzesco
The Museum of Musical Instruments in the Castello Sforzesco
Castello Sforzesco, Piazza Castello, 20121 Milan, Italy
Tel. (39) 02 8693071
Tue-Sun 9.30am-5.30pm

Neapolitan organ,
18th century
*Museo degli Strumenti
musicali (Rome)*

Among the Commune di Milano's museums is one of the larger collections of musical instruments in Italy. The core was purchased from the collector and teacher, Natale Gallini. There are splendid examples of violins, violas, cellos, and double basses. The viola built in 1662 by Gionvanni Grancino is an unusual shape by modern standards – it is one of the few in the world to retain its baroque neck.

Museo teatrale alla Scala
The Theatre Museum at La Scala
Via Filodrammatici 2, 20121 Milan, Italy
Tel. (39) 02 8053418   www.museoteatrale.com
May-Oct: daily 8.30am-12.30pm, 2-5.30pm. Nov-Apr: Mon-Sat 8.30am-12.30pm, 2-5.30pm

The majority of the museum's instrument collection originates from the purchase of the Sambon Collection in Paris in 1911. Other acquisitions followed, including 56 of the 135 instruments from the museum of the Guiseppe Verdi Conservatory of Music, much of which was transferred in 1914 to escape the war. Highlights include Verdi's Erard piano and the spinet he used at the age of eight, and Franz Liszt's Steinway piano.

Tropenmuseum
The Museum of the Tropics
Linnaeusstraat 2, 1092 AD, Amsterdam, The Netherlands
Tel. (31) 20 5688215   www.kit.nl
Mon-Fri 10am-5pm, Sat-Sun noon-5pm

The driving force behind the ethnomusicology collections of the Tropenmuseum was Jaap Kunst, who, in the 1920s, worked as a civil servant in the Indian archipelago. In 1934, he became curator of the Colonial Institute (later the Tropenmuseum), devoting the rest of his life to the field of ethnomusicology. At the museum, Kunst gathered together a rich collection. 150 objects came from the East Flores, including a flute orchestra of 53 transverse flutes and 33 ring-stop flutes; a pair of buzzers and a Jew's harp came from Nias. The collection grew through gifts and acquisitions from the official collectors for the museum, including the collector in Dutch New Guinea, who, in the 1950s, amassed drums and horns used during headhunting, as well as bullroarers. The Swiss anthropologist, Paul Wirtz, working in Papua New Guinea, also donated his instruments. A five-tone gamelan from Java was acquired and is now known as 'the Rembrandt' of the Tropenmuseum, displayed alongside a seven-tone gamelan.

Horn gramophone and records
Royal Museum of Scotland

Victorian Reed Organ & Harmonium Museum
Victorian Hall, Victoria Road, Saltaire Village, Shipley, West Yorkshire BD18 4PS, UK
Tel. (44) 1274 585601
Mon-Thu, Sun 11am-4pm

The Victorian Hall in the 'model' village built by Sir Titus Salt for his mill and workers (who produced Alpaca, the cloth that made him famous), now houses the Fluke collection of around 85 instruments and related materials. Among the many fine and even unique instruments is a specially carved oak harmonium with two manuals and pedal board, which was entered in the 1862 London Exhibition and which won a prize for its splendid case.

PHONOGRAPHS AND GRAMOPHONES

The British Library National Sound Archive
22 Micawber Street, London N1 7TB, UK
Tel. (44) 20 7412 7410   www.bl.uk
Open to researchers by appt. only

Though ninety per cent of the British Library's outstanding collection of early phonographs and recording machines remains in storage, some of the most significant items can be seen by appointment. These include equipment amassed by distinguished collector, George Frow (which included one of the best collections of Edisons to be found anywhere); 1930s furniture-style radio gramophones; portable gramophones and domestic tape recorders; and a unique collection of experimental items, particularly early tape dictation machines. Especially fascinating are the American attempts on re-recording discs, amongst other designs. Pre-tape equipment is also represented by several portable small cutting laths.

Edison Ford Winter Estates
2350 McGregor Boulevard, Fort Myers, Florida 33901, USA
Tel. (1) 941 334 7419   www.edison-ford-estate.com
Mon-Sat 9am-5.30pm

Ford met Edison while working at the Detroit Edison Illuminating Company. They soon became good friends, and to share ideas and time together Ford purchased Mangoes, a home next door to Edison's Seminole Lodge. Both houses, including Edison's botanical gardens and laboratory, are open to the public, along with a riveting museum displaying numerous inventions, ranging from the Model T Ford to a superb collection of over 200 original Edison phonographs.

Edison National Historic Site

Main Street and Lakeside Avenue, West Orange, New Jersey 07052, USA
Tel. (1) 973 736 0550   www.nps.gov
Wed-Fri noon-5pm, Sat-Sun 9am-5pm

An outstanding selection of some of Edison's earliest phonograph prototypes and sound recordings are on permanent display at this world-famous national historic site. Serious researchers can also access the massive archive and an artefact collection of around 400,000 objects, which includes hundreds of phonographs and a unique sound recording collection of over 37,000 discs and cylinders produced at the laboratory between 1888 and 1929.

*Edison Home
phonograph B, c. 1901
(above right)
Phonomuseum (Austria)*

*Morning Glory
phonographs in the
Edison Museum
(above left)
Edison Ford Winter Estates*

EMI Archives

EMI Group plc., Central Research Lab, Dawley Road, Hayes, Middlesex UB3 1HH, UK
Tel. (44) 20 8848 2000
Open to researchers by appt. only

This is one of the world's largest and most diverse music collections, with fifteen miles of archives, discs, and master tapes dating back to 1897, when William Barry Owen, Director of the National Gramophone Company in New York, arrived to set up business in Britain.

Mechanical Music and Doll Collection

Church Road, Portfield, Chichester, West Sussex PO19 4HN, UK
Tel. (44) 1243 372646
Jul-Sep: Wed 1-4pm (or by appt.)

As well as mechanical instruments and dolls, this private museum houses a unique collection of Edison phonographs and HMV gramophones.

*Two Pathé phonographs:
a recorder (left) and
reproducer (right)
Musée de la Musique
mécanique*

Musée de la Musique mécanique
The Museum of Mechanical Music

La Reposance, 74260 Les Gets, France
Tel. (33) 4 50 79 85 75
Mon-Sun 2.30-7.30pm

The museum houses an extensive collection of phonographs illustrating the evolution of the gramophone and the role it played in the demise of earlier mechanical music. Early developments are represented by a polyphon and its forty metal discs, the herophon with square discs that were read from below, or the famous German ariston.

Klingsor gramophone,
1908 (right)
The Science Museum

Edison cabinet model
'Amberola' Model A
phonograph, 1909
(far right)
The Science Museum

Luxurious horn
gramophone
by the Deustche
Grammophongesellschaft,
Berlin, *c.* 1913 (below)
Phonomuseum (Austria)

Pavek Museum of Broadcasting
3515 Raleigh Avenue, St. Louis Park, Minnesota 55416, USA
Tel. (1) 952 926 8198   www.pavekmuseum.org
Tue-Fri 10am-6pm, Sat 9am-5pm

Alongside the core collection of radio receivers and transmitters belonging to Joseph Pavek, is the Mullin Collection amassed by tape and video recording pioneer, John 'Jack' Mullin. Mullin's magnificent collection of early phonograph and recording equipment was given to the museum in 1990 and represents 125 years of audio recording technology.

Phono Museum
Hauptstrasse 9 / Rathaus, 78112 St Georgen, Germany
Tel. (49) 7724 87194
Mon-Fri 9am-12.30pm, 2-5pm (Thu until 6pm) (May-Sep also
Sat 10am-noon)

This small German town has had close links with the gramophone industry ever since the Steidinger brothers opened a phonograph factory here in 1906. Founded in 1972, the fascinating museum chronicles a complete history of sound recording, from the first phonograph produced in 1877 by Edison, to the advent of hi-fi.

Musée du Phonographe et de la Musique mécanique
The Museum of the Phonograph and Mechanical Music
Hôtel de la Paix, 25 place Jourdan, 87000 Limoges, France
Tel. (33) 5 55 343600
Please call for opening times

Claude Crenn's rare phonograph collection includes

original Edison wax cylinders and exhibits documenting the phonographic investigations made by Frenchman, Charles Cros, who attempted to register a patent for his speaking apparatus in Paris just two days after Thomas Edison had already registered his invention.

Phonomuseum
Mollardgasse 8/2, 1060 Vienna, Austria
Tel. (43) 1 5811159
Wed 6-8pm, Sun 10am-noon

This comprehensive history of the phonograph and gramophone has exhibitions on Edison's heritage, and rare examples of Edison's first tin foil and glass phonographs.

Musée de la Reproduction du son
The Museum of Sound Reproduction
Place de l'Hôtel de Ville, 89179 Saint Fargeau, France
Tel. (33) 3 86 741306
Apr-Oct: Daily 10am-noon, 2-6pm. Nov-Mar: by appt. only

Housed in a 17th-century convent, this museum shows an eclectic selection of early musical reproduction devices. The magnificent phonograph collection includes early devices produced by Edison, Bell, and Pathé, and over 400 phonographs.

Royal Museum of Scotland
Chambers Street, Edinburgh EH1 1JF, Scotland, UK
Tel. (44) 131 2257534 www.nms.ac.uk
Mon-Sat 10am-5pm (Thu until 8pm), Sun noon-5pm

The museum houses a representative selection of around 650 phonographs, gramophones, and magnetic tape recorders. The collection includes cylinder and disc recordings. Of particular interest is a rare cabinet recorder, produced in 1937, which used optically-read tapes.

Berliner gramophone, *c.* 1893 (below)
Phonomuseum (Austria)

Berliner gramophone, *c.* 1891 (bottom)
The Science Museum

The Science Museum
Exhibition Road, South Kensington, London SW7 2DD, UK
Tel. (44) 870 870 4771 www.sciencemuseum.org.uk
Daily 10am-6pm

The museum's magnificent sound reproduction collection consists of 65 rare phonographs, 100 gramophones, 60 tape recorders, 20 record players, and various miscellaneous objects including a telegraphone, auxetophone, stentorphone, and the only copy in the world of Queen Victoria's voice on a recording cylinder.

Van muziekdoos tot grammofoon
From the Music Box to the Gramophone
Museumcomplex Zwiggershoek, 9100 Sint-Niklaas, Belgium
Tel. (32) 3 7772942
Tue-Sat 2-5pm, Sun 10am-5pm

Jozef De Caluwé's magnificent private collection traces the history of mechanical music devices, from the first music boxes, to the production of the Ideal Mixte – a combination phonograph and gramophone which could play cylinders as well as records.

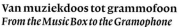

435

POLAR AND OCEANOGRAPHIC EXPLORATION

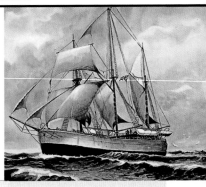

Theodolite used in polar
expedition (above)
Fram-Museet

The polar vessel (right)
Fram-Museet

Andréemuseet
The Andrée Museum
Brahegatan 38, 563 22 Gränna, Sweden
Tel. (46) 390 41015 www.grm.se
Please call for opening times

This extraordinary archive displays the equipment, developed film, and other objects discovered by hunters on White Island in 1930,
33 years after Salomon Andrée, Nils Strindberg
and Knut Fraenkel died during their heroic
attempt to reach the North Pole by balloon.

Fram-Museet
The Fram Museum
Bygdøynesveien, Oslo, Norway
Tel. (47) 22 438370 www.fram.museum.no
Please call for opening times

Standing in its own purpose-built building, the *Fram* remains one of the most famous
vessels in the history of polar exploration. A series of displays describe the most important expeditions made by the three-masted schooner, including Nansen's dramatic
attempt to ski to the North Pole after drifting across the Polar Sea embedded in pack ice
in 1893, Otto Sverdrup's expedition to the Northwest of Greenland (1898-1902), and
Roald Amundsen's epic race against Scott to reach the South Pole.

Mystic Aquarium / Institute for Exploration
55 Coogan Boulevard, Mystic Connecticut 06355-1997, USA
Tel. (1) 860 572 5955 www.mysticaquarium.org
Please call for opening times

This vast marine complex houses the internationally renowned
Institute for Exploration (IFE). It is headed by Dr Robert Ballard,
the oceanographer responsible for a string of important discoveries,
including the wrecks of the *Titanic* and *Bismarck*, and a graveyard of warships and planes from the Battle of Midway. His recent exploits combine
pioneering equipment, archaeologists, and oceanographers, and involve
developing technologies and methodologies for the newly developing
field of archaeology in deep water. Exhibits show the advanced
underwater imaging systems and associated technology used in
the Institute's expeditions in the Black Sea and off the coast of
Israel, near Ashkelon, where two Phoenician shipwrecks and
their cargos, dating from 750 BC, were discovered.

Navy one man one
atmosphere dive system
'Jim suit' (above left)
Naval Undersea Museum

Roald Amundsen,
1872-1928 (above right)
Fram-Museet

Statue of Fridtjof Nansen
by Per Hung (right)
Fram-Museet

Museo nazionale dell'Antartide
The National Museum of the Antarctic
Palazzo Millo, Porto Antico, 16128 Genoa, Italy
Tel. (39) 010 2543690 www.mna.it
Tue-Sat 9.45am-6.15pm, Sun 10am-7pm

Supported by the universities of Genoa, Siena, and Trieste,
this comprehensive museum focuses on every aspect of the
Antarctic, from its geology, biology, and ecology to the
history of its exploration.

Observatoriemuseet
The Observatory Museum
Drottninggatan 120, Observatorielunden, 11360 Stockholm, Sweden
Tel. (46) 8 315810   www.observatoriet.kva.se
Sat-Sun guided tours at noon, 1pm, 2pm, 6pm (Oct-Apr: also Tue guided tour at 6pm)

A room is dedicated to Adolf Erik Nordenskiöld, the famed Finnish Arctic explorer who conducted ten scientific expeditions between 1858 and 1904, and provided the Royal Swedish Academy of Sciences with a host of unique Arctic and Asian Arctic material.

Musée océanographique de Monaco
The Oceanographic Museum of Monaco
Avenue St-Martin, 98000 Monte Carlo, Principality of Monaco
Tel. (377) 93 153600
www.oceano.org
Apr-Oct: daily 9am-7pm.
Nov-Mar: daily 10am-6pm

Marine chronometer and deck-watch by Charles Frodsham, 1857
Observatoriemuseet

With its research laboratories and extensive library, this palatial institution, founded in 1910 by Prince Albert I of Monaco, is a world leader in oceanographic research. The museum houses displays on applied and physical oceanography, an aquarium, and a Whale Room. The wealth of curious marine artefacts includes fossil fish, fish preserved in bottles, and stuffed fish (including a giant lobster).

The Peary-MacMillan Arctic Museum and Arctic Studies Center
Hubbard Hall, Bowdoin College, Brunswick, Maine 04011, USA
Tel. (1) 207 725 3416   www.bowdoin.edu
Tue-Sat 10am-5pm, Sun 2-5pm

Named after the Arctic explorers, Robert Edwin Peary and Donald MacMillian, this lively research centre and museum is dedicated to the natural environment and cultures of the Arctic region. It includes original equipment used by the explorers, including the sledge, compasses, alcohol stove, and telegrams from Peary's 1909 North Pole expedition.

The Naval Undersea Museum
610 Dowell Street, Keyport, Washington 98345, USA
Tel. (1) 360 396 4148   num.kpt.nuwc.
Jun-Sep: daily 10am-4pm. Oct-May: Mon-Sat 10am-4pm

Located in the grounds of a division of the Naval Undersea Warfare Center, there's hardly an aspect concerning the sea that this museum does not address. Best exhibits are those exploring the plethora of technology used to illuminate man's understanding of this massive world, from the first diving bells and aqua-lungs, to remotely operated vehicles, submersibles, and high-tech diving suits. Forthcoming displays include those on nautical archaeology and the history of underwater exploration.

Museo polare Silvio Zavatti
The Silvio Zavatti Polar Museum
Villa Vitali, viale Trento 29, 63023 Fermo, Italy
Tel. (39) 0734 226166
Mon-Fri 9am-1pm, 4-7pm, Sat 9am-1pm

Situated in an elegant 19th-century villa, the museum houses a complete archive of scientific and ethnographic material relating to Zavatti's expeditions to the Arctic and Antarctic. In addition there are displays of photographs, newspapers, sleighs, pulkas, and tents from various other polar expeditions, including those of Amundsen, Scott, Umberto Nobile, and Carlo Bondavalli.

Polarmuseet i Tromsø
Polar Museum in Tromsø
Søndre Tollbugt 11, 9001 Tromsø., Norway
Tel. (47) 77 684373   troms.kulturnett.no
Please call for opening times

Submersible *Alvin 3*
Woods Hole Oceanographic
Institution

Tromsø has been the setting-off point for many Norwegian expeditions to the Arctic, including those of Fridjof Nansen and Roald Amundsen. The museum explores the history of polar exploration and the men behind it, while additional galleries focus on other Arctic activities such as polar bear and fox trapping, seal and walrus hunting, and the controversial topic of whaling.

Roald Amundsen Senter
The Roald Amundsen Centre
Framveien 7, 1659 Torp, Norway
Tel. (47) 69 348326
Daily 11am-4pm

The unassuming late Empire house where Roald Amundsen was born and brought up now contains a museum documenting all his expeditions, from his first expedition in 1897 to the Magnetic South Pole to his death in the Arctic Ocean during a mission to rescue the Italia expedition.

Rossiiskii gosudarstvennyi muzei arktiki i antarktiki
The Russian State Museum of the Arctic and Antarctic
Ulitsa Marata 24a, 191040 St Petersburg, Russian Federation
Tel (7) 812 1131998   www.polarmuseum.sp.ru
Wed-Sun 10am-5pm

This is one of the largest museums in the world devoted to the economy, culture, natural environment, and history of the polar regions. The centrepiece is a large relief model of the Northern hemisphere, showing the land, sea, and geographical borders of the Arctic. Around this, some 75,000 exhibits explore the economy, culture, natural environment, and history of the polar regions, with displays and dioramas ranging from stuffed wildlife to the paintings and art produced by their indigenous peoples.

ROV Jason being launched
Woods Hole Oceanographic
Institution

Musée du Scaphandre
The Museum of the Diving Suit
Rue Droite, 12500 Espalion, France
Tel. (33) 5 65 440918
May, Jun, Sep: Mon-Sat 2-5.30pm
Jul, Aug: daily 10am-noon, 2-6.45pm (or by appt.)

Dedicated to Benoit Rouquayrol, who invented the first self-contained underwater breathing apparatus in 1864, this is one of the few museums entirely devoted to the history of aqualungs and diving suits. The museum now houses over 200 items relating to diving, ranging from Rouquayrol's original suits (a design immortalized in Jules Verne's *20,000*

Leagues Under the Sea of 1870), to the acrylic plastic LAMA helmets designed by Yves Lamasson in the 1970s.

Scott Polar Research Institute

University of Cambridge, Lensfield Road, Cambridge, Cambridgeshire CB2 1ER, UK
Tel. (44) 1223 336540 www.spri.cam.ac.uk
Mon-Fri 2.30-4pm

The institute was originally founded in 1920 as a memorial to the five men who perished on Scott's second and last expedition to the Antarctic in 1910. As well as displaying an array of moving objects (including Scott's journals and the original black flag which Amundsen planted at the South Pole), the museum houses the Shackleton Memorial Library and the Thomas Manning Polar Archives, two of the world's largest collections of manuscripts and other unpublished material relating to the polar regions. Displayed in the library is a section of the mast pole from one of the whalers on the *Endurance*. This was the only surviving section of Shackleton's ill-fated ship, and he gave it to his head gardener on his return.

Extendable telescopes: Dollond, London, *c.* 1760 (left); Leonardo Semitecolo, Venice, mid 18th century (centre); manufacturer unknown, 19th century (right)
Optisches Museum der Ernst-Abbe-Stiftung

Museo storico dell'Aeronautica militare
The Museum of Aeronautical Military History
Aeroporto L. Bourlot, 00062 Vigna di Valle, Italy
Tel. (39) 06 9024034 www.aeronautica.difesa.it
Apr-Sep: Tue-Sun 9.30am-5.30pm. Oct-Mar: Tue-Sun 9.30am-4.30pm

An annexe to the main museum houses the Umberto Nobile Documentation Centre, founded in 1980 and commemorating the work of the Italian aeronautical engineer and pioneer who flew across the North Pole with Amundsen and Ellsworth in the *Norge 1* in 1926. The growing collection documents polar exploration in both the Arctic and Antarctic, with special emphasis on Greenland, Spitsbergen (now Svalbard), Siberia, and Alaska.

Woods Hole Oceanographic Institution
15 School Street, Woods Hole, Massachusetts, USA
Tel (1) 508 289 2252 www.whoi.edu
Please call for opening times

This is the premier centre for marine research, where leading-edge oceanographic research is conducted with teams of scientists and engineers who specialize in sub-mersible technology. Perhaps best known for developing the deep submersible *Alvin*, used by Dr Robert Ballard to discover the wreck of the *Titanic*, the group participates in dozens of underwater archaeological, geological, and marine biological expeditions every year. The Exhibit Center allow visitors to step inside a full-sized model of the inner sphere of *Alvin*, and audiovisuals explain the institute's research projects.

SCIENTIFIC INSTRUMENTS

Musée des Arts et Métiers
The Museum of Arts and Crafts
60 rue Réaumur, 75003 Paris, France
Tel. (33) 1 53 01 82 00 www.cnam.fr
Tue-Sun 10am-6pm, Thu 10am-9.30pm

This collection of scientific instruments is one of the best in the world. Items include Charlemagne's battery, which Lefrevre-Gibeau used in 1799 to determine the value of the kilogramme in old units. There is Burgi's sphere of 1580, a masterpiece of watch-making mechanics, and Janvier's regulator of 1800, one of the main instruments of measuring in the museum.

Museum für Astronomie und Technikgeschichte
The Museum of Astronomy and Technical History
Orangerie, An der Karlsaue 20 C, 34121 Kassel, Germany
Tel. (49) 561 715435
Tue-Sun 10am-5pm

The museum's centrepiece is the Hall of Astronomy with its superb collection of royal astronomical and horological instruments, including gauges, measuring instruments, and records of the first observatories (most notably of the observatory built by Wilhelm IV in 1560).

Planetary clockwork with celestial globe by E. Baldewein. H. Diepel, L. Wilhelm IV, 1561 (above)
Museum für Astronomie und Technikgeschichte

Spring balance for kitchen use, Germany, early 20th century (above right)
Museo della Bilancia

The observatory room with the quadrant by John Bird, 1757, and a telescope by William Cary (below)
Observatoriemuseet

Museo della Bilancia
The Museum of Scales
Via Garibaldi 34 A, 41011 Campogalliano, Italy
Tel. (39) 059 527133
Mon-Fri by appt. only, Sat-Sun 10-12.30pm, 3-6.30pm

The collection comprises more than 9,000 objects and related items which trace the history of weighing from the Middle Ages to the present day. On display are balances, platform scales, steel yards, and a rich collection of documentary material such as catalogues, posters, original prints, and photographic reproductions of antique objects and documents.

Museum Boerhaave
The Boerhaave Museum
Lange Sint Agnietenstraat 10, 2312 WC Leiden, The Netherlands
Tel. (31) 71 5214224 www.museumboerhaave.nl
Tue-Sat 10am-5pm, Sun noon-5pm

This museum was founded by two scientists at the University of Leiden in 1928 when they noticed old instruments languishing in cupboards and attics. Named after the famous Leiden professor, Herman Boerhaave, the collections are housed in a former convent and hospital, and are arranged in 23 rooms which cover five centuries of science. Among the outstanding pieces are three out of ten existing microscopes by the most famous 17th-century microscopist of his day, Antoni van Leeuwenhoek. These tiny instruments, the size of a matchbox, allowed him to investigate everything from dental

tartar to the eye of a whale. There is also a fine collection of astronomical instruments and clocks, some obtained from the observatory, built in Leiden in 1860. Among the many notable pieces is a 16th-century astronomical quadrant for measuring the circumference of the earth (made for Snellius by Willem Janszoon Blaeu).

Burton Constable Hall
Burton Constable, East Yorkshire HU11 4LN, UK
Tel. (44) 1964 562400
www.burtonconstable.com
Easter-Oct: Mon-Thu, Sat-Sun 1-5pm

Inside this magnificent 16th-century house are several rooms brimming with William Constable's collections of geological specimens, shells, his travelling medicine chest which he took on three Grand Tours, guns, and joyful oddities. Among these, his collection of scientific instruments are carefully displayed, one of the finest to be found in any English country house.

Cavendish Laboratory Museum
University of Cambridge, Department of Physics, Cavendish Laboratory, Madingley Road, Cambridge, Cambridgeshire CB3 0HE, UK
Tel. (44) 1223 337420 www.phy.cam.ac.uk
Mon-Fri 9am-5pm

Since its establishment in 1871, this laboratory has been the scene of several of the most important scientific discoveries of modern times. J. J. Thomson discovered the electron herein 1897, C. T. R. Wilson was awarded the Nobel Prize for his invention of the cloud chamber in 1927, Rutherford investigated the disintegration of the nucleus, and the structure of DNA was determined by Crick and Watson in 1953. Early apparatus associated with these major classical discoveries is on display.

An achromatic refractor by John Dollond, 1760 (above left)
Observatoriemuseet

17th-century sundial by Stauislaus Leszczyn (above right)
Muzeum Przypkowskich w Jedrzejowie

Faraday Museum
The Royal Institution of Great Britain, 21 Albemarle Street, London W1X 4BS, UK
Tel. (44) 20 7409 2992 www.ri.ac.uk
Mon-Fri 10am-4.30pm

Son of a blacksmith, Faraday started his professional life as a bookbinder but went on to become England's greatest physicist since Newton. Housed here, at the Royal Institution where Faraday lived and made many of his fundamental contributions to chemistry and physics, are displays of his apparatus, manuscripts, pictures, and personal memorabilia. Among these are the world's first transformer, as well as the first sample of Benzene which he discovered. He worked on projects to improve steel, was appointed scientific advisor to the Admiralty, made great improvements to the lighthouse service, including the introduction of electric light in the 1850s, and performed pioneering work on the liquifaction of gases.

Museu de Fisica da Universidade de Coimbra
The Museum of Physics of the University of Coimbra
Praça Marquês de Pmbal, 3004 Coimbra, Portugal
Tel. (351) 39 410600 www.fis.uc.pt
Mon-Thu 2.30-5.30pm

A superb collection of scientific and didactic instruments from the 18th and 19th centuries, used exclusively by the university's Physics Cabinet since its origin in 1772. It is exhibited in two large rooms, one of which is a reconstruction of a cabinet from the second half of the 18th century.

Museum voor de Geschiedenis van de Wetenschappen
The Museum of the History of Science
Universiteit Gent, Campus Wetenschappen, Krijgslaan 281 (S30), 9000 Gent, Belgium
Tel. (32) 9 2644930
Mon-Fri 10am-12.30pm, 1.30-5pm. Guided tours by appt.
Here there is a fine and comprehensive

Exterior of the museum
Museo della Bilancia

collection of instruments used for routine measurements, including simple microscopes, volt and ampere meters. Fields covered include physics, chemistry, mathematics, and topography. The museum also houses a rich collection of laboratory glass and cameras.

The William Herschel Museum
19 New King Street, Bath, Somerset BA1 2BL, UK
Tel. (44) 1225 311342
www.bath-preservation-trust.org.uk
Daily 2–5pm

This immaculately restored Georgian town house was home to the distinguished astronomer, scientist, and musician, William Herschel, and his sister Caroline, who was a talented astronomer in her own right. In 1781, using a home-made telescope, the pair discovered the planet Uranus. Later they were to discover several of its satellites. The garden where they saw the seventh planet shining dimly in the night sky has also been pristinely restored.

Musée d'Histoire des Sciences – Villa Bartholoni
The Museum of the History of Science – Villa Bartholoni
128 rue de Lausanne, 1202 Geneva, Switzerland
Tel. (41) 22 731 6985 www.ville-ge.ch
Mon, Wed–Sun 1–5pm

Set in this exquisite park is one of the city's most stunning neo-classical houses, built in 1828 with Pompeiian style wall painting. Displayed within is a large collection of scientific instruments which once belonged to Geneva's wealthy scholars and scientists, who acquired them from the finest manufacturers all over Europe.

Globe electrical machine in a vacuum-pump bell jar
Museum Boerhaave

Historische Sammlung physikalischer Apparate - Georg-August-Universität
The Historical Collection of Physical Instruments - Georg-August-University
First Institute of Physics, Bunsenstrasse 9, 37073 Göttingen, Germany
Tel. (49) 551 397602 www.ph1.physik.uni-goettingen.de
By appt. only

Most of this collection had been used for teaching at the university. Some of the oldest instruments were introduced by George Christoph Lichtenberg in 1778, who was the professor of experimental physics at the time. Originally, this was his private collection, kept at home where he performed his experiments.

Museum of the History of Science
Broad Street, Oxford, Oxfordshire OX1 3AZ, UK
Tel. (44) 1865 277280 www.mhs.ox.ac.uk
Tue–Sat noon–4pm

Opened in 1683, this was the first purpose-built museum in the world set up to display the collection of rarities donated by Elias Ashmole. Since 1924, it has been home to a premier collection of some 10,000 scientific instruments spanning all aspects of science from ancient times to the early 20th century. By far the best are the astrolabes (some 150-plus examples), including an Eastern Islamic instrument dating from 1480 (the only spherical astrolabe in the world); over 700 sundials; and early mathematical and optical instruments. A popular exhibit is the blackboard bearing equations chalked by Einstein, when on 16 May, 1931 he lectured in Oxford on the theory of relativity. To round it all off, there is also an outstanding library, rehoused in a newly completed extension.

Letter scales
Museo della Bilancia

Mathematisch-Physikalischer Salon
The Salon of Mathematics and Physics
Zwinger, Sophienstrasse 2, 01067 Dresden, Germany
Tel. (49) 351 4914622 www.staatl-kunstsammlungen-dresden.de
Mon-Wed, Fri-Sun 10am-6pm

The collections date from 1560, when the Elector August of Saxony founded the Dresdner Kunstkammer. By 1587 it contained 1,000 mathematic-technical instruments. The collection has pre-Industrial scientific instruments from the 16th to the 19th centuries; instruments to determine mathematical and physical measures such as length, mass, temperature, and pressure; and thermometers showing the scales of the physicians Fahrenheit, Celsius, Réaumur, and Delisle (De Lisle).

Národní Technické Muzeum
The National Technical Museum
Kostelní 42, 170 78 Prague 7, Czech Republic
Tel. (420) 2 20399111 www.ntm.cz
Tue-Sun 9am-5pm

During his reign, the mercurial Habsburg emperor Rudolf II (1576-1612) surrounded himself with a kaleidoscope of scientific talents from across the continent, including the brilliant Danish astronomer Tycho Brahe and his student Johannes Kepler (now chiefly remembered for discovering the three laws of planetary motion that bear his name). This magnificent museum houses an unparalleled collection of astronomic, mathematical, and survey instruments from the period, many made by some of the city's master craftsmen, including Bürgi, Stolle, Emmoser, and Habermel.

National Maritime Museum & Royal Observatory
Romney Road, Greenwich, London SE10 9NF, UK
Tel. (44) 20 8858 4422 www.nmm.ac.uk
Daily 10am-5pm

This comprehensive collection of historic navigational instruments, from medieval times to the present includes the Ramsden of London sextant used by Captain Cook on his third voyage to the Pacific, and the many marine timekeepers used by John Harrison in his struggle to measure longitude at sea.

Musée national de la Renaissance
The National Museum of the Renaissance
Château d'Ecouen, 95440 Ecouen, France
Tel. (33) 1 34 38 38 50 www.musexpo.com
Mon, Wed-Sun 9.45am-12.30pm, 2-5.15pm

Housed in the castle of Ecouen, this vast museum includes an outstanding collection of historic astronomical instruments shown in a reconstructed 16th-century scientist's room. Standing out among the many magnificent clocks and watches, astronomical instruments, and automata, are a gilded celestial globe made in Rome in 1502, a clock in the shape of a ship by Hans Schlottheim, and an astrolabe by Michel Lasne.

Observatoriemuseet
The Observatory Museum
Drottninggatan 120, Observatorielunden, 11360 Stockholm, Sweden
Tel. (46) 8 315810   www.observatoriet.kva.se
Sat-Sun: guided tours at noon, 1pm, 2pm, 6pm
(Oct-Apr: also Tue guided tour at 6pm)

Stockholm's historic observatory today houses a museum dedicated to the history of 18th- and 19th-century astronomy, meteorology, and geography. The displays include a fascinating reconstruction of the study belonging to one of Sweden's most important astronomers, Pehr Wilhelm Wargentin. He moved to the observatory in 1753, and lived and worked there until his death thirty years later.

Baroque microscope after a design by the Duke of Chaulnes, Paris, c. 1760
Optisches Museum der Ernst-Abbe-Stiftung

Optisches Museum der Ernst-Abbe-Stiftung
The Optical Museum of the Ernst Abbe Foundation
Carl-Zeiss-Platz 12, 07743 Jena, Germany
Tel. (49) 3641 443165   www.ernst-abbe-stiftung.de
Tue-Fri 10am-5pm, Sat 1-4.30pm, Sun 9.30am-1pm

This science and technology museum, founded in 1922, documents over five centuries of history, and specifically the technical development of optical instruments. Alongside a great collection of precision optical devices, it offers an insight into the lives and works of Ernst Abbe, Otto Schott, and Carl Zeiss, whose historic workshop from 1866 has been reconstructed. Their collaboration proved to be the foundation stone for the production of optical instruments of all sorts in Jena.

Porter Thermometer Museum
49 Zarahelma Road, Onset, Massachusetts 02558, USA
Tel. (1) 508 2955504
Please call for opening times

This museum contains a record collection of 3,000 thermometers gathered from all over the world. Of the more unusual are two handsome chandelier thermometers that

Vacuum pump from the workshop of Count Haus von Loser, c.1750
Mathematisch-Physikalischer Salon

were attached to lighting fixtures in railroad dining cars in the late 1800s. They can be read from any direction.

Muzeum Przypkowskich w Jedrzejowie
The Przypkowski Museum in Jedrzejów

Plac Tadeusza Kosciuszki 7-8,
28-3000 Jedrzejów, Poland
Tel. (48) 41 3862445
Tue-Sun 8am-3pm

The Przypkowski family began collecting scientific instruments in the 16th century, but it was Feliks Przypkowski, a doctor, who made the most significant contribution, and who in 1895, opened this museum in the family home. Alongside the astronomical instruments is a remarkable collection of mostly Polish, German, and French sundials dating from the 15th century to the present day.

Metal thermometer
by J. G. Zimmer, 1748
(above left)
*Mathematisch-
Physikalischer Salon*

Real Observatorio de Madrid
The Royal Observatory of Madrid

Calle Alfonso XII 3, 28014 Madrid, Spain
Tel. (34) 91 5270107   www.oan.es
Mon-Fri 9am-2pm

Telescope by Johann
Gottlob Rudolph, c.1750
(above right)
*Mathematisch-
Physikalischer Salon*

As well as a library, the observatory houses a magnificent museum of astronomical instruments and small instrumentation.

The Science Museum

Exhibition Road, South Kensington, London SW7 2DD, UK
Tel. (44) 870 8704771 www.sciencemuseum.org.uk
Daily 10am-6pm

An unrivalled collection of 18th-century scientific instruments and apparatus, commissioned from the instrument maker George Adams by King George III for the purpose of teaching his children. Each one of these is a work of art. A second group is made up of the apparatus assembled during the 1750s by Stephen Demainbray for use in his lectures to the public. Collections also include Caroline Herschel's telescope and William Herschel's prism and mirror (c.1800), used by him to make the first investigations of the solar spectrum beyond the visible region.

Museo della Specola
The Museum of the Observatory

Università di Bologna, via Zamboni 33, 40126 Bologna, Italy
Tel. (39) 051 2095701   www.bo.astro.it
Please call for opening times

Astronomy was taught at Bologna as early as the 13th century, and, at the instigation of Luigi Ferdinando Marsili, an observatory tower was added in the early 18th century. The collections have been significantly extended since, and today the museum exhibits over 100 of the most important astronomical instruments used by Bolognese astronomers from 1702 to the beginning of the 19th century.

Exterior of the museum
Optisches Museum der Ernst-Abbe-Stiftung

Museo di Storia della Scienza
The Museum of the History of Science
Piazza dei Giudici 1, 50122
Florence, Italy
Tel. (39) 055 2398876
galileo.imss.firenze.it
Tue, Thu, Sat 9.30am-1pm,
Mon, Wed, Fri also 2-5pm

This superb museum, tracing the history of science, houses a unique collection of astronomical apparatus owned by the Medicis. It includes such remarkable instruments as a device for measuring distance, engraved by Baldassare Lanci di Urbino (1557); numerous 16th-century nocturnal and solar-powered clocks; and the great Ptolemaic armillary sphere built in 1588 by Antonio Santucci, cosmographer to Ferdinand I of Medici. The museum's centrepiece is a gallery dedicated to Galileo, filled with displays of his instruments, such as the telescope he modified to observe the moon, and the lens with which he discovered the four satellites of Jupiter.

Teylers Museum
The Teylers Museum
Spaarne 16, 2011 CH Haarlem, The Netherlands
Tel. (31) 23 5319010 www.teylersmuseum.nl
Tue-Sat 10am-5pm, Sun noon-5pm

The Instrument Gallery contains a diverse collection of over 1,200 scientific instruments and chemistry equipment, assembled between 1784 and 1909. They were used primarily for research and demonstration.

18th-century telescope by Willliam Cary
Observatoriemuseet

Muzeum Uniwersytetu Jagielloñskiego
The Jagiellonian University Museum
Collegium Maius, ulica Jagielloñska 15, 31-010 Cracow, Poland
Tel. (48) 12 4220549
Daily 11am-3pm (Sat until 2pm)

Established by Kazimir the Great in 1364 (with authorization from Pope Urban V), this jewel of Gothic architecture originally had only three faculties: Arts, Medicine, and Law. The univerisity's most famous pupil, Nicolaus Copernicus, attended the Arts Faculty from 1491-95, studying astronomy from an observatory on a platform on the roof. Today, the university museum houses a superlative collection of astronomical instruments dating from the same period. Besides its collections of astronomical instruments and globes, there are collections of mathematical instruments, rules, slide rules, compasses, and surveying instruments from the 18th and 19th centuries, as well as a very large collection of 18th- and 19th-century chemical glassware.

Whipple Museum of the History of Science

Department of History and Philosophy of Science, Free School Lane, Cambridge,
Cambridgeshire CB2 3RH, UK
Tel. (44) 1223 330906 www.hps.cam.ac.uk
Mon-Fri 1.30-4.30pm. (The museum is not always open during university vacations, so
check beforehand.)

A designated collection packed with rarities, the core of which were donated to the
university by Robert Stewart Whipple, along with around 1,000 books. Today, it contains
a delightful spread of European and American instruments from the 16th to the 20th
centuries. Its strengths are early mathematical instruments, sundials, and astronomy
and optical instruments.

Special edition of Virgil's
Maronis Opera, 1719, with
whalebone clamp rim
spectacles (*c.* 1700) set
into the cover (above)
*Optisches Museum der Ernst-
Abbe-Stiftung*

16th-century sundial
by Erasmus Habermel
(far left)
*Muzeum Przypkowskich w
Jedrzejowie*

Tachymetre leveller by
F. W. Breithaupt & Son,
1913 (left)
*Museum für Astronomie
und Technikgeschichte*

TECHNOLOGY COLLECTIONS AND LIBRARIES

American Precision Museum

196 Main Street, Windsor, Vermont 05089, USA
Tel. (1) 802 674 5781 www.americanprecision.org
Memorial Day-Nov: daily 10am-5pm

This is the most significant collection of early machine tools in the US. The local
gunmakers Robbins, Kendall, and Lawrence were the brains behind some of these
machines. In 1851 this obscure armoury and machine shop, based in the woods of
Windsor, shook the manufacturing world when they took their guns and machines
to London's Great Exhibition in 1851, displaying for the first time parts which were
truly interchangeable. After the Civil War, the tools and techniques of precision manufacture were applied to the production of industrial and consumer goods, from sewing
machines to typewriters. Many of the earliest models are on display. The Edwin A.
Battison Library, containing volumes on the precision tool industry, tool catalogues,
photographs, and shop manuals, can be accessed by appointment.

Hagley Museum and Library

Route 141, Wilmington, Delaware 19807-0630, USA
Tel. (1) 302 658 2400 www.hagley.lib.de.us
Mid Mar-Dec: daily 9.30am-4.30pm
Jan-mid Mar: Mon-Fri: guided tours only, Sat-Sun 9.30am-4.30pm

Located on the site of the du Pont black powder works, and set among acres of gardens,
is this first-rate business and history of technology repository, consisting of a library,
historical museum, and a centre for advanced study. The library's main strength is in
the Middle Atlantic region, but the scope of collecting includes records of and works

about business organisations and companies with national impact. Notable are the manuscript collections containing the records of more than 1,000 firms, as well as the personal papers of the entrepreneurs who helped build them. Major railroad companies are documented, as are energy, iron, and steel companies, and those involved in computer and feedback technologies, including Sperry Corporation's Gyroscope and Aerospace divisions.

E. I. Du Pont household account book, *c.* 1821
Hagley Museum and Library

Muzei-arkhiv D. I. Mendeleeva
The Mendeleev Museum and Archives
St Petersburg State University, Mendeleevskaia liniia 2, 199034 St Petersburg, Russian Federation
Tel. (7) 812 3289744
Mon-Fri 11am-4pm

Mendeleev, the Russian genius of chemistry, not only managed to set out the Periodic Table, but during his lifetime filled in many of the gaps as more elements were discovered. These collections are housed in what used to be a flat specially designed for the professor of chemistry. It was here that many of his scientific writings were created, and where in 1869, he discovered periodic law and constructed his famous Table. His library consists of about 20,000 titles pertaining to almost all divisions of knowledge, including chemistry, physics, economics, history, and history of art. On a special bookshelf the visitor can see the work Mendeleev published in his own lifetime.

Planing machine, dated 1865, made at the New York Steam Engine Works
American Precision Museum

Musée des Arts et Métiers
The Museum of Arts and Crafts
60 rue Réaumur, 75003 Paris, France
Tel. (33) 1 53 01 82 00   www.cnam.fr
Tue-Sun 10am-6pm (Thu until 9.30pm)

The museum is part of the Conservatoire National des Arts et Métiers (CNAM), created in 1794 for the conservation of machines, tools, drawings, books, etc. used in the craft industry. The nucleus of the collection was a group of machines used in the silk industry. The Parisian institution advanced the case for a comparative international system for measures and weights in the 19th century. It therefore houses old standards of weights and measures, such as the late 15th-century Charlemagne's 'pile', used to determine the 'value' of kilograms in old units. The most prestigious objects, such as Foucault's Pendulum or Bollée's Obéissante, are displayed in the listed 12th-century chapel of the old Saint-Martin-des-Champs abbey, alongside the plane in which Blériot crossed the Channel on July 25th, 1909.

Národní Technické Muzeum
The National Technical Museum
Kostelní 42, 170 78 Prague 7, Czech Republic
Tel. (420) 2 2039 9111
Tue-Sun 9am-5pm

Although not in the limelight like its sisters in Central and Western Europe (or equal in size), this is undoubtedly one of the best technical museums in the world. Since its foundation in 1908, its goal has always been to document the

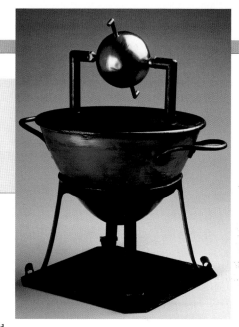

nation's (and elsewhere to a lesser extent) technical and cultural contributions, and to be an inspirational source to all. Today, its aims have been amply met, both as a national institution for scientific research and as a repository for artefacts from the 15th century to the present day. Future plans include the displaying of treasures currently in store, and providing global access to the collections via the Internet.

Muzej Nikole Tesle
The Nikola Tesla Museum
Proleterskih brigada 51, 11000 Belgrade, Yugoslavia
Tel. (381) 11 433886 www.yurope.com
Tue-Fri 10am-noon, 4-6pm, Sat-Sun 10am-1pm

Tesla gave us alternating current, Tesla coils, and a host of other inventions. A genius to many, he died penniless and relatively unrecognized, although he had 700 patents to his credit. Shown here are his personal belongings, collected and transferred to Belgrade after his death in New York in 1943 thanks to the efforts of his nephew, Sava Kosanovic. The archive material, consisting of more than 150,000 documents, pays tribute to his life and his wealth of creative work, alongside displays of his significant inventions.

Hero of Alexandria's aeolipile and steam boiler; a working model based on 16th-century manuscripts
The Science Museum

Birmingham Central Library
Chamberlain Square, Birmingham, West Midlands, B3 3HQ, UK
Tel. (44) 121 303 4217 www.ramesis.com
Mon-Fri 9am-8pm, Sat until 5pm (by appt. only for items in the special collections)

The archive of the steam engine partnership of Matthew Boulton and James Watt can be found in the archive rooms on the seventh floor. Dating from its formation in 1774 until the firm's closure in the 1890s, it comprises around 550 volumes of letter books, order books, and account and pattern books, a staggering 29,000 engine drawings, and upwards of 20,000 incoming letters from customers.

Deutsches Museum
The German Museum
Museumsinsel 1, 80538 Munich, Germany
Tel. (49) 89 21791 www.deutsches-museum.de
Daily 9am-5pm

Rated as one of the world's foremost museums of science and technology, this museum has something for everyone, from historic cars, locomotives, and musical instruments, to aircraft and an outstanding collection of 2,000 scientific instruments originating from the Bavarian Academy of Sciences. There are over 20km of displays, with whole halls devoted to bicycles, boats, space, and other topics.

The Dibner Institute for the History of Science and Technology
Dibner Building, Massachusetts Institute of Technology, E56-100, 38 Memorial Drive, Cambridge, Massachusetts 02139, USA
Tel. (1) 617 253 8721 dibinst.mit.edu
By appt. only

A stunning display of light bulbs and early electrical equipment greets you as you enter this temple to the history of science and technology. A national centre, it is also home to the Burndy Library, both founded by the industrial entrepreneur, Bern Dibner, who believed scholars needed to be able to reach rapidly and easily for their tools.

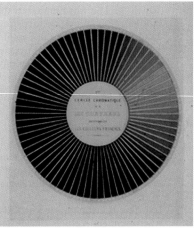

Wimshurst's Electrostatic
Machine, 1882 (above)
The Science Museum

A colour wheel from the
1860s (above right)
*The Dibner Institute for the
History of Science and
Technology*

At its core are extensive holdings of primary sources in electricity and magnetism,
electro-technology, 17th- to 19th-century mechanics, mathematics and optics, and
early modern chemistry and metallurgy. Unusual sidelines include its extensive
holdings in the history and transportation of obelisks, a subject for which Dibner
had a particular penchant, and a small, but rare selection of 18th- and 19th-century
Japanese works on Western science, including unique manuscript material. Significant
additions include the Grace K. Babson collection of Newtoniana, and The Mulhern
Weston Collection of early American electrical meters, gathered by Charles Mulhern
who worked for the Weston Company (founded by inventor Edward Weston).

Electropolis - Musée de l'Energie électrique
Electropolis - Museum of Electrical Energy
55 rue du Pâturage, 68200 Mulhouse, France
Tel. (33) 3 89 324860 www.electropolis.tm.fr
Jul, Aug: daily 10am-6pm. Sep-Jun: Tue-Sun 10am-6pm

Electropolis is the only European museum to be entirely dedicated to electricity, and it
aims at covering the scientific and social history of electricity production and use. More
of an attraction centre than a collection, the museum's collections nevertheless feature
over 10,000 objects.

Kew Bridge Steam Museum
Green Dragon Lane, Brentford, Middlesex TW8 0EN, UK
Tel. (44) 20 8568 4757 www.kbsm.org
Daily 11am-5pm (the engines are in steam Sat-Sun)

A gargantuan example of the best of Victorian engineering. The museum's prize is
the *Grand Junction 90* (2.3 metre wide) Cornish beam engine, the world's largest working
example, built in 1845. Used for over 100 years to pump water to the whole of West
London, it now rises and falls for only half an hour every Saturday and Sunday, setting
in motion its huge cylinder. To keep it pumping 24 hours a day, stokers tended its fourteen boilers while a greaser oiled its bearings non-stop.

Kirkaldy Testing Works
99 Southwark Street, London SE1 0JF, UK
Tel. (44) 1322 332195 www.eastside.ndirect.co.uk
Open 1st Sunday of every month (at other times by appt. only)

The Industrial Revolution brought about a vast increase in demand for metals, particularly iron and steel. However, the rate of fracture in these materials is high. David Kirkaldy built one of the most notable testing laboratories, and his work came to be so highly recognized that the test mark of Kirkaldy's Testing and Experimenting works became the first quality mark, and was highly respected. The museum is devoted to recounting the history of this remarkable man and his involvement in this area of engineering. The museum holds the original 48 foot-long load-testing machine.

MIT Museum

265 Massachusetts Avenue, Cambridge,
Massachusetts 02139, USA
Tel. (1) 617 253 4444 web.mit.edu
Tue-Fri 10am-5pm, Sat-Sun noon-5pm

The contribution MIT has made to the history of modern science and technology is significant indeed. The aim of the museum is to preserve that legacy, as well as to exhibit it and make it available for study. Spread over several areas are constantly changing exhibits drawing on its extensive collections of art, artefacts, holography (the largest holdings in the world acquired from the Museum of Holography), architectural material, and nautical drawings and models. Added to this are the displays dedicated to the scientific visionary, Harold 'Doc' Edgerton (1903-90), best known for his development of the electronic stroboscope which allowed us to see what we were never able to see before. Strobe Alley also highlights his sonar and underwater photography contributions, while the archives hold his expansive notebooks and diaries from the early 1930s until his death.

Nina de Angeli Walls

The New England Wireless and Steam Museum

1300 Frenchtown Road, East Greenwich, Rhode Island 02818, USA
Tel. (1) 401 885 0545 users.ids.net
By appt. only

Besides the wireless collection, this museum is dedicated to the beginnings of steam power, with many items in working order. In 1875, Rhode Island was the world centre of the stationary steam industry. One entire building is dedicated to the stationary steam engine collection, and includes the only surviving George H. Corliss engine running under steam today, plus steam engines from the state's manufacturers.

Royal Society of Chemistry Library and Information Centre

Burlington House, Piccadilly, London W1V 0BN, UK
Tel. (44) 20 7437 8656 www.chemsoc.org
By appt. only

The Royal Society of Chemistry has the longest tradition of any chemical society in the world. The Library and Information Centre contains an extensive collection of books dating back as far as the 16th century, dealing mainly with the history of firearms and explosives. The library also has a wide selection of prints and photographs, glass lantern slides, and

The cover of a guide to Hagley's collection of trade catalogues (top)
Hagley Museum and Library

A Victorian trade card celebrating the obelisk trade (above)
The Dibner Institute for the History of Science and Technology

A Victorian trade card celebrating the obelisks in London and New York (left)
The Dibner Institute for the History of Science and Technology

book illustrations, as well as an extensive range of images of notable chemists from the 15th century onwards, such as Agrippa, Priestly, and Pasteur.

The Science Museum

Exhibition Road, South Kensington, London sw7 2DD, UK
Tel. (44) 870 870 4771
www.sciencemuseum.org.uk
Daily 10am-6pm

This museum is one of the largest establishments in the world documenting scientific, medical, and technological advancements. As such, it is in a constant state of flux as new discoveries and inventions are made. 'Making the Modern World' is one of its latest displays. Covering the period 1750–2000, it includes Stephenson's *Rocket*, a Model-T Ford, a V2 missile, and the *Apollo 10* command module. Giant aircraft hangars housing unseen collections from a number of national museums, including this one, are based at a former aerodrome in the village of Wroughton.

Museo della Tecnica Electtrica
Museum of Electrical Technology`
Department of Electrical Engineering, University of Pavia, via Ferrata 1, 27100 Pavia, Italy
Tel. (39) 0382 505250 etabeta.unipv.it
Due to open in 2002

Tigirl, a reflection hologram by Margaret Benyon (above)
MIT Museum

Shooting the apple by Harold E. Edgerton, 1964 (right)
MIT Museum

This collection contains numerous items relating to the origins of the discovery of electricity and magnetism, plus old industrial equipment and documents. The collections have been enriched by objects from electrical companies such as the Italian Electricity Board, which donated its entire Museum of Electric Energy. In it there is a large selection of apparatus from over 125 pieces invented or used by Alessandro Volta. He become a Professor and Rector at the University of Pavia, and was the inventor of the voltaic pile – the electric battery.

CRICKET, BASEBALL AND BOWLING

GOLF

HORSE, SADDLERY AND RACING

HUNTING, SHOOTING AND FISHING

MOTORCAR RACING

OLYMPIC AND SPORT COLLECTIONS

RUGBY, FOOTBALL AND BOXING

SKIING, ALPINE AND WINTER SPORTS

TENNIS, SQUASH AND RELATED SPORTS

WATER SPORTS

CRICKET, BASEBALL AND BOWLING

Art Athletic Center – Fondazione Walter Rontani
The Art Athletic Centre – Walter Rontani Foundation
Via Maggio 39, 50125 Florence, Italy
Tel. (39) 055 217294
Every 2nd Sun of the month 4-8pm

This museum covers more than 75 sports. Particularly impressive are the items associated with the ancient games of *gioco del pallone col bracciale* and *pallamaglio*, the forerunner of sports such as cricket and baseball. *Gioco del pallone col bracciale* (game with ball and bracer) was first mentioned in 1555 and was played until around 1950 in northern and central Italy. The aim was to hit a leather ball as far as possible by knocking it with a wooden bracer which protected the arm and enabled the player to use extra force.

International Bowling Museum and Hall of Fame
111 Stadium Plaza, St Louis, Missouri 63102, USA
Tel. (1) 314 231 6340   www.bowlingmuseum.com
Apr-Sep: Mon-Sat 9am-5pm, Sun noon-5pm. Oct-Mar: daily 11am-4pm

The history of bowling is documented here through various exhibits. They include a replica of a stone bowling game found in a child's grave in Egypt dating back to 3200BC; life-sized dioramas of colonists bowling nine-pins on Bowling Green, New York; and an Aubusson tapestry from 1729 depicting the French playing skittles, or one of the many related games. One special item, a full-sized bowling pin car, attests to the sport's growing popularity at the beginning of the 20th century. Built in the 1930s by an enterprising bowling proprietor on a Studabaker frame, the car was designed for street use with the intention of raising awareness, which it did with great success.

Joyce Sports Research Collection
Department of Special Collections, 102 Hesburgh Library, University of Notre Dame, Notre Dame, Indiana 46556, USA
Tel. (1) 219 631 6506   www.sports.nd.edu
Mon-Fri 8am-5pm

A resource teeming with baseball monographs, annuals, periodicals, yearbooks, scrapbooks and, open reel audio tapes. Consult the complete holdings of *The Sporting News* (1886-) the erstwhile 'bible of baseball'; *Baseball Magazine*, the premier baseball monthly of the first half of the 20th century; and the collection of around 2,300 major league and 2,000 minor league programmes and scorecards going back to the 19th century.

Exterior view of the museum
International Bowling Museum and Hall of Fame

Kent County Cricket Club Museum
St Lawrence Ground, Old Dover Road, Canterbury, Kent CT1 3NZ, UK
Tel. (44) 1227 456886   www.kentcountycricket.co.uk
Access to collections only on days when cricket is being played. Other times by appt.

An original *Vanity Fair* cartoon watercolour of the famous Kent and England player Colin Blyth is a real beauty, but be sure to see the bats marking team performances and individual achievements. These include one used in a single wicket match in 1838 by Alfred Mynn, an early Kent Cricketer, and the one signed by the Kent Eleven of 1901. There are cricket balls too, including the one presented to the first-class cricketer A. P. Freeman (known as 'Titch'), who took 300 wickets in the 1928 season, and another he used in 1929 to take all ten wickets in an innings against Lancashire.

Koninklijke Bibliotheek
The Royal Library
Prins Willem-Alexanderhof 5, 2529 BE The
Hague, The Netherlands
Tel. (31) 70 3140911 www.konbib.nl
Mon-Fri 9am-5pm, Sat 9am-1pm

Tournament poster
(above)
*International Bowling
Museum and Hall of Fame*

'Old-Time' alleys, replete
with pinboys (above left)
*International Bowling
Museum and Hall of Fame*

Buried deep within this library are 1,200 books
on cricket, owned by the Royal Dutch Cricket
Association but placed here for safe keeping. The
association was founded in 1883, almost a decade
after cricket had been introduced to the
Netherlands by English school boys. When the occupied forces forbade cricket to be
played, a 'Save Dutch Cricket Fund' was established in England so that equipment could
be sent over, and Dutch cricketers could begin playing again in 1949. Books in English and
Dutch intermingle on the shelves and include a selection by one of England's greatest
cricket commentators, John Arlot.

Lancashire County Cricket Club Museum
Lancashire County Cricket Club, Old Trafford, Manchester M16 0RA, UK
Tel. (44) 161 2824000 www.lccc.co.uk
Open all 1st XI and International Match days

The Manchester Cricket Club, formed at the beginning of the 1800s, moved to Old Trafford
in 1857. The collection includes trophies presented to players from the 1820s, as well as
several early silver tankards, one dating from 1738. Remarkably, they also have some of
the oldest cricket statistics in existence – a goldmine for the earnest enthusiast.
Lancashire County Cricket Club, founded in 1864, also displays its memorabilia here.
Items associated with W. G. Grace make up part of the collections, but without a doubt it's
the cap presented to Richard Barlow by the Australian Captain, Murdoch, that should not
be missed. It was presented during the match between the North of England and the
Australians in 1884. Barlow, facing the demon bowler Spofforth, scored a century, took
ten Australian wickets and was even cheered from the field. So impressed was the Captain,
that he took off his cap and presented it to Barlow. The press went wild with the story and
the well-known saying 'I take my hat off to you' originates from that momentous occasion.

Louisville Slugger Museum
800 West Main Street, Louisville, Kentucky 40292, USA
Tel. (1) 502 588 7326 www.slugger.com
Mon-Sat 9am-5pm

Home to the factory famous for producing Louisville Sluggers – the bats fashioned out
of northern white ash which have graced most major league ball parks and beyond. In
the Oval room, bats of Cobb, Rose, and Aaron are displayed; you can read about the history of the game; or spend hours poring over George Herman (Babe) Ruth memorabilia.
Ruth's Louisville Slugger, used by him for much of his record-setting 1927 season, is held
here, complete with the 21 notches carved by him for each home run he hit with it.

Marylebone Cricket Club Library
Lord's Cricket Ground, London NW8 8QN, UK
Tel. (44) 20 7432 1033 www.lords.org
By appt. only

Along with the museum (see separate entry), the MCC library is heaven for cricket fans.
Its 12,000 volumes make up one of the leading collections in existence. Outstanding
examples include the collection given by Lady Cahn after Sir Julien Cahn's death. A

noted cricket captain, Sir Julien amassed more than 4,000 cricket books to which he added a similar number when he bought cricketing author Frederick Samuel Ashley-Cooper's library in 1931. Other donations have come from Alfred Lawson Ford in 1930, and Evelyn Rockley Wilson, who donated around 1,000 books and other collectables.

Marylebone Cricket Club Museum
Lord's Cricket Ground, London NW8 8QN, UK
Tel. (44) 20 7432 1033   www.lords.org
Tours daily at noon and 2pm (may vary)

Undisputedly the home of cricket in England. The museum, which charts the evolution of the game over the past 400 years, owes its origins to one man, Sir Spencer Ponsonby Fane, who started amassing pictures, scorecards, and implements for the club in 1864. Dr W. G. Grace looms large – arguably the most famous cricketer ever and in most people's minds, Britain's first national sporting hero. In the Long Room (part of the tour, but not part of the museum) is a portrait of Grace painted by Archibald Stuart Wortley, showing him at the wicket at Lord's wearing an MCC cap. Among the more famous exhibits within the museum is a stuffed sparrow, 'bowled out' by Jehangir Khan in 1936 and, of course, the Ashes, which are kept safely in a terracotta urn and which are rarely removed, whether it is England or Australia who hold them.

The C. C. Morris Cricket Library and Collection
Haverford College, Haverford, Pennsylvania 19041, USA
Tel. (1) 610 896 1162   www.haverford.edu
Mon, Fri 1-4pm, Sat 9am-noon

The first recorded American cricket match was played in New York in 1751 on the site of what is now the Fulton Fish market in downtown New York City. There's even a journal entry by General Washington referring to his troops at Valley Forge having played a game of 'wickets' in 1778. It was, however, Philadelphia which became the focus for the game, not only due to the influx of Lancashire and Yorkshire hosiery and mill-workers in the 1840s, but also thanks to the enthusiasm of William Rotch Wister, who became known as 'the father of Philadelphia cricket'. It was at Haverford College in Haverford, Pennsylvania, that the game was introduced to the young college students by the English landscape gardener, William Carvill, in 1834. The C. C. Morris Cricket Library was founded in 1969 and is the largest and best repository of cricket books and memorabilia in the US.

Hall of Fame building (top)
The National Baseball Hall of Fame

Babe Ruth Room (middle)
The National Baseball Hall of Fame

Ball Parks (above)
The National Baseball Hall of Fame

National Baseball Hall of Fame logo (right)
The National Baseball Hall of Fame

The National Baseball Hall of Fame
25 Main Street, Cooperstown, New York 13326, USA
Tel. (1) 607 547 7200   www.baseballhalloffame.org
Daily 9am-5pm (until 9pm in summer)

This tiny town, northwest of the Big Apple, has, since 1939, been home to the Hall of Fame of this most beloved of America's pastimes. The museum traces the developments made in the equipment used in the game: see the first catcher's mask worn at Harvard in 1876, or the fingerless gloves from the 1880s. In the Hall of Fame's timeline a wealth of bats, balls, gloves, and uniforms associated with great games and players are on display. Special displays include Women in Baseball, or tell the tragic stories of players like Clemente, the native of Puerto Rico who died in a plane crash while participating in an earthquake-relief mission to Nicaragua in 1972. And if baseball cards are your passion, there are thousands on display.

Negro Leagues Baseball Museum
1616 East 18th Street, Kansas City, Missouri 64108, USA
Tel. (1) 816 221 1920   www.nlbm.com
Tue-Sat 9am-6pm, Sun noon-6pm

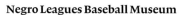

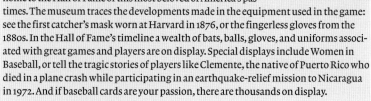

Although African-Americans began playing baseball during the Civil War and were part of professional white leagues until 1900, racism soon prohibited them joining these teams, and it wasn't until 1945 that an African-American was recruited onto a major league white team. This prompted Andrew Foster to establish the Negro National League in 1920, which lasted until the early 1960s. This museum is dedicated to them and celebrates their legacy. A vast array of memorabilia documents the history of African-American baseball from around 1860-1950.

The Babe Ruth Birthplace and Orioles Museum

216 Emory Street, Baltimore, Maryland 21230, USA
Tel. (1) 410 727 1539 www.baberuthmuseum.com
Please call for opening times

A homespun museum which salutes the national hero, George Herman 'Babe' Ruth. The displays cover his early life in Baltimore (up to the age of around 19), and include his boyhood bat, his inscribed hymnal, the official scorebook from his first professional game, and some unique photos of the man at training.

Hall of Fame Gallery
The National Baseball Hall of Fame

St Louis Cardinals Hall of Fame

111 Stadium Plaza, St Louis, Missouri 63102, USA
Tel. (1) 314 231 6340 www.bowlingmuseum.com
Apr-Sep: Mon-Sat 9am-5pm, Sun noon-5pm. Oct-Mar: daily 11am-4pm

Separate from, but located within, the International Bowling Museum is this 5,000-square-foot area devoted to this major league baseball team. On display is the '62 'Cardinal Red' Corvette given to Mark McGwire on the night of 8 September 1998, when he made history by shattering Roger Maris' single season home run record by hitting more than 62 off Steve Trachel of the Chicago Cubs. There are also items from the Barry Halper Collection and the entire personal collection of the Polish immigrant turned baseball star, Stan Musial. Voted three times the national league's most valuable player, Musial's donation includes items dating back to 1892 - the year the team made their debut as the St Louise Brown Stockings of the National League.

Somerset Cricket Museum

7 Priory Avenue, Taunton, Somerset TA1 1XX, UK
Tel. (44) 1823 275893
Apr-Oct: Mon-Fri 10am-4pm

The cricketing memorabilia here relates mostly to Somerset's cricket club. Displayed with affection and reverence are a collection of county caps of the eighteen first-class counties, photographs of famous Somerset teams, and bronzes of famous players. Pride of place goes to Ian Botham's bat, which he used to hit a match-winning 149 not out off the Australians at Headingley in July 1981.

Surrey County Cricket Club – The Oval

Kennington, London SE11 5SS, UK
Tel. (44) 20 7582 6660 www.surreyccc.co.uk
Open when matches are in play; tours at other times by appt.

Memorabilia includes a bat that once belonged to the tremendous batsman, Sir Jack Hobbs, who played for England and Surrey; various items donated by Ian Botham; and the oldest cricket bat (1729) known to exist. There are cricket balls galore and an additional nine or so bats, including one taken by Britain's former Prime Minister, John Major (and the club's current President) to a G7 conference where it was signed by all attending heads of state.

Trent Bridge Museum and Archives
Trent Bridge, Nottingham, Nottinghamshire NG2 6AG, UK
Tel. (44) 115 9821525
Open every match day; other times by appt.

Second only to Lord's in the quantity of material it holds in its library, this ground has come a long way from its beginnings in 1835, when it staged its first bona fide inter-county Nottinghamshire game against Sussex. The library has a huge volume of cricketing literature, including a complete run of Wisden's *Almanack* dating back to 1864. The highlight among the balls, stumps, trophies, and clothing in the museum is what must be the largest collection of cricket bats owned by any ground. The majority of the bats were collected before World War I, between 1890 and 1914, by a Mr Charles Green Pratt, who wrote to all the very best players asking if they would donate a winning bat in exchange for a new one. Most of the bats are signed, and on the reverse state in which match the bat was used.

Replica of the British Amateur Championship Cup, presented to Bobby Jones by members of the Royal and Ancient Golf Club of St. Andrews, Scotland, in 1930
Atlanta History Center

Bronze sculpture of Bobby Jones cast by the Gorham Silver Company in 1931 (right)
Atlanta History Center

Vimpelin pesäpallomuseo
The Vimpeli Museum of Finnish Baseball
Kangastie 7, 62800 Vimpeli, Finland
Tel. (358) 6565 1127
Jun, Jul, Aug; please call for opening times

There are many similarities between the Finnish game of *pesäpallo* and American baseball. Introduced to Finland in 1922 by Lauri Pihkala after he visited the US in 1907, it is played by more than ten per cent of the Finnish population. The collection consists of some 2,500 objects, most of which are items of equipment such as balls, mitts, bats, spikes, and various teams' uniforms and prizes.

GOLF

Atlanta History Center
130 West Paces Ferry Road NW, Atlanta, Georgia 30305-1366, USA
Tel. (1) 404 8144000 www.atlhist.org
Mon-Sat 10am-5.30pm, Sun noon-5.30pm

Honoured here is one of the great ambassadors of golf, Robert Tyre Jones, Jr. Born in Atlanta in 1902, his remarkable career includes winning thirteen national titles between 1923 and 1930. He went on to co-design the Augusta National Golf Course and establish the Masters there in 1934. His accolades include induction into the Georgia Golf Hall of Fame and being made an Honorary Burgess of St Andrews, Scotland (Ben Franklin is the only other American to share the honour). The exhibit 'Down the Fairway with Bobby Jones' traces the development of golf and focuses on his achievements.

The British Golf Museum
Bruce Embankment, St Andrews, Fife KY16 9AB, Scotland, UK
Tel. (44) 1334 478880 www.britishgolfmuseum.co.uk
Easter-mid Oct: daily 9.30am-5.30pm. Mid-Oct-Easter: Mon, Thu-Sun 11am-3pm

Though there are several rivals, such as Dutch *Kolf* and the French *Jeu de Mail*, which lay claim to be the forerunners of golf, there is little doubt that the Scottish pastime dating back the Middle Ages, which used a hole in the ground as a target, is the rightful ancestor of the modern game. In fact, the game's history is about as Scottish as you can get. Golf was banned by King James II of Scotland because it distracted his subjects from vital archery practice, and it is probable that the game was being played in St Andrews long before the university was founded in 1411. The museum draws on this rich his-tory to produce a collection that not only tells the story of golf, but imparts much of the enthusiasm felt by the people who have played it. As well as answering many questions (why is a 'birdie' so called and what does it mean to play a 'foozle') the museum has pictures of many golfers (some famous, some forgotten), trophies, collections of golfing art, and weird and wonderful clubs, many of which later became illegal.

The Heritage of Golf
West Links Road, Gullane, East Lothian, EH31 2BB, Scotland, UK
Tel. (44) 1875 870277
By appt. only

This is the private collection of Archie Baird, avid collector of golf memorabilia. While hunting for cheap furniture one day, he came across a bag of very old golf clubs and bought those instead. He caught the bug, and went on to amass a huge collection of early books from antiquarian book dealers in Edinburgh, golf paintings and watercolours, and some early equipment, including a collection of vintage balls.

James River Country Club Museum
1500 Country Club Road, Newport News, Virginia 23606, USA
Tel. (1) 757 595 3327
Tue-Thu 9am-9pm, Fri, Sat 9am-10pm (advisable to call before visiting)

Reputed to be the first golf museum in the world, this impressive club lies a few miles from downtown Newport News, on the historic James River. It was founded in 1932 by Archer M. Huntington, who never played golf but was an obsessive collector. He selected a curator, Mr John Campbell, a golf-playing Scot, who set sail for Scotland in 1932. Thanks to the Depression and a lack of interest in purchasing items associated with golf, he was able to return with numerous clubs, balls, paintings, photographs, and books. Contained in the collection is the oldest identifiable club of its kind in the world: a wooden putter made around 1790 by Simon Cossar of Leith, Scotland, a celebrated club-maker of the day.

Painting of Robert Tyre 'Bobby' Jones Jr. (top)
Atlanta History Center

Augusta National member's green jacket (above)
Atlanta History Center

Ouimet Museum - Francis Ouimet Scholarship Fund
The Golf House, 190 Park Road, Weston, Massachusetts 02493-2256, USA
Tel. (1) 781 891 6400 www.ouimet.org
Mon-Fri 9am-5pm (please call ahead to arrange access)

Son of a gardener, Francis Ouimet rose from his job as a caddie to make golfing history with his incredible win in 1913 over Harry Vardon and Ted Ray. It was a glorious achieve-ment and set Ouimet on course to become a national hero, winning the US Amateur twice and elected the first American captain of the Royal and Ancient in 1951. Besides celebrating his life with a selection of photographs and golfing equipment, the office administers the Francis Ouimet Caddie Scholarship Fund, the second largest caddie fund in the US, described by Ouimet as his greatest honour.

Royal North Devon Golf Club
Westward Ho!, Bideford, Devon EX39 1HD, UK
Tel. (44) 1237 473817 www.north-devon-golf.freeserve.co.uk
Open to members only. Non-members by appt.

Lots of firsts for this club. Established in 1864, it is the oldest golf course in existence in England. It was also the first golf club in England to be home to a golf museum. The museum traces the history of the club and the history of golf in Britain. There are more than 200 ancient golf clubs dating from 1840, together with many items of golfing memorabilia. The collection of old golf balls is particularly fine.

The United States Golf Association Museum and Library
Liberty Corner Road, Far Hills, New Jersey 07931, USA
Tel. (1) 908 234 2300   www.usga.org
Mon-Fri 9am-5pm, Sat-Sun 10am-4pm

Golfing memorabilia and a library of books and periodicals regarded as the largest
public collection in the world solely dedicated to golf. Three entire rooms are devoted
to the subject of golf balls. Learn about the exact methods involved in producing the
first feather-stuffed, leather-stitched golf ball, or about the advent of the gutta-percha
balls used from around 1848 to 1900. Displays celebrate 300 years of women's golf and
include The Robert Cox Cup donated by Cox, a member of British Parliament for the
1896 Women's Amateur contest. This resplendent silver trophy is the oldest of the
USGA's original trophies, as both the Havemeyer and US Open trophies were destroyed
by fire. In the Clubs of Champions Room, there is an array of famous clubs and the specially crafted moon club Alan Shepard brought on the Apollo 14 mission. Watch vintage
footage of famous golfing moments and visit the room dedicated to the evolution of the
golf tee which was first patented by Dr George F. Grant, a Boston dentist, in 1899.

Exterior of the museum
(top)
Atlanta History Center

Dorothy 'Dot' Kirby
(above)
Atlanta History Center

Spirit of the Morgan Horse by
Gwen Reardon (right)
*National Museum of the
Morgan Horse*

The Performance Gallery
(below)
*American Quarter Horse
Heritage Center and Museum*

The Women Golfers' Museum Archives and Library
National Museums of Scotland Library, Chambers Street, Edinburgh EH1 1JF, Scotland, UK
Tel. (44) 131 247 4137   www.nms.ac.uk
Mon-Fri 10am-12.30pm, 2-5pm

The Women Golfers' Museum, founded in 1938, was the brainchild of Cecil Leitch,
British Ladies Champion in 1914, 1920, 1921, and 1926. Sadly, the collections
are no longer self-contained – instead golf equipment, trophies, costumes
and all other non-paper items are on loan to the British Golf Museum,
while the library/archive is housed in the NMS library. The
NMS collection includes twenty photographic albums
illustrating the history of women's golf in the late 19th
and early 20th centuries.

HORSE, SADDLERY AND RACING

American Quarter Horse Heritage Center and Museum
2601 I-40 East, Amarillo, Texas 79104, USA
Tel. (1) 806 376 5181   www.aqha.com
Mon-Sat 9am-5pm, Sun noon-5.30pm (library open Mon-Fri only)

Everything relating to the most popular breed of horse in the world is covered here.
The American Quarter Horse is named for its speed in racing a quarter-mile, but besides
being a superb racing animal, it is used in rodeos, ranching, and showing. The
Performance Gallery features fibreglass replicas of 'America's Fastest Athlete' and traces
the history of the breed, from
colonial racing days to the
present. Superb displays of
saddles and tack from the 16th
century to the present day
pack the cases. The extensive
archival and library facilities
contain equine and agriculture publications, books on
veterinary medicine and horse
shoeing, photographs, reels
of film, and slides.

Cheltenham Hall of Fame

Cheltenham Racecourse, Prestbury Park, Cheltenham, Gloucestershire
GL50 4SH, UK
Tel. (44) 1242 513014 www.cheltenham.co.uk
Open to Tattersalls and Club visitors on racedays, plus Mon-Fri 9.30am-
4.30pm, Sat-Sun 10am-2pm

The Asian Section
Musée du Cheval (France)

Cheltenham Racecourse is home to some of England's most prestigious
races, including the Champion Hurdle, the Gold Cup and, since 1980,
The Queen Mother Champion Chase. Its Hall of Fame has a collection of archive footage,
memorabilia and studies of various aspects of racing life from Cheltenham and around
the world. Alongside pictures and profiles of top riders, find out about horse transportation (race horses once had to walk to the course with their groom), and the role of the
press, TV, and radio.

Musée du Cheval
Museum of the Horse

Château de Saumur, 49400 Saumur, France
Tel. (33) 2 41 40 24 40
Apr-May: daily 9.30am-noon, 2-5.30pm. Jun-Sep: daily 9am-6pm
Oct-Mar: Mon, Wed-Sun 9.30am-noon, 2-5.30pm

Housed in the magnificently timbered attics of the castle is this collection, created in 1911 by
Veterinary Officer Joly, director of veterinary studies at the Cavalry School, and by Dr Peton,
mayor of Saumur. Fossilized remains and skeletons take you back to the earliest ancestors
of the horse. The antiquity section, with artefacts on loan from the Louvre which include a
9th-8th century BC Luristan bit, examines the early domestication of the horse. The medieval
section's centrepiece is a large display of stirrups and spurs from the 10th to the 15th centuries. There is a showcase of early hoof protectors, and in the Renaissance Room, pieces of
cavalry armour, including a fine Italian Chamfron from the 16th century. A large selection
of saddles include Chinese and Tibetan examples decorated with ivory inlay and gilded
bronze, Japanese Samurai saddles, and European and American military examples.

Musée du Cheval
Museum of the Horse

Château de la Sarraz, 1315 La Sarraz, Switzerland
Tel. (41) 21 8666423 www.aseb.ch
Jun, Jul: Tue-Sun 1-5pm. Mid-end Apr, Sep, Oct: Sat-Sun 1-5pm

A museum that celebrates the horse not only for its usefulness to mankind, but also for
its beauty and power. Worth noting among the collection of carriages, harnesses, collars,
and saddles is the handsome yellow and black Grimsel Postal Stagecoach, constructed in
1895 by the blacksmith, Hans Moser, in Bern. The coach travelled between Meiringen
and Gletsch until 1922. Other exhibits are dedicated to the horse and its role on the farm,
in the army, and in sport and racing.

Gestütsmuseum
The Stud Farm Museum

Gestüt Altefeld, St.-Georg-Strasse 15, 37293 Herleshausen, Germany
Tel. (49) 5654 6563
By appt. only

The Altefeld stud farm has a long tradition of horse breeding. It was founded in 1913 by
Burchard von Oettingen, who had been the manager of the famous stud in Trakehnen
since 1892. The museum traces the history of breeding, focusing on this stud estate. As
well as paintings depicting horses that have been bred in Altefeld, there are saddles and

bridles, and sculptures commemorating famous race horses. Highlights include saddles from the French National Stud Farm called 'Saumure', and those of German production for use in the military.

Harness Racing Hall Museum and Hall of Fame

240 Main Street, Goshen, New York 10924, USA
Tel. (1) 914 294 6330 www.harnessmuseum.com
Daily 10am-6pm

Back in 1801, the English thoroughbred, Imported Messenger, found himself in the stable of Anthony Dobbin's Stagecoach Inn at Goshen, New York State. This fine horse was put, as they say, 'into service', and the perky trotting gait of his offspring soon brought fame to Goshen and the surrounding area. Since then, Goshen has played host to great harness races, and the surrounding Standardbred farms still produce top champions (many of whom are descended from Imported Messenger). Housed in what was once a stable, the collection includes Currier and Ives trotting prints, exhibits and displays featuring the harness horse, ephemera such as tickets, programmes and scrapbooks, as well as 5,000 photographs, 300 jackets, caps and helmets, and 200 trophies.

Horse skeletons (above)
The International Museum of the Horse

Calumet Farm trophies of the Triple Crown (above right)
The International Museum of the Horse

The Hubbard Museum of the American West

Ruidoso Downs, New Mexico 88346, USA
Tel. (1) 505 378 4142
www.zianet.com
Daily 10am-5pm

The museum is really three collections rolled into one. It is home to the Ruidoso Downs Race Horse Hall of Fame, with its walls of cases displaying a collection of rare photographs and trophies celebrating the famous jockeys and horses who have participated in the legendary races over the past six decades. The other collections include the Anne C. Stradling Collection of more than 10,000 bits, spurs, bridles, and saddles from around the world, collected by the horse-mad Anne Stradling since 1919. The museum has also acquired the collections of the Museum of the Horse which pay tribute to the horse and its role in the exploration and expansion of the cultures of the world, particularly the West.

The International Museum of the Horse

4089 Iron Works Pike, Lexington, Kentucky 40511, USA
Tel. (1) 859 259 4231 www.imh.org
Mid Mar-Oct: daily 9am-5pm. Nov-mid Mar: Wed-Sun 9am-5pm

Taking up more than 1,000 acres of an educational theme park, the Kentucky Horse Park is home to this museum, as well as the American Saddle Horse Museum, the Polo Museum, and the headquarters of the Pony Club of America. It is the largest and most comprehensive equestrian museum of them all, documenting the prehistory of the animal and the relationship between horse and man throughout 5,000 years of domestication.

W. K. Kellogg Arabian Horse Library

3801 W Temple Avenue, Pomona, California 91768, USA
Tel. (1) 909 869 3081 www.csupomona.edu
Open during buiness hours

A little-known passion of W. K. Kellogg ('King of the Cornflake') was breeding Arabian horses. In 1925, the great inventor and businessman invested in 377 acres of land in Pomana, California, as the site for an Arabian horse ranch. Today the ranch is part of the

California State University but the link has been maintained, with a collection of books and periodicals devoted to the Arabian horse.

Lipizzaner Museum
The Lipizzan Museum
Stallburg/Hofburg, Reitschulgasse 2, 1010 Vienna, Austria
Tel. (43) 1 5337811 www.lipizzaner.at
Daily 9am-6pm

The Lipizzan horse gets its name from the original stud farm of Lipizza in Slovenia which was used by archduke Karl II to breed Spanish horses. Through engravings, drawings, photographs, and paraphernalia, the museum tells the story of the Imperial stable from the 1600s to the present day. The focal point of the exhibition is the training of the horses and the skill with which they are ridden, although the high point for many visitors may be getting a glimpse of day-to-day life in the stables through two large glass windows.

Horsesleigh, for outings
*Musée du Cheval
(Switzerland)*

Musée lorrain du Cheval
The Horse Museum of the Lorraine
La Tour, rue Saint-Blaise, 55130 Gondrecourt-le-Château, France
Tel. (33) 3 29 89 72 35
Jul-Aug: Tue-Sun 2.30-6pm (groups at other times by appt.)

The museum is housed in a 14th-century tower (which used to be part of a fortified building), and in a contiguous 18th–19th-century building. It holds an extensive selection of old horseshoes, along with numerous saddles, both civilian and military. Don't miss the complete range of saddlery tools and one of the key exhibits – a late 19th-century English sewing machine used for stitching leather.

Muzeum Lowiectwa i Jezdziectwa
The Museum of Hunting and Horsemanship
Lazienki Królewskie w Warszawie ulica Szwolezerów 900-464 Warsaw, Poland
Tel. (48) 22 628 4205 www.muz-low.com.pl
Mon-Fri 10am-5pm, Sat-Sun 10am-6pm

A museum of hunting as well as horsemanship, the exhibition space devoted to the horse is housed in the stables (also called the horseshoe) built between 1825 and 1826. The majority of items in the exhibition are Polish objects or those used in areas which formally belonged to Poland, and date from the early 20th century. In addition, there are items from Russia, Germany, Austria, France, the US and the UK. There are wartime papers documenting attempts to 'enlist' Polish horses for use by the occupying army; Janusz Komorowski's polo shoes used by this eminent player in Argentina during the pre-war period; regional harnesses; and racing memorabilia including medals, light racing saddles made in England and Germany, as well as programmes, ribbons, and diplomas from competitions before and after the war.

The National Horseracing Museum
99 High Street, Newmarket, Suffolk CB8 8JL, UK
Tel. (44) 1638 667333 www.nhrm.co.uk
Mid-Apr-end Oct: Tue-Sun 10am-5pm (Jul, Aug daily 10am-5pm)

Known as the 'Headquarters', the Suffolk town of Newmarket's association with racing began with James I's arrival from Scotland in 1603. Although his interests focused on hunting and hawking, the king did own two racehorses and attended a race there in 1619. From these rather modest beginnings Newmarket grew to become one of Britain's

most famous racecourses. The permanent galleries here tell the story of this sport of kings, from the great royal races, to the horses who run them and the jockeys who race.

National Museum of the Morgan Horse
122 Bostwick Road, Shelburne,
Vermont 05482, USA
Tel. (1) 802 985 8665 www.morganmuseum.org
Mon-Fri 9am-4pm
(research centre by appt. only)

Calumet Farm trophies
The International Museum
of the Horse

The Morgan breed of horses have played a unique and highly significant role in America's history. A descendent from a prepotent stallion named Figure, who was foaled in 1789, Morgan horses helped clear land for pioneers' farms and served as transportation for the family. This, and the work they did hauling Concord stagecoaches on northern New England's primitive roads, earned them a reputation for stamina and endurance, qualities which went on to stand them in good stead as livery and business horses throughout the 19th century.

National Museum of Racing and Hall of Fame
191 Union Avenue, Saratoga Springs, New York 12866-3566, USA
Tel. (1) 518 5840400 www.racingmuseum.org
Mon-Sat 10am-4.30pm, Sun noon-4.30pm

An impressive collection of paintings and sculpture contains work by well-known equine artists such as Edward Troye and Vaughn Flannery (early studies have the horse with all four hooves off the ground at the same time). As well as silks from days past and present, much silver- and gold-ware is on display in the trophy room.

Newmarket Library
1a The Rookery, Newmarket, Suffolk CB8 8EQ, UK
Tel. (44) 1638 661216 www.suffolkcc.gov.uk
Tue, Thu, Sat 9am-5pm, Wed 9am-1pm, Fri 9am-7.30pm

The Racing Collection, established in 1973, is a special collection within the library. A useful online listing of its holdings of nearly 800 volumes reveals subjects ranging from flat racing history, steeple-chasing, and the anatomy of horses, to sporting memoirs and bibliographies. The periodicals date mainly from the 19th and 20th centuries.

Musée Vivant du Cheval
The Living Horse Museum
Grandes Écuries, BP 242, 60631 Chantilly, France
Tel. (33) 3 44 57 13 13
www.musee-vivant-du-cheval.fr
Apr-Oct: Mon-Fri 10.30am-5.30pm, Sat-Sun 10.30am-6pm
Nov-Mar: Mon-Fri 2-5pm, Sat-Sun 10.30am-5.30pm

As legend would have it, the 7th Prince de Conde, Louis-Henri de Bourbon, believed he would be reincarnated as a horse. Ever the pragmatist, he commissioned the architect Jean Aubert to design and build a stable outside Paris so he would have somewhere regal to reside once the transformation had taken place. The stables, set in 8,000 hectares of forest, are a masterpiece of 18th-century architecture. In their heyday, they housed some 250 horses and 500 hounds and were also the setting for lavish entertainment. Today, the buildings, racecourse, and grounds make up the museum where horses are groomed and trained. Demonstrations are given daily, with the riders in period costumes, and there are 31 rooms packed with art work depicting horses.

HUNTING, SHOOTING AND FISHING

The American Museum of Fly Fishing
3657 Main Street, Manchester, Vermont 05254, USA
Tel. (1) 802 362 3300 www.amff.com
Daily 10am–4pm

Containing one of the largest collections of angling and angling-related objects, this museum aims to document the evolution of fly fishing as a sport, art form, craft and industry in the US and abroad, from around the 16th century to the present. You name it, they've got it – everything from rods, reels, and flies, to photographs, manuscripts, and books. Treasures range from the fly fishing tackle of many famous Americans, including Dwight Eisenhower, Andrew Carnegie, and Ernest Hemingway, as well as flies by America's best fly tiers. The institution supports a significant publication programme which includes *The American Fly Fisher*.

Statue of man fishing
Catskill Fly Fishing Center and Museum

Musée de l'Armée
The Army Museum
Hôtel National des Invalides, 129 rue de Grenelle, 75007 Paris, France
Tel. (33) 1 44 42 37 72 www.invalides.org
Apr-Sep: daily 10am-6pm. Oct-Mar: daily 10am-5pm

The department of Arms and Armour here houses a significant collection of hunting weapons, including a stone thrower belonging to Catherine de Médicis, of French or Florentine workmanship (*c.* 1550); a wheel-lock harquebus belonging to Louis XIII, of French workmanship (*c.* 1615-20); a 17th-century wheel-lock harquebus from the Munich School, made by some of the great masters; and a pair of flint pistols from the Baroque period, Maastricht (1660-70).

Musée d'Art et d'Industrie
The Museum of Art and Industry
2 place Louis-Comte, 42000 Saint-Etienne, France
Tel. (33) 4 77 33 04 85 www.mairie-st-etienne.fr
Mon, Wed-Sun 10am-noon, 2-6pm

Grizzly bear, North America
Deutsches Jagd- und Fischerei-Museum

Saint-Etienne was a centre for arms manufacturing from the 16th century, and by the 19th century the industrial revolution had turned it into one of France's leading cities. Having built a reputation for its expertise, the city prudently began to diversify its activities and develop new industries. It was then that the famous arms manufacturer, Manufrance, was founded. The museum's collection of hunting weapons is considered to be one of the best in France, not only from a technical point of view but from an aesthetic one too.

Catskill Fly Fishing Center and Museum
5447 Old Route 17, Livingston Manor, New York, New York 12758, USA
Tel. (1) 914 439 4810 www.cffcm.org
Apr-Oct: 10am-4pm
Nov-Mar: Tue-Fri 10am-1pm, Sat 10am-4pm

Known as the birthplace of dry fly fishing, most of the famous American tackle makers and anglers have a connection with the area. The fly collection (tens of thousands of them) is one of the best in the world. A number of prize flies by Gordon are worth going to see in themselves, but don't ignore others from the 1920s and 1930s. Vintage rods and trout and salmon reels are also on display.

Musée de la Chasse et de la Nature
The Museum of Hunting and Wildlife
60 rue des Archives, 75003 Paris, France
Tel. (33) 1 53 01 92 40
Mon, Wed-Sun 10am-12.30pm, 1.30-5.30pm

Hunting sleighs with view of the White Hall Deutsches Jagd- und Fischerei-Museum

On dispay is large selection of weapons from the François Sommer collection and the Pauilhac collection. Among the most remarkable pieces are Frederic I, King of Sweden's gun; a gun given by Marie-Antoinette to her mother; a hunting gun offered by the town of Liège to Bonaparte during the first consulate; and guns which belonged to Joachim Murat, the former King of Naples.

Deutsches Jagd- und Fischerei-Museum
The German Hunting and Fishing Museum
Neuhauser Strasse 2, 80331 Munich, Germany
Tel. (49) 89 220522
Mon, Tue 9.30am-9pm, Wed-Sun 9.30am-5pm

Located in the former Augustinian church, one of Munich's most important buildings, is an exhibition documenting the evolution of hunting techniques and equipment. It contains not only a fine weapon collection and the famous antler-trophy collection of Count Arco, but also a number of significant artistic and cultural treasures. One of the centrepieces is the huge collection of antique hunting weapons, rods, reels, and lures. There is a substantial collection of hunting rifles, boar spears, and crossbows, and several elaborate royal hunting sleds from the 17th and 18th centuries.

George Eastman House - International Museum of Photography and Film
900 East Avenue, Rochester, New York 14607, USA
Tel. (1) 716 271 3361   www.eastman.org
Tue-Sat 10am-4.30pm, Sun 1-4.30pm

An avid sportsman, Eastman enjoyed many of the popular outdoor pursuits of the day, including fishing. Along with the many items of vintage sporting equipment, there are catalogues and correspondence by turn-of-the-century sporting supply companies, as well as photographs of the equipment in use. Eastman's fly fishing reel and case is a rare and early example of Edward von Hofe's hand-built salmon fishing reel, on the front of which is engraved Eastman's name and a serial number.

Stairwell with view of the White Hall (above) Deutsches Jagd- und Fischerei-Museum

Wild Boar; bronze sculpture by Martin Mayer (right) Deutsches Jagd- und Fischerei-Museum

The Flyfishers' Club
69 Brook Street, London W 1 Y 2ER, UK
Tel. (44) 20 7629 5958
Mon-Fri 10.30am-11pm to members only or by appt. to researchers and writers

One of the largest libraries of its kind anywhere, holding some 3,000 volumes. What makes it particularly special is the fact that a good number of the volumes have some close association with the famous anglers or authors who wrote them; some of them are, or were, members, and donated their inscribed copies to the club. Not surprisingly for a club founded in 1884 'for the social intercourse of gentlemen interested in the art of Flyfishing', there is some fine memorabilia, including what is believed to be Isaac Walton's reel and a Greenwell's Glory tied by Canon Greenwell.

Forge Mill Needle Museum
Needle Mill Lane, Riverside, Redditch, Worcestershire B98 8HY, UK
Tel. (44) 1527 62509 www.redditchbc.gov.uk
Easter-Sep: Mon-Fri 11am-4pm, Sat-Sun 2-5pm
Feb-Easter, Oct, Nov: Mon-Thu 11am-4pm, Sun 2-5pm

Besides needle making (at one time, 90 per cent of the world's needles were made here), Redditch was renowned as a major fishing tackle manufacturing centre, a trade which owes it origins to the needle industry – fish hooks are in effect a curved needle with a barb. One of the town's most famous companies was S. Allcock & Sons, which flourished from around 1880 to the 1960s. Besides a comprehensive collection of Allcock fishing tackle and fishing tackle catalogues, there is a fine selection of other brands of Redditch fishing gear, including reels, rods, hooks, and lures.

Musée international de la Chasse
The International Hunting Museum
Château de Gien, 45500 Gien, France
Tel. (33) 2 38 67 69 69
Jan-May, Oct-Dec: daily 9am-noon, 2-6pm. Jun-Sep: daily 9am-6pm

A dream of a museum housed in a castle overlooking the Loire, originally part of the royal estate in the 14th century. It contains more than 2,500 objects and works of art relating to hunting, including arms and works illustrating hunting techniques, as well as the animals that were hunted. Follow the evolution of the hunting weapon from pre-history to the Middle Ages, when it became part of the Seigneur's leisure. Illustrations of hunting are provided by the Flemish painter, Jan van der Straet, known as Stradanus.

The International Fly Fishing Center and Fly Fishing Museum
215 East Lewis Street, Livingston, Montana 59047, USA
Tel. (1) 406 222 9369 www.fedflyfishers.org
Jun-Sep: 10am-6pm. Oct-May: 10am-4pm

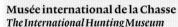

The history of fishing is documented room by room in a converted 1910 schoolhouse. The significant rod collection contains some beauties, like the split cane rods by Hiram Leonard of Bangor Maine, Edward Payne; and Fred Thomas, and an example by Stimpson & Lambuth of the rare twisted cane rod. The well stocked Lewis A. Bell Memorial Fly Fishing Library welcomes visitors.

International Game Fish Association Fishing Hall of Fame & Museum
300 Gulf Stream Way, Dania Beach, Florida 33004, USA
Tel. (1) 954 9224212 www.igfa.org
Daily 10am-6pm

A monster of a museum covering all aspects of recreational fishing. Life-sized mounts of world-record sport fish greet you in the Hall of Fame, which is filled with memorabilia commemorating the leaders in this sport. The best exhibits in the museum are the antique and contemporary reels, rods, lures, and flies, but for some light relief head to The Fish Gallery, where you can learn what it is like to be a fish (yes – really!).

Muzeum Lowiectwa i Jezdziectwa
The Museum of Hunting and Horsemanship
Lazienki Królewskie w Warszawie ulica Szwolezerów 9, 00-464 Warsaw, Poland
Tel. (48) 22 628 42 05 www.muz-low.com.pl
Mon-Fri 10am-5pm, Sat-Sun 10am-6pm

The former barracks and stables in the Royal Baths, at one time a zoological garden,

Target *The Fool Invites the Riflemen's Wives to a Joint Meal*, 1766 (top)
Schützenscheiben-Museum Scheibbs

Allegorical target from the Chartreuse of Gaming, 1762 (middle)
Schützenscheiben-Museum Scheibbs

Reconciliation target between the Chartreuse of Gaming and the Town of Scheibbs (above)
Schützenscheiben-Museum Scheibbs

houses this museum, which combines collections from hunters and the Polish Hunting Association with those of horse lovers. Together, the collections number some 10,000 items, many of considerable value. In the Polish Hunting Salon, is an array of hunting souvenirs, trophies, roebuck and red deer antlers, knives, and racks of hunting guns dating from the 16th to the 20th centuries.

Mátra Museum

Kossuth utca 40, 32 Gyöngyös, Hungary
Tel. (36) 37 311 447
Please call for opening times

The highest peak in Hungary, Kékestető, is in Mátra, and its surrounding forests once teemed with game of all sorts, making it a popular destination with hunters from both home and abroad. The exhibition on hunting shows only a selection of the museum's 1,692 objects. The first hall is dedicated to game keeping, while another contains firearms, bows and arrows, arrowheads, spears for hunting, hunting knives, and hunting accessories.

The Mitchell Library

The Reid Memorial Angling Collection, North Street, Glasgow G3 7DN, Scotland, UK
Tel. (44) 141 2872934   www.mitchelllibrary.org
Mon-Thu 9am-8pm, Fri, Sat 9am-5pm

A medical doctor with an enthusiasm for salmon fishing, Dr William L. Reid amassed a library of more than 850 volumes on all aspects of angling. Several notable publications dating from before 1800 include Thomas Barker's *The Art of Angling* annexed to *The Countryman's Recreation* (1654) and Thomas Fairfax's *The Complete Sportsman* (1760).

Minnesota Fishing Museum and Educational Facility

304 W Broadway, Little Falls, Minnesota 56345, USA
Tel. (1) 320 6162011   www.fallsnet.com
Summer: Tue-Fri 10am-6pm, Sat 9am-6pm, Sun 11am-4pm

Hunting rifles and guns
(top to bottom)
Odder Museum

A state full of rivers and lakes, Minnesota is steeped in fishing history. A point to keep in mind when viewing this collection is that all the items are the former possessions of individuals from across the state who were, and some who still are, part of the legacy of freshwater fishing in Minnesota. The collection holds over 4,000 fishing related items, from classic and antique outboard motors, to brass spearing decoys, plugs and spoons, and rods and reels.

National Freshwater Fishing Hall of Fame

1 Hall of Fame Drive, Hayward, Wisconsin 54843, USA
Tel. (1) 715 634 4440   www.pressenter.com
Mid Apr-end Oct: daily 10am-5pm

The list of items on display reads more like an entry in the *Guinness Book of Records* than a museum inventory list: 500 outboard motors; 300 fishing rods; 25,000 reels; 9,000 collectible lures, from early wooden and metal ones to examples of the later plastic ones; ten or eleven boats; an 88,000-gallon-pool stocked with live fish; 2,000 hooks; a gaggle of fishing nets; a mound of tackle boxes in leather, wood, and plastic; and 400 mounted fish representing around 200 species, among a plethora of other fishing related items. Researchers say coming here is like finding the Holy Grail. The movie industry is a frequent borrower, as are those in the advertising business.

Norsk Skogbruksmuseum
The Norwegian Forestry Museum
2401 Elverum, Norway
Tel. (47) 62 410299   www.skogbruk.museum.no
Mid Jun-mid Aug: daily 10am-6pm. Mid August-early Jun: daily 10am-4pm

This museum explores every aspect of Norway's natural resources, from forestry, hunting, trapping, and fishing, to the utilisation of moss and lichen. Exhibits illustrate the development of hunting implements, from bows up to modern sporting guns and rifles. Some of the earliest examples date from around 1550. One of the highlights is the collection of 300 Norwegian knives from the various counties (only 150 are on display at any one time). Fashioned from wood with steel blades, they are distinguished by their often elaborate carving. Many of them are not only used for hunting and fishing, but also as decorative accessories on folk costumes.

Odder Museum

Rosensgade 84, 833 Odder, Denmark
Tel. (45) 86 54 13 90 www.oddermuseum.dk
Mon-Fri 1-4pm, Sat-Sun & public holidays 1-5pm

Bringing home the last shot bear in Bavaria, near Ruhpolding, October 24 1835, painting after Heinrich Bürkel (above)
Deutsches Jagd- und Fischerei-Museum

The summer of 1988 saw the opening of this museum's new permanent collection based on the theme 'Weapons, Hunting and the Hunter'. The core of the selection on view is from the private collection of hunting weapons and accessories collected over more than 50 years by Sigfred Rasmussen of Ørtig.

Museo provinciale della Caccia e della Pesca
The Provincial Museum of Hunting and Fishing
Castel Wolfsthurn, 39040 Mareta, Italy
Tel. (39) 0472 758121
Apr-mid Nov: Tue-Sat 9.30am-5.30pm, Sun 1-5pm

The beautiful Castello Wolfsthurn, built by Baron von Sternbach, houses this museum. Special reference is made to the Emperor Maximilian I and Archduke Ferdinand II (1566-95) who both organised traditional hunting trips in honour of state visitors and diplomats. Hunting weapons from different periods include shotguns, iron-traps, and cages for capturing birds. Also trophies, amulets, tapestries, and paintings. Collections of documents and equipment recount the Tyrolian fishing tradition, which for centuries was the exclusive privilege of nobility, clergy, and the municipality. The Rudolf Reichel Collection of beautifully crafted flies is remarkable.

Royal Armouries Museum

Armouries Drive, Leeds, West Yorkshire LS10 1LT, UK
Tel. (44) 113 2201999 www.armouries.org.uk
Apr-Oct: daily 10.30am-5.30pm
Nov-Apr: Mon-Fri 10.30am-4.30pm, Sat-Sun 10.30am-5.30pm

Falconry by Arazzo, 1730 (above)
Museo provinciale della Caccia e della Pesca

Return from Hunting by Ignaz Stolz (below)
Museo provinciale della Caccia e della Pesca

This is the only museum in the UK that actively collects hunting and sporting weapons. It is home to a vast collection of arms and armour, as well as associated paintings, books, and engravings. The collections are arranged by theme and include a section on hunting. From spears and harpoons for hunting whales, to crossbows, longbows and decorated rifles, and from prints illustrating hog hunting in Lower Bengal to scenes of professional wildfowlers hunting birds in skips on the marshes of estuaries in the 1920s, there's hardly an aspect of hunting that is not covered.

469

Plaque *Hares Carrying the Hunter*, 1598
Museo provinciale della Caccia e della Pesca

Schützenscheiben-Museum Scheibbs
The Target Museum of Scheibbs
Rathausplatz 10, 3270 Scheibbs, Austria
Tel. (43) 7482 425110
May-Oct: Sat-Sun 10am-noon, 2-4pm

Housed in an historical building are 240 targets dating from 1680 to 1941, used by the Scheibbs Guild since the 17th century. Most were made and painted by artists from the area and from the Chartreuse of Gaming in Vienna. Exhibits recount the history of shooting clubs and display collections of riflemen's badges, decorations, and their rifles and guns.

Schweizer Jagdmuseum – Schloss Landshut
The Swiss Hunting Museum – Landshut Castle
Schloss Landshut, 3427 Utzenstorf, Switzerland
Tel. (41) 32 6654027
Mid May-mid Oct: Tue-Sat 2-5pm, Sun 10am-5pm

Surrounded by water, Castle Landshut is one of Switzerland's most beautiful castles. It houses the country's only hunting museum, containing an impressive collection of historical hunting weapons, the core of which was collected by Dr René La Roche. Besides local hunting traditions, with an emphasis on falconry, the exhibitions offer an insight into the indigenous fauna of the area.

Shelburne Museum
US Route 7, Shelburne, Vermont 05482, USA
Tel. (1) 802 985 3346   www.shelburnemuseum.org
Late May-late Oct: daily 10am-5pm

In this part of the world, the use of guns and hunting equipment, once necessary for survival, gave way to farming in the 19th century before becoming a commercial pursuit for professionals as well as a key recreational activity. Shotguns, rifles, large-bore punt guns, small boats for hunting ducks and other animals, and a selection of fishing tackle complement the museum's collection of decoys and hunting trophies.

Suomen metsästysmuseo
The Hunting Museum of Finland
Tehtaankatu 23 A, 11910 Riihimäki, Finland
Tel. (358) 19 722294   www.kolumbus.fi
May-Aug: daily 10am-6pm. Sep-Apr: Tue-Sun 10am-6pm (closed Jan)

Some 11,000 items relating to all aspects of hunting and fishing. Besides the usual collection of stuffed game trophies, there is a fascinating collection of hunting amulets. Highlights are the 900 or so firearms, from muzzleloaded flintlocks to modern hunting weapons.

Musée de la Vénerie
The Museum of Venery
Château Royal, 60300 Senlis, France
Tel. (33) 3 44 53 00 80
Mon, Wed-Sun 10am-noon, 2-6pm (Nov-Jan until 5pm)

Among paintings by François Desportes, Alfred de Dreux, Van der Meulen, Jean-Baptiste Oudry, and many more, are objects relating to the royal activity of hunting, to which the museum is entirely devoted. The splendid collections include hunting knives, horns, royal and imperial equipages (including the Empress Eugénie's hunting garments), along with hunting weapons and trophies.

MOTORCAR RACING

Antique Auto and Race Car Museum
Stone City Mall, 3348 16th Street, Bedford,
Indiana 47421, USA
Tel. (1) 812 275 0556
www.autoracemuseum.com
Apr-end Dec: Mon-Sat noon-6pm (extended
hours in summer)

This museum is a pot-pourri of antiques
and race cars put together by Eddie Evans,
the owner and curator. Indy 500 fans are
well represented, and among the collection
can be found A. J. Foyt's 1969 Sheraton,
Pancho Carter's 1978 Eagle and Gordon

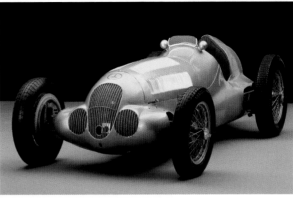

Mecerdes-Benz Formula
Racing Car W125, 1937
Mercedes-Benz Museum

Johncock's 1982 Wildcat. Alongside these are special interest cars such as Mustangs and
Corvettes, midget racers, go-carts, and other collectibles. Classic car enthusiasts will
enjoy the Rolls-Royces from the early 1930s, an even older Oldsmobile, as well as Model
'T' and Model 'A' Fords and an original Ford Paddy Wagon. There's even a fire truck
from 1927.

Museo dell'Automobile Carlo Biscaretti di Ruffia
The Carlo Buscaretti di Ruffia Automobile Museum
Corso Unità d'Italia 40, 10126 Turin, Italy
Tel. (39) 011 677666
Tue-Sun 10am-6.30pm

The Italians love to race and especially love to race cars. No surprise, then, that one of
the most spectacular collections of racing cars should be in Italy. The location, to be
more specific, is Turin, home to Fiat and also to the Carlo Biscaretti di Ruffia, a gem
among museums with a history as old as Italian motoring itself. All kinds of models are
represented here, from the very earliest days of racing onwards. There is Fiat's 130 HP
Grand Prix, which Felice Nazzaro drove to win the 1907 French Grand Prix. From the
same year, there is 'Pechino' in which Prince Scipione Borghese and Ettore Guissardi
won the Peking to Paris race sponsored by the Paris daily, *Le Matin*.

Musée Automobile de la Sarthe
The Car Museum of Sarthe

Mercedes-Benz 300 SL,
6 cylinder, 1952
Mercedes-Benz Museum

Circuit des 24 heures du Mans, 72009
Le Mans, France
Tel. (33) 2 43 72 72 24 www.sarthe.com
Jun-Sep: daily 10am-7pm
Oct-May: daily 10am-6pm

Motorcar racing enthusiasts' hearts skip a beat when
they utter the words 'Le Mans'. A city steeped in
history, this shrine of
motor racing is
the epicentre
of this
world.
Situated at
the main
entrance of
the Le Mans is
its museum, with

around 120 vehicles on display, from the early days of racing to the present. The display of around thirty racing cars are amazing. Of these, fourteen have won Le Mans.

Mercedes-Benz Formula Racing Car W25, 1934 (above)
Mercedes-Benz Museum

At Brooklands (right)
Brooklands Museum

Mecerdes-Benz Formula 1 Racing Car W196, 1954 (below right)
Mercedes-Benz Museum

Brooklands Museum
Brooklands Road, Weybridge, Surrey KT13 0QN, UK
Tel. (44) 1932 857381 www.motor-software.co.uk
Tue–Sun 10am–5pm (until 4pm in winter)

Brooklands, constructed in 1907, is the oldest racing circuit in the world, pipping Indianapolis to the post by just one year. Back then, there were no rules for the sport and, in the absence of anything better, regulations from horse racing were adopted, including 'handicapping' the cars by weighing them down, and requiring the drivers to wear silks as a means of identification. In its heyday, during the 1920s and 1930s, the

track, designed by record-breaker Malcolm Campbell, was dubbed the 'Ascot' of motor racing because of the 'high society' people who flocked there. Today, many of the cars and bikes that whizzed around its circuit are on display and much of the track and many of its original buildings and features have survived, including the Clubhouse, now an Ancient Monument.

The Donington Grand Prix Collection
Donington Park, Castle Donington, Derbyshire DE74 2RP, UK
Tel. (44) 1332 811027 www.donington.com
Summer: daily 9.30–5.30pm. Winter: daily 10am–4pm

The history of Donington race track stretches back to 1931 when one Fred Craner of the Derby and District Motor Club was granted the right to build a motorcycle racing circuit in and through the woods of Donington Park, near Castle Donington. These races proved so popular that the track was widened the same year to accommodate cars, and in 1935 the first Donington Grand Prix was held. Two years later the race had full international status and, until the start of World War II, the track saw some of the greatest battles in motor racing's history. Donington was abandoned in 1956 after being used as a vehicle depot by the War Office and would probably have vanished altogether had it not been for Tom Wheatcroft, who had first come to Donington in its heyday in 1935. His collection includes Ascari's Ferrari, Jim Clark's Lotus 23, and Nigel Mansell's Williams. There are also American midget racers, veteran and vintage models, and the world's only complete collection of Vanwells. Donington is also home to the world's largest collection of helmets. Heady stuff, indeed!

Espace automobiles Matra
Matra Motorcar Room
17 rue des Capucins, 41200
Romorantin-Lanthenay, France
Tel. (33) 2 54 94 55 55
Mon-Sat 9am-noon, 2-6pm,
Sun 10am-noon, 2-5pm

A joint effort by the town of
Romorantin-Lanthenay and the Motor
Company, Matra, founded this collec-
tion in 1974. Matra (Mechanique Aviation et TRAaction) was established in 1941, and over the years produced a series of roadcars. In the mid 1960s they bought the small racing car company of René Bonnetto, especially well known for its Panhard Le Mans prototypes, and fast cars soon gave the company a higher profile. The collection here traces the company's successes with road, race, and sports racing cars from 1963.

Classical racing cars
Brooklands Museum

Galleria Ferrari
The Ferrari Gallery
Via Dino Ferrari 43, 41053 Maranello, Italy
Tel. (39) 0536 943204 www.commune.maranello.modena.it
Tue-Sun 9.30am-12.30pm, 3-6pm

Ninety-two years after the birth of Enzo Ferrari, the Galleria Ferrari was opened at Maranello, also the headquarters of the company today. The exhibition includes both classic racing cars as well as perfectly preserved road models. A number of trophies are on display, including some won by Enzo Ferrari himself, while upstairs is a recreation of the 'Grand Old Gentleman's' study from which Ferrari used to watch his cars being tested on the track outside.

Indianapolis Motor Speedway Hall of Fame Museum
4790 West 16th Street, Indianapolis, Indiana 46222, USA
Tel. (1) 317 484 6747 www.indy500.com
Daily 9am-5pm

The Indy 500 attracts a million visitors each May, a third of whom come just for the day of the race itself – Memorial Day. The Hall of Fame was created in 1952 as a memorial to racing personalities and the development of the automobile industry. The museum sits in the track's infield and houses more than 75 cars, including 34 Indy winners, plus paintings, trophies, and photographs.

International Motorsports Hall of Fame
Speedway Blvd, off I-20, Talladega, Alabama 35160, USA
Tel. (1) 256 362 5002 www.motorsportshalloffame.com
Daily 8am-5pm

The Talladega Superspeedway, home to the Winston 500 and the DieHard 500 races, claims to be the fastest track in the world. The museum complex comprises five show-rooms. In the Daytona Room is Bill Elliott's 1985 Ford Thunderbird, which won the Winston 500 in 1985 as well as the world record for the fastest 500-mile race ever run (at 186.288mph average speed). Talladega has its fair share of eccentricities, including the Budweiser Rocket. More of a missile than a car, the Rocket is 39 feet long (it's only twenty

inches wide), it can accelerate from 1 to 140mph in just one second, and it achieved 739.666 mph at Edwards Air Force Base on 17 December, 1979.

Mercedes-Benz Museum

Mercedesstrasse 137,
70322 Stuttgart,
Germany
Tel. (49) 711 1722578
www.mercedes-benz.com
Tue-Sun 9am-5pm

Mecerdes Racing Car,
6 cylinder, 1906
Mercedes-Benz Museum

More than 110 years of automotive history are on display here. Beautifully crafted cars, like the world's first motor vehicles by Karl Benz (1886 Benz Patent Motor Car) and Gottlieb Daimler's motorised carriage, are historic pieces not to be missed. The early Benz racing car of 1899, produced before Benz & Cie and Daimler-Motoren-Gesellschaft merged in 1926, are mounted like trophies in a display area simulating a racetrack winding itself over several floors. Walking up the 'racetrack' you'll encounter sport cars from the 1920s and 1930s, like the 1924 Mercedes race car and the 1937 Mercedes-Benz W 125 Formula race car that in one year tallied up 27 victories. Photographs, a collection of winners' cups from several decades of racing, and films of famous races complement the collection.

Motor-Sport-Museum Hockenheimring
The Hockenheimring Motorsport Museum
Am Hockenheimring, 68754 Hockenheimring, Baden, Germany
Tel. (49) 6205 6005   www.hockenheimring.de
Daily 10am-5pm

Ever since 1938, when the Motodrom racing circuit was built, Hockenheim in Germany has been a racing town of the first order. At its Motorsport Museum an overview of the history of motorcycle racing is presented, emphasising Motodrom with references to designers, the machines, and a clutch of famous German riders. The heart of the collection was acquired in 1982, when Walter Brandstetter, chief mechanic for Daimler-Benz and a committed racing enthusiast, sold his collection. Among these are a good selection of English bikes, including early Sunbeams, Nortons, Triumphs, and BSAs, plus German BMWs and Italian Moto-Guzzis and Ducatis.

Motorsports Hall of Fame of America
Novi Expo Center, Water Tower, I-96 at Novi Road, Novi, Michigan 4837, USA
Tel. (1) 248 349 7223 www.mshf.com
Daily 10am-5pm

This is a showcase for everything to do with motor racing, and has photos of the personalities, drivers, and manufacturers; racing videos; drivers uniforms; memorabilia; and a collection of cars of all kinds, including Indy cars, stock cars, sports cars, dragsters, race trucks; and openwheelers, as well as champion and record holding race vehicles. Among the highlights is the Ford 999, the oldest vehicle in the collection, which was used to race in 1902. Despite only having one seat, a 'mechanician' was usually kept busy at the back, clinging on for dear life as he oiled bearings and made adjustments during the race. The 999's sister car was the Arrow, which Henry Ford drove across a frozen lake in 1904 at a speed of 91.37mph to take the land speed record. A little before his death, Ford

Horse, end of
19th century
Sportmuseum Vlaanderen

remarked to one of his drivers, Barney Oldfield, 'You made me and I made you'. Oldfield disagreed: 'Old 999 made both of us.'

The National Motor Museum

John Montagu Building, Beaulieu, Hampshire SO42 7ZN, UK
Tel. (44) 1590 612345 www.beaulieu.co.uk
May-Sep: daily 10am-6pm. Oct-Apr: daily 10am-5pm

Anyone with a taste for fast cars is in for a treat at Beaulieu. As well as the hundreds of classic petrol-guzzling sportsters and superbikes, the museum has its fair share of racing machines. These super-charged beasts of the track stretch back to the earliest days of racing, when it was still a gentleman's sport, up to the present day, when it takes big business and a bank balance the size of a Zeppelin airship to even compete. Among the collection are a 1922 Aston Martin 1.5 litre, built for the French Grand Prix at Strasbourg, with a top speed of 95mph, and world record breakers like Bluebird and Golden Arrow.

NHRA Motorsport Museum

Fairplex Gate, 1101 West McKinley Avenue, Ponoma, California 91768, USA
Tel. (1) 909 622 2133
Wed-Sun 10am-5pm

This museum is the dreamchild of 85-year-old Wally Parks, a true dragcar racing enthusiast if ever there was one. Having opened in 1998 after many years of planning, the collection here comprises some fifty vintage and historical racing cars ,as well as trophies, helmets, uniforms, paintings, and other memorabilia which, together, tell the story of American drag racing.

Porsche Automuseum Helmut Pfeifhofer
The Helmut Pfeifhofer Porsche Car Museum

Riesertratte 4a, 9853 Gmünd, Kärnten, Austria
Tel. (43) 4732 2471 www.erlebnis.net
Mid-May-mid-Oct: daily 9am-6pm. Mid-Oct-mid-May: daily 10am-4pm

Grown men have been known to weep when they enter this private Porsche museum opened by Helmut Pfeifhofer in 1982. In 1959, Pfeifhofer bought his first Porsche 356 and arduously restored it. Hooked by the beauty and speed of these cars, his collection grew quickly. The centrepiece of the collection is a Porsche from the very first Gmünd series, with its hand-beaten aluminium body work and chassis number 20. Besides the prize exhibit, the collection contains a fine selection of cars Porsche designed for the firms Austro-Daimler, Steyr, and VW, along with other Porsche racing cars that have performed on race tracks all over the world.

OLYMPIC AND SPORT COLLECTIONS

Amateur Athletic Foundation

2141 West Adams Boulevard, Los Angeles, California 90018, USA
Tel. (1) 323 730 4600
www.aafla.org
Library: Mon-Fri 10am-5pm, Wed 10am-7.30pm, first and last Sat of each month 10am-3pm

An amazing resource spread over three buildings. Among the library's strengths

Medal, pressed into
cardboard, from
Olympic tournament
held at the prisoner of
war camp at Gross Born
in 1944
*Muzeum Sportu i Turystyk*i

are its Olympic holdings. You'll find the official report of every modern Olympic games, as well as dozens of oral histories. The library's collection of sports artefacts is equally impressive, with items from the Olympics making up the largest section. Besides works of art and sporting memorabilia, it contains a wealth of sporting ephemera, posters of the Olympic Games, a philatelic collection of Olympic stamps from around the world, and a number of objects from the Los Angeles Olympic Games of 1932 and 1984.

Basketball Hall of Fame
1150 West Columbus Avenue, Springfield, Massachusetts 01101, USA
Tel. (1) 413 781 6500 www.masslive.com
Daily 9.30am-5.30pm

Oil painting of Lili Kronberger (1890-1974), first Hungarian world champion of figure skating (above)
Testnevelési és Sportmúzeum

Sabre Fencing Challenge Trophy awarded to the gold medal team at the 1912 Stockholm Olympic Games (above right)
Testnevelési és Sportmúzeum

Brass fruit dish awarded to the boxing champion of the first competition of the Hungarian Athletic Club in 1875 (right))
Testnevelési és Sportmúzeum

Basketball was invented by James Naismith in 1891 when he was asked to find a way of alleviating the boredom students at the local YMCA experienced during winter. Up went two peach baskets at approximately ten feet, so the more aggressive players could not just hurl the ball into them. Backboards were added, as well as chicken wire around the playing space to keep wildly enthusiastic fans out. The birthplace of the sport is a fitting place for this museum. Besides honouring the game's greats, there are displays of early baskets, including those where you had to pull a rope to get the ball out.

British Olympic Association
1 Wandsworth Plain, London SW18 1HE, UK
Tel. (44) 20 8871 2677 www.olympics.org.uk
Mon-Fri 9am-5pm by appt. only

A collection of approximately 1,500 volumes, mostly official reports of the Olympics, including papers appertaining to proceedings. Memorabilia relating to the history of the Olympics includes items from the games hosted in Britain in 1908 and 1948, among which is a rugby ball from the 1908 games, the flag from the same year, and the torch from the 1948 games.

Deutsches Sport- und Olympia-Museum
The German Sports and Olympic Museum
Rheinauhafen 1, 50678 Cologne, Germany
Tel. (49) 221 3360953
www.sportmuseum.koeln.de
Tue, Wed, Fri 10am-6pm, Thu 10am-8pm, Sat-Sun 11am-7pm

The museum is situated in a former customs and storehouse in the docks of Cologne. Its permanent exhibition takes the visitor on a journey through more than 100 years of sport, from the sport of ancient Greece to the German gymnastic movement, from the development of English sport to the modern Olympic Games and the contemporary world of sports. The collections include 100,000 sporting items ranging from sportswear, equipment, medals, certificates and awards, to posters, objects, graphic art, photographs, and much more.

Musée de l'Escrime Charles Debeur
The Charles Debeur Museum of Fencing
12 rue Général Thys, 1050 Brussels, Belgium
Tel. (32) 2 6486932 www.synec-doc.be
By appt. only

The museum is dedicated to sport-fencing and exhibits some of the first electrical scoring apparatus, masks, and gloves, as well as old sport-fencing weapons including the three types; foils, epées, and sabres. Five hundred posters, mounds of archival material, and well over 1,000 medals, complete the collection.

Fundación Pedro Ferrándiz
The Pedro Ferrándiz Foundation
Edificio 'Borislav Stankovic', Avenida de la Guindalera 22, Arroyo de la Vega, 28100 Alcobendas, Madrid, Spain
Tel. (34) 91 662 1913   www.leader.es
Mon-Fri 9.30am-1pm, 3-8pm

Conceived by Pedro Ferrándiz, the Real Madrid club coach during the 1960s and 70s, a unique architectural complex dedicated to basketball was built for the study and promotion of the sport. The world's biggest library on basketball is housed here, filled with thousands of books and specialist magazines, as well as a newspaper archive, a photographic archive (with some 100,000 images), and a videotape library. It contains the oldest basketball book in the world, written in 1897.

Het Kaatsmuseum
The Pelota Museum
Voorstraat 2, 8801 Franeker, The Netherlands
Tel. (31) 517 393910
www.knkb.nl
May-Oct: Tue-Sat 1-5pm
(groups by appt. all year)

Played since the end of the Middle Ages in Holland and France (there known as *jeu de paume*) pelota was originally a sport for the nobility. Soon, the common man discovered the fun he was missing out on and started playing in the streets and squares of the town. When the noise from playing began to disturb church services, and mis-thrown balls broke one too many church windows, the game was prohibited on Sundays. Opened in 1972, this museum is the oldest sports museum in Holland.

Arte dell'Armi, work on fencing by Achille Marozzo, Venice, 1568 (top)
The Schmitter Fencing Collection

From the fencing book *L'école des armes* by Domenico Angelo, London, 1763 (above)
The Schmitter Fencing Collection

Musée national du Sport
The National Museum of Sport
Parc des Princes, 24 rue de Commandant-Guilbaud, 75016 Paris, France
Tel. (33) 1 40 45 99 12   www.paris.org
Mon-Sat 9.30am-12.30pm, 2-5pm, Sun 10.30am-12.30pm, 2-6pm

Founded in 1988 by the French collector and sportsman, Jean Durry, the collections are extremely diverse and number nearly 100,000 items. Strengths of the collection include: a unique set of around 200 books on fencing from the 16th to the 18th centuries; a remarkable poster collection dating from 1850 to the present day, with examples by a number of artists, including Toulouse-Lautrec; a significant tennis collection; and a periodic collection of 1,400 titles, together with photographs and a large collection of stamps and autographs by sporting heroes.

Nederlands Sportmuseum
The Dutch Sports Museum
Museumweg 10, 8242 PD Lelystad, The Netherlands
Tel. (31) 320 261010   www.gokids.nl
Tue-Fri 10am-5pm, Sat-Sun noon-5pm

Many of the items in this collection are private gifts and include thousands of photos (250,000), books (40,000), sports awards (1,500), advertising material, films (1,500), newspaper articles, shirts, shoes, hats, hockey sticks, tennis rackets, and football shoes. A general overview of Dutch sport is provided, in addition to exhibits on the Olympics.

Musée Olympique
The Olympic Museum
1 quai d'Ouchy, 1001 Lausanne, Switzerland
Tel. (41) 21 621 6511 www.museum.olympic.org
Tue-Sun 9am-6pm (Thu until 8pm) plus Mon 9am-6pm from May-Sep only

Over five floors the visitor can acquire a vision of the Games which is both global and, at the same time, detailed. A room dedicated to Ancient Greece illustrates the modest origins of the event and recalls the most famous athletes, the main sporting events, and the ceremonies of the time. The exhibition follows the evolution of the Games up to the

founding of the IOC in 1894 and the celebration, two years later, of the first modern Olympic Games. The rich and varied collection includes 1,300 autographs of medallists, the torches used to carry the flame, as well as medals, flags, and certificates.

The Schmitter Fencing Collection
Michigan State University Libraries, Special Collections Division, 100 Library, East Lansing, Michigan 48824, USA
Tel. (1) 517 355-3770 www.lib.msu.edu
Mon-Fri 9am-5pm

Olympic poster by
Zygmunt Kaminski, 1928
(above)
Muzeum Sportu i Turistyki

From the poster *The
Football Player* by Alfred
Ost (below right)
Sportmuseum Vlaanderen

The Charles and Ruth Schmitter Fencing Collection is the gift of Charles Schmitter, the university's retired fencing coach. It numbers almost 1,000 titles in thirteen languages, spanning four centuries. Highlights of the collection include works by two of the great 16th-century Italian fencing masters. Achille Marozzo's *Opera Nova*, which first appeared in 1536, was the first work to attempt to fix uniform rules for the use of weapons. Notable English works include two titles by the 'Scots Fencing Master' Sir William Hope, whose treatises *The Compleat Fencing Master* (1692) and *A New, Short, and Easy Method of Fencing* (1707) were among the most celebrated English fencing works of the late 17th and early 18th centuries.

Sportmuseum Berlin
The Berlin Sports Museum
Hanns-Braun-Strasse, 14053 Berlin, Charlottenburg, Germany
Tel. (49) 30 3058390 www.stadtmuseum.de
By appt. only

Contained here is the largest and most varied holding on the history of German sport. Comprising some 45,000 items, it represents the history of athletics, sports and games in Berlin, when it was an Olympic city, and the development of sports both nationally and internationally. Focal points include the Olympic movement, the history of athletics and gymnastics, as well as the history of sports in Eastern Germany and the Jewish sports movement.

Muzei sporta 'Luzhniki'
The Museum of Sport 'Luzhniki'
Luzhniki 24,
119048 Moscow,
Russian
Federation
Tel. (7) 095 2010072
Mon-Fri 10am-5pm

The museum,
which was
founded in 1957
during the 6th
World Youth and
Students Festival in Moscow, is situated underneath the eastern stand of the sports arena at Luzhniki. It houses the biggest collection of sporting memorabilia in the country. The museum owns a unique collection of prizes and medals won by sportsmen in international competitions and world and European championships.

Challenge trophy of
Buschbach (far left)
Testnevelési és Sportmúzeum

Photograph of Alf
Goullet (left)
The US Bicycling Hall of Fame

Sportmuseum Vlaanderen
The Sports Museum in Flanders
Tervuursevest 101, 3001 Leuven, Belgium
Tel. (32) 16 225438   www.sportimonium.be
By appt. only

Started more than twenty years ago with a research programme at the University of Leuven to preserve sports heritage, it has since joined with the Vlaamse Volkssport Centrales which studies and promotes traditional games. Their mission is to conserve sporting material and use these objects to tell the story of sport, both in Flanders and internationally. More than 6,000 objects have been amassed, from sporting equipment to trophies, posters, books, photographs, and paintings.

Muzeum Sportu i Turystyki
The Museum of Sports and Tourism
Ulitsa Wawelska 5, Stadion, 02034 Warsaw, Poland
Tel. (48) 22 8254851
Tue-Sun 10am-6pm

At last count, the collections consisted of more than 43,000 exhibits, most connected with Polish sport. Besides the trophies, medals, badges, plaques, sport and tourist badges, coins, banners, flags, emblems, and posters there are sport clothes, related art, and postage stamps. Among these are the jacket worn by the hockey player Kazimierz Sokolowski in the 12th Olympic Games in Lake Placid in 1932, and souvenirs from the Olympic Games organised in prisoner of war camps in 1940 and 1944 which encapsulate the true spirit of the games.

Suomen Urheilumuseo
The Sports Museum of Finland
Olympia Stadion, 00250 Helsinki, Finland
Tel. (358) 9 4342250   www.stadion.fi
Mon-Fri 11am-5pm, Sat-Sun noon-4pm. Photography archives: Mon-Fri 8am-4pm

The core of the museum's extensive collection are the skis gathered together by the Finns at the beginning of the 1930s, numbering around 1,000 pairs. Other major groups

of articles are prize and remembrance medals, awards, and badges representing innumerable sports. A notable special collection comprises items related to the Helsinki Olympic Games of 1952 and includes photographs, prints, and books. The museum's best known objects are the gilded spike and stopwatch of nine-time Olympic winner, Paavo Nurmi.

Gold-plated commemorative medal of the 1896 Games
Modern Olympic Games Museum

Mouséio synchronon olympiakon agonon
Modern Olympic Games Museum
270 65 Ancient Olympia, Greece
Tel. (30) 1 6878 809 13 www.ioa.org.gr
Mon-Sat 8am-3.30pm, Sun & public holidays 9am-2.30pm

Founder Georgios Papastephanou-Provatakis was an art-lover, philatelist, and sportsman who gathered documents, records, and anything relating to the Olympic games over the course of many years. So abundant was his collection and his desire to share it with others that, in 1961, he purchased an old primary school building and dedicated his life to transforming it into exhibition space. The collection excels in commemorative items, including one of the most exhaustive collections of stamps issued for the Olympic Games.

Testnevelési és Sportmúzeum
The Museum of Physical Education and Sports
Dózsa György út 3, 1143 Budapest, Hungary
Tel. (36) 1 2521696 www.sportmuzeum.hu
Tue-Thu, Sat-Sun 10am-4.30pm

Early 19th-century collections were destroyed during World War II, however today, the collections contain more than 350,000 items. Numerous highlights include objects associated with sabre fencing, a sport in which Hungary excels and has won 32 Olympic gold medals. A prized item is the sabre fencing Challenge Trophy awarded to the gold medal team at the Stockholm Olympic Games (1912) which was sculpted by Ede Teltsch (1872-1948). Besides prizes, the vast collection contains portraits and memorabilia of great sportsmen across all sporting events.

The US Bicycling Hall of Fame
166 West Main Street, Sommerville, New Jersey 08876, USA
Tel. (1) 908 722 3620 www.usbhof.com
Mon-Fri noon-3pm

The spotlight here is on both competitive and recreational cycling. Bicycles, trophies, medals, news clips, photographs, and jerseys (including Greg LeMond's yellow jersey from his first Tour de France in 1986) commemorate the sport's most significant athletes. To date, 58 bicycling luminaries have been inducted into the Hall. A special exhibition area is dedicated to Frank Louis Kramer, who devoted 25 years to the sport, sweeping up medals and trophies, setting records, and basically dominating the sport for most of his career.

RUGBY, FOOTBALL AND BOXING

Ajax Museum
Arena Boulevard 29, 1101 AX Amsterdam Zuidoost,
The Netherlands
Tel. (31) 20 311 13 36 www.ajax.nl
Daily 9am-6pm (times vary during major events in the arena)

This high-tech, multi-functional stadium with a retractable glass roof (tours can be booked to visit the stadium), is home to Ajax football club. A leading European team with an outstanding record, the museum focuses on the team's illustrious history, tracing the development of the club from the 1890s to the present day. Pictures of one of the three founders, Han Dade, kitted out in the first red and white outfit of the team, serve as an introduction to the part of the museum dealing with the early years.

College Football Hall of Fame
111 South St Joseph Street, South Bend, Indiana 44601, USA
Tel. (1) 219 2359999 www.collegefootball.org
Jan-May: daily 10am-5pm. Jun-Dec: daily 10am-7pm

Collected by the National Football Foundation for nearly thirty years before a museum opened, items on display include footballs, uniforms, trophies, and an assortment of personal pieces of memorabilia. The most prized possessions are a jersey worn by Red Grange of Illinois, and the helmet of Jay Berwanger, the first Heisman Trophy winner.

Degerfors Fotbollsmuseum
The Degerfors Football Museum
Degerfors kommun, Lundmark/Berger, Nämndhuset, 69380 Degerfors, Sweden
Tel. (46) 5 8648399 www.degerforsif.se
May-Aug: Tue-Fri, Sun 1-5pm

Ajax Football Club coat of arms
Ajax Museum

Proudly presented through vintage photographs, old football boots, posters, and club badges, is the history of this club which began in 1907. So pleased were they with their newly acquired Premier Division standing, that the museum opened just hours before Degerfors played their first Premier Division home match on 18 April, 1993. As the only museum of its type in the country, it also shines light on other aspects of Swedish football.

Deutsches Boxsportmuseum Sagard
The German Boxing Museum of Sagard

Han Dade and his brother, Johan, c. 1900
Ajax Museum

August-Bebel-Strasse 36, 18551 Sagard, Insel Rügen, Germany
Tel. (49) 38302 2121
Apr-mid Oct: daily 10am-5pm
Mid Oct-Mar: Tue-Fri 10am-5pm, Sat 10am-1pm

Situated in the small village of Sagard on the island of Rügen on the Baltic (population 3,500), this museum is definitely a 'special' attraction. It is the private collection of the passionate collector, Leo Weichbrodt, who proudly states that since opening in 1991, the museum has already had guests from all five continents to admire its 19,000 items. The museum specialises in the history of boxing in Germany and the DDR, but also contains material on international boxing, as well as items owned by famous boxers, including Muhammad Ali.

481

FA Premier League Hall of Fame
County Hall, Riverside Building, Westminster Bridge
Road, London SE1 7PB, UK
Tel. (44) 20 7928 1800 www.hall-of-fame.co.uk
Daily 10am–6pm

Cap and the oldest jersey
in existence
*Museum of Rugby,
Twickenham*

County Hall's FA Premier League of Fame opened in 1999 with the aim
of telling the story of football from the Middle Ages to the present day.
The collection includes videos, photographs, waxworks, and trophies and also a number
of kits donated by famous players such as Bobby Moore and Pele. As well as the obvious
range of exhibits, the collection comprises a fascinating selection of more bizarre trivia:
a Victorian shin pad; cigarette cards from the 1890s; a player's contract from 1910, sign-
ing up Andrew Jackson to Middlesbrough FC for £4 a week; a World War I trench football game; a 1926 biscuit tin showing football scenes and results; and a copy of the
original Subbuteo game, then called 'Newfotty Table Soccer'.

Museu del Futbol Club Barcelona
The Museum of the Football Club Barcelona
Camp Nou Stadium, Aristides Maillol 12–18, 08028 Barcelona, Spain
Tel. (34) 93 4963600
Mon-Sat 10am–6.30pm, Sun 10am–2pm

One of the most famous and successful football clubs in the world, FC Barcelona has its
own museum in the stadium's main grandstand. The first floor traces the course of the
club's history and exhibits the main trophies won by the different sections, as well as
badges, membership cards, sportswear, former players' contracts, and much more. The
second floor contains the FC Barcelona art collection, built up from the two biennials
organised by the club and by donations from the country's leading artists.

James Gilbert Rugby Football Museum
5 St Mathews Street, Rugby, Warwickshire CV21 3BY, UK
Tel. (44) 1788 333888 www.rugby-museum.com
Mon-Fri 9am–5.30pm, Sat 9am–5pm

In 1823, when William Webb Ellis famously took the ball in his arms and ran with it, so
inventing the game of rugby, the chances are that the ball he ran with was made by
William Gilbert, bootmaker to Rugby School, who then had a sideline in manufacturing
sports equipment. The museum, opposite Rugby School, is housed in the old workshop
and contains a huge selection of rugby footballs, from the earliest examples (which
used to be inflated by lung power alone), to high pressure modern laminates. Besides
these, there is 'temple to rugby', fashioned from leather and created for the Great
Exhibition of 1851, plus 4,000 or so items of rugby memorabilia collected by William

England v. New Zealand
official programme, 1936
*Museum of Rugby,
Twickenham*

Gilbert's great, great nephew James Gilbert, who took
over the company after World War I.

International Boxing Hall of Fame
1 Hall of Fame Drive, Canastota, New York 13032, USA
Tel. (1) 315 6977095 www.ibhof.com
Daily 9am–5pm

This Hall of Fame originated from a small town's
desire to honour one of its own sons, Carmen Basillio,
who beat Sugar Ray Robinson in the late 1950s to
become middleweight champion. The museum has
gloves from the beginning of the 20th century, trophies
and fist-casts (visitors can compare their fist with that

of Jack Dempsey or Barney Ross), plus world championship belts, trunks, shoes, and robes which once belonged to legends like Joe Lewis, Willie Pep, and Joe Frazier.

The Calcutta Cup
Museum of Rugby,
Twickeham

Joyce Sports Research Collection

Department of Special Collections, 102 Hesburgh Library, University of Notre Dame, Notre Dame, Indiana 46556, USA
Tel. (1) 219 631 6506   www.sports.nd.edu
Mon-Fri 8am-5pm

These holdings cover a wide range of sports, from American football to boxing and wrestling. The football holdings include monographs, periodicals, annuals, programmes, yearbooks, and microfilmed papers. The *Australian Ring Digest, Big Book of Boxing,* and *The Ring*, among others, can be viewed in the Alanson and Mary Eddy Boxing and Wrestling Collection acquired by the University in 1992. More than 7,500 additional boxing-related images are held in The Harry El. Winkler Photographic Collection, while the Jack Pfefer Wrestling Collection consists of an array of materials gathered over a lifetime by professional wrestling promoter Jacob (Jack) Pfefer.

The Library and Collections of the Scottish Rugby Union

Scottish Rugby Union, Murrayfield, Edinburgh EH12 5PJ, Scotland, UK
Tel. (44) 131 346 5073
Mon-Fri 9am-5pm (collections by appt. only)

Areas for study and research are set aside within the library for those wishing to consult more than 800 books, scrapbooks, and related ephemera primarily associated with Scottish rugby. Several items are quite unique, including a sombre book that records all the home-nation players who fell in World War I, complete with sizeable entries about each one and photos too. Foresight on behalf of the Union meant that collections of memorabilia started coming in as the first international match was played in 1871. Sadly, although there was a museum on the grounds up until 1992, its entire contents, including a replica of the famous Calcutta Cup, a remarkable collection of programmes, boots, balls, and a mound of international rugby shirts are held in store.

Manchester United Museum

Old Trafford, Manchester M16 0RA, UK
Tel. (44) 161 868 8631   www.manutd.com
Daily 9.30am-5pm

Man U's dedicated museum traces the history of the world's most famous club, from its humble origins as a Lancashire railway workers team back in 1878, up to the present day. The museum, opened by Pele in 1998, is brimming with history. As well as a largish collection of memorabilia, including shirts, international caps, medals, ticket stubs, tour blazers, and the club's well-stocked Trophy Room, there are exhibits on the Munich air disaster, a legends gallery, and a room devoted to the club's huge number of fans.

The National Football Museum

Deepdale Stadium, Deepdale, Preston, Lancashire PR1 6RU, UK
Tel. (44) 1772 711600   www.nationalfootballmuseum.com
Tue-Sat 10am-5pm (match days until 7.30pm), Sun & public holidays 11am-5pm

Deepdale Stadium, steeped in football history, was chosen as the location for this new museum, because Preston North End FC were the first winners of the world's oldest professional football league in 1888-89. Two of the new stands in the refurbished stadium house eight distinct collections numbering more than 14,000 objects. A cornerstone of the collection is the FIFA (Fédération Internationale de Football Association) Museum Collection. A varied collection of more than 4,000 items reflects all aspects of the history of English football and contains items like the world's oldest football game (made in Preston, 1884) as well as a collection of more than 500 'Baines Cards' from the 1880s. Recently acquired is the Harry Langton Collection, which includes Arnold Kirke Smith's jersey and cap from the world's first international match between England and Scotland in 1872.

Musée national du Sport
The National Museum of Sport
Parc des Princes, 24 rue de Commandant-Guilbaud, 75016 Paris, France
Tel. (33) 1 40 459912 www.paris.org
Mon-Fri 9.30am-12.30pm, 2-5pm, Sun 10.30am-12.30pm, 2-6pm

The French Committee which organised the 1998 World Cup, together with the National Museum of Sport, gathered together a series of objects manufactured for this enormously popular event. Included in the display is the ball used during the final against Brazil, acquired at Christie's in Glasgow.

Museum of Rugby, Twickenham
Twickenham Stadium, Rugby Road, Twickenham, Middlesex TW1 1DZ, UK
Tel. (44) 208 892 8877 www.rfu.com
Tue-Sat 10am-5pm, Sun 2-5pm

This museum displays and preserves the world's largest and most comprehensive collection of Rugby Union memorabilia. From the time of its formation in 1871 as the world's first national rugby union, the RFU has amassed a large quantity of ephemera, including gifts presented to the England team on their travels around the world, books collected by members of the Union, copies of all Twickenham match programmes, and match tickets. Although many famous items are contained within the collection, pride of place belongs to the most famous rugby trophy in the world – the Calcutta Cup. This wonderful piece of Indian craftsmanship was created in 1877, when the Calcutta Rugby Club in India disbanded and melted down their remaining funds (270 silver rupees) to be turned into a competition prize. This was offered to the RFU to be used as a challenge cup, and ever since 1879 the winning captain of the annual England versus Scotland match has been presented with it. Another great rarity is the only known surviving jersey from the first ever international rugby match played between Scotland and England in 1871.

Scottish Football Museum
Hampden Park, Mount Florida, Glasgow GT42 9BA, Scotland, UK
Tel. (44) 141 332 6372 www.scottishfa.co.uk
Mon-Sat 9am-5pm

Housed in a 4,000-square-metre space in the new South Stand at Hampden Park, Glasgow, the Scottish Football Museum is ambitious in its aims, which are to explore the social history of football. In an effort to answer the question, 'Why is football the most popular game on earth?', the museum looks at a huge range of topics (the origins of the game, commercialism, professional football, junior and women's football, advertising, the fans etc.), as well as collecting together an historically significant array of football-related items. Among the artefacts on display are: the caps prepared for the Estonia v Scotland match on 9 October, 1996, which lasted all of three seconds when Estonia failed to show; issues of *Sick as a Parrot*, one of the first fanzines, which took an irreverent look at the game from the fans' point of view in the 1980s; and the 1900 Rosebery shirt (the primrose and pink racing colours of Archibald Philip Primrose, Lord Rosebery) worn by Scotland on at least nine occasions between 1881 and 1951.

SKIING, ALPINE AND WINTER SPORTS

The Alpine Club

55 Charlotte Road, London EC2A 3QF, UK
Tel. (44) 20 7613 0755 www.alpine-club.org.uk
(Access to archives by appt. only)

The English were the first of the great mountaineers. In fact, it was William Wills from Birmingham who first thought of climbing an alp just for the fun of it. In 1854, he scaled the Wetterhorn and later, with his peers, set about establishing the Alpine Club in 1857 – the first club of its kind in the world and the one upon which all others are modelled. As early as 1858, the club started acquiring reports of expeditions and ascents in the Alps, as well as maps, and now there are some 40,000 items in the collection (25,000 of which are books) spanning the geographical area from pole to pole and everywhere in between. Writers, historians, climbers, and genealogists find the collections indispensable. Memorabilia includes ice picks, boots, odd bits of mountaineering clothing, and the tent belonging to the British mountain climber, writer, and illustrator, Edward Whymper, which he used while climbing the Matterhorn in 1865.

Alpinmuseum Kempten
The Kempten Alpine Museum

Landwehrstrasse, 87439 Kempten, Germany

Tel. (49) 831 15957 www.bayerisches-nationalmuseum.de
Tue-Sun 10am-4pm

The museum, housed in the former royal stables, illustrates man's relationship with the mountains, from the earliest periods of human existence to the first permanent settlements in the Alps. Images and texts from early accounts, descriptions of scientific exploration, as well as artistic, photographic, and cinematic records offer a great impression of the area. There are maps, a herbarium, stuffed animals, and collections of rocks, as well as models of huts, furniture, and equipment.

The American Alpine Club Library

The American Mountaineering Center, 710 Tenth Street, Golden, Colorado 80401, USA
Tel. (1) 303 384 0112 www.americanalpineclub.org
Wed, Fri 8.30am-4.40pm, Tue, Thu noon-7pm

This is the oldest alpine research facility in the US and one of the largest in the world. More than 150 journal titles can be accessed, many acquired through exchanges for the club's publication, the *American Alpine Journal*. There is also a rare book room containing some 4,000 volumes dating from the

Clog skates (top)
*Het Eerste Friese
Schaatsmusem*

Memorabilia celebrating
Norway's ski-jumping
history and successes
(above)
Kongsberg Skimuseum

Norwegian skis made
from ash and bamboo
sticks, *c.* 1850 (left)
*Museo nazionale della
Montagna 'Duca degli
Abruzzi'*

15th century. Artefacts relating to mountaineering in the US and worldwide, including the American flag carried to the summit on the first ascent of Mount Whitney, will soon be on display in the building adjacent to the library, in the yet-to-be-built American Alpine Museum.

Wooden sleigh,
18th century (above)
Museo nazionale della Montagna 'Duca degli Abruzzi'

Wood model showing old technique of climbing (above right)
Museo nazionale della Montagna 'Duca degli Abruzzi'

Fantôme bobsleigh by Duffaud & Sting, probably after 1910 (below)
Schweizer Sportmuseum

Club alpin Français d'Ile-de-France
The French Alpine Club of Ile-de-France
24 av de Laumière, 75019 Paris, France
Tel. (33) 1 53 72 87 13   www.clubalpin.idf.free.fr
Tue, Wed 1.30-6.30pm, Thu 1.30-8pm, Fri 1.30-5.30pm, Sat 8.30am-12.30pm

The club's documentation centre is a gold mine of information. Since 1981, when it replaced the original library which was established at the time of the club's foundation in 1874, it has offered a wide range of material and literature to club members and the public alike. The library contains more than 10,000 volumes (some from before 1874) on alpinism and canyonism throughout the world.

Musée dauphinois
The Dauphin Museum
30 rue Maurice Gignoux, 38000 Grenoble, France
Tel. (33) 4 76 85 19 01   www.musee-dauphinois.fr
May-Oct: Mon, Wed-Sun 10am-7pm. Nov-Apr: Mon, Wed-Sun 10am-6pm

The museum is housed in the magnificent listed buildings of the former convent of Sainte-Marie-d'en-Haut (1604). It was founded at the beginning of the 20th century by Hippolyte Müller who wished to establish in Grenoble a regional ethnographical museum reflecting local customs and history, of which the winter sport collections are an essential part. The remarkable collection was amassed by Gilbert Merlin, who had

been collecting skis for more than forty years when he decided to sell his collection to the French manufacturers, Rossignol. Subsequently, he was asked by the company to design a display and the result was entitled 'The Great History of Skiing'. Eschewing chronological displays, Merlin opted to take an ethnographic approach and demonstrate the development of the shapes and uses of skis. Did you know that the snowboard was in use 200 years ago?

Het Eerste Friese Schaatsmuseum
The First Frisian Skating Museum
Kleine Weide 1-3, 8713 KZ Hindeloopen, The Netherlands
Tel. (31) 514 521683
Mon-Sat 10am-6pm, Sun 1-5pm

G. Bootsma's passion for collecting anything and everything related to skating is likely to have something to do with the fact that his home town, Hindeloopen, is one of the cities of the famous Efstedentocht (Eleven City Tour) skating event. This is a 200-km skating tour along the frozen canals of Friesland, whose extreme difficulty is only surpassed by its popularity. The race is held only when conditions are cold enough to freeze the canals to sufficient thickness – since it started in 1909 there have been only fifteen races, the last one in 1979. The collection encompasses every aspect of the sport.

Bobsleigh made in Davos, end of 19th / beginning of 20th century
Wintersport Museum

Hiihtomuseo
The Ski Museum
Urheilukeskus, PL 113, 15111 Lahti, Finland
Tel. (358) 3 8144523 www.lahti.fi
Mon-Fri 10am-5pm, Sat-Sun 11am-5pm

Located at the foot of the three majestic ski jumps in the Sports Center of Lahti is this recently renovated museum, designed by Professor Pekka Salminen. There is something for every ski-crazed fan here, from the new exhibition entitled 'Ski Game Spirit and Glistening Snow!' (an historical slice through Finnish competitive skiing), to the evolution of competitive cross-country skiing, and ski jumping as set forth in a presentation of the Lahti Ski Games.

Kongsberg Skimuseum
The Kongsberg Ski Museum
Hyttegata 3, 3602 Kongsberg, Norway
Tel. (47) 32 723200 www.bvm.museum.no
Mid May-Aug: daily 10am-4pm (Jul-mid Aug until 5pm). Sep: daily noon-4pm
Oct-mid May: Sun noon-3pm

One of several museums under the auspices of the Norwegian Mining Museum, it is housed in the old smelting works' premises of the Kongsberg Silver Mines. It celebrates the ski-jumping successes of Kongsberg's sons and daughters on the ski slopes of the world, with display cases crammed with trophies and medals, among which are the awards won by brothers Birger and Sigmund Ruud and Petter Hugsted. Row upon row of skis, along with mannequins dressed in period ski wear, tell of the significant role skiing has played in the history of Norway.

Museo nazionale della Montagna 'Duca degli Abruzzi'
The 'Duke of the Abruzzi' National Museum of the Mountains
Via G Giardino 39, Monte dei Cappuccini, 10131 Turin, Italy
Tel. (39) 011 6604104 www.museomontagna.org
Tue-Fri 8.30am-7.15pm, Sat-Sun 9am-noon, 2-7.15pm

The idea for this museum arose in 1874, when the first members of the Italian Alpine

Club installed an observation post and observatory. In 1901, Prince Luigi of Savoy, Duke of the Abruzzi and honorary president of the local branch, donated to the museum selected items and equipment used on his expedition to the North Pole, and the collections were further enriched by material collected at the International Exhibition held in Turin in 1911. Since then, the museum has been refurbished several times, and in 1981, after a complete renovation, the museum re-opened its doors to the public.

New England Ski Museum

Parkway exit 2, Franconia Notch State Park, Franconia, New Hampshire 03580-0267, USA
Tel. (1) 603 8237177 www.skimuseum.org
Late May-mid Oct: daily noon-5pm. Dec-Mar: Mon, Tue, Fri-Sun noon-5pm

Opened in 1977, this museum contains the largest collection of ski equipment, literature and art in the northeastern US. The artefacts fall into various classes, and include vintage ski equipment and clothing, equipment catalogues and other assorted documents, and photographs. There are around 400 films, from home movies to professionally produced pieces, and a collection of records, awards, and trophies.

Royal Caledonian Curling Club

Carnie House, Avenue K. Ingliston Showground, Newbridge, Edinburgh EH28 2NB, Scotland, UK
Tel. (44) 131 3333003
By appt. only

Founded in 1838, the club's boardroom displays several pictures, including one commemorating the Grand Match played in 1848 between the north and south of Scotland. Assembled on the frozen loch are all the notable curling players with the Royal Palace in the background. There are also a dozen or so curling stones, but the real thrill comes from stepping inside this historic club.

Schweizer Sportmuseum
The Swiss Sports Museum

Missionsstrasse 28, 4003 Basle, Switzerland
Tel. (41) 61 2611221 www.swiss-sports-museum.ch
Mon-Fri 10am-noon, 2-5pm, Sat 1-5pm, Sun 11am-5pm

The museum contains a vast collection of items related to almost every type of sport played in Switzerland, including a vast collection of ski advertising, assorted posters and programmes, as well as items related to other alpine sport competitions and championships. Particularly rare is the museum's collection of telemark posters. On display are several fine old-fashioned examples of skis and ski clothing, including a jumper worn by a member of the 1932 Swiss ski team.

Ice skate from the beginning of the 20th century
Wintersport Museum

Schweizerisches Alpines Museum
The Swiss Alpine Museum

Helvetiaplatz 4, 3005 Berne, Switzerland
Tel. (41) 31 3510434 www.alpinesmuseum.ch
Mon 2-5pm, Tue-Sun 10am-5pm

Founded in 1903 and located north of the Swiss Alps, this museum pays tribute to the mountainous regions of a country that has close associations with skiing and mountaineering. There is an important collection of skis and mountaineering equipment dating from the time of the first winter sports, as well as the equipment used by the pioneer explorers of this magnificent region.

Musée du Ski
The Ski Museum
Maison de la Reine Margot, 63610 Besse-et-Saint-Anastaise, France
Tel. (33) 4 73 79 57 30
Daily 9am-noon, 2-7pm

The museum occupies one room in the Queen Margot House and is crammed full of wooden skis from all over Europe, as well as sledges, ice skates, bobsleighs, and luges. The collection of skis consists of around 120 pairs dating from 1840 to 1940, of which fifty are on display.

Le Musée du Ski et du Bobsleigh
The Ski and Bobsleigh Museum
Centre d'Accueil, Grand Téras, 39220 Les Rousses, France
Tel. (33) 384 60 51 13
Tue, Thu 5-7pm

Ski wear, skis and bindings from the end of the 19th century
Wintersport Museum

Les Rousses on the Franco-Swiss border is the heart of the Jura, which claims to be the birthplace of skiing (although so does Norway). The private collection houses a small but fine selection of some 300 pairs of skis and seven bobsleighs, with the earliest objects dating back to the beginning of the 20th century. The collection is documented with a fine selection of photographs.

Ski-Museum
The Ski Museum
Bangarten 10, 9490 Vaduz, Principality of Liechtenstein
Tel. (423) 75 2321502
Mon-Fri 2-6pm

More than 100 years of skiing history, from its origins to the present day, are represented in this museum owned by Noldi Beck, a former ski racer and expert on the sport. Some 4,000 items, from the first snow-shoes and primitive skis of farmers and hunters, up to the most up-to-date equipment of Olympic and championship racers are on display.

Ski und Heimatmuseum
The Ski and Regional Museum
Karlsbader Strasse 3, 09484 Oberwiesenthal, Germany
Tel. (49) 37348 7521 www.museen-in-sachsen.smwk.de
Mon-Fri 2-5pm, Sat-Sun 10am-noon, 2-5pm

The preparations for the 450-year anniversary procession of Oberwiesenthal uncovered a great number of objects linked with the history of the town and its winter sports' activities. It took a little imagination to go one step further, and in 1983 this museum opened its doors to the public. The exhibition chronicles the development of winter sports through photographs and documents, as well as old skis and equipment, many from their Olympic winners, including Jens Weissflog.

Skimuseet i Holmenkollen
The Ski Museum in Holmenkollen
Kongeveien 5, 0787 Oslo, Norway
Tel. (47) 22 923200 www.skiforeningen.no
Oct-Apr: daily 10am-4pm. Jun-Aug: daily 9am-8pm. May, Sep: daily 10am-5pm

Founded in 1923, this museum is one of the oldest in the world specialising in the history of skiing. As well as a unique set of approximately 2,000 pairs of Norwegian skis from the 20th century, are a number of exhibits featuring the equipment used by Fridtjof

Nansen on his expedition to Greenland in 1888 and by Roald Amundsen who famously beat Scott to the South Pole in 1910-12. Scott's skis, donated by a pioneer Norwegian airman, Trygve Gran, are exhibited in the museum.

'Swan skates'
Het Eerste Friese
Schaatsmuseum

Skøytemuseet
The Ice Skating Museum
At Frogner Stadium, Middelthunsgt. 26, 0302 Oslo, Norway
Tel. (47) 22 434920
Tue, Thu 10am-2pm, Sun 11am-2pm

One of the very few permanent museums in the world dedicated to skating, and the only one in Norway. Cases are crammed full of skates and trophies from all of Norway's skating greats. Documents and photographs provide background information on the triumphs of Norwegian speed skaters. The trophies and medals are a sight to behold; one particularly spectacular trophy, won by a Norwegian skater in St Petersburg during the 1870s, is encrusted with rubies and was awarded by the Tsar of Russia.

Suomen Jääkiekkomuseo
The Finnish Ice Hockey Museum
Museokeskus Vapriikki, Veturinaukio 4, 33101 Tampere, Finland
Tel. (358) 3 31465303
Tue, Thu, Fri, Sat-Sun 10am-6pm, Wed 11am-8pm

A collection of around 10,000 items, from uniforms (more than 500 from across the globe) to sticks. The real treasure is the original Canada Trophy donated in 1950 to the Finnish Ice Hockey Association and played for annually. Other objects include the World Championship Trophy won by Finland in Stockholm in 1995, and an unusual collection of 116 wooden skates from the 19th and early 20th centuries.

Trøndelag Folkemuseum
The Troendelag Folk Museum
Sverresborg alle, 7020 Trondheim, Norway
Tel. (47) 73 890100
Mid May-Aug: daily 11am-6pm. Sep, Dec: Sun noon-4pm

This idyllic open-air museum, with views of the Trondeheimsfjord, is home to more than sixty historic buildings crammed with artefacts mainly from the 18th and 19th centuries. Displays on the history of skiing both as a competitive sport and as a means of transport are housed on the top floor of the old pharmacy building. A pair of skis from the Sami people, dating back 1,000 years, sit side by side with modern trophies and equipment.

Vimpelin suksitehdasmuseo
The Vimpeli Ski Factory Museum
Kangastie 7, 62800 Vimpeli, Finland
Tel. (358) 6 565 1231
Jun-Aug: please call for opening times

The museum describes the ski manufacturing industry of the area between 1919 and 1960. Housed in a former ski factory (operational between 1935-56) the museum's exhibitions include a display of ski manufacturing machines. The extensive collection of skis covers the development of the Finnish ski from the 1910s to the1980s, and has a small selection of military skis, including a pair from World War II (used by a parachute jumper) which could be folded in half.

Wintersport Museum
The Museum of Winter Sports
Promenade 43, 7270 Davos Platz, Switzerland
Tel. (41) 81 4132484
Tue, Thu, Sat 4.30-6.30pm (closed Sat in summer)

The first attempts at skiing in Davos were made as early as 1873; a mere 20 years later the Branger brothers crossed the Maienfelder Pass to Arosa on skis. Ski clothes, skis, and bindings from this period form the central part of the museum's collection, and include Carl Spengler's Lapland skis from 1873. They are unusual in that the right ski measures 285 cm and the left 258 cm – the left is equipped with a bronze point as a defence against wild animals. Davos is also known for the international sport of sledging; the first official race was held here in 1883, thanks to the author John Addington Symonds, who came to cure his tuberculosis in 1877. The world-famous 'Davos' sledge, which became the sledge for unmade runs, and has been copied ever since is also on display. Quite a large area is reserved for the history of ice hockey, including Davos's Hockey Club, and is documented with photographs and early equipment.

Yosemite Climbing Archives
Ahwahnee Hotel, Yosemite National Park, California 95389, USA
Tel. (1) 209 3728396
Daily during hotel hours

Climbing historian and big wall veteran climber, Mike Corbett, is founder and curator of this private collection of climbing memorabilia spanning more than sixty years. Cases in the hotel are crammed with rock climbing equipment, newspaper articles, and books highlighting epic ascents in the park. Learn about John Salathé's climb with Ax Nelson in 1946; they climbed the southwest face of Half Dome in twenty hours with no bolts. Displayed on the walls are pitons and carabiners used by Spanish, French, and Austrian climbers.

Pair of skis, late 19th century
Wintersport Museum

Zentralbibliothek des Schweizer Alpen-Clubs
The Central Library of the Swiss Alpine Club
Zentralbibliothek Zürich, Zähringerplatz 6, 8025 Zurich, Switzerland
Tel. (41) 1 268310   www-zb.unizh.ch
Reading room: Mon-Fri 8am-8pm, Sat 8am-4pm. Map collection: Mon-Fri 2-6pm, Sat 2-4pm

The history of alpine literature began in the mid 19th century with the foundation of alpine organisations all over Europe. These organisations published magazines and reports of expeditions and ascents, meeting the increasing demand by the Victorians for alpine literature. The Central Library of the Swiss Alpine Club was founded in 1890 and, despite its humble beginnings, it became one of the six greatest alpine libraries in the world. Books and magazines were acquired in exchange for the library's own publications, and added to these were donations from well-known alpinists. The purchase of the library of W. A. B. Coolidge (an eccentric American who climbed the Alps with his aunt and a dog in the 1870s) has further enhanced the collection.

TENNIS, SQUASH AND RELATED SPORTS

Collection of the Honorary Custodian of the Squash Racquet ssociation & National Squash Library
Ian Wright, 50 Tredegar Road, Wilminton, Dartford, Kent DA2 7AZ, UK
Tel. (44) 1322 272200
By appt. only

For the passionate squash enthusiast this is the collection to consult, and Mr Wright is the man. This complete collection of squash books amassed by Wright is one-of-a-kind. Among his favourite volumes is that written in 1929 by Charles Read, the first British Open Champion. It focuses on the unspoken etiquette of the game. He writes, 'If your opponent hits you in your private parts, just turn and politely smile back, for it was undoubtedly an accident, rather than a shot done with this in mind.'

Various early tilt top rackets, including the only know example (far left) of the Henry V model lawn tennis racket, 1878 *The Jaeger Tennis Heritage Collection*

The Gurney Collection

Gerald Gurney, Guildhall Orchard, Mary Lane North, Great Bromley, Colchester, Essex CO7 7TU, UK
Tel. (44) 1206 230330
By appt. only

Mention Mr Gerald Gurney to keen collectors of racket sport memorabilia and, if they have not met him, they will certainly known of him. As founder of the Tennis Collectors' Society in 1988, he has signed up more than 200 members worldwide and publishes a journal several times a year to keep them informed of the market and the history surrounding the sport. He displays his collection around the house. Thankfully his wife, who is also a collector, but a collector of swimming costumes, can relate to his obsession and tolerates having tennis items dominating every wall and corner.

International Tennis Hall of Fame Museum

194 Bellevue Avenue, Newport, Rhode Island 02840, USA
Tel. (1) 401 8493990   www.tennisfame.org
Daily 9.30am–5pm

Originally a casino for the Rhode Island's fabulously wealthy set, millions of pounds have since turned this Hall of Fame into a 13,000-square-foot masterpiece, complete with player memorabilia, audiovisuals, and hands-on interactives. The Early Tennis Galleries display early lawn tennis equipment and the elegant costumes of the Victorian era, while the Court Tennis Gallery shows the evolution of the game from courtyards in French monasteries to the walled game of court, or real tennis.

The Jaeger Tennis Heritage Collection

Costa Mesa, California 92628, USA
Tel. (1) 714 662 0937 www.tennisheritage.com

A travelling exhibit which the owner, Rolf Jaeger, makes available to tennis enthusiasts worldwide. He has achieved his goal, 'to keep the memory of the sport alive', by amassing, over the last thirty years, thousands of items relating to the game. There are 1,300 original rackets, including one dating from 1860, and a tilt-top racket from around 1878. There's a selection of rackets with unusual handles and stringing variations, demonstrating the continual ingenuity of the makers.

Sveriges Tennismuseum
National Tennis Museum
Köpmansgatan 2, 26935 Båstad, Sweden
Tel. (46) 4 3171672   www.bastad.se
Summer: daily 10am-6pm. Rest of year: groups by appt. only

The museum records the early days of the sport in Sweden and moves through the
intervening decades to bring the visitor up-to-date with tennis on an international level.
Photographs, clothes, trophies, books, and rackets from the Swedish tennis wonders
Björn Borg and Stefan Edberg grace the displays, while the archives hold more than
12,000 photographs relating to the sport. It is by far the largest collection in Sweden.

Mats Wilander
Sveriges Tennismuseum

Musée du Tennis
The Tennis Museum
Stade de Roland-Garros, 2 ave Gordon Bennett, 75016
Paris, France
Tel. (33) 1 47 434800   www.fft.fr
Opening in 2002; please call for details

This new museum is housed in the famous Roland
Garros stadium in Paris. Set up by a foundation that is
part of the French Tennis Federation, most of the items
have come via private donations and acquisitions from
auctions, or are loans. The collection features approximately 500 rackets and a large collection of posters.
Among the more curious items is an Andy Warhol
portrait of Chris Evert.

The Tennis Court
Lord's Ground, St John's Wood, London NW8 8QN, UK
Tel. (44) 20 7432 1013

Adjacent to the MCC Museum is a real (royal) tennis court opened in 1900. Played at
Lords since 1838, the original court was on the site of the present Mound Stand. Watch
players from the comfort of leather armchairs that line the room, have a cup a tea or
peruse the plaques listing the champions of the sport, among them, J. M. Heathcote, one
of the great players who won the Gold Racquet between 1867-79. Ask to see the Dedans
Display area where cases of real tennis trophies are on display.

Wimbledon Lawn Tennis Museum
The All England Lawn Tennis & Croquet Club, Church Road, Wimbledon, London
SW19 5AE, UK
Tel. (44) 20 8946 6131
www.wimbledon.org
Daily 10.30am-5pm
(open only to tourna-
ment visitors during
the Championships)

A museum rich in
tennis memorabilia,
including Boris
Becker's autograph
and a headband worn
by Pat Cash, the high-
light for some visitors

Early Horsman
lawn tennis set
*International Tennis
Hall of Fame Museum*

Artefacts and documentation of the game, both past and present (above)
International Tennis Hall of Fame Museum

The Golden Era Gallery celebrating champions from the 1920s and 30s with Suzanne Lenglen (above right)
International Tennis Hall of Fame Museum

will be the simple fact that they are standing on the site of the world-famous Wimbledon championships. The social and sporting history of the game is described through mock-ups of an Edwardian garden tennis party, a racket maker's workshop, an original gentlemen's dressing room, and a Victorian parlour with a collection of tennis objects. The Ladies' Costume Gallery demonstrates the radical changes that have taken place in women's tennis fashion, with examples ranging from the 1880s to the present day.

WATER SPORTS

Henley Royal Regatta Library and Collections

Regatta Headquarters, Henley-on-Thames, Oxfordshire RG9 2LY, UK
Tel. (44) 1491 572153 www.hrr.co.uk
By appt. only

The first Henley Regatta was held in 1839, originally as a public attraction along with a fair. Today, this most popular sport is serious business for the town, with crews from more than 86 countries competing in seventeen events for an array of trophies. The focal points of the library include a collection of books, mostly from the 20th century, on the Henley Royal Regatta and other key English rowing races, along with schools' rowing records, many of which go back to the beginning of the 19th century and earlier. There are also displays of winners' medals, and a trophy room jam-packed with regatta trophies.

International Surfing Museum

411 Olive Avenue, Huntington Beach, California 92648, USA
Tel. (1) 714 9603483 www.surfingmuseum.org
Mon, Wed-Sun noon-5pm (Wed-Sun only in winter)

For some, surfing is not merely a passion, it's a way of life, a reason for existing. That seems to be the case for the people here, who have put together a collection of some of the sport's most significant artefacts. Surfing originated in Hawaii and it was an Hawaiian, Duke Kahanamoku (an Olympic swimming champion), who became the sport's first ambassador, doing much to popularise it in the early 1920s. The museum has several of his trophies and also one of his wooden surfboards. Alongside these, visitors can see how the surfboard has developed from the centuries-old hardwood boards (planks, really) of the Hawaiian Islands, to the finned, fibreglass, balsa and foam boards of today.

International Swimming Hall of Fame
One Hall of Fame Drive, Fort Lauderdale, Florida 33316, USA
Tel. (1) 954 462 6536   www.ishof.org
Mon-Fri 9am-7pm, Sat-Sun 9am-5pm

A showcase for all aquatic sports, from swimming and diving to water polo and even synchronised swimming, this museum is filled with memorabilia, books, and manuscripts. In an elevated, wave-shaped building set along the ocean, swimsuits, goggles, pins, badges, diplomas, certificates, and more than sixty Olympic, national and club uniforms and warm-ups recall the sportsmen and women who have made their name in the sport. Technically-minded visitors will enjoy seeing the first automatic timing machine developed by Max Ritter in 1955.

Leander Club
Henley-on Thames, Oxfordshire RG9 2LP, UK
Tel. (44) 1491 575782   www.museums.reading.ac.uk
By appt. only

One of the oldest rowing clubs in Britain, its first home in 1818 was opposite the Houses of Parliament, where several other schools sited their clubhouses. It was in 1897 that they moved to their permanent home at Henley. Inside the club, a painting of their original home sets the scene for this most historic collection. Apart from data on the regatta, there are almanacs, membership lists, school records, books on the Thames, and a selection of photographs of various crews.

The National Rowing Foundation and the G. W. Blunt White Library
Mystic Seaport, Mystic, Connecticut 06355, USA
Tel. (1) 860 572 5367   www.mysticseaport.org
Mon-Fri 10.30am-5pm, Sat 11am-4pm

The library is home to the National Rowing Foundation's E.G.H. Moody's collection of books. Moody was a retired editor and publisher who rowed at Henley in the 1930s and later became a coach and Steward. It includes a large number of volumes on English rowing by classic rowing authors, including Cook, Dodd, Fairbairn, Page, and Woodgate.

The Rowing Gallery
River and Rowing Museum

River and Rowing Museum
Mill Meadows, Henley-on-Thames, Oxfordshire RG9 1BF, UK
Tel. (44) 1491 415600   www.rrm.co.uk
Apr-Oct: Mon-Sat 10am-5pm, Sun 11am-5pm
Nov-Mar: Mon-Sat 10am-4pm, Sun 11am-4pm

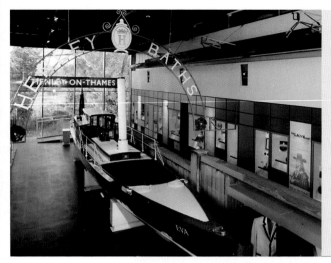

Housed in a building which looks much like an upturned boathouse on stilts, this museum fits perfectly into its picturesque river setting along the Thames. Using a unique collection of rowing boats and related rowing items, three interlinked topics are explored: the Thames; the sport of rowing; and the history of Henley, which includes a detailed account of its celebrated regatta. The ceiling of one gallery is hung with racing sculls and boats, old and new, including the gold-medal-winning boat powered by Steve Redgrave and Matthew Pinsent at the 1996 Olympic Games in Atlanta, and the boat which won the first Oxford and Cambridge boat race at Henley in 1829.

The Henley Gallery
(above)
River and Rowing Museum

Commemorative oar
(right)
River and Rowing Museum

The Museum of Yachting

Fort Adams State Park, Newport, Rhode Island 02840, USA
Tel. (1) 401 847 1018   www.moy.org
Mid May-Oct: daily 10am-5pm (off season by appt.)

This is the heart of New England's yachting scene, rich with maritime traditions reaching back to the founding of the state. The museum is proud to have as its flagship the two-time America's Cup winner, *Courageous*. There is a display of restored classic yachts dating from 1890-1955, including a collection of Beetle Cats and *Bris*, a Swedish pocket cruiser which sailed single-handed across the Atlantic. Inside, the Small Craft Gallery displays classic one-design, sail and power boats. Photographs, models, and related artefacts describe more than 140 years of the America Cup races held in Newport waters from 1930-1983.

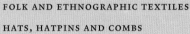

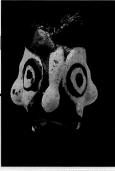

BEADS

Allard Pierson Museum
Oude Turfmarkt 127, 1012 GC, Amsterdam,
The Netherlands
Tel. (31) 20 5252556 www.uba.uva.nl
Tue-Fri 10am-5pm, Sat-Sun 1-5pm

Five Phoenican 'face
beads' (above left)
Allard Pierson Museum

Two of the four faces of an
Egyptian 'face bead' from
Carthage (above right and
below)
Allard Pierson Museum

This museum houses a study collection of 20,000 beads that once belonged to Dr W. G. N. van der Sleen and also possesses collars of beads from Egypt, Iran, and the Graeco-Roman world. This worldwide collection encompasses all periods. Especially well represented are beads from Africa, India, and Indonesia.

The Bead Museum and Study Centre
400 7th Street NW, Washington, DC 20004, USA
Tel. (1) 202 624 4500 www.thebeadmuseum.org
Mon-Wed, Fri 11am-4pm, Sun 1-4pm

Founded in 1994, the museum has been building its permanent collection of beads, reference, and study materials. Additions include a large six-layer, blue, red and white Venetian chevron bead from Zaire, a round blue Ptolemic or Roman bead found in Mali, and a fine two-tone glass bead with mosaic eyes found in the Djenne digs of central Mali.

The Bead Museum
5754 W Glenn Drive, Glendale, Arizona 85301, USA
Tel. (1) 623 931 2737 www.thebeadmuseum.com
Mon-Sat 10am-5pm (Thu until 8pm), Sun 11am-4pm

A gigantic collection of beads and adornments originating from cultures past and present. Displays are arranged thematically and include necklaces made of organic materials (wood, nuts, seeds, shells, amber, and animal teeth) which have been used as trade objects, forms of currency, or in rituals (the word 'bead' is derived from the Anglo-Saxon *beade* or *bede* and refers to prayer).

The Corning Museum of Glass
One Museum Way, Corning, New York 14830, USA
Tel. (1) 607 974 8274 www.cmog.org
Daily 9am-5pm (Jul, Aug until 8pm)

No glass collection worth its salt would be without examples of beads, and this collection, one of the most comprehensive in the world, contains the Lamb and Oliphant trade bead collections as well as examples of ancient beads.

Denver Museum of Nature and Science
2001 Colorado Boulevard, Denver, Colorado 80205, USA
Tel. (1) 303 322 7009 www.dmns.org
Daily 9am-5pm

An outstanding holding of beads which includes excavated specimens, some of them among America's oldest. The Crane collection has a superior collection of beadwork. An unusual wampum belt is a prized holding. The collection continues to grow through donations, and the museum has founded a Bead Study Group.

Pascack Historical Society Museum
19 Ridge Avenue, Park Ridge, New Jersey, USA
Tel. (1) 201 573 0307
Sun 2-4.30pm

Pascack was the site of a wampum mint from 1775 until 1889, set up by John W. Campbell. These cylindrical beads, made from the ends of shells, were traded for furs with the North American Indians, and made into ornaments and jewellery. Most wampum was laboriously manufactured by hand, but the Campbells invented a machine capable of drilling holes through six long shells at once, which greatly increased production, enabling them to produce up to 400 a day. The museum possesses what is believed to be the only wampum machine remaining in the US.

Picard Trade Bead Museum

27885 Berwick Drive, Carmel, California 93923, USA
Tel. (1) 831 624 4138 www.picardbeads.com
Mon-Sat 11am-5pm

A massive collection of beads dedicated to
the history and aesthetics of the bead
trade in Africa through the
centuries, amassed by
world collectors John
and Ruth Picard. Although
the main emphasis is on Venetian
and African beads, there are examples from
Bohemia, Holland, France, and Germany.

Skive Museum

Havnevej 14, 7800 Skive, Denmark
Tel. (45) 9752 6933
Mon-Fri 11-5pm, Sat-Sun 2-5pm

A large amber bead-find dating from the Neolithic period, discovered in the moors near Mollerup during World War II. Originally, this hoard of 1,300 beads would have been buried as an offering to the gods.

Millefiori beads from the
West African Trade
Picard Trade Bead Museum

Tropenmuseum
The Museum of the Tropics

Linnaeusstraat 2, 1092 AD, Amsterdam, The Netherlands
Tel. (31) 20 5688215 www.kit.nl
Mon-Fri 10am-5pm, Sat-Sun noon-5pm (bead collection by appt. only)

Ten thousand different Venetian beads, originally the samples of Silk & Co., were given to the museum when they closed their Amsterdam branch in 1920. Many of these beads did not come into general production and are, therefore, extremely rare. All are in mint condition.

Museo vetrario di Murano - Sezione antico
The Murano Glass Museum - Antique Section

Palazzo Giustinian, Fondamenta Giustinian 8, 30141 Venice, Italy
Tel. (39) 041 739586
Apr-Sep: Mon-Tue, Thu-Sun 10am-5pm. Oct-Mar: Mon-Tue, Thu-Sun 10am-4pm

The museum offers a fine selection of Venetian glass beads, a tradition taken over from the Romans and then by the Bohemians. Apart from the mirrors which became a major Murano export during the 15th century, they produced small beads of glass. Many of these were taken to Africa by white traders as barter for gold, ivory, or palm-nut oil. Alongside some exquisite beaded necklaces there is also a selection of *paternostri* (Italian glass prayer beads).

CARPETS AND RUGS

Fragment of knotted vase carpet
Österreichisches Museum für angewandte Kunst

Museo Stephano Bardini
The Stephano Bardini Museum
Piazza dei Mozzi 1, 50125 Florence, Italy
Tel. (39) 055 2342427
Thu-Tue, 9am-2pm, public holidays 8am-1pm

The dealer Stephano Bardini assembled a collection of objects of widely varying periods and quality. His remarkable palace is worth examining for he has incorporated doors, windows, and mouldings fragments from abandoned churches and villas. The Oriental carpet collection contains endless rarities, including fragments of a noted Mamluk blazon carpet from the 15th century (the matching fragments can be found in the Textile Museum in Washington, DC), and a splendid Persian carpet fragment from 16th-century Kashan or Esfahan, with elaborate landscapes, animals, and calligraphy.

The Burrell Collection
2060 Pollokshaws Road, Glasgow, G43 1AT, Scotland, UK
Tel. (44) 141 649 7151
Mon-Sat 10am-5pm, Sun 11am-5pm

A small but fine collection of Near Eastern carpets from Turkey, India, Persia, Central Asia, and the Caucasus, illustrating Burrell's passion for Oriental art. There is a fascinating fragment, previously in the Imperial Collections at Vienna, of what must have been a large Indian carpet, showing flowers and grotesque animals (16th-17th century). The most famous exhibit is the 17th-century Wagner Garden Carpet, depicting a traditional Persian garden with trees, pools, flowers, and birds.

Museum of Fine Arts
465 Huntington Avenue, Boston, Massachusetts 02115-5519, USA
Tel. (1) 617 267 9300 www.mfa.org
Mon-Tue 10am-5.45pm, Wed-Fri 10am-9.45pm.
West Wing: Thu-Fri after 5pm, Sat-Sun 10am-5.45pm

Although not a very large collection, its strength lies is its quality. In 1893, the museum acquired its first important carpet, an action-packed pictorial rug woven during the reign of the Mughal Indian emperor Akbar (1556-1605). Spanning a geographic range from Spain to India, there are other rare, pre-1800 carpets and carpet fragments in the permanent collection that are worth seeing.

Gosudarstvennyi muzei iskusstva narodov vostoka
The State Museum of Oriental Art
Nikitskii bul'var 12a, 121019 Moscow, Russian Federation
Tel. (7) 095 2024555
Tue-Sun 10am-8pm

A fine collection of Karakalpak rugs, mainly from Uzbekistan. The major part of this collection consists of *karshins* and *eshik kases*. The *karshin* is a bag for garments and other cloth articles. It is placed in the lower part of the bedding, which is set on a trunk. The *eshik kas* is a decorative rug for the inside, upper area of the yurt entrance.

Museo Marciano
St Mark's Museum
Basilica di San Marco, piazza San Marco, 30100 Venice, Italy

Tel. (39) 041 5225205
Summer: daily 9.45am-5.30pm. Winter: daily 9.45am-4.30pm

A modern and climate-controlled space in the frescoed Banqueting Hall of the
Procuratorial Palace adjacent to the cathedral, houses this famous group of Safavid silk-
and metal-thread carpets from the 17th century. Also on display are splendid Venetian
tapestries and a group of 15th-17th century church vestments, mainly of Italian cut velvet.

Náprstkovo muzeum asijských, afrických a amerických kultur
Náprstek Museum of Asian, African and American Cultures
Libechov Castle, Betlémské námesti 1 , 110 00 Prague 1, Czech Republic
Tel. (420) 222 221416 www.aconet.cz
Museum: Tue-Sun 9am-noon, 1.45-5.30pm. Castle: Tue-Sun 9am-5pm

More than 200 Anatolian 18th- and 19th-century kilims and carpets are on display.
These rugs, formerly used in prayer five times a day, come from the carpet production
areas including Bergama, Gördes, Kula, Ladik, Mucur, and Malatya.

Museo nazionale del Bargello
The National Museum of Bargello
Via del Proconsolo 4, 50122 Florence, Italy
Tel. (39) 055 2388606
Tue-Sat 8.30am-3pm

Silk knotted Mamluk
carpet, Egypt, 1700s
*Österreichisches Museum
für angewandte Kunst*

One of the oldest and most beautiful buildings in Florence (1255) was once a prison
and is now home to one of two major carpet collections in the city. Although the
collection is not large, all the Islamic pieces are of the highest quality, thanks to the
19th-century Franchetti and Carrand donations. The geographical range of the
collection is equally remarkable: Byzantine *samites*, Spanish and Indian *lampas* from
the 14th to the 16th century, an Ottoman 16th-century *çatma* from Turkey, and delicate
European animal silks from the 14th century.

The New de Young Museum
75 Tea Garden Drive, Golden Gate Park, San Francisco, California, USA
Tel. (1) 415 863 3330 www.thinker.org
Expected completion of the new building by June 2005. Please call for opening times

Recent major donations from the Middle East and Central Asia have resulted in a
pre-eminent collection of rugs. There are a group of early Turkish carpet fragments
and about thirty rugs and other pile textiles produced by the Turkoman tribes of
Central Asia. A superb piece is a fragment of a Turkish 'animal carpet' dating to the
13th century. Another important exhibit is the white-ground wedding trappings
from the Chodor Turkmen, the only known examples of their kind.

Musée Nissim de Camondo
The Nissim de Camondo Museum
63 rue de Monceau, 75008 Paris, France
Tel. (33) 1 53 89 06 50
Wed-Sun 10am-5pm

One of the best collection of carpets from the Royal Manufactory of the Savonnerie
was gathered by Count Moïse de Camondo. The collection's highlight is the carpet in
the Salon Doré, one of the 93 carpets from the Savonnerie commissioned by Louis XIV
for the Great Gallery of the Louvre Palace.

Österreichisches Museum für angewandte Kunst
The Austrian Museum of Applied Arts

Silk knotted hunting carpet, central Persia, 1700s
Österreichisches Museum für angewandte Kunst

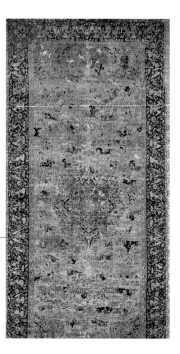

Stubenring 5, 1010 Vienna, Austria
Tel. (43) 1 71136 www.mak.at
Tue-Sun 10am-6pm (Thu until 9pm)

A fine collection of early 16th-century Egyptian knotted Mamluk carpets, including those dating from the Ottoman period beginning in Egypt after 1514. Especially notable is a silk-knotted Mamluk carpet from Cairo, the only example in its group made from silk. The most famous Islamic carpet in the collection is a silk carpet with a lively hunting scene from Kashan, central Persia (16th century). It is so finely knotted that a group of experts in the 19th century wrongly concluded that it was not woven but made from velvet.

Shelburne Museum
US Route 7, Shelburne, Vermont 05482, USA
Tel. (1) 802 985 3346
www.shelburnemuseum.org
Late May-late Oct: daily 10am-5pm
(walking tours available all year, reservations recommended)

In colonial America, rugs and carpets were considered a luxury, particularly the Oriental rugs which were kept as table coverings. Many women made their own rugs, using needlepoint, shirring, 'yarn-sewn' embroidery, braiding, and hooking. This collection, encompassing over 400 pieces, focuses on these handmade rugs.

St Louis Museum of Art
1 Fine Arts Drive, St Louis, Missouri 63110-1380, USA
Tel. (1) 314 721 0072 www.slam.org
Tue 1.30-8.30pm, Wed-Sun 10am-5pm (Fri until 9pm)

James F. Ballard, a prominent American collector of Oriental carpets, began collecting in 1905 and transformed his home into a gallery. The collection reflects his love of Turkish carpets, along with other important styles. Rare examples include a 16th-century Mamluk carpet, a 15th-century Spanish carpet, several prayer rugs, and early Turkish pieces known as Holbein and Lotto rugs, named because these artists depicted this style of carpet in their paintings.

Musée du Tapis et des Arts textiles
Museum of Carpets and Textile Arts
45 rue Ballainvilliers, 63000 Clermont-Ferrand, France
Tel. (33) 4 73 90 57 48
Tue-Sun 10am-6pm

The only museum in France to be solely devoted to carpets. Its permanent holdings include 110 carpets from Persia, Iran, Caucasus, Anatolia, Central Asia, Afghanistan, and Tibet, but the museum hosts many temporary exhibitions with carpets on loan from larger museums.

The Textile Museum
2320 S Street, NW, Washington, DC 20008-4088, USA
Tel. (1) 202 667 044 www.textilemuseum.org
Mon-Sat 10am-5pm, Sun 1-5pm

This is one of the most important research collections of Oriental carpets in the world, distinguished by both its range and depth. This museum also has important holdings of 15th-century Mamluk carpets, Spanish rugs, classical Indian carpet fragments, and a large number of Turkish rugs, which includes an excellent small selection of Ottoman Cairene rugs, together with a large collection of central Asian rugs, predominantly Turkmen.

Türk ve Islam Eserleri Müzesi
Museum of Turkish and Islamic Arts
At Meydani 46, Sultanahmet, Istanbul, Turkey
Tel. (90) 212 518 1906
Tue-Sun 10am-5pm

The carpet section forms one of the richest collections of carpet art in the world. Besides rare Seljuk carpets, prayer rugs, and animal-figure carpets belonging to the 15th century, there are carpets produced in Anatolia between the 15th and 17th centuries.

Victoria and Albert Museum
Cromwell Road, South Kensington, London sw7 2rl, UK
Tel. (44) 20 7942 2000 www.vam.ac.uk
Daily 10am-5.45pm (Wed & last Fri of the month 10am-10pm)

This is home to the most famous carpet in the world, the Ardabil Carpet. With its matching pair, it adorned the floors of the Ardabil Mosque in northwest Persia. These huge carpets, made in 1539-40 for the shrine of Sheikh Safi, the founder of the Safavid Dynasty, have been beautifully restored. The most beautiful of the pair is held here, the other in Los Angeles County Museum of Art. Other renowned Oriental carpets in this 1,600-piece collection include the Chelsea Carpet (Persia, 16th century) and the Fremlin Carpet (India, 17th century).

Temple spectacles - 'Dr Johnson's', believed to have belonged to Samuel Johnson (below)
British Optical Association Museum

Reading glass, early 19th century (bottom)
British Optical Association Museum

EYEGLASSES AND OPERA GLASSES

British Optical Association Museum
College of Optometrists, 42 Craven Street, London wc2n 5ng, UK
Tel. (44) 20 7839 6000 www.college-optometrists.org
Due to open 2003 (viewing by appt. only)

Among the vast collection of spectacles and sun-spectacles are examples with frames of a varied range of materials, including leather, wood, whalebone, ivory, bone, horn, tortoiseshell, gold, rolled gold, silver, iron, brass, blued steel, aluminium, cellulose nitrate and cellulose acetate. The collection is particularly strong in English silver spectacles of the 18th and 19th century and in antique oriental spectacles.

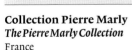

Collection Pierre Marly
The Pierre Marly Collection
France

A collection gathered by the optician Pierre Marly, once held at the Musée des Lunettes et des Lorgnettes de Jadis in Paris. The collection is currently waiting to be relocated and there is a strong possibility that it will end up in the Musée de la Lunetterie in Morez (see entry).

503

The collection of over 3,000 pieces includes eyeglasses from the 15th century, a pair of rather curious glasses made from bottles and worn by the Inuit, and the first binoculars in the world, made by Pierre Chérubin d'Orléans in 1719.

Bow spectacles, 17th century, with contemporary carved wooden case
British Optical Association Museum

18th-century spyglasses (right)
British Optical Association Museum

Collezione Ottiche & Occhiali
Collection of Optical Instruments and Eyeglasses
Corso Patrioti, 3 - 32021 Agordo, Italy
Tel. (39) 0437 62641
By appt. only

This collection is the work of two enthusiasts: Fritz Rathschüler, a Genoese optician who over 65 years of his life searched for objects relating to his profession, and Leonardo Del Vecchio, head of the Luxottica Group (a leading producer of eyeglass frames) who bought the optician's collection, added his pieces and set up the museum. Though a few items date from the 1500s, the majority of eyeglasses are from the 18th century and range from bow-glasses with whalebone frames, to early Venetian sunglasses (*c.* 1750) in horn, fitted with silk side protection. The fascinating telescope section includes English, French, Chinese, and Italian makes, among which is the eight-metre telescope by G. Campani (1682).

Galleria Guglielmo Tabacchi
Guglielmo Tabacchi Gallery
VII strada 15, 35129 Padova, Italy
Tel. (39) 049 8295311
www.safilo.com
By appt. only

The futuristic appearance of this gallery was inspired by the spectacles it displays. Tabacchi has been assembling his collection of eyeglasses for decades. Today, it comprises thousands of items and ranges from celebrity spectacles (see eyewear belonging to Elvis Presley, Peggy Guggenheim, and Bono from U2), to rare Italian steel hat spectacles (16th century) engraved with the owner's family motto and crest.

Lågdalsmuseet
Lågdal Museum
Tillischbakken 8-10, 3613 Kongsberg, Norway
Tel. (47) 32 7333468
End Jun-mid Aug: Mon-Fri 11am-5pm. Sep-Jun: Mon-Fri 11am-3.30pm

Besides being famous for silver and skiing, Kongsberg is considered the optical centre of Norway. Although two of the oldest eyeglasses in Norway are on display, the collection contains mostly foreign examples, including a Chinese handmade pair from around 1700 and a pair of European spectacles of the same date.

Musée de la Lunetterie
Museum of Eye-Glass Making
5 rue Lamartine, 39400 Morez, France (will relocate in 2002)
Tel. (33) 3 84 33 39 30
Wed-Sun 3-6.30pm

The museum is appropriately situated in Morez, the French capital of eyeglass manufacture. There are no real rare or precious items in this collection of 2,500 objects; instead it perfectly illustrates the history of eyeglass making and its link with social and fashion history in the 19th and 20th centuries.

Folding lorgnette, by
Baudin Freres, Geneva,
mid 19th century (above)
*British Optical Association
Museum*

Het Nationaal Brilmuseum
The National Museum of Spectacles
Gasthuismolensteeg 7, 1016 AM Amsterdam, The Netherlands
Tel. (31) 20 4212414 www.brilmuseumamsterdam.nl
Wed-Fri noon-5.30pm, Sat noon-5pm

This is part-museum, part-shop, as some of the exhibits are for sale. See examples of spyglasses built invisibly into fans; jewellery; walking sticks; railway spectacles with extra side pieces that unfold; the ultimate status-symbol opera glasses; optical toys; binoculars for sea and sport; monocles; goggles; and a whole array of bizarre one-offs handmade for celebrities.

Museo dell'Occhiale
Museum of Eyeglasses
Via degli Alpini 39, Pieve di Cadore, Italy
Tel. (39) 0435 500213 www.sunrise.it
Tue-Sun 9am-noon, 3-6pm

It would be unspeakable if the city at the heart of the Italian optical industry were without a museum to show off its remarkable contribution. This museum features collections bought by Vittorio Tabacchi, including that of the Belgian George Bodart. The 16,000 items from Bodart were amalgamated with the pre-existing De Lotto collection and range from eyeglasses, monocles, and telescopes, to binoculars and spyglasses concealed in anything from fans and perfume bottles, to walking sticks and parasols.

Otto Hallauer Sammlung - Medizinhistorisches Museum
The Otto Hallauer Collection - History of Medicine Museum
Bühlstrasse 26, 3000 Berne, Switzerland
Tel. (41) 31 6318486
Mon-Fri 8.30am-noon, 2-4.45pm

A representative selection of this important collection is accessible to the public. Among the many spectacles there are some magnificent examples of scissors-glasses, quizzing glasses, fine lorgnettes, and pince-nez spectacles.

Ivory painted fan, 1900s
(below left)
The Fan Museum

Wedding morning fan
The Fan Museum
(below)

FANS

British Museum
Great Russell Street, London WC1B 3DG, UK
Tel. (44) 20 7636 1555 www.british-museum.ac.uk
Mon-Sat 10am-5pm, Sun 2.30-6pm

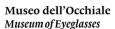

To view Lady Charlotte Schreiber's fan collection, you must make an appointment with the department of Prints and Drawings. The collection consists of over 600 pieces from England, France, Italy, Spain, Germany, Holland, North America, and the Far East, and reflects her main interests in history, politics, and social events. Don't miss the commemorative fans or those concerned with marriage, a rich source of subject matter which was both celebrated and satirized in the 18th century.

Ivory fan, Germany, c.1870
(above)
Musée de l'Eventail

The Orangery at The Fan
Museum (below)
The Fan Museum

British Optical Association Museum
College of Optometrists
42 Craven Street, London WC2N 5NG, UK
Tel. (44) 20 7839 6000 www.college-optometrists.org
Due to open in 2003 (viewing by appt. only)

The collection includes a small but beautiful selection of nine optical fans, which feature either a miniature spyglass or a quizzing glass so that the user might spy on neighbours and acquaintances on social occasions without being observed.

Museum of the City of New York
Fifth Avenue at 103rd Street, New York, New York 10029, USA
Tel. (1) 212 534 1672 www.netresource.com
Wed-Sat 10am-5pm, Sun 1-5 pm. Group tours: Tue 10am-2pm

The collection holds over 850 fans, from printed, painted, and brisé fans to those made of feathers. Many are in fragile condition, hence there is a reluctance to have them on long-term show. As a result, the museum offers the opportunity to view a selection online.

Museum of Costume
Assembly Rooms, Bennett Street, Bath, Somerset BA1 2QH, UK
Tel. (44) 1225 477752 www.museumofcostume.co.uk
Mon-Sat 10am-5pm, Sun 11am-5pm

Opened in 1963, the Museum of Costume is now one of the largest and finest of its kind in the UK. The collection ranges from inexpensive fans from the 18th century, with printed paper leaves and plain wooden sticks bought as souvenirs, to more sophisticated, highly decorated examples.

Musée du Costume et de la Dentelle
The Costume and Lace Museum
4-6 rue de la Violette, 1000 Brussels, Belgium
Tel. (32) 2 5127709 www.brussels-online.be
Apr-Sep: Mon, Tue, Thu, Fri 10am-12.30pm, 1.30-5pm
Oct-Mar: Mon, Tue, Thu, Fri 10am-12.30pm, 1.30-4pm, Sat-Sun 2-4.30pm

Started in 1979, the collection focuses on sumptuous European fans dating from the 17th to the 20th centuries. A fine example of the city's own tradition of fan making is a fan from 1880-90 with eighteen sticks and rivets made of pink mother-of-pearl and leaves of Brussels lace. Another magnificent fan is Cantonese (1840) with black-lacquered wooden sticks decorated in yellow and green gold, depicting a garden scene framed by flowers, insects, and Chinese objects.

Musée de l'Eventail
The Fan Museum
2 blvd de Strasbourg, 75010 Paris, France
Tel. (33) 1 42 08 19 89
Tue 2-5pm (group visits by appt. only)

Opened in 1993 by Anne Hoguet (France's only surviving fan-maker), the museum is set in the very same showroom where the Belle Epoque's most famous fan-maker, Lepault et Deberge worked. The collection is rotated to display the best of French fans from the 18th, 19th and

20th centuries. The history of fan-making is well explained through tools of the trade, the materials that went into fan making, as well as engravings of the many craftsmen who performed the time-consuming tasks involved.

Children's Game; fan on white mother-of-pearl mounting
Musée de l'Eventail

The Fan Museum

12 Crooms Hill, Greenwich, London SE10 8ER, UK
Tel. (44) 20 8305 1441 www.fan-museum.org
Tue-Sat 11am-5pm, Sun noon-5pm

This museum is devoted entirely to all aspects of the ancient art and craft of the fan and was the brainchild of Hélène Alexander, whose collection of over 2,000 fans, fan leaves, and related material forms the core of this museum's holdings. This collection is particularly strong on European fans from the 18th and 19th centuries, however there are also fans dating from the 17th century. Craft workshops for fan-making, conservation, and restoration facilities, study and research resources, including a reference library, are all available by appointment.

Museum of Fine Arts

465 Huntington Avenue, Boston, Massachusetts 02115-5519, USA
Tel. (1) 617 2679300 www.mfa.org
Mon, Tue 10am-4.45pm, Wed-Fri 10am-9.45pm
(West Wing: Thu-Fri after 5pm only, Sat-Sun 10am-5.45pm)

Masterpieces include an early 19th-century silver *brisé* fan with its original leather case previously belonging to Marie-Louise, the second wife of Napoleon, and a lovely lace fan, from 1775, with point d'Argentan lace, believed to have been made for the wedding of a princess of the house of Orléans. All of this collection was donated by Esther Oldham, a well-known fan collector and author.

An artist's impression of the museum by Barbara Dorf (above)
The Fan Museum

The *Greenwich Millennium Fan* (left)
The Fan Museum

Fitzwilliam Museum

Trumpington Street, Cambridge, Cambridgeshire CB2 1RB, UK
Tel. (44) 1223 332900
www.fitzmuseum.cam.ac.uk
Tue-Sat 10am-5pm, Sun 2.15-5pm

The superb collection of over 600 fans is overseen by the Print Department. The Fan Gallery displays approximately 150 fans at any one time, mainly Oriental, and holds a fine collection of unmounted fan leaves.

Historisches Museum Basel
The History Museum of Basle

Steinenberg 4, 4051 Basle, Switzerland
Tel. (41) 61 2710505 www.historischesmuseumbasel.ch
Mon, Wed-Sun 10am-5pm

The collection houses about 170 fans, including several with fine decoration and precious stones. A curious paper and rosewood fan from the late 18th century depicts the life of Guiseppe Balsamo, alias Count Alexander Cagliostro, and his wife. A convincing and charismatic charlatan, Balsamo's exploits are admired in the fan's inscription.

Romantic scenes on ivory mounting
Musée de l'Eventail

Manchester City Art Galleries

Platt Hall, Rusholme, Manchester M14 5LL, UK
Tel. (44) 161 224 5217 www.cityartgalleries.org.uk
Mar-Oct: daily 10am-5.30pm. Nov-Feb: daily 10am-4pm

Besides a good selection of handbags and umbrellas, there are over 300 fans in the reserve collection, which can be accessed by prior appointment only.

The Metropolitan Museum of Art

1000 Fifth Avenue at 82nd Street, 10028 New York, New York, USA
Tel. (1) 212 535 7710 www.metmuseum.org
Tue-Thu, Sun 9.30am-5.30pm, Fri, Sat 9.30am-9pm

As with all the collections here, this is impressive, with 800 examples from 17th-century Italy to 18th- and 19th-century France. Other examples are from China, Japan, Holland, and Tzarist Russia.

Victoria and Albert Museum

Cromwell Road, South Kensington, London SW7 2RL, UK
Tel. (44) 20 7942 2000 www.vam.ac.uk
Daily 10am-5.45pm (Wed & last Fri of every month 10am-10pm)

Among the dress collection is a spectacular collection of European folding fans from the 17th century to the present day. Most of the fans can only be viewed by appointment. The earliest examples are probably Italian dating from the 1620s. Worth viewing are the examples of exquisite Italian miniature paintings of classical scenes painted with watercolours on kid leather. One such fan, dating from the early 18th century, illustrates the subject of Venus and Adonis and is taken from the painting by Francesco Albani in the Villa Borghese and signed by Leonardo Germo of Rome. The fan has the added interest of having once been owned by the American painter Benjamin West who became President of the Royal Academy in 1792.

Waddesdon Manor - The Rothschild Collection

Waddesdon, Aylesbury, Buckinghamshire HP18 0JH, UK
Tel. (44) 1296 653211 www.waddesdon.org.uk
House: end Mar-mid Oct: Thu-Sat 12.30-6pm, Sun 11am-6.30pm. Jul-Aug: Wed also.
Grounds: Wed-Sun 11am-5pm

Waddesdon houses a little-known but extremely fine collection of 18th-century court fans. The whole collection is never on show, however two fans, which are on display for the 2001 season, show the exterior and interior of a milliners' shop, and an unmounted fan leaf depicting Louis XV and his family dining in Versailles.

The Seven Stages in the Bamboo Game, a Japanese brise fan, c. 1880
The Fan Museum

Wenham Museum

132 Main Street, Wenham, Massachusetts 01984, USA
Tel. (1) 978 468 2377
www.wenhammuseum.org
Tue-Sun 10am-4pm

A collection of over 400 fans from France, China, Japan, England, and the US. The largest holdings are paper fans that have been made in

numerous countries. Fans made with feathers from bird plumage, including ostrich and peacock, account for the next largest category with fifty outstanding pieces. Ivory and lace examples, cloth, advertising, and even oddities such as a fan from chicken skin, round off the collection.

'Hiogi', a Japanese Court fan around 1880
The Fan Museum

FOLK AND ETHNOGRAPHIC TEXTILES

American Museum of Natural History

Central Park West at 79th Street, New York, New York 10024, USA
Tel. (1) 212 769 5100 www.amnh.org
Mon-Thu, Sun 10am-5.45pm, Fri, Sat 10am-8.45pm

Most of the exhibits reached the museum through archaeological or ethnographic expeditions, often led by leading scholars dispatched by the museum. More items are gradually put on display in the various athropology departments, or can be accessed via the internet. There is a major collection of ancient fabrics from Peru from 2500BC onwards (Huaca Prieta), a major modern textile collection from Guatemala and 400 Navaho rugs from American India. The Asian holdings make it one of the world's finest collections.

Bankfield Museum

Boothtown Road, Halifax, West Yorkshire HX3 6HG, UK
Tel. (44) 1422 354823
Tue-Sat & public holidays 10am-5pm, Sun 2-5pm

One of the most important holdings is Mary Edith Durham's collections of Eastern European costume and embroideries which were collected between 1880 and 1910 while travelling around Albania and the lands which until recently formed Yugoslavia. In addition to gathering an astounding collection of costume and textiles, Durham sketched, photographed and studied the people and their customs. Every artefact came with an attached hand-written label with instructions on how it was worn or where it was bought.

Detail of an embroidered Japangi, Scutari, Albania
Bankfield Museum

British Museum

Great Russell Street, London WC1B 3DG, UK
Tel. (44) 20 7636 1555 www.thebritishmuseum.ac.uk
Mon-Sat 10am-5pm, Sun noon-6pm

A massive collection with thousands of textiles from Europe and Asia such as batik, ikat, and tie-dye fabrics from Indonesia and India. There are brocades from Malaysia, ikats from Sumba, woven and embroidered cloths from the Turkoman region, and woven fabrics from Greece, Turkey, and Cyprus. The collection from the Americas is one of the largest and is thought to have at least 5,000 items, including an extensive collection from Peru. There are a large number of items from the Pacific region as well as Africa, especially from Nigeria and Sierra Leone.

The Brooklyn Museum of Art

200 Eastern Parkway, Brooklyn, New York, New York 11238-6052, USA
Tel. (1) 718 638 5000 www.brooklynart.org
Wed-Fri 10am-5pm, Sat-Sun 11am-6pm (11am-11pm first Sat of every month)

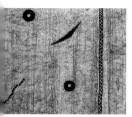

Bark cloth, Fiji, early 20th
century
Bankfield Museum

An extensive collection of textiles and costumes, including unique Andean pieces
such as the Paracas Textile from southwest Peru, thought to date from the 4th century
BC. The group of Native American holdings is among the finest in the world, as is the
collection of Russian folk textiles.

Musée du Feutre
The Museum of Felt
Place du Colombier, 08210 Mouzon, France
Tel. (33) 3 24 26 19 91
Apr, Oct: Wed-Thu 2-6pm. May, Sep: daily 4-6pm. Jun: 3-7pm
Jul, Aug: 10am-noon, 3-7pm

This museum explains the history, industry, and evolution of felt-making techniques.
The tradition has its roots in the nomadic lifestyle of people from Central Asia, who
brought with them their techniques, which then spread to many parts of Europe.
Displayed are carpets, coats, and boots made using traditional felt processes and a vast
selection of hats, capes, and jackets from Romania, Albania, Yugoslavia, and Greek
Macedonia.

Germanisches Nationalmuseum
The Germanic National Museum
Kartäusergasse 1, 90402 Nuremberg, Germany
Tel. (49) 911 13310 www.gnm.de
Tue-Sun 10am-5pm (Wed until 9pm)

Traditional regional costumes of 19th-century rural Germany (known as the Oskar
Kling Collection) are displayed as well as clothing worn over the past three centuries.

Indonesian batik sarong,
mid 19th century
Tropenmuseum

Musée de l'Homme
The Museum of Mankind
Palais de Chaillot, 17 place du
Trocadéro, 75016 Paris, France
Tel. (33) 1 44 05 72 72 www.mnhn.fr
Mon, Wed-Sun 9.45am-5.15pm

Endless amounts of objects grace the
storerooms and galleries here. Over
thirty European folk cultures are
represented in the collection of 19th-
and 20th-century peasant costumes
with excellent representation from
Yugoslavia, Albania, Bulgaria,
Czechoslovakia, Estonia, Greece,
Hungary, Portugal, and Romania.

Indianapolis Museum of Art
1200 W 38th Street, Indianapolis,
Indiana 46208-4196, USA
Tel. (1) 317 920 2660 www.ima-art.org
Tue-Sat 10am-5pm (Thu until 8.30pm),
Sun noon-5pm

Claims to be one of the first art institutions in the US to collect textiles. Its
6,000-piece collection represents virtually all of the world's traditions in
fabric.

Museum of International Folk Art

Museum of New Mexico, 706 Camino Lejo, Santa Fe, New Mexico, 87505, USA
Tel. (1) 505 476 1200   www.moifa.org
Tue-Sun 10am-5pm

The focus is on local and regional examples and contains significant selections of Mexican and Guatemalan Indian costumes. Examples from elsewhere including the Andes, the Atlas mountains of north Africa, the Carpathian range in Europe, Burma, Bhutan, Nepal, China, Uzbekistan, and the mountains of northern New Mexico.

Batik men's headdress,
Indonesia, 20th century
Tropenmuseum

Mouseío istorías tes ellenikés endumasías
The Museum of the History of Greek Costume

Dimokritou 7, 106 71 Athens, Greece
Tel. (30) 1 3629513
Jan-Jul, Sep-Dec: Mon, Wed, Fri 10am-1pm

Highlights include a costume from Siphnos, dating from the 18th or early 19th century, which is one of the very few costumes from the Cyclades that survives.

Museum der Kulturen
The Museum of Cultures

Augustinergasse 2, 4051 Basle, Switzerland
Tel. (41) 61 266 55 00   www.mkb.ch
Tue-Sun 2-5pm

A comprehensive collection of more than 20,000 textiles. Changing exhibitions focus on specific textile techniques or types of textiles, from batik and embroidery from southwest China, to east European floral embroidery, or Kuba raffia appliqué.

Museu nacional do Traje
The National Costume Museum

Largo Julio de Castillo, Luminar, 1600 Lisbon, Portugal
Tel. (351) 21 7590318
Please call for opening times.

The definitive museum for the study of Portuguese regional costumes. A unique collection.

Ethnikó isturikó mouseió
National Historical Museum

The Old Parliament Building, Odós Stadíou, 105 61 Athens, Greece
Tel. (30) 1 3237617
Tue-Sun 9am-2pm

Among the ethnographic collections are traditional regional costumes, jewellery, embroidery, textiles, as well as metal, ceramic, and wooden objects. The vast collection of traditional, popular costumes are from both ordinary people and craftsmen.

Nordiska Museet
The Nordic Museum

Djurgården, 115 93 Stockholm, Sweden
Tel. (46) 8 51956000   www.nordm.se
Tue-Sun 10am-5pm (Tue, Thu until 8pm)

Artur Hazelius, founder and first director, was passionate about the rural past and future of the Nordic countries and noted how traditional crafts and farming cultures were losing out to industrialization. This began an obsession to acquire folk

Indonesian batik cloth,
19th century
Tropenmuseum

costumes and peasant items. Hazelius amassed costumes from the Nordic world and the Baltic states, in particular the Swedish peasant costumes. With more than 1.3 million objects, there is a broad range of clothing, from wedding and mourning dress, and fine Swedish brocades, to working and everyday wear.

Norsk Folkemuseum
Norwegian Folk Museum
Museumsveien 10, 0287 Oslo, Norway
Tel. (47) 22 123700
www.norskfolke.museum.no
May-Sep: daily 10am-6pm. Oct-Apr: daily 11am-4pm

A unique folk-dress collection with a large selection on show in their permanent exhibition, which reflects the life's work of Aagot Noss, a former curator at the museum. Noss started her research in 1956, and she was able to interview many traditional users of folk dress. The main emphasis is on festive clothing ,such as wedding and baptismal clothes, or items that were worn on Sundays. The folk dress silver, consisting mostly of brooches, is substantial.

Peabody Museum of Archaeology and Ethnology
Harvard University, 11 Divinity Avenue, Cambridge, Massachusetts 02138, USA
Tel. (1) 617 495 9125 www.peabody.harvard.edu
Daily 9am-5pm

An enormous collection of flat textiles and costumes with strong examples from Peru, modern Guatemala, North America, India, Southeast Asia, and Polynesia. Treat yourself to some real rarities including skin-fish appliqué from Siberia, and early *molas* from Panama.

The Pitt Rivers Museum
South Parks Road, Oxford, Oxfordshire OX1 3PP, UK
Tel. (44) 1865 270927 www.prm.ox.ac.uk
Mon-Sat 1-4.30pm, Sun 2-4.30pm

The collection includes the most amazing objects you can find in any museum. Eskimo raincoats made of seal intestine, a blue silk Manchu lady's jacket, textiles of grass fibre from Sierra Leone, primitive looms from Formosa or Borneo, painted deerskins of the Cherokee Indians, and fabrics from Guatemala and Mexico.

Rossiiskii etnograficheskii muzei
The Russian Museum of Ethnography
Inzhenernaia ulitsa 4/1, 191011 St Petersburg, Russian Federation
Tel. (7) 812 2191710 www.ethnomuseum.ru
Tue-Sun 11am-6pm (closed last Fri of each month)

The museum boasts a large quantity of costumes, jewellery, accessories, and textiles. It holds one of the most spectacular displays of folk costume in the world. Most notable are the collections of ethnic Russian peasant dress and items from other former republics, including a spectacular Chukchi (eastern Siberian) Shaman's garment and some beautiful Tartar robes with highly ornate embroidery. If you have extra cash and time, there are two other displays: one in the Gold Hall, housing highly valuable jewellery and jewel-encrusted costume accessories, the other a rotating exhibition in the Marble Hall.

The Scottish Tartans Society
Port-na-Craig Road, Pitlochry, Perth and Kinross PH16 5ND, Scotland, UK
Tel. (44) 1796 474079 www.tartans.electricscotland.com
By appt. only

This is the only archive in Scotland dedicated to tartan and Highland dress with a register of all known tartans (over 2,500). A first-class collection of reference books is available in the library, including sample books and correspondence from many tartan-producing companies. Defined as a chequered pattern associated with a specific clan, the word 'tartan' is derived from the French *tiretaine* and the Spanish *tiritana*, meaning a light woollen material of any colour.

The Textile Museum
2320 S Street, NW, Washington, DC 20008-4088, USA
Tel. (1) 202 667 0441 www.textilemuseum.org
Mon-Sat 10am-5pm, Sun 1-5pm

The pre-Hispanic Peruvian textiles are particularly outstanding and include a collection of some seventy Chavin textiles from ancient Peru (1500-500BC). The textiles are painted onto cotton plainweave using outline and infill, or woven using a variety of techniques including slit-tapestry, warp-wrapping, and wrapped looping. Some exhibit the earliest-known use of tie-dye. There are also Ocucaje, Paracas, and early Nasca, late Nasca and Nasca-Huari, Huari, Ica style, Chancay style, Chimu style, Inca and Inca-influenced textiles. Also, shawls from Kashmir and India, and Mughal sashes and furnishings.

Textilmuseum Mindelheim
The Mindelheim Textile Museum
Ehemaliger Jesuitenkolleg, Hermelestrasse 4, 87719 Mindelheim, Germany
Tel. (49) 8261 991556 www.mindelheim.de
Tue-Sun 10am-noon, 2-4pm

Huipil or upper body garment, Guatemala
The Textile Museum

The majority of the collection consists of embroidered altar pieces, bishop robes, and tapestries (from as early as the 15th century). It also holds a beautiful collection of ethnographic textiles, including a section dedicated to Africa, which contains a fine range of Coptic woven textiles, Plangi and Tritik batiks and embroideries, as well as fine pieces from China, Japan, Indonesia, India, and Persia.

Tropenmuseum
The Museum of the Tropics
Linnaeusstraat 2, 1092 AD, Amsterdam, The Netherlands
Tel. (31) 20 5688215 www.kit.nl
Mon-Fri 10am-5pm, Sat-Sun noon-5pm

Excellent early textiles, with a strong emphasis on the Southeast Asian collections, including the world-renowned Tillmann collection of Indonesian textiles.

University Museum of Archaeology and Anthropology
Downing Street, Cambridge, Cambridgeshire CB2 3DZ, UK
Tel. (44) 1223 337733 www.cam.ac.uk
Mon-Fri 2-4pm, Sat 10am-12.30pm

Textiles from Peru dating from the first millennium BC and modern pieces from the Chancay, Ica, Nazca, and Tiahuananca.

HATS, HATPINS AND COMBS

The American Museum in Britain
Claverton Manor, Bath, Somerset BA2 7BD, UK
Tel. (44) 1225 460503 www.americanmuseum.org
Museum: Tue-Sun 2-5pm. Garden: Tue-Sun 1-6pm

A delightful 18th-century Dutch summer house, decorated in crisp blue and white, is the setting for the milliner's shop display. Every kind of costume accessory is displayed (beads, feathers, buttons, and other baubles). The highlight is the remarkable collection of bandboxes which line the walls.

British Museum
Great Russell Street, London WC1B 3DG, UK
Tel. (44) 20 7636 1555 www.thebritishmuseum.ac.uk
Mon-Sat 10am-5pm, Sun noon-6pm

Comb from the 1920s
The Miller Comb Museum

The well-known Hull Grundy gift of jewellery was put together by Anne Hull Grundy, who was born in Nuremberg and came to Britain as a child where she started collecting at a young age. Her discerning eye and collecting precept was, 'If you don't fall in love, don't buy it.' As a result the collection not only illustrates the best of the jewellers' art, but with its well-documented pieces, many in their original cases, also serves as an invaluable research tool for the historian, and ranges from 6th-century Byzantium to the 1950s. Among the beauties are numerous hair accessories and Victorian diamond jewellery fittings for combs and tiaras.

Musée du Chapeau
The Hat Museum
16 route de Saint-Galmier, 42140 Chazelles-sur-Lyon, France
Tel. (33) 4 77 94 23 29 www.museeduchapeau.com
Mon, Wed-Sat 2-6pm, Sun & public holidays 2.30-6.30pm

This small town became very rich, thanks in part to the felt-hat industry dating back to the 16th century. Opened in 1983, the museum displays hats from the 18th century onwards, including eccesiastical, colonial, military, and famous chefs' hats. There are hats worn by Grace Kelly, Marie Curie, Maurice Chevalier, François Mitterrand, and Jacques-Yves Cousteau.

Silver tulip hatpin representing Spring, France, c. 1900 (above)
Hutmuseum der Stadt Homburg

Silver maple hatpin representing Autumn France, c. 1900 (right)
Hutmuseum der Stadt Homburg

Musée de la Chapellerie
The Museum of Hat-Making
3 rue Bergerie, 11120 Le Somail, France
Tel. (33) 4 68 46 19 26
May-Sep: daily 9am-noon, 2-7pm. Oct-Apr: 2-6pm, Sun & public holidays 2-7pm

An eclectic collection of 6,500 headdresses covering 84 countries, gathered by Antoine Ramoneda who began collecting at the age of fourteen. What makes this holding unique is its diversity.

The Museum at the Fashion Institute of Technology
27th Street at Seventh Avenue, New York, New York 10001, USA
Tel. (1) 212 217 5700 www.fitnyc.edu
Tue-Fri noon-8pm, Sat 10am-5pm

The museum's enormous teaching and research holdings contain an accessories collection of 20,000 pieces. The hat section is particularly strong, from the late 19th century through to the early 1970s, with examples for both men and women. Highlights include hats by milliners such as Adolfo, Balenciaga, Emme, Halston, John Frederics, Lily Dache, Mr John, and Stetson. There is also a fine collection of contemporary hats by milliners, Patricia Underwood and Philip Treacy.

Haircomb with blue feather decoration
The Miller Comb Museum

The Field School Museum
17 School Street, Leominster, Massachusetts 01453, USA
Tel. (1) 978 537 5424
Tue, Thu, Sat 9am-noon (times may vary, please call for details)

Leominster Historical Society oversees a massive comb collection consisting primarily of three holdings collected by wives of husbands involved in the comb-making industry of Leominster, once known as the 'comb city of the world'. There are at any one time 500 or so on display fashioned from steel, longhorn, wood, ivory, gold, and cellulose, the largest part of which includes the nationally known Alice Sawyer Collection.

Hutmuseum der Stadt Bad Homburg
The Hat Museum of Bad Homburg
Museum im Gotischen Haus, Tannenwaldweg 102, 61350 Bad Homburg vd Höhe, Germany
Tel. (49) 6172 37618
Tue, Thu, Sat 2-5pm, Wed 2-7pm, Fri 9am-noon, 2-5pm, Sun 10am-noon, 2-5pm

The Homburg was created here about 100 years ago by Edward VII. The collection includes hats for working; courtly and military headgear; judges, professors, and clergymen's caps identifying their status, profession or religion; and Chancellor Adenauer's Homburg. The amazing collection of hatpins contains everything from simple sheet-metal pins to the most elaborate works of art.

The Merry Widow, hatpin from around 1910
Hutmuseum der Stadt Homburg

Kalap és Sipkamúzeum
The Hat and Cap Museum
Kossuth utca 32, 7044 Nagydorog, Hungary
Tel. (36) 75 332062 www.almanach.hu
Mon-Fri 8am-4pm, Sat-Sun & public holidays on request

More than 100 hats and caps from various parts of the world. The collection is particularly rich in headgear from Central Asia. The lively guided tour from elderly ladies of the village is a must.

The Miller Comb Museum
60860 Little Fireweed Lane, Homer, Alaska, USA
Tel. (1) 907 235 8819
Summer: by appt. only

The tip of the Kenai Peninsula is probably the last place you'd expect to find what most in the field consider to be one of the largest collections of ornamental hair combs and other hair-related objects in existence – 3,800 pieces dating from 300BC to around 1940. Several of the more eclectic examples collected by the husband-and-

wife-team, Ralph and Betty Miller, include those decorated with Blue Kingfisher feathers and Eskimo combs.

Musée du Peigne et de la Plasturgie
The Comb and Plastic Museum
Centre Culturel Aragon, place Georges Pompidou, 01100 Oyonnax, France
Tel. (33) 4 74 81 96 82
Jul, Aug: Mon-Sat 2.30-6.30pm. Sep-Jun: Tue-Sat 2-6pm

This museum, founded in 1977, is entirely devoted to the origins of the local industry of plastic combs, one of the city's core businesses. It dates back to the day one of the king's councillors had an accident in his carriage near Oyonnax. The local inhabitants helped him repair his carriage and gave him several combs as presents. Once back in Paris, the councillor granted the residents of Oyonnax the comb making monopoly. To this day, there are still more than twenty comb makers in the city.

Schweizerisches Kamm-Museum
The Swiss Comb Museum
Bürgerhaus, Brüggliweg 724, 4717 Mümliswil, Switzerland
Tel. (41) 62 3912901
Every 1st and 3rd Sun of the month 2-5pm

Mümliswil has a 200-year-old tradition of comb-making, which, after industrialization, turned into a flourishing industry. The exhibition recounts the development and trends of this city's key industry.

Half-mourning, hatpin from around 1910 (top)
Hutmuseum der Stadt Homburg

Silver calla hatpin representing Summer, France, *c.*1900 (above)
Hutmuseum der Stadt Homburg

Silver mistletoe hatpin representing Winter France, *c.*1900 (right)
Hutmuseum der Stadt Homburg

Shelburne Museum
US Route 7, Shelburne, Vermont 05482, USA
Tel. (1) 802 985 3346 www.shelburnemuseum.org
Late May-late Oct: daily 10am-5pm. Nov-Apr: reserved tours available

Hatboxes became very popular in the 19th century as steamboat and train travel increased. The collection includes a large selection of hat and bandboxes made by Hannah Davis, one of the most well-known local craftspeople.

HAUTE COUTURE AND CONTEMPORARY STREET CLOTHING

Musée d'Art et d'Industrie
Museum of Art and Industry
24 rue de l'Espérance, 59100 Roubaix, France
Tel. (33) 3 20 69 23 60
Daily 1-6pm

Roubaix, together with Tourcoing, has been the centre of the country's woollen industry since 1469, when Charles the Reckless (Duke of Burgundy 1467-77) awarded Roubaix a charter authorising it to weave cloth from wool. This museum has recently reopened in an old Art Deco swimming pool built between 1927-32 by the local architect Albert Baer (at one time considered to be the most beautiful of its kind in France). The collection's broad palette extends to include an exceptional 30,000 textile pieces, ranging from the Coptic period to the present. There is an extremely rich collection of haute-couture clothing and accessories by Courrèges, de Castelbajac, Myaké, Colona, Yves Saint-Laurent, Comme des Garçons, Ysa du Piré, Isaac Mizrahi, Christian Astuguevieille, Dior, Cardin, Chanel, and Patou, among others.

Centraal Museum
The Central Museum
Nicolaaskerkhof 10, 3512 XC Utrecht, The Netherlands
Tel. (31) 30 2362362 www.centraalmuseum.box.nl
Tue-Sun 11am-5pm

This museum's textile collection covers fashion trends from 1760 up to the present, with an increasing focus on contemporary Dutch fashion designers from World War II onwards.

Musée de la Chemiserie et de l'Elégance masculine
The Museum of Shirtmaking and Masculine Elegance
Rue Charles Brillaud, 36200 Argenton-sur-Creuse, France
Tel. (33) 2 54 24 34 69
Tue-Sun 9.30am-noon, 2-6pm

This fascinating museum in the heart of the French shirtmaking industry is dedicated to the history of men's fashion and shirt making. 'La Chemise fait l'homme' (the shirt makes the man) said the 18th-century French author de Buffon (the author could only start work after putting on a clean white shirt). Located in a one-time shirt factory, the museum's collection presents the history of shirtmaking from medieval times up to the present. One of the museum's attractions is an electronic fitting room where you can choose to be dressed up as a Renaissance aristocrat or a director of a multi-national company.

Rose de France, dress by Dior, 1956
Musée Christian Dior

The Chicago Historical Society - The Hope B. McCormick Costume Center
Clark Street at North Avenue, Chicago, Illinois 60614-6099, USA
Tel. (1) 312 642 4600 www.chicagohistory.org
By appt. only

This extensive costume collection includes suits worn by George Washington, John Adams, Abraham, and Mary Todd Lincoln, as well as clothing of prominent Chicagoans, including Michael Jordan's basketball uniform and Mahalia Jackson's choir robe. There is also an extensive designer collection.

The Les Rhumbs villa
Musée Christian Dior

Musée Christian Dior
The Christian Dior Museum
Villa Les Rhumbs, Jardin Public Christian Dior, 50400 Granville, France
Tel. (33) 2 33 61 48 21
May-Sep: daily 10am-12.30pm, 2-6.30pm

Christian Dior's childhood villa, Les Rhumbs, was transformed into a fashion museum in 1977. The core collection consists of numerous donations made by Dior's friends and family, including family portraits and photographs, along with the couturier's scissors. Acquired along the way are his watercolour costume sketches.

The Fashion and Textile Museum
83 Bermondsey Street, London SE1 3XF, UK
Tel. (44) 20 7403 0222 www.ftmmuseum.org
Due to open in 2002

Shirt by Jean-Claude de
Castelbajac
*Musée de la Chemiserie et de
l'Elégance masculine*

Zandra Rhodes, the fashion designer famous for her audacious
use of textiles, haute couture, punk imagery, and ever-changing
hair tone, has founded a museum with the aim of promoting
and recording the work of outstanding British designers from
the 1950s to the present day. Housed in a late-1950s cash-and-carry
warehouse, the museum (which has been transformed by Mexican
architect Ricardo Legorreta) is yet another reason, along with
the Tate Modern, the Design Museum, and Shakespeare's Globe,
to visit the south side of the Thames.

The Museum at the Fashion Institute of Technology

27th Street at Seventh Avenue, New York, New York 10001, USA
Tel. (1) 212 217 5700 www.fitnyc.edu
Please call for opening times

This is one of the largest holdings of 20th-century design in the world and was founded
in 1967 as a study collection. Of the 30,000 garments in the costume collection, the focus
is on 20th-century designer wear for both couture and ready-to-wear. Notable pieces
include those by Adrian Coco Chanel, Cristobal Balenciaga (200 pieces), Claire McCardell,
and Charles James. The photography archive includes the work of Louise Dahl-Wolfe,
Hermann Landshoff, and John Rawlings. The Halston Archives are equally important.

Flanders Fashion Institute

Eiermarkt 13, 2000 Antwerp, Belgium
Tel. (32) 3 226 1447
Due to open in March 2002

During the last decade, Belgian fashion designers have acquired a reputation at
world level, thanks to the Antwerp Royal Academy of Fine Arts and the 'Antwerp Six':
Walter van Beirendonck, Dirk van Saene, Dries van Noten, Dirk Bikkembergs, Ann
Demeulemeester, and Marina Yee. The collection's core is made up of textiles from
western Europe, which date from the 18th to the 20th century, and is particularly
strong in costumes featuring Belgian lace, as well as costumes, bags and shoes (two
of the major strengths of Belgian fashion designers).

Gemeentemuseum
The City Museum

Stadhouderslaan 41, 2501 CB The Hague, The Netherlands
Tel. (31) 70 3381111 www.gemeentemuseum.nl
Tue-Sun 11am-5pm

The core of this collection was formed with the purchase of actor Cruys Voorbergh's
costume collection, which ranges from 19th-century haute couture to 1980s punk
outfits.

Historisches Museum - Modesammlung
The Historical Museum - Fashion Collection

Schloss Hetzendorf, Hetzendorferstrasse 79, 1120 Vienna, Austria
Tel. (43) 1 5058747 www.museum.vienna.at
Mon-Fri 8am-4pm

After World War II, Professor Alfred Kunz, the first director of the fashion school of
Vienna, founded the Fashion Collection in Hetzendorf Castle. The focus is on evening
and ball dresses, but lingerie from the 1920s, Biedermeier shoes, and accessories such
as hats, shoes, gloves, clutch-bags, umbrellas, stockings, and jewellery also feature.

The Metropolitan Museum of Art
1000 Fifth Avenue at 82nd Street, New York, New York 10028, USA
Tel. (1) 212 535 7710 www.metmuseum.org
Tue-Thu, Sun 9.30am-5.30pm, Fri-Sat 9.30am-9pm

Tucked away on the ground floor of this museum is the famed Costume Institute. The collection has more than 85,000 costumes and accessories from seven centuries and five continents and is particularly strong in 20th-century haute couture, especially from France, as well as post-war American sportswear and contemporary fashion.

Musée de la Mode et du Costume
The Museum of Fashion and Costume
Palais Galliéra, 10 ave. Pierre 1er de Serbie, 75016 Paris, France
Tel. (33) 1 47 20 85 23
Tue-Sun 10am-5.40pm

Another exceptional Parisian collection, which competes with the Musée de la Mode et du Textile at the Louvre for the rank of world's largest clothing collection: over 100,000 pieces, consisting of approximately 30,000 costumes and 70,000 accessories. Obviously not on show all at one time, the collection includes the work of the great couturiers of the 20th century.

Fashion engraving,
The Progress, 1880 (top)
Musée de la Chemiserie et de l'Elégance masculine

Shirt worn by Frank Sinatra (above)
Musée de la Chemiserie et de l'Elégance masculine

Musée de la Mode et du Textile
The Fashion and Textile Museum
Palais du Louvre, 107 rue de Rivoli, 75001 Paris, France
Tel. (33) 1 44 55 59 54 www.udac.fr
Tue-Fri 11am-6pm (Wed until 9pm), Sat-Sun 10am-6pm

Shirts by René Straub (left)
Musée de la Chemiserie et de l'Elégance masculine

In 1997 the museum moved to three floors in the Rohan wing of the Louvre where two permanent galleries show collections which are rotated every six months. Clothes are selected from 16,000 costumes and 35,000 accessories from the 18th century to the present forming the third largest collection in the world. French designers are extremely well represented with items by Lanvin, Chanel, Dior, Courrèges, Paco Rabanne, Guy Laroche, Yves Saint Laurent, Patou, Lacroix, Jean-Louis Scherer. Of particular note is the Vicomtesse Bernard de Bonneval's collection, which was acquired in 1948. Men's, women's and children's clothes, dressing gowns, lingerie, accessories, shawls – the 1,033 items span two centuries up to 1900 and are a testimony to fashion history.

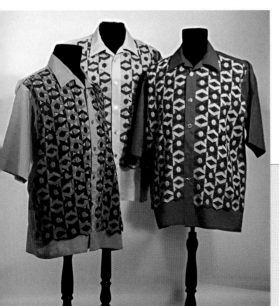

Philadelphia Museum of Art
26th Street and the Benjamin Franklin Parkway, Philadelphia, Pennsylvania 19130, USA
Tel. (1) 215 763 8100
www.philamuseum.org
Tue-Sun 10am-5pm (Wed until 8.45pm)

Linen shirt from around 1880
Musée de la Chemiserie et de l'Elégance masculine

Less well known than other collections in the country, it is nevertheless considered one of the best textile collections in the US, noteworthy for its collection of haute-couture clothing, which goes back to the 19th-century high-style designers. This includes important late 19th-century gowns designed by great Parisian couturiers, including Charles Frederick Worth. The museum also owns the wedding dress worn by Grace Kelly when she married Prince Rainier of Monaco in 1956.

Victoria and Albert Museum

Cromwell Road, South Kensington, London SW7 2RL, UK
Tel. (44) 20 7942 2000 www.vam.ac.uk
Daily 10am-5.45pm (Wed & last Fri of every month 10am-10pm)

Approximately a third of this colossal dress collection is made up of fashion from the 20th century. Particularly noteworthy is the collection formed by Cecil Beaton. Among recent accessions are 200 outfits donated by Jill Ritblat, a unique testimony of style and fashion from Christian Dior to the grunge fashion of London's trendy King's Road.

ISLAMIC AND ORIENTAL TEXTILES

Museum of Anthropology

University of Michigan, Natural Science Museum Building, 1109 Geddes Avenue, Ann Arbor, Michigan 48109-1079, USA
Tel. (1) 734 764 0485 www.umma.lsa.umich.edu
Mon-Fri 8am-5pm (by appt. only)

This large and diverse collection of textiles, amassed in the early 1930s by Dr Walter Koelz, contains several outstanding pieces documenting the sophisticated textile arts of South and Central Asia and Iran. The Stevens collection, donated in 1926, is also extremely valuable with more than 250 textiles, including a range of garments and accessories such as fans, fan cases, purses, hats, and shoes, as well as embroidered panels, tapestries, and brocades designed for making clothing, providing an excellent overview of the art of the early 20th-century Chinese weaving and needlework.

The Art Institute of Chicago

111 South Michigan Avenue, Chicago, Illinois 60603, USA
Tel. (1) 312 443 3600 www.artic.edu
Mon-Fri 10.30am-4.30pm (Tue until 8pm), Sat 10am-5pm, Sun noon-5pm

The Chinese textile collection is exceptional in quality and scope and features Imperial Court textiles used for various ceremonial and religious rituals, as well as rich textiles for use in homes.

Ashmolean Museum

Beaumont Street, Oxford, Oxfordshire OX1 2PH, UK
Tel. (44) 1865 278000 www.ashmol.ox.ac.uk
Tue-Sat 10am-5pm, Sun 2-5pm (except the Cast Gallery), most public holidays 2-5pm

The Ashmolean contains a notable collection of silk Ikat coats from Central Asia, collected in 1868-69 by merchant and explorer Robert Shaw, who was the first

Englishman to visit Yarkand and Kashgar in Chinese Turkestan. These spectacular dyed garments, patterned by the complex Ikat resist technique, were characteristic of Bukhara, Tashkent, and Samarkand. The Department of Eastern Art also has an exceptional collection of Islamic embroideries (the Newberry collection), mostly dating from the Fatimid, Ayyubid, and Mamluk periods. Apart from some caps and a fragile child's tunic, virtually all this material is fragmentary.

Association pour l'Etude et la Documentation des Textiles d'Asie
The Association for the Study and Documentation of Asian Textiles
60 bis ave. de Breteuil, 75007 Paris, France
Tel. (33) 1 45 67 94 01
By appt. only

Founded in 1979 by Krishna and Jean Riboud, who have been meticulously studying and collecting ancient Asian textiles for decades. When their collection had grown to overwhelming proportions they decided to found this study centre. Under Krishna's leadership it has amassed an impressive collection that includes several thousand textiles dating from the 15th through to the 20th century, including Indian shawls from the 18th century, kimonos from the Edo period, as well as Japanese textiles and Liao-period costume (907-1125).

Bankfield Museum
Boothtown Road, Halifax,
West Yorkshire HX3 6HG, UK
Tel. (44) 1422 354823
Mon 10am-5pm, Tue-Sat &
public holidays, Sun 2-5pm

Calderdale is part of the rich textile heritage of the West Yorkshire textile manufacturing belt begun in the 16th century. Hidden away here is this little museum set in what was once the home of Edward Akroyd, a prominent local textile owner. Highlights are items from China such as mandarin costumes and embroideries, including shoes for bound feet and what is probably the finest collection of Burmese textiles in Britain (around 880 items).

Linen hanging embroidered with coloured silks, Asia Minor, 18th century
Royal Museum of Scotland

Cooper-Hewitt National Design Museum
Smithsonian Institution, Fifth Avenue at 91st Street, New York, New York 10028, USA
Tel. (1) 212 849 8400 www.si.edu
Tue 10am-9pm, Wed-Sat 10am-5pm, Sun noon-5pm

An encyclopedic collection of Islamic textiles representing the Mediterranean and the Middle East from the 8th to the 13th century.

Field Museum of Natural History
1400 S Lake Shore Drive, Chicago, Illinois 60605-2496, USA
Tel. (1) 312 922 9410 www.fieldmuseum.org
Daily 9am-5pm

Perhaps not the first place you'd think of finding an array of important textiles, but the museum was founded to house both the biological and anthropological collections assembled for the World's Colombian Exposition of 1893. These objects form the core of the collections which have expanded through worldwide expeditions, exchange, purchase, and gifts to house over twenty million specimens. With more than 3,000 Chinese textiles, out of a collection of 6,000 ethnographic textiles, this museum has one of the top collections in the US.

Museum of Fine Arts

465 Huntington Avenue, Boston, Massachusetts 02115-5519, USA
Tel. (1) 617 267 9300 www.mfa.org
Mon-Tue 10am-4.45pm, Wed-Fri 10am-9.45pm (West Wing: Thu-Fri after 5pm only),
Sat-Sun 10am-5.45pm

The museum's Persian, Indian and Indonesian silk weavings are of exceptional quality, as is the collection of central Asian and Indonesian ikats. A Persian velvet tent ceiling with hunters and animals of the Safavid period, said to have been captured by the Ottoman Sultan Sulayman the Magnificent during one of his invasions of Persia in 1543-45, is an outstanding example of Persian 16th-century silk weaving.

Musée Guimet - Musée National des Arts Asiatiques
The Guimet Museum - National Museum for Asian Arts
6 place d'Iéna, 75016 Paris, France
Tel. (33) 1 56 52 53 00 www.museeguimet.fr
Mon, Wed-Sun 10am-6pm

The small but rich textile collection holds rare Chinese silk pieces. Some date back as far as the Han Dynasty (206BC-AD221) and were unearthed in tombs at Tuan-Huang near the Gobi Desert. These ancient fabrics are believed to be among the only preserved testimonies to the commercial Chinese silks of these times, which were then as precious as gold and jewels.

Indianapolis Museum of Art
1200 W 38th Street, Indianapolis, Indiana 46208-4196, USA
Tel. (1) 317 920 2660 www.ima-art.org
Tue-Sat 10am-5pm (Thu until 8.30pm), Sun noon-5pm

This part of the collection is probably less well known than those at other American museums, but is nonetheless worth a visit. Fine Persian embroideries and costumes, pile rugs and kilims, Turkish velvets, Greek Island embroideries, central Asian ikats and embroideries, Moorish textiles, Tunisian and Moroccan costumes, Moroccan wedding belts, embroideries, and rugs of many types.

Length of velvet *catma*, Turkish, late 15th to 16th century
Royal Museum of Scotland

Museum Kunst Palast
The Museum Art Palace
Ehrenhof 5, 40479
Dusseldorf, Germany
Tel. (49) 211 8992460
www.museum-kunstpalast.de
Tue-Sun 11am-6pm

The museum's collection comprises some 6,000

textiles representing most techniques from all European and many Eastern countries. A particular strength of the collection is its very fine selection of Islamic textiles. The silk-satin lampas fragments from Iran (16th century) and Turkey, (15th century) are particularly striking.

Los Angeles County Museum of Art (LACMA)
5905 Wiltshire Boulevard, Los Angeles, California 90036, USA
Tel. (1) 323 857 6000   www.lacma.org
Please call for opening times

More than 50,000 textiles and related objects in the textile department representing more than 100 cultures and 2,000 years of human civilization. Not only is there a collection of Edo and Momyana fragments from Japan and Japanese ecclesiastical vestments, but also a significant collection of Islamic fabrics from Persia, Turkey, and India. Smaller holdings from China, Tibet, and Korea, and Coptic tapestry weaving round up this part of the textile collection.

The Metropolitan Museum of Art
1000 Fifth Avenue at 82nd Street, New York, New York 10028, USA
Tel. (1) 212 535 7710   www.metmuseum.org
Tue-Thu, Sun 9.30am-5.30pm, Fri-Sat 9.30am-9pm

Thousands of textiles from China and Japan, including costumes and accessories such as kimonos, obis, wrestlers' costumes, and a rare collection of Noh costumes. The Chinese collection goes back to the T'ang Dynasty (AD618-907) and has over 2,000 pieces, including embroidered banners and woven silk tapestries. A large number of costumes, which include imperial court robes, are among the best of their kind in the West.

Minneapolis Institute of Arts
2400 Third Avenue South, Minneapolis, Minnesota 55404, USA
(1) 612 870 3131   www.artsmia.org
Tue-Wed, Sat 10am-5pm, Thu-Fri 10am-9pm, Sun noon-5pm

The largest Chinese robe collection in the US, with 350 robes from the early and late Ch'ing Dynasty (1644-1912), and imperial robes.

Nelson-Atkins Museum of Art
4525 Oak Street, Kansas City, Missouri 64111-1873, USA
Tel. (1) 816 561 4000   www.nelson-atkins.org
Tue-Thu 10am-4pm, Fri 10am-9pm, Sat 10am-5pm, Sun noon-5pm

A remarkable collection of Chinese textiles, with ancient pieces including early T'ang Dynasty (pattern-weave gauze fabrics), imperial costumes from the Ming Dynasty, and textile pieces from the tomb of Kuo Ch'in Wang, the 17th son of the K'ang Hsi emperor.

Philadelphia Museum of Art
26th Street and the Benjamin Franklin Parkway, Philadelphia, Pennsylvania 19130, USA
Tel. (1) 215 763 8100   www.philamuseum.org
Tue-Sun 10am-5pm (Wed until 8.45pm)

This prized collection of Chinese textiles includes over 2,000 pieces from the Han Dynasty (206BC-AD221) to the end of the Ch'ing Dynasty in 1911, and is one of the largest and finest in the US. The 22 Han Dynasty fragments, excavated by the Russian archaeologist P. K. Kozlov at Noin-ula in northern Mongolia in 1924-25, are among the only Han textiles in an American museum collection and are masterpieces of silk weaving. Key components of the Japanese collections (700 items) are Buddhist vestments and temple furnishings.

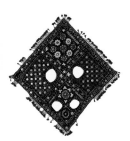

Andhani, a camel's head covering, Pakistan, early 20th century
The Textile Museum

The Royal Museum of Scotland
Chambers Street, Edinburgh EH1 1JF, Scotland, UK
Tel. (44) 131 2257534 www.nms.ac.uk
Mon-Sat 10am-5pm (Tue until 8pm), Sun noon-5pm

Outside of London, these collections are among the richest in the UK. Costumes and textiles of all sorts originate mainly from the Islamic regions of Arabia, Kuwait, Oman, Egypt, North Africa, Syria, Turkey, Iran, and Afghanistan. Notable are the examples of silk brocades and embroideries from Turkey, children's clothing from the early 17th century, along with complete costumes from the wardrobes of fashionable women from the 19th century.

The Textile Museum
2320 S Street, NW, Washington, DC 20008-4088, USA
Tel. (1) 202 667 0441 www.textilemuseum.org
Mon-Sat 10am-5pm, Sun 1-5pm

There is an important collection of *abbasid tiraz* (inscribed textiles) from Iraq, as well as a collection of around twenty inscribed cotton ikat from Yemen made in the 9th and 10th centuries. Although a small collection, it is in fact one of the largest such holdings in the world. Chinese textiles include garments and garment components such as rank badges. The Japanese collection also includes some 45 kimonos ranging from the mid-19th century to mid-20th century. Strong holdings of Javanese batik, Sumatra pieces, and Minangkabau textiles.

Musée des Tissus
The Museum of Fabrics
34 rue de la Charité, 69002 Lyon, France
Tel. (33) 4 78 37 15 05 www.lyon.cci.fr
Tue-Sun 10am-5.30pm

A wonderful display of Oriental and Islamic textiles with rare and fine examples. Highlights include Coptic tapestries; early Samanid Persian fabrics, featuring a superb green horseman's mantle; Byzantine textiles, including the Mozac Textile from the 8th century; and Persian and Turkish brocades and cut velvets.

Trésor de la Cathédrale
The Cathedral Treasure
6 rue Bonne Fortune, 4000 Liège, Belgium
Tel. (32) 4 232 6132
Tue-Sun 2-5pm

An outstanding exhibit of historic textiles and liturgical ornaments which includes a fine collection of medieval Oriental silk textiles dating back to the 6th century. Treasured by Liège's churches from as early as the Merovingian period, these silks bear witness to the good relations with the Orient prior to the Crusades.

Trésor de la Cathédrale de Sens
The Sens Cathedral Treasure
135 rue des Déportés de la Résistance, 89100 Sens, France
Tel. (33) 3 86 64 46 22
Oct-May: Mon, Thu-Fri 2-6pm, Wed, Sat-Sun 10am-noon, 2-6pm
Jun-Sep: daily 10am-noon, 2-6pm.

Many of the items in this ancient textile collection date back to the Middle Ages. Most of them escaped the turmoil of the French Revolution by being separated from their precious frames or reliquaries. There are many fragments, together with an exceptional group of shrouds and reliquary covers. There are Persian, Byzantine, Coptic, and Hispano-Mauresque pieces, most of them made of silk. Highlights include St Ebbon's chasuble and St Siviard's shroud in 8th-century Byzantine silk, St Léon's shroud in 11th- and 12th-century Byzantine silk, and St Victor's shroud in Persian silk, probably brought back from Agauna in 769 together with the martyr's body.

Victoria and Albert Museum
Cromwell Road, South Kensington, London SW7 2RL, UK
Tel. (44) 20 7942 2000
www.vam.ac.uk
Daily 10am-5.45pm (Wed & last Fri of every month 10am-10pm)

A museum with a very broad palette that embraces a variety of textiles holdings, including early Egyptian Islamic pieces, an enormous collection of Chinese textiles with thousands of items of woven and embroidered fabrics, and items from Japan such as priest robes, richly coloured kimonos from the Edo period, and Noh drama costumes. One of its greatest collections is made up of fabrics from the Ching Dynasty (1644-1912) such as velvets and brocades, and over 200 ceremonial robes. Notable, also, are 16th- and 17th-century Turkish velvets with designs showing traces of Italian influences, silks with ogival lattice patterns, and a child's silk kaftan with tiger stripes, said to have been removed from a royal tomb in Istanbul or Bursa. Early Islamic textile fragments are equally important. Among the most coveted is a silk cloth piece with woven patterns of circles containing bunches of grapes and flowers, along with an inscription embroidered in yellow silk with a reference to an Umayyad caliph. This is one of the oldest extant inscriptions of the official factories which played a part in the textile production of the Islamic world.

Zamek królewski na Wawelu
The Wawel Royal Castle
Wawel 5, 31-001 Crzcow, Poland
Tel. (48) 12 4225155
Tue-Sat 9.30am-3pm (Fri until 4pm), Sun 10am-3pm

An early traveller wrote, 'The Ottomans lodge more grandly in the field than at home.' Naturally, the sultan's tents were among the most lavish with embroidered silks and decorative quilting lining the walls and silk cord windows. Although the largest collection of Ottoman tents are to be found in the Topkapi Palace, Istanbul, they are for the most part held in storage. Here the visitor can enter the tents and enjoy their breathtaking beauty. The Royal Castle houses five complete pasha's tents, the largest of which has a wall height of 3.7 metres and a length of almost 24 metres. All these, along with a number of other items to be found at the Cracow National Museum, were captured at the Battle of Vienna in 1683.

Wereldmuseum
Willemskade 25, 3016 DM Rotterdam, The Netherlands
Tel. (31) 10 2707172   www.wereldmuseum.rotterdam.nl
Tue-Sun 10am-5pm

This museum's fine textile collection comprises some 11,000 examples, including archaeological fragments, from all of the world's civilizations and from almost every period in history. Indonesian batik predominates, amassed by the Dutch Missionary Society, active there since 1813. There is also a selection of Persian fabrics, Indian and Chinese embroidery, Japanese gold-thread kimonos and ikats, and ceremonial and theatre costumes.

JEWELLERY

Antikensammlung
The Collection of Antiquities

Schlossstrasse 1, 14059 Berlin, Germany
Tel. (49) 30 32091215
Mon-Thu 9am-5pm, Sat-Sun 10am-5pm

This museum possesses a fine collection of Greek and Roman decorative arts, including a treasury comprising an astonishing selection of antique objects in gold and silver, including gems from the Mediterranean basin. One of the finest collections of Scythian gold jewellery, including a gold fish weighing more than 600g (1.3lb).

Bracelet by Marion
Herbst, 1969
Museum Het Kruithuis

Museo archeologico nazionale di Firenze
The Florence National Archaeological Museum

Via della colonna 38, 50100 Florence, Italy
Tel. (39) 055 247864
Tue-Sat 9am-2pm, Sun 9am-1pm

This outstanding collection of precious stones (accessed only by special permission) contains gems of every description, cameos, the Unguent Box of Torrita, and the seal-ring of Augustus, in gold and jasper, found in his mausoleum in Rome.

Museo degli Argenti
The Silverware Museum

Palazzo Pitti, piazza Pitti, 50125 Florence, Italy
Tel. (39) 055 2388709
Daily 8.30am-3.30pm

Situated in the ground-floor rooms of Palazzo Pitti, this museum is packed to overflowing with precious objects of all kinds. Its lack of unity reflects the diversity of tastes, fashions, and working methods of the four centuries of collecting and patronage which make up this collection. Engravers of crystal, cameos, gold, and silver all competed in displays of invention and superb technique to produce the objects which are at the core of the museum. Of particular interest are the so-called *galaterie gioiellate* of Anna Maria Luisa de' Medici (18th century) who commissioned precious jewellery throughout Europe; the collections belonging to Mary Magdalene of Austria and Prince Ferdinando; and those belonging to the Palatine Electress.

The Arizona State Museum

The University of Arizona, Tucson, Arizona 85721-0026, USA
Tel. (1) 520 621 6281 www.statemuseum.arizona.edu
Mon-Sat 10am-5pm, Sun noon-5pm

American Indian silver jewellery from the Navaho, Hopi, and Zuni tribes, decorated with turquoise and other semiprecious stones. Traders were in awe of the beauty of these bold decorative pieces and a number of the earliest examples came from the trader John Wetherill. Others, such as Mexican crosses and glass-bead necklaces, came to the museum when Donald Cordry donated his collections.

Musée des Arts Décoratifs
The Museum of Decorative Arts

Palais du Louvre, 107 rue de Rivoli, 75001 Paris, France
Tel. (33) 1 44 55 57 50 www.ucad.fr
Due to re-open 2003

A splendid jewellery collection, of which two items stand out: the Lalique collection of some eighty objects includes the *Peigne aux Ombelles* in horn, silver, enamel, and patinal, and the *Broche Paon* made of moon stone and translucent blue enamel.

Il Museo del Bijou di Casalmaggiore
The Jewellery Museum of Casalmaggiore
Via A. Porzio, 9, 26041 Casalmaggiore, Italy
Tel. (39) 0375 42309
Sat-Sun 3.30-6.30pm

More than 5,000 items of 20th-century costume jewellery. Reconstructed workshops come complete with jewellery-making equipment and instruments. Among the most remarkable collections are the Art Deco and Art Nouveau gilded jewels.

British Museum
Great Russell Street, London WC1B 3DG, UK
Tel. (44) 20 7636 1555 ww.thebritishmuseum.ac.uk
Mon-Sat 10am-5pm, Sun noon-6pm

This extensive collection includes Byzantine, Anglo-Saxon, Medieval, Renaissance, and later goldsmith's work and jewellery. The national collection of engraved gems are on display, many of which came from the Sir Hans Sloane collection. There are a large number of objects from the *Sutton Hoo* ship burial. The Hull Grundy gift of jewellery ranges from 6th-century Byzantium to the 1950s, neatly extending the collection to the mid 20th century. It is particularly strong in the period 1700 to 1950 and includes a great variety of pieces worn by levels of society below the very rich.

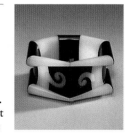

Bracelet of carved black and white jade, set with gold by Charlotte de Syllas, 1999
Worshipful Company of Goldsmiths

Cabinet des Médailles et Antiques
The Cabinet of Medals and Ancient Works of Art
Bibliothèque nationale de France, 58 rue de Richelieu, 75002 Paris, France
Tel. (33) 1 47 03 83 30
Daily 1-5pm

Housed in an old building of the national library, this is one of France's treasure troves. The collection of cameos (4,000 items) is one of the leading collections in the world, not only for the extraordinary variety and quality of its pieces, but also because it holds the Roman *Grand Camée* or *Apothéose de Germanicus*, the world's largest cameo (30cm) from the treasury of the Sainte-Chapelle. The collection of ancient cameos is astounding and contains a unique example representing Alexander the Great, which is thought to be the work of Pyrgoteles, one of the few artists allowed to represent him.

Museu Calouste Gulbenkian
The Calouste Gulbenkian Museum
Ave. de Berna 45a, 1067 Lisbon, Portugal
Tel. (351) 21 7823000 www.gulbenkian.pt
Tue 2-6pm, Wed-Sun 10am-6pm

A friend of Lalique for fifty years, Gulbenkian amassed a rich collection of jewellery, glass and other works. Perhaps one the best known of Gulbenkian's treasures is a brooch depicting a fanciful hybrid dragonfly, which was so stunning that it was the centre of attention at the 1900 World Exhibition in Paris.

Ermitazh
The Hermitage
Dvortsovskaia naberezhnaia 34-36, 191065 St Petersburg, Russian Federation
Tel. (7) 812 1109079 www.hermitage.ru
Tue-Sat 10.30am-6pm, Sun 10.30am-5pm

An exceptional collection of ancient Greek jewellery, including a gold pendant from the burial-mound of Kul-Oba near Kerch (5th century BC), on which is reproduced the famous head of Athena Parthenos by Phidias. Also on display is a gilded cover from a Scythian quiver, decorated with scenes from the life of Achilles (4th century BC). Masterpieces of modern jewellery are displayed in the Treasure Chamber and include many pieces that previously belonged to the Tsarinas.

Gosudarstvennoi istoriko-kul'turnyi muzei-zapovednik 'Moskovskii Kreml'-Oruzheinaia palata
The State Historical-Cultural Museum-Preserve 'Moscow Kremlin' - The Armoury
Krasnaia ploshchad', 103073 Moscow, Russian Federation
Tel. (7) 095 2023776   www.kremlin.museum.ru
Mon-Wed, Fri-Sun 10am-4pm

In 1709, after the Battle of Poltava, Peter the Great ordered that all trophy weapons and banners should be transferred to the Armoury to form a museum of military glory. The Armoury became a Russian treasure house where military trophies, the Tzars' regalia and items used in church services would be displayed. It also houses Russia's diamond treasury, which contains the Imperial crowns and regalia from the reign of Ivan the Terrible to the 19th century.

Bracelet by Emmy van Leersum, 1968
Museum Het Kruithuis

Headley-Whitney Museum
4435 Old Frankfort Pike, Lexington, Kentucky 40510, USA
Tel. (1) 606 255 6653   www.headley-whitney.org
Tue-Fri 10am-5pm, Sat-Sun noon-5pm

The Jewel Room features over 35 jewelled objects designed by George W. Headley between the 1940s and the 1970s. Headley, who studied at the Beaux-Arts,was influenced by both Benvenuto Cellini and Carl Fabergé.

Mouseío istorías tes ellenikés endumasías
The Museum of the History of Greek Costume
Dimokritou 7, 106 71 Athens, Greece
Tel. (30) 1 3629513
Mon, Wed, Fri 10am-1pm

The ornament is an indispensable accessory of Greek costume and there are fine specimens of Greek gold and silver work, in which one can discern the influences of both East and West.

Museum Het Kruithuis
The Kruithuis Museum
5211 LX 's-Hertogenbosch, The Netherlands
Tel. (31) 73 6122588   www.fku.nl
Wed-Sun 1-5pm

An international collection of contemporary jewellery from the 1940s to the present day. The museum has a conceptual approach to jewellery, which it places as equal to other applied arts such as ceramics, and attention is given to its contemporary developments. It showcases 500 works by over 25 artists and traces how the

Netherlands became an international pioneer in the development of avant-garde jewellery in the period after World War II.

Museum of London
London Wall, London EC2Y 5HN, UK
Tel. (44) 20 7600 3699 www.museumoflondon.org.uk
Mon-Sat 10am-5.50pm, Sun noon-5.50pm

Of the jewellery here, the Cheapside hoard of Elizabethan and Jacobean items is exceptional, as is the fine collection of mourning and costume jewellery.

Musée du Louvre
The Louvre
Palais du Louvre, 34-6 quai du Louvre, 75001 Paris, France
Tel. (33) 1 40 20 53 17 www.louvre.fr
Mon, Wed 9am-9.15pm, Thu-Sun 9am-5.30pm

Among the most famous items of the French crown jewels are the crowns of Louis XV (1772) and that of Charlemagne, and the Empress Josephine's pearl earrings. The Crown Diamonds include the 137-carat Regent, the 105-carat Cote de Bretagne ruby, the 20-carat Hortensia pink diamond, and the 56-carat Sancy diamond.

Double heart brooch of silver by A. Stewart, Inverness, late 18th century
Royal Museum of Scotland

Magyar nemzeti múzeum
The Hungarian National Museum
Múzeum körút 14-16, 1088 Budapest, Hungary
Tel. (36) 1 3382122 www.origo.hnm.hu
Mid Mar-Nov: daily 10am-6pm. Nov-mid Mar:daily 10am-5pm

The showcase of the museum, founded by Count Ferenc Széchényi in 1802, is the fine collection of jewellery dating from the Middle Ages to the 19th century. Unique items include the crown of the Emperor Constantinos Monomachos IX (11th century), a masterpiece of the imperial workshop assembled of golden plates with cloisonné enamel; and a 13th-century burial crown with breathtaking fleur-de-lys ornamentation.

Mpenaki mouseío
The Benaki Museum
Odós Koumbari 1, 10674 Athens, Greece
Tel. (30) 1 3611000 www.benaki.gr
Mon, Wed, Fri, Sat 9am-5pm, Thu 9am-midnight, Sun 9am-3pm

This exceptional collection of jewellery has been gathered from northern and central Greece, Attica, the Dodecanese, the Cyclades, the Ionian Islands, and Asia Minor. The most well known pieces include the three-masted caravels and the golden necklaces from Siphnos and Patmos; the gold ear-drops from Kos; the dazzling display of Mycenaean gold jewels discovered in a 'royal' burial in Thebes; and the Treasure of Thessaly.

National Museum of Natural History
Smithsonian Institution, 10th Street and Constitution Avenue, NW Washington, DC 20560, USA
Tel. (1) 202 357 2700 www.mnh.si.edu
Daily 10am-5.30pm

The gem and mineral collections contain exceptional pieces of historic jewellery, including a Spanish Inquisition necklace set with emeralds and diamonds; Marie-Antoinette's ear rings, given to her by Louis XVI and seized when she fled the Tuileries during the French Revolution; and the crown given to the Empress Marie-Louise by Napoleon, a masterpiece of 950 diamonds weighing 700 carats.

Porvoon Museo
The City Museum of Porvoo
Välikatu 11, 06100 Porvoo, Finland
Tel. (358) 19 5747589
May-Aug: daily 11am-4pm. Sep-Apr: Wed-Sun noon-4pm

Modest, but worth noting, is the collection of jewellery made of human hair, including necklaces, bracelets, ear rings, and watch chains – popular mementoes of loved ones during the romantic period of the early 19th century.

Provinciaal Diamantmuseum
The Provincial Museum of Diamonds
Lange Herentalsestraat 31-33, 2018 Antwerp, Belgium
Tel. (32) 3 202 4890
Daily 10am-5pm

Located in the heart of Antwerp's diamond quarter, in the middle of the Jewish district, every aspect of the diamond business is shown, including beautiful examples from the 17th and 18th centuries. A 19th-century diamond workshop has been reconstructed, where on Saturdays (or weekdays by appointment) you can watch a diamond cutter at work.

Royal Museum of Scotland
National Museums of Scotland, Chambers Street, Edinburgh EH1 1JF, Scotland, UK
Tel. (44) 131 225 7534 www.nms.ac.uk
Mon-Sat 10am-5pm (Tue until 8pm), Sun noon-5pm

More than 2,500 examples of 19th- and 20th-century European jewellery, including 220 pieces of 19th-century sentiment jewellery from the collection of Lady Binning. Work your way around the early material but look also at the internationally important collection of 20th-century costume jewellery. Particular strengths include Arts and Crafts jewellery and works of the 1970s. There is also a small collection of jewellery designed by Picasso, Cocteau, and Braque.

Necklace of silver, amethysts, and green and white enamel, English, *c.*1910
Royal Museum of Scotland

Tower of London
Tower Hill, London
EC3N 4AB, UK
Tel. (44) 20 7709 0765
www.tower-of-london.com
Mar-Oct: Mon-Sat 9am-5pm, Sun 10am-5pm. Nov-Feb: Tue-Sat 9am-4pm, Sun, Mon 10am-4pm

During medieval times, Crown Jewels were the personal property of the sovereign. Most were kept at the Tower, particularly when the sovereign was in residence there, although the Coronation Regalia was held at Westminster Abbey. Among the most fascinating pieces are the crowns, orbs, and sceptres, including the Imperial State Crown, Queen Victoria's small crown, and the lovely crown and diadem of Mary of Modena. Most date from the 17th century or later, but some, such as the Ampulla and Spoon used for the anointing of the new Sovereign with holy oil, are from the 12th century and late 14th century.

Victoria and Albert Museum
Cromwell Road, South Kensington, London SW7 2RL, UK
Tel. (44) 20 7942 2000 www.vam.ac.uk
Daily 10am-5.45pm (Wed & last Fri of every month 10am-10pm)

An impressive group of 18th- and 19th-century jewellery, and a medieval and Renaissance collection. Also on display is part of Napoleon's marriage gift in 1806 to Stephanie de Beauharnais (the future Grand Duchess of Baden). Contemporary examples by the world's current designers are continually being added to the collection.

The Walters Art Museum
600 N Charles Street, Baltimore, Maryland 21201, USA
Tel. (1) 410 547 9000 www.thewalters.org
Tue-Fri 10am-4pm (until 8pm first Thu of every month), Sat-Sun 11am-5pm

Henry Walters, unlike his collecting contemporaries Freer and Frick, who concentrated on one subject or one particular era, wanted a collection which would represent a cross-section of the world's jewellery. The result is astonishing; masterpieces abound from the 3rd millennium BC to the early 20th century.

Worshipful Company of Goldsmiths
Goldsmiths' Hall, Foster Lane, London EC2V 6BN, UK
Tel. (44) 20 7606 7010 www.thegoldsmiths.co.uk
By appt. only

Started in 1961, the collection of jewellery celebrates the work of British artist-jewellers, including many who are internationally famous, such as Andrew Grima, Gerda Flöckinger, and David Thomas. The library's archives dating from the 14th century are open by appointment.

LACE

The Art Institute of Chicago
111 S Michigan Avenue, Chicago, Illinois 60603, USA
Tel. (1) 312 443 3600 www.artic.edu
Mon-Fri 10.30am-4.30pm (Tue until 8pm), Sat 10am-5pm, Sun noon-5pm

Just short of around 1,000 pieces from all over the world, (especially Italy, Flanders, Belgium, and England), dating from the 17th to the 19th centuries, form part of this extensive collection of textiles. Needle and bobbin lace of endless types are represented, including a fine late 16th- to early 17th-century border made into a collar, and an inscribed border fragment that is a superb example of part lace (a form of bobbin lace where individual motifs are made and stitched together).

Musée des Beaux-Arts et de la Dentelle
The Museum of Fine Arts and Lace
12 rue Charles Aveline, 61000 Alençon, France
Tel. (33) 2 33 32 40 07 www.ville-alencon.fr
Tue-Sun 10am-noon, 2-6pm (closed Jul, Aug)

One of the best features of the collection is the display of the *Point d'Alençon* which is particular to the town of Alençon. The collection looks at lace from the 12th century to the present day and displays examples from the main lace-making centres in Europe: Venice, Bruges, Brussels, Chantilly, Le Puy, Malines, Valencia, and England as well as Russia and Eastern Europe.

Musée des Beaux-Arts et de la Dentelle
The Museum of Fine Arts and Lace
25 rue Richelieu, 62100 Calais, France
Tel. (33) 3 21 46 48 40
Mon, Wed-Sun 10am-noon, 2-5.30pm

Calais has been a centre of industrial lace since the mid-19th century. The museum has a collection of about 300,000 lace samples from here and other lace centres.

Brangwyn Museum
Dijver 16, 8000 Bruges, Belgium
Tel. (32) 5 044 8711
Apr-Sep: daily 9.30am-5pm. Oct-Mar: Mon, Wed-Sun 9.30am-12.30pm, 2-5pm

18th-century Burano needlepoint lace (from the Esther Oldham Collection)
Wellesley Historical Society

One of the star attractions is an early 18th-century Benediction Veil in Brussels bobbin lace and fine Brabantine clothing lace, including caps, flounces, and albs. The better part of the needlepoint section consists of Italian and more particularly Venetian work, with some fine pieces of Van Dyck lace. Interspersed between the displays are paintings, such as a full-length picture of Empress Maria Theresa dressed in Brussels lace (18th century), which dramatically illustrates the use of lace as costume decoration.

Musée du Costume et de la Dentelle
The Costume and Lace Museum
4-6 rue de la Violette, 1000 Brussels, Belgium
Tel. (32) 2 512 7709 www.brussels-online.be
Apr-Sep: Mon-Tue, Thu-Fri 10am-noon, 1.30-5pm, Sat-Sun 2-4.30pm. Oct-Mar: Mon-Tue, Thu-Fri 10am-12.30pm, 1.30-4pm, Sat-Sun 2-4.30pm

Charmingly located in two 18th-century gabled houses, its major collections of lace, costumes, and accessories from the 18th century to the present pay homage to one of the city's cornerstones of economic activity. The museum features new and old lace collections with special emphasis on 16th- to 19th-century lace from Brussels and the Belgium provinces. Outstanding examples of Brussels appliqué, such as shawls, flounces or christening and bridal veils, a magnificent ceremonial court skirt made from tulle with applied bobbin lace for Empress Eugénie, and a stunning Art Nouveau-inspired gala evening skirt (*c.* 1900) for the Duchess of Castro-Enrique, are just a selection of some of the highlights.

Museum of Costumes and Textiles
51 Castle Gate, Nottingham, Nottinghamshire NG1 6AF, UK
Tel. (44) 115 9153500
Daily 10am-5pm

The museum traces the history and development of clothing, fashion, and textiles from the 18th to the mid-20th century. It naturally concentrates on Nottingham's extensive lace-making industry.

Csipkemúzeum
The Lace Museum
Kossuth utca 37a, 6400 Kiskunhalas, Hungary
Tel. (36) 77 421797
Daily 10am-noon, 1-4pm

Kiskunhalas is the only town in Hungary which has a century-old history of lace-making. Halas lace has grown to compete seriously with the famous lace of Brussels. In Kiskunhalas you also have a chance to visit the actual workshop and witness the birth of this fine lace.

Harzer Klöppelmuseum
The Harz Museum of Pillow Lace
Haus des Gastes, 38678 Buntenbock, Germany
Tel. (49) 5323 3583
Daily 10am-5pm

With its exhibition of lace, lace pillows, bobbins, and patterns, this charming museum recounts the long tradition and history of Harz lace-making from the early 17th century onwards.

Cecil Higgins Art Gallery and Museum
Castle Close, Bedford, Bedfordshire MK40 3NY, UK
Tel. (44) 1234 211222
Tue-Sat 11am-5 pm, Sun 2-5pm

A collection of lace with the emphasis on English lace from Bedfordshire, Buckinghamshire, and Honiton in Devon. The large collection of Bedfordshire lace includes pieces worked in the 'point-ground' style, where pattern and ground were created together.

Hillwood Museum and Gardens
4155 Linnean Avenue NW, Washington, DC 20008, USA
Tel. (1) 202 686 5807 www.hillwoodmuseum.org
Jan, Mar-Dec: Tue-Sat 9am-5pm

Marjorie Merriweather Post's eclectic interests led her to collect a wide variety of objects, including lace, which she particularly loved. The collection contains several hundred pieces that can be divided into three categories: personal (wearable), household (utilitarian, for domestic use), and antique (collectible).

Musées historique et du Vieux Courseulles
The Historic Museum of Old Courseulles
17 rue Amiral-Robert, 14470 Courseulles-sur-Mer, France
Tel. (33) 2 31 37 70 00
Easter-Sep: daily 2.30-6.30pm

Exceptionally rich collection of bobbin lace made locally between 1822 and 1922 which includes a shawl in silk Chantilly, lace made from gold and silver threads, and unique motifs made from polychrome Chantilly.

Kantcentrum
The Lace Centre
Peperstraat 3A, 8000 Bruges, Belgium
Tel. (32) 5 033 0072 www.brugge.be
Mon-Fri 10am-noon, 2-6pm, Sat 10am-noon, 2-5pm

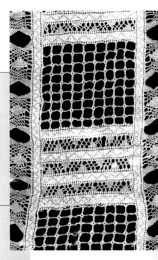

18th-century *reticello* work (from the Esther Oldham Collection)
(below)
Wellesley Historical Society

Detail of an Italian *mezzo punto* cuff from a scrapbook page (from the Esther Oldham Collection)
(bottom)
Wellesley Historical Society

The small museum's collection comprises early passement work from the late 16th century; opulent baroque Flemish clothing lace from the 17th century; and highly refined lace types such as Brussels, Mechelen, Valenciennes, Chantilly, Lille, and Paris lace produced in the southern Netherlands and northern France in the 18th and 19th centuries.

Museo del Merletto
The Lace Museum
Piazza Galuppi 187, 30012 Burano, Venice, Italy
Tel. (39) 041 730034
Apr-Oct: Mon, Wed-Sun 10am-5pm. Nov-Mar: Mon, Wed-Sun 10am-4pm

The 14th-century Palazzo Rodotà houses a collection of Burano and Venetian lace from the late 19th century to the early 20th century. Wonderful, are the fans and gloves made in Burano lace.

The Metropolitan Museum of Art
1000 Fifth Avenue at 82nd Street, New York, New York 10028, USA
Tel. (1) 212 535 7710   www.metmuseum.org
Tue-Thu, Sun 9.30am-5.30pm, Fri-Sat 9.30am-9pm

A massive lace collection with many thousands of examples covering the 16th through to the 20th century and revealing the history of lace-making virtually across the globe.

National Museum of Ireland
Kildare Street, Dublin 2, Ireland
Tel. (353) 1 6777444
Tue-Sat 10am-5pm, Sun 2-5pm

The lace collection includes a wide array of all types, mainly from Ireland but also from important European centres for lace-making from the 17th century to the present day. These include appliqué and guipure lace from Carrickmacross, and tambour and runwork from Limerick.

Detail of a skirt front of Carrickmacross lace designed by Alice Jacob
National Museum of Ireland

Museo del Pizzo e del Tombolo
The Bobbin Lace Museum
Villa Tigullio, Parco Casale, viale G. Maggio, 16035 Rapallo, Italy
Tel. (39) 0185 63305
Tue, Wed, Fri, Sat 3-6pm, Thu 10am-noon

The museum contains a rich collection of lace, documents, patterns and tools that illustrate the works of the lace-makers of Rapallo.

Royal Albert Memorial Museum
Queen Street, Exeter, Devon EX4 3RX, UK
Tel. (44) 1392 665858
www.exeter.gov.uk
Mon-Sat 10am-5pm

In the mid-19th century there was a general revival of interest in antique laces and Mrs Bury Palliser, sister of the novelist Captain Marryat, was an early collector and writer on this subject. The museum holds her collections and that of two other earlier collectors.

Royal Museum of Scotland

Chambers Street, Edinburgh EH1 1JF, Scotland, UK
Tel. (44) 131 2257534 www.nms.ac.uk
Mon-Sat 10am-5pm, Tue 10am-8pm, Sun noon-5pm

Around 1,200 items of lace are on display (not including lace on garments) dating from the 16th century onwards.

Tønder Museum

Kongevej 51, 6270 Tønder, Denmark
Tel. (45) 74 722657 www.tonder-net.dk
Jun-Aug: daily 10am-5pm. Sep-May: Tue-Sun 10am-5pm

The lace collection bears witness to the rich tradition of lace-making throughout western Schleswig. It can be divided into four types according to date and source of inspiration: the Flemish laces, also called Schleswig laces because they were produced in the whole of Schleswig (1550-1700); the Binche/Valencienne laces (1700-1800); the Lille laces (1800-50), and the Torchon laces (1850-1900). Tønder's exquisite products were peddled by 'lace postmen', who travelled to parts of Germany and Scandinavia selling the lace which they carried in leather bags.

Valentine Museum

Richmond History Center, 1015 East Clay Street, Richmond, Virginia 23219, USA
Tel. (1) 804 649 0711 www.valentinemuseum.com
Please call for opening times

A substantial costume-lace collection within a massive holding of costumes and textiles all originating from Virginia. There are several thousand pieces, mostly fragments, from all the main lace-producing countries.

Victoria and Albert Museum

Cromwell Road, South Kensington, London SW7 2RL, UK
Tel. (44) 20 7942 2000 www.vam.ac.uk
Daily 10am-5.45pm (Wed & last Fri of every month 10am-10pm)

This 2,000-plus-piece lace collection is extremely rich in Italian needle lace of the 17th century, with excellent examples of bobbin lace from Brussels (primarily 18th century). The collection also includes peasant laces from all over the world.

Wellesley Historical Society

229 Washington Street, Wellesley, Massachusetts, USA
Tel. (1) 781 235 6690 www.wellesleyhsoc.com
Mon, Wed 2-4.30pm, Thu 4.30-7.30pm, Sat 1.30-3.30pm (other times by appt.)

Fine examples of Italian workmanship from the 1500s, including the earliest form of needlepoint lace, known as *reticella*; an array of laces from England, France, Belgium, and Spain, with additional smaller holdings of examples from Malta, Ireland, Germany, and Scandinavia. Notable subsections include displays of Ipswich lace made by emigrants from the East Midlands counties of England as early as the 17th century. Knotted lace, sun lace, filet lace, *punto in aria* lace and early machine lace are all represented, along with lace pillows and bobbins, including several inscribed with romantic mottos. As well as the lace holdings, Esther Oldham donated her reference library containing dozens of volumes and scrapbooks she kept on lace and lace-making.

The Whitworth Art Gallery

University of Manchester, Oxford Road, Manchester M15 6ER, UK
Tel. (1) 161 2757450 www.man.ac.uk
Mon-Sat 10am-5pm, Sun 2-5pm

A textile and costume collection which almost matches that of the Victoria and Albert
Museum. Its particular strengths are early 16th- and 17th-century European lace –
mainly ecclesiastical rather than fashion-based examples.

QUILTS AND COVERLETS

The American Museum in Britain

Claverton Manor, Bath, Somerset BA2 7BD, UK
Tel. (44) 1225 460503 www.americanmuseum.org
Gardens: Tue-Fri 1-6pm, Sat-Sun noon-6pm, public holidays 11am-6pm
Museum: Tue-Sun 2-5pm, public holidays 11am-6pm

This impressive collection of more than 200 American quilts and woven coverlets
from the last two centuries is considered to be one of the finest in Europe. It includes
examples of patchwork, appliqué, quilting, candlewick, and embroidered spreads, as
well as *trapunto*, hooked rugs, samplers and examples of Navaho weaving. One of the
most extraordinary quilts on display was made by the slaves of the Mimosa Hall
Plantation in Texas for an Anglican bishop who toured the plantations each year to
baptise, confirm and marry.

The Art Institute of Chicago

111 South Michigan Avenue, Chicago, Illinois 60603, USA
Tel. (1) 312 443 3600 www.artic.edu
Mon-Fri 10.30am-4.30pm (Tue until 8pm), Sat 10am-5pm, Sun noon-5pm

Besides American bedcoverings, the museum's collection has had a significant
number of important additions over the past twenty years that range in date from the

Detail of a quilt
Shelburne Museum

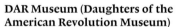

mid-16th to the 20th century. Among these are Chinese bedcovers tailored for export to English, French, or Dutch markets, a Portuguese example with densely placed needlework depicting the five senses, as well as an Indian bedcover executed using a resist-printing technique that was further embellished with painted elements.

Detail of a quilt
Shelburne Museum

Le Musée de Château-Gombert
The Gombert-Castle Museum
5 place des Héros, 13013 Marseille, France
Tel. (33) 4 91 68 14 38 www.enprovence.com
Mon-Fri 9am-noon, 2-6.30pm, Sat-Sun 2-6.30pm

Lion and Beavers, an American Waldoboro hooked rug, second half of 19th century
The American Museum in Britain

Local mason Jean-Baptiste Julien-Pignol amassed objects from his building sites and in 1928 displayed them in the museum's first exhibit of a Provençal kitchen. Growth of the collection has been phenomenal and now consists of thousands of local items that are shown over eight period rooms. Provençal urban and rural women's costumes from the 17th to the 20th century range from a late 17th-century quilted *cotillon* (petticoat), made from an imported indienne, an 18th-century corded-work camisole of delicate beauty to 19th-century quilted aprons and bedcovers.

DAR Museum (Daughters of the American Revolution Museum)
1776 D Street, NW, Washington, DC 20006-5392, USA
Tel. (1) 202 879 3241 www.dar.org
Mon-Fri 8.30am-4pm, Sun 1-5pm

Several period rooms and two galleries display one of the most historic quilt collections in the US with over 350 American quilts. The majority have documented histories and most were made prior to 1860.

Embroiderers' Guild
Apartment 41, Hampton Court Palace, Surrey KT8 9AU, UK
Tel. (44) 20 8943 1229
Mon-Fri 10.30am-4 pm

This collection is particularly magnificent as it has been donated by embroiderers as inspiration to others. Founded in 1906 the pioneers of the Guild started accumulating fragments of old British and foreign embroideries so that others could borrow and learn from them. There is a good representation of American patchwork quilts from the 19th century. Exquisite Persian covers, including the elaborate quilted bedcovers given to Bess of Hardwick by her son following a visit to Persia, are among many other gems.

Musée européen du Patchwork
The European Patchwork Museum
Le Bourg, 27500 Bourneville, France
Tel. (33) 2 32 57 40 41
Mar-Jun: Mon, Wed-Sun 2-6.30pm. Jul-Aug: daily 1.30-6.30pm. Sep-Oct: Mon, Wed-Sun 2-6pm. Nov-Dec: Sat, Sun 2-6pm

A unique patchwork collection of period pieces representing a wide range of designs and techniques with special emphasis on French and local production. There is a good collection of handmade old patchwork quilts and rag rugs as well as a fine selection of domestic items, such as cushions, blankets, and bedcovers.

Fenimore Art Museum
Lake Road, Route 80, Cooperstown, New York 13326, USA
Tel. (1) 607 547 1400 www.fenimoreartmuseum.org
Apr-May, Oct-Dec: Tue-Sun 10am-4pm. Jun-Sep: daily 10am-5pm

The New York State Historical Association's collection of textiles is extensive and includes 140 coverlets and a number of well-documented New York State quilts, representative of the weavers and techniques used in New York during the period 1790-1860.

Museum of Florida History
500 S Bronough Street, Tallahassee, Florida 32399-0250, USA
Tel. (1) 850 488 1484 www.dhr.dos.state.fl.us
Mon-Fri 9am-4.30pm, Sat 10am-4.30pm, Sun & public holidays noon-4.30pm

A small, but focused collection of around fifty quilts made in Florida, spanning its
history from the Territorial period to the present. It also maintains files on more than
5,000 quilts registered by the Florida Quilt Heritage Project.

The Kentucky Museum
The Kentucky Building, Western Kentucky University, One Big Red Way, Bowling
Green, Kentucky 42101, USA
Tel. (1) 270 745 2592 www.wku.edu
Tue-Sat 9.30am-4pm, Sun 1-4pm (times may vary please call for details; access to
museum artefacts by appt. only)

Quilts make up the most important single collection in the museum, established along
with the Kentucky Library in 1939 to preserve Kentucky's history and heritage. Today,
the quilt collection contains nearly 170 examples, made in the 19th century.

Michigan State University Museum
West Circle Drive, East Lansing, Michigan 48824-1045, USA
Tel. (1) 517 432 3800 www.museum.cl.msu.edu
Mon-Fri 9am-5pm, Sat 10am-5pm, Sun 1-5pm

Among the five hundred quilts, blocks and related items (including 5,000 files on
Michigan quilts and quilters), the focus of this collection is on Native American and
African American quilts. As the Plains Indians ran out of buffalo hides, they started
quilt-making based on lone-star patterns, or adaptations. The oldest Native
American quilt in the collection dates from the 1920s.

A selection of quilts
Shelburne Museum

National Museum of American History
14th Street and Constitution Avenue, NW, Smithsonian Institution, Washington, DC
20560 USA
Tel. (1) 202 357 2700 www.americanhistory.si.edu
Daily 10am-3.30pm

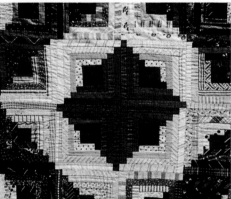

Over 600, mainly American, 18th to 20th-century bed covers, including whole cloth, pieced, and appliquéd quilts, hand-and-power woven coverlets and bedspreads. Highlights of the 18th-century bed covers include dated overshot coverlets, an all white New York quilt dated 1760, a linen counterpane with linen embroidery in shades of blue, and a quilt of printed cottons with crewel-embroidered borders and centre.

Two quilts from the Hat and Fragrance Textile Gallery
Shelburne Museum

The New England Quilt Museum

18 Shattuck Street, Lowell, Massachusetts, USA
Tel. (1) 978 452 4207
www.nequiltmuseum.org
Jan-Apr: Tue-Sat 10am-4pm.
May-Dec: Tue-Sat 10am-4pm,
Sun noon-4pm

This museum was founded in 1980 by the New England Quilter's Guild and is now in a landmark savings-bank building constructed in 1845 in the heart of Lowell. During the 19th century this was America's textile centre and besides this collection, there is, within walking distance, the American Textile History Museum. A permanent exhibition area showcases a rotating selection of four or five examples of quilts from their core collection numbering some 130 antique and contemporary quilts.

Pascack Historical Society Museum
19 Ridge Avenue, Park Ridge, New Jersey, USA
Tel. (1) 201 573 0307
Sun 2-4.30pm

This wonderful collection of quilts and coverlets includes the Tice quilt, made from the wedding dress of Harriet Van Riper Tice's great-great grandmother who was married in 1880. It is an example of the British 'double strike' copperplate printing developed by Joseph and Mary Ware (*c.* 1770). This is one of only two examples known to exist, the other was purchased by a British collection in 1957.

The People's Place Quilt Museum
3510 Old Philadelphia Pike, Intercourse, Pennsylvania 17534, USA
Tel. (1) 800 828 8218
Apr-Oct: Mon-Sat 9am-5pm

Considering the importance of the art of quilting to the Amish and Mennonite peoples, it is surprising that this is the only museum dedicated to this extraordinary art in Lancaster County. The museum holds no collections of its own, instead it features a new exhibit each year specializing in antique (pre-1940) Amish and Mennonite quilts loaned from a number of national museums and personal collections.

Shelburne Museum

US Route 7, Shelburne, Vermont 05482, USA
Tel. (1) 802 985 3346 www.shelburnemuseum.org
Late May-late Oct: daily 10am-5pm. Rest of year: tours by appt. at 1pm daily

Quilts and bed coverings provided much needed warmth and were often the only decoration in sparsely furnished 17th- and 18th-century homes. More than 700 examples are on display here.

Textilmuseum Max Berk
The Max Berk Textile Museum

Brahmsstrasse 8, 69118 Heidelberg-Ziegelshausen, Germany
Tel. (49) 6221 800317
Wed, Sat, Sun 1-6pm

The collection is dominated by a large stock of ladies costumes and accessories spanning three centuries. Additionally, one of the highlights is an important and extensive collection of antique patchwork quilts from the UK and the US from the 19th and 20th centuries. The museum has gained international recognition through hosting the Quilt Biennial, a unique forum for quilt-art enthusiasts from German-speaking countries.

Valentine Museum

Richmond History Centre, 1015 East Clay Street, Richmond, Virginia 23219, USA
Tel. (1) 804 649 0711 www.valentinemuseum.com
Mon-Sat 10am-5pm, Sun noon-5pm

One of the largest collections of costumes and textiles in the south (35,000 items), its focus is on clothes worn in this part of America from the 18th century onwards, but it also contains substantial holdings of bed accessories, including coverlets, appliquéd quilts and bed curtains, as well as blankets and robes from the 18th to the 20th century.

Wenham Museum

132 Main Street, Wenham, Massachusetts 01984, USA
Tel. (1) 978 468 2377 www.wenhammuseum.org
Tue-Sun 10am-4pm

Within the textile collections there is a significant collection of quilts, coverlets, quilt blocks, bedding and general household linens. The whole-cloth quilts constitute a collection from the late 18th to the early 19th centuries that includes a rare 18th-century example in yellow silk backed with yellow linen. Other quilts date from the mid-19th to the early 20th centuries. One of the most significant holdings in the textile department is the rare 1724 bed rug, said to be the finest piece of folk art north of Boston.

Winterthur Museum, Garden and Library

Route 52, Winterthur, Denver, Colorado 19735, USA
Tel. (1) 302 888 4600 www.winterthur.org
Mon-Sat 9am-5pm, Sun noon-5pm

Lovingly cared for by four generations of du Ponts this country estate cannot fail to inspire. Founder, Henry Francis du Pont, collector and horticulturist, created an unrivalled collection of early American decorative arts (1640-1860). Their major collection consists of several hundred patchwork, appliqué, and embroidered quilts and woven coverlets. One recent notable acquisition is a brilliantly coloured quilt made in 1827 by Philadelphia Quaker Rebecca Scattergood Savery. A staggering 6,708 diamond-shape pieces of cotton were stitched together in the starburst pattern to make this quilt and, because it was never washed, it still has its original glaze on the roller-printed fabric.

Worthing Museum and Art Gallery

Chapel Road, Worthing, West Sussex BN11 1HP, UK
Tel. (44) 1903 239999
Mon-Sat 10am-5pm

The domestic part of the textile collections contains cushions, tablecloths and even bell ropes, but the most popular aspect of this section is the collection of patchwork and quilted bedcovers. The earliest pieces date from 1800 and the most recent was completed in 1992. Pride of place is the 'Jubilee Quilt' made between 1887 and 1888 to mark Queen Victoria's Golden Jubilee.

SAMPLERS, EMBROIDERY AND NEEDLEWORK

The Art Institute of Chicago

111 South Michigan Avenue, Chicago, Illinois 60603, USA
Tel. (1) 312 443 3600 www.artic.edu
Please call for opening times

Magnificent Thuringian sampler, 1788
Das Deutsche Stickmuster-Museum

The holdings of 16th- and 17th-century English embroideries are particularly strong and include a partially assembled woman's cap embellished with coloured silks and gold and silver thread; a casket made by Rebecca Stonier Plaisted dated 1668; an embroidered mirror-glass frame with images of kings and queens; and an 18th-century panel from a settee with chinoiserie motifs.

Ashmolean Museum

Beaumont Street, Oxford, Oxfordshire OX1 2PH, UK
Tel. (44) 1865 278000 www.ashmol.ox.ac.uk
Tue-Sat 10am-5pm, Sun & public holidays 2-5pm (except the Cast Gallery)

On display are fine examples of *opus anglicanum* embroidery (AD1500) featuring mainly church vestments finely worked in silk and gold thread by highly skilled embroiderers.

The Burrell Collection

2060 Pollokshaws Road, Glasgow G43 1AT, Scotland, UK
Tel. (44) 141 6497151
Mon-Sat 10am-5pm, Sun 11am-5pm

Burrell's collection of textile pieces are of the highest quality. The items from the golden age of embroidered clothes in England (the Elizabethan era to the middle of the 17th century) are noteable. There are also stunning examples of later work, such as an English embroidered casket dating from the end of the 17th century, and small, embroidered pictures and mirror frames. This is not a static collection; the Lochleven hangings, among the earliest extant Scottish wall hangings, have recently been added.

Concord Museum

200 Lexington Road, Concord, Massachusetts, USA
Tel. (1) 978 369 9763 www.concordmuseum.org
Jan-Mar: Mon-Sat 11am-4pm, Sun 1-4pm. Apr-Dec: Mon-Sat 9am-5pm, Sun noon-5pm

This is the town where the first official battle of the Revolutionary War took place. It was also home to Emerson, Thoreau, Hawthorne, and Louisa May Alcott. Highlights

of the collection are the samplers and needlework pictures originating mainly from Concord and other parts of New England.

Das Deutsche Stickmuster-Museum
The German Sampler Museum
Palais in Prinzengarten, 29223 Celle, Germany
Tel. (49) 5141 382626
Feb-Dec: Tue-Thu, Sat-Sun 10am-5pm

Elfi and Hans-Joachim Connemann have been collecting samplers and needle arts since buying a small Danish sampler at auction in 1975. Since then they have amassed some 2,000 examples of these delicately embroidered works of art, covering four centuries.

South German sampler, 1763
Das Deutsche Stickmuster-Museum

Dean Castle
Dean Road, Kilmarnock, Ayrshire, Scotland, UK
Tel. (44) 1563 554704
Easter-Oct: daily noon-5pm. Nov-Easter: Sat-Sun noon-5pm

During the first half of the 19th century in Ayrshire, an important cottage industry grew up, perhaps encouraged by the demise of hand spinning. At its height, it employed thousands of female workers, who produced translucent, delicate muslins decorated with the finest of sewing threads, to produce a distinctive white-on-white embroidery, apparently inspired by a robe brought back from France by a daughter of the Earl of Eglinton. A growing collection of Ayrshire needlework is held at the Castle and includes samplers, christening robes, children's day dresses, and bonnets.

Embroiderers' Guild
Apartment 41, Hampton Court Palace, Surrey KT8 9AU, UK
Tel. (44) 20 8943 1229
Mon-Fri 10.30am-4pm

Danish sampler, 1808
Das Deutsche Stickmuster-Museum

This exquisite international collection is filled with many fine examples of embroidery, samplers, and needlework. The British collection spans four centuries to the present with an English coif from the early 17th century, a crewelwork hanging from the 18th century, and a superb 18th-century silk velvet Englishman's suit. The collection also benefits from a good representation of 20th-century embroidery. From the Native Americans are fine textiles and outstanding examples of quillwork, moosehair and beadwork embroidery on costumes and accessories. In addition, there is a unique collection of eastern Mediterranean embroideries on Turkish towels (*havlu*), a magnificent 19th-century Turkish ceremonial shaving robe and red silk velvet slippers, and fine Persian covers, quilts, costumes, and bridal shawls.

Museum of Fine Arts
465 Huntington Avenue, Boston, Massachusetts 02115-5519, USA
Tel. (1) 617 267 9300 www.mfa.org
Mon-Tue 10am-4.45pm, Wed-Fri 10am-9.45pm, Sat-Sun 10am-5.45pm

A remarkable collection of European embroidery dating from the 14th to

the 18th centuries, mainly from England, France, Italy, and Spain, including a late 14th-century Italian polychrome silk of The Crucifixion, from Florence. The Greek and Turkish embroidery holdings are world-famous. Well represented is New England embroidery as well as that from the Greek Islands (one of the most extensive collections in the US). There are also over 300 samplers, the oldest of which is a group worked by professional embroiderers in Mamluk Egypt from the 13th to the 16th centuries, but the strengths of this section are those from the 17th and 18th centuries, as highlighted by examples from the New World.

Interior of the museum
Das Deutsche Stickmuster-Museum

Fitzwilliam Museum

Trumpington Street, Cambridge, Cambridgeshire CB2 1RB, UK
Tel. (44) 1223 332900 www.fitzmuseum.cam.ac.uk
Tue-Sat 10am-5pm, Sun 2.15-5pm

Most of the 384 samplers in the collection are English. The earliest, dating from 1629, entered the museum with the Glaister and Longman bequests. Exhibits include a pattern darning sampler from Mamluk Egypt (15th century), a remarkable Ottoman sampler from the 18th century, which is covered with motifs found on Turkish domestic linen and costume, and different examples of map samplers, which became popular with teachers across Europe at the end of the 18th century. Embroidery pieces from the 16th to the 19th centuries include an important collection of Greek Island embroidery.

Manchester City Art Galleries

Gallery of Costume, Platt Hall, Rusholme, Manchester M14 5LL, UK
Tel. (44) 161 2245217 www.cityartgalleries.org.uk
Mar-Oct: daily 10am-5.30pm. Nov-Feb: daily 10am-4pm

An elegant 18th-century textile merchant's house contains one of the largest collections of clothing and fashion accessories in Britain, with around 20,000 items illustrating trends in British clothing for women, men, and children from 1600 to the present. One of the strengths of the collection is 18th-century British needlework and outstanding embroidery on aprons, men's waistcoats, undergarments, and shoes.

The Metropolitan Museum of Art

1000 Fifth Avenue at 82nd Street, New York, New York 10028, USA
Tel. (1) 212 535 7710 www.metmuseum.org
Tue-Thu, Sun 9.30am-5.30pm, Fri-Sat 9.30am-9pm

The embroidery collection has several thousand pieces from 14th-century Italy to 20th-century Hungary and Russia, with a large selection of English domestic embroideries. There is a substantial collection of samplers dating from the 17th to the 19th centuries representing numerous countries including Scandinavia and Holland.

Mpenaki mouseío
The Benaki Museum

Odós Koumbari 1, 10674 Athens, Greece
Tel. (30) 1 3611000 www.benaki.gr
Mon, Wed, Fri, Sat 9am-5pm, Thu 9am-midnight, Sun 9am-3pm

The collection of Greek embroideries in the Benaki Museum, founded in 1930, is particularly remarkable. They come from various regions of Greece and mostly date from the 17th and 18th centuries. The motifs show both Eastern and Western influence while retaining specific regional characteristics. The museum displays a fine selection of Cretan shift borders embroidered in coloured silks; a superb and colourful bedspread from Janina; and embroideries from Skyros, whose technique is remarkable, that include one of the earliest and best-known examples, the famous *goletta* (17th century).

543

Novgorodskii gosudarstvennyi muzei-zapovednik
The Novgorod State Museum-Preserve
Kreml' 11, 173007 Novgorod, Russian Federation
Tel. (7) 816 2273608 www.eng.novgorod-museum.ru
Mon, Wed-Sun 10am-6pm

A magnificent collection of medieval Russian embroidery and needlework. It ranges
from various shrouds and covers, to festive garments of the clergy and mitres,
each one with gold, silver and silk threads, pearls, and precious stones.

Musée du Pays rabastinois
The Rabastens Museum
Hôtel de la Fite, 2 rue Amédée Clausade, 81800 Rabastens, France
Tel. (33) 5 63 40 65 65
Apr-Nov: Tue-Sun 10am-noon, 3-5pm. Nov-Apr: Sat 10am-noon, 2.30-6pm, Sun 2.30-
6pm (groups at other times by appt. only)

The highlight of the museum is the René Bégué collection of embroideries. 'Rébé' was
the great Parisian haute-couture embroiderer who worked for the house of Dior and
donated to his native town more than 1,500 items, which he made throughout his career.

Philadelphia Museum of Art
26th Street and Benjamin Franklin Parkway, Philadelphia, Pennsylvania 19130, USA
Tel. (1) 215 763 8100 www.philamuseum.org
Tue-Sun 10am-5pm (Wed until 8.45pm)

Seven hundred samplers and embroidered pictures from Europe and the Americas,
of which nearly a third are European, with the greatest number from England and
Germany. As might be expected, the largest group of American samplers is from
Pennsylvania. Fine examples of Greek and Persian needlework, richly embroidered
Renaissance vestments, notable Lesage items by Schiaparelli, and Indian embroideries
containing the largest and most significant group of kantha embroideries outside of
India and Bangladesh.

The Pitt Rivers Museum
South Parks Road, Oxford, Oxfordshire OX1 3PP, UK
Tel. (44) 1865 270927 www.prm.ox.ac.uk
Mon-Sat 1-4.30pm, Sun 2-4.30pm

A densely packed collector's paradise. On display are examples from the rare and
curious collection of embroidery made with hair, mostly from Siberia and North America, as well as outstanding Naga textiles, including striped shawls worn by hunters.

Royal Museum of Scotland
Chambers Street, Edinburgh EH1 1JF, Scotland, UK
Tel. (44) 131 2257534 www.nms.ac.uk
Mon-Sat 10am-5pm (Tue until 8pm), Sun noon-5pm

British embroideries dominate the group. However, countries throughout the whole
world are represented. There are approximately 2,700 items of embroidery including
a fine collection of 200 samplers dating from the early 18th century to the present, of
which at least 150 are Scottish. The earliest pieces of embroidery are the *opus
anglicanum* (*c.* 1330), while Scottish pieces of particular importance include the
Fetternear banner (*c.* 1520), the sole remaining piece of pre-Reformation embroidery;
two early 17th-century panels of wall hangings from Lochleven Castle and
Linlithgow Palace; and a set of wall hangings by a Jacobite sympathizer, dated 1719.

Sárközi néprajzi ház
The Sárköz Ethnographical House
Kossuth Lajos utca 34-36, 7144 Decs, Hungary
Tel. (36) 74 495320
Mon-Fri 10am-6pm (Sat-Sun by appt. only)

The Sárköz on the west side of the Danube is a region of great ethnic variety. Agriculture made local peasants amazingly rich. Their wealth showed up in their handwoven embroidered textiles and embroideries in general. Three local enthusiasts, two parish priests and an artist, started collecting Sárköz embroidery and textiles, and the first ever exhibition was organized in Budapest in 1926. The Ethnographical House was opened in 1955 and remains the richest and most spectacular ethnographical museum in Hungary.

Textilmuseum
The Textile Museum
Vadianstrasse 2, 9000 St Gallen, Switzerland
Tel. (41) 71 2221744 www.textilmuseum.ch
Apr-Oct: Mon-Fri 10am-noon, 2-5pm, Sat 10am-5pm

A school for embroidery designers was established here in 1867 in order to train new designers in the wake of the rapid industrialisation which was revolutionizing the embroidery industry. The collection begins with a sumptuous display of exotic textiles, discovered in Egyptian tombs, and a number of historical embroideries that date from the 14th century including some manual and whitework embroidery from eastern Switzerland.

Victoria and Albert Museum
Cromwell Road, South Kensington, London SW7 2RL, UK
Tel. (44) 20 7942 2000 www.vam.ac.uk
Daily 10am-5.45pm (Wed & last Fri of every month 10am-10pm)

This diverse collection of embroidery concentrates on items from Western Europe ranging from pin cushions to wall hangings. The wealth of items in the collection is staggering as is the quality. The Dress Gallery has spectacular examples of embroidered clothing, from men's waistcoats to women's jackets. The same is true in the European Galleries, where superb examples of medieval ecclesiastical embroidery from their unrivalled collection of *opus anglicanum* (or 'English work') can always be viewed. Among the large collection of English embroidery from the 16th and 17th centuries are embroidered pictures. Featured in the new British Galleries are the museum's finest 18th-century English embroideries, known as the Stoke Edith Hangings, depicting formal garden scenes laid out in late 17th-century Anglo-Dutch style. Embroidered on linen canvas using silk and wool, they were intended to bring the garden inside the house.

Vserossiiskii muzei dekorativno-prikladnogo i narodnogo iskusstva
The All Russian Museum of Decorative-Applied and Folk Art
Delegatskaia ulitsa 3, 101000 Moscow, Russian Federation
Tel. (7) 095 9210139
Mon-Thu, Sat-Sun 10am-6pm

Embroidery has long been the treasure-store of the earliest Russian imagery. The museum boasts embroideries by craftswomen from all over Russia. One of the highlights is a magnificent north Russian 19th-century valance. The technique of the peoples of the Volga region is noted for its colour scheme. Tarusa embroidery (Kaluga region) with its profusion of ornamental motifs is done with a mesh, which is solidly coated with coloured thread. The Mstiora style, from the Vladimir region, employs the traditional rose pattern in white or coloured satin-stitch.

The Whitworth Art Gallery
University of Manchester, Oxford Road, Manchester M15 6ER, UK
Tel. (44) 161 275 7450 www.man.ac.uk
Mon-Sat 10am-5pm, Sun 2-5pm

The collection, tucked away in this provincial museum, is well worth a trip for its wealth of Persian, Turkish, and central Asian needlework. Highlights are a Shahrisyabz *ruijo* from Uzbekistan, with silk and wool embroidery on cotton, which would have been used as a sheet for the bridal bed; a Tekke Turkman *chyrpy*; and a number of Uzbek *suzanis*.

SHOES AND ACCESSORIES

Archäologisches Landesmuseum der Christian-Albrechts-Universität zu Kiel
The Regional Archaeological Museum of the Christian Albrecht University of Kiel
Schloss Gottorf, 24837 Schleswig, Germany
Tel. (49) 4621 813300
Mar-Oct: daily 9am-5pm. Nov-Feb: Tue-Sun 9.30am-4pm

Shoes of Pope John XXIII (right)
Museo della Calzatura

American boots, beginning of the 20th century (below)
Museo della Calzatura

This is one of the oldest archaeological museums in Germany, documenting the region's history from the Stone Age to the Middle Ages. There are some 1,500 pairs of excavated shoes of the Roman and Medieval periods. Preserved for centuries in the peat, they are in remarkable condition.

Musée d'Art et d'Industrie
The Museum of Art and Industry
2 place Louis Comte, 42 000 Saint-Étienne, France
Tel. (33) 4 77 33 04 85
Due to reopen end 2001 (please call for details)

The textile collections include 1.5 million samples of ribbons, illustrating the inventiveness of this region of France, which has been the world centre for ribbon-making since the end of the 18th century.

Musée des Arts Décoratifs
The Museum of Decorative Arts
Palais du Louvre, 107 rue de Rivoli, 75001 Paris, France
Tel. (33) 1 44 55 57 50 www.ucad.fr
Due to reopen 2003 (please call for details)

This remarkable collection of cane tops made of faïence, porcelain, and chased/carved gold, was donated by Félix Doisteau in 1934.

Museum of Childhood at Bethnal Green
Cambridge Heath Road, London E2 9PA, UK
Tel. (44) 20 8983 5200 www.vam.ac.uk
Mon-Thu, Sat-Sun 10am-5.50pm

Rare examples of children's footwear. Typical shoes from the past three centuries can even be tried on.

Greek clog, 19th century
Museo della Calzatura

Musée de la Bonneterie
The Museum of Hosiery
4 rue de Vauluisant, 10000 Troyes, France
Tel. (33) 3 25 42 33 33
Mon, Wed, Fri-Sun 10am-noon, 2-6pm

The only museum of its kind in France looks at the history of hosiery-making in the Troyes area, still one of the premier textile regions of France.

Museo della Calzatura
The Museum of Footwear
Piazza Matteotti, 8, 63019 Sant' Elpidio a Mare, Italy
Tel. (39) 0734 819668
Tue 4-8pm, Wed 4.30-7.30pm, Thu 9am-1pm, Fri 10am-1pm, Sat 4-7pm, Sun 9am-noon

Boots, sandals, clogs, slippers, and shoes from China, India, Tunisia, Argentina, the US, and Europe. Famous footwear includes shoes from Pope Leo XIII, Cardinal Achille Ratti, and the Duchess Aldegonda d'este, as well as sport shoes from the cyclist Francesco Moser, the motorbike racer Valentino Rossi, and the Formula 1 driver Eddie Irvine. Also postcards, shoehorns, and 400 miniature shoes in metal, ceramic, and fabric.

Central Museum and Art Gallery
Guildhall Road, Northampton, Northamptonshire NN1 1DP, UK
Tel. (44) 1604 238548   www.northampton.gov.uk
Mon-Sat 10am-5pm, Sun 2-5pm

The largest collection of footwear in the UK, and one of the most important in the world, from ancient Egypt to the present day. (It includes Queen Victoria's wedding slippers.) There is also a specialist reference library, shoemaking tools, machines, and accessories.

Musée de la Chemiserie et de l'Elégance masculine
The Museum of Shirtmaking and Masculine Elegance
Rue Charles Brillaud, 36200 Argenton-sur-Creuse, France
Tel. (33) 2 54 24 34 69
Tue-Sun 9am-noon, 2-6pm

English razor and strop,
19th century
Collezione 'G. Lorenzi' -
Museo del Rasoio

A museum entirely devoted to men's fashion, with accessories dating from the 17th century to the present day, including cuff links, tie pins, rings, and ear rings.

Museo Civico Correr
The Correr Town Museum
Piazza San Marco 52, 30124 Venice, Italy
Tel. (39) 041 25625
Mon, Wed-Sun 10am-6pm

The Correr, a long, sprawling museum that covers two sides of St Mark's Square, is without doubt the most interesting museum in Venice. Among great paintings, armour, ship models, and a fine collection of robes worn by successive doges is a collection of Venetian shoes. In the 16th century the Venetians took the platform sole to extraordinary heights (some soles are one and a half metres high).

Sandal with cork wedge covered with gold mosaic, 1936, by Carmen Miranda
Museo Salvatore Ferragamo

Collezione 'G. Lorenzi' - Museo del Rasoio
The 'G. Lorenzi' Collection - Museum of Shaving
18 via Montenapoleone, 20121 Milan, Italy
Tel. (39) 02 76022848 www.g.lorenzi.it
Daily 9-10.30am, 3-7.30pm by appt. only

Thanks to Giovanni Lorenzi, the founder of a cutlery shop in Milan, we now have one of the few collections of shaving equipment in the world. It includes over 2,000 safety razors (among them the original patented by the Kampfe brothers in 1880), 'cut-throat' blades, 'straight razors', as well as the first electric razor, produced by Shick in 1930.

Brown suede woman's shoe, 1996 (right)
Museo Salvatore Ferragamo

Museum of Costume
Assembly Rooms, Bennett Street,
Bath, Somerset BA1 2QH, UK
Tel. (44) 1225 477789 www.museumofcostume.co.uk
Daily 10am-5pm

One of the largest and most comprehensive collections in Britain of women's and children's costume, illustrating the evolution of clothing and the social history of the country through four centuries of fashion. It holds a very fine collection of over 100 pairs of gloves, including some early decorative ones.

Deutsches Klingenmuseum Solingen
The German Blade Museum of Solingen
Klosterhof 4, 42653 Solingen, Germany
Tel. (49) 212 59822 www.solingen.de
Tue-Thu, Sat-Sun 10am-5pm, Fri 2-5pm

This museum, which is most famous for its swords, also possesses a fine collection of razors and razor blades. The oldest razor in the collection (17th century) is a silver pocket razor with a handle made from silver, mother-of-pearl, and tortoiseshell.

Wooden woman's sandal with red suede strips
Museo Salvatore Ferragamo

Deutsches Ledermuseum - Schuhmuseum Offenbach
German Leather Museum - Shoe Museum of Offenbach
Frankfurter Strasse 86, 63067 Offenbach, Germany
Tel. (49) 6982 9798 www.dhm.de
Mon 10am-1pm, Tue-Sun 10am-5pm (Wed until 8pm)

With 5,000 pairs forming a worldwide ethnographic collection, there are also 5,000 pairs of European shoes from all periods. Among those on display are fine silk shoes of the 18th century; 16th-century 'horn and cow mouth' shoes; and shoes from ancient Egypt (1400BC), 5th-century Peru, and ancient Persia.

The Museum at the Fashion Institute of Technology
27th Street at Seventh Avenue, New York, New York 10001, USA
Tel. (1) 212 217 5700 www.fitnyc.edu
Tue-Fri noon-8pm, Sat 10am-5pm

The accessories collection comprises about 20,000 pieces, with shoes and bags as major categories. Highlights include shoes by Perugia, Roger Vivier, Manolo Blahnik, and Christian Louboutin, as well as early beaded bags, and designer bags from Gucci to Pucci.

Museo Salvatore Ferragamo
The Salvatore Ferragamo Museum
Palazzo Spini Feroni, via dei Tornabuoni 2, 50123 Florence, Italy
Tel. (39) 055 3360476
Mon-Fri 9am-1pm, 2-6pm (by appt. only)

Set in a medieval palazzo in the heart of Florence, this museum is
dedicated to the life and work of the man who became known both as
'Shoemaker of Dreams' and 'Shoemaker to the Stars'. Salvatore
Ferragamo left his small town in southern Italy in 1914 and headed for
Hollywood, where he found a job making boots for the early Westerns,
and shoes for lavish costume epics, going on to create shoes for some
of Hollywood's most glittering stars. There are over 10,000 exhibits,
highlights of which include a pair of 18-carat gold shoes, and the
dizzyingly high stiletto-heel shoes preferred by Marilyn Monroe.

Gold coloured Dr Marten
boot designed by Red or
Dead, London, 1992
The Horniman Museums and
Gardens

Frederick's of Hollywood Lingerie Museum
6608 Hollywood Boulevard, Los Angeles, California 90028, USA
Tel. (1) 323 466 8506
Mon-Thu 10am-9pm, Fri 10am-6pm, Sat-Sun noon-5pm

This collection of lingerie is housed in a purple and pink 1935 landmark art-deco
building, the original flagship store for Frederick Mellinger's lingerie chain. Items on
display include: Marilyn Monroe's bra from *Let's Make Love*, Lana Turner's black
camisole from *Merry Widow*, and Tony Curtis's black-lace bra from *Some Like It Hot*.

The Horniman Museum and Gardens
100 London Road, Forest Hill, London SE23 3PQ, UK
Tel. (44) 20 8699 1872 www.horniman.demon.co.uk
Mon-Sat 10.30am-5.30pm, Sun 2-5.30pm

The collection contains boots and shoes from more than sixty countries across the
world, with Asia particularly well represented. Most date from the 19th century
onwards although there are a few archaeological examples from ancient Egypt and
Roman Britain.

Musée international de la Chaussure
The International Shoe Museum
2 rue Sainte-Marie, 26100 Romans-sur-
Isère, France
Tel. (33) 4 75 05 81 30
Jan-Jun, Sep-Dec: Tue-Sat 9-
11.45am,
2-5.45pm, Sun 2.30-6pm

Housed in an old convent there
are remarkable examples of a
10,000-strong collection of shoes over
four floors. Romans-sur-Isère is now the
shoe capital of France.

Pair of Chinese women's
shoes for bound feet
The Horniman Museum and
Gardens

Kenwood House - The Iveagh Bequest
Hampstead Lane, London NW3 7JR, UK
Tel. (44) 20 8348 1286
Apr-Sep: daily 10am-6pm. Oct: daily 10am-5pm. Nov-Mar: daily 10am-4pm

Housed in one of Robert Adam's finest villas, a stunning collection of 1,300 18th- and 19th-century shoe buckles from France, England, Spain, and Holland bequeathed by Lady Maufe (1884-1976). The buckles range from bone and inlaid ivory to paste, including very fine French examples, and silver and gilt ones.

Klompenmuseum Gebr Wietzes
The Wietzes Bros Wooden Shoe Museum
Wolfhorn 1a, 9761 BA Eelde, The Netherlands
Tel. (31) 50 3091181 www.klompenmuseum.nl
Apr-Oct: Tue-Sun 2-5pm

Sandal from Uganda made from rhino hide and leopard fur
The Horniman Museum and Gardens

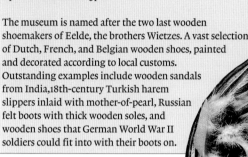

The museum is named after the two last wooden shoemakers of Eelde, the brothers Wietzes. A vast selection of Dutch, French, and Belgian wooden shoes, painted and decorated according to local customs. Outstanding examples include wooden sandals from India, 18th-century Turkish harem slippers inlaid with mother-of-pearl, Russian felt boots with thick wooden soles, and wooden shoes that German World War II soldiers could fit into with their boots on.

LaCrasia Gloves
304 Fifth Avenue, New York, New York 10001, USA
Tel. (1) 212 594 2223 www.wegloveyou.com
By appt. only

This private collection (housed in the LaCrasia boutique) spans over four centuries of glove fashion. The oldest piece on display is an embroidered gauntlet dating from around 1600, still in pristine condition.

Lambert Howarth Footwear Museum
Greenbridge Factory, Bocholt Way, Rawtenstall, Rossendale, Lancashire BB44 7NX, UK
Tel. (44) 1706 211621 www.lhsafety.co.uk
Mon-Fri 10am-5pm, Sat 9.30am-3.30pm

The museum, housed in an early 19th-century boardroom, outlines the development of the slipper and footwear industry in Lancashire. The oldest item is a slipper from around 1874, a time when anything from remnants of felt and carpet ends, to used railway-carriage seating, were used to make them.

Museum of London
London Wall, London EC2Y 5HN, UK
Tel. (44) 20 7600 3699 www.museumoflondon.org.uk
Mon-Sat 10am-5.50pm, Sun noon-5.50pm

Some of the best-preserved objects in the collections are made from organic materials such as wood or leather. The reserve collection holds 1,500 items of Roman leather, a few complete shoes as well as shoe components and off-cuts. The most famous Roman leather objects on display are two so-called 'bikini briefs', thought to have been worn by young female acrobats.

The Metropolitan Museum of Art
1000 Fifth Avenue at 82nd Street, New York, New York 10028, USA
Tel. (1) 212 535 7710 www.metmuseum.org
Tue-Thu, Sun 9.30am-5.30pm, Fri, Sat 9.30am-9pm

The world-renowned Costume Institute possesses more than 75,000 costumes and accessories from seven centuries and five continents. Hats, shoes, gloves, and buttons stand out above the rest of the accessories.

Footwear, end of 18th century
Museo della Calzatura

Minnesota Historical Society
345 W Kellogg Boulevard, St Paul, Minnesota 55102-1906, USA
Tel. (1) 651 296 1956 www.mnhs.org
Tue 10am-8pm, Wed-Sat 10am-5pm, Sun noon-5pm

This society preserves 3,500 pieces covering a century of undergarment production and fashion, from the 1880s to the 1980s donated by the locally based company Munsingwear. The collection demonstrates that the use of fabrics has become increasingly diversified and shows how underwear can be used to express political ideas as well as fashion trends.

Musée de la Mode et du Costume
The Museum of Fashion and Costume
Palais Galliéra, 10 ave. Pierre 1er de Serbie, 75016 Paris, France
Tel. (33) 1 47 20 85 23
Tue-Sun 10am-5.40pm

There are more than 70,000 accessories in this 100,000-piece clothing collection. Hats, scarves, canes, fans, gloves, umbrellas (including Queen Victoria's), combs, belt buckles (mainly from the 18th and 19th centuries), and Sarah Bernhardt's fan and gloves.

Museo dell'Ombrello e dei Parasole
The Umbrella and Parasol Museum
Via Golf Panorama, 2, 28040 Gignese, Italy
Tel. (39) 0323 208064 www.lagodorta.net
Apr-Sep: Tue-Sun 10am-noon, 3-6pm

Chinese court dignitaries' slipper, 19th century
Museo della Calzatura

Umbrellas, parasols, and walking canes from the 17th to the 19th centuries, presenting the fashion history of the umbrella, with various original and eccentric pieces once belonging to doges, popes, kings and queens, actors, and politicians.

Paisley Museum and Art Galleries
High Street , Paisley, Renfrewshire, PA1 2BA, Scotland, UK
Tel. (44) 1418 893151
Tue-Sat & public holidays 10am-5pm, Sun 2-5pm

A large selection of typical Paisley pine motif shawls, as well as the 1850 Amli type, or a Blue style, shawl, very popular around 1845-50.

Musée du Sabotier
The Sabot Maker Museum
6 rue des Sabotiers, 57960 Soucht, France
Tel. (33) 3 87 96 91 52
Easter-Oct: Sat-Sun 2-6pm

An excellent collection of 200 clogs from around the world, located in this French village, where there used to be up to sixty clog-makers before World War II.

Museo dello Scarpone
The Museum of the Climbing Boot
Villa Zuccareda Binetti, vicolo Zuccareda 5, 31044 Montebelluna, Italy
Tel. (39) 0423 303282 www.museoscarpone.it
Mon-Sat 9am-noon, 3-6pm, Sun 9am-noon, 3-7pm

Housed in a 16th-century villa, this unusual museum tells the story of the activity that made Montebelluna one of the most important centres for mountaineering boots.

Pearl-knitted purse with
floral design, Göppingen,
*c.*1920
*Städtisches Museum
Göppingen*

The Shoe Museum
C. and J. Clark Ltd, High Street, Street,
Somerset BA16 0YA, UK
Tel. (44) 1458 443131
Mon-Fri 10am-4.45pm, Sat 10am-5pm,
Sun 11am-5pm

Over 1,000 shoes from all over the world, from Roman times to the present day. Also 19th-century hand tools, machinery, advertising material, fashion plates, and a collection of 18th-century shoe buckles.

Städtisches Museum Göppingen
The Town Museum of Göppingen
Im Storchen, Wühlestrasse 36, 73033
Göppingen, Germany
Tel. (49) 7161 686375
Wed, Sat-Sun 10am-noon, 2-5pm

Arts and crafts using glass beads have a long tradition in Göppingen. During the first decades of the 20th century, the area was the centre of pearl knitting in southern Germany. A lovely collection of local pearl-knitted (rather than embroidered) items.

Umbrella from the 1930s
Várműzeum

TUSPM Shoe Museum
8th and Race Street, Philadelphia, Pennsylvania 19107, USA
Tel. (1) 215 625 5243 www.pcpm.edu
By appt. only

Eight hundred pairs of footwear from various periods of history and various countries are on display, even burial sandals from ancient Egypt. One of the most bizarre shoe fashions is represented in the museum's collection of Chinese lily shoes. An illustration shows the twisted and deformed structure of a bound lily foot as compared with a normal one. Based on a 1,000-year-old Chinese custom, the feet of young girls were tightly wrapped in cloth from the age of five until the arch was broken and the toes turned under, producing a foot about half the normal size. In addition to crippling girls for life and accentuating their economic uselessness, it emphasized the wealth of the men who could afford such obviously handicapped women.

Várműzeum
The Castle Museum
Vajda János tér, Vár, 7800 Siklós, Hungary
Tel. (36) 72 351433
Daily 10am-6pm

The management of the Hunor Glove Factory founded this atmospheric museum, which traces the history of the glove trade and commemorates the work of the factory founded in 1861 (the gloves for George VI's coronation were made here in 1936). The displays of kid gloves made in Grenoble, France, are second to none. Hats, fans, dresses, and parasols complement the displays, highlighting the various changes in glove fashion, starting from the late 19th century.

TAPESTRIES

Musée des Arts Décoratifs
The Museum of Decorative Arts
Palais du Louvre, 107 rue de Rivoli, 75001 Paris, France
Tel. (33) 1 44 55 57 50 www.ucad.fr
Due to reopen 2001 (please call for details)

One of the finest and largest collections of tapestries in France. Highlights include the Charles de Maximilien, Brussels, 1528-1533, and the History of Scipio, 1688-90.

Musée des Beaux-Arts
The Museum of Fine Arts
22 rue Paul-Doumer, 62000 Arras, France
Tel. (33) 3 21 71 26 43
Apr-Oct: Mon, Wed-Sun 10am-noon, 2-6pm.
Nov-Mar: Mon, Wed-Fri 10am-noon, 2-5pm, Sat-Sun 10am-noon, 2-6pm

Epiphany tapestry, Tournai or Brussels, *c.*1440/55
Bernisches Historisches Museum

In Shakespearean England 'arras' meant tapestry. Several pieces, such as St Vaast and the Bear from the end of the 15th century provide a unique and rare insight into the splendours of the town.

Bernisches Historisches Museum
The Historical Museum of Berne
Helvetiaplatz 5, 3000 Berne, Switzerland
Tel. (41) 31 3507711
Tue-Sun 10am-5pm

This neo-Gothic castle contains a magnificent series of Flemish tapestries, exemplifying the sumptuous style of the late Middle Ages in Burgundy and the Republic of Berne. A tapestry called The Thousand Flowers and four others telling the story of Julius Caesar once belonged to the dukes of Burgundy and the bishops of Lausanne.

The Burrell Collection
2060 Pollokshaws Road, Glasgow G43 1AT, Scotland, UK
Tel. (44) 141 649 7151
Mon-Sat 10am-5pm, Sun 11am-5pm

Tapestry showing St Francis receiving the stigmatae, Landrieve Studio, Aubusson, 1716
Musée de la Tapisserie (France)

Sir William Burrell, with some justification, regarded his tapestries as the most valuable part of his collection. There are more than 150 examples, most of which date from the late 15th to the early 16th century, representing all the major centres of production. The earliest dates from about 1300 and is part of the furnishings from an altar.

The Cloisters Museum

Fort Tryon Park, New York, New York, USA
Tel. (1) 212 923 3700
Tue-Sun 9.30am-5.15pm

*Detail of Aeneas and Dido –
the Encounter, Aubusson,
17th century (above)
Musée de la Tapisserie
(France)*

*Alaric or Conquered Rome:
The Battle between
Amalasontha and the
Princess Laponne,
Aubusson, 17th century
(right)
Musée de la Tapisserie
(France)*

This part of the Metropolitan Museum of Art is devoted exclusively to European art of the Middle Ages. Its most famous tapestries are the *Seven Unicorn*, designed in Paris and woven in Brussels (*c.* 1500).

Dean Castle

Dean Road, Kilmarnock, Ayrshire, Scotland, UK
Tel. (44) 1563 554704
Easter-end Oct: daily noon-5pm. Winter: Sat-Sun only

Lord Howard de Walden's gift to Kilmarnock includes grand Brussels tapestries from the 16th century, which adorn the great hall of the castle keep. The collection also contains 17th-century Brussels and Antwerp tapestries, as well as Flemish verdure tapestries from the 17th to the early 18th centuries, both complete and fragmentary.

Museum of Fine Arts

465 Huntington Avenue, Boston, Massachusetts 02115-5519, USA
Tel. (1) 617 267 9300 www.mfa.org
Mon, Tue 10am-4.45pm, Wed-Fri 10am-9.45pm

Fabulous tapestries from the 14th to the 16th century, including the masterpiece *Narcissus*, a millefleurs tapestry of French or Flemish origin, dating from the late 15th or early 16th century. The collection presents a balanced survey of the entire development of the art in western Europe and colonial Peru, which few collections in the US are able to match.

*Traian and Herkinbald,
detail showing the
Emperor Traian's
entourage, Tournai, c.1450
Bernisches Hisorisches
Museum*

Galerie de l'Apocalypse
The Apocalypse Gallery

Château, prom. du Bout-du-Monde, 49100 Angers, France
Tel. (33) 2 41 87 43 47
Jun-mid Sep: daily 9am-7pm. Mid Sep-May: daily 9.30am-12.30pm, 2-6pm

The highlight of this collection of medieval tapestries is the masterpiece *Apocalypse* by Jean de Bruges and Nicolas Bataille, which measures more than 100m long by 5.5m wide. This great work set a precedent for other medieval tapestries to follow. It was commissioned by Louis I of Anjou and was woven by Nicolas Bataille, the most famous weaver of the period in Paris, between 1373 and 1379.

Gruuthuse Museum

Dijver 17, 8000 Bruges, Belgium
Tel. (32) 50 448711
Apr-Sep: daily 9.30am-5pm.
Oct-Mar: Mon, Wed-Sun 9.30am-12.30pm, 2-5pm

The 17th-century tapestries woven in Bruges include the popular series of the *History of Gombaut and Macée* and the *Seven Liberal Arts*.

Musée du Louvre
The Louvre
Palais du Louvre, 34-6 quai du Louvre, 75001 Paris, France
Tel. (33) 1 40 20 53 17   www.louvre.fr
Mon, Wed 9am-9.15pm, Thu-Sun 9am-5.30pm

Certainly the best collection in France, and high up on the list of the best in the world, it provides an outstanding overview of tapestry weaving in Europe from the 15th to the 17th centuries. In the Anne of Bretagne Room there is a collection of mostly Belgian tapestries. The Renaissance collections include the remarkable *Tapestry of St Mammès,* made in Paris in 1544 after Jean Cousin. The Millefleurs Room contains the *Noble Pastorale* Tapestries, and two allegorical tapestries from the Martin Le Roy Collection, with English tapestries from the Mortlake workshop from the 17th century as well as Italian tapestries from Florence and Ferrara. The highlights of the collection are the twelve pieces of the *Hunts of Maximilian*, woven in Brussels in 1530, which were reunited in 1938 and recently given pride of place on the first floor of the Richelieu wing.

Mobilier National
1 rue Berbier-du-Mets, 75013 Paris, France
Tel. (33) 1 44 08 52 00
Tue-Thu for tours 2pm, 2.45pm

This national repository for furnishings from French royal households from the old Garde-meuble Royal and the Mobilier Imperial is not open to the general public, but available for research. A centre for restoration, it houses over 1,000 tapestries, including Flemish, English, Spanish, German, and Italian examples.

Greenery, de la Marche Studios, 17th century (top)
Musée de la Tapisserie (France)

The History of Aeneas: Dido's Death, de la Marche Studios, 17th century (above)
Musée de la Tapisserie (France)

Musée national du Château
The National Castle Museum
Château, 64000 Pau, France
Tel. (33) 5 59 82 38 19
Daily 9.30-11.45am, 2-5.15pm

One of the richest tapestry collections in France with most examples from the reign of Louis XIV. Every wall in the castle is covered with magnificent tapestries, many woven after designs by Poussin, Le Brun, and Mignard as well as *The Story of Henry IV* (*c.* 1780) by Vincent.

Musée national du Moyen Age - Thermes et Hôtel de Cluny
The National Museum of the Middle Ages - The Cluny Baths and Hôtel
6 place Paul-Painlevé, 75005 Paris, France
Tel. (33) 1 53 73 78 00
Mon, Wed-Sun 9.15am-5.45pm

Room XI is a circular gallery built especially for the six panels of the *Lady with the Unicorn*. This tapestry has inspired universal fascination and elicited numerous interpretations. We now know that it was probably woven in one of the northern cities of France or in Belgium, where the millefleurs technique was a particular specialisation at the beginning of the 16th century. The tapestry was made for Lady Claude Le Viste. Five of

Gobelin tapestry, late 17th
century, probably Brussels
Schlossmuseum Jever

the six panels illustrate the five senses, while
the sixth panel and its inscription *A mon seul
désir* ('To my only desire') remains enigmatic.

Palacio Real
The Royal Palace
Calle Bailén s/n, 28071 Madrid, Spain
Tel. (34) 91 5420059
Apr-Sep: Mon-Sat 9am-6pm.
Oct-Mar: Mon-Sat 9.30am-5pm, Sun 9am-3pm

The grand tour through the Palace is long, but,
even so, it barely allows time to contemplate the
extraordinary opulence of acres of Flemish
and Spanish tapestries. There is a unique
collection, woven in Brussels, depicting the
story of the Apostles designed by Raphael,
which decorate the dining room. Don't miss the newly restored series of nine monumental Flemish tapestries depicting kingly virtues and vices commissioned from the Brussels
workshops of Pieter Van Aelst at the time of Charles' coronation in Aachen in 1520.

Musée Saint-Rémi
The Saint-Rémi Museum
53 rue Simon, 51100 Reims, France
Tel. (33) 3 26 85 23 36
Mon-Fri 2-6.30pm, Sat-Sun 2-7pm

The museum is housed in the grandiose building of the former royal abbey of St
Remy. The 12th-century chapter-house is particularly stunning. Ten remarkable
tapestries, executed between 1523 and 1531, depict the life of St Remy.

Schlossmuseum Jever
The Castle Museum of Jever
Schlossplatz, 26441 Jever, Germany
Tel. (49) 4461 2106 www.schlossmuseum.de
Tue-Sun 10am-6pm

The Gobelin Hall of the castle displays some magnificent tapestries, woven from silk
and wool (*c.* 1700). The two largest show in great detail spacious Baroque gardens and
parkland with groups of people playing games or music.

Tapestry showing Judith
before Holophernes,
Aubusson, 17th century
*Musée de la Tapisserie
(France)*

Musée de la Tapisserie
The Tapestry Museum
9 place Reine Astride, 7500 Tournai, Belgium
Tel. (32) 69 842073
Mon, Wed-Sun 10am-noon, 2-5.30pm

The 15th century represents Tournai's Golden
Age when, for nearly a century, the town
became the European centre for tapestry.
Pasquier Grenier, a 15th-century businessman,
devoted his life to the export of Tournai
tapestries. As early as 1449 he was in contact
with French tapestry dealers and later initiated
commercial relations with Louis XI. Soon the
kings of Spain, England, Scotland, France,
and Naples all owned tapestries made here.

Musée de la Tapisserie
The Tapestry Museum
10 ave. des Lissiers, 23200 Aubusson, France
Tel. (33) 5 55 66 33 06
Jul & Aug: daily 10am-6pm. Sep-Jun: Mon, Wed-Sun 9.30am-noon, 2-6pm

Opened in 1981 the museum illustrates the history of Aubusson tapestries from the 17th to the 20th centuries.

Tapisserie de Bayeux
The Bayeux Tapestry
Centre Guillaume-le-Conquérant, 13 rue de Nesmond, 14400 Bayeux, France
Tel. (33) 2 31 51 25 55
Daily 9.30am-12.30pm, 2-6pm

Scene from the *St Vincent Tapestry* showing him going to school, 1515 (left)
Bernisches Historisches Museum

Jever Castle (below left)
Schlossmuseum Jever

The *Bayeux Tapestry* was originally commissioned for Bayeux Cathedral by the half-brother of William the Conqueror, Bishop of Bayeux, who became Earl of Kent in 1067. It is widely believed to have been made in England. The tapestry is over 230 feet long and 19.75 inches in height (70.34m x 65cm) and is woven from wool of eight colours on eight lengths of bleached linen, which were subsequently joined together. The wealth of information provided by the tapestry, tells us not only about Duke William of Normandy's conquest of England in 1066 but also reveals aspects of life during the 11th century.

Victoria and Albert Museum
Cromwell Road, South Kensington, London sw7 2RL, UK
Tel. (44) 20 7942 2000 www.vam.ac.uk
Daily 10am-5.45pm (Wed & last Fri of every month 10am-10pm)

Several hundred tapestries, the earliest from the 15th century, together with modern examples. No one should miss the Raphael Gallery, consisting of seven massive

cartoons by Raphael for the tapestries of the *Acts of the Apostles*, considered to be among the most important surviving examples of Renaissance art in the world.

Zeeuws Museum
The Zeeland Museum
Abdij, 4331 KB Middelburg, The Netherlands
Tel. (31) 118 626655
www.zeeuwsmuseum.nl
Mon-Sat 10am-5pm, Sun & public holidays noon-5pm

The series of 16th-century tapestries illustrate the battle between Zeeland's *geuzen* (Protestant fighters) and the Spanish on the Schelde rivers during the Eighty Years' War (1568-1648) and were woven in Delft and Middelburg.

THIMBLES, BUTTONS AND SEWING TOOLS

Hand-engraved silver
thimble (top)
Fingerhutmuseum

Thimble of silver and
enamel (above)
Fingerhutmuseum

Golden thimble from a
French sewing school
(right)
Fingerhutmuseum

Museum of Art

Munson-Williams-Proctor Arts Institute, 310 Genesee Street, Utica, New York 13502,
USA
Tel. (1) 315 797 0000 www.mwpi.edu
Tue-Sat 10am-5pm, Sun 1-5pm

Part of the vast Proctor Collection's holdings consist of thimbles gathered by the wives of
two of the Institute's founders as they travelled for pleasure between the 1880s and 1915.
Among 150 examples are those made of enamel, gold, glass, and other precious metals.

Alaska State Museum

395 Whittier, Juneau, Alaska 99801-1718, USA
Tel. (1) 907 465 2901 www.museums.state.ak.us
May-Sep: Mon-Fri 9am-6pm, Sat-Sun 10am-6pm. Oct-Apr: Tue-Sat 10am-4pm

Necessity is often the mother of invention and her handiwork can be seen in this
collection of over 200 sewing implements, including needles, thimbles, and needle-
cases, fashioned by Alaska's Native peoples in the 19th and 20th century. Survival in
the harsh climate dictated that garments, such as parkas of bird skins and waterproof
clothing made from seal intestines, were not only sewn with special stitches to be
effective but also had to be well fitted to be warm. This collection of needles and
other sewing tools, made primarily of natural materials such as sea mammals and
fish bones, were fashioned for the task at hand.

Birmingham Museum & Art Gallery

Chamberlain Square, Birmingham, West
Midlands B3 3DH, UK
Tel. (44) 121 303 2834
www.birmingham.gov.uk
Mon-Thu, Sat 10am-5pm, Fri 10.30am-5pm,
Sun 12.30-5pm

During the 18th and 19th centuries,
approximately a fifth of the population of
Birmingham was employed in the button
industry, and the bulk of British buttons,
both civilian and military, were
manufactured here or nearby. The Luckcock
Button Collection of over 500 buttons is
unique and was mainly compiled in the late
18th and early 19th century by a Birmingham
jeweller, Luckcock, whose particular skill lay
in setting precious stones in buttons.

Musée de la Chemiserie et de l'Elégance masculine

The Museum of Shirtmaking and Masculine Elegance
Rue Charles Brillaud, 36200 Argenton-sur-Creuse, France
Tel. (33) 2 54 24 34 69
Mid Feb-Dec: Tue-Sun 9am-noon, 2-6pm

This extensive collection contains 400 sewing machines, dating from 1860 to 1980. A
workshop has been reconstructed showing the steps undertaken when making a shirt,
from its design to its packaging.

Deutsches Klingenmuseum Solingen
The German Blade Museum of Solingen
Klosterhof 4, 42653 Solingen, Germany
Tel. (49) 212 59822 www.solingen.de
Tue-Thu, Sat-Sun 10am-5pm, Fri 2-5pm

The first scissors were forged from one piece, and
were in use from the Bronze Age to the end of the
16th century. The museum possesses such an example
from 16th-century Germany. By the end of the 16th
century, scissors with joints, as we know them today,
started to appear.

Fingerhutmuseum
The Thimble Museum
Kohlesmühle 6, 97993 Creglingen, Germany
Tel. (49) 7933 370
Apr-Oct: daily 9am-6pm. Nov-Mar: daily 1-4pm

Exterior of the museum
Forge Mill Needle Museum

An impressive and rare collection of more than 3,000 thimbles of every conceivable
material including leather, bone, ivory, glass, porcelain, mother-of-pearl, stone, and
wood, as well as metals, such as bronze, brass, iron, aluminium, silver and gold,
volcanic ash from St Helena, and even kangaroo leather.

Forge Mill Needle Museum
Needle Mill Lane, Riverside, Redditch, Worcester, Worcestershire B98 8HY, UK
Tel. (44) 1527 62509 www.redditchbc.gov.uk
Mon-Fri 11am-4pm, Sat-Sun 2-5pm

In 1700, Redditch became world famous for the production of steel needles. By 1870,
it is estimated that the Redditch needle-making district was manufacturing 3,500
million needles of all types per year, exporting them to the colonies and elsewhere.
The museum, housed in a restored 18th-century needle mill (the only water-powered
scouring mill left in the world) tells the story of the Redditch needle industry.

Historic Costume and Textiles Collection at the Ohio State University
The Geraldine Schottenstein Wing, 175 Campbell Hall, 1787 Neil Avenue, Columbus,
Ohio 43210-1295, USA
Tel. (1) 614 292 3090
Wed-Sat 11am-4pm

Known among button aficionados as one of the most complete holdings of button-
related material in the US, the Rudolph Collection includes an unusual set of dies
used to manufacture buttons and equipment, and artefacts related to button use.

Historisches Nähmaschinenmuseum
The Historic Sewing Machine Museum
Heimeranstrasse 68-70, 80339 Munich,
Germany
Tel. (49) 89 51088111
Mon-Fri 9am-5pm

Gold thimbles, *c.*1850
Fingerhutmuseum

The museum's collections integrate the
manufacture of safety bicycles and high-
wheelers with garment industry implements
and drawings, patent specifications, and

posters to illustrate industrial history. The collection, retracing the history and development of garment-making, comprises more than 200 sewing machines, including a reconstruction of the first sewing machine built by Balthasar Krems in 1800.

Keep Homestead Museum

35 Ely Road, Monson, Massachusetts 01057, USA
Tel. (1) 413 267 4137 www.keephomesteadmuseum.org
Apr-Dec: daily 1-3pm

A large collection of vintage buttons is exhibited on a rotating basis. On permanent display is a selection of mosaic buttons depicting flowers, birds, animals, people, and building scenes, with fine examples of Roman and Florentine mosaics mostly from the 1850s.

Mattatuck Museum

144 West Main Street, Waterbury, Connecticut 06702, USA
Tel. (1) 203 753 0381 www.mattatuckmuseum.org
Tue-Sat 10am-5pm, Sun noon-5pm

Known in the 19th century as the 'brass capital of the world', a major part of Waterbury's history can be traced through the manufacture of brass products, including buttons. Recently placed on permanent display is a collection of 10,000 buttons from all over the world. Founded in 1812, the Waterbury Company crafted buttons for both sides of the Civil War, from brass to those made from shell, gold plate and silver, as well as military buttons, for which the company is best known.

Table swift
(above)
Whaling Museum

Thread winders
(right)
Whaling Museum

The Strong Museum

One Manhatten Square, Rochester, New York 14607, USA
Tel. (1) 716 263 2700 www.strongmuseum.org
Mon-Thu, Sat 10am-5pm (Fri until 10pm), Sun noon-5pm

The largest and most diverse collection of buttons (1750-1970) to be found in any American museum. It numbers more than 200,000 buttons, made from all types of materials and in a range of styles that encompasses production for all economic levels of society.

Textilmuseum
The Textile Museum

Vadianstrasse 2, 9000 St Gallen, Switzerland
Tel. (41) 71 2221744 www.textilmuseum.ch
Apr-Oct: Mon-Fri 10am-noon, 2-5pm, Sat 10am-5pm

This wonderful collection of needlework accessories, from darners and needle cases to knitting needles and scissors, spans more than three centuries; the earliest implements date from the 18th century.

Waddesdon Manor - The Rothschild Collection

Waddesdon, Aylesbury, Buckinghamshire HP18 0JH, UK
Tel. (44) 1296 653211 www.waddesdon.org.uk
End Mar-mid Oct: Thu-Sat 12.30-6pm, Sun 11am-6.30pm

While the Rothschilds were accumulating money, Baroness Edmond de Rothschild was amassing buttons. And it is no ordinary collection, ranging from buttons made of steel, to those made of enamel, tortoiseshell, silver, ceramic, and mother-of-pearl. All

65 sets making up this incredible collection are on view, handsomely displayed in black-lacquer boxes which the Baroness chose herself to keep them safe.

Whaling Museum

Nantucket Historical Association, 13 Broad Street, Nantucket Town, Nantucket, Massachusetts 02554, USA
Tel. (1) 508 228 1894 www.nha.org
Oct-Nov: daily 11am-3pm

Silver thimbles, Germany, end of 19th century
Fingerhutmuseum

To occupy their time on whaling voyages lasting three to five years, the men turned their hand to scrimshanding. Besides making decorative objects from whale teeth and bone, they would also produce utilitarian items for their wives back home, among them thimbles, pins, needlework tools, thread winders, and knitting-needle holders, of which there are numerous examples in the scrimshaw collection.

WATCHES

British Museum

Great Russell Street, London WC1B 3DG, UK
Tel. (44) 20 7636 1555 www.thebritishmuseum.ac.uk
Mon-Sat 10am-5pm, Sun noon-6pm

Only a small part of the 2,500 strong watch collection is on display, but they are all wound regularly to keep them in full working order. Besides George III's watch, which he made himself, all the leading watchmakers are represented in the museum, covering more than four centuries of watchmaking.

Rolex pocket watch, *c*.1930
Musée de l'Horlogerie et de l'Emaillerie

Collection and Library of the Worshipful Company of Clockmakers

The Clock Room, Guildhall Library, Aldermanbury, London EC2P 2EJ, UK
Tel. (44) 20 7606 3030 www.clockmakers.org
Mon-Fri 9.30am-4.30pm

The Clockmakers' Company, founded by Royal Charter in 1631, was set up to regulate as well as encourage the art of clockmaking, and this is the oldest collection devoted to clocks and watches in the world. The majority of the collection was made between 1600 and 1800, and there are over 600 English and European watches, thirty clocks and fifteen marine timekeepers on display. Among the prize exhibits are John Harrison's 5th Marine timekeeper, which finally made it possible for ships to chart their exact position while at sea, and the watch worn by Edmund Hillary during his ascent of Everest in 1953.

Alfred Dunhill Museum and Archive

48 Jermyn Street, London SW1Y 6DL, UK
Tel. (44) 20 7838 8233
Mon-Fri 9.30am-6pm, Sat 10am-6pm (by appt. only)

A fascinating collection of timepieces, from the belt watch, which at the press of a button, flipped open to reveal a hidden timepiece, to *La captive* – a watch introduced in 1929 for the handbag or bedside with a mechanism at the side that tipped open a protective flap to reveal the face.

Musée Paul Dupuy
The Paul Dupuy Museum

13 rue de la Pleau, 31000 Toulouse, France
Tel. (33) 5 61 14 65 50
Mon, Wed-Sun 10am-5pm (Jun-Sep until 6pm)

An outstanding display of clocks and watches offering a cross section through the history of watchmaking. There is a selection of watches that belonged to Louis XV with decorations by such artists as Van Loo and Greuze. The museum also displays a remarkable collection of 'onion' watches by Huyghens from the 18th century, and watches of a more sober design, but greater precision, that appeared towards the end of the 18th and the beginning of the 19th century by Abraham-Louis Bréguet, Charles Oudin, and Louis Berthoud.

Musée d'Horlogerie
The Museum of Watch- and Clock-Making
Château des Monts, 2400 Le Locle, Switzerland
Tel. (41) 32 9311680
Tue-Sun 10am-5pm

Among many precious pieces is an early watch made in Stuttgart around 1560; a crystal rock watch in the shape of a crucifix, made in Germany in the middle of the 17th century; and a watch signed by Goudron (Paris, *c.* 1680) with a beautifully decorated case showing two pilgrims on their way to St Jacques de Compostelle.

Interior of the museum
Musée de la Montre

Musée de l'Horlogerie et de l'Emaillerie
The Museum of Watch- and Clock-Making and Enamelling
15 route de Malagnou, 1208 Geneva, Switzerland
Tel. (41) 22 4186470 www.mah.ville-ge.ch
Mon, Wed-Sun 10am-5pm

Now one of the best watch collections in the world, having been enriched with more than 1,000 pieces during the last 25 years. One of the most impressive window cases in the first room is devoted to the development of watchmaking between 1550 and 1995, illustrating the changes of fashion and technological evolution. Most of the exhibits are devoted to Genevan watchmaking. Don't miss the Geneva-made bee-shaped brooch-watch, decorated with niello, pierced white gold, rubies, emeralds, diamonds, and black enamel.

Musée international d'Horlogerie
The International Watch- and Clock-Making Museum
29 rue des Musées, 2301 La Chaux-de-Fonds, Switzerland
Tel. (41) 32 9676861
Jun-Sep: 10am-5pm. Oct-May: 10am-noon, 2-5pm

Most of the museum is built underground with a dramatic entrance through the side of a cliff. For those who admire contemporary architecture, this building in itself is worth a visit apart from the museum's impressive displays. The collection includes remarkable objects such as a watch bearing the portrait of Philippe IV (*c.* 1665), a rock crystal watch, and 'astronomical' watches from the 17th century. For collectors of 20th-century watches this significant holding contains works by Patek Philippe, Vacheron Constantin, and Paul Ditisheim. Also on display is the watch created by Omega in 1965 for astronauts going to the moon, and a Pop Art watch designed by Andy Warhol.

Manor House Museum
Honey Hill, Bury St Edmunds, Suffolk IP33 1HF, UK
Tel. (44) 1284 757072 www.stedmunds.co.uk
Please call for opening times

This is one of the world's outstanding collections of timepieces, from portable sundials, Renaissance clocks, watches of all periods, and even clockmakers' equipment. The watch collection's focus is on English watches and their makers, from the beginnings of the craft in Britain during the late 16th century, to the transformation of the industry in 1670, when English makers invented the balance spring.

Musée de la Montre
The Watch and Clock Museum
5 rue P. Berçot, 25130 Villers-le-Lac, France
Tel. (33) 3 81 68 08 00 montres.fc-net.fr
Jun-Sep: 10am-noon, 3-6pm. Oct-May: Sun 3-6pm

More than 1,000 outstanding pieces are on display and include everything related to watches, from watch keys, chronometers, and wristwatches to tools and automata. A showcase is devoted to chronometers explaining how the rivalry between the two great maritime powers of the 18th century, France and England, developed new techniques in time measuring in order to enable them to locate the enemy's ships and obtain supremacy at sea.

L'Amour instruit l'innocence,
Empire watch by Breguet
& Fils
Musée de la Montre

Museum of Art
Munson-Williams-Proctor Arts Institute, 310 Genesee Street, Utica, New York 13502, USA
Tel. (1) 315 797 0000 www.mwpi.edu
Tue-Sat 10am-5pm, Sun 1-5pm

The brothers Thomas and Fredrick Proctor, founders of the Institute, assembled during the late 19th and early 20th century an enviable watch collection despite competition from H. J. Heinz and Pierpont Morgan, who were also at the time collecting watches. Selectively they purchased rare and extraordinary examples of decorative watches from the early 17th to the early 20th century. Special exhibitions display a large portion of the collection.

Watch by Joseph Mirror,
c.1750
*Musée de l'Horlogerie
et de l'Emaillerie*

The National Watch and Clock Museum
514 Poplar Street, Columbia, Pennsylvania 17512-2130, USA
Tel. (1) 717 684 8261 www.nawcc.org
Tue-Sat 10am-5pm, Sun noon-4pm

Recently renovated, this astounding collection has expanded by leaps and bounds since it officially opened to the public in 1977 and today contains 12,000 items. Although it prides itself on 19th-century American watches, it also has superb examples of 18th- and 19th-century French timepieces and 19th- and 20th-century Swiss tools. Don't miss the Breguet Quarter Repeater sold to Caroline Bonaparte, Queen of Naples, in 1814. It took twenty artisans seven years to produce it.

Prescot Museum
34 Church Street, Prescot, Merseyside L34 3LA, UK
Tel. (44) 151 4307787
Tue-Sat 10am-5pm, Sun 2-5pm

From the mid-1600s to the beginning of the 20th century, this medieval Market town was a centre for clock and watch making. In addition to the collection of 600 or 700 watches, there are 280 clocks, files on over 21,000 makers from the Lancashire area, and a nationally important collection of watch making tools, which are displayed in several workshop reconstructions.

Portable polychrome
wooden watch showing
Neptune and the sea
gods, 18th century
Musée de la Montre

Taft Museum

316 Pike Street, Cincinnati, Ohio 45202, USA
Tel. (1) 513 241 0343 www.taftmuseum.org
Mon-Sat 10am-5pm, Sun 1-5pm

These 17th- and 18th-century decorative watches are in pristine condition, mainly untouched by restoration and with the movements unaltered. The collection ranks high on the list of the finest small art museums in the US. The earliest of the Taft watches illustrate the transformations in design which have taken place over the centuries. The real strength of the collection lies in its group of painted enamel watchcases dating from the middle of the 17th to the end of the 18th century.

Musée du Temps
The Museum of Time

Palais Granvelle, 96 Grande-Rue, 25000 Besançon, France
Tel. (33) 3 81 81 45 14
Due to open in 2002 (please call for details)

An encyclopedic collection of time apparatus focusing not only on the objects themselves but also on the relationship between mankind and time measurement, as well as key figures of the past who played a part, from clockmakers to physicists and engineers. This is a massive collection of several thousand clocks and watches, which includes pendulums, egg timers, and sundials, as well as more advanced scientific equipment.

Selection of 1930s Dunhill
timepieces
*Alfred Dunhill Museum and
Archive*

Usher Gallery

Lindum Road, Lincoln, Lincolnshire LN2 1NN, UK
Tel. (44) 1522 527980
Mon-Sat 10am-5.30pm, Sun 2.30-5pm

Jeweller and collector James Ward Usher left his collection of decorative arts to the city as well as funds to build this museum. His taste extended to exquisite workmanship, and many of the watches in this substantial collection have beautifully made cases.

ATLASES, MAPS, AND GLOBES

The American Museum in Britain
Claverton Manor, Bath, Somerset BA2 7BD, UK
Tel. (44) 1225 460503 www.americanmuseum.org
Tue-Sun 2-5pm, public holidays 11am-5pm

Dallas Pratt donated this renowned collection of early world maps and related
items in Europe, most of which are early printed or manuscript maps. The collection
contains a high proportion of recorded world maps; among them are several rare
16th-century Italian maps, such as a four-sheet world map by Michele Tramezzino
and a large heart-shaped map by Hadjii Ahmed. One of the most spectacular exhibits
is the 'fool's cap map', a late 16th-century copperplate map, set within a jester's face.

Birmingham Central Library
Chamberlain Square, Birmingham, West Midlands B3 3HQ, UK
Tel. (44) 121 3034217 www.ramesis.com
Mon-Fri 9am-8pm, Sat 9am-5pm

The library has a huge collection of early atlases, including a number of early editions of
Ptolemy dating from the Venetian edition of 1475; a Mercator atlas of 1613; *Le Nouvel Atlas*
by Jean Jansson in six volumes (1650-56), the earliest English marine atlas; and a French
marine atlas, *Le Neptune français* (1693). Also within the collection are two unique items:
a copy of Christopher Saxton's wall map of Great Britain (1583) and his atlas of maps of
England and Wales (1579).

Museum Boerhaave
Lange Sint Agnietenstraat 10, 2312 WC Leiden, The Netherlands
Tel. (31) 71 5214224 www.museumboerhaave.nl
Tue-Sat 10am-5pm, Sun & public holidays noon-5pm

Although there is a small map collection located in the museum's library, it is the holding
of early Dutch globes that is most notable. Examples by Gerard Valk and Jacob Floris
van Langren are displayed, together with pairs of globes by Willem Janszoon Blaeu and
Joan Blaeu. Globes were always made in pairs: one terrestrial and one celestial.

Portolan Chart, *c.* 1325
Royal Geographical Society

Germanisches Nationalmuseum
The Germanic National Museum
Kartäusergasse 1, 90402 Nuremberg, Germany
Tel. (49) 911 13310 www.gnm.de
Tue, Thu-Sun 10am-5pm, Wed 10am-9pm

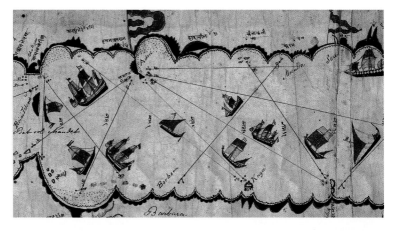

Pride of place here is the so-called Behaim terrestrial globe (1492-93). Also nicknamed the *Erdapfel* (Potato), it is the oldest surviving depiction of the earth in globe form. Even if Australia and the Americas are missing, it is remarkably accurate and was based on the latest charts supplied by Portuguese navigators and Ptolemy's map of the 2nd century AD.

Globenmuseum
The Globe Museum
Österreichische Nationalbibliothek, Josefsplatz 1, 1015 Vienna, Austria
Tel. (43) 1 53 410297 www.onb.ac.at
Mon-Wed, Thu 2-3pm, Fri 11am-noon,

This museum is part of the Austrian National Library. It contains more than 210 globes and relevant scientific instruments such as armillary spheres, telluria, and planetaria, the core of which have come from the former Habsburg family library. Emphasis in the collection is placed on terrestrial and celestial globes made before 1850, and includes the globe made by Mercator for the Emperor Karl V in 1541. Equally stunning is the celestial globe produced by Eimmart, decorated with pictorial symbols which represent the constellations of the zodiac. Probably the most important treasure is the *Atlas Blaeu-Van der Hem*, a Baroque anthology of fifty volumes.

Frontispiece to account the progress of an expedition to Central Africa, 1850-53
Royal Geographical Society

Harvard Map Collection
Nathan Marsh Pusey Library, Harvard Yard, Cambridge, Massachusetts 02138, USA
Tel. (1) 617 495 2417 www.hcl.harvard.edu
Mon-Fri 9am-4.45pm

One of the largest and most comprehensive cartographic collections in the US, it now encompasses 400,000 maps, 6,000 atlases, and 5,000 reference books. The Library's collections include rare editions of Mercator, Ortelius, and Ptolemaic atlases, as well as large-scale current topographic maps for geographic areas throughout the world.

The Library of Congress
Room LM B01, James Madison Memorial Building, 101 Independence Ave. SE, Washington, D.C. 20540-4650, USA
Tel. (1) 212 707 6277 www.loc.gov
Mon-Fri 8.30am-5pm

Well represented in the massive holdings are more than 300 terrestrial and celestial globes, armillary spheres, and 150 globe gores (paper segments used in the construction of globes) in all shapes and sizes, from pocket globes enclosed in fish-skin cases, to dissected globes, and folding examples such as R. Buckminster Fuller's Dymaxion Globe. The oldest item in the collection is a small, manuscript, terrestrial globe, housed within a series of eleven interlocking armillary rings produced in 1543 by Caspar Vopell, a Cologne mathematician and geographer.

Magyar Földrajzi Múzeum
The Hungarian Geographical Museum
Budai út 4, 2030 Érd, Hungary
Tel. (36) 23 365132
Tue-Fri 2-6pm, Sat-Sun 10am-6pm

This museum was set up to commemorate Hungarian exploration. The most spectacular item is the map upon which the routes of 28 Hungarian explorers are marked. The first detailed map of Hungary (with over 1,400 places marked on it) is held here and was drawn by Lázár Deák in 1528. Visitors can see the Jomard prize-winning *Atlas of Japan* by Pál Teleki, who also happened to hold the post of prime minister, or the folding boat of Lajos Lóczy (who made the first modern geological map of Hungary in 1890), which is displayed in the Cholnoky Room.

Relief of the Bernese Oberland by S. Simon
Schweizerisches Alpines Museum

Museu de Marinha
The Maritime Museum
Praça do Império, 1400 Lisbon, Portugal
Tel. (351) 21 3620010   www.museumarinha.pt
Oct-Mar: Tue-Sun 10am-5pm. Rest of year: Tue-Sun 10am-6pm

A large planisphere shows the principal voyages made by the Portuguese between the 15th and 18th centuries, and the line, agreed by the Crowns of Spain and Portugal at the Treaty of Tordesillas, which divided the unknown world into two areas of expansion – one for Spain, the other for Portugal. The museum also houses the first isogonic chart showing the lines of equal magnetic deviation, made by Luis Teixeira (*c.* 1585), which shows the location of the Solomon Islands for the first time. Further highlights include a collection of oriental cartography and two magnificent globes, manufactured in the 17th century by the celebrated Dutch Master Willem Jans Blaeu.

Maritiem Museum Prins Hendrik
The Prince Hendrik Maritime Museum
Leuvehaven 1, 3011 EA Rotterdam, The Netherlands
Tel. (31) 10 4132680   www.mmph.nl
Tue-Sat 10am-5pm, Sun & public holidays 11am-5pm

Rotterdam's maritime museum holds an exceptional collection of rare nautical charts and atlases (300 atlases and 1,000 maps), including a hand-coloured engraving from a map of the Indonesian archipelago, drawn for trade purposes by Petrus Plancius and dated 1592.

Museo Maritim
The Maritime Museum
Avinguda de les Drassanes 1, 08001 Barcelona, Spain
Tel. (34) 93 3429920   www.almogaver.com
Daily 10am-7pm

Apart from its outstanding collection of ship models and nautical vessels, the museum offers a fine exhibition of nautical maps and charts which provide an invaluable means of understanding the evolution of seafaring, with particular attention to Catalan's nautical heritage. The outstanding collection of maps includes eleven portolanos, drawn by the most important artists of the Mallorcan Cartographic School between the 15th and 17th centuries.

Mathematisch-Physikalischer Salon
The Salon of Mathematics and Physics
Zwinger, Sophienstrasse 2, 01067 Dresden, Germany
Tel. (49) 351 4914622 www.staatl-kunstsammlungen-dresden.de
Fri-Wed 10am-6pm

The collection offers an insight into the work of the southern German globe makers, including a star globe from Damascus decorated in silver and gold (1279), a most remarkable specimen of Persian-Arabic instrument making and astronomical knowledge.

Musée Mercator
The Mercator Museum
Zamanstraat 49, Museumcomplex, Zwijgershoek, 9100 Sint-Niklaas, Belgium
Tel. (32) 3 7772942
Tue-Sat 2-5pm, Sun 10am-5pm

Drawing on the rich Mercator Collection of the Royal Archaeological Society of the Land of Waas, the museum offers an introduction to the history of cartography before and after Gerard Mercator. Among the items on display in the Treasure Room are the original terrestrial and celestial globes made by the great man himself in 1541 and 1551 – Mercator's map of Europe from 1554 and his planisphere *Ad usum navigantium* (for the use of sailors) from 1569.

National Maritime Museum
Romney Road, Greenwich, London SE10 9NF, UK
Tel. (44) 20 88584422 www.nmm.ac.uk
Daily 10am-5pm

The collection of globes and armillary spheres is one of the finest anywhere and includes a copy of the earliest surviving terrestrial globe by Martin Behaim (1491-93), as well as Ptolemy's *Cosmographia* (1482), which shows Africa joined to an unknown Southern continent. The museum also houses an outstanding collection of 100,000 charts, as well as 50,000 prints and drawings, including the illustrations found in the journal of Edward Barlow (17th century), one of the most graphic accounts of early seafaring to survive.

Jagiellonian Globe with an island on the Indian Ocean called *America, Noviter Reperta*, gilded brass, c. 1520
Muzeum Uniwersytetu Jagiellońskiego

Nederlands Scheepvaartmuseum
The Dutch Maritime Museum
Kattenburgerplein 1, 1018 KK Amsterdam, The Netherlands
Tel. (31) 20 5232222 www.generali.nl
Mon-Sat 10am-5pm, Sun noon-5pm

Thanks to a transaction with Anton Mensing in 1921, the museum's library of atlases and maps is now one of the most important of its kind in the world. The collection includes a celestial globe from 1613, made by the Amsterdam cartographers Jodocus Hondius and Adriaan Veen.

Plantin-Moretus Museum
Vrijdagmarkt 22, 2000 Antwerp, Belgium
Tel. (32) 3 2211450 www.dma.be
Tue-Sun 10am-4.45pm

The Geography Room contains 16th-century atlases by Gemma-Frisius, Mercator, and Ortelius. The collection of maps of Antwerp includes a large plan of 1565 by Virgilius Boloniensis and Cornelis Grapheus.

Royal Geographical Society
1 Kensington Gore, London SW7 2AR, UK
Tel. (44) 20 75913050 www.rgs.org
By appt. only

The map room here contains one of the largest private collections of maps and related material in the world. There are 1,000,000 maps and charts, 2,600 atlases, forty globes, and 700 gazetteers comprising the core. Among the subjects here are ice thickness in Antarctica, a navigational atlas for the Yenisey River, trekking maps for Nepal, vegetation maps of Brazil, and satellite imagery maps.

Schweizerisches Alpines Museum
The Swiss Alpine Museum
Helvetiaplatz 4, 3005 Berne, Switzerland
Tel. (41) 31 3510434 www.alpinesmuseum.ch
Mon 2-5pm, Tue-Sun 10am-5pm (mid Oct-mid May closed noon-2pm)

Especially noteworthy is the museum's collection of reliefs, with masterpieces by Eduard Imhof, Xaver Imfeld, Carl Meili, Albert Heim, and Anton Mair. The collection of maps also includes the first wall-map, hand-made by H. Kuemmerli.

Museo della Specola
The Museum of the Observatory
Università di Bologna, via Zamboni 33, 40126 Bologna, Italy
Tel. (39) 051 2095701 www.bo.astro.it
Mon-Fri 8.30am-5.30pm (times may vary, please call for details)

The map collection comprises some fine nautical examples by Giulio di Cesare Petrucci and Banet Panadès. In addition, there are several illustrations of celestial phenomena painted by Maria Clara Eimmart, the daughter of Georg Christoph Eimmart (17th century). Geographical maps include works by the French cartographer Charles Hubert Alexis Jaillot (17th-18th century), and the *Carta Geografica Completa di tutti i Regni del Mundo*, drawn up in 1602 at Bejing by Matteo Ricci.

Sterling Memorial Library Map Collection
Yale University Library, 120 High Street, New Haven, Connecticut 06520, USA
Tel. (1) 203 432 2798 www.library.yale.edu
Mon-Fri 10am-noon, 1-5pm

This collection comprises over 200,000 map sheets, 3,000 atlases, and 900 reference books from around the world. It also houses approximately 15,000 rare (pre-1850) sheet maps, mostly pertaining to North America. Of special interest is the Lanman Globe Collection amassed by alumnus Dr Jonathan Lanman, as well as several fine globes by the Venetian Franciscan monk and cartographer, Vincenzo Coronelli.

Universiteitsbibliotheek Amsterdam
The Amsterdam University Library
Singel 425, 1012 WP Amsterdam, The Netherlands
Tel. (31) 20 5252354 www.uba.uva.nl
Tue-Fri 1-5pm

The Library contains some 4,500 atlases, about 500 of which date from before 1800, such as a Ptolemaic from 1511, an extensive range from the Antwerp period (second half of 16th century), and examples from the height of Amsterdam map-making in the 17th and 18th centuries. Highlights of rare broadsheet and manuscript maps include Cornelis Anthoniszoon's woodcut map of Amsterdam (1544), J.J.

Beeldsnijder's map of North Holland (1575), and Willem Jansz Blaeu's maps of the Seventeen Provinces (1604).

Muzeum Uniwersytetu Jagielloñskiego
The Jagiellonian University Museum
Collegium Maius, ulica Jagielloñska 15, 31-010 Cracow, Poland
Tel. (48) 12 4220549
Mon-Fri, Sun 11am-3pm, Sat 11am-2pm

Among this collection is the Gold Jagiellonian Globe, a mechanical armillary sphere with a Latin inscription on an Indian Ocean Island: *America Noviter Reperta* (America newly discovered). There are also a pair of globes by the globe maker, G. Mercator: the terrestrial globe is dated 1541 and the celestial globe is dated 1551.

CARRIAGES, SLEIGHS AND CARTS

Arlington Court
Arlington, near Barnstaple, Devon EX31 4LP, UK
Tel. (44) 1271 850296   www.nationaltrust.org.uk
Mon, Wed-Sun, 11am-5.30pm

This fine collection comprises nearly fifty vehicles and accompanying harnesses, including eight carriages donated by the Marquess of Bute. The finest vehicles are the State Coach from Knowle in Kent and Lord Craven's State Chariot of 1850, complete with silver-plated harness. Curious items range from dog carts, to General Tom Thumb's (of Barnum's Circus) Miniature Coach (*c.* 1897).

Gilt-covered wooden sledge showing Neptune riding a dolphin, *c.* 1700
Kunstsammlungen der Veste Coburg

Musée de Calèches
The Museum of Open Carriages
49A rue de Crautheim, 3390 Peppange, Grand Duchy of Luxembourg
Tel. (352) 510906   www.luxembourg.co.uk
Tue-Sun 2-5pm

A small but beautiful collection of carriages in both their original and restored states, built between 1850 and 1910. Apart from the coupé of the Grand Duke of Luxembourg, there is also a Mylord, a Landau, and a Berline Omnibus. Not to be missed is a fully operational coach workshop, equipped with tools and accessories, such as harnesses and travel cases.

Ceremonial carriage, 1586
Kunstsammlungen der Veste Coburg

Musée des Carrosses
The Museum of Carriages
Grande Ecurie du Roi, 1 avenue de Paris, 78000 Versailles, France
Tel. (33) 1 30 21 54 82
Jul, Aug: Sun 2-4.30pm

The collection comprises sedan chairs and 17th- and 18th-century carts and carriages, including Napoleon and Marie-Louise's wedding carriage (1810). One of the most utstanding items is the carriage of Charles X (1825), which was made for the baptism of the imperial prince in 1856.

THE CARRIAGE DEALERS JOURNAL

Vol. X.   NOVEMBER, 1899.   No. 7.

'The Carriage Dealers
Journal'
*The Long Island Museum of
American Art, History and
Carriages*

Museo delle Carrozze
The Museum of Carriages
Villa Trieste, frazione Siano, 88100 Catanzaro, Italy
Tel. (39) 0961 469546
Mon–Fri 8.30am–noon, 3.30–6pm

The exhibition comprises Baron de Paola's collection of 25 period carriages, including a fine cabriolet with a concertina hood and a 17th-century state coach. You will also see the carriage of Pope Clement XIV, and the late 19th-century carriage which appeared in the Hollywood blockbuster *Gone with the Wind*.

Museu dos Coches
The Museum of Carriages
Praça Afonso de Albuquerque, 1300 Lisbon, Portugal
Tel. (351) 21 3610850
Tue–Sun 10am–5.30pm

This museum houses vehicles from the royal household and from the Patriarch of Lisbon's collection. The main display is in the Salão Nobre, a beautifully decorated room which houses three carriages of King João V. The oldest carriage dates from the 17th century and belonged to King Philip II of Portugal.

Musée des Equipages
The Museum of Equipages
Château de Vaux-le-Vicomte, 77950 Maincy, France
Tel. (33) 1 64 14 41 90
Daily 10am–6pm

Basket phaeton
*The Long Island Museum of
American Art, History and
Carriages*

The collection comprises 18th- and 19th-century town carriages and travelling carriages such as park drag, omnibus, and diligence models. Some of the most interesting items include a Gala coupé with eight springs (1830), an open carriage by Ehrler, and a coupé by Mulbacher.

Berlin coach
*The Long Island Museum of
American Art, History and
Carriages*

Hedmarksmuseet og Domkirkeodden
The Hedmark Museum at Cathedral Point
Strandveien 100, 2305 Hamar, Norway
Tel. (47) 62 542700 www.hedmarksmuseet.museum.no
Mid May–mid Jun, mid Aug–mid Sep: 10am–4pm
Mid Jun–mid Aug: 10am–6pm

Most of the colourfully painted and carved sledges exhibited here date from 1750 to 1850. One particularly stunning example is embellished with carved lions and Rococo paintings on its back, and side panels depicting elegantly dressed ladies.

Historisches Museum
The Historical Museum
Pferdestrasse 6, 30159 Hanover, Germany
Tel. (49) 511 1683052
Wed-Fri 10am-4pm, Tue 10am-10pm, Sat-Sun 10am-6pm

This museum has a remarkable collection of carriages and harnesses, including the superb golden coupé of the Prince of Wales, dating from 1783.

Historisches Museum Basel
The Historical Museum of Basle
Steinenberg 4, 4051 Basle, Switzerland
Tel. (41) 61 2058600 www.historischesmu-seumbasel.ch
Mon, Wed-Sun 10am-5pm

Of the extensive collection, there is only room to show pieces of particular historical interest to the city. The ornate Diana sleigh is one of the loveliest, and dates from the Baroque period when 'carousel' sleigh rides (where the sleighs would form elaborate figures, to music) were a popular pastime.

Advertisement for the Columbia Carriage Company
The Long Island Museum of American Art, History and Carriages

Kunstsammlungen der Veste Coburg
The Art Collections of the Coburg Citadel
Veste Coburg, 96450 Coburg, Germany
Tel. (49) 9561 8790
www.kunstsammlungen-coburg.de
Apr-Oct: Tue-Sun 10am-5pm
Nov-Mar: Tue-Sun 1-4pm

This museum contains two magnificent gilt 16th-century carriages which were each used only once on the occasion of Duke Johann Casimir's two marriages. Both are regarded as among the oldest ceremonial carriages of such splendour in Europe. Also quite splendid are the displays of thirteen rather unusual 17th- and 18th-century tournament sledges, including the Carousel, staged by ladies at the Coburg Court.

The Long Island Museum of American Art, History and Carriages
1200 Route 25A, Stony Brook, New York 11790-1992, USA
Tel. (1) 631 751 0066 www.longislandmuseum.org
Wed-Sat 10am-5pm, Sun & public holidays noon-5pm

The carriage collection, comprising 250 horse-drawn vehicles, is the largest and most comprehensive in the US. There is an 18th-century phaeton that belonged to revolutionary war hero, General Peter Gansevoort. There are also carriage-making tools, harnesses, stable fixtures and vehicle accoutrements. In addition, the museum has a significant holding of pre-1850 trade literature that is especially rare.

Marstallmuseum
The Royal Stables Museum
Schloss Nymphenburg, 80638 Munich, Germany
Tel. (49) 89 179080
Apr-Sep: daily 9am-noon, 1-5pm. Oct-Mar: daily 10am-noon, 1-4pm

An array of royal sleighs and carriages, alongside 18th- and 19th-century harnesses, broughams, sledges, and sedan chairs used by the Wittelsbachs. Not to be missed are luxuriously ornamented exhibits such as the coronation coach of the Emperor Karl VII and the state coach and personal sleigh of Ludwig II.

Porvoon Museo
The Museum of Porvoo
Välikatu 11, 06100 Porvoo, Finland
Tel. (358) 19 5747589
May-Aug: daily 11am-4pm. Sep-Apr: Wed-Sun noon-4pm

Sleighs in abundance, including two that are known to have been used by Russian emperors during their travels in Finland.

The Royal Mews
Buckingham Palace, London SW1A 1AA, UK
Tel. (44) 20 78391377 www.btconnect.co.uk
Daily 9.30am-5pm

These are the finest working stables in existence and provide transport for the Queen and members of the Royal Family. It's home to horses, state motor-cars, and an array of carriages, each one seemingly gilt with more gold than the next. It includes the magnificent Gold State Coach used for Coronations, and carriages used for Royal and State occasions, weddings, and the State Opening of Parliament. Also displayed are collections of historic, ornate harnesses and presentation saddles.

Drawing of the first manned gas balloon on December 1, 1783
Ballon-Museum Gersthofen

Shelburne Museum
US Route 7, Shelburne, Vermont 05482, USA
Tel. (1) 802 985 3346 www.shelburnemuseum.org
End May-end Oct: daily 10am-5pm

This is one of the most comprehensive collections of horse-drawn vehicles in the US. It contains 225 examples, from a pair of fine, custom-made carriages (by Million et Guiet of Paris) and a fairytale Victoria sleigh, to a number of less luxurious vehicles, including several commercial wagons.

Stockwood Craft Museum & Gardens and Mossman Collection
Stockwood Country Park, Farley Hill, Luton, Bedfordshire, LU1 4BH, UK
Tel. (44) 1582 738714
Tue-Sun & public holidays
10am-4.45pm

The George Mossman Collection of horse-drawn vehicles is among the largest display of its kind in the UK. Exhibits trace the story of transport before the advent of the motor car, and there is also a section devoted to modern vehicles, including a Luton tram and vintage cars.

Tyrwhitt-Drake Museum of Carriages
Mill Street, Maidstone, Kent, UK
Tel. (44) 1622 663006
Apr-Oct: daily 10.30am-5.30pm. Nov-Mar: daily noon-5.30pm

Housed in the medieval stables of the nearby Archbishops' Palace, the exhibition, started by Sir Garrard Tyrwhitt-Drake, offers a wonderful collection of vehicles, including state and official carriages, horse-drawn sledges, baby carriages, and sedan chairs.

Zamek w Lañcucie
The Lancut Castle
Ulica Zamkowa 1, 37-100 Lañcut, Poland
Tel. (48) 17 2252008
Daily 9am-3pm

Lancut Castle contains an internationally renowned collection of horse-drawn vehicles consisting of 55 items. Many were made by the best European carriage manufacturers with the majority from the famous Viennese companies, Marius or Lohner, or from Paris by Binder and Rothschild.

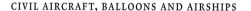

CIVIL AIRCRAFT, BALLOONS AND AIRSHIPS

Musée de l'Air et de l'Espace
The Air and Space Museum
Aéroport du Bourget BP 173, 93352 Le Bourget, France
Tel. (33) 1 49 92 71 99   www.mae.org
May-Oct: Tue-Sun 10am-6pm. Rest of year: Tue-Sun 10am-6pm

1918 Avro 504K
Shuttleworth Collection

In this museum, on the sight of Charles Lindbergh's historic landing, are 175 historic planes, many of which pay tribute to early pioneers. They include the Massia-Biot glider, a strange, bird-like contraption dating back to 1879. The prototype Concorde 001 and a number of other commercial airplanes developed between the two wars are also exhibited.

Anderson-Abruzzo International Balloon Museum
Maxie L. Anderson Foundation, Albuquerque, New Mexico 87191, USA
Tel. (1) 505 271 2119
Opening in 2003, please call for details

This museum traces the history of the balloon from the Montgolfier brothers to the present day, from scientific applications (i.e. the discovery of radiation belts), to balloons used for high altitude reconnaissance and adventure.

Ballon-Museum Gersthofen
The Gersthofen Balloon Museum
Bahnhofstrasse 10, 86368 Gersthofen, Germany
Tel. (49) 8212 491135
Sat-Sun 10am-6pm (other days by group appt. only)

This museum, housed in a former water-tower, celebrates ballooning achievements, particularly in Gersthofen, with models of the first balloons. Also included are instruments recounting the story of how man conquered the sky (including plans by Leonardo da Vinci), and a special exhibit dedicated to Pilatre de Rozier and the Marquis d'Arlande, who became the first men to fly in a balloon on November 21, 1783.

Musée des Ballons
The Balloon Museum
Château de Balleroy, 14490 Balleroy, France
Tel. (33) 2 31 21 60 61 www.chateau-balleroy.com
Mid Mar-mid Oct: daily 9am-6pm

The late Malcolm Forbes converted the stables of this château in Normandy into the world's first museum dedicated to ballooning. Paintings, miniatures, prints, documents, stamps, navigational instruments, old postcards, and balloon artefacts trace the development of this form of air travel and its uses.

Museum of Flying
2772 Donald Douglas Loop North, Santa Monica, California 90405, USA
Tel. (1) 310 392 8822 www.museumofflying.com
Wed-Sun 10am-5pm

1936 Dh87b Hornet Moth
Shuttleworth Collection

On display are over 45 propeller- and jet-powered aircraft, including a restored Beacley Little Looper from 1914, which achieved the first ever loop-the-loop in the US, and the smallest jet-powered aircraft in the world, Bede BD-5J Micro (1973), from the James Bond film *Octopussy*.

Musée historique de l'Hydraviation
Historic Museum of Marine Aviation
332 ave. Louis Breguet, 40600 Biscarrosse, France
Tel. (33) 5 58 78 00 65 www.latecoere.com
Apr-Jun, Sep: daily 3pm-7pm. Jul, Aug, Oct-Mar: daily 10am-7pm

Between 1930 and 1955, Biscarrosse was where Latécoère seaplanes were assembled and tested. Recounting the history are documents, files, recorded memories of the pilots, models, engines, and propellers, along with several restored seaplanes.

Exterior of the museum
Zeppelin-Museum
Friedrichschafen

National Air and Space Museum - Smithsonian Institution
7th and Independence Avenue SW, Washington, DC 20560, USA
Tel. (1) 202 357 2700 www.nasm.si.edu
Daily 10am-5.30pm

This museum's 23 galleries record the entire history of human attempts at flight. Suspended from the ceiling are dozens of aircraft, from a 1903 Wright Flyer that Wilbur Wright piloted over the sands of North Carolina, to Charles Lindbergh's *Spirit of St. Louis,* and the X-1 rocket plane in which Chuck Yeager broke the sound barrier.

Navy Lakehurst Historical Society & Naval Air Engineering Station
Highway 547, Lakehurst, New Jersey 08733-5041, USA
Tel. (1) 732 818 7520 www.nlhs.com
By appt. only

This famous dirigible field, founded in 1919, saw the USS *Shenandoah* (ZR-1) fly here in 1923, and later the commercial transatlantic flights of the Hindenburg (which crashed here in 1937), and the *Graf Zeppelin*. Still serving as the Naval Air Engineering Station, tours conducted by the Society take visitors to Hanger 1 (built to house the US Navy's rigid airships), to the Hindenburg crash site marked with a memorial plaque, and to Hangers 5 and 6, which were used to house blimps during World War II.

Old Rhinebeck Aerodrome
Stone Church Road, Rhinebeck, New York 12572, USA
Tel. (1) 845 752 3200 www.oldrhinebeck.org
Mid May-Oct: daily 10am-5pm

On display here is a unique and vast collection of early aircraft (and vintage vehicles), including the 1930 Aeromarine Klemm, which was built of wood. Cast your eyes to the sky to watch historic planes roar through the air, or hitch a ride in a classic 1929 New Standard open-cockpit biplane.

Reconstruction of a 33-metre-long section of the *LZ 129 Hindenburg Zeppelin-Museum Friedrichschafen*

Repüléstörténeti és ûrhajózási állandó kiállítás
The Permanent Exhibition of Aviation and Space Flight
Petôfi Csarnok, Zichy M. út, Városliget, 1146 Budapest, Hungary
Tel. (36) 343 0009
Tue-Fri 10am-5pm, Sat-Sun 10am-6pm

Planes, engines, and documents dating back to 1910 trace the development of aviation in Hungary. They focus mainly on civil aviation advances, although there are military exhibits, as well as items connected to Hungary's participation in space exploration.

Shuttleworth Collection
Old Warden Park, Biggleswade, Bedfordshire SG18 9EP, UK
Tel. (44) 1767 627288 www.shuttleworth.org
Apr-Oct: daily 10am-5pm. Nov-Mar: daily 10am-4pm

One of the few remaining all-grass aerodromes, with eight hangars packed with over forty planes amassed by Richard Shuttleworth, all maintained in full-flying condition. The collection traces the evolution of aviation from the heady days of Edwardian flying machines, illustrated by a 1909 Blériot, to their use as machines of war, as exemplified by a 1942 Spitfire.

Zeppelin-Museum Friedrichshafen
The Friedrichshafen Zeppelin Museum
Seestrasse 22, 88045 Friedrichshafen, Germany
Tel. (49) 7541 38010 www.zeppelin-museum.de
May-Oct: Tue-Sun 10am-6pm. Nov-Apr: Tue-Sun 10am-5pm

This museum presents the world's greatest repository of objects on the history of airship flight and technology, from its beginnings to the invention of the new Zeppelin NT. The library holds a comprehensive section on the history of airships, which is supplemented by the archives of the Luftschiffbau Zeppelin.

CYCLES AND MOTORCYCLES

Quadrant tricycle, Birmingham, 1886
Nationaal Fietsmuseum - Velorama

Musée d'Art et d'Industrie
The Museum of Art and Industry
2 place Louis Comte, 42000 Saint-Etienne, France
Tel. (33) 4 77 33 0485
Mon, Wed-Sun 10am-noon, 2-6pm

This museum holds an important and well-documen ted collection of over 150 bicycles, some of which are very rare. Also on display are more than 200 posters related to cycles, dating from the end of the 19th century.

The Bicycle Museum of America
7 West Monroe Street, New Bremen, Ohio 45869, USA
Tel. (1) 419 629 9249   www.bicyclemuseum.com
Mon-Fri 11am-5pm, Sat 11am-2pm

This museum comprises a fascinating array of early cycles, including the 1870s Shire Boneshaker and many other complicated, brakeless contraptions. Recent exhibits include the 1952 Huffy Dial-A-Ride in which, with a simple twist of the wrist, the cyclist could adjust the suspension. Also included are many weird and wonderful examples, notably the 1950s Gene Autry in rodeo-brown finish, with jewelled fenders and a pony's head on the fork.

British Cycling Museum
The Old Station, Camelford, Cornwall, PL32 9TZ, UK
Tel. (44) 1840 212811
Mon-Thu, Sun 10am-5pm

This museum comprises over 1,000 cycling medals, fobs, club badges from 1881, 400 cycles, 400 enamel advertising signs, posters, and an enormous library. Of particular interest is the American Star, a bike with a small wheel in front and a large one at the back. Rare examples of lighting equipment are a real treat; they include a hub light that originally fitted a penny farthing, as well as an example of the first cycle oil lamp.

Centre de l'Automobile ancienne
The Veteran Car Centre
10 square de Labédoyère, 02310 Nogent-l'Artaud, France
Tel. (33) 3 23 70 11 10
Daily 10am-noon, 2-6pm

The Centre contains some sixty motorbikes, including examples by Koehler, Escoffier, Terrot, Alcyon, and New-Map. Also on show are several micro cars, such as the Messerschmitt KR 175, Kabineraoller, Vespa 400, Autobianchi Lutece, Mochet, and Isetta Velam, as well as a two-wheeled skate made for Japanese schools by Honda.

Deutsches Zweirad- und NSU-Museum
The German Two-Wheeler and NSU Museum
Urbanstrasse 11, 74172 Neckarsulm, Germany
Tel. (49) 7132 35271   www.zweirad-museum.de
Tue-Sun 9am-5pm (Thu until 7pm)

This museum specializes in motorcycles and is one of
Germany's largest. Of the 300 vehicles permanently
on display, forty bicycles illustrate the history of their
development, from the very first trailing wheel of the
Baron of Drais (1817) and the French Michaux cycles,
to present-day bicycles. As well as a copy of Daimler's
first motorcycle (1885) there are early historic vehicles,
such as the first mass-produced motorcycle by
Hildebrand & Wolfmüller.

Il Museo del Falegname Tino Sana
The Tino Sana Carpentry Museum
Via Aldo Moro 6, 24030 Almenno San Bartolomeo, Italy
Tel. (39) 035 554411   www.tinosana.com
Sat 3-6pm, Sun 9.30am-noon, 3-6pm (closed Aug)

On display are rare examples of wooden bicycles, some
of them unique, like the Draisina from 1820, which is
without pedals and had to be propelled by pushing
with one's legs. There is also the famous Michandina
from 1861, the first model with pedals. Other exhibits
include an iron velocipede and tricycles from 1880, as
well as bicycles that belonged to cycling champions
like Coppi and Gimondi.

The First Penny Farthing Museum
92 King Street, Knutsford, Cheshire, WA16 6ED, UK
Tel. (44) 1565 652497
Daily 10am-5pm

This collection holds many examples of various Penny Farthings, from the Special
Challenge, which came complete with suspension saddle, oil tin, and spanners, to the
Paragon, which had a roller-brake on the back wheel and elaborate spring-loaded foot
rests on the front forks. A vast amount of additional paraphernalia also exists, from special clothing and hub lamps for night-time riding, to bugles to warn pedestrians to get
out of the way, and cyclometers that measured in furlongs, with a bell to ring out for
every mile travelled.

Tom Norton Snr, one
of the founders of the
collection (top)
National Cycle Exhibition

Interior of the museum
(above)
*Nationaal Fietsmuseum -
Velorama*

Indian Scout motorcycle,
1920 (left)
*Stubbekøbing Motorcykel- og
Radiomuseum*

Harley Davidson Museum
1148 Soquel Avenue, Santa Cruz, California 95062, USA
Tel. (1) 831 421 9600   www.santacruzharley.com
Mon-Fri 10am-6pm, Sat 9am-5pm, Sun 10am-5pm

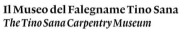

Exhibits include vintage motorcycles, memorabilia,
and photos from the Harley Davidson archives.
Among the highlights are a 1930 VL with side-
car, a 1993 FXRP Police motorcycle, and a
1929 JDH two-cam twin, which in its day
was the fastest road bike. There is even a
Harley Davidson 1918 girl's bicycle.

Metz Bicycle Museum

54 West Main Street, Freehold, New Jersey 07728, USA
Tel. (1) 732 462 7363   www.metzbicyclemuseum.com
Please call for opening times

A prized collection of several hundred antique bikes dating from the 1850s to the 1950s, collected by enthusiast Dave Metz. There is the rare 1885 Coventry Club Tandem Quadricycle and many oddities, including the 1894 Lamplighter (eight feet high), used for lighting gas lamps in New York City. There is even a watercycle (1910) with two pontoons that would hold the rider afloat while sailing down rivers.

Motorradmuseum
The Motorcycle Museum

Schloss Augustusburg, 09573 Augustusburg, Germany
Tel. (49) 37291 6528
Apr-Oct: daily 9am-6pm. Nov-Mar: daily 10am-5pm

This remarkable collection is one of the most comprehensive in Europe. Some 300 exhibits illustrate motorcycle history and its technical development from the early days. It is especially strong in two-stroke-engine motorcycles and racing motorcycles. Most of them are originals and include some rather special pieces, such as a Hildebrand & Wolfmüller's first mass-produced motorcycle (1894), two Böhmerland (longest mass-produced motorcycle, 1928), and two Megolas with five-cylinder radial engines (1922).

N.S.U. 326 ccm, 1914
Stubbekøbing Motorcykel- og Radiomuseum

Motorrad-Museum Krems-Egelsee
The Museum of Motorcycles Krems-Egelsee

Ziegelofengasse 1, 3500 Krems-Egelsee, Austria
Tel. (43) 2732 41624
Mar-Oct: daily 9am-5pm

Most of the 150 motorcycles here are German, British or Austrian and date from 1907 to 1977. Highlights include a 1895 De Dion Bouton, a 1906 Block & Hollender, a 1908 Laurin & Klement, and a 1910 Ormonde. There is a Triumph (1915), a NSU (1927), and a 1928 York. More than 200 engines from 1895 to 1960 are on display too, together with carburettors, timings, photographs, posters, and brochures. A special section is dedicated to the historical documentation of old Austrian motorcycles.

Humber tricycle,
Nottingham, 1889
Nationaal Fietsmuseum - Velorama

Nationaal Fietsmuseum – Velorama
The National Bicycle Museum - Velorama

Waalkade 107, 6511 XR Nijmegen, The Netherlands
Tel. (31) 24 3225851   www.velorama.nl
Mon-Sat 10am-5pm, Sun 11am-5pm

Over 250 cycles trace the development of the bicycle, tricycle, and quadricycle, from the very first examples to the latest models. A separate room is devoted to the Dutch bicycle industry, which sprang up around 1890, and for researchers there is the Wietske De Vries library containing archives on the Netherland's leading bicycle manufacturers.

National Cycle Exhibition

The Automobile Palace, Temple Street, Llandrindod Wells, Powys LD1 5DL, Wales, UK
Tel. (44) 1597 825 531
Daily 10am-4pm

With over 250 cycles on display, this is the largest collection of cycles in the UK, covering every aspect of cycling, from its earliest days of hobby-horses and boneshakers through to the latest in lightweight alloys. Among the exhibits are early velocipedes (1867-69), with wooden wheels and iron tyres, and the first safety bicycle (1888), which was chain-driven and included such refinements as a sprung seat, sloping forks, and improved frame design in the shape of a diamond. The collection also includes some 2,000 papers relating to the life of J. B. Dunlop and his invention (or reinvention) of the pneumatic tyre.

Penny Farthing
Nationaal Fietsmuseum - Velorama

The National Motor Museum

John Montagu Building, Beaulieu,
Hampshire, SO42 7ZN, UK
Tel. (44) 1590 612345 www.beaulieu.co.uk
Daily 10am-6pm

Pride of place in the exhibition goes to the British motorcycle industry (BSA, Triumph, Norton, Sunbeam, and Vincent), which enjoyed world leadership in the first half of the 20th century. Classic bikes from other nations are also well represented. There is everything from the gigantic touring monsters of BMW, to the little two-stroke scooters from Lambretta.

Pedaling History Bicycling Museum

3943 North Buffalo Road, Orchard Park, New York 14127, USA
Tel. (1) 716 662 3853 www.pedalinghistory.com
Please call for opening times

The 'walking machine' (1817), propelled by pushing your feet against the ground, was the invention of Baron von Drais, who wanted to get around his gardens faster. At the museum this and other early cycles can be seen in all their Heath-Robinsonesque finery. Among the most recent exhibits is an Otto Bicycle from 1883, in which the rider would sit between two large wheels, one on either side. Another interesting exhibit is from the 1890s: a collection of three military bicycles, armed with rifles, pistols, and a Colt machine gun.

Schweizer Sportmuseum Basel
The Swiss Sports Museum of Basle

Missionsstrasse 28, 4003 Basle, Switzerland
Tel. (41) 61 2611221 www.swiss-sports-museum.ch
Mon-Fri 10am-noon, 2-5pm, Sat 1-5pm, Sun 11-5pm

One of the museum's highlights is the Star Bicycle, a rare Penny Farthing manufactured in 1879-80 by Smith Machine Co. in New Jersey, US; it belonged to the expatriate Swiss cyclist Nick Kaufmann, a champion bike acrobat. Other cycle rarities include the four-seater Quadruplet (produced around 1896-97 in England), a chaircycle or Hirondelle, and even an exercise bike from around 1905.

Advertising clock
Museo Fisogni

Stubbekøbing Motorcykel- og Radiomuseum
The Stubbekøbing Motorcycle and Radio Museum
Nykøbingvej 54, 4850 Stubbekøbing, Denmark
Tel. (45) 54 442222
Please call for opening times

Among the exceptional models on display are the Excelsior 1000 (built in 1915), a smart Harley Davidson model 11. F (c. 1915), and the Pierce Arrow 600 (made in 1912). There is also a display of twenty mopeds, placed in the museum by the Danish Veteran Moped Club.

Musée du Vélocipède
The Velocipede Museum
Rue principale, 24480 Cadouin, France
Tel. (33) 5 53 63 46 60
Daily 10am-7pm

Gérard Buisset, a shop-window decorator, was asked to find old bicycles for a large Parisian store, a request that brought about this collection. The rare, wooden bicycle from 1870 was found by Buisset in a garage after his car broke down. The Grand Bi, one of the most precious items in the collection, was rescued on its way to the tip. But the highlight of the museum has to be the unique and sought-after collection of Draisiennes.

HISTORIC CARS AND AUTOMOBILIA

Petrol pumps
Museo Fisogni

Museo dell'Automobile Carlo Biscaretti di Ruffia
The Carlo Buscaretti di Ruffia Automobile Museum
Corso Unità d'Italia 40, 10126 Turin, Italy
Tel. (39) 011 677666
Tue-Sun 10am-6.30pm

The exhibition is arranged chronologically and begins in 1769 with a 7:10 scale reproduction of the world's first ever self-propelled vehicle – a wooden, steam-powered artillery tractor designed in Paris by Nicolas Joseph Cugnot. In addition, there is the Victoria, designed by Karl Benz, which was produced with only slight modifications until 1898. There are also some famous names here, including the first Fiat (1899), the first Oldsmobile (1904), and Ferdinand Porsche's Volkswagen.

Packard Super-Eight 1501,
USA, 1937
Museo dell'Automobile Carlo Biscaretti di Ruffia

Autoworld
11 parc du Cinquantenaire, 1000 Brussels, Belgium
Tel. (32) 27 364165 www.autoworld.be
Apr-Sep: daily 10am-6pm. Oct-Mar: daily 10am-5pm

Contained in this amazing collection of nearly 1,000 cars dating from 1886 to the 1970s are classic and sport models, as well as a selection of around thirty fire fighting cars in perfect condition, the bulk of which are Belgian. Furthermore, there is the Thiry Marcel Collection of motorcycles and Autoworld's exceptional library, containing periodicals, catalogues, and car manuals.

Centre de l'Automobile ancienne
The Veteran Car Centre
10 square de Labédoyère 02310 Nogent-l'Artaud, France
Tel. (33) 3 23 70 11 10
Daily 10am-noon, 2-6pm

This important assemblage of cars was collected by Francois Jeanson. The oldest piece is a tricycle called *le Nef* (1902) from Lacroix de Laville. Also included are pre- and post-war American cars such as the Lincoln Convertible, the Eldorado Cadillac, Ford Thunderbird, and Buick Roadmaster.

Fiat 4HP, Italy, 1899
(above)
Museo dell'Automobile Carlo Biscaretti di Ruffia

Ferrari 246 F1, Italy, 1960
(below)
Museo dell'Automobile Carlo Biscaretti di Ruffia

Centre historique de l'Automobile française
The Historical Centre of French Cars
84 ave. George Clémenceau, 51100 Reims, France
Tel. (33) 3 26 82 83 84
Mar-Nov: Mon, Wed-Sun 10am-noon, 2-7pm
(times may vary please call for details)

This is the only collection in France to concentrate on French-made cars. Famous models include a Marne taxi from 1912 by Renault (famous for transporting soldiers during World War I), Marshall Petain's Renault Vivastella (1938), and a Delaunay-Belleville that once belonged to the Tsar of Russia.

Alfred Dunhill Museum
48 Jermyn Street, London SW1Y 6DL, UK
Tel. (44) 20 783882 33
Mon-Fri 9.30am-6pm, Sat 10am-6pm

Alfred Dunhill's company famously sold everything for the motor car. His catalogues advertised between 1,300-1,400 items, from leather driving coats, dashboard clocks and valises, to caps and leather goggles.

Museo Fisogni
The Fisogni Museum
Palazzolo Milanese, via Tirano 14, 20030 Milan, Italy
Tel. (39) 02 990013306
www.museo-fisogni.org
By appt. only

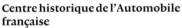

This is a substantial collection of gasoline pumps (200 and growing), oil cans, technical drawings, and other related items. The majority of Fisogni's pumps are Italian and date from the 1950s and 60s, though a number are also from France, Britain, and the US. All are placed side by side, lovingly restored and with gleaming new paint work.

583

Musée international de l'Automobile
The International Museum of the Automobile
40 voie-des-Traz, 1218 Grand-Saconnex, Switzerland
Tel. (41) 22 7888484
Tue-Sun 10am-6.30pm

Some of the prize exhibits include Fangio's 1954
Maserati F-250, Graham Hill's BRM Formula 1,
and Franco Sbarro's 1996 Alfa-Romeo prototype,
the Issima. Other attractions include King Hussein
of Jordan's Mercedes Benz 300 S roadster and an
armoured limousine from 1950 which once
protected Joseph Stalin.

Petrol pump (above)
Museo Fisogni

Interior of the museum
(above right)
Lakeland Motor Museum

Museo internazionale del Sidecar
International Sidecar Museum
Via Valcarecce 13, 62011 Cingoli, Italy
Tel. (39) 0733 602651   www.arcadianet.net
By appt. only

The collection of over 100 exhibits traces the history of the sidecar. There is a wide
selection of touring sidecars, scooter- and bicycle-sidecars, as well as ones that belonged
to famous people or appeared in films. Among the various exhibits is the longest sidecar
ever built, as well as the widest, the smallest, and the biggest.

Lakeland Motor Museum
Holker Hall, Cark-in-Cartment, Grange-over-Sands, South Lakeland, Cumbria,
LA11 7PL, UK
Tel. (44) 1539 558509
Apr-Oct: Mon-Fri, Sun 10.30am-4.45pm

Fiat 8 HP, Italy, 1901
Museo dell'Automobile Carlo
Biscaretti di Ruffia

Displayed are vintage vehicles, bikes and scooters, as well as tractors, fire engines,
micro cars, bicycles, model cars, and tricycles. Other attractions include a pre-war
dodgem car, one of the largest collections of petrol pump globes (illuminated lamps
that adorned the top of petrol pumps), a German amphibian car that went into
production in 1965, and an Indian rickshaw. There is also a special exhibition devoted
to the British heroes Sir Malcolm Campbell and his son Donald
who, between them, notched up 21 world
land- and water-speed records.

Mercedez-Benz Museum
Mercedesstrasse 137, 70322 Stuttgart Bad
Cannstatt/Untertürkheim,
Germany
Tel. (49) 711 1722578
www.mercedes-benz.com
Tue-Sun 9am-4pm

It was Karl Benz
who virtually
invented the
modern car, and
at the Mercedes-Benz
Museum visitors can
get close to historic

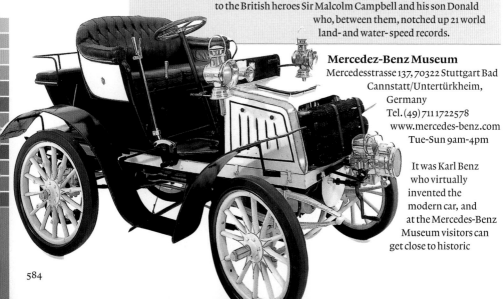

vehicles, from the very earliest (including the first petrol-driven motorcycle),
to the racing models (sleek unpainted Silver Arrows) of the 1930s, right up to
the ultra modern Smart Car.

The Patrick Motor Museum
180 Lifford Lane, Kings Norton, Birmingham, West Midlands B30 3NT, UK
Tel. (44) 1214 599111
By appt. only

This collection of classic cars numbers over 200 vehicles dating from
1904 to the present day. Displayed in a former 19th-century paper-mill
are over eighty cars, from a 1963 Daimler Dart sports car and a rare Rapport Forte
(based on Jaguar V12 running gear), to the unmistakable VW Beetle. In The Mansell
Hall are performance cars, including Nigel Mansell's Formula 1 Lotus 92.

Myreton Motor Museum
Aberlady, East Lothian, EH32 0PZ, Scotland, UK
Tel. (44) 1875 870288
Oct-Easter: 10am-5pm. Easter-Oct: 10am-6pm

Among the museum's historic cars are a 1934 Singer TT which has raced at Le Mans,
Donington and Silverstone and, at the slow end, a Scamp Electric Car, one of only twelve
manufactured by the Scottish Aviation Company. Also included are such oddities as the
Itera plastic bicycle, a General Electric car
from 1900, a steam-driven Locomobile,
and an 1896 Leon Boolee trike, once the
property of the Hon. C. S. Rolls
(of Rolls-Royce).

1967 Ford Lotus 49 R3
(above)
The National Motor Museum

Fuel gauges (left)
Museo Fisogni

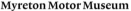

Musée national de l'Automobile - Collection Schlumpf
The National Car Museum – the Schlumpf Collection

192 avenue de Colmar, 68100 Mulhouse, France
Tel. (33) 3 89 33 23 23   www.musee-auto-schlumpf.asso.fr
Daily 10am-6pm

This collection provides a complete overview of car history. Early models include
a Jacquot (1878), a Benz Victoria (1893), and a Peugeot 1893. More recent developments
include a MacLaren-Peugeot (1994) and a Porsche 959 Paris-Dakar (1986). Amassed
by Fritz Schlumpf, this fabulous collection of more than 500 cars contains many
exceptional models.

The National Motor Museum
John Montagu Building, Beaulieu, Hampshire, SO42 7ZN, UK
Tel. (44) 1590 612345   www.beaulieu.co.uk
Daily 10am-6pm

Some of the famous World Land Speed Record cars are here, including the 4,100bhp
jet-powered Bluebird in which Donald Cambell broke 400mph at Lake Eyre, South
Australia (1964), as well as Thrust SCC, Richard Noble's rocket-powered monster, which
became the first car to break the sound barrier. Besides the many classic sportsters (Aston
Martin, Bugatti, Ferrari, and the rest) and the hi-octane Formula racing cars, Beaulieu
has a good selection of less prestigious but no less-loved models. These include Chitty
Chitty Bang Bang, one of only three; a 1903 Cadillac Model A – the first Cadillac to be
brought to Britain; and the first £100 car, the Morris Minor of 1931.

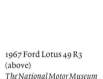

A limousine in the museum's Classic Collection
Mercedes-Benz Museum

National Corvette Museum

350 Corvette Drive, Bowling Green,
Kentucky 42101, USA
Tel. (1) 270 781 7973
www.corvettemuseum.com
Oct-May: daily 8am-5pm. Jun-Sep: 8am-6pm

The success of the Corvette is celebrated with a collection of cars from all eras plus thousands of items of memorabilia, including adverts, related photos, and scale models. The convertible and the famous 'split window' coupé are 'on sale' in a 1960s Chevrolet dealer showroom, while on a mocked-up assembly line visitors can see how these kings of Route 66 were put together.

The Petersen Automotive Museum

6060 Wilshire Blvd, Los Angeles, California 90036, USA
Tel. (1) 213 930 2277
Tue-Sun 10am-6pm

A massive, innovative museum which traces the evolution of the car through the 20th century. You will find everything from classics, movie cars, early motorcycles and racing cars, to prototypes, technology, design, and marketing paraphernalia. In the Hollywood Gallery there are displays called 'cars of the stars' and 'cars as stars'. Among the cars on display are a 1925 Lincoln, owned by Greta Garbo, and a 1956 Mercedes 300SC coupé that once belonged to Clark Gable.

Skoda Auto Muzeum
The Skoda Auto Museum

Tr. Václava Klementa 294, 293 60 Mladá Boleslav, Czech Republic
Tel. (420) 326 831139   www.skoda-auto.cz
Daily 9am-5pm

To celebrate the 100th anniversary of one of the oldest European car factories, this stunning museum, housed in modern premises, was opened in 1995. Exhibits include original models, photographs, and related ephemera tracing the history of one of the country's most successful enterprises.

Early Skoda car
Skoda Auto Muzeum

Musée Jean Tua de l'Automobile, de la Moto et du Cycle
The Jean Tua Museum of the Automobile, Motorcycle and Cycle

28-30 rue des Bains, 1205 Geneva,
Switzerland
Tel. (41) 22 3213637
Wed-Sun 2-6pm

Over 140 or so vintage cars dating from 1877 to 1939 are housed in this old factory. Among the rare models on display are a Hispano-Suiza, built by Parisians Fernandez and Darrin in 1936, an avant-gardist Citroën from 1938, with bodywork by Swiss designer Bernarth, and a 1932 Bugatti Type 49, with bodywork by Rucksthul.

Uudenkaupungin Automuseo
Uusikaupunki Car Museum
Autotehtaankatu 14, 23501 Uusikaupunki, Finland
Tel. (358) 2 2557645
Please call for opening times

Petrol pumps
Museo Fisogni

This museum is composed of three outstanding collections. The first is a general collection containing a good cross section of cars and motorcycles from the beginning of the 20th century to the 1960s. Within this is the unique Gardner Sport coupé (1928); as far as is known, this car is the only surviving one in the whole of Europe. The second houses the most comprehensive collection of Saabs in the world, and the last displays the products of the Valmet Automotive factory and its predecessor, Oy Saab-Valmet Ab.

Volvo Museet
The Volvo Museum
Avd. 1670 ARU, 405 08 Gothenburg, Sweden
Tel. (46) 31 664814   www.volvo.se
Tue-Fri noon-5pm, Sat-Sun 11am-4pm

Among the prize exhibits are the ÖV4 (Volvo's first car), a Volvo fire engine from 1934, and a sleek PV61 from 1949 which once belonged to the Swedish Nobel Prize winner, Selma Lagerlöff. There are many other historic cars and trucks to admire, as well as a J35 Draken aircraft – a military jet powered by the Volvo Aero engine.

Musée des Arts et Métiers
Museum of Arts and Crafts
60 rue Réaumur, 75003 Paris, France
Tel. (33) 1 53 01 82 00   www.cnam.fr
Tue-Sun 10am-6pm (Thu until 9.30pm)

This museum has a collection of early vehicles that include Cugnot's *Fardier*, the first mechanical vehicle to be propelled by its own steam engine; the 1840 Hawthorn Locomotive, which linked Paris to Versailles; and Seguin's Locomotive (1829), the first locomotive ever to be built in France.

Bressingham Steam Museum Trust
Bressingham, Diss, Norfolk IP22 2AB, UK
Tel. (44) 1379 687386   www.bressingham.co.uk
Summer: 10am-5.30pm. Winter: 10.30am-4pm

Saloon car in the Emperor's train (above right)
Suomen Rautatie Museo

The Empress' car in the Emperor's train (above left)
Suomen Rautatie Museo

Pride of place goes to the standard gauge locomotives. Many of these are brought out for display on the museum's 1/4-mile demonstration line and include 'little phutters' such as the 1893 Granville, through to the Royal Scot, used on the west-coast express service from London to Glasgow. Also of note is the Oliver Cromwell, which in 1968 became the last steam loco to haul a British passenger train.

California State Railroad Museum
125 1 Street, Old Sacramento, California 95814-2265, USA
Tel. (1) 916 445 6645   www.csrmf.org
Daily 10am-5pm

One of the great railroad museums in the US, it consists of six original, reconstructed buildings crammed with beautifully restored railroad cars and locomotives illustrating the railroad history of California and the West. The roster of steam locomotives is impressive and includes a total of nineteen dating from 1862 to 1944.

No. 990 Henry Oakley
Great Northern Railway
Bressingham Steam
Museum Trust

The Danish Railway Museum

Dannebrogsgade 24, 5000 Odense C, Denmark
Tel. (45) 66 13 66 30 www.jernbanemuseum.dk
Daily 10am-4pm

This small but significant collection takes a look at the history of rail travel in Denmark. It includes model railways, mini-train rides, and carriages and engines (both steam and diesel) dating from the 1850s onwards.

Das Deutsche Bahn Museum - Verkehrsmuseum
The German Railways Museum - Traffic Museum

Lessingstrasse 6, 90443 Nuremberg, Germany
Tel. (49) 911 2 19 24 28 www.dbmuseum.de
Tue-Sun 9am-5pm

There are a large number of original and historical engines and vehicles, including a replica of the first German train, the *Adler* (Eagle), which ran from Nuremberg to Fürth (1935), and two state coaches from King Ludwig II of Bavaria's Royal Train.

Railway diorama
STEAM - Museum of the
Great Western Railway

Deutsches Technikmuseum Berlin
The German Museum of Technology in Berlin

Trebbiner Strasse 9, 10963 Berlin, Germany
Tel. (49) 30 25 48 40 www.dtmb.de
Tue-Fri 9am-5.30pm, Sat-Sun 10am-6pm

This exhibition illustrates the history of trains and the lives of the everyday people who were involved in the railways. Its largest exhibit is the historical locomotive shed

complex dating back to 1874, which houses forty original rail vehicles on 34 tracks, as well as a large number of models.

Musée français du Chemin de Fer
The French Railway Museum
2 rue Alfred de Glehn, 68200 Mulhouse, France
Tel. (33) 3 89 42 83 33
Apr-Sep: daily 9am-6pm
Oct-Mar: daily 9am-5pm

This award-winning collection of more than 100 locomotives, carriages, and trains illustrates the technological, economic, and social history of the French railway. Of particular note is the *Buddicom*, built in 1844, which hauled passenger trains between Paris and Rouen for nearly seventy years. Also on display is the *PR1* (Presidential Car no. 1), dating from 1913 and decorated in Art Deco style with Lalique glass panels.

Muzeum Kolejnictwa w Warszawie
The Railway Museum in Warsaw
Ulica Towarowa 1, 00-958 Warsaw, Poland
Tel. (48) 22 5245758
Tue-Sun 10am-3pm

The Mallard, watercolour painting by Phil Belbin (top)
National Railway Museum

Mallard 4-6-2 steam lomotive, 1938 (above)
National Railway Museum

The collection focuses on locomotives built in Poland during the inter-war period. A unique highlight is the only surviving complete, armoured, military train which was manufactured in Germany in 1943. Several rooms are dedicated to related railway memorabilia, including railway association banners, watches, commemorative medals, paintings, and posters.

Národní Technické Muzeum
The National Technical Museum
Kostelní 42, 170 78 Prague 7, Czech Republic
Tel. (420) 2039 9111   www.ntm.cz
Tue-Sun 9am-5pm

The first horse-drawn railway in Europe was constructed here. Begun in 1825, it ran from České Budejovice, Bohemia, to Linz, Austria. A replica of the carriage Hannibal (1848) takes pride of place, surrounded by twelve other railway carriages, including one used in the court saloon train for Emperor Francis Joseph I (1891).

National Railway Museum
Leeman Road, York, North Yorkshire YO26 4XJ, UK
Tel. (44) 1904 621261   www.nrm.org.uk
Daily 10am-6pm

This award-winning museum has a huge main hall which contains about fifty locomotives dating from 1829 onwards, including the Mallard, which became the fastest steam engine in the world when it achieved 126mph in 1938. Some trains can be seen running at the museum; others take special trips all over the country during the summer. There is also an elaborate royal carriage once belonging to Edward VII, which contrasts sharply with the Spartan accommodation of a third-class Victorian coach.

The salon coach of the Royal Bavarian Train of Ludwig II
Das Deustche Bahn Museum - Verkehrsmuseum

Het Nederlands Spoorwegmuseum
The Dutch Railway Museum
Maliebaanstation 16, 3581 XW Utrecht,
The Netherlands
Tel. (31) 30 2306206 www.spoorwegmuseum.nl
Tue-Fri 10am-5pm

Staff hats, uniforms, documents, models and, paintings guide visitors through Dutch railway history. There are also displays relating to the railway network in Indonesia when it was a Dutch colony; these include the Indonesian *Sri Gunung* (Queen of the Mountain), which was used on the mountainous rail track and was donated by the Indonesian government in 1981.

Railway Museum of Pennsylvania
Paradise Lane, Strasburg, Pennsylvania 17579, USA
Tel. (1) 717 687 8628 www.rrmuseumpa.org
Apr-Oct: Mon-Sat 9am-5pm, Sun noon-5pm. Nov-May: Tue-Sat 9am-5pm, Sun noon-5pm

Here, in seventeen thematic zones, you can learn about various aspects of railroading history, from the No. 460 locomotive, which raced newsreel footage of Charles Lindbergh's triumphal 1927 return to the United States from Washington, DC to New York City, to people, like the engineers, firemen, blacksmiths, machinists, clerks, and dispatchers who made the railroads run. The massive library holdings can be accessed by appointment and visits can be made to the outdoor restoration yard.

STEAM – Museum of the Great Western Railway
Kemble Drive, Swindon, Wiltshire SN2 2TA, UK
Tel. (44) 1793 466646 www.swindonweb.com
Daily 10am-6pm (Thu until 8pm)

A series of lively reconstructions using original equipment, video, and interactive displays depict what life was like for some of the 12,000 workforce employed by the GWR in its heyday before World War I. At the finish, visitors are confronted by the product of all this combined effort – the express passenger locomotive *Caerphilly Castle* in ex-works condition, with gleaming paint and brass.

Suomen Rautatie Museo
The Finnish Railway Museum
Hyvinkääkatu 9, 05800 Hyvinkää, Finland
Tel. (358) 307 25241 www.rautatie.org
Jun-Aug: daily 11am-5pm. Sep-May: Tue-Sat noon-3pm, Sun noon-5pm

The museum holds a collection of trains illustrating the history of the railways in Finland. The finest exhibit is undoubtedly the set of coaches which once belonged to Nicholas II, the last Tsar of Russia.

SHIP MODELS

Arlington Court
Arlington, near Barnstaple, Devon EX31 4LP, UK
Tel. (44) 1271 850296 www.nationaltrust.org.uk
Mon, Wed-Sun 11am-5.30pm

Almost everywhere you look there are model ships displayed in cases, from Miss Rosalie Chichester's 200-strong collection, including a rare ivory model made in Dieppe for the Comte de Chambord in the early 19th century. Also displayed are a dozen 'Little Ships', which rescued the British Army from the beaches of Dunkirk in 1940.

Bergens Sjøfartsmuseum
The Bergen Maritime Museum
Haakon Sheteligs Plass 15, 5026 Bergen, Norway
Tel. (47) 55 327980
Jun-Aug: Mon-Fri, Sun 11am-3pm Sep-May: Mon-Fri, Sun 11am-2pm

Among the models of ancient vessels is the oldest Norwegian find, the Halsnøy boat (*c.* 200BC) and Viking vessels such as the *Gokstad*, *Oseberg* and *Kvalsund* (a number of original timbers from this boat are also here). Not to be missed is the frame-timber section of a model Nordic medieval ship, which is based on finds from the same period in Kalmar, Sweden.

H. Reynyhout, a spritsail-rigged Arnemuiden *hoogaars*, 1934 *Nationaal scheepvaartmuseum*

Dartmouth Museum
The Butterwalk, Duke Street,
Dartmouth, Devon TQ6 9PZ, UK
Tel. (44) 1803 832923
Mon-Sat 11am-5pm

This magnificent collection of ship models includes the Lewis Stock Collection, which is displayed in three rooms of an old merchant's house dated 1640. There's a fine model of the *Golden Hind*, ivory models of Chinese pleasure-boats, and bone models of the line made by French prisoners of war between 1802 and 1814.

Deutsches Schiffahrtsmuseum
The German Museum of Navigation
Hans-Scharoun-Platz 1, 27568 Bremerhaven, Germany
Tel. (49) 471 482070 www.dsm.de
Apr-Oct: daily 10am-6pm. Nov-Mar: Tue-Sun 10am-6pm

This museum comprises some 500 model ships, including European fleets from antiquity. There is a miniature harbour with remote-controlled model ships, and a large model of the convoy vessel *Wappen von Hamburg* (1720), which was the first German state ship to be built following English naval construction principles.

Wax model of 'Elephant' figurehead *Orlogsmuseet*

Hart Nautical Collections
MIT Museum, 265 Massachusetts Avenue, Cambridge,
Massachusetts 02139, USA
Tel. (1) 617 253 5942 web.mit.edu
Daily 9am-8pm

These collections consist of plans, books, models, photographs, and marine art, the core of which date from mid 19th- to 20th-century New England, as well as around 500 full- and half-ship models. Among these are those from former professors, and smaller

holdings from boat manufacturers and designers, such as Frank C. Paine, one of the most important yacht designers of the first half of the 20th century.

Mariners' Museum

100 Museum Drive, Newport News, Virginia 23606, USA
Tel. (1) 757 596-2222
www.mariner.org
Daily 10am-5pm

The museum contains a substantial and diverse collection of 1,800 ship models, including builders' and boardroom models; World War II warship recognition training models; and exquisite handcrafted miniature models from the August F. Crabtree Collection. Well over 100 are on display, but serious researchers should book ahead to see items held in store.

Model of Captain James Cook's famous ship, HM Bark *Endeavour*, by R. A. Lightly, 1975
National Maritime Museum

Museu de Marinha
The Maritime Museum

Praça do Império, 1400 Lisbon, Portugal
Tel. (351) 21 3620010 www.museumarinha.pt
Apr-Sep: Tue-Sun 10am-6pm: Oct-Mar: Tue-Sun 10am-5pm

This museum's vast collection of ship models ranges from traditional craft used in river traffic, to oriental ships, and models from the golden age of Portuguese voyages and discoveries. The museum houses a model of the *St Gabriel*, flagship of Vasco da Gama. There is also a unique collection of models of royal barges, as well as several pleasure craft which belonged to the royal household.

Maritiem Museum Prins Hendrik
The Prince Hendrik Maritime Museum

Leuvehaven 1, 3011 EA Rotterdam, The Netherlands
Tel. (31) 10 4132680 www.mmph.nl
Tue-Sat 10am-5pm, Sun 11am-5pm

This museum possesses a vast collection of ship models, including an outstanding group of Dutch sailing vessels for inland navigation. One object in the collection, the model of a Spanish caravel, also known as the *Coca de Matarò*, is internationally renowned.

Museu Maritim
The Maritime Museum

Avinguda de les Drassanes 1, 08001 Barcelona, Spain
Tel. (34) 93 3429920 www.almogaver.com
Daily 10am-7pm

The half-hull models, made up largely of 19th-century Catalan sailing ships, form one of the most important collections of its type in the world. The museum also stands out for its collection of models constructed in the museum's own workshops, which include John of Austria's remarkable Royal Galley and copies of Christopher Columbus' three ships.

Merseyside Maritime Museum

Albert Dock, Liverpool, Merseyside L3 4AQ, UK
Tel. (44) 151 478 4499 www.nmgm.org.uk
Daily 10am-5pm

Of national note is the museum's stunning group of over 1,000 ship models which range
from miniature models less than one inch long, to a twenty-foot builder's model of the
Titanic. Notable are a group of eighty fishing boat models and the Pilkington collection of
39 miniature warship models. The collection of British merchant ships built between 1850
and 1950 (especially steam ships) is second only to that of the Science Museum in London.

Mystic Seaport

75 Greenmanville Avenue, Mystic, Connecticut 06355-0990, USA
Tel. (1) 860 572 0711 www.mysticseaport.org
Daily 10am-4pm

Exterior of the museum
(above)
Orlogsmuseet

Exterior of the museum
(left)
Maritiem Museum Prins Hendrik

There is a diverse collection of ship models representing many significant makers, of
which 200 out of a total of over 1,300 are on display. The half-hull collection is equally
significant and numbers over 1,000 examples, not all of which are on display.

Nationaal scheepvaart-museum
The National Maritime Museum

Steenplein 1, 2000
Antwerp, Belgium
Tel. (32) 3 201 93 40
www.scheepvaartmu-
seum.nl
Tue-Sun 10am-4.45pm

This collection of ship
models includes a
9th-century boat
from Osenberg, an
official yacht from the
18th century, and a steam yacht dated 1883. There is also a model of Napoleon's ceremonial barge (1810), an extensive collection of models of the Belgian Naval Force, including
their training ships, and a unique collection of model Chinese junks.

Musée national de la Marine
The National Navy Museum

17 place du Trocadéro, 75116 Paris, France
Tel. (33) 1 53 65 69 69 www.musee-marine.fr
Mon, Wed-Sun 10am-6pm

This is one of the oldest and most prestigious collections of its type in the world. The
museum was formed with the donation by Henri-Louis Duhamel du Monceau to Louis
XV of a collection of model ships. Today it contains 3,000 models which provide a
remarkable panorama of naval history from the 17th century to the present day.

National Maritime Museum

Romney Road, Greenwich, London SE10 9NF, UK
Tel. (44) 20 8858 4422 www.nmm.ac.uk
Daily 10am-5pm

The core of this first-rate collection consists of Navy Board models from the mid 17th century to the age of Nelson. The most coveted is the model of the *Royal George*, a flagship sunk at anchor with the loss of 900 lives, in 1782. A section dedicated to cargo ships displays a model of the cargo liner *Bamenda Palm*, built in 1956 to trade between Britain and West Africa; and the *MV Orange*, launched in 1973 as one of the first ships to be designed specially for the orange juice trade.

Nederlands Scheepvaartmuseum
The Dutch Maritime Museum
Kattenburgerplein 1, 1018 KK Amsterdam, The Netherlands
Tel. (31) 20 5232222 www.generali.nl
Mon-Sat 10am-5pm, Sun noon-5pm

This museum holds an important collection of ship models that date from the 17th to the 19th

Regular service *tjalk* with sprit-rigging for freight and passenger transport, *c.*1800
Nationaal scheepvaartmuseum

centuries, including old sailing vessels, luxury passenger ships, and giant container ships. The collection of more recent objects includes contemporary models by Ernst Crone and the model of the *Maaslloyd*, a general cargo vessel built in the 1950s.

Norsk Sjøfartsmuseum
The Norwegian Museum of Navigation
Bygdøynesveien 37, 0286 Oslo, Norway
Tel. (47) 22 438240 www.museumsnett.no
Daily 10am-6pm

This museum comprises a collection of model ships that range from Viking ships and other ancient and medieval Scandinavian craft, to ships associated with discovery, colonialism or warfare, as well as the more recent merchant fleet of the 19th and 20th centuries.

Orlogsmuseet
The Royal Naval Museum
Overgaden oven Vandet 58, 1415 Copenhagen, Denmark
Tel. (45) 32 546363 www.kulturnet.dk
Tue-Sun noon-4pm

This museum's main attraction is its historic collection of ship models dating back to the time of King Christian III. One of the oldest models is of a warship made in the late 17th century during the time of Niels Juel (Lord High Admiral in the Danish Navy 1675); it was most likely designed as a votive ship for church use.

The Science Museum
Exhibition Road, London SW7 2DD, UK
Tel. (44) 870 870 4771 www.sciencemuseum.org.uk
Daily 10am-6pm

This is the best and most comprehensive collection of marine-steam engines anywhere, from the earliest examples up to around the 1860s. There are considerable holdings of Navy Board models, as well as a fine series of Chinese junks which were commissioned by Sir Frederick Maze; he served at the Chinese Maritime Customs throughout the 1920s. Other highlights include models of the *Cutty Sark* and *Victory* which were made in the 1940s by Dr. Longridge, and the original model of the HMS *Prince*, an English first-rank three-decker armed with 100 guns and built in 1670.

Sjöhistoriska museet
The Maritime Museum
Djurgårdsbrunnvägen 24, 102 52 Stockholm, Sweden
Tel. (46) 8 51954900 www.sjohistoriska.nu
Daily 10am-5pm

With an assemblage of more than 100,000 artefacts, this museum covers most aspects of civil and naval seafaring and its collections of some 1,500 ship models include some of the oldest and most valuable pieces still in existence.

F20 Tigershark jet air craft in vertical accelera-tion
California Science Center

Tsentral'nyi voenno-morskoi muzei
The Central Navy Museum
Birzhevaia ploshchad' 4, 199034 Saint Petersburg, Russian Federation
Tel. (7) 812 3282701 www.museum.navy.ru
Wed-Sun 11am-6pm

The collection includes artworks of outstanding craftsmanship, some of them made of the most exquisite material such as ivory, tortoiseshell, and wood, decorated with precious stones and metals. Among the priceless items on display are ship models that were given to Peter the Great by the English monarch William III, and a model of a Maltese galley from 1568, one of the oldest ship models in the world.

SPACE OBJECTS AND COLLECTIBLES

California Science Center
700 State Drive, Los Angeles, California 90037, USA
Tel. (1) 323 724 3623 www.casciencectr.org
Daily 10am-5pm

The Apollo 16 crew
California Science Center

Highlights of the existing collection include actual flown space capsules, Gemini 11 and Mercury MR-2 (1961), Astronaut Ken Mattingley's Apollo 16 spacesuit, a full-scale model of the solar-system explorer Pioneer 10, and the sole-surviving F-20 Tigershark jet aircraft. However, the landmark Frank Gehry building which houses the Air and Space Gallery, is currently being refurbished and will re-open in 2002. Out of hiding will come a model of the first X-ray astronomy satellite *Uhuru*, a real Aerobee Sounding Rocket payload, and an Orion Sounding Rocket.

Cité de l'Espace
Space City
Ave. Jean-Gonord, 31506 Toulouse, France
Tel. (33) 5 62 71 64 80
www.cite-espace.com
Tue-Fri 9.30am-6pm,
Sat, Sun 9am-7pm

Dominating this museum is a replica of the *Ariane 5* standing 55 metres high. Interactive displays allow you to watch the satellite lift-off, participate in the exploration of Mars, observe the Earth from space, or view the display of a genuine Vulcan engine stripped down to display its inner workings.

Historisch-Technisches Informationszentrum
Historic-Technical Information Centre
Bahnhofstrasse 28, 17449 Peenemüende, Germany
Tel. (49) 3837 120573 www.all-in-all.com
Apr-Oct: Tue-Sun 9am-6pm (Jun-Sep: daily 9am-6pm). Nov-Mar: Tue-Sun 10am-4pm

The American Thor Able Rocket inside the 42-metre-high tower
National Space Centre

The museum here, comprising several buildings and an outdoor exhibition space, sets forth the technical solutions achieved at this development centre, and the evolution of the V1 and V2 missiles and the thousands of lives lost in the process. Exhibition halls show parts of engines, rockets, aircraft, and rocket ships, some unceremoniously lit, others unlabelled.

La Coupole - Centre d'Histoire de la Guerre et des Fusées
The Cupola - Centre for the History of War and Rocketry
Rue Mont à Cars, 62570 Helfaut, France
Tel. (33) 3 21 930707 www.lacoupole.com
Apr-Sep: daily 9am-7pm. Oct-Mar: daily 10am-6pm

This is a former underground launch centre for the V2 rocket. Built in 1943 and made bomb-proof by means of a huge concrete dome, this was Hitler's second attempt at a launching base. Abandoned in 1944, the site was turned into a memorial in 1987 and ten years later opened as a centre on the history of war and rocketry. Inside, audiovisuals tell the story of life in northern France under German occupation.

The Rocket Tower by architect Nicholas Grimshaw
National Space Centre

Memoral'nyi muzei kosmonavtiki
The Memorial Museum of Cosmonautics
Prospekt Mira 111, 129515 Moscow, Russian Federation
Tel. (7) 095 2827398 www.museum.ru
Tue-Sun 10am-7pm

October 4, 1957, the Soviet Union launched the world's first satellite – *Sputnik 1* – and took the lead in the space race between two superpowers. This event is marked by the majestic monument, erected in 1964, of a silver rocket resting on a stream of titanium. The remaining apparatus from Gagarin's craft *Vostok*, and his original life-saving suit, commemorates his flight. Displayed here are the moon probes *Luna 1* (or *Lunik*) and *Luna 3*, the lunar rover *Lunokhod 1*, and the return apparatus of the station *Luna 16* with its samples of moon soil. There is also a section dedicated to international collaboration, displaying satellite *Intercosmos 1*, as well as the docking device of the spaceship *Soiuz 19*.

Musée de l'Air et de l'Espace
The Air and Space Museum
Aéroport du Bourget BP 173, 93352 Le Bourget, France
Tel. (33) 1 49 92 71 99 www.mae.org
Tue-Sun 10am-5pm

The museum's collections are outstanding and comprise a remarkable selection of original items that cover the history of space exploration, with items from France, Europe, and the US. On display are H1 engines used by NASA as early as 1961; the Vexin engine of 1965, which made France the third 'spatial' power; 1:1 models of *Sputnik 1*, *Vostok*, which in 1961 transported the first cosmonaut Gagarin; and *Venera 3*, launched to reach Venus but unfortunately lost.

Commemoratives marking Soviet space exploration (above and left) *Memoral'nyi muzei kosmonavtiki*

National Air and Space Museum

Independence Avenue and 6th Street, SW, Washington, DC, USA
Tel. (1) 202 357 2700 www.nasm.edu
Daily 10am-5.30pm

Over 8,500 artefacts document the history of space exploration in the US since the late 1950s and range from complete spacecraft such as the historic *Apollo 11* command capsule, to spacefood, components of satellites, rockets, and other items. The museum's warehouses (Paul E. Garber Facility in suburban Maryland), full of flight-related artefacts, can be toured by booking in advance. A new ten-storey-high Dulles annexe, displaying over 100 major space artefacts and aircraft, will open in 2003.

National Space Centre

Exploration Drive, Leicester, Leicestershire LE4 5NS, UK
Tel. (44) 870 6077223 www.nssc.co.uk
Tue-Sun 9.30am-4pm

A 'Rocket Tower' designed by Nicholas Grimshaw houses the UK's only museum dedicated to space science. It displays a British-built Blue Streak rocket, an American Thor Able rocket, one of only two Soyuz capsules, and an array of satellites. Galleries explore what it takes to be an astronaut, the future of the International Space Station, and the distant stars of the galaxy; they also display moon rock and Martian meteorites. The specially produced video shows are impressive, and the mission control/space station 'simulator' is the only one outside the US.

Repüléstörténeti és ûrhajózási állandó kiállítás
The Permanent Exhibition of Aviataion and Space Flight
Petôfi Csarnok, Zichy M. út, Városliget, 1146 Budapest, Hungary
Tel. (36) 343 0009
Tue-Fri 10am-5pm, Sat-Sun 10am-6pm

Hungary's contribution to space research began with Zoltán Bay (1900-92), where an echo from the moon was received with an experimental radar installation in 1946. Displayed in the former Hall of Industries in the City Park, just 200 metres from the main museum building, is a permanent exhibition on space flights, which highlights Hungary's contributions. Exhibited is the space capsule *Soyuz*, used by Bertalan Farkas, the first and only Hungarian cosmonaut who in 1980 carried out experiments on board the Soviet space station during his flight.

597

Unmanned interplanetary station *Venera-4*, which transmitted the first scientific information about the planet Venera in October, 1967
Memoral'nyi muzei kosmonavtiki

U. S. Air Force Museum

Wright-Patterson Air Force Base, 1100 Spaatz Street, Dayton, Ohio 45433-7102, USA
Tel. (1) 937 255 3284   www.wpafb.af.mil
Daily 9am-5pm

Displayed are the *Apollo 15* command module, McDonnell *Gemini* spacecraft, *Mercury* spacecraft and the Martin X-24A. Equal billing is given to space suit design and men who made it all happen, such as Dr Robert H. Goddard, known as 'the father of modern rocketry'.

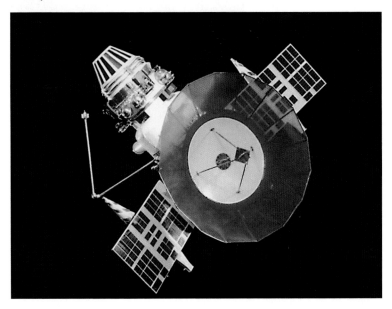

Zvezdnyi gorodok - Tsentr podgotovki kosmonavtov im. Iuriia Gagarina
Star City - The Yuri Gagarin Cosmonauts Training Centre
Dom kosmonavtov, near Moscow, Russian Federation

The Museum of Cosmonauts Training Centre was founded on the initiative of Yuri Gagarin in 1967. It contains one of the largest collections of documents and materials pertaining to the history of the space programme in Russia, including Gagarin's space suit and leather boots. Displays recount the various stages of manned space flights, from the first in *Vostok* to the recent demise of the *Mir* space station. On show are spacecraft, simulators, space suits, scientific equipment, and devices. Do not miss the reconstruction of Gagarin's study, which is traditionally visited by Russian and international crews on the eve of their space flights.

ECLECTIC AND ECCENTRIC COLLECTIONS

EROTIC ART

MAGIC AND ILLUSION

ECLECTIC AND ECCENTRIC COLLECTIONS

Musée de l'Automate
The Museum of the Automaton
Place de l'Abbaye, 46200 Souillac, France
Tel. (33) 5 65 37 07 07 www.souillac.net
Jan-Mar, Nov: Wed-Sun 2-5pm.
Apr-May, Oct: Tue-Sun 10am-noon, 3-8pm.
Jun-Sep: daily 10am-7pm (Jun, Sep until 6pm)

When this national centre for automata
opened in 1988 with over 3,000 objects, it was
the first of its kind in France. A comprehensive
collection, it contains mechanisms and
archives documenting the development
of automata from the mid 19th century to the
present. The heart of the collection comes from
the famous Roullet-Decamps automata
factory, founded in 1889. Among the best
known pieces on display are *Le petit jardinier with a wheelbarrow*, which was displayed
at the Universal Exposition of 1867, and *Le Pifferaro playing the harp* (1870), whose
intricate head was made by the French doll maker, Jumeau.

Luxurious sarcophogus
Bestattungsmuseum

Bestattungsmuseum
The Undertakers' Museum
Goldeggasse 19, 1041 Vienna, Austria
Tel. (43) 1 501 954227, www.wienerstadtwerke.at
Mon-Fri noon-3pm by appt. only

Run by a state funeral company, this collection offers elaborate costumes and
uniforms of undertakers worn through the years, along with their banners and
équipage. There is a large collection of palls, the oldest dating back to 1844, as well
as a number of urns and coffins. Among these are a painted wooden coffin from
the Viennese St Michael's tomb; a reusable 'flap coffin' with a trapdoor bottom;
and the *Rettungwecker* ('alarm clock'), a very popular device designed to prevent
people from being buried alive. There are also some wonderful examples of
funeral merchandising, including matches, photo albums, toy cars and, best
of all, undertakers' cigarettes with the motto 'smoking guarantees work'.

Museo Civico di Gallipoli
The Civic Museum of Gallipoli
Via Antonietta de Pace 118, 73014 Gallipoli, Italy
Tel. (39) 08 33264224
Jun-Sep: Mon-Sat 9.30am-12.30pm, 5-8pm.
Oct-May: Tue-Sat 9am-1pm, 4-7pm

Collection of stuffed dogs
Státní hrad Bítov

This museum, a relic from a different age, was made in the days when collections
were put together to enchant. Everything in this eclectic collection was found locally,
from rusty cannons to World War II
land mines, and from fossilized and
stuffed fish to obsolete bank notes in
denominations which include
literally dozens of zeros. Cabinets
contain a mixture of coins, corals,
shells and stones. There is a wonderful
selection of Greek pots with barnacles
and coral still clinging to them.

Museum of Death
6340 Hollywood Boulevard, Hollywood, California 90028, USA
Tel. (1) 323 4668011
Daily noon-8pm

This macabre museum on death, organised by Cathee Shultz and J.D. Healy, grew
from an annual art gallery show consisting of serial-killer art and letters. Hand-carved
Tibetan funerary skulls and a wooden embalming table from the 1880s are objects of
historic merit. However, the photographs of suicide, homicide and car-crash victims,
the bloodstained T-shirt worn by a murderer while being executed in the electric
chair, and the room dedicated to the Jonestown massacre, are just bad taste.

Deutsches Vogelbauermuseum
German Birdcage Museum
Vogelpark Walsrode, Am Rieselbach, 29664 Walsrode, Germany
Tel. (49) 5161 2015
www.vogelpark-walsrode.de
Mar-Oct: daily 9am-7pm

This extensive collection, started in the early 1960s by the entrepreneur Josef Voss,

documents four centuries of bird-
cages from Europe, Asia, and the
US. Among the attractions is a
birdcage in the shape of a cathedral,
and a German cage from 1850 made
completely out of glass, both of
which serve more of a decorative
rather than a functional purpose.
Another curiosity is a beautifully
crafted 19th-century French
wardrobe trunk used for transporting canaries, which contains
thirty compartments complete
with food and water facilities.

Bítov State Castle
Státní hrad Bítov

Dog Collar Museum
Leeds Castle, Maidstone, Kent ME17 1PL, UK
Tel. (44) 1622 765400   www.leeds-castle.co.uk
Mar-Oct: daily 10am-5pm. Nov-Feb: daily 10am-3pm.

This museum's unequalled collection of antique dog collars spans four centuries and
contains over 100 examples of canine neckwear. Early (15th- to 17th-century) collars
tended to be made from iron, with fearsome spikes designed to protect the throats
of hunting dogs against attacks. Other exhibits include collars displaying great
artistic crafts-manship that were intended purely for decoration and identification.

Fairbanks Ice Museum
Second & Lacey, Fairbanks, Alaska, USA
Tel. (1) 907 451 8222   www.fairbanks-alaska.com
Daily 10am-9pm

Each winter, sculptors from far and wide head to Fairbanks to sculpt what are
generally recognised as the world's largest blocks of ice into a myriad of forms.
They converge chiefly in March, when the ice festival takes place. Housed in a historic
downtown theatre, the museum offers a slide show on ice sculpting, and carvings
can be seen in a walk-in display case.

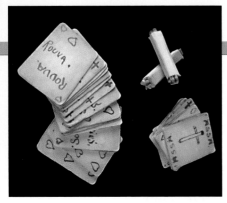

Improvised self-made
playing cards, confiscated
from prisons
Vankilamuseo

Forbes Magazine Galleries
62 5th Avenue at 12th Street, New York, New York 10011, USA
Tel. (1) 212 206 5548
Tue, Wed, Fri, Sat 10am-4pm

Perhaps the most fascinating part of this collection, amassed
by the publishing magnate the late Malcom S. Forbes, is a
room full of trophies that commemorate every conceivable
occasion. A miniature silver palace, given to King George V and Queen Mary by
residents of the North-West Frontier Province to mark a visit they paid to Peshawar,
sits alongside more than 200 trophies and commemoratives marking minor triumphs
in minor lives.

Hidíslenska Redasafn
The Icelandic Phallological Museum
Laugavegur 24, 101 Reykjavik, Iceland
Tel. (354) 566 8668 www.ismennt.is
May-Aug: Tue-Sat 2pm-5pm. Sep-Apr: Tue, Sat 2pm-5pm

Sigurdur Hjartarson began his collection at the age of fifteen when he was given
a whip with a handle made from a bull's penis. Since then, he has amassed nearly
100 penises from almost every kind of land and sea mammal in Iceland, including
one particularly prized specimen taken from a rogue polar bear. The museum also
lists some of the uses that penises and scrotums have been put to in the past, such
as a purse made from the skin of a ram's scrotum, a smoked horse's penis (a popular
snack in the 1930s), and an 85cm bull's penis which has been dried and transformed
into a walking stick.

Muséum d'Histoire naturelle
The Museum of Natural History
28 rue Albert 1er, 17000 La Rochelle, France
Tel. (33) 5 46 41 18 25
Tue-Fri 10am-noon, 1.30-5.30pm (mid Jun-mid Sep until 6pm), Sat-Sun 2-6pm

18th-century harpsichord,
Patricia Herbillon, France
(below)
Musée de la Miniature

Georgian Bureau,
John Davenport, UK
(below right)
Musée de la Miniature

Among the few natural history museums in France whose creation dates back to the 18th
century, this one teems with curiosities, from giraffes' skulls to cases groaning with
shells, fossils, and mounted birds. One room of the museum is devoted to Clément de
Lafaille's cabinet of curiosities which was first installed in La Rochelle's town hall and
later moved to its present home, an 18th-century townhouse just a few hundred yards
from the old harbour of La Rochelle. It was preserved as part of the museum's main collection of natural artefacts. In its heyday, in 1756, it contained many more specimens and
was arranged in a larger space, however the 1791 Revolution saw the collections reduced
substantially. Still, many of
his purpose-made cases and
chests lined with blue silk
have been restored to their
original ivory and saffron
colours and display Lafaille's
collections of corals, birds,
fish, shells, crystals, pickled
specimens, and other natural
rarities. Where there were
once numerous stuffed fish
and reptiles suspended from
the ceiling, there is now only
one lonely crocodile.

Jukeboxen Museum
The Jukebox Museum
Landgoed Den Hulst, Hulst 10, 5492 SB Sint Oedenrode, The Netherlands
Tel. (31) 413 476666 www.jukeboxen.nl
Sun 1–5pm (other times and groups by appt.)

For over 25 years, owner Christ Boelens has been avidly collecting jukeboxes, and not just one by one, but by the container-full, from the US and elsewhere. What he doesn't know about these spectacular creations his two technicians do, as not only is this the place to see jukeboxes (250 or so and counting) but it's here they come to be restored to working order using only original parts. Nostalgic for the carefree days of 1950s and 60s America? Besides jukeboxes, Boelens fell in love with and bought curvy American refrigerators in pastel shades, petrol pumps, traffic lights, posters, and 1950s diner furniture (also in pastel shades). A large collection of neon signs illuminate the collections of one-armed bandits, fifty Coca-Cola vending machines found along the highways and byways of the US, rows of pin ball machines, and stacks of gramophone records.

Earthenware chamber pot, Bohemia, *c*. 1850 (top)
Nachttopf-Museum-Zentrum für Aussergewöhnliche Museen

Kunstkammera
The Chamber of Curiosities
Muzei antropologii i etnografii im. Petra Velikogo, Universitetskaia naberezhnaia 3, 199034 Saint Petersburg, Russian Federation
Tel. (7) 812 3281412 www.win.kunstkamera.lanck.ru
Tue–Sun 11am–5.45pm (closed last Wed of the month)

Urinal flask, glass, Rome, 1st century BC (above)
Nachttopf-Museum-Zentrum für Aussergewöhnliche Museen

A passionate collector, Peter the Great was particularly fond of the unusual, and his personal collection displays a diverse array of both natural and human oddities. The centrepiece is a unique collection of some 2,000 anatomical preparations of foetuses and organs made by Frederik Ruysch, the leading anatomy specialist of the time. There are siamese twins, a two-headed calf, the skeleton of French giant Nicolas Bourgeois, surgical tools, a display of human teeth (all pulled personally by the Tsar), a mounted elephant, and endless other marvels.

A 'palm squeezer pistol' with a seven-shot revolving cartridge magazine made by the Fire Arms Co., Chicago, mid 19th century, known in the trade as The Protector (left)
Vankilamuseo

Maison de la Musique mécanique
The House of Mechanical Music
24 rue Chanzy, 88500 Mirecourt, France
Tel. (33) 3 29 37 51 13
May–Sep: Daily 10am–noon, 2–7pm
Oct–Apr: Wed, Sat 10am–noon, 2–6pm, Sun 2–6pm (groups by appt.)

The town of Mirecourt is the home of cylinder organs and holds one of the finest collections of its kind in France. It was here where serinettes, musical boxes for the training of singing canaries, were originally produced. In the middle of the 19th century, Mirecourt was producing five church organs, 450 'salon' organs, and 2,600 serinettes each year. The museum's collection of 200 instruments brilliantly illustrates the development of local but also foreign production, ranging from an 18th-century serinette to a monumental dance organ made in 1939.

Musée de la Miniature
The Museum of the Miniature
19 rue Pierre Julien, 26200 Montélimar, France
Tel. (33) 4 75 53 79 24
Please call for opening times

Opened in 1995 in the old chapel of a hospital, among the museum's *tours de force* are the insects made of a 25cm-square piece of paper folded 200 times; a gold ancient chariot in the eye of a needle; and an icon of Christ in a grain of rice. It is also the showcase for French contemporary artists in the art of model making, as well as a meeting place for foreign artists and collectors.

Nachttopf-Museum - Zentrum für Aussergewöhnliche Museen
The Chamber Pot Museum - Centre of Extraordinary Museums
Westenriederstrasse 41, 80331 Munich, Germany
Tel. (49) 89 2904121k
Daily 10am-5pm

A collection of some 2,000 chamber pots includes examples from the Roman period to the Art Deco era, alongside delicate Chinese porcelain pots with lids. Made from a variety of materials, some were owned by royal and imperial personages. The collection takes the visitor through two millennia of the fascinating history of these items.

Státní hrad Bítov
Bítov State Castle
67 110 Bítov, Czech Republic
Tel. (420) 624 294622
Please call for opening times

Prison guards' badges
from various decades
(above and below)
Vankilamuseo

Bítov is one of the oldest and most romantic castles in the Czech Republic, with a history stretching back to the 11th century. Today, it is filled with fine paintings and artistic treasures. Most famous is the last owner Baron Jirí Haas' enormous taxidermy collection, comprising an extensive display of fifty stuffed dogs, the largest collection of its kind in the world.

Tattoo Museum
Oudezijds Achterburgwal 130, 1012 DT Amsterdam, The Netherlands
Tel. (31) 20 6251565   www.tattoomuseum.com
Tue-Sun noon-6pm

This museum offers a well-researched and serious survey
of the history of tatooing and body art, and manages to convey the extraordinary popularity of tattooing across history
and various cultures. There are examples of tattoos from all around the world, as well as tattoo designs known as 'flashes'. Besides these fine examples (including tattoos from places as far-flung as India, Thailand, Burma, and New Zealand), the collection also features tattooing equipment: a travelling tattoo shop from India is displayed alongside a machine made from a ballpoint pen which was used in a Russian jail during the Stalin era. For those who are not squeamish, there are strips of human skin, including a 2,000 year-old piece of mummified arm from Peru, and the underarm of a drowned sailor who drifted ashore in Java in the 1920s.

Vakoilumuseo
Spy Museum
Hatanpään puistokuja 32, Tampere, Finland
Tel. (358) 3 2123 007   www.vakoilumuseo.fi
Mon-Fri noon-6pm, Sat-Sun 10am-4pm

In true Bond fashion the exhibits expose the world
of espionage and intelligence by recounting personal actions and displaying related equipment, including modern and old bugging/phone tapping devices, agents' guns, night vision apparatus, code breaking and radio transmission equipment, lie

detectors, medals, and maps, as well as numerous other instruments. Visitors are even allowed to try out some of the devices. The museum has proudly amassed a very large collection of restraints, and there is a special display of old and new handcuffs and chains from all over the world owned by Finnish escape artist, Timo Tuomivaara

Vankilamuseo
Prison Museum
Hämeenlinnan kaupungin historiallinen museo, Kustaa III:n katu 8, 13100
Hämeenlinna, Finland
Tel. (358) 3 621 2977 www.hth.fi
Daily 11am-5pm

Inspired by a French exhibition on the subject of prisons, prison staff started to collect objects related to imprisonment as early as the 1890s, picking up objects related to daily life in prison. There are pieces of interior decoration, cutlery, prisoners' and guards' uniforms, fetters, and objects made by the working prisoners, as well as items and letters confiscated from prisoners. A fascinating array of objects made from wire by prisoners originally at the Turku Penitentiary have found a home here, and include bread baskets, a letter rack, and a toy boat. The museum also maintains a picture collection and archive and there are even 10,000 uncatalogued objects.

Clément Lafaille's
Cabinet of Curiosities,
18th century (above)
Muséum d'Histoire naturelle

The prisoner Wilhelm
Seppänen's picture and
the texts he wrote during
his imprisionment in the
1880s (left)
Vankilamuseo

Villa Lattes
Via N. Sauro 23-24, 31036 Istrana, Italy
(39) 0422 658442
Late Mar-late Nov: Tue, Fri 9am-noon, Sat-Sun 9am-noon, 3-6pm

Housed in this Palladian villa are the whimsical collections of its last owner, the lawyer Bruno Lattes. Among the most charming pieces in the collection are the clockwork toys and music boxes. In his autobiography, whose title is best translated as Memoirs of an Optimistic Lawyer, Lattes says that he wished to 'collect anything of a happy, serene, curious or playful origin; and to exclude everything or almost everything with painful or unfortunate sources'.

The Museum of Westminster Abbey
Westminster Abbey, London SW1P 3PA, UK
Tel. (44) 20 7233 0019 www.westminster-abbey.org
Daily 10.30am-4pm

In the cloisters of Westminster Abbey lies a remarkable collection of eighteen English funeral effigies of kings, queens and distinguished public figures, known as the Ragged Regiment. These bizarre bods are survivors of a curious custom which dates back to Roman times, when wax masks of nobles were brought to their gravesides. The earliest surviving effigy is that of Edward III (buried in 1377), with eyebrows

made from the hair of a small dog. The last was Horatio Nelson's effigy made in 1806, dressed in his own clothes and hat, including the shoe buckles he was wearing when he fell.

Zászlómúzeum - Balogh Gyûjtemény
The Flag Museum - Balogh Collection
József körút 68, 1085 Budapest, Hungary
Tel. (36) 1 3340159
Tue-Sun 11am-6pm

Clément Lafaille's
Cabinet of Curiosities,
18th century
Muséum d'Histoire naturelle

The collector, László Balogh, has created a collection which contains the flag and arms of every country and administrative area, all obtained by correspondence and many from the heads of state. Among them is the flag of Chechnya sent by the former president, Dudajev; a flag accompanied by a letter from the late Mrs Indira Gandhi; and one from the former president of Croatia, the late Mr Tudjman, who sent a dedicated photograph with the flag and arms of his country.

EROTIC ART

Museo Archeologico Nazionale
The National Archaeological Museum
Via Museo 19, 80135 Naples, Italy
Tel. (39) 081 440166
Mon-Wed, Fri, 9am-7.30pm, Sat 9am-midnight, Sun 9am-8pm

A large part of this collection consists of male genitali – images of the organ both gigantic and minuscule from the Roman sites of Pompeii and Herculaneum. Among these are statues, paintings, and mosaics depicting sexual themes – all fine examples of erotic taste in the Roman world.

Paris-Hollywood cover
page; the most exclusive
french magazine of the
1950s
Museum Erotica

British Museum
Great Russell Street, London WC1B 3DG, UK
Tel. (44) 20 7636 1555,
www.thebritishmuseum.ac.uk
Mon-Sat 10am-5pm, Sun noon-6pm

This 'secret' collection owes much to the donation made by George Witt of 434 diverse objects described as 'symbols of the early worship of mankind.' Of great interest are the nine leather bound albums which contain sketches, water-colours, pioneer photographs, and descriptions of other objects held in both public and private collections. Also highly intriguing is Witt's correspondence with fellow collectors of phallic objects.

Erotic Museum
Oudezijds Achterburgwal 54,
Amsterdam, The Netherlands
Tel. (31) 20 624 7303
Mon-Thu, Sun 11am-1am, Fri,
Sat 11am-2am

This is not an easy place to miss; at the entrance to the museum is a life-sized female mannequin riding a bicycle, and the action of the pedals forces a dildo up and down through a hole in the saddle. This collection is the usual mix of the banal and the vulgar, leavened with an attempt to depict art.

Museu de l'Eròtica
The Museum of Eroticism
Rambla 96, 08002 Barcelona, Spain
Tel. (34) 93 3189865 www.eroticamuseum.com
Daily 10am-midnight

This is an establishment that genuinely endeavours to relate sex to culture, approaching the art of love on various continents with serious intent. Their large and varied collection is far more stimulating than museums that set out to exploit sex and sexual deviation to bring in the crowds.

Museum Erotica
Købmagergade 24, 1150 Copenhagen, Denmark
Tel. (45) 33 120 311 www.museum-erotica.dk
May-Sep: daily 10am-11pm. Oct-Apr: daily 11am-8pm

Here, one can learn about the sex lives of Freud, Nietzsche, and more surprisingly, Duke Ellington. The exhibits range from the subdued to the explicit, and include erotic Indian miniatures and sex toys.

Erotic Art Museum
Reeperbahn-Nobistor 10 a, 22767 Hamburg, Germany
Tel. (49) 40 31784126 www.erotic-art-museum.hamburg.de
Mon, Thu, Sun 10am-midnight, Fri, Sat 10am-1am

This collection contains much that can truly be called art. Several fine paintings by Allen Jones and a set of Japanese erotic prints are well worth looking at. However, the remainder is the sort of art that leaves little to the imagination.

Musée de l'Erotisme
Erotic Museum
72 blvd de Clichy, 75009 Paris, France
Tel. (33) 1 42582873
Daily 10am-2am

In this collection there are over 2,000 sexual objects, from phalluses to prints showing couples in various positions. Far more interesting, however, are the 19th-century French pornographic postcards.

Museu Nacional Arqueològic de Tarragona
National Archaeological Museum of Tarragona
Plaça del Rei, 5, 43003 Tarragona Spain
Tel. (34) 977 236209 www.mnat.es
Jun-Sep: Tue-Sat 10am-8pm, Sun 10am-2pm. Oct-May: Tue-Sat 10am-1.30pm, 4pm-7pm, Sun 10am-2pm

A collection that is largely concerned with fertility and eroticism, with objects dating from prehistory to the Greek and Roman cultures. Exhibits demonstrate that great art occasionally emerges from the enthusiasm for sex and the need for fertility.

Drawing by Felicien Rops (below left)
Erotic Art Museum

The Interior of a Harem, unknown French artist, *c.* 1840 (below right)
Erotic Art Museum

Photo of a brothel (bottom)
Musée de l'Erotisme

607

Diabolical Charges and Discharges, Eugène le Poiterin
Erotic Art Museum

Sexmuseum Amsterdam

'Venustempel' Damrak 18, 1012 LH
Amsterdam, The Netherlands
Tel. (31) 20 6228376
Daily 10am-11.30pm

This display is more salacious than most sex museums. Erotic lithographs, etchings, oil paintings, bronzes, porcelain, ivories, clay and marble figures, as well as photographs and films are all on display. The artistic level is low, the sexual level high.

MAGIC AND ILLUSION

American Museum of Magic

107 East Michigan Avenue, Marshall, Michigan 49068-1543, USA
Tel. (1) 616 781 7666
By appt. only

A young Harry Houdini posing for a publicity photo (date unknown)
Outagamie Museum & Houdini Historical Center

This immaculately restored 1868 house contains the largest publicly displayed, privately owned collection of magic-related memorabilia in the world. It includes hundreds of showbills, thousands of heralds, handbills, window cards and programmes, and tens of thousands of books, magazines, photographs, and correspondence from many of the famous magicians of the 19th and 20th centuries. In rooms papered with posters and broadsheets are displayed magic sets (including 500 children's sets), performer's scrapbooks, and the 'Milk Can' and the 'Overboard Packing Case' escape equipment used by Harry Houdini. The basement store, packed with filing cabinets containing artefacts and original documents acknowledging thousands of little-known conjurers, is an indispensable resource.

Musée de la Curiosité et de la Magie
The Museum of Curiosa and Magic

Ecole de la Magie, 11 rue Saint Paul, 75004 Paris, France
Tel. (33) 1 42 72 13 26 www.paris.org
Wed, Sat-Sun 2-7pm (magic show 2.30-6pm)

There are 300 fascinating objects on display here, dedicated to the history of magic in France. Among them are the famous automaton which stood for a time at the entrance of a movie theatre on the Place Pigalle, and the very first coffin-sized box used for sawing a woman in two, once owned by the American magician Henry Thurston (who became known for his stage illusions such as the 'floating lady'). Other paraphernalia is associated with conjuring, like the items used by George Proust, the spiritual founder of the museum, to perform tricks devised by himself. This collection also includes items used to create optical illusions.

Houdini Museum

1433 North Main, Scranton, Pennsylvania 18508, USA
Tel. (1) 570 342 5555 www.houdini.org
Jun: Sat-Sun 12.30-4pm. Jul, Aug: daily 12.30-4pm
Rest of year: hours vary; please call for details

Scranton was a proving ground for vaudeville performers eager to get the backing needed to take their acts on the road and into the big cities. Harry Houdini was one of countless travelling acts that passed through the area in the early 1900s, making numerous appearances at the former Poli Theatre and other venues. The rather cramped museum celebrates the achievements of the legendary Houdini. Copies of birth records and early family records as well as artefacts from his stage career and private life are intermingled with photos to trace this famous magician's career which later included producing silent films.

The Magic Circle

12 Stephenson Way, Euston, London NW1 2HD, UK
Tel. (44) 20 7387 2222 www.themagiccircle.co.uk
Open to members only but special open days organized throughout the year; please call for details

A dilapidated warehouse near London's Euston Station has been transformed into a four-storey centre for Britain's largest group of conjurors, the Magic Circle. Besides containing a theatre, it houses a library and a museum containing magical apparatus of bygone eras, along with a collection of posters of famous magicians, both past and present.

Maison de la Magie
The House of Magic

1 place du Château, 41000 Blois, France
Tel. (33) 2 54 55 26 26
Jun-Oct: Wed, Thu, Sat-Sun 10am-12.30pm, 2-5.30pm

The House of Magic was created by Jack Lang in 1989 and is dedicated to Jean Eugène Robert-Houdin (1805-71) who was born in Blois. It delves into the history of magic and describes Houdin's life and his incredible career. Items of special note include the top hat and magic wand belonging to Houdin, a bronze replica of the table which appeared centre stage for many of his performances, and a diploma in Arabic and French given to the magician for a performance in 1856 in Algeria, where he was sent by the French government to discredit native priests using magic to stir up trouble.

Houdini poses in restraints for a publicity photo, *c.* 1918 (below left)
Outagamie Museum & Houdini Historical Center

Milk can filled with sixty gallons of milk from which Houdini escaped in 1908 (below right)
Outagamie Museum & Houdini Historical Center

Outagamie Museum & Houdini Historical Center

330 East College Avenue, Appleton, Wisconsin 54911, USA
Tel. (1) 920 733 8445 www.foxvalleyhistory.org
Tue-Sat 10am-5pm, Sun noon-5pm, plus Mon 10am-5pm during Jun, Jul, Aug

Houdini and his family moved to Appleton when he was a child. He once said, 'the greatest escape I ever made was when I left Appleton, Wisconsin.' Despite his feelings, the Sidney H. Radner Collection of Houdini memorabilia, consisting of 125 artefacts and 150 classic photographic images, posters, and handbills, is among the finest

collections in the world dedicated to this master illusionist. Featuring Houdini's handcuffs, personal letters, leg irons, and lock picks, other highlights of the collection include the Guiteau handcuffs which held President Garfield's assassin and from which Houdini escaped, and Houdini's first performance contract.

Vent Haven Museum

33 West Maple Avenue, Fort Mitchell, Kentucky 41011, USA
Tel. (1) 859 341 0461 www.venthaven.com
May-Sep: tours by appt.

This is the only museum solely dedicated to the art of ventriloquism. Nowhere else will you find an entire cabinet of Edgar Bergen memorabilia, or a Vent's Hall of Fame that commemorates, among others, Bergen, Shari Lewis, and Jimmy Nelson. There are papier-mâché figures of George, Nettie, Happy and Old Mia (*c*. 1910) used by Jules Vernon, the blind vaudeville ventriloquist whose audience never knew he couldn't see. The collection numbers around 500 ventriloquist figures and contains thousands of pieces of related memorabilia. Talking canes, drinking glasses, clocks that turn into dummies, and a painting with a moveable mouth jostle for space among a gallery of over 1,000 autographed pictures of vents.

Harry Houdini all locked up in Germany, *c*. 1904
Outagamie Museum & Houdini Historical Center

PICTURE CREDITS

p. 14 Bwa plank mask (The Horniman Museum and Gardens) © Photo: Stephen Brayne.

p. 16 Haitian voodoo altar (The Horniman Museum and Gardens) © Photo: Heini Schneebeli.

p. 16 Bwa mask (The Horniman Museum and Gardens) © Photo: Stephen Brayne.

p. 20 Panathenaic amphora (Musée Antoine Vivenel) © Photo: C. Vatin.

p. 21 Attic lecythus; Attic psykter (Musée Antoine Vivenel) © Photo: C. Vatin.

p. 22 Attic bowl (Musée Antoine Vivenel) © Photo: C. Vatin.

p. 24 Central roundel from the *Cupid on a Dolphin* mosaic (Fishbourne Roman Palace) © Sussex Archaeological Society / Fishbourne Roman Palace.

p. 25 Seahorse from the *Cupid on a Dolphin* mosaic (Fishbourne Roman Palace) © Sussex Archaeological Society / Fishbourne Roman Palace.

p. 31 Terracotta male statue (Medelhavsmuseet) © Medelhavsmuseet/ Photo: M. Sjöblom.

p. 36 Main entrance and the Wiebengahal (Bonnefantenmuseum) © Photo: Kim Zwarts.

p. 40 Virgin and Child statue (Musée du Louvre) © Photo: Réunion des Musées Nationaux Photo: C. Jean.

p. 49 Bead net dress (Petrie Museum of Egyptian Archaeology) © Petrie Museum of Egyptian Archaeology, University College London/UC17743.

p. 50 *The Ebony Egress* (Petrie Museum of Egyptian Archaeology) © Petrie Museum of Egyptian Archaeology, University College London.

p. 51 Faience counterpoise with the head of a goddess (Myers Museum) Reproduced by permission of the Provost and Fellows of Eton College.

p. 52 Mummy portrait of woman in blue robe (Petrie Museum of Egyptian Archaeology) © Petrie Museum of Egyptian Archaeology, University College London/ UC14692.

p. 52 Earliest known linen dress (Petrie Museum of Egyptian Archaeology) © Petrie Museum of Egyptian Archaeology, University College London/UC286141B.

p. 53 Wooden painted shabti figure (Petrie Museum of Egyptian Archaeology) © Petrie Museum of Egyptian Archaeology, University College London/UC8824.

p. 54 Red jasper face inlay (Myers Museum) Reproduced by permission of the Provost and Fellows of Eton College.

p. 55 Footprints on part of a roof tile (Fishbourne RomanPalace) © Sussex Archaeological Society/ Fishbourne Roman Palace.

p. 62 Marble head of a boy (Fishbourne RomanPalace) © Sussex Archaeological Society / Fishbourne Roman Palace.

p. 64 Attic amphora with red figures (Musée du Louvre) © Photo: Réunion desMusées Nationaux (H. Lewandowski).

p. 64 Pergamon altar (Pergamon Museum) © Staatliche Museen zu Berlin - Preussischer Kulturbesitz, Antikensammlung/ Photo: Jürgen Liepe.

p. 65 Detail of Pergamon altar (Pergamon Museum) © Staatliche Museen zu Berlin - Preussischer Kulturbesitz, Antikensammlung/ Photo: Johannes Laurentius.

p. 66 *Aphrodite*; cult statue of a Goddess (J. Paul Getty Museum) © John Paul Getty Trust.

p. 71 Tall vase, cloisonné enamel on cast bronze (The Crow Collection of Asian Art) © The Trammell & Margaret Crow Collection of Asian Art/Photo: Michael Bodycomb.

p. 78 Prayer niche (Museu Calouste Gulbenkian) © Fundaçao Calouste Gulbenkian.

p. 79 Silk fragment; jade jug (Museu Calouste Gulbenkian) © Fundaçao Calouste Gulbenkian.

p. 82 Two folios from the *Divan* of Hafiz (Arthur M. Sackler Museum) © Harvard University Art Museums / Arthur M. Sackler Museum.

p. 87 Blackfeet Tepee camp; Reservation Era House (Plains Indian Museum) © Buffalo Bill Historical Center, Cody, Wyoming, June 2000.

p. 100 Early Bronze Age beaker; bronze 'Picardy' pin (Dover Museum) © Dover Bronze Age Boat Gallery.

p. 102 Early Bronze Age spear head; Iron Age gold stater (Dover Museum) © Dover Bronze Age Boat Gallery.

p. 103 Small decorated hanging urn (Dover Museum) © Dover Bronze Age Boat Gallery.

p. 107 Interior and aerial views of Mnajdra Megalithic temple (National Museum of Archaeology) © Malta Tourism Authority.

p. 118 Selection of Balzac's books and manuscripts (La Maison de Balzac) © PMVP. Photo: D. Lifermann.

p. 119 Astronomic clock (Goethe Haus und Museum) © Freies Deutsches Hochstift, Frankfurter Goethe Museum.

p. 119 Joyce death mask (James Joyce Museum) © Dublin Tourism.

p. 120 Corrected proofs of *La Vieille Fille*. (La Maison de Balzac) © Karin Maucotel.

p. 120 Portrait of Balzac (La Maison de Balzac) © PMVP.

p. 121 D. H. Lawrence and Frieda Lawrence in Chapala, Mexico; D. H. Lawrence in Sante Fe, Mexico (University of Nottingham Library) © University of Nottingham Department of Manuscripts and Special Collections.

p. 124 Botanical prints (Hunt Institute for Botanical Documentation) © Courtesy of Torner Collection of Sesse and Mocino Biological Illustrations, Hunt Institute for Botanical Documentation, Carnegie Mellon University, Pittsburgh, PA, USA.

p. 125 Botanical prints (Hunt Institute for Botanical Documentation) © Courtesy of Torner Collection of Sesse and Mocino Biological Illustrations, Hunt Institute for Botanical Documentation, Carnegie Mellon University, Pittsburgh, PA, USA.

Richmond/Bequest of Lillian Thomas Pratt/Photo: Katherine Wetzel.

p. 250 Round faced clock (Musée de Sarreguemines) © Coll. Musées de Sarreguemines/Photo Ch. Thévenin.

p. 251 Faience decorative plate; faience vase (Musée de Sarreguemines) © Coll. Musées de Sarreguemines/Photo Ch. Théveni.

p. 259 Museum entrance hall (The J. Paul Getty Museum) © Photo: Scott/Frances/Esto

p. 268 Amulet perfume; advertisement for Escape perfume (Alfred Dunhill Museum) © Photo: 'Alfred Dunhill Museum & Archive'.

p. 271 Romano-British wine or water carafe (The Museum of British Pewter) © Shakespeare Birthplace Trust. Two Communion flagons (Städtisches Museum Göppingen) © Photo: Dieter Dehnert, Göppingen.

p. 272 Octagonal flask, bowl, and tankard (Städtisches Museum Göppingen) © Photo: Dieter Dehnert, Göppingen.

p. 275 Vase (Cooper-Hewitt, National Design Museum) © Cooper-Hewitt, National Design Museum, Smithsonian Institution/ Art Resource USA. Gift of Ely Jacques Kahn, 1962-227-2/Photo: John White.

p. 277 Double trophy (Hiekan tadmuseo) © Photo: Petri Nuutinen.

p. 284 Four tiles (Keramieknuseum het Princessehof) © Photo: Johan v.d.Veer.

p. 287 Detail of panoramic wallpaper; wallpaper with flower motif (Deutsches Tapetenmuseum) © Staatliche Museen Kassel.

p. 288 Drawing room; textile (The Museum of Domestic Design and Architecture) © MoDA/ Middlesex University.

p. 289 The Practical House Holder (The Museum of Domestic Design and Architecture) © MoDA/Middlesex University.

p. 290 Wallpaper design, 1941; wallpaper (The Museum of Domestic Design and Architecture) © MoDA/Middlesex University.

p. 295 Spitfire IX EN199 (Malta Aviation Museum) © Photo: Frederick R. Galea. Part of Iraqi Supergun (Fort Nelson) © Royal Armouries, Fort Nelson.

p. 299 Turkish sabre; Nepalese kukri; Chinese sword (Royal Armouries Museum) © Royal Armouries, Leeds.

p. 300 Indian punch-dagger (Royal Armouries Museum) © Royal Armouries, Leeds.

p. 301 Armour (Royal Armouries Museum) © Royal Armouries, Leeds.

p. 302 Horned helmet; King Henry VIII's armour (Royal Armouries Museum) © Royal Armouries, Leeds.

p. 303 Tail piece of horse armour (Royal Armouries Museum) © Royal Armouries, Leeds. Armour for Prince Henry and James II (Tower of London) © Royal Armouries, Tower of London.

p. 304 Burgundian Bard horse (Royal Armouries Museum) © Royal Armouries, Leeds.

p. 305 Model of Italian export armour (Royal Armouries Museum) © Royal Armouries, Leeds.

p. 306 Earl of Worcester armour (Tower of London) © Royal Armouries, Tower of London.

p. 307 German Gothic style armour (Royal Armouries Museum) © Royal Armouries, Leeds.

p. 308 'Turning Point: The American Civil War' (Atlanta History Center) Photo: Jonathan Hillyer. Parker side-by-side; Sharps M18151 (Cody Firearms Museum) © Cody Firearms Museum, Buffalo Bill Historical Center.

p. 309 Erickson case Derringers (Cody Firearms Museum) © Cody Firearms Museum, Buffalo Bill Historical Center.

p. 310 Prussian pistol (Waffenmuseum Suhl) © Photo: R. Fetzer.

p. 311 Exterior of museum (Waffenmuseum Suhl) © Photo: W. Richter / J. Hopf. Japanese gift armour (Royal Armouries Museum) © Royal Armouries, Leeds.

p. 312 Indian quilted armour (Royal Armouries Museum) © Royal Armouries, Leeds.

p. 313 Quoit turban; Mongol helmet

(Royal Armouries Museum) © Royal Armouries, Leeds.

p. 314 Elephant armour (Royal Armouries Museum) © Royal Armouries, Leeds.

p. 315 Royal Navy Gold Medal; Glengarry Fencibles colours (The National War Museum of Scotland) © The Trustees of the National Museums of Scotland.

p. 316 Various medals (The National War Museum of Scotland) © The Trustees of the National Museums of Scotland.

p. 318 Grus leucogeranus (Musée cantonal de Zoologie) © Museum of Zoology of Lausanne, Switzerland. Preserved specimen of the Limulus (Grant Museum of Zoology and Comparative Anatomy) © Fred Langford Edwards.

p. 319 Exhibtion Room; Mergus cucullatus; Haeliaeetus leucocephalus (Musée cantonal de Zoologie) © Museum of Zoology of Lausanne, Switzerland.

p. 321 Carriage drawn by zebra (Walter Rothschild Zoological Museum) © The Natural History Museum.

p. 322 'Noctifer'; 'Martin Luther after his fall'; 'The Nondescript'; bird from the collection (Wakefield Museum) © Wakefield MDC Musuems& Arts.

p. 324 Butterflies (Booth Museum of Natural History) © The Royal Pavilion, Libraries and Museums, Brighton.

p. 328 Ice crystal; spectrolite; fossilised coral (Tampereen Kivimuseo) © Paavo Korhonen.

p. 329 Fossilised ammonite (Tampereen Kivimuseo) © Paavo Korhonen. Watercolour by de la Beche of Mary Anning (Lyme Regis Philpot Museum) By permission of Mr Roderick Gordon and Mrs. Diana Harman/© Buckland Papers.

p. 331 The 'Fahrkunst' lift; the mine train (Norsk Bergverksmuseum) © Norsk Bergverksmuseum, Norway/Photo: H. Rock Løwer.

p. 332 Machine drilling; silver miners in the King's Mine (Norsk Bergverksmuseum)© Norsk

Bergverksmuseum, Norway. The silver mines at Saggrenda (Norsk Bergverksmuseum) © Norsk Bergverksmuseum, Norway/Photo: Nystuen. Exterior of Norsk Bremuseum (Norsk Bremuseum) © Aune Forlag AS, Trondheim/Photo: Finn Loftesnes.

p. 333 Mine train entering the Christian VII audit (Norsk Bergverksmuseum) © Norsk Bergverksmuseum, Norway.

p. 334 Magnolia flower © Botanischer Garten und Botanisches Museum Berlin-Dahlem, I. Haas

p. 334 Pride of California flower (The Botanical Museum - Harvard Museum of Natural History) © Photo: Hillel Burger.

p. 336 Tropical Pavilion © Botanischer Garten und Botanisches Museum Berlin-Dahlem.

p. 342 Auto sardine can (Norsk Hermetikkmuseum) © NMKS - JGJ.

p. 343 Prince Olav sardine can; sardine cans by Dom... (Norsk Hermetikkmuseum) © NMKS - JGJ.

p. 345 Lapis Lazuli snuff bottle (The Chester Beatty Library) Reproduced by kind permission of the Trustees of the Chester Beatty Library, Dublin.

p. 348 Lewis chess figures (Royal Museum of Scotland) © The Trustees of the National Museums of Scotland.

p. 349 Walrus tusk chessman (Royal Museum of Scotland) © The Trustees of the National Museums of Scotland.

P. 355 Table clock (Nederlands Goud-, Zilver- en Klokkenmuseum) © Rob Glastra Fotografie.

p. 356 Table clock by Martinot. Paris (Musée Paul Dupuy) © Toulouse, musée Paul-Dupuy ou Toulouse/Photo: S.T.C.

p. 357 Alarm clocks (Nederlands Goud-, Zilver- en Klokkenmuseum) © Rob Glastra Fotografie.

p. 358 *Gnadenpfenning* (Staatliche Münzsammlung) © Praun-Kunstverlag.

p. 359 Tetradrachma showing Arethusa; silver medal by Hans Krafft; tetradrachma showing Athena; *Septimus Severus* (Staatliche Münzsammlung) © Praun-Kunstverlag.

p. 360 Velvet purse with silver thread embroidery (Musée de la Monnaie) © Musée de la Monnaie, Paris, France, 2001/ Photo: Jean Jacques Castaing.

p. 362 Silver medallion; five-ducat (Staatliche Münzsammlung) © Praun-Kunstverlag.

p. 365 *Buffalo Runners, Big Horn Basin*; black and silver chaps and vest (Sid Richardson Collection of Western Art) © Courtesy Sid Richardson Collection of Western Art, Fort Worth.

p. 366 Building donated by The Stanley Works; *Knox Bridge* painting; tool collection (Sloane-Stanley Museum) © Photo: F. McAuliffe.

p. 367 Eric Sloane's Warren studio; Eric Sloane believed Early American tools were works of art (Sloane-Stanley Museum) © Photo: F. McAuliffe.

p. 368 Buckets (Billings Farm and Museum) © Photo: Jon Gilbert Fox.

p. 369 Farm implements (Billings Farm and Museum) © Photo: Jon Gilbert Fox.

p. 371 Rhyton in shape of a ram's head (Museo Martini di Storia dell'Enologia) © Museo Martini di Storia dell'Enologia di Pessione di Chieri.

p. 374 All pictures (Museo Martini di Storia dell'Enologia) © Museo Martini di Storia dell'Enologia di Pessione di Chieri.

p. 375 Hall displaying goblets and glasses; two goblets (Museo Martini di Storia dell'Enologia) © Museo Martini di Storia dell'Enologia di Pessione di Chieri.

p. 375 Interior of production area (Norsk Hermetikkmuseum) © Photo: Johnsrud/Tveit.

p. 376 Late 18th-century copper wari (The National Museum of Gardening) © Trevarno Estate Gardens and National Museum of Gardening. Museum felling

and pruning display (Harlow Carr Museum of Gardening) © Photo: C Bower.

p. 377 Tin plate clockwork child's toy (The National Museum of Gardening) © Trevarno Estate Gardens and National Museum of Gardening.

p. 378 Box set of Victorian garden syringe and nozzles; advertising sign (The National Museum of Gardening) © Trevarno Estate Gardens and National Museum of Gardening. Ceramic plant labels (Harlow Carr Museum of Gardening) © Photo: C Bower.

p. 379 Rare seed cabinet; rare seed catalogue (The National Museum of Gardening) © Trevarno Estate Gardens and National Museum of Gardening.

p. 382 Sea monster crimper [S8191]; unicorn pie crimper [S9196] (Whaling Museum) © Nantucket Historical Association.

p. 383 The Albert Lock (The Lock Museum) © Photo: Brian Gamson.

p. 383 Dessert service (Cooper-Hewitt National Design Museum) © Cooper-Hewitt, National Design Museum, Smithsonian Institution/ Art Resource, NY, USA. Sarah Cooper Hewitt Fund, The Decorative Arts Association Acquisitions Fund and Smithsonian Regents Collections Aquisition Program Fund, 1996-56-1/83. Photo: Andrew Garn.

p. 384 Facsimile key (The Lock Museum) © Photo: Brian Gamson.

p. 385 Door lock (Cooper-Hewitt National Design Museum) © Cooper-Hewitt, National Design Museum, Smithsonian Institution/ Art Resource, NY, USA, Gift of the Museum Council, 1910-30-49-a,b. Photo: Hiro Ihara.

p. 391 Design and result; shaker, ice bucket and ice thongs; La conica coffee maker (The Alessi Factory) © Alessi s.p.a., Crusinallo, Italy.

p. 392 The 5070 condiment set (The Alessi Factory) © Alessi s.p.a., Crusinallo, Italy.

p. 392 Red lips sofa (Brighton Museum and Art Gallery)

© 'The Royal Pavilion, Libraries & Museums, Brighton'.

p. 393 Clock (The Alessi Factory) © Alessi s.p.a., Crusinallo, Italy.

p. 397 Dunhill-Namiki fountain pen (Alfred Dunhill Museum) © Photo: 'Alfred Dunhill Museum & Archive'.

p. 399 Twisted harpoon (Whaling Museum) © Nantucket Historical Association.

p. 403 Exterior of the museum (Salem Witch Museum) © Photo: Paul Lyden.

p. 410 Enigma Rotor Cypher; cyberbikes (Heinz Nixdorf Museumsforum) © Photo Jan Braun, Heinz Nixdorf Museumforum.

p. 411 Hansen's 'writing ball' (Heinz Nixdorf Museumsforum) © Heinz Nixdorf Museumforum/Photo: Jan Braun.

p. 413 Löwe economy tubes (Radiomuseum) © Radiofreunde Rottenburg e.V.

p. 414 Telegraph (Telegalleria) © The Finnish Museum's Association 1999.

p. 415 The Glass Woman (Deutsches Hygiene-Museum) © Stiftung. Deutsches-Hygiene Museum/ Photo: Volker Kreidler.

p. 416 Exterior of the museum (Deutsches Hygiene-Museum) © Stiftung. Deutsches-Hygiene Museum. Photo: Volker Kreidler.

p. 417 Pregnancy calendar; painting of pharmacy; Alpine wooden figure of Roccus (Medizinhistorisches Museum der Universität Zürich) © Photo: Eva Schnyder.

p. 418 Doctor's homepathic kit (Medizinhistorisches Museum der Universität Zürich) © Photo: Eva Schnyder.

p. 419 Early 19th-century trepanning set (The Old Operating Theatre, Museum and Herb Garret) © The Old Operating Theatre, Museum and Herb Garret, Southwark.

p. 420 The Herb Garret (The Old Operating Theatre, Museum and Herb Garret) © The Old Operating Theatre, Museum and Herb Garret, Southwark.

p. 422 *Pardessus de Viole* (The Horniman Museum and Gardens) © Horniman Public Museum and Public Park Trust.

p. 423 Bow harp (The Horniman Museum and Gardens) © Horniman Public Museum and Public Park Trust.

p. 425 Xylophone (The Horniman Museum and Gardens) © Horniman Public Museum and Public Park Trust.

p. 432 Horn gramophone and records (Royal Museum of Scotland) © The Trustees of the National Museums of Scotland, UK.

p. 434 Klingsor gramophone; 'Amberola' Model A phonograph (Science Museum) © Science Museum/Science and Society Picture Library.

p. 435 Berliner gramophone (Science Museum) © Science Museum/Science and Society Picture Library.

p. 436 The polar vessel *Fram* (Fram-Museet) © Normann. / Per Andersen. Roald Amundsen (Fram-Museet) © Normann. Fridjof Nansen (Fram-Museet) © Normann. / Henry van der Weyde.

p. 437 Marine chronometer and deck-watch (Observatorirmuseet) © Photo: Mats Landin. Observatoriemuseet, Sweden.

p. 438 Submersible *Alvin3* (Woods Hole Oceanographic Institution) © Photo: Rod Catanach.

p. 440 Planetary clockwork with celestial globe (Museum für Astronomie und Technikgeschichte) © Museum für Astronomie und Technikgeschichte, Staatliche Museen Kassel, Orangerie, Kassel.

p. 440 Spring balance for kitchen use (Museo della Bilancia) © Museo della Bilancia, Campogalliano, Italy. The observatory room with the quadrant (Observatorirmuseet) © Photo: Susanna Asklöf/ Observatoriemuseet, Sweden.

p. 441 Achromatic refractor (Observatorirmuseet) © Photo: SusannaAsklöf/Observatoriemuseet, Sweden.

p. 442 Exterior of the museum (Museo della Bilancia) © Museo della Bilancia, Campogalliano, Italy.

p. 443 Letter scales (Museo della Bilancia) © Museo della Bilancia, Campogalliano, Italy.

p. 444 Vacuum punp (Matematish-Physikalishcer Salon) © Staatliche Kunstsammlungen Dresden, Mathematisch-Physikalischer Salon/Photo: Karpinski.

p. 445 Metal thermometer; telescope (Matematish-Physikalishcer Salon) © Staatliche Kunstsammlungen Dresden, Mathematisch-Physikalischer Salon/Photo: Karpinski.

p. 446 18th-century telescope (Observatorirmuseet) © Photo: Susanna Asklöf/ Observatoriemuseet, Sweden.

p. 447 Tachymetre leveller (Museum für Astronomie undTechnikgeschichte) © Museum für Astronomie und Technikgeschichte, Staatliche Museen Kassel, Orangerie, Kassel.

p. 449 Hero's aeolipile and steam boiler (The Science Museum) © Science Museum/Science and Society Picture Library.

p. 450 Wimshurst's Electrostatic Machine (The Science Museum) © Science Museum/Science and Society Picture Library.

p. 452 *Shooting the Apple* (MIT Museum) © The Harold E. Edgerton Trust.

p. 465 Statue of man fishing (Catskill Fly Fishing Center and Museum) © Fred Bennet. Grizzly bear (Deutsches Jagd- und Fischereimuseum) © Deutsches Jagd- und Fischereimuseum München.

p. 466 Hunting sleighs with view of the White Hall; stairwell with view of the White Hall; *Wild Boar* (Deutsches Jagd- und Fischereimuseum) © Deutsches Jagd- und Fischereimuseum München.

p. 469 *Bringing home the last shot bear in Bavaria, near Ruhpolding, October 24, 1835* (Deutsches Jagd- und Fischereimuseum) © Deutsches Jagd- und Fischereimuseum München.*Falconry; Return from*

© Photo: KJanusz Kozina and Grzegorz Zygier.

p. 575 1918 Avro 504K (Shuttleworth Collection) © Photo: Steven Jefferson.

p. 576 1936 Dh87b Hornet Moth (Shuttleworth Collection) © Photo: Steven Jefferson.

p. 578 Quadrant tricycle (Nationaal Fietsmuseum - Velorama) © Veldkamp Nijmegen.

p. 579 Interior of the museum (Nationaal Fietsmuseum-Velorama) © Veldkamp Nijmegen.

p. 580 Humber tricycle (Nationaal Fietsmuseum - Velorama) © Veldkamp Nijmegen.

p. 581 Penny Farthing (Nationaal Fietsmuseum - Velorama) © Veldkamp Nijmegen.

p. 586 Limousine in the Classic Collection (Mercedes-Benz Museum) © DaimlerChrysler Konzernarchiv.

p. 587 Saloon car in the Emperor's train; the Empress' car in the Emperor's train(Suomen Rautatie Museo) © The Finnish Museums Association 1999.

p. 588 No. 990 *Henry Oakley* (Bressingham Steam Museum Trust) © Bressingham Steam Museum Trust, UK/Photo: Steve Allen.

p. 589 *The Mallard* watercolour; Mallard 4-6-2 steam locomotive (National Railway Museum) © National Railway Museum/ Science & Society Picture Library.

p. 591 Wax model of 'Elephant' figurehead (Orlogsmuseet) © Orlogsmuseet, Copenhagen, Denmark.

p. 592 Model of Captain James Cook's famous ship, HM Bark *Endeavour* (National Maritime Museum) © National Maritime Museum, Greenwich.

p. 593 Exterior of the museum (Orlogsmuseet) © Photo: Finn Christoffersen.

p. 595 F20 Tigershark jet aircraft (California Science Center) © Courtesy of the California Science Center; Apollo 16 crew (California Science Center) © Photo: NASA/JSC.

p. 600 Luxurious sarcophogus (Bestattungsmuseum) © Bestattungsmuseum, Austria.

p. 602 18th-century harpsichord (Musée de la Miniature) © Photo: Daniel Dupont, Montélimar. Georgian Bureau (Musée de la Miniature) © Photo: Studio L'oeil écoute, Bernard Coste-Montelimar,

p. 606 *Paris-Hollywood* cover page (Museum Erotica) © Museum Erotica, Copenhagen, Denmark.

p. 608 Young Harry Houdini photo (Outagamie Museum & Houdini Historica Center) © Courtesy of the Sidney H. Radner Collection, Houdini Historical Center, Appleton, WI.

p. 609 Houdini in restraints; milk can (Outagamie Museum & Houdini Historical Center) © Courtesy of the Sidney H. Radner Collection, Houdini Historical Center, Appleton, WI.

p. 610 Harry Houdin all locked up in Germany (Outagamie Museum & Houdini Historical Center) © Courtesy of the Sidney H. Radner Collection, Houdini Historical Center, Appleton, WI.

INDEX

The index is organised alphabetically within each country. You can either search for the museum's original name or for its translation into English.

USA